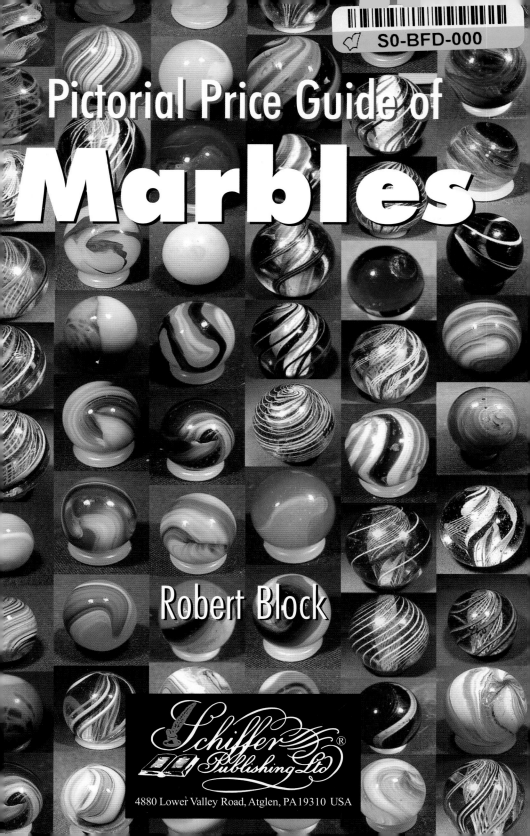

Pictorial Price Guide of
Marbles

Robert Block

Schiffer ®
Publishing Ltd

4880 Lower Valley Road, Atglen, PA 19310 USA

Dedication

This book is dedicated to my wife, Sarah, and my sons, Kevin and Benjamin, as well as to marble collectors everywhere, who have turned a childhood game into a full-fledged hobby.

Copyright © 2002 by Robert Block
Library of Congress Control Number: 2002101781

Designed by John P. Cheek
Cover design by Bruce M. Waters
Type set in Zapf Chancery Bd BT/Zapf Humanist BT

ISBN: 0-7643-1633-8

Printed in China

Published by Schiffer Publishing Ltd.
4880 Lower Valley Road
Atglen, PA 19310
Phone: (610) 593-1777
Fax: (610) 593-2002
E-mail: Schifferbk@aol.com
Please visit our web site catalog at
www.schifferbooks.com

In Europe, Schiffer books are distributed by Bushwood Books
6 Marksbury Ave. Kew Gardens
Surrey TW9 4JF England
Phone: 44 (0)20-8392-8585
Fax: 44 (0)20-8392-9876
E-mail: Bushwd@aol.com
Free postage in the UK. Europe: air mail at cost

This book may be purchased from the publisher.
Include $3.95 for shipping.
Please try your bookstore first.
We are always looking for people to write books on new and related subjects. If you have an idea for a book please contact us at the above address.
You may write for a free catalog.

Contents

Introduction

All marble books currently in print list the author's best estimate of the approximate value for average examples. They do not tell you the prices for which marbles have actually been sold. The actual price of a marble depends on a number of factors. In a perfect marketplace, the true value of a marble would be determined by its rarity, size, and condition. These factors are fairly objective and can be quantified with relative ease by collectors with a little practice and experience. However, every marble is different (they are not commodity items), and the antique and collectible marketplace is inherently imperfect. The price of a marble at any particular point in time is determined not solely by factors such as rarity, size, and condition, but by eye appeal and the emotions of the persons trying to purchase and sell it. This book reports the realized prices for individual marbles at auction.

The actual realized prices for 8,000 individual marbles are reported in this book. This price record encompasses individual marbles sold in A Chip Off The Old Block's Internet CyberAuctions during the year 2000 (CyberAuctions #330 through #508). In addition, A Chip Off The Old Block sold nearly 7,000 lots of multiple marbles. Those lots that consisted of more than one marble are not listed in this book, or included in the subsequent statistical analysis.

The catalogues for A Chip Off The Old Block CyberAuctions use the following categories (and subcategories):

Table 1 - Marble Categories and Subcategories

AKRO AGATE COMPANY	Lemonade	Swirl
Ade	Lemonade oxblood	Swirl oxblood
Ade hybrid	Limeade	Tri-color
Advertising marble	Milky oxblood	
Akroware	Moonie	**CHRISTENSEN AGATE**
Blue oxblood	Moss Agate	**COMPANY**
Carnelian	Orangeade	American Agate
Carnelian oxblood	Original package	Bloodie
Cherryade	Oxblood corkscrew	Cyclone/Cobra
Chocolate oxblood	Oxblood swirl	Flame swirl
Corkscrew	Patch	Guinea
Cornelian	Patch oxblood	Guinea-Cobra
Cullet	Popeye corkscrew	Handgathered
Egg yolk oxblood	Popeye patch	Pastel
Flintie	Ringer	Slag
Hero	Silver oxblood	Striped opaque
Hybrid Ade	Slag	Striped transparent
Imperial	Sparkler	Swirl

CONTEMPORARY HANDMADE

Andy Davis
Beetem Design Glassworks
Bob Hamon
Bob Olsen
Bob Powers
Boyd Miller
Boyer Glass
Brian Lonsway
Brookside Glass
Bruce Breslow/Moon Marble
    Company
California Glass Studios
Chatham Glass
Chris Robinson
Chuck Pound
Crystal Myths
Cuneo Furnace/Steve Maslach
Dale Danowski
David Grant Maul
David Rosenfeld
Davis Handmade Marbles
Douglas Ferguson
Douglas Sweet/Karuna Glass
Drew Fritts
Dudley Giberson
Francis Coupal
Fritz Glass
Fulton-Parker Glass
Gibson Glass
Greg Hoglin
Harry Besset/Vermont Glass
Hart's of Glass
J. Fine Glass
Jim Davis (IN)
Joe St. Clair
John Hamon Miller
John Talmage
Josh Simpson
Karen Federici
Lundberg Studios
Matthews Art Glass
Monty Fritts
Nadine Macdonald
Noble Effort
Phil McGlothlin
Richard Dinardo
Robert Brown
Rolf and Genie Wald
Salazar Art Glass
Sam Hogue
Sara Creekmore
Scott Patrick
Shane Caswell
William Murray

END-OF-DAY

Banded
Blizzard
Cloud
Coreless
Joseph Coat
Onionskin
Onionskin Mist
Panelled cloud
Panelled onionskin
Ribbon onionskin

LUTZ

Banded
End-of-day onionskin
Indian
Mist
Ribbon
Ribbon core

M.F. CHRISTENSEN & SON COMPANY

Brick
Opaque
Oxblood slag
Slag

MARBLE KING, INC.

Berry Pink
Blended
Bumblebee
Catseye
Cub Scout
Dragonfly
Girl Scout
Opaque
Original package
Premium
Rainbow
Tiger
Wasp

MASTER MARBLE/MASTER GLASS COMPANY

Catseye
Comet
Moonie
Original package
Patch
Sunburst
Tigereye

NON-GLASS HANDMADE

Bakelite
Bennington
Carpet Ball
China

Clay
Crockery
Limestone
Mocha ware
Opaque
Original package
Paper mache
Pottery
Steelie
Stone
Stoneware

OTHER HANDMADE

Banded opaque
Cased clambroth
Clambroth
Clearie
Indian
Mica
Mist
Opaque
Paperweight
Slag
Submarine

OTHER MACHINE MADE

Alley Agate
Aventurine
Cairo Novelty
Catseye
Champion Agate
Czechoslovakian
Foreign sparkler
German
Heaton Agate Company
Jackson Marble Company
Metallic
Original package
Swirl
Vacor de Mexico
Wire Pull

PELTIER GLASS COMPANY

Banana
Bloodie
Blue Galaxy
Blue Zebra
Bumblebee
Champion Jr.
Chocolate Cow
Christmas Tree
Clear Rainbo
Flaming Dragon
Golden Rebel
Graycoat
Ketchup and Mustard
Liberty

Miller swirl
Multicolor
National Line Rainbo
Original package
Patch
Peerless Patch
Picture Marble - comic
Rainbo
Rebel
Red Zebra
Slag
Superboy
Superman
Tiger
Tricolor
Wasp
Zebra

RAVENSWOOD NOVELTY WORKS

SULPHIDE

SWIRL
Banded
Butterscotch
Caramel
Coreless
Cornhusk
Custard
Divided core
Gooseberry
Joseph Coat
Latticinio core
Peppermint
Peppermint with mica
Ribbon core
Solid core

TRANSITIONAL
Bullet Mold

Crease pontil
Fold pontil
Ground pontil
Leighton
Melted pontil
Pinch pontil
Regular pontil

VITRO AGATE COMPANY
All-Red
Catseye
Original package
Oxblood
Parrot
Patch
Patch and ribbon
Ribbon
Tigereye
Whitie

This book consists of two major parts and two indices. Part One lists 460 individual marbles, with their actual price and with a color picture of each marble. These marbles include the top selling item in each of the categories and subcategories as listed above (approximately 250), along with nearly 200 of the highest selling marbles not already included in that 250. In this section, I tried to include the widest possible variety of marbles, so that you could see pictures of a great many different types of marbles, rather than numerous pictures of the same marble type.

Part Two lists every example of an individual marble sold during 2000 and reports the actual price realized at auction. Part Two is sorted by category and subcategory as listed above. Each lot entry includes the CyberAuction number and lot number from the original catalogue. In addition, each listing in Part Two is sequentially numbered from 1 to 7,996. This section is laid out by category and then sorted by subcategory within the category. For example, under Akro Agates, all the Swirl Oxbloods are grouped together. This way, if you are interested in seeing the range of prices for one particular type of marble, the information is easily accessible.

There are two indices following Part Two. The first index lists each CyberAuction/Lot in chronological order with a cross-reference to the sequential listing number in Part Two. The second index lists each of the categories/ subcategories shown above, along with the range of sequential numbers from Part Two that apply to each. Using this index, you can quickly find any type of marble. Lastly, the pictures in Part One retain the same sequential numbers used in the Part Two listings, as well as the indices. These indices and the use of the sequential listing numbers alleviate the problem with cross-referencing that occurred in *Marbles Illustrated Prices at Auction*, Volume I.

A Chip Off The Old Block

A Chip Off The Old Block has been an innovator in the use of the Internet to conduct auctions. Marble "CyberAuctions" are conducted two to four nights a week. These auctions are held completely live in an Internet chat room. These CyberAuctions are the oldest "live" auctions on the Internet. Only eBay™ has been conducting any form of auction on the Internet for a longer period of time, and that is a "proxy" auction, not a live auction. A Chip Off The Old Block featured the first auctioneer conducting auctions completely in real time on the Internet. In 1995 A Chip Off The Old Block also conducted the first simultaneous live Internet/on-site auction at the Philadelphia MarbleFest™. Additional information about A Chip Off The Old Block and "CyberAuctions" may be found at www.marblecollecting.com.

2000 Analysis

The year 2000 saw a continuation of the maturing process that has been noted over the past couple of years within the hobby. The year also saw a marked increase in the supply of marbles in general that are readily available to collectors at all levels. The rise of marble trading on the Internet indicates that there are now more people than ever collecting marbles and that there are more collectible marbles available now than ever before.

The marble market consists of several segments. The first tier segmentation of the total market is comprised of handmade marbles, machine made marbles, non-glass marbles, and contemporary marbles sub-markets. Each of these sub-markets can be further subdivided into smaller markets. Generally, handmade marbles are classified by type of construction, i.e., Swirl, end-of-day, etc.; machine made marbles are classified by manufacturer (Akro Agate Company, etc.); and contemporary marbles are classified as hot glass, torchwork, or by artist.

For each lot in A Chip Off The Old Block's auctions, a value estimate is published in the catalogue. Catalogue estimates are consistently applied across lots in each auction. Further, catalogue estimates most often lag behind changes in overall marble pricing. Since it is not known whether a price change is a temporary increase or decrease, or permanent, catalogue estimates can be slow to respond, or even lag behind market changes. Measuring the realized prices against catalogue estimates can provide a guide of segments of the market that are strong and others that are soft.

During 2000, the number of bidders participating in CyberAuctions was higher than in 1998. Therefore, any softening of relative prices between 1998 and 2000 is likely due to bidder sentiment, not a drop in bidder volume.

Table 2 - Price Analysis by Type

Segment	2000 % of Estimate	1998 % of Estimate
Akro Agate Company	108%	123%
Christensen Agate Company	90%	117%
Contemporary Handmade	93%	111%

Segment	2000 % of Estimate	1998 % of Estimate
End-of-day	84%	108%
Lutz	80%	94%
M.F. Christensen and Company	107%	126%
Marble King, Inc.	85%	111%
Master Marble/Glass Company	91%	116%
Non-Glass Handmade	80%	114%
Other Handmade	91%	114%
Other Machine Made	90%	101%
Peltier Glass Company	89%	115%
Sulphide	66%	98%
Swirl	81%	108%
Transitional	89%	109%

During 2000, only the marbles of Akro Agate and M.F. Christensen & Son Company have performed better than auction estimate. This is significantly different than two years ago. As more and more collectible marbles have become available on the Internet, prices are not increasing as quickly as they were in year's past. This can be read as a sign of maturity within the marble collecting hobby. At the other end of the spectrum, sulphides have been selling, on average, at two-thirds of catalogue estimate. A significant slowdown in interest in this type of marble has occurred. The slowdown in price increases is not necessarily viewed as an ominous occurance, but rather, it reflects more stability and predictability within the market. However, it also means that collectors who are buying for investment need to be more discerning in what they acquire.

This leads directly into the second analysis, which is how prices have been performing based on condition.

Table 3 - Price Analysis by Condition

Condition	2000 % of Estimate	1998 % of Estimate
Mint 9.7+	101%	124%
Mint	86%	114%
Near Mint 8.7+	83%	101%
Near Mint	74%	93%
Good	64%	85%

As Table 3 indicates, the better the condition, the better the actual realized price relative to estimate. As the hobby has matured, collectors have become more and more condition conscious. The adage "Quality sells, the rest dwells" continues to hold true.

The trends of the next year or two will be most interesting to follow.

Part One

1. AKRO AGATE COMPANY,
Ade hybrid. 5/8". 9.90.
CyberAuction #330, Lot #45.
Final Bid: $120.

51. AKRO AGATE COMPANY,
Blue oxblood. 25/32". 9.00.
CyberAuction #498, Lot #73.
Final Bid: $310.

85. AKRO AGATE COMPANY,
Carnelian oxblood. 3/4". 9.90.
CyberAuction #356, Lot #55.
Final Bid: $240.

4. AKRO AGATE COMPANY,
Advertising marble. 21/32". 8.90.
CyberAuction #339, Lot #5.
Final Bid: $44.

52. AKRO AGATE COMPANY,
Blue oxblood. 11/16". 9.00.
CyberAuction #459, Lot #56.
Final Bid: $55.

95. AKRO AGATE COMPANY,
Cherryade. 1". 8.60.
CyberAuction #403, Lot #18.
Final Bid: $80.

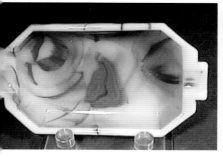

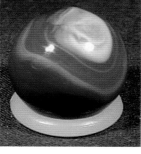

8. AKRO AGATE COMPANY, Akroware.
CyberAuction #508, Lot #42. Final Bid: $150.

63. AKRO AGATE COMPANY,
Carnelian. 3/4". 9.90.
CyberAuction #418, Lot #50.
Final Bid: $75.

98. AKRO AGATE COMPANY,
Chocolate oxblood. 3/4". 8.70.
CyberAuction #342, Lot #49.
Final Bid: $110.

99. AKRO AGATE COMPANY, Corkscrew. 5/8". 9.70. CyberAuction #491, Lot #23. Final Bid: $17.

589. AKRO AGATE COMPANY, Cullet. CyberAuction #339, Lot #35. Final Bid: $23.

606. AKRO AGATE COMPANY, Flintie. 5/8". 9.60. CyberAuction #448, Lot #37. Final Bid: $25.

584. AKRO AGATE COMPANY, Cornelian. 25/32". 9.70. CyberAuction #499, Lot #40. Final Bid: $150.

592. AKRO AGATE COMPANY, Egg yolk oxblood. 3/4". 9.20. CyberAuction #351, Lot #59. Final Bid: $335.

611. AKRO AGATE COMPANY, Hero. 19/32". 9.90. CyberAuction #378, Lot #57. Final Bid: $28.

588. AKRO AGATE COMPANY, Cornelian oxblood. 21/32". 9.90. CyberAuction #498, Lot #68. Final Bid: $410.

593. AKRO AGATE COMPANY, Egg yolk oxblood. 23/32". 9.90. CyberAuction #356, Lot #57. Final Bid: $325.

615. AKRO AGATE COMPANY, Hybrid Ade. 5/8". 8.90. CyberAuction #504, Lot #65. Final Bid: $95.

616. AKRO AGATE COMPANY,
Imperial. 21/32". 9.80.
CyberAuction #381, Lot #32.
Final Bid: $33.

654. AKRO AGATE COMPANY,
Limeade. 21/32". 9.80.
CyberAuction #459, Lot #32.
Final Bid: $70.

676. AKRO AGATE COMPANY,
Moonie. 25/32". 9.60.
CyberAuction #417, Lot #33.
Final Bid: $19.

618. AKRO AGATE COMPANY,
Lemonade. 5/8". 9.70.
CyberAuction #425, Lot #49.
Final Bid: $37.

671. AKRO AGATE COMPANY,
Marble bag. CyberAuction
#502, Lot #17. Final Bid:
$150.

680. AKRO AGATE COMPANY,
Moss Agate. 29/32". 9.90.
CyberAuction #414, Lot #11.
Final Bid: $25.

639. AKRO AGATE COMPANY,
Lemonade oxblood. 3/4". 9.10.
CyberAuction #500, Lot #57.
Final Bid: $235.

672. AKRO AGATE COMPANY,
Milky oxblood. 5/8". 9.70.
CyberAuction #382, Lot #57.
Final Bid: $38.

685. AKRO AGATE COMPANY,
Orangeade. 5/8". 9.80.
CyberAuction #500, Lot #19.
Final Bid: $120.

688. AKRO AGATE COMPANY, Original box. CyberAuction #406, Lot #33. Final Bid: $500.

689. AKRO AGATE COMPANY, Original box. CyberAuction #491, Lot #56. Final Bid: $500.

690. AKRO AGATE COMPANY, Original package. CyberAuction #359, Lot #28. Final Bid: $110.

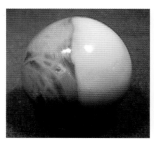

706. AKRO AGATE COMPANY, Patch. 1-1/8". 9.80. CyberAuction #448, Lot #59. Final Bid: $270.

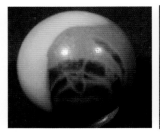

707. AKRO AGATE COMPANY, Patch. 1-1/16". 9.00. CyberAuction #508, Lot #72. Final Bid: $250.

712. AKRO AGATE COMPANY, Patch oxblood. 3/4". 8.70. CyberAuction #379, Lot #44. Final Bid: $85.

734. AKRO AGATE COMPANY, Popeye corkscrew. 5/8". 9.00. CyberAuction #369, Lot #40. Final Bid: $550.

735. AKRO AGATE COMPANY, Popeye corkscrew. 19/32". 9.90. CyberAuction #377, Lot #49. Final Bid: $370.

736. AKRO AGATE COMPANY Popeye corkscrew. 5/8". 9.80. CyberAuction #376, Lot #59. Final Bid: $360.

737. AKRO AGATE COMPANY Popeye corkscrew. 5/8". 9.90. CyberAuction #487, Lot #58. Final Bid: $335.

738. AKRO AGATE COMPANY Popeye corkscrew. 5/8". 9.90. CyberAuction #387, Lot #58. Final Bid: $320.

739. AKRO AGATE COMPANY Popeye corkscrew. 5/8". 9.60. CyberAuction #459, Lot #54. Final Bid: $270.

740. AKRO AGATE COMPANY, Popeye corkscrew. 5/8". 9.50. CyberAuction #357, Lot #57. Final Bid: $260.

957. AKRO AGATE COMPANY, Popeye patch. 3/4". 8.30. CyberAuction #502, Lot #72. Final Bid: $50.

1070. AKRO AGATE COMPANY, Sparkler. 5/8". 8.60. CyberAuction #489, Lot #9. Final Bid: $35.

741. AKRO AGATE COMPANY, Popeye corkscrew. 3/4". 8.80. CyberAuction #381, Lot #49. Final Bid: $260.

959. AKRO AGATE COMPANY, Ringer. 5/8". 8.70. CyberAuction #465, Lot #24. Final Bid: $13.

1075. AKRO AGATE COMPANY, Swirl. 25/32". 9. CyberAuction #366, Lot #47. Final Bid: $46.

742. AKRO AGATE COMPANY, Popeye corkscrew. 21/32". 9.10. CyberAuction #504, Lot #48. Final Bid: $260.

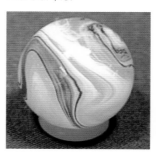

960. AKRO AGATE COMPANY, Silver oxblood. 25/32". 9.90. CyberAuction #448, Lot #54. Final Bid: $200.

1093. AKRO AGATE COMPANY, Swirl oxblood. 5/8". 9.90. CyberAuction #451, Lot #50. Final Bid: $47.

743. AKRO AGATE COMPANY, Popeye corkscrew. 21/32". 8.90. CyberAuction #406, Lot #59. Final Bid: $235.

996. AKRO AGATE COMPANY, Slag. 1-13/16". 8.10. CyberAuction #392, Lot #55. Final Bid: $210.

1155. AKRO AGATE COMPANY, Tri-color. 5/8". 9.90. CyberAuction #446, Lot #14. Final Bid: $7.

1157. CHRISTENSEN AGATE COMPANY, American Agate. 11/16". 9.70. CyberAuction #330, Lot #47. Final Bid: $70.

1172. CHRISTENSEN AGATE COMPANY, Flame swirl. 19/32". 9.90. CyberAuction #377, Lot #54. Final Bid: $575.

1195. CHRISTENSEN AGATE COMPANY, Guinea. 5/8". 9.90. CyberAuction #504, Lot #69. Final Bid: $525.

1164. CHRISTENSEN AGATE COMPANY, Bloodie. 19/32". 9.90. CyberAuction #424, Lot #43. Final Bid: $130.

1174. CHRISTENSEN AGATE COMPANY, Flame swirl. 21/32". 9.20. CyberAuction #508, Lot #70. Final Bid: $280.

1196. CHRISTENSEN AGATE COMPANY, Guinea. 17/32". 9.80. CyberAuction #373, Lot #57. Final Bid: $500.

1171. CHRISTENSEN AGATE COMPANY, Cyclone, half. CyberAuction #448, Lot #7. Final Bid: $42.

1175. CHRISTENSEN AGATE COMPANY, Flame swirl. 5/8". 9.00. CyberAuction #421, Lot #58. Final Bid: $240.

1197. CHRISTENSEN AGATE COMPANY, Guinea. 21/32". 9.60. CyberAuction #385, Lot #57. Final Bid: $485.

1198. CHRISTENSEN AGATE COMPANY, Guinea. 11/16". 9.80. CyberAuction #377, Lot #51. Final Bid: $465.

1201. CHRISTENSEN AGATE COMPANY, Guinea. 19/32". 9.70. CyberAuction #381, Lot #56. Final Bid: $440.

1205. CHRISTENSEN AGATE COMPANY, Guinea. 11/16". 9.70. CyberAuction #491, Lot #54. Final Bid: $410.

1199. CHRISTENSEN AGATE COMPANY, Guinea. 21/32". 9.80. CyberAuction #475, Lot #58. Final Bid: $460.

1206. CHRISTENSEN AGATE COMPANY, Guinea. 9/16". 9.80. CyberAuction #400, Lot #12. Final Bid: $400.

1203. CHRISTENSEN AGATE COMPANY, Guinea. 9/16". 9.90. CyberAuction #388, Lot #59. Final Bid: $410.

1200. CHRISTENSEN AGATE COMPANY, Guinea. 19/32". 9.70. CyberAuction #453, Lot #60. Final Bid: $450.

1207. CHRISTENSEN AGATE COMPANY, Guinea. 19/32". 9.70. CyberAuction #414, Lot #60. Final Bid: $400.

1204. CHRISTENSEN AGATE COMPANY, Guinea. 11/16". 9.80. CyberAuction #392, Lot #61. Final Bid: $410.

1208. CHRISTENSEN AGATE COMPANY, Guinea. 11/16". 9.80. CyberAuction #440, Lot #37. Final Bid: $310.

1211. CHRISTENSEN AGATE COMPANY, Guinea. 5/8". 8.90. CyberAuction #424, Lot #60. Final Bid: $285.

1219. CHRISTENSEN AGATE COMPANY, Pastel. 11/16". 9.60. CyberAuction #504, Lot #7. Final Bid: $110.

1209. CHRISTENSEN AGATE COMPANY, Guinea. 9/16". 9.90. CyberAuction #440, Lot #59. Final Bid: $310.

1215. CHRISTENSEN AGATE COMPANY, Guinea/Cobra. 21/32". 9.70. CyberAuction #501, Lot #74. Final Bid: $430.

1222. CHRISTENSEN AGATE COMPANY, Slag. 5/8". 9.90. CyberAuction #433, Lot #53. Final Bid: $140.

1210. CHRISTENSEN AGATE COMPANY, Guinea. 9/16". 9.60. CyberAuction #502, Lot #74. Final Bid: $310.

1216. CHRISTENSEN AGATE COMPANY, Hand-gathered. 9/16". 9. CyberAuction #483, Lot #55. Final Bid: $460.

1273. CHRISTENSEN AGATE COMPANY, Striped opaque. 19/32". 9.90. CyberAuction #400, Lot #55. Final Bid: $410.

1302. CHRISTENSEN AGATE COMPANY, Striped transparent. 19/32". 9.50. CyberAuction #373, Lot #54. Final Bid: $210.

1312. CHRISTENSEN AGATE COMPANY, Swirl. 23/32". 9.80. CyberAuction #500, Lot #48. Final Bid: $950.

1313. CHRISTENSEN AGATE COMPANY, Swirl. 11/16". 9.90. CyberAuction #381, Lot #60. Final Bid: $460.

1314. CHRISTENSEN AGATE COMPANY, Swirl. 5/8". 9.90. CyberAuction #369, Lot #51. Final Bid: $310.

1315. CHRISTENSEN AGATE COMPANY, Swirl. 5/8". 9.90. CyberAuction #396, Lot #55. Final Bid: $270.

1446. CONTEMPORARY HANDMADE, Andrew Davis. 1-1/2". 9.90. CyberAuction #344, Lot #49. Final Bid: $27.

1450. CONTEMPORARY HANDMADE, Beetem Design Glassworks. 1-5/8". 9.90. CyberAuction #348, Lot #48. Final Bid: $170.

1460. CONTEMPORARY HANDMADE, Beetem Design Glassworks. 1-7/16". 9.90. CyberAuction #501, Lot #45. Final Bid: $70.

1503. CONTEMPORARY HANDMADE, Bob Hamon. 29/32". 9.90. CyberAuction #408, Lot #20. Final Bid: $10.

17

1507. CONTEMPORARY HANDMADE, Bob Olsen. 25/32". 9.90. CyberAuction #337, Lot #59. Final Bid: $23.

1546. CONTEMPORARY HANDMADE, Boyd Miller/Tom Thornburgh. 1-7/8". 9.90. CyberAuction #410, Lot #55. Final Bid: $70.

1556. CONTEMPORARY HANDMADE, Bruce Breslow/ Moon Marble Company. 1-3/16". 9.90. CyberAuction #485, Lot #30. Final Bid: $15.

1513. CONTEMPORARY HANDMADE, Bob Powers. 31/32". 9.90. CyberAuction #354, Lot #10. Final Bid: $40.

1547. CONTEMPORARY HANDMADE, Boyer Glass. 1-7/8". 9.90. CyberAuction #356, Lot #31. Final Bid: $160.

1562. CONTEMPORARY HANDMADE, California Glass Studios. 1-7/8". 9.90. CyberAuction #422, Lot #58. Final Bid: $65.

1522. CONTEMPORARY HANDMADE, Bob "Doc" Powers. 31/32". 9.90. CyberAuction #481, Lot #15. Final Bid: $15.

1552. CONTEMPORARY HANDMADE, Brian Lonsway. 2-5/8". 9.90. CyberAuction #385, Lot #35. Final Bid: $285.

1578. CONTEMPORARY HANDMADE, Chatham Glass. 1-5/8". 9.90. CyberAuction #491, Lot #11. Final Bid: $32.

1531. CONTEMPORARY HANDMADE, Boyd Miller. 1-5/8". 9.90. CyberAuction #443, Lot #27. Final Bid: $37.

1553. CONTEMPORARY HANDMADE, Brookside Glass. 1-5/8". 9.90. CyberAuction #367, Lot #28. Final Bid: $38.

1581. CONTEMPORARY HANDMADE, Chris Robinson. 15/16". 9.90. CyberAuction #467, Lot #13. Final Bid: $80.

1583. CONTEMPORARY HANDMADE, Chuck Pound. 1-3/8". 9.90. CyberAuction #471, Lot #28. Final Bid: $42.

1588. CONTEMPORARY HANDMADE, Crystal Myths. 1-9/16". 9.90. CyberAuction #489, Lot #57. Final Bid: $50.

1593. CONTEMPORARY HANDMADE, Cuneo Furnace/ Steve Maslach. CyberAuction #436, Lot #28. Final Bid: $32.

1610. CONTEMPORARY HANDMADE, Dale Danowski. 1-9/16". 9.90. CyberAuction #360, Lot #33. Final Bid: $33.

1624. CONTEMPORARY HANDMADE, David Grant Maul. 1-5/8". 9.90. CyberAuction #505, Lot #30. Final Bid: $40.

1627. CONTEMPORARY HANDMADE, Davis Handmade Marbles. 1-1/2". 9.90. CyberAuction #414, Lot #32. Final Bid: $33.

1669. CONTEMPORARY HANDMADE, Douglas Ferguson. 1-3/16". 9.90. CyberAuction #463, Lot #42. Final Bid: $47.

1694. CONTEMPORARY HANDMADE, Francis Coupal. 1-15/16". 9.90. CyberAuction #418, Lot #29. Final Bid: $85.

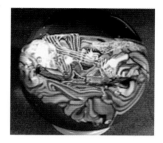

1676. CONTEMPORARY HANDMADE, Douglas Sweet/ Karuna Glass. 1-7/8". 9.90. CyberAuction #369, Lot #36. Final Bid: $60.

1680. CONTEMPORARY HANDMADE, Drew Fritts. 1-7/8". 9.90. CyberAuction #495, Lot #35. Final Bid: $70.

1693. CONTEMPORARY HANDMADE, Dudley Giberson. 1-5/8". 9.90. CyberAuction #501, Lot #7. Final Bid: $45.

1709. CONTEMPORARY HANDMADE, Fritz Glass. 1-5/8". 9.90. CyberAuction #351, Lot #46. Final Bid: $130.

1824. CONTEMPORARY HANDMADE, Greg Hoglin. 1-1/16". 9.90. CyberAuction #438, Lot #33. Final Bid: $27.

1861. CONTEMPORARY HANDMADE, Jim Davis (IN). 1-13/16". 9.90. CyberAuction #355, Lot #34. Final Bid: $55.

1799. CONTEMPORARY HANDMADE, Fulton-Parker Glass. 1-7/8". 9.90. CyberAuction #480, Lot #38. Final Bid: $40.

1827. CONTEMPORARY HANDMADE, Hart's of Glass. 1-9/16". 9.90. CyberAuction #473, Lot #24. Final Bid: $32.

1865. CONTEMPORARY HANDMADE, Joe St. Clair. 1-15/16". 8.90. CyberAuction #448, Lot #29. Final Bid: $55.

1808. CONTEMPORARY HANDMADE, Gibson Glass. 1-7/8". 9.90. CyberAuction #506, Lot #23. Final Bid: $45.

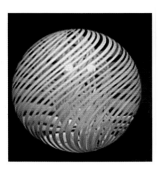

1830. CONTEMPORARY HANDMADE, J. Fine Glass. 1-5/16". 9.90. CyberAuction #462, Lot #8. Final Bid: $40.

1870. CONTEMPORARY HANDMADE, John Hamon Miller. 2-1/4". 9.90. CyberAuction #374, Lot #59. Final Bid: $38.

1899. CONTEMPORARY
HANDMADE, John Talmadge.
1-1/2". 9.90. CyberAuction
#366, Lot #24. Final Bid: $42.

1900. CONTEMPORARY
HANDMADE, Josh Simpson.
1-15/16". 9.90. CyberAuction
#388, Lot #57. Final Bid: $140.

1915. CONTEMPORARY
HANDMADE, Karen Federici.
31/32". 9.90. CyberAuction
#380, Lot #55. Final Bid: $39.

1917. CONTEMPORARY
HANDMADE, Lundberg
Studios. 2-3/8". 9.90.
CyberAuction #369, Lot #60.
Final Bid: $375.

1918. CONTEMPORARY
HANDMADE, Lundberg
Studios. 4". 9.90. CyberAuction
#348, Lot #59. Final Bid:
$300.

1919. CONTEMPORARY
HANDMADE, Matthews Art
Glass. 2-1/8". 9.90.
CyberAuction #459, Lot #60.
Final Bid: $500.

1920. CONTEMPORARY
HANDMADE, Matthews Art
Glass. 2-1/2". 9.90.
CyberAuction #508, Lot #75.
Final Bid: $460.

1921. CONTEMPORARY
HANDMADE, Matthews Art
Glass. 3". 9.90. CyberAuction
#440, Lot #60. Final Bid:
$410.

1922. CONTEMPORARY
HANDMADE, Matthews Art
Glass. 1-9/16". 9.90.
CyberAuction #504, Lot #72.
Final Bid: $330.

1923. CONTEMPORARY HANDMADE, Matthews Art Glass. 1-3/4". 9.80. CyberAuction #450, Lot #41. Final Bid: $260.

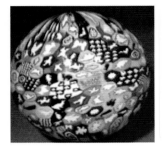

1990. CONTEMPORARY HANDMADE, Noble Effort. 2-5/16". 9.90. CyberAuction #491, Lot #59. Final Bid: $625.

1998. CONTEMPORARY HANDMADE, Rolf and Genie Wald. 1-7/16". 9.90. CyberAuction #376, Lot #18. Final Bid: $65.

1924. CONTEMPORARY HANDMADE, Matthews Art Glass. 3". 9.90. CyberAuction #455, Lot #59. Final Bid: $230.

1991. CONTEMPORARY HANDMADE, Phil McGlothlin. 1-1/16". 9.90. CyberAuction #371, Lot #32. Final Bid: $35.

2022. CONTEMPORARY HANDMADE, Salazar Art Glass. 1-7/16". 9.90. CyberAuction #356, Lot #58. Final Bid: $270.

1943. CONTEMPORARY HANDMADE, Monty Fritts. 27/32". 9.90. CyberAuction #360, Lot #2. Final Bid: $22.

1995. CONTEMPORARY HANDMADE, Richard Dinardo. 2-1/2". 9.90. CyberAuction #400, Lot #31. Final Bid: $140.

2065. CONTEMPORARY HANDMADE, Sam Hogue. 1-3/4". 9.90. CyberAuction #410, Lot #35. Final Bid: $37.

1985. CONTEMPORARY HANDMADE, Nadine MacDonald. 1-1/8". 9.90. CyberAuction #462, Lot #26. Final Bid: $25.

1996. CONTEMPORARY HANDMADE, Robert Brown. 7/8". 9.90. CyberAuction #354, Lot #6. Final Bid: $19.

2067. CONTEMPORARY HANDMADE, Sara Creekmore. 1-13/16". 9.90. CyberAuction #473, Lot #59. Final Bid: $32.

2068. CONTEMPORARY HANDMADE, Scott Patrick. 7/8". 9.90. CyberAuction #400, Lot #38. Final Bid: $110.

2132. CONTEMPORARY HANDMADE, William Murray. 1-5/8". 9.90. CyberAuction #372, Lot #35. Final Bid: $42.

2159. END-OF-DAY, Cloud. 1-1/4". 9.90. CyberAuction #505, Lot #75. Final Bid: $1,150.

2109. CONTEMPORARY HANDMADE, Shane Caswell. 1-5/16". 9.90. CyberAuction #377, Lot #58. Final Bid: $50.

2152. END-OF-DAY, Banded. 27/32". 8.60. CyberAuction #502, Lot #57. Final Bid: $40.

2160. END-OF-DAY, Cloud. 2-1/4". 8.40. CyberAuction #353, Lot #60. Final Bid: $1,050.

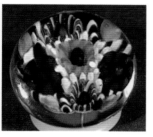

2116. CONTEMPORARY HANDMADE, David Rosenfeld. 1-5/16". 9.90. CyberAuction #504, Lot #22. Final Bid: $40.

2153. END-OF-DAY, Blizzard. ½ marble missing. CyberAuction #416, Lot #27. Final Bid: $17.

2161. END-OF-DAY, Cloud. 1-5/8". 9.00. CyberAuction #414, Lot #55. Final Bid: $585.

2123. CONTEMPORARY HANDMADE, Harry Besset. 1-9/16". 9.90. CyberAuction #363, Lot #36. Final Bid: $60.

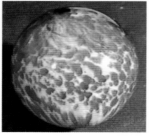

2158. END-OF-DAY, Cloud. 2-1/8". 9.70. CyberAuction #500, Lot #58. Final Bid: $1,950.

2162. END-OF-DAY, Cloud. 13/16". 9.90. CyberAuction #363, Lot #60. Final Bid: $575.

2163. END-OF-DAY, Cloud.
3/4". 9.10. CyberAuction
#500, Lot #54.
Final Bid: $500.

2166. END-OF-DAY, Cloud.
13/16". 8.90. CyberAuction
#506, Lot #49.
Final Bid: $320.

2169. END-OF-DAY, Cloud.
5/8". 9.90. CyberAuction
#366, Lot #56.
Final Bid: $240.

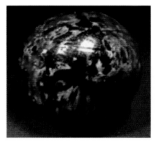

2164. END-OF-DAY, Cloud.
1-7/8". 8.10. CyberAuction
#455, Lot #42.
Final Bid: $485.

2167. END-OF-DAY, Cloud.
1-3/4". 7.90. CyberAuction
#388, Lot #35.
Final Bid: $310.

2188. END-OF-DAY, Coreless.
CyberAuction #396, Lot #29.
Final Bid: $165.

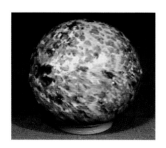

2165. END-OF-DAY, Cloud.
1-5/8". 7.70. CyberAuction
#414, Lot #25.
Final Bid: $385.

2168. END-OF-DAY, Cloud.
13/16". 8.90. CyberAuction
#495, Lot #56. Final Bid: $285.

2199. END-OF-DAY, Joseph
Coat. 19/32". 9.70.
CyberAuction #500, Lot #18.
Final Bid: $235.

2201. END-OF-DAY, Onion-skin Mist. 27/32". 9.00. CyberAuction #357, Lot #48. Final Bid: $260.

2203. END-OF-DAY, Onionskin. 1-5/8". 9.90. CyberAuction #483, Lot #60. Final Bid: $4,050.

2204. END-OF-DAY, Onionskin. 11/16". 9.90. CyberAuction #462, Lot #54. Final Bid: $525.

2205. END-OF-DAY, Onionskin. 25/32". 9.70. CyberAuction #467, Lot #54. Final Bid: $510.

2206. END-OF-DAY, Onionskin. 1-5/16". 9.80. CyberAuction #330, Lot #48. Final Bid: $450.

2207. END-OF-DAY, Onionskin. 1-13/16". 8.70. CyberAuction #501, Lot #75. Final Bid: $335.

2208. END-OF-DAY, Onion-skin. 25/32". 9.60. CyberAuction #508, Lot #65. Final Bid: $300.

2209. END-OF-DAY, Onionskin. 5/8". 9.70. CyberAuction #483, Lot #57. Final Bid: $290.

2210. END-OF-DAY, Onionskin. 1-5/8". Buffed. CyberAuction #397, Lot #58. Final Bid: $285.

2211. END-OF-DAY, Onionskin. 1-3/8". 9.20. CyberAuction #504, Lot #66. Final Bid: $260.

2214. END-OF-DAY, Onionskin. 1". 8.90. CyberAuction #357, Lot #52. Final Bid: $230.

2212. END-OF-DAY, Onionskin. 7/8". 9.50. CyberAuction #467, Lot #56. Final Bid: $235.

2559. END-OF-DAY, Panelled cloud. 3/4". 8.90. CyberAuction #348, Lot #1. Final Bid: $185.

2213. END-OF-DAY, Onionskin. 29/32". 9.80. CyberAuction #495, Lot #54. Final Bid: $235.

2560. END-OF-DAY, Panelled onionskin. 1-11/16". 9.10. CyberAuction #471, Lot #60. Final Bid: $1,775.

2561. END-OF-DAY, Panelled onionskin. 1-9/16". 9.90. CyberAuction #360, Lot #60. Final Bid: $1,200.

2562. END-OF-DAY, Panelled onionskin. 1-11/16". 9.10. CyberAuction #400, Lot #59. Final Bid: $700.

2563. END-OF-DAY, Panelled onionskin. 1-1/2". 8.70. CyberAuction #491, Lot #60. Final Bid: $650.

2564. END-OF-DAY, Panelled onionskin. 1-3/8". 8.90. CyberAuction #483, Lot #33. Final Bid: $435.

2567. END-OF-DAY, Panelled onionskin. 13/16". 9.80. CyberAuction #462, Lot #32. Final Bid: $335.

2570. END-OF-DAY, Panelled onionskin. 7/8". 9.20. CyberAuction #508, Lot #73. Final Bid: $310.

2565. END-OF-DAY, Panelled onionskin. 1-7/16". 9.10. CyberAuction #385, Lot #60. Final Bid: $400.

2568. END-OF-DAY, Panelled onionskin. 1-7/16". 9.20. CyberAuction #495, Lot #58. Final Bid: $335.

2571. END-OF-DAY, Panelled onionskin. 13/16". 9.80. CyberAuction #507, Lot #58. Final Bid: $300.

2566. END-OF-DAY, Panelled onionskin. 2-5/16". 8.60. CyberAuction #508, Lot #38. Final Bid: $360.

2569. END-OF-DAY, Panelled onionskin. 23/32". 9.90. CyberAuction #467, Lot #17. Final Bid: $310.

2572. END-OF-DAY, Panelled onionskin. 1-5/16". 9.70. CyberAuction #487, Lot #59. Final Bid: $290.

2573. END-OF-DAY, Panelled onionskin. 13/16". 9.80. CyberAuction #498, Lot #67. Final Bid: $285.

2576. END-OF-DAY, Panelled onionskin. 25/32". 9.00. CyberAuction #467, Lot #34. Final Bid: $260.

2900. END-OF-DAY, Ribbon onionskin. 21/32". 9.20. CyberAuction #491, Lot #50. Final Bid: $250.

2574. END-OF-DAY, Panelled onionskin. 1-9/16". 8.60. CyberAuction #498, Lot #72. Final Bid: $270.

2577. END-OF-DAY, Panelled onionskin. 1-5/8". Polished. CyberAuction #345, Lot #57. Final Bid: $235.

2901. END-OF-DAY, Ribbon onionskin. 25/32". 9.10. CyberAuction #498, Lot #69. Final Bid: $230.

2575. END-OF-DAY, Panelled onionskin. 13/16". 8.90. CyberAuction #360, Lot #52. Final Bid: $260.

2578. END-OF-DAY, Panelled onionskin. 1-5/16". 8.90. CyberAuction #352, Lot #59. Final Bid: $230.

2904. LUTZ, Banded. 11/16". 9.90. CyberAuction #336, Lot #57. Final Bid: $430.

2905. LUTZ, Banded. 1-3/16".
9.00. CyberAuction #487, Lot
#57. Final Bid: $410.

2966. LUTZ, END-OF-DAY
onionskin. 1-13/16". 8.90.
CyberAuction #500, Lot #60.
Final Bid: $3,275.

2969. LUTZ, END-OF-DAY
onionskin. 11/16". 9.40.
CyberAuction #357, Lot #60.
Final Bid: $360.

2906. LUTZ, Banded. 19/32".
9.70. CyberAuction #330, Lot
#60. Final Bid: $325.

2967. LUTZ, END-OF-DAY
onionskin. 7/8". 9.80.
CyberAuction #430, Lot #2.
Final Bid: $470.

2970. LUTZ, END-OF-DAY
onionskin. 21/32". 9.90.
CyberAuction #342, Lot #57.
Final Bid: $265.

2907. LUTZ, Banded. 7/8".
Buffed. CyberAuction #490,
Lot #43. Final Bid: $260.

2968. LUTZ, END-OF-DAY
onionskin. 7/8". 9.80.
CyberAuction #398, Lot #36.
Final Bid: $455.

2971. LUTZ, END-OF-DAY
onionskin. 3/4". 9.00.
CyberAuction #495, Lot #38.
Final Bid: $235.

3012. LUTZ, Indian. 13/16". 9.70.
CyberAuction #479, Lot #60.
Final Bid: $1,500.

3024. LUTZ, Ribbon. 11/16
9.00. CyberAuction #466,
#44. Final Bid: $335.

3019. LUTZ, Mist. 3/4". Buffed.
CyberAuction #405, Lot #56.
Final Bid: $65.

3013. LUTZ, Mist. 25/32".
9.00. CyberAuction #410, Lot
#59. Final Bid: $410.

3020. LUTZ, Ribbon core.
11/16". 9.70. CyberAuction
#414, Lot #59. Final Bid: $525.

3025. LUTZ, Ribbon. 19/32
9.00. CyberAuction #385,
#58. Final Bid: $310.

3014. LUTZ, Mist. 21/32".
8.50. CyberAuction #413, Lot
#51. Final Bid: $270.

3022. LUTZ, Ribbon. 11/16".
9.00. CyberAuction #406, Lot
#60. Final Bid: $335.

3026. LUTZ, Ribbon. 19/32
9.00. CyberAuction #345,
#61. Final Bid: $260.

3027. LUTZ, Ribbon. 1-3/16".
7.90. CyberAuction #504, Lot
#55. Final Bid: $260.

3041. M.F. CHRISTENSEN &
SON COMPANY, Brick. 29/32".
8.80. CyberAuction #330, Lot
#55. Final Bid: $600.

3044. M.F. CHRISTENSEN &
SON COMPANY, Brick. 27/32".
9.80. CyberAuction #336, Lot
#58. Final Bid: $260.

3028. LUTZ, Ribbon. 19/32".
8.90. CyberAuction #348, Lot
#60. Final Bid: $240.

3042. M.F. CHRISTENSEN &
SON COMPANY, Brick. 11/16".
9.90. CyberAuction #450, Lot
#49. Final Bid: $470.

3045. M.F. CHRISTENSEN &
SON COMPANY, Brick. 21/32".
9.70. CyberAuction #459, Lot
#50. Final Bid: $250.

3029. LUTZ, Ribbon. 9/16".
9.00. CyberAuction #375, Lot
#45. Final Bid: $235.

3043. M.F. CHRISTENSEN &
SON COMPANY, Brick. 27/32".
9.90. CyberAuction #507, Lot
#60. Final Bid: $440.

3101. M.F. CHRISTENSEN &
SON COMPANY, Opaque. 5/8".
9.90. CyberAuction #363, Lot
#57. Final Bid: $335.

3106. M.F. CHRISTENSEN & SON COMPANY, Oxblood slag. 5/8". 9.70. CyberAuction #500, Lot #11. Final Bid: $310.

3154. MARBLE KING, INC., Berry Pink. 1". 8.90. CyberAuction #373, Lot #46. Final Bid: $140.

3176. MARBLE KING, INC., Catseye. 29/32". 8.90. CyberAuction #381, Lot #11. Final Bid: $23.

3107. M.F. CHRISTENSEN & SON COMPANY, Oxblood slag. 21/32". 9.90. CyberAuction #504, Lot #46. Final Bid: $290.

3162. MARBLE KING, INC., Blended. 9/16". 9.90. CyberAuction #359, Lot #50. Final Bid: $32.

3188. MARBLE KING, INC., Cub Scout. 19/32". 9.90. CyberAuction #334, Lot #51. Final Bid: $20.

3109. M.F. CHRISTENSEN & SON COMPANY, Slag. 1-7/8". 8.50. CyberAuction #491, Lot #58. Final Bid: $725.

3166. MARBLE KING, INC., Bumblebee. 15/16". 9.40. CyberAuction #432, Lot #10. Final Bid: $24.

3199. MARBLE KING, INC., Dragonfly. 19/32". 9.90. CyberAuction #418, Lot #52. Final Bid: $100.

3201. MARBLE KING, INC., Girl Scout. 5/8". 9.70. CyberAuction #348, Lot #28. Final Bid: $14.

3222. MARBLE KING, INC., Premium. CyberAuction #497, Lot #36. Final Bid: $3.

3250. MASTER MARBLE/ GLASS COMPANY, Catseye. 5/8". 8.90. CyberAuction #351, Lot #16. Final Bid: $6.

3203. MARBLE KING, INC., Opaque. 19/32". 9.90. CyberAuction #340, Lot #45. Final Bid: $3.

3223. MARBLE KING, INC., Rainbow. 19/32". 9.70. CyberAuction #428, Lot #37. Final Bid: $24.

3251. MASTER MARBLE/GLASS COMPANY, Comet. 5/8". 9.90. CyberAuction #357, Lot #50. Final Bid: $19.

3207. MARBLE KING, INC., Original package. CyberAuction #341, Lot #31. Final Bid: $26.

3235. MARBLE KING, INC., Tiger. 3/4". 9.90. CyberAuction #348, Lot #54. Final Bid: $90.

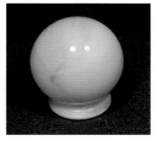

3253. MASTER MARBLE/GLASS COMPANY, Moonie. 23/32". 9.90. CyberAuction #334, Lot #23. Final Bid: $29.

33

3254. MASTER MARBLE/GLASS COMPANY, Original box. CyberAuction #405, Lot #60. Final Bid: $150.

3262. MASTER MARBLE/GLASS COMPANY, Patch. 3/4". 8.90. CyberAuction #420, Lot #9. Final Bid: $3.

3300. MISCELLANEOUS, Agate. 15/16". 9.90. CyberAuction #388, Lot #60. Final Bid: $875.

3304. MISCELLANEOUS, Agate. 1-1/4". 9.00. CyberAuction #385, Lot #37. Final Bid: $360.

3263. MASTER MARBLE/GLASS COMPANY, Sunburst. 23/32". 9.80. CyberAuction #413, Lot #56. Final Bid: $33.

3301. MISCELLANEOUS, Agate. 3/4". 9.90. CyberAuction #400, Lot #54. Final Bid: $410.

3306. MISCELLANEOUS, Agate. 7/8". 9.90. CyberAuction #403, Lot #46. Final Bid: $350.

3303. MISCELLANEO
Agate. 29/32". 9.00.
CyberAuction #385, |
#44. Final Bid: $385.

3293. MASTER MARBLE/GLASS COMPANY, Tigereye. 5/8". 9.30. CyberAuction #458, Lot #57. Final Bid: $32.

3307. MISCELLANEOUS, Agate. 23/32". 8.90. CyberAuction #403, Lot #57. Final Bid: $350.

3310. MISCELLANEOUS, Agate. 7/8". 9.90. CyberAuction #339, Lot #56. Final Bid: $330.

3313. MISCELLANEOUS, Agate. 13/16". 9.60. CyberAuction #388, Lot #14. Final Bid: $310.

3308. MISCELLANEOUS, Agate. 13/16". 9.60. CyberAuction #410, Lot #52. Final Bid: $350.

3311. MISCELLANEOUS, Agate. 17/32". 9.90. CyberAuction #392, Lot #53. Final Bid: $330.

3314. MISCELLANEOUS, Agate. 23/32". 9.90. CyberAuction #330, Lot #53. Final Bid: $285.

3309. MISCELLANEOUS, Agate. 9/16". 9.90. CyberAuction #486, Lot #43. Final Bid: $335.

3312. MISCELLANEOUS, Agate. 3/4". 9.90. CyberAuction #353, Lot #59. Final Bid: $325.

3315. MISCELLANEOUS, Agate. 13/16". 9.60. CyberAuction #426, Lot #54. Final Bid: $285.

3316. MISCELLANEOUS, Agate. 23/32". 9.90. CyberAuction #425, Lot #54. Final Bid: $280.

3318. MISCELLANEOUS, Agate. 1-7/16". 9.90. CyberAuction #400, Lot #47. Final Bid: $250.

3489. MISCELLANEOUS, Bottle stopper. CyberAuction #418, Lot #60. Final Bid: $230.

3517. MISCELLANEOUS, Cigarette card. CyberAuction #356, Lot #33. Final Bid: $65.

3484. MISCELLANEOUS, Ballot Box. CyberAuction #394, Lot #14. Final Bid: $33.

3488. MISCELLANEOUS, Bottle stopper. CyberAuction #425, Lot #59. Final Bid: $370.

3491. MISCELLANEOUS, Character marble. 1". 9.90. CyberAuction #354, Lot #32. Final Bid: $27.

3520. MISCELLANEOUS, Fisher Jewel Tray. 3-1/4". 9.50. CyberAuction #392, Lot #32. Final Bid: $34.

3529. MISCELLANEOUS, Fortune telling. 1-1/16". 9.70. CyberAuction #482, Lot #39. Final Bid: $25.

3559. MISCELLANEOUS,
Golden rule marble.
CyberAuction #388, Lot #33.
Final Bid: $17.

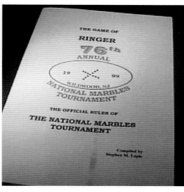

3633. MISCELLANEOUS, Rule book.
CyberAuction #354, Lot #35.
Final Bid: $12.

3656. MISCELLANEOUS,
Tournament medal.
CyberAuction #354, Lot #59.
Final Bid: $285.

3657. MISCELLANEOUS,
Tournament medal.
CyberAuction #379, Lot #45.
Final Bid: $235.

3577. MISCELLANEOUS,
Marble pouch. CyberAuction
#373, Lot #26. Final Bid: $29.

3635. MISCELLANEOUS,
Postcard. CyberAuction
#354, Lot #34.
Final Bid: $6.

3589. MISCELLANEOUS,
Marble shooter. CyberAuction
#477, Lot #35. Final Bid: $17.

3655. MISCELLANEOUS,
Tournament medal.
CyberAuction #333, Lot #60.
Final Bid: $285.

3658. MISCELLANEOUS,
Tournament medal.
CyberAuction #406, Lot #56.
Final Bid: $235.

3659. MISCELLANEOUS, Tournament medal. CyberAuction #474, Lot #45. Final Bid: $235.

3685. NON-GLASS HAND-MADE, Carpet Ball. 3-1/4". 9.90. CyberAuction #414, Lot #51. Final Bid: $460.

3694. NON-GLASS HAND-MADE, China. 1-13/16". 8.70. CyberAuction #356, Lot #60. Final Bid: $700.

3670. NON-GLASS HAND-MADE, Bakelite. 27/32". 9.90. CyberAuction #496, Lot #6. Final Bid: $17.

3686. MISCELLANEOUS, Carpet Ball. 3-1/4". 8.90. CyberAuction #400, Lot #35. Final Bid: $255.

3695. NON-GLASS HAND-MADE, China. 1-3/4". 8.60. CyberAuction #366, Lot #60. Final Bid: $675.

3671. NON-GLASS HAND-MADE, Bennington. 13/16". 9.90. CyberAuction #368, Lot #54. Final Bid: $100.

3693. NON-GLASS HAND-MADE, China. 1-11/16". 8.90. CyberAuction #493, Lot #60. Final Bid: $875.

3778. NON-GLASS HAND-MADE, Clay. 2-1/8". 9.90. CyberAuction #387, Lot #31. Final Bid: $44.

3779. NON-GLASS HAND-MADE, Crockery. 1-1/16". 9.70. CyberAuction #462, Lot #55. Final Bid: $125.

3800. NON-GLASS HANDMADE, Original box. CyberAuction #498, Lot #30. Final Bid: $260.

3796. NON-GLASS HAND-MADE, Limestone. 11/16". 9.50. CyberAuction #487, Lot #34. Final Bid: $17.

3801. NON-GLASS HAND-MADE, Pottery. 1-9/16". 9.90. CyberAuction #503, Lot #69. Final Bid: $321.

3803. NON-GLASS HAND-MADE, Stone. 13/16". 9.50. CyberAuction #359, Lot #8. Final Bid: $20.

3797. NON-GLASS HAND-MADE, Mocha ware. 3/4". 9.50. CyberAuction #426, Lot #58. Final Bid: $135.

3802. NON-GLASS HAND-MADE, Steelie. 1". 9.90. CyberAuction #497, Lot #43. Final Bid: $44.

3806. NON-GLASS HAND-MADE, Stoneware. 1". 9.90. CyberAuction #381, Lot #57. Final Bid: $55.

3813. OTHER HANDMADE, Banded Opaque. 25/32". 9.70. CyberAuction #363, Lot #56. Final Bid: $310.

3859. OTHER HANDMADE,
Cased clambroth. 11/16". 8.40.
CyberAuction #375, Lot #44.
Final Bid: $80.

3860. OTHER HANDMADE,
Clambroth. 13/16". 9.90.
CyberAuction #356, Lot #59.
Final Bid: $650.

3861. OTHER HANDMADE,
Clambroth. 25/32". 9.60.
CyberAuction #333, Lot #56.
Final Bid: $300.

3862. OTHER HANDMADE,
Clambroth. 3/4". 9.70.
CyberAuction #479, Lot #56.
Final Bid: $275.

3863. OTHER HANDMADE,
Clambroth. 23/32". 9.20.
CyberAuction #500, Lot #45.
Final Bid: $240.

3890. OTHER HANDMADE,
Clearie. 11/16". 7.90.
CyberAuction #375, Lot #16.
Final Bid: $55.

3920. OTHER HANDMADE,
Indian. 23/32". 9.70.
CyberAuction #503, Lot #22.
Final Bid: $435.

3921. OTHER HANDMADE,
Indian. 11/16". 9.90.
CyberAuction #503, Lot #64.
Final Bid: $400.

3922. OTHER HANDMADE,
Indian. 11/16". 9.50.
CyberAuction #502, Lot #75.
Final Bid: $340.

3923. OTHER HANDMADE,
Indian. 11/16". 9.70.
CyberAuction #507, Lot #1.
Final Bid: $310.

3926. OTHER HANDMADE,
Indian. 11/16". 9.50.
CyberAuction #507, Lot #48.
Final Bid: $285.

3929. OTHER HANDMADE,
Indian. 13/16". 9.70.
CyberAuction #450, Lot #47.
Final Bid: $255.

3924. OTHER HANDMADE,
Indian. 11/16". 9.70.
CyberAuction #507, Lot #59.
Final Bid: $310.

3927. OTHER HANDMADE,
Indian. 13/16". 9.70.
CyberAuction #486, Lot #32.
Final Bid: $270.

3930. OTHER HANDMADE,
Indian. 9/16". 9.90.
CyberAuction #366, Lot #50.
Final Bid: $240.

3925. OTHER HANDMADE,
Indian. 11/16". 9.80.
CyberAuction #505, Lot #73.
Final Bid: $300.

3928. OTHER HANDMADE,
Indian. 11/16". 9.90.
CyberAuction #504, Lot #68.
Final Bid: $260.

4036. OTHER HANDMADE,
Mica. 31/32". 9.50.
CyberAuction #373, Lot #60.
Final Bid: $2,250.

4037. OTHER HANDMADE,
Mica. 13/16". 8.60.
CyberAuction #410, Lot #60.
Final Bid: $985.

4041. OTHER HANDMADE,
Mica. 31/32". 8.70.
CyberAuction #403, Lot #58.
Final Bid: $485.

4044. OTHER HANDMADE,
Mica. 1-3/8". Polished.
CyberAuction #425, Lot #37.
Final Bid: $290.

4039. OTHER HANDMADE,
Mica. 15/32". 9.90.
CyberAuction #357, Lot #42.
Final Bid: $525.

4042. OTHER HANDMADE,
Mica. 1-9/16". 8.10.
CyberAuction #487, Lot #54.
Final Bid: $410.

4045. OTHER HANDMADE,
Mica. 25/32". 9.70.
CyberAuction #501, Lot #68.
Final Bid: $240.

4040. OTHER HANDMADE,
Mica. 1-9/16". 8.00.
CyberAuction #498, Lot #75.
Final Bid: $500.

4043. OTHER HANDMADE,
Mica. 21/32". 9.90.
CyberAuction #357, Lot #15.
Final Bid: $350.

4360. OTHER HANDMADE,
Mist. 1-3/16". 9.60.
CyberAuction #400, Lot #52.
Final Bid: $385.

4361. OTHER HANDMADE, Mist. 1-3/16". 9.90. CyberAuction #487, Lot #60. Final Bid: $300.

4393. OTHER HANDMADE, Opaque. 7/8". 8.90. CyberAuction #347, Lot #59. Final Bid: $140.

4430. OTHER HANDMADE, Paper mache. 7/8". 9.20. CyberAuction #366, Lot #55. Final Bid: $350.

4362. OTHER HANDMADE, Mist. 1-3/16". 9.00. CyberAuction #403, Lot #56. Final Bid: $235.

4425. NON-GLASS HAND-MADE, Opaque. 9/16". 9.80. CyberAuction #439, Lot #51. Final Bid: $7.

4432. OTHER HANDMADE, Paperweight. 1-3/16". 9.60. CyberAuction #504, Lot #75. Final Bid: $1,500.

4392. OTHER HANDMADE, Moonie. 9/16". 9.00. CyberAuction #429, Lot #1. Final Bid: $47.

4429. OTHER HANDMADE, Paper mache. 3/4". 9.70. CyberAuction #339, Lot #59. Final Bid: $365.

4433. OTHER HANDMADE, Slag. 3/4". 9.50. CyberAuction #479, Lot #52. Final Bid: $150.

4446. OTHER HANDMADE, Submarine. 25/32". 9.00. CyberAuction #340, Lot #56. Final Bid: $550.

4479. OTHER HANDMADE, Aventurine. 5/8". 8.60. CyberAuction #372, Lot #39. Final Bid: $6.

4548. OTHER MACHINE MADE, Sparkler. 3/4". 9.50. CyberAuction #418, Lot #12. Final Bid: $44.

4458. OTHER MACHINE MADE, Alley Agate. 3/4". 9.90. CyberAuction #357, Lot #27. Final Bid: $23.

4483. OTHER MACHINE MADE, Cairo Novelty. 21/32". 9.30. CyberAuction #449, Lot #38. Final Bid: $13.

4552. OTHER MACHINE MADE, Foreign sparkler. 19/32". 8.70. CyberAuction #351, Lot #43. Final Bid: $14.

4460. OTHER MACHINE MADE, Aventurine. 21/32". 9.90. CyberAuction #333, Lot #12. Final Bid: $35.

4545. OTHER MACHINE MADE, Czechoslovakian. 17/32". 8.90. CyberAuction #433, Lot #55. Final Bid: $175.

4564. OTHER MACHINE MADE, German. 27/32". 9.20. CyberAuction #401, Lot #55. Final Bid: $28.

4591. OTHER MACHINE MADE, Heaton Agate Company. CyberAuction #398, Lot #23. Final Bid: $23.

4608. OTHER MACHINE MADE, Original bag. CyberAuction #339, Lot #31. Final Bid: $12.

4643. OTHER MACHINE MADE, Vacor de Mexico. 1-1/16". 8.90. CyberAuction #358, Lot #1. Final Bid: $9.

4595. OTHER MACHINE MADE, Metallic. 21/32". 9.90. CyberAuction #330, Lot #39. Final Bid: $100.

4621. OTHER MACHINE MADE, Oxblood. 5/8". 9.90. CyberAuction #470, Lot #12. Final Bid: $27.

4644. OTHER MACHINE MADE, Wire Pull. 29/32". 9.70. CyberAuction #346, Lot #40. Final Bid: $12.

4600. OTHER MACHINE MADE, Original box. CyberAuction #433, Lot #29. Final Bid: $110.

4624. OTHER MACHINE MADE, Swirl. 5/8". 9.90. CyberAuction #373, Lot #10. Final Bid: $65.

4653. PELTIER GLASS COMPANY, Banana. 9/16". 9.90. CyberAuction #365, Lot #48. Final Bid: $65.

4655. PELTIER GLASS COMPANY, Bloodie. 3/4". 9.60. CyberAuction #444, Lot #5. Final Bid: $55.

4662. PELTIER GLASS COMPANY, Blue Zebra. 21/32". 9.90. CyberAuction #500, Lot #26. Final Bid: $46.

4675. PELTIER GLASS COMPANY, Chocolate Cow. 5/8". 8.30. CyberAuction #347, Lot #22. Final Bid: $70.

4660. PELTIER GLASS COMPANY, Blue Galaxy. 21/32". 8.60. CyberAuction #504, Lot #74. Final Bid: $950.

4663. PELTIER GLASS COMPANY, Bumblebee. 5/8". 9.90. CyberAuction #396, Lot #53. Final Bid: $130.

4676. PELTIER GLASS COMPANY, Christmas Tree. 23/32". 9.80. CyberAuction #366, Lot #59. Final Bid: $270.

4661. PELTIER GLASS COMPANY, Blue Galaxy. 21/32". 9.00. CyberAuction #475, Lot #60. Final Bid: $725.

4673. PELTIER GLASS COMPANY, Champion Jr. 19/32". 9.90. CyberAuction #421, Lot #4. Final Bid: $23.

4703. PELTIER GLASS COMPANY, Clear Rainbo. 19/32". 9.00. CyberAuction #339, Lot #13. Final Bid: $60.

4715. PELTIER GLASS COMPANY, Flaming Dragon. 21/32". 9.70. CyberAuction #330, Lot #6. Final Bid: $110.

4720. PELTIER GLASS COMPANY, Graycoat. 23/32". 9.90. CyberAuction #381, Lot #58. Final Bid: $430.

4751. PELTIER GLASS COMPANY, Liberty/Rebel hybrid. 23/32". 8.90. CyberAuction #500, Lot #53. Final Bid: $325.

4716. PELTIER GLASS COMPANY, Golden Rebel. 19/32". 8.70. CyberAuction #498, Lot #71. Final Bid: $525.

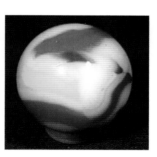

4721. PELTIER GLASS COMPANY, Ketchup and Mustard. 29/32". 8.80. CyberAuction #373, Lot #56. Final Bid: $420.

4752. PELTIER GLASS COMPANY, Miller swirl. 23/32". 9.20. CyberAuction #425, Lot #18. Final Bid: $180.

4717. PELTIER GLASS COMPANY, Golden Rebel. 19/32". 8.90. CyberAuction #377, Lot #56. Final Bid: $370.

4734. PELTIER GLASS COMPANY, Liberty. 19/32". 9.90. CyberAuction #355, Lot #52. Final Bid: $75.

4754. PELTIER GLASS COMPANY, Multicolor. 5/8". 9.90. CyberAuction #342, Lot #28. Final Bid: $65.

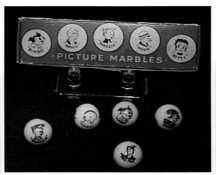

4875. PELTIER GLASS COMPANY, Original box. CyberAuction #425, Lot #60. Final Bid: $825.

4815. PELTIER GLASS COMPANY, National Line Rainbo. 29/32". 9.90. CyberAuction #381, Lot #51. Final Bid: $410.

4890. PELTIER GLASS COMPANY, Patch. 19/32". 9.90. CyberAuction #473, Lot #37. Final Bid: $3.

4876. PELTIER GLASS COMPANY, Original box. CyberAuction #400, Lot #60. Final Bid: $810.

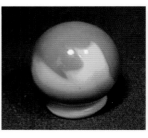

4816. PELTIER GLASS COMPANY, National Line Rainbo. 5/8". 9.60. CyberAuction #441, Lot #60. Final Bid: $370.

4891. PELTIER GLASS COMPANY, Peerless Patch. 23/32". 9.70. CyberAuction #333, Lot #14. Final Bid: $29.

4885. PELTIER GLASS COMPANY, Original package. CyberAuction #456, Lot #32. Final Bid: $15.

4818. PELTIER GLASS COMPANY, National Line Rainbo. 7/8". 8.90. CyberAuction #385, Lot #33. Final Bid: $260.

4925. PELTIER GLASS COMPANY, Picture Marble - comic. 21/32". 9.70. CyberAuction #428, Lot #60. Final Bid: $400.

4949. PELTIER GLASS
COMPANY, Picture Marble -
comic. 21/32". 9.70.
CyberAuction #508, Lot #29.
Final Bid: $100.

4930. PELTIER GLASS
COMPANY, Picture Marble -
comic. 21/32". 9.90.
CyberAuction #429, Lot #53.
Final Bid: $295.

4934. PELTIER GLASS
COMPANY, Picture Marble -
comic. 21/32". 9.70.
CyberAuction #429, Lot #11.
Final Bid: $275.

4927. PELTIER GLASS
COMPANY, Picture Marble -
comic. 21/32". 9.70.
CyberAuction #455, Lot #12.
Final Bid: $345.

4932. PELTIER GLASS
COMPANY, Picture Marble -
comic. 21/32". 9.70.
CyberAuction #438, Lot #48.
Final Bid: $285.

4935. PELTIER GLASS
COMPANY, Picture Marble -
comic. 21/32". 9.90.
CyberAuction #450, Lot #15.
Final Bid: $250.

4928. PELTIER GLASS
COMPANY, Picture marble -
comic. 21/32". 9.50.
CyberAuction #449, Lot #60.
Final Bid: $335.

4933. PELTIER GLASS
COMPANY, Picture marble -
comic. 21/32". 9.90.
CyberAuction #406, Lot #52.
Final Bid: $275.

4946. PELTIER GLASS
COMPANY, Picture Marble -
comic. 21/32". 9.90.
CyberAuction #425, Lot #50.
Final Bid: $125.

4954. PELTIER GLASS COMPANY, Picture marble - comic. 11/16". 9.70. CyberAuction #359, Lot #59. Final Bid: $80.

5027. PELTIER GLASS COMPANY, Red Zebra. 27/32". 9.90. CyberAuction #418, Lot #58. Final Bid: $260.

5061. PELTIER GLASS COMPANY, Superman. 23/32". 8.70. CyberAuction #373, Lot #52. Final Bid: $320.

4998. PELTIER GLASS COMPANY, Rainbo. 11/16". 9.70. CyberAuction #502, Lot #3. Final Bid: $38.

5032. PELTIER GLASS COMPANY, Slag. 5/8". 9.90. CyberAuction #330, Lot #26. Final Bid: $44.

5062. PELTIER GLASS COMPANY, Superman. 21/32". 9.80. CyberAuction #475, Lot #54. Final Bid: $235.

5015. PELTIER GLASS COMPANY, Rebel. 23/32". 9.70. CyberAuction #471, Lot #58. Final Bid: $300.

5059. PELTIER GLASS COMPANY, Superboy. 5/8". 8.80. CyberAuction #333, Lot #59. Final Bid: $100.

5080. PELTIER GLASS COMPANY, Tiger. 11/16". 9.70. CyberAuction #373, Lot #37. Final Bid: $80.

5090. PELTIER GLASS COMPANY, Tricolor. 21/32". 8.70. CyberAuction #381, Lot #16. Final Bid: $2.

5091. PELTIER GLASS COMPANY, Wasp. 19/32". 9.90. CyberAuction #498, Lot #61. Final Bid: $95.

5098. PELTIER GLASS COMPANY, Zebra. 5/8". 9.90. CyberAuction #368, Lot #12. Final Bid: $42.

5130. RAVENSWOOD NOVELTY WORKS, Swirl. 19/32". 9.90. CyberAuction #483, Lot #45. Final Bid: $30.

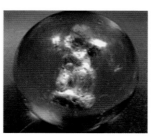

5144. SULPHIDE. 1-7/16". 8.20. CyberAuction #436, Lot #60. Final Bid: $1,700.

5145. SULPHIDE. 1-11/16". 9.00. CyberAuction #504, Lot #71. Final Bid: $1,700.

5146. SULPHIDE. 1-5/8". 9.20. CyberAuction #479, Lot #59. Final Bid: $1,650.

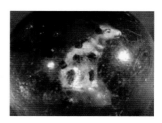

5147. SULPHIDE. 2-1/16". 7.50. CyberAuction #500, Lot #56. Final Bid: $1,275.

5148. SULPHIDE. 2-1/4". 8.70. CyberAuction #373, Lot #58. Final Bid: $1,225.

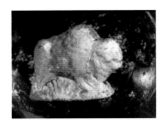

5149. SULPHIDE. 2". 8.00. CyberAuction #503, Lot #61. Final Bid: $1,200.

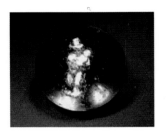

5153. SULPHIDE. 1-11/16". 8.10. CyberAuction #455, Lot #58. Final Bid: $675.

5156. SULPHIDE. 1-1/2". 8.50. CyberAuction #351, Lot #60. Final Bid: $435.

5151. SULPHIDE. 1-3/4". Buffed. CyberAuction #457, Lot #50. Final Bid: $750.

5154. SULPHIDE. 1-5/8". 9.20. CyberAuction #421, Lot #59. Final Bid: $555.

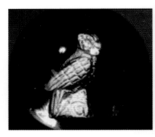

5157. SULPHIDE. 2-1/16". 9.20. CyberAuction #467, Lot #33. Final Bid: $435.

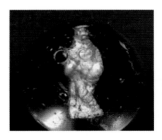

5152. SULPHIDE. 1-7/16". CyberAuction #467, Lot #29. Final Bid: $750.

5155. SULPHIDE. 1-3/4". Polished. CyberAuction #424, Lot #59. Final Bid: $500.

5158. SULPHIDE. 1-1/4". 8.80. CyberAuction #430, Lot #24. Final Bid: $430.

5159. SULPHIDE. 2". Buffed.
CyberAuction #345, Lot #34.
Final Bid: $410.

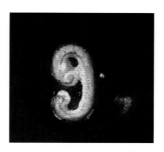

5162. SULPHIDE. 1-9/16".
9.90. CyberAuction #444, Lot
#24. Final Bid: $410.

5167. SULPHIDE. 1-3/4".
Polished. CyberAuction #429,
Lot #34. Final Bid: $360.

5160. SULPHIDE. 1-1/4". 8.80.
CyberAuction #410, Lot #38.
Final Bid: $410.

5163. SULPHIDE. 2-1/16".
7.30. CyberAuction #444, Lot
#29. Final Bid: $410.

5168. SULPHIDE. 1-13/16".
9.50. CyberAuction #432, Lot
#33. Final Bid: $360.

5161. SULPHIDE.
CyberAuction #443, Lot #60.
Final Bid: $410.

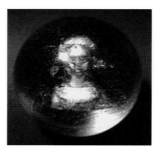

5165. SULPHIDE. 1-11/16".
8.00. CyberAuction #433, Lot
#60. Final Bid: $385.

5169. SULPHIDE. 1-7/8".
Polished. CyberAuction #406,
Lot #49. Final Bid: $335.

5171. SULPHIDE. 1-3/4".
Polished. CyberAuction #454,
Lot #21. Final Bid: $311.

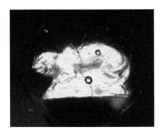

5174. SULPHIDE. 1-7/8. 9.90.
CyberAuction #414, Lot #29.
Final Bid: $285.

5177. SULPHIDE. 1-13/16".
8.20. CyberAuction #468, Lot
#46. Final Bid: $275.

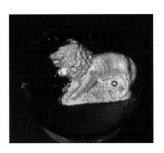

5172. SULPHIDE. 1-7/16".
9.40. CyberAuction #442, Lot
#35. Final Bid: $310.

5175. SULPHIDE. 1-7/8". 8.00.
CyberAuction #374, Lot #60.
Final Bid: $280.

5178. SULPHIDE. 1-1/2". 7.90.
CyberAuction #471, Lot #27.
Final Bid: $275.

5173. SULPHIDE. 2-1/16".
9.20. CyberAuction #421, Lot
#49. Final Bid: $300.

5273. SULPHIDE. 11/16".
8.80. CyberAuction #428, Lot
#34. Final Bid: $110.

5179. SULPHIDE. 2-3/8". 9.80.
CyberAuction #385, Lot #45.
Final Bid: $260.

5180. SULPHIDE. 1-3/4". 8.90. CyberAuction #414, Lot #56. Final Bid: $260.

5183. SULPHIDE. 1-5/8". Buffed. CyberAuction #469, Lot #33. Final Bid: $260.

5186. SULPHIDE. 1-3/16". 8.60. CyberAuction #413, Lot #50. Final Bid: $250.

5181. SULPHIDE. 1-9/16". 8.40. CyberAuction #429, Lot #57. Final Bid: $260.

5184. SULPHIDE. 1-3/4". Polished. CyberAuction #479, Lot #35. Final Bid: $260.

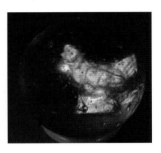

5187. SULPHIDE. 1-7/16". 7.50. CyberAuction #448, Lot #28. Final Bid: $250.

5182. SULPHIDE. 1-3/4". 7.90. CyberAuction #442, Lot #23. Final Bid: $260.

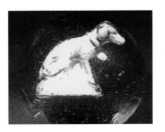

5185. SULPHIDE. 1-31/32". 9.00. CyberAuction #412, Lot #44. Final Bid: $250.

5190. SULPHIDE. 1-9/16". 9.90. CyberAuction #472, Lot #45. Final Bid: $235.

5191. SULPHIDE. 1-1/4". 7.90. CyberAuction #413, Lot #20. Final Bid: $230.

5546. SWIRL, Caramel. 15/16". Buffed. CyberAuction #406, Lot #48. Final Bid: $150.

5616. SWIRL, Custard. 5/8". 8.10. CyberAuction #487, Lot #14. Final Bid: $27.

5396. SWIRL, Banded. 1-5/16". 8.90. CyberAuction #422, Lot #57. Final Bid: $180.

5572. SWIRL, Coreless. 19/32". 8.90. CyberAuction #388, Lot #48. Final Bid: $235.

5617. SWIRL, Divided core. 2-1/8". 8.20. CyberAuction #432, Lot #19. Final Bid: $320.

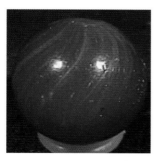

5519. SWIRL, Butterscotch. 23/32". 9.70. CyberAuction #386, Lot #14. Final Bid: $95.

5603. SWIRL, Cornhusk. 11/16". 9.50. CyberAuction #445, Lot #55. Final Bid: $120.

5618. SWIRL, Divided core. 2-3/8". 8.10. CyberAuction #424, Lot #47. Final Bid: $315.

5619. SWIRL, Divided core. 2".
8.70. CyberAuction #508, Lot
#37. Final Bid: $285.

6139. SWIRL, Gooseberry.
11/16". 9.20. CyberAuction
#330, Lot #17. Final Bid: $90.

6149. SWIRL, Joseph Coat.
15/16". 9.80. CyberAuction
#429, Lot #55. Final Bid: $375.

5620. SWIRL, Divided core.
1-7/8". 8.60. CyberAuction
#414, Lot #28. Final Bid:
$260.

6147. SWIRL, Joseph Coat. 1".
9.20. CyberAuction #500, Lot
#22. Final Bid: $700.

6263. SWIRL, Latticinio core.
2-1/16". 9.00. CyberAuction
#467, Lot #31. Final Bid: $710.

5621. SWIRL, Divided core.
1-7/16". 9.40. CyberAuction
#338, Lot #59. Final Bid:
$230.

6148. SWIRL, Joseph Coat.
25/32". 9.20. CyberAuction
#462, Lot #53. Final Bid: $450.

6264. SWIRL, Latticinio core.
25/32". 9.00. CyberAuction
#500, Lot #52. Final Bid: $505.

6265. SWIRL, Latticinio core. 1-1/2". 8.90. CyberAuction #342, Lot #60. Final Bid: $310.

6268. SWIRL, Latticinio core. 2". 9.00. CyberAuction #410, Lot #36. Final Bid: $300.

6271. SWIRL, Latticinio core. 2-1/2". 7.90. CyberAuction #421, Lot #36. Final Bid: $270.

6266. SWIRL, Latticinio core. 2-1/8". 9.70. CyberAuction #388, Lot #54. Final Bid: $310.

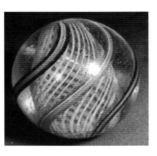

6269. SWIRL, Latticinio core. 2-1/8". 8.90. CyberAuction #495, Lot #60. Final Bid: $285.

6272. SWIRL, Latticinio core. 2-3/8". 8.00. CyberAuction #469, Lot #32. Final Bid: $260.

6267. SWIRL, Latticinio core. 1-9/16". 9.00. CyberAuction #400, Lot #57. Final Bid: $310.

6270. SWIRL, Latticinio core. 2-3/8". 8.30. CyberAuction #418, Lot #53. Final Bid: $270.

6273. SWIRL, Latticinio core. 2-1/2". 7.50. CyberAuction #420, Lot #35. Final Bid: $235.

6274. SWIRL, Latticinio core. 2-1/8". 8.00. CyberAuction #413, Lot #38. Final Bid: $230.

7019. SWIRL, Peppermint. 11/16". 8.60. CyberAuction #360, Lot #38. Final Bid: $210.

7052. SWIRL, Ribbon core. 1-11/16". 8.90. CyberAuction #504, Lot #70. Final Bid: $500.

6275. SWIRL, Latticinio core. 2-3/8". 8.30. CyberAuction #421, Lot #35. Final Bid: $230.

7050. SWIRL, Ribbon core. 1-13/16". 8.30. CyberAuction #385, Lot #39. Final Bid: $875.

7053. SWIRL, Ribbon core. 1-15/16". 8.20. CyberAuction #431, Lot #14. Final Bid: $352.

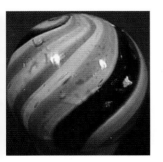

7018. SWIRL, Peppermint with mica. 7/8". Polished. CyberAuction #386, Lot #43. Final Bid: $325.

7051. SWIRL, Ribbon core. 27/32". 9.70. CyberAuction #503, Lot #75. Final Bid: $775.

7054. SWIRL, Ribbon core. 2-1/16". 8.00. CyberAuction #430, Lot #34. Final Bid: $325.

7055. SWIRL, Ribbon core.
2-1/8". 8.60. CyberAuction
#412, Lot #43. Final Bid: $300.

7208. SWIRL, Solid core.
2-5/16". 8.20. CyberAuction
#455, Lot #33. Final Bid: $360.

7212. SWIRL, Solid core.
2-1/16". 8.20. CyberAuction
#418, Lot #25. Final Bid: $260.

7057. SWIRL, Ribbon core.
1-3/4". 9.00. CyberAuction
#489, Lot #49. Final Bid: $285.

7209. SWIRL, Solid core.
2-3/8". 8.20. CyberAuction
#453, Lot #27. Final Bid: $285.

7214. SWIRL, Solid core.
1-7/8". 8.10. CyberAuction
#467, Lot #30. Final Bid: $250.

7207. SWIRL, Solid core. 2-3/16".
9.20. CyberAuction #505, Lot
#69. Final Bid: $825.

7210. SWIRL, Solid core.
2-1/16". 8.20. CyberAuction
#468, Lot #12. Final Bid: $285.

7215. SWIRL, Solid core.
1-13/16". 8.80. CyberAuction
#491, Lot #57. Final Bid: $250.

7793. TRANSITIONAL, Bullet Mold. 3/4". 8.90. CyberAuction #506, Lot #36. Final Bid: $33.

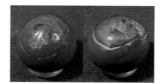

7850. TRANSITIONAL, Leighton. 27/32". 9.70. CyberAuction #483, Lot #59. Final Bid: $2,100.

7853. TRANSITIONAL, Leighton. 25/32". 9.90. CyberAuction #434, Lot #60. Final Bid: $985.

7820. TRANSITIONAL, Ground pontil. 13/16". 9.90. CyberAuction #336, Lot #60. Final Bid: $230.

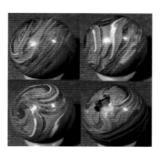

7851. TRANSITIONAL, Leighton. 3/4". 9.90. CyberAuction #377, Lot #60. Final Bid: $2,050.

7873. TRANSITIONAL, Leighton. 27/32". 8.60. CyberAuction #395, Lot #58. Final Bid: $150.

7849. TRANSITIONAL, Leighton. 3/4". 9.90. CyberAuction #500, Lot #59. Final Bid: $2,550.

7852. TRANSITIONAL, Leighton. 7/8". 9.60. CyberAuction #445, Lot #60. Final Bid: $1,100.

7856. TRANSITIONAL, Leighton. 15/16". 8.80. CyberAuction #436, Lot #58. Final Bid: $710.

7857. TRANSITIONAL,
Leighton. 31/32". 9.00.
CyberAuction #508, Lot #74.
Final Bid: $485.

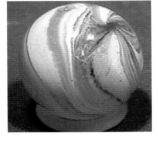

7860. TRANSITIONAL,
Leighton. 31/32". 9.00.
CyberAuction #406, Lot #54.
Final Bid: $410.

7863. TRANSITIONAL,
Leighton. 29/32". 8.60.
CyberAuction #421, Lot #60.
Final Bid: $320.

7858. TRANSITIONAL,
Leighton. 21/32". 9.40.
CyberAuction #373, Lot #59.
Final Bid: $470.

7861. TRANSITIONAL,
Leighton. 27/32". 9.20.
CyberAuction #424, Lot #58.
Final Bid: $400.

7864. TRANSITIONAL,
Leighton. 13/16". 9.80.
CyberAuction #330, Lot #59.
Final Bid: $310.

7859. TRANSITIONAL,
Leighton. 1-1/16". 8.90.
CyberAuction #475, Lot #55.
Final Bid: $435.

7862. TRANSITIONAL,
Leighton. 3/4". 9.60.
CyberAuction #439, Lot #60.
Final Bid: $360.

7865. TRANSITIONAL,
Leighton. 15/16". 9.00.
CyberAuction #465, Lot #60.
Final Bid: $310.

7866. TRANSITIONAL,
Leighton. 29/32". 8.90.
CyberAuction #450, Lot #46.
Final Bid: $300.

7869. TRANSITIONAL,
Leighton. 27/32". 9.20.
CyberAuction #414, Lot #54.
Final Bid: $260.

7934. TRANSITIONAL, Regular
pontil. 11/16". 9.00.
CyberAuction #339, Lot #48.
Final Bid: $50.

7867. TRANSITIONAL,
Leighton. 29/32". 8.90.
CyberAuction #466, Lot #45.
Final Bid: $300.

7870. TRANSITIONAL,
Leighton. 9/16". 9.70.
CyberAuction #504, Lot #60.
Final Bid: $250.

7936. VITRO AGATE COM-
PANY, All-Red. 7/8". 9.90.
CyberAuction #380, Lot #5.
Final Bid: $15.

7868. TRANSITIONAL,
Leighton. 15/16". 8.80.
CyberAuction #357, Lot #59.
Final Bid: $260.

7903. TRANSITIONAL, Pinch
pontil. 5/8". 9.90.
CyberAuction #335, Lot #9.
Final Bid: $27.

7937. VITRO AGATE COM-
PANY, Catseye. 7/8". 9.90.
CyberAuction #381, Lot #47.
Final Bid: $37.

7948. JABO-VITRO AGATE COMPANY, Original package. CyberAuction #429, Lot #32. Final Bid: $23.

7949. VITRO AGATE COMPANY, Original bag. CyberAuction #390, Lot #24. Final Bid: $21.

7966. VITRO AGATE COMPANY, Oxblood patch. 15/16". 8.00. CyberAuction #505, Lot #41. Final Bid: $17.

7967. VITRO AGATE COMPANY, Parrot. 29/32". 9.00. CyberAuction #426, Lot #52. Final Bid: $38.

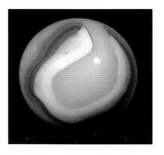

7975. VITRO AGATE COMPANY, Patch. 31/32". 9.70. CyberAuction #374, Lot #56. Final Bid: $60.

7988. VITRO AGATE COMPANY, Patch and ribbon. 19/32". 9.90. CyberAuction #443, Lot #9. Final Bid: $3.

7989. VITRO AGATE COMPANY, Patch oxblood. 7/8". 9.80. CyberAuction #465, Lot #40. Final Bid: $40.

7991. VITRO AGATE COMPANY, Ribbon. 19/32". 9.90. CyberAuction #481, Lot #53. Final Bid: $70.

7994. VITRO AGATE COMPANY, Tigereye. 19/32". 9.70. CyberAuction #365, Lot #42. Final Bid: $3.

1. AKRO AGATE COMPANY. Ade hybrid. Lemonade/limeade hybrid. Fluorescent translucent ade base. Lots of wispy white in it. Yellow corkscrew with a thin green corkscrew next to it. Rare marble. Clarksburg, WV, circa 1925-1935. 5/8". Mint (9.9). Price: $120. CyberAuction #330, Lot #45.

2. AKRO AGATE COMPANY. Ade hybrid. Very rare marble. This is a lemonade with an additional swirl of blue. Super marble. Very lightly buffed. Clarksburg, WV, circa 1927-1935. 9/16". Price: $70. CyberAuction #353, Lot #54.

3. AKRO AGATE COMPANY. Ade hybrid. Very rare hybrid ade marble. Cherryade/lemonade hybrid. Semi-opaque very fluorescent ade base with wispy white swirls. Semi-opaque red and semi-opaque yellow swirl on the surface. Some pits and an annealing fracture. Clarksburg, WV, circa 1927-1935. 21/32". Near Mint(+) (8.7). Price: $55. CyberAuction #407, Lot #42.

4. AKRO AGATE COMPANY. Advertising marble. Translucent yellow marble printed "-PORCELFRIT-". Some sparkles on the marble. 21/32". Near Mint(+) (8.9). The base marble is Akro, although the printing may have been done by someone else. They are believed to be 1930s or 1940s and are from Western Pennsylvania. Price: $44. CyberAuction #339, Lot #5.

5. AKRO AGATE COMPANY. Advertising marble. Translucent yellow marble printed "-PORCELFRIT-". Some sparkles on the marble. 21/32". Near Mint(+) (8.9). The base marble is Akro, although the printing may have been done by someone else. They are believed to be 1930s or 1940s and are from Western Pennsylvania. Price: $44. CyberAuction #494, Lot #41.

6. AKRO AGATE COMPANY. Advertising marble. Translucent yellow marble printed "-PORCELFRIT-". Some sparkles on the marble. 21/32". Near Mint(+)(8.9). The base marble is Akro, although the printing may have been done by someone else. They are believed to be 1930s or 1940s and are from Western Pennsylvania. Price: $42. CyberAuction #375, Lot #32.

7. AKRO AGATE COMPANY. Advertising marble. Translucent yellow marble printed "-PORCELFRIT-". Some sparkles on the marble. 21/32". Near Mint(+)(8.9). The base marble is Akro, although the printing may have been done by someone else. They are believed to be 1930s or 1940s and are from Western Pennsylvania. Price: $42. CyberAuction #445, Lot #59.

8. AKRO AGATE COMPANY. Akroware. No. 249 Rectangular Ashtray, with short tabs. Fluorescent cream with loads of aventurine green and oxblood swirling. Stunning ashtray. 3-1/2". Mint (9.9). Price: $150. CyberAuction #508, Lot #42.

9. AKRO AGATE COMPANY. Akroware. Cup and saucer. Gorgeous fluorescent lemonade oxblood. Very hard to find. Octagonal panelled cup, closed handle. About 2-1/4" in diameter. Akro logo on the bottom. Octagonal panel saucer. About 3-1/4" in diameter. Akro logo on bottom. Price: $95. CyberAuction #429, Lot #59.

10. AKRO AGATE COMPANY. Akroware. No. 249 Rectangular Ashtray, with long tabs. Marbleized fiery aventurine green, some wispy oxblood swirling. Stamped on bottom with the Akro crow and Made In USA. This coloring is very unusual. 3-3/4". Mint (9.9). Price: $85. CyberAuction #342, Lot #36.

11. AKRO AGATE COMPANY. Akroware. No. 249 Rectangular Ashtray, with short tabs. Cream with loads of green and oxblood swirling. Stunning ashtray. 3-1/2". Mint (9.9). Price: $60. CyberAuction #479, Lot #36.

12. AKRO AGATE COMPANY. Akroware. Fluted planter. Beaded design. Outstanding very fluorescent creamy white with tons of oxblood. Super!!!! Akro logo and "Made in U.S.A." on bottom. About 3-3/4" high. 2" wide at bottom, flaring to 3-1/4" wide at top. Mint (9.9). Price: $55. CyberAuction #418, Lot #36.

13. AKRO AGATE COMPANY. Akroware. Fluted bowl. Dart pattern. Oxblood and fluorescent creamy white. Gorgeous. Marked on bottom with Akro logo and "Made in U.S.A.". Stunning. About 3-1/2" high, 4-1/2" wide at top (about 2" wide at bottom). Mint. Price: $55. CyberAuction #425, Lot #30.

14. AKRO AGATE COMPANY. Akroware. No. 249 Rectangular Ashtray, with short tabs. White with some green and with lots of oxblood swirling. 3-1/2". Mint (9.9). Price: $49. CyberAuction #345, Lot #35.

15. AKRO AGATE COMPANY. Akroware. Small octagonal plate. Gorgeous fluorescent lemonade oxblood. Very hard to find. Akro logo on the bottom. About 4-1/4" diameter. Price: $47. CyberAuction #429, Lot #30.

16. AKRO AGATE COMPANY. Akroware. No. 249 Rectangular Ashtray,

with short tabs. White with green and oxblood swirling. 3-1/2". Mint (9.9). Price: $35. CyberAuction #339, Lot #34.

17. AKRO AGATE COMPANY. Akroware. No. 764 hand planter. Lady's hand rising from the base, holding a planter. Opalescent white and orange. Akro logo on bottom with model number. About 3-1/2" high and 2" wide. Mint (9.9). Price: $35. CyberAuction #418, Lot #32.

18. AKRO AGATE COMPANY. Akroware. Fluted planter. Dart pattern. Yellow. Very interesting. Bottom reads "Akro Agate Co. Clarksburg, W. Va." and Akro logo. About 3" tall, 2-1/4" wide at top. Mint. Price: $30. CyberAuction #421, Lot #28.

19. AKRO AGATE COMPANY. Akroware. Small handle-less cup (?). Dart pattern. Very fluorescent creamy white with tons of oxblood. Akro logo on bottom. 2" high. 1-1/2" wide base tapered up to a 2-1/4" rim. Mint (9.9). Price: $26. CyberAuction #418, Lot #33.

20. AKRO AGATE COMPANY. Akroware. No. 765 Cornucopia planter. Opalescent white base with orange, blue and dark yellow swirls. Gorgeous. Akro logo and model number on bottom. About 3-1/2" x 3". Mint (9.9). Price: $26. CyberAuction #418, Lot #34.

21. AKRO AGATE COMPANY. Akroware. No. 657 Lily Planter. Marbleized blue and white. Model number, "Made in USA" and Akro crow on the base. 4-1/4". Mint (9.9). Price: $25. CyberAuction #358, Lot #24.

22. AKRO AGATE COMPANY. Akroware. No. 657 Lily Planter. Marbleized orange and white. Akro logo on the base. 4-1/4". Mint (9.9). Price: $22. CyberAuction #425, Lot #28.

23. AKRO AGATE COMPANY. Akroware. Grecian urn planter. Blue and white slag. Bottom has Akro logo and "764"(?). About 2-3/4" tall. Mint. Price: $21. CyberAuction #421, Lot #30.

24. AKRO AGATE COMPANY. Akroware. Planter cup. Orange and fluorescent white. Dart pattern. 2" wide. 1-1/2" diameter at bottom, fluting up to 2-1/4" diameter at top. Akro logo on the bottom. Mint. Price: $21. CyberAuction #429, Lot #28.

25. AKRO AGATE COMPANY. Akroware. Small pot. Fluorescent opaque creamy white. Beauty. About 2-1/4" high. Price: $19. CyberAuction #357, Lot #31.

26. AKRO AGATE COMPANY. Akroware. Small flower pot. Fluorescent white and green. About 4" high. Price: $17. CyberAuction #355, Lot #31.

27. AKRO AGATE COMPANY. Akroware. No. 657 Lily Planter. Marbleized green and white. Model number, "Made in USA" and Akro crow on the base. 4-1/4". Mint (9.9). Price: $17. CyberAuction #359, Lot #29.

28. AKRO AGATE COMPANY. Akroware. No. 657 Lily Planter. Marbleized blue and white. Model number, "Made in USA" and Akro crow on the base. 4-1/4". Mint (9.9). Price: $17. CyberAuction #398, Lot #21.

29. AKRO AGATE COMPANY. Akroware. No. 658 Lily planter. Dull orange and white slag. Bottom reads "Made in U.S.A. 658". About 4" tall. Mint. Price: $17. CyberAuction #421, Lot #27.

30. AKRO AGATE COMPANY. Akroware. Oval planter. Green. Akro logo on bottom, with "Made in U.S.A." About 6" x 3" x 3". Mint. Price: $17. CyberAuction #425, Lot #25.

31. AKRO AGATE COMPANY. Akroware. Grecian Urn, No. 764. Small planter. Marbleized white, green and blue. About 4" tall. Mint. Price: $16. CyberAuction #361, Lot #37.

32. AKRO AGATE COMPANY. Akroware. Lily planter No. 657. Green and white slag. "Made in U.S.A.", Akro logo and model number on bottom. About 5" x 2-3/4" x 2". Mint. Price: $15. CyberAuction #429, Lot #29.

33. AKRO AGATE COMPANY. Akroware. No. 657 Lily Planter. Marbleized green and white. Model number, "Made in USA" and Akro crow on the base. 4-1/4". Mint (9.9). Price: $14. CyberAuction #399, Lot #36.

34. AKRO AGATE COMPANY. Akroware. No. 246 leaf ashtray. Blue slag. Opalescent. Akro logo on bottom. About 3" long. Mint (9.9). Price: $14. CyberAuction #508, Lot #41.

35. AKRO AGATE COMPANY. Akroware. Small handled cup. White and caramel brown swirls. Akro logo on bottom. 2-1/4" wide. Mint (9.9). Price: $13. CyberAuction #418, Lot #35.

36. AKRO AGATE COMPANY. Akroware. Fluted No 297 planter. In light blue. Not sure of the pattern name. Beaded and crescent rim, if that helps. Bottom reads "Made in U.S.A. 297" and has Akro logo. About 3-1/4" high, 2-3/4" wide at top. Mint. Price: $13. CyberAuction #421, Lot #29.

37. AKRO AGATE COMPANY. Akroware. No. 656 planter. White and green slag. "Made in U.S.A.", Akro logo and model number on the bottom. About 6" x 3" x 3". Mint. Price: $13. CyberAuction #429, Lot #25.

38. AKRO AGATE COMPANY. Akroware. No. 658 Lily Planter. Marbleized orange and white. Model number, "Made in USA" and Akro crow on the base. Tiny rim chip. 4-1/4". Near Mint(+) (8.9). Price: $12. CyberAuction #362, Lot #36.

39. AKRO AGATE COMPANY. Akroware. Small planter. No number on bottom. The hole is punched out. Green and white slag, with a little oxblood. 1-7/8" high. 1-7/8" white at top. Near Mint(+). Price: $12. CyberAuction #421, Lot #24.

40. AKRO AGATE COMPANY. Akroware. Cornucopia. Hard to find opaque blue (usually they are slag). No markings on the bottom, but it is Akro. About 3-1/2" high. Mint. Price: $12. CyberAuction #429, Lot #27.

41. AKRO AGATE COMPANY. Akroware. Small planter. Semi-opaque green. Reeded rim. Bottom reads "Made in U.S.A. 13 300F" and Akro logo. About 3" high, 2-1/2" wide at top. Mint. Price: $10. CyberAuction #421, Lot #31.

42. AKRO AGATE COMPANY. Akroware. Grecian urn planter. White with a little green. Nothing on bottom. About 2-3/4" tall. Mint. Price: $10. CyberAuction #425, Lot #27.

43. AKRO AGATE COMPANY. Akroware. Small flower pot. Marked on bottom with Akro logo, "Made in U.S.A.", and "300F". About 3-1/2" tall, 2-1/2" wide at top. Mint. Price: $9. CyberAuction #425, Lot #26.

44. AKRO AGATE COMPANY. Akroware. Small flower pot. Fluorescent white and green. About 4" high. This one was used. The bottom hole is punched out, resulting in a tiny fracture in the bottom, and a piece of glass missing from the inside bottom. Price: $8. CyberAuction #359, Lot #30.

45. AKRO AGATE COMPANY. Akroware. Grecian Urn No. 764. Opalescent white and green. About 3-3/4" tall. Akro logo on bottom, and model number. Mint. Price: $8. CyberAuction #429, Lot #26.

46. AKRO AGATE COMPANY. Akroware. Small square ashtray. Semi-opaque opalescent white with lime green swirls. About 3" width. Price: $7. CyberAuction #357, Lot #32.

47. AKRO AGATE COMPANY. Akroware. Mimic of an Akroware slag glass Cornucopia planter. Marked on bottom "Vogue Merc Co. NYC". About 3" tall. Mint. Price: $6. CyberAuction #465, Lot #28.

48. AKRO AGATE COMPANY. Akroware. Cup saucer. Orange and white slag. Akro logo on bottom. About 4" diameter. Mint. Price: $5. CyberAuction #460, Lot #32.

49. AKRO AGATE COMPANY. Akroware. Cup saucer. Orange and white slag. Akro logo on bottom. About 4" diameter. Mint. Price: $4. CyberAuction #425, Lot #29.

50. AKRO AGATE COMPANY. Akroware. Octagonal small cake plate. Opaque white. About 3-1/4" diameter. Price: $3. CyberAuction #456, Lot #35.

51. AKRO AGATE COMPANY. Blue oxblood. Stunning example. Shooter. Translucent milky white base. Spiral of wide oxblood and spiral of wide blue, painted on the surface. Exceptional. One pit. Clarksburg, WV, circa 1927-1935. 25/32". Mint(-) (9.0). Price: $310. CyberAuction #498, Lot #73.

52. AKRO AGATE COMPANY. Blue oxblood. Super shooter marble. Translucent milky base with a corkscrew of translucent blue spiral and a spiral of oxblood on the surface. Beauty. One tiny sparkle. Clarksburg, WV, circa 1928-1935. 11/16". Mint(-) (9.0). Price: $55. CyberAuction #459, Lot #56.

53. AKRO AGATE COMPANY. Blue oxblood. Translucent milky white base. Swirl of translucent blue. Swirl of oxblood. A beauty. One tiny chip, some pits and tiny subsurface moons. Clarksburg, WV, circa 1925-1935. 21/32". Near Mint (8.6). Price: $43. CyberAuction #351, Lot #56.

54. AKRO AGATE COMPANY. Blue oxblood. Super shooter marble. Translucent milky base with a corkscrew of translucent blue spiral and a spiral of oxblood on the surface. Several Small subsurface moon, a couple of tiny pits. Clarksburg, WV, circa 1928-1935. 25/32". Near Mint (8.6). Price: $40. CyberAuction #461, Lot #50.

55. AKRO AGATE COMPANY. Blue oxblood. Super shooter marble. Translucent milky white base with a corkscrew of translucent blue spiral and a spiral of oxblood on the surface. Several small chips and subsurface moons, some roughness. Clarksburg, WV, circa 1928-1935. 25/32". Good (7.6). Price: $36. CyberAuction #375, Lot #2.

56. AKRO AGATE COMPANY. Blue oxblood. Translucent milky white base. Swirl of translucent blue. Thinner swirl of burnt oxblood. Several tiny subsurface moons. Clarksburg, WV, circa 1925-1935. 19/32". Near Mint (8.5). Price: $32. CyberAuction #338, Lot #3.

57. AKRO AGATE COMPANY. Blue oxblood. Translucent milky white base. Swirl of translucent blue and swirl of oxblood. Several small chips and tiny subsurface moons. Clarksburg, WV, circa 1925-1935. 11/16". Good(+) (7.9). Price: $32. CyberAuction #446, Lot #8.

58. AKRO AGATE COMPANY. Blue oxblood. Translucent milky white base. Swirl of translucent blue and swirl of oxblood. Several small chips and tiny subsurface moons. Clarksburg, WV, circa 1925-1935. 11/16". Good(+) (7.9). Price: $22. CyberAuction #482, Lot #8.

59. AKRO AGATE COMPANY. Blue oxblood. Translucent milky white base. Swirl of translucent blue and swirl of oxblood. Several small chips and tiny subsurface moons. Clarksburg, WV, circa 1925-1935. 11/16". Good(+) (7.9). Price: $22. CyberAuction #499, Lot #15.

60. AKRO AGATE COMPANY. Blue oxblood. Translucent milky white base. Swirl of translucent blue. Thinner swirl of burnt oxblood. Several tiny subsurface moons. Clarksburg, WV, circa 1925-1935. 11/16". Near Mint (8.3). Price: $17. CyberAuction #421, Lot #10.

61. AKRO AGATE COMPANY. Blue oxblood. Translucent milky white base. Swirl of translucent blue. Thin swirls of burnt oxblood. A couple of tiny subsurface moons. Clarksburg, WV, circa 1925-1935. 11/16". Near Mint (8.6). Price: $17. CyberAuction #421, Lot #44.

62. AKRO AGATE COMPANY. Blue oxblood. Milky white base. Swirl of dark blue and dark oxblood. Tiny pitting, tiny chips and tiny subsurface moons. Clarksburg, WV, circa 1927-1935. 19/32". Good (7.5). Price: $13. CyberAuction #353, Lot #38.

63. AKRO AGATE COMPANY. Carnelian. Shooter. Akro Agate Carnelian. Very fluorescent. Ade base, translucent brown and semi-opaque white. Clarksburg, WV, circa 1925-1935. 3/4". Mint (9.9). Price: $75. CyberAuction #418, Lot #50.

64. AKRO AGATE COMPANY. Carnelian. Akro Agate Carnelian. Very fluorescent, corkscrew pattern. Stunning. Clarksburg, WV, circa 1925-1935. 11/16". Mint (9.8). Price: $46. CyberAuction #500, Lot #5.

65. AKRO AGATE COMPANY. Carnelian. Akro Agate Carnelian. Very fluorescent, corkscrew pattern. Super. One tiny pinprick. Clarksburg, WV, circa 1925-1935. 3/4". Mint(-) (9.2). Price: $43. CyberAuction #504, Lot #51.

66. AKRO AGATE COMPANY. Carnelian. Akro Agate Carnelian. Very fluorescent, corkscrew pattern. Super, but very little wispy white. Clarksburg, WV, circa 1925-1935. 11/16". Mint (9.8). Price: $37. CyberAuction #501, Lot #49.

67. AKRO AGATE COMPANY. Carnelian. Akro Agate Carnelian. Very fluorescent, corkscrew pattern. Clarksburg, WV, circa 1925-1935. 23/32". Mint (9.8). Price: $32. CyberAuction #355, Lot #45.

68. AKRO AGATE COMPANY. Carnelian. Akro Agate Carnelian. Very fluorescent, corkscrew pattern. Clarksburg, WV, circa 1925-1935. 21/32". Mint (9.9). Price: $30. CyberAuction #443, Lot #43.

69. AKRO AGATE COMPANY. Carnelian. Fluorescent "ade" base. Wispy white and a nice wide corkscrew of semi-opaque brown. Beauty. Clarksburg, WV, circa 1927-1935. 21/32". Mint (9.9). Price: $22. CyberAuction #363, Lot #15.

70. AKRO AGATE COMPANY. Carnelian. Akro Agate Carnelian. Very fluorescent, corkscrew pattern. Clarksburg, WV, circa 1925-1935. 21/32". Mint (9.9). Price: $22. CyberAuction #365, Lot #7.

71. AKRO AGATE COMPANY. Carnelian. Akro Agate Carnelian. Very fluorescent, corkscrew pattern. Super, but very little wispy white. Clarksburg, WV, circa 1925-1935. 21/32". Mint (9.8). Price: $22. CyberAuction #425, Lot #3.

72. AKRO AGATE COMPANY. Carnelian. Akro Agate Carnelian. Very fluorescent, corkscrew pattern. Super, but very little wispy white. Clarksburg, WV, circa 1925-1935. 19/32". Mint (9.6). Price: $21. CyberAuction #501, Lot #57.

73. AKRO AGATE COMPANY. Carnelian. Akro Agate Carnelian. Very fluorescent, corkscrew pattern. Some pitting. Clarksburg, WV, circa 1925-1935. 23/32". Near Mint (8.6). Price: $19. CyberAuction #332, Lot #3.

74. AKRO AGATE COMPANY. Carnelian. Akro Agate Carnelian. Very fluorescent, corkscrew pattern. Some pitting. Clarksburg, WV, circa 1925-1935. 21/32". Mint (9.9). Price: $15. CyberAuction #406, Lot #42.

75. AKRO AGATE COMPANY. Carnelian. Shooter. Akro Agate Carnelian. Very fluorescent. Ade base, translucent brown and semi-opaque white. One tiny sparkle. Clarksburg, WV, circa 1925-1935. 21/32". Mint(-) (9.2). Price: $15. CyberAuction #429, Lot #19.

76. AKRO AGATE COMPANY. Carnelian. Akro Agate Carnelian. Very fluorescent, corkscrew pattern. Clarksburg, WV, circa 1925-1935. 21/32". Mint (9.7). Price: $15. CyberAuction #479, Lot #26.

77. AKRO AGATE COMPANY. Carnelian. Akro Agate Carnelian. Very fluorescent, corkscrew pattern. One sparkle. Clarksburg, WV, circa 1925-1935. 11/16". Mint(-) (9.0). Price: $14. CyberAuction #378, Lot #53.

78. AKRO AGATE COMPANY. Carnelian. Akro Agate Carnelian. Very fluorescent. Ade base, translucent brown and semi-opaque white. Two very tiny flakes. Clarksburg, WV, circa 1925-1935. 11/16". Near Mint(+) (8.7). Price: $12. CyberAuction #360, Lot #4.

79. AKRO AGATE COMPANY. Carnelian. Akro Agate Carnelian. Very fluorescent, corkscrew pattern. One tiny subsurface moon. Clarksburg, WV, circa 1925-1935. 23/32". Near Mint(+) (8.9). Price: $12. CyberAuction #407, Lot #31.

80. AKRO AGATE COMPANY. Carnelian. Fluorescent ade base. Semi-opaque white swirls, translucent brown swirls. A couple of tiny sparkles. Clarksburg, WV, circa 1925-1935. 11/16". Near Mint(+) (8.9). Price: $10. CyberAuction #358, Lot #8.

81. AKRO AGATE COMPANY. Carnelian. Akro Agate Carnelian. Very fluorescent. One tiny flake. Clarksburg, WV, circa 1925-1935. 5/8". Near Mint(+) (8.9). Price: $9. CyberAuction #464, Lot #7.

82. AKRO AGATE COMPANY. Carnelian. Akro Agate Carnelian. Very fluorescent, corkscrew pattern. Some pitting. Clarksburg, WV, circa 1925-1935. 3/4". Near Mint(+) (8.7). Price: $7. CyberAuction #469, Lot #55.

83. AKRO AGATE COMPANY. Carnelian. Akro Agate Carnelian. Very fluorescent, corkscrew pattern. Some tiny sparkles. Clarksburg, WV, circa 1925-1935. 19/32". Near Mint(+) (8.8). Price: $5. CyberAuction #485, Lot #27.

84. AKRO AGATE COMPANY. Carnelian. Akro Agate Carnelian. Very fluorescent, corkscrew pattern. A few subsurface moons. Clarksburg, WV, circa 1925-1935. 3/4". Good(+) (7.9). Price: $3. CyberAuction #344, Lot #41.

85. AKRO AGATE COMPANY. Carnelian oxblood. Translucent milky white base. Transparent brown corkscrew in the marble. Nice oxblood corkscrew on the surface. Exceptional example. Superb. Clarksburg, WV, circa 1928-1935. 3/4". Mint (9.9). Price: $240. CyberAuction #356, Lot #55.

86. AKRO AGATE COMPANY. Carnelian oxblood. Translucent milky white base. Lots of transparent brown swirling in the marble. Nice oxblood swirl on the surface. Exceptional surface. Clarksburg, WV, circa 1928-1935. 3/4". Mint (9.7). Price: $200. CyberAuction #505, Lot #70.

87. AKRO AGATE COMPANY. Carnelian oxblood. Translucent milky white base. Lots of transparent brown swirling in the marble. Nice oxblood swirl on the surface. Exceptional surface. Clarksburg, WV, circa 1928-1935. 5/8". Mint (9.9). Price: $135. CyberAuction #400, Lot #53.

88. AKRO AGATE COMPANY. Carnelian oxblood. Translucent milky white base. Lots of transparent brown swirling in the marble. Nice oxblood swirl on the surface. Exceptional surface. Clarksburg, WV, circa 1928-1935. 19/32". Mint (9.9). Price: $95. CyberAuction #351, Lot #18.

9. AKRO AGATE COMPANY. Carnelian oxblood. Translucent milky white ase. Transparent brown spiral and narrow oxblood spiral. Beautiful sur-ace. Clarksburg, WV, circa 1928-1935. 19/32". Mint (9.6). Price: $75. CyberAuction #363, Lot #52.

0. AKRO AGATE COMPANY. Carnelian oxblood. Translucent milky white ase. Lots of transparent brown swirling in the marble. Nice oxblood swirl n the surface. Two tiny subsurface moons. Clarksburg, WV, circa 1928-935. 11/16". Near Mint(+) (8.8). Price: $35. CyberAuction #412, Lot #40.

1. AKRO AGATE COMPANY. Carnelian oxblood. Translucent milky white ase. Wispy white swirls. Very dark oxblood corkscrew with translucent rown next to it. Some sparkles. Clarksburg, WV, circa 1927-1935. 19/32". Near Mint (8.6). Price: $31. CyberAuction #501, Lot #41.

2. AKRO AGATE COMPANY. Carnelian oxblood. Interesting marble. Milky white base. Very dark oxblood spiral, and a translucent brown spiral. Sub-urface moon and several sparkles. Clarksburg, WV, circa 1925-1935. 3/4". Near Mint(-) (8.2). Price: $23. CyberAuction #485, Lot #42.

4. AKRO AGATE COMPANY. Carnelian oxblood. Translucent milky white ase. Transparent brown swirling in the marble. Thin oxblood swirl on the urface. Sparkles. Clarksburg, WV, circa 1928-1935. 19/32". Near Mint 8.3). Price: $17. CyberAuction #501, Lot #51.

5. AKRO AGATE COMPANY. Cherryade. Hard to find shooter. Fluores-ent ade base. Opaque white and translucent red surface swirls. Two tiny reas of roughness. Clarksburg, WV, circa 1927-1935. ". Near Mint (8.6). Price: $80. CyberAuction #403, Lot #18.

6. AKRO AGATE COMPANY. Cherryade. Hard to find shooter. Fluores-ent ade base. Opaque white and translucent red surface swirls. Two tiny reas of roughness. Clarksburg, WV, circa 1927-1935. 3/4". Near Mint(+) 8.7). Price: $55. CyberAuction #462, Lot #10.

7. AKRO AGATE COMPANY. Cherryade. Hard to find shooter. Fluores-ent ade base. Opaque white and translucent red surface swirls. Tiny chips, ome pitting. Clarksburg, WV, circa 1927-1935. 1". Near Mint(-) (8.0). Price: 30. CyberAuction #485, Lot #45.

8. AKRO AGATE COMPANY. Chocolate oxblood. Rare marble. Opaque rown/gray base. Patch of oxblood covering about one-third of the marble. las a couple of sparkles. Clarksburg, WV, circa 1930-1945. 3/4". Near Aint(+) (8.7). Price: $110. CyberAuction #342, Lot #49.

9. AKRO AGATE COMPANY. Corkscrew. Transparent clear base. Opaque ght blue snake. Narrower translucent wispy white snake on the clear. larksburg, WV, circa 1927-1935. 5/8". Mint (9.7). Price: $17. CyberAuction 491, Lot #23.

00. AKRO AGATE COMPANY. Corkscrew. Very hard to find marble. Opaque yellow base. Orange/red snake on the surface. Oxblood snake on he surface. Air hole in the orange/red. A couple of pinpricks. Clarksburg, WV, circa 1927-1935. 23/32". Near Mint(+) (8.9). Price: $165. CyberAuction 357, Lot #51.

01. AKRO AGATE COMPANY. Corkscrew. Rare marble. White with dark lue spiral. Dark oxblood spiral under the blue. Gorgeous. Clarksburg, WV, rca 1927-1935. 5/8". Mint (9.7). Price: $120. CyberAuction #392, Lot 59.

02. AKRO AGATE COMPANY. Corkscrew. Gorgeous blue and red cork-crew. Early corkscrew. The red is semi-opaque and edged by black. Super xample. Clarksburg, WV, circa 1925-1930. 3/4". Mint (9.8). Price: 110. CyberAuction #330, Lot #20.

03. AKRO AGATE COMPANY. Corkscrew. Superb shooter marble. Equal ze spirals of orange and green. Very thin red where the orange and reen. Superb and hard to find. Clarksburg, WV, circa 1927-1935. 3/4". Aint (9.9). Price: $110. CyberAuction #330, Lot #22.

04. AKRO AGATE COMPANY. Corkscrew. Rare marble!!!! Huge five color orkscrew. Semi-opaque white base. Wide snakes on the surface of or-nge, yellow, blue and green. Large subsurface moon one side (1/2"). Not oo distracting, and the surface itself is pristine. Clarksburg, WV, circa 1927-935. 1". Near Mint(+) (8.7). Price: $110. CyberAuction #359, Lot #13.

05. AKRO AGATE COMPANY. Corkscrew. Hard to find oxblood ribbon orkscrew. Transparent clear bubble filled base. Two semi-opaque dark xblood ribbon corkscrews. In great shape. It's hard to find these without ome damage on them. Clarksburg, WV, circa 1927-1935. 9/16". Mint (9.9). rice: $110. CyberAuction #400, Lot #15.

06. AKRO AGATE COMPANY. Corkscrew. Rare five-color corkscrew. Opaque white base. Spirals of clear, orange, yellow and blue. Very nice xample. Clarksburg, WV, circa 1927-1935. 5/8". Mint (9.9). Price: $110. yberAuction #504, Lot #13.

07. AKRO AGATE COMPANY. Corkscrew. Interesting. Transparent milky white base. Spiral of translucent orange/brown. Spiral of burnt oxblood on he orange. Beauty. Clarksburg, WV, circa 1927-1935. 5/8". Mint (9.6). rice: $95. CyberAuction #366, Lot #33.

08. AKRO AGATE COMPANY. Corkscrew. Very rare. Black spiral on dark lue. Wow. Clarksburg, WV, circa 1927-1935. 5/8". Mint (9.6). Price: $95. yberAuction #377, Lot #22.

09. AKRO AGATE COMPANY. Corkscrew. Rare five-color corkscrew. Wide piral of transparent and a couple of semi-opaque white. Narrow opaque ellow spiral, very narrow transparent red spiral. On about half the clear is pirit of translucent gray/black. Superb. Clarksburg, WV, circa 1927-1935. /8". Mint (9.7). Price: $95. CyberAuction #504, Lot #10.

10. AKRO AGATE COMPANY. Corkscrew. Three-color Indian Blanket. ellow, black, red. Excellent example!!! Clarksburg, WV, circa 1927-1935. 3/32". Mint (9.7). Price: $90. CyberAuction #507, Lot #57.

111. AKRO AGATE COMPANY. Corkscrew. Four color corkscrew. Beauty. Translucent red spiral, opaque black spiral, narrow white spiral, narrow gray spiral. 11/16". Mint (9.7). Price: $85. CyberAuction #487, Lot #46.

112. AKRO AGATE COMPANY. Corkscrew. Light green, red and yellow. Shooter. Very nice. Clarksburg, WV, circa 1927-1935. 25/32". Mint (9.8). Price: $80. CyberAuction #413, Lot #14.

113. AKRO AGATE COMPANY. Corkscrew. Red spiral on royal blue. Very hard coloring to find. One sparkle. Clarksburg, WV, circa 1927-1935. 23/32". Mint(-) (9.0). Price: $80. CyberAuction #464, Lot #44.

114. AKRO AGATE COMPANY. Corkscrew. Very unusual three-color. Wide pale orange spiral and white spiral. Narrow cherry red spiral on one side of the orange. Gorgeous and rare coloring. Clarksburg, WV, circa 1927-1935. 23/32". Mint (9.6). Price: $76. CyberAuction #429, Lot #49.

115. AKRO AGATE COMPANY. Corkscrew. Indian Blanket three-color. Opaque yellow, transparent dark red, opaque black. Beauty. Clarksburg, WV, circa 1927-19.35. 21/32". Mint (9.9). Price: $75. CyberAuction #333, Lot #25.

116. AKRO AGATE COMPANY. Corkscrew. Odd coloring. Yellow and or-ange. Beautiful shooter. Clarksburg, WV, circa 1927-1935. 31/32". Mint (9.9). Price: $75. CyberAuction #342, Lot #52.

117. AKRO AGATE COMPANY. Corkscrew. Very rare corkscrew. Transpar-ent cobalt blue base. with a double twisted opaque orange snake. I've never seen this color combination before. One small subsurface moon. Clarksburg, WV, circa 1927-1935. 5/8". Near Mint(+) (8.8). Price: $70. CyberAuction #340, Lot #50.

118. AKRO AGATE COMPANY. Corkscrew. Very rare corkscrew. Transpar-ent cobalt blue base. with a double twisted opaque orange snake. I've never seen this color combination before. One small subsurface moon. Clarksburg, WV, circa 1927-1935. 5/8". Near Mint(+) (8.8). Price: $70. CyberAuction #441, Lot #54.

119. AKRO AGATE COMPANY. Corkscrew. Extremely rare marble. Trans-lucent green and wispy white base. Double twist snake of light blue. Stun-ning. Some manufacturing marks, but no damage. Clarksburg, WV, circa 1927-1935. 11/16". Mint (9.7). Price: $70. CyberAuction #450, Lot #39.

120. AKRO AGATE COMPANY. Corkscrew. Hard to find shooter Ace. Milky white base. Red snake on it. Clarksburg, WV, circa 1927-1935. 31/32". Mint (9.8). Price: $70. CyberAuction #462, Lot #42.

121. AKRO AGATE COMPANY. Corkscrew. Beautiful four-color corkscrew. White, blue, red, light green. Gorgeous. A tiny sparkle. Clarksburg, WV, circa 1927-1935. 5/8". Mint (-) (9.2). Price: $70. CyberAuction #487, Lot #49.

122. AKRO AGATE COMPANY. Corkscrew. Red and yellow Popeye. Clarksburg, WV, circa 1927-1935. 3/4". Mint (9.7). Price: $70. CyberAuction #501, Lot #62.

123. AKRO AGATE COMPANY. Corkscrew. And yet another interesting corkscrew. Translucent milky white base. Orange spiral and a black spiral on the surface, next to each other. Very nice. In great shape. Clarksburg, WV, circa 1927-1935. 19/32". Mint (9.5). Price: $65. CyberAuction #336, Lot #32.

124. AKRO AGATE COMPANY. Corkscrew. Four-color corkscrew. Very hard to find. White, red, narrow light green, narrow light blue. Gorgeous. Clarksburg, WV, circa 1927-1935. 5/8". Mint (9.8). Price: $65. CyberAuction #421, Lot #53.

125. AKRO AGATE COMPANY. Corkscrew. Three-color corkscrew. Type of Indian Blanket. Opaque white, opaque black and transparent red spi-rals. Clarksburg, WV, circa 1927-1935. 23/32". Mint (9.7). Price: $65. CyberAuction #440, Lot #29.

126. AKRO AGATE COMPANY. Corkscrew. Oddly colored Ace. Translu-cent milky white base. Translucent brown and burnt oxblood corkscrew. Very nice. Hard to find. Clarksburg, WV, circa 1927-1935. 1". Mint (9.7). Price: $65. CyberAuction #448, Lot #10.

127. AKRO AGATE COMPANY. Corkscrew. Five color corkscrew, some-times categorized as a snake Popeye. Transparent clear base. Four snakes on the surface. White, red, light green, narrow yellow. Rare marble. Dimple on one side, some tiny chips. Clarksburg, WV, circa 1927-1935. 3/4". Near Mint (8.6). Price: $65. CyberAuction #461, Lot #25.

128. AKRO AGATE COMPANY. Corkscrew. Superb tiny marble. Salmon pink, red and yellow spirals. All about the same width. Outstanding ex-ample. Rare size. Clarksburg, WV, circa 1927-1935. 17/32". Mint (9.8). Price: $60. CyberAuction #336, Lot #53.

129. AKRO AGATE COMPANY. Corkscrew. Three color corkscrew. Gor-geous. Half light green and half light yellow. Red spiral on the yellow. Su-perb. Clarksburg, WV, circa 1927-1935. 5/8". Mint (9.9). Price: $60. CyberAuction #366, Lot #3.

130. AKRO AGATE COMPANY. Corkscrew. Excellent four-color corkscrew. White, yellow and red on top of blue. Some pinpricks. Clarksburg, WV, circa 1927-1935. 5/8". Mint(-) (9.0). Price: $60. CyberAuction #418, Lot #46.

131. AKRO AGATE COMPANY. Corkscrew. Very rare shooter. Black snake on mottled red. You rarely see this as a 5/8"-size marble, I have never seen it as a shooter. Very rare. Some sparkles. Clarksburg, WV, circa 1927-1935. 25/32". Near Mint(+) (8.8). Price: $60. CyberAuction #436, Lot #34.

132. AKRO AGATE COMPANY. Corkscrew. Gorgeous three color. White, light green, orange/red. Each spiral about the same width. Clarksburg, WV, circa 1927-1935. 13/16". Mint (9.7). Price: $57. CyberAuction #371, Lot #6.

133. AKRO AGATE COMPANY. Corkscrew. Very interesting coloring. Trans-lucent, almost vitreous orange with a translucent white spiral. Superb marble. Clarksburg, WV, circa 1927-1935. 5/8". Mint (9.9). Price: $55. CyberAuction #353, Lot #41.

134. AKRO AGATE COMPANY. Corkscrew. Mixture of predominately lav-

ender with some white. Wide spiral of red. Beautiful!!!! Clarksburg, WV, circa 1927-1935. 29/32". Mint (9.9). Price: $55. CyberAuction #363, Lot #5.

135. AKRO AGATE COMPANY. Corkscrew. Orange snake on white. Very nice. Clarksburg, WV, circa 1927-1935. 31/32". Mint (9.8). Price: $55. CyberAuction #458, Lot #19.

136. AKRO AGATE COMPANY. Corkscrew. Orange and light blue. Hard coloring to find. Beautiful. Clarksburg, WV, circa 1927-1935. 5/8". Mint (9.9). Price: $55. CyberAuction #459, Lot #52.

137. AKRO AGATE COMPANY. Corkscrew. Translucent red snake on opaque white. Triple twist. Clarksburg, WV, circa 1927-1935. 23/32". Mint (9.9). Price: $50. CyberAuction #410, Lot #22.

138. AKRO AGATE COMPANY. Corkscrew. Stunning. Very lightly tinted blue base, with a snake of light blue and a snake of blue. So, three shades of blue spiral. Gorgeous. Clarksburg, WV, circa 1927-1935. 5/8". Mint (9.9). Price: $49. CyberAuction #365, Lot #9.

139. AKRO AGATE COMPANY. Corkscrew. Very odd two color. Pale orange and baby blue. Very unusual coloring. Clarksburg, WV, circa 1927-1935. 9/16". Mint (9.9). Price: $48. CyberAuction #330, Lot #25.

140. AKRO AGATE COMPANY. Corkscrew. Four-color corkscrew. White, semi-opaque mustard yellow, semi-opaque orange, and a thin spiral of clear. Gorgeous marble. Clarksburg, WV, circa 1927-1935. 23/32". Mint (9.7). Price: $48. CyberAuction #455, Lot #34.

141. AKRO AGATE COMPANY. Corkscrew. Black spiral on semi-opaque light blue. Rare. One sparkle. Clarksburg, WV, circa 1927-1935. 9/16". Mint (9.4). Price: $48. CyberAuction #500, Lot #41.

142. AKRO AGATE COMPANY. Corkscrew. Very odd shooter corkscrew. Black base with yellow spiral. The yellow is smeared with the black and has some transparent clear in it. Very odd. Clarksburg, WV, circa 1927-1935. 3/4". Mint (9.6). Price: $47. CyberAuction #336, Lot #27.

143. AKRO AGATE COMPANY. Corkscrew. Gorgeous. Transparent bubble filled base. Double twist ribbon of pale blue. Faint white snake of wispy white. Clarksburg, WV, circa 1927-1935. 5/8". Mint (9.9). Price: $47. CyberAuction #357, Lot #45.

144. AKRO AGATE COMPANY. Corkscrew. Rare coloring. Yellow and lavender. Very unusual. One tiny flake. Clarksburg, WV, circa 1927-1935. 21/32". Near Mint(+) (8.9). Price: $47. CyberAuction #462, Lot #3.

145. AKRO AGATE COMPANY. Corkscrew. Nice three-color corkscrew. White, orange/red and light green. Clarksburg, WV, circa 1927-1935. 5/8". Mint (9.9). Price: $47. CyberAuction #465, Lot #3.

146. AKRO AGATE COMPANY. Corkscrew. Four color corkscrew. Blue, orange, brown and gray/black. Very nice. Clarksburg, WV, circa 1927-1935. 5/8". Mint (9.7). Price: $46. CyberAuction #332, Lot #12.

147. AKRO AGATE COMPANY. Corkscrew. Nice five-color corkscrew. White, red, blue, light green, light gray. Very nice. Clarksburg, WV, circa 1927-1935. 5/8". Mint (9.8). Price: $46. CyberAuction #505, Lot #58.

148. AKRO AGATE COMPANY. Corkscrew. Red, light green and white shooter corkscrew. Clarksburg, WV, circa 1927-1935. 13/16". Mint (9.9). Price: $45. CyberAuction #433, Lot #32.

149. AKRO AGATE COMPANY. Corkscrew. Red, yellow and white shooter corkscrew. Clarksburg, WV, circa 1927-1935. 23/32". Mint (9.9). Price: $43. CyberAuction #433, Lot #19.

150. AKRO AGATE COMPANY. Corkscrew. Transparent peach base with opaque white ribbon. Rare color for a corkscrew. Clarksburg, WV, circa 1927-1935. 5/8". Mint (9.7). Price: $42. CyberAuction #388, Lot #7.

151. AKRO AGATE COMPANY. Corkscrew. White base. Wide peach spiral, with an orange spiral, edged by yellow. One tiny pit. Large shooter, hard to find, rare coloring. Clarksburg, WV, circa 1927-1935. 29/32". Mint(-) (9.0). Price: $42. CyberAuction #389, Lot #56.

152. AKRO AGATE COMPANY. Corkscrew. Very unusual corkscrew. White with a deep root beer brown snake spiral. Blue spiral on the white. Very odd coloring. Clarksburg, WV, circa 1927-1935. 9/16". Mint (9.6). Price: $42. CyberAuction #391, Lot #57.

153. AKRO AGATE COMPANY. Corkscrew. Nice shooter. Semi-opaque creamy base. Orange and red spirals. Beauty. Clarksburg, WV, circa 1927-1935. 13/16". Mint (9.7). Price: $42. CyberAuction #497, Lot #56.

154. AKRO AGATE COMPANY. Corkscrew. Very interesting double twist shooter. Predominately red, with a white and black spiral. A little smearing of the black and white. Twisted two and one-half times. A rough area and some sparkles. Clarksburg, WV, circa 1927-1935. 23/32". Near Mint (8.6). Price: $41. CyberAuction #337, Lot #21.

155. AKRO AGATE COMPANY. Corkscrew. Three-color corkscrew, called an Indian Blanket. Spirals of black, yellow and red. One tiny pinprick. Excellent example. Clarksburg, WV, circa 1927-1935. 21/32". Mint(-) (9.2). Price: $41. CyberAuction #503, Lot #15.

156. AKRO AGATE COMPANY. Corkscrew. Red and light green. Nice shooter. Clarksburg, WV, circa 1927-1935. 15/16". Mint (9.7). Price: $40. CyberAuction #352, Lot #43.

157. AKRO AGATE COMPANY. Corkscrew. Transparent bubble-filled green base. Opaque white snake. Clarksburg, WV, circa 1927-1935. 3/4". Mint (9.7). Price: $40. CyberAuction #487, Lot #22.

158. AKRO AGATE COMPANY. Corkscrew. Four-color. Salmon, white, red and lavender. One tiny subsurface moon. Clarksburg, WV, circa 1927-1935. 21/32". Near Mint(+) (8.9). Price: $40. CyberAuction #500, Lot #32.

159. AKRO AGATE COMPANY. Corkscrew. Translucent milky white base. Semi-opaque red spiral and translucent brown with black spiral. Clarksburg, WV, circa 1927-1935. 5/8". Mint (9.9). Price: $39. CyberAuction #364, Lot #18.

160. AKRO AGATE COMPANY. Corkscrew. Semi-opaque lightly green tinted white base with a nice blue spiral. Beauty. Clarksburg, WV, circa 1927-1935. 11/16". Mint (9.8). Price: $39. CyberAuction #377, Lot #37.

161. AKRO AGATE COMPANY. Corkscrew. Semi-opaque light blue base with darker blue spiral on it. Superb. Very hard to find. Stunning. Clarksburg, WV, circa 1927-1935. 9/16". Mint (9.9). Price: $38. CyberAuction #333, Lot #38.

162. AKRO AGATE COMPANY. Corkscrew. Super Ace shooter corkscrew. Semi-opaque milky white base. Nice snake of orange. One melt spot. Beautiful example, in great shape. Clarksburg, WV, circa 1927-1935. 1". Mint(-) (9.2). Price: $38. CyberAuction #400, Lot #23.

163. AKRO AGATE COMPANY. Corkscrew. Nice three-color. White, light green and translucent red. Super marble. Clarksburg, WV, circa 1927-1935. 7/8". Mint (9.9). Price: $38. CyberAuction #404, Lot #16.

164. AKRO AGATE COMPANY. Corkscrew. Very interesting coloring. Translucent, almost vitreous orange with a translucent white spiral. Superb marble. Clarksburg, WV, circa 1927-1935. 5/8". Mint (9.9). Price: $38. CyberAuction #443, Lot #26.

165. AKRO AGATE COMPANY. Corkscrew. Beauty. Opaque white, translucent orange/red and transparent very dark purple. Excellent. Clarksburg, WV, circa 1927-1935. 5/8". Mint (9.9). Price: $38. CyberAuction #485, Lot #56.

166. AKRO AGATE COMPANY. Corkscrew. Reddish base with a black spiral on the surface. Beauty. Shooter. Clarksburg, WV, circa 1927-1935. 23/32". Mint (9.7). Price: $37. CyberAuction #336, Lot #6.

167. AKRO AGATE COMPANY. Corkscrew. Three color corkscrew, commonly referred to as an Indian Blanket. White, red and black corkscrew. Two tiny sparkles. Clarksburg, WV, circa 1927-1935. 23/32". Mint(-) (9.0). Price: $37. CyberAuction #356, Lot #19.

168. AKRO AGATE COMPANY. Corkscrew. Red, yellow and light green. Clarksburg, WV, circa 1927-1935. 25/32". Mint (9.5). Price: $37. CyberAuction #403, Lot #50.

169. AKRO AGATE COMPANY. Corkscrew. Three-color shooter corkscrew. Red, light blue, white. Small pinprick. Gorgeous. Clarksburg, WV, circa 1927-1935. 13/16". Mint(-) (9.0). Price: $37. CyberAuction #448, Lot #13.

170. AKRO AGATE COMPANY. Corkscrew. Very hard to find colors. Ribbon corkscrew. Transparent lavender base, with loads of air bubbles, opaque yellow ribbon. Beauty. Clarksburg, WV, circa 1927-1935. 5/8". Mint (9.8). Price: $37. CyberAuction #451, Lot #14.

171. AKRO AGATE COMPANY. Corkscrew. Super marble. Transparent green base. Semi-opaque white ribbon. Snake of transparent brown on the surface. Very unusual. Clarksburg, WV, circa 1927-1935. 19/32". Mint (9.9). Price: $37. CyberAuction #459, Lot #3.

172. AKRO AGATE COMPANY. Corkscrew. Very odd five-color corkscrew. Rare. Transparent clear base. Separate spirals of opaque yellow, opaque white, translucent red and semi-opaque peach. Very rare coloring. Some roughness, scratching and pits. Clarksburg, WV, circa 1927-1935. 5/8". Near Mint (8.6). Price: $36. CyberAuction #436, Lot #44.

173. AKRO AGATE COMPANY. Corkscrew. Hard to find snake/ribbon cork. This is an exceptional example. Transparent clear base. Opaque yellow ribbon. In the clear space is an opaque white snake. One of the most nicely formed examples I have seen. Clarksburg, WV, circa 1927-1935. 5/8". Mint (9.9). Price: $35. CyberAuction #339, Lot #8.

174. AKRO AGATE COMPANY. Corkscrew. Superb. Triple twisted white ribbon in transparent green. Shooter. Has been lightly buffed. Clarksburg, WV, circa 1927-1935. 7/8". Mint (9.9). Price: $35. CyberAuction #357, Lot #44.

175. AKRO AGATE COMPANY. Corkscrew. Lot of two marbles. Odd Popeye type. Spiral of clear with white wisps. One has a brown and burnt orange spiral, other has a brown and very pale green spiral. Both have minor damage. 19/32". Near Mint(+) (8.8 & Near Mint (8.4). Price: $35. CyberAuction #394, Lot #34.

176. AKRO AGATE COMPANY. Corkscrew. Rare. Very fluorescent semi-opaque creamy white base with opaque orange spiral. Gorgeous. Clarksburg, WV, circa 1927-1935. 5/8". Mint (9.7). Price: $35. CyberAuction #428, Lot #51.

177. AKRO AGATE COMPANY. Corkscrew. Three-color. Milky white base. Dark translucent blue spiral and a translucent egg yolk yellow spiral. Superb. One very tiny rub spot. Clarksburg, WV, circa 1927-1935. 5/8". Mint(-) (9.2). Price: $35. CyberAuction #429, Lot #51.

178. AKRO AGATE COMPANY. Corkscrew. Narrow pale green, narrow white, wide orange. Beauty. Clarksburg, WV, circa 1927-1935. 5/8". Mint (9.9). Price: $35. CyberAuction #432, Lot #1.

179. AKRO AGATE COMPANY. Corkscrew. Beautiful three-color Indian Blanket corkscrew. Opaque yellow, opaque black, translucent red. One tiny pit. Beauty. Clarksburg, WV, circa 1927-1935. 19/32". Mint(-) (9.2). Price: $35. CyberAuction #496, Lot #39.

180. AKRO AGATE COMPANY. Corkscrew. Transparent bubble-filled green base. Opaque white snake. Clarksburg, WV, circa 1927-1935. 23/32". Mint (9.7). Price: $34.50. CyberAuction #487, Lot #42.

181. AKRO AGATE COMPANY. Corkscrew. Very nice marble. Translucent milky white base. Semi-opaque yellow and blue corkscrew. Some blending of the yellow and blue to create green. A couple of tiny sparkles. Clarksburg, WV, circa 1927-1935. 3/4". Mint(-) (9.0). Price: $34. CyberAuction #356, Lot #8.

182. AKRO AGATE COMPANY. Corkscrew. Odd coloring. Lavender, blue white, red. Small scratch and small sparkles. Clarksburg, WV, circa 1927-1935. 5/8". Near Mint (8.6). Price: $34. CyberAuction #370, Lot #49.

183. AKRO AGATE COMPANY. Corkscrew. Yellow, orange and light green. Clarksburg, WV, circa 1927-1935. 23/32". Mint (9.9). Price: $34. CyberAuction #505, Lot #51.

184. AKRO AGATE COMPANY. Corkscrew. Orange, blue and black/brown

Very nice. One tiny scratch. Clarksburg, WV, circa 1927-1935. 5/8". Mint(-) (9.2). Price: $33. CyberAuction #421, Lot #1.

185. AKRO AGATE COMPANY. Corkscrew. Gorgeous. Transparent bubble-filled emerald green base. Two and a half twist narrow white snake on the surface. One sparkle. Clarksburg, WV, circa 1927-1935. 11/16". Mint(-) (9.2). Price: $32. CyberAuction #352, Lot #60.

186. AKRO AGATE COMPANY. Corkscrew. Three-color corkscrew. Type of Indian Blanket. Opaque white, opaque black and transparent red spirals. Clarksburg, WV, circa 1927-1935. 23/32". Mint (9.7). Price: $32. CyberAuction #369, Lot #38.

187. AKRO AGATE COMPANY. Corkscrew. Orange and light blue. Harder to find color combination. One tiny subsurface moon. Clarksburg, WV, circa 1927-1935. 11/16". Near Mint(+) (8.8). Price: $32. CyberAuction #373, Lot #23.

188. AKRO AGATE COMPANY. Corkscrew. Gray, green and orange. Nice. Clarksburg, WV, circa 1927-1935. 17/32". Mint (9.7). Price: $32. CyberAuction #376, Lot #11.

189. AKRO AGATE COMPANY. Corkscrew. Nice three-color. Creamy white base. Transparent red deep spiral. Thin blue spiral lying on the white spiral. Double twist. A couple of sparkles. Clarksburg, WV, circa 1927-1935. 21/32". Near Mint(+) (8.9). Price: $32. CyberAuction #377, Lot #12.

190. AKRO AGATE COMPANY. Corkscrew. Lavender with some white, with a nice dark red spiral. Gorgeous. Clarksburg, WV, circa 1927-1935. 5/8". Mint (9.8). Price: $32. CyberAuction #388, Lot #24.

191. AKRO AGATE COMPANY. Corkscrew. Three color. Yellow, light blue, gray. Clarksburg, WV, circa 1927-1935. 5/8". Mint (9.7). Price: $32. CyberAuction #417, Lot #28.

192. AKRO AGATE COMPANY. Corkscrew. Large red and yellow corkscrew. Clarksburg, WV, circa 1927-1935. 31/32". Mint (9.7). Price: $32. CyberAuction #428, Lot #5.

193. AKRO AGATE COMPANY. Corkscrew. Transparent clear base. Double twist semi-opaque red ribbon. Clarksburg, WV, circa 1927-1935. 5/8". Mint (9.7). Price: $32. CyberAuction #465, Lot #44.

194. AKRO AGATE COMPANY. Corkscrew. Very pale blue spiral on yellow. Gorgeous. Clarksburg, WV, circa 1927-1935. 5/8". Mint (9.9). Price: $32. CyberAuction #467, Lot #20.

195. AKRO AGATE COMPANY. Corkscrew. Orange with light green and brown spirals. Clarksburg, WV, circa 1927-1935. 5/8". Mint (9.9). Price: $32. CyberAuction #505, Lot #20.

196. AKRO AGATE COMPANY. Corkscrew. Black snake on orange, with a narrow salmon spiral. Clarksburg, WV, circa 1927-1935. 19/32". Mint (9.8). Price: $32. CyberAuction #505, Lot #24.

197. AKRO AGATE COMPANY. Corkscrew. Orange base. Spiral of black, covered by oxblood. Hard to find. Tiny flake at one end. Clarksburg, WV, circa 1927-1935. 5/8". Near Mint(+) (8.8). Price: $32. CyberAuction #508, Lot #17.

198. AKRO AGATE COMPANY. Corkscrew. Beauty. Lavender, white and orange/red. Very pretty. Clarksburg, WV, circa 1927-1935. 5/8". Mint (9.9). Two marbles available, you are bidding on one. Winner has choice of either or both, remainder to under. Price: $31. CyberAuction #340, Lot #21.

199. AKRO AGATE COMPANY. Corkscrew. Gorgeous four-color. Orange, red, gray and creamy white. One tiny air hole. Superb. Clarksburg, WV, circa 1927-1935. 21/32". Mint (9.5). Consignor note: C22. Price: $31. CyberAuction #424, Lot #16.

200. AKRO AGATE COMPANY. Corkscrew. Very unusual ribbon corkscrew. Translucent light orange base. There are three ribbons, or perhaps it's a three-vaned ribbon of translucent white in the marble, with the white spirals on the surface. One sparkle. Clarksburg, WV, circa 1927-1935. 5/8". Near Mint(+) (8.9). Price: $30. CyberAuction #336, Lot #31.

201. AKRO AGATE COMPANY. Corkscrew. Milky white base. Two wide surface spirals of semi-opaque red, one thin spiral of black. Some cold roll lines. Clarksburg, WV, circa 1927-1935. 3/4". Mint (9.5). Price: $30. CyberAuction #341, Lot #43.

202. AKRO AGATE COMPANY. Corkscrew. Very unusual ribbon corkscrew. Transparent clear base. Ribbon is opaque green with a ribbon of opaque blue right next to it. Odd. Has a sparkle. Clarksburg, WV, circa 1927-1935. 5/8". Mint(-) (9.0). Price: $30. CyberAuction #344, Lot #43.

203. AKRO AGATE COMPANY. Corkscrew. Unusual coloring. Translucent milky white base. Snake of translucent orange/brown, with a snake of black on it. Clarksburg, WV, circa 1927-1935. 5/8". Mint (9.8). Price: $30. CyberAuction #344, Lot #45.

204. AKRO AGATE COMPANY. Corkscrew. Rare marble. Green milky base with a very wide snake of black on it. One tiny subsurface moon. Clarksburg, WV, circa 1927-1935. 5/8". Near Mint(+) (8.9). Price: $30. CyberAuction #369, Lot #15.

205. AKRO AGATE COMPANY. Corkscrew. Ribbon corkscrew. Semi-opaque white ribbon in transparent dark aqua base. Triple twist. Clarksburg, WV, circa 1927-1935. 19/32". Mint (9.6). Price: $30. CyberAuction #381, Lot #5.

206. AKRO AGATE COMPANY. Corkscrew. Yellow base with a translucent orange/red spiral on it. Thin black spiral next to it. Looks like oxblood, but it isn't. Very nice. Clarksburg, WV, circa 1927-1935. 11/16". Mint (9.8). Price: $30. CyberAuction #387, Lot #55.

207. AKRO AGATE COMPANY. Corkscrew. Wide dark red, wide light green, very narrow yellow. Clarksburg, WV, circa 1927-1935. 5/8". Mint (9.7). Price: $30. CyberAuction #413, Lot #1.

208. AKRO AGATE COMPANY. Corkscrew. Orange, light blue, gray. Clarksburg, WV, circa 1927-1935. 5/8". Mint (9.7). Price: $30. CyberAuction #505, Lot #39.

209. AKRO AGATE COMPANY. Corkscrew. Interesting orange and green.

Very nice marble. Clarksburg, WV, circa 1927-1935. 5/8". Mint (9.7). Price: $28. CyberAuction #348, Lot #42.

210. AKRO AGATE COMPANY. Corkscrew. Yellow and blue corkscrew. Beauty. Clarksburg, WV, circa 1927-1935. 3/4". Mint (9.9). Price: $28. CyberAuction #369, Lot #9.

211. AKRO AGATE COMPANY. Corkscrew. Light blue and narrow yellow. Double twist. Two tiny subsurface moons. Clarksburg, WV, circa 1927-1935. 11/16". Near Mint(+) (8.8). Price: $28. CyberAuction #373, Lot #18.

212. AKRO AGATE COMPANY. Corkscrew. Very odd four color corkscrew. Transparent clear base. Ribbon of opaque yellow with a snake of opaque blue on top of it. The blue is edged by a narrow snake of black. Very odd. Several chips and an annealing fracture. Rare. Clarksburg, WV, circa 1927-1935. 5/8". Mint(-) (8.0). Price: $28. CyberAuction #388, Lot #2.

213. AKRO AGATE COMPANY. Corkscrew. Rare marble. Opalescent milky white base with a translucent dark purple snake on it. Very nice. Clarksburg, WV, circa 1927-1935. 19/32". Mint (9.9). Price: $28. CyberAuction #396, Lot #38.

214. AKRO AGATE COMPANY. Corkscrew. Yellow base with a translucent orange/red spiral on it. Thin black spiral next to it. Looks like oxblood, but it isn't. Very nice. Clarksburg, WV, circa 1927-1935. 11/16". Mint (9.8). Price: $28. CyberAuction #441, Lot #48.

215. AKRO AGATE COMPANY. Corkscrew. Very interesting corkscrew. Milky white base. Snake of transparent orange/red, edged by a spiral of wispy olive green. Odd. Clarksburg, WV, circa 1927-1935. 21/32". Mint (9.8). Price: $28. CyberAuction #464, Lot #11.

216. AKRO AGATE COMPANY. Corkscrew. Double twist. Thin red and yellow spiral. Shooter. Superb. Clarksburg, WV, circa 1927-1935. 25/32". Mint (9.7). Price: $28. CyberAuction #500, Lot #39.

217. AKRO AGATE COMPANY. Corkscrew. Snake. Fluorescent transparent very lightly Vaseline base. Snake of orange and red on it. One tiny annealing fracture. Clarksburg, WV, circa 1927-1935. 5/8". Mint(-) (9.0). Price: $27. CyberAuction #341, Lot #40.

218. AKRO AGATE COMPANY. Corkscrew. Double ingot Indian Blanket. Opaque black base with translucent red and opaque yellow spirals. Two corkscrews melted together. Some annealing fractures. Clarksburg, WV, circa 1927-1935. 25/32". Mint(-) (9.0). Price: $27. CyberAuction #345, Lot #23.

219. AKRO AGATE COMPANY. Corkscrew. Four-color corkscrew. Light green, yellow, transparent red and transparent orange. One sparkle and a scratch. Clarksburg, WV, circa 1927-1935. 5/8". Near Mint(+) (8.8). Price: $27. CyberAuction #385, Lot #5.

220. AKRO AGATE COMPANY. Corkscrew. Pale lavender, white and orange. Beauty. Clarksburg, WV, circa 1927-1935. 11/16". Mint (9.9). Price: $27. CyberAuction #392, Lot #11.

221. AKRO AGATE COMPANY. Corkscrew. Light blue base with pale yellow spiral. Wispy brown snake on the surface. Nice. Clarksburg, WV, circa 1927-1935. 21/32". Mint (9.8). Price: $27. CyberAuction #425, Lot #7.

222. AKRO AGATE COMPANY. Corkscrew. White and yellow corkscrew. Wispy snake of black on the white. Nice. Clarksburg, WV, circa 1927-1935. 5/8". Mint (9.7). Price: $27. CyberAuction #425, Lot #12.

223. AKRO AGATE COMPANY. Corkscrew. Light green and red corkscrew. Very dark red narrow spiral next to the lighter red. Wispy dark red/brown spiral on the light green. One pinprick. Gorgeous. Clarksburg, WV, circa 1927-1935. 3/4". Mint(-) (9.2). Price: $27. CyberAuction #425, Lot #20.

224. AKRO AGATE COMPANY. Corkscrew. Double twist white snake in transparent light red. Outstanding example. Clarksburg, WV, circa 1927-1935. 19/32". Mint (9.9). Price: $27. CyberAuction #462, Lot #19.

225. AKRO AGATE COMPANY. Corkscrew. Light green base. Almost completely covered by transparent brown and translucent gray. A sparkle. Clarksburg, WV, circa 1927-1935. 19/32". Mint(-) (9.1). Price: $27. CyberAuction #498, Lot #33.

226. AKRO AGATE COMPANY. Corkscrew. Wide black snake on opaque bright orange. Beauty. Clarksburg, WV, circa 1927-1935. 5/8". Mint (9.6). Price: $27. CyberAuction #498, Lot #41.

227. AKRO AGATE COMPANY. Corkscrew. Another interesting corkscrew. Translucent milky white base. Opaque dark blue spiral and an opaque egg yolk yellow spiral. Several tiny subsurface moons and sparkles, but a large marble. Clarksburg, WV, circa 1927-1935. 31/32". Near Mint(+) (8.7). Price: $26. CyberAuction #336, Lot #28.

228. AKRO AGATE COMPANY. Corkscrew. Nice ribbon. Transparent red base. Opaque white ribbon. Shooter. Clarksburg, WV, circa 1927-1935. 3/4". Mint (9.9). Price: $26. CyberAuction #339, Lot #11.

229. AKRO AGATE COMPANY. Corkscrew. Orange base with a black snake on the surface. Gorgeous. Clarksburg, WV, circa 1927-1935. 21/32". Mint (9.9). Price: $26. CyberAuction #351, Lot #41.

230. AKRO AGATE COMPANY. Corkscrew. Transparent very dark green base. Opaque white ribbon. Nice. Clarksburg, WV, circa 1927-1935. 3/4". Mint (9.5). Price: $26. CyberAuction #458, Lot #16.

231. AKRO AGATE COMPANY. Corkscrew. Triple twist black spiral in yellow. Clarksburg, WV, circa 1927-1935. 11/16". Mint (9.8). Price: $26. CyberAuction #461, Lot #47.

232. AKRO AGATE COMPANY. Corkscrew. Nice snake corkscrew. Fluorescent transparent Vaseline yellow base. Double twist opaque white snake on surface. Clarksburg, WV, circa 1927-1935. 11/16". Mint (9.9). Price: $25. CyberAuction #342, Lot #6.

233. AKRO AGATE COMPANY. Corkscrew. Interesting three-color. Orange and creamy white corkscrew. Black snake on the white. Clarksburg, WV, circa 1927-1935. 9/16". Mint (9.9). Price: $25. CyberAuction #352, Lot #52.

234. AKRO AGATE COMPANY. Corkscrew. Superb snake corkscrew. Triple twisted opaque white snake on fluorescent Vaseline yellow base. Beauty. A couple of pits and some scratching. Clarksburg, WV, circa 1927-1935. 11/16". Near Mint(+) (8.9). Price: $25. CyberAuction #359, Lot #52.

235. AKRO AGATE COMPANY. Corkscrew. Very nice snake. Transparent clear base. Orange snake. One tiny chip. 5/8". Near Mint(+) (8.9). Price: $25. CyberAuction #360, Lot #37.

236. AKRO AGATE COMPANY. Corkscrew. Yellow base with wide transparent red spiral. Clarksburg, WV, circa 1927-1935. 29/32". Mint (9.9). Price: $25. CyberAuction #366, Lot #21.

237. AKRO AGATE COMPANY. Corkscrew. Ribbon corkscrew. Transparent orange/red base. Opaque white ribbon. Brown edge to the ribbon. Double twist. Clarksburg, WV, circa 1927-1935. 5/8". Mint (9.7). Price: $25. CyberAuction #373, Lot #32.

238. AKRO AGATE COMPANY. Corkscrew. Transparent cherry red base. Opaque white snake. Gorgeous. Clarksburg, WV, circa 1927-1935. 5/8". Mint (9.9). Price: $25. CyberAuction #403, Lot #14.

239. AKRO AGATE COMPANY. Corkscrew. Ribbon corkscrew. Double twist. Opaque white ribbon in transparent light green. Beauty. Clarksburg, WV, circa 1927-1935. 11/16". Mint (9.9). Price: $25. CyberAuction #429, Lot #45.

240. AKRO AGATE COMPANY. Corkscrew. Double ingot shooter. Transparent red and white. Clarksburg, WV, circa 1927-1935. 13/16". Mint (9.7). Price: $25. CyberAuction #436, Lot #5.

241. AKRO AGATE COMPANY. Corkscrew. Red, blue and white corkscrew. Cold dimples and lines. Clarksburg, WV, circa 1927-1935. 13/16". Mint (9.5). Price: $25. CyberAuction #450, Lot #21.

242. AKRO AGATE COMPANY. Corkscrew. Three-color corkscrew. Orange/red, yellow, light green. Very nice. Clarksburg, WV, circa 1927-1935. 25/32". Mint (9.7). Price: $25. CyberAuction #508, Lot #57.

243. AKRO AGATE COMPANY. Corkscrew. Opaque yellow and translucent red. A beauty. Clarksburg, WV, circa 1927-1935. 1". Mint (9.7). Price: $24. CyberAuction #333, Lot #27.

244. AKRO AGATE COMPANY. Corkscrew. Three color. Nice. White base with blue spiral. Spiral is on green. Interesting. Some scratches and pits. Clarksburg, WV, circa 1927-1935. 23/32". Near Mint(+) (8.8). Price: $24. CyberAuction #337, Lot #6.

245. AKRO AGATE COMPANY. Corkscrew. Interesting four-color. Opaque white base. Spiral of light lavender, spiral of very faint light green, spiral of semi-opaque brown/red. One tiny pit. Clarksburg, WV, circa 1927-1935. 19/32". Mint(-) (9.1). Price: $24. CyberAuction #365, Lot #51.

246. AKRO AGATE COMPANY. Corkscrew. Gorgeous snake. Transparent clear base. Double twist white snake, with a wispy white double twist snake in the clear spiral. Very nice. Clarksburg, WV, circa 1927-1935. 5/8". Mint (9.9). Price: $24. CyberAuction #396, Lot #27.

247. AKRO AGATE COMPANY. Corkscrew. Red and yellow. Beauty. Clarksburg, WV, circa 1927-1935. 15/16". Mint(-) (9.1). Price: $24. CyberAuction #403, Lot #11.

248. AKRO AGATE COMPANY. Corkscrew. White snake on transparent brown. Very nice. Clarksburg, WV, circa 1927-1935. 3/4". Mint (9.7). Price: $24. CyberAuction #465, Lot #42.

249. AKRO AGATE COMPANY. Corkscrew. Four color. Black, red, salmon and white. Tiny flake and tiny sparkle. Clarksburg, WV, circa 1927-1935. 21/32". Near Mint(+) (8.8). Price: $24. CyberAuction #501, Lot #38.

250. AKRO AGATE COMPANY. Corkscrew. Type of Indian Blanket threecolor. Opaque white, transparent dark red, opaque black. One tiny scratch. Clarksburg, WV, circa 1927-19.35. 21/32". Mint(-) (9.2). Price: $23. CyberAuction #333, Lot #21.

251. AKRO AGATE COMPANY. Corkscrew. Beauty. Four color corkscrew. Semi-opaque white base. Three snakes on the surface. One is black. Edged by thin blue. Other is semi-opaque orange. Some pitting. Clarksburg, WV, circa 1927-1935. 19/32". Near Mint (8.6). Price: $23. CyberAuction #339, Lot #20.

252. AKRO AGATE COMPANY. Corkscrew. Ribbon corkscrew. Transparent orange base with opaque white ribbon. Superb marble. Clarksburg, WV, circa 1927-1935. 5/8". Mint (9.7). Price: $23. CyberAuction #356, Lot #11.

253. AKRO AGATE COMPANY. Corkscrew. Lemonade corkscrew. Fluorescent ade base, white spiral and a yellow spiral. One subsurface moon. Clarksburg, WV, circa 1927-1935. 31/32". Near Mint(+) (8.8). Price: $23. CyberAuction #367, Lot #49.

254. AKRO AGATE COMPANY. Corkscrew. Yellow and black corkscrew. Some pitting. Tiny flake and tiny sparkle. Clarksburg, WV, circa 1927-1935. 1". Mint(-) (9.0). Price: $23. CyberAuction #368, Lot #46.

255. AKRO AGATE COMPANY. Corkscrew. White base. Transparent red spiral, lavender on the remaining white. Clarksburg, WV, circa 1927-1935. 5/8". Mint (9.9). Price: $23. CyberAuction #380, Lot #44.

256. AKRO AGATE COMPANY. Corkscrew. Two-color shooter corkscrew. Mocha brown and red. Beauty. A couple of pinpricks. Clarksburg, WV, circa 1927-1935. 29/32". Mint(-) (9.2). Price: $23. CyberAuction #400, Lot #4.

257. AKRO AGATE COMPANY. Corkscrew. Pale green, yellow and red. Shooter. Some tiny subsurface moons. Clarksburg, WV, circa 1927-1935. 13/16". Near Mint (8.6). Price: $23. CyberAuction #421, Lot #13.

258. AKRO AGATE COMPANY. Corkscrew. Odd color. Opaque light blue base. Semi-opaque yellow spiral on it, but is smeared into the blue to create a light green. Clarksburg, WV, circa 1927-1935. 5/8". Mint (9.9). Price: $23. CyberAuction #432, Lot #55.

259. AKRO AGATE COMPANY. Corkscrew. Ribbon corkscrew. Transparent brown base with translucent white ribbon. Beauty. Clarksburg, WV, circa 1927-1935. 19/32". Mint (9.9). Price: $23. CyberAuction #443, Lot #16.

260. AKRO AGATE COMPANY. Corkscrew. Double ingot corkscrew. Red spirals on yellow. Two tiny rough spots. Clarksburg, WV, circa 1928-1935. 13/16". Near Mint(+) (8.9). Price: $23. CyberAuction #445, Lot #41.

261. AKRO AGATE COMPANY. Corkscrew. Three-color corkscrew. Yellow, light green and light orange/red. Clarksburg, WV, circa 1927-1935. 5/8". Mint (9.8). Price: $23. CyberAuction #498, Lot #37.

262. AKRO AGATE COMPANY. Corkscrew. Ribbon corkscrew. Transparent clear base. Opaque yellow ribbon, edged by red. Very nice. One sparkle. Clarksburg, WV, circa 1927-1935. 19/32". Mint(-) (9.2). Price: $22. CyberAuction #341, Lot #14.

263. AKRO AGATE COMPANY. Corkscrew. Gorgeous three-color. Opaque white with lavender bands mixed in. Spiral of semi-opaque red. One tiny fracture. Clarksburg, WV, circa 1927-1935. 23/32". Mint(-) (9.0). Price: $22. CyberAuction #341, Lot #51.

264. AKRO AGATE COMPANY. Corkscrew. Yellow and creamy white corkscrew. Bright yellow. Super. Clarksburg, WV, circa 1927-1935. 5/8". Mint (9.9). Price: $22. CyberAuction #347, Lot #52.

265. AKRO AGATE COMPANY. Corkscrew. Opaque yellow base with a black snake. Beautiful. Clarksburg, WV, circa 1927-1935. 11/16". Mint (9.9). Price: $22. CyberAuction #365, Lot #17.

266. AKRO AGATE COMPANY. Corkscrew. Three color corkscrew. Referred to as an Indian Blanket. Red, white, black. One tiny subsurface moon. Clarksburg, WV, circa 1927-1935. 21/32". Near Mint(+) (8.8). Price: $22. CyberAuction #367, Lot #60.

267. AKRO AGATE COMPANY. Corkscrew. Very odd marble. Very early corkscrew. Translucent white base. There is a yellow spiral inside the marble. The surface is covered with wispy white spirals. A couple of tiny subsurface moons. Clarksburg, WV, circa 1925-1930. 3/4". Near Mint(+) (8.8). Price: $22. CyberAuction #369, Lot #53.

268. AKRO AGATE COMPANY. Corkscrew. Error marble. Dumbbell type (well, half the dumbbell). Creamy white and orange spiral. Too much glass came down into the rollers and there is a long nub at each end. Melt spot and small flake on the marble. Probably dug at the plant site. Originally from Roger and Claudia Hardy. Clarksburg, WV, circa 1927-1935. 13/16" 1-1/16". Near Mint(+) (8.7). Price: $22. CyberAuction #374, Lot #10.

269. AKRO AGATE COMPANY. Corkscrew. Opaque white base. Two spirals of mustard yellow and one of black on it. Very odd colors. A couple of sparkles and one cold roll area. Clarksburg, WV, circa 1927-1935. 21/32". Near Mint(+) (8.8). Price: $22. CyberAuction #377, Lot #14.

270. AKRO AGATE COMPANY. Corkscrew. Superb shooter. Opaque white base. Narrow double twist spiral of orange and of yellow. One tiny subsurface moon, one sparkle. Clarksburg, WV, circa 1927-1935. 23/32". Near Mint(+) (8.8). Price: $22. CyberAuction #379, Lot #37.

271. AKRO AGATE COMPANY. Corkscrew. White, light blue and transparent red. Creased design, but not a double ingot. Pinprick. Clarksburg, WV, circa 1927-1935. 23/32". Mint(-) (9.2). Price: $22. CyberAuction #381, Lot #15.

272. AKRO AGATE COMPANY. Corkscrew. Very unusual corkscrew. Semi opaque green base with unmelted sand in it. Orange snake on it. Clarksburg, WV, circa 1927-1935. 21/32". Mint (9.7). Price: $22. CyberAuction #425, Lot #5.

273. AKRO AGATE COMPANY. Corkscrew. Three-color corkscrew. Transparent red, opaque yellow, opaque white. Clarksburg, WV, circa 1927-1935. 5/8". Mint (9.7). Price: $22. CyberAuction #425, Lot #40.

274. AKRO AGATE COMPANY. Corkscrew. White, orange and lavender. Pretty. Clarksburg, WV, circa 1927-1935. 11/16". Mint (9.9). Price: $22. CyberAuction #461, Lot #11.

275. AKRO AGATE COMPANY. Corkscrew. Transparent red and opaque white corkscrew. Lavender on the white. Clarksburg, WV, circa 1927-1935. 19/32". Mint (9.9). Price: $22. CyberAuction #462, Lot #23.

276. AKRO AGATE COMPANY. Corkscrew. Transparent bubble-filled brown base with opaque yellow spiral. Gorgeous. Clarksburg, WV, circa 1927-1935. 5/8". Mint (9.8). Price: $22. CyberAuction #464, Lot #13.

277. AKRO AGATE COMPANY. Corkscrew. Very nice marble. Opaque orange spiral in opaque white. Narrow transparent red spiral next to the orange. Clarksburg, WV, circa 1927-1935. 5/8". Mint (9.9). Price: $22. CyberAuction #471, Lot #3.

278. AKRO AGATE COMPANY. Corkscrew. Hard to find snake/ribbon base. This is an exceptional example. Transparent clear base. Opaque yellow ribbon. In the clear space is an opaque white snake. One of the most nicely formed examples I have seen. Clarksburg, WV, circa 1927-1935. 5/8". Mint (9.9). Price: $22. CyberAuction #479, Lot #2.

279. AKRO AGATE COMPANY. Corkscrew. Creamy white base, yellow spiral, wide very dark cobalt blue spiral. One tiny flake. Clarksburg, WV, circa 1927-1935. 19/32". Near Mint(+) (8.8). Price: $22. CyberAuction #503, Lot #72.

280. AKRO AGATE COMPANY. Corkscrew. Very interesting marble. Milky white base. Opaque yellow spiral, covered by transparent green. One tiny subsurface moon. Very nice. Clarksburg, WV, circa 1927-1935. 19/32". Near Mint(+) (8.9). Price: $21. CyberAuction #348, Lot #18.

281. AKRO AGATE COMPANY. Corkscrew. Imperial. Translucent milky white base with some opaque white in it. Nice spiral of translucent brown on the surface. A beauty. Excellent marble. Clarksburg, WV, circa 1927-1935. 5/8". Mint (9.9). Price: $21. CyberAuction #359, Lot #56.

282. AKRO AGATE COMPANY. Corkscrew. Orange/brown corkscrew on yellow. Shooter. Nice. Clarksburg, WV, circa 1927-1935. 3/4". Mint (9.7). Price: $21. CyberAuction #420, Lot #5.

283. AKRO AGATE COMPANY. Corkscrew. Transparent red spiral in creamy white. Interesting. Clarksburg, WV, circa 1927-1935. 3/4". Mint (9.9). Price: $21. CyberAuction #420, Lot #47.

284. AKRO AGATE COMPANY. Corkscrew. Rare three-color. Black snake on white. Thin orange/yellow next to the black. Clarksburg, WV, circa 1927-1935. 21/32". Mint (9.9). Price: $21. CyberAuction #448, Lot #23.

285. AKRO AGATE COMPANY. Corkscrew. Transparent light brown base. Semi-opaque white ribbon. Beautiful example. Clarksburg, WV, circa 1927-1935. 5/8". Mint (9.9). Price: $21. CyberAuction #455, Lot #19.

286. AKRO AGATE COMPANY. Corkscrew. Three-color Indian Blanket. Black, red and yellow. Very nice. Has two tiny flakes. Clarksburg, WV, circa 1927-1935. 21/32". Near Mint(+) (8.7). Price: $21. CyberAuction #458, Lot #54.

287. AKRO AGATE COMPANY. Corkscrew. Orange and green spiral. Nice color, hard to find. Shooter. Several sparkles. Clarksburg, WV, circa 1927-1935. 3/4". Near Mint(+) (8.8). Price: $21. CyberAuction #479, Lot #46.

288. AKRO AGATE COMPANY. Corkscrew. Black on red. Hard to find. Clarksburg, WV, circa 1927-1935. 5/8". Mint (9.8). Price: $21. CyberAuction #481, Lot #28.

289. AKRO AGATE COMPANY. Corkscrew. Double twist ribbon/snake. Transparent dark red base with opaque creamy white ribbon. Narrow gray snake running beside the ribbon. Clarksburg, WV, circa 1927-1935. 5/8". Mint (9.7). Price: $21. CyberAuction #483, Lot #5.

290. AKRO AGATE COMPANY. Corkscrew. Opaque white with several spirals of bright red and olive gray. One tiny rough spot. Clarksburg, WV, circa 1927-1935. 21/32". Near Mint(+) (8.9). Price: $21. CyberAuction #498, Lot #21.

291. AKRO AGATE COMPANY. Corkscrew. Milky white base. Spiral of brown and a narrow spiral that looks like burnt oxblood. Overall scratches. Clarksburg, WV, circa 1927-1935. 5/8". Near Mint(+) (8.9). Price: $20. CyberAuction #395, Lot #5.

292. AKRO AGATE COMPANY. Corkscrew. Green, brown and orange. Clarksburg, WV, circa 1927-1935. 5/8". Mint (9.9). Price: $20. CyberAuction #399, Lot #23.

293. AKRO AGATE COMPANY. Corkscrew. Black snake on red. One tiny sparkle. Clarksburg, WV, circa 1927-1935. 21/32". Mint(-) (9.2). Price: $20. CyberAuction #462, Lot #11.

294. AKRO AGATE COMPANY. Corkscrew. Opaque white, transparent cherry red, transparent light brown. The brown is narrower than the other two colors. Very rare coloring. Small sparkle. Clarksburg, WV, circa 1927-1935. 23/32". Near Mint(+) (8.9). Price: $20. CyberAuction #487, Lot #5.

295. AKRO AGATE COMPANY. Corkscrew. Light opaque green, opaque yellow, transparent red, transparent brown. Overall tiny pits and pinpricks. A couple of tiny chips. Clarksburg, WV, circa 1927-1935. 5/8". Near Mint(-) (8.0). Price: $20. CyberAuction #498, Lot #27.

296. AKRO AGATE COMPANY. Corkscrew. White, lavender and transparent red. Clarksburg, WV, circa 1927-1935. 5/8". Mint (9.6). Price: $20. CyberAuction #505, Lot #22.

297. AKRO AGATE COMPANY. Corkscrew. Double ingot corkscrew. White with transparent brown spirals. Shooter. Very nice. Clarksburg, WV, circa 1927-1935. 13/16". Mint (9.9). Price: $19. CyberAuction #350, Lot #43.

298. AKRO AGATE COMPANY. Corkscrew. Double ingot corkscrew. Each half is a red and blue. One sparkle. Clarksburg, WV, circa 1927-1935. 25/32". Mint(-) (9.1). Price: $19. CyberAuction #351, Lot #47.

299. AKRO AGATE COMPANY. Corkscrew. Superb ribbon corkscrew. Very fluorescent. Vaseline yellow transparent base with a translucent white ribbon in it. Two very tiny subsurface moons, one tiny flake. Hard to find. Clarksburg, WV, circa 1927-1935. 11/16". Near Mint(+) (8.8). Price: $19. CyberAuction #359, Lot #6.

300. AKRO AGATE COMPANY. Corkscrew. Nice shooter. Yellow and blue. Narrow yellow. Some annealing fractures. Clarksburg, WV, circa 1927-1935. 29/32". Mint(-) (9.0). Price: $19. CyberAuction #360, Lot #15.

301. AKRO AGATE COMPANY. Corkscrew. Snake corkscrew. Transparent red base. Triple twist opaque white snake. Clarksburg, WV, circa 1927-1935. 5/8". Mint (9.9). Price: $19. CyberAuction #369, Lot #33.

302. AKRO AGATE COMPANY. Corkscrew. Semi-opaque milky white base. Snake of orange, brown and black, mixed. Clarksburg, WV, circa 1927-1935. 11/16". Mint (9.7). Price: $19. CyberAuction #378, Lot #50.

303. AKRO AGATE COMPANY. Corkscrew. Yellow and orange shooter. Some pinpricking. Clarksburg, WV, circa 1927-1935. 13/16". Mint(-) (9.0). Price: $19. CyberAuction #384, Lot #41.

304. AKRO AGATE COMPANY. Corkscrew. Light blue, yellow and thin black corkscrew. Beauty. Clarksburg, WV, circa 1927-1935. 21/32". Mint (9.8). Price: $19. CyberAuction #396, Lot #42.

305. AKRO AGATE COMPANY. Corkscrew. Lavender with red spiral. Very nice. Clarksburg, WV, circa 1927-1935. 5/8". Mint (9.9). Price: $19. CyberAuction #403, Lot #35.

306. AKRO AGATE COMPANY. Corkscrew. Red/brown, blue. Some narrow gray. Clarksburg, WV, circa 1927-1935. 5/8". Mint (9.7). Price: $19. CyberAuction #421, Lot #21.

307. AKRO AGATE COMPANY. Corkscrew. Three color. Red, white and blue. One pinprick. Clarksburg, WV, circa 1927-1935. 5/8". Mint(-) (9.2). Price: $19. CyberAuction #427, Lot #38.

308. AKRO AGATE COMPANY. Corkscrew. Three color. Dark red, orange and white. Odd. One sparkle. Clarksburg, WV, circa 1927-1935. 11/16". Mint(-) (9.0). Price: $19. CyberAuction #427, Lot #40.

309. AKRO AGATE COMPANY. Corkscrew. Odd marble. Oxblood-like red spiral on black. Some cold creasing. Clarksburg, WV, circa 1927-1935. 5/8". Mint (9.6). Price: $19. CyberAuction #481, Lot #39.

310. AKRO AGATE COMPANY. Corkscrew. Four-color corkscrew, but odd. Opaque white, two separate spirals of red, light green, light brown. One very tiny flake. Clarksburg, WV, circa 1927-1935. 5/8". Near Mint(+) (8.9). Price: $19. CyberAuction #491, Lot #31.

311. AKRO AGATE COMPANY. Corkscrew. Double twist shooter. Trans-

parent red on purple. Tiny pinprick. Clarksburg, WV, circa 1927-1935. 3/4". Mint(-) (9.2). Price: $19. CyberAuction #496, Lot #36.

312. AKRO AGATE COMPANY. Corkscrew. Excellent marble. Translucent milky white base. Opaque white snake on top of opaque white spiral. Superb. Clarksburg, WV, circa 1927-1935. 5/8". Mint (9.7). Price: $19. CyberAuction #501, Lot #43.

313. AKRO AGATE COMPANY. Corkscrew. Shooter. Double twist blue spiral on yellow. Very nice. Clarksburg, WV, circa 1927-1935. 11/16". Mint (9.7). Price: $18. CyberAuction #368, Lot #5.

314. AKRO AGATE COMPANY. Corkscrew. Three color corkscrew. White base. Very wide lavender spiral. Narrower red spiral. Nice. Clarksburg, WV, circa 1927-1935. 23/32". Mint (9.9). Price: $18. CyberAuction #369, Lot #5.

315. AKRO AGATE COMPANY. Corkscrew. Opaque yellow and transparent red. Double twist. Beautiful. Clarksburg, WV, circa 1927-1935. 5/8". Mint (9.7). Price: $18. CyberAuction #388, Lot #40.

316. AKRO AGATE COMPANY. Corkscrew. Yellow base. Light blue spiral, gray spiral. Clarksburg, WV, circa 1927-1935. 11/16". Mint (9.7). Price: $18. CyberAuction #505, Lot #18.

317. AKRO AGATE COMPANY. Corkscrew. Blue and yellow. Very nice. Clarksburg, WV, circa 1927-1935. 5/8". Mint (9.7). Price: $17. CyberAuction #342, Lot #10.

318. AKRO AGATE COMPANY. Corkscrew. Nice ribbon corkscrew. Transparent clear base. Double twist opaque yellow ribbon. Clarksburg, WV, circa 1927-1935. 5/8". Mint (9.7). Price: $17. CyberAuction #343, Lot #15.

319. AKRO AGATE COMPANY. Corkscrew. Interesting ribbon corkscrew. Transparent fluorescent Vaseline yellow base. Double twisted white ribbon. Clarksburg, WV, circa 1927-1935. 5/8". Mint (9.9). Price: $17. CyberAuction #344, Lot #8.

320. AKRO AGATE COMPANY. Corkscrew. Orange base with a black snake. One tiny subsurface moon. Clarksburg, WV, circa 1927-1935. 9/16". Near Mint(+) (8.7). Price: $17. CyberAuction #348, Lot #40.

321. AKRO AGATE COMPANY. Corkscrew. Light blue base with dark blue spiral. Beauty. One tiny scratching spot. Clarksburg, WV, circa 1927-1935. 21/32". Mint(-) (9.0). Price: $17. CyberAuction #351, Lot #29.

322. AKRO AGATE COMPANY. Corkscrew. Black snake on orange. Beauty. Clarksburg, WV, circa 1927-1935. 5/8". Mint (9.8). Price: $17. CyberAuction #354, Lot #23.

323. AKRO AGATE COMPANY. Corkscrew. Blue and yellow, with a wide blend of green. Clarksburg, WV, circa 1927-1935. 11/16". Mint (9.9). Price: $17. CyberAuction #365, Lot #5.

324. AKRO AGATE COMPANY. Corkscrew. Double ingot corkscrew. Red spirals on yellow. Two tiny rough spots. Clarksburg, WV, circa 1928-1935. 13/16". Near Mint(+) (8.9). Price: $17. CyberAuction #374, Lot #1.

325. AKRO AGATE COMPANY. Corkscrew. Imperial. Translucent milky white base with some opaque white in it. Nice spiral of translucent brown on the surface. A beauty. Excellent marble. Clarksburg, WV, circa 1927-1935. 5/8". Mint (9.7). Price: $17. CyberAuction #378, Lot #20.

326. AKRO AGATE COMPANY. Corkscrew. Interesting. Opaque white base. Transparent dark royal blue snake on the surface. There is a thin oxblood spiral under the blue, that you can see with a light. A couple of tiny sparkles. Clarksburg, WV, circa 1927-1935. 5/8". Mint(-) (9.0). Price: $17. CyberAuction #378, Lot #59.

327. AKRO AGATE COMPANY. Corkscrew. Creamy white base with a bright orange spiral. Odd. Clarksburg, WV, circa 1927-1935. 11/16". Mint (9.7). Price: $17. CyberAuction #381, Lot #21.

328. AKRO AGATE COMPANY. Corkscrew. Transparent red base with a double twisted opaque white snake. Clarksburg, WV, circa 1927-1935. 5/8". Mint (9.9). Price: $17. CyberAuction #388, Lot #11.

329. AKRO AGATE COMPANY. Corkscrew. Double ingot corkscrew. Translucent red and opaque white. Slightly malformed. Clarksburg, WV, circa 1927-1935. 29/32". Mint (9.5). Price: $17. CyberAuction #390, Lot #40.

330. AKRO AGATE COMPANY. Corkscrew. Hard to find. Opalescent moonie base. Black snake spiral. One air hole, a couple of tiny scratches. Clarksburg, WV, circa 1927-1935. 5/8". Mint(-) (9.0). Price: $17. CyberAuction #395, Lot #56.

331. AKRO AGATE COMPANY. Corkscrew. Transparent dark purple base with wide opaque white spiral. One sparkle. Clarksburg, WV, circa 1927-1935. 11/16". Mint(-) (9.0). Price: $17. CyberAuction #403, Lot #5.

332. AKRO AGATE COMPANY. Corkscrew. Purple mixed with white, with a red spiral. Very nice. Clarksburg, WV, circa 1927-1935. 5/8". Mint (9.7). Price: $17. CyberAuction #416, Lot #24.

333. AKRO AGATE COMPANY. Corkscrew. Red snake on white, with thin yellow. Clarksburg, WV, circa 1927-1935. 5/8". Mint (9.9). Price: $17. CyberAuction #416, Lot #31.

334. AKRO AGATE COMPANY. Corkscrew. Black spiral on yellow. Gorgeous. Clarksburg, WV, circa 1927-1935. 11/16". Mint (9.7). Price: $17. CyberAuction #424, Lot #39.

335. AKRO AGATE COMPANY. Corkscrew. Yellow and blue. Clarksburg, WV, circa 1927-1935. 9/16". Mint (9.9). Price: $17. CyberAuction #427, Lot #3.

336. AKRO AGATE COMPANY. Corkscrew. Two and one-half twist snake corkscrew. Transparent cherry red base with opaque white snake. Clarksburg, WV, circa 1927-1935. 5/8". Mint (9.8). Price: $17. CyberAuction #448, Lot #14.

337. AKRO AGATE COMPANY. Corkscrew. Three color corkscrew. Blue and yellow snakes on semi-opaque white. Beauty. Clarksburg, WV, circa 1927-1935. 5/8". Mint (9.9). Price: $17. CyberAuction #458, Lot #34.

338. AKRO AGATE COMPANY. Corkscrew. Orange and green, with brown edging. Clarksburg, WV, circa 1927-1935. 19/32". Mint (9.9). Price: $17. CyberAuction #461, Lot #30.

339. AKRO AGATE COMPANY. Corkscrew. Three-color corkscrew. Indian Blanket. Red, black and yellow. Some light oxidation on the black. Clarksburg, WV, circa 1927-1935. 5/8". Near Mint(+) (8.9). Price: $17. CyberAuction #463, Lot #20.

340. AKRO AGATE COMPANY. Corkscrew. Opaque white ribbon in transparent brown, with transparent red on part of the transparent brown. Odd. Clarksburg, WV, circa 1927-1935. 5/8". Mint (9.9). Price: $17. CyberAuction #463, Lot #48.

341. AKRO AGATE COMPANY. Corkscrew. Very nice shooter. Translucent milky white base. Semi-opaque white swirls. Translucent blue swirls. Very nice. Some tiny pinpricks. Clarksburg, WV, circa 1927-1935. 31/32". Mint(-) (9.0). Price: $17. CyberAuction #469, Lot #60.

342. AKRO AGATE COMPANY. Corkscrew. Lavender with some white, with a nice dark red spiral. Gorgeous. Clarksburg, WV, circa 1927-1935. 5/8". Mint (9.8). Price: $17. CyberAuction #470, Lot #18.

343. AKRO AGATE COMPANY. Corkscrew. White, gray and orange. Very nice. Clarksburg, WV, circa 1927-1935. 5/8". Mint (9.9). Price: $17. CyberAuction #473, Lot #16.

344. AKRO AGATE COMPANY. Corkscrew. Double ingot red and white corkscrew. Probably dug. Clarksburg, WV, circa 1927-1935. 25/32". Mint(-) (9.0). Price: $17. CyberAuction #473, Lot #26.

345. AKRO AGATE COMPANY. Corkscrew. Opaque yellow base. Two spirals of transparent red. Beauty. Clarksburg, WV, circa 1927-1935. 11/16". Mint (9.7). Price: $17. CyberAuction #498, Lot #55.

346. AKRO AGATE COMPANY. Corkscrew. Pale yellow base with black snake. Some pits. Clarksburg, WV, circa 1927-1935. 5/8". Mint(-) (9.0). Price: $17. CyberAuction #501, Lot #53.

347. AKRO AGATE COMPANY. Corkscrew. Similar to a Popeye, but it is a snake. Transparent clear base. Opaque white snake on it, with a narrow yellow spiral and a narrow red spiral, on the white. One tiny chip. Clarksburg, WV, circa 1927-1935. 5/8". Near Mint(+) (8.9). Price: $17. CyberAuction #507, Lot #23.

348. AKRO AGATE COMPANY. Corkscrew. Translucent milky white base. Opaque white spiral with opaque yellow on top of it. Translucent wispy black spiral on the clear spiral. Clarksburg, WV, circa 1927-1935. 5/8". Mint (9.8). Price: $17. CyberAuction #508, Lot #25.

349. AKRO AGATE COMPANY. Corkscrew. Orange and light blue. Very nice marble. One barely visible subsurface moon. Clarksburg, WV, circa 1927-1935. 5/8". Near Mint(+) (8.9). Price: $15. CyberAuction #332, Lot #38.

350. AKRO AGATE COMPANY. Corkscrew. Snake. Fluorescent Vaseline green base. Opaque white snake. Clarksburg, WV, circa 1927-1935. 21/32". Mint (9.8). Price: $15. CyberAuction #333, Lot #29.

351. AKRO AGATE COMPANY. Corkscrew. Odd mix of white and black. Clarksburg, WV, circa 1927-1935. 19/32". Mint (9.6). Price: $15. CyberAuction #340, Lot #57.

352. AKRO AGATE COMPANY. Corkscrew. Unusual coloring. Smeared and blended ruddy orange, black and brown. Very odd. Several tiny and small subsurface moons. Clarksburg, WV, circa 1927-1935. 5/8". Near Mint (8.4). Price: $15. CyberAuction #341, Lot #55.

353. AKRO AGATE COMPANY. Corkscrew. Very nice three color corkscrew. Light green, yellow and dark red. Oddly jumbled. Buffed. Clarksburg, WV, circa 1927-1935. 23/32". Price: $15. CyberAuction #343, Lot #54.

354. AKRO AGATE COMPANY. Corkscrew. Milky white base. Snake of semi-opaque brown/orange, with a snake of burnt oxblood next to it. One tiny subsurface moon. Clarksburg, WV, circa 1927-1935. 5/8". Near Mint(+) (8.9). Price: $15. CyberAuction #364, Lot #50.

355. AKRO AGATE COMPANY. Corkscrew. Very odd ribbon corkscrew. Transparent clear base. Opaque white ribbon. Yellow spiral inside the ribbon (odd). Wispy white snake on clear offsetting the ribbon. Clarksburg, WV, circa 1927-1935. 5/8". Mint (9.5). Price: $15. CyberAuction #380, Lot #22.

356. AKRO AGATE COMPANY. Corkscrew. White, red and light green. One sparkle. Clarksburg, WV, circa 1927-1935. 13/16". Mint(-) (9.0). Price: $15. CyberAuction #403, Lot #32.

357. AKRO AGATE COMPANY. Corkscrew. Very unusual corkscrew. Transparent clear base. Double twist green snake on surface. Another green spiral inside the core. One sparkle. Clarksburg, WV, circa 1927-1935. 5/8". Near Mint(+) (8.9). Price: $15. CyberAuction #409, Lot #50.

358. AKRO AGATE COMPANY. Corkscrew. Double twist. Blue snake on top of white, on clear. Nice. Clarksburg, WV, circa 1927-1935. 5/8". Mint (9.9). Price: $15. CyberAuction #424, Lot #56.

359. AKRO AGATE COMPANY. Corkscrew. Black and yellow. Clarksburg, WV, circa 1927-1935. 5/8". Mint (9.9). Price: $15. CyberAuction #428, Lot #47.

360. AKRO AGATE COMPANY. Corkscrew. Light green and orange. Clarksburg, WV, circa 1927-1935. 5/8". Mint (9.9). Price: $15. CyberAuction #435, Lot #41.

361. AKRO AGATE COMPANY. Corkscrew. Ribbon corkscrew. Double twist. Opaque white ribbon in transparent orange. Clarksburg, WV, circa 1927-1935. 5/8". Mint (9.8). Price: $15. CyberAuction #436, Lot #40.

362. AKRO AGATE COMPANY. Corkscrew. Two-color shooter. Light green and translucent dark red. One very tiny subsurface moon, a couple of tiny pits. Clarksburg, WV, circa 1927-1935. 15/16". Near Mint(+) (8.7). Price: $15. CyberAuction #451, Lot #9.

363. AKRO AGATE COMPANY. Corkscrew. Opaque orange ribbon in transparent clear. Wispy white snake on the surface. One tiny flake. Clarksburg, WV, circa 1927-1935. 5/8". Near Mint(+) (8.9). Price: $15. CyberAuction #462, Lot #15.

364. AKRO AGATE COMPANY. Corkscrew. Augur style ribbon core. Opaque white ribbon in transparent orange. Rare. Two tiny chips. Clarksburg, WV, circa 1927-1935. 11/16". Near Mint(+) (8.8). Price: $15. CyberAuction #463, Lot #40.

365. AKRO AGATE COMPANY. Corkscrew. Very unusual. Fluorescent creamy base. Spiral of dark blue and spiral of light blue, next to each other. Several very tiny pinpricks. Clarksburg, WV, circa 1927-1935. 11/16". Near Mint(+) (8.9). Price: $15. CyberAuction #485, Lot #13.

366. AKRO AGATE COMPANY. Corkscrew. Beautiful snake corkscrew. Transparent bubble-filled aqua base. Opaque white snake on the surface. One very tiny sparkle. Clarksburg, WV, circa 1927-1935. 5/8". Mint (9.9). Price: $15. CyberAuction #487, Lot #16.

367. AKRO AGATE COMPANY. Corkscrew. Superb snake. Dark Vaseline yellow base. Wispy white surface snake. One tiny annealing fracture. Clarksburg, WV, circa 1927-1935. 21/32". Mint(-) (9.2). Price: $15. CyberAuction #491, Lot #19.

368. AKRO AGATE COMPANY. Corkscrew. Translucent light red and mocha tan. Shooter. Clarksburg, WV, circa 1927-1935. 29/32". Mint(-) (9.2). Price: $15. CyberAuction #497, Lot #49.

369. AKRO AGATE COMPANY. Corkscrew. Double ingot corkscrew. Yellow and light blue. Clarksburg, WV, circa 1927-1935. 25/32". Mint (9.5). Price: $15. CyberAuction #505, Lot #33.

370. AKRO AGATE COMPANY. Corkscrew. I believe this is a Popeye from near an end of the run. Base is Popeye of clear and white mixture. Red spiral. Space for a yellow or blue spiral, but it is missing (maybe some very, very faint yellow, if you use your imagination). Clarksburg, WV, circa 1927-1935. 5/8". Mint (9.7). Price: $14. CyberAuction #363, Lot #2.

371. AKRO AGATE COMPANY. Corkscrew. Semi-opaque white base. Snake of black. Clarksburg, WV, circa 1927-1935. 11/16". Mint (9.9). Price: $14. CyberAuction #369, Lot #29.

372. AKRO AGATE COMPANY. Corkscrew. Blue and yellow. Gorgeous. Clarksburg, WV, circa 1927-1935. 5/8". Mint (9.9). Price: $14. CyberAuction #403, Lot #7.

373. AKRO AGATE COMPANY. Corkscrew. Red spiral, edged by dark gray, on blue. Beauty. Clarksburg, WV, circa 1927-1935. 5/8". Mint (9.8). Price: $14. CyberAuction #438, Lot #17.

374. AKRO AGATE COMPANY. Corkscrew. Rare coloring. Light blue spiral in light green. Super. Not quite wet and has a sparkle and a pit. Clarksburg, WV, circa 1927-1935. 5/8". Near Mint(+) (8.9). Price: $14. CyberAuction #464, Lot #5.

375. AKRO AGATE COMPANY. Corkscrew. Light blue and orange corkscrew. Thin red spiral on the orange. Clarksburg, WV, circa 1927-1935. 5/8". Mint (9.7). Price: $14. CyberAuction #464, Lot #37.

376. AKRO AGATE COMPANY. Corkscrew. Very nice three color shooter. Light blue, red, yellow. Several tiny flakes. Clarksburg, WV, circa 1927-1935. 3/4". Near Mint (8.6). Price: $13. CyberAuction #340, Lot #23.

377. AKRO AGATE COMPANY. Corkscrew. Translucent milky white base. Swirling corkscrew of translucent blue and semi-opaque pale yellow egg yolk. A couple of pinpricks. Clarksburg, WV, circa 1927-1935. 19/32". Mint(-) (9.0). Price: $13. CyberAuction #357, Lot #12.

378. AKRO AGATE COMPANY. Corkscrew. Snake corkscrew. Transparent blue base with opaque white ribbon. One sparkle. Clarksburg, WV, circa 1927-1935. 9/16". Near Mint(+) (8.9). Price: $13. CyberAuction #364, Lot #55.

379. AKRO AGATE COMPANY. Corkscrew. Very nice three color. Opaque white with opaque yellow spiral. Red spiral on top of the yellow. Two tiny pits. Clarksburg, WV, circa 1927-1935. 11/16". Near Mint(+) (8.9). Price: $13. CyberAuction #366, Lot #14.

380. AKRO AGATE COMPANY. Corkscrew. Nice shooter. Light green and dark red. Appears to be a dug marble, has some marks on the surface. Clarksburg, WV, circa 1928-1935. 29/32". Mint(-) (9.0). Price: $13. CyberAuction #368, Lot #17.

381. AKRO AGATE COMPANY. Corkscrew. White and green corkscrew, with a thin spiral of blue. One tiny melt spot. Clarksburg, WV, circa 1927-1935. 5/8". Mint (9.5). Price: $13. CyberAuction #369, Lot #42.

382. AKRO AGATE COMPANY. Corkscrew. Orange base with a shiny black snake on it. Gorgeous. Clarksburg, WV, circa 1927-1935. 5/8". Mint (9.9). Price: $13. CyberAuction #377, Lot #41.

383. AKRO AGATE COMPANY. Corkscrew. Three color corkscrew. Pale red and yellow snakes on white. Nice. Clarksburg, WV, circa 1927-1935. 5/8". Mint (9.7). There are three marbles available. You are bidding on one. Winner has choice of any or all. Remainder to under. Price: $13. CyberAuction #386, Lot #11.

384. AKRO AGATE COMPANY. Corkscrew. Light blue with yellow spiral. Some gray. Shooter. One tiny subsurface moon. Clarksburg, WV, circa 1927-1935. 25/32". Near Mint(+) (8.9). Price: $13. CyberAuction #414, Lot #23.

385. AKRO AGATE COMPANY. Corkscrew. White ribbon in emerald green. A couple of pinpricks. Clarksburg, WV, circa 1927-1935. 19/32". Mint(-) (9.1). Price: $13. CyberAuction #427, Lot #17.

386. AKRO AGATE COMPANY. Corkscrew. Ringer. Translucent milky white base. Semi-opaque white corkscrew. Opaque red snake. Very nice. Clarksburg, WV, circa 1927-1935. 5/8". Mint (9.8). Price: $13. CyberAuction #435, Lot #16.

387. AKRO AGATE COMPANY. Corkscrew. Three color shooter. Red, light green and white. Very nice. A few tiny pinpricks. Clarksburg, WV, circa 1927-1935. 25/32". Mint(-) (9.0). Price: $13. CyberAuction #457, Lot #30.

388. AKRO AGATE COMPANY. Corkscrew. Three-color corkscrew. Yellow, light green and light orange/red. A couple of sparkles. Clarksburg, WV, circa 1927-1935. 5/8". Mint(-) (9.0). Price: $13. CyberAuction #498, Lot #23.

389. AKRO AGATE COMPANY. Corkscrew. Transparent clear base. Opaque yellow ribbon with wispy green edge. Double twist. Clarksburg, WV, circa 1927-1935. 19/32". Mint (9.9). Price: $13. CyberAuction #501, Lot #18.

390. AKRO AGATE COMPANY. Corkscrew. Milky white semi-opaque base with a snake of orange/yellow. Overall tiny subsurface moons. Clarksburg, WV, circa 1927-1935. 5/8". Near Mint(-) (8.1). Price: $12. CyberAuction #341, Lot #20.

391. AKRO AGATE COMPANY. Corkscrew. Red, yellow and light blue. Sparkles and scratches. Clarksburg, WV, circa 1927-1935. 13/16". Near Mint (8.6). There are four marbles available, you are bidding on one. Winner has choice of any or all, remainder to under. Price: $12. CyberAuction #395, Lot #32.

392. AKRO AGATE COMPANY. Corkscrew. Blue and yellow. Beauty. Just a couple of tiny pits in one spot. Clarksburg, WV, circa 1927-1935. 13/16". Near Mint(+) (8.9). Price: $12. CyberAuction #412, Lot #34.

393. AKRO AGATE COMPANY. Corkscrew. Double ingot shooter. Opaque white and transparent root beer brown. Super example. Clarksburg, WV, circa 1927-1935. 27/32". Mint (9.9). Price: $12. CyberAuction #429, Lot #56.

394. AKRO AGATE COMPANY. Corkscrew. Indian Blanket. Black, yellow and red. Some pinpricks and overall wear. Clarksburg, WV, circa 1927-1935. 23/32". Near Mint (8.3). Price: $12. CyberAuction #431, Lot #1.

395. AKRO AGATE COMPANY. Corkscrew. Narrow bright yellow spiral on white. Clarksburg, WV, circa 1927-1935. 19/32". Mint (9.8). Price: $12. CyberAuction #438, Lot #41.

396. AKRO AGATE COMPANY. Corkscrew. Lavender with some white, with a nice dark red spiral. Gorgeous. Clarksburg, WV, circa 1927-1935. 5/8". Mint (9.8). Price: $12. CyberAuction #453, Lot #42.

397. AKRO AGATE COMPANY. Corkscrew. Black snake on orange. Clarksburg, WV, circa 1927-1935. 5/8". Mint (9.9). Price: $12. CyberAuction #461, Lot #45.

398. AKRO AGATE COMPANY. Corkscrew. Light blue and yellow with a narrow black spiral. Clarksburg, WV, circa 1927-1935. 11/16". Mint (9.7). There are two marbles, from the same run, you are bidding on one. Winner has choice of either or both, remainder to under. Price: $12. CyberAuction #480, Lot #44.

399. AKRO AGATE COMPANY. Corkscrew. White, light green, light red. Very nice. Two tiny sparkles. Clarksburg, WV, circa 1927-1935. 21/32". Mint(-) (9.2). Price: $12. CyberAuction #505, Lot #26.

400. AKRO AGATE COMPANY. Corkscrew. Ringer. Translucent white with wispy semi-opaque white swirls. Translucent red snake. Clarksburg, WV, circa 1927-1935. 5/8". Mint (9.7). Price: $12. CyberAuction #508, Lot #55.

401. AKRO AGATE COMPANY. Corkscrew. Ribbon corkscrew. Transparent red base with opaque white ribbon. Several sparkles and a tiny subsurface moon. Clarksburg, WV, circa 1927-1935. 25/32". Near Mint (8.6). Price: $11. CyberAuction #338, Lot #8.

402. AKRO AGATE COMPANY. Corkscrew. White base. Yellow snake. Narrow red next to the yellow on one side. Clarksburg, WV, circa 1927-1935. 9/16". Mint (9.9). Price: $11. CyberAuction #350, Lot #47.

403. AKRO AGATE COMPANY. Corkscrew. Three color corkscrew. White base. Green spiral, edged by blue. Very nice. Clarksburg, WV, circa 1927-1935. 19/32". Mint (9.9). Price: $11. CyberAuction #352, Lot #56.

404. AKRO AGATE COMPANY. Corkscrew. Gray/green spiral and yellow spiral. A sparkle. Clarksburg, WV, circa 1927-1935. 9/16". Near Mint(+) (8.9). Price: $11. CyberAuction #377, Lot #26.

405. AKRO AGATE COMPANY. Corkscrew. Brown and green corkscrew. Clarksburg, WV, circa 1927-1935. 21/32". Mint (9.9). Price: $11. CyberAuction #399, Lot #42.

406. AKRO AGATE COMPANY. Corkscrew. Black, narrow creamy white, orange. Very nice. Two sparkles. Clarksburg, WV, circa 1927-1935. 5/8". Near Mint(+) (8.8). Consignor note: F6. Price: $11. CyberAuction #423, Lot #41.

407. AKRO AGATE COMPANY. Corkscrew. Red and yellow. Clarksburg, WV, circa 1927-1935. 9/16". Mint (9.9). Price: $11. CyberAuction #427, Lot #9.

408. AKRO AGATE COMPANY. Corkscrew. Red and yellow corkscrew. Very nice. Clarksburg, WV, circa 1927-1935. 5/8". Mint (9.9). Price: $11. CyberAuction #428, Lot #19.

409. AKRO AGATE COMPANY. Corkscrew. Double ingot two-color corkscrew. Translucent red and creamy white. Clarksburg, WV, circa 1927-1935. 13/16". Mint (9.5). Price: $11. CyberAuction #448, Lot #15.

410. AKRO AGATE COMPANY. Corkscrew. Three-color corkscrew. Light blue and yellow with transparent red on the yellow. Some crazing and annealing fractures. Clarksburg, WV, circa 1927-1935. 13/16". Near Mint (8.6). Price: $11. CyberAuction #451, Lot #16.

411. AKRO AGATE COMPANY. Corkscrew. Translucent red, opaque white and opaque light lavender. Some pinpricks. Clarksburg, WV, circa 1927-1935. 11/16". Mint(-) (9.0). Price: $11. CyberAuction #452, Lot #16.

412. AKRO AGATE COMPANY. Corkscrew. Double twist snake. Transparent dark red base. Opaque white snake. Price: $. CyberAuction #457, Lot #26.

413. AKRO AGATE COMPANY. Corkscrew. Four-color corkscrew. Light blue, green, red and white. Small annealing fracture. Some tiny pinpricking. Clarksburg, WV, circa 1927-1935. 11/16". Near Mint (8.6). Price: $11. CyberAuction #463, Lot #35.

414. AKRO AGATE COMPANY. Corkscrew. Blue and yellow corkscrew. Clarksburg, WV, circa 1927-1935. 19/32". Mint (9.9). Price: $11. CyberAuction #473, Lot #7.

415. AKRO AGATE COMPANY. Corkscrew. Light blue, creamy white, narrow gray. Clarksburg, WV, circa 1927-1935. 19/32". Mint (9.7). Price: $11. CyberAuction #475, Lot #2.

416. AKRO AGATE COMPANY. Corkscrew. Blue and yellow, with some very narrow black edging. One tiny sparkle. Clarksburg, WV, circa 1927-1935. 11/16". Mint(-) (9.2). Price: $11. CyberAuction #483, Lot #20.

417. AKRO AGATE COMPANY. Corkscrew. Translucent light red spiral on opaque white with light lavender. A couple of sparkles. Clarksburg, WV, circa 1927-1935. 23/32". Near Mint(+) (8.9). Price: $11. CyberAuction #487, Lot #38.

418. AKRO AGATE COMPANY. Corkscrew. Translucent milky white base. Opaque green spiral. Clarksburg, WV, circa 1927-1935. 19/32". Mint (9.8). Price: $11. CyberAuction #508, Lot #31.

419. AKRO AGATE COMPANY. Corkscrew. Lavender, red and yellow. Very nice. Some pits. Clarksburg, WV, circa 1927-1935. 5/8". Near Mint(+) (8.7). Price: $10. CyberAuction #361, Lot #56.

420. AKRO AGATE COMPANY. Corkscrew. Red, white and blue corkscrew. No damage, but not wet mint. Clarksburg, WV, circa 1927-1935. 5/8". Mint (9.3). Price: $10. CyberAuction #370, Lot #51.

421. AKRO AGATE COMPANY. Corkscrew. Pale green, yellow and red. Shooter. Some tiny subsurface moons. Clarksburg, WV, circa 1927-1935. 13/16". Near Mint (8.6). Price: $10. CyberAuction #376, Lot #8.

422. AKRO AGATE COMPANY. Corkscrew. Transparent pale amethyst base with an opaque yellow ribbon. Double twist. One small chip. Clarksburg, WV, circa 1927-1935. 5/8". Near Mint(+) (8.9). Price: $10. CyberAuction #377, Lot #8.

423. AKRO AGATE COMPANY. Corkscrew. Yellow spiral on white. Odd coloring. Clarksburg, WV, circa 1927-1935. 21/32". Mint (9.7). Price: $10. CyberAuction #389, Lot #52.

424. AKRO AGATE COMPANY. Corkscrew. White base with a root beer brown spiral. One small fold crease at the equator, but not a double ingot. A couple of pinpricks. Clarksburg, WV, circa 1927-1935. 25/32". Mint(-) (9.2). Price: $10. CyberAuction #391, Lot #47.

425. AKRO AGATE COMPANY. Corkscrew. Purple with very narrow light green covered by very narrow transparent orange. Clarksburg, WV, circa 1927-1935. 5/8". Mint (9.8). Price: $10. CyberAuction #403, Lot #25.

426. AKRO AGATE COMPANY. Corkscrew. Semi-opaque white base with light blue snake. Clarksburg, WV, circa 1927-1935. 5/8". Mint (9.9). Price: $10. CyberAuction #433, Lot #4.

427. AKRO AGATE COMPANY. Corkscrew. Double ingot. Red/brown spiral and light green. Clarksburg, WV, circa 1927-1935. 7/8". Mint (9.6). Price: $10. CyberAuction #438, Lot #22.

428. AKRO AGATE COMPANY. Corkscrew. Orange and blue corkscrew. Very nice. Clarksburg, WV, circa 1927-1935. 21/32". Mint (9.8). Price: $10. CyberAuction #463, Lot #12.

429. AKRO AGATE COMPANY. Corkscrew. Semi-opaque white base with green spiral. Clarksburg, WV, circa 1927-1935. 5/8". Mint (9.9). Price: $10. CyberAuction #479, Lot #29.

430. AKRO AGATE COMPANY. Corkscrew. Opaque yellow and translucent red. Nice. Clarksburg, WV, circa 1927-1935. 19/32". Mint (9.7). Price: $9. CyberAuction #338, Lot #19.

431. AKRO AGATE COMPANY. Corkscrew. Interesting ribbon/snake corkscrew. Transparent clear base. Opaque yellow ribbon. Narrow white snake ringing the clear part of the surface. One sparkle. Clarksburg, WV, circa 1927-1935. 5/8". Near Mint(+) (8.9). Price: $9. CyberAuction #348, Lot #3.

432. AKRO AGATE COMPANY. Corkscrew. Blue and yellow. Nice. Clarksburg, WV, circa 1927-1935. 21/32". Mint (9.7). Price: $9. CyberAuction #351, Lot #1.

433. AKRO AGATE COMPANY. Corkscrew. Error corkscrew. Blue and yellow. Football shape. About 5/8". Mint (9.9). Price: $9. CyberAuction #351, Lot #5.

434. AKRO AGATE COMPANY. Corkscrew. Translucent milky white base. Snake of translucent red on it. A couple of tiny pinpricks. Clarksburg, WV, circa 1927-1935. 5/8". Mint(-) (9.0). Price: $9. CyberAuction #353, Lot #4.

435. AKRO AGATE COMPANY. Corkscrew. Three color corkscrew. Light blue, red and white. One subsurface moon. Clarksburg, WV, circa 1927-1935. 23/32". Near Mint(+) (8.8). Price: $9. CyberAuction #353, Lot #35.

436. AKRO AGATE COMPANY. Corkscrew. Double twist ribbon corkscrew. Opaque white ribbon in transparent root beer brown. One sparkle. Clarksburg, WV, circa 1927-1935. 19/32". Mint(-) (9.2). Price: $9. CyberAuction #365, Lot #13.

437. AKRO AGATE COMPANY. Corkscrew. Opaque white with transparent dark purple spiral. Very odd. Small chip. Clarksburg, WV, circa 1927-1935. 11/16". Near Mint(+) (8.7). Price: $9. CyberAuction #389, Lot #50.

438. AKRO AGATE COMPANY. Corkscrew. Double ingot ribbon. Opaque white ribbon in transparent root beer brown. One pit. Clarksburg, WV, circa 1927-1935. 13/16". Near Mint(+) (8.9). Price: $9. CyberAuction #393, Lot #49.

439. AKRO AGATE COMPANY. Corkscrew. Yellow and light blue. Clarksburg, WV, circa 1927-1935. 5/8". Mint (9.9). Price: $9. CyberAuction #399, Lot #45.

440. AKRO AGATE COMPANY. Corkscrew. Red and yellow. Small sparkle, small annealing fracture. Clarksburg, WV, circa 1927-1935. 29/32". Near Mint(+) (8.8). Price: $9. CyberAuction #406, Lot #4.

441. AKRO AGATE COMPANY. Corkscrew. Opaque white with transparent dark purple spiral. Very odd. Small chip. Clarksburg, WV, circa 1927-1935. 11/16". Near Mint(+) (8.7). Price: $9. CyberAuction #408, Lot #3.

442. AKRO AGATE COMPANY. Corkscrew. Double twist ribbon corkscrew. Yellow ribbon in clear. Nice. Clarksburg, WV, circa 1927-1935. 5/8". Mint (9.5). Price: $9. CyberAuction #424, Lot #50.

443. AKRO AGATE COMPANY. Corkscrew. Opaque white with transparent dark purple spiral. Very odd. Small chip. Clarksburg, WV, circa 1927-1935. 11/16". Near Mint(+) (8.7). Price: $9. CyberAuction #426, Lot #7.

73

444. AKRO AGATE COMPANY. Corkscrew. Odd color. Very dark purple snake on opaque white. One sparkle. Clarksburg, WV, circa 1927-1935. 5/8". Mint(-) (9.0). Price: $9. CyberAuction #452, Lot #2.

445. AKRO AGATE COMPANY. Corkscrew. Very nice three-color. Orange, green and white. One tiny melt hole. Clarksburg, WV, circa 1927-1935. 11/16". Mint(-) (9.1). Price: $9. CyberAuction #457, Lot #39.

446. AKRO AGATE COMPANY. Corkscrew. Interesting corkscrew. Milky white base. Snake of opaque ruddy red. Wispy snake of lavender. One tiny flake. Clarksburg, WV, circa 1927-1935. 5/8". Near Mint(+) (8.9). Price: $9. CyberAuction #465, Lot #5.

447. AKRO AGATE COMPANY. Corkscrew. Opaque black with very thin white spiral in it. Odd. Clarksburg, WV, circa 1927-1935. 11/16". Mint (9.7). Three available, you are bidding on one. Winner has choice of any or all, remainder to under. Price: $9. CyberAuction #465, Lot #45.

448. AKRO AGATE COMPANY. Corkscrew. Dark blue snake on semi-opaque white. Very nice. Clarksburg, WV, circa 1927-1935. 5/8". Mint (9.9). Price: $9. CyberAuction #467, Lot #42.

449. AKRO AGATE COMPANY. Corkscrew. Transparent brown spiral on mocha tan. Clarksburg, WV, circa 1927-1935. 11/16". Mint (9.9). Price: $9. CyberAuction #479, Lot #19.

450. AKRO AGATE COMPANY. Corkscrew. Three-color. Red, light green and yellow. Beautiful colors. One small flake. Clarksburg, WV, circa 1927-1935. 5/8". Near Mint(+) (8.7). Price: $9. CyberAuction #483, Lot #3.

451. AKRO AGATE COMPANY. Corkscrew. Opaque white with transparent dark purple spiral. Very odd. Small chip. Clarksburg, WV, circa 1927-1935. 11/16". Near Mint(+) (8.7). Price: $9. CyberAuction #486, Lot #37.

452. AKRO AGATE COMPANY. Corkscrew. Three color corkscrew. White, yellow, orange. Very nice. Clarksburg, WV, circa 1927-1935. 5/8". Mint (9.6). Price: $9. CyberAuction #492, Lot #29.

453. AKRO AGATE COMPANY. Corkscrew. Gorgeous snake corkscrew. Transparent clear base with tiny air bubbles. Translucent strawberry red snake. Beauty. Clarksburg, WV, circa 1927-1935. 19/32". Mint (9.7). There are three marbles available, you are bidding on one. Winner has choice of any or all, remainder to under. Price: $9. CyberAuction #501, Lot #2.

454. AKRO AGATE COMPANY. Corkscrew. Looks like a Popeye, but minimal clear. Green, yellow and white (with a little clear). Clarksburg, WV, circa 1927-1929. 19/32". Mint (9.5). Price: $9. CyberAuction #501, Lot #15.

455. AKRO AGATE COMPANY. Corkscrew. Interesting. Translucent milky white base. Subsurface spiral of wispy white. Surface spiral of semi-opaque brown/red. Some sparkles and pits. Clarksburg, WV, circa 1927-1935. 3/4". Near Mint (8.6). Price: $8. CyberAuction #338, Lot #24.

456. AKRO AGATE COMPANY. Corkscrew. Very nice marble. Predominately red with a narrow blue spiral. A few sparkles. Clarksburg, WV, circa 1927-1935. 19/32". Mint(-) (9.0). Price: $8. CyberAuction #351, Lot #2.

457. AKRO AGATE COMPANY. Corkscrew. Three-color. Opaque white base. Two wide snakes of red and snake of blue on the surface. One pit, some dulling. Clarksburg, WV, circa 1927-1935. 21/32". Near Mint(+) (8.9). Price: $8. CyberAuction #352, Lot #50.

458. AKRO AGATE COMPANY. Corkscrew. Three color corkscrew shooter. White, light blue, transparent red. Cold roll lines. Clarksburg, WV, circa 1927-1935. 25/32". Mint(-) (9.2). Price: $8. CyberAuction #361, Lot #51.

459. AKRO AGATE COMPANY. Corkscrew. Translucent wispy opalescent base with a semi-opaque blue snake. One sparkle, but nice. Clarksburg, WV, circa 1927-1935. 19/32". Near Mint(+) (8.9). Price: $8. CyberAuction #364, Lot #42.

460. AKRO AGATE COMPANY. Corkscrew. Lavender and red spirals, on white (or mixed with white). One tiny chip, some sparkles. Clarksburg, WV, circa 1927-1935. 11/16". Near Mint (8.6). Price: $8. CyberAuction #376, Lot #10.

461. AKRO AGATE COMPANY. Corkscrew. Transparent red base with a wide opaque creamy white ribbon. Beauty. Clarksburg, WV, circa 1927-1935. 21/32". Mint(-) (9.0). Price: $8. CyberAuction #382, Lot #11.

462. AKRO AGATE COMPANY. Corkscrew. Ribbon corkscrew. Transparent bubble filled clear base. Shallow pale yellow ribbon with blue snake on it. Black next to the blue. One small flake. Clarksburg, WV, circa 1927-1935. 5/8". Near Mint(+) (8.7). Price: $8. CyberAuction #392, Lot #37.

463. AKRO AGATE COMPANY. Corkscrew. Double twist ribbon. Opaque white ribbon in transparent root beer brown. One pit. Clarksburg, WV, circa 1927-1935. 13/16". Near Mint(+) (8.9). Price: $8. CyberAuction #393, Lot #46.

464. AKRO AGATE COMPANY. Corkscrew. Four-color. Light blue, red, green and yellow. Buffed. 9/16". Price: $8. CyberAuction #395, Lot #14.

465. AKRO AGATE COMPANY. Corkscrew. Three color. White base. Black snake. Narrow green snake. One tiny flake. Clarksburg, WV, circa 1927-1935. 5/8". Mint(-) (8.8). Price: $8. CyberAuction #396, Lot #7.

466. AKRO AGATE COMPANY. Corkscrew. Three-color. Opaque white, semi-opaque brown/red, translucent brown/gray. Clarksburg, WV, circa 1927-1935. 5/8". Mint (9.7). Price: $8. CyberAuction #406, Lot #21.

467. AKRO AGATE COMPANY. Corkscrew. Dark red spiral on light green. One subsurface moon. Clarksburg, WV, circa 1927-1935. 29/32". Near Mint(+) (8.7). Price: $8. CyberAuction #420, Lot #19.

468. AKRO AGATE COMPANY. Corkscrew. Nice snake. Transparent amber base. White snake. Clarksburg, WV, circa 1927-1935. 5/8". Mint (9.9). Price: $8. CyberAuction #421, Lot #3.

469. AKRO AGATE COMPANY. Corkscrew. Snake corkscrew. Transparent green base. Narrow white snake. Clarksburg, WV, circa 1927-1935. 5/8". Mint (9.7). Price: $8. CyberAuction #428, Lot #44.

470. AKRO AGATE COMPANY. Corkscrew. Yellow spiral in black. Clarksburg, WV, circa 1927-1935. 21/32". Mint (9.7). Price: $8. CyberAuction #436, Lot #4.

471. AKRO AGATE COMPANY. Corkscrew. Bright yellow and light blue corkscrew. Beauty. Clarksburg, WV, circa 1927-1935. 19/32". Mint (9.9). Price: $8. CyberAuction #438, Lot #19.

472. AKRO AGATE COMPANY. Corkscrew. Black and orange/red corkscrew. The black disappears into the marble on the equator. Clarksburg, WV, circa 1927-1935. 5/8". Mint (9.7). Price: $8. CyberAuction #438, Lot #23.

473. AKRO AGATE COMPANY. Corkscrew. Semi-opaque opalescent white base with blue snake. Clarksburg, WV, circa 1927-1935. 9/16". Mint (9.9). Price: $8. CyberAuction #447, Lot #10.

474. AKRO AGATE COMPANY. Corkscrew. Black snake on white base. Very nice. Clarksburg, WV, circa 1927-1935. 5/8". Mint (9.9). Price: $8. CyberAuction #448, Lot #45.

475. AKRO AGATE COMPANY. Corkscrew. Three-color. Milky white base. Dark translucent blue spiral and a translucent egg yolk yellow spiral. Some scratches and tiny sparkles. Clarksburg, WV, circa 1927-1935. 5/8". Near Mint(+) (8.9). Price: $8. CyberAuction #455, Lot #29.

476. AKRO AGATE COMPANY. Corkscrew. Opaque white with transparent dark purple spiral. Very odd. Small chip. Clarksburg, WV, circa 1927-1935. 11/16". Near Mint(+) (8.7). Price: $8. CyberAuction #450, Lot #50.

477. AKRO AGATE COMPANY. Corkscrew. Opaque white ribbon in dark transparent red. Two very tiny flakes. Clarksburg, WV, circa 1927-1935. 25/32". Near Mint(+) (8.9). Price: $8. CyberAuction #463, Lot #4.

478. AKRO AGATE COMPANY. Corkscrew. Black double-twist snake on semi-opaque white base. Gorgeous. Clarksburg, WV, circa 1927-1935. 11/16". Mint (9.8). Price: $8. CyberAuction #466, Lot #30.

479. AKRO AGATE COMPANY. Corkscrew. Transparent clear base. Semi-opaque brown/orange ribbon, edged by burnt oxblood. Some pits. Clarksburg, WV, circa 1927-1935. 5/8". Near Mint (8.6). Price: $8. CyberAuction #469, Lot #59.

480. AKRO AGATE COMPANY. Corkscrew. Transparent orange/red spiral in opaque white. Clarksburg, WV, circa 1927-19345. 3/4". Mint (9.8). Price: $8. CyberAuction #497, Lot #23.

481. AKRO AGATE COMPANY. Corkscrew. Translucent milky white snake in blue. Beauty. Clarksburg, WV, circa 1927-1935. 5/8". Mint(-) (9.2). Price: $8. CyberAuction #497, Lot #52.

482. AKRO AGATE COMPANY. Corkscrew. Milky white base with light red snake. Several tiny sparkles. Clarksburg, WV, circa 1927-1935. 5/8". Mint(-) (9.0). Price: $8. CyberAuction #505, Lot #55.

483. AKRO AGATE COMPANY. Corkscrew. Opaque white base. Spiral of light baby blue, spiral of orange. One subsurface moon. Clarksburg, WV, circa 1927-1935. 9/16". Near Mint(+) (8.8). Price: $8. CyberAuction #508, Lot #19.

484. AKRO AGATE COMPANY. Corkscrew. Orange base with a black snake. One sparkle. Nice. Clarksburg, WV, circa 1927-1935. 5/8". Mint(-) (9.0). Price: $7. CyberAuction #330, Lot #3.

485. AKRO AGATE COMPANY. Corkscrew. Opaque yellow base with a wide translucent orange spiral. Very nice. Clarksburg, WV, circa 1927-1935. 11/16". Mint (9.9). Price: $7. CyberAuction #342, Lot #4.

486. AKRO AGATE COMPANY. Corkscrew. Snake corkscrew. Yellow snake on clear. Clarksburg, WV, circa 1927-1935. 5/8". Mint (9.7). Price: $7. CyberAuction #348, Lot #26.

487. AKRO AGATE COMPANY. Corkscrew. Ringer. Translucent white with wispy semi-opaque white swirls. Translucent red snake. One sparkle. Clarksburg, WV, circa 1927-1935. 5/8". Near Mint(+) (8.9). Price: $7. CyberAuction #355, Lot #25.

488. AKRO AGATE COMPANY. Corkscrew. Ringer. Translucent white with wispy semi-opaque white swirls. Translucent red snake. Clarksburg, WV, circa 1927-1935. 5/8". Mint (9.7). Price: $7. CyberAuction #395, Lot #41.

489. AKRO AGATE COMPANY. Corkscrew. Light blue and yellow. Clarksburg, WV, circa 1927-1935. 5/8". Mint (9.7). Price: $7. CyberAuction #396, Lot #2.

490. AKRO AGATE COMPANY. Corkscrew. Ringer. Translucent white with wispy semi-opaque white swirls. Translucent red snake. One tiny sparkle. Clarksburg, WV, circa 1927-1935. 5/8". Mint(-) (9.1). Price: $7. CyberAuction #425, Lot #1.

491. AKRO AGATE COMPANY. Corkscrew. Odd coloring. Wide spiral of smeared orange and yellow, narrow spiral of translucent light green on white. Very pretty. A tiny sparkle. Clarksburg, WV, circa 1927-1935. 5/8". Mint(-) (9.0). There are two marbles available, you are bidding on one. Winner has choice of either or both, remainder to under. Price: $7. CyberAuction #432, Lot #18.

492. AKRO AGATE COMPANY. Corkscrew. Orange, lavender and creamy white corkscrew. One tiny flake. Clarksburg, WV, circa 1927-1935. 5/8". Near Mint(+) (8.9). Price: $7. CyberAuction #433, Lot #23.

493. AKRO AGATE COMPANY. Corkscrew. Nice Ace. Translucent milky white base. Double twist translucent red/orange snake. Beauty. Clarksburg, WV, circa 1927-1935. 5/8". Mint (9.7). Price: $7. CyberAuction #448, Lot #39.

494. AKRO AGATE COMPANY. Corkscrew. Black snake on orange. Clarksburg, WV, circa 1927-1935. 5/8". Mint (9.8). Price: $7. CyberAuction #465, Lot #7.

495. AKRO AGATE COMPANY. Corkscrew. Very nice marble. Predominately red with a narrow blue spiral. A few sparkles. Clarksburg, WV, circa 1927-1935. 19/32". Mint(-) (9.0). Price: $7. CyberAuction #470, Lot #26.

496. AKRO AGATE COMPANY. Corkscrew. Shooter. Transparent light red on opaque yellow. Some haze. Clarksburg, WV, circa 1927-1935. 31/32". Near Mint(-) (8.2). Price: $7. CyberAuction #472, Lot #31.

497. AKRO AGATE COMPANY. Corkscrew. Red, white and blue. Some annealing fractures and sparkles. Shooter. Clarksburg, WV, circa 1927-1935. 25/32". Near Mint(+) (8.9). There are three marbles available. Appear to be same run. All have similar damage. You are bidding on one. Winner has choice of any or all, remainder to under. Price: $7. CyberAuction #481, Lot #19.

498. AKRO AGATE COMPANY. Corkscrew. Snake corkscrew. Opaque yellow snake on transparent bubble suffused dark amber base. Clarksburg, WV, circa 1927-1935. 19/32". Mint (9.6). Price: $7. CyberAuction #498, Lot #3.

499. AKRO AGATE COMPANY. Corkscrew. Translucent milky white base with a translucent green spiral. One sparkle. Clarksburg, WV, circa 1927-1935. 19/32". Mint(-) (9.0). Price: $7. CyberAuction #507, Lot #11.

500. AKRO AGATE COMPANY. Corkscrew. Ribbon corkscrew. Transparent clear base. Semi-opaque light green ribbon. Clarksburg, WV, circa 1927-1935. 5/8". Mint (9.7). Price: $6. CyberAuction #346, Lot #9.

501. AKRO AGATE COMPANY. Corkscrew. Very nice ribbon corkscrew. Transparent clear base. Double twist red ribbon. Beautiful. Several pits on the surface. Clarksburg, WV, circa 1927-1935. 19/32". Near Mint (8.6). Price: $6. CyberAuction #351, Lot #22.

502. AKRO AGATE COMPANY. Corkscrew. Ribbon corkscrew. Transparent blue base with a semi-opaque white ribbon. A couple of sparkles. Clarksburg, WV, circa 1927-1935. 5/8". Near Mint(+) (8.8). Price: $6. CyberAuction #372, Lot #12.

503. AKRO AGATE COMPANY. Corkscrew. Blue spiral on light blue. Subsurface moon. Clarksburg, WV, circa 1927-1935. 11/16". Near Mint(+) (8.9). Price: $6. CyberAuction #380, Lot #42.

504. AKRO AGATE COMPANY. Corkscrew. Orange and light green. Some brown edging the green. A couple of tiny chips. Clarksburg, WV, circa 1927-1935. 11/16". Near Mint(+) (8.7). Price: $6. CyberAuction #382, Lot #4.

505. AKRO AGATE COMPANY. Corkscrew. Light transparent red base with an opaque white snake. Clarksburg, WV, circa 1927-1935. 5/8". Mint (9.7). Price: $6. CyberAuction #396, Lot #19.

506. AKRO AGATE COMPANY. Corkscrew. Red and blue corkscrew, with some white. Some minor damage. Clarksburg, WV, circa 1927-1935. 27/32". Near Mint (8.6). Price: $6. CyberAuction #403, Lot #44.

507. AKRO AGATE COMPANY. Corkscrew. Ribbon corkscrew. Four-twist ribbon. White ribbon in aqua. Two tiny sparkles. Clarksburg, WV, circa 1927-1935. 19/32". Near Mint(+) (8.9). Price: $6. CyberAuction #428, Lot #1.

508. AKRO AGATE COMPANY. Corkscrew. Three-color corkscrew. Red, yellow, light blue. Some subsurface moons. 13/16". Near Mint(-) (8.0). Price: $6. CyberAuction #430, Lot #55.

509. AKRO AGATE COMPANY. Corkscrew. Semi-opaque white base with bright opaque yellow spiral. Clarksburg, WV, circa 1927-1935. 5/8". Mint (9.9). Price: $6. CyberAuction #432, Lot #3.

510. AKRO AGATE COMPANY. Corkscrew. Blue spiral on light blue. Subsurface moon. Clarksburg, WV, circa 1927-1935. 11/16". Near Mint(+) (8.9). Price: $6. CyberAuction #440, Lot #12.

511. AKRO AGATE COMPANY. Corkscrew. Translucent white base, blue snake. Several small subsurface moons. Clarksburg, WV, circa 1927-1935. 15/16". Near Mint (8.4). Price: $6. CyberAuction #441, Lot #49.

512. AKRO AGATE COMPANY. Corkscrew. Opaque white ribbon in transparent cherry red. Orange spiral on the white. Several sparkles. Clarksburg, WV, circa 1927-1935. 11/16". Near Mint(+) (8.8). Price: $6. CyberAuction #448, Lot #5.

513. AKRO AGATE COMPANY. Corkscrew. Orange and blue. Harder to find color combination. Two tiny subsurface moons. Clarksburg, WV, circa 1927-1935. 19/32". Near Mint (8.5). Price: $6. CyberAuction #470, Lot #35.

514. AKRO AGATE COMPANY. Corkscrew. Ringer. Translucent white with wispy semi-opaque white swirls. Translucent red snake. Some sparkles and tiny subsurface moons. Clarksburg, WV, circa 1925-1935. 3/4". Near Mint (8.5). Price: $6. CyberAuction #505, Lot #14.

515. AKRO AGATE COMPANY. Corkscrew. Very pale blue with orange snake. Minor pits and tiny subsurface moon. Clarksburg, WV, circa 1927-1935. 5/8". Near Mint (8.6). There are two marbles available. You are bidding on one. Winner has choice of either or both, remainder to under. Price: $5. CyberAuction #355, Lot #5.

516. AKRO AGATE COMPANY. Corkscrew. Three-color corkscrew. Red, yellow, light blue. Some subsurface moons. 13/16". Near Mint(-) (8.0). There are five marbles available. All the same size and same relative condition. You are bidding on one. Winner has choice of any or all, remainder to under. Price: $5. CyberAuction #361, Lot #14.

517. AKRO AGATE COMPANY. Corkscrew. Semi-opaque milky white base. Wide spiral of translucent brown with a dark brown line in it. One small chip. Clarksburg, WV, circa 1927-1935. 11/16". Near Mint(+) (8.7). Price: $5. CyberAuction #376, Lot #31.

518. AKRO AGATE COMPANY. Corkscrew. Three color. Buffed. 9/16". Price: $5. CyberAuction #378, Lot #3.

519. AKRO AGATE COMPANY. Corkscrew. Nice snake. Transparent amber base. White snake. Clarksburg, WV, circa 1927-1935. 5/8". Mint (9.9). Price: $5. CyberAuction #381, Lot #28.

520. AKRO AGATE COMPANY. Corkscrew. Baby blue opaque with wide spiral of black. Some tiny subsurface moons. Clarksburg, WV, circa 1927-1935. 5/8". Near Mint(+) (8.8). Price: $5. CyberAuction #395, Lot #6.

521. AKRO AGATE COMPANY. Corkscrew. Orange and blue. Harder to find color combination. Two tiny subsurface moons. Clarksburg, WV, circa 1927-1935. 19/32". Near Mint (8.5). Price: $5. CyberAuction #395, Lot #39.

522. AKRO AGATE COMPANY. Corkscrew. Three-color corkscrew. Red, yellow, light blue. Some subsurface moons. 13/16". Near Mint(-) (8.0). Price: $5. CyberAuction #398, Lot #41.

523. AKRO AGATE COMPANY. Corkscrew. Translucent milky white base.

Swirling corkscrew of translucent blue and semi-opaque pale yellow egg yolk. A couple of pinpricks. Clarksburg, WV, circa 1927-1935. 19/32". Mint(-) (9.0). Price: $5. CyberAuction #418, Lot #15.

524. AKRO AGATE COMPANY. Corkscrew. Opaque white ribbon in very fluorescent transparent yellow. Gorgeous. Two very tiny subsurface moons. Clarksburg, WV, circa 1927-1935. 21/32". Near Mint(+) (8.7). Price: $5. CyberAuction #429, Lot #8.

525. AKRO AGATE COMPANY. Corkscrew. Black and white corkscrew. Very nice. Clarksburg, WV, circa 1927-1935. 5/8". Mint (9.9). Price: $5. CyberAuction #436, Lot #36.

526. AKRO AGATE COMPANY. Corkscrew. Semi-opaque milky white base. Snake of orange, brown and black, mixed. Clarksburg, WV, circa 1927-1935. 11/16". Mint (9.7). Price: $5. CyberAuction #444, Lot #20.

527. AKRO AGATE COMPANY. Corkscrew. Narrow white spiral in butterscotch brown. Small dimple in one side. Clarksburg, WV, circa 1870-1915. 21/32". Mint(-) (9.0). Price: $5. CyberAuction #475, Lot #26.

528. AKRO AGATE COMPANY. Corkscrew. Interesting ribbon/snake corkscrew. Transparent clear base. Opaque white ribbon. Narrow white snake ringing the clear part of the surface. One sparkle. Clarksburg, WV, circa 1927-1935. 5/8". Near Mint(+) (8.9). Price: $5. CyberAuction #478, Lot #40.

529. AKRO AGATE COMPANY. Corkscrew. Shooter. Red and yellow. Annealing fractures. Clarksburg, WV, circa 1927-1935. 29/32". Mint(-) (9.0). Price: $5. CyberAuction #481, Lot #32.

530. AKRO AGATE COMPANY. Corkscrew. Blue and yellow corkscrew. Two sparkles. Clarksburg, WV, circa 1927-1935. 3/4". Mint(-) (9.0). Price: $5. CyberAuction #487, Lot #28.

531. AKRO AGATE COMPANY. Corkscrew. Dark transparent red on light green. Some sparkles. Clarksburg, WV, circa 1927-1935. 13/16". Near Mint(+) (8.9). Price: $5. CyberAuction #497, Lot #37.

532. AKRO AGATE COMPANY. Corkscrew. Ribbon corkscrew. Fluorescent Vaseline base. Opaque white ribbon edged by an opaque white snake. Interesting. A few tiny chips. Clarksburg, WV, circa 1927-1935. 11/16". Near Mint (8.4). Price: $4. CyberAuction #332, Lot #7.

533. AKRO AGATE COMPANY. Corkscrew. Translucent white base, blue snake. Several small subsurface moons. Clarksburg, WV, circa 1927-1935. 15/16". Near Mint (8.4). Price: $4. CyberAuction #355, Lot #39.

534. AKRO AGATE COMPANY. Corkscrew. Pale green and red. Nice. Clarksburg, WV, circa 1927-1935. 5/8". Mint (9.9). Price: $4. CyberAuction #368, Lot #44.

535. AKRO AGATE COMPANY. Corkscrew. Three-color corkscrew. Orange/red, light green, white. One pit. Clarksburg, WV, circa 1927-1935. 5/8". Near Mint(+) (8.9). Price: $4. CyberAuction #406, Lot #8.

536. AKRO AGATE COMPANY. Corkscrew. Blue snake on light blue base. A couple of tiny subsurface moons, in the same area. Clarksburg, WV, circa 1927-1935. 5/8". Near Mint(+) (8.7). Price: $4. CyberAuction #410, Lot #27.

537. AKRO AGATE COMPANY. Corkscrew. Black snake on white. Some pits. Clarksburg, WV, circa 1927-1935. 3/4". Near Mint(+) (8.7). Price: $4. CyberAuction #413, Lot #54.

538. AKRO AGATE COMPANY. Corkscrew. Transparent clear base. Double twist ribbon of semi-opaque red. Very nice. Some scratches. Clarksburg, WV, circa 1927-1935. 5/8". Near Mint(+) (8.9). Price: $4. CyberAuction #415, Lot #56.

539. AKRO AGATE COMPANY. Corkscrew. Snake corkscrew. Blue snake on transparent clear. A couple of pits. Clarksburg, WV, circa 1927-1935. 5/8". Near Mint(+) (8.9). Price: $4. CyberAuction #421, Lot #45.

540. AKRO AGATE COMPANY. Corkscrew. Semi-opaque opalescent white base. Opaque green spiral. Tiny sparkle. Clarksburg, WV, circa 1927-1935. 5/8". Mint(-) (9.1). There are three marbles available, you are bidding on one. Winner has choice of any or all, remainder to under. Price: $4. CyberAuction #432, Lot #16.

541. AKRO AGATE COMPANY. Corkscrew. Ringer. Translucent white with wispy semi-opaque white swirls. Translucent red snake. One sparkle. Clarksburg, WV, circa 1927-1935. 5/8". Mint(-) (9.0). Price: $4. CyberAuction #433, Lot #1.

542. AKRO AGATE COMPANY. Corkscrew. Ribbon corkscrew. Transparent light green base. Opaque white ribbon. One very tiny flake. Clarksburg, WV, circa 1927-1935. 11/16". Near Mint(+) (8.9). Price: $4. CyberAuction #433, Lot #8.

543. AKRO AGATE COMPANY. Corkscrew. Orange, white and black. One subsurface moon. Clarksburg, WV, circa 1927-1935. 11/16". Near Mint(+) (8.7). Price: $4. CyberAuction #435, Lot #37.

544. AKRO AGATE COMPANY. Corkscrew. Black double-twist snake on semi-opaque white base. Gorgeous. Clarksburg, WV, circa 1927-1935. 11/16". Mint (9.8). Price: $4. CyberAuction #450, Lot #6.

545. AKRO AGATE COMPANY. Corkscrew. Black snake on white. Beauty. Clarksburg, WV, circa 1927-1935. 9/16". Mint (9.9). Price: $4. CyberAuction #459, Lot #19.

546. AKRO AGATE COMPANY. Corkscrew. Orange and blue corkscrew. Clarksburg, WV, circa 1927-1929. 19/32". Mint (9.9). Price: $4. CyberAuction #461, Lot #6.

547. AKRO AGATE COMPANY. Corkscrew. Blue spirals on yellow. Odd design. Some light haze. Clarksburg, WV, circa 1927-1935. 5/8". Near Mint (8.6). Price: $4. CyberAuction #463, Lot #11.

548. AKRO AGATE COMPANY. Corkscrew. Snake corkscrew. Light red snake on clear. Two tiny sparkles. Clarksburg, WV, circa 1927-1935. 19/32". Mint(-) (9.0). Price: $4. CyberAuction #463, Lot #22.

549. AKRO AGATE COMPANY. Corkscrew. Ringer. Translucent white with wispy semi-opaque white swirls. Translucent red snake. Several tiny scrapes. Clarksburg, WV, circa 1927-1935. 5/8". Near Mint(+) (8.8). Price: $4. CyberAuction #475, Lot #41.

550. AKRO AGATE COMPANY. Corkscrew. Wispy red/brown on mustard yellow. Clarksburg, WV, circa 1927-1935. 5/8". Mint (9.7). Price: $4. CyberAuction #493, Lot #8.

551. AKRO AGATE COMPANY. Corkscrew. Very pale semi-opaque green base. Brown and gray spiral. Not wet, but no damage. Clarksburg, WV, circa 1927-1935. 19/32". Mint(-) (9.0). Price: $4. CyberAuction #497, Lot #21.

552. AKRO AGATE COMPANY. Corkscrew. Double twist ribbon corkscrew. Beautiful. Transparent light blue base with an opaque white ribbon. Two tiny pits. Clarksburg, WV, circa 1927-1935. 5/8". Near Mint(+) (8.8). Price: $4. CyberAuction #498, Lot #12.

553. AKRO AGATE COMPANY. Corkscrew. Dark red and light green. One tiny sparkle. Clarksburg, WV, circa 1927-1935. 19/32". Mint(-) (9.2). Price: $4. CyberAuction #504, Lot #34.

554. AKRO AGATE COMPANY. Corkscrew. Black and white. One sparkle. Clarksburg, WV, circa 1927-1935. 21/32". Near Mint(+) (8.9). Price: $3. CyberAuction #351, Lot #3.

555. AKRO AGATE COMPANY. Corkscrew. Fluorescent semi-opaque white base. Opaque green spiral. Some pitting. Clarksburg, WV, circa 1927-1935. 19/32". Mint(-) (9.0). Price: $3. CyberAuction #351, Lot #39.

556. AKRO AGATE COMPANY. Corkscrew. Three-color corkscrew. Red, yellow, light blue. Some subsurface moons. 13/16". Near Mint(-) (8.0). There are five marbles available. All the same size and same relative condition. You are bidding on one. Winner has choice of any or all, remainder to under. Price: $3. CyberAuction #362, Lot #22.

557. AKRO AGATE COMPANY. Corkscrew. Interesting ribbon/snake corkscrew. Transparent clear base. Opaque yellow ribbon. Narrow white snake ringing the clear part of the surface. One sparkle. Clarksburg, WV, circa 1927-1935. 5/8". Near Mint(+) (8.9). Price: $3. CyberAuction #395, Lot #3.

558. AKRO AGATE COMPANY. Corkscrew. Three-color. Milky white base. Dark translucent blue spiral and a translucent egg yolk yellow spiral. Some pitting and tiny subsurface moons. Clarksburg, WV, circa 1927-1935. 5/8". Near Mint (8.3). Price: $3. CyberAuction #395, Lot #8.

559. AKRO AGATE COMPANY. Corkscrew. Semi-opaque opalescent white base with blue snake. Clarksburg, WV, circa 1927-1935. 9/16". Mint (9.9). There are four marbles available, you are bidding on one. Winner has choice of any or all, remainder to under. Price: $3. CyberAuction #412, Lot #2.

560. AKRO AGATE COMPANY. Corkscrew. Ringer. Translucent white with wispy semi-opaque white swirls. Translucent red swirl. One sparkle. Clarksburg, WV, circa 1927-1935. 21/32". Mint(-) (9.0). Price: $3. CyberAuction #412, Lot #31.

561. AKRO AGATE COMPANY. Corkscrew. Nice Ace. Translucent milky white base. Red snake. One pit. Clarksburg, WV, circa 1927-1935. 21/32". Mint(-) (9.0). Price: $3. CyberAuction #413, Lot #5.

562. AKRO AGATE COMPANY. Corkscrew. Translucent milky white base. Swirling corkscrew of translucent blue and semi-opaque pale yellow egg yolk. A couple of small subsurface moons. Clarksburg, WV, circa 1927-1935. 5/8". Near Mint (8.3). Price: $3. CyberAuction #419, Lot #47.

563. AKRO AGATE COMPANY. Corkscrew. Double twist ribbon corkscrew. Cherry red transparent base. Opaque white corkscrew. A couple of tiny chips. Clarksburg, WV, circa 1927-1935. 11/16". Near Mint (8.6). Price: $3. CyberAuction #431, Lot #20.

564. AKRO AGATE COMPANY. Corkscrew. Orange and green. Very nice. Tiny sparkle. Clarksburg, WV, circa 1927-1935. 19/32". Mint(-) (9.0). Price: $3. CyberAuction #436, Lot #1.

565. AKRO AGATE COMPANY. Corkscrew. Dark blue snake on light blue opaque base. One small rough spot. Clarksburg, WV, circa 1927-1935. 5/8". Near Mint(+) (8.7). Price: $3. CyberAuction #459, Lot #5.

566. AKRO AGATE COMPANY. Corkscrew. Dark blue spiral on light blue. One tiny subsurface moon. Clarksburg, WV, circa 1927-1935. 5/8". Near Mint(+) (8.9). Price: $3. CyberAuction #467, Lot #47.

567. AKRO AGATE COMPANY. Corkscrew. Ringer. Translucent white with wispy semi-opaque white swirls. Translucent red snake. Clarksburg, WV, circa 1927-1935. 5/8". Mint (9.7). Price: $3. CyberAuction #469, Lot #1.

568. AKRO AGATE COMPANY. Corkscrew. Black snake on white. One pit. Clarksburg, WV, circa 1927-1935. 5/8". Near Mint(+) (8.9). Price: $3. CyberAuction #471, Lot #16.

569. AKRO AGATE COMPANY. Corkscrew. Dark translucent red on yellow. Shooter. Some sparkles and annealing fractures. Clarksburg, WV, circa 1927-1935. 27/32". Near Mint (8.6). There are two marbles available, you are bidding on one. Winner has choice of either or both, remainder to under. Price: $3. CyberAuction #485, Lot #41.

570. AKRO AGATE COMPANY. Corkscrew. Blue and yellow corkscrew. Some sparkles. Clarksburg, WV, circa 1927-1935. 23/32". Near Mint(+) (8.9). Price: $3. CyberAuction #497, Lot #13.

571. AKRO AGATE COMPANY. Corkscrew. Snake corkscrew. Opaque orange snake on transparent clear. A couple of tiny pits. Clarksburg, WV, circa 1927-1935. 5/8". Near Mint(+) (8.7). Price: $3. CyberAuction #498, Lot #19.

572. AKRO AGATE COMPANY. Corkscrew. Transparent very light brown with opaque white fat ribbon. Clarksburg, WV, circa 1927-1935. 11/16". Mint (9.7). Price: $3. CyberAuction #503, Lot #7.

573. AKRO AGATE COMPANY. Corkscrew. Very interesting marble. Ringer type. Translucent milky white base. Spiral of opaque white. Spiral of opaque yellow. Some tiny chipping. Clarksburg, WV, circa 1927-1935. 21/32". Near Mint (8.4). Price: $2. CyberAuction #332, Lot #18.

574. AKRO AGATE COMPANY. Corkscrew. Red and white corkscrew. Clarksburg, WV, circa 1927-1935. 5/8". Mint (9.8). Price: $2. CyberAuction #351, Lot #14.

575. AKRO AGATE COMPANY. Corkscrew. Transparent brown base with

white snake. Clarksburg, WV, circa 1927-1935. 5/8". Mint (9.3). Price: $2. CyberAuction #417, Lot #15.

576. AKRO AGATE COMPANY. Corkscrew. Light orange snake on yellow. One pit. Clarksburg, WV, circa 1927-1935. 21/32". Near Mint(+) (8.9). Price: $2. CyberAuction #433, Lot #16.

577. AKRO AGATE COMPANY. Corkscrew. White base with a light blue spiral. Thin black spiral under the blue. One tiny chip. Clarksburg, WV, circa 1927-1935. 5/8". Near Mint(+) (8.8). Price: $2. CyberAuction #438, Lot #25.

578. AKRO AGATE COMPANY. Corkscrew. Light green and brown/red corkscrew. One tiny flake. Clarksburg, WV, circa 1927-1935. 5/8". Near Mint(+) (8.8). Price: $2. CyberAuction #461, Lot #38.

579. AKRO AGATE COMPANY. Corkscrew. Translucent red spiral on mocha tan. Clarksburg, WV, circa 1870-1915. 5/8". Mint (9.7). Price: $2. CyberAuction #497, Lot #39.

580. AKRO AGATE COMPANY. Corkscrew. Three-color corkscrew. White base. Blue spiral on a yellow spiral (or next to it). One very tiny subsurface moon. Clarksburg, WV, circa 1927-1935. 19/32". Near Mint(+) (8.9). Price: $2. CyberAuction #503, Lot #4.

581. AKRO AGATE COMPANY. Corkscrew. Opalescent semi-opaque white base. Opaque black snake. One air hole, a couple of tiny sparkles. Clarksburg, WV, circa 1927-1935. 5/8". Near Mint(+) (8.9). Price: $1. CyberAuction #438, Lot #14.

582. AKRO AGATE COMPANY. Corkscrew. Light red and green shooter. Pitting. Clarksburg, WV, circa 1927-1935. 15/16". Near Mint (8.5). Price: $1. CyberAuction #468, Lot #39.

583. AKRO AGATE COMPANY. Corkscrew. Semi-opaque milky white base. Snake of orange, brown and black, mixed. Two tiny sparkles, tiny subsurface moon. Clarksburg, WV, circa 1927-1935. 11/16". Near Mint(+) (8.7). Price: $1. CyberAuction #495, Lot #28.

584. AKRO AGATE COMPANY. Cornelian. Rare large Akro Cornelian. Red base with thin white swirls. Cornelians are very hard to find. This is one of the largest I have ever seen and it is great shape. Clarksburg, WV, circa 1922-1927. 25/32". Mint (9.7). Price: $150. CyberAuction #499, Lot #40.

585. AKRO AGATE COMPANY. Cornelian. Rare large Akro Cornelian. Red base with thin white swirls. Cornelians are very hard to find. This is one of the largest I have ever seen and it is great shape. Clarksburg, WV, circa 1922-1927. 25/32". Mint (9.7). Price: $110. CyberAuction #450, Lot #44.

586. AKRO AGATE COMPANY. Cornelian. Rare large Akro Cornelian. Red base with thin white swirls. Cornelians are very hard to find. This is one of the largest I have ever seen and it is great shape. Clarksburg, WV, circa 1922-1927. 25/32". Mint (9.7). Price: $110. CyberAuction #470, Lot #39.

587. AKRO AGATE COMPANY. Cornelian. Rare large Akro Cornelian. Red base with thin white swirls. Cornelians are very hard to find. A few small subsurface moons. Clarksburg, WV, circa 1922-1927. 13/16". Near Mint (8.5). Price: $37. CyberAuction #393, Lot #50.

588. AKRO AGATE COMPANY. Cornelian oxblood. Extremely rare marble. This is an Akro Cornelian with oxblood mixed in. Mixture of semi-opaque red swirled with white. Oxblood swirling on it. Extremely rare. Clarksburg, WV, circa 1925-1930. 21/32". Mint (9.9). Price: $410. CyberAuction #498, Lot #68.

589. AKRO AGATE COMPANY. Cullet. Nice large piece of yellow and blue swirled cullet. Excellent addition to any Akro collection, especially since this color corkscrew is not too hard to find. About 5" x 3" x 3" (sight). Price: $23. CyberAuction #339, Lot #35.

590. AKRO AGATE COMPANY. Cullet. Piece of blue and yellow cullet. Nice. Would look good displayed with a corkscrew of the same color. About 3" x 2" x 2". Mint. Price: $22. CyberAuction #387, Lot #54.

591. AKRO AGATE COMPANY. Cullet. Piece of cullet glass. Red and yellow. Would look great next to the corkscrews of the same color. About 3" x 1" x 1". Mint. Price: $17. CyberAuction #340, Lot #52.

592. AKRO AGATE COMPANY. Egg yolk oxblood. Shooter. Beautiful egg yolk oxblood. Semi-opaque white base. Nice spiral of opaque yellow and a nice spiral of oxblood. Gorgeous. Cold roll dimple. Clarksburg, WV, circa 1928-1938. 3/4". Mint(-) (9.2). Price: $335. CyberAuction #351, Lot #59.

593. AKRO AGATE COMPANY. Egg yolk oxblood. Shooter. Beautiful egg yolk oxblood. Semi-opaque white base. Nice swirls of semi-opaque yellow and oxblood. Gorgeous. Superb. Clarksburg, WV, circa 1928-1938. 23/32". Mint (9.9). Price: $325. CyberAuction #356, Lot #57.

594. AKRO AGATE COMPANY. Egg yolk oxblood. Beautiful egg yolk oxblood. Semi-opaque white base. Nice swirl of opaque yellow and a nice swirl of oxblood. Very nice. Clarksburg, WV, circa 1928-1938. 21/32". Mint (9.7). Price: $130. CyberAuction #491, Lot #51.

595. AKRO AGATE COMPANY. Egg yolk oxblood. Very rare and outstanding error experimental egg yolk oxblood. Two early experimental egg yolk oxbloods stuck together in a melted cluster. Both are translucent white, with translucent bright egg yolk yellow and nice rich oxblood. Corkscrew patterns. Slightly flattened. No damage. Originally from Roger and Claudia Hardy. See Page 18 of their book, upper picture, second row, second marble from the left for an almost identical example. Clarksburg, WV, circa 1925-1927. 13/16" x 1-1/2". Mint (9.7). Price: $110. CyberAuction #394, Lot #44.

596. AKRO AGATE COMPANY. Egg yolk oxblood. Milky white base. Swirl of yellow and very nice oxblood. Clarksburg, WV, circa 1927-1935. 5/8". Mint (9.7). Price: $95. CyberAuction #462, Lot #47.

597. AKRO AGATE COMPANY. Egg yolk oxblood. Beautiful egg yolk oxblood. Semi-opaque white base. Nice spiral of opaque yellow and a nice spiral of oxblood. Gorgeous. One tiny sparkle. Clarksburg, WV, circa 1928-1938. 5/8". Mint(-) (9.2). Price: $95. CyberAuction #483, Lot #52.

598. AKRO AGATE COMPANY. Egg yolk oxblood. Small marble. Translucent white base with oxblood spiral next to an egg yolk and brown spiral. Interesting example. One sparkle, one elongated air hole. Clarksburg, WV, circa 1928-1935. 19/32". Mint(-) (9.0). Price: $55. CyberAuction #376, Lot #57.

599. AKRO AGATE COMPANY. Egg yolk oxblood. Very nice egg yolk oxblood. Semi-opaque milky white base. Nice corkscrew of semi-opaque yellow and oxblood. One tiny chip. Clarksburg, WV, circa 1928-1938. 11/16". Near Mint(+) (8.8). Price: $55. CyberAuction #465, Lot #47.

600. AKRO AGATE COMPANY. Egg yolk oxblood. Shooter. Milky white base. Nice egg yolk yellow and rich oxblood swirls. Small subsurface moon, some pitting and some sparkles. Clarksburg, WV, circa 1925-1935. 3/4". Good(+) (7.7). Price: $50. CyberAuction #397, Lot #55.

601. AKRO AGATE COMPANY. Egg yolk oxblood. Very nice egg yolk oxblood. Semi-opaque milky white base. Nice swirls of semi-opaque yellow and oxblood. Two subsurface moons, some pits. Clarksburg, WV, circa 1928-1938. 19/32". Near Mint(-) (8.1). Price: $35. CyberAuction #387, Lot #50.

602. AKRO AGATE COMPANY. Egg yolk oxblood. Milky white base. Swirl of yellow and very nice oxblood. Small flake, tiny chip. Clarksburg, WV, circa 1927-1935. 23/32". Near Mint (8.6). Price: $25. CyberAuction #426, Lot #56.

603. AKRO AGATE COMPANY. Egg yolk oxblood. Milky white base. Swirl of yellow and very nice oxblood. Some tiny chips, overall haziness. Clarksburg, WV, circa 1927-1935. 19/32". Good (7.6). Price: $21. CyberAuction #353, Lot #45.

604. AKRO AGATE COMPANY. Egg yolk oxblood. Milky white base. Swirl of yellow and very nice oxblood. Small flake, tiny chip. Clarksburg, WV, circa 1927-1935. 23/32". Near Mint (8.6). Price: $21. CyberAuction #408, Lot #26.

605. AKRO AGATE COMPANY. Egg yolk oxblood. Three-quarters of one, at least. This is the early experimental type. Milky white base, deep oxblood swirl, "sick" translucent egg yolk. Misshapen and missing part of the marble. 23/32". Price: $15. CyberAuction #481, Lot #22.

606. AKRO AGATE COMPANY. Flintie. Brown Flintie. Opalescent semi-opaque brown marble. Clarksburg, WV, circa 1925-1930. 5/8". Mint (9.6). There are three marbles available, you are bidding on one. Winner has choice of any or all, remainder to under. Price: $25. CyberAuction #448, Lot #37.

607. AKRO AGATE COMPANY. Flintie. Brown Flintie. Opalescent semi-opaque brown marble. Clarksburg, WV, circa 1925-1930. 5/8". Mint (9.6). There are four marbles available, you are bidding on one. Winner has choice of any or all, remainder to under. Price: $17. CyberAuction #455, Lot #9.

608. AKRO AGATE COMPANY. Flintie. Brown Flintie. Opalescent semi-opaque brown marble. Minor scratches. Clarksburg, WV, circa 1925-1930. 19/32". Mint(-) (9.0). Price: $13. CyberAuction #484, Lot #8.

609. AKRO AGATE COMPANY. Flintie. Brown Flintie. Opalescent semi-opaque brown marble. Clarksburg, WV, circa 1925-1930. 5/8". Mint (9.6). There are three marbles available, you are bidding on one. Winner has choice of any or all, remainder to under. Price: $12. CyberAuction #486, Lot #29.

610. AKRO AGATE COMPANY. Flintie. Brown Flintie. Opalescent semi-opaque brown marble. Clarksburg, WV, circa 1925-1930. 5/8". Mint (9.6). There are four marbles available, you are bidding on one. Winner has choice of any or all, remainder to under. Price: $5. CyberAuction #450, Lot #27.

611. AKRO AGATE COMPANY. Hero. Type of Hero patch. Creamy white base. Orange/red patch on the top. Nice feathering at the seams. Early Akro. Clarksburg, WV, circa 1922-1927. 19/32". Mint (9.7). There are two examples available, you are bidding on one. Winner has choice of either or both, remainder to under. Price: $28. CyberAuction #378, Lot #57.

612. AKRO AGATE COMPANY. Hero. Type of Hero patch. Creamy white base. Wispy orange/red patch on the top. Nice feathering at the seams. Early Akro. Clarksburg, WV, circa 1922-1927. 5/8". Mint (9.9). Price: $22. CyberAuction #381, Lot #38.

613. AKRO AGATE COMPANY. Hero. Opaque white base with semi-opaque orange/red patch. Nice example. Clarksburg, WV, circa 1922-1927. 5/8". Mint (9.9). Price: $21. CyberAuction #432, Lot #7.

614. AKRO AGATE COMPANY. Hero. Hero patch. Creamy white base. Wispy orange patch on the top. Nice feathering at the seams. One tiny flake. Early Akro. Clarksburg, WV, circa 1922-1927. 23/32". Near Mint(+) (8.9). Price: $17. CyberAuction #388, Lot #47.

615. AKRO AGATE COMPANY. Hybrid Ade. Cherryade/Lemonade hybrid. Fluorescent milky white base. Wispy opaque white swirls. Semi-opaque orange and semi-opaque yellow swirls. Rare. Tiny subsurface moon. Clarksburg, WV, circa 1927-1935. 5/8". Near Mint (8.9). Price: $95. CyberAuction #504, Lot #65.

616. AKRO AGATE COMPANY. Imperial. Very interesting. Opalescent base of clear with wispy white. One wispy spiral of brown on the surface. Clarksburg, WV, circa 1927-1929. 21/32". Mint (9.8). Price: $33. CyberAuction #381, Lot #32.

617. AKRO AGATE COMPANY. Imperial. Translucent white base of clear with wispy white. Spiral of brown on the surface. A couple of pinpricks. Clarksburg, WV, circa 1927-1929. 5/8". Mint(-) (9.2). Price: $5. CyberAuction #428, Lot #22.

618. AKRO AGATE COMPANY. Lemonade. Lemonade corkscrew. Very fluorescent. Clarksburg, WV, circa 1928-1935. 5/8". Mint (9.7). Price: $37. CyberAuction #425, Lot #49.

619. AKRO AGATE COMPANY. Lemonade. Lemonade corkscrew. Very fluorescent. Stunning example. Clarksburg, WV, circa 1928-1935. 21/32". Mint (9.9). Price: $36. CyberAuction #498, Lot #53.

620. AKRO AGATE COMPANY. Lemonade. Lemonade corkscrew. Very fluorescent. One tiny pit. Clarksburg, WV, circa 1928-1935. 5/8". Mint(-) (9.1). Price: $35. CyberAuction #362, Lot #55.

621. AKRO AGATE COMPANY. Lemonade. Gorgeous lemonade swirl. Fluorescent yellow ade base. Wide opaque yellow swirl, narrower opaque white swirl. Stunning. Clarksburg, WV, circa 1925-1935. 19/32". Mint (9.9). Price: $33. CyberAuction #357, Lot #47.

622. AKRO AGATE COMPANY. Lemonade. Lemonade corkscrew. Fluorescent ade base. Yellow and white spirals. Gorgeous. Clarksburg, WV, circa 1927-1935. 5/8". Mint (9.7). Price: $25. CyberAuction #388, Lot #22.

623. AKRO AGATE COMPANY. Lemonade. Lemonade swirl. Very fluorescent "ade" base. Swirl of opaque wispy white and swirl of opaque yellow. Clarksburg, WV, circa 1928-1935. 19/32". Mint (9.7). Price: $23. CyberAuction #373, Lot #30.

624. AKRO AGATE COMPANY. Lemonade. Shooter lemonade corkscrew. Very fluorescent. A couple of sparkles, one tiny pit area, some annealing fractures in the yellow. Clarksburg, WV, circa 1928-1935. 1". Near Mint(+) (8.9). Price: $22. CyberAuction #479, Lot #34.

625. AKRO AGATE COMPANY. Lemonade. Corkscrew. Fluorescent ade base, wispy white spiral, egg yolk yellow spiral. Some sparkles and pinpricks, but still is nice. Clarksburg, WV, circa 1925-1935. 3/4". Near Mint(+) (8.8). Price: $22. CyberAuction #505, Lot #1.

626. AKRO AGATE COMPANY. Lemonade. Lemonade swirl. Very fluorescent "ade" base. Swirl of opaque wispy white and swirl of opaque yellow. Superb. One tiny "seed". Clarksburg, WV, circa 1928-1935. 21/32". Mint (9.7). Price: $21. CyberAuction #348, Lot #44.

627. AKRO AGATE COMPANY. Lemonade. Lemonade swirl. Very fluorescent. Melt air hole. Clarksburg, WV, circa 1928-1935. 5/8". Mint (9.7). Price: $17. CyberAuction #429, Lot #21.

628. AKRO AGATE COMPANY. Lemonade. Lemonade corkscrew. Very fluorescent. Clarksburg, WV, circa 1928-1935. 5/8". Mint (9.9). Price: $16. CyberAuction #380, Lot #53.

629. AKRO AGATE COMPANY. Lemonade. Lemonade swirl. Very fluorescent. Clarksburg, WV, circa 1928-1935. 5/8". Mint (9.7). There are three marbles available, you are bidding on one. Winner has choice of any or all, remainder to under. Price: $14. CyberAuction #384, Lot #57.

630. AKRO AGATE COMPANY. Lemonade. Corkscrew. Very fluorescent. Several tiny chips. Clarksburg, WV, circa 1925-1935. 19/32". Near Mint(+) (8.7). Price: $12. CyberAuction #477, Lot #52.

631. AKRO AGATE COMPANY. Lemonade. Lemonade corkscrew. Very fluorescent. Clarksburg, WV, circa 1928-1935. 19/32". Mint (9.7). Price: $11. CyberAuction #436, Lot #14.

632. AKRO AGATE COMPANY. Lemonade. Lemonade corkscrew. Very fluorescent. One sparkle. Clarksburg, WV, circa 1928-1935. 5/8". Mint(-) (9.1). Price: $10. CyberAuction #378, Lot #5.

633. AKRO AGATE COMPANY. Lemonade. Lemonade corkscrew. Very fluorescent. One sparkle. Clarksburg, WV, circa 1928-1935. 5/8". Mint(-) (9.1). Price: $10. CyberAuction #428, Lot #17.

634. AKRO AGATE COMPANY. Lemonade. Lemonade corkscrew. Fluorescent Ade base. Opaque white and opaque yellow corkscrew. Several tiny subsurface moons and sparkles. Clarksburg, WV, circa 1927-1935. 15/16". Near Mint (8.6). Price: $8. CyberAuction #419, Lot #45.

635. AKRO AGATE COMPANY. Lemonade. Lemonade swirl. Ade base. Opaque yellow and opaque white swirls. Several tiny subsurface moons and tiny chips. Clarksburg, WV, circa 1927-1935. 27/32". Near Mint (8.4). Price: $6. CyberAuction #389, Lot #57.

636. AKRO AGATE COMPANY. Lemonade. Lemonade swirl. Very fluorescent "ade" base. Swirl of opaque wispy white and swirl of opaque yellow. Some pits and sparkles. Clarksburg, WV, circa 1928-1935. 19/32". Near Mint (8.5).. Price: $6. CyberAuction #395, Lot #37.

637. AKRO AGATE COMPANY. Lemonade. Lemonade corkscrew. Fluorescent "ade" base. Opaque white corkscrew and opaque yellow corkscrew. Tiny subsurface moon, two sparkles. Clarksburg, WV, circa 1925-1935. 5/8". Near Mint(+) (8.9). Price: $6. CyberAuction #483, Lot #24.

638. AKRO AGATE COMPANY. Lemonade. Lemonade swirl. Very fluorescent. A couple of tiny chips. Clarksburg, WV, circa 1928-1935. 19/32". Near Mint (8.6). Price: $3. CyberAuction #457, Lot #42.

639. AKRO AGATE COMPANY. Lemonade oxblood. Superior shooter. Fluorescent Vaseline lemonade base with wispy white swirls in it, and an oxblood corkscrew brushed on the surface. Stunning. Two melt spots. 3/4". Mint(-) (9.1). Price: $235. CyberAuction #500, Lot #57.

640. AKRO AGATE COMPANY. Lemonade oxblood. I've categorized this as a lemonade oxblood, for lack of a better category. Fluorescent Vaseline translucent base with lots of white swirls. Wispy oxblood corkscrew. One tiny melt spot. 3/4". Mint(-) (9.2). Price: $110. CyberAuction #459, Lot #36.

641. AKRO AGATE COMPANY. Lemonade oxblood. Outstanding shooter lemonade oxblood. Semi-opaque "ade" greenish base. with swirls of translucent white in it. Excellent oxblood swirling on the surface. One tiny rough spot and a few tiny sparkles. Clarksburg, WV, circa 1927-1935. 3/4"-. Near Mint(+) (8.9). Price: $80. CyberAuction #351, Lot #7.

642. AKRO AGATE COMPANY. Lemonade oxblood. Very interesting example. Very pale Vaseline base. Fluorescent. Almost a greenish tinge to it. Very light. Wispy translucent white swirls. Nice oxblood swirling on the surface. Clarksburg, WV, circa 1927-1935. 21/32". Mint (9.6). Price: $60. CyberAuction #334, Lot #59.

643. AKRO AGATE COMPANY. Lemonade oxblood. Shooter corkscrew lemonade oxblood. Hard to find. Base is yellow/green ade. Very fluorescent. Corkscrew spiral of oxblood brushed on the surface. One small blown out area that looks like a mint chip. Clarksburg, WV, circa 1927-1935. 3/4". Mint(-) (9.0). Price: $55. CyberAuction #332, Lot #20.

644. AKRO AGATE COMPANY. Lemonade oxblood. Fluorescent Vaseline lemonade base with wispy white swirls and nice oxblood. 19/32". Mint (9.8). Price: $55. CyberAuction #376, Lot #52.

645. AKRO AGATE COMPANY. Lemonade oxblood. Fluorescent Vaseline lemonade base with wispy swirls and nice oxblood. Tiny sparkle. 5/8". Mint (9.3). Price: $55. CyberAuction #392, Lot #39.

646. AKRO AGATE COMPANY. Lemonade oxblood. Very interesting marble. Lemonade oxblood patch. Fluorescent Vaseline lemonade base. Translucent white patch with wispy oxblood patch. 19/32". Mint (9.9). Price: $50. CyberAuction #356, Lot #6.

647. AKRO AGATE COMPANY. Lemonade oxblood. Fluorescent Vaseline lemonade base with corkscrew of wispy white and oxblood. Several tiny pinpricks and sparkles. 19/32". Near Mint(+) (8.7). Price: $42. CyberAuction #471, Lot #51.

648. AKRO AGATE COMPANY. Lemonade oxblood. Fluorescent Vaseline lemonade base with wispy white swirls and nice oxblood. One sparkle. 11/16". Near Mint(+) (8.9). Price: $41. CyberAuction #433, Lot #57.

649. AKRO AGATE COMPANY. Lemonade oxblood. Fluorescent Vaseline lemonade base with wispy white swirls and nice oxblood. Several tiny subsurface moons, pits and sparkles. 11/16". Near Mint (8.3). Price: $35. CyberAuction #397, Lot #57.

650. AKRO AGATE COMPANY. Lemonade oxblood. Fluorescent Vaseline lemonade base with wispy white swirls and nice oxblood. Several tiny subsurface moons. 5/8". Near Mint(+) (8.7). Price: $31. CyberAuction #337, Lot #4.

651. AKRO AGATE COMPANY. Lemonade oxblood. Shooter lemonade oxblood. Very fluorescent. Nice oxblood. Several tiny pits, not wet. Clarksburg, WV, circa 1925-1935. 23/32". Near Mint (8.6). Consignor note: D14. Price: $30. CyberAuction #344, Lot #20.

652. AKRO AGATE COMPANY. Lemonade oxblood. Fluorescent Vaseline lemonade base with wispy white swirls and nice oxblood. Pinprick and tiny subsurface moon. 19/32". Near Mint(+) (8.8). Price: $29. CyberAuction #455, Lot #54.

653. AKRO AGATE COMPANY. Lemonade oxblood. Shooter lemonade oxblood. Very fluorescent. Nice oxblood. Small chipping and roughness. Clarksburg, WV, circa 1925-1935. 23/32". Good (7.6). Consignor note: D13. Price: $21. CyberAuction #343, Lot #39.

654. AKRO AGATE COMPANY. Limeade. Beautiful limeade corkscrew. Fluorescent "ade" base. Wispy white and translucent green corkscrew. In great shape. Clarksburg, WV, circa 1927-1935. 21/32". Mint (9.8). Price: $70. CyberAuction #459, Lot #32.

655. AKRO AGATE COMPANY. Limeade. Limeade swirl. Fluorescent "ade" base. Opaque white and translucent green swirls. Very narrow faint burnt oxblood swirl. Gorgeous. Clarksburg, WV, circa 1925-1935. 5/8". Mint (9.9). Price: $55. CyberAuction #481, Lot #48.

656. AKRO AGATE COMPANY. Limeade. Limeade swirl. Fluorescent "ade" base. Opaque white and opaque green swirl. Beauty. Clarksburg, WV, circa 1925-1935. 5/8". Mint (9.9). Price: $55. CyberAuction #483, Lot #43.

657. AKRO AGATE COMPANY. Limeade. Beautiful limeade corkscrew. Fluorescent "ade" base. Wispy white and translucent green corkscrew. In great shape. Clarksburg, WV, circa 1927-1935. 19/32". Mint (9.8). Price: $40. CyberAuction #461, Lot #17.

658. AKRO AGATE COMPANY. Limeade. Beautiful limeade swirl. Fluorescent "ade" base. Wispy white and translucent green swirls. In great shape. Clarksburg, WV, circa 1927-1935. 5/8". Mint (9.7). Price: $36. CyberAuction #417, Lot #45.

659. AKRO AGATE COMPANY. Limeade. Beautiful limeade corkscrew. Fluorescent "ade" base. Wispy white and translucent green corkscrew. In great shape. Clarksburg, WV, circa 1927-1935. 5/8". Mint (9.8). Price: $35. CyberAuction #502, Lot #67.

660. AKRO AGATE COMPANY. Limeade. Beautiful limeade corkscrew. Fluorescent "ade" base. Wispy white and translucent green corkscrew. In great shape. Clarksburg, WV, circa 1927-1935. 5/8". Mint (9.7). Price: $32. CyberAuction #363, Lot #24.

661. AKRO AGATE COMPANY. Limeade. Beautiful limeade corkscrew. Fluorescent "ade" base. Wispy white and translucent green corkscrew. In great shape. Clarksburg, WV, circa 1927-1935. 5/8". Mint (9.8). Price: $29. CyberAuction #504, Lot #23.

662. AKRO AGATE COMPANY. Limeade. Beautiful limeade swirl. Fluorescent "ade" base. Wispy white and translucent green swirl. In great shape. Clarksburg, WV, circa 1927-1935. 19/32". Mint (9.8). Price: $27. CyberAuction #501, Lot #16.

663. AKRO AGATE COMPANY. Limeade. Beautiful limeade corkscrew. Fluorescent "ade" base. Wispy white and translucent green corkscrew. In great shape. Clarksburg, WV, circa 1927-1935. 5/8". Mint (9.8). Price: $25. CyberAuction #503, Lot #55.

664. AKRO AGATE COMPANY. Limeade. Beautiful limeade swirl. Fluorescent "ade" base. Wispy white and translucent green swirls. In great shape. Clarksburg, WV, circa 1927-1935. 5/8". Mint (9.7). There are two marbles available, you are bidding on one. Winner has choice of either or both, remainder to under. Price: $21. CyberAuction #384, Lot #48.

665. AKRO AGATE COMPANY. Limeade. Corkscrew. Fluorescent ade base. Wispy white corkscrew and a green spiral. A couple of pits. Clarksburg, WV, circa 1927-1935. 5/8". Near Mint(+) (8.9). Price: $20. CyberAuction #476, Lot #38.

666. AKRO AGATE COMPANY. Limeade. Beautiful limeade swirl. Fluorescent "ade" base. Wispy white and translucent green swirls. One sparkle. Clarksburg, WV, circa 1927-1935. 5/8". Mint(-) (9.2). Price: $19. CyberAuction #408, Lot #37.

667. AKRO AGATE COMPANY. Limeade. Beautiful limeade swirl. One sparkle. Clarksburg, WV, circa 1925-1935. 5/8". Mint(-) (9.0). Price: $17. CyberAuction #339, Lot #38.

668. AKRO AGATE COMPANY. Limeade. Beautiful limeade swirl. Fluorescent "ade" base. Wispy white and translucent green swirls. Subsurface moon.

Clarksburg, WV, circa 1927-1935. 19/32". Near Mint(+) (8.8). Price: $8. CyberAuction #407, Lot #33.

669. AKRO AGATE COMPANY. Limeade. Very nice. Ade base with wispy white swirls and translucent green swirls. Several small subsurface moons. Clarksburg, WV, circa 1927-1935. 5/8". Near Mint (8.4). There are two marbles available, you are bidding on one. Winner has choice of either or both, remainder to other. Price: $7. CyberAuction #382, Lot #39.

670. AKRO AGATE COMPANY. Limeade. Limeade corkscrew. Fluorescent ade base. Wispy white spiral. Opaque green spiral. Some sparkles and very tiny subsurface moons. Clarksburg, WV, circa 1925-1935. 23/32". Near Mint (8.5). Price: $7. CyberAuction #505, Lot #11.

671. AKRO AGATE COMPANY. Marble bag. Hard to find buckskin Akro Agate marble pouch. Double walled yellow buckskin bag. With the Akro logo on it. Original drawstring. Two pinholes at bottom, small tear at top. Bag is dirty but could be cleaned up. Needed for Akro tins and boxes. Very hard to find. Near Mint(+) (8.9). Price: $150. CyberAuction #502, Lot #17.

672. AKRO AGATE COMPANY. Milky oxblood. Semi-opaque white base. Nice swirl of semi-opaque oxblood on it. Beauty. Clarksburg, WV, circa 1930-1935. 5/8". Mint (9.7). Price: $38. CyberAuction #382, Lot #44.

673. AKRO AGATE COMPANY. Milky oxblood. Semi-opaque white base with nice oxblood swirls. Clarksburg, WV, circa 1930-1945. 5/8". Mint (9.9). Price: $32. CyberAuction #387, Lot #48.

674. AKRO AGATE COMPANY. Milky oxblood. Semi-opaque white base. Loads of oxblood swirls. Some cold lines. Beauty and hard to find. Clarksburg, WV, circa 1930-1945. 9/16". Mint (9.5). Price: $27. CyberAuction #459, Lot #29.

675. AKRO AGATE COMPANY. Milky oxblood. Semi-opaque to translucent white base. Swirls of oxblood on it. Several very tiny chips. Clarksburg, WV, circa 1925-1935. 5/8". Near Mint(+) (8.7). Price: $6. CyberAuction #420, Lot #12.

676. AKRO AGATE COMPANY. Moonie. Semi-opaque opalescent white marble. Beauty. Clarksburg, WV, circa 1920-1930. 25/32". Mint (9.6). Price: $19. CyberAuction #417, Lot #33.

677. AKRO AGATE COMPANY. Moonie. Semi-opaque opalescent white marble. Nice orange glow. Clarksburg, WV, circa 1925-1930. 23/32". Mint (9.9). Price: $13. CyberAuction #481, Lot #26.

678. AKRO AGATE COMPANY. Moonie. Akro Moonie. Opalescent semi-opaque white marble. Clarksburg, WV, circa 1925-1930. 19/32". Mint (9.9). Price: $6. CyberAuction #372, Lot #47.

679. AKRO AGATE COMPANY. Moonie. Semi-opaque opalescent white marble. Nice orange glow and lots of tiny air bubbles. Clarksburg, WV, circa 1925-1930. 21/32". Mint (9.9). Price: $4. CyberAuction #407, Lot #10.

680. AKRO AGATE COMPANY. Moss Agate. Large Moss Agate. Fluorescent "ade" base. Large opaque yellow patch. Clarksburg, WV, circa 1922-1927. 29/32". Mint (9.9). Price: $25. CyberAuction #414, Lot #11.

681. AKRO AGATE COMPANY. Moss Agate. Large Moss Agate. Fluorescent "ade" base. Large opaque yellow patch. One tiny pit. Clarksburg, WV, circa 1922-1927. 1". Mint(-) (9.0). Price: $25. CyberAuction #417, Lot #51.

682. AKRO AGATE COMPANY. Moss Agate. Fluorescent yellowish semi-opaque base, opaque yellow patch. Clarksburg, WV, circa 1925-1935. 3/4". Mint (9.7). Price: $13. CyberAuction #431, Lot #33.

683. AKRO AGATE COMPANY. Moss Agate. A type of Moss Agate patch. Would have been a Helmet Patch if there were a stripe on the patch. Fluorescent yellow ade base. Wide white/yellow patch, helmet style. Super example. Clarksburg, WV, circa 1925-1930. 3/4". Mint (9.9). Price: $12. CyberAuction #330, Lot #1.

684. AKRO AGATE COMPANY. Moss Agate. Very unusual example. Semi-opaque fluorescent ade base. Patch covering about have the marble. Patch is about orange/red and half yellow, with some blue smeared into the yellow. Very unusual. Tiny subsurface moon. 21/32". Near Mint(+) (8.9). Price: $6. CyberAuction #420, Lot #49.

685. AKRO AGATE COMPANY. Orangeade. Orangeade corkscrew. Semi-opaque fluorescent "ade" base. Wide opaque white spiral and a wide translucent orange spiral. Rare. Clarksburg, WV, circa 1925-1935. 5/8". Mint (9.8). Price: $120. CyberAuction #500, Lot #19.

686. AKRO AGATE COMPANY. Orangeade. Orangeade corkscrew. Semi-opaque fluorescent "ade" base. Wide opaque white spiral and a wide translucent orange spiral. Rare. Several subsurface moons. Clarksburg, WV, circa 1925-1935. 11/16". Near Mint (8.5). Consignor note: H40. Price: $42. CyberAuction #378, Lot #51.

687. AKRO AGATE COMPANY. Orangeade. Orangeade corkscrew. Semi-opaque fluorescent "ade" base. Wide opaque white spiral and a wide translucent orange spiral. Rare. Several subsurface moons. Clarksburg, WV, circa 1925-1935. 5/8". Near Mint (8.5). Price: $30. CyberAuction #395, Lot #4.

688. AKRO AGATE COMPANY. Original package. Hard to find box. "100 Assorted Royal Akro Agate Marbles No. 0". Cardboard marbleized tan and brown box. Early Akro logo on the top. Dark graphic, well-centered. Box top has a missing corner. A tiny puncture on the right edge and a small puncture on the bottom edge. Paper label pasted on the edge identifying it as Akro Royals. Bottom is Mint. Includes one hundred 5/8" Akro Royals in five colors. Marbles are Mint. Box top is Near Mint. Clarksburg, WV, circa 1922-1927. Very hard to find. Price: $500. CyberAuction #406, Lot #33.

689. AKRO AGATE COMPANY. Original package. Original box of 25 No. 0 Cardinal Red. Box is in great shape, with just a tiny bit of rubbing. Marbles are Mint. Stunning set and getting very hard to find. Box is Mint. Price: $500. CyberAuction #491, Lot #56.

690. AKRO AGATE COMPANY. Original package. Rare advertising package. No. 16 cardboard box containing five slags. Printed, in red, on the

78

back is "This Box of Marbles FREE with a Package of "MALT-O-MEAL Breakfast Cereal". Marbles are Mint. Box has one torn flap (all pieces are present, graded as Near Mint (8.5). Very hard to find. Price: $110. CyberAuction #359, Lot #28.

691. AKRO AGATE COMPANY. Original package. Original No. 16 box with original slags. This is the blue cardboard sleeve. Very nice. Slight crushing on one end with a tiny tear in the one oval. Contains a green, orange, brown, yellow and blue slag. Sleeve is about 3-1/2" x 11/16" x 11/16". Marbles are about 11/16". Box is Mint(-) (9.0). Marbles are Mint (9.9-9.0). Price: $75. CyberAuction #495, Lot #32.

692. AKRO AGATE COMPANY. Original package. Original Akro Agate Chinese Checkers box. Tan box. Has full complement of marbles. In nice shape with just a little rubbing around the edges. Graphic off-center. Two split corners. No fading. Near Mint(+) (8.9). Price: $21. CyberAuction #341, Lot #28.

693. AKRO AGATE COMPANY. Original package. Original "60 Game Marbles No. 00" "Akro Agate Chinese Checkers". Tan box. Blue graphic. Small puncture in box top. Full complement of marbles. Marbles are Mint. Box is Near Mint (8.6). Price: $20. CyberAuction #445, Lot #25.

694. AKRO AGATE COMPANY. Original package. Original "60 Game Marbles No. 00" "Akro Agate Chinese Checkers". Tan box. Blue graphic. Small puncture in box top. Full complement of marbles. Marbles are Mint. Box is Near Mint (8.6). Price: $15. CyberAuction #413, Lot #30.

695. AKRO AGATE COMPANY. Oxblood corkscrew. Orange base. Black spiral on top of dark oxblood. Clarksburg, WV, circa 1927-1935. 5/8". Mint (9.8). Price: $100. CyberAuction #435, Lot #7.

696. AKRO AGATE COMPANY. Oxblood corkscrew. Transparent bubble filled clear base. Double twist semi-opaque oxblood ribbon in the marble. Superb. Clarksburg, WV, circa 1927-1935. 17/32". Mint (9.6). Price: $80. CyberAuction #429, Lot #43.

697. AKRO AGATE COMPANY. Oxblood corkscrew. Transparent bubble filled clear base. Double twist semi-opaque oxblood ribbon in the marble. Clarksburg, WV, circa 1927-1935. 19/32". Mint (9.8). Price: $71. CyberAuction #500, Lot #1.

698. AKRO AGATE COMPANY. Oxblood corkscrew. Transparent bubble filled clear base. Double twist semi-opaque oxblood ribbon in the marble. One very tiny rub spot. Clarksburg, WV, circa 1927-1935. 19/32". Mint(-) (9.2). Price: $70. CyberAuction #455, Lot #45.

699. AKRO AGATE COMPANY. Oxblood corkscrew. Rare example. Dark oxblood spiral on bright orange. Some pitting. Clarksburg, WV, circa 1927-1935. 11/16". Near Mint(+) (8.8). Price: $65. CyberAuction #499, Lot #32.

700. AKRO AGATE COMPANY. Oxblood corkscrew. Opaque white base. Spiral of oxblood on top of a spiral of black. Two pits. Clarksburg, WV, circa 1927-1935. 5/8". Mint(-) (9.0). Price: $50. CyberAuction #403, Lot #37.

701. AKRO AGATE COMPANY. Oxblood corkscrew. Semi-opaque white base. Oxblood snake on black snake. Outstanding example! Clarksburg, WV, circa 1927-1935. 5/8". Mint. (9.9). Price: $50. CyberAuction #493, Lot #53.

702. AKRO AGATE COMPANY. Oxblood corkscrew. Transparent bubble filled clear base. Double twist semi-opaque oxblood ribbon in the marble. A couple of small flakes. Clarksburg, WV, circa 1927-1935. 21/32". Near Mint (8.6). There are two marbles available, you are bidding on one. Winner has choice of either or both, remainder to under. Price: $42. CyberAuction #443, Lot #46.

703. AKRO AGATE COMPANY. Oxblood corkscrew. Semi-opaque white base. Oxblood snake on black snake. Outstanding example! Clarksburg, WV, circa 1927-1935. 5/8". Mint (9.9). Price: $32. CyberAuction #462, Lot #5.

704. AKRO AGATE COMPANY. Oxblood corkscrew. Transparent bubble filled clear base. Double twist semi-opaque oxblood ribbon in the marble. A couple of small flakes. Clarksburg, WV, circa 1927-1935. 9/16". Near Mint (8.6). There are two marbles available, you are bidding on one. Winner has choice of either or both, remainder to under. Price: $26. CyberAuction #438, Lot #9.

705. AKRO AGATE COMPANY. Oxblood corkscrew. Transparent bubble filled clear base. Double twist semi-opaque oxblood ribbon in the marble. A couple of small flakes. Clarksburg, WV, circa 1927-1935. 9/16". Near Mint (8.6). Price: $20. CyberAuction #444, Lot #19.

706. AKRO AGATE COMPANY. Patch. Very rare experimental patch. Bright orange and bright mottled blue. These popped up a few years ago and were quickly snapped up. They have been almost impossible to find since. Probably experimental marbles. Slightly out of round. Clarksburg, WV, circa 1922-1927. 1-1/8". Mint (9.8). Price: $270. CyberAuction #448, Lot #59.

707. AKRO AGATE COMPANY. Patch. Very rare experimental patch. Bright orange and bright mottled blue. A couple of tiny pinpricks. These popped up a few years ago and were quickly snapped up. They have been almost impossible to find since. Probably experimental marbles. Clarksburg, WV, circa 1922-1927. 1-1/16". Mint(+) (9.0). Price: $250. CyberAuction #508, Lot #72.

708. AKRO AGATE COMPANY. Patch. Experimental Akro patch. Transparent green base with a little wispy white in it and lots of air bubbles. Streaky yellow patch on the top. These popped up about six or seven years ago from Roger and Claudia Hardy. Early experimentals. Clarksburg, WV, circa 1922-1927. 11/16". Mint (9.9). There are two examples available, you are bidding on one. Winner has choice of either or both, remainder to under. Price: $40. CyberAuction #407, Lot #53.

709. AKRO AGATE COMPANY. Patch. Moss Agate type patch. The base is not fluorescent. Milky white base. Bright orange patch. Clarksburg, WV, circa 1925-1930. 11/16". Mint (9.9). Price: $6. CyberAuction #351, Lot #33.

710. AKRO AGATE COMPANY. Patch. Translucent white base. Green patch. Several tiny subsurface moons. Clarksburg, WV, circa 1927-1935. 15/16". Near Mint (8.5). Price: $4. CyberAuction #355, Lot #41.

711. AKRO AGATE COMPANY. Patch. Translucent white base. Green patch. Several tiny subsurface moons. Clarksburg, WV, circa 1927-1935. 15/16". Near Mint (8.5). Price: $1. CyberAuction #440, Lot #22.

712. AKRO AGATE COMPANY. Patch oxblood. Very rare Royal patch oxblood. Translucent milky white base with translucent red patch covering about one-third of it (Royal). Very rich oxblood patch covering about one-third of the marble, next to the red patch. Several tiny flakes and pinpricks on the red patch. Very rare. Clarksburg, WV, circa 1927-1935. 3/4". Near Mint(+) (8.7). Price: $85. CyberAuction #379, Lot #44.

713. AKRO AGATE COMPANY. Patch oxblood. Very rare Royal patch oxblood. Translucent milky white base with translucent red patch covering about one-third of it (Royal). Very rich oxblood patch covering about one-third of the marble, next to the red patch. Several tiny flakes and pinpricks on the red patch. Very rare. Clarksburg, WV, circa 1927-1935. 3/4". Near Mint(+) (8.7). Price: $85. CyberAuction #446, Lot #59.

714. AKRO AGATE COMPANY. Patch oxblood. Transparent dark brown base. Nice band of oxblood on the surface. Very hard to find marble. Clarksburg, WV, circa 1930-1950. 21/32". Mint (9.7). Price: $60. CyberAuction #351, Lot #12.

715. AKRO AGATE COMPANY. Patch oxblood. Opaque white base. Wide patch of blue, narrow patch of green, wide patch of oxblood. Very nice example of a shooter. Clarksburg, WV, circa 1930-1945. 31/32". Mint (9.9). Price: $55. CyberAuction #356, Lot #42.

716. AKRO AGATE COMPANY. Patch oxblood. Very interesting. Opaque white base. Nice patch of transparent yellow (transparent clear patch under half of it, nice effect). Nice patch of oxblood. Clarksburg, WV, circa 1930-1945. 21/32". Mint (9.9). Price: $46. CyberAuction #356, Lot #51.

717. AKRO AGATE COMPANY. Patch oxblood. Very rare marble. Opalescent white moonie base. Small patch of translucent blue and small patch of dark oxblood. Clarksburg, WV, circa 1930-1945. 19/32". Mint (9.7). Price: $39. CyberAuction #498, Lot #58.

718. AKRO AGATE COMPANY. Patch oxblood. Shooter size marble. Interesting. Opaque white base. Wide patch of green. Two patches of oxblood. Clarksburg, WV, circa 1930-1945. 7/8". Mint (9.9). Price: $37. CyberAuction #351, Lot #24.

719. AKRO AGATE COMPANY. Patch oxblood. Probably Vitro Agate. Brushed patch of oxblood covering about half a marble. American, circa 1940-1950. 23/32". Mint (9.6). Price: $32. CyberAuction #469, Lot #50.

720. AKRO AGATE COMPANY. Patch oxblood. Shooter. Opaque white base. Green patch on one side, oxblood patch on other. One sparkle, on pinprick area. Clarksburg, WV, circa 1930-1945. 7/8". Near Mint(+) (8.9). Price: $17. CyberAuction #462, Lot #36.

721. AKRO AGATE COMPANY. Patch oxblood. Shooter. Opaque white base. Oxblood band and green band. A couple of pits. Clarksburg, WV, circa 1930-1945. 25/32". Near Mint(+) (8.7). Price: $15. CyberAuction #380, Lot #38.

722. AKRO AGATE COMPANY. Patch oxblood. Semi-opaque white base. Thin patch, edged by a thin oxblood patch. Mostly white. Clarksburg, WV, circa 1930-1945. 7/8". Mint (9.9). Price: $15. CyberAuction #387, Lot #36.

723. AKRO AGATE COMPANY. Patch oxblood. Opaque white base. Nice oxblood patch. Next to it is a mixed patch of oxblood and green. Large dimple with dirt in it. Clarksburg, WV, circa 1930-1945. 23/32". Near Mint(+) (8.9). Price: $13. CyberAuction #357, Lot #6.

724. AKRO AGATE COMPANY. Patch oxblood. Semi-opaque white base. Oxblood patch on one side, green patch on the other. Clarksburg, WV, circa 1935-1945. 9/16". Mint (9.9). Price: $12. CyberAuction #350, Lot #44.

725. AKRO AGATE COMPANY. Patch oxblood. Semi-opaque white base. Green band on one side, oxblood band on the other. Clarksburg, WV, circa 1930-1945. 9/16". Mint (9.9). Price: $12. CyberAuction #364, Lot #37.

726. AKRO AGATE COMPANY. Patch oxblood. Opaque white base. Nice oxblood patch. Blue patch on other side. Clarksburg, WV, circa 1930-1945. 19/32". Mint (9.9). Price: $12. CyberAuction #435, Lot #2.

727. AKRO AGATE COMPANY. Patch oxblood. Semi-opaque white base. Green band on one side, oxblood band on the other. Clarksburg, WV, circa 1930-1945. 9/16". Mint (9.9). Price: $10. CyberAuction #443, Lot #45.

728. AKRO AGATE COMPANY. Patch oxblood. White base. Oxblood patch on one side, green patch on the other. Clarksburg, WV, circa 1930-1945. 9/16". Mint (9.8). There are four examples available, you are bidding on one. Winner has choice of any or all, remainder to under. Price: $7. CyberAuction #465, Lot #1.

729. AKRO AGATE COMPANY. Patch oxblood. White base. Oxblood patch on one side, green patch on the other. Clarksburg, WV, circa 1930-1945. 9/16". Mint (9.8). There are four. Price: $. CyberAuction #467, Lot #16.

730. AKRO AGATE COMPANY. Patch oxblood. White base. Oxblood patch on one side, green patch on the other. Clarksburg, WV, circa 1930-1945. 9/16". Mint (9.8). There are two examples available, you are bidding on one. Winner has choice of any or all, remainder to under. Price: $5. CyberAuction #472, Lot #28.

731. AKRO AGATE COMPANY. Patch oxblood. White base. Oxblood patch on one side, green and blue patch on the other. Clarksburg, WV, circa 1930-1945. 9/16". Mint (9.8). There are two examples available, you are bidding on one. Winner has choice of any or all, remainder to under. Price: $5. CyberAuction #473, Lot #1.

732. AKRO AGATE COMPANY. Patch oxblood. Semi-opaque white base. Thin blue patch on one side. Wide oxblood patch on the other. One tiny sparkle. Clarksburg, WV, circa 1930-1935. 19/32". Mint(-) (9.2). Price: $3. CyberAuction #406, Lot #18.

733. AKRO AGATE COMPANY. Patch oxblood. Semi-opaque white base. Oxblood band on one side, translucent green band on other. Clarksburg, WV, circa 1927-1935. 9/16". Mint (9.8). Two marbles available, you are bidding on one. Winner has choice of either or both, remainder to under. Price: $3. CyberAuction #493, Lot #31.

734. AKRO AGATE COMPANY. Popeye corkscrew. Hybrid Popeye corkscrew. Blue and yellow, with a narrow green spiral and a narrow orange spiral. Hard to find six-color. A couple of pinpricks. Rare. Clarksburg, WV, circa 1927-1935. 5/8". Mint(-) (9.0). Price: $550. CyberAuction #369, Lot #40.

735. AKRO AGATE COMPANY. Popeye corkscrew. Red, yellow and green hybrid Popeye. Gorgeous. Exceptional example. Clarksburg, WV, circa 1927-1935. 19/32". Mint (9.9). Price: $370. CyberAuction #377, Lot #49.

736. AKRO AGATE COMPANY. Popeye corkscrew. Gorgeous hybrid Popeye. Red, blue and yellow. The yellow is below the two surface spirals. Gorgeous colors!!!! In superb shape. Clarksburg, WV, circa 1927-1935. 5/8". Mint (9.8). Price: $360. CyberAuction #376, Lot #59.

737. AKRO AGATE COMPANY. Popeye corkscrew. Gorgeous hybrid Popeye corkscrew. Light orange, green and yellow. Exceptional example!!!! Clarksburg, WV, circa 1927-1935. 5/8". Mint (9.9). Price: $335. CyberAuction #487, Lot #58.

738. AKRO AGATE COMPANY. Popeye corkscrew. Hybrid Popeye corkscrew. Red, yellow, green and blue. The red is wide, the yellow is typical width, the yellow is narrow and the blue is very thin. A beauty and very hard to find this many colors in a hybrid. Clarksburg, WV, circa 1927-1935. 5/8". Mint (9.9). Price: $320. CyberAuction #387, Lot #58.

739. AKRO AGATE COMPANY. Popeye corkscrew. Superb hybrid Popeye corkscrew. Navy blue, green and yellow. The green is not a blend. Outstanding. Clarksburg, WV, circa 1927-1935. 5/8". Mint (9.6). Price: $270. CyberAuction #459, Lot #54.

740. AKRO AGATE COMPANY. Popeye corkscrew. Hybrid Popeye. Gorgeous example. Lots of white in the clear. Wide spiral of yellow. Two spirals of purple, one on each side of the yellow. Thin spiral of transparent orange. One tiny manufacturing melt spot, else the surface is pristine. Exceptional example. Clarksburg, WV, circa 1927-1935. 5/8". Mint (9.5). Price: $260. CyberAuction #357, Lot #57.

741. AKRO AGATE COMPANY. Popeye corkscrew. Shooter hybrid Popeye. Rare! Red, green and yellow. Tiny subsurface moon and some pits (possibly manufacturing). Clarksburg, WV, circa 1927-1935. 3/4". Near Mint(+) (8.8). Price: $260. CyberAuction #381, Lot #49.

742. AKRO AGATE COMPANY. Popeye corkscrew. Hybrid. Red and blue, with a thin green spiral. Superb marble. One tiny pit. Clarksburg, WV, circa 1927-1935. 21/32". Mint(-) (9.1). Price: $260. CyberAuction #504, Lot #48.

743. AKRO AGATE COMPANY. Popeye corkscrew. Superb hybrid Popeye. Green, red, blue and yellow. One tiny flake. Stunning. Clarksburg, WV, circa 1927-1935. 21/32". Near Mint(+) (8.9). Price: $235. CyberAuction #406, Lot #59.

744. AKRO AGATE COMPANY. Popeye corkscrew. Very nice hybrid Popeye corkscrew. Red and green Popeye with a spiral of yellow in the core. The red and green are on the surface. One sparkle. Super marble. Clarksburg, WV, circa 1927-1935. 23/32". Mint(-) (9.1). Price: $200. CyberAuction #385, Lot #53.

745. AKRO AGATE COMPANY. Popeye corkscrew. Red and blue Popeye. Superb snake type. Gorgeous. Clarksburg, WV, circa 1927-1935. 19/32". Mint (9.9). Price: $180. CyberAuction #400, Lot #50.

746. AKRO AGATE COMPANY. Popeye corkscrew. Purple and yellow. Very nice shooter. A couple of tiny pinpricks. Clarksburg, WV, circa 1927-1935. 3/4". Mint(-) (9.1). Price: $170. CyberAuction #418, Lot #44.

747. AKRO AGATE COMPANY. Popeye corkscrew. Purple and yellow. Very nice shooter. A couple of tiny pinpricks. Clarksburg, WV, circa 1927-1935. 3/4". Mint(-) (9.1). Price: $160. CyberAuction #455, Lot #27.

748. AKRO AGATE COMPANY. Popeye corkscrew. Hybrid Popeye corkscrew. Green and yellow with narrow red. Clarksburg, WV, circa 1927-1935. 5/8". Mint (9.9). Price: $160. CyberAuction #498, Lot #44.

749. AKRO AGATE COMPANY. Popeye corkscrew. Red and blue Popeye. Gorgeous. Clarksburg, WV, circa 1927-1935. 21/32". Mint (9.7). Price: $140. CyberAuction #373, Lot #39.

750. AKRO AGATE COMPANY. Popeye corkscrew. Very nice hybrid Popeye. White and clear base. Spirals of green, red and yellow. The yellow is narrow and between the green and red. Two tiny rough spots at one end. Very nicely formed. Clarksburg, WV, circa 1927-1935. 5/8". Near Mint(+) (8.9). Price: $135. CyberAuction #508, Lot #21.

751. AKRO AGATE COMPANY. Popeye corkscrew. Dark purple and yellow Popeye. Beauty. Clarksburg, WV, circa 1927-1935. 5/8". Mint (9.9). Price: $130. CyberAuction #330, Lot #28.

752. AKRO AGATE COMPANY. Popeye corkscrew. Rare shooter fluorescent green and yellow. Very rarely seen this large. One sparkle. Stunning. Clarksburg, WV, circa 1927-1935. 3/4". Mint(-) (9.0). Price: $130. CyberAuction #381, Lot #54.

753. AKRO AGATE COMPANY. Popeye corkscrew. Shooter. Light blue and yellow. Lots of white. Super marble. Clarksburg, WV, circa 1927-1935. 3/4". Mint (9.7). Price: $120. CyberAuction #366, Lot #9.

754. AKRO AGATE COMPANY. Popeye corkscrew. Hard to find. Orange and red. Orange is a thin spiral. Clarksburg, WV, circa 1927-1935. 5/8". Mint (9.9). Price: $120. CyberAuction #381, Lot #7.

755. AKRO AGATE COMPANY. Popeye corkscrew. Purple and yellow shooter. Two very tiny chips. Clarksburg, WV, circa 1927-1935. 23/32". Near Mint(+) (8.9). Price: $120. CyberAuction #483, Lot #56.

756. AKRO AGATE COMPANY. Popeye corkscrew. Light purple and yellow Popeye. Beauty. Clarksburg, WV, circa 1927-1935. 5/8". Mint (9.9). Price: $110. CyberAuction #330, Lot #49.

757. AKRO AGATE COMPANY. Popeye corkscrew. Hybrid Popeye. Red and yellow with very thin blue. A couple of tiny sparkles. Clarksburg, WV, circa 1927-1935. 23/32". Mint(-) (9.0). Price: $110. CyberAuction #432, Lot #43.

758. AKRO AGATE COMPANY. Popeye corkscrew. Shooter Popeye. Purple and yellow Popeye. Sparkle and tiny subsurface moon. Clarksburg, WV, circa 1927-1935. 3/4". Near Mint(+) (8.7). Price: $100. CyberAuction #348, Lot #56.

759. AKRO AGATE COMPANY. Popeye corkscrew. Purple and yellow Popeye. Gorgeous. Clarksburg, WV, circa 1927-1935. 19/32". Mint (9.9). Price: $100. CyberAuction #400, Lot #48.

760. AKRO AGATE COMPANY. Popeye corkscrew. Gorgeous purple and yellow Popeye. Outstanding. Clarksburg, WV, circa 1927-1935. 11/16". Mint (9.9). Price: $100. CyberAuction #407, Lot #2.

761. AKRO AGATE COMPANY. Popeye corkscrew. Purple and yellow Popeye. In great shape. Clarksburg, WV, circa 1927-1935. 11/16". Mint (9.8). Price: $95. CyberAuction #407, Lot #11.

762. AKRO AGATE COMPANY. Popeye corkscrew. Purple and yellow Popeye. Beauty. Clarksburg, WV, circa 1927-1935. 11/16". Mint (9.9). Price: $95. CyberAuction #443, Lot #57.

763. AKRO AGATE COMPANY. Popeye corkscrew. Blue and yellow shooter. Gorgeous. Clarksburg, WV, circa 1927-1935. 3/4". Mint (9.9). Price: $90. CyberAuction #388, Lot #51.

764. AKRO AGATE COMPANY. Popeye corkscrew. Red and yellow Popeye shooter. Clarksburg, WV, circa 1927-1935. 25/32". Mint (9.7). Price: $90. CyberAuction #405, Lot #49.

765. AKRO AGATE COMPANY. Popeye corkscrew. Purple and yellow Popeye. Shooter!!! A pit and a scratch. Clarksburg, WV, circa 1927-1935. 23/32". Near Mint(+) (8.7). Price: $85. CyberAuction #337, Lot #17.

766. AKRO AGATE COMPANY. Popeye corkscrew. Hybrid Popeye. Red and yellow with very thin blue. Clarksburg, WV, circa 1927-1935. 23/32". Mint (9.9). Price: $80. CyberAuction #392, Lot #24.

767. AKRO AGATE COMPANY. Popeye corkscrew. Purple and yellow Popeye. Beauty. Clarksburg, WV, circa 1927-1935. 11/16". Mint (9.9). Price: $80. CyberAuction #392, Lot #52.

768. AKRO AGATE COMPANY. Popeye corkscrew. Purple and yellow Popeye. Two purple spirals. Stunning. Clarksburg, WV, circa 1927-1935. 5/8". Mint (9.9). Price: $80. CyberAuction #502, Lot #63.

769. AKRO AGATE COMPANY. Popeye corkscrew. Hybrid Popeye shooter. Yellow, narrow green, very narrow red. One tiny subsurface moon. Clarksburg, WV, circa 1927-1935. 23/32". Near Mint(+) (8.9). Price: $80. CyberAuction #505, Lot #66.

770. AKRO AGATE COMPANY. Popeye corkscrew. Fluorescent green and yellow Popeye. Excellent example, hard to find. Clarksburg, WV, circa 1927-1935. 11/16". Mint (9.7). Price: $70. CyberAuction #414, Lot #57.

771. AKRO AGATE COMPANY. Popeye corkscrew. Purple and yellow shooter. Wide purple spiral. Very nice coloring. Some pits on it. Clarksburg, WV, circa 1927-1935. 3/4". Near Mint (8.5). Price: $65. CyberAuction #332, Lot #9.

772. AKRO AGATE COMPANY. Popeye corkscrew. Hybrid. Green and yellow Popeye with a very thin spiral of transparent red. A couple of sparkles. Clarksburg, WV, circa 1927-1935. 21/32". Mint(-) (9.0). Price: $65. CyberAuction #463, Lot #55.

773. AKRO AGATE COMPANY. Popeye corkscrew. Dark purple and pale yellow Popeye. Two sparkles. Gorgeous marble. Clarksburg, WV, circa 1927-1935. 11/16". Mint(-) (9.1). Price: $65. CyberAuction #493, Lot #50.

774. AKRO AGATE COMPANY. Popeye corkscrew. Fluorescent green and yellow Popeye. Excellent example, hard to find. Clarksburg, WV, circa 1927-1935. 11/16". Mint (9.7). Price: $60. CyberAuction #373, Lot #12.

775. AKRO AGATE COMPANY. Popeye corkscrew. Red and green Popeye. Gorgeous. Clarksburg, WV, circa 1927-1935. 11/16". Mint (9.9). Price: $60. CyberAuction #373, Lot #36.

776. AKRO AGATE COMPANY. Popeye corkscrew. Light blue and yellow Popeye. Very nice. Clarksburg, WV, circa 1927-1935. 11/16". Mint (9.9). Price: $60. CyberAuction #396, Lot #13.

777. AKRO AGATE COMPANY. Popeye corkscrew. Baby blue and yellow Popeye. This is from near an end of the run. Wispy white. Thin pale yellow, thin baby blue. Lots of clear. Very nice. Clarksburg, WV, circa 1927-1935. 5/8". Mint (9.7). Price: $56. CyberAuction #336, Lot #39.

778. AKRO AGATE COMPANY. Popeye corkscrew. Orange/red and green Popeye. One sparkle. Clarksburg, WV, circa 1927-1935. 5/8". Mint(-) (9.2). Price: $56. CyberAuction #396, Lot #4.

779. AKRO AGATE COMPANY. Popeye corkscrew. Interesting corkscrew. Transparent clear base. Even sized snakes of red, green and white on the surface. Beauty. Clarksburg, WV, circa 1927-1935. 11/16". Mint (9.7). Price: $55. CyberAuction #366, Lot #23.

780. AKRO AGATE COMPANY. Popeye corkscrew. Hybrid Popeye. Red, yellow and blue. The yellow and blue are wide, the red is very thin and is lying on the yellow. Several very tiny chips (just a little bigger than pits). Clarksburg, WV, circa 1927-1935. 23/32". Near Mint(-) (8.0). Price: $55. CyberAuction #391, Lot #8.

781. AKRO AGATE COMPANY. Popeye corkscrew. Shooter blue and yellow Popeye. Three sparkles in one area. Clarksburg, WV, circa 1927-1935. 3/4". Near Mint(+) (8.9). Price: $55. CyberAuction #408, Lot #42.

782. AKRO AGATE COMPANY. Popeye corkscrew. Blue and yellow Popeye. Gorgeous. Clarksburg, WV, circa 1927-1935. 5/8". Mint (9.9). Price: $55. CyberAuction #483, Lot #37.

783. AKRO AGATE COMPANY. Popeye corkscrew. Purple and yellow Popeye. Beautiful colors. A couple of tiny pinpricks. Clarksburg, WV, circa 1927-1935. 5/8". Mint(-) (9.0). Price: $55. CyberAuction #485, Lot #52.

784. AKRO AGATE COMPANY. Popeye corkscrew. Odd marble. Green and yellow shooter. Blob of brown glass in the clear/white. Clarksburg, WV, circa 1927-1935. 3/4". Mint (9.8). Price: $55. CyberAuction #505, Lot #72.

785. AKRO AGATE COMPANY. Popeye corkscrew. Blue and yellow Popeye. Very nice. Clarksburg, WV, circa 1927-1935. 5/8". Mint (9.9). Price: $50. CyberAuction #418, Lot #22.

786. AKRO AGATE COMPANY. Popeye corkscrew. Blue and yellow Popeye. Clarksburg, WV, circa 1927-1935. 5/8". Mint (9.9). Price: $50. CyberAuction #435, Lot #47.

787. AKRO AGATE COMPANY. Popeye corkscrew. Hybrid Popeye. Red and yellow with very thin blue. A couple of tiny sparkles. Clarksburg, WV, circa 1927-1935. 23/32". Mint(-) (9.0). Price: $50. CyberAuction #457, Lot #9.

788. AKRO AGATE COMPANY. Popeye corkscrew. Blue and yellow. Beauty. Clarksburg, WV, circa 1927-1935. 11/16". Mint (9.7). Price: $50. CyberAuction #481, Lot #55.

789. AKRO AGATE COMPANY. Popeye corkscrew. Interesting hybrid Popeye corkscrew. Red spiral, very light blue, very narrow light yellow. The blue lies on the yellow, so the yellow appears to be light green. Several pit and very tiny rough spots. Clarksburg, WV, circa 1927-1935. 21/32". Near Mint (8.4). Price: $50. CyberAuction #485, Lot #58.

790. AKRO AGATE COMPANY. Popeye corkscrew. Purple and yellow Popeye. Clarksburg, WV, circa 1927-1935. 5/8". Mint (9.8). Price: $50. CyberAuction #493, Lot #46.

791. AKRO AGATE COMPANY. Popeye corkscrew. Fluorescent green and yellow Popeye. Excellent example, hard to find. One sparkle. Clarksburg, WV, circa 1927-1935. 5/8". Mint(-) (9.0). Price: $49. CyberAuction #432, Lot #38.

792. AKRO AGATE COMPANY. Popeye corkscrew. Navy blue and yellow Popeye. Very jumbled, swirled marble. Excellent! Clarksburg, WV, circa 1927-1935. 23/32". Mint (9.9). Price: $48. CyberAuction #344, Lot #55.

793. AKRO AGATE COMPANY. Popeye corkscrew. Purple Popeye. Missing the yellow. Has a wide spiral of light purple and a narrow spiral of dark purple. Unusual. A couple of very tiny chips in one spot. Clarksburg, WV, circa 1927-1935. 19/32". Near Mint (8.6). Price: $48. CyberAuction #375, Lot #43.

794. AKRO AGATE COMPANY. Popeye corkscrew. Red and yellow Popeye. Has an additional thin spiral of brown. Two tiny chips. Nice shooter. Clarksburg, WV, circa 1927-1935. 25/32". Near Mint (8.6). Price: $47. CyberAuction #404, Lot #40.

795. AKRO AGATE COMPANY. Popeye corkscrew. Interesting hybrid. Wide red spiral, narrow orange spiral and a completely separate thin yellow spiral. Odd. Small flake. Clarksburg, WV, circa 1927-1935. 21/32". Near Mint (8.6). Price: $47. CyberAuction #505, Lot #5.

796. AKRO AGATE COMPANY. Popeye corkscrew. Navy blue and yellow. Open clear panel. Nice white cushion. Gorgeous. Clarksburg, WV, circa 1927-1935. 11/16". Mint (9.9). Price: $46. CyberAuction #475, Lot #52.

797. AKRO AGATE COMPANY. Popeye corkscrew. Navy blue and yellow Popeye. Clarksburg, WV, circa 1927-1935. 5/8". Mint (9.9). Price: $46. CyberAuction #487, Lot #30.

798. AKRO AGATE COMPANY. Popeye corkscrew. Purple and yellow shooter. Gorgeous. Buffed surface. One pit remains. Clarksburg, WV, circa 1927-1935. 23/32". Mint (9.9). Price: $45. CyberAuction #360, Lot #56.

799. AKRO AGATE COMPANY. Popeye corkscrew. Navy blue and yellow Popeye. Wide clear open panel. Clarksburg, WV, circa 1927-1935. 23/32". Mint (9.9). Price: $45. CyberAuction #369, Lot #11.

800. AKRO AGATE COMPANY. Popeye corkscrew. Purple and yellow Popeye. Two sparkles. Clarksburg, WV, circa 1927-1935. 11/16". Near Mint(+) (8.8). Price: $44. CyberAuction #396, Lot #49.

801. AKRO AGATE COMPANY. Popeye corkscrew. Red and green Popeye. Gorgeous example. Clarksburg, WV, circa 1927-1935. 23/32". Mint (9.8). Price: $44. CyberAuction #498, Lot #9.

802. AKRO AGATE COMPANY. Popeye corkscrew. Transparent red and opaque orange/yellow Popeye. Super marble. Clarksburg, WV, circa 1927-1935. 5/8". Mint (9.8). Price: $43. CyberAuction #452, Lot #11.

803. AKRO AGATE COMPANY. Popeye corkscrew. Fluorescent green and yellow Popeye. Nice example. One tiny subsurface moon. Clarksburg, WV, circa 1927-1935. 21/32". Near Mint(+) (8.9). Price: $42. CyberAuction #376, Lot #51.

804. AKRO AGATE COMPANY. Popeye corkscrew. Purple and ruddy yellow Popeye. One small subsurface moon, a couple of pits. Clarksburg, WV, circa 1927-1935. 5/8". Near Mint (8.6). Price: $42. CyberAuction #391, Lot #15.

805. AKRO AGATE COMPANY. Popeye corkscrew. Light blue and yellow Popeye. Very nice. Clarksburg, WV, circa 1927-1935. 5/8". Mint (9.7). Price: $42. CyberAuction #396, Lot #22.

806. AKRO AGATE COMPANY. Popeye corkscrew. Red and yellow Popeye. Very nice. Clarksburg, WV, circa 1927-1935. 5/8". Mint (9.7). Price: $42. CyberAuction #410, Lot #37.

807. AKRO AGATE COMPANY. Popeye corkscrew. Blue and yellow Popeye. Clarksburg, WV, circa 1927-1935. 11/16". Mint (9.9). Price: $42. CyberAuction #451, Lot #54.

808. AKRO AGATE COMPANY. Popeye corkscrew. Red and green Popeye. Beautiful marble. Clarksburg, WV, circa 1927-1935. 21/32". Mint (9.9). Price: $42. CyberAuction #483, Lot #7.

809. AKRO AGATE COMPANY. Popeye corkscrew. Exceptional example!!! Ribbon of opaque yellow in the center. Narrow white. Wide snake of trans-

---

lucent red on the surface. Stunning. Clarksburg, WV, circa 1927-1935. 19/32". Mint (9.9). Price: $42. CyberAuction #505, Lot #9.

810. AKRO AGATE COMPANY. Popeye corkscrew. Navy blue and yellow Popeye. Beauty. Clarksburg, WV, circa 1927-1935. 21/32". Mint (9.9). Price: $41. CyberAuction #500, Lot #7.

811. AKRO AGATE COMPANY. Popeye corkscrew. Blue and yellow Popeye. Shooter. Tiny flake on it. Clarksburg, WV, circa 1927-1935. 3/4". Near Mint(+) (8.7). Price: $40. CyberAuction #339, Lot #45.

812. AKRO AGATE COMPANY. Popeye corkscrew. Red and yellow Popeye. Has an additional thin spiral of brown. Two tiny chips. Nice shooter. Clarksburg, WV, circa 1927-1935. 25/32". Near Mint (8.6). Price: $40. CyberAuction #348, Lot #46.

813. AKRO AGATE COMPANY. Popeye corkscrew. Blue and yellow Popeye. Very nice. Clarksburg, WV, circa 1927-1935. 5/8". Mint (9.6). Price: $40. CyberAuction #366, Lot #29.

814. AKRO AGATE COMPANY. Popeye corkscrew. Fluorescent green and yellow Popeye. Excellent example, hard to find. Clarksburg, WV, circa 1927-1935. 5/8". Mint (9.7). Price: $40. CyberAuction #387, Lot #56.

815. AKRO AGATE COMPANY. Popeye corkscrew. Red and yellow Popeye. Very nice. Clarksburg, WV, circa 1927-1935. 5/8". Mint (9.9). Price: $40. CyberAuction #396, Lot #15.

816. AKRO AGATE COMPANY. Popeye corkscrew. Blue and yellow Popeye. Clarksburg, WV, circa 1927-1935. 5/8". Mint (9.9). Price: $40. CyberAuction #414, Lot #2.

817. AKRO AGATE COMPANY. Popeye corkscrew. Blue and yellow Popeye. Clarksburg, WV, circa 1927-1935. 11/16". Mint (9.7). Price: $40. CyberAuction #415, Lot #58.

818. AKRO AGATE COMPANY. Popeye corkscrew. Blue and yellow Popeye. Clarksburg, WV, circa 1927-1935. 11/16". Mint (9.9). Price: $40. CyberAuction #416, Lot #40.

819. AKRO AGATE COMPANY. Popeye corkscrew. Red and yellow Popeye. Beauty. Clarksburg, WV, circa 1927-1935. 5/8". Mint (9.9). Price: $40. CyberAuction #418, Lot #10.

820. AKRO AGATE COMPANY. Popeye corkscrew. Red and yellow Popeye. Clarksburg, WV, circa 1927-1935. 5/8". Mint (9.7). Price: $40. CyberAuction #421, Lot #8.

821. AKRO AGATE COMPANY. Popeye corkscrew. Red and yellow Popeye. Gorgeous. Clarksburg, WV, circa 1927-1935. 5/8". Mint (9.9). Price: $40. CyberAuction #483, Lot #31.

822. AKRO AGATE COMPANY. Popeye corkscrew. Green and yellow Popeye. Wide brown blend. Clarksburg, WV, circa 1927-1935. 5/8". Mint (9.8). Price: $40. CyberAuction #491, Lot #21.

823. AKRO AGATE COMPANY. Popeye corkscrew. Purple and yellow Popeye. Two tiny sparkles and a pinprick. Clarksburg, WV, circa 1927-1935. 11/16". Near Mint(+) (8.9). Price: $40. CyberAuction #503, Lot #29.

824. AKRO AGATE COMPANY. Popeye corkscrew. Green and yellow Popeye. Gorgeous. Clarksburg, WV, circa 1927-1935. 11/16". Mint (9.9). Price: $40. CyberAuction #504, Lot #26.

825. AKRO AGATE COMPANY. Popeye corkscrew. Green and yellow. Very nice. Clarksburg, WV, circa 1927-1935. 5/8". Mint (9.9). Price: $39. CyberAuction #363, Lot #38.

826. AKRO AGATE COMPANY. Popeye corkscrew. Red and green Popeye corkscrew. Beauty. Clarksburg, WV, circa 1927-1935. 5/8". Mint (9.9). Price: $38. CyberAuction #388, Lot #20.

827. AKRO AGATE COMPANY. Popeye corkscrew. Red and navy blue Popeye. A number of pits, scratches, tiny pits and sparkles. Clarksburg, WV, circa 1927-1935. 3/4". Near Mint(-) (8.0). Price: $38. CyberAuction #434, Lot #58.

828. AKRO AGATE COMPANY. Popeye corkscrew. Green and yellow, with a wide brown blend. Wide open clear panel too. One sparkle. Clarksburg, WV, circa 1927-1935. 21/32". Mint(-)(9.1). Price: $38. CyberAuction #443, Lot #41.

829. AKRO AGATE COMPANY. Popeye corkscrew. Green and yellow Popeye. Beauty. Clarksburg, WV, circa 1927-1935. 11/16". Mint (9.9). Price: $38. CyberAuction #462, Lot #51.

830. AKRO AGATE COMPANY. Popeye corkscrew. Blue and yellow Popeye. Clarksburg, WV, circa 1927-1935. 21/32". Mint (9.9). Price: $37. CyberAuction #403, Lot #3.

831. AKRO AGATE COMPANY. Popeye corkscrew. Purple and yellow Popeye. One sparkle, a couple of tiny pinpricks. Clarksburg, WV, circa 1927-1935. 19/32". Near Mint(+) (8.9). Price: $37. CyberAuction #505, Lot #3.

832. AKRO AGATE COMPANY. Popeye corkscrew. Red and yellow Popeye shooter. Some tiny sparkles and pinpricks. Clarksburg, WV, circa 1927-1935. 3/4". Near Mint(+) (8.8). Price: $37. CyberAuction #505, Lot #35.

833. AKRO AGATE COMPANY. Popeye corkscrew. Red and green Popeye. Clarksburg, WV, circa 1927-1935. 5/8". Mint (9.8). Price: $36. CyberAuction #452, Lot #26.

834. AKRO AGATE COMPANY. Popeye corkscrew. Yellow and green, with wide brown blend. Clarksburg, WV, circa 1927-1935. 11/16". Mint (9.9). Price: $36. CyberAuction #503, Lot #23.

835. AKRO AGATE COMPANY. Popeye corkscrew. Dark blue and yellow Popeye. Narrow blue. Wide clear panel. Couple of sparkles. Clarksburg, WV, circa 1927-1935. 23/32". Mint(-) (9.0). Price: $35. CyberAuction #395, Lot #50.

836. AKRO AGATE COMPANY. Popeye corkscrew. Red and navy blue Popeye. A number of pits, scratches, tiny pits and sparkles. Clarksburg, WV, circa 1927-1935. 3/4". Near Mint(-) (8.0). Price: $35. CyberAuction #397, Lot #59.

837. AKRO AGATE COMPANY. Popeye corkscrew. Red and green. Gorgeous. Clarksburg, WV, circa 1927-1935. 5/8". Mint (9.9). Price: $35. CyberAuction #429, Lot #42.

838. AKRO AGATE COMPANY. Popeye corkscrew. Green and yellow Popeye. Loads of white, almost no clear. Clarksburg, WV, circa 1927-1935. 5/8". Mint (9.9). Price: $34. CyberAuction #330, Lot #22.

839. AKRO AGATE COMPANY. Popeye corkscrew. Red and blue Popeye. Several very tiny chips. Clarksburg, WV, circa 1927-1935. 5/8". Near Mint (8.5). Price: $34. CyberAuction #462, Lot #46.

840. AKRO AGATE COMPANY. Popeye corkscrew. Red and green. The colors are snakes on the surface. Clarksburg, WV, circa 1927-1935. 5/8". Mint (9.8). Price: $34. CyberAuction #500, Lot #14.

841. AKRO AGATE COMPANY. Popeye corkscrew. Blue and yellow Popeye. Gorgeous. Clarksburg, WV, circa 1927-1935. 21/32". Mint (9.9). Price: $33. CyberAuction #335, Lot #57.

842. AKRO AGATE COMPANY. Popeye corkscrew. Green and yellow Popeye. Brown blend. Very nice. Clarksburg, WV, circa 1927-1935. 5/8". Mint (9.7). Price: $33. CyberAuction #489, Lot #37.

843. AKRO AGATE COMPANY. Popeye corkscrew. Red and green Popeye. Gorgeous. Clarksburg, WV, circa 1927-1935. 5/8". Mint (9.9). Price: $33. CyberAuction #504, Lot #16.

844. AKRO AGATE COMPANY. Popeye corkscrew. Green and yellow Popeye. Two tiny melt air holes. Clarksburg, WV, circa 1927-1935. 5/8". Mint (9.7). Price: $32. CyberAuction #341, Lot #46.

845. AKRO AGATE COMPANY. Popeye corkscrew. Hybrid. Red and green Popeye. Narrow yellow spiral. A couple of tiny pits and a couple of tiny chips. Clarksburg, WV, circa 1927-1935. 21/32". Near Mint (8.5). Price: $32. CyberAuction #349, Lot #11.

846. AKRO AGATE COMPANY. Popeye corkscrew. Red and green Popeye. Super marble. Clarksburg, WV, circa 1927-1935. 11/16". Mint (9.8). Price: $32. CyberAuction #459, Lot #4.

847. AKRO AGATE COMPANY. Popeye corkscrew. Blue and yellow Popeye. Clarksburg, WV, circa 1927-1935. 5/8". Mint (9.8). Price: $32. CyberAuction #485, Lot #24.

848. AKRO AGATE COMPANY. Popeye corkscrew. Red and yellow Popeye. Clarksburg, WV, circa 1927-1935. 5/8". Mint (9.9). Price: $30. CyberAuction #362, Lot #53.

849. AKRO AGATE COMPANY. Popeye corkscrew. Red and yellow Popeye. Clarksburg, WV, circa 1927-1935. 5/8". Mint (9.8). Price: $30. CyberAuction #368, Lot #59.

850. AKRO AGATE COMPANY. Popeye corkscrew. Purple and yellow Popeye. Small air hole, some tiny pits. Clarksburg, WV, circa 1927-1935. 11/16". Near Mint(+) (8.7). Price: $30. CyberAuction #406, Lot #2.

851. AKRO AGATE COMPANY. Popeye corkscrew. Red and yellow shooter. One very tiny flake. Clarksburg, WV, circa 1927-1935. 3/4". Near Mint(+) (8.9). Price: $30. CyberAuction #407, Lot #21.

852. AKRO AGATE COMPANY. Popeye corkscrew. Green and yellow. Almost no clear, mostly white. Clarksburg, WV, circa 1927-1935. 5/8". Mint (9.8). Price: $30. CyberAuction #418, Lot #5.

853. AKRO AGATE COMPANY. Popeye corkscrew. Light green and yellow, with a brown blend. One tiny sparkle. Clarksburg, WV, circa 1927-1935. 5/8". Mint(-) (9.2). Price: $30. CyberAuction #500, Lot #17.

854. AKRO AGATE COMPANY. Popeye corkscrew. Blue and yellow Popeye. Clarksburg, WV, circa 1927-1935. 5/8". Mint (9.9). Price: $30. CyberAuction #501, Lot #29.

855. AKRO AGATE COMPANY. Popeye corkscrew. Green and yellow with a brown blend. Very nice. Clarksburg, WV, circa 1927-1935. 5/8". Mint (9.9). Price: $30. CyberAuction #502, Lot #55.

856. AKRO AGATE COMPANY. Popeye corkscrew. Green and yellow. Some brown blend. Superb! Clarksburg, WV, circa 1927-1935. 11/16". Mint (9.9). Price: $30. CyberAuction #504, Lot #53.

857. AKRO AGATE COMPANY. Popeye corkscrew. Red and green Popeye corkscrew. Beauty. One very tiny sparkle. Clarksburg, WV, circa 1927-1935. 5/8". Mint(-) (9.2). Price: $29. CyberAuction #432, Lot #5.

858. AKRO AGATE COMPANY. Popeye corkscrew. Red and yellow. Narrow brown blend. Gorgeous. Clarksburg, WV, circa 1927-1935. 11/16". Mint (9.8). Price: $29. CyberAuction #507, Lot #13.

859. AKRO AGATE COMPANY. Popeye corkscrew. Red and green. Clarksburg, WV, circa 1927-1935. 23/32". Mint (9.4). Two marbles available. You are bidding on one. Winner has choice of either or both, remainder to under. Price: $28. CyberAuction #415, Lot #46.

860. AKRO AGATE COMPANY. Popeye corkscrew. Red and green Popeye. Very nice. Clarksburg, WV, circa 1927-1935. 5/8". Mint (9.8). Price: $27. CyberAuction #330, Lot #12.

861. AKRO AGATE COMPANY. Popeye corkscrew. Red and yellow. Very nice. Clarksburg, WV, circa 1927-1935. 11/16". Mint (9.7). Price: $27. CyberAuction #388, Lot #7.

862. AKRO AGATE COMPANY. Popeye corkscrew. Blue and yellow Popeye. A tiny sparkle. Clarksburg, WV, circa 1927-1935. 11/16". Mint(-) (9.1). Price: $27. CyberAuction #407, Lot #44.

863. AKRO AGATE COMPANY. Popeye corkscrew. Red and green Popeye. Beauty. Clarksburg, WV, circa 1927-1935. 5/8". Mint (9.7). Price: $27. CyberAuction #491, Lot #35.

864. AKRO AGATE COMPANY. Popeye corkscrew. Blue and yellow. Clarksburg, WV, circa 1927-1935. 11/16". Mint (9.9). Price: $27. CyberAuction #503, Lot #70.

865. AKRO AGATE COMPANY. Popeye corkscrew. Red and yellow Popeye. Ribbon type. Hard to find. Several tiny sparkles. Clarksburg, WV, circa 1927-1935. 5/8". Mint(-) (9.0). Price: $25. CyberAuction #373, Lot #13.

866. AKRO AGATE COMPANY. Popeye corkscrew. Green and yellow, with a wide brown blend. Wide open clear panel too. One sparkle.

Clarksburg, WV, circa 1927-1935. 21/32". Mint(-)(9.1). Price: $25. CyberAuction #380, Lot #56.

867. AKRO AGATE COMPANY. Popeye corkscrew. Shooter. Navy blue and pale yellow. Several sparkles. Clarksburg, WV, circa 1927-1935. 23/32". Near Mint(+) (8.9). Price: $25. CyberAuction #381, Lot #42.

868. AKRO AGATE COMPANY. Popeye corkscrew. Blue and yellow shooter. Some green blend. Several tiny subsurface moons. Clarksburg, WV, circa 1927-1935. 3/4". Near Mint (8.6). Price: $25. CyberAuction #407, Lot #14.

869. AKRO AGATE COMPANY. Popeye corkscrew. Red and yellow with an orange blend. One tiny sparkle. Clarksburg, WV, circa 1927-1935. 11/16". Mint(-) (9.2). Price: $25. CyberAuction #507, Lot #6.

870. AKRO AGATE COMPANY. Popeye corkscrew. Purple and yellow Popeye. Several tiny chips. Clarksburg, WV, circa 1927-1935. 5/8". Near Mint (8.3). Price: $24. CyberAuction #368, Lot #52.

871. AKRO AGATE COMPANY. Popeye corkscrew. Fluorescent green and yellow Popeye. Piece of unmelted sand on it. Clarksburg, WV, circa 1927-1935. 5/8". Mint(-) (9.1). Price: $24. CyberAuction #417, Lot #48.

872. AKRO AGATE COMPANY. Popeye corkscrew. Fluorescent green and yellow Popeye. Piece of unmelted sand on it. Clarksburg, WV, circa 1927-1935. 5/8". Mint(-) (9.1). Price: $24. CyberAuction #455, Lot #57.

873. AKRO AGATE COMPANY. Popeye corkscrew. Red and yellow Popeye. Some minor scratches on the surface. Clarksburg, WV, circa 1927-1935. 21/32". Mint(-) (9.2). Price: $24. CyberAuction #481, Lot #8.

874. AKRO AGATE COMPANY. Popeye corkscrew. Red and yellow Popeye. Beauty. Clarksburg, WV, circa 1927-1935. 21/32". Mint (9.8). Price: $24. CyberAuction #503, Lot #19.

875. AKRO AGATE COMPANY. Popeye corkscrew. Fluorescent green and yellow Popeye. A couple of small subsurface moons. Clarksburg, WV, circa 1927-1935. 5/8". Near Mint (8.3). Price: $23. CyberAuction #338, Lot #53.

876. AKRO AGATE COMPANY. Popeye corkscrew. Yellow and green Popeye. Very thin green. One sparkle. Very nice. Clarksburg, WV, circa 1927-1935. 11/16". Mint(-) (9.0). Price: $23. CyberAuction #342, Lot #50.

877. AKRO AGATE COMPANY. Popeye corkscrew. Blue and yellow Popeye. Some sparkles. Clarksburg, WV, circa 1927-1935. 11/16". Mint(-) (9.0). Price: $23. CyberAuction #433, Lot #10.

878. AKRO AGATE COMPANY. Popeye corkscrew. Blue and yellow Popeye. One pinprick. Clarksburg, WV, circa 1927-1935. 5/8". Mint(-) (9.1). Price: $23. CyberAuction #503, Lot #59.

879. AKRO AGATE COMPANY. Popeye corkscrew. Blue and yellow Popeye. Pretty much folded in half, messed up corkscrew design. Interesting. One tiny subsurface moon. Clarksburg, WV, circa 1927-1935. 21/32". Near Mint(+) (8.9). Price: $22. CyberAuction #341, Lot #53.

880. AKRO AGATE COMPANY. Popeye corkscrew. Red and yellow Popeye. Shooter. Several tiny flakes and rough spots. Clarksburg, WV, circa 1927-1935. 3/4". Near Mint (8.4). Price: $22. CyberAuction #354, Lot #2.

881. AKRO AGATE COMPANY. Popeye corkscrew. Red and yellow. Very nice. A couple of pinpricks. Clarksburg, WV, circa 1927-1935. 11/16". Mint (9.4). Price: $22. CyberAuction #396, Lot #6.

882. AKRO AGATE COMPANY. Popeye corkscrew. Green and yellow Popeye. Odd design. Opaque yellow ribbon, translucent green snake, wispy white snake. One air hole. Clarksburg, WV, circa 1927-1935. 19/32". Mint(-) (9.2). Price: $22. CyberAuction #400, Lot #17.

883. AKRO AGATE COMPANY. Popeye corkscrew. Red and yellow. One sparkle. Clarksburg, WV, circa 1927-1935. 5/8". Mint(-) (9.0). Price: $22. CyberAuction #433, Lot #26.

884. AKRO AGATE COMPANY. Popeye corkscrew. Red and green Popeye. Clarksburg, WV, circa 1927-1935. 21/32". Mint (9.7). Price: $22. CyberAuction #501, Lot #34.

885. AKRO AGATE COMPANY. Popeye corkscrew. Green and yellow with a brown blend. Clarksburg, WV, circa 1927-1935. 5/8". Mint (9.7). Price: $22. CyberAuction #502, Lot #7.

886. AKRO AGATE COMPANY. Popeye corkscrew. Pale yellow and nice green. Nice white wispy spiral too. Excellent example. Clarksburg, WV, circa 1927-1935. 19/32". Mint (9.8). Price: $22. CyberAuction #502, Lot #52.

887. AKRO AGATE COMPANY. Popeye corkscrew. Red and green. A tiny scratch. Clarksburg, WV, circa 1297-1935. 5/8". Mint(-) (9.0). Price: $21. CyberAuction #339, Lot #2.

888. AKRO AGATE COMPANY. Popeye corkscrew. Red and green Popeye. Beauty. One sparkle. Clarksburg, WV, circa 1927-1935. 5/8". Mint(-) (9.0). Price: $21. CyberAuction #403, Lot #30.

889. AKRO AGATE COMPANY. Popeye corkscrew. Blue and yellow. Two tiny sparkles. Clarksburg, WV, circa 1927-1935. 5/8". Mint(-) (9.0). Price: $21. CyberAuction #435, Lot #52.

890. AKRO AGATE COMPANY. Popeye corkscrew. Red and yellow Popeye. One sparkle. Clarksburg, WV, circa 1927-1935. 5/8". Mint(-) (9.0). Price: $21. CyberAuction #458, Lot #11.

891. AKRO AGATE COMPANY. Popeye corkscrew. Green, yellow, and brown Popeye. Nice. Some sparkles. Clarksburg, WV, circa 1927-1935. 5/8". Near Mint(+) (8.9). Price: $21. CyberAuction #458, Lot #50.

892. AKRO AGATE COMPANY. Popeye corkscrew. Blue and yellow Popeye. Clarksburg, WV, circa 1927-1929. 19/32". Mint (9.8). Price: $21. CyberAuction #503, Lot #47.

893. AKRO AGATE COMPANY. Popeye corkscrew. Red and yellow Popeye. Beauty. Almost no white. Nice red and yellow spirals. Clarksburg, WV, circa 1927-1935. 5/8". Mint (9.7). Price: $20. CyberAuction #333, Lot #23.

894. AKRO AGATE COMPANY. Popeye corkscrew. Red and yellow Popeye. Clarksburg, WV, circa 1927-1935. 19/32". Mint (9.9). Price: $20.

895. AKRO AGATE COMPANY. Popeye corkscrew. Red and yellow Popeye. Beauty. One pinprick, slight flat spot. Clarksburg, WV, circa 1927-1935. 1/16". Mint(-) (9.0). Price: $20. CyberAuction #400, Lot #7.

896. AKRO AGATE COMPANY. Popeye corkscrew. Blue and yellow Popeye. One tiny flake. Clarksburg, WV, circa 1927-1935. 5/8". Near Mint(+)(8.8). Price: $20. CyberAuction #498, Lot #36.

897. AKRO AGATE COMPANY. Popeye corkscrew. Red and yellow. Has a sparkle. Clarksburg, WV, circa 1927-1935. 5/8". Mint(-) (9.0). There are three marbles available. You are bidding on one. Winner has choice of any or all, remainder to under. Price: $19. CyberAuction #332, Lot #5.

898. AKRO AGATE COMPANY. Popeye corkscrew. Red and yellow. Has a sparkle. Clarksburg, WV, circa 1927-1935. 5/8". Mint(-) (9.0). There are five marbles available. You are bidding on one. Winner has choice of any or all, remainder to under. Price: $19. CyberAuction #332, Lot #32.

899. AKRO AGATE COMPANY. Popeye corkscrew. Red and yellow Popeye. One tiny subsurface moon. Clarksburg, WV, circa 1927-1935. 21/32". Near Mint(+) (8.9). Price: $19. CyberAuction #359, Lot #4.

900. AKRO AGATE COMPANY. Popeye corkscrew. Red and green Popeye. A couple of pinpricks. Clarksburg, WV, circa 1927-1935. 5/8". Mint(-) (9.0). Price: $19. CyberAuction #489, Lot #22.

901. AKRO AGATE COMPANY. Popeye corkscrew. Light blue and yellow shooter Popeye. Two tiny subsurface moons. Clarksburg, WV, circa 1927-1935. 23/32". Near Mint(+)(8.7). Price: $19. CyberAuction #493, Lot #42.

902. AKRO AGATE COMPANY. Popeye corkscrew. Red and yellow. Clarksburg, WV, circa 1927-1935. 11/16". Near Mint(+) (8.9). Price: $18. CyberAuction #500, Lot #21.

903. AKRO AGATE COMPANY. Popeye corkscrew. Red and green. Some blending to create black. Small annealing fracture. Clarksburg, WV, circa 1927-1935. 5/8". Mint(-) (9.0). There are two marbles available. You are bidding on one. Winner has choice of either or both, remainder to under. Price: $17. CyberAuction #331, Lot #37.

904. AKRO AGATE COMPANY. Popeye corkscrew. Red and yellow Popeye. Beautiful. Clarksburg, WV, circa 1927-1935. 5/8". Mint (9.9). Price: $17. CyberAuction #332, Lot #43.

905. AKRO AGATE COMPANY. Popeye corkscrew. Red and green Popeye. Has a small subsurface moon. Clarksburg, WV, circa 1927-1935. 5/8". Near Mint(+) (8.8). There are three marbles available. You are bidding on one. Winner has choice of any or all, remainder to under. Price: $17. CyberAuction #344, Lot #12.

906. AKRO AGATE COMPANY. Popeye corkscrew. Red and yellow Popeye. Gorgeous. One tiny pinprick. Clarksburg, WV, circa 1927-1935. 21/32". Mint (9.4). Price: $17. CyberAuction #365, Lot #38.

907. AKRO AGATE COMPANY. Popeye corkscrew. Blue and yellow. Ribbon type. Very nice. A little scratching on it. Clarksburg, WV, circa 1927-1935. 5/8". Mint(-) (9.0). Price: $17. CyberAuction #368, Lot #33.

908. AKRO AGATE COMPANY. Popeye corkscrew. Fluorescent green and yellow Popeye. A couple of tiny subsurface moons. Clarksburg, WV, circa 1927-1935. 5/8". Near Mint (8.6). Price: $17. CyberAuction #402, Lot #58.

909. AKRO AGATE COMPANY. Popeye corkscrew. Red and green shooter Popeye. Several tiny chips and a rust stain on it. Clarksburg, WV, circa 1927-1935. 3/4". Near Mint (8.5). Price: $17. CyberAuction #412, Lot #39.

910. AKRO AGATE COMPANY. Popeye corkscrew. Fluorescent green and yellow Popeye. Buffed surface. Clarksburg, WV, circa 1927-1935. 9/16". Price: $17. CyberAuction #455, Lot #39.

911. AKRO AGATE COMPANY. Popeye corkscrew. Red and green Popeye. Two chips. Clarksburg, WV, circa 1927-1935. 21/32". Near Mint (8.6). Price: $17. CyberAuction #482, Lot #17.

912. AKRO AGATE COMPANY. Popeye corkscrew. Green and yellow with thin brown blend. One sparkle. Clarksburg, WV, circa 1927-1935. 5/8". Near Mint(+) (8.9). Price: $17. CyberAuction #507, Lot #4.

913. AKRO AGATE COMPANY. Popeye corkscrew. Red and yellow Popeye. Beautiful. Clarksburg, WV, circa 1927-1935. 5/8". Mint (9.9). There are three marbles available. You are bidding on one. Winner has choice of any or all, remainder to under. Price: $15. CyberAuction #331, Lot #4.

914. AKRO AGATE COMPANY. Popeye corkscrew. Red and yellow Popeye. Beauty. Almost no white. Nice red and yellow spirals. One sparkle. Clarksburg, WV, circa 1927-1935. 5/8". Mint(-) (9.0). Price: $15. CyberAuction #333, Lot #46.

915. AKRO AGATE COMPANY. Popeye corkscrew. Green and yellow. Some brown blend. One subsurface moon, one small chip. Clarksburg, WV, circa 1927-1935. 11/16". Near Mint(-) (8.1). Price: $15. CyberAuction #355, Lot #18.

916. AKRO AGATE COMPANY. Popeye corkscrew. Red and yellow. Sparkles and tiny subsurface moons. Clarksburg, WV, circa 1927-1935. 5/8". Near Mint (8.6). There are two marbles available. You are bidding on one. Winner has choice of either or both, remainder to under. Price: $15. CyberAuction #374, Lot #12.

917. AKRO AGATE COMPANY. Popeye corkscrew. Red/orange and yellow. A pinprick. Clarksburg, WV, circa 1927-1935. 5/8". Mint(-) (9.0). Price: $15. CyberAuction #421, Lot #15.

918. AKRO AGATE COMPANY. Popeye corkscrew. Red and yellow. Small annealing fracture. Very nice. Clarksburg, WV, circa 1927-1935. 21/32". Mint(-) (9.0). Price: $14. CyberAuction #331, Lot #31.

919. AKRO AGATE COMPANY. Popeye corkscrew. Red and green. A subsurface moon. Clarksburg, WV, circa 1297-1935. 21/32". Near Mint(+) (8.8). Price: $14. CyberAuction #332, Lot #1.

920. AKRO AGATE COMPANY. Popeye corkscrew. Green and yellow Popeye. Tiny subsurface moon, some pitting. Clarksburg, WV, circa 1927-

1935. 11/16". Near Mint (8.6). Price: $14. CyberAuction #396, Lot #18.

921. AKRO AGATE COMPANY. Popeye corkscrew. Red and green Popeye. Some sparkles. Clarksburg, WV, circa 1927-1935. 19/32". Near Mint(+) (8.9). Price: $14. CyberAuction #438, Lot #40.

922. AKRO AGATE COMPANY. Popeye corkscrew. Blue and yellow. Some pitting and light haze. Clarksburg, WV, circa 1927-1935. 5/8". Near Mint (8.6). Price: $13. CyberAuction #337, Lot #40.

923. AKRO AGATE COMPANY. Popeye corkscrew. Light blue and yellow Popeye. One fracture. Clarksburg, WV, circa 1927-1935. 5/8". Near Mint (8.5). Price: $13. CyberAuction #367, Lot #54.

924. AKRO AGATE COMPANY. Popeye corkscrew. Green and yellow Popeye. One sparkle. Clarksburg, WV, circa 1927-1935. 11/16". Mint(-) (9.1). Price: $13. CyberAuction #391, Lot #49.

925. AKRO AGATE COMPANY. Popeye corkscrew. Green and yellow Popeye. One very tiny subsurface moon. Clarksburg, WV, circa 1927-1935. 5/8". Near Mint(+) (8.7). Price: $13. CyberAuction #420, Lot #43.

926. AKRO AGATE COMPANY. Popeye corkscrew. Red and yellow Popeye. Has a pit. Clarksburg, WV, circa 1927-1935. 19/32". Near Mint(+) (8.9). Price: $13. CyberAuction #502, Lot #27.

927. AKRO AGATE COMPANY. Popeye corkscrew. Red and green Popeye. Has a small subsurface moon. Clarksburg, WV, circa 1927-1935. 5/8". Near Mint(+) (8.8). There are two marbles available. You are bidding on one. Winner has choice of either or both, remainder to under. Price: $12. CyberAuction #342, Lot #14.

928. AKRO AGATE COMPANY. Popeye corkscrew. Blue and yellow Popeye. Sparkle and a small annealing fracture. Clarksburg, WV, circa 1927-1935. 11/16". Near Mint(+) (8.7). Price: $12. CyberAuction #405, Lot #18.

929. AKRO AGATE COMPANY. Popeye corkscrew. Red and green Popeye. One pit. Clarksburg, WV, circa 1927-1935. 21/32". Near Mint(+) (8.9). Price: $12. CyberAuction #420, Lot #23.

930. AKRO AGATE COMPANY. Popeye corkscrew. Red and yellow Popeye. Small annealing fracture, tiny flake and a tiny subsurface moon. Clarksburg, WV, circa 1927-1935. 5/8". Near Mint (8.6). Price: $12. CyberAuction #455, Lot #4.

931. AKRO AGATE COMPANY. Popeye corkscrew. Green and yellow. Small annealing fracture and some minor sparkles. Clarksburg, WV, circa 1927-1935. 19/32". Near Mint(+) (8.8). Price: $12. CyberAuction #501, Lot #9.

932. AKRO AGATE COMPANY. Popeye corkscrew. Red and green. Some blending to create black. Sparkle and annealing fracture. Clarksburg, WV, circa 1927-1935. 5/8". Near Mint(+) (8.7). There are two marbles available. You are bidding on one. Winner has choice of either or both, remainder to under. Price: $11. CyberAuction #332, Lot #36.

933. AKRO AGATE COMPANY. Popeye corkscrew. Green and yellow Popeye. Two tiny sparkles. Clarksburg, WV, circa 1927-1935. 11/16". Near Mint(+) (8.9). Price: $11. CyberAuction #392, Lot #2.

934. AKRO AGATE COMPANY. Popeye corkscrew. Red and yellow Popeye. Several tiny subsurface moons. Clarksburg, WV, circa 1927-1935. 5/8". Near Mint (8.6). Price: $11. CyberAuction #406, Lot #12.

935. AKRO AGATE COMPANY. Popeye corkscrew. Red and yellow. Tiny subsurface moon. Clarksburg, WV, circa 1927-1935. 5/8". Near Mint(+) (8.9). Price: $11. CyberAuction #408, Lot #28.

936. AKRO AGATE COMPANY. Popeye corkscrew. Blue and yellow Popeye. Clarksburg, WV, circa 1927-1935. 11/16". Buffed. Price: $11. CyberAuction #412, Lot #28.

937. AKRO AGATE COMPANY. Popeye corkscrew. Red and blue Popeye. Clarksburg, WV, circa 1927-1935. 23/32". Good (7.6). Price: $11. CyberAuction #415, Lot #48.

938. AKRO AGATE COMPANY. Popeye corkscrew. Blue and yellow Popeye. Some tiny subsurface moons. Clarksburg, WV, circa 1927-1935. 5/8". Near Mint(-) (8.6). Price: $11. CyberAuction #420, Lot #2.

939. AKRO AGATE COMPANY. Popeye corkscrew. Red and yellow Popeye. Small subsurface moon. Clarksburg, WV, circa 1927-1935. 5/8". Near Mint(+) (8.9). There are five marbles available. You are bidding on one. Winner has choice of any or all, remainder to under. Price: $10. CyberAuction #342, Lot #33.

940. AKRO AGATE COMPANY. Popeye corkscrew. Red and yellow Popeye. Some tiny chips. Clarksburg, WV, circa 1927-1935. 5/8". Near Mint(-) (8.2). Price: $10. CyberAuction #399, Lot #21.

941. AKRO AGATE COMPANY. Popeye corkscrew. Red and yellow Popeye. Small subsurface moon. Clarksburg, WV, circa 1927-1935. 5/8". Near Mint(+) (8.9). There are three marbles available. You are bidding on one. Winner has choice of one or both, remainder to under. Price: $10. CyberAuction #404, Lot #23.

942. AKRO AGATE COMPANY. Popeye corkscrew. Blue and yellow Popeye. Very nice. One small flake. Clarksburg, WV, circa 1927-1935. 5/8". Near Mint(+) (8.8). Price: $10. CyberAuction #419, Lot #59.

943. AKRO AGATE COMPANY. Popeye corkscrew. Green and yellow Popeye. Wide clear panel. Some tiny pits. Clarksburg, WV, circa 1927-1935. 5/8". Near Mint(+) (8.8). Price: $9. CyberAuction #336, Lot #5.

944. AKRO AGATE COMPANY. Popeye corkscrew. Red and yellow Popeye. Two tiny chips. Clarksburg, WV, circa 1927-1935. 5/8". Near Mint (8.6). Price: $9. CyberAuction #392, Lot #16.

945. AKRO AGATE COMPANY. Popeye corkscrew. Red and green Popeye. Couple of tiny subsurface moons and some tiny pits. Clarksburg, WV, circa 1927-1935. 11/16". Near Mint (8.4). Price: $9. CyberAuction #399, Lot #47.

946. AKRO AGATE COMPANY. Popeye corkscrew. Blue and yellow Popeye. Pitting. Clarksburg, WV, circa 1927-1935. 11/16". Near Mint(-) (8.1). Price: $9. CyberAuction #401, Lot #11.

947. AKRO AGATE COMPANY. Popeye corkscrew. Blue and yellow Popeye. Buffed. 5/8". Price: $9. CyberAuction #502, Lot #18.

948. AKRO AGATE COMPANY. Popeye corkscrew. Green and yellow Popeye. Buffed. 19/32". Price: $8. CyberAuction #350, Lot #12.

949. AKRO AGATE COMPANY. Popeye corkscrew. Red and green Popeye. Small annealing fracture, tiny flake and a tiny subsurface moon. Clarksburg, WV, circa 1927-1935. 5/8". Near Mint (8.6). Price: $8. CyberAuction #405, Lot #58.

950. AKRO AGATE COMPANY. Popeye corkscrew. Purple and yellow. Overall tiny chips. Clarksburg, WV, circa 1927-1935. 5/8". Good (7.6). Price: $8. CyberAuction #407, Lot #8.

951. AKRO AGATE COMPANY. Popeye corkscrew. Red and green Popeye. Some pitting. Clarksburg, WV, circa 1928-1935. 5/8". Near Mint(+) (8.8). Price: $8. CyberAuction #436, Lot #48.

952. AKRO AGATE COMPANY. Popeye corkscrew. Red and yellow Popeye. Pitting. Clarksburg, WV, circa 1927-1935. 5/8". Near Mint (8.3). Price: $5. CyberAuction #419, Lot #7.

953. AKRO AGATE COMPANY. Popeye corkscrew. Red and green Popeye. Two chips. Clarksburg, WV, circa 1927-1935. 21/32". Near Mint (8.6). Price: $5. CyberAuction #457, Lot #2.

954. AKRO AGATE COMPANY. Popeye corkscrew. Blue and yellow. One subsurface moon, a couple of sparkles. Clarksburg, WV, circa 1927-1935. 5/8". Near Mint (8.6). Price: $4. CyberAuction #419, Lot #22.

955. AKRO AGATE COMPANY. Popeye corkscrew. Navy blue and white. Overall tiny chips and flakes. Clarksburg, WV, circa 1927-1935. 5/8". Good (7.5). Price: $3. CyberAuction #435, Lot #22.

956. AKRO AGATE COMPANY. Popeye corkscrew. Red and yellow Popeye. Overall tiny chipping and tiny flaking. Clarksburg, WV, circa 1927-1935. 5/8". Good(+) (7.9). Price: $3. CyberAuction #435, Lot #26.

957. AKRO AGATE COMPANY. Popeye patch. Very rare Popeye Patch. This is genuine, not a Vitro mimic. Red and green, almost impossible to true Popeye patch. Some pits. Clarksburg, WV, circa 1927-1935. 3/4". Near Mint (8.3). Price: $50. CyberAuction #502, Lot #72.

958. AKRO AGATE COMPANY. Popeye patch. Very rare Popeye Patch. This is genuine, not a Vitro mimic. Purple and yellow, almost impossible to find in a Popeye patch. Overall pitting. Clarksburg, WV, circa 1927-1935. 21/32". Good(+) (7.9). Price: $30. CyberAuction #407, Lot #37.

959. AKRO AGATE COMPANY. Ringer. Very unusual Ringer. Milky white base. Wispy white swirl. Translucent light red swirl and translucent light yellow swirl. Tiny subsurface moons and sparkles. Clarksburg, WV, circa 1927-1935. 5/8". Near Mint(+) (8.7). There are two marbles available, you are bidding on one. Winner has choice of either or both, remainder to under. Price: $13. CyberAuction #465, Lot #24.

960. AKRO AGATE COMPANY. Silver oxblood. Stunning shooter. Translucent milky white base. Semi-opaque white swirls. Nice oxblood swirl on the top. Rare in this size. Clarksburg, WV, circa 1925-1935. 25/32". Mint (9.9). Price: $200. CyberAuction #448, Lot #54.

961. AKRO AGATE COMPANY. Silver oxblood. Hard to find shooter. Translucent milky white base. Semi-opaque white swirls. Nice oxblood swirl on the top. One tiny pit. Gorgeous. Clarksburg, WV, circa 1925-1935. 3/4". Mint(-) (9.2). Price: $185. CyberAuction #450, Lot #42.

962. AKRO AGATE COMPANY. Silver oxblood. Shooter. Translucent milky white base. Semi-opaque white swirls. Nice oxblood swirl on the top. Gorgeous. Clarksburg, WV, circa 1925-1935. 3/4". Mint (9.9). Price: $160. CyberAuction #376, Lot #22.

963. AKRO AGATE COMPANY. Silver oxblood. Corkscrew. Superior example. Translucent milky white base. Opaque white corkscrew. Rich oxblood corkscrew. Excellent example. Clarksburg, WV, circa 1925-1935. 5/8". Mint (9.8). Price: $120. CyberAuction #351, Lot #48.

964. AKRO AGATE COMPANY. Silver oxblood. Translucent milky white base. Semi-opaque white swirls. Nice oxblood swirl on the top. Exceptional example. Clarksburg, WV, circa 1925-1935. 5/8". Mint (9.9). Price: $95. CyberAuction #356, Lot #29.

965. AKRO AGATE COMPANY. Silver oxblood. Translucent milky white base. Semi-opaque wide white swirls. Nice oxblood swirl on the top. Stunning. Clarksburg, WV, circa 1925-1935. 5/8". Mint (9.9). Price: $56. CyberAuction #498, Lot #49.

966. AKRO AGATE COMPANY. Silver oxblood. Translucent milky white base. Semi-opaque white swirls. Nice oxblood swirl on the top. Excellent example. Clarksburg, WV, circa 1925-1935. 5/8". Mint (9.9). Price: $55. CyberAuction #356, Lot #21.

967. AKRO AGATE COMPANY. Silver oxblood. Semi-opaque milky white base. Nice oxblood swirl on the top. Excellent example. Clarksburg, WV, circa 1925-1935. 19/32". Mint (9.9). Price: $47. CyberAuction #462, Lot #52.

968. AKRO AGATE COMPANY. Silver oxblood. Translucent milky white base. Semi-opaque white swirls. Nice wispy oxblood swirl on the top. Excellent example. Clarksburg, WV, circa 1925-1935. 21/32". Mint (9.9). Price: $42. CyberAuction #341, Lot #49.

969. AKRO AGATE COMPANY. Silver oxblood. Translucent milky white base. Semi-opaque white swirls. Nice oxblood swirl on the top. Clarksburg, WV, circa 1925-1935. 5/8". Mint (9.9). Price: $42. CyberAuction #400, Lot #42.

970. AKRO AGATE COMPANY. Silver oxblood. Translucent milky white base. Semi-opaque white swirls. Nice oxblood swirl on the top. Clarksburg, WV, circa 1925-1935. 21/32". Mint (9.6). Price: $40. CyberAuction #376, Lot #35.

971. AKRO AGATE COMPANY. Silver oxblood. Translucent milky white base. Semi-opaque white swirls. Nice oxblood swirl on the top. Excellent example. Clarksburg, WV, circa 1925-1935. 5/8". Mint (9.9). Price: $37. CyberAuction #465, Lot #43.

972. AKRO AGATE COMPANY. Silver oxblood. Semi-opaque milky white base. Nice oxblood swirl on the top. Excellent example. Clarksburg, WV, circa 1925-1935. 11/16". Mint (9.7). Price: $35. CyberAuction #414, Lot #7.

973. AKRO AGATE COMPANY. Silver oxblood. Semi-opaque milky white base. Wispy white swirl. Nice rich oxblood swirl on the top. Excellent example. Clarksburg, WV, circa 1925-1935. 5/8". Mint (9.9). Price: $34. CyberAuction #505, Lot #56.

974. AKRO AGATE COMPANY. Silver oxblood. Translucent milky white base. Semi-opaque white swirls. Nice oxblood swirl on the top. One tiny sparkle. Excellent example. Clarksburg, WV, circa 1925-1935. 19/32". Mint (9.4). Price: $32. CyberAuction #351, Lot #45.

975. AKRO AGATE COMPANY. Silver oxblood. Translucent milky white base. Semi-opaque white swirls. Nice oxblood swirl on the top. Tiny subsurface moons and tiny pits. Clarksburg, WV, circa 1925-1935. 5/8". Mint (8.6).. Price: $32. CyberAuction #470, Lot #37.

976. AKRO AGATE COMPANY. Silver oxblood. Semi-opaque milky white base. Nice oxblood swirl on the top. Excellent example. Clarksburg, WV, circa 1925-1935. 11/16". Mint (9.7). Price: $32. CyberAuction #500, Lot #3.

977. AKRO AGATE COMPANY. Silver oxblood. Translucent milky white base. Semi-opaque white swirls. Nice oxblood swirl on the top. Rough spot and some pits. Clarksburg, WV, circa 1925-1935. 3/4". Near Mint (8.6). Price: $31. CyberAuction #354, Lot #12.

978. AKRO AGATE COMPANY. Silver oxblood. Semi-opaque milky white base. Nice oxblood swirl on the top. Excellent example. Clarksburg, WV, circa 1925-1935. 11/16". Mint (9.7). Price: $31. CyberAuction #508, Lot #50.

979. AKRO AGATE COMPANY. Silver oxblood. Semi-opaque milky white base. Nice oxblood swirl on the top. Excellent example. Clarksburg, WV, circa 1925-1935. 5/8". Mint (9.7). Price: $30. CyberAuction #379, Lot #39.

980. AKRO AGATE COMPANY. Silver oxblood. Translucent milky white base. Semi-opaque white swirls. Nice oxblood swirl on the top. Clarksburg, WV, circa 1925-1935. 19/32". Mint (9.9). Price: $30. CyberAuction #388, Lot #55.

981. AKRO AGATE COMPANY. Silver oxblood. Translucent milky white base. Semi-opaque white swirls. Nice oxblood swirl on the top. Some pitting. Clarksburg, WV, circa 1925-1935. 5/8". Near Mint(+) (8.8). Price: $30. CyberAuction #420, Lot #58.

982. AKRO AGATE COMPANY. Silver oxblood. Translucent milky white base. Semi-opaque white swirls. Nice oxblood swirl on the top. Excellent example. Clarksburg, WV, circa 1925-1935. 19/32". Mint (9.9). Price: $28. CyberAuction #346, Lot #52.

983. AKRO AGATE COMPANY. Silver oxblood. Semi-opaque milky white base. Nice oxblood swirl on the top. Excellent example. Clarksburg, WV, circa 1925-1935. 5/8". Mint (9.7). Price: $28. CyberAuction #348, Lot #11.

984. AKRO AGATE COMPANY. Silver oxblood. Translucent milky white base. Semi-opaque white swirls. Nice oxblood swirl on the top. Pitting and sparkles. Clarksburg, WV, circa 1925-1935. 11/16". Near Mint(-) (8.1). Price: $27. CyberAuction #443, Lot #55.

985. AKRO AGATE COMPANY. Silver oxblood. Translucent milky white base. Semi-opaque white swirls. Nice oxblood swirl on the top. One tiny sparkle. Clarksburg, WV, circa 1925-1935. 5/8". Mint(-) (9.2). Price: $27. CyberAuction #452, Lot #42.

986. AKRO AGATE COMPANY. Silver oxblood. Translucent milky white base. Semi-opaque white swirls. Nice oxblood swirl on the top. A couple of very tiny sparkles. Clarksburg, WV, circa 1925-1935. 19/32". Mint(-) (9.0). Price: $26. CyberAuction #337, Lot #43.

987. AKRO AGATE COMPANY. Silver oxblood. Translucent milky white base. Semi-opaque white swirls. Nice oxblood swirl on the top. Tiny subsurface moons and tiny pits. Clarksburg, WV, circa 1925-1935. 5/8". Near Mint (8.6).. Price: $26. CyberAuction #395, Lot #52.

988. AKRO AGATE COMPANY. Silver oxblood. Translucent milky white base. Semi-opaque white swirls. Nice oxblood swirl on the top. Clarksburg, WV, circa 1925-1935. 19/32". Mint (9.7). Price: $25. CyberAuction #390, Lot #50.

989. AKRO AGATE COMPANY. Silver oxblood. Translucent milky white base. Semi-opaque white swirls. Nice oxblood swirl on the top. Clarksburg, WV, circa 1925-1935. 5/8". Mint (9.9). Price: $25. CyberAuction #470, Lot #39.

990. AKRO AGATE COMPANY. Silver oxblood. Translucent milky white base. Semi-opaque white swirls. Nice oxblood swirl on the top. One sparkle. Clarksburg, WV, circa 1925-1935. 5/8". Mint(-) (9.0). Price: $22. CyberAuction #455, Lot #52.

991. AKRO AGATE COMPANY. Silver oxblood. Translucent milky white base. Semi-opaque white swirls. Nice oxblood swirl on the top. Pitting and sparkles. Clarksburg, WV, circa 1925-1935. 11/16". Near Mint(-) (8.1). Price: $21. CyberAuction #397, Lot #50.

992. AKRO AGATE COMPANY. Silver oxblood. Shooter size. Translucent milky white base. Semi-opaque white swirls. Nice oxblood swirl on the top. Subsurface moon. 23/32". Near Mint(+) (8.8). Price: $19. CyberAuction #441, Lot #52.

993. AKRO AGATE COMPANY. Silver oxblood. Semi-opaque milky white base. Nice oxblood swirl on the top. Excellent example. Clarksburg, WV, circa 1925-1935. 17/32". Mint (9.7). Price: $19. CyberAuction #459, Lot #21.

994. AKRO AGATE COMPANY. Silver oxblood. Translucent milky white base. Semi-opaque white swirls. Nice oxblood swirl on the top. One rough spot. Clarksburg, WV, circa 1925-1935. 19/32". Near Mint(+) (8.9). Price: $15. CyberAuction #373, Lot #2.

995. AKRO AGATE COMPANY. Silver oxblood. Translucent milky white base. Semi-opaque white swirls. Nice oxblood swirl on the top. Pitting. Clarksburg, WV, circa 1925-1935. 19/32". Near Mint(+) (8.7). Price: $12. CyberAuction #355, Lot #59.

996. AKRO AGATE COMPANY. Slag. Very early, huge, Akro green slag. Hand gathered. One tiny flake, one tiny chip, several tiny subsurface moons, some sparkles. Still, rare. Clarksburg, WV, circa 1920-1925. 1-13/16". Near Mint(-) (8.1). Price: $210. CyberAuction #392, Lot #55.

997. AKRO AGATE COMPANY. Slag. Large brown slag. Early example. Some cold lines, one very tiny subsurface moon, two tiny melt spots. Clarksburg, WV, circa 1922-1927. 1-3/16". Near Mint(+) (8.9). Price: $70. CyberAuction #391, Lot #32.

998. AKRO AGATE COMPANY. Slag. Rare, very early, "true" orange slag. Lots of white, gorgeous orange. Exceptional. One very tiny sparkle. Rare. Akron, OH, circa 1917-1925. 19/32". Mint (9.4). Price: $59. CyberAuction #485, Lot #54.

999. AKRO AGATE COMPANY. Slag. Shooter green slag. Gorgeous. Clarksburg, WV, circa 1925-1930. 27/32". Mint (9.9). Price: $45. CyberAuction #413, Lot #49.

1000. AKRO AGATE COMPANY. Slag. Very early purple slag. Superb pattern, stunning marble. Clarksburg, WV, circa 1920-1925. 23/32". Mint (9.6). Price: $39. CyberAuction #347, Lot #24.

1001. AKRO AGATE COMPANY. Slag. Aqua slag with an "oxblood" color in it. Clarksburg, WV, circa 1925-1930. 5/8". Mint (9.7). Price: $32. CyberAuction #414, Lot #21.

1002. AKRO AGATE COMPANY. Slag. Brown slag. Clarksburg, WV, circa 1925-1935. 27/32". Mint (9.9). Price: $30. CyberAuction #414, Lot #37.

1003. AKRO AGATE COMPANY. Slag. Fluorescent yellow slag. Little bit of green near the apparent cutoff spot. Gorgeous example. Clarksburg, WV, circa 1922-1927. 11/16". Mint (9.9). Price: $30. CyberAuction #496, Lot #40.

1004. AKRO AGATE COMPANY. Slag. Early brown slag. Large. One tiny pit on it. Clarksburg, WV, circa 1922-1927. 1". Mint(-) (9.0). Price: $27. CyberAuction #412, Lot #38.

1005. AKRO AGATE COMPANY. Slag. Shooter green slag. Clarksburg, WV, circa 1925-1930. 15/16". Mint (9.8). Price: $27. CyberAuction #413, Lot #58.

1006. AKRO AGATE COMPANY. Slag. Purple slag. Beautiful shooter. Clarksburg, WV, circa 1925-1930. 27/32". Mint (9.7). Price: $24. CyberAuction #386, Lot #32.

1007. AKRO AGATE COMPANY. Slag. Early red slag. Very nice. Clarksburg, WV, circa 1922-1927. 21/32". Mint (9.8). Price: $24. CyberAuction #473, Lot #44.

1008. AKRO AGATE COMPANY. Slag. Yellow slag. Pale yellow. Very fluorescent. Very interesting marble, appears to be early. Clarksburg, WV, circa 1922-1927. 3/4". Mint (9.5). Price: $22. CyberAuction #338, Lot #1.

1009. AKRO AGATE COMPANY. Slag. Red slag. Very nice. One tiny sparkle. Clarksburg, WV, circa 1925-1930. 11/16". Mint (9.4). Price: $22. CyberAuction #373, Lot #21.

1010. AKRO AGATE COMPANY. Slag. Early shooter brown slag. Clarksburg, WV, circa 1922-1927. 1-1/16". Near Mint(+) (8.9). Price: $22. CyberAuction #392, Lot #41.

1011. AKRO AGATE COMPANY. Slag. Gorgeous red slag. Early and a beauty. Clarksburg, WV, circa 1922-1927. 5/8". Mint (9.9). Price: $22. CyberAuction #467, Lot #36.

1012. AKRO AGATE COMPANY. Slag. Very early Akro red slag. One seam mark. Clarksburg, WV, circa 1922-1927. 19/32". Mint (9.9). Price: $21. CyberAuction #479, Lot #12.

1013. AKRO AGATE COMPANY. Slag. Shooter purple slag. Very nice. Clarksburg, WV, circa 1925-1935. 15/16". Mint (9.5). Price: $20. CyberAuction #368, Lot #29.

1014. AKRO AGATE COMPANY. Slag. Fluorescent pale yellow slag. Very nice. Clarksburg, WV, circa 1925-1930. 5/8". Mint (9.7). Price: $20. CyberAuction #448, Lot #24.

1015. AKRO AGATE COMPANY. Slag. Very early red slag. Has a seam on the bottom. One sparkle. Nice. Clarksburg, WV, circa 1920-1925. 19/32". Mint(-) (9.2). Price: $20. CyberAuction #455, Lot #15.

1016. AKRO AGATE COMPANY. Slag. Early Akro slag. Blue. Hand gathered. Nice "9", tail and seam. Clarksburg, WV, circa 1920-1925. 5/8". Mint (9.9). Price: $19. CyberAuction #340, Lot #47.

1017. AKRO AGATE COMPANY. Slag. Very early red slag. Loads of white. Some orange in it too. Hand gathered. Two tiny subsurface moons. Hard to find. Clarksburg, WV, circa 1922-1927. 25/32". Near Mint(+) (8.9). Price: $19. CyberAuction #459, Lot #25.

1018. AKRO AGATE COMPANY. Slag. Early hand gathered Akro slag. Light amber with loads of white. Nice "9", trailing tail and seam. Clarksburg, WV, circa 1922-1925. 11/16". Mint (9.7). Price: $18. CyberAuction #377, Lot #35.

1019. AKRO AGATE COMPANY. Slag. Hand gathered blue slag. Early. Nice "9". Clarksburg, WV, circa 1920-1925. 5/8". Mint (9.9). Price: $17. CyberAuction #392, Lot #44.

1020. AKRO AGATE COMPANY. Slag. Lavender slag. Gorgeous. Clarksburg, WV, circa 1925-1935. 5/8". Mint (9.9). Price: $17. CyberAuction #435, Lot #5.

1021. AKRO AGATE COMPANY. Slag. Shooter brown slag. One sparkle. Clarksburg, WV, circa 1925-1930. 27/32". Mint(-) (9.0). Price: $17. CyberAuction #488, Lot #13.

1022. AKRO AGATE COMPANY. Slag. Clear slag. White swirls in transparent clear. Clarksburg, WV, circa 1925-1935. 3/4". Mint (9.7). Price: $15. CyberAuction #435, Lot #49.

1023. AKRO AGATE COMPANY. Slag. Aqua slag. Clarksburg, WV, circa 1925-1935. 5/8". Mint (9.7). Price: $13. CyberAuction #351, Lot #20.

1024. AKRO AGATE COMPANY. Slag. Gorgeous green slag. Clarksburg, WV, circa 1925-1930. 3/4". Mint (9.9). Two marbles available. You are bidding on one. Winner has choice of either or both, remainder to under. Price: $13. CyberAuction #365, Lot #46.

1025. AKRO AGATE COMPANY. Slag. Early very light brown slag. One sparkle, couple of pits. Clarksburg, WV, circa 1922-1927. 15/16". Near Mint(+) (8.9). Price: $13. CyberAuction #425, Lot #29.

1026. AKRO AGATE COMPANY. Slag. Early very light lavender slag. Very hard color to find. One tiny rust stain on it. Akron, OH, circa 1922-1927. 5/8". Mint (9.5). Price: $13. CyberAuction #425, Lot #45.

1027. AKRO AGATE COMPANY. Slag. Nice red slag. Lots of white. Clarksburg, WV, circa 1925-1930. 5/8". Mint (9.9). Price: $12. CyberAuction #377, Lot #39.

1028. AKRO AGATE COMPANY. Slag. Early aqua slag. Clarksburg, WV, circa 1922-1927. 5/8". Mint (9.9). Price: $12. CyberAuction #415, Lot #53.

1029. AKRO AGATE COMPANY. Slag. Red slag. Very nice early example. Clarksburg, WV, circa 1922-1927. 5/8". Mint (9.9). Price: $12. CyberAuction #420, Lot #45.

1030. AKRO AGATE COMPANY. Slag. Brown slag. Gorgeous marble. Clarksburg, WV, circa 1925-1935. 25/32". Mint (9.8). Price: $12. CyberAuction #436, Lot #19.

1031. AKRO AGATE COMPANY. Slag. Aqua slag. Beauty Clarksburg, WV, circa 1925-1930. 5/8". Mint (9.9). Price: $12. CyberAuction #450, Lot #8.

1032. AKRO AGATE COMPANY. Slag. Shooter green slag. Hand gathered. Some tiny flakes and some roughness. Clarksburg, WV, circa 1922-1927. 29/32". Good(+) (7.9). Price: $11. CyberAuction #337, Lot #49.

1033. AKRO AGATE COMPANY. Slag. Cardinal Red. Shooter red slag. Some sparkles. Clarksburg, WV, circa 1922-1927. 23/32". Near Mint(+) (8.9). Price: $11. CyberAuction #364, Lot #23.

1034. AKRO AGATE COMPANY. Slag. Clear slag. Early. Several tiny subsurface moons and sparkles. Clarksburg, WV, circa 1922-1927. 29/32". Near Mint (8.4). Price: $11. CyberAuction #421, Lot #19.

1035. AKRO AGATE COMPANY. Slag. Shooter blue slag. Some subsurface moons. Clarksburg, WV, circa 1927-1935. 31/32". Near Mint(-) (8.0). Price: $10. CyberAuction #337, Lot #33.

1036. AKRO AGATE COMPANY. Slag. Blue. Gorgeous. Clarksburg, WV, circa 1925-1935. 23/32". Mint (9.9). Price: $10. CyberAuction #365, Lot #1.

1037. AKRO AGATE COMPANY. Slag. Shooter brown slag. One sparkle. Clarksburg, WV, circa 1925-1930. 27/32". Mint(-) (9.0). Price: $10. CyberAuction #413, Lot #44.

1038. AKRO AGATE COMPANY. Slag. Early green slag. Poor "9". Very nice whiptail and seam. Sand seed on the surface. Clarksburg, WV, circa 1925-1930. 25/32". Mint (9.6). Price: $10. CyberAuction #436, Lot #17.

1039. AKRO AGATE COMPANY. Slag. Large green slag. Hand gathered. Beautiful pattern. Two large chips at the top, a couple of tiny subsurface moons and sparkles. Clarksburg, WV, circa 1922-1927. 1-3/16". Good(+) (7.9). Price: $10. CyberAuction #442, Lot #18.

1040. AKRO AGATE COMPANY. Slag. Shooter brown slag. Two tiny subsurface moons. Clarksburg, WV, circa 1925-1930. 15/16". Near Mint(+) (8.7). Price: $10. CyberAuction #494, Lot #9.

1041. AKRO AGATE COMPANY. Slag. Very fluorescent yellow slag. Beauty. One tiny sparkle. Clarksburg, WV, circa 1925-1930. 21/32". Mint(-) (9.0). Price: $9. CyberAuction #450, Lot #1.

1042. AKRO AGATE COMPANY. Slag. Early purple slag. Gorgeous color. One tiny air hole. Clarksburg, WV, circa 1925-1935. 5/8". Mint (9.6). Price: $8. CyberAuction #438, Lot #15.

1043. AKRO AGATE COMPANY. Slag. Pretty blue slag. Wispy white blankets and swirls. One melt spot. Clarksburg, WV, circa 1925-1935. 13/16". Mint (9.7). Price: $8. CyberAuction #438, Lot #18.

1044. AKRO AGATE COMPANY. Slag. Brown slag. Very early. Nice hand gathered pattern. A couple of tiny subsurface moons. Clarksburg, WV, circa 1922-1927. 7/8". Near Mint(+) (8.8). Price: $8. CyberAuction #439, Lot #37.

1045. AKRO AGATE COMPANY. Slag. Shooter brown slag. One sparkle. Clarksburg, WV, circa 1925-1930. 27/32". Mint(-) (9.0). Price: $8. CyberAuction #457, Lot #8.

1046. AKRO AGATE COMPANY. Slag. Orange slag. Some sparkles. Clarksburg, WV, circa 1922-1927. 5/8". Near Mint(+) (8.7). Price: $7. CyberAuction #365, Lot #49.

1047. AKRO AGATE COMPANY. Slag. Yellow slag. Very fluorescent. Several sparkles. Clarksburg, WV, circa 1927-1935. 21/32". Near Mint(+) (8.9). Price: $7. CyberAuction #399, Lot #49.

1048. AKRO AGATE COMPANY. Slag. Very early aqua slag. Nice pattern. One tiny sparkle. Clarksburg, WV, circa 1920-1925. 21/32". Mint(-) (9.2). Price: $7. CyberAuction #433, Lot #3.

1049. AKRO AGATE COMPANY. Slag. Shooter brown slag. Two tiny subsurface moons. Clarksburg, WV, circa 1925-1930. 15/16". Near Mint(+) (8.7). Price: $7. CyberAuction #461, Lot #26.

1050. AKRO AGATE COMPANY. Slag. Early brown slag. Very nice. One tiny pit. Clarksburg, WV, circa 1922-1927. 19/32". Mint(-) (9.2). Price: $7. CyberAuction #471, Lot #48.

1051. AKRO AGATE COMPANY. Slag. Clear slag. Nice marble. Clarksburg, WV, circa 1922-1927. 21/32". Mint (9.7). Price: $7. CyberAuction #476, Lot #42.

1052. AKRO AGATE COMPANY. Slag. Early purple slag. One seam. Has a melt dimple on it. Nice. Clarksburg, WV, circa 1920-1925. 19/32". Mint(-) (9.0). Price: $6. CyberAuction #481, Lot #30.

1053. AKRO AGATE COMPANY. Slag. Red slag. Some sparkles. Clarksburg,

WV, circa 1927-1935. 11/16". Near Mint(+) (8.9). Price: $5. CyberAuction #495, Lot #26.

1054. AKRO AGATE COMPANY. Slag. Early Akro slag. Blue. One tiny sub-surface moon. Clarksburg, WV, circa 1922-1927. 21/32". Near Mint(+) (8.8). Price: $4. CyberAuction #345, Lot #11.

1055. AKRO AGATE COMPANY. Slag. Nice early Akro slag. Brown. Clarksburg, WV, circa 1922-1927. 11/16". Mint (9.6). Price: $4. CyberAuction #345, Lot #27.

1056. AKRO AGATE COMPANY. Slag. Aqua slag. Subsurface moon. Clarksburg, WV, circa 1922-1927. 21/32". Near Mint(+) (8.7). Price: $4. CyberAuction #448, Lot #4.

1057. AKRO AGATE COMPANY. Slag. Green slag. One tiny sparkle. Clarksburg, WV, circa 1922-1927. 21/32". Mint(-) (9.2). Price: $4. CyberAuction #484, Lot #31.

1058. AKRO AGATE COMPANY. Slag. Clear slag. A couple of tiny flakes. Clarksburg, WV, circa 1922-1927. 5/8". Near Mint (8.5). Price: $4. CyberAuction #488, Lot #34.

1059. AKRO AGATE COMPANY. Slag. Shooter green slag. A couple of tiny subsurface moons. Clarksburg, WV, circa 1927-1935. 13/16". Near Mint(+) (8.7). Price: $4. CyberAuction #494, Lot #4.

1060. AKRO AGATE COMPANY. Slag. Very early orange Akro slag. One flake. Clarksburg, WV, circa 1917-1922. 9/16". Near Mint (8.6). Price: $3. CyberAuction #381, Lot #3.

1061. AKRO AGATE COMPANY. Slag. Red slag, almost orange. One sparkle. Early. Clarksburg, WV, circa 1922-1925. 21/32". Mint(-) (9.0). Price: $3. CyberAuction #391, Lot #7.

1062. AKRO AGATE COMPANY. Slag. Red slag. Clarksburg, WV, circa 1925-1935. 11/16". Mint (9.7). Price: $3. CyberAuction #421, Lot #37.

1063. AKRO AGATE COMPANY. Slag. Fluorescent yellow slag. Tiny sub-surface moon. Out of round. Clarksburg, WV, circa 1925-1935. 11/16". Near Mint(+) (8.9). Price: $3. CyberAuction #473, Lot #14.

1064. AKRO AGATE COMPANY. Slag. Early purple slag. One tiny sparkle. Clarksburg, WV, circa 1922-1927. 11/16". Mint(-) (9.1). Price: $3. CyberAuction #497, Lot #41.

1065. AKRO AGATE COMPANY. Slag. Yellow slag. One tiny sparkle. Clarksburg, WV, circa 1925-1930. 5/8". Mint(-) (9.2). Price: $2. CyberAuction #406, Lot #16.

1066. AKRO AGATE COMPANY. Slag. Blue slag. Early example. Several annealing fractures and a tiny subsurface moon. Clarksburg, WV, circa 1922-1927. 5/8". Near Mint (8.6). Price: $2. CyberAuction #455, Lot #13.

1067. AKRO AGATE COMPANY. Slag. Yellow slag. One tiny sparkle. Clarksburg, WV, circa 1925-1930. 5/8". Mint(-) (9.2). Price: $2. CyberAuction #457, Lot #28.

1068. AKRO AGATE COMPANY. Slag. Green slag. One tiny sparkle. Clarksburg, WV, circa 1922-1927. 21/32". Mint(-) (9.2). Price: $1. CyberAuction #457, Lot #6.

1069. AKRO AGATE COMPANY. Slag. Clear slag. A couple of tiny flakes. Clarksburg, WV, circa 1922-1927. 5/8". Near Mint (8.5). Price: $.50. CyberAuction #417, Lot #40.

1070. AKRO AGATE COMPANY. Sparkler. Ribbon of white, yellow, black, brown, light blue. Wide core, loads of color. Flat at one end, tiny subsurface moon. Clarksburg, WV, circa 1925-1930. 5/8". Near Mint (8.6). Price: $35. CyberAuction #489, Lot #9.

1071. AKRO AGATE COMPANY. Sparkler. Core of white, yellow, black, brown, light blue. Wide core, loads of color. A couple of tiny subsurface moons. Clarksburg, WV, circa 1925-1930. 5/8". Near Mint(+) (8.7). Price: $21. CyberAuction #355, Lot #55.

1072. AKRO AGATE COMPANY. Sparkler. Core of white, yellow, black, brown, light blue. Wide core, loads of color. A couple of tiny subsurface moons. Clarksburg, WV, circa 1925-1930. 5/8". Near Mint (8.6). Price: $19. CyberAuction #340, Lot #55.

1073. AKRO AGATE COMPANY. Sparkler. Ribbon of white, yellow, black, brown, light blue. Wide core, loads of color. One small flake. Clarksburg, WV, circa 1925-1930. 5/8". Near Mint (8.6). Price: $14. CyberAuction #465, Lot #15.

1074. AKRO AGATE COMPANY. Sparkler. Nice coloring. Subsurface moon and flat on one side. Clarksburg, WV, circa 1925-1930. 5/8". Near Mint(-) (8.0). There are two examples available, you are bidding on one. Winner has choice of either or both, remainder to under. Price: $10. CyberAuction #399, Lot #17.

1075. AKRO AGATE COMPANY. Swirl. Experimental swirl. Transparent bubble-filled light green glass, swirled with brick-red and opaque white. One small air hole. This is one of the marble recently dug from under a building adjacent to the Akro Agate property in Clarksburg WV. Clarksburg, WV, circa 1925-1935. 25/32". Mint(-) (9.0). Price: $46. CyberAuction #366, Lot #47.

1076. AKRO AGATE COMPANY. Swirl. Experimental swirl. Transparent bubble-filled light brown glass, swirled with red and opaque white. This is one of the marble recently dug from under a building adjacent to the Akro Agate property in Clarksburg WV. Clarksburg, WV, circa 1925-1935. 13/16". Mint (9.7). Price: $37. CyberAuction #330, Lot #14.

1077. AKRO AGATE COMPANY. Swirl. Experimental swirl. Transparent bubble-filled light brown glass, swirled with oxblood-like red and opaque white. This is one of the marble recently dug from under a building adjacent to the Akro Agate property in Clarksburg WV. Clarksburg, WV, circa 1925-1935. 13/16". Mint(-) (9.1). There are two marbles available, you are bidding on one. Winner has choice of either or both, remainder to under. Price: $36. CyberAuction #436, Lot #27.

1078. AKRO AGATE COMPANY. Swirl. Experimental swirl. Transparent bubble-filled light brown glass, swirled with red and opaque white. This is one of the marble recently dug from under a building adjacent to the Akro

Agate property in Clarksburg WV. Several small melt spots. Clarksburg, WV, circa 1925-1935. 13/16". Mint(-) (9.0). Price: $32. CyberAuction #429, Lot #54.

1079. AKRO AGATE COMPANY. Swirl. Experimental swirl. Transparent bubble-filled light brown glass, swirled with oxblood-like red and opaque white. This is one of the marble recently dug from under a building adjacent to the Akro Agate property in Clarksburg WV. Clarksburg, WV, circa 1925-1935. 13/16". Mint(-) (9.1). Price: $30. CyberAuction #433, Lot #22.

1080. AKRO AGATE COMPANY. Swirl. Experimental swirl. Transparent bubble-filled light brown glass, swirled with oxblood-like red and opaque white. This is one of the marble recently dug from under a building adjacent to the Akro Agate property in Clarksburg WV. Clarksburg, WV, circa 1925-1935. 13/16". Mint(-) (9.1). Price: $30. CyberAuction #453, Lot #52.

1081. AKRO AGATE COMPANY. Swirl. Experimental swirl. Transparent bubble-filled light brown glass, swirled with oxblood-like red and opaque white. This is one of the marble recently dug from under a building adjacent to the Akro Agate property in Clarksburg WV. Clarksburg, WV, circa 1925-1935. 13/16". Mint(-) (9.0). There are three small marbles (last three from this consignment), you are bidding on one. Winner has choice of any or all remainder to under. Price: $28. CyberAuction #443, Lot #21.

1082. AKRO AGATE COMPANY. Swirl. Experimental swirl. Transparent bubble-filled light brown glass, swirled with oxblood-like red and opaque white. This is one of the marble recently dug from under a building adjacent to the Akro Agate property in Clarksburg WV. Clarksburg, WV, circa 1925-1935. 19/32". Mint (9.8). Price: $28. CyberAuction #465, Lot #20.

1083. AKRO AGATE COMPANY. Swirl. Experimental swirl. Transparent bubble-filled light brown glass, swirled with oxblood-like red and opaque white. This is one of the marble recently dug from under a building adjacent to the Akro Agate property in Clarksburg WV. Clarksburg, WV, circa 1925-1935. 13/16". Mint(-) (9.1). Price: $28. CyberAuction #496, Lot #10.

1084. AKRO AGATE COMPANY. Swirl. Experimental swirl. Transparent bubble-filled light brown glass, swirled with oxblood-like red and opaque white. This is one of the marble recently dug from under a building adjacent to the Akro Agate property in Clarksburg WV. Clarksburg, WV, circa 1925-1935. 13/16". Mint(-) (9.0). Price: $25. CyberAuction #438, Lot #7.

1085. AKRO AGATE COMPANY. Swirl. Experimental swirl. Transparent bubble-filled light brown glass, swirled with oxblood-like red and opaque white. This is one of the marble recently dug from under a building adjacent to the Akro Agate property in Clarksburg WV. Clarksburg, WV, circa 1925-1935. 13/16". Mint(-) (9.1). Price: $24. CyberAuction #435, Lot #18.

1086. AKRO AGATE COMPANY. Swirl. Three color. Milky white base blue swirl, pale yellow swirl. Clarksburg, WV, circa 1925-1935. 19/32". Mint (9.7). Price: $22. CyberAuction #435, Lot #54.

1087. AKRO AGATE COMPANY. Swirl. Experimental swirl. Transparent bubble-filled light brown glass, swirled with oxblood-like red and opaque white. This is one of the marble recently dug from under a building adjacent to the Akro Agate property in Clarksburg WV. Clarksburg, WV, circa 1925-1935. 25/32". Near Mint(+) (8.8). Price: $22. CyberAuction #444, Lot #22.

1088. AKRO AGATE COMPANY. Swirl. Experimental swirl. Transparent bubble-filled light brown glass, swirled with oxblood-like red and opaque white. This is one of the marble recently dug from under a building adjacent to the Akro Agate property in Clarksburg WV. Clarksburg, WV, circa 1925-1935. 13/16". Mint(-) (9.1). Price: $22. CyberAuction #474, Lot #41.

1089. AKRO AGATE COMPANY. Swirl. Three color. Translucent milky white base. Opaque pale egg yolk yellow swirl. Translucent dark blue swirl Pinprick. Beauty. Clarksburg, WV, circa 1927-1935. 19/32". Mint (9.6). Price: $17. CyberAuction #475, Lot #21.

1090. AKRO AGATE COMPANY. Swirl. Very unusual and rare hybrid swirl Ace/Imperial hybrid. Translucent white base with lots of semi-opaque white swirled in. On the surface is a swirl of translucent brown with some translucent yellow. Very unusual. Clarksburg, WV, circa 1927-1935. 5/8". Min (9.8). Price: $17. CyberAuction #501, Lot #4.

1091. AKRO AGATE COMPANY. Swirl. Unusual example. Milky white base, lots of wispy opaque white, nice opaque yellow swirl. Annealing fracture. Clarksburg, WV, circa 1927-1935. 21/32". Near Mint (8.5). Price $5. CyberAuction #477, Lot #19.

1092. AKRO AGATE COMPANY. Swirl. Three color. Milky white base blue swirl, pale yellow swirl. Tiny chip. Clarksburg, WV, circa 1925-1935 5/8". Near Mint(+) (8.7). Price: $4. CyberAuction #416, Lot #12.

1093. AKRO AGATE COMPANY. Swirl oxblood. Opaque white base with swirls of oxblood. Very nice. Clarksburg, WV, circa 1930-1935. 5/8". Min (9.9). Price: $47. CyberAuction #451, Lot #50.

1094. AKRO AGATE COMPANY. Swirl oxblood. Opaque white. Nice swir of oxblood on it. Clarksburg, WV, circa 1930-1940. 21/32". Mint (9.8) Price: $46. CyberAuction #347, Lot #56.

1095. AKRO AGATE COMPANY. Swirl oxblood. Opaque white base with swirls of oxblood. Very nice. Clarksburg, WV, circa 1930-1935. 5/8". Mint (9.9). Price: $42. CyberAuction #333, Lot #42.

1096. AKRO AGATE COMPANY. Swirl oxblood. Interesting early oxblood swirl. Opaque white base. Swirls of oxblood on one side of the marble Distinct "Master-type" seams on the marble. Slightly out of round Clarksburg, WV, circa 1930-1940. 3/4". Mint (9.7). Price: $40. CyberAuction #470, Lot #30.

1097. AKRO AGATE COMPANY. Swirl oxblood. Opaque white base with swirls of oxblood. Very nice. Clarksburg, WV, circa 1930-1935. 5/8". Mint (9.9). Price: $35. CyberAuction #467, Lot #40.

1098. AKRO AGATE COMPANY. Swirl oxblood. Opaque white base with some clear swirls in it. Nice oxblood swirling. Clarksburg, WV, circa 1930-1945. 5/8". Mint (9.9). Price: $34. CyberAuction #372, Lot #53.

1099. AKRO AGATE COMPANY. Swirl oxblood. Opaque white base with swirls of oxblood. Very nice. Clarksburg, WV, circa 1930-1935. 5/8". Mint (9.9). Price: $32. CyberAuction #369, Lot #19.

1100. AKRO AGATE COMPANY. Swirl oxblood. Opaque white base. Actually, this is a patch type marble. Oxblood covering about forty percent of the surface. One tiny flake spot, but there is where the veneer came off the surface. Clarksburg, WV, circa 1930-1945. 23/32". Mint(-) (9.0). Price: $30. CyberAuction #355, Lot #14.

1101. AKRO AGATE COMPANY. Swirl oxblood. Opaque white base with swirls of oxblood. Very nice. Clarksburg, WV, circa 1930-1935. 5/8". Mint (9.6). Price: $30. CyberAuction #421, Lot #5.

1102. AKRO AGATE COMPANY. Swirl oxblood. Shooter. Opaque white. Nice swirl of oxblood on one side. Clarksburg, WV, circa 1930-1940. 3/4". Mint (9.6). Price: $29. CyberAuction #347, Lot #50.

1103. AKRO AGATE COMPANY. Swirl oxblood. Swirl oxblood with two seams. Opaque white with oxblood red swirls. May very well be Vitro Agate. Nice though. American, circa 1930-1945. 3/4". Mint (9.9). Price: $29. CyberAuction #485, Lot #43.

1104. AKRO AGATE COMPANY. Swirl oxblood. Opaque white base with wide covering of rich oxblood. Clarksburg, WV, circa 1930-1940. 5/8". Mint (9.9). Price: $28. CyberAuction #381, Lot #26.

1105. AKRO AGATE COMPANY. Swirl oxblood. Semi-opaque white base with rich oxblood swirls. Clarksburg, WV, circa 1930-1945. 5/8". Mint (9.9). Price: $27. CyberAuction #381, Lot #34.

1106. AKRO AGATE COMPANY. Swirl oxblood. Opaque white base with swirls of oxblood. Very nice. One cold roll dimple. Clarksburg, WV, circa 1930-1935. 5/8". Mint (9.6). Price: $27. CyberAuction #456, Lot #20.

1107. AKRO AGATE COMPANY. Swirl oxblood. Opaque white base with swirls of oxblood. Very nice. Clarksburg, WV, circa 1930-1935. 5/8". Mint (9.9). Price: $26. CyberAuction #339, Lot #42.

1108. AKRO AGATE COMPANY. Swirl oxblood. Opaque white base. Nice swirls of rich oxblood. Clarksburg, WV, circa 1930-1945. 19/32". Mint (9.9). Price: $24. CyberAuction #505, Lot #47.

1109. AKRO AGATE COMPANY. Swirl oxblood. Opaque white base. Lots of oxblood swirling. Gorgeous. One very tiny pinprick. Clarksburg, WV, circa 1927-1935. 5/8". Mint(-) (9.0). Price: $23. CyberAuction #357, Lot #3.

1110. AKRO AGATE COMPANY. Swirl oxblood. Opaque white base with swirls of oxblood. Very nice. Clarksburg, WV, circa 1930-1935. 5/8". Mint (9.9). Price: $22. CyberAuction #342, Lot #18.

1111. AKRO AGATE COMPANY. Swirl oxblood. Opaque white base. Very nice oxblood swirls. Clarksburg, WV, circa 1930-1940. 19/32". Mint (9.9). Two marbles available. Virtually identical. You are bidding on one. Winner has choice of either or both, remainder to under. Price: $22. CyberAuction #352, Lot #10.

1112. AKRO AGATE COMPANY. Swirl oxblood. Opaque white base with swirls of oxblood. Very nice. Clarksburg, WV, circa 1930-1935. 5/8". Mint (9.8). Price: $22. CyberAuction #446, Lot #55.

1113. AKRO AGATE COMPANY. Swirl oxblood. Opaque white base with swirls of oxblood. Very nice. Clarksburg, WV, circa 1930-1935. 5/8". Mint (9.9). Price: $21. CyberAuction #348, Lot #16.

1114. AKRO AGATE COMPANY. Swirl oxblood. Opaque white base with swirls of oxblood. Very nice. One cold roll dimple. Clarksburg, WV, circa 1930-1935. 5/8". Mint (9.6). Price: $21. CyberAuction #433, Lot #45.

1115. AKRO AGATE COMPANY. Swirl oxblood. Opaque white base with swirls of oxblood. Very nice. Clarksburg, WV, circa 1930-1935. 5/8". Mint (9.8). Price: $21. CyberAuction #438, Lot #6.

1116. AKRO AGATE COMPANY. Swirl oxblood. Opaque white base with swirls of oxblood. Very nice. Clarksburg, WV, circa 1930-1935. 5/8". Mint (9.9). Price: $20. CyberAuction #334, Lot #53.

1117. AKRO AGATE COMPANY. Swirl oxblood. Opaque white base with swirls of oxblood. Very nice. Clarksburg, WV, circa 1930-1935. 5/8". Mint (9.9). Price: $19. CyberAuction #342, Lot #38.

1118. AKRO AGATE COMPANY. Swirl oxblood. Opaque white base with swirls of oxblood. Very nice. One cold roll dimple. Clarksburg, WV, circa 1930-1935. 5/8". Mint (9.6). Price: $19. CyberAuction #435, Lot #10.

1119. AKRO AGATE COMPANY. Swirl oxblood. Opaque white base. Swirls of oxblood on it. Slightly out of round. Clarksburg, WV, circa 1930-1945. 23/32". Mint(-) (9.2). Price: $19. CyberAuction #455, Lot #7.

1120. AKRO AGATE COMPANY. Swirl oxblood. Opaque white base. Two wide stripes of oxblood. Clarksburg, WV, circa 1930-1940. 23/32". Mint (9.9). Price: $19. CyberAuction #471, Lot #37.

1121. AKRO AGATE COMPANY. Swirl oxblood. Opaque white base. Several oxblood swirls. One cold roll line. Clarksburg, WV, circa 1930-1945. 11/16". Mint (9.5). Price: $19. CyberAuction #473, Lot #10.

1122. AKRO AGATE COMPANY. Swirl oxblood. Opaque white base with swirls of oxblood. Very nice. Clarksburg, WV, circa 1930-1935. 5/8". Mint (9.9). Price: $17. CyberAuction #334, Lot #1.

1123. AKRO AGATE COMPANY. Swirl oxblood. Opaque white base with wispy swirls of oxblood. Very nice. Clarksburg, WV, circa 1930-1935. 5/8". Mint (9.9). Price: $17. CyberAuction #335, Lot #31.

1124. AKRO AGATE COMPANY. Swirl oxblood. Opaque white base with thin swirls of oxblood. Very nice. Clarksburg, WV, circa 1930-1935. 19/32". Mint (9.9). Price: $17. CyberAuction #375, Lot #39.

1125. AKRO AGATE COMPANY. Swirl oxblood. Opaque white with oxblood swirls. Clarksburg, WV, circa 1930-1945. 19/32". Mint (9.9). Price: $17. CyberAuction #489, Lot #28.

1126. AKRO AGATE COMPANY. Swirl oxblood. Opaque white base with swirls of oxblood. Very nice. Clarksburg, WV, circa 1930-1935. 5/8". Mint (9.9). Price: $15. CyberAuction #335, Lot #26.

1127. AKRO AGATE COMPANY. Swirl oxblood. Opaque white base with swirls of oxblood. One tiny flake. Clarksburg, WV, circa 1930-1935. 5/8". Near Mint(+) (8.9). Price: $15. CyberAuction #349, Lot #54.

1128. AKRO AGATE COMPANY. Swirl oxblood. Opaque white base with nice oxblood swirls. A few smalls sparkles. Clarksburg, WV, circa 1930-1945. 19/32". Near Mint(+) (8.7). Price: $15. CyberAuction #359, Lot #46.

1129. AKRO AGATE COMPANY. Swirl oxblood. Opaque white base with nice oxblood swirling. Clarksburg, WV, circa 1927-1935. 19/32". Mint (9.9). Price: $15. CyberAuction #389, Lot #55.

1130. AKRO AGATE COMPANY. Swirl oxblood. Opaque white base with swirls of oxblood. Very nice. Clarksburg, WV, circa 1930-1935. 5/8". Mint (9.9). Price: $15. CyberAuction #461, Lot #43.

1131. AKRO AGATE COMPANY. Swirl oxblood. Opaque white base. Nice oxblood swirls. One pinprick. Clarksburg, WV, circa 1930-1940. 19/32". Mint(-) (9.2). Price: $15. CyberAuction #477, Lot #40.

1132. AKRO AGATE COMPANY. Swirl oxblood. Opaque white base with swirls of rich oxblood. Very nice. Clarksburg, WV, circa 1930-1935. 5/8". Mint (9.9). Price: $15. CyberAuction #493, Lot #40.

1133. AKRO AGATE COMPANY. Swirl oxblood. Opaque white base with swirls of oxblood. Very nice. Clarksburg, WV, circa 1930-1935. 5/8". Mint (9.9). Price: $14. CyberAuction #333, Lot #2.

1134. AKRO AGATE COMPANY. Swirl oxblood. Opaque white base with swirls of oxblood. Very nice. One cold roll dimple. Clarksburg, WV, circa 1930-1935. 5/8". Mint (9.6). Price: $14. CyberAuction #438, Lot #39.

1135. AKRO AGATE COMPANY. Swirl oxblood. Opaque white base with swirls of oxblood. Some tiny chipping. Clarksburg, WV, circa 1930-1935. 5/8". Near Mint (8.6). Price: $13. CyberAuction #334, Lot #46.

1136. AKRO AGATE COMPANY. Swirl oxblood. Opaque white base. Thin oxblood swirls on it. Clarksburg, WV, circa 1930-1940. 19/32". Mint (9.9). Price: $13. CyberAuction #374, Lot #49.

1137. AKRO AGATE COMPANY. Swirl oxblood. Opaque white base, thin oxblood swirls. Very nice. Clarksburg, WV, circa 1927-1935. 5/8". Mint (9.9). Price: $13. CyberAuction #483, Lot #17.

1138. AKRO AGATE COMPANY. Swirl oxblood. Opaque white base with some clear swirling. Nice oxblood swirl on it. Some tiny flakes and tiny chips. Clarksburg, WV, circa 1927-1935. 19/32". Near Mint (8.6). Price: $12. CyberAuction #353, Lot #17.

1139. AKRO AGATE COMPANY. Swirl oxblood. Opaque white base. Thin oxblood swirls on it. Clarksburg, WV, circa 1930-1940. 19/32". Mint (9.9). Price: $12. CyberAuction #354, Lot #45.

1140. AKRO AGATE COMPANY. Swirl oxblood. Opaque white base. Nice oxblood swirls on some of the surface. Clarksburg, WV, circa 1930-1945. 19/32". Mint (9.7). There are six marbles available, you are bidding on one. Winner has choice of any or all, remainder to under. Price: $12. CyberAuction #384, Lot #19.

1141. AKRO AGATE COMPANY. Swirl oxblood. Nice oxblood swirls on opaque white. Deep crease on one side. Clarksburg, WV, circa 1930-1945. 5/8". Mint(-) (9.1). Price: $12. CyberAuction #429, Lot #38.

1142. AKRO AGATE COMPANY. Swirl oxblood. Opaque white base with swirls of oxblood. Very nice. One cold roll dimple. Clarksburg, WV, circa 1930-1935. 5/8". Mint (9.6). Price: $12. CyberAuction #433, Lot #9.

1143. AKRO AGATE COMPANY. Swirl oxblood. Error marble. Large swirl oxblood with a nub at one end. Very nice. Clarksburg, WV, circa 1927-1935. 13/16". Mint (9.5). Price: $12. CyberAuction #457, Lot #33.

1144. AKRO AGATE COMPANY. Swirl oxblood. Opaque white base. Nice oxblood swirls. Clarksburg, WV, circa 1930-1945. 21/32". Mint (9.9). Price: $12. CyberAuction #481, Lot #11.

1145. AKRO AGATE COMPANY. Swirl oxblood. Error marble. Large swirl oxblood with a nub at one end. Very nice. Clarksburg, WV, circa 1927-1935. 13/16". Mint (9.5). Price: $12. CyberAuction #488, Lot #19.

1146. AKRO AGATE COMPANY. Swirl oxblood. Error marble. Large swirl oxblood with a nub at one end. Very nice. Clarksburg, WV, circa 1927-1935. 13/16". Mint (9.5). Price: $12. CyberAuction #506, Lot #8.

1147. AKRO AGATE COMPANY. Swirl oxblood. Opaque white base with swirls of oxblood. Very nice. One cold roll dimple. Clarksburg, WV, circa 1930-1935. 5/8". Mint (9.6). Price: $11. CyberAuction #436, Lot #8.

1148. AKRO AGATE COMPANY. Swirl oxblood. Thin oxblood stripes on opaque white. One small melt/nub on the surface. Clarksburg, WV, circa 1930-1945. 21/32". Mint(-) (9.2). Price: $11. CyberAuction #475, Lot #28.

1149. AKRO AGATE COMPANY. Swirl oxblood. Opaque white base with some oxblood swirls. Two melt glass spots on it. Clarksburg, WV, circa 1930-1945. 19/32". Mint (9.5). Price: $11. CyberAuction #489, Lot #19.

1150. AKRO AGATE COMPANY. Swirl oxblood. Thin oxblood swirls on white. Very nice. Clarksburg, WV, circa 1930-1940. 19/32". Mint (9.9). Price: $10. CyberAuction #355, Lot #16.

1151. AKRO AGATE COMPANY. Swirl oxblood. Thin oxblood swirls on opaque white. Clarksburg, WV, circa 1930-1945. 5/8". Mint (9.9). Price: $10. CyberAuction #481, Lot #35.

1152. AKRO AGATE COMPANY. Swirl oxblood. Opaque white base with swirls of oxblood. Very nice. Several tiny sparkles. Clarksburg, WV, circa 1930-1935. 5/8". Mint(-) (9.0). Price: $9. CyberAuction #362, Lot #38.

1153. AKRO AGATE COMPANY. Swirl oxblood. Opaque white base with some clear swirls in it. Rich oxblood swirls on surface. Some minor haze. Clarksburg, WV, circa 1930-1945. 19/32". Near Mint (8.6). Price: $9. CyberAuction #387, Lot #53.

1154. AKRO AGATE COMPANY. Swirl oxblood. Opaque white base with swirls of oxblood. Very nice. Small dimple and a tiny dimple. Clarksburg, WV, circa 1930-1935. 5/8". Near Mint(+) (8.9). Price: $6. CyberAuction #485, Lot #21.

1155. AKRO AGATE COMPANY. Tri-color. Tri-color Agate. Opaque white base. Blue patch and yellow patch. You almost never see these out of the original box. Clarksburg, WV, circa 1925-1930. 5/8". Mint (9.9). Price: $7. CyberAuction #446, Lot #14.

1156. AKRO AGATE COMPANY. Tri-color. Tri-color Agate. Opaque white base. Blue patch and yellow patch. You almost never see these out of the original box. Clarksburg, WV, circa 1925-1930. 5/8". Mint (9.9). There are four marbles available. You are bidding on one. Winner has choice of any or all, remainder to under. Price: $2. CyberAuction #376, Lot #16.

1157. CHRISTENSEN AGATE COMPANY. American Agate. Interesting variant. Translucent white base. Very thin electric red swirling on the surface. Almost all white. Possibly hand gathered. Poor "9" and has a crease pontil. Cambridge, OH, circa 1927-1929. 11/16". Mint (9.7). Price: $70. CyberAuction #330, Lot #47.

1158. CHRISTENSEN AGATE COMPANY. American Agate. Semi-opaque opalescent milky white with translucent electric red swirls. Cambridge, OH, circa 1927-1929. 19/32". Mint (9.9). Price: $42. CyberAuction #501, Lot #22.

1159. CHRISTENSEN AGATE COMPANY. American Agate. Semi-opaque milky white with translucent electric red swirls. Cambridge, OH, circa 1927-1929. 11/16". Mint (9.8). Price: $42. CyberAuction #502, Lot #61.

1160. CHRISTENSEN AGATE COMPANY. American Agate. Semi-opaque white with semi-opaque electric red swirls. Cambridge, OH, circa 1927-1929. 5/8". Mint (9.9). Price: $40. CyberAuction #498, Lot #59.

1161. CHRISTENSEN AGATE COMPANY. American Agate. Semi-opaque milky white with translucent electric red swirls. Cambridge, OH, circa 1927-1929. 19/32". Mint (9.5). Price: $36. CyberAuction #371, Lot #3.

1162. CHRISTENSEN AGATE COMPANY. American Agate. Ruddy electric red on white. Some tiny pits. Appears hand gathered. Cambridge, OH, circa 1927-1929. 11/16". Near Mint (8.8). Price: $29. CyberAuction #473, Lot #42.

1163. CHRISTENSEN AGATE COMPANY. American Agate. Semi-opaque milky white with translucent very light red swirls. Cambridge, OH, circa 1927-1929. 5/8". Mint (9.5). Price: $19. CyberAuction #499, Lot #58.

1164. CHRISTENSEN AGATE COMPANY. Bloodie. Stunning Bloodie. Super example. Opaque white, translucent brown and transparent dark red. Equal amounts of each color. Super pattern. Cambridge, OH, circa 1927-1929. 19/32". Mint (9.9). Price: $130. CyberAuction #424, Lot #43.

1165. CHRISTENSEN AGATE COMPANY. Bloodie. Opaque white base. Transparent red and translucent brown swirls. Superb example. Cambridge, OH, circa 1927-1929. 19/32". Mint (9.8). Price: $95. CyberAuction #491, Lot #25.

1166. CHRISTENSEN AGATE COMPANY. Bloodie. Opaque white base. Transparent red and translucent brown swirls. Superb example. Cambridge, OH, circa 1927-1929. 21/32". Mint (9.8). Price: $80. CyberAuction #455, Lot #11.

1167. CHRISTENSEN AGATE COMPANY. Bloodie. Nice Bloodie. Opaque white base. Transparent red and translucent brown swirls. Beauty, hard to find. Cambridge, OH, circa 1927-1929. 5/8". Mint (9.7). Price: $65. CyberAuction #400, Lot #46.

1168. CHRISTENSEN AGATE COMPANY. Bloodie. Opaque white base with transparent red swirls and translucent brown swirls. This one has some flame tips and a poor turkey head. Very little white. Stunning. Cambridge, OH, circa 1927-1929. 19/32". Mint (9.9). Price: $60. CyberAuction #499, Lot #42.

1169. CHRISTENSEN AGATE COMPANY. Bloodie. Opaque white base. Transparent red and translucent brown swirls. Some pitting. Cambridge, OH, circa 1927-1929. 19/32". Near Mint(+) (8.7). Price: $26. CyberAuction #452, Lot #28.

1170. CHRISTENSEN AGATE COMPANY. Bloodie. Opaque white base with transparent red and translucent brown swirls. This one has some flame tips and a poor turkey head. Very little white. One small flake, some pitting. Cambridge, OH, circa 1927-1929. 5/8". Near Mint(-) (8.1). Price: $9. CyberAuction #485, Lot #9.

1171. CHRISTENSEN AGATE COMPANY. Cyclone. One-half a Cyclone. Was a purple and yellow cyclone in clear. Nice piece for jewelry. Cambridge, OH, circa 1927-1929. 11/16". Mint (9.7). Price: $42. CyberAuction #448, Lot #7.

1172. CHRISTENSEN AGATE COMPANY. Flame swirl. Stunning marble. Opaque white base. Light green and transparent dark red swirls. Exceptional swirling and flaming. Exceptional marble!!!! Rarer than a Guinea. Cambridge, OH, circa 1927-1929. 19/32". Mint (9.9). Price: $575. CyberAuction #377, Lot #54.

1173. CHRISTENSEN AGATE COMPANY. Flame swirl. Pale salmon pink swirls in opaque white. Over a dozen flame tips. Outstanding pattern. Exceptional marble. Cambridge, OH, circa 1927-1929. 21/32". Mint (9.9). Price: $335. CyberAuction #342, Lot #53.

1174. CHRISTENSEN AGATE COMPANY. Flame swirl. Orange/red swirls in light green. About fifteen flame tips. Superb. One tiny sparkle. Cambridge, OH, circa 1927-1929. 21/32". Mint(-) (9.2). Price: $280. CyberAuction #508, Lot #70.

1175. CHRISTENSEN AGATE COMPANY. Flame swirl. Light blue base. Yellow flame swirls, with some red highlights. A couple of sparkles. Very pretty. Great pattern. Cambridge, OH, circa 1927-1929. 5/8". Mint(-) (9.0). Price: $240. CyberAuction #421, Lot #58.

1176. CHRISTENSEN AGATE COMPANY. Flame swirl. Light blue base. Ruddy red and gray/brown flame swirls. Super pattern. Gorgeous marble. One very tiny chip. Cambridge, OH, circa 1927-1929. 5/8". Near Mint(+) (8.9). Price: $210. CyberAuction #462, Lot #54.

1177. CHRISTENSEN AGATE COMPANY. Flame swirl. Yellow base. Light red swirls with white highlights. Nice swirling, some flame tips. Gorgeous. Cambridge, OH, circa 1927-1929. 21/32". Mint (9.9). Price: $200. CyberAuction #436, Lot #57.

1178. CHRISTENSEN AGATE COMPANY. Flame swirl. Very dark transparent red and some translucent brown flames in white. A Bloodie flame?

Gorgeous. Cambridge, OH, circa 1927-1929. 5/8". Mint (9.9). Price: $200. CyberAuction #459, Lot #58.

1179. CHRISTENSEN AGATE COMPANY. Flame swirl. Light and dark red swirls in orange base. Rare coloring. About a half dozen flame tips. Gorgeous marble. Cambridge, OH, circa 1927-1929. 5/8". Mint (9.8). Price: $200. CyberAuction #467, Lot #57.

1180. CHRISTENSEN AGATE COMPANY. Flame swirl. Opaque white base. Semi-opaque black swirls. Some nice flame tips. Nice pattern. Beautiful marble. Cambridge, OH, circa 1927-1929. 11/16". Mint (9.7). Price: $190. CyberAuction #505, Lot #74.

1181. CHRISTENSEN AGATE COMPANY. Flame swirl. Superb flame swirl. Opaque white with orange and gray flames. About ten flame tips. One tiny sparkle. Unusual color. Cambridge, OH, circa 1927-1929. 21/32". Mint(-) (9.2). Price: $150. CyberAuction #495, Lot #59.

1182. CHRISTENSEN AGATE COMPANY. Flame swirl. Orange flames in white. Super pattern with numerous narrow flames. Some cold roll spots. Cambridge, OH, circa 1927-1929. 11/16". Mint (9.7). Price: $150. CyberAuction #499, Lot #44.

1183. CHRISTENSEN AGATE COMPANY. Flame swirl. Superb flame swirl. Opaque white with orange and gray flames. About ten flame tips. One tiny sparkle. Unusual color. Cambridge, OH, circa 1927-1929. 21/32". Mint(-) (9.2). Price: $150. CyberAuction #506, Lot #48.

1184. CHRISTENSEN AGATE COMPANY. Flame swirl. Red flame swirls on light blue. Some flame tips, but not well defined. Has a melted piece of glass on it. Cambridge, OH, circa 1927-1929. 21/32". Mint (9.6). Price: $100. CyberAuction #438, Lot #50.

1185. CHRISTENSEN AGATE COMPANY. Flame swirl. Light blue base with light red and gray swirls. Several flame tips. A couple of very tiny sparkles. Cambridge, OH, circa 1927-1929. 5/8". Mint(-) (9.0). Price: $100. CyberAuction #485, Lot #1.

1186. CHRISTENSEN AGATE COMPANY. Flame swirl. Red swirls in yellow. Some nice flame tips. Cambridge, OH, circa 1927-1935. 11/16". Mint (9.6). Price: $95. CyberAuction #453, Lot #58.

1187. CHRISTENSEN AGATE COMPANY. Flame swirl. Red flame swirls on light blue. Some flame tips, but not well defined. Has a melted piece of glass on it. Cambridge, OH, circa 1927-1929. 21/32". Mint (9.6). Price: $90. CyberAuction #456, Lot #60.

1188. CHRISTENSEN AGATE COMPANY. Flame swirl. Yellow and gray flame swirls on light blue. Nice pattern. Cambridge, OH, circa 1927-1929. 19/32". Mint (9.7). Price: $90. CyberAuction #479, Lot #50.

1189. CHRISTENSEN AGATE COMPANY. Flame swirl. Orange flames in white. Super pattern with numerous narrow flames. Some cold roll spots. Cambridge, OH, circa 1927-1929. 11/16". Mint (9.7). Price: $85. CyberAuction #479, Lot #57.

1190. CHRISTENSEN AGATE COMPANY. Flame swirl. Red swirls in yellow. Some nice flame tips. Cambridge, OH, circa 1927-1935. 11/16". Mint (9.6). Price: $80. CyberAuction #435, Lot #60.

1191. CHRISTENSEN AGATE COMPANY. Flame swirl. White base with orange flame swirls. Outstanding pattern and a superb example. Cambridge, OH, circa 1927-1929. 21/32". Mint (9.9). Price: $80. CyberAuction #443, Lot #59.

1192. CHRISTENSEN AGATE COMPANY. Flame swirl. Interesting example. Light blue base. Flame swirls of brown and black. Buffed. Cambridge, OH, circa 1927-1929. 23/32". Price: $55. CyberAuction #359, Lot #40.

1193. CHRISTENSEN AGATE COMPANY. Flame swirl. Nice example. Black flame swirls on white. Some broad flames tips. Some pitting. Cambridge, OH, circa 1927-1929. 11/16". Near Mint(+) (8.7). Price: $46. CyberAuction #332, Lot #50.

1194. CHRISTENSEN AGATE COMPANY. Flame swirl. Orange/red swirls on white. Nice pattern. Some tiny pits. Cambridge, OH, circa 1927-1929. 19/32". Near Mint (8.6). Price: $32. CyberAuction #473, Lot #40.

1195. CHRISTENSEN AGATE COMPANY. Guinea. Amber base. Surface is three-quarters covered with bright splotches, except for one open panel. Gorgeous. Cambridge, OH, circa 1927-1929. 5/8". Mint (9.9). Price: $525. CyberAuction #504, Lot #69.

1196. CHRISTENSEN AGATE COMPANY. Guinea. Transparent blue base. Single seam. Flecks of light blue, green , yellow, orange, lavender and white. Almost completely covered by color. A little bit of melted dirt. Superb. Cambridge, OH, circa 1927-1929. 17/32". Mint (9.8). Price: $500. CyberAuction #373, Lot #57.

1197. CHRISTENSEN AGATE COMPANY. Guinea. Clear base Guinea. Two seam. Lavender, orange, yellow, black, green and blue spots. In great shape. Two tiny melt spots. There is also color inside the marble. A beauty!!!! This is guaranteed authentic! Cambridge, OH, circa 1927-1928. 21/32". Mint (9.6). Price: $485. CyberAuction #385, Lot #57.

1198. CHRISTENSEN AGATE COMPANY. Guinea. Clear base Guinea. Two seam. Lavender, orange, yellow and blue spots. In great shape. A beauty!!!! This is guaranteed authentic! Cambridge, OH, circa 1927-1928. 19/32". Mint (9.8). Price: $465. CyberAuction #377, Lot #51.

1199. CHRISTENSEN AGATE COMPANY. Guinea. Two seam beauty. Transparent clear base. Stretched yellow, orange, light blue, light green, dark purple on it. Some color inside. Gorgeous. Cambridge, OH, circa 1927-1929. 21/32". Mint (9.8). Price: $460. CyberAuction #475, Lot #58.

1200. CHRISTENSEN AGATE COMPANY. Guinea. Cobalt base Guinea. Light blue, orange, lavender, black, yellow and green spots. Two seam. One piece of oven brick. In great shape. A beauty!!!! This is guaranteed authentic! Cambridge, OH, circa 1927-1928. 19/32". Mint (9.7). Price: $450. CyberAuction #453, Lot #60.

1201. CHRISTENSEN AGATE COMPANY. Guinea. Transparent blue base. Double seam. Flecks of light blue, green , yellow, orange, lavender and white. Completely covered by color. One tiny dirt spot. Cambridge, OH, circa 1927-1929. 19/32". Mint (9.7). Price: $440. CyberAuction #381, Lot #56.

1202. CHRISTENSEN AGATE COMPANY. Guinea. Cobalt base Guinea. Light blue, orange, yellow, lavender and green spots. In great shape. A beauty!!!! This is guaranteed authentic! Cambridge, OH, circa 1927-1928. 9/16". Mint (9.8). Price: $420. CyberAuction #417, Lot #60.

1203. CHRISTENSEN AGATE COMPANY. Guinea. Transparent blue base. Single seam. Flecks of light blue, green, yellow, orange, lavender and white. Almost completely covered by color. Cambridge, OH, circa 1927-1929. 9/16". Mint (9.9). Price: $410. CyberAuction #388, Lot #59.

1204. CHRISTENSEN AGATE COMPANY. Guinea. Clear base Guinea. Two seam. Lavender, orange, yellow and blue spots. In great shape. A beauty!!!! This is guaranteed authentic! Cambridge, OH, circa 1927-1928. 19/32". Mint (9.8). Originally sold as Lot #51 in CyberAuction #377, the winning bidder has informed me that he cannot pay for it, so it is being re-offered here. Price: $410. CyberAuction #392, Lot #61.

1205. CHRISTENSEN AGATE COMPANY. Guinea. Cobalt blue base. Two seam. About three-quarters covered by spot soft light green, lavender, bright orange, yellow. Gorgeous. Cambridge, OH, circa 1927-1929. 11/16". Mint (9.7). Price: $410. CyberAuction #491, Lot #54.

1206. CHRISTENSEN AGATE COMPANY. Guinea. Cobalt base Guinea. Light blue, orange, yellow and green spots. In great shape. A beauty!!!! Very odd four seam design, might be two Guineas that ended up fused together. This is guaranteed authentic! Cambridge, OH, circa 1927-1928. 9/16". Mint (9.8). Price: $400. CyberAuction #400, Lot #12.

1207. CHRISTENSEN AGATE COMPANY. Guinea. Cobalt base Guinea. Light blue, orange, lavender, black, yellow and green spots. Two seam. One piece of oven brick. In great shape. A beauty!!!! This is guaranteed authentic! Cambridge, OH, circa 1927-1928. 19/32". Mint (9.7). Price: $400. CyberAuction #414, Lot #60.

1208. CHRISTENSEN AGATE COMPANY. Guinea. Clear base Guinea. Two seam. Lavender, orange, yellow and blue spots. In great shape. A beauty!!!! This is guaranteed authentic! Cambridge, OH, circa 1927-1928. 19/32". Mint (9.8). Price: $310. CyberAuction #440, Lot #37.

1209. CHRISTENSEN AGATE COMPANY. Guinea. Transparent blue base. Single seam. Flecks of light blue, green, yellow, orange, lavender and white. Almost completely covered by color. Cambridge, OH, circa 1927-1929. 9/16". Mint (9.9). Price: $310. CyberAuction #440, Lot #59.

1210. CHRISTENSEN AGATE COMPANY. Guinea. Two seam. Transparent clear base. Covered by mostly green with some light blue, orange, lavender and yellow. Cambridge, OH, circa 1927-1929. 9/16". Mint (9.6). Price: $310. CyberAuction #502, Lot #74.

1211. CHRISTENSEN AGATE COMPANY. Guinea. Transparent clear base. Overall splotches of yellow, green, orange, light blue, black. Open panel on one side. Very tiny subsurface moon on the open panel. Cambridge, OH, circa 1927-1929. 5/8". Near Mint(+) (8.9). Price: $285. CyberAuction #424, Lot #60.

1212. CHRISTENSEN AGATE COMPANY. Guinea. One-half a Guinea. Amber base Guinea. Gorgeous piece for jewelry. Cambridge, OH, circa 1927-1929. 5/8". Mint. Price: $31. CyberAuction #448, Lot #20.

1213. CHRISTENSEN AGATE COMPANY. Guinea. One-half a Guinea. Amber base Guinea. Gorgeous piece for jewelry. Cambridge, OH, circa 1927-1929. 23/32". Mint. Price: $19. CyberAuction #455, Lot #8.

1214. CHRISTENSEN AGATE COMPANY. Guinea. One-half a Guinea. Amber base Guinea. Gorgeous piece for jewelry. Cambridge, OH, circa 1927-1929. 5/8". Mint. Price: $17. CyberAuction #457, Lot #7.

1215. CHRISTENSEN AGATE COMPANY. Guinea/Cobra. Transparent clear base. Two seams. Completely covered by yellow, lavender, light blue, orange. One tiny clear spot and you can see the interior is filled with color. Cambridge, OH, circa 1927-1929. 21/32". Mint (9.7). Price: $430. CyberAuction #501, Lot #74.

1216. CHRISTENSEN AGATE COMPANY. Hand gathered. Exceptional and extremely rare marble. This is a hand gathered swirl of electric yellow and transparent cobalt blue. Nice "9", good tail, nice seam. Unbelievable. Has one tiny spot on it that may be a flat spot or may be a very tiny flake. Extremely rare marble. Cambridge, OH, circa 1927. 9/16". Mint(-) (9.0). Price: $460. CyberAuction #483, Lot #55.

1217. CHRISTENSEN AGATE COMPANY. Hand gathered. Yellow with red swirl. Hand gathered. Poor "9", trailing tail. Some tiny pits and rough spots. Cambridge, OH, circa 1927-1929. 11/16". Near Mint (8.6). Price: $80. CyberAuction #342, Lot #58.

1218. CHRISTENSEN AGATE COMPANY. Hand gathered. Very hard to find hand gathered swirl. Semi-opaque white base with faint swirls of light pink. Nice "9" at the top, cut-off line at bottom. Early Christensen Agate. Some bits of melted dirt. Cambridge, OH, circa 1927. 5/8". Mint (9.5). Price: $80. CyberAuction #508, Lot #59.

1219. CHRISTENSEN AGATE COMPANY. Pastel. Salmon pastel swirl. Single seam. Two shades of salmon. Rare. One tiny air hole. Cambridge, OH, circa 1927-1929. 11/16". Mint (9.6). From the same group as CyberAuction #500, Lot 37. Price: $110. CyberAuction #504, Lot #3.

1220. CHRISTENSEN AGATE COMPANY. Pastel. Pastel blue double-seam marble. Very light blue base with some slightly dark blue bands. Gorgeous. Very hard to find. Cambridge, OH, circa 1927-1935. 5/8". Mint (9.8). Price: $75. CyberAuction #498, Lot #66.

1221. CHRISTENSEN AGATE COMPANY. Pastel. Salmon pastel swirl. Single seam. Two shades of salmon. Rare. Cambridge, OH, circa 1927-1929. 9/16". Mint (9.9). Price: $75. CyberAuction #500, Lot #37.

1222. CHRISTENSEN AGATE COMPANY. Slag. Electric yellow slag. Two-seam. Transparent electric yellow base. White swirls. Cambridge, OH, circa 1927-1929. 5/8". Mint (9.9). Price: $140. CyberAuction #433, Lot #53.

1223. CHRISTENSEN AGATE COMPANY. Slag. Electric yellow slag. Two-seam. Transparent electric yellow base. White swirls. Cambridge, OH, circa 1927-1929. 5/8". Mint (9.9). Price: $75. CyberAuction #433, Lot #31.

1224. CHRISTENSEN AGATE COMPANY. Slag. Two seam slag. Transparent electric yellow, with white. Nice, hard to find. Cambridge, OH, circa 1927-1929. 5/8". Mint (9.9). Price: $55. CyberAuction #377, Lot #49.

1225. CHRISTENSEN AGATE COMPANY. Slag. Single seam, diaper fold. Bright aqua slag. Gorgeous. Cambridge, OH, circa 1927-1929. 9/16". Mint (9.9). Price: $55. CyberAuction #508, Lot #63.

1226. CHRISTENSEN AGATE COMPANY. Slag. Red slag. Two seam. Great color. In super shape. Cambridge, OH, circa 1927-1929. 5/8". Mint (9.9). Price: $44. CyberAuction #400, Lot #29.

1227. CHRISTENSEN AGATE COMPANY. Slag. Fluorescent yellow/green slag. Peewee. Two seam. Very hard to find. Cambridge, OH, circa 1927-1929. 1/2". Mint (9.9). Price: $40. CyberAuction #333, Lot #32.

1228. CHRISTENSEN AGATE COMPANY. Slag. Orange slag. Peewee. Two seam. Very hard to find. Cambridge, OH, circa 1927-1929. 1/2". Mint (9.9). Price: $38. CyberAuction #338, Lot #23.

1229. CHRISTENSEN AGATE COMPANY. Slag. Clear slag. Two seam. Super white swirls in transparent clear. Hard to find marble. Cambridge, OH, circa 1927-1929. 19/32". Mint (9.9). Price: $36. CyberAuction #435, Lot #14.

1230. CHRISTENSEN AGATE COMPANY. Slag. Yellow slag. Two seam. Gorgeous pale yellow with white swirling. Superb. Cambridge, OH, circa 1927-1929. 5/8". Mint (9.9). Price: $36. CyberAuction #436, Lot #46.

1231. CHRISTENSEN AGATE COMPANY. Slag. Aqua slag. Two seams. Gorgeous. Cambridge, OH, circa 1927-1929. 21/32". Mint (9.9). Price: $35. CyberAuction #360, Lot #42.

1232. CHRISTENSEN AGATE COMPANY. Slag. Very pale amber slag with loads of white. Two-seam example. Gorgeous marble. Cambridge, OH, circa 1927-1929. 5/8". Mint (9.9). Price: $35. CyberAuction #396, Lot #26.

1233. CHRISTENSEN AGATE COMPANY. Slag. Brown slag Two seam. Beauty. Cambridge, OH, circa 1927-1929. 23/32". Mint (9.9). Price: $34. CyberAuction #333, Lot #44.

1234. CHRISTENSEN AGATE COMPANY. Slag. Very nice bright yellow slag. Two seam. One tiny flake. Cambridge, OH, circa 1927-1929. 19/32". Near Mint(+) (8.9). Price: $31. CyberAuction #438, Lot #42.

1235. CHRISTENSEN AGATE COMPANY. Slag. Electric yellow slag. Electric yellow translucent base. White swirling. One seam. Two sparkles. Cambridge, OH, circa 1927-1929. 5/8". Near Mint(+) (8.9). Price: $28. CyberAuction #374, Lot #51.

1236. CHRISTENSEN AGATE COMPANY. Slag. Very hard to find single seam diaper fold slag. Red slag. Super cherry color. Cambridge, OH, circa 1927-1929. 19/32". Mint (9.7). Price: $27. CyberAuction #396, Lot #46.

1237. CHRISTENSEN AGATE COMPANY. Slag. Electric yellow slag. Electric yellow translucent base. White swirling. One seam. Two sparkles. Cambridge, OH, circa 1927-1929. 5/8". Near Mint(+) (8.9). Price: $26. CyberAuction #351, Lot #31.

1238. CHRISTENSEN AGATE COMPANY. Slag. Hard to find orange slag. Two-seam. Translucent orange filled with opaque white. Surface is not wet, but no damage. Cambridge, OH, circa 1927-1929. 21/32". Near Mint(+) (8.9). Price: $23. CyberAuction #355, Lot #10.

1239. CHRISTENSEN AGATE COMPANY. Slag. Purple slag. Two seam. Cambridge, OH, circa 1927-1929. 19/32". Mint (9.5). Price: $22. CyberAuction #470, Lot #41.

1240. CHRISTENSEN AGATE COMPANY. Slag. Very light olive green slag. These are very unusual slags, due to their design. They came out of Cambridge OH with some Guineas. We had a bunch of these in absentee auction about ten years ago from the same consignor. It is my opinion that they are very early hand gathered Christensen Agate slags. They bear the same pattern as hand gathered Christensen Agate swirls. 5/8". Mint (9.9). There are six marbles available, you are bidding on one. Winner has choice of any or all, remainder to under. Price: $21. CyberAuction #417, Lot #11.

1241. CHRISTENSEN AGATE COMPANY. Slag. Brown slag. Two seam. Wispy white swirls in transparent brown. Cambridge, OH, circa 1927-1929. 19/32". Mint (9.9). Price: $20. CyberAuction #435, Lot #20.

1242. CHRISTENSEN AGATE COMPANY. Slag. Red slag. Two seam. Gorgeous red color. Wispy white. Cambridge, OH, circa 1927-1929. 5/8". Mint (9.8). Price: $19. CyberAuction #396, Lot #23.

1243. CHRISTENSEN AGATE COMPANY. Slag. Green slag. Two seam. Bright. Cambridge, OH, circa 1927-1929. 19/32". Mint (9.7). Price: $17. CyberAuction #395, Lot #44.

1244. CHRISTENSEN AGATE COMPANY. Slag. Light amber slag. Loads of white. Two seam. One tiny subsurface moon. Cambridge, OH, circa 1927-1929. 21/32". Near Mint(+) (8.9). Price: $17. CyberAuction #399, Lot #55.

1245. CHRISTENSEN AGATE COMPANY. Slag. Brown slag. These are very unusual slags, due to their design. They came out of Cambridge OH with some Guineas. We had a bunch of these in absentee auction about ten years ago from the same consignor. It is my opinion that they are very early hand gathered Christensen Agate slags. They bear the same pattern as hand gathered Christensen Agate swirls. 5/8". Mint (9.9). There are four marbles available, you are bidding on one. Winner has choice of any or all, remainder to under. Price: $17. CyberAuction #414, Lot #42.

1246. CHRISTENSEN AGATE COMPANY. Slag. Red slag. Single seam. One tiny flake. Cambridge, OH, circa 1927-1929. 19/32". Near Mint(+) (8.9). Price: $17. CyberAuction #449, Lot #61.

1247. CHRISTENSEN AGATE COMPANY. Slag. Two-seam slag. Transparent green base with white. Cambridge, OH, circa 1927-1929. 9/16". Mint (9.9). Price: $15. CyberAuction #365, Lot #57.

1248. CHRISTENSEN AGATE COMPANY. Slag. Two-seam. Brown slag.

Very nice. Some scratching and pinpricks. Cambridge, OH, circa 1927-1929. 5/8". Near Mint(+) (8.9). Price: $15. CyberAuction #436, Lot #31.

1249. CHRISTENSEN AGATE COMPANY. Slag. Green slag. Single seam. Beauty. Cambridge, OH, circa 1927-1929. 19/32". Mint (9.8). Price: $15. CyberAuction #438, Lot #31.

1250. CHRISTENSEN AGATE COMPANY. Slag. Two-seam marble. Bright yellow with opaque white. Very nice. One tiny chip. Cambridge, OH, circa 1927-1929. 5/8". Near Mint(+) (8.7). Price: $14. CyberAuction #376, Lot #43.

1251. CHRISTENSEN AGATE COMPANY. Slag. Very fluorescent light green slag. Two seam design. Small. Has two small subsurface moons. Cambridge, OH, circa 1927-1935. 1/2". Near Mint (8.6). Price: $14. CyberAuction #425, Lot #42.

1252. CHRISTENSEN AGATE COMPANY. Slag. Pale green fluorescent slag. One seam. Loads of white. One tiny flake and a couple of pits. Cambridge, OH, circa 1927-1929. 1/2". Near Mint(+) (8.7). Price: $14. CyberAuction #481, Lot #37.

1253. CHRISTENSEN AGATE COMPANY. Slag. Clear slag. Loads of white. Two seam. Two tiny flakes. Cambridge, OH, circa 1927-1929. 21/32". Near Mint (8.6). Price: $13. CyberAuction #399, Lot #49.

1254. CHRISTENSEN AGATE COMPANY. Slag. Very light olive green slag. These are very unusual slags, due to their design. They came out of Cambridge OH about ten years ago from the same consignor. It is my opinion that they are very early hand gathered Christensen Agate slags. They bear the same pattern as hand gathered Christensen Agate swirls. Annealing fractures. 5/8". Mint(-) (9.1). Price: $13. CyberAuction #455, Lot #51.

1255. CHRISTENSEN AGATE COMPANY. Slag. Very light olive green slag. These are very unusual slags, due to their design. They came out of Cambridge OH about ten years ago from the same consignor. It is my opinion that they are very early hand gathered Christensen Agate slags. They bear the same pattern as hand gathered Christensen Agate swirls. 5/8". Mint (9.9). Price: $13. CyberAuction #460, Lot #33.

1256. CHRISTENSEN AGATE COMPANY. Slag. Single seam orange slag. Almost all white. Hard to find. One melt spot on it. Cambridge, OH, circa 1927-1929. 9/16". Mint(-) (9.0). Price: $12. CyberAuction #455, Lot #1.

1257. CHRISTENSEN AGATE COMPANY. Slag. Brown slag. Two seam. Very nice marble. One sparkle. Cambridge, OH, circa 1927-1929. 5/8". Near Mint(+) (8.9). Price: $12. CyberAuction #483, Lot #2.

1258. CHRISTENSEN AGATE COMPANY. Slag. Clear slag. Two seam. Tiny subsurface moon. Cambridge, OH, circa 1927-1929. 19/32". Near Mint(+) (8.9). Price: $12. CyberAuction #507, Lot #44.

1259. CHRISTENSEN AGATE COMPANY. Slag. Purple slag. Two seam. Cambridge, OH, circa 1927-1929. 19/32". Mint (9.5). Price: $11. CyberAuction #395, Lot #45.

1260. CHRISTENSEN AGATE COMPANY. Slag. Very light olive green slag. These are very unusual slags, due to their design. They came out of Cambridge OH with some Guineas. We had a bunch of these in absentee auction about ten years ago from the same consignor. It is my opinion that they are very early hand gathered Christensen Agate slags. Annealing fractures. 5/8". Mint(-) (9.2). Price: $11. CyberAuction #457, Lot #18.

1261. CHRISTENSEN AGATE COMPANY. Slag. Red slag. Two seam. Loads of white. Cambridge, OH, circa 1927-1929. 9/16". Mint (9.9). Price: $10. CyberAuction #467, Lot #24.

1262. CHRISTENSEN AGATE COMPANY. Slag. Blue slag. Two seam. Nice. One pit. Cambridge, OH, circa 1927-1929. 19/32". Mint(-) (9.0). Price: $10. CyberAuction #470, Lot #4.

1263. CHRISTENSEN AGATE COMPANY. Slag. Blue slag. Two seam. Nice. One pit. Cambridge, OH, circa 1927-1929. 19/32". Mint(-) (9.0). Price: $9. CyberAuction #395, Lot #43.

1264. CHRISTENSEN AGATE COMPANY. Slag. Red slag. One seam. Some tiny chips. Cambridge, OH, circa 1927-1929. 9/16". Near Mint(-) (8.0). Price: $8. CyberAuction #481, Lot #5.

1265. CHRISTENSEN AGATE COMPANY. Slag. Brown slag. Single seam. One pit. Cambridge, OH, circa 1927-1929. 19/32". Mint(-) (9.0). Price: $7. CyberAuction #395, Lot #46.

1266. CHRISTENSEN AGATE COMPANY. Slag. Red slag. Single seam. One tiny flake. Cambridge, OH, circa 1927-1929. 19/32". Near Mint(+) (8.9). Price: $6. CyberAuction #395, Lot #47.

1267. CHRISTENSEN AGATE COMPANY. Slag. Bright green slag. Transparent bright green with white swirls. Two-seam. Several very tiny flakes. Cambridge, OH, circa 1927-1929. 19/32". Near Mint (8.6). Price: $6. CyberAuction #436, Lot #52.

1268. CHRISTENSEN AGATE COMPANY. Slag. Amber brown slag. Two seam. Very nice. One tiny subsurface moon. Cambridge, OH, circa 1927-1935. 5/8". Near Mint(+) (8.9). Price: $5. CyberAuction #400, Lot #13.

1269. CHRISTENSEN AGATE COMPANY. Slag. Blue slag. Two seam. Loads of white. One pit and one tiny subsurface moon. Cambridge, OH, circa 1927-1929. 5/8". Near Mint(+) (8.8). Price: $5. CyberAuction #420, Lot #54.

1270. CHRISTENSEN AGATE COMPANY. Slag. Blue slag. Single seam. Several tiny flakes. Cambridge, OH, circa 1927-1929. 19/32". Near Mint(-) (8.2). Price: $5. CyberAuction #435, Lot #8.

1271. CHRISTENSEN AGATE COMPANY. Slag. Aqua slag. Two seam. Very pretty. One sparkle. Cambridge, OH, circa 1927-1929. 5/8". Near Mint(+) (8.9). Price: $4. CyberAuction #428, Lot #9.

1272. CHRISTENSEN AGATE COMPANY. Slag. Aqua slag. Two seam. Some tiny chips. Cambridge, OH, circa 1927-1929. 19/32". Near Mint (8.4). Price: $2. CyberAuction #405, Lot #53.

1273. CHRISTENSEN AGATE COMPANY. Striped opaque. Stunning three-color striped opaque. Light blue base. Two seam. Loads of bands and swirls of electric orange and burnt oxblood brown on the surface. One of the finest examples of this type that I have ever seen. Stunning. Cambridge, OH, circa 1927-1929. 19/32". Mint (9.9). Price: $410. CyberAuction #400, Lot #55.

1274. CHRISTENSEN AGATE COMPANY. Striped opaque. Single seam, diaper fold design. Stunning colors. Bright light and dark blue base. Bands of electric orange on it. Pristine. Stunning. Cambridge, OH, circa 1927-1929. 9/16". Mint (9.9). Price: $210. CyberAuction #366, Lot #57.

1275. CHRISTENSEN AGATE COMPANY. Striped opaque. Lace type striped opaque. Transparent dark purple on white. Two seam. In exceptionally good shape. Super marble. Cambridge, OH, circa 1927-1929. 23/32". Mint (9.9). Price: $175. CyberAuction #396, Lot #59.

1276. CHRISTENSEN AGATE COMPANY. Striped opaque. Rare coloring. Two seam. Bright yellow base. Wispy electric red bands on both sides. Cambridge, OH, circa 1927-1929. 19/32". Mint (9.9). Price: $175. CyberAuction #503, Lot #74.

1277. CHRISTENSEN AGATE COMPANY. Striped opaque. Exceptional marble. Single seam. Light blue base. Bands of electric yellow on it. The yellow is semi-opaque, it has a slightly green hue to it, from the blue. Outstanding. Cambridge, OH, circa 1927-1929. 9/16". Mint (9.8). Price: $165. CyberAuction #504, Lot #58.

1278. CHRISTENSEN AGATE COMPANY. Striped opaque. Opaque white base. About half covered with bands and blankets of opaque electric orange. Simply, an outstanding example. Stunning marble. Single seam. Cambridge, OH, circa 1927-1929. 5/8". Mint (9.8). Price: $150. CyberAuction #348, Lot #53.

1279. CHRISTENSEN AGATE COMPANY. Striped opaque. Bright electric orange bands on light blue. Single seam. Stunning. Cambridge, OH, circa 1927-1929. 9/16". Mint (9.8). Price: $130. CyberAuction #500, Lot #51.

1280. CHRISTENSEN AGATE COMPANY. Striped opaque. Similar to an American Agate. Semi-opaque bright white base. Bands of electric red on it. Single seam. One tiny sparkle. Cambridge, OH, circa 1927-1929. 5/8". Mint(-) (9.2). Price: $130. CyberAuction #504, Lot #67.

1281. CHRISTENSEN AGATE COMPANY. Striped opaque. Gorgeous marble. Opaque white base. Bright electric orange bands. Two-seam marble. Some tiny annealing fractures on the marble. Stunning. Cambridge, OH, circa 1927-1929. 5/8". Mint(-) (9.2). Price: $120. CyberAuction #400, Lot #21.

1282. CHRISTENSEN AGATE COMPANY. Striped opaque. Two seam marble. Base is light blue. Strands and loops of the brown oxblood striping. Very nice. One melt pit, has some brown in it. Beauty. Cambridge, OH, circa 1927-1929. 11/16". Mint (9.6). Price: $110. CyberAuction #399, Lot #59.

1283. CHRISTENSEN AGATE COMPANY. Striped opaque. Rare striped opaque. Light blue base. Thin ribbons of oxblood on it. This is often misidentified as the M.F. Christensen Persion Oxblood. One tiny pinprick. Cambridge, OH, circa 1927-1929. 5/8". Mint (9.5). Price: $100. CyberAuction #467, Lot #50.

1284. CHRISTENSEN AGATE COMPANY. Striped opaque. Opaque electric orange on light green. Stunning marble!!!! Two seam. One melted air hole. Cambridge, OH, circa 1927-1929. 5/8". Mint (9.7). Price: $95. CyberAuction #498, Lot #51.

1285. CHRISTENSEN AGATE COMPANY. Striped opaque. Gorgeous marble. Opaque white base. Bright electric orange bands. Two-seam marble. Some tiny annealing fractures on the marble. Stunning. Cambridge, OH, circa 1927-1929. 5/8". Mint(-) (9.2). Price: $80. CyberAuction #437, Lot #60.

1286. CHRISTENSEN AGATE COMPANY. Striped opaque. Single seam. Blue base. Lots of bands of electric orange. Super looking marble. One tiny air hole. Cambridge, OH, circa 1927-1929. 5/8". Mint (9.5). Price: $80. CyberAuction #467, Lot #59.

1287. CHRISTENSEN AGATE COMPANY. Striped opaque. Black base. Electric yellow/green bands and laces on it. Two-seam. Cambridge, OH, circa 1927-1935. 21/32". Mint (9.8). Price: $70. CyberAuction #448, Lot #52.

1288. CHRISTENSEN AGATE COMPANY. Striped opaque. Loads of electric yellow swirled on opaque black. Gorgeous marble. Probably hand gathered. Poor turkey head. Single seam. One air hole. Superb, bright color. Cambridge, OH, circa 1927-1929. 19/32". Mint(-) (9.2). Price: $70. CyberAuction #498, Lot #17.

1289. CHRISTENSEN AGATE COMPANY. Striped opaque. Blue base with electric orange bands. Single seam. Nice colors. Tiny sparkle. Clarksburg, WV, circa 1927-1929. 9/16". Mint(-) (9.0). Price: $70. CyberAuction #502, Lot #65.

1290. CHRISTENSEN AGATE COMPANY. Striped opaque. Black base. Electric yellow/green bands and laces on it. Two-seam. Cambridge, OH, circa 1927-1935. 21/32". Mint (9.8). Price: $59. CyberAuction #474, Lot #7.

1291. CHRISTENSEN AGATE COMPANY. Striped opaque. Very rare coloring. Opaque salmon peach base with thin translucent orange swirls. Two seam. Several tiny chips. Rare colors. Cambridge, OH, circa 1927-1929. 17/32". Near Mint (8.5). Price: $55. CyberAuction #405, Lot #55.

1292. CHRISTENSEN AGATE COMPANY. Striped opaque. Gorgeous marble. Opaque white base. Bright electric orange bands. Two-seam marble. Some tiny annealing fractures on the marble. Stunning. Cambridge, OH, circa 1927-1929. 5/8". Mint(-) (9.2). Price: $55. CyberAuction #456, Lot #58.

1293. CHRISTENSEN AGATE COMPANY. Striped opaque. Two seam example. Electric orange bands and stripes on opaque white. A couple of tiny pinpricks. Outstanding coloring. Cambridge, OH, circa 1927-1929. 5/8". Mint(-) (9.0). Price: $50. CyberAuction #441, Lot #58.

1294. CHRISTENSEN AGATE COMPANY. Striped opaque. Electric yellow bands on black. Two seam. Cambridge, OH, circa 1927-1929. 9/16". Mint (9.9). Price: $44. CyberAuction #475, Lot #50.

1295. CHRISTENSEN AGATE COMPANY. Striped opaque. Light blue base with striping of gray and black. One tiny moon. Super looking. Cambridge, OH, circa 1927-1929. 5/8". Near Mint(+) (8.8). Price: $42. CyberAuction #333, Lot #51.

1296. CHRISTENSEN AGATE COMPANY. Striped opaque. Dark purple banding on opaque white. Two seam. Cambridge, OH, circa 1927-1929. 9/16". Mint (9.9). Price: $42. CyberAuction #498, Lot #56.

1297. CHRISTENSEN AGATE COMPANY. Striped opaque. Two seam. Opaque black base. Wispy bands of electric green. Cambridge, OH, circa 1927-1929. 19/32". Mint (9.6). Price: $37. CyberAuction #435, Lot #43.

1298. CHRISTENSEN AGATE COMPANY. Striped opaque. Opaque black base with striped dark green on one side. Two seam. A couple of air holes and some wear. Cambridge, OH, circa 1927-1929. 19/32". Near Mint(+) (8.9). Price: $31. CyberAuction #336, Lot #16.

1299. CHRISTENSEN AGATE COMPANY. Striped opaque. Opaque black base. Orange bands. Single seam. Cambridge, OH, circa 1927-1929. 9/16". Mint (9.9). Price: $31. CyberAuction #501, Lot #24.

1300. CHRISTENSEN AGATE COMPANY. Striped opaque. Opaque black base. Electric yellow lace swirls and loops on the surface. Two pits. Cambridge, OH, circa 1927-1929. 9/16". Near Mint(+) (8.9). Price: $26. CyberAuction #347, Lot #42.

1301. CHRISTENSEN AGATE COMPANY. Striped opaque. Opaque black base. Two seam. Loopings of electric orange on one side. One chip, some pitting. Cambridge, OH, circa 1927-1929. 5/8". Near Mint(-) (8.0). Price: $17. CyberAuction #343, Lot #13.

1302. CHRISTENSEN AGATE COMPANY. Striped transparent. Rare coloring and pattern. Transparent amber base. Bright baby blue bands in a lace pattern on one side. Two seam. Stunning. One melt pit. Cambridge, OH, circa 1927-1929. 19/32". Mint (9.5). Price: $210. CyberAuction #373, Lot #54.

1303. CHRISTENSEN AGATE COMPANY. Striped transparent. Superb and rare marble. Transparent dark green base. Two seam. One side is completely covered by electric yellow. Other side has some electric yellow bands in a lace pattern. Stunning. Rare size. Cambridge, OH, circa 1927-1929. 1/2". Mint (9.9). Price: $160. CyberAuction #400, Lot #40.

1304. CHRISTENSEN AGATE COMPANY. Striped transparent. Electric yellow striped transparent. Two-seam. Opaque white bands on one side. Cambridge, OH, circa 1927-1929. 19/32". Mint (9.9). Price: $110. CyberAuction #438, Lot #46.

1305. CHRISTENSEN AGATE COMPANY. Striped transparent. Rare marble, but not Mint. Transparent green base. Double seam diaper fold design. Some opaque white bands in the marble. Surface is covered with loads of very electric orange bands and strands. Pretty. One small are of roughness and tiny flakes. Cambridge, OH, circa 1927-1929. 5/8". Near Mint (8.6). Price: $100. CyberAuction #340, Lot #60.

1306. CHRISTENSEN AGATE COMPANY. Striped transparent. Transparent fluorescent yellow base. Two seam. One side has lace bands of semi-opaque white on it. Rare. Cambridge, OH, circa 1927-1929. 19/32". Mint (9.7). Price: $90. CyberAuction #373, Lot #14.

1307. CHRISTENSEN AGATE COMPANY. Striped transparent. Superb. Electric transparent green base. Bands and strands of white covering about half the marble. Two-seam. Superb. Cambridge, OH, circa 1927-1929. 19/32". Mint (9.9). Price: $80. CyberAuction #381, Lot #9.

1308. CHRISTENSEN AGATE COMPANY. Striped transparent. Very unusual coloring. Transparent very dark olive green base. Small lace band of light opaque blue. Cambridge, OH, circa 1927-1929. 19/32". Mint (9.6). Price: $80. CyberAuction #505, Lot #63.

1309. CHRISTENSEN AGATE COMPANY. Striped transparent. Two seam. Bright transparent green. Three-quarters covered by white, with some white inside. Cambridge, OH, circa 1927-1929. 19/32". Mint (9.9). Price: $32. CyberAuction #486, Lot #18.

1310. CHRISTENSEN AGATE COMPANY. Striped transparent. Transparent green base. Two seam. White blanketing on one side. Some wispy white inside. Sparkling. Cambridge, OH, circa 1927-1935. 19/32". Near Mint(+) (8.9). Price: $22. CyberAuction #342, Lot #30.

1311. CHRISTENSEN AGATE COMPANY. Striped transparent. Two seam. Bright transparent green. Three-quarters covered by white, with some white inside. Cambridge, OH, circa 1927-1929. 19/32". Mint (9.9). Price: $22. CyberAuction #469, Lot #53.

1312. CHRISTENSEN AGATE COMPANY. Swirl. One of the most amazing Christensen Agate swirls I've ever seen. I have to call it a "brain swirl" for lack of a better term. Red and brown, swirled in black. Looks like a brain. Exceptional marble. In great shape. Cambridge, OH, circa 1927-1929. 23/32". Mint (9.8). Price: $950. CyberAuction #500, Lot #48.

1313. CHRISTENSEN AGATE COMPANY. Swirl. Very hard to find four-color swirl. Wow!!! White base. Wide swirls of green, gray and red/brown. Stunning marble. Cambridge, OH, circa 1927-1929. 11/16". Mint (9.9). Price: $460. CyberAuction #381, Lot #60.

1314. CHRISTENSEN AGATE COMPANY. Swirl. Stunning three-color swirl. Yellow, orange and red. Gorgeous. Cambridge, OH, circa 1927-1929. 5/8". Mint (9.9). Price: $310. CyberAuction #369, Lot #51.

1315. CHRISTENSEN AGATE COMPANY. Swirl. Superior three color swirl. Predominately black, with light blue and yellow swirls. Gorgeous. Cambridge, OH, circa 1927-1929. 5/8". Mint (9.9). Price: $270. CyberAuction #396, Lot #55.

1316. CHRISTENSEN AGATE COMPANY. Swirl. Four-color swirl. Outstand-

ing example. Opaque white base. Wide swirls of yellow and red, with some thin brown mixed in the red. Superb. A couple of tiny sparkles. Cambridge, OH, circa 1927-1929. 11/16". Mint(-) (9.2). Price: $185. CyberAuction #504, Lot #62.

1317. CHRISTENSEN AGATE COMPANY. Swirl. Nice shooter. Ruddy red and yellow swirls in black. Only a couple of wide flame tips. One tiny flake. Cambridge, OH, circa 1927-1929. 3/4". Near Mint(+) (8.8). Price: $185. CyberAuction #508, Lot #10.

1318. CHRISTENSEN AGATE COMPANY. Swirl. Very unusual swirl. Gray swirls in black. Early Christensen Agate, possibly hand gathered. Slightly misshapen. Cambridge, OH, circa 1927-1929. 5/8". Mint (9.8). Price: $150. CyberAuction #399, Lot #51.

1319. CHRISTENSEN AGATE COMPANY. Swirl. Super looking swirl. Red and brown/gray swirls on light blue. Super pattern. Cambridge, OH, circa 1927-1929. 5/8". Mint (9.9). Price: $130. CyberAuction #479, Lot #42.

1320. CHRISTENSEN AGATE COMPANY. Swirl. Purple base with yellow swirls. Superb. Cambridge, OH, circa 1927-1929. 5/8". Mint (9.9). Price: $110. CyberAuction #363, Lot #31.

1321. CHRISTENSEN AGATE COMPANY. Swirl. Three color swirl. Opaque white base. Salmon pink and yellow swirls. Slightly out of round. Beauty. Some tiny sparkles. Clarksburg, WV, circa 1927-1929. 11/16". Mint(-) (9.0). Price: $110. CyberAuction #406, Lot #39.

1322. CHRISTENSEN AGATE COMPANY. Swirl. Hard to find coloring. Light green base. Swirls of dark brown and light brown. Very nice marble. Cambridge, OH, circa 1927-1929. 5/8". Mint (9.8). Price: $110. CyberAuction #478, Lot #44.

1323. CHRISTENSEN AGATE COMPANY. Swirl. Very unusual three color swirl. Opaque white base with some gray in it. Wide swirl of black, edged by salmon. Very unusual. Cambridge, OH, circa 1927-1929. 11/16". Mint (9.7). Price: $100. CyberAuction #339, Lot #53.

1324. CHRISTENSEN AGATE COMPANY. Swirl. Interesting swirl of salmons and pinks in white. Almost no white. Beauty. Cambridge, OH, circa 1927-1929. 21/32". Mint (9.9). Price: $100. CyberAuction #358, Lot #60.

1325. CHRISTENSEN AGATE COMPANY. Swirl. Red swirls in yellow. Gorgeous marble!!! Cambridge, OH, circa 1927-1929. 19/32". Mint (9.8). Price: $100. CyberAuction #376, Lot #55.

1326. CHRISTENSEN AGATE COMPANY. Swirl. Three color. Brown and black/gray swirls on blue. Very nice. Cambridge, OH, circa 1927-1929. 5/8". Mint (9.9). Price: $100. CyberAuction #381, Lot #31.

1327. CHRISTENSEN AGATE COMPANY. Swirl. Light blue base. Yellow and gray swirls. Nice pattern. Cambridge, OH, circa 1927-1929. 5/8". Mint (9.9). Price: $95. CyberAuction #503, Lot #52.

1328. CHRISTENSEN AGATE COMPANY. Swirl. Three color swirl. Green base. Orange/brown and black/gray swirls. One tiny air hole. Great pattern. Super marble. Cambridge, OH, circa 1927-1929. 21/32". Mint (9.5). Price: $80. CyberAuction #391, Lot #60.

1329. CHRISTENSEN AGATE COMPANY. Swirl. Two color swirl. Yellow swirls in various shades of gray. Cambridge, OH, circa 1927-1929. 5/8". Mint (9.8). Price: $80. CyberAuction #455, Lot #41.

1330. CHRISTENSEN AGATE COMPANY. Swirl. Super swirl. Yellow swirls on light blue. Bright colors. Super pattern with some flaming. Cambridge, OH, circa 1927-1929. 21/32". Mint (9.8). Price: $75. CyberAuction #332, Lot #45.

1331. CHRISTENSEN AGATE COMPANY. Swirl. Orange and black swirl. Gorgeous. Cambridge, OH, circa 1927-1935. 21/32". Mint (9.9). Price: $75. CyberAuction #396, Lot #51.

1332. CHRISTENSEN AGATE COMPANY. Swirl. Hard to find coloring. Light green base. Swirls of dark brown and light brown. Very nice marble. Cambridge, OH, circa 1927-1929. 5/8". Mint (9.8). Price: $75. CyberAuction #450, Lot #19.

1333. CHRISTENSEN AGATE COMPANY. Swirl. These are being referred to as "Graybacks" by some collectors. They recently surfaced from a plant site dig and were probably experimental. Two-seam opaque swirl in various shades of gray. Nice turkey head. Cambridge, OH, circa 1927-1929. 5/8". Mint (9.9). Price: $75. CyberAuction #467, Lot #53.

1334. CHRISTENSEN AGATE COMPANY. Swirl. Three color swirl. Red edged by brown/gray on light blue. Stunning. Cambridge, OH, circa 1927-1929. 5/8". Mint (9.9). Price: $70. CyberAuction #357, Lot #24.

1335. CHRISTENSEN AGATE COMPANY. Swirl. Light blue base. Red/brown, brown and gray swirls. Little blue showing. Nice patterns. Cambridge, OH, circa 192-1929. 21/32". Mint (9.7). Price: $70. CyberAuction #503, Lot #63.

1336. CHRISTENSEN AGATE COMPANY. Swirl. Light blue base with yellow swirls. Some green blending. This is a beauty!!! Cambridge, OH, circa 1927-1929. 21/32". Mint (9.8). Price: $65. CyberAuction #345, Lot #24.

1337. CHRISTENSEN AGATE COMPANY. Swirl. Bright yellow, light green. Gorgeous. Small turkey head in the green. Cambridge, OH, circa 1927-1929. 5/8". Mint (9.8). Price: $65. CyberAuction #373, Lot #34.

1338. CHRISTENSEN AGATE COMPANY. Swirl. Yellow and some gray swirls in light blue. Nice patterns. Cambridge, OH, circa 1927-1929. 19/32". Mint (9.8). Price: $65. CyberAuction #471, Lot #21.

1339. CHRISTENSEN AGATE COMPANY. Swirl. Three-color swirl. Light blue base. Ruddy red and gray swirls. Little blue showing. Great patterns. Cambridge, OH, circa 1927-1929. 5/8". Mint (9.8). Price: $65. CyberAuction #489, Lot #52.

1340. CHRISTENSEN AGATE COMPANY. Swirl. Green swirls on yellow. Gorgeous. Cambridge, OH, circa 1927-1929. 19/32". Mint (9.9). Price: $65. CyberAuction #507, Lot #41.

1341. CHRISTENSEN AGATE COMPANY. Swirl. Gray/red on light blue. Nice pattern. Beauty. Cambridge, OH, circa 1927-1929. 11/16". Mint (9.9). Price: $61. CyberAuction #410, Lot #18.

1342. CHRISTENSEN AGATE COMPANY. Swirl. Light green and brown/gray swirls on yellow. Gorgeous. Cambridge, OH, circa 1927-1929. 5/8". Mint (9.7). Price: $60. CyberAuction #377, Lot #31.

1343. CHRISTENSEN AGATE COMPANY. Swirl. Nice salmon swirls on white. Very interesting swirling. Not a flame or turkey pattern, but that style. Two pits. Cambridge, OH, circa 1927-1935. 5/8". Mint (-) (9.0). Price: $60. CyberAuction #391, Lot #55.

1344. CHRISTENSEN AGATE COMPANY. Swirl. Black and white swirl. Very nice. In great shape. Cambridge, OH, circa 1927-1929. 11/16". Mint (9.9). Price: $60. CyberAuction #400, Lot #10.

1345. CHRISTENSEN AGATE COMPANY. Swirl. Opaque white base. Small black and brown swirls. Odd coloring. A couple of tiny chips. Cambridge, OH, circa 1927-1929. 23/32". Near Mint (8.5). Price: $60. CyberAuction #463, Lot #4.

1346. CHRISTENSEN AGATE COMPANY. Swirl. Mustard yellow swirls on black. Cambridge, OH, circa 1927-1935. 21/32". Mint (9.9). Price: $55. CyberAuction #347, Lot #54.

1347. CHRISTENSEN AGATE COMPANY. Swirl. Single seam. Baby blue base with black swirls. Rare coloring. Some pits. Cambridge, OH, circa 1927-1929. 5/8". Near Mint (8.6). Price: $55. CyberAuction #350, Lot #21.

1348. CHRISTENSEN AGATE COMPANY. Swirl. Purple base with yellow swirls. Two tiny pits and a tiny sparkle. Very nice. Cambridge, OH, circa 1927-1929. 5/8". Near Mint(+) (8.9). Price: $55. CyberAuction #373, Lot #50.

1349. CHRISTENSEN AGATE COMPANY. Swirl. Orange and black swirl. Gorgeous. Cambridge, OH, circa 1927-1935. 19/32". Mint (9.9). Price: $55. CyberAuction #436, Lot #32.

1350. CHRISTENSEN AGATE COMPANY. Swirl. These are being referred to as "Graybacks" by some collectors. They recently surfaced from a plant site dig and were probably experimental. Two-seam opaque swirl in various shades of gray. Cold dimple. Cambridge, OH, circa 1927-1929. 5/8". Mint (9.5). Price: $55. CyberAuction #478, Lot #42.

1351. CHRISTENSEN AGATE COMPANY. Swirl. Light green base. Swirls of red and brown. Very nice shooter. One tiny scratch. Cambridge, OH, circa 1927-1929. 23/32". Mint(-) (9.1). Price: $55. CyberAuction #503, Lot #36.

1352. CHRISTENSEN AGATE COMPANY. Swirl. Three color swirl. Opaque white. Lots of red swirls with gray edging. Cambridge, OH, circa 1927-1929. 21/32". Mint (9.9). Price: $52. CyberAuction #356, Lot #15.

1353. CHRISTENSEN AGATE COMPANY. Swirl. Orange and black swirl. Very nice. Cambridge, OH, circa 1927-1929. 19/32". Mint (9.9). Price: $50. CyberAuction #433, Lot #51.

1354. CHRISTENSEN AGATE COMPANY. Swirl. These are being referred to as "Graybacks" by some collectors. They recently surfaced from a plant site dig and were probably experimental. Two-seam opaque swirl in various shades of gray. Cold dimple. Cambridge, OH, circa 1927-1929. 5/8". Mint (9.5). There are two examples available, you are bidding on one. Winner has choice of one or both, remainder to under. Price: $50. CyberAuction #448, Lot #46.

1355. CHRISTENSEN AGATE COMPANY. Swirl. These are being referred to as "Graybacks" by some collectors. They recently surfaced from a plant site dig and were probably experimental. Single-seam opaque swirl in various shades of gray. Some turkey heads. Cambridge, OH, circa 1927-1929. 21/32". Mint (9.3). Price: $50. CyberAuction #489, Lot #44.

1356. CHRISTENSEN AGATE COMPANY. Swirl. Very nice three-color swirl. Lots of ruddy red and gray on light blue. Nice turkey head in the blue. Beauty. Cambridge, OH, circa 1927-1929. 5/8". Mint. Price: $50. CyberAuction #491, Lot #3.

1357. CHRISTENSEN AGATE COMPANY. Swirl. Light green base. Ruddy red and black swirls. Very nice. Sparkle. Cambridge, OH, circa 1927-1929. 23/32". Mint(-) (9.0). Price: $50. CyberAuction #495, Lot #39.

1358. CHRISTENSEN AGATE COMPANY. Swirl. These are being referred to as "Graybacks" by some collectors. They recently surfaced from a plant site dig and were probably experimental. Single-seam opaque swirl in various shades of gray. Cold dimple, tiny marks. Cambridge, OH, circa 1927-1929. 23/32". Mint(-) (9.0). Price: $50. CyberAuction #502, Lot #49.

1359. CHRISTENSEN AGATE COMPANY. Swirl. These are being referred to as "Graybacks" by some collectors. They recently surfaced from a plant site dig and were probably experimental. Several poor turkey heads. Larger one. Cambridge, OH, circa 1927-1929. 3/4". Mint (9.8). Price: $49. CyberAuction #491, Lot #39.

1360. CHRISTENSEN AGATE COMPANY. Swirl. Yellow swirls in black. Cambridge, OH, circa 1927-1929. 21/32". Mint (9.9). Price: $48. CyberAuction #436, Lot #49.

1361. CHRISTENSEN AGATE COMPANY. Swirl. Three color swirl. Green base with red swirls, edged with some brown. One sparkle. Beauty. Cambridge, OH, circa 1927-1935. 21/32". Mint(-) (9.1). Price: $46. CyberAuction #345, Lot #26.

1362. CHRISTENSEN AGATE COMPANY. Swirl. Yellow and gray swirls in light blue. Cambridge, OH, circa 1927-1929. 19/32". Mint (9.9). Price: $45. CyberAuction #376, Lot #19.

1363. CHRISTENSEN AGATE COMPANY. Swirl. Dark red swirls in blue. Cambridge, OH, circa 1927-1929. 5/8". Mint (9.9). Price: $42. CyberAuction #392, Lot #45.

1364. CHRISTENSEN AGATE COMPANY. Swirl. Beauty. Dark brown swirls in light blue. Cambridge, OH, circa 1927-1929. 5/8". Mint (9.8). Price: $42. CyberAuction #452, Lot #9.

1365. CHRISTENSEN AGATE COMPANY. Swirl. These are being referred to as "Graybacks" by some collectors. They recently surfaced from a plant site dig and were probably experimental. Single-seam opaque swirl in various shades of gray. Cambridge, OH, circa 1927-1929. 5/8". Mint (9.9). Price: $42. CyberAuction #505, Lot #53.

1366. CHRISTENSEN AGATE COMPANY. Swirl. Blue swirls on yellow. Cambridge, OH, circa 1927-1935. 19/32". Mint (9.9). Price: $41. CyberAuction #387, Lot #47.

1367. CHRISTENSEN AGATE COMPANY. Swirl. Yellow and brown swirls in light blue. Cambridge, OH, circa 1927-1929. 19/32". Mint (9.9). Price: $41. CyberAuction #438, Lot #1.

1368. CHRISTENSEN AGATE COMPANY. Swirl. Three-color swirl. Ruddy red and gray swirls on blue. Wide turkey head. Some rust on the marble. Cambridge, OH, circa 1927-1929. 21/32". Mint (9.6). Price: $40. CyberAuction #473, Lot #54.

1369. CHRISTENSEN AGATE COMPANY. Swirl. Two colored swirl. Orange swirls on yellow. Cambridge, OH, circa 1927-1929. 19/32". Mint (9.8). Price: $37. CyberAuction #347, Lot #47.

1370. CHRISTENSEN AGATE COMPANY. Swirl. Green swirls on yellow. Cambridge, OH, circa 1927-1935. 19/32". Mint (9.9). Price: $37. CyberAuction #387, Lot #42.

1371. CHRISTENSEN AGATE COMPANY. Swirl. Transparent black swirls in white. Odd coloring. Cambridge, OH, circa 1927-1929. 19/32". Mint (9.6). Price: $37. CyberAuction #496, Lot #41.

1372. CHRISTENSEN AGATE COMPANY. Swirl. Light blue base. Opaque yellow and transparent brown swirls. Some cold roll lines. Cambridge, OH, circa 1927-1935. 19/32". Mint (9.7). Price: $36. CyberAuction #433, Lot #18.

1373. CHRISTENSEN AGATE COMPANY. Swirl. Three-color swirl. Yellow base. Red and gray swirls. Average turkey head pattern. Cambridge, OH, circa 1927-1929. 9/16". Mint (9.9). Price: $36. CyberAuction #435, Lot #15.

1374. CHRISTENSEN AGATE COMPANY. Swirl. These are being referred to as "Graybacks" by some collectors. They recently surfaced from a plant site dig and were probably experimental. Single-seam opaque swirl in various shades of gray. Cold dimple. Cambridge, OH, circa 1927-1929. 5/8". Mint (9.3). Compare to Lot #41 in this auction, which is the same base with a yellow swirl in it. Price: $36. CyberAuction #455, Lot #56.

1375. CHRISTENSEN AGATE COMPANY. Swirl. Yellow swirl on black. A little larger than you usually find. Nice. One sparkle. Cambridge, OH, 1927-1929. 11/16". Mint(-) (9.0). Price: $34. CyberAuction #336, Lot #8.

1376. CHRISTENSEN AGATE COMPANY. Swirl. Red, edge by gray, swirled on light green. Very nice patterns, with a couple of lazy turkey heads. Slightly out of round. Cambridge, OH, circa 1927-1929. 23/32". Mint (9.7). Price: $34. CyberAuction #491, Lot #47.

1377. CHRISTENSEN AGATE COMPANY. Swirl. Bright yellow swirled in bright yellow. Gorgeous. Cambridge, OH, circa 1927-1929. 19/32". Mint (9.9). Price: $34. CyberAuction #508, Lot #8.

1378. CHRISTENSEN AGATE COMPANY. Swirl. Three-color swirl. Light blue base. Red and gray swirls. Average turkey head pattern. Cambridge, OH, circa 1927-1929. 9/16". Mint (9.9). Price: $33. CyberAuction #433, Lot #12.

1379. CHRISTENSEN AGATE COMPANY. Swirl. Red swirls in black. Cambridge, OH, circa 1927-1929. 5/8". Mint (9.5). Price: $32. CyberAuction #382, Lot #53.

1380. CHRISTENSEN AGATE COMPANY. Swirl. Green and yellow. Stunning. Cambridge, OH, circa 1927-1929. 11/16". Mint (9.9). Price: $32. CyberAuction #500, Lot #23.

1381. CHRISTENSEN AGATE COMPANY. Swirl. Ruddy red and gray swirls on light green. Beauty. Cambridge, OH, circa 1927-1929. 19/32". Mint (9.9). Price: $32. CyberAuction #502, Lot #11.

1382. CHRISTENSEN AGATE COMPANY. Swirl. Red swirls in blue. Very nice. Cambridge, OH, circa 1927-1929. 21/32". Mint (9.7). Price: $31. CyberAuction #382, Lot #27.

1383. CHRISTENSEN AGATE COMPANY. Swirl. Gray/red on light blue. Nice pattern. One sparkle. Beauty. Cambridge, OH, circa 1927-1929. 5/8". Mint(-) (9.2). Price: $31. CyberAuction #410, Lot #44.

1384. CHRISTENSEN AGATE COMPANY. Swirl. Light red and nice yellow swirl. Cambridge, OH, circa 1927-1929. 19/32". Mint (9.8). Price: $31. CyberAuction #452, Lot #18.

1385. CHRISTENSEN AGATE COMPANY. Swirl. Yellow swirl on blue. Some gray edging. Cambridge, OH, circa 1927-1929. 5/8". Mint (9.9). Price: $31. CyberAuction #479, Lot #8.

1386. CHRISTENSEN AGATE COMPANY. Swirl. Interesting three color swirl. Blue base. Light red swirls, edged in black. Very nice pattern. One small subsurface moon. Cambridge, OH, circa 1927-1929. 21/32". Near Mint(+) (8.7). Price: $30. CyberAuction #342, Lot #47.

1387. CHRISTENSEN AGATE COMPANY. Swirl. Red swirls in blue. Beauty. One tiny pit. Cambridge, OH, circa 1927-1929. 19/32". Mint(-) (9.0). Price: $29. CyberAuction #489, Lot #40.

1388. CHRISTENSEN AGATE COMPANY. Swirl. Yellow swirls on blue. Cambridge, OH, circa 1927-1935. 23/32". Mint (9.8). Price: $28. CyberAuction #495, Lot #21.

1389. CHRISTENSEN AGATE COMPANY. Swirl. Yellow swirls on light blue. Cambridge, OH, circa 1927-1929. 5/8". Mint (9.9). Price: $27. CyberAuction #399, Lot #53.

1390. CHRISTENSEN AGATE COMPANY. Swirl. Red and gray swirls on light green. Out of round. Cambridge, OH, circa 1927-1929. 21/32". Mint (9.5). Price: $27. CyberAuction #438, Lot #44.

1391. CHRISTENSEN AGATE COMPANY. Swirl. Red swirls in black. Cambridge, OH, circa 1927-1929. 9/16". Mint (9.7). Price: $27. CyberAuction #463, Lot #1.

1392. CHRISTENSEN AGATE COMPANY. Swirl. Light mustard yellow swirl on black. Cambridge, OH, circa 1927-1929. 5/8". Mint (9.9). Price: $26. CyberAuction #502, Lot #14.

1393. CHRISTENSEN AGATE COMPANY. Swirl. Two color swirl. Red swirls on green. A few tiny pits. Cambridge, OH, circa 1927-1929. 5/8". Mint(-) (9.0). Price: $25. CyberAuction #343, Lot #49.

1394. CHRISTENSEN AGATE COMPANY. Swirl. Yellow swirls in light blue. Cambridge, OH, circa 1927-1929. 5/8". Mint (9.9). Price: $25. CyberAuction #435, Lot #17.

1395. CHRISTENSEN AGATE COMPANY. Swirl. These are being referred to as "Graybacks" by some collectors. They recently surfaced from a plant site dig and were probably experimental. Single-seam opaque swirl in various shades of gray. Cold dimple, tiny chip. Cambridge, OH, circa 1927-1929. 5/8". Near Mint(+) (8.7). Two examples available, you are bidding on one. Winner has choice of either or both, remainder to under. Price: $25. CyberAuction #485, Lot #23.

1396. CHRISTENSEN AGATE COMPANY. Swirl. Light blue base, almost completely covered in ruddy red and brown/gray swirls. One sparkle. Cambridge, OH, circa 1927-1929. 5/8". Mint(-) (9.0). Price: $25. CyberAuction #495, Lot #53.

1397. CHRISTENSEN AGATE COMPANY. Swirl. Yellow swirls on light blue. One pit. Cambridge, OH, circa 1927-1929. 5/8". Mint(-) (9.1). Price: $24. CyberAuction #432, Lot #51.

1398. CHRISTENSEN AGATE COMPANY. Swirl. Red swirl on yellow. Poor turkey head design. A couple of very tiny sparkles. Cambridge, OH, circa 1927-1929. 21/32". Mint(-) (9.0). Price: $23. CyberAuction #429, Lot #5.

1399. CHRISTENSEN AGATE COMPANY. Swirl. Yellow base. Light green and brown swirls. Poor turkey head. Cambridge, OH, circa 1927-1929. 9/16". Mint (9.9). Price: $23. CyberAuction #433, Lot #38.

1400. CHRISTENSEN AGATE COMPANY. Swirl. Three color. Brown and gray swirls on light blue. One small chip. Cambridge, OH, circa 1927-1929. 9/16". Near Mint (8.6). Price: $22. CyberAuction #352, Lot #54.

1401. CHRISTENSEN AGATE COMPANY. Swirl. This is a hand gathered two-color swirl. Bright green and blue. Buffed, some damage remains. Cambridge, OH, circa 1927-1929. 21/32". Buffed. Price: $22. CyberAuction #408, Lot #15.

1402. CHRISTENSEN AGATE COMPANY. Swirl. Green and gray on yellow. Cambridge, OH, circa 1927-1929. 9/16". Mint (9.7). Price: $22. CyberAuction #435, Lot #45.

1403. CHRISTENSEN AGATE COMPANY. Swirl. Transparent black swirls in white. Odd coloring. Cambridge, OH, circa 1927-1929. 19/32". Mint (9.6). Price: $22. CyberAuction #469, Lot #49.

1404. CHRISTENSEN AGATE COMPANY. Swirl. Three color swirl. Orange and gray on white. Poor turkey head. Some tiny pinpricks. Cambridge, OH, circa 1927-1929. 19/32". Mint(-) (9.0). Price: $22. CyberAuction #471, Lot #52.

1405. CHRISTENSEN AGATE COMPANY. Swirl. Two color swirl. Red/brown swirls on light blue. One sparkle. Cambridge, OH, circa 1927-1929. 9/16". Mint(-) (9.0). Price: $21. CyberAuction #336, Lot #37.

1406. CHRISTENSEN AGATE COMPANY. Swirl. Blue base with brown and gray-edged swirl. A sparkle. Cambridge, OH, circa 1927-1929. 11/16". Mint(-) (9.0). Price: $21. CyberAuction #360, Lot #29.

1407. CHRISTENSEN AGATE COMPANY. Swirl. Yellow swirls on black. Some minor rubbing. Cambridge, OH, circa 1927-1929. 19/32". Near Mint(+) (8.9). Price: $21. CyberAuction #371, Lot #44.

1408. CHRISTENSEN AGATE COMPANY. Swirl. Green and yellow swirl. Poor turkey head. Very nice. Cambridge, OH, circa 1927-1929. 9/16". Mint (9.9). Price: $21. CyberAuction #438, Lot #35.

1409. CHRISTENSEN AGATE COMPANY. Swirl. Blue base with ruddy red and brown swirls. Nice marble. Cambridge, OH, circa 1927-1929. 5/8". Mint (9.6). Price: $21. CyberAuction #462, Lot #43.

1410. CHRISTENSEN AGATE COMPANY. Swirl. Red swirls in light green. Some pits. Cambridge, OH, circa 1927-1929. 11/16". Near Mint(+) (8.9). Price: $21. CyberAuction #465, Lot #57.

1411. CHRISTENSEN AGATE COMPANY. Swirl. Red and gray swirls on light blue. Poor turkey head. Cambridge, OH, circa 1927-1929. 9/16". Mint (9.9). There are five examples available, you are bidding on one. Winner has choice of any or all, remainder to under. Price: $20. CyberAuction #438, Lot #21.

1412. CHRISTENSEN AGATE COMPANY. Swirl. Two color swirl. Red swirls on yellow. Very nice. Cambridge, OH, circa 1927-1929. 19/32". Mint (9.7). Price: $19. CyberAuction #334, Lot #57.

1413. CHRISTENSEN AGATE COMPANY. Swirl. Three color swirl. Green base. Red and black/gray swirls. A couple of tiny chips. Nice. Cambridge, OH, circa 1927-1929. 5/8". Near Mint(+) (8.1). Price: $19. CyberAuction #343, Lot #44.

1414. CHRISTENSEN AGATE COMPANY. Swirl. Red swirls on green. Cambridge, OH, circa 1927-1929. 19/32". Mint (9.8). Price: $19. CyberAuction #375, Lot #41.

1415. CHRISTENSEN AGATE COMPANY. Swirl. Yellow swirls on light blue. Nice pattern. A couple of sparkles. Cambridge, OH, circa 1927-1929. 5/8". Mint(-) (9.0). Price: $19. CyberAuction #431, Lot #42.

1416. CHRISTENSEN AGATE COMPANY. Swirl. Three-color swirl. Light blue base. Red and gray swirls. Average turkey head pattern. Cambridge, OH, circa 1927-1929. 9/16". Mint (9.9). Price: $19. CyberAuction #435, Lot #11.

1417. CHRISTENSEN AGATE COMPANY. Swirl. Red and gray swirls on light blue. Poor turkey head. Cambridge, OH, circa 1927-1929. 9/16". Mint (9.9). There are four examples available, you are bidding on one. Winner has choice of any or all, remainder to under. Price: $19. CyberAuction #436, Lot #9.

1418. CHRISTENSEN AGATE COMPANY. Swirl. Orange and yellow swirl. Poor turkey head. Very nice. Cambridge, OH, circa 1927-1929. 9/16". Mint (9.9). Price: $19. CyberAuction #438, Lot #24.

1419. CHRISTENSEN AGATE COMPANY. Swirl. Green and yellow swirl. Poor turkey head. Very nice. Cambridge, OH, circa 1927-1929. 9/16". Mint (9.9). Price: $19. CyberAuction #438, Lot #28.

1420. CHRISTENSEN AGATE COMPANY. Swirl. Light blue base. Yellow swirls. Some smearing to create green. Tiny chip. Cambridge, OH, circa 1927-1929. 5/8". Near Mint(+) (8.8). Price: $19. CyberAuction #461, Lot #15.

1421. CHRISTENSEN AGATE COMPANY. Swirl. Red and yellow blended swirl on blue. Wide colors. One tiny sparkle. Cambridge, OH, circa 1927-1929. 5/8". Mint(-) (9.2). Price: $19. CyberAuction #495, Lot #18.

1422. CHRISTENSEN AGATE COMPANY. Swirl. Red swirls on yellow. Cambridge, OH, circa 1927-1929. 19/32". Mint (9.9). Price: $18. CyberAuction #413, Lot #52.

1423. CHRISTENSEN AGATE COMPANY. Swirl. Very odd marble. Basic yellow swirls with some gray edging on light blue. However, has some very wispy red and very light metallic swirls on it too. Also, the marble was apparently cleaned with some sort of liquid at some point. There are a large number of very, very tiny subsurface moons where the liquid steeped under the surface of them and colored them dark. Unusual. Cambridge, OH, circa 1927-1935. 21/32". Mint(-) (9.0). Price: $17. CyberAuction #493, Lot #55.

1424. CHRISTENSEN AGATE COMPANY. Swirl. Ruddy mustard swirls on black. Nice pattern. Cambridge, OH, circa 1927-1929. 19/32". Mint (9.7). Price: $17. CyberAuction #503, Lot #11.

1425. CHRISTENSEN AGATE COMPANY. Swirl. Black and white swirl. One tiny flake. Cambridge, OH, circa 1927-1929. 19/32". Near Mint(+) (8.9). Price: $15. CyberAuction #369, Lot #25.

1426. CHRISTENSEN AGATE COMPANY. Swirl. Two-color swirl. Red swirls on green. Some pits. Cambridge, OH, circa 1927-1929. 11/16". Near Mint(+) (8.7). Price: $15. CyberAuction #377, Lot #19.

1427. CHRISTENSEN AGATE COMPANY. Swirl. This is a hand gathered two-color swirl. Bright green and blue. Buffed, some damage remains. Cambridge, OH, circa 1927-1929. 21/32". Buffed. Price: $15. CyberAuction #391, Lot #45.

1428. CHRISTENSEN AGATE COMPANY. Swirl. Almost a Bloodie, but it has no brown. Transparent red swirls in opaque white. Some surface wear. Cambridge, OH, circa 1927-1929. 19/32". Near Mint(+) (8.9). Price: $15. CyberAuction #473, Lot #47.

1429. CHRISTENSEN AGATE COMPANY. Swirl. Green swirls on yellow. One chip. Cambridge, OH, circa 1927-1929. 5/8". Near Mint(+) (8.7). Price: $15. CyberAuction #477, Lot #48.

1430. CHRISTENSEN AGATE COMPANY. Swirl. Red and gray swirl in yellow. One small flake. Cambridge, OH, circa 1927-1929. 9/16". Near Mint(+) (8.7). Price: $14. CyberAuction #436, Lot #54.

1431. CHRISTENSEN AGATE COMPANY. Swirl. Error marble. Brown/red and green swirl attached to small piece of cullet. About 1" long, 11/16" wide. Cambridge, OH, circa 1927-1929. Price: $14. CyberAuction #448, Lot #22.

1432. CHRISTENSEN AGATE COMPANY. Swirl. Green and some gray swirl on yellow. Very poor turkey head. Cambridge, OH, circa 1927-1929. 19/32". Mint (9.8). Price: $13. CyberAuction #436, Lot #16.

1433. CHRISTENSEN AGATE COMPANY. Swirl. Two color swirl. Light red/orange on yellow. Very nice. Cambridge, OH, circa 1927-1929. 5/8". Mint (9.7). Price: $12. CyberAuction #346, Lot #57.

1434. CHRISTENSEN AGATE COMPANY. Swirl. Orange swirls on cream. Slightly out of round. Some cold rolls. Cambridge, OH, circa 1927-1929. 11/16". Mint(-) (9.1). Price: $11. CyberAuction #452, Lot #20.

1435. CHRISTENSEN AGATE COMPANY. Swirl. Yellow swirls on black. Minor flame pattern. One tiny flake. Cambridge, OH, circa 1927-1929. 19/32". Near Mint(+) (8.7). Price: $11. CyberAuction #477, Lot #50.

1436. CHRISTENSEN AGATE COMPANY. Swirl. Wispy dark orange swirls on light green. One seam. A small flake and some tiny flakes. Cambridge, OH, circa 1927-1929. 23/32". Near Mint(-) (8.0). Price: $10. CyberAuction #355, Lot #22.

1437. CHRISTENSEN AGATE COMPANY. Swirl. Yellow swirls on light blue. Tiny chip, or blown out air hole, and a number of small pits. Large. Cambridge, OH, circa 1927-1929. 3/4". Near Mint(+) (8.2). Price: $10. CyberAuction #485, Lot #5.

1438. CHRISTENSEN AGATE COMPANY. Swirl. Error. Blue and white swirl marble attached to a misshapen piece of cullet. Not formed properly in machine. about 1" x 19/32". Mint(-). Price: $9. CyberAuction #452, Lot #6.

1439. CHRISTENSEN AGATE COMPANY. Swirl. Yellow and gray swirls on light blue. One tiny pit. Cambridge, OH, circa 1927-1935. 19/32". Mint(-) (9.2). Price: $9. CyberAuction #495, Lot #8.

1440. CHRISTENSEN AGATE COMPANY. Swirl. Yellow swirls on black. Some minor rubbing. Cambridge, OH, circa 1927-1929. 19/32". Near Mint(+) (8.9). Price: $8. CyberAuction #457, Lot #16.

1441. CHRISTENSEN AGATE COMPANY. Swirl. Light blue base. Yellow swirls with gray edging. Subsurface moon and small fracture. Cambridge, OH, circa 1927-1929. 5/8". Near Mint (8.5). Price: $5. CyberAuction #350, Lot #54.

1442. CHRISTENSEN AGATE COMPANY. Swirl. Red/orange on green. One small chip. Cambridge, OH, circa 1927-1929. 21/32". Near Mint (8.6). Price: $5. CyberAuction #399, Lot #15.

1443. CHRISTENSEN AGATE COMPANY. Swirl. Red and gray swirls on light blue. Overall pitting. Cambridge, OH, circa 1927-1929. 21/32". Near Mint (8.5). Price: $5. CyberAuction #439, Lot #36.

1444. CHRISTENSEN AGATE COMPANY. Swirl. Brown swirls on light blue. Some pitting. Cambridge, OH, circa 1927-1929. 19/32". Near Mint (8.6). Price: $2. CyberAuction #464, Lot #40.

1445. CHRISTENSEN AGATE COMPANY. Swirl. Half a yellow on light blue swirl. From a recent dig. 5/8". Mint (9.9). Price: $1. CyberAuction #472, Lot #11.

1446. CONTEMPORARY HANDMADE. Andrew Davis. Blizzard end of day onionskin. Transparent clear base. Core is onionskin blue, red and black. Subsurface layer of mica. Signed "a.D." 1-1/2". Mint (9.9). Price: $27. CyberAuction #344, Lot #49.

1447. CONTEMPORARY HANDMADE. Andrew Davis. Sulphide. Standing squirrel. Marble is signed "a. D". 1-15/16". Mint (9.9). Price: $27. CyberAuction #371, Lot #23.

1448. CONTEMPORARY HANDMADE. Andrew Davis. Nice red band clambroth on black. Signed "a.D.". 1-5/8". Mint (9.9). Price: $21. CyberAuction #452, Lot #14.

1449. CONTEMPORARY HANDMADE. Andrew Davis. Blue and red onionskin core. Subsurface layer is controlled air bubbles and mica. Signed "a. D.". Pretty. 1-5/8". Mint (9.9). Price: $13. CyberAuction #450, Lot #10.

1450. CONTEMPORARY HANDMADE. Beetem Design Glassworks. Prototype fillegrana. Transparent clear base. Subsurface red layer. Eight bands of yellow fillegrana strands on dichroic blue. Separated by sets of yellow fillegrana. This was a prototype for the series that Beetem eventually produced. Signed "G Beetem P 99c". 1-5/8". Mint (9.9). Price: $170. CyberAuction #348, Lot #48.

1451. CONTEMPORARY HANDMADE. Beetem Design Glassworks. Early Beetem Globe. Transparent clear base. Opaque blue core. Green dichroic land masses. White clouds. Gorgeous. Signed "G. D. Beetem 1995 c 0113". The 113th globe he produced. 1-7/16". Mint (9.9). Price: $135. CyberAuction #487, Lot #52.

1452. CONTEMPORARY HANDMADE. Beetem Design Glassworks. Globe marble. Opaque blue core. Green/red dichroic landmasses. Gorgeous opaque white clouds above the globe. Clear outer layer. Gorgeous. Signed on the bottom "Geoffrey D. Beetem c99 1097". Stunning. American. 1-7/8". Mint (9.9). Price: $120. CyberAuction #345, Lot #54.

1453. CONTEMPORARY HANDMADE. Beetem Design Glassworks. Gorgeous ribbon core. Transparent clear base. Double twisted translucent cranberry red ribbon, with dichroic on the faces, and lutz edges. Signed "Beetem P 99c". This is a prototype marble, not in production. American, circa 1999. 1-9/16". Mint (9.9). Price: $120. CyberAuction #357, Lot #34.

1454. CONTEMPORARY HANDMADE. Beetem Design Glassworks. Absolutely outstanding marble. Air-twist core. Transparent clear base. Four trapped air bands in the center of the marble. Double twisted. Each band is the same width and length. Excellent effect. Exceptional piece of workmanship. Signed on bottom "Beetem 2000". He doesn't make too many of these. 2-1/8". Mint (9.9). Price: $120. CyberAuction #396, Lot #57.

1455. CONTEMPORARY HANDMADE. Beetem Design Glassworks. Limited edition. Swirl of various colors with dichroic bands. Very nice. Production was limited to 15 pieces. This is number 1. Signed "G Beetem P99 c 1" (Geoffrey Beetem Prototype 1999 copyright number 1). 1-3/8". Mint (9.9). Price: $90. CyberAuction #467, Lot #25.

1456. CONTEMPORARY HANDMADE. Beetem Design Glassworks. Globe marble. Opaque blue core. Green/red dichroic landmasses. Gorgeous opaque white clouds above the globe. Clear outer layer. Gorgeous. Signed on the bottom "Geoffrey D. Beetem c99 1046". Stunning. American. 1-5/8". Mint (9.9). Price: $85. CyberAuction #389, Lot #60.

1457. CONTEMPORARY HANDMADE. Beetem Design Glassworks. Stardust V-lobe swirl. Transparent clear base. Blue ribbon core. Two red and gold dichroic outer bands, in the lobes. Edges by orange and brown bands. Signed "Beetem 99". American, circa 1993-1998. 1-11/16". Mint (9.9). Price: $75. CyberAuction #360, Lot #53.

1458. CONTEMPORARY HANDMADE. Beetem Design Glassworks. Absolutely outstanding marble. Air-twist core. Transparent clear base. Four trapped air bands in the center of the marble. Double twisted. Each band is the same width and length. Excellent effect. Exceptional piece of workmanship. Signed on bottom "Beetem". This one is a little older. He doesn't make too many of these. 1-13/16". Mint (9.9). Price: $75. CyberAuction #503, Lot #60.

1459. CONTEMPORARY HANDMADE. Beetem Design Glassworks. Beetem clambroth. Transparent amethyst core. Subsurface layer of green dichroic with blue strands. Gorgeous. Signed "Beetem". 1-5/8". Mint (9.9). Price: $70. CyberAuction #372, Lot #60.

1460. CONTEMPORARY HANDMADE. Beetem Design Glassworks. Dichroic cranberry ribbon core swirl. Blue edging. Signed "Beetem P 99 c". ("P" signifies Prototype). 1-7/16". Mint (9.9). Price: $70. CyberAuction #501, Lot #45.

1461. CONTEMPORARY HANDMADE. Beetem Design Glassworks. Ribbon core swirl. Pink center, gold lutz, lavender, blue and yellow bands. Signed on bottom "Beetem 99". American, circa 1990-1998. 1-7/16". Mint (9.9). Price: $62. CyberAuction #359, Lot #54.

1462. CONTEMPORARY HANDMADE. Beetem Design Glassworks. Beetem clambroth. Transparent amethyst core. Subsurface layer of alternating green and blue dichroic bands with red and yellow strands. Gorgeous. Signed "Beetem 2000c". 1-7/8". Mint (9.9). Price: $60. CyberAuction #426, Lot #47.

1463. CONTEMPORARY HANDMADE. Beetem Design Glassworks. Single ribbon core. Bands forming rainbow. Nicely twisted. Super marble. Signed on bottom "Beetem 99". American, circa 1990-1998. 1-9/16". Mint (9.9). Price: $55. CyberAuction #332, Lot #44.

1464. CONTEMPORARY HANDMADE. Beetem Design Glassworks. Beetem clambroth. Transparent amethyst core. Subsurface layer of alternating green and blue dichroic bands with red and yellow strands. Gorgeous. Signed "Beetem 2000c". 1-7/8". Mint (9.9). Price: $55. CyberAuction #409, Lot #59.

1465. CONTEMPORARY HANDMADE. Beetem Design Glassworks.

Stardust Clambroth. Alternating blue and green dichroic bands, separated by alternating yellow and orange strands. Large one. Signed "Beetem c 2000". 1-13/16". Mint (9.9). Price: $55. CyberAuction #493, Lot #30.

1466. CONTEMPORARY HANDMADE. Beetem Design Glassworks. Ribbon core swirl. Purple band center, green, aqua and yellow bands. Signed on bottom "Beetem 99". American, circa 1990-1998. 1-7/16". Mint (9.9). Price: $54. CyberAuction #356, Lot #40.

1467. CONTEMPORARY HANDMADE. Beetem Design Glassworks. Ribbon core swirl. Yellow latticinio center, purple lutz, pink, blue and yellow bands. Signed on bottom "Beetem 99". American, circa 1990-1998. 1-9/16". Mint (9.9). Price: $51. CyberAuction #346, Lot #59.

1468. CONTEMPORARY HANDMADE. Beetem Design Glassworks. Stardust V-lobe swirl. Transparent clear base. Baby blue ribbon. Dichroic in the lobes. Outer bands of green and blue. Signed "Beetem 99". American, circa 1993-1998. 1-11/16". Mint (9.9). Price: $50. CyberAuction #333, Lot #49.

1469. CONTEMPORARY HANDMADE. Beetem Design Glassworks. Beetem clambroth. Transparent amethyst core. Subsurface layer of alternating green and blue dichroic bands with orange strands. Gorgeous. Signed "Beetem 2000c". 1-7/8". Mint (9.9). Price: $47. CyberAuction #381, Lot #46.

1470. CONTEMPORARY HANDMADE. Beetem Design Glassworks. Beetem clambroth. Transparent amethyst core. Subsurface layer of red dichroic with green strands. Gorgeous. Signed "Beetem 2000c". 1-5/8". Mint (9.9). Price: $47. CyberAuction #392, Lot #35.

1471. CONTEMPORARY HANDMADE. Beetem Design Glassworks. Beetem clambroth. Transparent amethyst core. Subsurface layer of red dichroic with green strands. Gorgeous. Signed "Beetem 2000c". 1-5/8". Mint (9.9). Price: $47. CyberAuction #446, Lot #51.

1472. CONTEMPORARY HANDMADE. Beetem Design Glassworks. Green aventurine core with blue and orange strands. Outer layer is three sets of blue bands. Signed "Beetem c 2000". 1-9/16". Mint (9.9). Price: $47. CyberAuction #496, Lot #27.

1473. CONTEMPORARY HANDMADE. Beetem Design Glassworks. Stardust V-lobe. Gorgeous green dichroic on baby blue. Signed "Beetem c 2000". 1-9/16". Mint (9.9). Price: $47. CyberAuction #504, Lot #30.

1474. CONTEMPORARY HANDMADE. Beetem Design Glassworks. Stardust V-lobe. Opaque orange ribbon core swirl. Dichroic on the ribbon. Ribbon edges are bands of red, blue and green. Signed "Beetem". Earlier Beetem marble. 1-7/8". Mint (9.9). Price: $47. CyberAuction #508, Lot #36.

1475. CONTEMPORARY HANDMADE. Beetem Design Glassworks. Ribbon core swirl. Gold lutz center, opaque pink and blue bands, and wide purple lutz. Superb. Signed on bottom "Beetem". American, circa 1990-1998. 1-5/16". Mint (9.9). Price: $45. CyberAuction #336, Lot #35.

1476. CONTEMPORARY HANDMADE. Beetem Design Glassworks. Ribbon core swirl. Yellow latticinio center, gold lutz, pink, green and yellow bands. Signed on bottom "Beetem". American, circa 1990-1998. 1-3/8". Mint (9.9). Price: $43. CyberAuction #353, Lot #58.

1477. CONTEMPORARY HANDMADE. Beetem Design Glassworks. Stardust V-lobe. Gorgeous gold and green dichroic. Signed "Beetem". 1-9/16". Mint (9.9). Price: $42. CyberAuction #500, Lot #10.

1478. CONTEMPORARY HANDMADE. Beetem Design Glassworks. Single ribbon core swirl. Superb. Signed "Beetem". 1-9/16". Mint (9.9). Price: $40. CyberAuction #502, Lot #64.

1479. CONTEMPORARY HANDMADE. Beetem Design Glassworks. Single ribbon core. Yellow latticinio core center. Blue, blue lutz, yellow and green bands. Gorgeous. Signed "Beetem". 1-7/8". Mint (9.9). Price: $39. CyberAuction #434, Lot #55.

1480. CONTEMPORARY HANDMADE. Beetem Design Glassworks. Ribbon core swirl. Red center, gold lutz, blue and orange bands. Signed on bottom "Beetem". American, circa 1990-1998. 1-9/16". Mint (9.9). Price: $38. CyberAuction #430, Lot #57.

1481. CONTEMPORARY HANDMADE. Beetem Design Glassworks. Stardust V-lobe. Nice coloring in the dichroic. Strong black, yellow and lavender outer bands. Signed "Beetem". This is an early Beetem, from an extensive old collection. The work is more primitive than more recent, established Beetem pieces. Has one small sparkle on it. 1-9/16". Mint(-) (9.0). Price: $38. CyberAuction #480, Lot #45.

1482. CONTEMPORARY HANDMADE. Beetem Design Glassworks. Stardust V-lobe swirl. Transparent clear base. Yellow ribbon core. Two green dichroic outer bands, in the lobes. Edges by orange and purple bands. Signed "Beetem". American, circa 1993-1998. 1-1/4". Mint (9.9). Price: $37. CyberAuction #376, Lot #49.

1483. CONTEMPORARY HANDMADE. Beetem Design Glassworks. Ribbon core swirl. Red center, gold lutz, blue and orange bands. Signed on bottom "Beetem". American, circa 1990-1998. 1-9/16". Mint (9.9). Price: $37. CyberAuction #399, Lot #60.

1484. CONTEMPORARY HANDMADE. Beetem Design Glassworks. Superb single ribbon swirl. Blue lutz interior. Various bands of blues, whites and browns. Signed "Beetem". 1-13/16". Mint (9.9). Price: $37. CyberAuction #464, Lot #46.

1485. CONTEMPORARY HANDMADE. Beetem Design Glassworks. Ribbon core swirl. Pink on white center, gold lutz, pink and green bands. Signed on bottom "Beetem". 1-3/8". Mint (9.9). Price: $37. CyberAuction #490, Lot #42.

1486. CONTEMPORARY HANDMADE. Beetem Design Glassworks. Ribbon core swirl. Yellow latticinio center, gold lutz, pink, blue and yellow bands. Signed on bottom "Beetem". American, circa 1990-1998. 1-7/16". Mint (9.9). Price: $36. CyberAuction #330, Lot #33.

1487. CONTEMPORARY HANDMADE. Beetem Design Glassworks.

Stardust Clambroth. This is a very early example. Dichroic green/blue with orange strands in it. Signed "Beetem". Very coarse dichroic. Probably early 1990s. 1-9/16". Mint (9.9). Price: $36. CyberAuction #498, Lot #46.

1488. CONTEMPORARY HANDMADE. Beetem Design Glassworks. Single ribbon lutz core swirl. Signed "Beetem". 1-7/16". Mint (9.9). Price: $34. CyberAuction #497, Lot #50.

1489. CONTEMPORARY HANDMADE. Beetem Design Glassworks. Ribbon core swirl. Yellow latticinio center. Outer bands are blue and pink on white. Signed on bottom "Beetem 99". American, circa 1990-1998. 1-5/16". Mint (9.9). Price: $33. CyberAuction #430, Lot #48.

1490. CONTEMPORARY HANDMADE. Beetem Design Glassworks. Stardust V-lobe swirl. Transparent clear base. Blue ribbon core. Two red dichroic outer bands, in the lobes. Edged by pink and green bands. Signed "Beetem 99 c". 1-9/16". Mint (9.9). Price: $32. CyberAuction #366, Lot #41.

1491. CONTEMPORARY HANDMADE. Beetem Design Glassworks. Ribbon core swirl. Pink on white center, gold lutz, pink and green bands. Signed on bottom "Beetem". 1-3/8". Mint (9.9). Price: $32. CyberAuction #384, Lot #58.

1492. CONTEMPORARY HANDMADE. Beetem Design Glassworks. Single ribbon core. Yellow latticinio core center. Blue, blue lutz, yellow and green bands. Gorgeous. Signed "Beetem". 1-7/16". Mint (9.9). Price: $32. CyberAuction #388, Lot #38.

1493. CONTEMPORARY HANDMADE. Beetem Design Glassworks. Stardust V-lobe swirl. Transparent clear base. Blue ribbon core. Two red dichroic outer bands, in the lobes. Edged by pink and green bands. Signed "Beetem 99 c". 1-9/16". Mint (9.9). Price: $32. CyberAuction #458, Lot #56.

1494. CONTEMPORARY HANDMADE. Beetem Design Glassworks. Ribbon core swirl. Yellow latticinio center. Outer bands are blue and pink on white. Signed on bottom "Beetem 99". American, circa 1990-1998. 1-5/16". Mint (9.9). Price: $30. CyberAuction #340, Lot #59.

1495. CONTEMPORARY HANDMADE. Beetem Design Glassworks. Ribbon core swirl. Yellow latticinio center. Outer bands are blue and pink on white. Signed on bottom "Beetem 99". American, circa 1990-1998. 1-5/16". Mint (9.9). Price: $30. CyberAuction #383, Lot #44.

1496. CONTEMPORARY HANDMADE. Beetem Design Glassworks. Ribbon core swirl. Pink on white center, gold lutz, pink and green bands. Signed on bottom "Beetem". 1-3/8". Mint (9.9). Price: $27. CyberAuction #437, Lot #54.

1497. CONTEMPORARY HANDMADE. Beetem Design Glassworks. V-lobe ribbon core. Gorgeous. Pink, green, lavender and lutz. Signed "Beetem 2000 c". 1-9/16". Mint (9.9). Price: $27. CyberAuction #473, Lot #29.

1498. CONTEMPORARY HANDMADE. Beetem Design Glassworks. Ribbon core swirl. Pink on white center, gold lutz, pink and green bands. Signed on bottom "Beetem". 1-3/8". Mint (9.9). Price: $26. CyberAuction #460, Lot #52.

1499. CONTEMPORARY HANDMADE. Beetem Design Glassworks. Gorgeous green aventurine solid core with some colored bands. Outer layer is three sets of blue and black bands. Nice design. Signed "Beetem 2000". 1-7/16". Mint (9.9). Price: $26. CyberAuction #475, Lot #37.

1500. CONTEMPORARY HANDMADE. Beetem Design Glassworks. Single ribbon core swirl. Signed "Beetem". 1-7/16". Mint (9.9). Price: $24. CyberAuction #479, Lot #16.

1501. CONTEMPORARY HANDMADE. Beetem Design Glassworks. Ribbon core swirl. Turquoise ribbon, covered by dichroic. Purple and pink bands. Signed "Beetem 2000 c". 1-1/2". Mint (9.9). Price: $22. CyberAuction #477, Lot #49.

1502. CONTEMPORARY HANDMADE. Beetem Design Glassworks. V-lobe. Light blue ribbon core with green dichroic. Outer bands are orange and green. Has a small subsurface moon. Signed "Beetem". 1-9/16". Near Mint(+) (8.9). Price: $22. CyberAuction #470, Lot #41.

1503. CONTEMPORARY HANDMADE. Bob Hamon. Corkscrew of orange, lutz and light blue in clear. Unsigned. 29/32". Mint (9.9). Price: $10. CyberAuction #408, Lot #20.

1504. CONTEMPORARY HANDMADE. Bob Hamon. Swirl of clear, white, light green, red. Unsigned. 31/32". Mint (9.9). Price: $9. CyberAuction #445, Lot #52.

1505. CONTEMPORARY HANDMADE. Bob Hamon. Swirl of clear, white, light green, red. Unsigned. 31/32". Mint (9.9). Price: $8. CyberAuction #365, Lot #44.

1506. CONTEMPORARY HANDMADE. Bob Hamon. Corkscrew of orange, lutz and light blue in clear. Unsigned. 29/32". Mint (9.9). Price: $8. CyberAuction #366, Lot #17.

1507. CONTEMPORARY HANDMADE. Bob Olsen. Banded opaque. Wide green bands on white. Nice mimic. I cannot find a signature on it, but the consignor states that it was made by Bob Olsen. 25/32". Mint (9.9). Price: $23. CyberAuction #337, Lot #59.

1508. CONTEMPORARY HANDMADE. Bob Olsen. Banded opaque. Wide green bands on white. Nice mimic. I cannot find a signature on it, but the consignor states that it was made by Bob Olsen. 25/32". Mint (9.9). Price: $21. CyberAuction #486, Lot #39.

1509. CONTEMPORARY HANDMADE. Bob Olsen. Clambroth. Multicolor. Nice mimic. I cannot find a signature on it, but the consignor states that it was made by Bob Olsen. 3/4". Mint (9.9). Price: $19. CyberAuction #359, Lot #17.

1510. CONTEMPORARY HANDMADE. Bob Olsen. Banded opaque. Wide green bands on white. Nice mimic. I cannot find a signature on it, but the consignor states that it was made by Bob Olsen. 25/32". Mint (9.9). Price: $17. CyberAuction #344, Lot #39.

1511. CONTEMPORARY HANDMADE. Bob Olsen. Banded opaque. Wide green bands on white. Nice mimic. I cannot find a signature on it, but the consignor states that it was made by Bob Olsen. 25/32". Mint (9.9). Price: $17. CyberAuction #386, Lot #34.

1512. CONTEMPORARY HANDMADE. Bob Olsen. Banded opaque. Wide green bands on white. Nice mimic. I cannot find a signature on it, but the consignor states that it was made by Bob Olsen. 25/32". Mint (9.9). Price: $17. CyberAuction #430, Lot #43.

1513. CONTEMPORARY HANDMADE. Bob Powers. This is a fascinating marble. Transparent blue base. Elongated wire thin air bubbles and tiny seed bubbles. Looks like steel wire running through it. Or the canals of Mars. Signed "BP 99" (the BP is a logo). 31/32". Mint (9.9). Price: $40. CyberAuction #354, Lot #10.

1514. CONTEMPORARY HANDMADE. Bob Powers. Torchwork. Banded lutz. Transparent clear base with four subsurface red bands alternating with four subsurface lutz bands. Signed "BP 99" (BP is a logo). 15/16". Mint (9.9). Price: $25. CyberAuction #352, Lot #47.

1515. CONTEMPORARY HANDMADE. Bob Powers. Dichroic bands in the bottom half of a clear sphere. Signed "BP98" (BP are a logo). 29/32". Mint (9.9). Price: $25. CyberAuction #358, Lot #46.

1516. CONTEMPORARY HANDMADE. Bob Powers. Gorgeous swirl of blues, reds, yellows and clear. Signed "BP 00" (the BP is a logo). 1-1/16". Mint (9.9). Price: $23. CyberAuction #494, Lot #25.

1517. CONTEMPORARY HANDMADE. Bob Powers. Torchwork. Marbre design of white on black. Signed "BP 99" (BP is a logo). 7/8". Mint (9.9). Price: $19. CyberAuction #331, Lot #12.

1518. CONTEMPORARY HANDMADE. Bob Powers. Torchwork. Solid core swirl type of various colors including a wide band of gold lutz. Signed "BP 98" (the BP are an interlocking logo). 1". Mint (9.9). Price: $19. CyberAuction #343, Lot #12.

1519. CONTEMPORARY HANDMADE. Bob Powers. Swirls of red, green, yellow and dichroic, in clear. Signed "BP 98" (BP is a logo). 1". Mint(9.9). Price: $18. CyberAuction #367, Lot #10.

1520. CONTEMPORARY HANDMADE. Bob Powers. Torchwork. Swirl of transparent clear, white, green aventurine and iridescent pearl. Super coloring. Signed "BP 99". The "BP" are an interlocking logo. 29/32". Mint (9.9). Price: $17. CyberAuction #386, Lot #7.

1521. CONTEMPORARY HANDMADE. Bob Powers. Swirls of red, green, yellow and dichroic, in clear. Signed "BP 98" (BP is a logo). 1". Mint(9.9). Price: $17. CyberAuction #458, Lot #42.

1522. CONTEMPORARY HANDMADE. Bob Powers. Nice clambroth. Black on orange. Signed "BP 00" (the BP is a logo). 31/32". Mint (9.9). Price: $15. CyberAuction #481, Lot #15.

1523. CONTEMPORARY HANDMADE. Bob Powers. Transparent cobalt blue with silver wire drizzled throughout it. Signed "BP 00" (BP is a logo). 31/32". Mint (9.9). Price: $15. CyberAuction #483, Lot #32.

1524. CONTEMPORARY HANDMADE. Bob Powers. Optical illusion whirlpool. Orange and dichroic in clear. Signed "BP 00" (the BP is a logo). 7/8". Mint (9.9). Price: $15. CyberAuction #488, Lot #41.

1525. CONTEMPORARY HANDMADE. Bob Powers. Marbre design of yellow and black. Signed "BP 00" (the BP is a logo). 15/16". Mint (9.9). Price: $15. CyberAuction #495, Lot #14.

1526. CONTEMPORARY HANDMADE. Bob Powers. Torchwork. Swirl of transparent clear, opaque white, green aventurine and iridescent pearl. Super coloring. Signed "BP 99". The "BP" are an interlocking logo. 29/32". Mint (9.9). Price: $14. CyberAuction #340, Lot #5.

1527. CONTEMPORARY HANDMADE. Bob Powers. Nice swirl of bright green and yellow, with large red splotches. Signed "BP 00" (BP is a logo). 1-1/16". Mint (9.9). Price: $14. CyberAuction #482, Lot #4.

1528. CONTEMPORARY HANDMADE. Bob Powers. Torchwork. Swirl of transparent clear, opaque white, green aventurine and iridescent pearl. Super coloring. Signed "BP 99". The "BP" are an interlocking logo. 29/32". Mint (9.9). Price: $12. CyberAuction #453, Lot #7.

1529. CONTEMPORARY HANDMADE. Bob Powers. Swirl of white and lutz in transparent blue. Signed "BP 00" (the BP is a logo). 1-1/16". Mint (9.9). Price: $12. CyberAuction #496, Lot #20.

1530. CONTEMPORARY HANDMADE. Bob Powers. Swirl of root beer and white. Nice. Signed "BP 00" (BP is a logo). 1". Mint (9.9). Price: $12. CyberAuction #497, Lot #47.

1531. CONTEMPORARY HANDMADE. Boyd Miller. Blue on white solid core with lutz bands. Outer layer is white strands. Signed "BAM". 1-5/8". Mint (9.9). Price: $37. CyberAuction #443, Lot #27.

1532. CONTEMPORARY HANDMADE. Boyd Miller. Four panel onionskin lutz. Very nice. Signed "BAM". 1-11/16". Mint (9.9). Price: $28. CyberAuction #453, Lot #31.

1533. CONTEMPORARY HANDMADE. Boyd Miller. Solid core with two outer bands. Signed "BAM". 1-3/4". Mint (9.9). Price: $27. CyberAuction #393, Lot #23.

1534. CONTEMPORARY HANDMADE. Boyd Miller. Four panel onionskin lutz. Very nice. Signed "BAM". 1-11/16". Mint (9.9). Price: $26. CyberAuction #387, Lot #22.

1535. CONTEMPORARY HANDMADE. Boyd Miller. Nice solid core swirl. Signed "BAM". 1-3/4". Mint (9.9). Price: $26. CyberAuction #415, Lot #27.

1536. CONTEMPORARY HANDMADE. Boyd Miller. Four panel onionskin lutz. Very nice. Signed "BAM". 1-11/16". Mint (9.9). Price: $26. CyberAuction #434, Lot #20.

1537. CONTEMPORARY HANDMADE. Boyd Miller. Red bands and lutz bands on black core. Signed "BAM". 1-7/8". Mint (9.9). Price: $25. CyberAuction #472, Lot #23.

1538. CONTEMPORARY HANDMADE. Boyd Miller. Swirl. White core. Two purple bands and two green. Separated by similar colors on white bands. Signed "BAM". 1-5/8". Mint (9.9). Price: $24. CyberAuction #382, Lot #36.

1539. CONTEMPORARY HANDMADE. Boyd Miller. Solid core swirl. Beauty. Signed "BAM". 1-13/16". Mint (9.9). Price: $23. CyberAuction #435, Lot #27.

1540. CONTEMPORARY HANDMADE. Boyd Miller. Solid core swirl with some lutz. Signed on bottom "BAM". 2". Mint (9.9). Price: $22. CyberAuction #384, Lot #23.

1541. CONTEMPORARY HANDMADE. Boyd Miller. Corkscrew of dark red, dark blue, black and lutz. Unsigned, probably Boyd Miller. 25/32". Mint (9.9). Price: $21. CyberAuction #360, Lot #28.

1542. CONTEMPORARY HANDMADE. Boyd Miller. Swirl of white, pink and lutz in transparent aqua. Unsigned, probably Boyd Miller. 1-1/16". Mint (9.9). Price: $19. CyberAuction #360, Lot #44.

1543. CONTEMPORARY HANDMADE. Boyd Miller. Clambroth. Yellow bands on green. Unsigned. 1-9/16". Mint (9.9). Price: $19. CyberAuction #468, Lot #34.

1544. CONTEMPORARY HANDMADE. Boyd Miller. Swirl of white, black, red, blue and yellow. Very nice. Unsigned, probably Boyd Miller. 1". Mint (9.9). Price: $17. CyberAuction #361, Lot #57.

1545. CONTEMPORARY HANDMADE. Boyd Miller. Wild swirl of red, yellow and light blue. Unsigned, probably Boyd Miller. 3/4". Mint (9.9). Price: $15. CyberAuction #361, Lot #52.

1546. CONTEMPORARY HANDMADE. Boyd Miller/Tom Thornburgh. Rare collaboration. The sulphide is a donut hole elephant, with great detail. The sulphide figure was hand carved from a piece of sulphide, not molded. It has black eyes and is sticking out its tongue. The sulphide figure is signed on the bottom "BM" and "TT". Outer glass is clear. 1-7/8". Mint (9.9). Price: $70. CyberAuction #410, Lot #55.

1547. CONTEMPORARY HANDMADE. Boyer Glass. Four panel onionskin. Blue and white. Signed "HB". This is a mid 1980s marble. 1-7/8". Mint (9.9). Price: $160. CyberAuction #356, Lot #31.

1548. CONTEMPORARY HANDMADE. Boyer Glass. Single flower with green leaves. Signed "Boyer". 1-3/8". Mint (9.9). Price: $46. CyberAuction #500, Lot #15.

1549. CONTEMPORARY HANDMADE. Boyer Glass. Opaque black core. Coating of thick lutz. Clear outer layer. Signed "Boyer". 1-3/8". Mint (9.9). Price: $36. CyberAuction #496, Lot #38.

1550. CONTEMPORARY HANDMADE. Boyer Glassworks. Hard to find type. Huge fillegrana. Gorgeous. Probably late 1980s, early 1990s. Signed "Boyer". 2-1/2". Mint (9.9). Price: $100. CyberAuction #392, Lot #49.

1551. CONTEMPORARY HANDMADE. Boyer Glassworks. Onionskin swirl. White core. pink, blue and green skin. Two wide panels of lutz. Left twist. Signed "Boyer". 1-5/8". Mint (9.9). Price: $32. CyberAuction #395, Lot #35.

1552. CONTEMPORARY HANDMADE. Brian Lonsway. Very hard to find maker. Yellow latticinio core swirl. Outer layer is a cage of orange and blue strands. Signed "Lonsway 86". Rare. 2-5/8". Mint (9.9). Price: $285. CyberAuction #385, Lot #35.

1553. CONTEMPORARY HANDMADE. Brookside Glass. Onionskin with mica. Very nice. Signed "JKT 00 BG" (John K. Talmadge). 1-5/8". Mint (9.9). Price: $38. CyberAuction #367, Lot #28.

1554. CONTEMPORARY HANDMADE. Brookside Glass. Mica. Transparent clear core. Subsurface layer of very dark purple with a layer of mica on it. Clear overglaze. Signed "BG 00 JKT" (John K. Talmadge). 1-7/16". Mint (9.9). Price: $37. CyberAuction #378, Lot #58.

1555. CONTEMPORARY HANDMADE. Brookside Glass. Transparent clear base. Pink onionskin core. Subsurface layer of blue bands with some lutz. Signed "BG 00 JKT" (John K. Talmadge). 1-5/8". Mint (9.9). Price: $29. CyberAuction #388, Lot #34.

1556. CONTEMPORARY HANDMADE. Bruce Breslow/Moon Marble Company. Mustard yellow, red and black swirl. Signed "BB 99". 1-3/16". Mint (9.9). Price: $15. CyberAuction #485, Lot #30.

1557. CONTEMPORARY HANDMADE. Bruce Breslow/Moon Marble Company. Yellow, green, black and red swirl. Signed "BB 99". 1-1/16". Mint (9.9). Price: $13. CyberAuction #489, Lot #15.

1558. CONTEMPORARY HANDMADE. Bruce Breslow/Moon Marble Company. Yellow on black clambroth. Signed "BB 99". 1-3/16". Mint (9.9). Price: $11. CyberAuction #492, Lot #33.

1559. CONTEMPORARY HANDMADE. Bruce Breslow/Moon Marble Company. Swirl of red, green and yellow on black. Unsigned. 1-1/16". Mint (9.9). Price: $10. CyberAuction #490, Lot #14.

1560. CONTEMPORARY HANDMADE. California Glass Studios. This is an individual marble from the "Autumn" portion of the Seasons series. The Season series is a set of twelve marbles, three representing each season, in colors evocative of the Southern California Pacific coast. This was a limited edition and there were only 12 sets created. This is marble number 1 from the 11th set. Transparent clear base. Transparent orange core with orange, gold and blue dichroic on it. Signed "CGS 2-3/11-12". I have no idea why there was only one marble consigned, but here it is. 1-13/16". Mint (9.9). Price: $110. CyberAuction #376, Lot #60.

1561. CONTEMPORARY HANDMADE. California Glass Studios. This is an individual marble from the "Autumn" portion of the Seasons series. The Season series is a set of twelve marbles, three representing each season, in colors evocative of the Southern California Pacific coast. This was a limited edition and there were only 12 sets created. This is marble number 3 from the 11th set. Transparent clear base. Transparent aqua core with orange, gold and blue dichroic on it. Signed "CGS 3-3/11-12". 1-13/16". Mint (9.9). Price: $70. CyberAuction #363, Lot #48.

1562. CONTEMPORARY HANDMADE. California Glass Studios. Very interesting Spiral. The ribbon spiral consists of three sections. One is blue

and white, one is baby blue and white, last is aqua and turquoise. Very, very odd. Usually the spiral is just one of the colors. First time I've seen this. Signed "CGS". 1-7/8". Mint (9.9). Price: $65. CyberAuction #422, Lot #58.

1563. CONTEMPORARY HANDMADE. California Glass Studios. Part of one of the Seasons, limited edition series. Spiral. Transparent clear base. Translucent purple spiral with dichroic splotches of red, green, gold and blue. Signed "CGS 99 3-3/5-12". 1-15/16". Mint (9.9). Price: $65. CyberAuction #426, Lot #55.

1564. CONTEMPORARY HANDMADE. California Glass Studios. This is an individual marble from the "Summer" portion of the Seasons series. The Season series is a set of twelve marbles, three representing each season, in colors evocative of the Southern California Pacific coast. This was a limited edition and there were only 12 sets created. This is marble number 2 from the 11th set. Transparent clear base. Transparent lime green core with orange, gold and blue dichroic on it. Signed "CGS 2-3/11-12". I have no idea why there was only one marble consigned, but here it is. 1-13/16". Mint (9.9). Price: $60. CyberAuction #357, Lot #58.

1565. CONTEMPORARY HANDMADE. California Glass Studios. Transparent clear base. Transparent currant purple with green, gold and blue dichroic on it. Consignor says that this is a limited edition, it is similar to the Seasons series they produced. Might have been a prototype for that series. Signed "CGS". 1-13/16". Mint (9.9). Price: $60. CyberAuction #391, Lot #17.

1566. CONTEMPORARY HANDMADE. California Glass Studios. This is an individual marble from the "Summer" portion of the Seasons series. The Season series is a set of twelve marbles, three representing each season, in colors evocative of the Southern California Pacific coast. This was a limited edition and there were only 12 sets created. This is marble number 1 from the 11th set. Transparent clear base. Transparent green core with orange, gold and blue dichroic on it. Signed "CGS 2-3/11-12". I have no idea why there was only one marble consigned, but here it is. 1-13/16". Mint (9.9). Price: $60. CyberAuction #417, Lot #56.

1567. CONTEMPORARY HANDMADE. California Glass Studios. This is an individual marble from Modern Artists series. The Modern Artist series is a set of three marbles, representing modern painters. This was a limited edition and there were only 12 sets created. This is marble number 1 from the 5th set. Transparent clear base. Light blue core with various colored dichroic on it. Signed "CGS '99 M/00 3-3 5-12". 1-13/16". Mint (9.9). Price: $55. CyberAuction #501, Lot #72.

1568. CONTEMPORARY HANDMADE. California Glass Studios. Very interesting Spiral. The ribbon spiral consists of three sections. One is blue and white, one is baby blue and white, last is aqua and turquoise. Very, very odd. Usually the spiral is just one of the colors. First time I've seen this. Signed "CGS". 1-7/8". Mint (9.9). Price: $50. CyberAuction #395, Lot #59.

1569. CONTEMPORARY HANDMADE. California Glass Studios. Part of one of the Seasons, limited edition series. Spiral. Transparent clear base. Translucent purple spiral with dichroic splotches of red, green, gold and blue. Signed "CGS 99 2-3/11-12". 1-15/16". Mint (9.9). Price: $50. CyberAuction #465, Lot #58.

1570. CONTEMPORARY HANDMADE. California Glass Studios. This is an individual marble from Modern Artists series. The Modern Artist series is a set of three marbles, representing modern painters. This was a limited edition and there were only 12 sets created. This is marble number 3 from the 5th set. Transparent clear base. Pink core with various colored dichroic on it. Signed "CGS '99 M/00 3-3 5-12". 1-13/16". Mint (9.9). Price: $48. CyberAuction #500, Lot #30.

1571. CONTEMPORARY HANDMADE. California Glass Studios. Beautiful. Silver Spiral. Iridescent silver bands with mauve, pink and black, in the form a ribbon. Signed "CGS". 1-7/8". Mint (9.9). Price: $47. CyberAuction #385, Lot #38.

1572. CONTEMPORARY HANDMADE. California Glass Studios. Part of one of the Seasons, limited edition series. Spiral. Transparent clear base. Translucent purple spiral with dichroic splotches of red, green, gold and blue. Signed "CGS 99 2-3/5-12". 1-15/16". Mint (9.9). Price: $47. CyberAuction #473, Lot #35.

1573. CONTEMPORARY HANDMADE. California Glass Studios. Part of one of the Seasons, limited edition series. Spiral. Transparent clear base. Translucent purple spiral with dichroic splotches of red, green, gold and blue. Signed "CGS 99 3-3/5-12". 1-15/16". Mint (9.9). Price: $46. CyberAuction #406, Lot #31.

1574. CONTEMPORARY HANDMADE. California Glass Studios. Beautiful. Silver Spiral. Iridescent silver bands with cranberry splotches, in the form a ribbon. Signed "CGS". 1-7/8". Mint (9.9). Price: $45. CyberAuction #494, Lot #44.

1575. CONTEMPORARY HANDMADE. California Glass Studios. Beautiful. Pink Spiral. Iridescent silver/green bands alternating with pink and black, in the form a ribbon. Signed "CGS". 1-7/8". Mint (9.9). Price: $38. CyberAuction #432, Lot #58.

1576. CONTEMPORARY HANDMADE. California Glass Studios. Beautiful. Silver Spiral. Iridescent silver bands with light blue, in the form a ribbon. Signed "CGS". 1-7/8". Mint (9.9). Price: $36. CyberAuction #443, Lot #47.

1577. CONTEMPORARY HANDMADE. California Glass Studios. Paperweight. Transparent clear. Swirled core of transparent dark purple covered by effervescent air bubbles of various sizes. Signed on bottom "CGS". Outstanding. American, circa 1998-1999. 3-3/8" x 1-7/8". Mint (9.9). Price: $28. CyberAuction #337, Lot #36.

1578. CONTEMPORARY HANDMADE. Chatham Glass. Three-layer swirl. Signed "Chatham Glass 00". 1-5/8". Mint (9.9). Price: $32. CyberAuction #491, Lot #11.

1579. CONTEMPORARY HANDMADE. Chatham Glass. Three layer. Ribbon is green on one side, blue on other. Middle layer is two sets of white strands, following the ribbon faces. Outer layer is four bands. Signed "Chatham Glass '00". 1-5/8". Mint (9.9). Price: $32. CyberAuction #498, Lot #57.

1580. CONTEMPORARY HANDMADE. Chatham Glass. Single ribbon core swirl. Exceptional symmetry. Great craftsmanship. Signed "Chatham Glass 00". 1-9/16". Mint (9.9). Price: $30. CyberAuction #487, Lot #9.

1581. CONTEMPORARY HANDMADE. Chris Robinson. Indian with lutz. Very nice. Unsigned (none of his are signed). He has stopped producing marbles. 15/16". Mint (9.9). Price: $80. CyberAuction #467, Lot #13.

1582. CONTEMPORARY HANDMADE. Chris Robinson. Indian. Opaque black base. Two panels on the surface covering about ninety percent. Grays, blue, orange, red. Unsigned. 1-1/16". Mint (9.9). Price: $25. CyberAuction #330, Lot #5.

1583. CONTEMPORARY HANDMADE. Chuck Pound. Very nice bright yellow swirls on very dark blue. Beauty. Signed "CP 00". 1-3/8". Mint (9.9). Price: $42. CyberAuction #471, Lot #28.

1584. CONTEMPORARY HANDMADE. Chuck Pound. Red and yellow corkscrew on black. Super looking. Signed "CP 00". 1-5/16". Mint (9.9). Price: $42. CyberAuction #472, Lot #12.

1585. CONTEMPORARY HANDMADE. Chuck Pound. Red, blue and white swirl on black. Signed "CP 00". 1-3/16". Mint (9.9). Price: $32. CyberAuction #473, Lot #21.

1586. CONTEMPORARY HANDMADE. Chuck Pound. Beautiful swirl of blues and whites in black. Signed "CP 00". 1-3/16". Mint (9.9). Price: $32. CyberAuction #475, Lot #24.

1587. CONTEMPORARY HANDMADE. Crystal Myths. Paperweight style. Transparent clear base. Pink speckled ground. Large green frog with black eyes. Bottom is ground pontil. Unsigned. It is Lewis and Jennifer Wilson, or Jennifer Wilson only. 1-1/2". Mint (9.9). Price: $55. CyberAuction #493, Lot #51.

1588. CONTEMPORARY HANDMADE. Crystal Myths. Paperweight style. Orange snake and blue flower on a lutz and colored pebble ground. Gorgeous. Signed "LJW 2000" (Lewis and Jennifer Wilson). 1-9/16". Mint (9.9). Price: $50. CyberAuction #489, Lot #57.

1589. CONTEMPORARY HANDMADE. Crystal Myths. Paperweight style. Multicolor bumblebee with lutz wings floating above a lutz ground. Beauty. Signed "LJW 97" (Lewis and Jennifer Wilson). 1-9/16". Mint (9.9). Price: $50. CyberAuction #495, Lot #23.

1590. CONTEMPORARY HANDMADE. Crystal Myths. Paperweight style marble. Green frog on jasper ground. Signed "LJW 2000" (Lewis and Jennifer Wilson). 1-1/2". Mint (9.9). Price: $47. CyberAuction #508, Lot #48.

1591. CONTEMPORARY HANDMADE. Crystal Myths. Dichroic "cave" on a paperweight jasper ground. Interesting contemporary design. Signed "LJW 2000" (Lewis and Jennifer Wilson). 1-13/16". Mint (9.9). Price: $42. CyberAuction #498, Lot #29.

1592. CONTEMPORARY HANDMADE. Crystal Myths. Paperweight style. Blue flower with a lutz rock, on a blue carpet ground. Handmade by Lewis and Jennifer Wilson (father and daughter). 1-9/16". Mint (9.9). Price: $40. CyberAuction #414, Lot #13.

1593. CONTEMPORARY HANDMADE. Cuneo Furnace/Steve Maslach. Heart paperweight. White ribbon core flattened and shaped into a heart. Purple and white in clear. Very nice. Perfect for your sweetheart. About 2" x 1-1/2". Mint (9.9). Price: $32. CyberAuction #436, Lot #28.

1594. CONTEMPORARY HANDMADE. Cuneo Furnace/Steve Maslach. Heart paperweight. Purple and white ribbon core with green and lavender latticinio. Flattened and shaped into a heart. Red and white in clear. Very nice. Perfect for your sweetheart. About 2-3/8" x 1-3/4". Mint (9.9). Price: $32. CyberAuction #451, Lot #32.

1595. CONTEMPORARY HANDMADE. Cuneo Furnace/Steve Maslach. Heart paperweight. White latticinio core flattened and shaped into a heart. Red and white in clear. Very nice. Perfect for your sweetheart. About 2-3/8" x 1-3/4". Mint (9.9). Price: $30. CyberAuction #378, Lot #49.

1596. CONTEMPORARY HANDMADE. Cuneo Furnace/Steve Maslach. Heart paperweight. Orange ribbon core with cage of purple bands. Flattened and shaped into a heart. Red and white in clear. Very nice. Perfect for your sweetheart. About 2-3/8" x 1-3/4". Mint (9.9). Price: $29. CyberAuction #422, Lot #50.

1597. CONTEMPORARY HANDMADE. Cuneo Furnace/Steve Maslach. Heart paperweight. Red and white ribbon core. Flattened and shaped into a heart. Very nice. Perfect for your sweetheart. About 2-3/8" x 1-3/4". Mint (9.9). Price: $29. CyberAuction #455, Lot #32.

1598. CONTEMPORARY HANDMADE. Cuneo Furnace/Steve Maslach. Heart paperweight. White ribbon core flattened and shaped into a heart. Purple and white in clear. Very nice. Perfect for your sweetheart. About 2" x 1-1/2". Mint (9.9). Price: $28. CyberAuction #477, Lot #24.

1599. CONTEMPORARY HANDMADE. Cuneo Furnace/Steve Maslach. Heart paperweight. White latticinio core flattened and shaped into a heart. Purple and white in clear. Very nice. Perfect for your sweetheart. About 2-3/8" x 1-3/4". Mint (9.9). Price: $27. CyberAuction #391, Lot #56.

1600. CONTEMPORARY HANDMADE. Cuneo Furnace/Steve Maslach. Heart paperweight. Orange ribbon core with cage of purple bands. Flattened and shaped into a heart. Red and white in clear. Very nice. Perfect for your sweetheart. About 2-3/8" x 1-3/4". Mint (9.9). Price: $27. CyberAuction #393, Lot #28.

1601. CONTEMPORARY HANDMADE. Cuneo Furnace/Steve Maslach. Heart paperweight. Purple and aventurine green ribbon core with white latticinio. Flattened and shaped into a heart. Red and white in clear. Very nice. Perfect for your sweetheart. About 2-3/8" x 1-3/4". Price: $27. CyberAuction #427, Lot #24.

1602. CONTEMPORARY HANDMADE. Cuneo Furnace/Steve Maslach.

1603. CONTEMPORARY HANDMADE. Cuneo Furnace/Steve Maslach. Heart paperweight. White latticinio core flattened and shaped into a heart. Purple and white in clear. Very nice. Perfect for your sweetheart. About 2-3/8" x 1-3/4". Mint (9.9). Price: $27. CyberAuction #447, Lot #48.

1604. CONTEMPORARY HANDMADE. Cuneo Furnace/Steve Maslach. Heart paperweight. White latticinio core flattened and shaped into a heart. Purple and white in clear. Very nice. Perfect for your sweetheart. About 2-3/8" x 1-3/4". Mint (9.9). Price: $27. CyberAuction #482, Lot #23.

1605. CONTEMPORARY HANDMADE. Cuneo Furnace/Steve Maslach. Heart paperweight. White latticinio core flattened and shaped into a heart. Purple and white in clear. Very nice. Perfect for your sweetheart. About 2-3/8" x 1-3/4". Mint (9.9). Price: $27. CyberAuction #499, Lot #21.

1605. CONTEMPORARY HANDMADE. Cuneo Furnace/Steve Maslach. Heart paperweight. Pink and aventurine green ribbon core with white latticinio. Flattened and shaped into a heart. Red and white in clear. Very nice. Perfect for your sweetheart. About 2-3/8" x 1-3/4". Mint (9.9). Price: $25. CyberAuction #469, Lot #35.

1606. CONTEMPORARY HANDMADE. Cuneo Furnace/Steve Maslach. Gorgeous ribbon core swirl. Handmade by Cuneo Furnace. 1-3/8". Mint (9.9). Price: $20. CyberAuction #409, Lot #41.

1607. CONTEMPORARY HANDMADE. Cuneo Furnace/Steve Maslach. Beautiful blue latticinio core swirl. Unsigned. 29/32". Mint (9.9). Price: $15. CyberAuction #448, Lot #26.

1608. CONTEMPORARY HANDMADE. Cuneo Furnace/Steve Maslach. Ribbon core swirl with cage outer layer. Outstanding. Unsigned. 1-1/16". Mint (9.9). Price: $12. CyberAuction #459, Lot #18.

1609. CONTEMPORARY HANDMADE. Cuneo Furnace/Steve Maslach. Ribbon core swirl with cage outer layer. Outstanding. Unsigned. 1-1/16". Mint (9.9). Price: $12. CyberAuction #496, Lot #2.

1610. CONTEMPORARY HANDMADE. Dale Danowski. Large onionskin. Signed on the bottom "DD" (logo). One of the largest Danowski's I've seen. 1-9/16". Mint (9.9). Price: $33. CyberAuction #360, Lot #33.

1611. CONTEMPORARY HANDMADE. Dale Danowski. Fascinating marble. Transparent brown gooseberry base. Two bands covering about sixty percent of the marble. Each is alternating yellow and lutz bands. Signed with "D" logo. 25/32". Mint (9.9). Price: $23. CyberAuction #353, Lot #23.

1612. CONTEMPORARY HANDMADE. Dale Danowski. Torchwork. Transparent aqua base with six white latticinio filigree bands in the surface. 27/32". Mint (9.9). Price: $22. CyberAuction #345, Lot #20.

1613. CONTEMPORARY HANDMADE. Dale Danowski. Torchwork. Indian mimic. Yellow and blue strands on black. Super mimic. Signed "DD" (logo). 25/32". Mint (9.9). Price: $22. CyberAuction #359, Lot #38.

1614. CONTEMPORARY HANDMADE. Dale Danowski. Nice banded lutz. Opaque brown base. Six yellow strands, two lutz bands. Signed "DD" (logo). 3/4". Mint (9.9). Price: $19. CyberAuction #360, Lot #12.

1615. CONTEMPORARY HANDMADE. Dale Danowski. Torchwork. Clambroth. Red base with yellow strands. Signed on bottom with the D logo. 25/32". Mint (9.9). Price: $17. CyberAuction #350, Lot #15.

1616. CONTEMPORARY HANDMADE. Dale Danowski. Transparent green glass. Swirls of lutz and white in it. Signed "DD" (logo). 25/32". Mint (9.9). Price: $17. CyberAuction #367, Lot #58.

1617. CONTEMPORARY HANDMADE. Dale Danowski. Torchwork. Panelled clambroth. Blue and red band panels on white. Signed on bottom with the D logo. 25/32". Mint (9.9). Price: $17. CyberAuction #404, Lot #17.

1618. CONTEMPORARY HANDMADE. Dale Danowski. Torchwork. Panelled clambroth. Blue and red band panels on white. Signed on bottom with the D logo. 25/32". Mint (9.9). Price: $15. CyberAuction #347, Lot #14.

1619. CONTEMPORARY HANDMADE. Dale Danowski. Transparent aqua base. Subsurface layer of light lutz. Surface layer of white strand cage. Signed "DD" (logo). 27/32". Mint (9.9). Price: $15. CyberAuction #358, Lot #56.

1620. CONTEMPORARY HANDMADE. Dale Danowski. Nice banded lutz. Opaque brown base. Two bands of yellow and lutz strands. Signed "DD" (logo). 27/32". Mint (9.9). Price: $15. CyberAuction #364, Lot #22.

1621. CONTEMPORARY HANDMADE. Dale Danowski. Nice banded lutz. Opaque brown base. Four sets of three yellow strands alternating with four lutz bands. Signed "DD" (logo). 13/16". Mint (9.9). Price: $15. CyberAuction #365, Lot #8.

1622. CONTEMPORARY HANDMADE. Dale Danowski. Torchwork. Transparent clear base with six black and white twisted bands on the surface. Signed with the D logo. 27/32". Mint (9.9). Price: $14. CyberAuction #346, Lot #44.

1623. CONTEMPORARY HANDMADE. Dale Danowski. Blue gooseberry with lutz. Very pretty. Handmade by Dale Danowski. Signed on a double-sided D. American, circa 1997-1998. 13/16". Mint (9.9). Price: $13. CyberAuction #440, Lot #9.

1624. CONTEMPORARY HANDMADE. David Grant Maul. Nice mushroom solid core. Signed "D G Maul 1993 U.S.A.". 1-5/8". Mint (9.9). Price: $40. CyberAuction #505, Lot #30.

1625. CONTEMPORARY HANDMADE. Davis Handmade Marbles. This is made by the Jim Davis from Indiana who no longer produces marbles, not the Jim Davis of West Virginia who is still currently producing. Jim Davis (IN) marbles are very hard to find. Red, white and clear slag. Very nice. Signed "JD 86". 1-13/16". Mint (9.9). Price: $70. CyberAuction #434, Lot #29.

1626. CONTEMPORARY HANDMADE. Davis Handmade Marbles. This is made by the Jim Davis from Indiana who no longer produces marbles, not the Jim Davis of West Virginia who is still currently producing. Jim Davis (IN) marbles are very hard to find. Red, white and clear slag. Very nice. Signed "JD 86". 1-13/16". Mint (9.9). Price: $47. CyberAuction #396, Lot #40.

1627. CONTEMPORARY HANDMADE. Davis Handmade Marbles. White core with a blue band and a red band on it. Outer layer is a blizzard of mica. Signed "Jim Davis". 1-1/2". Mint (9.9). Price: $33. CyberAuction #414, Lot #32.

1628. CONTEMPORARY HANDMADE. Davis Handmade Marbles. Transparent clear base. Blue, pink and white onionskin with six very deep lobes. Gorgeous. Signed "Jim Davis". 1-1/2". Mint (9.9). Price: $28. CyberAuction #420, Lot #34.

1629. CONTEMPORARY HANDMADE. Davis Handmade Marbles. Beautiful banded solid core. Very similar in color and design to the Mark Matthews pastel 7-lobe solid core swirls of last year. Signed "Jim Davis". 1-7/16". Mint (9.9). Price: $28. CyberAuction #429, Lot #14.

1630. CONTEMPORARY HANDMADE. Davis Handmade Marbles. Peacock. Blue, white and red. Very nice. Signed "Jim Davis". 1-1/2". Mint (9.9). Price: $28. CyberAuction #471, Lot #30.

1631. CONTEMPORARY HANDMADE. Davis Handmade Marbles. Four panel Peacock. Very interesting. Signed "Jim Davis". 1-9/16". Mint (9.9). Price: $23. CyberAuction #479, Lot #32.

1632. CONTEMPORARY HANDMADE. Davis Handmade Marbles. Onionskin type that is two orange panels on black. Nice Halloween marble. Signed "Jim Davis". Earlier Davis marble. 1-1/2". Mint (9.5) (bottom pontil has some scratches). Price: $22. CyberAuction #437, Lot #18.

1633. CONTEMPORARY HANDMADE. Davis Handmade Marbles. Four panel onionskin. Signed "Jim Davis". 1-9/16". Mint (9.9). Price: $21. CyberAuction #364, Lot #49.

1634. CONTEMPORARY HANDMADE. Davis Handmade Marbles. Banded swirl. Seven blue bands, seven onionskin bands. Signed "Jim Davis". 1-9/16". Mint (9.9). Price: $21. CyberAuction #501, Lot #40.

1635. CONTEMPORARY HANDMADE. Davis Handmade Marbles. Panelled onionskin. Fourteen panels. Signed "Jim Davis". 1-7/16". Mint (9.9). Price: $19. CyberAuction #378, Lot #12.

1636. CONTEMPORARY HANDMADE. Davis Handmade Marbles. Balloon. Very nice pink and green on white. Lobed. Signed "Jim Davis". 1-1/2". Mint (9.9). Price: $19. CyberAuction #380, Lot #35.

1637. CONTEMPORARY HANDMADE. Davis Handmade Marbles. Three panel onionskin with mica. Very nice. Signed "Jim Davis". 1-1/2". Mint (9.9). Price: $19. CyberAuction #425, Lot #31.

1638. CONTEMPORARY HANDMADE. Davis Handmade Marbles. Sulphide. Painted penguin. Black and white with black eyes and yellow beak. Signed "Jim Davis". 2". Mint (9.9). Price: $17. CyberAuction #335, Lot #36.

1639. CONTEMPORARY HANDMADE. Davis Handmade Marbles. Transparent clear base. Subsurface snakeskin pattern of white and slate blue. Unsigned. 1-9/16". Mint (9.9). Price: $17. CyberAuction #340, Lot #31.

1640. CONTEMPORARY HANDMADE. Davis Handmade Marbles. Transparent clear. Random pattern of white, green and green aventurine. Signed "Jim Davis". 1-1/2". Mint (9.9). Price: $17. CyberAuction #362, Lot #20.

1641. CONTEMPORARY HANDMADE. Davis Handmade Marbles. Onionskin type that is two orange panels on black. Nice Halloween marble. Signed "Jim Davis". Earlier Davis marble. 1-1/2". Mint (9.5) (bottom pontil has some scratches). Price: $17. CyberAuction #400, Lot #9.

1642. CONTEMPORARY HANDMADE. Davis Handmade Marbles. Four panel onionskin. Beautiful. Signed "Jim Davis". 1-7/16". Mint (9.9). Price: $17. CyberAuction #431, Lot #13.

1643. CONTEMPORARY HANDMADE. Davis Handmade Marbles. Balloon. Very nice blue and yellow on white. Lobed. Signed "Jim Davis". 1-1/2". Mint (9.9). Price: $17. CyberAuction #434, Lot #8.

1644. CONTEMPORARY HANDMADE. Davis Handmade Marbles. Balloon. Signed "Jim Davis". 1-1/2". Mint (9.9). Price: $17. CyberAuction #476, Lot #19.

1645. CONTEMPORARY HANDMADE. Davis Handmade Marbles. Peacock. Pink on white, in clear. Signed "Jim Davis". 1-5/8". Mint (9.9). Price: $17. CyberAuction #505, Lot #12.

1646. CONTEMPORARY HANDMADE. Davis Handmade Marbles. Peacock. Green, blue, pink and white. Signed "Jim Davis". 1-5/8". Mint (9.9). Price: $16. CyberAuction #361, Lot #43.

1647. CONTEMPORARY HANDMADE. Davis Handmade Marbles. Lobed onionskin. Signed "Jim Davis". 1-1/2". Mint (9.9). Price: $16. CyberAuction #475, Lot #32.

1648. CONTEMPORARY HANDMADE. Davis Handmade Marbles. Transparent clear base. Three subsurface panels. One each of white, blue and red. Unsigned. 1-7/16". Mint (9.9). Price: $15. CyberAuction #340, Lot #12.

1649. CONTEMPORARY HANDMADE. Davis Handmade Marbles. Interesting lobed onionskin. Signed "Jim Davis". 1-1/2". Mint (9.9). Price: $15. CyberAuction #382, Lot #24.

1650. CONTEMPORARY HANDMADE. Davis Handmade Marbles. Very nice onionskin. Earthy tones. Signed "Jim Davis". 1-1/2". Mint (9.9). Price: $15. CyberAuction #415, Lot #54.

1651. CONTEMPORARY HANDMADE. Davis Handmade Marbles. Peacock. Purple on white. Signed "Jim Davis". 1-9/16". Mint (9.9). Price: $15. CyberAuction #417, Lot #23.

1652. CONTEMPORARY HANDMADE. Davis Handmade Marbles. Peacock. Earthy tones with lutz. Signed "Jim Davis". 1-1/2". Mint (9.9). Price: $15. CyberAuction #419, Lot #35.

1653. CONTEMPORARY HANDMADE. Davis Handmade Marbles. Onionskin of blue, pink and green. Signed "Jim Davis". 1-7/16". Mint (9.9). Price: $14. CyberAuction #368, Lot #19.

1654. CONTEMPORARY HANDMADE. Davis Handmade Marbles. Multipanel onionskin. Nice. Signed "Jim Davis". 1-7/16". Mint (9.9). Price: $14. CyberAuction #421, Lot #12.

1655. CONTEMPORARY HANDMADE. Davis Handmade Marbles. Peacock. Blue and yellows. Signed "Jim Davis". 1-1/2". Mint (9.9). Price: $14. CyberAuction #468, Lot #7.

1656. CONTEMPORARY HANDMADE. Davis Handmade Marbles. Transparent clear base with narrow wavy strands of various colors. Signed "Jim Davis". 1-1/2". Mint (9.9). Price: $13. CyberAuction #360, Lot #6.

1657. CONTEMPORARY HANDMADE. Davis Handmade Marbles. Onionskin lutz. Mostly onionskin. Signed "Jim Davis". 1-5/8". Mint (9.9). Price: $13. CyberAuction #366, Lot #35.

1658. CONTEMPORARY HANDMADE. Davis Handmade Marbles. Sulphide of a reclining lamb. Black eyes and nose. Signed "Jim Davis". 1-15/16". Mint (9.9). Price: $13. CyberAuction #379, Lot #34.

1659. CONTEMPORARY HANDMADE. Davis Handmade Marbles. Random onionskin of blues, whites, oranges and other dark colors. Signed "Jim Davis". 1-7/16". Mint (9.9). Price: $13. CyberAuction #445, Lot #7.

1660. CONTEMPORARY HANDMADE. Davis Handmade Marbles. Multipanel onionskin. Nice. Signed "Jim Davis". 1-7/16". Mint (9.9). Price: $13. CyberAuction #456, Lot #10.

1661. CONTEMPORARY HANDMADE. Davis Handmade Marbles. Random onionskin of blues, whites, oranges and other dark colors. Signed "Jim Davis". 1-7/16". Mint (9.9). Price: $12. CyberAuction #365, Lot #39.

1662. CONTEMPORARY HANDMADE. Davis Handmade Marbles. Balloon. Very nice blue and yellow on white. Lobed. Signed "Jim Davis". 1-1/2". Mint (9.9). Price: $12. CyberAuction #389, Lot #24.

1663. CONTEMPORARY HANDMADE. Davis Handmade Marbles. Onionskin with lutz. Very pretty. Unsigned. Subsurface moon. 1-1/2". Near Mint(+) (8.7). Price: $12. CyberAuction #412, Lot #42.

1664. CONTEMPORARY HANDMADE. Davis Handmade Marbles. Four panel onionskin. Signed "Jim Davis". 1-9/16". Mint (9.9). Price: $12. CyberAuction #441, Lot #41.

1665. CONTEMPORARY HANDMADE. Davis Handmade Marbles. Transparent clear. Random pattern of white, green and green aventurine. Signed "Jim Davis". 1-1/2". Mint (9.9). Price: $12. CyberAuction #451, Lot #26.

1666. CONTEMPORARY HANDMADE. Davis Handmade Marbles. Transparent clear. Random pattern of white, green and green aventurine. Signed "Jim Davis". 1-1/2". Mint (9.9). Price: $12. CyberAuction #470, Lot #10.

1667. CONTEMPORARY HANDMADE. Davis Handmade Marbles. Blue and pink onionskin with pink bands on it. Signed "Jim Davis". 1-1/2". Mint (9.9). Price: $12. CyberAuction #472, Lot #30.

1668. CONTEMPORARY HANDMADE. Davis Handmade Marbles. Onionskin of pink on white, with a sprinkling of lutz. Signed "Jim Davis". 1-1/2". Mint (9.9). Price: $11. CyberAuction #413, Lot #32.

1669. CONTEMPORARY HANDMADE. Douglas Ferguson. "Coral Reef". Jumbled cane sections in the center to resemble a coral reef. Beauty. Unsigned. 1-3/16". Mint (9.9). Price: $47. CyberAuction #463, Lot #42.

1670. CONTEMPORARY HANDMADE. Douglas Ferguson. Nice red, yellow, aventurine blue and blue. Marbie design, lobed. Signed "DMF 00". 1-3/8". Mint (9.9). Price: $45. CyberAuction #410, Lot #40.

1671. CONTEMPORARY HANDMADE. Douglas Ferguson. Interesting lazy marbrie design. Signed "DMF 2000". 1-3/8". Mint (9.9). Price: $35. CyberAuction #432, Lot #48.

1672. CONTEMPORARY HANDMADE. Douglas Ferguson. Interesting lazy marbrie design. Coral, tan and aventurine light blue. Signed "DMF 2000". 1-5/16". Mint (9.9). Price: $26. CyberAuction #495, Lot #11.

1673. CONTEMPORARY HANDMADE. Douglas Ferguson. Interesting lazy marbrie design. Signed "DMF 2000". 1-3/8". Mint (9.9). Price: $22. CyberAuction #428, Lot #45.

1674. CONTEMPORARY HANDMADE. Douglas Ferguson. Transparent clear base. Stretched splotches of olive green and gray. Signed "DMF 2000". 1-3/8". Mint (9.9). Price: $22. CyberAuction #443, Lot #23.

1675. CONTEMPORARY HANDMADE. Douglas Ferguson. Transparent clear base. Stretched splotches of olive green and gray. Signed "DMF 2000". 1-3/8". Mint (9.9). Price: $22. CyberAuction #454, Lot #11.

1676. CONTEMPORARY HANDMADE. Douglas Sweet/Karuna Glass. Very nice Douglas Sweet "Orb". Excellent example. Signed "Sweet". American, circa 1992-1997. 1-7/8". Mint (9.9). Price: $60. CyberAuction #369, Lot #36.

1677. CONTEMPORARY HANDMADE. Douglas Sweet/Karuna Glass. Early Sweet planet. Signed "Sweet". From an old contemporary collection. 1-5/8". Mint (9.9). Price: $60. CyberAuction #483, Lot #47.

1678. CONTEMPORARY HANDMADE. Douglas Sweet/Karuna Glass. Orb. Paperweight style. Transparent black base. Dark jasper ground with scattered canes in it. Upper half is clear. Signed "Sweet". 2". Mint (9.9). Price: $45. CyberAuction #504, Lot #43.

1679. CONTEMPORARY HANDMADE. Douglas Sweet/Karuna Glass. Fairydust Orb. Transparent clear base. Subsurface layer of transparent dark purple, covered with dichroic flakes. Signed "Sweet". 2". Mint (9.9). Price: $39. CyberAuction #471, Lot #49.

1680. CONTEMPORARY HANDMADE. Drew Fritts. Black core with various dichroic bands on it. Clear outer casing. Signed "AF 2000 10". The "AF" is a logo. 1-7/8". Mint (9.9). Price: $70. CyberAuction #495, Lot #35.

1681. CONTEMPORARY HANDMADE. Drew Fritts. Excellent marble. Stained Glass Tiger. Signed "AF 1999". The AF is a logo. Rare discontinued style. 1-3/16". Mint (9.9). Price: $65. CyberAuction #490, Lot #36.

1682. CONTEMPORARY HANDMADE. Drew Fritts. Stained Glass Tiger. Blue and black swirls in orange. According to consignor, this is a one of kind from Drew's experimental bin. Signed "AF 1999" (AF is a logo). 1-5/16". Mint (9.9). Price: $60. CyberAuction #489, Lot #38.

1683. CONTEMPORARY HANDMADE. Drew Fritts. Excellent marble. Amethyst Tiger. Signed "AF 1999". The AF is a logo. Discontinued style. 1 5/16". Mint (9.9). Price: $55. CyberAuction #492, Lot #45.

684. CONTEMPORARY HANDMADE. Drew Fritts. Excellent marble. Iberian Tiger. Signed "AF 1999". The AF is a logo. Discontinued style. 1-3/6". Mint (9.9). Price: $55. CyberAuction #493, Lot #45.

685. CONTEMPORARY HANDMADE. Drew Fritts. "Raspberry lambroth". Blue bands on very light blue white base. Signed "AF 2000 1" AF is a logo). 31/32". Mint (9.9). This is the last Drew Fritts marble from this collection. Price: $55. CyberAuction #493, Lot #54.

686. CONTEMPORARY HANDMADE. Drew Fritts. Transparent green ore. Four panel marbrie lutz lines. Clear outer casing. Signed "AF 2000" (AF is a logo). 1-3/4". Mint (9.9). Price: $55. CyberAuction #503, Lot 49.

687. CONTEMPORARY HANDMADE. Drew Fritts. "Blueberry lambroth". Blue bands on very light blue white base. Signed "AF 2000 1" AF is a logo). 31/32". Mint (9.9). Price: $50. CyberAuction #489, Lot #55.

688. CONTEMPORARY HANDMADE. Drew Fritts. Excellent marble. olden Tiger. Signed "AF 1999". The AF is a logo. Discontinued style. 1-5/6". Mint (9.9). Price: $47. CyberAuction #490, Lot #20.

689. CONTEMPORARY HANDMADE. Drew Fritts. Limited edition. orchwork. Butterfly. Very colorful marbre marble. Signed "DF 1999 18/ 8 "(DF logo). 1-1/4". Mint (9.9). Price: $43. CyberAuction #336, Lot 43.

690. CONTEMPORARY HANDMADE. Drew Fritts. Excellent marble. Peppermint swirl. Signed "AF 2000 1". The AF is a logo. Discontinued style. 1". Mint (9.9). Price: $42. CyberAuction #485, Lot #32.

691. CONTEMPORARY HANDMADE. Drew Fritts. Excellent marble. aramel Tiger. Signed "AF 1999". The AF is a logo. Discontinued style. 1-3/ 6". Mint (9.9). Price: $42. CyberAuction #485, Lot #59.

692. CONTEMPORARY HANDMADE. Drew Fritts. Torchwork. Transarent clear base. Green and white end of day core. Six bands of stretched right orange/yellow on top. Signed "DF"(DF logo). 1-3/8". Mint (9.9). Price: 27. CyberAuction #365, Lot #54.

693. CONTEMPORARY HANDMADE. Dudley Giberson. Lobed solid ore swirl. Nice. Signed "Giberson". He no longer makes marbles. 1-5/8". Mint (9.9). Price: $45. CyberAuction #501, Lot #7.

694. CONTEMPORARY HANDMADE. Francis Coupal. Called a "Canaian Mist". Transparent clear base. White latticinio core. Subsurface layer f transparent dark blue bands with loads of mica. 1-15/16". Mint (9.9). Price: $85. CyberAuction #418, Lot #29.

695. CONTEMPORARY HANDMADE. Francis Coupal. Red core, nineanel onionskin. Gorgeous. Signed "fc" (logo). 1-7/16". Mint (9.9). Price: 75. CyberAuction #377, Lot #52.

696. CONTEMPORARY HANDMADE. Francis Coupal. Part of the "Fire nd Ice" Series. Opaque blue core. End of day stretched bands of orange nd yellow, separated by light green bands. Signed "fc". 1-11/16". Mint .9). Price: $75. CyberAuction #498, Lot #40.

697. CONTEMPORARY HANDMADE. Francis Coupal. Canadian artist. ery nice lobed solid core. Transparent clear base. Core is transparent dark lue with mica. Deeply lobed by six bands of orange and red. Signed "fc". -15/16". Mint (9.9). Price: $70. CyberAuction #421, Lot #38.

698. CONTEMPORARY HANDMADE. Francis Coupal. Canadian artist. ransparent clear base. Opaque blue core. Panels of stretched yellow plotches, separated by orange strands, on the core. Signed "fc". Very nice. -3/4". Mint (9.9). Price: $70. CyberAuction #424, Lot #57.

699. CONTEMPORARY HANDMADE. Francis Coupal. Gorgeous marble. paque purple core. Three purple panels and three bright orange and right yellow panels, all separated by red bands, on the core. Clear outer yer. Stunning. Signed "fc" (logo). 2". Mint (9.9). Price: $70. CyberAuction 491, Lot #43.

700. CONTEMPORARY HANDMADE. Francis Coupal. Interesting marble. our lobe white solid core. Subsurface layer of transparent color bands with ica. Ten transparent lavender bands alternating with ten transparent pink ands. Loads of mica. Signed "fc". Gorgeous marble. 1-13/16". Mint (9.9). rice: $60. CyberAuction #487, Lot #36.

701. CONTEMPORARY HANDMADE. Francis Coupal. Part of the "Fire nd Ice" Series. Opaque blue core. End of day stretched bands of orange nd green, separated by yellow bands. Signed "fc". 1-3/4". Mint (9.9). Price: 60. CyberAuction #501, Lot #64.

702. CONTEMPORARY HANDMADE. Francis Coupal. Opaque white ore. Core is pink with blue bands, and overall mica. Very nice. igned "fc" (logo). 1-9/16". Mint (9.9). Price: $60. CyberAuction #505, Lot 45.

703. CONTEMPORARY HANDMADE. Francis Coupal. Part of his Fire nd Ice series. Transparent clear base. Currant core. Outer layer is red and range bands. Covered by mica. Signed "fc". Canadian. 1-7/8". Mint (9.9). rice: $55. CyberAuction #436, Lot #22.

704. CONTEMPORARY HANDMADE. Francis Coupal. Excellent modrn interpretation of a submarine with mica. Transparent clear base. Two ubsurface panels of red, yellow, orange and green. Two core panels of the ame coloring. There is heavy mica in the clear panels above the core anels. Gorgeous. Signed "fc" (logo). 1-3/4". Mint (9.9). Price: $55. yberAuction #495, Lot #50.

705. CONTEMPORARY HANDMADE. Francis Coupal. Part of his "Fire nd Ice series. Transparent clear base. White core. Outer layer is alternatng translucent blue and transparent pink bands. Covered by mica. Signed fc". Canadian. 1-13/16". Mint (9.9). Price: $42. CyberAuction #433, ot #35.

706. CONTEMPORARY HANDMADE. Francis Coupal. Part of the "Fire nd Ice" Series. Opaque blue core. End of day stretched bands of orange nd yellow, separated by lavender bands. Signed "fc". 1-1/2". Mint (9.9). rice: $39. CyberAuction #454, Lot #45.

707. CONTEMPORARY HANDMADE. Francis Coupal. Torchwork. Trans-

parent clear base. Green and white end of day core. Six bands of stretched bright orange/yellow on top. Signed "fc". 1-3/8". Mint (9.9). Price: $38. CyberAuction #463, Lot #58.

1708. CONTEMPORARY HANDMADE. Francis Coupal. Part of the "Fire and Ice" Series. Opaque blue core. End of day stretched bands of orange and yellow, separated by lavender strands. Signed "fc". 1-1/2". Mint (9.9). Price: $36. CyberAuction #442, Lot #24.

1709. CONTEMPORARY HANDMADE. Fritz Glass. "Half and Half" marble. Very rare example, made from the ends of three canes. Top half is a Joseph Coat, middle is a ribbon core swirl, bottom is a tiny solid core. Handmade and signed "Fritz 1998 1-1". "1-1" signifies that Fritz only made one like this, because it contained the end of the canes. American. 1-5/8". Mint (9.9). Price: $130. CyberAuction #351, Lot #46.

1710. CONTEMPORARY HANDMADE. Fritz Glass. Joseph Coat. Rainbow of subsurface bands in clear. Made by Fritz Lauenstein. American, circa 1999. Large marble. Fritz hardly ever makes marbles over 2" diameter. 2-1/8". Mint (9.9). Price: $110. CyberAuction #332, Lot #51.

1711. CONTEMPORARY HANDMADE. Fritz Glass. "Half and Half" marble. Top is a ribbon, bottom is a Joseph Coat. Handmade and signed "Fritz 98 1-1". "1-1" signifies that Fritz only made one like this, because it contained the end of the canes. American. 1-5/8". Mint (9.9). Price: $110. CyberAuction #377, Lot #20.

1712. CONTEMPORARY HANDMADE. Fritz Glass. Limited Edition marble. Transparent clear base. Subsurface layer of lavender with spaced light blue bands, and one yellow band. Left-twist, reverse twist top. Signed "F 99 2-P". Second artist proof. Rare. American. 1-9/16". Mint (9.9). Price: $90. CyberAuction #338, Lot #58.

1713. CONTEMPORARY HANDMADE. Fritz Glass. Rare. Confetti with a signature cane. Transparent clear base. Surface dots of transparent brown. "F" signature cane in top pole. Signed "Fritz 1998 1-1" (only one made). 1-9/16". Mint (9.9). Price: $77. CyberAuction #393, Lot #60.

1714. CONTEMPORARY HANDMADE. Fritz Glass. Stunning five-twist naked single ribbon core swirl. Signed "Fritz 2000". Harder to find larger size. 2". Mint (9.9). Price: $75. CyberAuction #421, Lot #55.

1715. CONTEMPORARY HANDMADE. Fritz Glass. "Half and Half" marble. Top is a Joseph Coat, bottom is a solid core. Handmade and signed "F 2000 1-1". "1-1" signifies that Fritz only made one like this, because it contained the end of the canes. American. 1-5/8". Mint (9.9). Price: $70. CyberAuction #423, Lot #27.

1716. CONTEMPORARY HANDMADE. Fritz Glass. Limited Edition marble. Transparent clear base. Subsurface layer of lavender with spaced light blue bands, and one yellow band. Left-twist, reverse twist top. Signed "F 99 18-20". Eighteenth of twenty. American. 1-9/16". Mint (9.9). Price: $65. CyberAuction #366, Lot #48.

1717. CONTEMPORARY HANDMADE. Fritz Glass. Beautiful Joseph Coat (?). White subsurface layer with variously colored transparent bands on it. Large. Signed "F2000". 2-1/16". Mint (9.9). Price: $65. CyberAuction #400, Lot #30.

1718. CONTEMPORARY HANDMADE. Fritz Glass. "Half and Half" marble. Top is a ribbon, bottom is a solid core swirl. Handmade and signed "Fritz 99 1-1". "1-1" signifies that Fritz only made one like this, because it contained the end of the canes. American. 1-5/8". Mint (9.9). Price: $65. CyberAuction #435, Lot #56.

1719. CONTEMPORARY HANDMADE. Fritz Glass. Super large marble. Core is a narrow lobed green and yellow solid core. Outer layer is a cage of blue bands. Reverse twist at top. Fritz does not produce too many of these larger ones. Signed "F 2000". 2-1/16". Mint (9.9). Price: $61. CyberAuction #391, Lot #26.

1720. CONTEMPORARY HANDMADE. Fritz Glass. Single ribbon core swirl. Multicolor ribbon. A beauty. Signed "Fritz 2000". 2-1/16". Mint (9.9). Price: $60. CyberAuction #403, Lot #24.

1721. CONTEMPORARY HANDMADE. Fritz Glass. Same marble as prior lot (CyberAuction 423, Lot #35). But a larger size. Excellent complement to the previous lots. Nice three-layer. Very narrow core of orange and blue. Middle layer is a cage of green strands. Outer layer is a cage of orange and blue mixed bands. Reverse twist top. Signed "Fritz 2000". 2-1/16". Mint (9.9). Price: $60. CyberAuction #423, Lot #36.

1722. CONTEMPORARY HANDMADE. Fritz Glass. Joseph Coat. Earthy colors. Signed "F 99". 1-5/8". Mint (9.9). Price: $55. CyberAuction #358, Lot #30.

1723. CONTEMPORARY HANDMADE. Fritz Glass. Large single ribbon swirl. Very pretty. Fritz hardly ever makes these big ones. Signed "F 2000". 2-1/16". Mint (9.9). Price: $55. CyberAuction #385, Lot #30.

1724. CONTEMPORARY HANDMADE. Fritz Glass. Half-and-Half marble. One half is a lavender and aventurine green bande swirl. Other half is a ribbon swirl. Signed "Fritz 2000 1-1". 1-5/8". Mint (9.9). Price: $55. CyberAuction #418, Lot #24.

1725. CONTEMPORARY HANDMADE. Fritz Glass. Experimental twocolor onionskin. Fritz says that he only made one cane of these. Signed "Fritz 1996". 1-9/16". Mint (9.9). Price: $50. CyberAuction #396, Lot #36.

1726. CONTEMPORARY HANDMADE. Fritz Glass. Nice Joseph Coat. Transparent clear base. Subsurface layer of closely pack alternating bands of yellow, green, red and blue. Signed "F 99". American. 1-5/8". Mint (9.9). Price: $49. CyberAuction #339, Lot #32.

1727. CONTEMPORARY HANDMADE. Fritz Glass. Gorgeous marble. Transparent clear base. Core is dark green and blue. Outer layer is a cage of orange strands. Signed "Fritz 2000". 1-7/8". Mint (9.9). Price: $49. CyberAuction #455, Lot #30.

1728. CONTEMPORARY HANDMADE. Fritz Glass. Outstanding wide naked single ribbon core swirl. Orange, yellow, teal and blue ribbon, edged by black. Signature reverse twist at the top. Signed "F 99". 1-5/8". Mint (9.9). Price: $46. CyberAuction #330, Lot #23.

1729. CONTEMPORARY HANDMADE. Fritz Glass. Superb Onionskin. This is a limited edition, Fritz did not make these for long. Superb. Signed "F98". 1-9/16". Mint (9.9). Price: $44. CyberAuction #473, Lot #50.

1730. CONTEMPORARY HANDMADE. Fritz Glass. Outstanding wide naked single ribbon core swirl. Bands are a rainbow of colors. Signature reverse twist at the top. Signed "F 99". 1-5/8". Mint (9.9). Price: $43. CyberAuction #331, Lot #50.

1731. CONTEMPORARY HANDMADE. Fritz Glass. Very interesting smaller Fritz marble. Opaque white core. Middle layer of transparent orange. Outer layer is a subsurface layer of transparent black bands. Reverse twist top. Signed "F 99". 1-1/16". Mint (9.9). Price: $42. CyberAuction #347, Lot #48.

1732. CONTEMPORARY HANDMADE. Fritz Glass. Fritz Onionskin. He makes very few of these. Beautiful. Signed "Fritz 2000". 1-9/16". Mint (9.9). Price: $42. CyberAuction #387, Lot #25.

1733. CONTEMPORARY HANDMADE. Fritz Glass. Half and Half. One half is an onionskin, other half is a ribbon. Two cane ends, fused together. Signed "Fritz 1-1". Not dated. 1-9/16". Mint (9.9). Price: $42. CyberAuction #406, Lot #28.

1734. CONTEMPORARY HANDMADE. Fritz Glass. Half and Half. One half is an onionskin, other half is a ribbon. Two cane ends, fused together. Signed "Fritz 1-1". Not dated. 1-9/16". Mint (9.9). Price: $42. CyberAuction #426, Lot #33.

1735. CONTEMPORARY HANDMADE. Fritz Glass. Ribbon core swirl. Ribbon is transparent blue with mica, pink and mustard yellow. Signed "F 99". 1-5/8". Mint (9.9). Price: $42. CyberAuction #440, Lot #33.

1736. CONTEMPORARY HANDMADE. Fritz Glass. Gorgeous. Single ribbon core. Rainbow of outer bands. Signed "Fritz 2000". 1-1/2". Mint (9.9). Price: $42. CyberAuction #443, Lot #33.

1737. CONTEMPORARY HANDMADE. Fritz Glass. Half-and-Half marble. One half is a lavender and aventurine green bande swirl. Other half is a ribbon swirl. Signed "Fritz 2000 1-1". 1-5/8". Mint (9.9). Price: $42. CyberAuction #460, Lot #59.

1738. CONTEMPORARY HANDMADE. Fritz Glass. Large lobed solid core. Signed "F99". 2-1/16". Mint (9.9). Price: $42. CyberAuction #489, Lot #35.

1739. CONTEMPORARY HANDMADE. Fritz Glass. Black and white four-vane ribbon swirl. Beauty. Signed "Fritz 2000". 1-1/2". Mint (9.9). Price: $41. CyberAuction #507, Lot #33.

1740. CONTEMPORARY HANDMADE. Fritz Glass. White solid core. Four outer vanes. Beauty. Signed "Fritz 2000". 2-1/16". Mint (9.9). Price: $40. CyberAuction #476, Lot #36.

1741. CONTEMPORARY HANDMADE. Fritz Glass. Fritz divided core swirl. Four band core. Outer layer is a cage of blue bands. Signed "F 99". 1-1/16". Mint (9.9). Price: $39. CyberAuction #441, Lot #50.

1742. CONTEMPORARY HANDMADE. Fritz Glass. Very nice marble. Blizzard mica core. Outer layer is four bands. One each of pink, green, yellow and blue. Reverse twist top. Signed "Fritz 2000". 1-9/16". Mint (9.9). Price: $39. CyberAuction #503, Lot #35.

1743. CONTEMPORARY HANDMADE. Fritz Glass. Smaller Fritz. St. Mary's catseye mimic!!! Two black vanes and two white vanes. Super! Signed "F 99". 1-1/16". Mint (9.9). Price: $38. CyberAuction #357, Lot #38.

1744. CONTEMPORARY HANDMADE. Fritz Glass. Solid core. Two panels of white, two of yellow, separated by red strands. Signed "Fritz 2000". 1-9/16". Mint (9.9). Price: $38. CyberAuction #420, Lot #48.

1745. CONTEMPORARY HANDMADE. Fritz Glass. Small Fritz ribbon core swirl. Single naked ribbon core swirl. Orange on one side and yellow on the other. Edged in blue. Signed "F 99". 1-1/16". Mint (9.9). Price: $37. CyberAuction #354, Lot #38.

1746. CONTEMPORARY HANDMADE. Fritz Glass. Small Fritz divided core swirl. Four band core. Outer layer is a cage of blue bands. Signed "F 99". 1-1/16". Mint (9.9). Price: $37. CyberAuction #359, Lot #48.

1747. CONTEMPORARY HANDMADE. Fritz Glass. Joseph Coat of orange and yellow bands. Signed "F 99". Small size. 1-1/16". Mint (9.9). Price: $37. CyberAuction #362, Lot #57.

1748. CONTEMPORARY HANDMADE. Fritz Glass. Gorgeous single ribbon core swirl. Ribbon is opaque white with purple on it. Red edges. Signed "Fritz 2000". 1-9/16". Mint (9.9). Price: $37. CyberAuction #413, Lot #60.

1749. CONTEMPORARY HANDMADE. Fritz Glass. Ribbon onionskin with outer bands. Very pretty. Signed "Fritz 2000". 1-1/2". Mint (9.9). Price: $37. CyberAuction #457, Lot #37.

1750. CONTEMPORARY HANDMADE. Fritz Glass. Outstanding wide naked single ribbon core swirl. pink, green, teal and blue ribbon, edged by black. Signature reverse twist at the top. Signed "F 99". 1-5/8". Mint (9.9). Price: $36. CyberAuction #342, Lot #35.

1751. CONTEMPORARY HANDMADE. Fritz Glass. Outstanding wide naked single ribbon core swirl. Orange ribbon, edged by white bands. Signature reverse twist at the top. Signed "F 99". 1-1/16". Mint (9.9). Price: $35. CyberAuction #363, Lot #22.

1752. CONTEMPORARY HANDMADE. Fritz Glass. Large single ribbon core swirl. Signed "Fritz 2000". One of the large Fritz marbles. 2-1/16". Mint (9.9). Price: $35. CyberAuction #448, Lot #36.

1753. CONTEMPORARY HANDMADE. Fritz Glass. Solid core. Middle layer is a cage of green. Outer layer is a cage of multicolor bands. Signed "Fritz 2000". 2-1/16". Mint (9.9). Price: $35. CyberAuction #463, Lot #25.

1754. CONTEMPORARY HANDMADE. Fritz Glass. Single ribbon core swirl. Multicolor ribbon. A beauty. Signed "Fritz 2000". 1-1/2". Mint (9.9). Price: $34. CyberAuction #400, Lot #5.

1755. CONTEMPORARY HANDMADE. Fritz Glass. Beautiful banded swirl with lutz. Signed "Fritz 2000". 1-1/2". Mint (9.9). Price: $34. CyberAuction #479, Lot #10.

1756. CONTEMPORARY HANDMADE. Fritz Glass. Fritz Onionskin. H makes very few of these. Beautiful. Signed "Fritz 2000". 1-9/16". Mint (9.9) Price: $33. CyberAuction #441, Lot #33.

1757. CONTEMPORARY HANDMADE. Fritz Glass. Beauty. Transpare clear base. Subsurface layer is a repeating pattern of black, lavender an light green bands. Signed "F 97". 1-5/8". Mint (9.9). Price: $32. CyberAuctic #338, Lot #22.

1758. CONTEMPORARY HANDMADE. Fritz Glass. Divided core swi Nice. Reverse twist top. Signed "F 99". 1-1/16". Mint (9.9). Price: $3. CyberAuction #368, Lot #42.

1759. CONTEMPORARY HANDMADE. Fritz Glass. Gorgeous single rit bon swirl with red outer strands. Signed "Fritz 2000". 1-9/16". Mint (9.9 Price: $32. CyberAuction #381, Lot #35.

1760. CONTEMPORARY HANDMADE. Fritz Glass. Ribbon core of re yellow and light green. Outer layer is a cage of transparent pink and tran parent yellow bands. Reverse twist on the top. Signed "Fritz 2000". Gor geous. 1-9/16". Mint (9.9). Price: $32. CyberAuction #428, Lot #30.

1761. CONTEMPORARY HANDMADE. Fritz Glass. Single ribbon core swirl. Gorgeous. Signed "F 2000". 2-1/16". Mint (9.9). Price: $3. CyberAuction #442, Lot #48.

1762. CONTEMPORARY HANDMADE. Fritz Glass. Four panel solid cor Signed "Fritz 2000". 1-1/2". Mint (9.9). Price: $32. CyberAuction #44 Lot #27.

1763. CONTEMPORARY HANDMADE. Fritz Glass. Half and Half. On half is an onionskin, other half is a ribbon. Two cane ends, fused togethe Signed "Fritz 1-1". Not dated. 1-9/16". Mint (9.9). Price: $32. CyberAuctic #456, Lot #28.

1764. CONTEMPORARY HANDMADE. Fritz Glass. Transparent clear bas Four vane ribbon core, pinks, turquoise and blues. Outer layer is a cage blue bands. Reverse twist top. Signed "F 99". 1-1/16". Mint (9.9). Pric $31. CyberAuction #352, Lot #53.

1765. CONTEMPORARY HANDMADE. Fritz Glass. Ribbon core swir Ribbon is transparent blue with mica, pink and mustard yellow. Signed " 99". 1-5/8". Mint (9.9). Price: $31. CyberAuction #370, Lot #59.

1766. CONTEMPORARY HANDMADE. Fritz Glass. Onionskin. Fritz usu ally makes swirls. Signed "F 99". 1-5/8". Mint (9.9). Price: $31. CyberAuctic #384, Lot #26.

1767. CONTEMPORARY HANDMADE. Fritz Glass. Single blue ribbc core, white edged. Outer layer is a cage of orange strands. Reverse twist c top. Signed "Fritz 2000". 1-9/16". Mint (9.9). Price: $30. CyberAuctic #416, Lot #20.

1768. CONTEMPORARY HANDMADE. Fritz Glass. Single ribbon cor swirl. Pink ribbon with white edges. Gorgeous. Signed "Fritz 2000". 1-9 16". Mint (9.9). Price: $30. CyberAuction #433, Lot #59.

1769. CONTEMPORARY HANDMADE. Fritz Glass. Red, white and blu solid core. Three outer bands of same color. Signed "Fritz 2000". 1-9/16 Mint (9.9). Price: $30. CyberAuction #471, Lot #34.

1770. CONTEMPORARY HANDMADE. Fritz Glass. Blue and orang banded core. Green cage around it. Outer layer is cage of orange and blu bands. Reverse twist top. Signed "Fritz 2000". 1-9/16". Mint (9.9). Pric $30. CyberAuction #472, Lot #43.

1771. CONTEMPORARY HANDMADE. Fritz Glass. Lobed solid core wi one outer band. Signed "Fritz 2000". 1-9/16". Mint (9.9). Price: $2 CyberAuction #392, Lot #31.

1772. CONTEMPORARY HANDMADE. Fritz Glass. Joseph Coat, most blue bands. Signed "Fritz 2000". 1-9/16". Mint (9.9). Price: $2 CyberAuction #436, Lot #21.

1773. CONTEMPORARY HANDMADE. Fritz Glass. Naked single ribbc swirl. Core is a rainbow formed of bands. Signed "F 99". 1-1/16". Mir (9.9). Price: $28. CyberAuction #345, Lot #45.

1774. CONTEMPORARY HANDMADE. Fritz Glass. Three lobed solid cor swirl. Gorgeous. Signed "Fritz 2000". 1-1/2". Mint (9.9). Price: $2 CyberAuction #438, Lot #43.

1775. CONTEMPORARY HANDMADE. Fritz Glass. Gorgeous. Blue ar white narrow core. Middle layer is a cage of black bands. Outer layer cage of red bands. Reverse twist top. Signed "Fritz 2000". 1-1/2". Mint (9.9). Price: $28. CyberAuction #491, Lot #29.

1776. CONTEMPORARY HANDMADE. Fritz Glass. Transparent clear bas Subsurface layer of black bands, alternating with strands of various brigł colors. Reverse twist at top. Signed "Fritz 2000". 1-9/16". Mint (9.9). Pric $28. CyberAuction #508, Lot #54.

1777. CONTEMPORARY HANDMADE. Fritz Glass. Divided core wit colored strands as the outside layer. Signed "F99". 1-5/8". Mint (9.9). Pric $27. CyberAuction #335, Lot #24.

1778. CONTEMPORARY HANDMADE. Fritz Glass. Gorgeous single rit bon core swirl. Light blue edged by red. Signed "Fritz 2000". 1-5/8". Mir (9.9). Price: $27. CyberAuction #450, Lot #30.

1779. CONTEMPORARY HANDMADE. Fritz Glass. Outstanding wid naked single ribbon core swirl. Orange ribbon, edged by green on whit bands. Signed "F 99". 1-1/16". Mint (9.9). Price: $26. CyberAuction #36 Lot #24.

1780. CONTEMPORARY HANDMADE. Fritz Glass. Gorgeous. Transpal ent blue solid core covered by olive. Outer layer is a cage of orange band Reverse twist on top. Signed "Fritz 2000". 1-1/2". Mint (9.9). Price: $2 CyberAuction #429, Lot #39.

1781. CONTEMPORARY HANDMADE. Fritz Glass. Gorgeous case clambroth. Transparent clear base. Core is bands of opaque white, alterna ing with dichroic red and dichroic green bands. Signed "Fritz 2000". 1-2". Mint (9.9). Price: $26. CyberAuction #432, Lot #32.

782. CONTEMPORARY HANDMADE. Fritz Glass. Four panel swirl. Very pretty. Signed "Fritz 2000". 1-9/16". Mint (9.9). Price: $26. CyberAuction #449, Lot #17.

783. CONTEMPORARY HANDMADE. Fritz Glass. Gorgeous. Transparent blue solid core covered by olive. Outer layer is a cage of orange bands. Reverse twist on top. Signed "Fritz 2000". 1-1/2". Mint (9.9). Price: $26. CyberAuction #466, Lot #18.

784. CONTEMPORARY HANDMADE. Fritz Glass. Nice three-layer. Very arrow core of orange and blue. Middle layer is a cage of green strands. Outer layer is a cage of orange and blue mixed bands. Reverse twist top. Signed "Fritz 2000". 1-9/16". Mint (9.9). Price: $25. CyberAuction #423, Lot #35.

785. CONTEMPORARY HANDMADE. Fritz Glass. Single ribbon core swirl. Gorgeous. Signed "Fritz 2000". 1-1/2". Mint (9.9). Price: $25. CyberAuction #424, Lot #45.

786. CONTEMPORARY HANDMADE. Fritz Glass. Transparent clear base. Four-vane ribbon. Each a different dark color. Signed "F99". 1-5/8". Mint (9.9). Price: $25. CyberAuction #469, Lot #30.

787. CONTEMPORARY HANDMADE. Fritz Glass. Double ribbon of black and white, tightly twisted. Signed "F99". 1-9/16". Mint (9.9). Price: $25. CyberAuction #475, Lot #14.

788. CONTEMPORARY HANDMADE. Fritz Glass. Beautiful ribbon core. Signed "Fritz 2000". 1-1/2". Mint (9.9). Price: $25. CyberAuction #476, Lot #26.

789. CONTEMPORARY HANDMADE. Fritz Glass. Outstanding wide naked single ribbon core swirl. Orange ribbon, edged by green on white bands. Signed "F 99". 1-1/16". Mint (9.9). Price: $24. CyberAuction #457, Lot #32.

790. CONTEMPORARY HANDMADE. Fritz Glass. Gorgeous single ribbon core swirl. Signed "Fritz 2000". 1-11/16". Mint (9.9). Price: $24. CyberAuction #479, Lot #24.

791. CONTEMPORARY HANDMADE. Fritz Glass. Solid core with green strand cage and two color outer layer bands. Signed "Fritz 2000". 1-9/16". Mint (9.9). Price: $24. CyberAuction #493, Lot #20.

792. CONTEMPORARY HANDMADE. Fritz Glass. Four panel lobed solid core. Signed "Fritz 2000". 1-1/2". Mint (9.9). Price: $24. CyberAuction #500, Lot #25.

793. CONTEMPORARY HANDMADE. Fritz Glass. Banded swirl of orange, green and blue. Signed "Fritz 2000". 1-9/16". Mint (9.9). Price: $24. CyberAuction #505, Lot #37.

794. CONTEMPORARY HANDMADE. Fritz Glass. Four panel swirl. Very pretty. Signed "Fritz 2000". 1-9/16". Mint (9.9). Price: $22. CyberAuction #399, Lot #32.

795. CONTEMPORARY HANDMADE. Fritz Glass. Narrow solid core. Middle layer is a cage of olive green bands. Outer layer is a cage of bands in blue and orange color schemes. Signed "Fritz 2000". 1-9/16". Mint (9.9). Price: $22. CyberAuction #431, Lot #35.

796. CONTEMPORARY HANDMADE. Fritz Glass. White core. Outer layer is two ribbons of blue and two of white, each edged by red, turned perpendicular to core. Signed "Fritz 2000". 1-5/8". Mint (9.9). Price: $22. CyberAuction #452, Lot #23.

797. CONTEMPORARY HANDMADE. Fritz Glass. Gorgeous cased lambroth. Transparent clear base. Core is bands of opaque white, alternating with dichroic red and dichroic green bands. Signed "Fritz 2000". 1-1/2". Mint (9.9). Price: $22. CyberAuction #453, Lot #34.

798. CONTEMPORARY HANDMADE. Fritz Glass. Blue solid core design. Unsigned. Looks like Fritz Glass work. One tiny subsurface moon. 1-1/2". Near Mint(+) (8.9). Price: $17. CyberAuction #451, Lot #47.

799. CONTEMPORARY HANDMADE. Fulton-Parker Glass. Banded swirl with wide lutz band. Signed "FP 94". 1-7/8". Mint (9.9). Price: $40. CyberAuction #480, Lot #38.

800. CONTEMPORARY HANDMADE. Fulton-Parker Glass. Ribbon core swirl. Transparent clear base. White single ribbon with gold lutz center. Triple twisted. Outer layer is two blue bands alternating with two narrower lighter blue bands that have lutz. Signed "FP 99". 3/4". Mint (9.9). Price: $26. CyberAuction #351, Lot #15.

801. CONTEMPORARY HANDMADE. Fulton-Parker Glass. Banded swirl. Nice. Signed "FP 99". 29/32". Mint (9.9). Price: $24. CyberAuction #427, Lot #32.

802. CONTEMPORARY HANDMADE. Fulton-Parker Glass. Narrow white core. Cased with lutz. Outer layer is a cage of blue bands. Signed "FP 98". 7/8". Mint (9.9). Price: $23. CyberAuction #431, Lot #39.

803. CONTEMPORARY HANDMADE. Fulton-Parker Glass. Transparent olive yellow marble. Six wide transparent yellow vanes in it. Signed "FP 98". 7/8". Mint (9.9). Price: $19. CyberAuction #434, Lot #10.

804. CONTEMPORARY HANDMADE. Fulton-Parker Glass. Transparent olive yellow marble. Six wide transparent yellow vanes in it. Signed "FP 98". 7/8". Mint (9.9). Price: $17. CyberAuction #334, Lot #49.

805. CONTEMPORARY HANDMADE. Fulton-Parker Glass. Transparent olive yellow marble. Six wide transparent yellow vanes in it. Signed "FP 98". 7/8". Mint (9.9). Price: $17. CyberAuction #386, Lot #4.

806. CONTEMPORARY HANDMADE. Fulton-Parker Glass. Pink and aventurine blue ribbon core swirl. Signed "FP 98". 13/16". Mint (9.9). Price: $17. CyberAuction #435, Lot #23.

807. CONTEMPORARY HANDMADE. Fulton-Parker Glass. Pink and aventurine blue ribbon core swirl. Signed "FP 98". 13/16". Mint (9.9). Price: $17. CyberAuction #453, Lot #14.

808. CONTEMPORARY HANDMADE. Gibson Glass. Older Gibson snakeskin. Gorgeous example. Unsigned. 1-7/8". Mint (9.9). Price: $45. CyberAuction #506, Lot #23.

809. CONTEMPORARY HANDMADE. Gibson Glass. Large Snakeskin. Blue and gray on white. Unsigned. 2-3/4". Mint (9.9). Price: $42. CyberAuction #502, Lot #13.

1810. CONTEMPORARY HANDMADE. Gibson Glass. Older Gibson marble. White onionskin core. Outer orange and red/yellow bands. Unsigned. 2-5/16". Mint (9.9). Price: $42. CyberAuction #508, Lot #33.

1811. CONTEMPORARY HANDMADE. Gibson Glass. Huge white latticinio core swirl. Earlier Gibson. About 2-3/4" long. Mint (9.9). Price: $37. CyberAuction #496, Lot #25.

1812. CONTEMPORARY HANDMADE. Gibson Glass. Older Gibson snakeskin. Gorgeous example. Unsigned. 1-7/8". Mint (9.9). Price: $34. CyberAuction #494, Lot #8.

1813. CONTEMPORARY HANDMADE. Gibson Glass. Snakeskin. Yellows, greens and blues, on a white base. Unsigned. 1-3/4". Mint (9.9). Price: $25. CyberAuction #364, Lot #34.

1814. CONTEMPORARY HANDMADE. Gibson Glass. Transparent clear base. White latticinio core. Wide outer bands of red, yellow and green. Unsigned. 1-7/8". Mint (9.9). Price: $25. CyberAuction #508, Lot #39.

1815. CONTEMPORARY HANDMADE. Gibson Glass. Snakeskin. Nice coloring. Unsigned. From the mid-1980s. 1-1/2". Mint (9.9). Price: $23. CyberAuction #471, Lot #26.

1816. CONTEMPORARY HANDMADE. Gibson Glass. Lobed onionskin. Gray on white. Unsigned. 1-13/16". Mint (9.9). Price: $22. CyberAuction #477, Lot #30.

1817. CONTEMPORARY HANDMADE. Gibson Glass. Purple on white onionskin. Older. 2-1/8". Mint (9.9). Price: $19. CyberAuction #480, Lot #9.

1818. CONTEMPORARY HANDMADE. Gibson Glass. Transparent clear base. Subsurface bands of translucent white and orange. Unsigned. 1-7/16". Mint (9.9). Price: $17. CyberAuction #341, Lot #35.

1819. CONTEMPORARY HANDMADE. Gibson Glass. Feather design. Lavender on white base. Large marble. One small subsurface moon. This is an early Gibson. From an old contemporary collection. 2-1/8". Near Mint(+) (8.9). Price: $17. CyberAuction #483, Lot #35.

1820. CONTEMPORARY HANDMADE. Gibson Glass. Feather pattern. Pink feathering on white. Unsigned. 1-1/4". Mint (9.9). Price: $15. CyberAuction #428, Lot #4.

1821. CONTEMPORARY HANDMADE. Gibson Glass. Green, brown and white snakeskin. 1-15/16". Mint (9.9). Price: $14. CyberAuction #402, Lot #32.

1822. CONTEMPORARY HANDMADE. Gibson Glass. Feather pattern. Pink feathering on white. Unsigned. 1-1/4". Mint (9.9). Price: $12. CyberAuction #455, Lot #2.

1823. CONTEMPORARY HANDMADE. Gibson Glass. Green eight-lobed onionskin in clear. Unsigned. 1-9/16". Mint (9.9). Price: $12. CyberAuction #472, Lot #5.

1824. CONTEMPORARY HANDMADE. Greg Hoglin. Yellow base with red, black and lutz bands. Nice. Signed "GH 99". 1-1/16". Mint (9.9). Price: $27. CyberAuction #438, Lot #33.

1825. CONTEMPORARY HANDMADE. Greg Hoglin. Yellow base with red, black and lutz bands. Nice. Signed "GH 99". 1-1/16". Mint (9.9). Price: $27. CyberAuction #454, Lot #9.

1826. CONTEMPORARY HANDMADE. Greg Hoglin. White core, covered by purple/pink. Loads of mica on the outer. Outer layer is white bands and lutz bands. Signed "GH 98". 1-1/8". Mint (9.9). Price: $22. CyberAuction #429, Lot #22.

1827. CONTEMPORARY HANDMADE. Hart's of Glass. Banded swirl of lutz, orange, white and yellow. Tightly swirled. Signed with a heart cane. 1-9/16". Mint (9.9). Price: $32. CyberAuction #473, Lot #24.

1828. CONTEMPORARY HANDMADE. Hart's of Glass. Reverse twist onionskin. With brown lutz. Has a heart cane in the bottom as the signature. 1-1/2". Mint (9.9). Price: $29. CyberAuction #469, Lot #56.

1829. CONTEMPORARY HANDMADE. Hart's of Glass. Super looking marble. Transparent aqua base filled with tiny air bubbles. Subsurface layer is a reverse twist pattern of alternating white and aventurine blue bands. Has a "heart" signature cane in one end. 1-7/16". Mint (9.9). Price: $22. CyberAuction #479, Lot #37.

1830. CONTEMPORARY HANDMADE. J. Fine Glass. Outstanding marble. Transparent clear base. Core is white latticinio. Middle layer is three bands of white latticinio. Outer layer is white strands. Unsigned. Superb. 1-5/16". Mint (9.9). Price: $40. CyberAuction #462, Lot #8.

1831. CONTEMPORARY HANDMADE. J. Fine Glass. Three vane ribbon core. Two are green stripes on white, one is aventurine green. Outer layer of one black and yellow band. Unsigned, but Jody Fine. 29/32". Mint (9.9). Price: $32. CyberAuction #349, Lot #53.

1832. CONTEMPORARY HANDMADE. J. Fine Glass. Large ribbon core swirl. Handmade by Jody Fine, but unsigned. 2-1/4". Mint (9.9). Price: $30. CyberAuction #409, Lot #55.

1833. CONTEMPORARY HANDMADE. J. Fine Glass. Lobed solid core. Very colorful. Outer layer is a cage of white bands and one multi-color band. Unsigned. 1-11/16". Mint (9.9). Price: $26. CyberAuction #497, Lot #33.

1834. CONTEMPORARY HANDMADE. J. Fine Glass. Latticinio core with outer bands. Tight twist. Gorgeous marble. Unsigned. 2-1/4". Mint (9.9). Price: $25. CyberAuction #508, Lot #2.

1835. CONTEMPORARY HANDMADE. J. Fine Glass. Large ribbon core swirl. Handmade by Jody Fine, but unsigned. 2-3/8". Mint (9.9). Price: $24. CyberAuction #409, Lot #32.

1836. CONTEMPORARY HANDMADE. J. Fine Glass. Banded swirl. Transparent clear base. Subsurface layer of six lavender bands and six orange strands, separated by twelve white bands. Gorgeous. Unsigned. 1-5/16". Mint (9.9). Price: $24. CyberAuction #487, Lot #19.

1837. CONTEMPORARY HANDMADE. J. Fine Glass. Rainbow single ribbon core. Outer layer is a cage of white strands. Unsigned. 1-11/16". Mint (9.9). Price: $23. CyberAuction #507, Lot #37.

1838. CONTEMPORARY HANDMADE. J. Fine Glass. Gorgeous three layer panelled banded swirl. Unsigned. 1-11/16". Mint (9.9). Price: $22. CyberAuction #489, Lot #24.

1839. CONTEMPORARY HANDMADE. J. Fine Glass. Single ribbon core swirl. Opaque white ribbon. Rainbow bands on one side. One green band as the outer layer. Unsigned. 1-5/16". Mint (9.9). Price: $17. CyberAuction #504, Lot #18.

1840. CONTEMPORARY HANDMADE. J. Fine Glass. Very nice Jody Fine swirl. Unsigned. 29/32". Mint (9.9). Price: $15. CyberAuction #459, Lot #33.

1841. CONTEMPORARY HANDMADE. J. Fine Glass. Ribbon swirl with outer cage. Unsigned. 1-3/8". Mint (9.9). Price: $14. CyberAuction #468, Lot #6.

1842. CONTEMPORARY HANDMADE. J. Fine Glass. Nice swirl. Handmade by Jody Fine, but unsigned. 1-1/8". Mint (9.9). Price: $13. CyberAuction #409, Lot #46.

1843. CONTEMPORARY HANDMADE. J. Fine Glass. Ribbon core swirl with chunky green aventurine. Unsigned, but it is Jody Fine. 1-3/16". Mint (9.9). Price: $13. CyberAuction #477, Lot #6.

1844. CONTEMPORARY HANDMADE. J. Fine Glass. Probably Jody Fine, possibly Steve Maslach. Nice swirl. 13/16". Mint (9.9). Price: $13. CyberAuction #488, Lot #38.

1845. CONTEMPORARY HANDMADE. J. Fine Glass. Nice swirl. Handmade by Jody Fine, but unsigned. 1-1/8". Mint (9.9). Price: $12. CyberAuction #409, Lot #52.

1846. CONTEMPORARY HANDMADE. J. Fine Glass. Probably Jody Fine, possibly Steve Maslach. Nice swirl. 13/16". Mint (9.9). Price: $12. CyberAuction #426, Lot #43.

1847. CONTEMPORARY HANDMADE. J. Fine Glass. Probably Jody Fine, possibly Steve Maslach. Nice swirl. 13/16". Mint (9.9). Price: $12. CyberAuction #426, Lot #50.

1848. CONTEMPORARY HANDMADE. J. Fine Glass. Ribbon core swirl with chunky green aventurine. Unsigned, but it is Jody Fine. Older contemporary, based on the collection is came out of. 1-3/16". Mint (9.9). Price: $12. CyberAuction #450, Lot #12.

1849. CONTEMPORARY HANDMADE. J. Fine Glass. Ribbon swirl. Unsigned, but Jody Fine. 7/8". Mint (-) (9.2). Price: $12. CyberAuction #454, Lot #8.

1850. CONTEMPORARY HANDMADE. J. Fine Glass. Probably Jody Fine, possibly Steve Maslach. Nice swirl. 13/16". Mint (9.9). Price: $12. CyberAuction #460, Lot #34.

1851. CONTEMPORARY HANDMADE. J. Fine Glass. Probably Jody Fine, possibly Steve Maslach. Nice swirl. 13/16". Mint (9.9). Price: $12. CyberAuction #484, Lot #33.

1852. CONTEMPORARY HANDMADE. J. Fine Glass. Nice ribbon core swirl with outer bands. Pretty. Handmade by Jody Fine, but unsigned. 1-1/8". Mint (9.9). Price: $11. CyberAuction #409, Lot #12.

1853. CONTEMPORARY HANDMADE. J. Fine Glass. Nice swirl. Handmade by Jody Fine, but unsigned. 1-1/8". Mint (9.9). Price: $10. CyberAuction #437, Lot #37.

1854. CONTEMPORARY HANDMADE. J. Fine Glass. Jody Fine swirl. Unsigned. 13/16". Mint (9.9). Price: $10. CyberAuction #456, Lot #5.

1855. CONTEMPORARY HANDMADE. J. Fine Glass. Nice swirl. Handmade by Jody Fine, but unsigned. 1-1/8". Mint (9.9). Price: $10. CyberAuction #456, Lot #42.

1856. CONTEMPORARY HANDMADE. J. Fine Glass. Nice ribbon core swirl with outer bands. Pretty. Handmade by Jody Fine, but unsigned. 1-1/8". Mint (9.9). Price: $10. CyberAuction #457, Lot #14.

1857. CONTEMPORARY HANDMADE. J. Fine Glass. Ribbon swirl. Unsigned, but Jody Fine. 7/8". Mint (-) (9.2). Price: $8. CyberAuction #401, Lot #49.

1858. CONTEMPORARY HANDMADE. J. Fine Glass. Ribbon swirl. Unsigned, but Jody Fine. 7/8". Mint (-) (9.2). Price: $8. CyberAuction #437, Lot #12.

1859. CONTEMPORARY HANDMADE. Jennifer Wilson. Paperweight style. One millefiori cane on a lutz ground on a blue background. Signed "J W 97". This is a rare marble. Jennifer Wilson usually makes marbles in conjunction with her father, Lewis Wilson of Crystal Myth. Those are signed "LJW". You almost never find marbles signed only by her. 25/32". Mint (9.9). Price: $31. CyberAuction #436, Lot #45.

1860. CONTEMPORARY HANDMADE. Jerry Park. Brown, blue and white swirl. Signed "JP 99". 1-5/16". Mint (9.9). Price: $17. CyberAuction #467, Lot #45.

1861. CONTEMPORARY HANDMADE. Jim Davis (IN). Type of onionskin. Signed "JD 1990". This was made by Jim Davis of Indiana. He has not made marbles in years. This is not the Jim Davis from West Virginia who is currently producing marbles. 1-13/16". Mint (9.9). Price: $55. CyberAuction #355, Lot #34.

1862. CONTEMPORARY HANDMADE. Jim Davis (IN). Transparent blue base. Blue subsurface layer with tan splotches. Evocative of a Monet lily pad painting. Signed "JD 1989". This is the Jim Davis from Indiana. He has not produced marbles in almost a decade. 1-15/16". Mint (9.9). Price: $45. CyberAuction #497, Lot #27.

1863. CONTEMPORARY HANDMADE. Jim Davis (IN). Banded swirl with mica. Signed "JD 1991". This is the Jim Davis from Indiana, not Jim Davis from West Virginia. This Jim Davis has not produced marbles in about ten years. 1-13/16". Mint (9.7). Price: $40. CyberAuction #500, Lot #36.

1864. CONTEMPORARY HANDMADE. Jim Davis (IN). Very interesting.

Transparent clear base filled with white onionskin. Two subsurface bands orange and two of green. Signed "JD 1991 XX". I am not sure if the X mean that it was an experimental piece, a numbered pieces, or if Jim was just sending kisses to someone. 1-15/16". Mint (9.9). Price: $40 CyberAuction #502, Lot #21.

1865. CONTEMPORARY HANDMADE. Joe St. Clair. Sulphide is a bust George Washington. Off-center. Unsigned, but it is Joe St. Clair. Tiny sub surface moon on the side of the marble, does not affect viewing the su phide. 1-15/16". Near Mint(+) (8.9). Price: $55. CyberAuction #448, Lot #29.

1866. CONTEMPORARY HANDMADE. Joe St. Clair. Sulphide of the n meral #4. Unsigned, but probably Joe St. Clair or his studio. Definitely a older contemporary, these haven't been made for quite some time, and came from an old contemporary collection. Small flake on the back. 1-8". Near Mint(+) (8.7). Price: $55. CyberAuction #450, Lot #20.

1867. CONTEMPORARY HANDMADE. Joe St. Clair. A paperweight, on a marble. Solid glass bell. Base has three flowers on white ground. Em bossed "Joe St. Clair". American, 1970s. About 3-3/4" tall. Mint (9.9). Pric $44. CyberAuction #503, Lot #42.

1868. CONTEMPORARY HANDMADE. Joe St. Clair. Sulphide of the n meral #9. Unsigned, but probably Joe St. Clair or his studio. Definitely a older contemporary, these haven't been made for quite some time, and came from an old contemporary collection. Small flake on the back. 1-8". Near Mint(+) (8.8). Price: $43. CyberAuction #484, Lot #45.

1869. CONTEMPORARY HANDMADE. Joe St. Clair. Sulphide of the n meral #9. Unsigned, but probably Joe St. Clair or his studio. Definitely a older contemporary, these haven't been made for quite some time, and came from an old contemporary collection. Small flake on the back. 1-8". Near Mint(+) (8.8). Price: $35. CyberAuction #452, Lot #30.

1870. CONTEMPORARY HANDMADE. John Hamon Miller. Transpare clear base. Outer layer is packed alternating opaque white, opaque re and transparent green bands. Signed "JHM 3/99". Very pretty. 2-1/4". Mi (9.9). Price: $38. CyberAuction #374, Lot #59.

1871. CONTEMPORARY HANDMADE. John Hamon Miller. Transpare clear base. Outer layer is packed alternating opaque white, opaque re and transparent green bands. Signed "JHM 3/99". Very pretty. 2-1/4". Mi (9.9). Price: $38. CyberAuction #434, Lot #24.

1872. CONTEMPORARY HANDMADE. John Hamon Miller. Onionsk lutz. Beauty. Unsigned. 1-1/2". Mint (9.9). Price: $36. CyberAuction #47 Lot #10.

1873. CONTEMPORARY HANDMADE. John Hamon Miller. Transpare clear base. Outer layer is packed alternating opaque white, opaque re and transparent green bands. Signed "JHM 3/99". Very pretty. 2-1/4". Mi (9.9). Price: $32. CyberAuction #335, Lot #49.

1874. CONTEMPORARY HANDMADE. John Hamon Miller. Lobed sol core with lutz. Signed "JHM". 1-15/16". Mint (9.9). Price: $32. CyberAuct #476, Lot #23.

1875. CONTEMPORARY HANDMADE. John Hamon Miller. Purple ar white onionskin with lutz. Gorgeous. Signed "JHM". 1-1/2". Mint (9.9 Price: $25. CyberAuction #450, Lot #5.

1876. CONTEMPORARY HANDMADE. John Hamon Miller. Swirl of orange, yellow, black and blue. Very nice. Signed "JHM". 15/16". Mi (9.9). Price: $17. CyberAuction #360, Lot #21.

1877. CONTEMPORARY HANDMADE. John Hamon Miller. Corkscrew of red, green, blue and lutz, in clear. Signed "JH". 13/16". Mint (9.9). Pric $17. CyberAuction #363, Lot #34.

1878. CONTEMPORARY HANDMADE. John Hamon Miller. Torchworke Onionskin lutz. White, red and purple core with lutz bands on it. Signe "JHM 3/99". 13/16". Mint (9.9). Price: $17. CyberAuction #434, Lot #4

1879. CONTEMPORARY HANDMADE. John Hamon Miller. Swirl of re light blue and dark blue. Unsigned. 15/16". Mint (9.9). Price: $1 CyberAuction #422, Lot #40.

1880. CONTEMPORARY HANDMADE. John Hamon Miller. Corkscrew of red, black, yellow and lutz, in clear. Unsigned. 7/8". Mint (9.9). Price $15. CyberAuction #364, Lot #44.

1881. CONTEMPORARY HANDMADE. John Hamon Miller. Swirl of lig blue, red and dark blue. Unsigned. 29/32". Mint (9.9). Price: $1 CyberAuction #367, Lot #22.

1882. CONTEMPORARY HANDMADE. John Hamon Miller. Torchworke Onionskin lutz. White, red and purple core with lutz bands on it. Signe "JHM 3/99". 13/16". Mint (9.9). Price: $15. CyberAuction #386, Lot #3

1883. CONTEMPORARY HANDMADE. John Hamon Miller. Corkscre of white, blue, black and red. Unsigned. 29/32". Mint (9.9). Price: $1 CyberAuction #362, Lot #48.

1884. CONTEMPORARY HANDMADE. John Hamon Miller. Swirl of c ange, blue, yellow and lutz. Unsigned. 27/32". Mint (9.9). Price: $1 CyberAuction #367, Lot #17.

1885. CONTEMPORARY HANDMADE. John Hamon Miller. Swirl of tran parent yellow, opaque white and lutz. Unsigned, probably John Hamc Miller. 31/32". Mint (9.9). Price: $13. CyberAuction #398, Lot #18.

1886. CONTEMPORARY HANDMADE. John Hamon Miller. Swirl of ye low, red, black and green. Unsigned, probably John Hamon Miller. 7/8 Mint (9.9). Price: $12. CyberAuction #361, Lot #5.

1887. CONTEMPORARY HANDMADE. John Hamon Miller. Corkscre of red, black, yellow and lutz, in clear. Unsigned. 1-1/16". Mint (9.9). Price $12. CyberAuction #362, Lot #8.

1888. CONTEMPORARY HANDMADE. John Hamon Miller. Nice lutz Opaque black base. Two red and yellow wide bands. Two narrow sets lutz. Gorgeous. Unsigned. 1-1/16". Mint (9.9). Price: $12. CyberAuctic #368, Lot #23.

1889. CONTEMPORARY HANDMADE. John Hamon Miller. Swirl of o ange, blue and yellow. Some manufacturing roughness. Unsigned. 15/16". Mint(-) (9.0). Price: $12. CyberAuction #368, Lot #56.

1890. CONTEMPORARY HANDMADE. John Hamon Miller. Swirl of light blue, dark blue, red. Unsigned, probably John Hamon Miller. 15/16". Mint (9.9). Price: $11. CyberAuction #361, Lot #9.

1891. CONTEMPORARY HANDMADE. John Hamon Miller. Corkscrew of light blue, orange, red and lutz. Unsigned. 3/4". Mint (9.9). Price: $11. CyberAuction #398, Lot #42.

1892. CONTEMPORARY HANDMADE. John Hamon Miller. Corkscrews of red, black, yellow and lutz, in clear. Unsigned. 13/16". Mint (9.9). Price: $11. CyberAuction #441, Lot #23.

1893. CONTEMPORARY HANDMADE. John Hamon Miller. Swirl of transparent yellow, opaque white and lutz. Unsigned, probably John Hamon Miller. 31/32". Mint (9.9). Price: $10. CyberAuction #361, Lot #16.

1894. CONTEMPORARY HANDMADE. John Hamon Miller. Corkscrew of light blue, orange, red and lutz. Unsigned. 3/4". Mint (9.9). Price: $10. CyberAuction #362, Lot #1.

1895. CONTEMPORARY HANDMADE. John Hamon Miller. Corkscrews of red, black, yellow and lutz, in clear. Unsigned. 13/16". Mint (9.9). Price: $10. CyberAuction #363, Lot #25.

1896. CONTEMPORARY HANDMADE. John Hamon Miller. Swirl of brown, orange and white. Unsigned. 1". Mint (9.9). Price: $9. CyberAuction #362, Lot #11.

1897. CONTEMPORARY HANDMADE. John Hamon Miller. Swirl of white, blue, yellow and some clear. Unsigned. 15/16". Mint (9.9). Price: $9. CyberAuction #362, Lot #17.

1898. CONTEMPORARY HANDMADE. John Hamon Miller. Swirl of red, light blue and dark blue. Unsigned. 15/16". Mint (9.9). Price: $8. CyberAuction #367, Lot #52.

1899. CONTEMPORARY HANDMADE. John Talmadge. Black based clambroth with white bands. Signed "JKT 00". 1-1/2". Mint (9.9). Price: $42. CyberAuction #366, Lot #24.

1900. CONTEMPORARY HANDMADE. Josh Simpson. "Graviton". Transparent clear base. Single fat ribbon filling the marble from side to side. Ribbon is cobalt blue covered on both sides with equidistantly spaced seed air bubbles. Stunning marble. Signed "JS 00". This is the first new marble design that Simpson has made in over twenty years. 1-15/16". Mint (9.9). Price: $140. CyberAuction #388, Lot #57.

1901. CONTEMPORARY HANDMADE. Josh Simpson. Planet type. "Uninhabited World". Excellent design with one satellite. Unsigned, earlier Simpson work. American, circa 1980-1990. 1-7/16". Mint (9.9). Price: $80. CyberAuction #400, Lot #43.

1902. CONTEMPORARY HANDMADE. Josh Simpson. Planet type. "Uninhabited World". Excellent design with one satellite. Unsigned, earlier Simpson work. American, circa 1980-1990. 1-7/8". Mint (9.9). Price: $80. CyberAuction #403, Lot #48.

1903. CONTEMPORARY HANDMADE. Josh Simpson. Planet type. "Attacked Inhabited World". Excellent design with a lutz edged satellite. Super looking marble, great example. Signed "JS 00". American, circa 1980-1990. 1-7/8". Mint (9.9). Price: $70. CyberAuction #392, Lot #58.

1904. CONTEMPORARY HANDMADE. Josh Simpson. "Graviton". Transparent clear base. Single fat ribbon filling the marble from side to side. Ribbon is cobalt blue covered on both sides with equidistantly spaced seed air bubbles. Stunning marble. Signed "JS 00". This is the first new marble design that Simpson has made in over twenty years. 1-15/16". Mint (9.9). Price: $70. CyberAuction #462, Lot #49.

1905. CONTEMPORARY HANDMADE. Josh Simpson. "Graviton". Transparent clear base. Single fat ribbon filling the marble from side to side. Ribbon is cobalt blue covered on both sides with equidistantly spaced seed air bubbles. Stunning marble. Signed "JS 00". This is the first new marble design that Simpson has made in over twenty years. 1-15/16". Mint (9.9). Price: $63. CyberAuction #497, Lot #58.

1906. CONTEMPORARY HANDMADE. Josh Simpson. Planet type. "Inhabited World". Excellent design including several red lava flows (unusual), a couple of tall mountains and a satellite. Super looking marble, great example. Signed "JS 99". American, circa 1980-1990. 1-9/16". Mint (9.9). Price: $60. CyberAuction #373, Lot #55.

1907. CONTEMPORARY HANDMADE. Josh Simpson. "Graviton". Transparent clear base. Single fat ribbon filling the marble from side to side. Ribbon is cobalt blue covered on both sides with equidistantly spaced seed air bubbles. Stunning marble. Signed "JS 00". This is the first new marble design that Simpson has made in over twenty years. 1-13/16". Mint (9.9). Price: $60. CyberAuction #429, Lot #58.

1908. CONTEMPORARY HANDMADE. Josh Simpson. Planet type. "Uninhabited World". Excellent design. Signed "JS98" 1-7/16". Mint (9.9). Price: $55. CyberAuction #414, Lot #58.

1909. CONTEMPORARY HANDMADE. Josh Simpson. Planet type. "Alien Inhabited World". Excellent design with one satellite. Exceptional detail and texture. Signed "JS 00". 1-13/16". Mint (9.9). Price: $55. CyberAuction #448, Lot #47.

1910. CONTEMPORARY HANDMADE. Josh Simpson. Planet type. "Uninhabited World". Excellent design with one moon. Signed "JS 00". American, circa 1980-1990. 1-5/8". Mint (9.9). Price: $50. CyberAuction #380, Lot #49.

1911. CONTEMPORARY HANDMADE. Josh Simpson. "Graviton". Transparent clear base. Single fat ribbon filling the marble from side to side. Ribbon is transparent covered on both sides with equidistantly spaced seed air bubbles. Stunning marble. Signed "JS 00". 1-13/16". Mint (9.9). Price: $50. CyberAuction #508, Lot #13.

1912. CONTEMPORARY HANDMADE. Josh Simpson. Planet type. "Alien Inhabited World". Excellent design with one satellite. Exceptional detail

and texture. Signed "JS 99". 1-7/8". Mint (9.9). Price: $48. CyberAuction #479, Lot #49.

1913. CONTEMPORARY HANDMADE. Josh Simpson. Planet type. "Alien Inhabited World". Excellent design with one satellite. Exceptional detail and texture. Signed "JS 00". American, circa 1980-1990. 1-9/16". Mint (9.9). Price: $41. CyberAuction #442, Lot #58.

1914. CONTEMPORARY HANDMADE. Josh Simpson. Planet type. "Alien Inhabited World". Excellent design with one satellite. Exceptional detail and texture. Signed "JS 00". American, circa 1980-1990. 1-9/16". Mint (9.9). Price: $36. CyberAuction #454, Lot #58.

1915. CONTEMPORARY HANDMADE. Karen Federici. Paperweight type. Red flower in clear. Signed "Karen Federici 00". 31/32". Mint (9.9). Price: $39. CyberAuction #380, Lot #55.

1916. CONTEMPORARY HANDMADE. Karen Federici. Paperweight type. Light blue flower in clear. Signed "Karen Federici 00". 31/32". Mint (9.9). Price: $35. CyberAuction #396, Lot #12.

1917. CONTEMPORARY HANDMADE. Lundberg Studios. Stunning marble. Huge pink flower with green petals and pink stamen. Intricately detailed yellow pistils. Gorgeous. Signed on bottom "Lundberg Studios Steve Lundberg 1989 051725". 2-3/8". Mint (9.9). Price: $375. CyberAuction #369, Lot #60.

1918. CONTEMPORARY HANDMADE. Lundberg Studios. Worldsphere. Absolutely gorgeous!!!! Transparent clear sphere. Subsurface layer of the continents in dichroic browns and greens. The oceans are a blues. White snow. Signed on bottom, "Lundberg Studios 103066 1998". With original certificate. Stunning. About 4" (about the size of a softball). Mint (9.9). Price: $300. CyberAuction #348, Lot #59.

1919. CONTEMPORARY HANDMADE. Matthews Art Glass. One of the Predator Series. This is the Cheetah. Stunning piece of art glass. Utilizing the Graal technique, Matthews has created a scale model of a Cheetah's abdomen. Absolutely exceptional work. Signed "Matthews 1996". This comes from an old-time collector who bought much of Matthew's work early on. This particular marble is a "premium piece". The consignor was a regular customer of Matthew's and received specific pieces that Mark held aside as exceptional quality. 2-1/8" diameter. Mint (9.9). Price: $500. CyberAuction #459, Lot #60.

1920. CONTEMPORARY HANDMADE. Matthews Art Glass. One of the Predator Series. This is the Leopard. Stunning piece of art glass. Utilizing the Graal technique, Matthews has created a scale model of a Leopard's abdomen. Absolutely exceptional work. Signed "Matthews 1996". This comes from an old-time collector who bought much of Matthew's work early on. The consignor was a regular customer of Matthew's and received specific pieces that Mark held aside as exceptional quality. 2-1/2" diameter. Mint (9.9). Price: $460. CyberAuction #508, Lot #75.

1921. CONTEMPORARY HANDMADE. Matthews Art Glass. One of the Predator Series. This is the Bengal Tiger. Stunning piece of art glass. Utilizing the Graal technique, Matthews has created a scale model of a Bengal Tiger's abdomen. Absolutely exceptional work. Signed "Matthews 1999". About 3" diameter. Mint (9.9). Price: $410. CyberAuction #440, Lot #60.

1922. CONTEMPORARY HANDMADE. Matthews Art Glass. Predator. This is the Snow Leopard. Gorgeous. Signed "Matthews 1997". 1-9/16". Mint (9.9). Price: $330. CyberAuction #504, Lot #72.

1923. CONTEMPORARY HANDMADE. Matthews Art Glass. Rare opportunity. Trapped air twist. Four trapped elongated air bubbles in transparent clear. Signed at one end "Matthews 1986". Some carbon at either end where Matthews fire polished the ends. Very early Matthews, this came from an old contemporary collection. Came from the group that was made for one of his first Population Portraits. 1-3/4". Mint (9.8). Price: $260. CyberAuction #450, Lot #41.

1924. CONTEMPORARY HANDMADE. Matthews Art Glass. Super Jetson II. Transparent ice blue. Four air trap saucers with air trap barbells through them. Beautiful marble. Nice example of Matthews air trap work. Signed "Matthews 1998". About 3" diameter (my template isn't big enough). Mint (9.9). Price: $230. CyberAuction #455, Lot #59.

1925. CONTEMPORARY HANDMADE. Matthews Art Glass. Banded lutz. Transparent clear base. Translucent Vaseline green subsurface layer. Two wide white-edged lutz bands. Each is separated by three opaque green bands. Signed "Matthews 1996". These are always stunning. 1-3/16". Mint (9.9). Price: $190. CyberAuction #347, Lot #60.

1926. CONTEMPORARY HANDMADE. Matthews Art Glass. Very rare marble This is an experimental for the 7-lobe solid core swirls. According to Mark Matthews, this is off the first cane he made and there were only five marbles made from that cane. Transparent clear base. Subsurface layer is white base with transparent bright colors on it. Lobed and looping. Stunning marble. Signed "Matthews 1999". 2-1/16". Mint (9.9). Price: $160. CyberAuction #400, Lot #56.

1927. CONTEMPORARY HANDMADE. Matthews Art Glass. Satin iridescent miniature classic "King Tut" pattern. Thick gold Aurene surface bands with ten fingerprint swirls. Signed "Matthews 1993". From an old contemporary collection. 1-15/16". Mint (9.9). Price: $160. CyberAuction #483, Lot #58.

1928. CONTEMPORARY HANDMADE. Matthews Art Glass. 7-lobe solid core swirl. Limited edition. Transparent clear base. Subsurface layer is white base with transparent bright colors on it. Lobed and looping. Stunning marble. Signed "Matthews 1999". 1-15/16". Mint (9.9). Price: $145. CyberAuction #339, Lot #60.

1929. CONTEMPORARY HANDMADE. Matthews Art Glass. Jetson in clear glass. Trapped air forming a ring which encircles the constriction of an hour glass shaped bubble. Signed "Matthews 1988". From a very early Matthews collection. Excellent marble. 2". Mint (9.9). Price: $140. CyberAuction #471, Lot #59.

1930. CONTEMPORARY HANDMADE. Matthews Art Glass. Early Matthews marble. Poorly fire polished pontil. Vaned ribbon swirl design. Gorgeous. Signed on bottom with the Matthews logo of an M over an M. 1-7/16". Mint (9.9). Price: $120. CyberAuction #452, Lot #48.

1931. CONTEMPORARY HANDMADE. Matthews Art Glass. Banded lutz. Transparent clear base. Translucent Vaseline green subsurface layer. Two wide white-edged lutz bands. Each is separated by three opaque green bands. Signed "Matthews 1993". These are always stunning. 1-3/16". Mint (9.9). Price: $120. CyberAuction #454, Lot #46.

1932. CONTEMPORARY HANDMADE. Matthews Art Glass. Hard to find, old design. Banded swirl. Transparent clear base. Two subsurface bands of translucent blue, edged by orange bands. Two clear spaces have some blue. Signed with the Matthews logo of an "M" within and "M". 1-1/2". Mint (9.9). Price: $110. CyberAuction #475, Lot #57.

1933. CONTEMPORARY HANDMADE. Matthews Art Glass. Early Matthews swirl. Transparent clear base. Subsurface layer of purple. Three bands of white on one side of the purple. Signed "Matthews 1986". From a very early Matthews collection. Excellent marble. 1-3/8". Mint (9.9). Price: $110. CyberAuction #479, Lot #58.

1934. CONTEMPORARY HANDMADE. Matthews Art Glass. Banded lutz. Transparent teal base. Six dark blue bands, two white-edged lutz bands. Gorgeous marble. From an old contemporary collection. Signed "Matthews 1994". 1-1/4". Mint (9.9). Price: $110. CyberAuction #481, Lot #57.

1935. CONTEMPORARY HANDMADE. Matthews Art Glass. Super marble. Type of cased clambroth. Transparent clear base. Milky opaque white subsurface layer. Seventeen lobes in that layer, well spaced. There is a light green band on the peak of each lobe. Clear casing. Stunning. Signed with the Matthews logo (M over M). Probably late 1980s to early 1990s. 1-5/16". Mint (9.9). Price: $100. CyberAuction #380, Lot #60.

1936. CONTEMPORARY HANDMADE. Matthews Art Glass. Transparent clear base. Four vane ribbon core. Two are transparent blue, two are pale white. Outer layer is two sets of orange and yellow strands. Signed "Matthews 1999". Beautiful marble. 1-5/8". Mint (9.9). Price: $90. CyberAuction #333, Lot #57.

1937. CONTEMPORARY HANDMADE. Matthews Art Glass. Fascinating. Transparent very fluorescent Vaseline yellow base. Subsurface layer of evenly spaced controlled air bubbles. Signed "Matthews 2000". 1-11/16". Mint (9.9). Price: $90. CyberAuction #369, Lot #49.

1938. CONTEMPORARY HANDMADE. Matthews Art Glass. Air Trap Number "0". Trapped air in shape of numeral "1" in transparent ice blue glass. From an early Matthews collection. Signed "Matthews 1991". 1-11/16". Mint (9.9). Price: $75. CyberAuction #462, Lot #59.

1939. CONTEMPORARY HANDMADE. Matthews Art Glass. Older Gumball. Larger than you usually see. Transparent clear base. Subsurface layer of olive green. Clear hole at either pole. Signed with Matthews logo of "M" in an "M". 1-1/2". Mint (9.9). Price: $75. CyberAuction #475, Lot #45.

1940. CONTEMPORARY HANDMADE. Matthews Art Glass. Beauty. Four vane ribbon core. Two are transparent currant purple, two are opaque white. Outer layer is two sets of white, grey and blue bands. Signed "Matthews 1999". 1-9/16". Mint (9.9). Price: $70. CyberAuction #344, Lot #60.

1941. CONTEMPORARY HANDMADE. Matthews Art Glass. Transparent clear base with trapped air bubble numeral. Beautiful marble. 1-11/16". Numerals 0 to 9 are available in the set. You are bidding on one, your choice of numeral(s). Signed "Matthews {date}". They are dated various 1998 to 2000, set is not dated the same. Winning bidder has choice, remainder to under(s). Price: $45. CyberAuction #487, Lot #56.

1942. CONTEMPORARY HANDMADE. Matthews Art Glass. Transparent clear base with trapped air bubble letter. Beautiful marble. 1-11/16". Most letters from the set are available, there are some duplicates. You are bidding on one, your choice of letter(s). Signed "Matthews 2000". Winning bidder has choice, remainder to under(s). Price: $37.50. CyberAuction #498, Lot #74.

1943. CONTEMPORARY HANDMADE. Monty Fritts. Torchwork. Swirl of transparent green, opaque yellow and lutz. Nice. Signed "MF 99". 27/32". Mint (9.9). Price: $22. CyberAuction #360, Lot #2.

1944. CONTEMPORARY HANDMADE. Monty Fritts. Swirl of light blue, green and yellow. Signed "MF 00". 31/32". Mint (9.9). Price: $17. CyberAuction #362, Lot #51.

1945. CONTEMPORARY HANDMADE. Monty Fritts. Swirl of yellow, blue, red, black and lutz. Gorgeous. Signed "MF 00". 1-3/16". Mint (9.9). Price: $17. CyberAuction #366, Lot #28.

1946. CONTEMPORARY HANDMADE. Monty Fritts. Swirl of black, red, yellow, blue and lutz. Signed "MF 00". 1-1/4". Mint (9.9). Price: $17. CyberAuction #368, Lot #32.

1947. CONTEMPORARY HANDMADE. Monty Fritts. Swirl of light blue, yellow and red. Signed "MF 99". 1". Mint (9.9). Price: $17. CyberAuction #470, Lot #32.

1948. CONTEMPORARY HANDMADE. Monty Fritts. Swirl of white and two shades of green. Signed "MF 00". 1-3/16". Mint (9.9). Price: $16. CyberAuction #402, Lot #17.

1949. CONTEMPORARY HANDMADE. Monty Fritts. Swirl of red, yellow, black and lutz. Signed "MF 00". 1-3/16". Mint (9.9). Price: $15. CyberAuction #367, Lot #47.

1950. CONTEMPORARY HANDMADE. Monty Fritts. Swirl of light blue, yellow and red. Signed "MF 99". 1". Mint (9.9). Price: $14. CyberAuction #380, Lot #40.

1951. CONTEMPORARY HANDMADE. Monty Fritts. Black ribbon edged by lutz, in clear. Signed "MF 00". 15/16". Mint (9.9). Price: $14. CyberAuction #385, Lot #22.

1952. CONTEMPORARY HANDMADE. Monty Fritts. Orange and red two-patch. Signed "MF 00". 7/8". Mint (9.9). Price: $12. CyberAuction #361 Lot #22.

1953. CONTEMPORARY HANDMADE. Monty Fritts. Swirl of blue and white. Torchwork. Signed "MF 00". 1-1/16". Mint (9.9). Price: $12 CyberAuction #362, Lot #45.

1954. CONTEMPORARY HANDMADE. Monty Fritts. Swirl of yellow, orange and brown. Signed "MF 99". 15/16". Mint (9.9). Price: $12. CyberAuction #378, Lot #56.

1955. CONTEMPORARY HANDMADE. Monty Fritts. Red, black, yellow and lutz swirl. Signed "MF 00". 1-3/16". Mint (9.9). Price: $12. CyberAuction #489, Lot #6.

1956. CONTEMPORARY HANDMADE. Monty Fritts. Swirl of white and electric transparent yellow. Signed "MF 99". 7/8". Mint (9.9). Price: $11. CyberAuction #380, Lot #3.

1957. CONTEMPORARY HANDMADE. Monty Fritts. Swirl of red, black, yellow and lutz. Signed "MF 00". 1-3/16". Mint (9.9). Price: $11. CyberAuction #384, Lot #51.

1958. CONTEMPORARY HANDMADE. Monty Fritts. Yellow, dark aventurine blue and light blue swirl. Signed "MF 00". 1-3/16". Mint (9.9). Price: $11. CyberAuction #385, Lot #4.

1959. CONTEMPORARY HANDMADE. Monty Fritts. Swirl of clear, yellow, white, red and green. Signed "MF 00". 1-1/4". Mint (9.9). Price: $11. CyberAuction #389, Lot #4.

1960. CONTEMPORARY HANDMADE. Monty Fritts. Black ribbon edged by lutz, in clear. Signed "MF 00". 15/16". Mint (9.9). Price: $11. CyberAuction #478, Lot #32.

1961. CONTEMPORARY HANDMADE. Monty Fritts. Swirl of white, red, green and yellow. Bright. Signed "MF 00". 1". Mint (9.9). Price: $10. CyberAuction #360, Lot #9.

1962. CONTEMPORARY HANDMADE. Monty Fritts. Swirl of opaque yellow and transparent green. Signed "MF 99". 7/8". Mint (9.9). Price: $10. CyberAuction #378, Lot #8.

1963. CONTEMPORARY HANDMADE. Monty Fritts. Swirl of red, yellow, light green and lutz in clear. Signed "MF 98". 1-1/16". Mint (9.9). Price: $10. CyberAuction #395, Lot #10.

1964. CONTEMPORARY HANDMADE. Monty Fritts. Swirls of yellow, red, white and lutz. Signed "MF 00". 1-5/16". Mint (9.9). Price: $10. CyberAuction #395, Lot #23.

1965. CONTEMPORARY HANDMADE. Monty Fritts. Red and green swirl. Signed "MF 00". 1-1/16". Mint (9.9). Price: $10. CyberAuction #401, Lot #5.

1966. CONTEMPORARY HANDMADE. Monty Fritts. Swirl of light blue, yellow and red. Signed "MF 99". 1". Mint (9.9). Price: $10. CyberAuction #442, Lot #44.

1967. CONTEMPORARY HANDMADE. Monty Fritts. Swirl of yellow, white, green, red, blue and aventurine black. Signed "MF 00". 1-3/16". Mint (9.9). Price: $10. CyberAuction #485, Lot #35.

1968. CONTEMPORARY HANDMADE. Monty Fritts. Blue, red and white swirl. Signed "MF 00". 1-1/4". Mint (9.9). Price: $9. CyberAuction #393, Lot #12.

1969. CONTEMPORARY HANDMADE. Monty Fritts. Clear, green and yellow swirl. Signed "MF 00". 1-3/16". Mint (9.9). Price: $9. CyberAuction #393, Lot #51.

1970. CONTEMPORARY HANDMADE. Monty Fritts. Brown and white slag. Signed "MF 99". 29/32". Mint (9.7). Price: $9. CyberAuction #402, Lot #21.

1971. CONTEMPORARY HANDMADE. Monty Fritts. Swirl of light blue, red and white. Signed "MF 00". 1". Mint (9.9). Price: $9. CyberAuction #441, Lot #16.

1972. CONTEMPORARY HANDMADE. Monty Fritts. Contemporary wire pull. Signed "MF 00". 27/32". Mint (9.9). Price: $8. CyberAuction #384, Lot #39.

1973. CONTEMPORARY HANDMADE. Monty Fritts. Swirl of dark blue, light blue and white. Signed "MF 00". 1-1/16". Mint (9.9). Price: $8. CyberAuction #389, Lot #54.

1974. CONTEMPORARY HANDMADE. Monty Fritts. Swirl of red, yellow and white. Signed "MF 00". 1-1/4". Mint (9.9). Price: $8. CyberAuction #391, Lot #40.

1975. CONTEMPORARY HANDMADE. Monty Fritts. Swirl of white, greens, yellow, orange and blue aventurine. Signed "MF 00". 1-1/4". Mint (9.9). Price: $8. CyberAuction #399, Lot #19.

1976. CONTEMPORARY HANDMADE. Monty Fritts. Black ribbon edged by lutz, in clear. Signed "MF 00". 15/16". Mint (9.9). Price: $8. CyberAuction #440, Lot #26.

1977. CONTEMPORARY HANDMADE. Monty Fritts. Swirl of orange, yellow, white and clear. Signed "MF 00". 29/32". Mint (9.9). Price: $8. CyberAuction #484, Lot #9.

1978. CONTEMPORARY HANDMADE. Monty Fritts. Swirl of yellow, light green, red, lutz and clear. Signed "MF 00". 1-1/16". Mint (9.9). Price: $8. CyberAuction #490, Lot #11.

1979. CONTEMPORARY HANDMADE. Monty Fritts. Swirl of white, green, red and blue. Unsigned. 1-1/16". Mint (9.9). Price: $8. CyberAuction #492, Lot #23.

1980. CONTEMPORARY HANDMADE. Monty Fritts. Swirl of light blue, red and white. Signed "MF 00". 1". Mint (9.9). Price: $7. CyberAuction #401, Lot #25.

1981. CONTEMPORARY HANDMADE. Monty Fritts. Swirl of orange, yellow, white and clear. Signed "MF 99". 29/32". Mint (9.9). Price: $7. CyberAuction #408, Lot #1.

1982. CONTEMPORARY HANDMADE. Monty Fritts. Swirl of orange, yellow, white and clear. Signed "MF 99". 29/32". Mint (9.9). Price: $7. CyberAuction #426, Lot #25.

1983. CONTEMPORARY HANDMADE. Monty Fritts. Swirl of green, yellow and clear. Signed "MF 00". 15/16". Mint (9.7). Price: $6. CyberAuction #399, Lot #38.

1984. CONTEMPORARY HANDMADE. Monty Fritts. Swirl of orange, yellow, white and clear. Signed "MF 99". 29/32". Mint (9.9). Price: $5. CyberAuction #391, Lot #34.

1985. CONTEMPORARY HANDMADE. Nadine MacDonald. Hand painted porcelain. Orange background. Incised jack-o-lantern with face on either side. Signed "N.M. 97". 1-1/8". Mint (9.9). Price: $25. CyberAuction #462, Lot #26.

1986. CONTEMPORARY HANDMADE. Nadine MacDonald. "Cape Cod Garden". Hand painted china. Pink flowers with green leaves and vines. Signed "NM 96". 1-1/16". Mint (9.9). Price: $24. CyberAuction #332, Lot #32.

1987. CONTEMPORARY HANDMADE. Nadine MacDonald. Hand painted porcelain. Orange marble. Incised with a jack-o-lantern. Signed "N.M.". 13/16". Mint (9.8). There are two marbles available, you are bidding on one. Winner has choice of either or both, remainder to under. Price: $12. CyberAuction #464, Lot #31.

1988. CONTEMPORARY HANDMADE. Nadine MacDonald. Hand painted pottery. Yellow base, purple and red swirls. Painted to resemble a Christensen Agate diaper fold swirl. Signed "N.M.". American, circa 1995-1998. 13/16". Mint (9.9). Price: $11. CyberAuction #350, Lot #40.

1989. CONTEMPORARY HANDMADE. Nadine MacDonald. Hand painted porcelain. Orange marble. Incised with a jack-o-lantern. Signed "N.M.". 13/16". Mint (9.8). Price: $8. CyberAuction #492, Lot #39.

1990. CONTEMPORARY HANDMADE. Noble Effort. Very hard to find. Noble Effort murrini marble. Transparent clear with subsurface layer of various silhouette and picture canes. Includes a cane that reads "c 1984 Noble Effort". Note, this is not one of the more recent Ro Purser murrinis. Ro Purser was half of Noble Effort, with Richard Marquis. Purser starting producing murrinis again about a year or so ago. His all have a cane in them reading "Ro" plus the date. Noble Effort was the company formed by Ro Purser and Richard Marquis, the first artists to produce contemporary marbles. They only produced for about a year or two. These are very hard to find. Current Purser murrinis retail in the $600 range. 2-5/16". Mint (9.9). Price: $625. CyberAuction #491, Lot #59.

1991. CONTEMPORARY HANDMADE. Phil McGlothlin. Nice looking planetoid. Light blue base with some black mottled in. "Canals" of red and yellow. Unsigned. American, circa 1998-1999. 1-1/16". Mint (9.9). Price: $35. CyberAuction #371, Lot #32.

1992. CONTEMPORARY HANDMADE. Phil McGlothlin. Torchwork. Looks like a Peltier National Line Rainbo. Blue base with black and lutz ribbons. Signed "Mac". 5/8". Mint (9.9). Price: $23. CyberAuction #375, Lot #42.

1993. CONTEMPORARY HANDMADE. Phil McGlothlin. Ribbon corkscrew. Transparent clear base. Triple twist ribbon of orange and dichroic. Beauty. Signed "mac". 25/32". Mint (9.9). Price: $10. CyberAuction #371, Lot #9.

1994. CONTEMPORARY HANDMADE. Phil McGlothlin. Ribbon corkscrew. Transparent clear base. Triple twist ribbon of orange and dichroic. Beauty. Signed "mac". 25/32". Mint (9.9). Price: $10. CyberAuction #430, Lot #25.

1995. CONTEMPORARY HANDMADE. Richard Dinardo. Very rare. This is a double ribbon core marble that he made into a paperweight, by grinding it flat. Dinardo marbles are hard to come by anyways, since he has not produced in about ten years. Super!!! Signed "Dinardo 1986". 2-1/2". Mint (9.9). Price: $140. CyberAuction #400, Lot #31.

1996. CONTEMPORARY HANDMADE. Robert Brown. Glazed hand painted china. Intersecting lines. Signed "Robert A. Brown 1990". 7/8". Mint (9.9). Price: $19. CyberAuction #354, Lot #6.

1997. CONTEMPORARY HANDMADE. Rolf and Genie Wald. Limited Edition "American Flag". Created by Rolf and Genie Wald. Ribbon core swirl. Blue base on one side, covered with gold lutz. Other side is seven red and six white bands to form that face. Ribbon has three yellow bands on either edge. Signed and numbered. "Wald 1999 98/100". 2". Mint (9.9). I spoke with Rolf and he has none of these left. They are only available on the secondary market now. Price: $200. CyberAuction #330, Lot #52.

1998. CONTEMPORARY HANDMADE. Rolf and Genie Wald. Onionskin with bronze color mica. Nice colors. Signed "Wald 98". 1-7/16". Mint (9.9). Price: $65. CyberAuction #376, Lot #18.

1999. CONTEMPORARY HANDMADE. Rolf and Genie Wald. Beautiful Wald Joseph Coat with lutz. Signed "Wald 99". 1-7/16". Mint (9.9). Price: $56. CyberAuction #372, Lot #57.

2000. CONTEMPORARY HANDMADE. Rolf and Genie Wald. Celebration marble. Transparent clear base. Subsurface golden lutz layer with alternating red, yellow and blue bands. Reverse twist on it. Signed "Wald 99". Gorgeous. 1-7/16". Mint (9.9). Price: $55. CyberAuction #495, Lot #47.

2001. CONTEMPORARY HANDMADE. Rolf and Genie Wald. Beach Ball. Orange, white, aventurine red, yellow, green, blue. Signed on bottom "Wald 99". 1-5/16". Mint (9.9). Price: $50. CyberAuction #381, Lot #50.

2002. CONTEMPORARY HANDMADE. Rolf and Genie Wald. Marble related item. Glass hand of variegated glass, shooting a peewee Wald Beach Ball. Signed "Wald 99". 1-1/4" x 1-3/8". Mint (9.9). Price: $45. CyberAuction #430, Lot #52.

2003. CONTEMPORARY HANDMADE. Rolf and Genie Wald. Marble related item. Glass hand of variegated glass, shooting a peewee Wald Beach Ball. Signed "Wald 99". 1-1/4" x 1-3/8". Mint (9.9). Price: $42. CyberAuction #464, Lot #38.

2004. CONTEMPORARY HANDMADE. Rolf and Genie Wald. Marble related item. Glass hand of variegated glass, shooting a peewee Wald Beach

2005. CONTEMPORARY HANDMADE. Rolf and Genie Wald. Spinner. Transparent dark blue lutz core. Colored strands on the core. Signed "Wald 99". 1-7/16". Mint (9.9). Price: $37. CyberAuction #435, Lot #35.

2006. CONTEMPORARY HANDMADE. Rolf and Genie Wald. Onionskin with bronze color mica. Nice colors. Signed "Wald 98". 1-1/16". Mint (9.9). Price: $35. CyberAuction #364, Lot #58.

2007. CONTEMPORARY HANDMADE. Rolf and Genie Wald. Very nice Joseph Coat swirl with lutz bands. Signed "Wald 99". 1-1/8". Mint (9.9). Price: $35. CyberAuction #370, Lot #47.

2008. CONTEMPORARY HANDMADE. Rolf and Genie Wald. Nice ribbon lutz. Single ribbon core. One side is gold lutz, other side is yellow. Colored strands floating above the yellow side. Colored strands edging the ribbon. Very pretty. Signed "Wald 95". 1-9/16". Mint (9.9). Price: $35. CyberAuction #387, Lot #49.

2009. CONTEMPORARY HANDMADE. Rolf and Genie Wald. Marble related item. Glass hand of variegated glass, shooting a peewee Wald Beach Ball. Signed "Wald 99". 1-1/4" x 1-3/8". Mint (9.9). Price: $35. CyberAuction #395, Lot #51.

2010. CONTEMPORARY HANDMADE. Rolf and Genie Wald. Nice ribbon lutz. Single ribbon core. One side is gold lutz, other side is yellow. Colored strands floating above the yellow side. Colored strands edging the ribbon. Very pretty. Signed "Wald 95". 1-9/16". Mint (9.9). Price: $35. CyberAuction #447, Lot #58.

2011. CONTEMPORARY HANDMADE. Rolf and Genie Wald. Beautiful single ribbon swirl. Signed "Wald 99". 1-1/8". Mint (9.9). Price: $32. CyberAuction #416, Lot #43.

2012. CONTEMPORARY HANDMADE. Rolf and Genie Wald. Spinner. Transparent dark blue lutz core. Colored strands on the core. Signed "Wald 99". 1-1/2". Mint (9.9). Price: $32. CyberAuction #425, Lot #48.

2013. CONTEMPORARY HANDMADE. Rolf and Genie Wald. Onionskin with bronze color mica. Nice colors. Signed "Wald 98". 1-1/16". Mint (9.9). Price: $32. CyberAuction #441, Lot #22.

2014. CONTEMPORARY HANDMADE. Rolf and Genie Wald. Marble related item. Glass hand of variegated glass, shooting a peewee Wald Beach Ball. Signed "Wald 99". 1-1/4" x 1-3/8". Mint (9.9). Price: $32. CyberAuction #461, Lot #20.

2015. CONTEMPORARY HANDMADE. Rolf and Genie Wald. Spinner. Transparent dark blue lutz core. Colored strands on the core. Signed "Wald 99". 1-1/2". Mint (9.9). Price: $32. CyberAuction #478, Lot #37.

2016. CONTEMPORARY HANDMADE. Rolf and Genie Wald. Interesting split ribbon lutz. Signed "Wald 93". 1-5/16". Mint (9.9). Price: $31. CyberAuction #505, Lot #16.

2017. CONTEMPORARY HANDMADE. Rolf and Genie Wald. Onionskin with bronze mica. Mostly blues. Signed "Wald 96". 1-1/2". Mint (9.9). Price: $30. CyberAuction #431, Lot #45.

2018. CONTEMPORARY HANDMADE. Rolf and Genie Wald. Spinner. Black core. Colored strands on the core. Signed "Wald 98". 1-7/16". Mint (9.9). Price: $27. CyberAuction #442, Lot #30.

2019. CONTEMPORARY HANDMADE. Rolf and Genie Wald. Spinner. Transparent dark purple lutz core. Colored strands on the core. Signed "Wald 97". 1-1/8". Mint (9.9). Price: $22. CyberAuction #382, Lot #55.

2020. CONTEMPORARY HANDMADE. Rolf and Genie Wald. Spinner. Black core. Colored strands on the core. Signed "Wald 98". 1-7/16". Mint (9.9). Price: $22. CyberAuction #466, Lot #43.

2021. CONTEMPORARY HANDMADE. Rolf and Genie Wald. A top that is made of onionskin lutz glass. Unsigned, but Wald. Very nice. About 1-1/2" long. Price: $12. CyberAuction #501, Lot #20.

2022. CONTEMPORARY HANDMADE. Salazar Art Glass. Earlier Salazar. Semi-opaque white base. Cobalt blue orchid. Pink stamen. Green stem and leaves. Virtually impossible to find these older Salazars. Signed "D.P. Salazar 88". 1-7/16". Mint (9.9). Price: $270. CyberAuction #356, Lot #58.

2023. CONTEMPORARY HANDMADE. Salazar Art Glass. Old Salazar. Butterfly and poppies on opaque white. He hasn't made this style in years. Signed "D P Salazar 86". 1-7/16". Mint (9.9). Price: $170. CyberAuction #500, Lot #55.

2024. CONTEMPORARY HANDMADE. Salazar Art Glass. Stars and Stripes. Blue base. Three red and three white outer bands. Top is crowned by nine white stars. Signed "D P Salazar 8/91". 1-5/8". Mint (9.9). Price: $95. CyberAuction #477, Lot #60.

2025. CONTEMPORARY HANDMADE. Salazar Art Glass. Bird of Paradise. Transparent clear base. Dichroic blue bottom. Large white moon on that. Purple and orange bird of paradise with green leaves and stem floating above that. Signed "D P Salazar 5/99". 1-3/4". Mint (9.9). Price: $90. CyberAuction #351, Lot #54.

2026. CONTEMPORARY HANDMADE. Salazar Art Glass. Orca. Blue base with white stars. An orca leaping above blue waves, with a yellow sun in background. Signed "D P Salazar 4/97". 1-11/16". Mint (9.9). Price: $90. CyberAuction #501, Lot #59.

2027. CONTEMPORARY HANDMADE. Salazar Art Glass. Orchid in moonlight. Dichroic blue background. Large white moon. Four orchids, one in bloom. Clear top. Signed "DP Salazar 2/99". 1-13/16". Mint (9.9). Price: $85. CyberAuction #505, Lot #59.

2028. CONTEMPORARY HANDMADE. Salazar Art Glass. Moon and stars. Opaque blue marble with overall white five-pointed stars and a yellow crescent moon. Signed "DP Salazar 1/00". 1-13/16". Mint (9.9). Price: $44. CyberAuction #428, Lot #56.

2029. CONTEMPORARY HANDMADE. Salazar Art Glass. Moon and Stars. His signature design. Opaque blue base. Orange moon, white stars. Early example. Signed "DPS 92". 1-7/16". Mint (9.9). Price: $40. CyberAuction #498, Lot #70.

2030. CONTEMPORARY HANDMADE. Salazar Art Glass. Beautiful marble. Transparent clear base. This onionskin ribbon core. Core is white with lots of clear spaces. Outer layer is a cage of colored bands on white, separated by transparent smoky end of day. Looks great. Signed "DPS 11/99". 1-7/16". Mint (9.9). Price: $34. CyberAuction #334, Lot #37.

2031. CONTEMPORARY HANDMADE. Salazar Art Glass. Beautiful marble. Transparent clear base. Translucent dichroic core. Outer layer is bands of green and white. Signed "DPS 11/99". American. 1-1/2". Mint (9.9). Price: $33. CyberAuction #340, Lot #49.

2032. CONTEMPORARY HANDMADE. Salazar Art Glass. Very unusual. Divided core of lutz in various greens and red. Signed "D P Salazar 4/00". 1-3/4". Mint (9.9). Price: $32. CyberAuction #424, Lot #36.

2033. CONTEMPORARY HANDMADE. Salazar Art Glass. Interesting, small onionskin. Four panel. Two are dichroic blue, two are wispy white on blue. Signed "DPSG 6/96". 1-1/4". Mint (9.9). Price: $30. CyberAuction #339, Lot #18.

2034. CONTEMPORARY HANDMADE. Salazar Art Glass. Multicolor smeared onionskin with a deep lobe. Signed "DPS 11/99". 1-7/16". Mint (9.9). Price: $30. CyberAuction #346, Lot #35.

2035. CONTEMPORARY HANDMADE. Salazar Art Glass. End of day variety in clear. Signed "D P Salazar 4/00". 1-5/8". Mint (9.9). Price: $30. CyberAuction #427, Lot #21.

2036. CONTEMPORARY HANDMADE. Salazar Art Glass. Mustard and white end of day core. Outer layer is bands of green aventurine and yellow and white. Signed "DP Salazar 4/00". 1-11/16". Mint (9.9). Price: $30. CyberAuction #433, Lot #33.

2037. CONTEMPORARY HANDMADE. Salazar Art Glass. Beautiful marble. Transparent clear base. Fat transparent currant purple core. Outer layer two sets of green, pink and white bands. Looks great. Signed "DPSG 5/98". 1-9/16". Mint (9.9). Price: $29. CyberAuction #341, Lot #45.

2038. CONTEMPORARY HANDMADE. Salazar Art Glass. Transparent clear base. White onionskin core. Outer layer is various bands of purple and light blue. Signed "D P Salazar 4/00". 1-5/8". Mint (9.9). Price: $29. CyberAuction #419, Lot #53.

2039. CONTEMPORARY HANDMADE. Salazar Art Glass. End of day variety in clear. Signed "D P Salazar 4/00". 1-5/8". Mint (9.9). Price: $29. CyberAuction #421, Lot #23.

2040. CONTEMPORARY HANDMADE. Salazar Art Glass. Transparent emerald green solid core. Middle layer is a couple of bands of white dichroic. Outer layer is three wide colored bands and a thin lutz band. Signed "DP Salazar 4/00". 1-3/4". Mint (9.9). Price: $26. CyberAuction #432, Lot #20.

2041. CONTEMPORARY HANDMADE. Salazar Art Glass. Transparent clear base. Outer layer is bands of aventurine green, yellow, pink and blue. Tightly swirled. Signed "D P Salazar 9/99". 1-9/16". Mint (9.9). Price: $25. CyberAuction #342, Lot #32.

2042. CONTEMPORARY HANDMADE. Salazar Art Glass. Nice swirl. Transparent clear base. Core is a twisted transparent purple lutz core. Outer layer is bands of various colors, including purple lutz. Very nice. Signed "DPS 11/99". 1-7/16". Mint (9.9). Price: $24. CyberAuction #350, Lot #31.

2043. CONTEMPORARY HANDMADE. Salazar Art Glass. Transparent clear base. Subsurface bands of pink, blue and white. Also, some brown lutz. Signed "DPS 9/99". 1-1/2". Mint (9.9). Price: $24. CyberAuction #352, Lot #19.

2044. CONTEMPORARY HANDMADE. Salazar Art Glass. Tight swirls of purple and white in clear. Signed "DP Salazar 4/00". 1-11/16". Mint (9.9). Price: $24. CyberAuction #417, Lot #26.

2045. CONTEMPORARY HANDMADE. Salazar Art Glass. Transparent emerald green solid core. Middle layer is a couple of bands of white dichroic. Outer layer is three wide colored bands and a thin lutz band. Signed "DP Salazar 4/00". 1-3/4". Mint (9.9). Price: $24. CyberAuction #454, Lot #23.

2046. CONTEMPORARY HANDMADE. Salazar Art Glass. Interesting type of cased clambroth. Transparent clear base. Subsurface layer of opaque white with embedded bands of blue, purple, green, teal, pink and lutz. Signed "DPS 11/98". 1-7/16". Mint (9.9). Price: $23. CyberAuction #338, Lot #4.

2047. CONTEMPORARY HANDMADE. Salazar Art Glass. Transparent dark purple base. Subsurface layer of green bands. Outer casing of transparent clear. Clambroth cased type. Signed "DPS 11/98". 1-9/16". Mint (9.9). Price: $22. CyberAuction #337, Lot #42.

2048. CONTEMPORARY HANDMADE. Salazar Art Glass. Transparent clear with narrow bands of blue, red and dichroic. Signed "DPS 5/00". 1-1/16". Mint (9.9). Price: $22. CyberAuction #452, Lot #37.

2049. CONTEMPORARY HANDMADE. Salazar Art Glass. Onionskin core. Three outer bands. Unsigned. 1-1/16". Mint (9.9). Price: $19. CyberAuction #462, Lot #20.

2050. CONTEMPORARY HANDMADE. Salazar Art Glass. Nice swirl of dark colors and lutz. Some air bubbles in it. Signed "DPS 2/00". 1-3/16". Mint (9.9). Price: $17. CyberAuction #450, Lot #23.

2051. CONTEMPORARY HANDMADE. Salazar Art Glass. Tiny onionskin core at bottom with three outer bands. Signed "DPS 3/00". 1-1/16". Mint (9.9). Price: $17. CyberAuction #465, Lot #31.

2052. CONTEMPORARY HANDMADE. Salazar Art Glass. Onionskin core. Three outer bands. Unsigned. 1-1/16". Mint (9.9). Price: $14. CyberAuction #461, Lot #4.

2053. CONTEMPORARY HANDMADE. Salazar Art Glass. Banded swirl. Signed "DPS 8/00". 1-1/16". Mint (9.9). Price: $14. CyberAuction #463, Lot #37.

2054. CONTEMPORARY HANDMADE. Salazar Art Glass. Salazar Baby Swirl. Banded swirl with lutz. Unsigned. 1-1/16". Mint (9.9). Price: $14. CyberAuction #490, Lot #26.

2055. CONTEMPORARY HANDMADE. Salazar Art Glass. Interesting marble. Unsigned, but from David Salazar. Transparent clear base. Very tiny onionskin core, just at the bottom. Outer layer is one wide band. Very nice. 1-1/16". Mint (9.9). Price: $13. CyberAuction #451, Lot #12.

2056. CONTEMPORARY HANDMADE. Salazar Art Glass. Interesting marble. Unsigned, but from David Salazar. Onionskin core with outer ribbons, including green aventurine. 1-1/16". Mint (9.9). Price: $13. CyberAuction #451, Lot #18.

2057. CONTEMPORARY HANDMADE. Salazar Art Glass. Nice beginning of cane-type onionskin. Signed "DPS 8/00". 1-1/16". Mint (9.9). Price: $13. CyberAuction #452, Lot #12.

2058. CONTEMPORARY HANDMADE. Salazar Art Glass. Blue and white end of cane onionskin design in clear. Unsigned, but it is a recent David Salazar marble. 1-1/16". Mint (9.9). Price: $12. CyberAuction #455, Lot #24.

2059. CONTEMPORARY HANDMADE. Salazar Art Glass. Small Salazar banded swirl. Signed "DPS 8/00". 1-1/16". Mint (9.9). Price: $12. CyberAuction #457, Lot #17.

2060. CONTEMPORARY HANDMADE. Salazar Art Glass. Joseph Coat with clear spaces. Pretty. Signed "DPS 7/00". 1-1/16". Mint (9.9). Price: $12. CyberAuction #458, Lot #35.

2061. CONTEMPORARY HANDMADE. Salazar Art Glass. Onionskin. Signed "DPS 6/00". 1-1/16". Mint (9.9). Price: $12. CyberAuction #461, Lot #21.

2062. CONTEMPORARY HANDMADE. Salazar Art Glass. Baby Onionskin. Signed "DPS 6/00". 1-1/16". Mint (9.9). Price: $12. CyberAuction #494, Lot #3.

2063. CONTEMPORARY HANDMADE. Salazar Art Glass. Banded swirl with lutz. Unsigned. 1-1/16". Mint (9.9). Price: $10. CyberAuction #459, Lot #24.

2064. CONTEMPORARY HANDMADE. Salazar Art Glass. Onionskin type. Signed "DPS 3/00". Large annealing fracture. 1-1/16". Mint(-) (9.0). Price: $6. CyberAuction #463, Lot #46.

2065. CONTEMPORARY HANDMADE. Sam Hogue. Slaggish end of day in clear type. Signed "SLH 96". Each has a tiny subsurface moon. One green/white, one blue/white, one green/pink/white. 1-7/8". Near Mint(+) (8.9). Price: $37. CyberAuction #410, Lot #35.

2066. CONTEMPORARY HANDMADE. Sam Hogue. Slaggish end of day in clear type. Signed "SLH 96". 1-7/8". Mint (9.9). There are four marbles available. You are bidding on one. You have choice of any or all, by color, remainder to under. 1-blue, 2-pink, 3-brown, 4-multicolor. Price: $29. CyberAuction #360, Lot #39.

2067. CONTEMPORARY HANDMADE. Sara Creekmore. Swirls of dichroic in clear. Unsigned. Sara Creekmore is no longer producing marbles. 1-13/16". Mint (9.9). Price: $32. CyberAuction #473, Lot #59.

2068. CONTEMPORARY HANDMADE. Scott Patrick. Very early Scott Patrick reworked oxblood. Transparent clear with a ribbon of opaque white and oxblood in it. Ground pontil. Made to mimic a Leighton transitional. These are the earliest Scott Patrick marbles, I don't think he's made them in a number of years. Hard to find. American, circa 1990-1995. 7/8". Mint (9.9). Price: $110. CyberAuction #400, Lot #38.

2069. CONTEMPORARY HANDMADE. Scott Patrick. Very early Scott Patrick reworked oxblood. Transparent clear with a ribbon of opaque white and oxblood in it. Ground pontil. Made to mimic a Leighton transitional. These are the earliest Scott Patrick marbles, I don't think he's made them in a number of years. Hard to find. American, circa 1990-1995. 7/8". Mint (9.9). Price: $110. CyberAuction #454, Lot #48.

2070. CONTEMPORARY HANDMADE. Scott Patrick. Very early Scott Patrick reworked oxblood. Transparent clear with a ribbon of opaque white and oxblood in it. Ground pontil. Made to mimic a Leighton transitional. These are the earliest Scott Patrick marbles, I don't think he's made them in a number of years. Hard to find. American, circa 1990-1995. 7/8". Mint (9.9). Price: $110. CyberAuction #470, Lot #44.

2071. CONTEMPORARY HANDMADE. Scott Patrick. Very early Scott Patrick reworked oxblood. Translucent milky white with egg yolk yellow and oxblood. Mimics an egg yolk oxblood. These are the earliest Scott Patrick marbles, I don't think he's made them in a number of years. Hard to find. American, circa 1990-1995. 21/32". Mint (9.9). Price: $80. CyberAuction #456, Lot #57.

2072. CONTEMPORARY HANDMADE. Scott Patrick. Very early Scott Patrick reworked oxblood. Translucent milky white with egg yolk yellow and oxblood. Mimics an egg yolk oxblood. These are the earliest Scott Patrick marbles, I don't think he's made them in a number of years. Hard to find. American, circa 1990-1995. 21/32". Mint (9.9). Price: $75. CyberAuction #425, Lot #16.

2073. CONTEMPORARY HANDMADE. Scott Patrick. Very early Scott Patrick reworked oxblood. Translucent milky white with egg yolk yellow and oxblood. Mimics an egg yolk oxblood. These are the earliest Scott Patrick marbles, I don't think he's made them in a number of years. Hard to find. American, circa 1990-1995. 3/4". Mint (9.9). Price: $75. CyberAuction #425, Lot #56.

2074. CONTEMPORARY HANDMADE. Scott Patrick. Very early Scott Patrick reworked oxblood. Transparent clear base with tons of oxblood in it. Ground pontil. Mimics a clear brick. This is one of the earliest Scott Patrick marbles, I don't think he's made them in a number of years. Last of a small collection. Hard to find. American, circa 1990-1995. 29/32". Mint (9.9). Price: $75. CyberAuction #429, Lot #46.

2075. CONTEMPORARY HANDMADE. Scott Patrick. Very early Scott

Patrick reworked oxblood. Translucent milky white with egg yolk yellow and oxblood. Mimics an egg yolk oxblood. These are the earliest Scott Patrick marbles, I don't think he's made them in a number of years. Hard to find. American, circa 1990-1995. 3/4". Mint (9.9). Price: $75. CyberAuction #484, Lot #44.

2076. CONTEMPORARY HANDMADE. Scott Patrick. Very early Scott Patrick reworked oxblood. Transparent clear spiraled egg yolk yellow and oxblood. Ground pontil. Made to mimic a Leighton transitional. These are the earliest Scott Patrick marbles, I don't think he's made them in a number of years. Hard to find. American, circa 1990-1995. 27/32". Mint (9.9). Price: $60. CyberAuction #471, Lot #50.

2077. CONTEMPORARY HANDMADE. Scott Patrick. Very early Scott Patrick reworked oxblood. Transparent clear base with tons of oxblood in it. Ground pontil. Mimics a clear brick. This is one of the earliest Scott Patrick marbles, I don't think he's made them in a number of years. Last of a small collection. Hard to find. American, circa 1990-1995. 29/32". Mint (9.9). Price: $55. CyberAuction #466, Lot #6.

2078. CONTEMPORARY HANDMADE. Scott Patrick. Early Scott Patrick reworked oxblood. Transparent clear base with tons of oxblood in it. Ground pontil. An early Scott Patrick marble, I don't think he's made them in a number of years. Part of a small collection. Hard to find. American, circa 1990-1995. 27/32". Mint (9.9). Price: $48. CyberAuction #475, Lot #39.

2079. CONTEMPORARY HANDMADE. Scott Patrick. Early Scott Patrick reworked oxblood. Transparent clear with a ribbon of opaque white, transparent green and oxblood in it. Ground pontil. Made to mimic a rare horizontal slag. These are the earliest Scott Patrick marbles, I don't think he's made them in a number of years. Hard to find. American, circa 1990-1995. 23/32". Mint (9.9). Price: $42. CyberAuction #467, Lot #49.

2080. CONTEMPORARY HANDMADE. Scott Patrick. Blue and yellow swirl. Christensen Agate swirl mimic. Unsigned. 5/8". Mint (9.9). Price: $30. CyberAuction #352, Lot #41.

2081. CONTEMPORARY HANDMADE. Scott Patrick. Early Scott Patrick Cobra. Multicolored core in clear. Beauty. Unsigned. 5/8". Mint (9.9). Price: $27. CyberAuction #400, Lot #14.

2082. CONTEMPORARY HANDMADE. Scott Patrick. Swirl of electric orange and blue. Mimics a Christensen Agate swirl. Handmade. Unsigned. 15/32". Mint (9.9). Price: $22. CyberAuction #435, Lot #39.

2083. CONTEMPORARY HANDMADE. Scott Patrick. Blue and red swirled in white. Mimicking a Peltier Liberty. Nice mimic. American, circa 1996-1998. 11/16". Mint (9.9). Price: $21. CyberAuction #352, Lot #4.

2084. CONTEMPORARY HANDMADE. Scott Patrick. Early attempt to mimic a Christensen Agate Cobra. Light blue and orange in clear. Unsigned. 21/32". Mint (9.9). Price: $20. CyberAuction #503, Lot #41.

2085. CONTEMPORARY HANDMADE. Scott Patrick. Torchwork. Oxblood-red, yellow and white swirl. Unsigned. 5/8". Mint (9.9). Price: $19. CyberAuction #351, Lot #25.

2086. CONTEMPORARY HANDMADE. Scott Patrick. Swirl of bright red and yellow in light blue. Mimics Christensen Agate swirl. Unsigned. 3/4". Mint (9.9). Price: $19. CyberAuction #498, Lot #14.

2087. CONTEMPORARY HANDMADE. Scott Patrick. Torchwork. Red, blue and yellow swirl. Christensen Agate swirl mimic. Unsigned. 5/8". Mint (9.9). Price: $17. CyberAuction #350, Lot #49.

2088. CONTEMPORARY HANDMADE. Scott Patrick. Torchwork. Guinea mimic. Transparent cobalt blue base. Covered by white splotches. Unsigned. 21/32". Mint (9.9). Price: $15. CyberAuction #350, Lot #19.

2089. CONTEMPORARY HANDMADE. Scott Patrick. Torchwork. Guinea mimic. Transparent cobalt blue base. Covered by white splotches. Unsigned. 21/32". Mint (9.9). Price: $15. CyberAuction #353, Lot #10.

2090. CONTEMPORARY HANDMADE. Scott Patrick. Tight swirl of oxblood red, black, yellow, brown, light blue. Signed "S". 13/16". Mint (9.7). Price: $15. CyberAuction #422, Lot #2.

2091. CONTEMPORARY HANDMADE. Scott Patrick. Peltier Golden Rebel mimic. 11/16". Mint (9.9). Two marbles available, you are bidding on one. Winner has choice of either or both, remainder to under. Price: $15. CyberAuction #472, Lot #25.

2092. CONTEMPORARY HANDMADE. Scott Patrick. Black and red swirled in white. Mimicking a Peltier Rebel. Excellent mimic. American, circa 1996-1998. 13/16". Mint (9.9). Price: $14. CyberAuction #338, Lot #6.

2093. CONTEMPORARY HANDMADE. Scott Patrick. Black and red swirled in yellow. Mimicking a Peltier Golden Rebel. Excellent mimic. American, circa 1996-1998. 1/2"-. Mint (9.9). Price: $13. CyberAuction #348, Lot #14.

2094. CONTEMPORARY HANDMADE. Scott Patrick. Tight swirl of oxblood red, black, yellow, brown, light blue. Signed "S". 13/16". Mint (9.7). Price: $13. CyberAuction #364, Lot #28.

2095. CONTEMPORARY HANDMADE. Scott Patrick. Swirl of electric orange and blue. Mimics a Christensen Agate swirl. Handmade. Unsigned. 7/16". Mint (9.9). Price: $13. CyberAuction #438, Lot #3.

2096. CONTEMPORARY HANDMADE. Scott Patrick. Torchwork. Guinea mimic. Transparent cobalt blue base. Covered by white splotches. Unsigned. 19/32". Mint (9.9). Price: $12. CyberAuction #383, Lot #16.

2097. CONTEMPORARY HANDMADE. Scott Patrick. Swirl of red, yellow and light blue. Unsigned. 23/32". Mint (9.9). There are two examples available, you are bidding on one. Winner has choice of either or both, remainder to under. Price: $12. CyberAuction #428, Lot #43.

2098. CONTEMPORARY HANDMADE. Scott Patrick. Early attempt of Scott Patrick's to make a Cyclone mimic. Transparent clear with orange, light green and lavender inside. Unsigned. 19/32". Mint (9.9). Price: $12. CyberAuction #481, Lot #43.

2099. CONTEMPORARY HANDMADE. Scott Patrick. Yellow swirls in very

light blue. Mimics a Christensen Agate swirl. Unsigned. 25/32". Mint (9.7). Price: $12. CyberAuction #498, Lot #35.

2100. CONTEMPORARY HANDMADE. Scott Patrick. Red and black swirled in yellow. Mimicking a Peltier Golden Rebel. Nice mimic. American, circa 1996-1998. 5/8". Mint (9.9). Price: $11. CyberAuction #363, Lot #19.

2101. CONTEMPORARY HANDMADE. Scott Patrick. Torchwork. Guinea mimic. Transparent cobalt blue base. Covered by white splotches. Unsigned. 21/32". Mint (9.9). Price: $11. CyberAuction #440, Lot #40.

2102. CONTEMPORARY HANDMADE. Scott Patrick. Black and yellow swirled in black. Mimicking a Peltier Golden Rebel. Excellent mimic. American, circa 1996-1998. 5/8". Mint (9.9). Price: $10. CyberAuction #337, Lot #29.

2103. CONTEMPORARY HANDMADE. Scott Patrick. Blue and red swirled in yellow. American, circa 1996-1998. 5/8". Mint (9.9). Two marbles available, bidding on one. Winner has choice of either or both, remainder to under. Price: $9. CyberAuction #496, Lot #7.

2104. CONTEMPORARY HANDMADE. Scott Patrick. Swirl of pink, black and light blue. Unsigned. 23/32". Mint (9.9). There are two examples available, you are bidding on one. Winner has choice of either or both, remainder to under. Price: $8. CyberAuction #427, Lot #12.

2105. CONTEMPORARY HANDMADE. Scott Patrick. Swirl of purple, white and lutz. Unsigned. 23/32". Mint (9.9). There are two examples available, you are bidding on one. Winner has choice of either or both, remainder to under. Price: $8. CyberAuction #427, Lot #26.

2106. CONTEMPORARY HANDMADE. Scott Patrick. Black and red swirled in yellow. Mimicking a Peltier Golden Rebel. Excellent mimic. American, circa 1996-1998. 19/32. Mint (9.9). Two marbles available, you are bidding on one. Winner has choice of either or both, remainder to under. Price: $8. CyberAuction #494, Lot #11.

2107. CONTEMPORARY HANDMADE. Scott Patrick. Yellow and white swirl. Christensen Agate swirl mimic. Unsigned. 5/8". Mint (9.9). Two marbles available, you are bidding on one. Winner has choice of either or both, remainder to under. Price: $8. CyberAuction #494, Lot #34.

2108. CONTEMPORARY HANDMADE. Scott Patrick. Peltier Rebel mimic. 11/16". Mint (9.9). Two marbles available, you are bidding on one. Winner has choice of either or both, remainder to under. Price: $6. CyberAuction #473, Lot #11.

2109. CONTEMPORARY HANDMADE. Shane Caswell. "Sea Floral". Looks like a rock outcropping of pale blue and white core, with pink centers. Super. Signed "SS K SS 98". 1-5/16". Mint (9.9). Price: $50. CyberAuction #377, Lot #58.

2110. CONTEMPORARY HANDMADE. Shane Caswell. "Sea Floral". Looks like a rock outcropping of pale blue and white core, with pink centers. Super. Unsigned. 1-9/16". Mint (9.9). Price: $40. CyberAuction #341, Lot #59.

2111. CONTEMPORARY HANDMADE. Shane Caswell. Sea Floral. Unsigned. 1-9/16". Mint (9.9). Price: $32. CyberAuction #491, Lot #15.

2112. CONTEMPORARY HANDMADE. Shane Caswell. Gorgeous "coral seascape" in clear glass. Unsigned. 1-3/16". Mint (9.9). Price: $26. CyberAuction #448, Lot #16.

2113. CONTEMPORARY HANDMADE. Shane Caswell. "Sea Floral". Looks like a rock outcropping of pale blue and white core, with pink centers. Small subsurface moon. Unsigned. 1-1/4". Near Mint(+) (8.9). Price: $18. CyberAuction #460, Lot #49.

2114. CONTEMPORARY HANDMADE. Shane Caswell. "Sea Floral". Looks like a rock outcropping of pale blue and white core, with pink centers. Small subsurface moon. Unsigned. 1-1/4". Near Mint(+) (8.9). Price: $15. CyberAuction #436, Lot #56.

2115. CONTEMPORARY HANDMADE. Shipwrecked Glass. Rosenfeld Orb. This is a hollow glass sphere, filled with glycerine, cane sections, small millefiori pieces and a seashell. Hole is plugged with a millefiori cane piece. The glass pieces float around in the glycerine, kind of a like a snow globe. Signed "D+D 7-99". David and Debbie Rosenfeld. 2-1/8". Mint (9.9). Price: $185. CyberAuction #385, Lot #46.

2116. CONTEMPORARY HANDMADE. Shipwrecked Glass. Translucent green swirl with dichroic flakes on it, encased in clear. Signed "NDR 2000". 1-5/16". Mint (9.9). Price: $40. CyberAuction #504, Lot #16.

2117. CONTEMPORARY HANDMADE. Shipwrecked Glass. Dichroic banded swirl with emerald green base. Signed "NDR 2000". 1-7/16". Mint (9.9). Price: $39. CyberAuction #489, Lot #46.

2118. CONTEMPORARY HANDMADE. Shipwrecked Glass. Translucent blue core with dichroic flakes on it, encased in clear. Signed "NDR 2000". 1-5/16". Mint (9.9). Price: $32. CyberAuction #494, Lot #20.

2119. CONTEMPORARY HANDMADE. TNT Glass. Very nice torchworked marble. Transparent clear with a snake torsade of brown/orange and light blue on the surface. Signed "TNT". 1-1/16". Mint (9.9). Price: $19. CyberAuction #440, Lot #39.

2120. CONTEMPORARY HANDMADE. TNT Glass. Swirl of yellow, black and lutz. Signed "TNT". 25/32". Mint (9.9). Price: $13. CyberAuction #495, Lot #5.

2121. CONTEMPORARY HANDMADE. TNT Glass. Very nice torchworked marble. Transparent clear with a snake torsade of brown/orange and light blue on the surface. Signed "TNT". 1-1/16". Mint (9.9). Price: $12. CyberAuction #482, Lot #10.

2122. CONTEMPORARY HANDMADE. Teign Valley Glass. White latticinio core swirl. Two sets of outer strands. Each set is one each of red, white and blue. Comes with a small cardboard display stand. England. 1-3/8". Mint (9.9). Price: $27. CyberAuction #390, Lot #23.

2123. CONTEMPORARY HANDMADE. Vermont Glass/Harry Besset. Star design. Transparent clear base that was overlaid with opaque blue. Then the blue was stripped away, except for a nice layer of five-point stars. Very pretty. Signed "Besset c". 1-9/16". Mint (9.9). Price: $60. CyberAuction #363, Lot #36.

2124. CONTEMPORARY HANDMADE. Vermont Glass/Harry Besset. Transparent clear base that had an overlay of blue. The overlay was then cut away leaving raised blue stars on the surface. Signed "Besset 00". 1-1/2". Mint (9.9). Price: $39. CyberAuction #501, Lot #13.

2125. CONTEMPORARY HANDMADE. Vermont Glass/Harry Besset. Star design. Transparent clear base that was overlaid with opaque black. Then the black was stripped away, except for a nice layer of five-point stars. Very pretty. Signed "Besset c". 1-9/16". Mint (9.9). Price: $38. CyberAuction #395, Lot #48.

2126. CONTEMPORARY HANDMADE. Vermont Glass/Harry Besset. A flying bird cut out of a sheet of mica, in clear glass. So, what would you call it? A mica, a sulphide, a micaphide? Artist calls it an "Eisenglass". Signed "Bessett c". 1-1/2". Mint (9.9). Price: $38. CyberAuction #447, Lot #28.

2127. CONTEMPORARY HANDMADE. Vermont Glass/Harry Besset. Cameo. Transparent clear base that had an overlay of yellow. The overlay was then cut away leaving raised alphabet and stars. Signed "Besset 00". 1-1/2". Mint (9.9). Price: $38. CyberAuction #507, Lot #46.

2128. CONTEMPORARY HANDMADE. Vermont Glass/Harry Besset. A five-point star cut out of a sheet of mica, in clear glass. So, what would you call it? A mica, a sulphide, a micaphide? Artist calls it an "Eisenglass". Signed "Bessett c". 1-1/2". Mint (9.9). Price: $37. CyberAuction #373, Lot #24.

2129. CONTEMPORARY HANDMADE. Vermont Glass/Harry Besset. Clear base. Overlay of black glass that has been etched away to form the alphabet spiraling around the marble with several stars. Beauty. Signed "Bessett 0". 1-1/2". Mint (9.9). Price: $36. CyberAuction #487, Lot #48.

2130. CONTEMPORARY HANDMADE. Vermont Glass/Harry Besset. A flying bird cut out of a sheet of mica, in clear glass. So, what would you call it? A mica, a sulphide, a micaphide? Artist calls it an "Eisenglass". Signed "Bessett c". 1-1/2". Mint (9.9). Price: $32. CyberAuction #389, Lot #53.

2131. CONTEMPORARY HANDMADE. Vermont Glass/Harry Besset. A five-point star cut out of a sheet of mica, in clear glass. So, what would you call it? A mica, a sulphide, a micaphide? Artist calls it an "Eisenglass". Signed "Bessett c". 1-1/2". Mint (9.9). Price: $32. CyberAuction #453, Lot #20.

2132. CONTEMPORARY HANDMADE. William Murray. transparent clear base. Opaque white core. Subsurface caged layer of color strands. Signed "WFM 99". 1-5/8". Mint (9.9). Price: $42. CyberAuction #372, Lot #35.

2133. CONTEMPORARY HANDMADE. William Murray. Beautiful ribbon core swirl. Signed "WFM 00". Super marble. 1-7/16". Mint (9.9). Price: $40. CyberAuction #462, Lot #40.

2134. CONTEMPORARY HANDMADE. William Murray. Transparent clear base. Core is transparent lavender on opaque white ribbon, coated with mica. Outer layer is two sets of green strands. Signed "WFM 98". 1-5/16". Mint (9.9). Price: $39. CyberAuction #336, Lot #34.

2135. CONTEMPORARY HANDMADE. William Murray. Transparent cobalt blue core, encrusted with mica. Gorgeous. Clear outer layer. Signed "WFM 98". 1-9/16". Mint (9.9). Price: $39. CyberAuction #354, Lot #50.

2136. CONTEMPORARY HANDMADE. William Murray. Transparent cobalt blue core, encrusted with mica. Three lobes, edged by red. Gorgeous. Clear outer layer. Signed "WFM 99". 1-7/16". Mint (9.9). Price: $36. CyberAuction #333, Lot #35.

2137. CONTEMPORARY HANDMADE. William Murray. Transparent cobalt blue core, encrusted with mica. Three lobes, edged by red. Gorgeous. Clear outer layer. Signed "WFM 99". 1-3/16". Mint (9.9). Price: $36. CyberAuction #353, Lot #51.

2138. CONTEMPORARY HANDMADE. William Murray. Transparent clear base. Core is transparent lavender on opaque white ribbon, coated with mica. Outer layer is two sets of green strands. Signed "WFM 99". 1-5/16". Mint (9.9). Price: $34. CyberAuction #51.

2139. CONTEMPORARY HANDMADE. William Murray. Transparent clear base. Core is transparent lavender on opaque white ribbon, edged by orange, coated with mica. Outer layer is two sets of green strands. Signed "WFM 99". 1-9/16". Mint (9.9). Price: $32. CyberAuction #339, Lot #36.

2140. CONTEMPORARY HANDMADE. William Murray. Transparent cobalt blue core, encrusted with mica. Outer layer is a cage of yellow strands. Gorgeous. Signed "WFM 98". 1-5/16". Mint (9.9). Price: $32. CyberAuction #343, Lot #59.

2141. CONTEMPORARY HANDMADE. William Murray. Transparent cobalt blue core, encrusted with mica. Outer layer is a cage of yellow strands. Gorgeous. Clear outer layer. Signed "WFM 00". 1-1/4". Mint (9.9). Price: $30. CyberAuction #427, Lot #42.

2142. CONTEMPORARY HANDMADE. William Murray. Transparent clear base. Core is transparent red ribbon coated with mica. Outer layer is three sets of yellow and pink strands. Signed "WFM 99". 1-1/2". Mint (9.9). Price: $27. CyberAuction #334, Lot #60.

2143. CONTEMPORARY HANDMADE. William Murray. Banded lutz on subsurface purple. Beauty. Signed "WFM 00". 1-5/16". Mint (9.9). Price: $27. CyberAuction #472, Lot #40.

2144. CONTEMPORARY HANDMADE. William Murray. Gorgeous. Blue latticinio core. Surrounded by two bands of white and blue. Outer layer is a cage of red and green strands. Signed "WFM 99". Stunning. 1-5/8". Mint (9.9). Price: $25. CyberAuction #467, Lot #8.

2145. CONTEMPORARY HANDMADE. William Murray. Opaque blue core. Outer layer is alternating orange, white and yellow bands and strands. Signed "WFM 00". 1-3/8". Mint (9.9). Price: $23. CyberAuction #433, Lot #44.

2146. CONTEMPORARY HANDMADE. William Murray. Red core, outer layer is a cage of narrow bands. Unsigned. My guess is that it is early Will-

iam Murray. Some melt spots. 1-3/8". Mint (9.5). Price: $22. CyberAuction #370, Lot #37.

2147. CONTEMPORARY HANDMADE. William Murray. Red core, outer layer is a cage of narrow bands. Unsigned. My guess is that it is early William Murray. Some melt spots. 1-3/8". Mint (9.5). Price: $22. CyberAuction #430, Lot #39.

2148. CONTEMPORARY HANDMADE. William Murray. Transparent green core, encrusted with mica. Gorgeous. Outer layer is a cage of orange and red. Three tiny chips. Signed "WFM 99". 1-5/16". Near Mint(+) (8.8). Price: $17. CyberAuction #368, Lot #10.

2149. CONTEMPORARY HANDMADE. William Murray. Red core, outer layer is a cage of narrow bands. Unsigned. My guess is that it is early William Murray. Some melt spots. 1-3/8". Mint (9.5). Price: $17. CyberAuction #466, Lot #4.

2150. CONTEMPORARY HANDMADE. William Murray. Red core, outer layer is a cage of narrow bands. Unsigned. My guess is that it is early William Murray. Some melt spots. 1-3/8". Mint (9.5). Price: $17. CyberAuction #490, Lot #22.

2151. CONTEMPORARY HANDMADE. William Murray. Transparent green core, encrusted with mica. Gorgeous. Outer layer is a cage of orange and red. Three tiny chips. Signed "WFM 99". 1-5/16". Near Mint(+) (8.8). Price: $14. CyberAuction #459, Lot #46.

2152. END-OF-DAY. Banded. Transparent cobalt blue base. One band of stretched splotches of white, yellow, blue and red. A couple of tiny subsurface moons. Germany, circa 1870-1915. 27/32". Near Mint (8.6). Price: $40. CyberAuction #502, Lot #57.

2153. END-OF-DAY. Blizzard. Well, half a blizzard (demi-blizzard?). The other half of the marble is missing. Appears to have had an internal flaw and it shattered. Transparent clear base. Core is a mixture of blue and red splotches and tons of mica. Would have been a beauty. There has been some grinding around the edges to smooth them. Interesting example. You can either use it as an example to show the construction of a marble, or have it trimmed and use it in a piece of jewelry. 1-5/16". Price: $17. CyberAuction #416, Lot #27.

2154. END-OF-DAY. Cane piece. Section of cane for making an end of day onionskin. Excellent!!! 2-3/4" long, 17/32" diameter. Mint (9.5). Price: $37. CyberAuction #365, Lot #16.

2155. END-OF-DAY. Cane piece. Rare piece. Cane section from an uncased onionskin. Clear base. Surface is coated with bumpy globs of red and very dark green. Fascinating. Germany, circa 1870-1915. About 2-1/4 long, 19/32" diameter. Price: $27. CyberAuction #364, Lot #24.

2156. END-OF-DAY. Cane piece. Rare piece. Uncased cane section from a four-panel onionskin. Clear base. Surface is coated with white with bumpy globs of red and green. Fascinating. Germany, circa 1870-1915. About 2" long, 19/32" diameter. Price: $21. CyberAuction #370, Lot #24.

2157. END-OF-DAY. Cane piece. The end of the cane (first end) of an onionskin. Clear glass ampoule with some end of day color at the very bottom. Interesting. Germany, circa 1870-1915. 25/32" x 1". Mint (9.9). Price: $10. CyberAuction #405, Lot #38.

2158. END-OF-DAY. Cloud. Exceptional single pontil huge cloud. Transparent clear base. Yellow and white mottled core. Covered by pink dots. Left twist. Color ends just before the top of the marble. Stunning marble. Very rare. Germany, circa 1870-1915. 2-1/8". Mint (9.7). Price: $1950. CyberAuction #500, Lot #58.

2159. END-OF-DAY. Cloud. Stunning single pontil cloud in pristine condition. Amazing marble. Transparent clear base. Opaque white core rising up the marble. Bumpy spots of blue, and a couple of pink and green, on the core. Nice texture. Stunning marble. Very rare. Germany, circa 1870-1915. 1-1/4". Mint (9.9). Price: $1150. CyberAuction #505, Lot #75.

2160. END-OF-DAY. Cloud. Very rare marble. Single-pontil cloud with three panels of floating blizzard cloud. Absolutely stunning!!!!! Transparent clear base. Mushroom cloud core. Core is yellow, consisting of flakes of yellow melted together, with some clear spaces at the top. Pink flecks melted on the yellow, with a few green flecks. Core ends about two-thirds up the marble. Floating in a layer are three bands of mica. Blizzards of mica. Nice layer of mica floating above the top of the core. A chip on one side. Chip is about 3/4". Also, small chip and small subsurface moon. Exceptional marble, stunning. Germany, circa 1870-1915. 2-1/4". Near Mint (8.4). Price: $1050. CyberAuction #353, Lot #60.

2161. END-OF-DAY. Cloud. Transparent clear base. Opaque white core with dark blue splotches on it. Some trapped air bubbles on the core that give it the look of mica. Initially, I thought the surface had been buffed. However, the surface is completely original. One small melt spot where it touched another marble or piece of glass while hot and one small sparkle. Outstanding example of this type and truly gorgeous. Germany, circa 1870-1915. 1-5/8". Mint(-) (9.0). Price: $585. CyberAuction #414, Lot #55.

2162. END-OF-DAY. Cloud. Stunning and extremely rare single pontil (hand gathered) Cloud in superb condition. Transparent clear base. Core of yellow and white, with pink and green splotches rising about half way up the marble. The red and green smear into the upper half. Almost looks like a Simpson Planet. Surface in superior shape. Stunning example!!! Germany, circa 1870-1915. 13/16". Mint (9.9). Price: $575. CyberAuction #363, Lot #60.

2163. END-OF-DAY. Cloud. Very rare marble. Transparent clear base. Core is stretched dots of white, olive green, black and orange. One tiny melt spot. England, possibly Germany, circa 1870-1915. 3/4". Mint(-) (9.1). Price: $500. CyberAuction #500, Lot #54.

2164. END-OF-DAY. Cloud. Rare marble. Single-pontil, four-panel, cloud. Transparent dark smoky base. Mushroom-cloud type core, rising from the pontil, about three-quarters of the way up the marble. Core is a yellow and white spots. On this are two panels of blue and two panels of pink. A little green too. Several tiny chips on the top. Some pinpricking. Very rare marble. Germany, circa 1870-1915. 1-7/8". Near Mint(-) (8.1). Price: $485. CyberAuction #455, Lot #42.

2165. END-OF-DAY. Cloud. Single-pontil four-panel cloud. Left-hand twist with mica. Gorgeous and rare. Transparent clear base. Core is two white panels and two yellow panels. The core ends about two-thirds of the way up the marble. Overall pink splotches with some blue and green. Nice sprinkling of mica. Surface has been lightly buffed. One small chip remains. Some other damage remains. Germany, circa 1870-1915. 2-1/8". Buffed. Price: $385. CyberAuction #414, Lot #25.

2166. END-OF-DAY. Cloud. Amazing three-panel, single pontil, first off cane Cloud. Transparent clear base. Subsurface layer of opaque white. Large clear hole at the top of that layer. Three panels, one each of blue, pink and green. Faceted pontil. Stunning marble. Tiny flake near the bottom. Germany, circa 1870-1915. 13/16". Near Mint(+) (8.9). Price: $320. CyberAuction #506, Lot #49.

2167. END-OF-DAY. Cloud. Stunning and large single pontil cloud. Transparent clear base. Core of white with two small panels of yellow. Almost completely fills the marble. Splotches of red, blue and green on the core. Surface has been polished, a little damage remains. Stunning marble!!!! Germany, circa 1870-1915. 1-13/16". Price: $310. CyberAuction #388, Lot #35.

2168. END-OF-DAY. Cloud. Amazing three-panel, single pontil, first off cane Cloud. Transparent clear base. Subsurface layer of opaque white. Large clear hole at the top of that layer. Three panels, one each of blue, pink and green. Faceted pontil. Stunning marble. Tiny flake near the bottom. Germany, circa 1870-1915. 13/16". Near Mint(+) (8.9). Price: $285. CyberAuction #495, Lot #56.

2169. END-OF-DAY. Cloud. Stunning marble from near an end of the cane. Transparent clear base. Yellow core with clouds of green and pink on it. Very shrunken on one side, lobed on the other, and one edge comes almost out of the surface. Pristine. Gorgeous. Germany, circa 1870-1915. 5/8". Mint (9.9). Price: $240. CyberAuction #366, Lot #56.

2170. END-OF-DAY. Cloud. Single pontil end of day cloud. Very hard to find. Transparent clear base. Opaque white core reaching about three-quarters of the way up the marble. Covered by pink splotches, with some blue and yellow splotches. Three shallow lobes. One small moon, several small subsurface moons, some haze. Still, very hard to find. Germany, circa 1870-1915. 1-9/16". Near Mint(-) (8.0). Price: $150. CyberAuction #430, Lot #54.

2171. END-OF-DAY. Cloud. Very rare marble. Single pontil cloud in light blue glass. Base is light blue. Three large splotches of opaque white, one of light blue, and one of red. Single pontil. One tiny flake, three tiny subsurface moons. Rare. Germany, circa 1870-1915. 9/16". Near Mint (8.6). Price: $140. CyberAuction #359, Lot #60.

2172. END-OF-DAY. Cloud. Single-pontil cloud. Outstanding example. Transparent clear base. Mushroom cloud of opaque white with pink splotches. In superior shape. Germany, circa 1870-1915. 9/16". Mint (9.9). Price: $140. CyberAuction #418, Lot #37.

2173. END-OF-DAY. Cloud. Single pontil end of day cloud. Transparent clear base. Core of white coming up about halfway through the marble. Two panels of green, two of pink. Gorgeous. Small flake, some pitting and haze. Germany, circa 1870-1915. 1-1/4". Near Mint(-) (8.1). Price: $135. CyberAuction #437, Lot #33.

2174. END-OF-DAY. Cloud. Stunning small cloud. Transparent very light blue glass. Core is stretched spots of orange, blue, white, yellow. Super and rare marble. One tiny flake. Germany, circa 1870-1915. 19/32". Near Mint(+) (8.9). Price: $120. CyberAuction #475, Lot #59.

2175. END-OF-DAY. Cloud. Single pontil end of day cloud. Very hard to find. Transparent clear base. Opaque white core reaching about three-quarters of the way up the marble. Covered by pink splotches, with some blue and yellow splotches. Three shallow lobes. One small moon, several small subsurface moons, some haze. Still, very hard to find. Germany, circa 1870-1915. 1-9/16". Near Mint(-) (8.0). Price: $111. CyberAuction #417, Lot #50.

2176. END-OF-DAY. Cloud. Rare ribbon cloud. English. Stunning. Transparent clear base. Core is a ribbon of splotches of bright greens and yellow. Gorgeous. One subsurface moon. England, circa 1870-1915. 25/32". Near Mint(+) (8.9). Price: $110. CyberAuction #473, Lot #56.

2177. END-OF-DAY. Cloud. Single pontil end of day cloud. Transparent clear base. Core of white coming up about halfway through the marble. Two panels of green, two of pink. Gorgeous. Small flake, some pitting and haze. Germany, circa 1870-1915. 1-1/4". Near Mint(-) (8.1). Price: $100. CyberAuction #406, Lot #29.

2178. END-OF-DAY. Cloud. Superb, very rare, first off cane, end of day cloud. Transparent clear base. Yellow core with two big clouds of pink on either side. Rises about two-thirds of the way up the marble. Large subsurface moon, a couple of tiny subsurface moons and a couple of tiny moons. Very nice. Germany, circa 1870-1915. 9/16". Good(+) (7.8). Price: $85. CyberAuction #374, Lot #45.

2179. END-OF-DAY. Cloud. Single pontil cloud. Transparent clear base. Splotches of red, blue, orange, white and green. Misshapen. Slightly hazy. Germany, circa 1870-1915. 1/2". Near Mint (8.6). Price: $55. CyberAuction #367, Lot #59.

2180. END-OF-DAY. Cloud. Single pontil cloud. Transparent clear base. Splotches of red, blue, orange, white and green. Misshapen. Slightly hazy. Germany, circa 1870-1915. 1/2". Near Mint (8.6). Price: $42. CyberAuction #422, Lot #22.

2181. END-OF-DAY. Cloud. Single pontil cloud. Transparent clear base. Splotches of red, blue, orange, white and green. Misshapen. Slightly hazy. Germany, circa 1870-1915. 1/2". Near Mint (8.6). Price: $42. CyberAuction #478, Lot #6.

2182. END-OF-DAY. Cloud. Transparent clear base. Flattened core of splotches of white with pink. Overall pinpricking. Odd. Germany, circa 1870-1915. 19/32". Near Mint (8.5). Price: $29. CyberAuction #420, Lot #14.

2183. END-OF-DAY. Cloud. Rare single pontil. Transparent clear base. About two-thirds filled with white covered transparent pink. Beauty. Unfortunately, a number of small subsurface moons. Germany, circa 1870-1915. 5/8". Good (7.5). Price: $25. CyberAuction #387, Lot #37.

2184. END-OF-DAY. Cloud. Transparent clear base. Opaque white core, shrunken on one side. Splotches of red, green and blue on the core. Surface has tiny chips. Germany, circa 1870-1915. 27/32". Good (7.5). Price: $19. CyberAuction #428, Lot #29.

2185. END-OF-DAY. Cloud. Single pontil cloud. Tiny. Transparent clear base. White mushroom cloud with blue dots. Hazy and misshapen. Germany, circa 1870-1915. 17/32". Good (7.6). Price: $15. CyberAuction #408, Lot #36.

2186. END-OF-DAY. Cloud. Transparent clear base. Opaque white core, shrunken on one side. Splotches of red, green and blue on the core. Surface has tiny chips. Germany, circa 1870-1915. 27/32". Good (7.5). Price: $15. CyberAuction #466, Lot #1.

2187. END-OF-DAY. Cloud. Single pontil cloud. Tiny. Transparent clear base. White mushroom cloud with blue dots. Hazy and misshapen. Germany, circa 1870-1915. 17/32". Good (7.6). Price: $12. CyberAuction #426, Lot #53.

2188. END-OF-DAY. Coreless. Stunning and very rare marble, but it's buffed. Transparent clear base. Three bright subsurface panels. One is stretched red, one is stretched blue, one is stretched light green. Lightly buffed, one small chip remains. Out of round. Germany, circa 1870-1915. 1-3/16". Price: $165. CyberAuction #396, Lot #29.

2189. END-OF-DAY. Coreless. Rare English panelled coreless onionskin. Stunning and very rare. Two-panel. Transparent clear base. One side is a subsurface layer of stretched light green bands. The other side is a subsurface layer of stretched red bands. Superior marble, very rare and in great shape with just one tiny melt spot (looks like a flake, but it's from manufacture). English, possibly Germany, circa 1870-1920. 21/32". Mint(-) (9.1). Price: $135. CyberAuction #400, Lot #49.

2190. END-OF-DAY. Coreless. Rare coreless onionskin. Two panel. Transparent clear base. Red strands, yellow strand, white band in core. Subsurface panel of bright blue and subsurface panel of bright yellow. Superb and rare. Surface has overall subsurface moons. England, possibly Germany, circa 1870-1915. 1-9/16". Good (7.3). Price: $90. CyberAuction #434, Lot #21.

2191. END-OF-DAY. Coreless. Rare coreless onionskin. Two panel. Transparent clear base. Red strands, yellow strand, white band in core. Subsurface panel of bright blue and subsurface panel of bright yellow. Superb and rare. Surface has overall subsurface moons. England, possibly Germany, circa 1870-1915. 1-9/16". Good (7.3). Price: $75. CyberAuction #401, Lot #54.

2192. END-OF-DAY. Coreless. Rare coreless onionskin. Two panel. Transparent clear base. Red strand, yellow strand, white band in core. Two subsurface panels of stretched bright red. Some white strands on the surface. Superb and rare. Surface has overall subsurface moons. England, possibly Germany, circa 1870-1915. 1-9/16". Good (7.3). Price: $75. CyberAuction #449, Lot #23.

2193. END-OF-DAY. Coreless. Rare coreless onionskin. Two panel. Transparent clear base. Red strand, yellow strand, white band in core. Two subsurface panels of stretched bright red. Some white strands on the surface. Superb and rare. Surface has overall subsurface moons. England, possibly Germany, circa 1870-1915. 1-9/16". Good (7.3). Price: $65. CyberAuction #401, Lot #50.

2194. END-OF-DAY. Coreless. Rare coreless onionskin. Two panel. Transparent clear base. Red strand, yellow strand, white band in core. Two subsurface panels of stretched bright red. Some white strands on the surface. Superb and rare. Surface has overall subsurface moons. England, possibly Germany, circa 1870-1915. 1-9/16". Good (7.3). Price: $65. CyberAuction #477, Lot #34.

2195. END-OF-DAY. Coreless. Small example of a coreless end of day. Transparent clear base. Three subsurface panels. One stretched bright orange, one stretched blue, one stretched light green. Small clear panel. Tiny subsurface moon, two small very shallow surface flakes. Germany, circa 1870-1915. 5/8". Near Mint(-) (8.1). Price: $38. CyberAuction #396, Lot #32.

2196. END-OF-DAY. Coreless. Small example of a coreless end of day. Transparent clear base. Three subsurface panels. One stretched bright orange, one stretched blue, one stretched light green. Small clear panel. Tiny subsurface moon, two small very shallow surface flakes. Germany, circa 1870-1915. 5/8". Near Mint(-) (8.1). Price: $32. CyberAuction #442, Lot #60.

2197. END-OF-DAY. Coreless. Small example of a coreless end of day. Transparent clear base. Three subsurface panels. One stretched bright orange, one stretched blue, one stretched light green. Small clear panel. Tiny subsurface moon, two small very shallow surface flakes. Germany, circa 1870-1915. 5/8". Near Mint(-) (8.1). Price: $27. CyberAuction #466, Lot #42.

2198. END-OF-DAY. Coreless. Small example of a coreless end of day. Transparent clear base. Three subsurface panels. One stretched bright orange, one stretched blue, one stretched light green. Small clear panel. Tiny subsurface moon, two small very shallow surface flakes. Germany, circa 1870-1915. 5/8". Near Mint(-) (8.1). Price: $27. CyberAuction #494, Lot #7.

2199. END-OF-DAY. Joseph Coat. Transparent clear base. Opaque white core. Stretched bands of multiple colors on the white. Includes two bands of oxblood-type red, and one band of fiery green aventurine. Rare. A couple of cold roll lines. Germany, circa 1870-1915. 19/32". Mint (9.7). Price: $235. CyberAuction #500, Lot #18.

2200. END-OF-DAY. Joseph Coat. End of day type of Joseph Coat. Transparent clear base. Core is packed bands of orange, red, green, yellow, blue and white. Bands do not run continuously from pole to pole, although there are no clear spaces. Overall light haze, a couple of very minor chips. A buff will bring out a true beauty. Germany, possibly England, circa 1870-1915. 1-1/4". Good(+) (7.9). Price: $80. CyberAuction #502, Lot #28.

2201. END-OF-DAY. Mist. Extremely rare marble. Transparent clear base. Core is a shrunken onionskin core of opaque white with pink skin. Subsurface outer layer of transparent bands of blue and green. Very rare!!! Surface in great shape, except for one small pit near the top pontil. Germany, circa 1870-1915. 27/32". Mint(-) (9.0). Price: $260. CyberAuction #357, Lot #48.

2202. END-OF-DAY. Mist. Very rare two-panel end of day Mist type. Transparent clear base. Core is transparent stretched blue on one side and translucent stretched white on the other. One very tiny flake near the bottom pontil. Stunning marble. Very rare. Germany, circa 1870-1915. 17/32". Near Mint(+) (8.9). Price: $110. CyberAuction #396, Lot #60.

2203. END-OF-DAY. Onionskin. One of the most unbelievable onionskins I have ever seen. Another extremely rare and important marble. Transparent clear base. Opaque white core. Core is covered with splotches of bright red, bright orange, bright yellow, bright blue. And I mean bright!!! Surface is pristine. Absolutely stunning marble. It will knock your socks off. Pictures cannot do this one justice. Amazing! Germany, possibly England, circa 1870-1915. 1-5/8". Mint (9.9) (as close to 10.0 as I have ever seen). Price: $4050. CyberAuction #483, Lot #60.

2204. END-OF-DAY. Onionskin. Stunning and extremely rare onionskin. Transparent clear base. Subsurface layer is overall electric opaque blue and electric opaque red. Stunning!!!! England, circa 1870-1920. 11/16". Mint (9.9). Price: $525. CyberAuction #462, Lot #54.

2205. END-OF-DAY. Onionskin. Stunning and rare English type onionskin. Transparent clear base. Subsurface layer is stretched bands of bright green, bright orange, yellow and blue. Some clear spaces. Gorgeous marble. England, circa 1870-1915. 25/32". Mint (9.7). Price: $510. CyberAuction #467, Lot #54.

2206. END-OF-DAY. Onionskin. Gorgeous onionskin with mica. Rare marble. Transparent clear base. Subsurface layer of opaque white. Broad splotches of dark blue and green covering the marble. Not much stretching. Nice sprinkling of finely ground mica. This is a beauty!!!! Germany, circa 1870-1915. 1-5/16". Mint (9.8). Price: $450. CyberAuction #330, Lot #48.

2207. END-OF-DAY. Onionskin. Three lobed onionskin. Transparent clear base. Yellow core. Pink skin, with some green. Three lobes. Very nice. Several shallow subsurface moons, not very visible. Still, a beauty. Germany, circa 1870-1915. 1-13/16". Near Mint(+) (8.7). Price: $335. CyberAuction #501, Lot #75.

2208. END-OF-DAY. Onionskin. Gorgeous English type onionskin. Transparent clear base. Subsurface layer of bright white. Some bands of orange, yellow, green and blue on it. One green band is fiery aventurine. One tiny dimple. Stunning. England, possibly Germany, circa 1870-1915. 25/32". Mint (9.6). Price: $300. CyberAuction #508, Lot #65.

2209. END-OF-DAY. Onionskin. Absolutely stunning marble. Transparent clear base. White core. The core is covered by splotches of pastel pink, pink, baby blue and dark blue. Germany, circa 1870-1915. 5/8". Mint (9.7). Price: $290. CyberAuction #483, Lot #57.

2210. END-OF-DAY. Onionskin. Gorgeous left-twist onionskin with mica. Transparent clear base. Yellow core. Stretched dots of pink, green and blue. Nice sprinkling of mica. Buffed. Pontils are completely intact, a little damage remains. Super looking marble, absolutely stunning. Germany, circa 1870-1915. 1-7/8". Price: $285. CyberAuction #397, Lot #58.

2211. END-OF-DAY. Onionskin. Rare example. Transparent blue tinted base. Mustard yellow core. Pink skin on the core. Some blue bands just under the surface. One tiny dirt spot and a tiny pinprick. Still has an inventory tag on the bottom pontil. Germany, circa 1870-1915. 1-3/8". Mint(-) (9.2). Price: $260. CyberAuction #504, Lot #66.

2212. END-OF-DAY. Onionskin. Hard to find lobed onionskin. Transparent clear base. Opaque yellow core with very nice green skin. There are four lobes. Three are fairly deep, one is very shallow. Reverse twist top. Two very tiny air holes, one very tiny pinprick. This is an outstanding example. Rare and very hard to find. Germany, circa 1870-1915. 7/8". Mint (9.5). Price: $235. CyberAuction #467, Lot #56.

2213. END-OF-DAY. Onionskin. Stunning panelled onionskin. Transparent clear base. Wispy bright blue bands in the core. Subsurface layer is two wide panels of bright orange and red. Two outer white bands. Very bright colors. Germany, possibly England, circa 1870-1915. 29/32". Mint (9.8). Price: $235. CyberAuction #495, Lot #54.

2214. END-OF-DAY. Onionskin. I think you would really call this an end of day Joseph Coat or a Joseph Coat onionskin. Very hard to find. Transparent clear base. Core is a multitude of stretched bright colors. Superb. One tiny subsurface moon near the bottom pontil, else surface is pristine. Germany, circa 1870-1915. 1". Near Mint(+) (8.9). Price: $230. CyberAuction #357, Lot #52.

2215. END-OF-DAY. Onionskin. Large onionskin with mica. Transparent clear base. Opaque yellow subsurface layer. Light pink skin. Nicely sprinkling of finely ground mica on it. Several small and tiny chips, and small subsurface moons. Still, a beauty. Germany, circa 1870-1915. 2-1/16". Good(+) (7.8). Price: $220. CyberAuction #359, Lot #49.

2216. END-OF-DAY. Onionskin. Exceptional left-twist onionskin. Transparent clear base. Opaque white core. Overall pink skin with three bands of green. One band is fairly wide. May have been intended as a six-panel. Nice left-twist. Gorgeous. Germany, circa 1870-1915. 27/32". Mint (9.8). Price: $200. CyberAuction #504, Lot #59.

2217. END-OF-DAY. Onionskin. Transparent very lightly tinted brown base. The consignor (an Englishman) told me that this color is referred to as "barleycorn" in England, and these are called "barleycorn marbles". Opaque white core with pink, green and blue bands. The consignor was quite enamored with this marble, and it was tough getting him to let go of it. Germany, circa 1870-1915. 7/8". Mint (9.9). Price: $190. CyberAuction #503, Lot #10.

2218. END-OF-DAY. Onionskin. Unusual example. Transparent clear base. Subsurface layer of stretched splotches of opaque white, transparent green, some pink, some blue. Lots of clear spaces. Surface is very lightly polished, some damage remains. Germany, circa 1870-1915. 1-5/8". Price: $180. CyberAuction #420, Lot #33.

2219. END-OF-DAY. Onionskin. Large onionskin with mica. Hard to find. Transparent clear base. Opaque yellow core with pink skin. A little bit of mica scattered on the core. Some tiny chips and pits, some very minor haze. Germany, circa 1870-1915. 1-3/4". Near Mint(-) (8.0). Price: $180. CyberAuction #421, Lot #32.

2220. END-OF-DAY. Onionskin. Stunning marble. Transparent clear base. Opaque white core. Stretched black and pink bands on it. Covered by "lumpy" bright yellow. A couple of cold roll lines. Germany, circa 1870-1915. 11/16". Mint (9.6). Price: $170. CyberAuction #502, Lot #73.

2221. END-OF-DAY. Onionskin. Gorgeous marble. Transparent clear base. Opaque white core. Stretched splotches of blue with a little pink. No twist. Superior and stunning marble. Germany, circa 1870-1915. 7/8". Mint (9.9). Price: $160. CyberAuction #450, Lot #45.

2222. END-OF-DAY. Onionskin. Large onionskin with mica. Hard to find. Transparent clear base. Opaque yellow core with pink skin. A little bit of mica scattered on the core. Some tiny chips and pits, some very minor haze. Germany, circa 1870-1915. 1-3/4". Near Mint(-) (8.0). Price: $160. CyberAuction #471, Lot #31.

2223. END-OF-DAY. Onionskin. Hard to find type. Transparent clear base. Predominately dark red subsurface layer, with white, yellow and blue mixed in. One small fracture spot, hard to see. Germany, circa 1870-1915. 7/8". Near Mint(+) (8.7). Price: $160. CyberAuction #506, Lot #50.

2224. END-OF-DAY. Onionskin. Hard to find type. Transparent clear base. Predominately dark red subsurface layer, with white, yellow and blue mixed in. One small fracture spot, hard to see. Germany, circa 1870-1915. 7/8". Near Mint(+) (8.7). Price: $150. CyberAuction #336, Lot #44.

2225. END-OF-DAY. Onionskin. Gorgeous English type onionskin. Transparent clear base. Subsurface layer of bright white. Some bands of orange, yellow, green and blue on it. One tiny dimple. Stunning. England, possibly Germany, circa 1870-1915. 25/32". Mint (9.6). Price: $150. CyberAuction #459, Lot #41.

2226. END-OF-DAY. Onionskin. Hard to find type. Transparent clear base. Predominately dark red subsurface layer, with white, yellow and blue mixed in. One small fracture spot, hard to see. Germany, circa 1870-1915. 7/8". Near Mint(+) (8.7). Price: $150. CyberAuction #495, Lot #45.

2227. END-OF-DAY. Onionskin. Rare first off cane onionskin with mica. Looped type. Transparent clear base. Yellow core with green skin. Marble is folded in half. First off the cane. Very rare. Excellent example. One tiny air hole. A few pits. Germany, circa 1870-1915. 11/16". Near Mint(+) (8.9). Price: $140. CyberAuction #330, Lot #58.

2228. END-OF-DAY. Onionskin. Four-lobed onionskin. Large. Transparent clear base. Opaque white core with blue skin. Four shallow lobes. Buffed. Pontils remain, as does some damage. Germany, circa 1870-1915. 1-7/8". Price: $140. CyberAuction #353, Lot #27.

2229. END-OF-DAY. Onionskin. Unusual example. Transparent clear base. Subsurface layer of stretched splotches of opaque white, transparent green, some pink, some blue. Lots of clear spaces. Surface is very lightly polished, some damage remains. Germany, circa 1870-1915. 1-5/8". Price: $135. CyberAuction #484, Lot #21.

2230. END-OF-DAY. Onionskin. Transparent clear base. Opaque white core. Transparent red skin. Some mica. Large. Surface has been very lightly polished, damage remains, pontils are gone. Germany, circa 1870-1915. 1-15/16". Price: $130. CyberAuction #416, Lot #44.

2231. END-OF-DAY. Onionskin. Rare marble. Transparent clear base. Subsurface layer is very dark "oxblood" red. Two white strands on the layer. Small chip, two tiny subsurface moons, some very light haze. Germany, circa 1870-1915. 9/16". Near Mint (8.6). Price: $120. CyberAuction #363, Lot #51.

2232. END-OF-DAY. Onionskin. Super onionskin with mica. Transparent clear base. Opaque white subsurface layer with turquoise skin. A little blue, and a nice sprinkling of small mica. In great shape. Superb marble. Germany, circa 1870-1915. 19/32". Mint (9.8). Price: $110. CyberAuction #336, Lot #52.

2233. END-OF-DAY. Onionskin. I think you would really call this an end of day Joseph Coat or a Joseph Coat onionskin. Very hard to find. Transparent clear base. Core is a multitude of stretched bright colors. Superb. One tiny subsurface moon near the bottom pontil, else surface is pristine. Germany, circa 1870-1915. 1". Near Mint(+) (8.9). Price: $110. CyberAuction #443, Lot #53.

2234. END-OF-DAY. Onionskin. Rare ribbon type onionskin. Transparent clear base. Opaque white core, blue skin. Shrunken on two sides to create single fat ribbon. Very nice. One small manufacturing pit near the top. Germany, circa 1870-1915. 13/16". Mint(-) (9.2). Price: $110. CyberAuction #464, Lot #50.

2235. END-OF-DAY. Onionskin. Hard to find onionskin in transparent blue glass. Core is white with yellow skin. Some rubbing on the surface. Germany, circa 1870-1915. 9/16". Mint(-) (9.0). Price: $100. CyberAuction #339, Lot #50.

2236. END-OF-DAY. Onionskin. From near the start of the cane. Very rare marble. Transparent clear base. Extremely thin core. Opaque white core with two panels of turquoise and two of pink. In great shape. Very rare. Germany, circa 1870-1915. 13/16". Mint (9.7). Price: $100. CyberAuction #406, Lot #45.

2237. END-OF-DAY. Onionskin. Transparent clear base. Yellow subsurface layer. Green skin. Some pink, blue and white. Beauty. Germany, circa 1870-1915. 3/4". Mint (9.8). Price: $95. CyberAuction #350, Lot #57.

2238. END-OF-DAY. Onionskin. Stunning left-twist onionskin with mica. Transparent clear base. Subsurface layer of white, covered by green, with some blue. Some mica. One tiny flake, one tiny subsurface moon. Some unmelted sand. Germany, circa 1870-1915. 23/32". Near Mint(+) (8.7). Price: $95. CyberAuction #369, Lot #56.

2239. END-OF-DAY. Onionskin. Stunning example. Transparent clear base. Subsurface layer of opaque white covered with transparent green and some transparent pink. Gorgeous. Germany, circa 1870-1915. 5/8". Mint (9.9). Price: $95. CyberAuction #396, Lot #45.

2240. END-OF-DAY. Onionskin. Transparent clear base. Opaque white core. Skin of blue and pink. Reverse twist top. One small manufacturing chip. Very nice. Germany, circa 1870-1915. 27/32". Mint(-) (9.0). Price: $90. CyberAuction #352, Lot #56.

2241. END-OF-DAY. Onionskin. Superb. Opaque white core. Almost completely covered by pink, with some green, blue and bright yellow. Melt spot, a couple of tiny chips. Germany, circa 1870-1915. 27/32". Near Mint(+) (8.7). Price: $90. CyberAuction #377, Lot #59.

2242. END-OF-DAY. Onionskin. Rare marble. Four-panel coreless onionskin. Transparent clear base. Two wide panels of ruddy red, with some white and blue. Lots of tiny clear spaces. Two narrow panels of blue. One tiny melt spot and a tiny sparkle. Germany, possibly England, circa 1870-1915. 3/4". Mint(-) (9.0). Price: $90. CyberAuction #471, Lot #42.

2243. END-OF-DAY. Onionskin. Onionskin with mica. Transparent clear base. Subsurface layer of opaque white with blue skin. Nice sprinkling of mica. Tiny flake and a pit. Germany, circa 1870-1915. 25/32". Near Mint(+) (8.7). Price: $90. CyberAuction #498, Lot #54.

2244. END-OF-DAY. Onionskin. Large. Transparent clear base. Opaque white core. Unstretched flecks of blue on it. Gorgeous. Some small chips and small subsurface moons. Germany, circa 1870-1915. 1-15/16". Good(+) 7.9). Price: $80. CyberAuction #359, Lot #35.

2245. END-OF-DAY. Onionskin. Transparent clear base. Subsurface yellow layer. Pink skin. Several flakes of mica. One very tiny melt chip. Germany, circa 1870-1915. 3/4". Mint(-) (9.1). Price: $80. CyberAuction #379, Lot #36.

2246. END-OF-DAY. Onionskin. Nice marble with mica. Left hand twist. Yellow subsurface layer. Covered by pink dots. A little blue. Some mica sprinkled on it. Heavily polished. Germany, circa 1870-1915. 1-1/2". Price: $80. CyberAuction #390, Lot #44.

2247. END-OF-DAY. Onionskin. Transparent clear base. Subsurface layer of stretched "oxblood" red and white, with some clear spaces. One tiny melt spot. Germany, possibly England, circa 1870-1915. 3/4". Mint (9.5). Price: $80. CyberAuction #479, Lot #45.

2248. END-OF-DAY. Onionskin. Transparent clear base. Yellow core, pink skin. Germany, circa 1870-1915. 3/4". Mint (9.7). Price: $80. CyberAuction #483, Lot #27.

2249. END-OF-DAY. Onionskin. Transparent clear base. Subsurface yellow layer. Pink skin. Several flakes of mica. One very tiny melt chip. Germany, circa 1870-1915. 3/4". Mint(-) (9.1). Price: $75. CyberAuction #351, Lot #51.

2250. END-OF-DAY. Onionskin. Transparent clear base. White core. Bright pink skin. Two mica flakes. Pristine. Germany, circa 1870-1915. 25/32". Mint (9.9). Price: $75. CyberAuction #360, Lot #55.

2251. END-OF-DAY. Onionskin. Transparent clear base. Opaque white core. Stretched blue, pink and turquoise. Left-hand twist. Superb marble. Germany, circa 1870-1915. 21/32". Mint (9.9). Price: $75. CyberAuction #483, Lot #38.

2252. END-OF-DAY. Onionskin. Could be called a coreless panelled onionskin, or maybe a submarine. Transparent clear base. Two subsurface bands covering about seventy five percent of the marble. One is wide and electric orange. Other is narrower and is white. A couple of tiny pinpricks. England, possibly Germany, circa 1870-1915. 23/32". Mint (9.4). Price: $75. CyberAuction #503, Lot #66.

2253. END-OF-DAY. Onionskin. Rare ribbon type onionskin. Transparent clear base. Opaque white core, blue skin. Shrunken on two sides to create single fat ribbon. Very nice. One small manufacturing pit near the top. Germany, circa 1870-1915. 13/16". Mint(-) (9.2). Price: $75. CyberAuction #507, Lot #53.

2254. END-OF-DAY. Onionskin. Very unusual onionskin. Transparent clear base. White core. Four panel subsurface white onionskin layer, with clear spaces. No color. Very odd. Germany, circa 1870-1915. 5/8". Mint (9.7). Price: $70. CyberAuction #459, Lot #38.

2255. END-OF-DAY. Onionskin. Transparent clear base. Opaque yellow subsurface layer. Pink skin. Beauty!!! Germany, circa 1870-1915. 3/4". Mint (9.9). Price: $70. CyberAuction #483, Lot #22.

2256. END-OF-DAY. Onionskin. Superb onionskin. Transparent clear base. Mustard yellow subsurface layer, with lots of small smeared pink bands and some green. Gorgeous marble. In pristine shape. Germany, circa 1870-1915. 11/16". Mint (9.9). Price: $65. CyberAuction #336, Lot #29.

2257. END-OF-DAY. Onionskin. Very pretty. Transparent clear base. Opaque white core. Smeared splotches of blue and turquoise. Gorgeous.

One very tiny flake, some manufacturing pits. Germany, circa 1870-1915. 11/16". Near Mint(+) (8.9). Price: $65. CyberAuction #377, Lot #38.

2258. END-OF-DAY. Onionskin. Nice onionskin. Transparent clear base. Mustard yellow core with pink skin. One large flake on one side, sparkle on the other. Views nicely from one side. Germany, circa 1870-1915. 1-1/2". Near Mint (8.4). Price: $65. CyberAuction #476, Lot #28.

2259. END-OF-DAY. Onionskin. Transparent clear base. Opaque white subsurface layer with gorgeous pink skin. Germany, circa 1870-1915. 21/32". Mint (9.9). Price: $65. CyberAuction #503, Lot #9.

2260. END-OF-DAY. Onionskin. Transparent clear base. Opaque white subsurface layer. Blue skin. Very pretty. Two tiny sparkles. Germany, circa 1870-1915. 11/16". Mint(-) (9.0). Price: $60. CyberAuction #365, Lot #52.

2261. END-OF-DAY. Onionskin. Transparent clear base. Yellow subsurface layer. Green skin. Some pink, blue and white. Beauty. One tiny pit. Germany, circa 1870-1915. 3/4". Mint(-) (9.2). Price: $60. CyberAuction #385, Lot #41.

2262. END-OF-DAY. Onionskin. Hard to find bright English onionskin. Transparent clear base. Subsurface layer is stretched splotches of bright orange, bright red and bright white. No clear spaces. A few tiny flakes and pits. England, possibly Germany, circa 1870-1920. 13/16". Near Mint(-) (8.2). Price: $60. CyberAuction #425, Lot #15.

2263. END-OF-DAY. Onionskin. Transparent clear base. Yellow core. Pink skin with a sprinkling of mica. Heavily polished, some damage remains. Germany, circa 1870-1915. 1-5/8". Price: $60. CyberAuction #427, Lot #25.

2264. END-OF-DAY. Onionskin. Very nice. Transparent clear base. Subsurface layer of white. Skin is pink, blue and green. Very nice marble. Germany, circa 1870-1915. 25/32". Mint (9.9). Price: $60. CyberAuction #465, Lot #52.

2265. END-OF-DAY. Onionskin. Gorgeous marble. Great colors. Transparent clear base. Opaque white core, shrunken on one side. Skin is pink, blue, turquoise and bright yellow. One tiny sparkle. Super. Germany, circa 1870-1915. 19/32". Mint(-) (9.1). Price: $60. CyberAuction #489, Lot #53.

2266. END-OF-DAY. Onionskin. Onionskin with mica. Nice marble. Needs a buff or very light polish. Opaque white subsurface layer. Skin of pink with some yellow and blue. Some scattered mica. Surface has a couple of shallow small chips, some tinier chipping and some haziness. Germany, circa 1870-1915. 1-1/4". Good (7.6). Price: $56. CyberAuction #394, Lot #35.

2267. END-OF-DAY. Onionskin. Transparent slightly smoky clear base. Opaque white core. Skin is smeared blue and pink dots. Odd coloring. Very slight haze to the surface, but no hits or missing glass. Germany, circa 1870-1915. 1-1/8". Near Mint (8.6). Price: $55. CyberAuction #334, Lot #24.

2268. END-OF-DAY. Onionskin. Very unusual. Transparent clear. Semiopaque white core with bands of green and lavender on it. Very odd coloring. Germany, circa 1870-1915. 5/8". Mint (9.9). Price: $55. CyberAuction #342, Lot #29.

2269. END-OF-DAY. Onionskin. Transparent very lightly tinted blue base. Core is white with some yellow. Pink skin with some blue and green. Polished, damage. Germany, circa 1870-1915. 1-11/16". Price: $55. CyberAuction #428, Lot #29.

2270. END-OF-DAY. Onionskin. Transparent clear base. Opaque white core. Blue skin with some pink. A couple of pieces of mica. Some minor surface scratching. Germany, circa 1870-1915. 15/16". Mint(-) (9.0). Price: $55. CyberAuction #501, Lot #54.

2271. END-OF-DAY. Onionskin. Transparent clear base. Subsurface layer of dark oxblood-type red. Some lines of yellow and blue on it. Tiny flat spot, piece of melted dirt, and is not quite wet. Very unusual. Germany, circa 1870-1915. 21/32". Mint(-) (9.0). Price: $55. CyberAuction #504, Lot #40.

2272. END-OF-DAY. Onionskin. End of cane. First off rod. Single pontil. Transparent clear base. Just a few wispy flakes of green at the very bottom. Some very light haze. Germany, circa 1870-1915. 11/16". Near Mint (8.6). Price: $52. CyberAuction #365, Lot #43.

2273. END-OF-DAY. Onionskin. Transparent clear base. Opaque yellow subsurface layer with green skin. Some red. Two tiny pits and a sparkle. Germany, circa 1870-1915. 25/32". Near Mint(+) (8.9). Price: $51. CyberAuction #348, Lot #7.

2274. END-OF-DAY. Onionskin. Transparent clear base. Opaque white core. Pink skin with a little blue. Super texture to the core. One tiny melt spot. Germany, circa 1870-1915. 11/16". Mint (9.9). Price: $50. CyberAuction #333, Lot #33.

2275. END-OF-DAY. Onionskin. Transparent clear base. Opaque yellow subsurface layer with green skin. Some red. Two tiny pits and a sparkle. Germany, circa 1870-1915. 25/32". Near Mint(+) (8.9). Price: $50. CyberAuction #371, Lot #45.

2276. END-OF-DAY. Onionskin. End of cane (first off cane) onionskin. Transparent clear base. Core of white with pink and blue on it. Partially looped over. Stunning. Appears to have received a buff. Germany, circa 1870-1915. 19/32". Price: $50. CyberAuction #372, Lot #6.

2277. END-OF-DAY. Onionskin. Very rare end of cane (first off cane) ribbon onionskin. Transparent clear base. Thin ribbon of stretched orange/yellow and blue that shoots out of the top of the marble. Slightly flattened. Two tiny subsurface moons at the bottom pontil. Germany, circa 1870-1915. 9/16". Near Mint(+) (8.7). Price: $50. CyberAuction #372, Lot #54.

2278. END-OF-DAY. Onionskin. Transparent clear base. Core is semiopaque white and transparent green. An odd reverse twist top. Germany, circa 1870-1915. 1/2". Mint (9.9). Price: $50. CyberAuction #373, Lot #7.

2279. END-OF-DAY. Onionskin. Yellow subsurface layer with pink skin. One blue dot. In great shape. Germany, circa 1870-1915. 23/32". Mint (9.8). Price: $50. CyberAuction #379, Lot #14.

2280. END-OF-DAY. Onionskin. Transparent clear base. Opaque yellow subsurface layer. Light pink skin. Beauty. One melt spot, a pinprick. Germany, circa 1870-1915. 5/8". Mint(-) (9.2). Price: $50. CyberAuction #396, Lot #39.

2281. END-OF-DAY. Onionskin. Transparent clear base. White core with pink skin. Several tiny chips, but beautiful. Germany, circa 1870-1915. 27/32". Near Mint (8.6). Price: $50. CyberAuction #403, Lot #10.

2282. END-OF-DAY. Onionskin. Transparent clear base. Opaque white subsurface layer. Blue and pink skin. One small flake. Beauty. Germany, circa 1870-1915. 13/16". Near Mint(+) (8.8). Price: $50. CyberAuction #403, Lot #49.

2283. END-OF-DAY. Onionskin. Transparent clear base. Peewee. White skin. Two panels of green, two of pink. Tiny. Germany, circa 1870-1915. 7/16". Mint (9.7). Price: $50. CyberAuction #441, Lot #51.

2284. END-OF-DAY. Onionskin. Very unusual. Was used on a hatpin. Transparent clear base. Opaque white core. Pink skin with lots of mica. Left-twist. The top pontil has a hole melted into it, for inserting on a hatpin. One small flake, some scratching. Germany, circa 1870-1915. 11/16". Near Mint(+) (8.7). Price: $50. CyberAuction #447, Lot #52.

2285. END-OF-DAY. Onionskin. Gorgeous marble. Transparent clear base. Subsurface layer of white and pink skin. Heavy coating of mica. Buffed surface. Pontils remain, and remnants of tiny subsurface moons. Germany, circa 1870-1915. 11/16". Price: $50. CyberAuction #491, Lot #45.

2286. END-OF-DAY. Onionskin. Transparent clear base. Opaque white core, pink overall skin. One air hole. Germany, circa 1870-1915. 11/16". Mint(-) (9.2). Price: $50. CyberAuction #493, Lot #56.

2287. END-OF-DAY. Onionskin. Transparent clear base. Subsurface mustard layer with green and pink skin. Germany, circa 1870-1915. 11/16". Mint (9.7). Price: $50. CyberAuction #504, Lot #8.

2288. END-OF-DAY. Onionskin. Transparent clear base. White subsurface layer with blue skin. Beauty. Germany, circa 1870-1915. 3/4". Mint (9.8). Price: $49. CyberAuction #462, Lot #44.

2289. END-OF-DAY. Onionskin. Transparent clear base. Pink skin, with a little green. Germany, circa 1870-1915. 1/2". Mint (9.7). Price: $48. CyberAuction #363, Lot #17.

2290. END-OF-DAY. Onionskin. Very nice onionskin. Transparent clear base. Subsurface semi-opaque white covered with blue skin. One tiny melt spot. Germany, circa 1870-1915. 27/32". Mint (9.5). Price: $48. CyberAuction #475, Lot #40.

2291. END-OF-DAY. Onionskin. Hard to find left-twist onionskin. Transparent clear base. Opaque white core. Pink skin. Left-twist. Beautiful marble!!! Germany, circa 1870-1915. 17/32". Mint (9.8). Price: $48. CyberAuction #487, Lot #17.

2292. END-OF-DAY. Onionskin. Transparent clear base. Yellow core. Transparent pink subsurface layer. Beauty. Germany, circa 1870-1915. 21/32". Mint (9.9). Price: $46. CyberAuction #332, Lot #46.

2293. END-OF-DAY. Onionskin. Transparent very lightly tinted blue base. Core is white with some yellow. Pink skin with some blue and green. Polished, damage. Germany, circa 1870-1915. 1-11/16". Price: $46. CyberAuction #470, Lot #25.

2294. END-OF-DAY. Onionskin. Transparent clear base. Opaque yellow core with pink skin. Germany, circa 1870-1915. 5/8". Mint (9.9). Price: $45. CyberAuction #330, Lot #38.

2295. END-OF-DAY. Onionskin. Very odd marble. Transparent clear base. Opaque white core with blue skin. Left-hand twist. Very shrunken on one side. Has two large pieces of unmelted sand in it. One melt spot. Germany, circa 1870-1915. 5/8". Mint(-) (9.0). Price: $45. CyberAuction #333, Lot #31.

2296. END-OF-DAY. Onionskin. Transparent dark blue base. White subsurface layer with some yellow. Germany, circa 1870-1915. 9/16". Mint (9.9). Price: $45. CyberAuction #335, Lot #54.

2297. END-OF-DAY. Onionskin. Transparent clear base. Opaque white subsurface layer with pink skin. Some light green bands on the pink. In nice shape. Germany, circa 1870-1915. 5/8". Mint (9.9). Price: $45. CyberAuction #336, Lot #33.

2298. END-OF-DAY. Onionskin. Transparent clear base. Subsurface layer of opaque white and transparent green. Germany, circa 1870-1915. 1/2". Mint (9.9). Price: $45. CyberAuction #369, Lot #32.

2299. END-OF-DAY. Onionskin. Transparent clear base. Opaque yellow subsurface layer. Dark green skin. Gorgeous. Germany, circa 1870-1915. 5/8". Mint (9.9). Price: $45. CyberAuction #371, Lot #12.

2300. END-OF-DAY. Onionskin. Another beauty. Transparent clear base. Subsurface translucent blue layer with some opaque white. One tiny sparkle. Very nice. Germany, circa 1870-1915. 21/32". Mint(-) (9.1). Price: $45. CyberAuction #396, Lot #43.

2301. END-OF-DAY. Onionskin. Very unusual. Was used on a hatpin. Transparent clear base. Opaque white core. Pink skin with lots of mica. Left-twist. The top pontil has a hole melted into it, for inserting on a hatpin. One small flake, some scratching. Germany, circa 1870-1915. 11/16". Near Mint(+) (8.7). Price: $45. CyberAuction #403, Lot #51.

2302. END-OF-DAY. Onionskin. Transparent clear base. Opaque white subsurface layer with blue and a little green skin. Germany, circa 1870-1915. 9/16". Mint (9.8). Price: $45. CyberAuction #443, Lot #25.

2303. END-OF-DAY. Onionskin. Transparent clear base. Opaque white core. Pink skin. Polished. Damage remains. 1-3/4". Germany, circa 1870-1915. Price: $45. CyberAuction #466, Lot #19.

2304. END-OF-DAY. Onionskin. Transparent clear base. White core encased by a floating layer of transparent pink. Some mica. One tiny flake. 9/16". Near Mint(+) (8.8). Price: $44. CyberAuction #383, Lot #18.

2305. END-OF-DAY. Onionskin. Transparent clear base. Core is stretched opaque white splotches with a skin of pink and green. Polished. Some

damage remains. Pretty. Germany, circa 1870-1915. 1-3/4". Price: $44. CyberAuction #428, Lot #27.

2306. END-OF-DAY. Onionskin. Transparent clear base. Opaque white subsurface layer, pink skin. Germany, circa 1870-1915. 15/32". Mint (9.8). Price: $44. CyberAuction #469, Lot #57.

2307. END-OF-DAY. Onionskin. Transparent clear base. Pink skin, with a little green. Germany, circa 1870-1915. 1/2". Mint (9.7). Price: $44. CyberAuction #506, Lot #39.

2308. END-OF-DAY. Onionskin. Transparent clear base. Yellow subsurface layer with transparent pink skin. Beauty. Germany, circa 1870-1915. 1/2". Mint (9.9). Price: $44. CyberAuction #508, Lot #16.

2309. END-OF-DAY. Onionskin. Transparent clear base. Opaque white subsurface layer is with light blue and a little green skin. Germany, circa 1870-1915. 17/32". Mint (9.9). Price: $43. CyberAuction #345, Lot #50.

2310. END-OF-DAY. Onionskin. Transparent clear base. Opaque white subsurface layer is with light blue and a little green skin. Germany, circa 1870-1915. 17/32". Mint (9.9). Price: $43. CyberAuction #444, Lot #48.

2311. END-OF-DAY. Onionskin. Transparent clear base. Opaque yellow core with nice green skin. Beauty. Germany, circa 1870-1915. 19/32". Mint (9.9). Price: $42. CyberAuction #330, Lot #21.

2312. END-OF-DAY. Onionskin. Transparent clear base. Opaque white core with pink and blue bands on it. Germany, circa 1870-1915. 11/16". Mint (9.9). Price: $42. CyberAuction #385, Lot #49.

2313. END-OF-DAY. Onionskin. Very interesting marble from near an end of the cane. Transparent slightly tinted blue base. Core is opaque white with lots of clear spaces, and stretched flecks of blue. Even has some blue melted into the surface. A few tiny pits. Germany, circa 1870-1915. 9/16". Near Mint(+) (8.7). Price: $42. CyberAuction #406, Lot #9.

2314. END-OF-DAY. Onionskin. Transparent clear base. Opaque white core with pink and blue skin. Shrunken on one side. Germany, circa 1870-1915. 5/8". Mint (9.9). Price: $42. CyberAuction #406, Lot #51.

2315. END-OF-DAY. Onionskin. Very pretty. Transparent clear base. Core is white, yellow and green. Some additional blue and red on it. A number of small chips on the marble. Germany, circa 1870-1915. 1-9/16". Good(+) (7.8). Price: $42. CyberAuction #427, Lot #23.

2316. END-OF-DAY. Onionskin. Transparent clear base. Yellow subsurface layer. Green skin. Some pink, blue and white. Beauty. One tiny pit. Germany, circa 1870-1915. 3/4". Mint(-) (9.2). Price: $42. CyberAuction #443, Lot #54.

2317. END-OF-DAY. Onionskin. Very odd marble. Transparent clear base. Opaque white subsurface layer. bands of lavender, blue, red, orange and green. Some cold roll lines. Very nice marble. Germany, circa 1870-1915. 21/32". Mint (9.6). Price: $42. CyberAuction #459, Lot #43.

2318. END-OF-DAY. Onionskin. Four-panel onionskin. Transparent clear base. Opaque white subsurface layer. Two pink panels, two panels of green and blue. Very nice. Germany, circa 1870-1915. 9/16". Mint (9.9). Price: $42. CyberAuction #465, Lot #49.

2319. END-OF-DAY. Onionskin. Very interesting marble from near an end of the cane. Transparent slightly tinted blue base. Core is opaque white with lots of clear spaces, and stretched flecks of blue. Even has some blue melted into the surface. A few tiny pits. Germany, circa 1870-1915. 9/16". Near Mint(+) (8.7). Price: $42. CyberAuction #474, Lot #44.

2320. END-OF-DAY. Onionskin. Transparent clear base. Translucent white subsurface layer with green skin of various bright shade. Beauty. One sparkle. Germany, circa 1870-1915. 3/4". Mint(-) (9.1). Price: $42. CyberAuction #475, Lot #23.

2321. END-OF-DAY. Onionskin. Very interesting marble from near an end of the cane. Transparent slightly tinted blue base. Core is opaque white, with lots of clear spaces, and stretched flecks of blue. Even has some blue melted into the surface. A few tiny pits. Germany, circa 1870-1915. 9/16". Near Mint(+) (8.7). Price: $42. CyberAuction #486, Lot #27.

2322. END-OF-DAY. Onionskin. Transparent clear base. Translucent white subsurface layer with green skin of various bright shade. Beauty. One sparkle. Germany, circa 1870-1915. 3/4". Mint(-) (9.1). Price: $42. CyberAuction #486, Lot #36.

2323. END-OF-DAY. Onionskin. Transparent clear base. Yellow core. Subsurface layer of white and blue, with some clear spaces. Beauty. Germany, circa 1870-1915. 25/32". Mint (9.8). Price: $42. CyberAuction #496, Lot #42.

2324. END-OF-DAY. Onionskin. Transparent clear base. Subsurface layer is stretched bands of various shades of an oxblood-type red. A melt chip and two tiny flakes. Rare coloring. Germany, circa 1870-1915. 11/16". Near Mint(+) (8.7). Price: $42. CyberAuction #504, Lot #12.

2325. END-OF-DAY. Onionskin. Transparent clear base. Opaque white subsurface layer. Blue skin. Germany, circa 1870-1915. 17/32". Mint (9.7). Price: $42. CyberAuction #506, Lot #32.

2326. END-OF-DAY. Onionskin. Interesting. Transparent clear base. Yellow core. Subsurface layer of white and blue. In great shape. Germany, circa 1870-1915. 21/32". Mint (9.9). Price: $41. CyberAuction #334, Lot #52.

2327. END-OF-DAY. Onionskin. Peewee. Blue skin on white. Tiny. Germany, circa 1870-1915. 7/16". Mint (9.9). Price: $41. CyberAuction #434, Lot #50.

2328. END-OF-DAY. Onionskin. Transparent clear base. Subsurface layer of white, with pink skin. Slightly shrunken on one side. Some cold rolling. Germany, circa 1870-1915. 5/8". Mint (9.6). Price: $40. CyberAuction #336, Lot #42.

2329. END-OF-DAY. Onionskin. Transparent clear base. Opaque yellow subsurface layer. Skin of green and some pink. Very light haze to surface. Some tiny chipping and subsurface moons. Germany, circa 1870-1915. 1-1/8". Good(+) (7.9). Price: $40. CyberAuction #350, Lot #9.

330. END-OF-DAY. Onionskin. Transparent green base. Opaque white subsurface layer. Skin is pink, blue and green. Gorgeous. Lightly buffed, pontils are intact. Germany, circa 1870-1915. 3/4". Price: $40. CyberAuction #364, Lot #54.

331. END-OF-DAY. Onionskin. Transparent clear base. White and pink subsurface layer with some yellow and blue. Beauty. Germany, circa 1870-1915. 9/16". Mint (9.9). Price: $40. CyberAuction #366, Lot #8.

332. END-OF-DAY. Onionskin. Stunning marble. Transparent clear base. Opaque white core with a skin of pink and blue. One manufacturing pit. Germany, circa 1870-1915. 5/8". Mint (9.6). Price: $40. CyberAuction #366, Lot #46.

333. END-OF-DAY. Onionskin. Transparent clear base. Subsurface layer of opaque white and transparent green. Beauty. Germany, circa 1870-1915. 5/8". Mint (9.8). Price: $40. CyberAuction #396, Lot #33.

334. END-OF-DAY. Onionskin. Transparent clear base. Pink and blue skin. Germany, circa 1870-1915. 1/2". Mint (9.7). Price: $40. CyberAuction #435, Lot #55.

335. END-OF-DAY. Onionskin. Transparent clear base. Subsurface white layer with green skin and some pink. Germany, circa 1870-1915. 9/16". Mint (9.9). Price: $40. CyberAuction #443, Lot #35.

336. END-OF-DAY. Onionskin. Transparent clear base. Subsurface layer of opaque white and transparent green. Germany, circa 1870-1915. 1/2". Mint (9.9). Price: $40. CyberAuction #444, Lot #15.

337. END-OF-DAY. Onionskin. Peewee. Blue skin on white. Tiny. Germany, circa 1870-1915. 7/16". Mint (9.9). Price: $40. CyberAuction #453, Lot #57.

338. END-OF-DAY. Onionskin. Transparent clear base. Subsurface opaque white layer with lime green skin. Two small annealing fractures, but a beauty. Germany, circa 1870-1915. 25/32". Near Mint(+) (8.9). Price: $40. CyberAuction #462, Lot #50.

339. END-OF-DAY. Onionskin. Transparent clear base. Subsurface layer of translucent to opaque white white blue skin. Very nice marble. One very tiny melt spot. Germany, circa 1870-1915. 13/16". Mint (9.6). Price: $40. CyberAuction #471, Lot #43.

340. END-OF-DAY. Onionskin. Transparent clear base. Subsurface layer of translucent to opaque white white blue skin. Very nice marble. One very tiny melt spot. Germany, circa 1870-1915. 13/16". Mint (9.6). Price: $40. CyberAuction #488, Lot #40.

341. END-OF-DAY. Onionskin. Transparent clear base. Yellow subsurface layer with green skin. Germany, circa 1870-1915. 5/8". Mint (9.9). Price: $40. CyberAuction #505, Lot #32.

342. END-OF-DAY. Onionskin. Transparent clear base. Yellow subsurface layer. Green skin with a little red. Germany, circa 1870-1915. 5/8". Mint (9.6). Price: $39. CyberAuction #372, Lot #48.

343. END-OF-DAY. Onionskin. End of cane onionskin. Transparent clear base. Core is a partial, white with pink spots. malformed. Haziness. Germany, circa 1870-1915. 19/32". Near Mint (8.3). Price: $38. CyberAuction #350, Lot #18.

344. END-OF-DAY. Onionskin. Transparent clear base. Subsurface layer of blue and white. Some pink. Really nice. Germany, circa 1870-1915. 11/16". Mint (9.8). Price: $38. CyberAuction #354, Lot #17.

345. END-OF-DAY. Onionskin. Transparent clear base. Subsurface white layer with green skin and some pink. Germany, circa 1870-1915. 9/16". Mint (9.8). Price: $38. CyberAuction #355, Lot #54.

346. END-OF-DAY. Onionskin. Transparent clear base. Opaque white subsurface layer. Pink and blue skin. Beauty. Germany, circa 1870-1915. 9/16". Mint (9.9). Price: $38. CyberAuction #467, Lot #26.

347. END-OF-DAY. Onionskin. Transparent clear base. Opaque white core. Blue skin. One small pink band. One tiny piece of mica. Germany, circa 1870-1915. 21/32". Mint (9.9). Price: $38. CyberAuction #473, Lot #51.

348. END-OF-DAY. Onionskin. Transparent clear base. Opaque white subsurface layer. Pink skin. Germany, circa 1870-1915. 1/2". Mint (9.9). Price: $38. CyberAuction #508, Lot #47.

349. END-OF-DAY. Onionskin. Transparent clear base. Opaque yellow subsurface layer. Dark green skin. Gorgeous. Germany, circa 1870-1915. 5/8". Mint (9.9). Price: $37. CyberAuction #351, Lot #32.

350. END-OF-DAY. Onionskin. Transparent clear base. Subsurface white layer. Blue, pink and green bands and strands on it. Germany, circa 1870-1915. 15/32". Mint (9.9). Price: $37. CyberAuction #366, Lot #27.

351. END-OF-DAY. Onionskin. Transparent clear base. Opaque white core. Blue skin. Slightly shrunken core on one side. One very tiny chip. Germany, circa 1870-1915. 5/8". Near Mint(+) (8.9). Price: $37. CyberAuction #373, Lot #33.

352. END-OF-DAY. Onionskin. Transparent clear base. Opaque white subsurface layer with green and pink skin. Several tiny flakes. Germany, circa 1870-1915. 9/16". Near Mint (8.3). Price: $37. CyberAuction #376, Lot #34.

353. END-OF-DAY. Onionskin. Peewee. Blue skin on white. Tiny. Germany, circa 1870-1915. 7/16". Mint (9.9). Price: $37. CyberAuction #390, Lot #3.

354. END-OF-DAY. Onionskin. Transparent clear base. Opaque white core. Dark blue skin. In great shape. Germany, circa 1870-1915. 21/32". Mint (9.8). Price: $37. CyberAuction #390, Lot #6.

355. END-OF-DAY. Onionskin. Transparent clear base. Opaque white subsurface layer. Skin of blue with a little red. Two melt spots. Germany, circa 1870-1915. 11/16". Mint (9.4). Price: $37. CyberAuction #425, Lot #51.

356. END-OF-DAY. Onionskin. Very interesting marble from near an end of the cane. Transparent slightly tinted blue base. Core is opaque white, with lots of clear spaces, and stretched flecks of blue. Even has some blue

melted into the surface. A few tiny pits. Germany, circa 1870-1915. 9/16". Near Mint(+) (8.7). Price: $37. CyberAuction #437, Lot #53.

2357. END-OF-DAY. Onionskin. End of cane. First off rod. Single pontil. Transparent clear base. Just a few wispy flakes of green at the very bottom. Some very light haze. Germany, circa 1870-1915. 11/16". Near Mint (8.6). Price: $37. CyberAuction #444, Lot #42.

2358. END-OF-DAY. Onionskin. Transparent clear base. Subsurface layer of blue and white. Some pink. Really nice. Germany, circa 1870-1915. 11/16". Mint (9.8). Price: $37. CyberAuction #444, Lot #51.

2359. END-OF-DAY. Onionskin. Very interesting marble from near an end of the cane. Transparent slightly tinted blue base. Core is opaque white, with lots of clear spaces, and stretched flecks of blue. Even has some blue melted into the surface. A few tiny pits. Germany, circa 1870-1915. 9/16". Near Mint(+) (8.7). Price: $37. CyberAuction #454, Lot #43.

2360. END-OF-DAY. Onionskin. Transparent clear base. Core is bright pastel orange and green stretched bands. Annealing fracture running length of marble on one side. England, possibly Germany, circa 1870-1915. 25/32". Mint(-) (9.0). Price: $37. CyberAuction #479, Lot #11.

2361. END-OF-DAY. Onionskin. End of cane. First off rod. Single pontil. Transparent clear base. Just a few wispy flakes of green at the very bottom. Some very light haze. Germany, circa 1870-1915. 11/16". Near Mint (8.6). Price: $37. CyberAuction #490, Lot #10.

2362. END-OF-DAY. Onionskin. End of cane. First off rod. Single pontil. Transparent clear base. Just a few wispy flakes of green at the very bottom. Some very light haze. Germany, circa 1870-1915. 11/16". Near Mint (8.6). Price: $37. CyberAuction #506, Lot #34.

2363. END-OF-DAY. Onionskin. Transparent clear base. Subsurface layer of white and pink. Germany, circa 1870-1915. 15/32". Mint (9.9). Price: $36. CyberAuction #339, Lot #24.

2364. END-OF-DAY. Onionskin. Transparent clear base. Mustard yellow core with pink skin. Reverse twist top. Germany, circa 1870-1915. 5/8". Mint (9.9). Price: $36. CyberAuction #385, Lot #22.

2365. END-OF-DAY. Onionskin. Opaque white subsurface layer. Skin of blue and red, with some yellow. One melt hole. Germany, circa 1870-1915. 21/32". Mint(-) (9.0). Price: $36. CyberAuction #393, Lot #53.

2366. END-OF-DAY. Onionskin. Transparent clear base. Opaque white core. Green, pink and blue skin. Germany, circa 1870-1915. 19/32". Mint (9.6). Price: $36. CyberAuction #403, Lot #43.

2367. END-OF-DAY. Onionskin. Transparent clear base. Pink skin, with a little green. Germany, circa 1870-1915. 1/2". Price: $36. CyberAuction #441, Lot #21.

2368. END-OF-DAY. Onionskin. Transparent clear base with loads of tiny air bubbles. Blue and white skin. Germany, circa 1870-1915. 9/16". Mint (9.9). Price: $36. CyberAuction #452, Lot #19.

2369. END-OF-DAY. Onionskin. Transparent clear base. Pink skin, with a little green. Germany, circa 1870-1915. 1/2". Mint (9.7). Price: $36. CyberAuction #490, Lot #35.

2370. END-OF-DAY. Onionskin. Transparent clear base. Very shrunken core. Yellow core. Three quarters covered with stretched green splotches, one-quarter with stretched pink splotches. Tiny annealing fracture on the core. Germany, circa 1870-1915. 11/16". Mint(-) (9.2). Price: $36. CyberAuction #503, Lot #25.

2371. END-OF-DAY. Onionskin. Transparent clear base. Subsurface layer of opaque white. Pink skin. Gorgeous. Germany, circa 1870-1915. 19/32". Mint (9.9). Price: $35. CyberAuction #348, Lot #4.

2372. END-OF-DAY. Onionskin. Transparent clear base. Opaque white subsurface layer with pink skin. One dirt line on it. Germany, circa 1870-1915. 21/32". Mint (9.6). Price: $35. CyberAuction #384, Lot #56.

2373. END-OF-DAY. Onionskin. Transparent clear base. Opaque white subsurface layer with blue skin. Germany, circa 1870-1915. 1/2". Mint (9.9). Price: $35. CyberAuction #385, Lot #47.

2374. END-OF-DAY. Onionskin. Transparent clear base. Yellow core with pink skin. Germany, circa 1870-1915. 19/32". Mint (9.8). Price: $35. CyberAuction #391, Lot #50.

2375. END-OF-DAY. Onionskin. Transparent clear base. Opaque white core with yellow and pink skin. Very shrunken on one side. One melt spot. Very nice. Germany, circa 1870-1915. 21/32". Mint(-) (9.2). Price: $35. CyberAuction #400, Lot #20.

2376. END-OF-DAY. Onionskin. Transparent clear base. Opaque white subsurface layer, dark blue skin. Germany, circa 1870-1915. 17/32". Mint (9.7). Price: $35. CyberAuction #439, Lot #49.

2377. END-OF-DAY. Onionskin. Transparent clear base. Opaque white subsurface layer with pink and blue skin. One piece of mica. One pit. Germany, circa 1870-1915. 1/2". Mint(-) (9.0). Price: $35. CyberAuction #479, Lot #9.

2378. END-OF-DAY. Onionskin. Transparent clear base. Opaque white core. Pink skin with a little blue. Germany, circa 1870-1915. 5/8". Mint (9.7). Price: $34. CyberAuction #338, Lot #20.

2379. END-OF-DAY. Onionskin. Transparent clear base. Core is white with blue skin. Germany, circa 1870-1915. 11/16". Mint (9.9). Price: $34. CyberAuction #357, Lot #4.

2380. END-OF-DAY. Onionskin. Transparent clear base. Subsurface base with pink and blue skin. Germany, circa 1870-1915. 1/2". Mint (9.9). Price: $34. CyberAuction #357, Lot #10.

2381. END-OF-DAY. Onionskin. Transparent clear base. White core with pink skin. Germany, circa 1870-1915. 23/32". Mint (9.7). Price: $34. CyberAuction #391, Lot #54.

2382. END-OF-DAY. Onionskin. Transparent clear base. White subsurface layer with lots of clear spaces. Pink skin with one blue band. Melt spot and cold roll line. Germany, circa 1870-1915. 17/32". Mint (9.5). Price: $34. CyberAuction #433, Lot #11.

2383. END-OF-DAY. Onionskin. Another beauty. Transparent clear base. Subsurface translucent blue layer with some opaque white. One tiny sparkle. Very nice. Germany, circa 1870-1915. 21/32". Mint(-) (9.1). Price: $34. CyberAuction #442, Lot #38.

2384. END-OF-DAY. Onionskin. Transparent clear base. Opaque yellow subsurface layer. Light pink skin. Beauty. One melt spot, a pinprick. Germany, circa 1870-1915. 5/8". Mint(+) (9.2). Price: $34. CyberAuction #442, Lot #54.

2385. END-OF-DAY. Onionskin. Transparent clear base. Subsurface white layer. Pale pink and some pale green on it. Nice. One tiny chip. Germany, circa 1870-1915. 23/32". Near Mint(+) (8.8). Price: $34. CyberAuction #443, Lot #30.

2386. END-OF-DAY. Onionskin. Transparent clear base. Opaque yellow subsurface layer. Dark green skin. Gorgeous. Germany, circa 1870-1915. 5/8". Mint (9.9). Price: $34. CyberAuction #444, Lot #18.

2387. END-OF-DAY. Onionskin. Transparent clear base. Subsurface mustard yellow with a pink skin. Broken off bottom pontil. Germany, circa 1870-1915. 5/8". Mint (9.9). Price: $34. CyberAuction #445, Lot #40.

2388. END-OF-DAY. Onionskin. Transparent clear base. Opaque white core with light pink skin. Gorgeous. Germany, circa 1870-1915. 21/32". Mint (9.7). Price: $34. CyberAuction #489, Lot #11.

2389. END-OF-DAY. Onionskin. Transparent clear base. Subsurface layer of white and blue. Germany, circa 1870-1915. 11/16". Mint (9.8). Price: $34. CyberAuction #504, Lot #27.

2390. END-OF-DAY. Onionskin. Transparent clear base. Opaque white subsurface layer with lime green skin. Tiny annealing fracture in the white, and a tiny pit. Germany, circa 1870-1915. 23/32". Mint (-) (9.0). Price: $34. CyberAuction #504, Lot #49.

2391. END-OF-DAY. Onionskin. Onionskin with mica. Transparent clear base. Yellow core. Pink skin. Some large mica flakes on it. Some tiny chips and haziness. Germany, circa 1870-1915. 5/8". Good(+) (7.8). Price: $33. CyberAuction #346, Lot #56.

2392. END-OF-DAY. Onionskin. Transparent green base. Yellow core with pink skin. Slightly shrunken on one side. One melted nub of glass on it. Germany, circa 1870-1915. 5/8". Mint (9.7). Price: $33. CyberAuction #375, Lot #3.

2393. END-OF-DAY. Onionskin. Transparent clear base. Yellow subsurface layer with pink skin. Slightly shrunken on one side. Very pretty marble. Germany, circa 1870-1915. 9/16". Mint (9.9). Price: $33. CyberAuction #398, Lot #7.

2394. END-OF-DAY. Onionskin. Transparent clear base. Subsurface white base with pink and green skin. Tiny melt spot. Germany, circa 1870-1915. 1/2". Mint(-) (9.2). Price: $33. CyberAuction #404, Lot #43.

2395. END-OF-DAY. Onionskin. Transparent clear base. White core with pink skin. One tiny pit. Germany, circa 1870-1915. 11/16". Mint(-) (9.0). Price: $33. CyberAuction #414, Lot #22.

2396. END-OF-DAY. Onionskin. Transparent clear base. Mustard yellow subsurface layer with green skin. One pit. Germany, circa 1870-1915. 1/2". Mint(-) (9.0). Price: $33. CyberAuction #445, Lot #12.

2397. END-OF-DAY. Onionskin. Transparent clear base. Opaque white subsurface layer with pink and blue skin. Germany, circa 1870-1915. 9/16". Mint (9.7). Price: $33. CyberAuction #448, Lot #6.

2398. END-OF-DAY. Onionskin. Transparent clear base. Subsurface layer of white with blue and pink. Germany, circa 1870-1915. 1/2". Mint (9.7). Price: $33. CyberAuction #490, Lot #7.

2399. END-OF-DAY. Onionskin. Transparent clear base. Opaque white subsurface layer with one small chip, some very minor haze. Germany, circa 1870-1915. 17/32". Near Mint (8.6). Price: $32. CyberAuction #331, Lot #44.

2400. END-OF-DAY. Onionskin. Transparent clear base. Yellow core with green skin. One tiny subsurface moon. Germany, circa 1870-1915. 5/8". Near Mint(+) (8.9). Price: $32. CyberAuction #341, Lot #56.

2401. END-OF-DAY. Onionskin. Transparent clear base. Subsurface white layer. Pale pink and some pale green on it. Nice. One tiny chip. Germany, circa 1870-1915. 23/32". Near Mint(+) (8.8). Price: $32. CyberAuction #365, Lot #31.

2402. END-OF-DAY. Onionskin. White core with pink skin. Germany, circa 1870-1915. 21/32". Mint (9.5). Price: $32. CyberAuction #374, Lot #9.

2403. END-OF-DAY. Onionskin. Transparent clear base. Opaque white core. Skin of an oddly hued green. One melt spot. Germany, circa 1870-1915. 21/32". Mint(-) (9.2). Price: $32. CyberAuction #418, Lot #41.

2404. END-OF-DAY. Onionskin. Transparent clear base. Opaque white core with pink skin. Small cold roll line. Germany, circa 1870-1915. 1/2". Mint (9.6). Price: $32. CyberAuction #436, Lot #13.

2405. END-OF-DAY. Onionskin. Transparent clear base. Opaque white core with blue skin. A couple of tiny chips, overall pinpricking. Germany, circa 1870-1915. 1-3/16". Near Mint(-) (8.0). Price: $32. CyberAuction #440, Lot #20.

2406. END-OF-DAY. Onionskin. Transparent clear base. Opaque white core. Pink skin. Polished. Damage remains. 1-3/4". Germany, circa 1870-1915. Price: $32. CyberAuction #447, Lot #34.

2407. END-OF-DAY. Onionskin. Transparent clear base. Opaque white subsurface layer with pink skin. Very slight haze. Germany, circa 1870-1915. 9/16". Near Mint(+) (8.8). Price: $32. CyberAuction #450, Lot #24.

2408. END-OF-DAY. Onionskin. Transparent clear base. Opaque yellow core. Green skin. Germany, circa 1870-1915. 19/32". Mint (9.8). Price: $32. CyberAuction #463, Lot #41.

2409. END-OF-DAY. Onionskin. Transparent clear base. Opaque yellow core, pink skin. Germany, circa 1870-1915. 19/32". Mint (9.8). Price: $32. CyberAuction #475, Lot #4.

2410. END-OF-DAY. Onionskin. Transparent clear base. White core. Dark blue and pink skin. A couple of melt spots, all on one side. Germany, circa 1870-1915. 11/16". Mint(-) (9.0). Price: $32. CyberAuction #488, Lot #29.

2411. END-OF-DAY. Onionskin. Transparent clear base. Subsurface layer of white, green skin. A little bit of pink. Germany, circa 1870-1915. 1/2". Mint (9.5). Price: $32. CyberAuction #508, Lot #15.

2412. END-OF-DAY. Onionskin. Transparent clear base. Opaque white subsurface layer with pink skin. One tiny manufacturing chip. Germany, circa 1870-1915. 11/16". Mint(-) (9.1). Price: $31. CyberAuction #338, Lot #52.

2413. END-OF-DAY. Onionskin. Transparent clear base. Opaque white subsurface layer with green skin. One tiny chip. Germany, circa 1870-1915. 19/32". Near Mint(+) (8.7). Price: $31. CyberAuction #342, Lot #15.

2414. END-OF-DAY. Onionskin. Transparent clear base. Yellow subsurface layer with pink skin. Slightly shrunken on one side. Very pretty marble. Germany, circa 1870-1915. 9/16". Mint (9.9). Price: $31. CyberAuction #345, Lot #3.

2415. END-OF-DAY. Onionskin. Transparent clear base. Thin green core. Subsurface layer of semi-opaque white with light turquoise skin. Germany, circa 1870-1915. 9/16". Mint (9.9). Price: $31. CyberAuction #345, Lot #19.

2416. END-OF-DAY. Onionskin. Transparent clear base. Mustard yellow subsurface layer with green skin. One pit. Germany, circa 1870-1915. 1/2". Mint(-) (9.0). Price: $31. CyberAuction #384, Lot #49.

2417. END-OF-DAY. Onionskin. Transparent clear base. Opaque white subsurface layer. Skin is pink, green and blue. Germany, circa 1870-1915. 1/2". Mint (9.7). Price: $31. CyberAuction #479, Lot #13.

2418. END-OF-DAY. Onionskin. Transparent clear base. Yellow core with green skin. One melt chip. Germany, circa 1870-1915. 5/8". Near Mint(+) (8.9). Price: $30. CyberAuction #337, Lot #12.

2419. END-OF-DAY. Onionskin. Transparent clear base. Opaque white subsurface layer. Skin is pink and green. Beautiful. Small nub bottom pontil. Germany, circa 1870-1915. 5/8". Mint (9.7). Price: $30. CyberAuction #339, Lot #3.

2420. END-OF-DAY. Onionskin. Transparent clear base. Subsurface layer of yellow, transparent green and a little red. Surface has some pinpricks. Germany, circa 1870-1915. 9/16". Near Mint(+) (8.9). Price: $30. CyberAuction #344, Lot #21.

2421. END-OF-DAY. Onionskin. Transparent clear base. Subsurface mustard yellow with a pink skin. Broken off bottom pontil. Germany, circa 1870-1915. 5/8". Mint (9.9). Price: $30. CyberAuction #388, Lot #21.

2422. END-OF-DAY. Onionskin. Transparent clear base. Opaque yellow core with some white. Pink and green skin. Shrunken on one side. Very nice. Germany, circa 1870-1915. 11/16". Mint (9.8). Price: $30. CyberAuction #418, Lot #4.

2423. END-OF-DAY. Onionskin. First of cane onionskin. Looped type. Transparent clear base. Small core of green on yellow, rising about halfway up the marble and looped over. Has a nub pontil. Small subsurface moon. Germany, circa 1870-1915. 19/32". Near Mint (8.6). Price: $30. CyberAuction #419, Lot #50.

2424. END-OF-DAY. Onionskin. Transparent clear base. Subsurface layer of white with blue and pink. Germany, circa 1870-1915. 1/2". Mint (9.7). Price: $30. CyberAuction #425, Lot #39.

2425. END-OF-DAY. Onionskin. Transparent clear base. Opaque white core with blue skin. A couple of tiny chips, overall pinpricking. Germany, circa 1870-1915. 1-3/16". Near Mint(-) (8.0). Price: $30. CyberAuction #427, Lot #31.

2426. END-OF-DAY. Onionskin. Transparent clear base. White core with light green skin and some pink and blue. Some light pinpricks. Germany, circa 1870-1915. 23/32". Mint(-) (9.0). Price: $30. CyberAuction #435, Lot #50.

2427. END-OF-DAY. Onionskin. Transparent clear base. Opaque white core with pink skin. Small cold roll line. Germany, circa 1870-1915. 1/2". Mint (9.6). Price: $30. CyberAuction #436, Lot #18.

2428. END-OF-DAY. Onionskin. Transparent clear base. Subsurface layer of opaque white. Green and blue bands on it. Germany, circa 1870-1915. 21/32". Mint (9.8). Price: $30. CyberAuction #459, Lot #31.

2429. END-OF-DAY. Onionskin. Transparent clear base. White core. Dark blue and pink skin. A couple of melt spots, all on one side. Germany, circa 1870-1915. 11/16". Mint(-) (9.0). Price: $30. CyberAuction #461, Lot #4.

2430. END-OF-DAY. Onionskin. Transparent clear base. Mustard yellow subsurface layer with pink skin. Germany, circa 1870-1915. 9/16". Mint (9.7). Price: $30. CyberAuction #461, Lot #23.

2431. END-OF-DAY. Onionskin. Transparent clear base. Subsurface white and lime green skin. Two subsurface moons, but the surface itself is wet. Gorgeous anyway. Germany, circa 1870-1915. 13/16". Near Mint(+) (8.8). Price: $30. CyberAuction #467, Lot #38.

2432. END-OF-DAY. Onionskin. First off cane onionskin. Looped type. Transparent clear base. Small core of green on yellow, rising about halfway up the marble and looped over. Has a nub pontil. Small subsurface moon. Germany, circa 1870-1915. 19/32". Near Mint (8.6). Price: $30. CyberAuction #482, Lot #38.

2433. END-OF-DAY. Onionskin. Transparent clear base. Opaque white core with pink skin. Small cold roll line. Germany, circa 1870-1915. 1/2". Mint (9.6). Price: $30. CyberAuction #484, Lot #38.

2434. END-OF-DAY. Onionskin. Transparent clear base. Opaque white core. Light green skin. A little blue. One melt chip. Germany, circa 1870-1915. 21/32". Mint(-) (9.2). Price: $30. CyberAuction #488, Lot #30.

2435. END-OF-DAY. Onionskin. Transparent clear base. Subsurface layer of opaque white. Green and blue bands on it. Germany, circa 1870-1915. 21/32". Mint (9.8). Price: $30. CyberAuction #490, Lot #19.

436. END-OF-DAY. Onionskin. First off cane onionskin. Looped type. Transparent clear base. Small core of green on yellow, rising about halfway up the marble and looped over. Has a nub pontil. Small subsurface moon. Germany, circa 1870-1915. 19/32". Near Mint (8.6). Price: $30. CyberAuction #499, Lot #8.

437. END-OF-DAY. Onionskin. Pink on yellow skin. Germany, circa 1870-1915. Mint (9.7). Price: $29. CyberAuction #392, Lot #6.

438. END-OF-DAY. Onionskin. Transparent green base. Opaque white subsurface layer. Skin is pink, blue and green. Gorgeous. Lightly buffed, pontils are intact. Germany, circa 1870-1915. 3/4". Price: $29. CyberAuction #444, Lot #43.

439. END-OF-DAY. Onionskin. Transparent clear base. Opaque white core with pink skin. Several pits, some light haze. Germany, circa 1870-1915. 1". Near Mint (8.3). Price: $29. CyberAuction #460, Lot #51.

440. END-OF-DAY. Onionskin. Transparent clear base. Subsurface layer with green bands and some red. Cold roll line. Germany, circa 1870-1915. 17/32". Mint (9.5). Price: $29. CyberAuction #462, Lot #6.

441. END-OF-DAY. Onionskin. Transparent clear base. Opaque white subsurface layer. Blue skin. Germany, circa 1870-1915. 17/32". Mint (9.9). Price: $29. CyberAuction #490, Lot #32.

442. END-OF-DAY. Onionskin. Transparent clear base. Subsurface layer of opaque white with pink skin. Several small chips and tiny pits. Germany, circa 1870-1915. 3/4". Near Mint (8.2. CyberAuction #343, Lot #55.

443. END-OF-DAY. Onionskin. Peewee onionskin. Transparent clear base. Opaque white core. Pink skin, with some blue. A couple of very tiny chips. Germany, circa 1870-1915. 15/32". Near Mint (8.6). Price: $28. CyberAuction #390, Lot #33.

444. END-OF-DAY. Onionskin. Transparent clear base. Subsurface white layer with pink skin. One tiny chip. Germany, circa 1870-1915. 5/8". Near Mint(+) (8.9). Price: $28. CyberAuction #414, Lot #8.

445. END-OF-DAY. Onionskin. Transparent clear base. Opaque white subsurface layer, green skin. Tiny annealing fracture, a couple of pits. Germany, circa 1870-1915. 23/32". Near Mint(+) (8.9). Price: $28. CyberAuction #432, Lot #59.

446. END-OF-DAY. Onionskin. Transparent clear base. Semi-opaque white subsurface layer with blue skin. Germany, circa 1870-1915. 9/16". Mint (9.7). Price: $28. CyberAuction #459, Lot #28.

447. END-OF-DAY. Onionskin. Transparent very lightly tinted blue base. Subsurface skin of translucent white and blue. Germany, circa 1870-1915. 9/32". Mint (9.7). Price: $28. CyberAuction #499, Lot #35.

448. END-OF-DAY. Onionskin. Transparent clear base. Subsurface layer of yellow with green skin. One blue band. A few pinpricks. Germany, circa 1870-1915. 9/16". Mint(-) (9.0). Price: $27. CyberAuction #334, Lot #56.

449. END-OF-DAY. Onionskin. Transparent green base. Yellow core with pink skin. Slightly shrunken on one side. One melted nub of glass on it. Germany, circa 1870-1915. 5/8". Mint (9.7). Price: $27. CyberAuction #345, Lot #42.

450. END-OF-DAY. Onionskin. Transparent clear base. Yellow subsurface layer with pink skin. Slightly shrunken on one side. Very pretty marble. Germany, circa 1870-1915. 9/16". Mint (9.9). Price: $27. CyberAuction #374, Lot #7.

451. END-OF-DAY. Onionskin. Transparent clear base. Subsurface layer of white with green skin. Some haze. Germany, circa 1870-1915. 15/32". Near Mint (8.6). Price: $27. CyberAuction #376, Lot #28.

452. END-OF-DAY. Onionskin. Lot of two marbles. One is a blue skin onionskin, 3/4", polished. Other is a four-panel, 23/32", Near Mint(-) (8.0). Price: $27. CyberAuction #387, Lot #3.

453. END-OF-DAY. Onionskin. Transparent clear base. Opaque white subsurface layer with blue skin. A couple of tiny chips. Germany, circa 1870-1915. 11/16". Near Mint (8.6). Price: $27. CyberAuction #419, Lot #2.

454. END-OF-DAY. Onionskin. Transparent clear base. Opaque white subsurface layer. Bands of pink, blue and yellow. One subsurface moon. Germany, circa 1870-1915. 17/32". Near Mint (8.6). Price: $27. CyberAuction #433, Lot #54.

455. END-OF-DAY. Onionskin. Transparent clear base. Subsurface layer with pink skin. One melt spot. Germany, circa 1870-1915. 1/2". Mint(-) (9.1). Price: $27. CyberAuction #438, Lot #47.

456. END-OF-DAY. Onionskin. Transparent clear base. Opaque white subsurface layer with pink skin. One tiny chip. Germany, circa 1870-1915. 1/2". Near Mint(+) (8.9). Price: $27. CyberAuction #443, Lot #5.

457. END-OF-DAY. Onionskin. Transparent clear base. Yellow subsurface layer, light pink skin. Cold dimple at bottom. Germany, circa 1870-1915. 9/16". Mint (9.6). Price: $27. CyberAuction #448, Lot #44.

458. END-OF-DAY. Onionskin. Transparent clear base. Blue and white skin. One tiny melt spot. Germany, circa 1870-1915. 9/16". Mint (9.5). Price: $27. CyberAuction #452, Lot #21.

459. END-OF-DAY. Onionskin. Transparent clear base. Opaque white subsurface layer. Almost completely covered by blue skin. One tiny melt spot. Germany, circa 1870-1915. 19/32". Mint(-) (9.2). Price: $27. CyberAuction #452, Lot #32.

460. END-OF-DAY. Onionskin. Transparent clear base. Opaque white subsurface layer. Blue skin. Germany, circa 1870-1915. 17/32". Mint (9.9). Price: $27. CyberAuction #459, Lot #11.

461. END-OF-DAY. Onionskin. Transparent clear base. Semi-opaque white subsurface layer with blue skin. Germany, circa 1870-1915. 9/16". Mint (9.7). Price: $27. CyberAuction #459, Lot #26.

462. END-OF-DAY. Onionskin. Transparent clear base. Opaque white subsurface layer. Blue skin. Germany, circa 1870-1915. 17/32". Mint (9.7). Price: $27. CyberAuction #461, Lot #32.

2463. END-OF-DAY. Onionskin. Transparent clear base. Yellow subsurface layer, light pink skin. Cold dimple at bottom. Germany, circa 1870-1915. 9/16". Mint (9.6). Price: $27. CyberAuction #466, Lot #27.

2464. END-OF-DAY. Onionskin. Transparent clear base. Blue and white skin. One tiny melt spot. Germany, circa 1870-1915. 9/16". Mint (9.5). Price: $27. CyberAuction #470, Lot #40.

2465. END-OF-DAY. Onionskin. Transparent clear base. Core of white with blue and green skin. Beautiful. One tiny melt chip. Very slightly flattened at ends. Germany, circa 1870-1915. 19/32". Mint (-) (9.0). Price: $27. CyberAuction #485, Lot #53.

2466. END-OF-DAY. Onionskin. Transparent clear base. Opaque white core. Light pink and dark blue skin. Gorgeous. Two melt spots near the bottom pontil. Germany, circa 1870-1915. 21/32". Mint(-) (9.0). Price: $27. CyberAuction #489, Lot #7.

2467. END-OF-DAY. Onionskin. Transparent clear base. Opaque white subsurface layer. Blue skin. Germany, circa 1870-1915. 17/32". Mint (9.7). Price: $27. CyberAuction #490, Lot #12.

2468. END-OF-DAY. Onionskin. Transparent clear base. Semi-opaque white subsurface layer with blue skin. Germany, circa 1870-1915. 9/16". Mint (9.7). Price: $27. CyberAuction #496, Lot #4.

2469. END-OF-DAY. Onionskin. Transparent clear base. Blue and white skin. One tiny melt spot. Germany, circa 1870-1915. 9/16". Mint (9.5). Price: $27. CyberAuction #496, Lot #5.

2470. END-OF-DAY. Onionskin. Very odd smeared colors. Transparent clear base. Opaque white core with lots of clear spaces. Smeared transparent blue and transparent red. Slight left twist. Some wear on the surface. Germany, circa 1870-1915. 19/32". Near Mint(+) (8.9). Price: $26. CyberAuction #331, Lot #11.

2471. END-OF-DAY. Onionskin. Transparent clear base. Opaque white base with some clear spaces. Skin is light blue, light green and light red. A couple of pits on the surface. Germany, circa 1870-1915. 9/16". Near Mint(+) (8.9). Price: $26. CyberAuction #345, Lot #14.

2472. END-OF-DAY. Onionskin. Four panel onionskin. Transparent clear base. Opaque white subsurface layer. Two narrow blue panels, two wide pink panels. Yellow band on one pink panel. Some pits. Germany, circa 1870-1915. 15/32". Near Mint (8.6). Price: $26. CyberAuction #357, Lot #7.

2473. END-OF-DAY. Onionskin. Transparent clear base. White subsurface layer with blue skin. Three small subsurface moons. Germany, circa 1870-1915. 11/16". Near Mint (8.5). Price: $26. CyberAuction #376, Lot #20.

2474. END-OF-DAY. Onionskin. Transparent clear base. Opaque white core with pink skin. Several pits, some light haze. Germany, circa 1870-1915. 1". Near Mint (8.3). Price: $26. CyberAuction #417, Lot #30.

2475. END-OF-DAY. Onionskin. Transparent clear base. Opaque white core. Light green skin. A little blue. One melt chip. Germany, circa 1870-1915. 21/32". Mint(-) (9.2). Price: $26. CyberAuction #431, Lot #38.

2476. END-OF-DAY. Onionskin. Transparent clear base. Opaque white core with pink skin. Small cold roll line. Germany, circa 1870-1915. 1/2". Mint (9.7). Price: $26. CyberAuction #454, Lot #13.

2477. END-OF-DAY. Onionskin. Transparent very lightly tinted blue base. Subsurface skin of translucent white and blue. Germany, circa 1870-1915. 19/32". Mint (9.7). Price: $26. CyberAuction #485, Lot #44.

2478. END-OF-DAY. Onionskin. Transparent clear base. Core is opaque white with lots of clear spaces. Covered by transparent green skin and a little blue. Has a small annealing fracture on the core. Germany, circa 1870-1915. 23/32". Mint(-) (9.0). Price: $25. CyberAuction #331, Lot #35.

2479. END-OF-DAY. Onionskin. Transparent clear base. Opaque yellow core with a skin of pink. Has an orange hue to it. Germany, circa 1870-1915. 17/32". Mint(-) (9.1). Price: $25. CyberAuction #341, Lot #21.

2480. END-OF-DAY. Onionskin. Transparent clear base. Opaque white core. Pink and green skin. Some pinpricks. Germany, circa 1870-1915. 9/16". Near Mint(+) (8.9). Price: $25. CyberAuction #376, Lot #41.

2481. END-OF-DAY. Onionskin. Transparent clear base. White subsurface layer, some scratching. Germany, circa 1870-1915. 3/4". Near Mint (8.6). Price: $25. CyberAuction #407, Lot #22.

2482. END-OF-DAY. Onionskin. Very unusual onionskin, probably from near the beginning of the cane. Transparent clear base. Opaque yellow core. Several bands and partial bands of pink, and one green band. Shrunken on one side. Some pits. Germany, circa 1870-1915. 17/32". Near Mint(+) (8.7). Price: $25. CyberAuction #450, Lot #3.

2483. END-OF-DAY. Onionskin. Transparent clear base. Opaque white subsurface layer, pink skin. One pit, one melt spot. Germany, circa 1870-1915. 21/32". Mint(-) (9.0). Price: $25. CyberAuction #454, Lot #18.

2484. END-OF-DAY. Onionskin. Very unusual. Transparent clear base Subsurface layer of stretched green and white, lots of clear. Large fracture. Germany, possibly English, circa 1870-1915. 25/32". Near Mint(-) (8.0). Price: $25. CyberAuction #461, Lot #41.

2485. END-OF-DAY. Onionskin. Transparent clear base. Opaque yellow core, pink skin. One melt flat spot. Germany, circa 1870-1915. 9/16". Mint(-) (9.0). Price: $25. CyberAuction #468, Lot #40.

2486. END-OF-DAY. Onionskin. Very unusual. Transparent clear base Subsurface layer of stretched green and white, lots of clear. Large fracture. Germany, possibly English, circa 1870-1915. 25/32". Near Mint(-) (8.0). Price: $25. CyberAuction #486, Lot #17.

2487. END-OF-DAY. Onionskin. Transparent clear base. Opaque white subsurface layer. Blue skin with some green. Two tiny pits. Germany, circa 1870-1915. 11/16". Near Mint(+) (8.9). Price: $25. CyberAuction #507, Lot #22.

2488. END-OF-DAY. Onionskin. Transparent clear base. Opaque white subsurface layer. Blue skin with a pink band. One tiny subsurface moon, one air hole. Germany, circa 1870-1915. 1/2". Near Mint(+) (8.9). Price: $25. CyberAuction #508, Lot #6.

2489. END-OF-DAY. Onionskin. Opaque white and transparent blue core. Subsurface moon, some pits. Germany, circa 1870-1915. 15/32". Near Mint (8.5). Price: $24. CyberAuction #359, Lot #47.

2490. END-OF-DAY. Onionskin. Transparent clear base. Opaque white subsurface layer. Pink and blue skin. Not wet, but no damage. Germany, circa 1870-1915. 19/32". Near Mint(+) (8.9). Price: $24. CyberAuction #465, Lot #8.

2491. END-OF-DAY. Onionskin. Very unusual onionskin, probably from near the beginning of the cane. Transparent clear base. Opaque yellow core. Several bands and partial bands of pink, and one green band. Shrunken on one side. Some pits. Germany, circa 1870-1915. 17/32". Near Mint(+) (8.7). Price: $24. CyberAuction #478, Lot #27.

2492. END-OF-DAY. Onionskin. Transparent clear base. Yellow core, pink skin. One small blown air hole. Germany, circa 1870-1915. 21/32". Mint(-) (9.1). Price: $24. CyberAuction #489, Lot #16.

2493. END-OF-DAY. Onionskin. Transparent clear base. Core is white with pink, blue and yellow splotches. Shoved over to one side of the marble. Some overall roughness. Germany, circa 1870-1915. 23/32". Good (7.5). Price: $23. CyberAuction #370, Lot #52.

2494. END-OF-DAY. Onionskin. Transparent clear base. Semi-opaque white core. Stretched spots of light blue. Small chip, several pits. Beauty though. Germany, circa 1870-1915. 13/16". Near Mint (8.6). Price: $23. CyberAuction #406, Lot #26.

2495. END-OF-DAY. Onionskin. Transparent clear base. Semi-opaque white core. Stretched spots of light blue. Small chip, several pits. Beauty though. Germany, circa 1870-1915. 13/16". Near Mint (8.6). Price: $23. CyberAuction #437, Lot #36.

2496. END-OF-DAY. Onionskin. Transparent clear base. Opaque white core, light blue skin. Some pitting. Germany, circa 1870-1915. 9/16". Near Mint(+) (8.8). Price: $23. CyberAuction #448, Lot #25.

2497. END-OF-DAY. Onionskin. Peewee. Blue skin on white. Two very tiny pits. Germany, circa 1870-1915. 15/32". Near Mint(+) (8.9). Price: $22. CyberAuction #386, Lot #35.

2498. END-OF-DAY. Onionskin. Transparent clear base. Opaque white core. Pink skin. One flake. Germany, circa 1870-1915. 9/16". Near Mint(+) (8.7). Price: $22. CyberAuction #397, Lot #36.

2499. END-OF-DAY. Onionskin. Transparent clear base. Yellow subsurface layer. Pink skin with some blue and white. Small subsurface moon and small melt chip. Germany, circa 1870-1915. 21/32". Near Mint (8.6). Price: $22. CyberAuction #401, Lot #20.

2500. END-OF-DAY. Onionskin. Transparent clear base. Opaque white subsurface layer, pink skin. One pit, one melt spot. Germany, circa 1870-1915. 21/32". Mint(-) (9.0). Price: $22. CyberAuction #414, Lot #45.

2501. END-OF-DAY. Onionskin. Transparent clear base. White subsurface layer with pink skin. A little yellow. A couple of pinpricks. Germany, circa 1870-1915. 19/32". Mint (9.5). Price: $22. CyberAuction #418, Lot #8.

2502. END-OF-DAY. Onionskin. Peewee. Blue skin on white. Two very tiny pits. Germany, circa 1870-1915. 15/32". Near Mint(+) (8.9). Price: $22. CyberAuction #430, Lot #50.

2503. END-OF-DAY. Onionskin. Transparent clear base. Subsurface yellow layer with pink skin. A couple of tiny sparkles. Germany, circa 1870-1915. 17/32". Mint(-) (9.1). Price: $22. CyberAuction #471, Lot #24.

2504. END-OF-DAY. Onionskin. Transparent clear base. Opaque white core. Light green skin. A little blue. One melt chip. Germany, circa 1870-1915. 21/32". Mint(-) (9.2). Price: $22. CyberAuction #474, Lot #36.

2505. END-OF-DAY. Onionskin. Transparent clear base. White and blue skin, just below the surface. Several tiny pits. Germany, circa 1870-1915. 15/32". Near Mint(+) (8.8). Price: $22. CyberAuction #487, Lot #6.

2506. END-OF-DAY. Onionskin. Transparent clear base. Subsurface yellow layer with pink skin. A couple of tiny sparkles. Germany, circa 1870-1915. 17/32". Mint(-) (9.1). Price: $22. CyberAuction #494, Lot #40.

2507. END-OF-DAY. Onionskin. Transparent clear base. Opaque yellow core, pink skin. A couple of tiny pieces of mica. One large elongated air holes. Germany, circa 1870-1915. 5/8". Near Mint (8.4). Price: $21. CyberAuction #382, Lot #42.

2508. END-OF-DAY. Onionskin. Transparent clear base. Opaque white subsurface layer. Almost completely covered by blue skin. One tiny melt spot. Germany, circa 1870-1915. 19/32". Mint(-) (9.2). Price: $21. CyberAuction #474, Lot #3.

2509. END-OF-DAY. Onionskin. Transparent clear base. Opaque white subsurface layer. Almost completely covered by blue skin. One tiny melt spot. Germany, circa 1870-1915. 19/32". Mint(-) (9.2). Price: $21. CyberAuction #496, Lot #9.

2510. END-OF-DAY. Onionskin. Transparent clear base. Opaque white subsurface layer. Bands of blue and green on it. One cold roll crease. Several pinpricks. Germany, circa 1870-1915. 21/32". Mint(-) (9.0). Price: $21. CyberAuction #505, Lot #23.

2511. END-OF-DAY. Onionskin. Transparent clear base. Opaque white core. Skin of pink and some green. Three shallow lobes. Small chip, several tiny chips and pits. Germany, circa 1870-1915. 13/16". Near Mint (8.6). Price: $20. CyberAuction #406, Lot #5.

2512. END-OF-DAY. Onionskin. Transparent clear base. Opaque bright white subsurface layer. Two panels of bright orange. One has a little blue. One small scratch. This is a match to Lot #8 in this auction. Germany, possibly English, circa 1870-1915. 21/32". Near Mint(+) (8.9).. Price: $20. CyberAuction #424, Lot #46.

2513. END-OF-DAY. Onionskin. Transparent clear base. Opaque yellow core, pink skin. One blue band. Two tiny chips. Germany, circa 1870-1915. 11/16". Near Mint(+) (8.8). Price: $20. CyberAuction #503, Lot #28.

2514. END-OF-DAY. Onionskin. White core with blue skin. Pretty. On[e] subsurface moon. Germany, circa 1870-1915. 19/32". Near Mint(+) (8.7[)] Price: $19. CyberAuction #340, Lot #46.

2515. END-OF-DAY. Onionskin. Small marble. Transparent clear bas[e] White subsurface layer with pink and green skin. Several sparkles and light haze. Germany, circa 1870-1915. 1/2". Near Mint (8.6). Price: $19 CyberAuction #370, Lot #54.

2516. END-OF-DAY. Onionskin. Transparent clear base. Opaque whi[te] core with dark pink skin. Subsurface moon. Germany, circa 1870-1915 17/32". Near Mint(+) (8.7). Price: $19. CyberAuction #394, Lot #39.

2517. END-OF-DAY. Onionskin. Transparent clear base. Opaque whi[te] core. Skin of pink and some green. Three shallow lobes. Small chip, sever[al] tiny chips and pits. Germany, circa 1870-1915. 13/16". Near Mint (8.6[)] Price: $19. CyberAuction #437, Lot #38.

2518. END-OF-DAY. Onionskin. Yellow subsurface layer with pink skin Heavily polished. Germany, circa 1870-1915. 7/8". Price: $19. CyberAuctio[n] #437, Lot #56.

2519. END-OF-DAY. Onionskin. Transparent clear base. White subsu[r]face layer, blue skin. Some minor haze. Germany, circa 1870-1915. 1[7/]32". Near Mint(+) (8.7). Price: $19. CyberAuction #455, Lot #6.

2520. END-OF-DAY. Onionskin. Transparent clear base. Subsurface laye[r] of mustard yellow, with some pink and green on it. Overall small chip[s] Germany, circa 1870-1915. 27/32". Good (7.5). Price: $17. CyberAuction #370, Lot #28.

2521. END-OF-DAY. Onionskin. Opaque white core with blue skin. [A] couple of very tiny chips. Germany, circa 1870-1915. 9/16". Near Mi[nt] (8.3). Price: $17. CyberAuction #390, Lot #19.

2522. END-OF-DAY. Onionskin. Odd onionskin. Transparent clear bas[e] Subsurface layer of red with some white bands. One open panel in the re[d] Overall tiny chips and moons. Germany, circa 1870-1915. 11/16". Goo[d] (7.5). Price: $17. CyberAuction #399, Lot #39.

2523. END-OF-DAY. Onionskin. Transparent clear base. Opaque whi[te] subsurface layer with turquoise skin. One piece of mica. Heavily polishe[d] Germany, circa 1870-1915. 27/32". Price: $17. CyberAuction #417, L[ot] #43.

2524. END-OF-DAY. Onionskin. Transparent clear base. Subsurface ye[l]low layer. Pink skin. Small fracture on one side. Germany, circa 1870-191[5] 11/16". Near Mint (8.8). Price: $17. CyberAuction #428, Lot #42.

2525. END-OF-DAY. Onionskin. Transparent clear base. Opaque whi[te] core. Pink and green skin. Some pinpricks. Germany, circa 1870-1915. [9/]16". Near Mint (8.9). Price: $17. CyberAuction #444, Lot #39.

2526. END-OF-DAY. Onionskin. Opaque white core with blue skin. [A] couple of very tiny chips. Germany, circa 1870-1915. 9/16". Near Mi[nt] (8.3). Price: $17. CyberAuction #445, Lot #9.

2527. END-OF-DAY. Onionskin. Transparent clear base. Opaque whi[te] subsurface layer with lime green skin. Three fractures. Germany, circa 187[0-]1915. 25/32". Near Mint (8.5). Price: $17. CyberAuction #477, Lot #5.

2528. END-OF-DAY. Onionskin. Opaque white core with blue skin. [A] couple of very tiny chips. Germany, circa 1870-1915. 9/16". Near Mi[nt] (8.3). Price: $17. CyberAuction #478, Lot #2.

2529. END-OF-DAY. Onionskin. Transparent clear base. White core wi[th] green skin. Some blue. Tiny flake. Germany, circa 1870-1915. 5/8". Nea[r] Mint(+) (8.8). Price: $17. CyberAuction #489, Lot #4.

2530. END-OF-DAY. Onionskin. Transparent clear base. Subsurface laye[r] of white, pink and blue. A number of pinpricks. Germany, circa 1870[-] 1915. 11/16". Near Mint(+) (8.8). Price: $17. CyberAuction #502, L[ot] #12.

2531. END-OF-DAY. Onionskin. Transparent clear base. Subsurface laye[r] of white with blue skin. Some small chips. Germany, circa 1870-1915. 2[5/] 32". Good (7.5). Price: $15. CyberAuction #361, Lot #55.

2532. END-OF-DAY. Onionskin. Transparent clear base. Opaque whi[te] core. Blue skin, with some pink. A couple of small chips and some haz[e] Germany, circa 1870-1915. 5/8". Good (7.5). Price: $15. CyberAuctio[n] #382, Lot #40.

2533. END-OF-DAY. Onionskin. Core is bands of yellow, white, blue an[d] pink. Shrunken on one side. Small chip, some tiny chips. Germany, circ[a] 1870-1915. 1-1/16". Good (7.4). Price: $15. CyberAuction #402, Lot #[4]

2534. END-OF-DAY. Onionskin. Transparent clear base. Subsurface whi[te] base with pink skin. Heavily polished. Germany, circa 1870-1915. 25/3[2"] Price: $15. CyberAuction #407, Lot #48.

2535. END-OF-DAY. Onionskin. Transparent clear base. Opaque whi[te] core, pink skin. One very deep lobe. Tight twist. One subsurface moo[n] at the top. Germany, circa 1870-1915. 9/16". Near Mint(+) (8.9). Price $15. CyberAuction #479, Lot #38.

2536. END-OF-DAY. Onionskin. Transparent clear base. Opaque whi[te] core with blue skin. Slight haze with some tiny chips. Germany, circa 187[0-] 1915. 7/8". Good(+) (7.9). Price: $15. CyberAuction #492, Lot #15.

2537. END-OF-DAY. Onionskin. Transparent clear base. Opaque whi[te] core with dark pink skin. Subsurface moon. Germany, circa 1870-191[5] 17/32". Near Mint(+) (8.7). Price: $14. CyberAuction #355, Lot #50.

2538. END-OF-DAY. Onionskin. Transparent clear base. Opaque whi[te] subsurface layer. Blue skin with some pink. One melt spot, one tiny chi[p] Germany, circa 1870-1915. 9/16". Near Mint (8.6). Price: $14. CyberAuctio[n] #452, Lot #27.

2539. END-OF-DAY. Onionskin. Transparent clear base with blue an[d] green skin. Overall haze, tiny chips and pitting. Germany, circa 1870-191[5] 23/32". Good (7.6). Price: $13. CyberAuction #454, Lot #45.

2540. END-OF-DAY. Onionskin. Opaque white core with pink skin. Slig[ht] haze. Germany, circa 1870-1915. 9/16". Near Mint (8.6). Price: $1[3] CyberAuction #350, Lot #51.

2541. END-OF-DAY. Onionskin. Transparent clear base. White subsu[...]

ce layer with blue skin. Two subsurface moons. Germany, circa 1870-915. 15/32". Near Mint (8.5). Price: $13. CyberAuction #388, Lot #10.

542. END-OF-DAY. Onionskin. Opaque white core with pink skin. Slight aze. Germany, circa 1870-1915. 9/16". Near Mint (8.6). Price: $13. yberAuction #451, Lot #53.

543. END-OF-DAY. Onionskin. Transparent clear base. Opaque white ore. Pink and green skin. Overall light scratching. Germany, circa 1870-915. 11/16". Near Mint (8.4). Price: $13. CyberAuction #499, Lot #31.

544. END-OF-DAY. Onionskin. Yellow subsurface layer with pink skin. Heavily polished. Germany, circa 1870-1915. 7/8". Price: $12. CyberAuction #401, Lot #4.

545. END-OF-DAY. Onionskin. Transparent clear base. Opaque white ore. Blue skin. One band of red. Overall haziness. Germany, circa 1870-915. 9/16". Good(+) (7.9). Price: $12. CyberAuction #446, Lot #16.

546. END-OF-DAY. Onionskin. Transparent clear base. Opaque white ore. Pink and green skin. Some pinpricks. Germany, circa 1870-1915. 9/6". Near Mint(+) (8.9). Price: $12. CyberAuction #477, Lot #55.

547. END-OF-DAY. Onionskin. Transparent clear base. Opaque white ore. Pink and green skin. Overall light scratching. Germany, circa 1870-915. 11/16". Near Mint (8.4). Price: $12. CyberAuction #485, Lot #4.

548. END-OF-DAY. Onionskin. Transparent clear base. Opaque white ore. Lime green skin. A couple of pink and blue bands. Annealing fractures above the core. Germany, circa 1870-1915. 21/32". Mint(-) (9.0). rice: $12. CyberAuction #503, Lot #14.

549. END-OF-DAY. Onionskin. Transparent clear base. Opaque white ore. Green skin. Germany, circa 1870-1915. Buffed. 5/8". Price: $11. yberAuction #414, Lot #36.

550. END-OF-DAY. Onionskin. Transparent clear base. White core, blue kin. Overall haze. Germany, circa 1870-1915. 31/32". Good (7.6). Price: 11. CyberAuction #477, Lot #7.

551. END-OF-DAY. Onionskin. Transparent clear base. Opaque yellow ubsurface layer, green skin. Slight haze on one side. Germany, circa 1870-915. 1/2". Near Mint (8.6). Price: $10. CyberAuction #455, Lot #55.

552. END-OF-DAY. Onionskin. Onionskin with mica. Transparent clear ase. Subsurface opaque white. Transparent pink skin. Nice sprinkling of nica. Large blown air hole on one side, some rough spots. Germany, circa 870-1915. 9/16". Good(+) (7.9). Price: $10. CyberAuction #458, Lot #14.

553. END-OF-DAY. Onionskin. Transparent clear base. White core with lue skin. Some clear spaces. Two subsurface moons. Germany, circa 1870-915. 25/32". Near Mint (8.1). Price: $9. CyberAuction #473, Lot #9.

554. END-OF-DAY. Onionskin. Transparent clear base. Opaque white ore. Pink skin. Overall tiny chips and pitting. Germany, circa 1870-1915. 5/32". Good(+) (7.9). Price: $8. CyberAuction #458, Lot #17.

555. END-OF-DAY. Onionskin. Transparent clear base. Opaque bright hite subsurface layer. Two panels of bright orange. One has a little blue. everal fractures. Germany, possibly English, circa 1870-1915. 21/32". Near Mint(-) (8.2). Price: $8. CyberAuction #460, Lot #57.

556. END-OF-DAY. Onionskin. Transparent clear base. Yellow core. Subsurface layer of opaque white and transparent blue skin. Fractures. Germany, circa 1870-1915. 25/32". Near Mint(-) (8.0). Price: $8. CyberAuction #476, Lot #18.

557. END-OF-DAY. Onionskin. Transparent clear base. Opaque bright hite subsurface layer. Two panels of bright orange. One has a little blue. everal fractures. Germany, possibly English, circa 1870-1915. 21/32". Near Mint(-) (8.2). Price: $7. CyberAuction #424, Lot #8.

558. END-OF-DAY. Onionskin. Transparent clear base. White subsurface layer. Blue skin. Polished, some damage remains. 19/32". Price: $5. CyberAuction #458, Lot #2.

559. END-OF-DAY. Panelled cloud. Super marble. Single pontil, left-twist, four-panel cloud with mica. Transparent clear base. Opaque white core going about three-quarters up the marble. Two panels of pink lots and two panels of blue dots. Overall coating of nice, finely ground mica. One large blown out air hole near the bottom. Marble shows some ubbing. Germany, circa 1870-1915. 3/4". Near Mint(+) (8.9). Price: $185. CyberAuction #348, Lot #1.

560. END-OF-DAY. Panelled onionskin. Extremely rare four-panel onionskin with mica in super shape. Transparent clear base. Opaque white ore with splotches of light yellow. Two turquoise panels and two pink nes. Nice layer of finely ground mica. A couple of tiny melt spots, one tiny parkle. Absolutely stunning marble. You almost never find them this clean. Gorgeous, it would be a centerpiece of any onionskin collection. Germany, circa 1870-1915. 1-11/16". Mint(-) (9.1). Price: $1775. CyberAuction #471, ot #60.

561. END-OF-DAY. Panelled onionskin. Stunning marble. Absolutely superb!!!! Four-panel onionskin in mica, in pristine condition. Transparent lear base. Opaque mustard yellow core. Two panels of stretched tiny pink pots and two of stretched tiny green dots. Some blue in the green panels. he red panels are very slightly lobed. All panels are about the width. Light prinkling of finely ground mica. Bottom pontil is nicely ground. Surface is ristine. Extremely rare, gorgeous marble. A superior addition to any collection. Germany, circa 1870-1915. 1-9/16". Mint (9.9). Price: $1200. CyberAuction #360, Lot #60.

562. END-OF-DAY. Panelled onionskin. Extremely rare four-panel onionskin with mica in super shape. Transparent clear base. Opaque white ore with splotches of light yellow. Two turquoise panels and two pink nes. Nice layer of finely ground mica. A couple of tiny melt spots, one tiny parkle. Absolutely stunning marble. You almost never find them this clean. Gorgeous, it would be a centerpiece of any onionskin collection. Germany, circa 1870-1915. 1-11/16". Mint(-) (9.1). Price: $700. CyberAuction #400, Lot #59.

2563. END-OF-DAY. Panelled onionskin. Stunning four-panel onionskin with loads of mica. Transparent clear base. Opaque yellow core. Two narrow green panels, two wide pink panels. Overall super coating of mica. Slightly shrunken on one side. Some tiny pinpricking and a couple of sparkles. Stunning marble. Very hard to find. Germany, circa 1870-1915. 1-1/2". Near Mint(+) (8.7). Price: $650. CyberAuction #491, Lot #60.

2564. END-OF-DAY. Panelled onionskin. Four-panel two-lobe onionskin. An outstanding marble! Transparent clear base. Opaque white core. Two pink on yellow panels. Two blue panels, with a little pink. Each blue panel is lobed. Two extremely tiny chips, and a cold roll line around part of the equator. Views exceptionally well, it is a shame to grade it less than Mint, it certainly looks Mint. Germany, circa 1870-1915. 1-3/8". Near Mint(+) (8.9). Price: $435. CyberAuction #483, Lot #33.

2565. END-OF-DAY. Panelled onionskin. Stunning example. Four-panel onionskin. Transparent clear base. Mustard yellow core with a few white dots mixed in. Two panels of dark green and two of red. Reverse twist at the equator. Surface has two melt spots with pits and a couple of other melt spots. It was resting against straw or other marbles while hot. Gorgeous marble, it's a winner!!! Germany, circa 1870-1915. 1-7/16". Mint(-) (9.1). Price: $400. CyberAuction #385, Lot #60.

2566. END-OF-DAY. Panelled onionskin. Large marble. Transparent clear base. White and yellow inner core. White subsurface layer. Two green panels and two pink panels. Bits of blue and green all over the white. Tiny moon, couple of tiny subsurface moons, a few sparkles. Germany, circa 1870-1915. 2-5/16". Near Mint (8.6). Price: $360. CyberAuction #508, Lot #38.

2567. END-OF-DAY. Panelled onionskin. Rare and gorgeous marble. Transparent clear base. Four-panel. Subsurface layer of stretched white. Two panels are mustard yellow, two are lime green and mustard yellow. Lots of clear spaces. England, possibly Germany, circa 1870-1915. 13/16". Mint (9.8). Price: $335. CyberAuction #462, Lot #32.

2568. END-OF-DAY. Panelled onionskin. Stunning example. Four-panel onionskin. Transparent clear base. Subsurface layer of white with some green. Two panels of blue, two of pink. Tight twist. Very clear and clean looking marble. One tiny melt chip. Superb. Germany, circa 1870-1915. 1-7/16". Mint(-) (9.2). Price: $335. CyberAuction #495, Lot #58.

2569. END-OF-DAY. Panelled onionskin. Gorgeous and rare onionskin. Four panel. Transparent clear base. Two panels are orange, yellow, green and white. Two panels are olive green and white. In great shape. Rare!! Germany, possibly England, circa 1870-1915. 23/32". Mint (9.9). Price: $310. CyberAuction #467, Lot #17.

2570. END-OF-DAY. Panelled onionskin. Four-panel onionskin. Very unusual marble. Transparent clear base. White core with some yellow mixed in. Two pink panels, two blue panels. One of the blue panels has a large air bubble on it. Inside the air bubble is a free-floating piece of the blue glass. If you rotate the marble, the piece of glass moves freely in it. Very unusual. Gorgeous marble anyhow. One tiny sparkle, one tiny melt spot. Germany, circa 1870-1915. 7/8". Mint(-) (9.2). Price: $310. CyberAuction #508, Lot #73.

2571. END-OF-DAY. Panelled onionskin. Stunning eight-panel onionskin. Transparent clear base. Opaque white core. Four panels of stretched color. One is brown/red. One brown/red, green and blue. Two brown/red and green. There are four white panels. In super shape. Stunning. England, possibly Germany, circa 1870-1915. 13/16". Mint (9.8). Price: $300. CyberAuction #507, Lot #58.

2572. END-OF-DAY. Panelled onionskin. Exceptional four-panel onionskin in superb shape. Transparent clear base. Core is two panels of dark blue on white and two panels of green on yellow. One tiny pinprick on the surface (probably manufacture). Gorgeous and exceptional example!!!! Germany, circa 1870-1915. 1-5/16". Mint (9.7). Price: $290. CyberAuction #487, Lot #59.

2573. END-OF-DAY. Panelled onionskin. Stunning eight-panel onionskin. Transparent clear base. Opaque white core. Four panels of stretched color. One is brown/red. One brown/red, green and blue. Two brown/red and green. There are four white panels. In super shape. Stunning. England, possibly Germany, circa 1870-1915. 13/16". Mint (9.8). Price: $285. CyberAuction #498, Lot #67.

2574. END-OF-DAY. Panelled onionskin. Transparent clear base. Opaque white core. Four panels. Two are narrow and stretched red. One of those has a lobe. The other two wide panels are tiny dots of stretched blue with some red and yellow. Some tiny pits and sparkles. Germany, circa 1870-1915. 1-9/16". Near Mint (8.6). Price: $270. CyberAuction #498, Lot #72.

2575. END-OF-DAY. Panelled onionskin. Another unbelievable onionskin. Four-panel, with a slight left-hand twist. Opaque white core. Each panel is the same width. Two are completely translucent pink, with a layer of very tiny air bubbles on them. Outstanding. Other two are slightly stretched blue dots. Slight left hand twist. Exceptional example!!! One very tiny moon. Germany, circa 1870-1915. 13/16". Near Mint(+) (8.9). Price: $260. CyberAuction #360, Lot #52.

2576. END-OF-DAY. Panelled onionskin. Stunning marble. Very rare. Transparent clear base. Yellow core. Outer layer is two panels of yellow with a little white and two panels of red. Two sparkle and tiny subsurface moon. Superb marble. England, possibly Germany, circa 1870-1915. 25/32". Mint(-) (9.0). Price: $260. CyberAuction #467, Lot #34.

2577. END-OF-DAY. Panelled onionskin. Four panel onionskin. Two panels are blue splotches on white, two are pink on yellow. Almost no twist. Germany, circa 1870-1915. Huge. Buffed, some damage remains. 2-1/4". Price: $235. CyberAuction #345, Lot #57.

2578. END-OF-DAY. Panelled onionskin. Stunning marble. Transparent clear base. Opaque white core. Two pink bands, two green bands. A little bit of yellow. Superb coloring. Has a tiny subsurface moon and a couple of

tiny sparkles. Germany, circa 1870-1915. 1-5/16". Near Mint(+) (8.9). Price: $230. CyberAuction #352, Lot #59.
2579. END-OF-DAY. Panelled onionskin. Four-panel onionskin. Transparent clear base. Core is two panels of white and two panels of white, "oxblood" red and yellow. Slightly shrunken on one side. Stunning and rare marble. Germany, possibly England, circa 1870-1915. 13/16". Mint (9.9). Price: $220. CyberAuction #483, Lot #54.
2580. END-OF-DAY. Panelled onionskin. Gorgeous and rare-colored onionskin. Transparent clear base. White core with clear spaces. Two panels of blue on pastel pink. Some pastel pink in the two other panels. Left-twist marble. Very rare and beautiful. Germany, circa 1870-1915. 21/32". Mint (9.7). Price: $210. CyberAuction #495, Lot #36.
2581. END-OF-DAY. Panelled onionskin. Very rare huge Four-panel onionskin with mica. Transparent clear base. Opaque white core. Two blue panels and two pink panels. Super overall sprinkling of mica. Absolutely no damage on the marble. However, there is a very large circular (1-3/8") annealing fracture on one side. I can find no impact point, so it was not caused by a hit. Rather it occurred during cooling. Marble is a superb viewer from three sides. Absolutely stunning and very rare. Germany, circa 1870-1915. 2-1/8". Near Mint (8.5). Price: $200. CyberAuction #447, Lot #29.
2582. END-OF-DAY. Panelled onionskin. Stunning and very rare marble. Transparent clear base. Subsurface onionskin layer. Two wide panels of stretched olive green with some clear spaces and some orange. Two narrow panels of smeared orange. Very rare. England, possibly Germany, circa 1870-1915. 25/32". Mint (9.9). Price: $200. CyberAuction #459, Lot #53.
2583. END-OF-DAY. Panelled onionskin. Phenomenal marble. Four-panel left-twist onionskin with a little mica. Transparent clear base. Opaque mustard core. Two panels of green and two of pink. The panels are the pale, smeared type, that I sometimes refer to as "watercoloured". Has a couple of tiny pieces of mica. Exceptional. Two tiny pits. Germany, circa 1870-1915. 27/32". Mint(-) (9.0). Price: $200. CyberAuction #504, Lot #47.
2584. END-OF-DAY. Panelled onionskin. Transparent clear base. Two panels of stretched bright green and yellow. Two panels of stretched bright red. Some clear spaces. Probably English, possibly German. Stunning and rare. 25/32". Mint (9.8). Price: $195. CyberAuction #459, Lot #59.
2585. END-OF-DAY. Panelled onionskin. Four-panel onionskin with mica. Transparent clear base. Core is two panels of blue on white and two of pink on yellow. Some mixing at the edges of each panel. Nice sprinkling of mica, especially on one side. Two tiny subsurface moons, a few pits and very tiny chips, some minor haze. Still, very nice. Germany, circa 1870-1915. 1-11/16". Near Mint(-) (8.0). Price: $190. CyberAuction #418, Lot #26.
2586. END-OF-DAY. Panelled onionskin. Another of the odd four-panel English onionskins. Transparent clear base. Subsurface layer of color. Stretched bands and strands, clear spaces. One panel is orange, white, yellow and green. One panel is orange and yellow. Two panels are very finely stretched blue and white. Super marble. England, possibly Germany, circa 1870-1915. 25/32". Mint (9.9). Price: $185. CyberAuction #481, Lot #60.
2587. END-OF-DAY. Panelled onionskin. Four-panel onionskin. Transparent clear base. Opaque white subsurface layer. Two panels of blue, two of pink. One side has several small moons and subsurface moons. Other side is clean. Germany, circa 1870-1915. 1-13/16". Near Mint (8.5). Price: $185. CyberAuction #507, Lot #30.
2588. END-OF-DAY. Panelled onionskin. Four panel onionskin. Core of lime green and blue. Outer layer is two panels of lime green and two panels of ruddy red and bright orange. Clear spaces in the panels. Cold roll line. England, possibly Germany, circa 1870-1915. 25/32". Mint (9.7). Price: $180. CyberAuction #506, Lot #15.
2589. END-OF-DAY. Panelled onionskin. Four-panel onionskin. Transparent clear base. Two panels of blue on white, two of pink on white and yellow. Overall scratching and pitting, but no major damage. Big. Germany, circa 1870-1915. 2-1/8". Good(+) (7.9). Price: $175. CyberAuction #430, Lot #31.
2590. END-OF-DAY. Panelled onionskin. Very rare huge Four-panel onionskin with mica. Transparent clear base. Opaque white core. Two blue panels and two pink panels. Super overall sprinkling of mica. Absolutely no damage on the marble. However, there is a very large circular (1-3/8") annealing fracture on one side. I can find no impact point, so it was not caused by a hit. Rather it occurred during cooling. Marble is a superb viewer from three sides. Absolutely stunning and very rare. Germany, circa 1870-1915. 2-1/8". Near Mint (8.5). Price: $170. CyberAuction #397, Lot #32.
2591. END-OF-DAY. Panelled onionskin. Four-panel. Transparent clear base. Opaque white core. Two wide bands of pink, two narrow bands of blue. Buffed, but still a beauty. Pontils are intact. Germany, circa 1870-1915. 1-9/16". Price: $160. CyberAuction #421, Lot #48.
2592. END-OF-DAY. Panelled onionskin. Four-panel. Transparent clear base. Opaque white core. Two wide bands of pink, two narrow bands of blue. Buffed, but still a beauty. Pontils are intact. Germany, circa 1870-1915. 1-9/16". Price: $160. CyberAuction #470, Lot #21.
2593. END-OF-DAY. Panelled onionskin. Four-panel onionskin. Transparent clear base. Opaque white core. Two panels of sparse blue. Two panels of mustard yellow with sparse pink. All panels are about the same width. Overall tiny chips and rough spots. Has received a very light buff. Pontils are intact. Very well-made. Germany, circa 1870-1915. 1-7/16". Price: $155. CyberAuction #378, Lot #60.
2594. END-OF-DAY. Panelled onionskin. Four-panel onionskin. Transparent clear base. Two panels of blue on white, two of pink on white and yellow. Overall scratching and pitting, but no major damage. Big. Germany, circa 1870-1915. 2-1/8". Good(+) (7.9). Price: $151. CyberAuction #397, Lot #51.
2595. END-OF-DAY. Panelled onionskin. Four-panel onionskin. Transparent clear base. Two panels of pink on yellow, two of blue on white. Buffed, damage remains. Bottom pontil pretty much intact. Germany, circa 1870-1915. 1-7/8". Price: $150. CyberAuction #428, Lot #33.
2596. END-OF-DAY. Panelled onionskin. Four panel onionskin. Core of lime green and blue. Outer layer is two panels of lime green and two panels of ruddy red and bright orange. Clear spaces in the panels. Cold roll line. England, possibly Germany, circa 1870-1915. 25/32". Mint (9.7). Price: $150. CyberAuction #471, Lot #54.
2597. END-OF-DAY. Panelled onionskin. Four panel onionskin. Core of lime green and blue. Outer layer is two panels of lime green and two panels of ruddy red and bright orange. Clear spaces in the panels. Cold roll line. England, possibly Germany, circa 1870-1915. 25/32". Mint (9.7). Price: $150. CyberAuction #488, Lot #45.
2598. END-OF-DAY. Panelled onionskin. Exceptional and rare marble. Transparent clear base. Shrunken core. Core is opaque white. Two panels of pink, two of green. No white showing. Very distinct left-hand twist!! Core is covered by tiny air bubbles (intentional). One tiny sparkle. Excellent marble. Germany, circa 1870-1915. 27/32". Mint(-) (9.2). Price: $150. CyberAuction #503, Lot #18.
2599. END-OF-DAY. Panelled onionskin. Four-panel onionskin. Left-twist. Transparent clear base. Opaque white core. Two wide pink panels and two narrow turquoise panels. A couple of tiny sparkles. Germany, circa 1870-1915. 7/8". Mint(-) (9.2). Price: $150. CyberAuction #505, Lot #67.
2600. END-OF-DAY. Panelled onionskin. Transparent clear base. Two panels of stretched bright green and yellow. Two panels of stretched bright red. Some clear spaces. Probably English, possibly German. Stunning and rare. 25/32". Mint (9.8). Price: $150. CyberAuction #507, Lot #56.
2601. END-OF-DAY. Panelled onionskin. Stunning four-panel onionskin with mica. Transparent clear base. Core is two panels of green on yellow, two of red on white. Overall excellent sprinkling of mica. Some pits and tiny chips, but views very well. Really nice looking marble. Germany, circa 1870-1915. 13/16". Near Mint(+) (8.7). Price: $145. CyberAuction #448, Lot #60.
2602. END-OF-DAY. Panelled onionskin. Superior and rare marble. Four-panel left-twist onionskin. Transparent clear base. Opaque white core. Two pink panels, one light blue panel, one light turquoise panel. A couple of flakes of mica. Slightly shrunken on one side. Stunning!!! Germany, circa 1870=1915. 11/16". Mint (9.7). Price: $140. CyberAuction #491, Lot #55.
2603. END-OF-DAY. Panelled onionskin. Stunning marble. Transparent clear base. Opaque white core. Two pink bands, two green bands. A little bit of yellow. Superb coloring. Has a tiny subsurface moon and a couple of tiny sparkles. Germany, circa 1870-1915. 1-5/16". Near Mint(+) (8.9). Price: $135. CyberAuction #444, Lot #58.
2604. END-OF-DAY. Panelled onionskin. Four-lobe, four-panel onionskin. Transparent clear base. Opaque white core. Two panels are blue, two are pink. Four very deep lobes, one in the center of each panel. Very well made. Polished surface, remnants of chips remain. Germany, circa 1870-1915. 1-9/16". Price: $135. CyberAuction #497, Lot #60.
2605. END-OF-DAY. Panelled onionskin. With mica. Transparent clear base. White core. Two panels of blue, two of green (with a little yellow). Excellent sprinkling of mica on the core. Some melt spots on the surface and a couple of very tiny rub spots. Outstanding! Germany, circa 1870-1915. 13/16". Near Mint(+) (8.9). Price: $130. CyberAuction #342, Lot #56.
2606. END-OF-DAY. Panelled onionskin. Stunning marble. Transparent clear base. Opaque white core. Two pink panels and two panels of stretched blue dots. Gorgeous. Germany, circa 1870-1915. 11/16". Mint (9.8). Price: $130. CyberAuction #385, Lot #56.
2607. END-OF-DAY. Panelled onionskin. Four panel onionskin. Two panels are orange/red, two are light olive green. Great coloring. Super marble. England, possibly Germany, circa 1870-1915. 25/32". Mint (9.9). Price: $130. CyberAuction #499, Lot #43.
2608. END-OF-DAY. Panelled onionskin. Rare three-panel onionskin, in pastel colors. Transparent clear base. Opaque white core. One panel each of yellow, blue and green. Superior example. Very rare. One melt spot. Germany, circa 1870-1915. 19/32". Mint (9.6). Price: $130. CyberAuction #501, Lot #73.
2609. END-OF-DAY. Panelled onionskin. Rare two-panel onionskin. Transparent clear base. Opaque white subsurface layer. One side is pink skin, other side is blue skin. Super example. Germany, circa 1870-1915. 9/16". Mint (9.9). Price: $120. CyberAuction #373, Lot #53.
2610. END-OF-DAY. Panelled onionskin. Outstanding four-panel left-twist onionskin. Transparent clear base. Core is white with loads of clear spaces. Two panels of turquoise, two panels of pink. Core is shrunken on one pink side. Nice left-twist. One tiny sparkle. Stunning marble. 21/32". Mint(-) (9.2). Price: $120. CyberAuction #383, Lot #2.
2611. END-OF-DAY. Panelled onionskin. Four panel. Gorgeous. Transparent clear base. Large trapped air bubble as the core. Outer layer is subsurface layer. Two panels are light bright green, two are light bright orange. Tiny clear spaces. One melt spot. Stunning. 25/32". England or Germany, circa 1870-1915. 25/32". Mint(-) (9.2). Price: $120. CyberAuction #496, Lot #45.
2612. END-OF-DAY. Panelled onionskin. Four-panel, left-twist onionskin. Superb marble. Transparent clear base. Core is two panels of blue on white and two panels of turquoise on yellow. Small flake, tiny subsurface moon, some tiny pitting at the bottom. Still, views very well and it's a great marble. Germany, circa 1870-1915. 1-1/8". Near Mint (8.4). Price: $111. CyberAuction #422, Lot #49.
2613. END-OF-DAY. Panelled onionskin. Rare end-of-cane (first-off-cane) four-panel onionskin. Two blue and white panels and two pink and white

panels. Lots of clear space at the top with very nice swirling. One small chip (might be manufacturing), rest of surface is original. Rare. Germany, circa 1870-1915. 25/32". Near Mint (8.6). Price: $110. CyberAuction #394, Lot #31.

2614. END-OF-DAY. Panelled onionskin. Transparent clear base. Opaque white subsurface layer. Two wide panels of red, two panels of blue. Some yellow. One small melt spot, one sparkle. Stunning!!! Germany, circa 1870-1915. 31/32". Mint(-) (9.0). Price: $110. CyberAuction #396, Lot #56.

2615. END-OF-DAY. Panelled onionskin. Very hard to find three-panel onionskin. Transparent clear base. Opaque white subsurface layer. One panel each of red, blue and green. A few pieces of mica in it. Some pits. Germany, circa 1870-1915. 11/16". Near Mint(+) (8.8). Price: $110. CyberAuction #398, Lot #27.

2616. END-OF-DAY. Panelled onionskin. Four-panel onionskin. Transparent clear base. Opaque white subsurface layer. Two panels of blue, two of pink. One side has several small moons and subsurface moons. Other side is clean. Germany, circa 1870-1915. 1-13/16". Near Mint (8.5). Price: $110. CyberAuction #415, Lot #60.

2617. END-OF-DAY. Panelled onionskin. Rare end-of-cane (first-off-cane) four-panel onionskin. Two blue and white panels and two pink and white panels. Lots of clear space at the top with very nice swirling. One small chip (might be manufacturing), rest of surface is original. Rare. Germany, circa 1870-1915. 25/32". Near Mint (8.6). Price: $110. CyberAuction #422, Lot #59.

2618. END-OF-DAY. Panelled onionskin. Four-panel onionskin. Transparent clear base. Opaque white subsurface layer. Two wide panels of red, two panels of blue. Some yellow. One small melt spot, one sparkle. Stunning!!! Germany, circa 1870-1915. 31/32". Mint(-) (9.0). Price: $110. CyberAuction #442, Lot #59.

2619. END-OF-DAY. Panelled onionskin. Four-panel onionskin. Transparent clear base. Opaque white subsurface layer. Two panels of blue, two of pink. One side has several small moons and subsurface moons. Other side is clean. Germany, circa 1870-1915. 1-13/16". Near Mint (8.5). Price: $110. CyberAuction #460, Lot #44.

2620. END-OF-DAY. Panelled onionskin. Four-panel. Transparent clear base. Yellow core. Two panels of green and two of pink. Some pitting, small chips and haze on the surface. Odd colors. Germany, circa 1870-1915. 1-3/4". Good(+) (7.7). Price: $110. CyberAuction #466, Lot #25.

2621. END-OF-DAY. Panelled onionskin. Super English coloring. Four panel onionskin. Transparent clear base. Subsurface layer of color. Two panels are stretched bright green, two panels are stretched duller green. Clear spaces, no white or yellow sublayer. Super coloring. England, possibly Germany, circa 1870-1915. One tiny melt pit. 25/32". Mint (9.6). Price: $110. CyberAuction #481, Lot #74.

2622. END-OF-DAY. Panelled onionskin. Rare end-of-cane (first-off-cane) four-panel onionskin. Two blue and white panels and two pink and white panels. Lots of clear space at the top with very nice swirling. One small chip (might be manufacturing), rest of surface is original. Rare. Germany, circa 1870-1915. 25/32". Near Mint (8.6). Price: $110. CyberAuction #484, Lot #43.

2623. END-OF-DAY. Panelled onionskin. Four-panel onionskin. Very similar to Lot #59 in this auction, possibly off the same cane. Left-twist. Transparent clear base. Opaque white core. Two pink panels and two turquoise panels. All panels about the same width. Nice left twist. One sparkle. Germany, circa 1870-1915. 27/32". Mint(-) (9.0). Price: $110. CyberAuction #504, Lot #63.

2624. END-OF-DAY. Panelled onionskin. Left-twist four-panel onionskin. Transparent clear base. Opaque white core. Two blue panels and two pink panels. Surface has been buffed. Pontils are missing, there are the remnants of chips. Germany, circa 1870-1915. 1-3/8". Price: $110. CyberAuction #508, Lot #35.

2625. END-OF-DAY. Panelled onionskin. Transparent clear base. Opaque white core. Two panels of pink and two of blue. Slightly shrunken on one side. One tiny melt spot. Germany, circa 1870-1915. 7/8". Mint (9.4). Price: $100. CyberAuction #351, Lot #26.

2626. END-OF-DAY. Panelled onionskin. Four panel onionskin. Transparent clear base. Opaque white core. Two blue panels and two pink panels. Surface has a couple of small subsurface moons, a few tiny chips, overall pitting and overall light haze. Germany, circa 1870-1915. 1-15/16". Good (7.5). Price: $100. CyberAuction #362, Lot #31.

2627. END-OF-DAY. Panelled onionskin. Base is very lightly tinted blue. Four-panel onionskin. Opaque white core. Two wide blue panels, two narrow pink panels. A few tiny chips, some tiny subsurface moons and some haziness. Germany, circa 1870-1915. 1-13/16". Good(+) (7.9). Price: $100. CyberAuction #374, Lot #32.

2628. END-OF-DAY. Panelled onionskin. Stunning four-panel onionskin. Transparent clear base. Opaque white core. Two panels of red, one of blue, one of green. Superior example. Germany, circa 1870-1915. 11/16". Mint (9.8). Price: $100. CyberAuction #388, Lot #56.

2629. END-OF-DAY. Panelled onionskin. Four-panel onionskin. Transparent clear base. Subsurface layer is two panels of yellow and two of white. Overall slab of pink. Green on the two white panels. Minor scratching and pits. Germany, circa 1870-1915. 1-1/8". Near Mint(+) (8.7). Price: $100. CyberAuction #403, Lot #41.

2630. END-OF-DAY. Panelled onionskin. Four-panel. Transparent clear base. Yellow core. Two panels of green and two of pink. Some pitting, small chips and haze on the surface. Odd colors. Germany, circa 1870-1915. 1-3/4". Good(+) (7.7). Price: $100. CyberAuction #428, Lot #31.

2631. END-OF-DAY. Panelled onionskin. Six-panel onionskin. Transparent clear base. Core is two white panels, two blue panels and two yellow

panels. Covered by blue skin. Very unusual. Germany, circa 1870-1915. 21/32". Mint (9.7). Price: $100. CyberAuction #430, Lot #5.

2632. END-OF-DAY. Panelled onionskin. Gorgeous marble. Rare. Four-panel onionskin. Transparent clear base. Core is opaque yellow with one white panel. Shrunken on the white side. Two narrow panels of pink, one on the white. Two wide panels of blue dots. Tiny chip on one side, a couple of pinpricks. Germany, circa 1870-1915. 27/32". Near Mint(+) (8.7). Price: $100. CyberAuction #450, Lot #50.

2633. END-OF-DAY. Panelled onionskin. Four panel. Gorgeous. Transparent clear base. Large trapped air bubble as the core. Outer layer is subsurface layer. Two panels are light bright green, two are light bright orange. Tiny clear spaces. One melt spot. Stunning. 25/32". England or Germany, circa 1870-1915. 25/32". Mint(-) (9.2). Price: $100. CyberAuction #475, Lot #56.

2634. END-OF-DAY. Panelled onionskin. Four-panel onionskin. Transparent clear base. Opaque white subsurface layer. Two panels of pink, two of blue. Stunning. Germany, circa 1870-1915. 27/32". Mint (9.7). Price: $100. CyberAuction #501, Lot #63.

2635. END-OF-DAY. Panelled onionskin. Four panel onionskin. Transparent clear base. White core. Two narrow pink panels, two wide turquoise panels. Almost no twist. Stunning. Germany, circa 1870-1915. 25/32". Mint (9.9). Price: $95. CyberAuction #356, Lot #52.

2636. END-OF-DAY. Panelled onionskin. Very hard to find three-panel onionskin. Transparent clear base. Opaque white subsurface layer. One panel each of red, blue and green. A few pieces of mica in it. Some pits. Germany, circa 1870-1915. 11/16". Near Mint(+) (8.8). Price: $90. CyberAuction #351, Lot #13.

2637. END-OF-DAY. Panelled onionskin. Transparent clear base. Opaque white core. Two panels of pink and two of blue. Slightly shrunken on one side. One tiny melt spot. Germany, circa 1870-1915. 7/8". Mint (9.4). Price: $90. CyberAuction #357, Lot #26.

2638. END-OF-DAY. Panelled onionskin. English colors. Transparent clear base. Opaque white core. Two panels of blue, two of pink/orange. Superb. England, possibly Germany, circa 1870-1915. 23/32". Mint (9.7). Price: $90. CyberAuction #418, Lot #55.

2639. END-OF-DAY. Panelled onionskin. Rare four-panel with mica. Opaque white core. Narrow blue panel, narrow turquoise panel, two wide pink panels. Excellent overall coating of mica. The marble has been remelted. 1-11/16". Price: $90. CyberAuction #434, Lot #14.

2640. END-OF-DAY. Panelled onionskin. Rare three-panel onionskin with mica. Almost no twist to the marble. Fat opaque white core. One panel of pink, one panel of blue dots, one panel of pink and blue dots on light yellow. Each panel is about the same width. Some mica on the core. Very lightly buffed, some very tiny damage remains. Pontils pretty much intact. A beauty and rare. Germany, circa 1927-1935. 27/32". Price: $90. CyberAuction #447, Lot #57.

2641. END-OF-DAY. Panelled onionskin. Base is very lightly tinted blue. Four-panel onionskin. Opaque white core. Two wide blue panels, two narrow pink panels. A few tiny chips, some tiny subsurface moons and some haziness. Germany, circa 1870-1915. 1-13/16". Good(+) (7.9). Price: $85. CyberAuction #353, Lot #34.

2642. END-OF-DAY. Panelled onionskin. Very hard to find three-panel onionskin. Transparent clear base. Opaque white subsurface layer. One panel each of red, blue and green. A few pieces of mica in it. Some pits. Germany, circa 1870-1915. 11/16". Near Mint(+) (8.8). Price: $85. CyberAuction #374, Lot #2.

2643. END-OF-DAY. Panelled onionskin. Four-panel onionskin. Transparent clear base. Opaque white core. Two blue cloud panels and two pink panels. Nice. Lightly polished. Pontils pretty much gone. Damage remains. Germany, circa 1870-1915. 1-5/8". Price: $85. CyberAuction #375, Lot #24.

2644. END-OF-DAY. Panelled onionskin. Transparent clear base. Two panels of pink. Two panels of turquoise on light yellow. Superb. Germany, circa 1870-1915. 21/32". Mint (9.9). Price: $85. CyberAuction #381, Lot #59.

2645. END-OF-DAY. Panelled onionskin. Hard to find six-panel onionskin. Peewee marble. Transparent clear base. The core is six panels. Two pink on white, two green on yellow, two blue on yellow. Beauty. Germany, circa 1870-1915. 1/2". Mint (9.7). Price: $85. CyberAuction #443, Lot #20.

2646. END-OF-DAY. Panelled onionskin. Outstanding design. Transparent clear base. Opaque white core. Two yellow panels. Two panels of green splotches and two of pink splotches. Splotched layer is smeared to the left. Very interesting. Polished surface, one filled hole. Germany, circa 1870-1915. 1-11/16". Price: $85. CyberAuction #480, Lot #47.

2647. END-OF-DAY. Panelled onionskin. Rare three-panel onionskin. Transparent clear base. Opaque white core. One panel is pink, one blue, one green. One elongated air hole. Superb!!! Germany, circa 1870-1915. 21/32". Mint(-) (9.1). Price: $81. CyberAuction #333, Lot #47.

2648. END-OF-DAY. Panelled onionskin. Transparent clear base. Opaque white core. Two wide pink panels, two narrow blue panels. 11/16". Mint (9.7). Price: $80. CyberAuction #377, Lot #28.

2649. END-OF-DAY. Panelled onionskin. Four panel onionskin. Transparent clear base. Two panels of pink on white. Two panels of green and pink on white. Little blending between panels. Almost no twist. Surface has an overall haziness. Germany, circa 1870-1915. 1-15/16". Good(+) (7.8). Price: $80. CyberAuction #382, Lot #34.

2650. END-OF-DAY. Panelled onionskin. Four panel onionskin. Transparent clear base. Two panels of blue on white, two panels of blue and pink, on yellow. A number of tiny chips and moons on the surface, one small area may have been lightly polished. Germany, circa 1870-1915. 1-11/16". Good (7.4). Price: $80. CyberAuction #387, Lot #26.

2651. END-OF-DAY. Panelled onionskin. Four-panel onionskin. Transparent clear base. Core is two panels of pink on white and two panels of pink and green on yellow. Shrunken core on one side. Polished, some damage remains. No pontils. A little mica. Germany, circa 1870-1915. 1-11/16". Price: $80. CyberAuction #441, Lot #32.

2652. END-OF-DAY. Panelled onionskin. Four panel onionskin. Transparent clear base. Two panels of pink on white. Two panels of green and pink on white. Little blending between panels. Almost no twist. Surface has an overall haziness. Germany, circa 1870-1915. 1-15/16". Good(+) (7.8). Price: $80. CyberAuction #446, Lot #32.

2653. END-OF-DAY. Panelled onionskin. Four panel onionskin. Two panels are orange/red, two are light olive green. Great coloring. Super marble. England, possibly Germany, circa 1870-1915. 25/32". Mint (9.9). Price: $80. CyberAuction #479, Lot #51.

2654. END-OF-DAY. Panelled onionskin. Transparent light blue base. Opaque white subsurface layer. Two blue panels, two pink panels. Gorgeous. A couple of tiny sparkles. Germany, circa 1870-1915. 3/4". Mint(-) (9.0). Price: $75. CyberAuction #347, Lot #49.

2655. END-OF-DAY. Panelled onionskin. End of cane (last off cane). Four panel onionskin. Transparent clear base. Yellow subsurface layer. Two green panels and two pink panels. The very bottom has a small bit of the nub from another marble melted into it. In great shape. Germany, circa 1870-1915. 21/32". Mint (9.8). Price: $75. CyberAuction #354, Lot #5.

2656. END-OF-DAY. Panelled onionskin. Hard to find six-panel onionskin. Peewee marble. Transparent clear base. The core is six panels. Two pink on white, two green on yellow, two blue on yellow. Beauty. Germany, circa 1870-1915. 1/2". Mint (9.7). Price: $75. CyberAuction #356, Lot #50.

2657. END-OF-DAY. Panelled onionskin. Very odd. Transparent clear base. Subsurface layer of white. Overall skin of pink. One side of the marble has a lot of green and some blue on it. Some small and tiny chips. Germany, circa 1870-1915. 1-1/2". Good(+) (7.9). Price: $75. CyberAuction #358, Lot #36.

2658. END-OF-DAY. Panelled onionskin. Six-panel onionskin. Transparent clear base. Core is two white panels, two blue panels and two yellow panels. Covered by blue skin. Very unusual. Germany, circa 1870-1915. 21/32". Mint (9.7). Price: $75. CyberAuction #369, Lot #4.

2659. END-OF-DAY. Panelled onionskin. Four-panel onionskin. Transparent clear base. White core. Two panels of pink, two of turquoise. The colors are smeared. From near an end of the cane. Some subsurface moons, overall haze. Germany, circa 1870-1915. 1-1/2". Good(+) (7.9). Price: $75. CyberAuction #375, Lot #22.

2660. END-OF-DAY. Panelled onionskin. Stunning marble. Transparent clear base. Opaque yellow core. White subsurface layer. Two panels of blue and two of pink on it. Ground bottom pontil. Gorgeous. Germany, circa 1870-1915. 19/32". Mint (9.8). Price: $75. CyberAuction #396, Lot #21.

2661. END-OF-DAY. Panelled onionskin. Interesting English onionskin. Transparent clear base. Two wide panels of bright green, two narrow panels of brighter green. Clear spaces. No base layer of yellow or white. Very narrow elongated air bubble, two tiny pits. Gorgeous. English, circa 1870-1915. 13/16". Near Mint(+) (8.9). Price: $75. CyberAuction #473, Lot #48.

2662. END-OF-DAY. Panelled onionskin. Four-panel onionskin. Transparent clear base. Subsurface layer is two panels of translucent blue and white, and two panels of translucent orange, yellow and white. Beauty. Germany, circa 1870-1915. 25/32". Mint (9.8). Price: $75. CyberAuction #479, Lot #18.

2663. END-OF-DAY. Panelled onionskin. Interesting English onionskin. Transparent clear base. Two panels of bright green, two narrow panels of brighter green. Clear spaces. No base layer of yellow or white. Very narrow elongated air bubble, two tiny pits. Gorgeous. English, circa 1870-1915. 13/16". Near Mint(+) (8.9). Price: $75. CyberAuction #494, Lot #43.

2664. END-OF-DAY. Panelled onionskin. Stunning marble. Transparent clear base. Opaque white core. Slightly shrunken. Two pink panels, two turquoise panels. Thick outer casing of clear. One very tiny melt flake. Germany, circa 1870-1915. 7/8". Mint(-) (9.0). Price: $75. CyberAuction #503, Lot #73.

2665. END-OF-DAY. Panelled onionskin. Transparent clear base. Two panels of pink on white. Two panels of green on yellow. Stunning. One pit and a cold roll mark right at the top. Germany, circa 1870-1915. 11/16". Mint(-) (9.0). Price: $72. CyberAuction #396, Lot #52.

2666. END-OF-DAY. Panelled onionskin. Four-panel left-hand twist onionskin. Gorgeous. Transparent clear base. Subsurface yellow layer. Two pink panels and two green panels. Cold roll seam at the bottom. Very nice. Germany, circa 1870-1915. 21/32". Mint (9.5). Price: $70. CyberAuction #333, Lot #5.

2667. END-OF-DAY. Panelled onionskin. Four-panel onionskin. Transparent clear base. Opaque white core. Two blue cloud panels and two pink panels. Nice. Lightly polished. Pontils pretty much gone. Damage remains. Germany, circa 1870-1915. 1-5/8". Price: $70. CyberAuction #353, Lot #28.

2668. END-OF-DAY. Panelled onionskin. Nice left-twist four-panel onionskin. Transparent clear base. Opaque yellow subsurface layer. Two panels of light green and two panels of light pink. One tiny flake, one tiny sparkle. Germany, circa 1870-1915. 5/8". Near Mint(+) (8.9). Price: $70. CyberAuction #377, Lot #44.

2669. END-OF-DAY. Panelled onionskin. Rare four-panel with mica. Opaque white core. Narrow blue panel, narrow turquoise panel, two wide pink panels. Excellent overall coating of mica. The marble has been remelted. 1-11/16". Price: $70. CyberAuction #393, Lot #29.

2670. END-OF-DAY. Panelled onionskin. Four-panel, left-twist onionskin. Superb marble. Transparent clear base. Core is two panels of blue on white and two panels of turquoise on yellow. Two sparkles, tiny subsurface moon, some tiny pitting at the bottom. Still, views very well and it's a great marble. Germany, circa 1870-1915. 1-1/8". Near Mint (8.4). Price: $70. CyberAuction #395, Lot #60.

2671. END-OF-DAY. Panelled onionskin. Four-panel onionskin. Transparent clear base. White subsurface layer. Two wide panels of pink with some yellow. Two narrow panels of blue. Sparkle, two pits and some pinpricks. Very pretty. Germany, circa 1870-1915. 1-1/16". Near Mint(+) (8.7). Price: $70. CyberAuction #403, Lot #4.

2672. END-OF-DAY. Panelled onionskin. Four-panel onionskin. Gorgeous. Transparent clear base. White subsurface layer. Two panels of pink, two of turquoise. Almost no twist. A couple of sparkles on the surface. Germany, circa 1870-1915. 7/8". Near Mint(+) (8.9). Price: $70. CyberAuction #502, Lot #62.

2673. END-OF-DAY. Panelled onionskin. Six-panel onionskin. Transparent clear base. Opaque white subsurface layer. Three blue panels and three pink. Germany, circa 1870-1915. 17/32". Mint (9.9). Price: $70. CyberAuction #504, Lot #1.

2674. END-OF-DAY. Panelled onionskin. Four panel onionskin. Opaque white core. Two light blue panels and two light red panels. One tiny subsurface moon, two tiny pits. Pretty. Germany, circa 1870-1915. 27/32". Near Mint (8.5). Price: $66. CyberAuction #434, Lot #40.

2675. END-OF-DAY. Panelled onionskin. Stunning marble. Transparent clear base. Opaque yellow core. White subsurface layer. Two panels of blue and two of pink on it. Ground bottom pontil. Gorgeous. Germany, circa 1870-1915. 19/32". Mint (9.8). Price: $66. CyberAuction #442, Lot #45.

2676. END-OF-DAY. Panelled onionskin. Four-panel onionskin. Transparent clear base. Two wide panels of blue on white, two narrow panels of pink on yellow. Super marble. Germany, circa 1870-1915. 23/32". Mint (9.7). Price: $65. CyberAuction #330, Lot #50.

2677. END-OF-DAY. Panelled onionskin. Nice larger marble. Transparent clear base. Subsurface opaque white layer. Two panels of pink and two of blue. Several small chips and some roughness and haziness. Germany, circa 1870-1915. 1-3/4". Good(+) (7.7). Price: $65. CyberAuction #344, Lot #34.

2678. END-OF-DAY. Panelled onionskin. Four panel onionskin. Transparent clear base. Opaque mustard yellow subsurface layer. Two panels of light pink, two panels of light turquoise. Beauty. Germany, circa 1870-1915. 11/16". Mint (9.7). Price: $65. CyberAuction #363, Lot #7.

2679. END-OF-DAY. Panelled onionskin. Transparent clear base. Yellow core. Two panels of pink, two of green. Very shrunken on one side. Ground bottom pontil. One dirt melt spot. Superior. Germany, circa 1870-1915. 9/16". Mint (9.7). Price: $65. CyberAuction #396, Lot #24.

2680. END-OF-DAY. Panelled onionskin. Four-panel onionskin. Transparent clear base. Subsurface white layer. Two panels of pink, two of blue. Gorgeous marble. Germany, circa 1870-1915. 5/8". Mint (9.7). Price: $65. CyberAuction #400, Lot #39.

2681. END-OF-DAY. Panelled onionskin. Gorgeous marble. Transparent clear base. Opaque white core. Two panels of blue. Germany, circa 1870-1915. 23/32". Mint (9.8). Price: $65. CyberAuction #421, Lot #52.

2682. END-OF-DAY. Panelled onionskin. Four panel onionskin. Transparent clear base. Two panels of blue on white. Two panels of blue and pink, on yellow. A number of tiny chips and moons on the surface, one small area may have been lightly polished. Germany, circa 1870-1915. 1-11/16". Good (7.4). Price: $65. CyberAuction #422, Lot #34.

2683. END-OF-DAY. Panelled onionskin. Four panel onionskin. Transparent clear base. Core is two panels of pink on white and two panels of pink and green on yellow. Shrunken core on one side. Polished, some damage remains. No pontils. A little mica. Germany, circa 1870-1915. 1-11/16". Price: $65. CyberAuction #427, Lot #20.

2684. END-OF-DAY. Panelled onionskin. Transparent clear base. Yellow and white mottled core. Two panels of green and two of pink. Unmelted sand floating in the marble. Stunning marble. Germany, circa 1870-1915. 23/32". Mint (9.9). Price: $61. CyberAuction #339, Lot #52.

2685. END-OF-DAY. Panelled onionskin. Four-panel onionskin. Transparent clear base. Opaque white core. Two pink panels, two turquoise panels. Germany, circa 1870-1915. 11/16". Mint (9.7). Price: $61. CyberAuction #501, Lot #44.

2686. END-OF-DAY. Panelled onionskin. Interesting. Transparent clear base. Opaque white core with overall light pink skin. Two panels of blue on top of that. A couple of melt pits, some light pitting. Germany, circa 1870-1915. 1-1/8". Near Mint (8.6). Price: $60. CyberAuction #332, Lot #39.

2687. END-OF-DAY. Panelled onionskin. Six-panel onionskin. Transparent clear base. Core is two panels of yellow and two of white. The yellow has turquoise on it. Each white panel has a panel of turquoise and a panel of pink on it. Beauty. Three tiny chips. Germany, circa 1870-1915. 25/32". Near Mint (8.5). Price: $60. CyberAuction #353, Lot #53.

2688. END-OF-DAY. Panelled onionskin. Four-panel onionskin. Transparent clear base. Opaque white core. Two narrow panels of blue, two wide panels of pink. Stunning. Germany, circa 1870-1915. 11/16". Mint (9.9). Price: $60. CyberAuction #388, Lot #41.

2689. END-OF-DAY. Panelled onionskin. Four-panel onionskin. Transparent clear base. Subsurface white layer. Two wide green panels, one narrow blue panel, one red panel. Colors are bright. Beauty. Germany, circa 1870-1915. 21/32". Mint (9.8). Price: $60. CyberAuction #425, Lot #44.

2690. END-OF-DAY. Panelled onionskin. Rare two-panel onionskin. Transparent clear base. Opaque white core. One side is pink, one side is light blue. Very nice example. Germany, circa 1870-1915. 9/16". Mint (9.7). Price: $60. CyberAuction #481, Lot #17.

2691. END-OF-DAY. Panelled onionskin. Four band core. Light blue base glass. Two panels are blue and white, two are pink on yellow. Gorgeous and rare marble. One tiny moon. Germany, circa 1870-1915. 11/16". Near Mint(+) (8.9). Price: $60. CyberAuction #493, Lot #32.

2692. END-OF-DAY. Panelled onionskin. Transparent clear base. Subsurface layer is two white panels and two yellow panels. Overall pink skin. Germany, circa 1870-1915. 9/16". Mint (9.7). Price: $59. CyberAuction #492, Lot #6.

2693. END-OF-DAY. Panelled onionskin. Four-panel three-lobe onionskin. Transparent clear base. Subsurface layer of white. Two wide pink panels, one blue panel, one turquoise panel. Three very deep lobes. Overall tiny chipping and very light haze. Germany, circa 1870-1915. 1-1/16". Good (7.3). Price: $55. CyberAuction #350, Lot #27.

2694. END-OF-DAY. Panelled onionskin. Four-panel onionskin. Transparent clear base. White core. Two panels of pink, two of turquoise. The colors are smeared. From near an end of the cane. Some subsurface moons, overall haze. Germany, circa 1870-1915. 1-1/2". Good(+) (7.9). Price: $55. CyberAuction #353, Lot #32.

2695. END-OF-DAY. Panelled onionskin. Gorgeous. Transparent clear base. Opaque white subsurface layer. Two panels of pastel pink and two of pastel blue. Two tiny chips. Germany, circa 1870-1915. 7/8". Near Mint (8.6). Price: $55. CyberAuction #355, Lot #58.

2696. END-OF-DAY. Panelled onionskin. Four panel onionskin. Left-hand twist. Small marble. Transparent clear base. Opaque white core. Two wide panels of pink, two narrow panels of blue. Shrunken on one side. Super marble. Germany, circa 1870-1915. 17/32". Mint (9.9). Price: $55. CyberAuction #356, Lot #41.

2697. END-OF-DAY. Panelled onionskin. Transparent clear base. Core is opaque white and yellow. Two panels of blue and two of turquoise. A stunning marble. One original pit. Germany, circa 1870-1915. 11/16". Mint (9.6). Price: $55. CyberAuction #388, Lot #15.

2698. END-OF-DAY. Panelled onionskin. Gorgeous. Transparent clear base. Subsurface white layer. Covered by a dark pink skin. Two narrow blue panels. One pit. Germany, circa 1870-1915. 23/32". Mint(-) (9.0). Price: $55. CyberAuction #396, Lot #37.

2699. END-OF-DAY. Panelled onionskin. Four-panel, left-twist onionskin with mica. Transparent clear base. Opaque white subsurface layer. Two panels of green and two of pink. Some nice mica flakes in it. One small chip. Very nice. Germany, circa 1870-1915. 3/4". Near Mint (8.6). Price: $55. CyberAuction #399, Lot #56.

2700. END-OF-DAY. Panelled onionskin. Four-panel onionskin. Two panels of turquoise on yellow, two of blue on white. Some pink. Has a small melt spot. Germany, circa 1870-1915. 13/16". Mint(-) (9.0). Price: $55. CyberAuction #403, Lot #34.

2701. END-OF-DAY. Panelled onionskin. Transparent light blue base. Opaque white subsurface layer. Two blue panels, two pink panels. Gorgeous. A couple of tiny sparkles. Germany, circa 1870-1915. 3/4". Mint(-) (9.0). Price: $55. CyberAuction #444, Lot #49.

2702. END-OF-DAY. Panelled onionskin. Four panel onionskin. Transparent clear base. Two panels of blue on white. Two panels of blue and pink, on yellow. A number of tiny chips and moons on the surface, one small area may have been lightly polished. Germany, circa 1870-1915. 1-11/16". Good (7.4). Price: $55. CyberAuction #456, Lot #30.

2703. END-OF-DAY. Panelled onionskin. Four-panel onionskin. Transparent clear base. Two panels of blue on white, two of pink on yellow. One tiny chip, several pits, overall very light scratching. Germany, circa 1870-1915. 1-7/16". Near Mint(+) (8.0). Price: $55. CyberAuction #487, Lot #35.

2704. END-OF-DAY. Panelled onionskin. Transparent clear base. Opaque white core. Two pink panels, two blue panels. No twist. One elongated subsurface air bubble. Beautiful example. Three tiny pits, may be air bubbles. Germany, circa 1870-1915. 13/16". Mint(-) (9.0). Price: $55. CyberAuction #490, Lot #4.

2705. END-OF-DAY. Panelled onionskin. Four-panel onionskin. Light blue base. Two panels of pink on yellow, two of blue on white. Beauty. Germany, circa 1870-1915. 21/32". Mint (9.8). Price: $55. CyberAuction #491, Lot #6.

2706. END-OF-DAY. Panelled onionskin. Transparent clear base. Opaque white core. Two pink panels and two turquoise panels. One very tiny sparkle. Gorgeous marble. Germany, circa 1870-1915. 3/4". Mint(-) (9.2). Price: $51. CyberAuction #487, Lot #12.

2707. END-OF-DAY. Panelled onionskin. Large marble. Transparent clear base. White subsurface layer. Two narrow green panels, two wide pink panels. Polished, damage remains. 1-5/8". Price: $50. CyberAuction #358, Lot #15.

2708. END-OF-DAY. Panelled onionskin. Transparent clear base. White subsurface layer. Two blue panels, two green panels. One melt spot. Gorgeous. Germany, circa 1870-1915. 21/32". Mint(-) (9.2). Price: $50. CyberAuction #360, Lot #50.

2709. END-OF-DAY. Panelled onionskin. Transparent clear base. Two panels of white, and two of yellow. Overall slightly stretched green spots. The surface was damaged and has now been coated with a polymer. 2-1/8". Reworked. Price: $50. CyberAuction #391, Lot #25.

2710. END-OF-DAY. Panelled onionskin. Four-panel onionskin. Two panels of red on yellow, two of pale green on white. Heavily polished. Germany, circa 1870-1915. 1-1/2". Polished. Price: $50. CyberAuction #391, Lot #31.

2711. END-OF-DAY. Panelled onionskin. Stunning marble. Four-panel onionskin. Transparent clear base. Opaque white core. Four very shallow lobes. Two panels of orange/red, two panels of blue. One melt chip. Germany, circa 1870-1915. 11/16". Mint (9.7). Price: $50. CyberAuction #421, Lot #57.

2712. END-OF-DAY. Panelled onionskin. Six-panel onionskin. White core. Two green panels, two pink panels, two pink and yellow panels. Polished, damage remains. Germany, circa 1870-1915. 1-3/4". Price: $50. CyberAuction #434, Lot #22.

2713. END-OF-DAY. Panelled onionskin. Transparent clear base. Opaque white subsurface layer. Two pink panels and two blue panels. One tiny chip. Germany, circa 1870-1915. 23/32". Near Mint(+) (8.9). Price: $50. CyberAuction #443, Lot #49.

2714. END-OF-DAY. Panelled onionskin. Transparent clear base. Opaque white core. Two pink panels, two blue panels. No twist. One elongated subsurface air bubble. Beautiful example. Three tiny pits, may be air bubbles. Germany, circa 1870-1915. 13/16". Mint(-) (9.0). Price: $50. CyberAuction #459, Lot #48.

2715. END-OF-DAY. Panelled onionskin. Very nice four-panel onionskin. Transparent clear base. Opaque white subsurface layer. Two pink panels, one green panel, one blue panel. One pinprick. Germany, circa 1870-1915. 19/32". Mint (9.5). Price: $50. CyberAuction #462, Lot #35.

2716. END-OF-DAY. Panelled onionskin. Four-panel onionskin. Transparent clear base. Panels are: pink, blue and green on white. Pink and green on yellow. No color on white. Pink and blue on yellow. Interesting. Some tiny and small chips. Germany, circa 1870-1915. 1-3/8". Good(+) (7.9). Price: $50. CyberAuction #493, Lot #26.

2717. END-OF-DAY. Panelled onionskin. Transparent clear base. Subsurface layer is yellow. Two panels of green, two of pink. Stunning. One very tiny flake. Germany, circa 1870-1915. 21/32". Near Mint(+) (8.9). Price: $50. CyberAuction #502, Lot #70.

2718. END-OF-DAY. Panelled onionskin. Four-panel onionskin. Transparent clear base. Subsurface layer is a mix of yellow and white. Two pink panels, two blue panels. One tiny melt spot, one tiny pinprick. Germany, circa 1870-1915. 25/32". Mint(-) (9.2). Price: $50. CyberAuction #505, Lot #57.

2719. END-OF-DAY. Panelled onionskin. Four-panel. Transparent clear base. White core. Two turquoise panels and two pink panels. One very deep lobe, shrunken on that side. Very pretty. One pit. Germany, circa 1870-1915. 23/32". Mint(-) (9.1). Price: $49. CyberAuction #392, Lot #48.

2720. END-OF-DAY. Panelled onionskin. Four-panel. Transparent clear base. White core. Two turquoise panels and two pink panels. One very deep lobe, shrunken on that side. Very pretty. One pit. Germany, circa 1870-1915. 23/32". Mint(-) (9.1). Price: $49. CyberAuction #408, Lot #7.

2721. END-OF-DAY. Panelled onionskin. Two-lobe, four-panel onionskin. Transparent clear base. Opaque white core. Two wide panels of turquoise and blue, two narrow panels of pink. Two lobes, in the pink. Small chip, several very tiny rough spots. Germany, circa 1870-1915. 23/32". Near Mint (8.6). Price: $48. CyberAuction #346, Lot #53.

2722. END-OF-DAY. Panelled onionskin. Four panel onionskin. Transparent clear base. Opaque white core. Two panels of green and two of pink. Very pretty. Germany, circa 1870-1915. 9/16". Mint (9.9). Price: $48. CyberAuction #369, Lot #18.

2723. END-OF-DAY. Panelled onionskin. Four panel onionskin. Two white panels with pink. Two yellow panels, one has a little pink and blue, one had pink. Left-hand twist. Two small chips. Germany, circa 1870-1915. 11/16". Near Mint (8.5). Price: $47. CyberAuction #355, Lot #17.

2724. END-OF-DAY. Panelled onionskin. Four-panel onionskin. Transparent clear base. Subsurface white layer. Two panels are pink and two are blue. Pristine. Germany, circa 1870-1915. 21/32". Mint (9.9). Price: $47. CyberAuction #366, Lot #53.

2725. END-OF-DAY. Panelled onionskin. Four-panel onionskin. Transparent clear base. Opaque white core. Two light blue panels and two light red panels. One tiny subsurface moon, two tiny pits. Pretty. Germany, circa 1870-1915. 27/32". Near Mint (8.5). Price: $47. CyberAuction #394, Lot #42.

2726. END-OF-DAY. Panelled onionskin. Four-panel onionskin. Transparent clear base. Opaque white core. Two wide panels of green and blue, two narrow panels of pink. Gorgeous. Germany, circa 1870-1915. 5/8". Mint (9.9). Price: $47. CyberAuction #473, Lot #45.

2727. END-OF-DAY. Panelled onionskin. Gorgeous onionskin. Transparent clear base. White core. Two pink panels and two blue panels. Tight twist. Beauty. A couple of very tiny pits, might be melt spots. Germany, circa 1870-1915. 25/32". Mint(-) (9.0). Price: $47. CyberAuction #488, Lot #43.

2728. END-OF-DAY. Panelled onionskin. Four panel onionskin. Transparent clear base. Two wide yellow panels, two white panels. All have a skin of pink on them. Nice marble. Germany, circa 1870-1915. 5/8". Mint (9.9). Price: $46. CyberAuction #337, Lot #30.

2729. END-OF-DAY. Panelled onionskin. Four panel onionskin. Two are blue on white, two are pink on yellow. Remelted. 2-1/8". Price: $45. CyberAuction #361, Lot #47.

2730. END-OF-DAY. Panelled onionskin. Four panel onionskin. Transparent clear base. Two panels of pink on white. Two panels of green on yellow. Stunning. One pit and a cold roll mark right at the top. Germany, circa 1870-1915. 11/16". Mint(-) (9.0). Price: $45. CyberAuction #442, Lot #56.

2731. END-OF-DAY. Panelled onionskin. Four-panel onionskin with mica. Transparent clear base. Opaque white core. Two narrow pink panels, two wide blue panels. Shrunken on one side. Nice sprinkling of mica. Several small chips. Germany, circa 1870-1915. 13/16". Near Mint (8.4). Price: $45. CyberAuction #446, Lot #43.

2732. END-OF-DAY. Panelled onionskin. Four panel onionskin. Transparent clear base. Opaque mustard yellow subsurface layer. Two narrow pink panels, two wide green panels. One very tiny subsurface moon. Germany, circa 1870-1915. 25/32". Near Mint(+) (8.9). Price: $44. CyberAuction #363, Lot #12.

2733. END-OF-DAY. Panelled onionskin. Four-panel onionskin. Yellow core. Two wide panels of pink, two narrow panels of blue. Beauty. Germany, circa 1870-1915. 5/8". Mint (9.9). Price: $44. CyberAuction #392, Lot #19.

2734. END-OF-DAY. Panelled onionskin. Transparent clear base. Opaque white core. Two panels of pink and two of blue. Each panel is slightly lobed, one actually shows no lobing. Perhaps from near and end of the cane. In great shape. Germany, circa 1870-1915. 9/16". Mint (9.8). Price: $44. CyberAuction #400, Lot #8.

2735. END-OF-DAY. Panelled onionskin. Lightly tinted blue base. Core is two panels of blue on white and two of green on yellow. Shrunken on one side. Heavily polished. Germany, circa 1870-1915. 29/32". Price: $44. CyberAuction #401, Lot #53.

2736. END-OF-DAY. Panelled onionskin. Lightly tinted blue base. Core is two panels of blue on white and two of green on yellow. Shrunken on one side. Heavily polished. Germany, circa 1870-1915. 29/32". Price: $44. CyberAuction #441, Lot #53.

2737. END-OF-DAY. Panelled onionskin. Four panel onionskin. Transparent clear base. Opaque white core. Two panels of yellow. Overall skin of pink. Very interesting. Melt spot, some melt pits. Tiny chip, some tiny subsurface moons. Germany, circa 1870-1915. 1-1/8". Near Mint(-) (8.0). Price: $43. CyberAuction #407, Lot #24.

2738. END-OF-DAY. Panelled onionskin. Four-panel onionskin. Two panels of blue on white, two of pink on yellow. Tiny chip and several open air holes. Very pretty. Germany, circa 1870-1915. 3/4". Near Mint(+) (8.8). Price: $42. CyberAuction #392, Lot #1.

2739. END-OF-DAY. Panelled onionskin. Six-panel onionskin. White core. Two green panels, two pink panels, two pink and yellow panels. Polished, damage remains. Germany, circa 1870-1915. 1-3/4". Price: $42. CyberAuction #393, Lot #21.

2740. END-OF-DAY. Panelled onionskin. Four-panel onionskin. Transparent clear base. White core. Two pink panels and two turquoise panels. Polished, some damage remains. Germany, circa 1870-1915. 1-11/16". Price: $42. CyberAuction #434, Lot #26.

2741. END-OF-DAY. Panelled onionskin. Transparent clear base. Opaque white core. Overall pink skin. Two blue panels. One rough spot. Germany, circa 1870-1915. 17/32". Near Mint(+) (8.7). Price: $42. CyberAuction #443, Lot #51.

2742. END-OF-DAY. Panelled onionskin. Four panel onionskin. Transparent clear base. Opaque white core. Two panels of green and two of red. Large chip on one side, some smaller chips around the marble. Germany, circa 1870-1915. 1-3/4". Good (7.3). Price: $42. CyberAuction #447, Lot #31.

2743. END-OF-DAY. Panelled onionskin. Four-panel onionskin. Transparent clear base. Two panels of pink on yellow, two of pink, blue and green on white. Germany, circa 1870-1915. 21/32". Mint (9.5). Price: $42. CyberAuction #450, Lot #31.

2744. END-OF-DAY. Panelled onionskin. Four-panel onionskin. Transparent clear base. Core is two panels of blue on white and two of pink on yellow. Slightly shrunken on one side. Three tiny flakes, some rubbing. Germany, circa 1870-1915. 29/32". Near Mint (8.6). Price: $42. CyberAuction #455, Lot #44.

2745. END-OF-DAY. Panelled onionskin. Four-panel. Transparent clear base. White core. Two turquoise panels and two pink panels. One very deep lobe, shrunken on that side. Very pretty. One pit. Germany, circa 1870-1915. 23/32". Mint(-) (9.1). Price: $42. CyberAuction #460, Lot #11.

2746. END-OF-DAY. Panelled onionskin. Four panel onionskin. Transparent clear base. Opaque white core. Two panels of green and two of red. Large chip on one side, some smaller chips around the marble. Germany, circa 1870-1915. 1-3/4". Good (7.3). Price: $42. CyberAuction #478, Lot #24.

2747. END-OF-DAY. Panelled onionskin. Transparent clear base. Opaque white core. Two narrow blue panels, two wide pink panels. Distinct left-hand twist. Small annealing fracture, cold roll line. Germany, circa 1870-1915. 21/32". Mint(-) (9.2). Price: $42. CyberAuction #503, Lot #30.

2748. END-OF-DAY. Panelled onionskin. Four-panel onionskin. Transparent clear base. Opaque white core. Overall light skin of pink. Two blue panels. One tiny moon, tiny subsurface moon. Germany, circa 1870-1915. 13/16". Near Mint(+) (8.9). Price: $41. CyberAuction #428, Lot #50.

2749. END-OF-DAY. Panelled onionskin. Four panel onionskin. Two panels are blue on white, two are pink on yellow. Overall haziness. A couple of small subsurface moons. Germany, circa 1870-1915. 1-7/16". Good(+) (7.7). Price: $41. CyberAuction #434, Lot #33.

2750. END-OF-DAY. Panelled onionskin. Transparent clear base. Opaque white core. Two pink panels, two blue panels. Gorgeous. Germany, circa 1870-1915. 5/8". Mint (9.9). Price: $41. CyberAuction #475, Lot #48.

2751. END-OF-DAY. Panelled onionskin. Four-panel onionskin. Transparent clear base. Opaque white subsurface layer with yellow mixed in. Overall pink skin. Two green panels. One manufacturing chip. Germany, circa 1870-1915. 19/32". Mint(-) (9.0). Price: $40. CyberAuction #371, Lot #15.

2752. END-OF-DAY. Panelled onionskin. Transparent clear base. Opaque yellow core. Two panels of pale green and two of pale pink. Germany, circa 1870-1915. 11/16". Mint (9.8). Price: $40. CyberAuction #381, Lot #40.

2753. END-OF-DAY. Panelled onionskin. Four-panel onionskin. Transparent clear base. Opaque white core. Two blue panels and two red. Germany, circa 1870-1915. 21/32". Mint (9.9). Price: $40. CyberAuction #381, Lot #53.

2754. END-OF-DAY. Panelled onionskin. Four-panel onionskin. Transparent clear base. White core. Two pink panels and two turquoise panels. Polished, some damage remains. Germany, circa 1870-1915. 1-11/16". Price: $40. CyberAuction #397, Lot #29.

2755. END-OF-DAY. Panelled onionskin. Six-panel onionskin. Transparent clear base. Opaque white subsurface layer. Two panels of pink on yellow, two panels of green on white, two panels of yellow on white. Two tiny scratch spots. Germany, circa 1870-1915. 11/16". Mint(-) (9.0). Price: $40. CyberAuction #399, Lot #58.

2756. END-OF-DAY. Panelled onionskin. Four-panel onionskin. Transparent clear base. Opaque white core. Two pink panels two turquoise and blue panels. Melt spot and tiny chip. Germany, circa 1870-1915. 27/32". Near Mint(+) (8.7). Price: $40. CyberAuction #403, Lot #27.

2757. END-OF-DAY. Panelled onionskin. Transparent clear base. Opaque yellow subsurface layer. Two green panels and two pink panels. Double twist on the top, and a cold roll line. 25/32". Mint (9.5). Price: $40. CyberAuction #419, Lot #19.

2758. END-OF-DAY. Panelled onionskin. Six-panel onionskin. Transparent clear base. Opaque white subsurface layer. Two panels of pink on yellow, two panels of green on white, two panels of yellow on white. Two tiny scratch spots. Germany, circa 1870-1915. 11/16". Mint(-) (9.0). Price: $40. CyberAuction #430, Lot #16.

2759. END-OF-DAY. Panelled onionskin. Transparent clear base. Yellow core. Two panels of pink, two of green. Very shrunken on one side. Ground bottom pontil. One dirt melt spot. Superior. Germany, circa 1870-1915. 9/16". Mint (9.7). Price: $40. CyberAuction #442, Lot #39.

2760. END-OF-DAY. Panelled onionskin. Four panel onionskin. Two panels are blue on white, two are pink on yellow. Overall haziness. A couple of small subsurface moons. Germany, circa 1870-1915. 1-7/16". Good(+) (7.7). Price: $40. CyberAuction #453, Lot #53.

2761. END-OF-DAY. Panelled onionskin. Four-panel onionskin. Transparent clear base. Subsurface white layer. Two panels of pink, two of blue. Gorgeous marble. Germany, circa 1870-1915. 5/8". Mint (9.9). Price: $40. CyberAuction #455, Lot #40.

2762. END-OF-DAY. Panelled onionskin. Stunning marble. Four-panel onionskin. Transparent clear base. Opaque white core. Four very shallow lobes. Two panels of orange/red, two panels of blue. One melt chip. Germany, circa 1870-1915. 11/16". Mint (9.7). Price: $40. CyberAuction #457, Lot #29.

2763. END-OF-DAY. Panelled onionskin. Gorgeous onionskin. Transparent clear base. White core. Two pink panels and two blue panels. Tight twist. Beauty. A couple of very tiny pits, might be melt spots. Germany, circa 1870-1915. 25/32". Mint(-) (9.0). Price: $40. CyberAuction #461, Lot #8.

2764. END-OF-DAY. Panelled onionskin. Four panel onionskin. Transparent clear base. Two panels of pink on yellow, two of blue on white. Germany, circa 1870-1915. 11/16". Mint (9.8). Price: $40. CyberAuction #461, Lot #37.

2765. END-OF-DAY. Panelled onionskin. Gorgeous marble. Four-panel onionskin. Transparent clear base. Mustard yellow core. Two pink panels and two green. Beauty. One moon. Germany, circa 1870-1915. 25/32". Near Mint(+) (8.9). Price: $40. CyberAuction #461, Lot #49.

2766. END-OF-DAY. Panelled onionskin. Transparent clear base. Yellow core. Two panels of pink, two of green. Very shrunken on one side. Ground bottom pontil. One dirt melt spot. Superior. Germany, circa 1870-1915. 9/16". Mint (9.7). Price: $40. CyberAuction #482, Lot #36.

2767. END-OF-DAY. Panelled onionskin. Four panel onionskin. Transparent clear base. Two panels of pink on yellow, two of blue on white. Germany, circa 1870-1915. 11/16". Mint (9.8). Price: $40. CyberAuction #496, Lot #13.

2768. END-OF-DAY. Panelled onionskin. Hard to find three-panel onionskin. Transparent clear base. Opaque white subsurface layer. One panel each of pink, blue, green. The pink and green have a nice lobe in them. Each panel is about the same width. Some haziness on one side. Small chip on the same side. Germany, circa 1870-1915. 13/16". Near Mint(-) (8.0). Price: $39. CyberAuction #365, Lot #60.

2769. END-OF-DAY. Panelled onionskin. Transparent clear base. Two panels of pink on yellow, two panels of green on white. Overall haze. Germany, circa 1870-1915. 7/8". Near Mint(-) (8.1). Price: $39. CyberAuction #407, Lot #43.

2770. END-OF-DAY. Panelled onionskin. Nice peewee. Transparent clear base. Opaque white subsurface layer. Two narrow green bands, two wide pink panels. Cold roll line. Germany, circa 1870-1915. 15/32". Mint (9.7). Price: $39. CyberAuction #429, Lot #35.

2771. END-OF-DAY. Panelled onionskin. Six-panel onionskin. Transparent clear base. Two panels of yellow, two of green on white, two of pink on white. Small chip and some pits. Germany, circa 1870-1915. 1-1/16". Mint (8.4). Price: $38. CyberAuction #426, Lot #18.

2772. END-OF-DAY. Panelled onionskin. Four-panel onionskin. Transparent clear base. Opaque white subsurface layer. Two narrow panels of blue, two wide panels of pink. One tiny pit. Germany, circa 1870-1915. 9/16". Mint (9.4). Price: $38. CyberAuction #445, Lot #11.

2773. END-OF-DAY. Panelled onionskin. Gorgeous four-panel onionskin. Semi-opaque white core. Opaque white subsurface layer is some clear spaces. Two pink panels, two turquoise green panels. Beautiful. One pinprick. Germany, circa 1870-1915. 21/32". Mint (9.3). Price: $38. CyberAuction #450, Lot #4.

2774. END-OF-DAY. Panelled onionskin. Four-panel onionskin. Transparent clear base. Opaque white subsurface layer. Two blue panels and two pink panels. Tiny sparkle and a tiny pinprick. Germany, circa 1870-1915. 13/16". Mint(-) (9.0). Price: $38. CyberAuction #463, Lot #50.

2775. END-OF-DAY. Panelled onionskin. Transparent clear base. Opaque white subsurface layer. Two narrow green and blue panels, two wide pink panels. One large crease. Germany, circa 1870-1915. 5/8". Mint (9.5). Price: $37. CyberAuction #360, Lot #8.

2776. END-OF-DAY. Panelled onionskin. Transparent clear base. Subsurface mustard yellow layer. Two light panels of pale pink, two light panels of pale green. A couple of tiny chips. Germany, circa 1870-1915. 11/16". Near Mint (8.6). Price: $37. CyberAuction #380, Lot #12.

2777. END-OF-DAY. Panelled onionskin. Four-panel onionskin. Transparent clear base. Opaque white subsurface layer. Two wide panels of pink, two narrow panels of green and blue. Overall light haze. Germany, circa 1870-1915. 31/32". Near Mint(-) (8.2). Price: $37. CyberAuction #420, Lot #59.

2778. END-OF-DAY. Panelled onionskin. Transparent clear base. White subsurface layer. Two wide pink bands, two narrow blue bands. Germany, circa 1870-1915. 1/2". Mint (9.7). Price: $37. CyberAuction #433, Lot #56.

2779. END-OF-DAY. Panelled onionskin. Six-panel onionskin. Transparent clear base. Core is two panels of yellow and two of white. The yellow has turquoise on it. Each white panel has a panel of turquoise and a panel of pink on it. Beauty. Three tiny chips. Germany, circa 1870-1915. 25/32". Near Mint (8.5). Price: $37. CyberAuction #444, Lot #21.

2780. END-OF-DAY. Panelled onionskin. Four panel onionskin. Left-hand twist. Small marble. Transparent clear base. Opaque white core. Two wide panels of pink, two narrow panels of blue. Shrunken on one side. Super marble. Germany, circa 1870-1915. 17/32". Mint (9.9). Price: $37. CyberAuction #444, Lot #46.

2781. END-OF-DAY. Panelled onionskin. Four panel onionskin. Two white panels with pink. Two yellow panels, one has a little pink and blue, one had pink. Left-hand twist. Two small chips. Germany, circa 1870-1915. 11/16". Near Mint (8.5). Price: $37. CyberAuction #444, Lot #55.

2782. END-OF-DAY. Panelled onionskin. Transparent clear base. Subsurface white layer. Two narrow blue panels, two wide pink panels. Very pretty. Germany, circa 1870-1915. 5/8". Mint (9.5). Price: $37. CyberAuction #481, Lot #50.

2783. END-OF-DAY. Panelled onionskin. Transparent clear base. Opaque white core. Two narrow blue panels, two wide pink on yellow panels. Two tiny chips on one side. Very pretty. Germany, circa 1870-1915. 3/4". Near Mint(+) (8.7). Price: $36. CyberAuction #359, Lot #45.

2784. END-OF-DAY. Panelled onionskin. Four panel onionskin. White core. Two blue panels, two pink panels. Several pits. Germany, circa 1870-1915. 1/2". Near Mint(+) (8.9). Price: $36. CyberAuction #379, Lot #38.

2785. END-OF-DAY. Panelled onionskin. Four-panel onionskin. Transparent clear base. Opaque white subsurface layer. Two wide pink panels, two narrow blue. Some haziness. Germany, circa 1870-1915. 21/32". Near Mint (8.6). Price: $36. CyberAuction #380, Lot #57.

2786. END-OF-DAY. Panelled onionskin. Six-panel onionskin. Transparent clear base. Two panels of yellow, two of green on white, two of pink on white. Small chip and some pits. Germany, circa 1870-1915. 1-1/16". Near Mint (8.4). Price: $36. CyberAuction #407, Lot #59.

2787. END-OF-DAY. Panelled onionskin. Transparent clear base. Opaque white subsurface layer. Two green panels, two blue panels. Two tiny flakes. Germany, circa 1870-1915. 21/32". Near Mint(+) (8.7). Price: $36. CyberAuction #501, Lot #58.

2788. END-OF-DAY. Panelled onionskin. Transparent clear base. Opaque white subsurface layer. Two blue panels, two narrow pink with white around them. One melt spot. Germany, circa 1870-1915. 21/32". Mint (9.6). Price: $36. CyberAuction #503, Lot #6.

2789. END-OF-DAY. Panelled onionskin. Four panel onionskin. Two pink on white panels, one blue on white, one green on white. Some melted glass on the surface. Very nice. Germany, circa 1870-1915. 11/16". Mint(-) (9.1). Price: $35. CyberAuction #374, Lot #55.

2790. END-OF-DAY. Panelled onionskin. Four panel onionskin. Two panels are blue on white, two are pink on yellow. Overall haziness. A couple of small subsurface moons. Germany, circa 1870-1915. 1-7/16". Good(+) (7.7). Price: $35. CyberAuction #393, Lot #16.

2791. END-OF-DAY. Panelled onionskin. Four panel onionskin. Two wide panels of pink on yellow, two narrow panels of blue on white. Overall tiny subsurface moons and sparkles. Germany, circa 1870-1915. 27/32". Near Mint(-) (8.0). Price: $34. CyberAuction #407, Lot #27.

2792. END-OF-DAY. Panelled onionskin. Four-panel onionskin. Transparent clear base. Opaque white core. Two panels of yellow. Overall skin of pink. Very interesting. Melt spot, some melt pits. Tiny chip, some tiny subsurface moons. Germany, circa 1870-1915. 1-1/8". Near Mint(-) (8.0). Price: $34. CyberAuction #432, Lot #57.

2793. END-OF-DAY. Panelled onionskin. Rare onionskin from near an end of the cane. Transparent clear base. Opaque white core. One pink panel, one blue panel. Lots of white showing. Beauty. One tiny flake. Germany, circa 1870-1915. 9/16". Near Mint(+) (8.7). Price: $34. CyberAuction #446, Lot #56.

2794. END-OF-DAY. Panelled onionskin. Beautiful marble. Transparent clear base. Opaque yellow subsurface layer. Two panels of light turquoise, two panels of light pink. A couple of sparkles. Very nice. Germany, circa 1870-1915. 21/32". Mint(-) (9.0). Price: $34. CyberAuction #450, Lot #49.

2795. END-OF-DAY. Panelled onionskin. Four-panel onionskin. Transparent clear base. Opaque yellow core. Two pink panels and two green panels. Some pits. Germany, circa 1870-1915. 27/32". Near Mint(+) (8.9). Price: $34. CyberAuction #472, Lot #29.

2796. END-OF-DAY. Panelled onionskin. Transparent clear base. Two panels of green on white, two panels of pink on yellow. Nice. One pit. Germany, circa 1870-1915. 9/16". Mint(-) (9.2). Price: $33. CyberAuction #464, Lot #4.

2797. END-OF-DAY. Panelled onionskin. Four panel onionskin. Transparent clear base. Two panels of blue on white, two of pink on yellow. One large manufacturing chip, some tiny chips. Germany, circa 1870-1915. 3/4". Near Mint (8.5). Price: $32. CyberAuction #343, Lot #51.

2798. END-OF-DAY. Panelled onionskin. Transparent clear base. Opaque white core. Two panels of blue, two of pink. One pit and some pinpricks. Germany, circa 1870-1915. 9/16". Mint(-) (9.0). Price: $32. CyberAuction #359, Lot #57.

2799. END-OF-DAY. Panelled onionskin. Four-panel onionskin. Transparent clear base. Opaque white subsurface layer. Two narrow panels of blue, two wide panels of pink. One tiny pit. Germany, circa 1870-1915. 9/16". Mint (9.4). Price: $32. CyberAuction #369, Lot #52.

2800. END-OF-DAY. Panelled onionskin. Transparent clear base. Opaque white subsurface layer. Two pink panels and two blue panels. One tiny chip. Germany, circa 1870-1915. 23/32". Near Mint(+) (8.9). Price: $32. CyberAuction #395, Lot #42.

2801. END-OF-DAY. Panelled onionskin. Four-panel. Transparent clear base. White core. Two turquoise panels and two pink panels. One very deep lobe, shrunken on that side. Very pretty. One pit. Germany, circa 1870-1915. 23/32". Mint(-) (9.1). Price: $32. CyberAuction #426, Lot #11.

2802. END-OF-DAY. Panelled onionskin. Beautiful four-panel onionskin. Transparent clear base. Opaque white subsurface layer with clear spaces. Two lime green panels, two dark pink panels. One melt spot of glass on the surface. Very pretty. Germany, circa 1870-1915. 5/8". Mint (9.5). Price: $32. CyberAuction #429, Lot #16.

2803. END-OF-DAY. Panelled onionskin. Transparent clear base. Opaque white subsurface layer with clear spaces. Two narrow blue panels, two wide pink panels. A small cold roll line. Germany, circa 1870-1915. 15/32". Mint (9.7). Price: $32. CyberAuction #429, Lot #52.

2804. END-OF-DAY. Panelled onionskin. Transparent clear base. Four panels. Two are green on white, two are pink on yellow. Some minor haziness and pitting. Germany, circa 1870-1915. 7/8". Near Mint(-) (8.0). Price: $32. CyberAuction #446, Lot #7.

2805. END-OF-DAY. Panelled onionskin. Transparent clear base. Subsurface layer is two white panels and two yellow panels. Overall skin pink. Germany, circa 1870-1915. 9/16". Mint (9.7). Price: $32. CyberAuction #464, Lot #48.

2806. END-OF-DAY. Panelled onionskin. Transparent clear base. Four panels. Two are green on white, two are pink on yellow. Some minor haziness and pitting. Germany, circa 1870-1915. 7/8". Near Mint(-) (8.0). Price: $32. CyberAuction #470, Lot #31.

2807. END-OF-DAY. Panelled onionskin. Gorgeous, shooter four-panel onionskin. Transparent clear base. Yellow core. Two wide pink panels, two narrow blue panels. Beauty. Tiny flake on top, one pit. Germany, circa 1870-1915. 13/16". Near Mint(+) (8.8). Price: $32. CyberAuction #489, Lot #45.

2808. END-OF-DAY. Panelled onionskin. Beautiful four-panel onionskin. Transparent clear base. Yellow core. Two panels of "bubbly" red, two of turquoise. Heavily polished but very pretty. Germany, circa 1870-1915. 1". Price: $31. CyberAuction #337, Lot #1.

2809. END-OF-DAY. Panelled onionskin. Four-panel onionskin. Transparent clear base. Opaque white subsurface layer. Two panels of pink, two of turquoise. Some minor pinpricks. Germany, circa 1870-1915. 25/32". Near Mint(+) (8.7). Price: $31. CyberAuction #407, Lot #41.

2810. END-OF-DAY. Panelled onionskin. Transparent clear base. Two white panels and two yellow panels, pink skin. One pit. Germany, circa 1870-1915. 9/16". Mint (9.4). Price: $30. CyberAuction #345, Lot #25.

2811. END-OF-DAY. Panelled onionskin. Four-panel onionskin. Transparent clear base. Opaque white subsurface layer with yellow mixed in. Overall pink skin. Two green panels. One manufacturing chip. Germany, circa 1870-1915. 19/32". Mint(-) (9.0). Price: $30. CyberAuction #348, Lot #47.

2812. END-OF-DAY. Panelled onionskin. Four panel onionskin. Two panels are blue with pink on white. Other two are pink on yellow. One tiny chip. Very nice. Germany, circa 1870-1915. 19/32". Near Mint(+) (8.9). Price: $30. CyberAuction #379, Lot #28.

2813. END-OF-DAY. Panelled onionskin. Transparent clear base. Subsurface layer of white. Two wide panels of pink, two narrow panels of blue with some green. Gorgeous. Very slightly oval. Germany, circa 1870-1915. 19/32". Mint (9.7). Price: $30. CyberAuction #420, Lot #20.

2814. END-OF-DAY. Panelled onionskin. Four-panel onionskin. Narrow blue and wide pink panels on white. Several tiny chips. Germany, circa 1870-1915. 11/16". Near Mint (8.5). Price: $30. CyberAuction #445, Lot #29.

2815. END-OF-DAY. Panelled onionskin. Transparent clear base. Opaque white core. Two wide pink panels, two narrow blue panels. Very nice marble. A couple of pinpricks. Germany, circa 1870-1915. 11/16". Mint(-) (9.2). Price: $30. CyberAuction #464, Lot #43.

2816. END-OF-DAY. Panelled onionskin. Transparent clear base. White subsurface layer. Two blue panels, two green panels. One melt spot. Gorgeous. Germany, circa 1870-1915. 21/32". Mint(-) (9.2). Price: $30. CyberAuction #470, Lot #14.

2817. END-OF-DAY. Panelled onionskin. Transparent clear base. Opaque white subsurface layer with clear spaces. Two narrow blue panels, two wide pink panels. A small cold roll line. Germany, circa 1870-1915. 15/32". Mint (9.7). Price: $30. CyberAuction #474, Lot #38.

2818. END-OF-DAY. Panelled onionskin. Transparent clear base. Four panel onionskin. Two panels are pink on yellow, other two are turquoise on white. Some tiny blue bands. Very shrunken on one side. Several small chips and a few tiny chips. Germany, circa 1870-1915. 13/16". Good(+) (7.9). Price: $29. CyberAuction #353, Lot #18.

2819. END-OF-DAY. Panelled onionskin. Four-panel onionskin. Transparent clear base. Two panels of blue on white, two of pink on yellow. Two tiny flakes. Germany, circa 1870-1915. 9/16". Near Mint (8.6). Price: $29. CyberAuction #369, Lot #24.

2820. END-OF-DAY. Panelled onionskin. Four panel onionskin. White core. Two panels of blue, one heavy blue, one light. Two panels of blue on yellow. One tiny flake. Germany, circa 1870-1915. 17/32". Near Mint(+) (8.9). Price: $29. CyberAuction #386, Lot #38.

2821. END-OF-DAY. Panelled onionskin. Four-panel onionskin. Two panels are blue with pink on white. Other two are pink on yellow. One tiny chip. Very nice. Germany, circa 1870-1915. 19/32". Near Mint(+) (8.9). Price: $29. CyberAuction #442, Lot #50.

2822. END-OF-DAY. Panelled onionskin. Four-panel onionskin. Transparent clear base. Opaque white subsurface layer, with some clear spaces. Two panels of pink and two of blue. Small annealing fracture. Germany, circa 1870-1915. 21/32". Mint(-) (9.0). Price: $29. CyberAuction #457, Lot #43.

2823. END-OF-DAY. Panelled onionskin. Four-panel onionskin. Transparent clear base. Subsurface layer of yellow. Two wide panels of pink, two narrow panels of green. Germany, circa 1870-1915. 9/16". Mint (9.5). Price: $29. CyberAuction #460, Lot #27.

2824. END-OF-DAY. Panelled onionskin. Four-panel onionskin. Transparent clear base. White core. Two pink panels and two light green. Some annealing crackling on the core. One tiny chip. Germany, circa 1870-1915. 3/4". Near Mint(+) (8.9). Price: $29. CyberAuction #481, Lot #14.

2825. END-OF-DAY. Panelled onionskin. Transparent clear base. Opaque white core. Overall pink skin. Two blue panels. One rough spot. Germany, circa 1870-1915. 17/32". Near Mint(+) (8.7). Price: $28. CyberAuction #353, Lot #48.

2826. END-OF-DAY. Panelled onionskin. Odd two panel. Transparent clear base. Subsurface layer is a wide panel of yellow with green skin (two-thirds of the marble) and a narrow panel of white (one-third). One very tiny subsurface moon. Germany, circa 1870-1915. 9/16". Near Mint(+) (8.9). Price: $28. CyberAuction #385, Lot #16.

2827. END-OF-DAY. Panelled onionskin. Four-panel onionskin. Transparent clear base. Core is white and yellow. Two panels of green, two panels of pink. Overall small and tiny subsurface moons. Germany, circa 1870-1915. 1-5/16". Good(+) (7.7). Price: $28. CyberAuction #440, Lot #10.

2828. END-OF-DAY. Panelled onionskin. Transparent clear base. White subsurface layer. Two blue panels, two green panels. One melt spot. Gorgeous. Germany, circa 1870-1915. 21/32". Mint(-) (9.2). Price: $28. CyberAuction #444, Lot #19.

2829. END-OF-DAY. Panelled onionskin. Transparent clear base. Opaque white core. Two panels are pink and two are green. Overall haze, but no chips. Germany, circa 1870-1915. 1-5/8". Good (7.3). Price: $28. CyberAuction #446, Lot #29.

2830. END-OF-DAY. Panelled onionskin. Four-panel onionskin. Two very wide panels of pink floating on yellow. Two narrow panels of blue floating on white. Very shrunken core on two sides, it is almost a ribbon onionskin. Several tiny subsurface moons and some tiny pinpricks. Germany, circa 1870-1915. 25/32". Good(+) (7.9). Price: $27. CyberAuction #407, Lot #15.

2831. END-OF-DAY. Panelled onionskin. Two-lobe, four-panel onionskin. Transparent clear base. Opaque white core. Two wide panels of turquoise and blue, two narrow panels of pink. Two lobes, in the pink. Small chip, several very tiny rough spots. Germany, circa 1870-1915. 23/32". Near Mint (8.6). Price: $27. CyberAuction #444, Lot #36.

2832. END-OF-DAY. Panelled onionskin. Four-panel onionskin. Transparent clear base. Opaque white subsurface layer. Two pink panels, one blue panel, one green panel. Some scratching. Germany, circa 1870-1915. 15/32". Mint(-) (9.0). Price: $27. CyberAuction #465, Lot #13.

2833. END-OF-DAY. Panelled onionskin. Four-panel onionskin. Transparent clear base. Opaque white core. Two blue panels and two pink panels. Overall haze and tiny chipping. Germany, circa 1870-1915. 1-5/16". Good (7.5). Price: $27. CyberAuction #469, Lot #42.

2834. END-OF-DAY. Panelled onionskin. Two-lobe, four-panel onionskin. Transparent clear base. Opaque white core. Two wide panels of turquoise and blue, two narrow panels of pink. Two lobes, in the pink. Small chip, several very tiny rough spots. Germany, circa 1870-1915. 23/32". Near Mint (8.6). Price: $27. CyberAuction #484, Lot #4.

2835. END-OF-DAY. Panelled onionskin. Super looking English type four-panel onionskin. Transparent clear base. One wide panel of bright yellow, one wide panel of bright red. Two clear panels. There are a couple of white bands hovering above the clear panels. One tiny flake. England, possibly Germany, circa 1870-1915. 1/2". Near Mint(+) (8.8). Price: $27. CyberAuction #487, Lot #4.

2836. END-OF-DAY. Panelled onionskin. Four-panel onionskin. Transparent clear base. Opaque white subsurface layer. Two pink panels, one blue panel, one green panel. Some scratching. Germany, circa 1870-1915. 15/32". Mint(-) (9.0). Price: $27. CyberAuction #496, Lot #37.

2837. END-OF-DAY. Panelled onionskin. Four-panel onionskin. Transparent clear base. Yellow core. Two green panels, two pink panels. One sparkle. Germany, circa 1870-1915. 11/16". Mint(-) (9.0). Price: $27. CyberAuction #503, Lot #3.

2838. END-OF-DAY. Panelled onionskin. Transparent clear base. Opaque white subsurface layer. Two blue panels and two pink panels. A couple of tiny flakes. Germany, circa 1870-1915. 25/32". Near Mint(+) (8.8). Price: $26. CyberAuction #332, Lot #25.

2839. END-OF-DAY. Panelled onionskin. Seven panel onionskin. Transparent clear base. Subsurface layer is the following panels: blue/white, white, pink/yellow, pink/white, green/yellow, pink/white, pink/yellow. Hazy surface. Germany, circa 1870-1915. 11/16". Near Mint (8.3). Price: $26. CyberAuction #364, Lot #11.

2840. END-OF-DAY. Panelled onionskin. Four panel onionskin. Very interesting marble. Transparent clear base. Opaque white core. Two pink panels. Two uncolored panels. Those two each have one band of blue. Some surface pitting. Germany, circa 1870-1915. 3/4". Near Mint (8.5). Price: $26. CyberAuction #383, Lot #20.

2841. END-OF-DAY. Panelled onionskin. Four-panel onionskin. Transparent clear base. Opaque white core. Two panels of green and two of blue. Surface is not quite wet, but no damage. Germany, circa 1870-1915. 19/32". Mint(-) (9.0). Price: $26. CyberAuction #388, Lot #50.

2842. END-OF-DAY. Panelled onionskin. Four-panel onionskin. Transparent clear base. Opaque white core. Two panels of green and two of blue. Surface is not quite wet, but no damage. Germany, circa 1870-1915. 19/32". Mint(-) (9.0). Price: $26. CyberAuction #445, Lot #42.

2843. END-OF-DAY. Panelled onionskin. Four-panel onionskin. Transparent clear base. Opaque white core. Two panels of green and two of blue. Surface is not quite wet, but no damage. Germany, circa 1870-1915. 19/32". Mint(-) (9.0). Price: $26. CyberAuction #482, Lot #33.

2844. END-OF-DAY. Panelled onionskin. Four-panel onionskin. Translucent white core. Two panels of transparent pink, two of transparent green, although one panel of green is pretty much missing. One tiny flake. Peewee. Germany, circa 1870-1915. 7/16". Near Mint(+) (8.7). Price: $25. CyberAuction #371, Lot #41.

2845. END-OF-DAY. Panelled onionskin. Four-panel onionskin. Transparent clear base. Subsurface layer of white with yellow mixed in. Two panels of pink, two narrow panels of green. Some small and tiny chips. Germany, circa 1870-1915. 25/32". Near Mint(-) (8.1). Price: $25. CyberAuction #380, Lot #51.

2846. END-OF-DAY. Panelled onionskin. Four-panel onionskin. Transparent clear base. Subsurface white layer. Two panels of blue and two of pink. Melt spot. Germany, circa 1870-1915. 19/32". Mint (-) (9.1). Price: $25. CyberAuction #410, Lot #56.

2847. END-OF-DAY. Panelled onionskin. Hard to find six-panel onionskin. Transparent clear base. Subsurface opaque white layer. Three blue panels, one orange/red panel, two white panels. Fracture in the orange/red panel. No surface damage. Super looking number. England, possibly Germany, circa 1870-1915. 11/16". Near Mint(+) (8.7). Price: $25. CyberAuction #432, Lot #13.

2848. END-OF-DAY. Panelled onionskin. Four-panel onionskin. Transparent clear base. Yellow subsurface layer. Two pink panels and two green panels. One very tiny subsurface moon. Germany, circa 1870-1915. 19/32". Near Mint(+) (8.9). Price: $25. CyberAuction #463, Lot #44.

2849. END-OF-DAY. Panelled onionskin. Four-panel onionskin. Two are pink on yellow, two are blue on white. Overall chipping. Germany, circa 1870-1915. 1-13/16". Collectible. Price: $24. CyberAuction #383, Lot #23.

2850. END-OF-DAY. Panelled onionskin. Oddly colored four-panel onionskin. Transparent clear base. White subsurface layer. Two green on yellow panels. Overall some blue and pink. Several tiny chips. Germany, circa 1870-1915. 27/32". Near Mint(-) (8.2). Price: $24. CyberAuction #407, Lot #55.

2851. END-OF-DAY. Panelled onionskin. Four-panel onionskin. Transparent clear base. Core is white and yellow. Two panels of green, two panels of pink. Overall small and tiny subsurface moons. Germany, circa 1870-1915. 1-5/16". Good(+) (7.7). Price: $24. CyberAuction #427, Lot #4.

2852. END-OF-DAY. Panelled onionskin. Four panel onionskin. Transparent clear base. Two panels of pink on mustard yellow, two of blue on white. Overall very light scratches. Germany, circa 1870-1915. 19/32". Near Mint(+) (8.9). Price: $24. CyberAuction #471, Lot #39.

2853. END-OF-DAY. Panelled onionskin. Transparent clear base. Subsurface mustard yellow layer. Two light panels of pale pink, two light panels of pale green. A couple of tiny chips. Germany, circa 1870-1915. 11/16". Near Mint (8.6). Price: $23. CyberAuction #444, Lot #41.

2854. END-OF-DAY. Panelled onionskin. Four-panel onionskin. Transparent clear base. Two panels of blue on white, two of pink on yellow. In great shape, just a couple of pits. Germany, circa 1870-1915. 9/16". Mint(-) (9.0). Price: $23. CyberAuction #481, Lot #6.

2855. END-OF-DAY. Panelled onionskin. Four-panel onionskin. Transparent clear base. Subsurface layer of yellow. Two wide panels of pink, two narrow panels of green. Germany, circa 1870-1915. 9/16". Mint (9.5). Price: $22. CyberAuction #420, Lot #46.

2856. END-OF-DAY. Panelled onionskin. Four-panel onionskin. Transparent clear base. Subsurface white layer. Two panels of blue and two of pink. Melt spot. Germany, circa 1870-1915. 19/32". Mint (-) (9.1). Price: $22. CyberAuction #441, Lot #6.

2857. END-OF-DAY. Panelled onionskin. Four-panel onionskin. White core. Two blue panels, two pink panels. Several pits. Germany, circa 1870-1915. 1/2". Near Mint(+) (8.9). Price: $22. CyberAuction #442, Lot #49.

2858. END-OF-DAY. Panelled onionskin. Four-panel onionskin. Transparent clear base. Opaque white subsurface layer. Two wide pink panels, two narrow blue. Some haziness. Germany, circa 1870-1915. 21/32". Near Mint (8.6). Price: $22. CyberAuction #442, Lot #52.

2859. END-OF-DAY. Panelled onionskin. Four-panel onionskin. Transparent clear base. Two panels of blue on white, two of pink on yellow. Two tiny flakes. Germany, circa 1870-1915. 9/16". Near Mint (8.6). Price: $22. CyberAuction #444, Lot #14.

2860. END-OF-DAY. Panelled onionskin. Transparent clear base. Opaque white subsurface layer. One panel of pink with a blue band on it, one panel of green with a blue band next to it, two panels of white. Two large melt spots. Unusual. Germany, circa 1870-1915. 9/16". Mint(-) (9.0). Price: $22. CyberAuction #459, Lot #9.

2861. END-OF-DAY. Panelled onionskin. Transparent clear base. Opaque white subsurface layer. One panel of pink with a blue band on it, one panel of green with a blue band next to it, two panels of white. Two large melt spots. Unusual. Germany, circa 1870-1915. 9/16". Mint(-) (9.0). Price: $22. CyberAuction #488, Lot #35.

2862. END-OF-DAY. Panelled onionskin. Four panel onionskin. Transparent clear base. Two panels of green on white, two of pink on yellow. One melt flat spot. Germany, circa 1870-1915. 9/16". Mint (-) (9.0). Price: $22. CyberAuction #499, Lot #11.

2863. END-OF-DAY. Panelled onionskir. Four-panel onionskin. Transparent clear base. Opaque white core. Two panels of green on yellow, two panels of blue. Small flake, a few tiny subsurface moons. Germany, circa 1870-1915. 25/32". Near Mint (8.4). Price: $21. CyberAuction #406, Lot #11.

2864. END-OF-DAY. Panelled onionskin. Four-panel onionskin. Two panels of blue on white, two of pink on yellow. Overall tiny subsurface moons. Germany, circa 1870-1915. 1-1/16". Good (7.3). Price: $21. CyberAuction #407, Lot #13.

2865. END-OF-DAY. Panelled onionskin. Four-panel onionskin. Transparent clear base. Opaque yellow core. Two pink panels and two green panels. Overall tiny and small chips and subsurface moons. Germany, circa 1870-1915. 1-13/16". Good (7.3). Price: $21. CyberAuction #497, Lot #26.

2866. END-OF-DAY. Panelled onionskin. Four panel onionskin. Transparent clear base. Opaque white core. Pink skin. Two blue panels on the pink. Some very tiny subsurface moons. Germany, circa 1870-1915. 23/32". Near Mint (8.6). Price: $21. CyberAuction #505, Lot #13.

2867. END-OF-DAY. Panelled onionskin. Four panel onionskin. Transparent clear base. White core. Two pink panels and two green panels. Several very tiny chips. Germany, circa 1870-1915. 13/16". Near Mint (8.6). Price: $20. CyberAuction #372, Lot #13.

2868. END-OF-DAY. Panelled onionskin. Four panel onionskin. Transparent clear base. Two panels of blue on white, two of pink on yellow. Two tiny flakes. Germany, circa 1870-1915. 9/16". Near Mint (8.6). Price: $20. CyberAuction #477, Lot #51.

2869. END-OF-DAY. Panelled onionskin. Four panel onionskin. Transparent clear base. Two panels of green on white, two of pink on yellow. One melt flat spot. Germany, circa 1870-1915. 9/16". Mint(-) (9.0). Price: $20. CyberAuction #481, Lot #40.

2870. END-OF-DAY. Panelled onionskin. Four panel. Transparent clear base. Core is overall white, yellow and green. Two narrow panels of red. A couple of pits. One very tiny subsurface moon. Germany, circa 1870-1915. 5/8". Near Mint(+) (8.8). Price: $19. CyberAuction #424, Lot #49.

2871. END-OF-DAY. Panelled onionskin. Four panel onionskin. Transparent clear base. Two panels are pink on white, two are green on yellow. Slightly oval. Cold roll lines and tiny rub spot. Germany, circa 1870-1915. 9/16". Near Mint(+) (8.9). Price: $19. CyberAuction #481, Lot #42.

2872. END-OF-DAY. Panelled onionskin. Four-panel onionskin. Transparent clear base. White core with lots of clear spaces. Two wide panels of light green, one narrow panel of pink, one narrow panel of pink and blue. Has a small chip. Germany, circa 1870-1915. 11/16". Near Mint (8.3). Price: $17. CyberAuction #331, Lot #8.

2873. END-OF-DAY. Panelled onionskin. Four-panel onionskin. Transparent clear base. Opaque white subsurface layer. Two panels of blue and two of red. Germany, circa 1870-1915. One tiny subsurface moon. 9/16". Near Mint(+) (8.7). Price: $17. CyberAuction #418, Lot #1.

2874. END-OF-DAY. Panelled onionskin. Four-panel onionskin. Transparent clear base. Two blue panels and two pink panels. A couple of tiny chips and pinpricks. Germany, circa 1870-1915. 23/32". Near Mint(-) (8.2). Price: $17. CyberAuction #427, Lot #39.

2875. END-OF-DAY. Panelled onionskin. Four panel onionskin. Transparent clear base. Two pink on yellow panels, two blue on white panels. Two tiny chips. Germany, circa 1870-1915. 21/32". Near Mint(+) (8.8). Price: $17. CyberAuction #497, Lot #53.

2876. END-OF-DAY. Panelled onionskin. Peewee. Transparent clear base. White subsurface layer. Two pink panels, two blue panels. Overall haze. Germany, circa 1870-1915. 1/2". Near Mint(-) (8.1). Price: $15. CyberAuction #403, Lot #1.

2877. END-OF-DAY. Panelled onionskin. Four panel onionskin. Transparent clear base. Opaque yellow core. Two pink panels and two green panels. Three small chips. Germany, circa 1870-1915. 27/32". Near Mint(-) (8.2). Price: $15. CyberAuction #476, Lot #39.

2878. END-OF-DAY. Panelled onionskin. Four-panel onionskin. Transparent clear base. White core. Two pink panels, two blue panels. Flat spot and some tiny scratching. Germany, circa 1870-1915. 19/32". Near Mint(+) (8.9). Price: $15. CyberAuction #489, Lot #20.

2879. END-OF-DAY. Panelled onionskin. Four-panel onionskin. Transparent clear base. White core. Two pink panels, two blue panels. Flat spot and some tiny scratching. Germany, circa 1870-1915. 19/32". Near Mint(+) (8.9). Price: $15. CyberAuction #506, Lot #18.

2880. END-OF-DAY. Panelled onionskin. Transparent clear base. White subsurface layer with some clear spaces. Two pink panels and two blue panels. Subsurface moon, small chip. Germany, circa 1870-1915. 9/16". Near Mint (8.3). Price: $14. CyberAuction #481, Lot #10.

2881. END-OF-DAY. Panelled onionskin. Four panel onionskin. Transparent clear base. Opaque white subsurface layer. Two green panels, two blue panels. A couple of pits and a couple of tiny sparkles. Germany, circa 1870-1915. 9/16". Near Mint (8.6). Price: $13. CyberAuction #485, Lot #10.

2882. END-OF-DAY. Panelled onionskin. Probably English. Four-panel onionskin. Transparent clear base. Yellow core. Two wide panels of bright orange/red, two narrow panels of green. Fracture, small subsurface moons, some tiny chips. Germany, circa 1870-1915. 5/8". Good (7.6). Price: $12. CyberAuction #460, Lot #54.

2883. END-OF-DAY. Panelled onionskin. Transparent clear base. Subsurface layer of two bright green panels and two bright light green panels. Overall fractures. Pretty marble though. England, possibly Germany, circa 1870-1915. 25/32". Near Mint(-) (8.0). Price: $12. CyberAuction #476, Lot #14.

2884. END-OF-DAY. Panelled onionskin. Four-panel onionskin. Transparent clear base. Two panels of blue on white, two of pink on yellow. Large blown air hole, several tiny chips. Germany, circa 1870-1915. 25/32". Good(+) (7.7). Price: $12. CyberAuction #496, Lot #12.

2885. END-OF-DAY. Panelled onionskin. Four-panel onionskin. Transparent clear base. Opaque white core. Two narrow blue panels, two wide pink panels. The pink panels are lobed. Some pits. Germany, circa 1870-1915. 21/32". Near Mint (8.6). Price: $12. CyberAuction #507, Lot #38.

2886. END-OF-DAY. Panelled onionskin. Four panel onionskin. Transparent clear base. Opaque white core. Two pink panels and two light blue panels. Overall haze. Germany, circa 1870-1915. 11/16". Near Mint(-) (8.0). Price: $11. CyberAuction #502, Lot #16.

2887. END-OF-DAY. Panelled onionskin. Probably English. Four-panel onionskin. Transparent clear base. Yellow core. Two wide panels of bright orange/red, two narrow panels of green. Fracture, small subsurface moons, some tiny chips. Germany, circa 1870-1915. 5/8". Good (7.6). Price: $10. CyberAuction #409, Lot #5.

2888. END-OF-DAY. Panelled onionskin. Four-panel onionskin. Transparent clear base. Two panels of blue on white, two of pink on yellow. Large blown air hole, several tiny chips. Germany, circa 1870-1915. 25/32". Good(+) (7.7). Price: $10. CyberAuction #409, Lot #7.

2889. END-OF-DAY. Panelled onionskin. Four-panel onionskin. Transparent clear base. Opaque white core. Two orange panels, one blue panel, one light green panel. Several fractures. Germany, circa 1870-1915. 21/32". Good (7.3). Price: $10. CyberAuction #431, Lot #23.

2890. END-OF-DAY. Panelled onionskin. Four-panel onionskin. Transparent clear base. Two panels of blue on white, two of pink on yellow. Large blown air hole, several tiny chips. Germany, circa 1870-1915. 25/32". Good(+) (7.7). Price: $10. CyberAuction #474, Lot #19.

2891. END-OF-DAY. Panelled onionskin. Transparent clear base. White core. Two narrow blue panels, two wide pink ones. Overall haziness. Germany, circa 1870-1915. 9/16". Good (7.6). Price: $9. CyberAuction #355, Lot #24.

2892. END-OF-DAY. Panelled onionskin. Transparent clear base. White core. Two narrow blue panels, two wide pink ones. Overall haziness. Germany, circa 1870-1915. 9/16". Good (7.6). Price: $9. CyberAuction #375, Lot #28.

2893. END-OF-DAY. Panelled onionskin. Transparent clear base. Subsurface layer of color. Two panels of bright green, two of orange. No base layer or white or yellow under it. Several large fractures. England, possibly Germany, circa 1870-1915. 25/32". Good(+) (7.9). Price: $9. CyberAuction #472, Lot #13.

2894. END-OF-DAY. Panelled onionskin. Transparent clear base. White core. Two narrow blue panels, two wide pink ones. Overall haziness. Germany, circa 1870-1915. 9/16". Good (7.6). Price: $9. CyberAuction #486, Lot #31.

2895. END-OF-DAY. Panelled onionskin. Probably English. Four-panel onionskin. Transparent clear base. Yellow core. Two wide panels of bright orange/red, two narrow panels of green. Fracture, small subsurface moons, some tiny chips. Germany, circa 1870-1915. 5/8". Good (7.6). Price: $8. CyberAuction #437, Lot #41.

2896. END-OF-DAY. Panelled onionskin. Four-panel onionskin. Transparent clear base. Two panels of blue on white, two of pink on yellow. Large blown air hole, several tiny chips. Germany, circa 1870-1915. 25/32". Good(+) (7.7). Price: $8. CyberAuction #437, Lot #50.

2897. END-OF-DAY. Panelled onionskin. Four panel onionskin. Transparent clear base. Opaque white subsurface layer. Two blue panels, two green panels. Small chip, some light haze. Germany, circa 1870-1915. 9/16". Good(+) (7.8). Price: $7. CyberAuction #463, Lot #16.

2898. END-OF-DAY. Panelled onionskin. Four-panel onionskin. Transparent clear base. Opaque yellow subsurface layer. Two panels of pink and two of green. Germany, circa 1870-1915. 11/16". Polished. Price: $6. CyberAuction #388, Lot #12.

2899. END-OF-DAY. Panelled onionskin. Transparent clear base. Opaque white subsurface layer. Two light blue panels, one pink panel, one no-color panel. Tiny chips and tiny subsurface moons. Germany, circa 1870-1915. 9/16". Good (7.5). Price: $6. CyberAuction #463, Lot #7.

2900. END-OF-DAY. Ribbon onionskin. Very rare marble. Double ribbon onionskin. Transparent clear base. Two panels. Each is white with spots of blue on it. A pink spot on one of them. One melt spot. Superb and very rare. Germany, circa 1870-1915. 21/32". Mint(-) (9.1). Price: $250. CyberAuction #491, Lot #50.

2901. END-OF-DAY. Ribbon onionskin. Rare marble. Transparent clear base. Core is stretched bands and splotches of opaque forest green. Slightly flattened on two sides to create a ribbon. On the unflattened sides are stretches spots of light green. Exceptional. Tiny melt chip. England, possibly Germany, circa 1870-1915. 25/32". Mint(-) (9.1). Price: $230. CyberAuction #498, Lot #69.

2902. END-OF-DAY. Ribbon onionskin. Rare example. Transparent clear base. Opaque white core in the form of a fat single ribbon. Pink on one side, a little yellow on the other. Very interesting. Germany, circa 1870-1915. 23/32". Mint (9.8). Price: $150. CyberAuction #495, Lot #52.

2903. END-OF-DAY. Ribbon onionskin. Very rare marble. Double ribbon onionskin. Transparent clear base. Core is two bands. Each is stretched pink on yellow. Superb!!! One pinprick. Germany, circa 1870-1915. 5/8". Mint(-) (9.2). Price: $100. CyberAuction #498, Lot #52.

2904. LUTZ. Banded. Rare marble, in outstanding condition. Very dark purple transparent base (maglite). Four gray bands and two white edged lutz bands. Dead Mint!!!! Superb. Germany, circa 1870-1915. 11/16". Mint (9.9). Price: $430. CyberAuction #336, Lot #57.

2905. LUTZ. Banded. Large banded lutz, in great shape. Transparent clear base. Four white-edged lutz bands. Four light blue bands. Small sparkle and one tiny scratched spot. Not wet, but not damaged. Germany, circa 1870-1915. 1-3/16". Mint(-) (9.0). Price: $410. CyberAuction #487, Lot #57.

2906. LUTZ. Banded. Opaque black base. Four blue bands, two white edged lutz bands. One tiny area of a couple of melt bubbles. Superb example, in great shape. Hard to find. Germany, circa 1870-1915. 19/32". Mint (9.7). Price: $325. CyberAuction #330, Lot #60.

2907. LUTZ. Banded. Very nice shooter. Semi-opaque white base. Four bright red bands, two white-edged lutz bands. Buffed, some minor damage remains. Germany, circa 1870-1915. 7/8". Price: $260. CyberAuction #490, Lot #43.

2908. LUTZ. Banded. Transparent clear base. Four orange/red bands and two white-edged lutz bands. Germany, circa 1870-1915. 1/2". Mint (9.9). Price: $210. CyberAuction #428, Lot #59.

2909. LUTZ. Banded. Large shooter. Transparent olive yellow base. Two white-edged lutz bands. Four other white bands. Two subsurface moons, some light haze. Still, views very well. Germany, circa 1870-1915. 1-1/16". Good(+) (7.9). Price: $186. CyberAuction #441, Lot #59.

2910. LUTZ. Banded. Large shooter. Transparent olive yellow base. Two white-edged lutz bands. Four other white bands. Two subsurface moons, some light haze. Still, views very well. Germany, circa 1870-1915. 1-1/16". Good(+) (7.9). Price: $180. CyberAuction #383, Lot #45.

2911. LUTZ. Banded. Opaque black core. Four light blue bands and two white edged lutz bands on it. Clear outer layer. Marble has been polished, but bottom pontil is intact. 13/16". Price: $165. CyberAuction #386, Lot #45.

2912. LUTZ. Banded. Opaque black core. Four light blue bands and two white edged lutz bands on it. Clear outer layer. Marble has been polished, but bottom pontil is intact. 13/16". Price: $165. CyberAuction #478, Lot #36.

2913. LUTZ. Banded. Transparent clear base. Four red bands, two white-edged lutz bands. Small chip, very tiny chip, some sparkles and surface wear. Nice sized shooter. Germany, circa 1870-1915. 1". Near Mint (8.4). Price: $160. CyberAuction #471, Lot #53.

2914. LUTZ. Banded. Opaque black core. Four light blue bands, two white-edged lutz bands. Clear outer casing. Buffed, pontils and some pits remain. Germany, circa 1870-1915. 21/32". Price: $160. CyberAuction #490, Lot #39.

2915. LUTZ. Banded. Transparent clear base. Two white-edged lutz bands, four yellow bands. Two pits. Germany, circa 1870-1915. 9/16". Near Mint(+) (8.9). Price: $160. CyberAuction #502, Lot #66.

2916. LUTZ. Banded. Transparent clear base. Four light blue bands. Two white-edged lutz bands. One tiny melt spot, one thin line of melted glass. Germany, circa 1870-1915. 25/32". Mint(-) (9.1). Price: $150. CyberAuction #462, Lot #57.

2917. LUTZ. Banded. Transparent clear base. Four light blue bands, two white-edged lutz bands. Gorgeous. Germany, circa 1870-1915. 21/32". Mint (9.7). Price: $140. CyberAuction #444, Lot #57.

2918. LUTZ. Banded. Opaque black core. Four light blue bands and two white edged lutz bands on it. Clear outer layer. Marble has been polished, but bottom pontil is intact. 13/16". Price: $130. CyberAuction #449, Lot #50.

2919. LUTZ. Banded. Transparent clear base. Four blue bands. Two white edged lutz bands. One tiny flake. Germany, circa 1870-1915. 13/16". Near Mint(+) (8.9). Price: $130. CyberAuction #482, Lot #40.

2920. LUTZ. Banded. Transparent clear base. Four light blue bands, two white-edged lutz bands. Lightly buffed, pontils are still intact, subsurface moon remains. Germany, circa 1870-1915. 7/8". Price: $125. CyberAuction #371, Lot #38.

2921. LUTZ. Banded. Transparent clear base. Four light blue bands, two white-edged lutz bands. Gorgeous. Germany, circa 1870-1915. 21/32". Mint (9.7). Price: $125. CyberAuction #382, Lot #60.

2922. LUTZ. Banded. Transparent clear base. Four light blue bands, two white-edged lutz bands. Super marble, in great shape. Germany, circa 1870-1915. 5/8". Mint (9.9). Price: $120. CyberAuction #400, Lot #44.

2923. LUTZ. Banded. Transparent clear base. Four blue bands. Two white edged lutz bands. One tiny flake. Germany, circa 1870-1915. 13/16". Near Mint(+) (8.9). Price: $120. CyberAuction #449, Lot #59.

2924. LUTZ. Banded. Transparent aqua blue base. Two white-edged lutz bands. Very lightly buffed, some minor damage remains. Pontils are intact. Germany, circa 1870-1915. 25/32". Price: $110. CyberAuction #341, Lot #37.

2925. LUTZ. Banded. Transparent clear base. Two white-edged lutz bands, four yellow bands. One tiny pit near the top pontil. Superb marble. Germany, circa 1870-1915. 11/16". Mint(-) (9.2). Price: $110. CyberAuction #396, Lot #58.

2926. LUTZ. Banded. Transparent clear base. Four red bands, two white-edged lutz bands. Small flake, tiny chips, some sparkles and surface wear. Nice sized shooter. Germany, circa 1870-1915. 15/16". Near Mint(-) (8.0). Price: $101. CyberAuction #489, Lot #48.

2927. LUTZ. Banded. Transparent clear base. Four light blue bands, two white edged lutz bands. One small flake, some scratching. Germany, circa 1870-1915. 11/16". Near Mint (8.6). Price: $100. CyberAuction #359, Lot #58.

2928. LUTZ. Banded. Transparent clear base. Four blue bands. Two white edged lutz bands. One tiny flake. Germany, circa 1870-1915. 13/16". Near Mint(+) (8.9). Price: $100. CyberAuction #392, Lot #57.

2929. LUTZ. Banded. Large. Transparent clear base. Four orange/red bands, two white-edged lutz bands. A couple of subsurface moons and some fractures. Germany, circa 1870-1915. 1-5/16". Good(+) (7.7). Price: $96. CyberAuction #500, Lot #47.

2930. LUTZ. Banded. Transparent clear base. Four light blue bands, two white-edged lutz bands. Lightly buffed, pontils are still intact, subsurface moon remains. Germany, circa 1870-1915. 7/8". Price: $95. CyberAuction #335, Lot #44.

2931. LUTZ. Banded. Transparent clear base. Four yellow bands, two white-edged lutz bands. Price: $. CyberAuction #443, Lot #58.

2932. LUTZ. Banded. Semi-opaque blue base. Four narrow white bands, two white-edged lutz bands. Buffed, pontils and damage remain. Germany, circa 1870-1915. 23/32". Price: $85. CyberAuction #374, Lot #51.

2933. LUTZ. Banded. Transparent clear base. Four orange bands, two white edged lutz bands. Two tiny flakes. Germany, circa 1870-1915. 11/16". Near Mint(+) (8.8). Price: $80. CyberAuction #403, Lot #54.

2934. LUTZ. Banded. Transparent clear base. Four blue bands, two white-edged lutz bands. Several tiny chips and haziness. Germany, circa 1870-1915. 7/8". Good (7.5). Price: $80. CyberAuction #440, Lot #49.

2935. LUTZ. Banded. Transparent clear base. Four blue bands, two white-edged lutz bands. Several tiny chips and haziness. Germany, circa 1870-1915. 7/8". Good (7.5). Price: $75. CyberAuction #401, Lot #52.

2936. LUTZ. Banded. Opaque black base. Four white bands. Two white edged lutz bands. Casing of clear. Overall small chips. Could be polished. Germany, circa 1870-1915. 11/16". Good (7.4). Price: $70. CyberAuction #358, Lot #55.

2937. LUTZ. Banded. Transparent clear base. Four yellow bands. Two white-edged lutz bands. Tiny subsurface moon and some scratching. Germany, circa 1870-1915. 21/32". Near Mint(+) (8.8). Price: $70. CyberAuction #388, Lot #58.

2938. LUTZ. Banded. Transparent banded lutz. Gorgeous amber brown base. Four white bands, two white-edged lutz bands. Small chip, tiny chip and a couple of small tiny subsurface moons. Very pretty though. Germany, circa 1870-1915. 11/16". Near Mint(-) (8.1). Price: $65. CyberAuction #394, Lot #43.

2939. LUTZ. Banded. Transparent clear base. Four yellow bands, two white-edged lutz bands. Price: $. CyberAuction #395, Lot #49.

2940. LUTZ. Banded. Light green base. Four yellow bands, two white-edged lutz bands. Some pitting and pinpricks. Germany, circa 1870-1195. 21/32". Good(+) (7.9). Price: $65. CyberAuction #419, Lot #60.

2941. LUTZ. Banded. Transparent clear base. Four light green bands. Two white-edged lutz bands. One melt spot, some tiny chips and pits. Germany, circa 1870-1915. 11/16". Near Mint (8.4). Price: $65. CyberAuction #440, Lot #54.

2942. LUTZ. Banded. Transparent clear base. Four orange/red bands and two white-edged lutz bands. Several tiny flakes. Germany, circa 1870-1915. 19/32". Near Mint(-) (8.0). Price: $60. CyberAuction #344, Lot #42.

2943. LUTZ. Banded. Large banded lutz. Transparent clear base. Four blue bands and two white-edged lutz bands. Heavily polished and there was a large elongated air hole in one band that is at the surface now. Germany, circa 1870-1915. 1-7/16". Polished. Price: $60. CyberAuction #391, Lot #30.

2944. LUTZ. Banded. Transparent clear base. Four orange bands, two white-edged lutz bands. Two tiny flakes, several tiny pits. Germany, circa 1870-1915. 5/8". Near Mint(-) (8.0). Price: $60. CyberAuction #397, Lot #25.

2945. LUTZ. Banded. Transparent banded lutz. Gorgeous amber brown base. Four white bands, two white-edged lutz bands. Small chip, tiny chip and a couple of small and tiny subsurface moons. Very pretty though. Germany, circa 1870-1915. 11/16". Near Mint(-) (8.1). Price: $60. CyberAuction #422, Lot #55.

2946. LUTZ. Banded. Opaque black base. Four blue bands, two white-edged lutz bands. Transparent clear outer layer. Flake off the top, some pitting and sparkles. Germany, circa 1870-1915. 11/16". Good (7.6). Price: $60. CyberAuction #430, Lot #58.

2947. LUTZ. Banded. Opaque black base. Four white bands, two white-edged lutz bands. Clear overglaze. Some small chips. Germany, circa 1870-1915. 5/8". Good(+) (7.9). Price: $60. CyberAuction #434, Lot #53.

2948. LUTZ. Banded. Transparent clear base. Four blue bands. Two white-edged lutz bands. Polished. Germany, circa 1870-1915. 17/32". Price: $60. CyberAuction #469, Lot #43.

2949. LUTZ. Banded. Transparent clear base. Four light blue bands. Two white bands and two white-edged lutz bands. Some tiny chips and pits. Germany, circa 1870-1915. 21/32". Good(+) (7.9). Price: $55. CyberAuction #334, Lot #25.

2950. LUTZ. Banded. Opaque black base. Four blue bands, two white-edged lutz bands. Transparent clear outer layer. Flake off the top, some pitting and sparkles. Germany, circa 1870-1915. 11/16". Good (7.6). Price: $55. CyberAuction #397, Lot #6.

2951. LUTZ. Banded. Transparent clear base. Four light green bands. Two white-edged lutz bands. One melt spot, some tiny chips and pits. Germany, circa 1870-1915. 11/16". Near Mint (8.4). Price: $50. CyberAuction #402, Lot #11.

2952. LUTZ. Banded. Transparent clear base. Four light blue bands, two white-edged lutz bands. Small chip, some tiny chips. Germany, circa 1870-1915. 11/16". Near Mint(+) (8.0). Price: $50. CyberAuction #446, Lot #60.

2953. LUTZ. Banded. Transparent clear base. Four blue bands, two sets of white edged lutz bands. Some tiny chips and overall pits. Germany, circa 1870-1915. 25/32". Near Mint(-) (8.0). Price: $50. CyberAuction #454, Lot #4.
2954. LUTZ. Banded. Transparent clear base. Two white-edged lutz bands, four yellow bands. Small chip, several tiny chips. Germany, circa 1870-1915. 11/16". Near Mint(-) (8.0). Price: $49. CyberAuction #430, Lot #22.
2955. LUTZ. Banded. Opaque black base. Four white bands, two white-edged lutz bands. Clear overglaze. Some small chips. Germany, circa 1870-1915. 5/8". Good(+) (7.9). Price: $48. CyberAuction #405, Lot #46.
2956. LUTZ. Banded. Transparent clear base. Four blue bands, two sets of white edged lutz bands. Some tiny chips and overall pits. Germany, circa 1870-1915. 25/32". Near Mint(-) (8.0). Price: $42. CyberAuction #411, Lot #60.
2957. LUTZ. Banded. Transparent clear base. Four light blue bands, two white edged lutz bands. Pitting. Germany, circa 1870-1915. 15/32". Near Mint (8.4). Price: $42. CyberAuction #489, Lot #17.
2958. LUTZ. Banded. Transparent clear base. Two white-edged lutz bands, four yellow bands. Small chip, several tiny chips. Germany, circa 1870-1915. 11/16". Near Mint(-) (8.0). Price: $40. CyberAuction #397, Lot #17.
2959. LUTZ. Banded. Transparent clear base. Four light blue bands, two white-edged lutz bands. Small chip, some tiny chips. Germany, circa 1870-1915. 11/16". Near Mint(+) (8.0). Price: $40. CyberAuction #405, Lot #52.
2960. LUTZ. Banded. Transparent clear base. Four light blue bands, two white-edged lutz bands. Chipping. Germany, circa 1870-1915. 13/16". Good(-) (7.1). Price: $38. CyberAuction #401, Lot #12.
2961. LUTZ. Banded. Transparent clear base. Four yellow bands, two white-edged lutz bands. Overall pitting and haze. Germany, circa 1870-1915. 21/32". Good(+) (7.7). Price: $34. CyberAuction #468, Lot #45.
2962. LUTZ. Banded. Very light transparent blue base. Four white base. Two white-edged lutz bands. Overall haziness and some tiny subsurface moons. Germany, circa 1870-1915. 25/32". Good (7.5). Price: $32. CyberAuction #439, Lot #29.
2963. LUTZ. Banded. Transparent clear base. Four light blue bands, two white-edged bands. Flakes and subsurface moons. Germany, circa 1870-1915. 11/16". Good (7.4). Price: $30. CyberAuction #411, Lot #16.
2964. LUTZ. Banded. Error marble. Transparent clear base. Three red bands, one white-edged lutz band. One red band and one lutz band missing. Overall tiny pits and very tiny chips. Germany, circa 1870-1915. 5/8". Good(+) (7.8). Price: $22. CyberAuction #497, Lot #15.
2965. LUTZ. Cane piece. Small cane piece from an onionskin lutz. Shaped like a teardrop.15/32" x 5/8". Mint (9.5). Price: $50. CyberAuction #366, Lot #10.
2966. LUTZ. End of day onionskin. One of the rarest lutzes I have ever seen. Huge. Transparent clear base. Opaque white core. Completely covered in lutz and stretched to create an onionskin effect. Some heavy bands, some stretched splotches. Amazing marble. Extremely rare!!!!! A tiny subsurface moon and two tiny sparkles bring it below Mint. But, it views much better than that. Surface is pristine, except for those three defects. Unbelievable marble. Germany, circa 1870-1915. 1-13/16". Near Mint(+) (8.9). Price: $3275. CyberAuction #500, Lot #60.
2967. LUTZ. End of day onionskin. Outstanding example! Two-panel onionskin. Transparent clear base. Core is stretched bands of semi-opaque white with loads of clear spaces. Transparent pink on one side and transparent blue on the other. One side is completely covered by lutz, the other side has a number of heavy bands. Not a lot of shimmering, but a rare example. Germany, circa 1870-1915. 7/8". Mint (9.8). Price: $470. CyberAuction #430, Lot #2.
2968. LUTZ. End of day onionskin. Outstanding example! Two-panel onionskin. Transparent clear base. Core is stretched bands of semi-opaque white with loads of clear spaces. Transparent pink on one side and transparent blue on the other. One side is completely covered by lutz, the other side has a number of heavy bands. Not a lot of shimmering, but a rare example. Germany, circa 1870-1915. 7/8". Mint (9.8). Price: $455. CyberAuction #398, Lot #36.
2969. LUTZ. End of day onionskin. Superb example. Transparent clear base. Subsurface layer of translucent green and white. Exceptional coating of lutz on the color. Surface has one tiny melt flat spot, else it is pristine. Stunning!!!! Germany, circa 1870-1915. 11/16". Mint (9.4). Price: $360. CyberAuction #357, Lot #60.
2970. LUTZ. End of day onionskin. Transparent clear base. Opaque white subsurface layer. Skin of transparent green. Nice layer of lutz. This is a beauty. Stunning. Germany, circa 1870-1915. 21/32". Mint (9.9). Price: $265. CyberAuction #342, Lot #57.
2971. LUTZ. End of day onionskin. Super example. Transparent clear base. Opaque white subsurface layer. Pink skin on that with a little blue. Covered by lutz bands. A couple of pinpricks. Germany, circa 1870-1915. 3/4". Mint(-) (9.0). Price: $235. CyberAuction #495, Lot #38.
2972. LUTZ. End of day onionskin. Transparent clear base. Subsurface layer of blue skin on white. Nice bands of heavy lutz on it. Exceptional and stunning example. Germany, circa 1870-1915. 9/16". Mint (9.9). Price: $225. CyberAuction #482, Lot #45.
2973. LUTZ. End of day onionskin. Transparent clear base. Subsurface layer of white and green, with loads of lutz. Gorgeous example. One tiny melt spot. Germany, circa 1870-1915. 21/32". Mint (9.5). Price: $220. CyberAuction #441, Lot #55.
2974. LUTZ. End of day onionskin. Transparent clear base. Opaque yellow skin. Gorgeous lutz layer. One small melt spot, one tiny flake. Germany, circa 1870-1915. 11/16". Near Mint(+) (8.8). Price: $210. CyberAuction #360, Lot #58.
2975. LUTZ. End of day onionskin. Transparent clear base. Subsurface layer of white and green, with loads of lutz. Gorgeous example. One tiny melt spot. Germany, circa 1870-1915. 21/32". Mint (9.5). Price: $210. CyberAuction #390, Lot #45.
2976. LUTZ. End of day onionskin. Nice yellow core, with some clear spaces. Some bands of lutz and an overall light sprinkling. 21/32". Mint (9.7). Price: $200. CyberAuction #422, Lot #1.
2977. LUTZ. End of day onionskin. Gorgeous onionskin lutz. Transparent clear base. Opaque white subsurface layer with bands of green and pink. There are several nice bands of lutz. A beauty. Germany, circa 1870-1915. 9/16". Mint (9.9). Price: $200. CyberAuction #422, Lot #52.
2978. LUTZ. End of day onionskin. Nice yellow core, with some clear spaces. Some bands of lutz and an overall light sprinkling. 21/32". Mint (9.7). Price: $195. CyberAuction #383, Lot #11.
2979. LUTZ. End of day onionskin. Gorgeous onionskin lutz. Transparent clear base. Opaque white subsurface layer with bands of green and pink. There are several nice bands of lutz. A beauty. Germany, circa 1870-1915. 9/16". Mint (9.9). Price: $195. CyberAuction #384, Lot #60.
2980. LUTZ. End of day onionskin. Transparent clear base. Subsurface layer of white and green, with loads of lutz. Gorgeous example. One tiny melt spot. Germany, circa 1870-1915. 21/32". Mint (9.5). Price: $185. CyberAuction #339, Lot #57.
2981. LUTZ. End of day onionskin. Transparent clear base. Opaque yellow core with some blue streaks. Excellent layer of heavy lutz. Two small chips, some pinpricking. Germany, circa 1870-1915. 25/32". Near Mint (8.3). Price: $170. CyberAuction #417, Lot #59.
2982. LUTZ. End of day onionskin. Transparent clear base. Opaque yellow core with some blue streaks. Excellent layer of heavy lutz. Two small chips, some pinpricking. Germany, circa 1870-1915. 25/32". Near Mint (8.3). Price: $170. CyberAuction #478, Lot #43.
2983. LUTZ. End of day onionskin. Shooter. Transparent clear base. Onionskin subsurface layer is green and white. Nice bands of lutz. A couple of small flakes and some haze. Germany, circa 1870-1915. 25/32". Near Mint(-) (8.0). Price: $160. CyberAuction #382, Lot #46.
2984. LUTZ. End of day onionskin. Shooter. Transparent clear base. Onionskin subsurface layer is green and white. Nice bands of lutz. A couple of small flakes and some haze. Germany, circa 1870-1915. 25/32". Near Mint(-) (8.0). Price: $160. CyberAuction #440, Lot #21.
2985. LUTZ. End of day onionskin. Nice yellow core, with some clear spaces. Some bands of lutz and an overall light sprinkling. 21/32". Mint (9.7). Price: $160. CyberAuction #456, Lot #15.
2986. LUTZ. End of day onionskin. Shooter. Transparent clear base. Onionskin subsurface layer is green and white. Nice bands of lutz. A couple of small flakes and some haze. Germany, circa 1870-1915. 25/32". Near Mint(-) (8.0). Price: $160. CyberAuction #460, Lot #23.
2987. LUTZ. End of day onionskin. Hard to find four-panel onionskin lutz. Transparent clear base. Two panels of yellow, two of white. Nice lutz on the core. One small subsurface moon. Germany, circa 1870-1915. 19/32". Near Mint (8.6). Price: $150. CyberAuction #355, Lot #57.
2988. LUTZ. End of day onionskin. Some collectors refer to this type as Mist. I've categorized it as a "floater" onionskin. Transparent clear base. Subsurface layer of transparent green on translucent white. Then a layer of clear. Floating on this layer of clear is a heavy coating of lutz bands. Then a clear casing. This one is unusual because it is larger than you usually find. Two small chips, some pitting and several fractures. 7/8". Near Mint(-) (8.0). Price: $120. CyberAuction #445, Lot #58.
2989. LUTZ. End of day onionskin. Transparent clear base. Subsurface layer of opaque yellow, with pink skin, covered by super lutz. Four very tiny chips. Germany, circa 1870-1915. 5/8". Near Mint (8.5). Price: $120. CyberAuction #499, Lot #45.
2990. LUTZ. End of day onionskin. Shooter. Transparent clear base. Onionskin subsurface layer is green and white. Nice bands of lutz. A couple of small flakes and some haze. Germany, circa 1870-1915. 25/32". Near Mint(-) (8.0). Price: $120. CyberAuction #507, Lot #55.
2991. LUTZ. End of day onionskin. Transparent clear base. Subsurface layer of opaque yellow, with pink skin, covered by super lutz. Four very tiny chips. Germany, circa 1870-1915. 5/8". Near Mint (8.5). Price: $90. CyberAuction #474, Lot #42.
2992. LUTZ. End of day onionskin. Hard to find four-panel onionskin lutz. Transparent clear base. Two panels of yellow, two of white. Nice lutz on the core. One small subsurface moon. Germany, circa 1870-1915. 19/32". Near Mint (8.6). Price: $80. CyberAuction #443, Lot #12.
2993. LUTZ. End of day onionskin. Transparent clear base. Subsurface layer of blue skin on white. Nice bands of heavy lutz on it. Two small chips, some pitting. Germany, circa 1870-1915. 5/8". Near Mint(-) (8.0). Price: $80. CyberAuction #447, Lot #59.
2994. LUTZ. End of day onionskin. Transparent clear base. Subsurface layer of white and green. Nice sprinkling of lutz. Surface has been lightly buffed. Pontils remain, as well as some minor damage. Germany, circa 1870-1915. 21/32". Price: $75. CyberAuction #387, Lot #59.
2995. LUTZ. End of day onionskin. Transparent clear base. Subsurface layer of blue skin on white. Nice bands of heavy lutz on it. Two small chips, some pitting. Germany, circa 1870-1915. 5/8". Near Mint(-) (8.0). Price: $75. CyberAuction #412, Lot #41.
2996. LUTZ. End of day onionskin. Four-panel onionskin with loads of lutz. Transparent clear base. Core is two panels of blue on white and two panels of pink on yellow. Nice layer of lutz. Surface has a couple of small chips, some tiny chips and some pits. Germany, circa 1870-1915. 9/16". Good(+) (7.9). Price: $75. CyberAuction #420, Lot #4.
2997. LUTZ. End of day onionskin. Transparent clear base. Subsurface layer of opaque yellow, with pink skin, covered by super lutz. Four very tiny

chips. Germany, circa 1870-1915. 5/8". Near Mint (8.5). Price: $75. CyberAuction #445, Lot #45.

2998. LUTZ. End of day onionskin. Four-panel onionskin with loads of lutz. Transparent clear base. Core is two panels of blue on white and two panels of pink on yellow. Nice layer of lutz. Surface has a couple of small chips, some tiny chips and some pits. Germany, circa 1870-1915. 9/16". Good(+) (7.9). Price: $70. CyberAuction #456, Lot #59.

2999. LUTZ. End of day onionskin. White core. Bands of lutz on the core. Two subsurface moons, pitting, several pinpricks. Germany, circa 1870-1915. 5/8". Near Mint(-) (8.0). Price: $70. CyberAuction #460, Lot #60.

3000. LUTZ. End of day onionskin. Nice onionskin lutz with loads of lutz. Transparent clear base. Subsurface layer is red, white, blue and teal. Covered by a heavy coating of lutz. A number of tiny chips and pits on the surface. Germany, circa 1870-1915. 11/16". Good (7.5). Price: $55. CyberAuction #370, Lot #44.

3001. LUTZ. End of day onionskin. White core. Bands of lutz on the core. Two subsurface moons, pitting, several pinpricks. Germany, circa 1870-1915. 5/8". Near Mint (8.0). Price: $55. CyberAuction #392, Lot #21.

3002. LUTZ. End of day onionskin. White core. Bands of lutz on the core. Two subsurface moons, pitting, several pinpricks. Germany, circa 1870-1915. 5/8". Near Mint (8.0). Price: $55. CyberAuction #440, Lot #7.

3003. LUTZ. End of day onionskin. Onionskin lutz. Transparent clear base. White core. Lutz skin. Pretty marble. Fractures and some tiny chips. Germany, circa 1870-1915. 13/16". Good (7.6). Price: $51. CyberAuction #441, Lot #20.

3004. LUTZ. End of day onionskin. Nice onionskin lutz with loads of lutz. Transparent clear base. Subsurface layer is red, white, blue and teal. Covered by a heavy coating of lutz. A number of tiny chips and pits on the surface. Germany, circa 1870-1915. 11/16". Good (7.5). Price: $41. CyberAuction #444, Lot #50.

3005. LUTZ. End of day onionskin. Yellow onionskin with nice lutz bands. A number of small subsurface moons. Germany, circa 1870-1915. 25/32". Good(+) (7.7). Price: $40. CyberAuction #439, Lot #31.

3006. LUTZ. End of day onionskin. Four-panel onionskin lutz. Transparent clear base. Opaque white core. Two pink panels and two green panels. Overall lutz. Surface is hazy with tiny flakes and a couple of chips. Germany, circa 1870-1915. 3/4". Good(-) (7.1). Price: $37. CyberAuction #411, Lot #12.

3007. LUTZ. End of day onionskin. Yellow and white subsurface layer. Some nice lutz bands. Heavily polished. Germany, circa 1870-1915. 21/32". Price: $35. CyberAuction #402, Lot #2.

3008. LUTZ. End of day onionskin. Onionskin lutz. Transparent clear base. White core. Lutz skin. Pretty marble. Fractures and some tiny chips. Germany, circa 1870-1915. 13/16". Good (7.6). Price: $35. CyberAuction #405, Lot #23.

3009. LUTZ. End of day onionskin. Yellow and white subsurface layer. Some nice lutz bands. Heavily polished. Germany, circa 1870-1915. 21/32". Price: $35. CyberAuction #440, Lot #41.

3010. LUTZ. End of day onionskin. Yellow and white subsurface layer. Some nice lutz bands. Heavily polished. Germany, circa 1870-1915. 21/32". Price: $32. CyberAuction #454, Lot #42.

3011. LUTZ. End of day onionskin. Well, half of one. Nice shimmering. Would be useful for a piece of jewelry. 11/16". Price: $10. CyberAuction #481, Lot #2.

3012. LUTZ. Indian. Extremely rare marble. Opaque black base. Two bands of color covering about seventy percent of the surface. Left-hand twist. One band is blue and white, one is red and yellow. There are two half-inch long narrow bands of lutz in the yellow. Very, very rare. Germany, circa 1870-1915. 13/16". Mint (9.7). Price: $1500. CyberAuction #479, Lot #60.

3013. LUTZ. Mist. Rare. Transparent clear base. Subsurface layer of lutz. Beautiful. One tiny sparkle, a couple of pinpricks. Super!!! Germany, circa 1870-1915. 25/32". Mint(-) (9.0). Price: $410. CyberAuction #410, Lot #59.

3014. LUTZ. Mist. Transparent clear base. Opaque black core. Layer of gorgeous lutz floating above the core. Clear outer layer. One small chip. Germany, circa 1870-1915. 21/32". Near Mint (8.5). Price: $270. CyberAuction #413, Lot #51.

3015. LUTZ. Mist. Transparent clear base. White core. Transparent green layer floating above the core. Layer of lutz floating just under the surface. Very hard to find. One small subsurface moon. Germany, circa 1870-1915. 21/32". Near Mint (8.5). Price: $121. CyberAuction #439, Lot #57.

3016. LUTZ. Mist. Hard to find type. Transparent clear base. Opaque white core. Covered by transparent green. Subsurface layer of floating lutz. Gorgeous. Small flake, some tiny chips, some pits. Germany, circa 1870-1915. 25/32". Good (7.6). Price: $115. CyberAuction #440, Lot #58.

3017. LUTZ. Mist. Hard to find type. Transparent clear base. Opaque white core. Covered by transparent green. Subsurface layer of floating lutz. Gorgeous. Small flake, some tiny chips, some pits. Germany, circa 1870-1915. 25/32". Good (7.6). Price: $110. CyberAuction #401, Lot #57.

3018. LUTZ. Mist. Transparent clear base. Opaque white core. Layer of transparent dark green floating above that. Layer of lutz floating above that. Polished, subsurface moon at top. Germany, circa 1870-1915. 5/8". Price: $105. CyberAuction #455, Lot #16.

3019. LUTZ. Mist. Transparent clear base. Opaque white core. Layer of transparent dark green floating above that. Layer of lutz floating above that. Polished. Germany, circa 1870-1915. 5/8". Price: $65. CyberAuction #405, Lot #56.

3020. LUTZ. Ribbon. Rare color. Opaque orange ribbon. Ribbon is edged on either side by a white-edged lutz band. In great shape. Superior example!!!! Germany, circa 1870-1915. 11/16". Mint (9.7). Price: $525. CyberAuction #414, Lot #59.

3021. LUTZ. Ribbon. Nice ribbon lutz. Ribbon is opaque yellow on one side and opaque light blue on the other. Each edge is a white-edged lutz band. In superb shape. Germany, circa 1870-1915. 9/16". Mint (9.9). Price: $405. CyberAuction #354, Lot #60.

3022. LUTZ. Ribbon. Gorgeous ribbon lutz. Ribbon is opaque yellow on one side and opaque light blue on the other. Each edge is a white-edged lutz band. Small scratch and two tiny pits. Germany, circa 1870-1915. 11 16". Mint(-) (9.0). Price: $335. CyberAuction #406, Lot #60.

3023. LUTZ. Ribbon. Gorgeous ribbon lutz. Ribbon is opaque yellow on one side and opaque light blue on the other. Each edge is a white-edged lutz band. Small scratch and two tiny pits. Germany, circa 1870-1915. 11 16". Mint(-) (9.0). Price: $335. CyberAuction #426, Lot #60.

3024. LUTZ. Ribbon. Gorgeous ribbon lutz. Ribbon is opaque yellow on one side and opaque light blue on the other. Each edge is a white-edged lutz band. Small scratch and two tiny pits. Germany, circa 1870-1915. 11 16". Mint(-) (9.0). Price: $335. CyberAuction #466, Lot #44.

3025. LUTZ. Ribbon. Nice ribbon lutz. Ribbon is opaque yellow on one side and opaque light blue on the other. Each edge is a white-edged lutz band. Melt spot and two tiny manufacturing pinpricks, near the bottom pontil. Germany, circa 1870-1915. 19/32"". Mint(-) (9.0). Price: $310. CyberAuction #385, Lot #58.

3026. LUTZ. Ribbon. Nice ribbon lutz. Ribbon is translucent yellow on one side and opaque blue on the other. Each edge is a white-edged lutz band. A couple of pinpricks. Stunning. Germany, circa 1870-1915. 19/32". Mint(-) (9.0). Price: $260. CyberAuction #345, Lot #61.

3027. LUTZ. Ribbon. Rarer large ribbon lutz. Ribbon is light green on one side, yellow on the other. Two white-edged lutz bands on the edges. Transparent clear base. Some overall tiny chips and tiny subsurface moons. Germany, circa 1870-1915. 1-3/16". Good(+) (7.9). Price: $260. CyberAuction #504, Lot #55.

3028. LUTZ. Ribbon. Nice ribbon lutz. Ribbon is translucent yellow on one side and opaque lavender on the other. Each edge is a white-edged lutz band. Tiny melt spot, sparkle and pinprick. Germany, circa 1870-1915 19/32". Near Mint(+) (8.9). Price: $240. CyberAuction #348, Lot #60.

3029. LUTZ. Ribbon. A beauty. Transparent emerald green glass. Opaque white ribbon. Edged by lutz. One tiny pinprick. Not wet, but in great shape. Germany, circa 1870-1915. 9/16". Mint(-) (9.0). Price: $235. CyberAuction #375, Lot #45.

3030. LUTZ. Ribbon. Nice ribbon lutz. Ribbon is opaque yellow on one side and opaque light blue on the other. Each edge is a white-edged lutz band. Several very tiny pits and very tiny chips. Germany, circa 1870-1915 9/16". Near Mint(+) (8.7). Price: $220. CyberAuction #351, Lot #58.

3031. LUTZ. Ribbon. Transparent clear base. Double ribbon. One is bright orange, one is light blue. Edged by one narrow band and one wide band of white edged lutz. Buffed surface. Pontils intact, some damage remains. Germany, circa 1870-1915. 23/32". Price: $220. CyberAuction #387, Lot #43.

3032. LUTZ. Ribbon. Nice ribbon lutz. Ribbon is translucent yellow on one side and opaque lavender on the other. Each edge is a white-edged lutz band. Tiny melt spot, sparkle and pinpricks. Germany, circa 1870-1915. 19/32". Near Mint(+) (8.7). Price: $210. CyberAuction #369, Lot #57.

3033. LUTZ. Ribbon. Single ribbon core. Transparent clear base. Opaque white ribbon. One face is blue, other is red. Edged by two wide white-edged lutz bands. Surface has chips, pits and haziness. Shooter size, though. Germany, circa 1870-1915. 7/8". Good(-) (7.2). Price: $180. CyberAuction #374, Lot #47.

3034. LUTZ. Ribbon. Unusual marble from near an end of the cane. Single opaque white ribbon. Faced on either side by transparent cranberry red. One edge has a wide white-edged lutz band. Other edge has just an extremely thin strand of lutz, no white edging. Two small subsurface moons and some wear. Germany, circa 1870-1915. 21/32". Near Mint(-) (8.1) Price: $160. CyberAuction #454, Lot #41.

3035. LUTZ. Ribbon. Nice ribbon lutz. Ribbon is translucent yellow on one side and opaque lavender on the other. Each edge is a white-edged lutz band. A couple of pinpricks and an annealing fracture. Germany, circa 1870-1915. 5/8". Near Mint(+) (8.7). Price: $135. CyberAuction #444, Lot #60.

3036. LUTZ. Ribbon. Transparent clear base. Transparent cranberry ribbon. Two white edged lutz bands. A number of tiny rough spots and chips. Germany, circa 1870-1915. 13/16". Good(+) (7.9). Price: $110. CyberAuction #404, Lot #8.

3037. LUTZ. Ribbon. Two ribbons. One is baby blue, other is yellow. Edged by white-edged lutz bands. Very lightly buffed, but retains overall pitting. Pontils are still completely intact. Germany, circa 1870-1915. 11/16". Price: $110. CyberAuction #445, Lot #54.

3038. LUTZ. Ribbon. Nice ribbon lutz. Ribbon is opaque yellow on one side and opaque light blue on the other. Each edge is a white-edged lutz band. Some tiny pitting and chipping. Germany, circa 1870-1915. 11/16". Near Mint(-) (8.1). Price: $100. CyberAuction #333, Lot #9.

3039. LUTZ. Ribbon. Unusual marble from near an end of the cane. Single opaque white ribbon. Faced on either side by transparent cranberry red. One edge has a wide white-edged lutz band. Other edge has just an extremely thin strand of lutz, no white edging. Two small subsurface moons and some wear. Germany, circa 1870-1915. 21/32". Near Mint(-) (8.1). Price: $100. CyberAuction #391, Lot #37.

3040. LUTZ. Ribbon. Double ribbon. Yellow and blue. White edged lutz bands. Lots of chips. Needs a good polish. Germany, circa 1870-1915. 11/16". Good(-) (7.0). Price: $46. CyberAuction #361, Lot #53.

3041. M.F. CHRISTENSEN & SON COMPANY. Brick. Very rare. The brick is swirls of oxblood red and white, in dark transparent green. Very rare!!!!

128

two tiny subsurface moons. Stunning shooter. Akron, OH, circa 1912-1917. 29/32". Near Mint(+) (8.8). Price: $600. CyberAuction #330, Lot #55.

3042. M.F. CHRISTENSEN & SON COMPANY. Brick. Exceptional marble of oxblood red and transparent dark green, with some white. Loads of green. Nice "9". Exceptional example. Akron, OH, circa 1912-1917. 11/16". Mint (9.8). Price: $470. CyberAuction #450, Lot #49.

3043. M.F. CHRISTENSEN & SON COMPANY. Brick. Exceptional, large brick. Oxblood red with some mottled black. Nice wide white swirled in. Excellent texture. In pristine condition. Unbelievable example!!!! Akron, OH, circa 1912-1917. 27/32". Mint (9.9). Price: $440. CyberAuction #507, Lot #60.

3044. M.F. CHRISTENSEN & SON COMPANY. Brick. Superior example. Dark brick. Dark oxblood red with swirls of white, black and transparent green. Lots of broad swirling. Has a small fold pontil (?) at one end. In superb condition. Exceptional. Akron, OH, circa 1912-1917. 27/32". Mint (9.8). Price: $260. CyberAuction #336, Lot #58.

3045. M.F. CHRISTENSEN & SON COMPANY. Brick. Exceptional Brick. Swirled oxblood red and green, with some black and a little white. Great pattern. Super coloring. Hand gathered. Outstanding. Akron, OH, circa 1912-1917. 21/32". Mint (9.7). Price: $250. CyberAuction #459, Lot #50.

3046. M.F. CHRISTENSEN & SON COMPANY. Brick. Exceptional hand gathered marble of oxblood red and transparent dark green, with some white. About half oxblood and half green. Nice "9". Exceptional example. Akron, OH, circa 1912-1917. 11/16". Mint (9.8). Price: $215. CyberAuction #495, Lot #57.

3047. M.F. CHRISTENSEN & SON COMPANY. Brick. Large shooter. Oxblood red with black smeared in. Hand gathered, excellent "9" on top. No damage at all. Rare. Akron, OH, circa 1912-1917. 27/32". Mint (9.8). Price: $210. CyberAuction #455, Lot #47.

3048. M.F. CHRISTENSEN & SON COMPANY. Brick. Stunning shooter. Oxblood red with mottled black. Nice "9". Gorgeous. Super example. Akron, OH, circa 1912-1917. 11/16". Mint (9.9). Price: $175. CyberAuction #448, Lot #56.

3049. M.F. CHRISTENSEN & SON COMPANY. Brick. Stunning Brick!!!! Oxblood red swirled with white, black and green. Incredible. Gorgeous. Tiny sparkle. Akron, OH, circa 1912-1917. 5/8". Mint (9.6). Price: $175. CyberAuction #489, Lot #59.

3050. M.F. CHRISTENSEN & SON COMPANY. Brick. Outstanding shooter brick. Oxblood red with some white swirling. Nice "9", tail and seam on it. Two tiny melt pits. Superb example!!! Akron, OH, circa 1912-1917. 25/32". Mint(+) (9.2). Price: $170. CyberAuction #418, Lot #56.

3051. M.F. CHRISTENSEN & SON COMPANY. Brick. Gorgeous shooter of black and dark oxblood. Excellent pattern. Superb. Small flake and a tiny flake. Akron, OH, circa 1912-1917. 3/4". Near Mint(+) (8.7). Price: $120. CyberAuction #401, Lot #59.

3052. M.F. CHRISTENSEN & SON COMPANY. Brick. Oxblood red, mottled with black. Gorgeous! Two tiny melt hole. Akron, OH, circa 1912-1917. 5/32". Mint (9.5). Price: $120. CyberAuction #473, Lot #60.

3053. M.F. CHRISTENSEN & SON COMPANY. Brick. Large brick. Oxblood red with nice black and white "9". Several tiny pits. Akron, OH, circa 1912-1917. 27/32". Mint(-) (9.0). Price: $120. CyberAuction #491, Lot #13.

3054. M.F. CHRISTENSEN & SON COMPANY. Brick. Gorgeous oxblood red, swirled with some black and dark green. Pristine surface. Akron, OH, circa 1912-1917. 9/16". Mint (9.9). Price: $110. CyberAuction #475, Lot #46.

3055. M.F. CHRISTENSEN & SON COMPANY. Brick. Oxblood red with some white and black. Large marble. Akron, OH, circa 1912-1917. 13/16". Mint (9.8). Price: $110. CyberAuction #479, Lot #53.

3056. M.F. CHRISTENSEN & SON COMPANY. Brick. Large shooter. Oxblood red with mottled black. Very nice. Two very tiny flakes, else superb. Stunning marble. Akron, circa 1912-1917. 7/8". Near Mint(+) (8.9). Price: $100. CyberAuction #360, Lot #54.

3057. M.F. CHRISTENSEN & SON COMPANY. Brick. Very dark oxblood mixed with white. Nice swirling. One small fold mark. Probably early Akro agate. Clarksburg, WV, circa 1917-1920. 11/16". Mint (9.7). Price: $100. CyberAuction #462, Lot #27.

3058. M.F. CHRISTENSEN & SON COMPANY. Brick. Oxblood red with black and red swirls. Super marble. Akron, OH, circa 1912-1917. 5/8". Mint (9.7). Price: $90. CyberAuction #348, Lot #8.

3059. M.F. CHRISTENSEN & SON COMPANY. Brick. Gorgeous brick. Dark oxblood red, with some black swirled in . Nice swirl of white. In great shape. Akron, OH, circa 1912-1917. 11/16". Mint (9.9). Price: $90. CyberAuction #363, Lot #13.

3060. M.F. CHRISTENSEN & SON COMPANY. Brick. Nice brick. Oxblood red swirled with white and a little black. Nice "9". Excellent texture. Akron, OH, circa 1912-1917. 5/8". Mint (9.9). Price: $85. CyberAuction #333, Lot #48.

3061. M.F. CHRISTENSEN & SON COMPANY. Brick. Oxblood red, swirled with black and white. Gorgeous Brick. One tiny dimple, a pinprick. Akron, OH, circa 1912-1917. 3/4". Mint(-) (9.2). Price: $80. CyberAuction #463, Lot #60.

3062. M.F. CHRISTENSEN & SON COMPANY. Brick. Gorgeous shooter of black and dark oxblood. Excellent pattern. Superb. A couple of tiny pinpricks. Akron, OH, circa 1912-1917. 3/4". Mint(-) (9.0). Price: $75. CyberAuction #444, Lot #59.

3063. M.F. CHRISTENSEN & SON COMPANY. Brick. Oxblood red with some black and white. Very pretty shooter. Akron, OH, circa 1912-1917. 23/32". Mint (9.6). Price: $70. CyberAuction #471, Lot #11.

3064. M.F. CHRISTENSEN & SON COMPANY. Brick. Oxblood red with some white and black swirling. Two very tiny melt spots. Akron, OH, circa 1912-1917. 21/32". Mint (9.6). Price: $70. CyberAuction #497, Lot #54.

3065. M.F. CHRISTENSEN & SON COMPANY. Brick. Oxblood red with black swirls. Superb. Akron, OH, circa 1912-1917. 9/16". Mint (9.9). Price: $70. CyberAuction #500, Lot #43.

3066. M.F. CHRISTENSEN & SON COMPANY. Brick. Oxblood red with a little green and white swirled in. Nice "9". Akron, OH, circa 1912-1917. 21/32". Mint (9.9). Price: $70. CyberAuction #503, Lot #67.

3067. M.F. CHRISTENSEN & SON COMPANY. Brick. Oxblood red with super white blanketing swirls. Poor "9", nice seam. Akron, OH, circa 1912-1917. 5/8". Mint (9.9). Price: $65. CyberAuction #502, Lot #69.

3068. M.F. CHRISTENSEN & SON COMPANY. Brick. Large, very nice brick. Nice "9" with a very nice tail, and a small seam. Small chip, some tiny pits and scratching. Akron, OH, circa 1912-1917. 27/32". Good(+) (7.9). Consignor note: D4. Price: $55. CyberAuction #343, Lot #55.

3069. M.F. CHRISTENSEN & SON COMPANY. Brick. Nice brick. Oxblood red with and black swirling. Couple of pinpricks. Very pretty. Akron, OH, circa 1912-1917. 5/8". Mint(-) (9.1). Price: $55. CyberAuction #392, Lot #47.

3070. M.F. CHRISTENSEN & SON COMPANY. Brick. White swirls in oxblood red. Poor "9". One tiny melt spot. Akron, OH, circa 1912-1917. 5/8". Mint (9.5). Price: $55. CyberAuction #483, Lot #41.

3071. M.F. CHRISTENSEN & SON COMPANY. Brick. Gorgeous swirls of white in oxblood red. One tiny pinprick. Akron, OH, circa 1912-1917. 21/32". Mint(-) (9.2). Price: $55. CyberAuction #504, Lot #20.

3072. M.F. CHRISTENSEN & SON COMPANY. Brick. Oxblood red with faint black and white swirls. One tiny air hole. Akron, OH, circa 1912-1917. 11/16". Mint (9.7). Price: $55. CyberAuction #508, Lot #64.

3073. M.F. CHRISTENSEN & SON COMPANY. Brick. Oxblood red with a nice green, black and white swirl. Akron, OH, circa 1912-1917. 19/32". Near Mint(+) (8.9). Price: $48. CyberAuction #495, Lot #4.

3074. M.F. CHRISTENSEN & SON COMPANY. Brick. Nice swirl of oxblood red. Shooter! Buffed. 27/32". Price: $47. CyberAuction #375, Lot #36.

3075. M.F. CHRISTENSEN & SON COMPANY. Brick. Large brick. Oxblood red with white and some black swirling. Several small chips, some pinpricking. Akron, OH, circa 1912-1917. 27/32". Good(+) (7.8). Price: $45. CyberAuction #476, Lot #33.

3076. M.F. CHRISTENSEN & SON COMPANY. Brick. Oxblood red with some black. A couple of pinpricks. Akron, OH, circa 1912-1917. 19/32". Mint (9.5). Price: $45. CyberAuction #477, Lot #59.

3077. M.F. CHRISTENSEN & SON COMPANY. Brick. Nice oxblood with black and some white swirling. Tiny chip and overall scratching. Akron, OH, circa 1912-1915. 23/32". Near Mint(-) (8.1). Price: $42. CyberAuction #395, Lot #9.

3078. M.F. CHRISTENSEN & SON COMPANY. Brick. Oxblood red and black. No pattern. Some pinpricks. Akron, OH, circa 1912-1917. 5/8". Near Mint(+) (8.9). Price: $42. CyberAuction #408, Lot #35.

3079. M.F. CHRISTENSEN & SON COMPANY. Brick. Gorgeous brick. Oxblood red with white and some black swirls. Nice pattern. One tiny sparkle. Akron, OH, circa 1912-1917. 5/8". Mint(-) (9.2). Price: $42. CyberAuction #457, Lot #44.

3080. M.F. CHRISTENSEN & SON COMPANY. Brick. Shooter brick. Oxblood red with some black swirled in. Some tiny chips and some pitting. Akron, OH, circa 1912-1917. 25/32". Good(+) (7.9). Price: $40. CyberAuction #391, Lot #41.

3081. M.F. CHRISTENSEN & SON COMPANY. Brick. Gorgeous brick. Oxblood red with white and black swirling. Some pinpricking and very tiny chips. Akron, OH, circa 1912-1917. 21/32". Near Mint (8.5). Price: $40. CyberAuction #451, Lot #6.

3082. M.F. CHRISTENSEN & SON COMPANY. Brick. Beautiful shooter brick. Oxblood red, some white and some black. Nicely swirled with a good "9" and tail. Small fold dimple near end of tail. Several pits and very tiny chips. Akron, OH, circa 1912-1917. 25/32'. Near Mint(+) (8.9). Price: $38. CyberAuction #485, Lot #50.

3083. M.F. CHRISTENSEN & SON COMPANY. Brick. Oxblood red with black swirls and some white. Two pinpricks. Akron, OH, circa 1912-1917. 19/32". Mint(-) (9.2). Price: $35. CyberAuction #393, Lot #54.

3084. M.F. CHRISTENSEN & SON COMPANY. Brick. Large brick. Oxblood red with white and some black swirling. Several small chips, some pinpricking. Akron, OH, circa 1912-1917. 27/32". Good(+) (7.8). Price: $32. CyberAuction #447, Lot #17.

3085. M.F. CHRISTENSEN & SON COMPANY. Brick. Shooter. Buffed. Nice black smeared in oxblood. 13/16". Price: $31. CyberAuction #384, Lot #41.

3086. M.F. CHRISTENSEN & SON COMPANY. Brick. Swirled pattern of oxblood red, white and some mottled black. Small chip, overall wear. Akron, OH, circa 1912-1917. 5/8". Near Mint(-) (8.1). Price: $30. CyberAuction #405, Lot #40.

3087. M.F. CHRISTENSEN & SON COMPANY. Brick. Nice black swirling in oxblood red. Two tiny flakes. Akron, OH, circa 1912-1917. 5/8". Near Mint(+) (8.7). Price: $28. CyberAuction #385, Lot #25.

3088. M.F. CHRISTENSEN & SON COMPANY. Brick. Nice brick. Oxblood red with some white and black swirling. Some pinpricking and damage. Akron, OH, circa 1912-1917. 11/16". Near Mint(+) (8.0). Price: $26. CyberAuction #387, Lot #4.

3089. M.F. CHRISTENSEN & SON COMPANY. Brick. Oxblood red with black swirls. Very nice. Pitting. Akron, OH, circa 1912-1917. 3/4". Near Mint (8.5). Price: $25. CyberAuction #472, Lot #44.

3090. M.F. CHRISTENSEN & SON COMPANY. Brick. Oxblood red with nice white swirling. A couple of tiny chips and some haze. Akron, OH, circa 1912-1917. 11/16". Good (7.5). Price: $22. CyberAuction #397, Lot #9.

3091. M.F. CHRISTENSEN & SON COMPANY. Brick. Nice swirling pattern of oxblood red, black and white. Large melt crease. Some chipping and pitting. Akron, OH, circa 1912-1917. 25/32". Good(+) (7.9). Price: $22. CyberAuction #405, Lot #6.

3092. M.F. CHRISTENSEN & SON COMPANY. Brick. Half a brick. Very dark. Beauty. Akron, OH, circa 1912-1917. 3/4". Mint (9.9). Price: $22. CyberAuction #467, Lot #14.

3093. M.F. CHRISTENSEN & SON COMPANY. Brick. Dark oxblood red with white swirls. Very nice patterns. Some chips. Akron, OH, circa 1912-1917. 3/4". Good(+) (7.9). Price: $20. CyberAuction #402, Lot #24.

3094. M.F. CHRISTENSEN & SON COMPANY. Brick. Dark oxblood red with lots of black and some white. Some pits and scratches. Akron, OH, circa 1912-1917. 5/8". Near Mint (8.6). Price: $19. CyberAuction #439, Lot #41.

3095. M.F. CHRISTENSEN & SON COMPANY. Brick. Oxblood red with black and white swirls. Small fold on one side. There is a small elongated cut or gash that was filled with a polymer. Some very light haziness. Akron, OH, circa 1912-1917. 3/4". Good(+) (7.9). Price: $17. CyberAuction #383, Lot #43.

3096. M.F. CHRISTENSEN & SON COMPANY. Brick. Oxblood red with some white and black. Excellent "9". Some tiny chips. Akron, OH, circa 1912-1917. 11/16". Good (7.6). Price: $16. CyberAuction #404, Lot #10.

3097. M.F. CHRISTENSEN & SON COMPANY. Brick. Oxblood red with black and white swirls. Small fold on one side. There is a small elongated cut or gash that was filled with a polymer. Some very light haziness. Akron, OH, circa 1912-1917. 3/4". Good(+) (7.9). Price: $15. CyberAuction #344, Lot #37.

3098. M.F. CHRISTENSEN & SON COMPANY. Brick. Oxblood red with some white and black. Excellent "9". Overall haze. Some tiny chips. Akron, OH, circa 1912-1917. 11/16". Good (7.6). Price: $15. CyberAuction #346, Lot #58.

3099. M.F. CHRISTENSEN & SON COMPANY. Brick. Oxblood red with black swirls. Polished. 25/32". Price: $15. CyberAuction #401, Lot #28.

3100. M.F. CHRISTENSEN & SON COMPANY. Brick. Half a brick. Very nice. 5/8". Price: $3. CyberAuction #469, Lot #45.

3101. M.F. CHRISTENSEN & SON COMPANY. Opaque. Hard to find Imperial Jade. Hand gathered opaque green marble. Pronounced "9" and whiptail. One of the best I have ever seen. Akron, OH, circa 1912-1917. 5/8". Mint (9.9). Price: $335. CyberAuction #363, Lot #57.

3102. M.F. CHRISTENSEN & SON COMPANY. Opaque. Rare marble. Hand-gathered opaque M.F. Christensen & Son marble. Powder blue. Very light blue with a pale white swirl. Hand-gathered very faint "9" on one end, and a pale cut-off seam at the other end. Hard spiral to see. Akron, OH, circa 1912-1917. 5/8". Mint (9.7). Price: $210. CyberAuction #471, Lot #56.

3103. M.F. CHRISTENSEN & SON COMPANY. Opaque. Rare marble. Hand-gathered opaque M.F. Christensen & Son marble. Powder blue. Very light blue with a pale white swirl. Hand-gathered faint "9" on one end, and a pale cut-off seam at the other end. Hard spiral to see. Some minor pinpricks. Akron, OH, circa 1912-1917. 3/4". Mint(-) (9.0). Price: $200. CyberAuction #338, Lot #60.

3104. M.F. CHRISTENSEN & SON COMPANY. Opaque. Rare marble. Hand-gathered opaque M.F. Christensen & Son marble. Light blue. Slightly darker blue spiral. Hand-gathered faint "9" on one end, and a pale cut-off seam at the other end. In superb shape. One very tiny pit. Akron, OH, circa 1912-1917. 21/32". Mint(-) (9.2). Price: $155. CyberAuction #479, Lot #55.

3105. M.F. CHRISTENSEN & SON COMPANY. Opaque. Hand gathered Imperial Jade opaque. Exceptional "9" and cutoff line. But has a large chip off one side. Akron, OH, circa 1912-1917. 23/32". Good(+) (7.8). Price: $13. CyberAuction #442, Lot #10.

3106. M.F. CHRISTENSEN & SON COMPANY. Oxblood slag. Very dark transparent green with oxblood swirled in. Superb example. Rare. Akron, OH, circa 1912-1917. 5/8". Mint (9.9). Price: $310. CyberAuction #500, Lot #11.

3107. M.F. CHRISTENSEN & SON COMPANY. Oxblood slag. Superior example. Transparent green base with loads of oxblood swirled in. Absolutely stunning, when you put a light to it. Akron, OH, circa 1912-1917. 21/32". Mint (9.9). Price: $290. CyberAuction #504, Lot #46.

3108. M.F. CHRISTENSEN & SON COMPANY. Oxblood slag. Very hard to find. Hand gathered. Very dark transparent green base with translucent white spiral. Nice "9" and tail. Nice cutoff seam. There is oxblood tracing the white. Very hard type to find. One tiny chip, one blown air hole, some wear. Akron, OH, circa 1912-1917. 5/8". Near Mint (8.6). Price: $90. CyberAuction #353, Lot #15.

3109. M.F. CHRISTENSEN & SON COMPANY. Slag. This has got to be one of the largest (non-transitional) slags that I have ever seen. Probably the largest size machine made marble that the M.F. Christensen company could make. Great white spiraling on green. Almost a horizontal!!! Unbelievably large. One tiny subsurface moon, some overall pinpricking (almost very light areas of haze). Not Mint, but how many have you ever seen that are even near this size, that are not covered with chips. The damage appears to come from it rolling around in a box with some other marbles or other items. I seriously doubt that this was ever really played with. Superb!!!! Akron, OH, circa 1912-1917. 1-7/8". Near Mint (8.5). Price: $725. CyberAuction #491, Lot #58.

3110. M.F. CHRISTENSEN & SON COMPANY. Slag. Huge brown slag. Hand gathered, indented seam on bottom. Nice whiptail. An air hole and some pitting. No chips, although some roughness. In remarkable shape, given its age. Rare. Akron, OH, circa 1910-1915. 1-5/8". Near Mint(+) (8.7). Price: $165. CyberAuction #400, Lot #33.

3111. M.F. CHRISTENSEN & SON COMPANY. Slag. Rare M.F. Christensen yellow slag. Almost an amber color, but definitely not brown. Superb "9" and a nice cut line. Exceptional example. Akron, OH, circa 1912-1917. 21/32". Mint (9.9). Price: $150. CyberAuction #373, Lot #6.

3112. M.F. CHRISTENSEN & SON COMPANY. Slag. Very large brown slag. Nice seam, good "9", nice whiptail. One sparkle. Gorgeous marble especially for the size. Akron, OH, circa 1912-1917. 1-5/16". Mint(-) (9.0). Price: $100. CyberAuction #493, Lot #57.

3113. M.F. CHRISTENSEN & SON COMPANY. Slag. Super example of a large slag. Hand gathered brown slag. Nice "9" and tail. Nice nice seam. Has a tiny subsurface moon and three very tiny chips. Akron, OH, circa 1910-1915. 1-1/4". Near Mint(+) (8.7). Price: $63. CyberAuction #356, Lot #38.

3114. M.F. CHRISTENSEN & SON COMPANY. Slag. Gorgeous shooter brown slag. Nice pattern, in great shape. Akron, OH, circa 1912-1917. 29/32". Mint (9.9). Price: $60. CyberAuction #408, Lot #39.

3115. M.F. CHRISTENSEN & SON COMPANY. Slag. Late M.F. Christensen brown slag. Dark brown. Nice cut-off seam, poor "9". Two very tiny subsurface moons, a couple of sparkles. Akron, OH, circa 1915-1917. 1-3/16". Near Mint(+) (8.7). Price: $48. CyberAuction #492, Lot #16.

3116. M.F. CHRISTENSEN & SON COMPANY. Slag. Gorgeous blue slag. Excellent "9", very nice seam. In great shape. Akron, OH, circa 1912-1917. 13/16". Mint (9.7). Price: $42. CyberAuction #440, Lot #16.

3117. M.F. CHRISTENSEN & SON COMPANY. Slag. Hard to find hybric. Top two-thirds is red, bottom is brown with a lot more white. Gorgeous. Akron, OH, circa 1912-1917. 11/16". Mint (9.7). Price: $40. CyberAuction #376, Lot #48.

3118. M.F. CHRISTENSEN & SON COMPANY. Slag. Hard to find M. Christensen red slag. Excellent "9" on the top. Super marble. Tiny sparkle. Akron, OH, circa 1912-1917. 19/32". Mint (9.4). Price: $35. CyberAuction #429, Lot #13.

3119. M.F. CHRISTENSEN & SON COMPANY. Slag. Shooter brown slag. Gorgeous "9" on it. Akron, OH, circa 1912-1917. 25/32". Mint (9.7). Price: $33. CyberAuction #481, Lot #33.

3120. M.F. CHRISTENSEN & SON COMPANY. Slag. Late M.F. Christensen slag. Purple. In great shape. Akron, OH, circa 1915-1917. 11/16". Mint (9.8). Price: $30. CyberAuction #452, Lot #4.

3121. M.F. CHRISTENSEN & SON COMPANY. Slag. Brown slag. Stunning. Excellent "9", nice seam. Super example!!! Akron, OH, circa 1912-1917. 5/8". Mint (9.9). Price: $29. CyberAuction #435, Lot #24.

3122. M.F. CHRISTENSEN & SON COMPANY. Slag. Excellent example in remarkable shape. Brown slag. Lazy "9" on the top, but long seam on the bottom. One tiny melt pit. Superb. Akron, OH, circa 1912-1917. 7/8". Mint (9.5). Price: $27. CyberAuction #410, Lot #47.

3123. M.F. CHRISTENSEN & SON COMPANY. Slag. Nice shooter slag. Very light brown. Loads of white. Very nice "9" with a good seam. Akron, OH, circa 1912-1917. 25/32". Mint (9.6). Price: $26. CyberAuction #330, Lot #37.

3124. M.F. CHRISTENSEN & SON COMPANY. Slag. Brown slag. Super example. Excellent "9" and bottom seam. Akron, OH, circa 1912-1915. 23/32". Mint (9.7). Price: $22. CyberAuction #338, Lot #50.

3125. M.F. CHRISTENSEN & SON COMPANY. Slag. Brown slag. Loads of white. Super "9" on it. Excellent. Akron, OH, circa 1912-1917. 11/16". Mint (9.6). Price: $21. CyberAuction #436, Lot #11.

3126. M.F. CHRISTENSEN & SON COMPANY. Slag. Gorgeous brown slag. Very nice "9". Akron, OH, circa 1912-1917. 23/32". Mint (9.7). Price: $21. CyberAuction #491, Lot #33.

3127. M.F. CHRISTENSEN & SON COMPANY. Slag. Blue slag. Exceptional "9". Akron, OH, circa 1912-1917. 5/8". Mint (9.9). Price: $19. CyberAuction #360, Lot #26.

3128. M.F. CHRISTENSEN & SON COMPANY. Slag. Superb shooter brown slag. Excellent "9" on the top. Very nice tail. This is a super example. One long air hole on one side and a small dirt spot. Akron, OH, circa 1912-1917. 27/32". Mint (9.5). Price: $19. CyberAuction #429, Lot #9.

3129. M.F. CHRISTENSEN & SON COMPANY. Slag. Brown slag. Very nice "9" with a trailing tail. One tiny subsurface moon. Akron, OH, circa 1912-1917. 25/32". Near Mint(+) (8.8). Price: $17. CyberAuction #330, Lot #10.

3130. M.F. CHRISTENSEN & SON COMPANY. Slag. Gorgeous amber slag with a fold on the bottom. Beauty. Akron, OH, circa 1910-1915. 27/32". Mint (9.7). Price: $17. CyberAuction #392, Lot #5.

3131. M.F. CHRISTENSEN & SON COMPANY. Slag. Green slag. Wide full "9". Akron, OH, circa 1912-1917. 21/32". Mint (9.7). Price: $17. CyberAuction #467, Lot #44.

3132. M.F. CHRISTENSEN & SON COMPANY. Slag. Late M.F. Christensen brown slag. Doesn't have a "9". One sparkle. Akron, OH, circa 1912-1917. 7/8". Mint(-) (9.0). Price: $15. CyberAuction #382, Lot #47.

3133. M.F. CHRISTENSEN & SON COMPANY. Slag. Very nice green slag. Nice "9" and seam. Akron, OH, circa 1912-1917. 11/16". Mint (9.7). Price: $15. CyberAuction #388, Lot #9.

3134. M.F. CHRISTENSEN & SON COMPANY. Slag. Hard to find M. Christensen red slag. Poor "9" on the top. A couple of tiny sparkles. Akron, OH, circa 1912-1917. 19/32". Near Mint(+) (8.8). Price: $15. CyberAuction #429, Lot #40.

3135. M.F. CHRISTENSEN & SON COMPANY. Slag. Green slag. Nice "9" and seam. Akron, OH, circa 1912-1917. 19/32". Mint (9.9). Price: $15. CyberAuction #508, Lot #27.

3136. M.F. CHRISTENSEN & SON COMPANY. Slag. Brown slag. Wide "9". Very nice. Akron, OH, circa 1912-1917. 5/8". Mint (9.9). Price: $15. CyberAuction #419, Lot #54.

3137. M.F. CHRISTENSEN & SON COMPANY. Slag. Hard to find MF ear slag. Hand gathered. Nice seam line, poor "9". Two small subsurface oons. Akron, OH, circa 1912-1917. 21/32". Near Mint(+) (8.8). Price: 2. CyberAuction #395, Lot #15.

38. M.F. CHRISTENSEN & SON COMPANY. Slag. Blue slag. Nice "9". Akron, OH, circa 1915-1917. 1-3/16". Good (7.4). Consignor ote: G5. Price: $12. CyberAuction #402, Lot #19.

39. M.F. CHRISTENSEN & SON COMPANY. Slag. Brown slag. Nice. oor "9". Overall pitting and tiny chips. Akron, OH, circa 1915-1917. 1-3/ ". Good(-) (7.2). Price: $11. CyberAuction #358, Lot #35.

40. M.F. CHRISTENSEN & SON COMPANY. Slag. Red slag. Lots of hite. Poor "9". In great shape. Akron, OH, circa 1912-1917. 9/16". Mint .9). Price: $11. CyberAuction #373, Lot #8.

41. M.F. CHRISTENSEN & SON COMPANY. Slag. Gorgeous small green g with a great melted trailing tail. Some tiny annealing fractures, but still tunning marble. Akron, OH, circa 1912-1917. 19/32". Mint (9.3). Price: 1. CyberAuction #446, Lot #44.

42. M.F. CHRISTENSEN & SON COMPANY. Slag. Brown slag. Nice ne. Akron, OH, circa 1912-1917. 11/16". Mint (9.9). Price: $11. /berAuction #448, Lot #18.

43. M.F. CHRISTENSEN & SON COMPANY. Slag. Gorgeous small green g with a great melted trailing tail. Some tiny annealing fractures, but still tunning marble. Akron, OH, circa 1912-1917. 19/32". Mint (9.3). Price: 0. CyberAuction #396, Lot #9.

44. M.F. CHRISTENSEN & SON COMPANY. Slag. Light orange slag. nusual coloring. Subsurface moon, some pits. Akron, OH, circa 1912- 17. 5/8". Near Mint(-) (8.0). Price: $9. CyberAuction #481, Lot #3.

45. M.F. CHRISTENSEN & SON COMPANY. Slag. Brown slag. Pale own. Interesting. Akron, OH, circa 1915-1917. 9/16". Mint (9.7). Two arbles available, you are bidding on one. Winner has choice of either or th, remainder to under. Price: $8. CyberAuction #349, Lot #2.

46. M.F. CHRISTENSEN & SON COMPANY. Slag. Green slag. Wide ", nice seam. One tiny melt pit. Akron, OH, circa 1912-1917. 3/4". Mint(- .0). Price: $8. CyberAuction #363, Lot #33.

47. M.F. CHRISTENSEN & SON COMPANY. Slag. Red slag. Poor "9", ce seam. Akron, OH, circa 1915-1917. 9/16". Mint (9.9). Price: $8. /berAuction #385, Lot #10.

48. M.F. CHRISTENSEN & SON COMPANY. Slag. Brown slag. Nice ". Good seam. Akron, OH, circa 1912-1917. 15/16'. Buffed. Price: $8. /berAuction #405, Lot #51.

49. M.F. CHRISTENSEN & SON COMPANY. Slag. Clear slag. Shooter. ce "9". Two small subsurface moons, some tiny pitting. Very hard to find lor. Akron, OH, circa 1912-1917. 7/8". Near Mint(-) (8.2). Price: $8. /berAuction #481, Lot #49.

50. M.F. CHRISTENSEN & SON COMPANY. Slag. Brown slag. Gor- ous. Nice "9", long tail. One tiny melt pit. Akron, OH, circa 1912-1917. /32". Mint (9.6). Price: $7. CyberAuction #420, Lot #39.

51. M.F. CHRISTENSEN & SON COMPANY. Slag. Brown slag. Poor ". Akron, OH, circa 1912-1917. 5/8". Mint (9.7). Price: $2. CyberAuction 457, Lot #46.

52. MARBLE KING, INC. Advertising package. Poly bag. Yellow header ads "With The Best Wishes of Elsie, The Cow". Contains fourteen Rain- ws, including three Bumblebees. 4" x 3". Mint (9.7). Price: $19. /berAuction #339, Lot #33.

53. MARBLE KING, INC. Bengal Tiger. Four color patch and ribbon inbow Bengal Tiger. Opaque white base. Black and yellow patch and bon, with red on the yellow. Some white showing on the bottom. One flake. Paden City WV, circa 1955-1970. 31/32". Near Mint(+) (8.9). ce: $80. CyberAuction #369, Lot #58.

54. MARBLE KING, INC. Berry Pink. Patch marble referred to by collec- s as a "Berry Pink". Transparent clear base, filled with satiny white. There a patch on about a quarter of the surface of blue and red. Two seams. cellent example. Several sparkles on the clear. Very hard to find. St. Mary's V, circa 1948-1953. 1". Near Mint(+) (8.9). Price: $140. CyberAuction 373, Lot #46.

55. MARBLE KING, INC. Berry Pink. Patch marble referred to by collec- s as a "Berry Pink". Transparent clear base, with satiny white patch. There a patch on about a quarter of the surface of blue and some red. Two ams. In great shape. Very hard to find. St. Mary's WV, circa 1948-1953. Mint (9.7). Price: $85. CyberAuction #444, Lot #56.

56. MARBLE KING, INC. Berry Pink. Patch marble referred to by collec- s as a "Berry Pink". Transparent clear base, with satiny white patch. There a patch on about a quarter of the surface of blue and some red. Two ams. A number of small sparkles. Very hard to find. St. Mary's WV, circa 48-1953. 1". Near Mint (8.5). Price: $70. CyberAuction #391, Lot #38.

57. MARBLE KING, INC. Berry Pink. Patch marble referred to by collec- s as a "Berry Pink". Transparent clear base, with satiny white patch. There a patch on about a quarter of the surface of blue and some red. Two ams. A number of small sparkles. Very hard to find. St. Mary's WV, circa 48-1953. 1". Near Mint (8.6). Price: $60. CyberAuction #441, Lot #14.

58. MARBLE KING, INC. Berry Pink. Patch marble referred to by collec- s as a "Berry Pink". Transparent clear base, with satiny white patch. There a patch on about a quarter of the surface of blue and some red. Two ams. A number of small sparkles. Very hard to find. St. Mary's WV, circa 48-1953. 1". Near Mint (8.5). Price: $51. CyberAuction #430, Lot #59.

59. MARBLE KING, INC. Berry Pink. Patch marble referred to by collec- s as a "Berry Pink". Transparent clear base, with satiny white patch. There a patch on about a quarter of the surface of blue and some red. Two ams. Several small sparkles. Very hard to find. St. Mary's WV, circa 1948- 53. 1". Near Mint(+) (8.7). Price: $50. CyberAuction #420, Lot #60.

60. MARBLE KING, INC. Berry Pink. Patch marble referred to by collec- s as a "Berry Pink". Transparent clear base, with satiny white patch. There

is a patch on about a quarter of the surface of blue and some red. Two seams. A number of small sparkles. Very hard to find. St. Mary's WV, circa 1948-1953. 1". Near Mint (8.5). Two marbles available, you are bidding on one. Winner has choice of either or both, remainder to under. Price: $47. CyberAuction #401, Lot #8.

3161. MARBLE KING, INC. Berry Pink. Patch marble referred to by collec- tors as a "Berry Pink". Transparent clear base, with satiny white patch. There is a patch on about a quarter of the surface of blue and some red. Two seams. A number of small sparkles. Very hard to find. St. Mary's WV, circa 1948-1953. 1". Near Mint (8.5). Price: $42. CyberAuction #395, Lot #18.

3162. MARBLE KING, INC. Blended. Blended Spiderman. Opaque white base covered by smeared ribbons of blue and red. Paden City WV, 1955- 1960. 19/32". Mint (9.9). Price: $32. CyberAuction #359, Lot #50.

3163. MARBLE KING, INC. Blended. Blended Spiderman. Opaque white base covered by smeared ribbons of blue and red. Paden City WV, age unknown although there is indication that they are mid to late 1950s. 9/ 16". Mint (9.9). Price: $27. CyberAuction #350, Lot #45.

3164. MARBLE KING, INC. Blended. Blended Spiderman. Opaque white base covered by smeared ribbons of blue and red. One small flake. Paden City WV, 195-1960. 9/16". Near Mint(+) (8.7). Price: $15. CyberAuction #354, Lot #47.

3165. MARBLE KING, INC. Blended. Blended Spiderman. Opaque white base covered by smeared ribbons of blue and red. One flake. Paden City WV, 1955-1960. 9/16". Near Mint(+) (8.8). Price: $14. CyberAuction #375, Lot #1.

3166. MARBLE KING, INC. Bumblebee. Three color patch and ribbon Rainbow Bumblebee. Opaque white base. Black and yellow patch and ribbon. Thin red on one yellow ribbon. Some white showing. A couple of very tiny sparkles. Paden City WV, circa 1955-1975. 15/16". Mint (9.4). Price: $24. CyberAuction #432, Lot #10.

3167. MARBLE KING, INC. Bumblebee. Three color patch and ribbon Rainbow Bumblebee. Opaque white base. Black and yellow patch and ribbon. Some white showing. Paden City WV, circa 1955-1975. 31/32". Mint (9.7).. Price: $13. CyberAuction #412, Lot #19.

3168. MARBLE KING, INC. Bumblebee. Three color patch and ribbon Rainbow Bumblebee. Opaque white base. Black and yellow patch and ribbon. Some white showing. Paden City WV, circa 1955-1975. 15/16". Mint (9.7).. Price: $10. CyberAuction #392, Lot #9.

3169. MARBLE KING, INC. Bumblebee. Shooter Bumblebee. Black and yellow patch and ribbon. Paden City WV, circa 1955-1975. 23/32". Mint (9.9). Price: $10. CyberAuction #441, Lot #45.

3170. MARBLE KING, INC. Bumblebee. Three color patch and ribbon Rainbow Bumblebee. Opaque white base. Black and yellow patch and ribbon. Some tiny air holes. Paden City WV, circa 1955-1975. 3/4". Mint (9.5). Price: $9. CyberAuction #350, Lot #10.

3171. MARBLE KING, INC. Bumblebee. Patch and ribbon Rainbow Bumblebee. Black and yellow patch and ribbon on opaque white. Shooter. 23/32". Mint (9.9). Price: $8. CyberAuction #449, Lot #34.

3172. MARBLE KING, INC. Bumblebee. Patch and ribbon Rainbow Bumblebee. Black and yellow patch and ribbon on opaque white. Shooter. 23/32". Mint (9.9). Price: $6. CyberAuction #394, Lot #37.

3173. MARBLE KING, INC. Bumblebee. Shooter two color patch and rib- bon Rainbow Bumblebee. Black and yellow patch and ribbon. Some sparkles. Paden City WV, circa 1955-1975. 31/32". Near Mint(+) (8.9). Price: $5. CyberAuction #340, Lot #19.

3174. MARBLE KING, INC. Bumblebee. Patch and ribbon Rainbow Bumblebee. Black and yellow patch and ribbon on opaque white. Shooter. 23/32". Mint (9.9). Price: $4. CyberAuction #466, Lot #7.

3175. MARBLE KING, INC. Bumblebee. Patch and ribbon Rainbow Bumblebee. Black and yellow patch and ribbon on opaque white. Shooter. 23/32". Mint (9.9). Price: $4. CyberAuction #492, Lot #26.

3176. MARBLE KING, INC. Catseye. Large St. Mary's catseye. Clear base. Four vanes of blue, edged by green. Some pits and sparkles. St. Mary WV, circa 1950-1955. 29/32". Near Mint(+) (8.9). Price: $23. CyberAuction #381, Lot #11.

3177. MARBLE KING, INC. Catseye. St. Mary's catseye. Two vanes of yellow, two of white. Harder to find than the blue/yellow. St. Marys, WV, circa 1950-1955. 5/8". Mint (9.4). Price: $13. CyberAuction #344, Lot #22.

3178. MARBLE KING, INC. Catseye. Interesting St. Mary's catseye. Trans- parent clear base. Four white vanes, edged by blue. Beauty. St. Mary's WV, circa 1950-1955. 5/8". Mint (9.7). Price: $11. CyberAuction #388, Lot #45.

3179. MARBLE KING, INC. Catseye. Yellow and white St. Mary's catseye. St. Mary's WV, circa 1948-1951. 5/8". Mint(-) (9.0). Price: $10. CyberAuction #331, Lot #48.

3180. MARBLE KING, INC. Catseye. Blue and white St. Mary's catseye. St. Mary's WV, circa 1950-1955. 5/8". Mint (9.9). Price: $10. CyberAuction #413, Lot #46.

3181. MARBLE KING, INC. Catseye. Blue and white St. Mary's catseye. Some rubbing. St. Mary's WV, circa 1948-1951. 5/8". Mint(-) (9.0). There are three marble available. You are bidding on one. Winner has choice of any or all, remainder to under. Price: $6. CyberAuction #332, Lot #24.

3182. MARBLE KING, INC. Catseye. Blue and white St. Mary's catseye. Has a pit. St. Mary's WV, circa 1948-1951. 5/8". Mint(-) (9.0). There are five marble available. You are bidding on one. Winner has choice of any or all, remainder to under. Price: $6. CyberAuction #382, Lot #29.

3183. MARBLE KING, INC. Catseye. Blue and white St. Mary's catseye. St. Mary's WV, circa 1948-1951. 5/8". Mint (9.7). There are four marble available. You are bidding on one. Winner has choice of any or all, remain- der to under. Price: $5. CyberAuction #370, Lot #33.

3184. MARBLE KING, INC. Catseye. Blue and yellow St. Mary's catseye. St. Mary's WV, circa 1948-1951. 5/8". Mint (9.7). There are four marble available. You are bidding on one. Winner has choice of any or all, remainder to under. Price: $5. CyberAuction #470, Lot #6.

3185. MARBLE KING, INC. Catseye. Blue and white St. Mary's catseye. Some cold roll lines. St. Mary's WV, circa 1948-1951. 5/8". Mint(-) (9.0). Price: $4. CyberAuction #334, Lot #9.

3186. MARBLE KING, INC. Catseye. Blue and yellow St. Mary's catseye. St. Mary's WV, circa 1948-1951. 5/8". Mint (9.7). There are four marble available. You are bidding on one. Winner has choice of any or all, remainder to under. Price: $3. CyberAuction #368, Lot #35.

3187. MARBLE KING, INC. Catseye. Blue and yellow St. Mary's catseye. St. Mary's WV, circa 1948-1951. 5/8". Mint (9.7). There are four marble available. You are bidding on one. Winner has choice of any or all, remainder to under. Price: $3. CyberAuction #444, Lot #38.

3188. MARBLE KING, INC. Cub Scout. Three color patch and ribbon Rainbow Cub Scout. Blue and yellow patch and ribbon. Has a red stripe in one yellow ribbon. Paden City WV, circa 1955-1975. 19/32". Mint (9.9). Price: $20. CyberAuction #334, Lot #51.

3189. MARBLE KING, INC. Cub Scout. Two color blue and yellow patch and ribbon Cub Scout shooter. Paden City, WV, circa 1955-1970. 27/32". Mint (9.7). Price: $20. CyberAuction #396, Lot #20.

3190. MARBLE KING, INC. Cub Scout. Four-color patch and ribbon Rainbow Cub Scout. Opaque white base. Patch and ribbon of blue and yellow. Red streak in the yellow patch and one yellow ribbon. Shooter. Paden City WV, circa 1955-1975. 31/32". Mint (9.7). Price: $19. CyberAuction #455, Lot #26.

3191. MARBLE KING, INC. Cub Scout. Two-color patch and ribbon Cub Scout. Blue and yellow patch and ribbon. Paden City WV, circa 1955-1975. 5/8". Mint (9.8). There are five marbles available. You are bidding on one. Winner has choice of any or all, remainder to under. Price: $4. CyberAuction #434, Lot #41.

3192. MARBLE KING, INC. Cub Scout. Two-color patch and ribbon Cub Scout. Blue and yellow patch and ribbon. Paden City WV, circa 1955-1975. 5/8". Mint (9.8). There are five marbles available. You are bidding on one. Winner has choice of any or all, remainder to under. Price: $3. CyberAuction #389, Lot #40.

3193. MARBLE KING, INC. Cub Scout. Two color blue and yellow patch and ribbon Cub Scout. Paden City, WV, circa 1955-1970. 19/32". Mint (9.7). There are four marbles available, you are bidding on one. Winner has choice of any or all, remainder to under. Price: $2. CyberAuction #396, Lot #16.

3194. MARBLE KING, INC. Cub Scout. Two color blue and yellow patch and ribbon Cub Scout. Paden City, WV, circa 1955-1970. 19/32". Mint (9.7). There are five marbles available, you are bidding on one. Winner has choice of any or all, remainder to under. Price: $2. CyberAuction #415, Lot #15.

3195. MARBLE KING, INC. Cub Scout. Two color blue and yellow patch and ribbon Cub Scout. Paden City, WV, circa 1955-1970. 19/32". Mint (9.7). There are five marbles available, you are bidding on one. Winner has choice of any or all, remainder to under. Price: $2. CyberAuction #417, Lot #17.

3196. MARBLE KING, INC. Cub Scout. Two color blue and yellow patch and ribbon Cub Scout. Paden City, WV, circa 1955-1970. 19/32". Mint (9.7). Price: $1. CyberAuction #368, Lot #31.

3197. MARBLE KING, INC. Cub Scout. Two color blue and yellow patch and ribbon Cub Scout. Paden City, WV, circa 1955-1970. 19/32". Mint (9.6). There are ten marbles available, you are bidding on one. Winner has choice of any or all, remainder to under. Price: $1. CyberAuction #457, Lot #20.

3198. MARBLE KING, INC. Cub Scout. Two color blue and yellow patch and ribbon Cub Scout. Paden City, WV, circa 1955-1970. 19/32". Mint (9.7). There are three marbles available, you are bidding on one. Winner has choice of any or all, remainder to under. Price: $1. CyberAuction #494, Lot #39.

3199. MARBLE KING, INC. Dragonfly. Patch and ribbon Rainbow. Opaque white base. Patch and ribbon of green and blue. Some smearing. Paden City WV, circa 1955-1970. 19/32". Mint (9.9). Price: $100. CyberAuction #418, Lot #52.

3200. MARBLE KING, INC. Dragonfly. Three-color patch and ribbon Rainbow Dragonfly. Opaque white base. Mostly blue veneer with a pale green patch and a pale green ribbon. Some blue mixed in the ribbon. Also, white shows through the green. Paden City WV, circa 1960-1975. 11/16". Mint (9.9). Price: $80. CyberAuction #373, Lot #19.

3201. MARBLE KING, INC. Girl Scout. Two color patch and ribbon Rainbow Girl Scout. Yellow and green patch and ribbon. Paden City WV, circa 1955-1965. 5/8". Mint (9.7). Price: $14. CyberAuction #348, Lot #28.

3202. MARBLE KING, INC. Girl Scout. Two color patch and ribbon Rainbow Girl Scout. Yellow and green patch and ribbon. Paden City WV, circa 1955-1965. 5/8". Mint (9.7). There are three marbles available, you are bidding on one. Winner has choice of any or all, remainder to under. Price: $6. CyberAuction #396, Lot #30.

3203. MARBLE KING, INC. National Marble Tournament. Opaque blue Marble King. These are the marbles used as the target marbles at the National Marbles Tournament in Wildwood. The consignor picked these up at the 1987 tournament. 19/32". Mint (9.9). There are two marbles available. You are bidding on one. Winner has choice of either or both, remainder to under. Price: $3. CyberAuction #340, Lot #45.

3204. MARBLE KING, INC. Original package. Original poly bag of "100 Rainbow Marble King Marbles". Nice bag, in great shape, as is the label. Has Bumblebees, Cub Scouts, as well as some tri colors. The rest are two color. Super bag. There are some very tiny pinholes in the bag and the label has folding. Still, hard to find. Paden City WV, circa 1950-1965. Mint(-) (9.1). Price: $82.50. CyberAuction #339, Lot #30.

3205. MARBLE KING, INC. Original package. Original cloth Marble King Tournament Assortment bag. Harder to find than the poly one. No marbles but uses drawstring. Berry Pink Industries. Some minor stains. no hole In very nice shape. 1950s. About 10" x 7". Mint(-). Price: $36. CyberAuction #499, Lot #23.

3206. MARBLE KING, INC. Original package. No. 65 Chinese Checker box. Berry Pink Inc. Yellow box. Sixty marbles. Has full complement c marbles. Box has a little crushing. Box is Mint(-). Marbles are Mint. 1930s 1940s. Price: $30. CyberAuction #339, Lot #28.

3207. MARBLE KING, INC. Original package. Poly bag of "40 Rainbow Marble King Marbles 40". Red label. Includes several Bumblebees and bunch of multi colors. Mint (9.5). Price: $26. CyberAuction #341, Lot #3

3208. MARBLE KING, INC. Original package. Original package of Marble King marbles given out at the 1998 National Marbles Tournament. Include fifteen modern Cub Scouts (5/8") and a commemorative shooter characte marble. Opaque blue marbles with white printing. "75th Anniversary Na tional Marbles Tournament Wildwood NJ 1998". 31/32". In original pol packet (no label). Consigned by The National Marbles Tournament. A proceeds go directly to the Tournament to defray costs. No commission being charged on this sale. Price: $26. CyberAuction #354, Lot #3

3209. MARBLE KING, INC. Original package. Berry Pink Chinko-Checke Marblo Box. With marbles. Some water staining on the top. Corners ar split. Has marbles. Near Mint (8.5). Price: $19. CyberAuction #346, Lot #29.

3210. MARBLE KING, INC. Original package. Poly bag of "19 Rainbow Marble King Marbles 19". Red printing on white. Includes several multicolor Paden City WV, circa 1960-1970. 5" x 3". Mint (9.9). Price: $19 CyberAuction #379, Lot #33.

3211. MARBLE KING, INC. Original package. Poly bag of "14 Rainbow Marble King Marbles 14". Red printing on white. Includes two Bumblebee and some multicolors. Paden City WV, circa 1960-1970. 5" x 3". Mint (9.9 Two bags available, you are bidding on one. Winner has choice of either c both, remainder to under. Price: $17. CyberAuction #339, Lot #29.

3212. MARBLE KING, INC. Original package. Poly bag of "19 Rainbow Marble King Marbles 19". Red printing on white. Includes a couple c multicolors. Paden City WV, circa 1960-1970. 5" x 3". Mint (9.9). Thre bags available, you are bidding on one. Winner has choice of any or al remainder to under. Price: $17. CyberAuction #341, Lot #25.

3213. MARBLE KING, INC. Original package. Original large poly bag wit red drawstring. "Marble King Tournament Assortment". Shows the crowne kid shooting marbles on the front. Contains an assortment of catseyes ar Rainbows. Still has the original price tag on it. Mid to late 1970s. Mint ((9.0). Price: $17. CyberAuction #344, Lot #30.

3214. MARBLE KING, INC. Original package. No. 65 Chinese Checker box. Berry Pink Inc. Yellow box. Sixty marbles. Has full complement c marbles. Box has lots of stains. Box is Near Mint(-) (8.0). Marbles are Min 1930s-1940s. Price: $15. CyberAuction #355, Lot #32.

3215. MARBLE KING, INC. Original package. Original cloth Marble King Tournament Assortment bag. Harder to find than the poly one. No marble but uses drawstring. Berry Pink Industries. Some minor stains. no hole In very nice shape. 1950s. About 10" x 7". Mint(-). Price: $15. CyberAuctio #439, Lot #13.

3216. MARBLE KING, INC. Original package. Poly bag. Header label white paper with a green print on white. Reads "60 Marine Crystals 60 Sixty green clearies. Paden City WV, circa 1950-1955. 8" x 3" (sight). Mi (9.5). Price: $12. CyberAuction #404, Lot #12.

3217. MARBLE KING, INC. Original package. Poly bag. Header label white paper with a green print on white. Reads "60 Marine Crystals 60 Sixty green clearies. Paden City WV, circa 1950-1955. 8" x 3" (sight). Mi (9.5). Price: $12. CyberAuction #446, Lot #1.

3218. MARBLE KING, INC. Original package. Poly bag of 3 catsey Shooters. Black and red label. 4" x 4". Mint. There are seven bags available You are bidding on one. Winner has choice of any or all, remainder under. Price: $10. CyberAuction #349, Lot #29.

3219. MARBLE KING, INC. Original package. Blister card. Sometim referred to as the J-card. Forty catseyes with a nylon mesh bag. Marb games on back. Fairly recent. Mint. Price: $5. CyberAuction #404, Lot #27.

3220. MARBLE KING, INC. Original package. Poly bag of twenty fiv clearies. Red and black, on white, label. 1970s. Mint (9.5). Price: $ CyberAuction #419, Lot #32.

3221. MARBLE KING, INC. Original package. Poly bag of twenty clearie Red printing on white header. Probably 1960s. About 4" x 5". Mint (9.0 Two packages available, you are bidding on one. Winner has choice either or both, remainder to under. Price: $3. CyberAuction #472, Lo #15.

3222. MARBLE KING, INC. Premium. Lid from a Dixie cup. Fro Heilemann's Sundae Cup. Advertises Marble King marbles. Send in the l and 25 cents and get a poly bag of 50 marbles. From 1963. You ar you are bidding on one. Winner has choice of either or both, remainder under. Price: $3. CyberAuction #497, Lot #36.

3223. MARBLE KING, INC. Rainbow. Odd Rainbow. Transparent dark blu base. Patch and ribbon of opaque red mixed with opaque white. Oth patch and ribbon is the blue showing through. Unusual. Paden City W 1955-1975. 19/32". Mint (9.7). Price: $24. CyberAuction #428, Lot #

3224. MARBLE KING, INC. Rainbow. Interesting. Opaque white bas Red patch on one pole, then black band, then very narrow yellow ban then wide red band, then white patch on bottom pole. Paden City W rca 1955-1975. 5/8". Mint (9.9). Price: $13. CyberAuction #350, Lot 6.

225. MARBLE KING, INC. Rainbow. Double ingot Rainbow. Green on hite. Hard to find. Paden City WV, circa 1955-1975. 3/4". Mint (9.7). ice: $12. CyberAuction #404, Lot #33.

226. MARBLE KING, INC. Rainbow. Double ingot Rainbow. Green on hite. Hard to find. Paden City WV, circa 1955-1975. 3/4". Mint (9.7). ice: $12. CyberAuction #453, Lot #4.

227. MARBLE KING, INC. Rainbow. Modern Rainbow. Girl Scout. Has me very faint blue aventurine too. A couple of sparkles. 5/8". Mint(-) .0). Price: $10. CyberAuction #368, Lot #6.

228. MARBLE KING, INC. Rainbow. Green patch and ribbons with some xblood ribbon too. Paden City WV, circa 1965-1975. 31/32". Mint (9.7). ice: $8. CyberAuction #370, Lot #39.

229. MARBLE KING, INC. Rainbow. Shooter old-style Rainbow. Patch d ribbon. Opaque white base. Fiery aventurine green patch and ribbon. few scratches and pits. Paden City WV, circa 1955-1975. 7/8". Near int(+) (8.9). Price: $5. CyberAuction #362, Lot #47.

230. MARBLE KING, INC. Rainbow. Double ingot Rainbow. Translucent een and white. 23/32". Mint (-) (9.0). Price: $3. CyberAuction #361, Lot 54.

231. MARBLE KING, INC. Rainbow. Four color Rainbows, white base. ne ribbon is a fiery aventurine green. Paden City WV, circa 1960-1975.)/32". Mint (9.9). Lot of four marbles available, you are bidding on one. inner has choice of any or all, remainder to under. Price: $2. CyberAuction 365, Lot #25.

232. MARBLE KING, INC. Rainbow. White base with an aventurine green atch and ribbon. 19/32". Mint (9.9). Two marbles available, you are bid- ng on one. Winner has choice of either or both, remainder to under. ice: $2. CyberAuction #370, Lot #27.

233. MARBLE KING, INC. Rainbow. Patch and ribbon Rainbow. Aventu- ne green patch and ribbon on white. Light aventurine. Paden City WV, rca 1965-1975. 5/8". Mint (9.7). Price: $2. CyberAuction #435, Lot #3.

234. MARBLE KING, INC. Rainbow. Four color Rainbows, white base. ne ribbon is a fiery aventurine green. Paden City WV, circa 1960-1975.)/32". Mint (9.9). Lot of two marbles available, you are bidding on one. inner has choice of any or all, remainder to under. Price: $2. CyberAuction 447, Lot #11.

235. MARBLE KING, INC. Tiger. Hard to find shooter two color Rainbow ger. Orange and black patch and ribbon. Paden City WV, circa 1955-)75. 3/4". Mint (9.9). Price: $90. CyberAuction #348, Lot #54.

236. MARBLE KING, INC. Tiger. Two color Rainbow Tiger. Orange and ack. Nice example. Air hole. Paden City WV, circa 1950-1965. 5/8". Mint(- 9.0). Price: $15. CyberAuction #344, Lot #47.

237. MARBLE KING, INC. Tiger. Three-color patch and ribbon Rainbow ger. Opaque white base. Black and orange patch and ribbon. Paden ty WV, circa 1955-1975. 19/32". Mint (9.8). There are two examples ailable, you are bidding on one. Winner has choice of either or both, mainder to under. Price: $12. CyberAuction #414, Lot #35.

238. MARBLE KING, INC. Tiger. Three-color patch and ribbon Rainbow ger. Opaque white base. Patch and ribbon of dark orange and black. den City WV, circa 1960-1975. 5/8". Mint (9.9). Price: $12. CyberAuction 452, Lot #31.

239. MARBLE KING, INC. Tiger. Two color Rainbow Tiger. Orange and ack. One moon. Paden City WV, circa 1950-1965. 5/8". Near Mint (8.6). ice: $8. CyberAuction #350, Lot #50.

240. MARBLE KING, INC. Tiger. Three-color patch and ribbon Rainbow ger. Opaque white base. Black and orange/red patch and ribbon. Paden ty WV, circa 1955-1975. 5/8". Mint (9.7). Price: $8. CyberAuction #451, t #4.

241. MARBLE KING, INC. Tiger. Three-color patch and ribbon Rainbow ger. Opaque white base. Black and orange/red patch and ribbon. Paden ty WV, circa 1955-1975. 19/32". Mint (9.8). There are two examples ailable, you are bidding on one. Winner has choice of either or both, mainder to under. Price: $7. CyberAuction #396, Lot #11.

242. MARBLE KING, INC. Wasp. Two color Rainbow Wasp. Black and d patch and ribbon. Paden City WV, circa 1955-1965. 19/32". Mint (9.9). ere are two marbles available. You are bidding on one. Winner has choice either or both, remainder to under. Price: $8. CyberAuction #359, Lot 20.

243. MARBLE KING, INC. Wasp. Two color Rainbow Wasp. Black and d patch and ribbon. Paden City WV, circa 1955-1965. 19/32". Mint (9.9). ere are two marbles available. You are bidding on one. Winner has choice either or both, remainder to under. Price: $6. CyberAuction #335, Lot 1.

244. MARBLE KING, INC. Wasp. Two color Rainbow Wasp. Black and d patch and ribbon. Tiny air hole. Paden City WV, circa 1955-1965. 19/ ". Mint (9.8). Price: $4. CyberAuction #404, Lot #35.

245. MARBLE KING, INC. Wasp. Two color Rainbow Wasp. Black and d patch and ribbon. Paden City WV, circa 1955-1965. 19/32". Near int(+) (8.7). Price: $3. CyberAuction #337, Lot #25.

246. MARBLE KING, INC. Wasp. Two color Rainbow Wasp. Black and d patch and ribbon. Paden City WV, circa 1955-1965. 19/32". Mint (9.9). ere are three marbles available. You are bidding on one. Winner has oice of any or all, remainder to under. Price: $3. CyberAuction #384, t #40.

247. MARBLE KING, INC. Wasp. Two color Rainbow Wasp. Black and d patch and ribbon. Paden City WV, circa 1955-1965. 19/32". Mint (9.9). ere are four marbles available. You are bidding on one. Winner has choice any or all, remainder to under. Price: $3. CyberAuction #396, Lot #14.

248. MARBLE KING, INC. Wasp. Two color Rainbow Wasp. Black and

red patch and ribbon. Paden City WV, circa 1955-1965. 19/32". Mint (9.9). There are four marbles available. You are bidding on one. Winner has choice of any or all, remainder to under. Price: $2. CyberAuction #403, Lot #22.

3249. MARBLE KING, INC. Wasp. Two color Rainbow Wasp. Black and red patch and ribbon. An additional brown narrow ribbon. Large air hole, some sparkles and surface fracture lines. Paden City WV, circa 1955-1965. 19/32". Near Mint (8.1). Price: $1. CyberAuction #364, Lot #20.

3250. MASTER MARBLE/GLASS COMPANY. Catseye. Early catseye in red glass. Transparent red glass. Flat vane of opaque white. One sparkle. Clarksburg, WV, circa 1945-1950. 5/8". Near Mint(+) (8.9). Price: $6. CyberAuction #351, Lot #16.

3251. MASTER MARBLE/GLASS COMPANY. Comet. Early Comet patch. Fascinating. Very similar in coloring to an Akro Cornelian, but a patch. Ruddy red base with a wispy white patch on it. Clarksburg, WV, circa 1931-1936. 5/8". Mint (9.9). Price: $19. CyberAuction #357, Lot #50.

3252. MASTER MARBLE/GLASS COMPANY. Comet. Orange patch on yellow. Clarksburg, WV, circa 1930-1940. 23/32". Mint (9.9). Price: $4. CyberAuction #424, Lot #13.

3253. MASTER MARBLE/GLASS COMPANY. Moonie. This is a Master Marble Company opalescent semi-opaque. Clarksburg, WV, circa 1931-1941. 23/32". Mint (9.9). Price: $29. CyberAuction #334, Lot #23.

3254. MASTER MARBLE/GLASS COMPANY. Original package. Original Master Marble counter display stock box. Brown cardboard. Black and yellow graphics. Depicts some marbles on the surface. Some extraneous cardboard on the top that peeled off the box that was stacked on it at one point. Interesting. Marked "100 Assorted Master Meteor Marbles No. 0" on one end. Contains ninety-nine Master opaques in three colors. Marbles are Mint. Box is Mint(-). Very nice item. Price: $150. CyberAuction #405, Lot #60.

3255. MASTER MARBLE/GLASS COMPANY. Original package. Original Master Marble No. 10 box. Double size of the more commonly seen No. 5 box. This contains brushed transparent marbles. Back is printed with the instructions for Ringer. Front has oval cut outs. Red, white and blue box. Hard to find. This one has two tears in the front ovals. Circa mid to late 1930s. Near Mint(+) (8.9). Price: $100. CyberAuction #385, Lot #28.

3256. MASTER MARBLE/GLASS COMPANY. Original package. Original Master Marble No. 10 box. Double size of the more commonly seen No. 5 box. This contains brushed transparent marbles. Back is printed with the instructions for Ringer. Front has oval cut outs. Red, white and blue box. Hard to find. This one has two tears in the front ovals. Circa mid to late 1930s. Near Mint(+) (8.9). Price: $90. CyberAuction #507, Lot #25.

3257. MASTER MARBLE/GLASS COMPANY. Original package. Original No. 13 Master Marble box. This is a rectangular box. Five oval cutouts in the top. Master "sunbeam design" box. Marked No. 13 on one end. The back has the Popsicle premium advertisement on it. Super box. Contains thirteen Comets and Cloudies. The box is Mint (9.8). The marbles are Mint (9.9). Price: $60. CyberAuction #357, Lot #36.

3258. MASTER MARBLE/GLASS COMPANY. Original package. Original Master Marble No. 10 box. Double size of the more commonly seen No. 5 box. This contains transparent marbles. Back is printed with the instructions for Ringer. Front has oval cut outs. Red, white and blue box. Hard to find. This one has some tears in the front ovals. Circa mid to late 1930s. Near Mint(+) (8.9). Price: $55. CyberAuction #396, Lot #31.

3259. MASTER MARBLE/GLASS COMPANY. Original package. Original No. 13 Master Marble box. This is a rectangular box. Five oval cutouts in the top. Master "sunbeam design" box. Marked No. 13 on one end. The back has the Popsicle premium advertisement on it. Super box. Contains thirteen Comets and Cloudies. The box has a torn flap at one end. The box is Near Mint(-). The marbles are Mint (9.9). Price: $25. CyberAuction #395, Lot #30.

3260. MASTER MARBLE/GLASS COMPANY. Original package. No. 5 Master Glass box. Contains Heaton and Champion Agates. Mint (9.7). Price: $10. CyberAuction #457, Lot #24.

3261. MASTER MARBLE/GLASS COMPANY. Patch. Master Glass patch. Translucent white and green patch. Clarksburg, WV, circa 1960-1970. 7/8". Mint (9.9). Price: $7. CyberAuction #461, Lot #35.

3262. MASTER MARBLE/GLASS COMPANY. Patch. Nice Comet patch. One side is brown/red. Other side is yellow. Sparkles. Clarksburg, WV, circa 1930-1940. 3/4". Near Mint(+) (8.9). Price: $3. CyberAuction #420, Lot #9.

3263. MASTER MARBLE/GLASS COMPANY. Sunburst. Clear Sunburst. Light blue, orange, yellow, in clear. Beauty. Clarksburg, WV, circa 1930-1940. 23/32". Mint (9.8). Price: $33. CyberAuction #413, Lot #56.

3264. MASTER MARBLE/GLASS COMPANY. Sunburst. Clear Sunburst. Transparent clear base with some bands of white, light green and orange/brown. Clarksburg, WV, circa 1931-1941. 21/32". Mint (9.9). Price: $25. CyberAuction #412, Lot #36.

3265. MASTER MARBLE/GLASS COMPANY. Sunburst. Clear Sunburst. Transparent clear base with some bands of white, light blue and orange. Clarksburg, WV, circa 1931-1941. 21/32". Mint (9.9). Price: $25. CyberAuction #414, Lot #40.

3266. MASTER MARBLE/GLASS COMPANY. Sunburst. Browns, grays, yellows, light red. Clarksburg, WV, circa 1930-1940. 23/32". Mint (9.9). Price: $22. CyberAuction #431, Lot #37.

3267. MASTER MARBLE/GLASS COMPANY. Sunburst. Dark Sunburst. Browns, reds, yellows, greens. Clarksburg, WV, circa 1931-1941. 3/4". Mint (9.7). Price: $20. CyberAuction #425, Lot #14.

3268. MASTER MARBLE/GLASS COMPANY. Sunburst. Gorgeous example. Clarksburg, WV, circa 1930-1940. 21/32". Mint (9.7). Price: $19. CyberAuction #424, Lot #41.

3269. MASTER MARBLE/GLASS COMPANY. Sunburst. Oddly colored early

Sunburst. Orange and light green on yellow base. Unusual. Clarksburg, WV, circa 1930-1940. 21/32". Mint (9.7). Price: $19. CyberAuction #428, Lot #13.

3270. MASTER MARBLE/GLASS COMPANY. Sunburst. Master Marble Sunburst shooter. Red and brown on green, mostly green. Clarksburg, WV, circa 1930-1940. 3/4". Mint (9.6). Price: $19. CyberAuction #432, Lot #40.

3271. MASTER MARBLE/GLASS COMPANY. Sunburst. Clear Sunburst. Transparent clear base with some bands of white, light yellow and orange/brown. Clarksburg, WV, circa 1931-1941. 21/32". Mint (9.9). Price: $17. CyberAuction #424, Lot #53.

3272. MASTER MARBLE/GLASS COMPANY. Sunburst. Nice marble. Red, gray, yellow and dark green. Clarksburg, WV, circa 1930-1940. 3/4". Mint (9.9). Price: $17. CyberAuction #427, Lot #34.

3273. MASTER MARBLE/GLASS COMPANY. Sunburst. Greens, blues and reds. Nice. Clarksburg, WV, circa 1931-1941. 11/16". Mint (9.7). Price: $17. CyberAuction #458, Lot #1.

3274. MASTER MARBLE/GLASS COMPANY. Sunburst. Mostly greens with some yellow and gray. Clarksburg, WV, circa 1931-1941. 23/32". Mint (9.6). Price: $15. CyberAuction #345, Lot #40.

3275. MASTER MARBLE/GLASS COMPANY. Sunburst. Dark Sunburst. Browns, blues, yellows, clears. Clarksburg, WV, circa 1931-1941. 3/4". Mint (9.7). Price: $15. CyberAuction #363, Lot #9.

3276. MASTER MARBLE/GLASS COMPANY. Sunburst. Light blue, red, dark green and gray. Shooter. Clarksburg, WV, circa 1931-1941. 3/4". Mint (9.9). Price: $15. CyberAuction #410, Lot #39.

3277. MASTER MARBLE/GLASS COMPANY. Sunburst. Nice Master Marble Sunburst. Shooter. Cocoa and red with some brown. One sparkle. Clarksburg, WV, circa 1930-1940. 23/32". Mint(-) (9.0). Price: $14. CyberAuction #412, Lot #22.

3278. MASTER MARBLE/GLASS COMPANY. Sunburst. Nice marble. Red, brown, gray and light green. Clarksburg, WV, circa 1930-1940. 23/32". Mint (9.7). Price: $14. CyberAuction #427, Lot #13.

3279. MASTER MARBLE/GLASS COMPANY. Sunburst. Nice marble. Red, brown, gray and light green. Clarksburg, WV, circa 1930-1940. 11/16". Mint (9.5). Price: $13. CyberAuction #413, Lot #12.

3280. MASTER MARBLE/GLASS COMPANY. Sunburst. Clear Sunburst. Transparent clear base. Filled with white with smeared light blue, and some orange. Clarksburg, WV, circa 1930-1940. 5/8". Mint (9.6). Price: $13. CyberAuction #432, Lot #45.

3281. MASTER MARBLE/GLASS COMPANY. Sunburst. Nice Sunburst. Late Master Marble. Clarksburg, WV, circa 1937-1941. 3/4". Mint (9.7). Price: $12. CyberAuction #424, Lot #20.

3282. MASTER MARBLE/GLASS COMPANY. Sunburst. Clear Sunburst. Transparent clear base almost completely filled with white, light green and orange/brown. Small chip and a sparkle. Clarksburg, WV, circa 1931-1941. 11/16". Near Mint (8.5). Price: $11. CyberAuction #387, Lot #52.

3283. MASTER MARBLE/GLASS COMPANY. Sunburst. Clear Sunburst. Transparent clear base with some bands of white, light green and orange/brown. Clarksburg, WV, circa 1931-1941. 21/32". Mint (9.9). Price: $11. CyberAuction #392, Lot #20.

3284. MASTER MARBLE/GLASS COMPANY. Sunburst. Dark Sunburst. Browns, blues, yellows, clears. Cold roll lines, some wear. Clarksburg, WV, circa 1931-1941. 3/4". Mint(-) (9.1). Price: $10. CyberAuction #404, Lot #31.

3285. MASTER MARBLE/GLASS COMPANY. Sunburst. Odd coloring. White, salmon, peach, pink, yellow, with a clear spot on the top and bottom. One tiny rough spot. Clarksburg, WV, circa 1930-1940. 3/4". Near Mint(+) (8.9). Price: $9. CyberAuction #431, Lot #9.

3286. MASTER MARBLE/GLASS COMPANY. Sunburst. Dark Sunburst. Browns, reds, yellows, greens. Clarksburg, WV, circa 1931-1941. 3/4". Mint (9.7). Price: $8.50. CyberAuction #470, Lot #2.

3287. MASTER MARBLE/GLASS COMPANY. Sunburst. Very nice example. Whites, greens and reds. Clarksburg, WV, circa 1935-1945. 3/4". Mint (9.7). Price: $7. CyberAuction #407, Lot #12.

3288. MASTER MARBLE/GLASS COMPANY. Sunburst. Greens, yellows and browns. A couple of sparkles. Clarksburg, WV, circa 1931-1941. 23/32". Near Mint(+) (8.8). Price: $6. CyberAuction #376, Lot #3.

3289. MASTER MARBLE/GLASS COMPANY. Sunburst. Opaque white, transparent red, faint blue, brown. A couple of sparkles. Clarksburg, WV, circa 1935-1945. 21/32". Near Mint(+) (8.9). Price: $3. CyberAuction #482, Lot #35.

3290. MASTER MARBLE/GLASS COMPANY. Sunburst. White, greens, browns, yellows and reds. Clarksburg, WV, circa 1931-1941. 23/32". Near Mint (8.5). Price: $2. CyberAuction #340, Lot #43.

3291. MASTER MARBLE/GLASS COMPANY. Sunburst. Clear Sunburst. Transparent clear base with some bands of white, light green and orange/brown. Some sparkles. Clarksburg, WV, circa 1931-1941. 5/8". Near Mint(+) (8.7). Price: $2. CyberAuction #345, Lot #32.

3292. MASTER MARBLE/GLASS COMPANY. Sunburst. Opaque white, transparent red, faint blue, brown. A couple of sparkles. Clarksburg, WV, circa 1935-1945. 21/32". Near Mint(+) (8.9). Price: $1. CyberAuction #420, Lot #17.

3293. MASTER MARBLE/GLASS COMPANY. Tigereye. Clear Sunburst. Transparent clear, opaque black, opaque white and translucent orange. Called a Tigereye. Excellent example, one tiny sparkle. Hard to find. Clarksburg, WV, circa 1931-1941. 5/8". Mint (9.3). Price: $32. CyberAuction #458, Lot #57.

3294. MASTER MARBLE/GLASS COMPANY. Tigereye. Clear Sunburst. Transparent clear, opaque black, opaque white and translucent orange. Called a Tigereye. Excellent example. Hard to find. Clarksburg, WV, circa 1931-1941. 5/8". Mint (9.6). Price: $24. CyberAuction #347, Lot #45.

3295. MASTER MARBLE/GLASS COMPANY. Tigereye. Clear Sunburst Transparent clear, opaque black, opaque white and translucent orang Called a Tigereye. Excellent example, one tiny sparkle. Hard to find. Clarksburg, WV, circa 1931-1941. 5/8". Mint (9.3). Price: $24. CyberAuctic #414, Lot #48.

3296. MASTER MARBLE/GLASS COMPANY. Tigereye. Clear Sunbur Transparent clear, opaque black, opaque white and translucent orang Called a Tigereye. Tiny subsurface moon at one pole. Hard to fin Clarksburg, WV, circa 1931-1941. 21/32". Near Mint(+) (8.9). Price: $2 CyberAuction #360, Lot #45.

3297. MASTER MARBLE/GLASS COMPANY. Tigereye. Clear Sunbur Transparent clear, opaque black, opaque white and translucent orang Called a Tigereye. Excellent example, one tiny sparkle. Hard to fin Clarksburg, WV, circa 1931-1941. 5/8". Mint (9.3). Price: $17. CyberAuctic #410, Lot #44.

3298. MASTER MARBLE/GLASS COMPANY. Tigereye. Clear Sunbur Transparent clear, opaque black, opaque white and translucent orang Called a Tigereye. A couple of tiny subsurface moons. Hard to fin Clarksburg, WV, circa 1931-1941. 5/8". Near Mint(+) (8.9). Price: $1 CyberAuction #485, Lot #37.

3299. MASTER MARBLE/GLASS COMPANY. Tigereye. Clear Sunbur Transparent clear, opaque black, opaque white and translucent red. Call a Tigereye. A couple of tiny subsurface moons. Hard to find. Clarksbu WV, circa 1931-1941. 5/8". Near Mint (8.6). Price: $2. CyberAuction #46 Lot #24.

3300. MISCELLANEOUS. Agate. Absolutely stunning and rare large ha cut dyed banded agate. Super faceting. Dyed so that it is blue on most the marble and turquoise at one end. The opposite end is a nice bulls ey Alternating blue and white bands. Fairly parallel lines with a little wavine Superior example!!!! Huge for a dyed hand cut agate. A centerpiece any agate collection. Germany, circa 1850-1920. 15/16". Mint (9.9). Price: $875. CyberAuction #388, Lot #60.

3301. MISCELLANEOUS. Agate. Hand cut dyed blue agate. Banded. E cellent faceting. Nice blue color with white bands. Great bulls eyes. G geous. Germany, circa 1870-1930. 3/4". Mint (9.9). Price: $41 CyberAuction #400, Lot #54.

3302. MISCELLANEOUS. Agate. Hand cut dyed blue agate. Banded. E cellent faceting. Nice blue color with white bands. Great bulls eyes. G geous. Germany, circa 1870-1930. 3/4". Mint (9.9). Price: $39 CyberAuction #422, Lot #56.

3303. MISCELLANEOUS. Agate. Superior and exceptional hand cut b eye banded agate. Perfectly parallel banding. Bulls eye on one end. Wh center with brown around it, then a wide white band to the equator. B tom half are bands of shades of brown and mocha cream. Has an intern flaw (original to stone), one tiny flat gouge (from manufacturer) and a ti hit mark. Exceptional marble. Germany, circa 1840-1890. 29/32". Mint (9.2). Price: $385. CyberAuction #385, Lot #44.

3304. MISCELLANEOUS. Agate. Super "eyeball" agate. Hand cut band agate. Brown and white. Excellent faceting. Two original gouges (the sphe was a cube originally) and one pit. Excellent example of an "eyeball" ty and very large for any hand cut agate. Germany, circa 1830-1880. 1-1/ Mint(-) (9.0). Price: $360. CyberAuction #385, Lot #37.

3305. MISCELLANEOUS. Agate. Very rare marble. Hand cut dyed band agate. Alternating bands of blue and light yellow. Very rare. Nice facetin Germany, circa 1850-1920. 9/16". Mint (9.9). Price: $360. CyberAucti #462, Lot #37.

3306. MISCELLANEOUS. Agate. Hand cut banded agate. Stunning marb Nice faceting. Excellent banding. Gorgeous. Germany, circa 1850-1920. 8". Mint (9.9). Price: $350. CyberAuction #403, Lot #46.

3307. MISCELLANEOUS. Agate. Hand cut dyed blue banded agate. G geous coloring and pattern. Nice faceting. A beauty. Two tiny hit marks one end. Germany, circa 1850-1920. 23/32". Near Mint(+)(8.9). Pric $350. CyberAuction #403, Lot #57.

3308. MISCELLANEOUS. Agate. Hand cut banded agate. Black dyed a ate. Great banding of white and black. Slight waviness. Crystal panel at o end. Nice faceting on parts of it. Super marble!!! Germany, circa 185 1920. 13/16". Mint (9.7). Price: $350. CyberAuction #410, Lot #52.

3309. MISCELLANEOUS. Agate. Very rare marble. Hand cut dyed band agate. Alternating bands of blue and light yellow. Very rare. Nice facetin Germany, circa 1850-1920. 9/16". Mint (9.9). Price: $335. CyberAucti #486, Lot #43.

3310. MISCELLANEOUS. Agate. Rare dyed agate. This is hand cut, w some faceting left on it. Bulls eye banded agate. Dyed blue. With wh bands. Crystal bulls eye on one end! Stunning. Probably Germany, cir 1860-1920. 7/8". Mint (9.9). Price: $330. CyberAuction #339, Lot #5

3311. MISCELLANEOUS. Agate. Hand cut dyed green banded agate. Ban of gorgeous green and white. Nice faceting. Iron inclusion near botto Gorgeous and very hard color to find. Germany, circa 1850-1920. 17/3 Mint (9.9). Price: $330. CyberAuction #392, Lot #53.

3312. MISCELLANEOUS. Agate. Rare dyed agate. This is hand cut, w some faceting left on it. Bulls eye banded agate. Dyed blue. With wh bands. Blue bulls eye on one end. Olive bulls eye on the other! Probal Germany, circa 1860-1920. 3/4". Mint (9.9). Price: $325. CyberAucti #353, Lot #59.

3313. MISCELLANEOUS. Agate. Gorgeous banded hand cut agate. N faceting on it, although somewhat polished. Super bulls eye at either en Very nice tight banding of white and salmon red. Fairly parallel bands w just a little waviness. One tiny fracture defect that is inherent in the origi stone. A beauty!!!! Germany, circa 1860-1920. 13/16". Mint (9.6). Pri $310. CyberAuction #388, Lot #14.

3314. MISCELLANEOUS. Agate. Very hard to find dyed hand cut aga

Highly polished, faceting is just barely visible in a couple of spots. Two white bands around the equator, slightly above it. Green semi-opaque patch on one pole. Other half of the marble is a brown bulls eye, with a green ring around it and then a brown ring between the green and the white. Hard to find coloring. Germany, circa 1860-1920. 23/32". Mint (9.9). Price: $285. CyberAuction #330, Lot #53.

3315. MISCELLANEOUS. Agate. Hand cut banded agate. Black dyed agate. Great banding of white and black. Slight waviness. Crystal panel at one end. Nice faceting on parts of it. Super marble!!! Germany, circa 1850-1920. 13/16". Mint (9.7). Price: $285. CyberAuction #426, Lot #54.

3316. MISCELLANEOUS. Agate. Hand cut dyed agate. Blue, white and green. Blue banding, with white, on most of the marble. Bottom has a translucent milky white patch with green inclusions. Very nice. Nice faceting. Super marble. Germany, circa 1850-1920. 23/32". Mint (9.9). Price: $280. CyberAuction #425, Lot #54.

3317. MISCELLANEOUS. Agate. Hand cut dyed agate. Blue, white and green. Blue banding, with white, on most of the marble. Bottom has a translucent milky white patch with green inclusions. Very nice. Nice faceting. Super marble. Germany, circa 1850-1920. 23/32". Mint (9.9). Price: $280. CyberAuction #482, Lot #41.

3318. MISCELLANEOUS. Agate. Large hand cut black dyed agate. Nice "eye" design. Large crystal panel on the top. Super faceting. This was original on the top of a cane, but it was converted to a marble a long time ago. There is a tiny hole on the bottom that has been filled with a reddish rubber-type substance. From the looks of it, the fill was done close to a hundred years ago. Very rare. Germany, circa 1850-1900. 1-7/16". Mint (9.9). Price: $250. CyberAuction #400, Lot #47.

3319. MISCELLANEOUS. Agate. Excellent example. Black agate (probably dyed). Hand cut, excellent faceting. One end is a crystal patch and a white band. Superb!!! Germany, circa 1870-1930. 13/16". Mint (9.9). Price: $220. CyberAuction #363, Lot #44.

3320. MISCELLANEOUS. Agate. Hand cut banded agate. Super pattern on it. Great faceting. Germany, circa 1850-1920. 15/16". Mint (9.7). Price: $220. CyberAuction #403, Lot #9.

3321. MISCELLANEOUS. Agate. Hand cut dyed green banded agate. Very nice. Pale green. Nice faceting and bands. Some tiny hit marks. Germany, circa 1850-1920. 21/32". Near Mint(+) (8.9). Price: $195. CyberAuction #403, Lot #39.

3322. MISCELLANEOUS. Agate. Hand cut banded agate. Nice faceting. Gorgeous banding. Large crystal panel on one end. Gorgeous. Germany, circa 1860-1920. 29/32". Mint (9.9). Price: $195. CyberAuction #406, Lot #38.

3323. MISCELLANEOUS. Agate. Black dyed banded agate. Hand cut, but then polished. Minimal faceting. Nice tight white and black bands though. Very nice. Germany, circa 1860-1920. 21/32". Mint (9.6). Price: $195. CyberAuction #406, Lot #53.

3324. MISCELLANEOUS. Agate. Hand cut faceted agate. Very nice "eye" pattern. Bands of black, gray, brown and white. Several manufacturing flat spots. Nice. Germany, circa 1850-1920. 29/32". Mint (9.5). Price: $185. CyberAuction #392, Lot #14.

3325. MISCELLANEOUS. Agate. Gorgeous hand cut banded bulls eye agate. Nice faceting. Brown and white equator. Large milky patch at one end, crystal panel at other. Germany, circa 1850-1920. 7/8". Mint (9.5). Price: $185. CyberAuction #395, Lot #21.

3326. MISCELLANEOUS. Agate. Hand cut black dyed banded agate. Stunning pattern. Two very tiny hit marks. Superb marble with great facets. Germany, circa 1850-1920. 13/16". Near Mint(+) (8.9). Price: $185. CyberAuction #424, Lot #44.

3327. MISCELLANEOUS. Agate. Hand cut dyed blue agate. Banded. Faceting is hard to see, but it is present. Nice blue color with white bands. Gorgeous. Germany, circa 1870-1930. 19/32". Mint (9.9). Price: $180. CyberAuction #363, Lot #53.

3328. MISCELLANEOUS. Agate. Hand cut dyed blue banded agate. Dark blue with white equatorial bands. Super faceting. Excellent marble. Germany, circa 1850-1920. 21/32". Mint (9.7). Price: $175. CyberAuction #436, Lot #53.

3329. MISCELLANEOUS. Agate. Superb hand cut agate. A truly outstanding banded agate. Clears, milkies, browns, blacks, whites and grays. Super pattern. Nicely faceted. Crystal panel at one end. Wow. Germany, circa 1860-1900. 1-1/16". Mint (9.6). Price: $170. CyberAuction #336, Lot #55.

3330. MISCELLANEOUS. Agate. Hand cut banded agate. Honey brown and translucent white. Polished after it was faceted, but old. Germany, circa 1860-1920. 1-1/16". Mint (9.7). Price: $160. CyberAuction #403, Lot #20.

3331. MISCELLANEOUS. Agate. Hand cut banded agate. Various shades of brown. Nice faceting. Great pattern. Germany, circa 1850-1920. 7/8". Mint (9.9). Price: $160. CyberAuction #425, Lot #47.

3332. MISCELLANEOUS. Agate. Hand cut dyed blue banded agate. Dark blue with white equatorial bands. Super faceting. Excellent marble. Germany, circa 1850-1920. 21/32". Mint (9.7). Price: $160. CyberAuction #470, Lot #43.

3333. MISCELLANEOUS. Agate. Hand cut dyed black banded agate. Beautiful faceting. Nice crystal panel at one end. Germany, circa 1850-1920. 17/32". Mint (9.9). Price: $150. CyberAuction #403, Lot #13.

3334. MISCELLANEOUS. Agate. Gorgeous hand cut banded agate. Superb faceting. Great pattern. Germany, circa 1850-1920. 1-1/16". Mint (9.8). Price: $150. CyberAuction #414, Lot #19.

3335. MISCELLANEOUS. Agate. Banded agate. Hand cut. Black, white. Super marble. Very hard to find these old ones with black. Excellent faceting. Germany, circa 1850-1900. 23/32". Mint (9.9). Price: $140. CyberAuction #341, Lot #60.

3336. MISCELLANEOUS. Agate. Hand cut banded agate. Black dyed agate. Great banding of white and black. Black panels at either end. Super marble!!! Germany, circa 1850-1920. 3/4". Mint (9.7). Price: $140. CyberAuction #417, Lot #57.

3337. MISCELLANEOUS. Agate. Hand cut agate. Honey brown color with some white. Several dark inclusion. Gorgeous faceting. Exceptional example. Germany, circa 1850-1920. 13/16". Mint (9.6). Price: $135. CyberAuction #400, Lot #1.

3338. MISCELLANEOUS. Agate. Very rare marble. Hand cut with nice faceting. Jet black with three narrow white bands. I do not believe that this is dyed, I think it is naturally pitch black. Very rare. In great shape. Germany, circa 1850-1920. 23/32". Mint (9.8). Price: $120. CyberAuction #348, Lot #43.

3339. MISCELLANEOUS. Agate. Dyed green agate. Probably modern, possibly hand ground. Not much faceting on it. Not antique. Very nice big one though. 1-3/4". Mint (9.7). Price: $110. CyberAuction #393, Lot #18.

3340. MISCELLANEOUS. Agate. Hand cut banded agate. Nice faceting. White and brown bulls eye at one end. Grays, browns and whites. Very nice. Germany, circa 1860-1920. 7/8". Mint (9.9). Price: $110. CyberAuction #396, Lot #54.

3341. MISCELLANEOUS. Agate. Exceptional hand cut bulls eye banded agate. Honey brown and white bands. Perfectly parallel bands. Super faceting. Germany, circa 1860-1920. 23/32". Mint (9.9). Price: $110. CyberAuction #400, Lot #28.

3342. MISCELLANEOUS. Agate. Very nice hand cut banded agate. Germany, circa 1850-1920. 27/32". Mint (9.9). Price: $110. CyberAuction #415, Lot #49.

3343. MISCELLANEOUS. Agate. Hand cut agate. Honey brown color with some white. Several dark inclusion. Gorgeous faceting. Exceptional example. Germany, circa 1850-1920. 13/16". Mint (9.6). Price: $110. CyberAuction #422, Lot #48.

3344. MISCELLANEOUS. Agate. Dyed green agate. Probably modern, possibly hand ground. Not much faceting left on it. Not antique. Very nice big one though. 1-3/4". Mint (9.7). Price: $110. CyberAuction #430, Lot #29.

3345. MISCELLANEOUS. Agate. Hand cut banded agate. Super pattern on it. Great faceting. Germany, circa 1850-1920. 15/16". Mint (9.7). Price: $110. CyberAuction #449, Lot #51.

3346. MISCELLANEOUS. Agate. Hand cut agate. Honey brown color with some white. Several dark inclusion. Gorgeous faceting. Exceptional example. Germany, circa 1850-1920. 13/16". Mint (9.6). Price: $110. CyberAuction #460, Lot #10.

3347. MISCELLANEOUS. Agate. Hand cut dyed black banded agate. Thin white concentric rings. Excellent faceting. One flat spot. Germany, circa 1850-1920. 11/16". Mint (9.5). Price: $110. CyberAuction #504, Lot #28.

3348. MISCELLANEOUS. Agate. Hand cut banded agate. Brown and white bands, with a large crystal patch at one pole. Germany, circa 1850-1920. 11/16". Mint (9.9). Price: $90. CyberAuction #347, Lot #58.

3349. MISCELLANEOUS. Agate. Beautiful hand cut agate. Finely polished. Banded agate. Brown and oranges with whites and creams. Large. This one is superb. Germany, circa 1860-1920. 15/16". Mint (9.9). Price: $85. CyberAuction #336, Lot #34.

3350. MISCELLANEOUS. Agate. Gorgeous, large hand cut agate. Banded. Reds, whites, grays, browns. Beauty and large. Germany, circa 1860-1920. 1". Mint (9.4). Price: $85. CyberAuction #339, Lot #37.

3351. MISCELLANEOUS. Agate. Hand cut banded agate. Superb banding and bulls eyes. Gorgeous. Nice faceting. Germany, circa 1850-1920. 11/16". Mint (9.9). Price: $85. CyberAuction #369, Lot #44.

3352. MISCELLANEOUS. Agate. Very nice hand cut agate. One half is orange/brown. Other half is milky white with some brown. Nice faceting. Small gouge line at one pole that was a fault in the stone itself. Germany, circa 1850-1920. 7/8". Mint(-) (9.2). Price: $80. CyberAuction #404, Lot #39.

3353. MISCELLANEOUS. Agate. Modern agate sphere. Mexican agate. Super red, brown, gray and white banding. Red eyeball on top. 2-3/4" (sight). Mint (9.9). Price: $80. CyberAuction #413, Lot #27.

3354. MISCELLANEOUS. Agate. Hand cut agate. Honey brown color with some white. Several dark inclusion. Gorgeous faceting. Exceptional example. Germany, circa 1850-1920. 13/16". Mint (9.6). Price: $80. CyberAuction #507, Lot #20.

3355. MISCELLANEOUS. Agate. Hand cut banded agate. Nice faceting. Nice parallel bands, with some minor waviness. Small bulls eye at one end. Two minor inclusions. Germany, circa 1860-1920. 11/16". Mint (9.6). Price: $75. CyberAuction #406, Lot #7.

3356. MISCELLANEOUS. Agate. Very nice hand cut banded agate. Germany, circa 1850-1920. 27/32". Mint (9.9). Price: $75. CyberAuction #441, Lot #56.

3357. MISCELLANEOUS. Agate. Very nice hand cut agate. One half is orange/brown. Other half is milky white with some brown. Nice faceting. Small gouge line at one pole that was a fault in the stone itself. Germany, circa 1850-1920. 7/8". Mint(-) (9.2). Price: $75. CyberAuction #499, Lot #28.

3358. MISCELLANEOUS. Agate. Rare yellow dyed agate. Not the best of examples, but very rare. The equator is opaque white, about three-quarters or so of the surface of the marble. There are several faint gray strands in it and two very faint ruddy yellow bands. One end is a poor crystal panel, the other end is a semi-translucent gray patch with ruddy yellow coloring where the patch meets the white. Some faceting. Overall wear and very tiny hits from use. Germany, circa 1830-1900. 23/32". Near Mint(-) (8.0). Price: $70. CyberAuction #387, Lot #40.

3359. MISCELLANEOUS. Agate. Superb hand cut black banded agate. Two thirds of the marble is banding in various transparent shades of tan and gray. One third is a bulls eye of opaque black and white banding. Excellent facets. Superb marble. Hard to find. Germany, circa 1850-1920. 19/32". Mint (9.7). Price: $70. CyberAuction #390, Lot #30.

3360. MISCELLANEOUS. Agate. Black dyed bulls eye agate. Hand cut, nice faceting. Almost completely black. White band around equator. Bulls eye of various banded shades of gray and black at one end. Super. Germany, circa 1850-1920. 1/2". Mint (9.9). Price: $70. CyberAuction #391, Lot #58.

3361. MISCELLANEOUS. Agate. Hand cut dyed black agate. Great pattern with a crystal panel. Nice faceting. Gorgeous. Germany, circa 1860-1920. 5/8". Mint (9.7). Price: $70. CyberAuction #444, Lot #6.

3362. MISCELLANEOUS. Agate. Hand cut dyed black banded agate. No faceting. Germany, circa 18750-1920. 19/32". Mint (9.9). Price: $65. CyberAuction #465, Lot #50.

3363. MISCELLANEOUS. Agate. Hand cut banded agate. Various shades of brown. Nice faceting. Great pattern. Germany, circa 1850-1920. 7/8". Mint (9.9). Price: $65. CyberAuction #478, Lot #38.

3364. MISCELLANEOUS. Agate. Hand cut dyed black banded agate. No faceting. Germany, circa 18750-1920. 19/32". Mint (9.9). Price: $65. CyberAuction #494, Lot #2.

3365. MISCELLANEOUS. Agate. Super bulls eye banded agate. Hand cut. Browns, grays and whites. Gorgeous. Germany, circa 1860-1920. 11/16". Mint (9.7). Price: $60. CyberAuction #391, Lot #49.

3366. MISCELLANEOUS. Agate. Very nice hand cut agate. One half is orange/brown. Other half is milky white with some brown. Nice faceting. Small gouge line at one pole that was a fault in the stone itself. Germany, circa 1850-1920. 7/8". Mint(-) (9.2). Price: $55. CyberAuction #441, Lot #35.

3367. MISCELLANEOUS. Agate. Hand cut banded agate. Various shades of brown. Nice faceting. Great pattern. Germany, circa 1850-1920. 7/8". Mint (9.9). Price: $55. CyberAuction #456, Lot #50.

3368. MISCELLANEOUS. Agate. Very nice hand cut agate. One half is orange/brown. Other half is milky white with some brown. Nice faceting. Small gouge line at one pole that was a fault in the stone itself. Germany, circa 1850-1920. 7/8". Mint(-) (9.2). Price: $55. CyberAuction #484, Lot #39.

3369. MISCELLANEOUS. Agate. Hand cut agate. Very lightly banded. Gorgeous marble, super faceting. Germany, circa 1860-1920. 27/32". Mint (9.9). Price: $50. CyberAuction #333, Lot #8.

3370. MISCELLANEOUS. Agate. Hand cut agate. Nice faceting. Bands of transparent, white and black. It may have been dyed. One manufacturing gouge. Germany, circa 1860-1920. 9/16". Mint(-) (9.1). Price: $50. CyberAuction #366, Lot #31.

3371. MISCELLANEOUS. Agate. Hand cut banded agate. Brown and creams. Crystal eyeball on one side. Germany, circa 1850-1920. 7/8". Mint (9.9). Price: $50. CyberAuction #479, Lot #31.

3372. MISCELLANEOUS. Agate. Hand cut dyed black banded agate. Super black and white bulls eye at one end. Grayish transparent on the rest. Great faceting. Germany, circa 1870-1915. 9/16". Mint (9.6). Price: $47. CyberAuction #421, Lot #46.

3373. MISCELLANEOUS. Agate. Hand cut banded agate. Black dyed agate. Great banding of white and black. White panel at one end. Two small gouges. Super marble!!! Germany, circa 1850-1920. 17/32". Mint (9.5). Price: $45. CyberAuction #414, Lot #33.

3374. MISCELLANEOUS. Agate. Hand cut banded agate. Browns and whites. Nice faceting. A little wear. Germany, circa 1850-1920. 13/16". Near Mint(+) (8.9). Price: $45. CyberAuction #421, Lot #14.

3375. MISCELLANEOUS. Agate. Hand cut banded agate. Super looking marble, very pretty. Nice faceting, a couple of original gouges. Germany, circa 1850-1920. 7/8". Mint (9.3). Price: $44. CyberAuction #439, Lot #53.

3376. MISCELLANEOUS. Agate. Hand cut banded agate. Very light faceting. White patch at one end. Dark brown at the other. Light brown in between. Some tiny hit marks. Germany, circa 1860-1920. 27/32". Near Mint(+) (8.9). Price: $42. CyberAuction #403, Lot #29.

3377. MISCELLANEOUS. Agate. Hand cut dyed black agate. Nice faceting. Germany, circa 1870-1920. 5/8". Mint (9.8). Price: $42. CyberAuction #439, Lot #32.

3378. MISCELLANEOUS. Agate. Carnelian hand cut agate with small bulls eye. Germany, circa 1850-1920. 25/32". Mint (9.9). Price: $42. CyberAuction #501, Lot #36.

3379. MISCELLANEOUS. Agate. Dyed hand cut dark brown banded agate. Some faceting. Nice patterns. Germany, circa 1850-1920. 3/4". Mint (9.9). Price: $42. CyberAuction #508, Lot #23.

3380. MISCELLANEOUS. Agate. Hand cut dyed black agate. Nice faceting. Germany, circa 1870-1915. 5/8". Mint (9.8). Price: $41. CyberAuction #482, Lot #19.

3381. MISCELLANEOUS. Agate. Hand cut carnelian agate. Very nice with some white mixed in. Pretty. Germany, circa 1860-1920. 23/32". Mint (9.9). Price: $37. CyberAuction #335, Lot #51.

3382. MISCELLANEOUS. Agate. Hand cut banded agate. Nice faceting. And nice bands. A beauty. Germany, circa 1860-1920. 3/4". Mint (9.6). Price: $37. CyberAuction #341, Lot #47.

3383. MISCELLANEOUS. Agate. Hand cut banded agate. Beauty. Germany, circa 1850-1920. 5/8". Mint (9.9). Price: $37. CyberAuction #414, Lot #9.

3384. MISCELLANEOUS. Agate. Large green agate. Not antique. Gorgeous sphere. Couple of tiny hit marks. Origin and age unknown. 1-1/2". Near Mint(+) (8.9). Price: $36. CyberAuction #375, Lot #20.

3385. MISCELLANEOUS. Agate. Hand cut gray agate. Older marble, not colored or dyed. Top half is a crystal panel. Bottom half is white and gray banding. Nice faceting. Germany, circa 1900-1950. 3/4". Mint(-) (9.0). Price: $35. CyberAuction #414, Lot #38.

3386. MISCELLANEOUS. Agate. Very nice hand cut agate. Subtle banding. Nice faceting. Germany, circa 1860-1920. 23/32". Mint (9.9). Price: $32. CyberAuction #347, Lot #38.

3387. MISCELLANEOUS. Agate. Hand cut banded agate. Very little faceting, mostly polished off, but a few flat spots. Nice coloring and pattern. Germany, circa 1850-1920. 3/4". Near Mint(+) (8.9). Price: $32. CyberAuction #410, Lot #42.

3388. MISCELLANEOUS. Agate. Modern banded. Gorgeous, almost Vaseline colors. Very nice. 1-1/4". Mint (9.9). Price: $32. CyberAuction #419, Lot #37.

3389. MISCELLANEOUS. Agate. Hand cut banded agate. Very light faceting. White patch at one end. Dark brown at the other. Light brown in between. Some tiny hit marks. Germany, circa 1860-1920. 27/32". Near Mint(+) (8.9). Price: $32. CyberAuction #440, Lot #57.

3390. MISCELLANEOUS. Agate. Hand cut dyed black agate. Nice faceting. Two original flat spots. Germany, circa 1870-1915. 3/4". Mint (9.6). Price: $32. CyberAuction #442, Lot #19.

3391. MISCELLANEOUS. Agate. Hand cut banded agate. Browns and white. Beauty. Germany, circa 1850-1920. 11/16". Mint (9.9). Price: $32. CyberAuction #475, Lot #47.

3392. MISCELLANEOUS. Agate. Carnelian hand cut agate with small bulls eye. Germany, circa 1850-1920. 23/32". Mint (9.9). Price: $32. CyberAuction #501, Lot #55.

3393. MISCELLANEOUS. Agate. Blue dyed agate. I cannot discern any faceting on it, so I cannot tell if it is hand cut or not. Probably highly polished. Looks old, but I can't offer an opinion on the age. White bulls eye at one end. Blue remainder with hints of green. 27/32". Mint (9.9). Price: $31. CyberAuction #365, Lot #59.

3394. MISCELLANEOUS. Agate. Hand cut agate. Nice faceting. Mostly orange/brown. White band near the equator. Brown patch at one pole. Germany, circa 1870-1915. 3/4". Mint (9.9). Price: $30. CyberAuction #353, Lot #21.

3395. MISCELLANEOUS. Agate. Hand cut banded agate. Some faceting on it, but it's been polished. Some hits. Germany, circa 1860-1910. 15/16". Near Mint (8.5). Price: $30. CyberAuction #407, Lot #50.

3396. MISCELLANEOUS. Agate. Hand cut banded agate. Some faceting on it, but it's been polished. Some hits. Germany, circa 1860-1910. 15/16". Near Mint (8.5). Price: $30. CyberAuction #506, Lot #6.

3397. MISCELLANEOUS. Agate. Hand cut agate. Very interesting. One side is translucent white/gray. Other side is a large crystal patch. There is a narrow orange/brown, and a opaque white, band in between. One tiny hit mark on the crystal. Nice faceting. Germany, circa 1850-1920. 25/32". Near Mint(+) (8.9). Price: $29. CyberAuction #383, Lot #29.

3398. MISCELLANEOUS. Agate. Hand cut banded dyed brown agate. Very nice. Germany, circa 1850-1920. 9/16". Mint (9.9). Price: $28. CyberAuction #508, Lot #11.

3399. MISCELLANEOUS. Agate. Hand cut banded agates. Bands of red/ browns and whites. Very nice banding. Highly polished. Germany, circa 1860-1920. 21/32". Mint (9.7). Price: $27. CyberAuction #345, Lot #51.

3400. MISCELLANEOUS. Agate. Hand cut agate. Bottom half is gray. Then a white band. Then upper half is crystal. Some small hits. Germany, circa 1860-1920. 3/4". Near Mint (8.6). Price: $27. CyberAuction #355, Lot #23.

3401. MISCELLANEOUS. Agate. Nice banded light brown and creamy white. Opaque brown patch at either pole. Nice faceting. Germany, circa 1860-1920. 3/4". Mint (9.9). Price: $25. CyberAuction #342, Lot #11.

3402. MISCELLANEOUS. Agate. Hand cut banded agate. Mostly brown. One end has white bulls eye. Germany, circa 1860-1920. 21/32". Mint (9.9). Price: $25. CyberAuction #345, Lot #29.

3403. MISCELLANEOUS. Agate. Hand cut dyed black banded agate from a hatpin. Has a small hole in the bottom. White and black banding. Germany, circa 1860-1920. 13/32". Mint (9.7). Price: $25. CyberAuction #411, Lot #8.

3404. MISCELLANEOUS. Agate. Hand cut banded agate. Nice faceting. Some subsurface hit marks. Germany, circa 1860-1920. 13/16". Near Mint (8.6). Price: $23. CyberAuction #341, Lot #52.

3405. MISCELLANEOUS. Agate. Hand cut banded agate. Creamy browns, brown/reds and white. Nice bulls eye on one end. One tiny subsurface hit spot. Germany, circa 1860-1920. 3/4". Near Mint(+) (8.9). Price: $23. CyberAuction #351, Lot #4.

3406. MISCELLANEOUS. Agate. Modern dyed banded agate. Machine cut. Crystal patch at one end. Nice dyed blue color. Large open hole in it. Origin and age unknown. 25/32". Mint (9.9). Price: $23. CyberAuction #352, Lot #57.

3407. MISCELLANEOUS. Agate. Hand cut banded agate. Whites and brown/oranges. Nice bulls eye and banding. Good faceting. Has some tiny hit marks on it. Germany, circa 1860-1920. 5/8". Near Mint (8.6). Price: $23. CyberAuction #359, Lot #2.

3408. MISCELLANEOUS. Agate. Banded agate. Hand cut. Nice faceting. Orange/brown and white bands. Germany, circa 1870-1915. 5/8". Mint (9.9). Price: $23. CyberAuction #382, Lot #8.

3409. MISCELLANEOUS. Agate. Very unusual hand cut agate. Creamy, almost peach color, with a brown/orange patch at one end. Small crystal inclusion on one side. Several original stone fractures and an original manufacturing gouge. Very unusual. Germany, circa 1850-1920. 7/8". Mint(-) (9.0). Price: $23. CyberAuction #449, Lot #55.

3410. MISCELLANEOUS. Agate. Hand cut banded agate. Mostly semi-opaque white, with some orange/brown bands on it. Very nice marble. Germany, circa 1860-1920. 25/32". Mint (9.9). Price: $22. CyberAuction #335, Lot #33.

3411. MISCELLANEOUS. Agate. Hand cut banded agate. Crystal at one end. White at other. Bands of white and orange/brown in the middle. 17/32". Mint (9.9). Price: $22. CyberAuction #348, Lot #35.

3412. MISCELLANEOUS. Agate. Hand cut banded agate. Creamy mocha brown and orange/red. Nice faceting. A beauty. Germany, circa 1860-1920. 3/4". Mint (9.9). Price: $22. CyberAuction #384, Lot #44.

3413. MISCELLANEOUS. Agate. Hand cut banded agate. Some faceting on it, but it's been polished. Some hits. Germany, circa 1860-1910. 15/16". Near Mint (8.5). Price: $22. CyberAuction #437, Lot #8.

3414. MISCELLANEOUS. Agate. Hand cut agate. Nice faceting. Nice banding of gray, white and orange/brown. 11/16". Mint (9.9). Price: $21. CyberAuction #348, Lot #23.

3415. MISCELLANEOUS. Agate. Hand cut agate. Brown at one end. White at other. Bands of white and orange/brown in the middle. 17/32". Mint (9.9). Price: $21. CyberAuction #350, Lot #4.

3416. MISCELLANEOUS. Agate. Hand cut agate. Banded. Nice oblong bulls eye at one end. Browns and whites. Germany, circa 1860-1920. 23/32". Mint (9.9). Price: $21. CyberAuction #354, Lot #18.

3417. MISCELLANEOUS. Agate. Black dyed banded agate. Highly polished. I do not believe it to be antique. Still, gorgeous marble. Origin and age unknown. 25/32". Mint (9.9). Price: $21. CyberAuction #369, Lot #55.

3418. MISCELLANEOUS. Agate. Very unusual hand cut agate. Creamy, almost peach color, with a brown/orange patch at one end. Small crystal inclusion on one side. Several original stone fractures and an original manufacturing gouge. Very unusual. Germany, circa 1850-1920. 7/8". Mint(-) (9.0). Price: $20. CyberAuction #389, Lot #58.

3419. MISCELLANEOUS. Agate. Hand cut carnelian agate. Nice. One flaw. Germany, circa 1860-1920. 5/8". Mint (9.5). Price: $19. CyberAuction #350, Lot #17.

3420. MISCELLANEOUS. Agate. Hand cut banded agate. Shades of white, with brown patch on top. Germany, circa 1850-1920. 17/32". Mint (9.5). Price: $19. CyberAuction #464, Lot #2.

3421. MISCELLANEOUS. Agate. Hand cut agate. Some faceting on it, but it's been polished. Some hits. Germany, circa 1860-1910. 15/16". Near Mint (8.5). Price: $19. CyberAuction #488, Lot #12.

3422. MISCELLANEOUS. Agate. Hand cut agate. Banded. Interesting coloring. Blue/gray with wide white panel at one end. Some white banded. Some tiny hit marks at the other end. Germany, circa 1860-1920. 3/4". Near Mint(+) (8.8). Price: $18. CyberAuction #351, Lot #23.

3423. MISCELLANEOUS. Agate. Hand cut agate. Very interesting. Translucent white stone. Has two layers of brown, one at either end. There is a layer of floating black inclusions also. Nice. Germany, circa 1860-1920. 19/32". Mint (9.9). Price: $17. CyberAuction #338, Lot #16.

3424. MISCELLANEOUS. Agate. Gray agate. Probably machine cut. 1-3/16". Mint (9.9). Price: $17. CyberAuction #347, Lot #18.

3425. MISCELLANEOUS. Agate. Hand cut banded agate. One half is white bands. One half is brown bands with a white bulls eye. Germany, circa 1860-1920. 9/16". Mint (9.8). Price: $17. CyberAuction #354, Lot #39.

3426. MISCELLANEOUS. Agate. Very interesting hand cut agate. Translucent gray sphere. Small brown patch on one end. Very interesting thin flat inclusion running through the marble. Germany, circa 1870-1915. 11/16". Mint (9.7). Price: $17. CyberAuction #389, Lot #51.

3427. MISCELLANEOUS. Agate. Hand cut banded agate. Light brown and white bands. Nice faceting. A beauty. Germany circa 1860-1920. 19/32". Mint (9.9). Price: $17. CyberAuction #396, Lot #5.

3428. MISCELLANEOUS. Agate. Hand cut banded agate. Not sure of it's age though. 7/8". Mint (9.7). Price: $17. CyberAuction #399, Lot #40.

3429. MISCELLANEOUS. Agate. Hand cut carnelian agate. Faint banding. Dark brown patch at either pole. Two small original gouges. Nice faceting. Germany, circa 1860-1920. 5/8". Mint(-) (9.0). Price: $17. CyberAuction #466, Lot #34.

3430. MISCELLANEOUS. Agate. Hand cut peewee banded agate. Very nice. Germany, circa 1860-1920. 15/32". Mint (9.7). Price: $15. CyberAuction #351, Lot #8.

3431. MISCELLANEOUS. Agate. Hand cut banded agate. Translucent milky white, orange/brown, white. Germany, circa 1860-1920. 21/32". Mint (9.8). Price: $15. CyberAuction #351, Lot #10.

3432. MISCELLANEOUS. Agate. Hand cut agate. Nice agate. Brown banded with a white patch at one pole. Germany, circa 1860-1920. 5/8". Mint (9.9). Price: $15. CyberAuction #355, Lot #44.

3433. MISCELLANEOUS. Agate. Hand cut agate. Nice light brown and white color. Almost orange. Nice patterns, some fractures that are natural to the stone. Germany, circa 1860-1920. 17/32". Mint(-) (9.1). Price: $15. CyberAuction #471, Lot #20.

3434. MISCELLANEOUS. Agate. Hand cut dyed agate. Dark brown. Nice banding. Large crystal panel at one end. Small inclusion at other end that shattered when it was cut. Germany, circa 1850-1920. 13/16". Mint(-) (9.0). Price: $15. CyberAuction #490, Lot #6.

3435. MISCELLANEOUS. Agate. Nice hand cut banded agate. Creamy whites, brown/oranges, brown/reds. Germany, circa 1860-1920. 5/8". Mint (9.7). Price: $14. CyberAuction #353, Lot #6.

3436. MISCELLANEOUS. Agate. Hand cut agate. Banded. Light orange/brown and white bands. Several tiny subsurface hits. Germany, circa 1860-1920. 23/32". Near Mint(+) (8.7). Price: $14. CyberAuction #356, Lot #17.

3437. MISCELLANEOUS. Agate. Hand cut banded bulls eye agate. Nice faceting. Brown and white. One small gouge. Beauty. Germany, circa 1850-1920. 5/8". Mint(-) (9.1). Price: $14. CyberAuction #395, Lot #19.

3438. MISCELLANEOUS. Agate. Hand cut banded agate. Light faceting. Very light brown, blending with off-white. Two inclusions. Germany, circa 1850-1920. 5/8". Mint (9.7). Price: $14. CyberAuction #474, Lot #18.

3439. MISCELLANEOUS. Agate. Hand cut agate. Orange/brown on one end, milky white on the other. One tiny sparkle. Germany, circa 1860-1920. 9/16". Mint(-) (9.0). Price: $13. CyberAuction #352, Lot #45.

3440. MISCELLANEOUS. Agate. Hand cut banded agate. Predominately whites, with a few brown bands. A couple of original gouges. Germany, circa 1870-1915. 5/8". Mint(-) (9.0). Price: $13. CyberAuction #356, Lot #13.

3441. MISCELLANEOUS. Agate. Hand cut banded agate. Various shades of light brown. Original gouge at either pole. Germany, circa 1860-1920. 9/16". Mint(-) (9.0). Price: $13. CyberAuction #375, Lot #14.

3442. MISCELLANEOUS. Agate. Hand cut peewee banded agate. Very nice. Some pits in one spot, part of original manufacturing. Germany, circa 1860-1920. 15/32". Mint(-) (9.0). Price: $13. CyberAuction #385, Lot #14.

3443. MISCELLANEOUS. Agate. Hand cut carnelian agate. One original gouge, nice faceting. Germany, circa 1850-1920. 11/16". Mint (9.5). Price: $13. CyberAuction #439, Lot #47.

3444. MISCELLANEOUS. Agate. Hand cut agate. Mostly brown creamy, with some slightly darker brown bands. White and brown bulls eye at one end. Germany, circa 1870-1915. 5/8". Mint (9.9). Consignor note: A7. Price: $12. CyberAuction #344, Lot #6.

3445. MISCELLANEOUS. Agate. Hand cut agate. Carnelian with a white bulls eye. Germany, circa 1860-1920. 21/32". Mint (9.9). Price: $12. CyberAuction #358, Lot #49.

3446. MISCELLANEOUS. Agate. Hand cut agate. Carnelian. White patch at one pole. Some hits. Germany, circa 1860-1920. 17/32". Near Mint (8.5). Price: $12. CyberAuction #360, Lot #40.

3447. MISCELLANEOUS. Agate. Hand cut agate. Brown bottom. White patch on one pole. Germany, circa 1850-1920. 1/2". Mint (9.9). Price: $12. CyberAuction #425, Lot #10.

3448. MISCELLANEOUS. Agate. Hand cut banded agate. Some faceting on it, but it's been polished. Some hits. Germany, circa 1860-1910. 15/16". Near Mint (8.5). Price: $12. CyberAuction #460, Lot #16.

3449. MISCELLANEOUS. Agate. Hand cut agate. Orange/brown and shades of white. Some original defects. Germany, circa 1860-1920. 5/8". Mint(-) (9.0). Price: $11. CyberAuction #352, Lot #39.

3450. MISCELLANEOUS. Agate. Hand cut banded agate. Very nice. Germany, circa 1850-1920. 7/16". Mint (9.6). Price: $11. CyberAuction #363, Lot #3.

3451. MISCELLANEOUS. Agate. Hand cut banded agate. Grey, brown and white. Germany, circa 1860-1920. 19/32". Mint(-) (9.1). Price: $11. CyberAuction #366, Lot #25.

3452. MISCELLANEOUS. Agate. Hand cut pale bulls eye agate. Nice faceting. One tiny gouge. Nice example. Germany, circa 1850-1900. 5/8". Mint (9.5). Price: $11. CyberAuction #387, Lot #9.

3453. MISCELLANEOUS. Agate. Powder blue dyed Brazilian lace agate. Modern. 29/32". Mint (9.8). Price: $11. CyberAuction #402, Lot #49.

3454. MISCELLANEOUS. Agate. Hand cut banded agate. Browns, grays and whites. Nice faceting. I'm not sure of the age. 1/2". Mint (9.9). Price: $11. CyberAuction #421, Lot #18.

3455. MISCELLANEOUS. Agate. Hand cut carnelian agate. Nice honey brown color. Some original gouges, nice faceting. Germany, circa 1850-1920. 3/4". Mint (9.3). Price: $11. CyberAuction #442, Lot #1.

3456. MISCELLANEOUS. Agate. Hand cut agate. Various shades of brown. Germany, circa 1850-1920. 5/8". Mint (9.5). Price: $11. CyberAuction #455, Lot #21.

3457. MISCELLANEOUS. Agate. Nice hand cut banded agate. One side is crystal. Other side is white and orange/brown banded. Very nice. One tiny flake. Germany, circa 1870-1915. 17/32". Near Mint(+) (8.9). Price: $10. CyberAuction #353, Lot #37.

3458. MISCELLANEOUS. Agate. Hand cut banded agate. Two manufacturing gouges and a small fracture. Nice banding and faceting. Germany, circa 1860-1920. 11/16". Near Mint(+) (8.8). Price: $10. CyberAuction #359, Lot #15.

3459. MISCELLANEOUS. Agate. Hand cut carnelian agate. Faint banding. Dark brown patch at either pole. Two small original gouges. Nice faceting. Germany, circa 1850-1920. 5/8". Mint(-) (9.0). Price: $10. CyberAuction #371, Lot #4.

3460. MISCELLANEOUS. Agate. Hand cut agate. Nice faceting. One manufacturing gouge at one end. Some subsurface moons. Well-loved. Nice example. Germany, circa 1850-1900. 13/16". Near Mint (8.6). Price: $10. CyberAuction #374, Lot #3.

3461. MISCELLANEOUS. Agate. Hand cut agate. Bands are various shades of honey brown. Some hit marks, it's been used. Germany, circa 1850-1920. 13/16". Near Mint(-) (8.0). Price: $10. CyberAuction #412, Lot #32.

3462. MISCELLANEOUS. Agate. Hand cut agate. Bands are various shades of honey brown. Some hit marks, it's been used. Germany, circa 1850-1920. 13/16". Near Mint(-) (8.0). Price: $10. CyberAuction #430, Lot #38.

3463. MISCELLANEOUS. Agate. Hand cut carnelian agate. Nice honey brown color. Some original gouges, nice faceting. Germany, circa 1850-1920. 25/32". Mint (9.3). Price: $10. CyberAuction #439, Lot #44.

3464. MISCELLANEOUS. Agate. Hand cut agate. Bands are various shades of honey brown. Some hit marks, it's been used. Germany, circa 1850-1920. 13/16". Near Mint(-) (8.0). Price: $10. CyberAuction #477, Lot #56.

3465. MISCELLANEOUS. Agate. Hand cut banded agate. Very nice. Some gouges. Germany, circa 1860-1920. 19/32". Mint (9.6). Price: $9. CyberAuction #334, Lot #17.

3466. MISCELLANEOUS. Agate. Hand cut carnelian agate. One tiny white spot. Nice faceting. A few original defects in the stone. Germany, circa 1850-1920. 23/32". Mint(-) (9.0). Price: $9. CyberAuction #340, Lot #10.

3467. MISCELLANEOUS. Agate. Hand cut carnelian agate. Some faceting. One rough spot. Germany, circa 180-1920. 19/32". Mint(-) (9.0). Price: $9. CyberAuction #344, Lot #13.

3468. MISCELLANEOUS. Agate. Hand cut agate. Banded. Browns with some pale white bands. A couple of gouges. Germany, circa 1860-1920. 17/32". Mint(-) (9.0). Price: $9. CyberAuction #374, Lot #21.

3469. MISCELLANEOUS. Agate. Hand cut banded agate. Shades of brown, white and cream. 1/2". Mint (9.9). Price: $9. CyberAuction #423, Lot #37.

3470. MISCELLANEOUS. Agate. Hand cut banded agate. Light faceting. Very light brown, blending with off-white. Two inclusions. Germany, circa 1850-1920. 5/8". Mint (9.7). Price: $8. CyberAuction #410, Lot #4.

3471. MISCELLANEOUS. Agate. Hand cut agate. Various shades of brown. Germany, circa 1850-1920. 5/8". Mint (9.5). Price: $8. CyberAuction #428, Lot #2.

3472. MISCELLANEOUS. Agate. Hand cut banded agate. Light faceting. Very light brown, blending with off-white. Two inclusions. Germany, circa 1850-1920. 5/8". Mint (9.7). Price: $8. CyberAuction #446, Lot #52.

3473. MISCELLANEOUS. Agate. Hand cut carnelian agate. Overall tiny subsurface hit marks. Germany, circa 1860-1920. 13/16". Near Mint (8.4). Price: $7. CyberAuction #331, Lot #14.

3474. MISCELLANEOUS. Agate. Hand cut agate. Banded. Browns with some pale white bands. A couple of gouges. Germany, circa 1860-1920. 17/32". Mint(-) (9.0). Price: $7. CyberAuction #354, Lot #7.

3475. MISCELLANEOUS. Agate. Hand cut banded agate. Nice faceting. Very nice light bulls eye at one end. One tiny hit mark, one original stone fracture. Germany, circa 1850-1920. 9/16". Near Mint(+) (8.9). Price: $7. CyberAuction #391, Lot #10.

3476. MISCELLANEOUS. Agate. Hand cut agate. Nice faceting. Mostly brown with wavy white ribbons. Several original defects. Beauty. Germany, circa 1870-1915. 19/32". Mint(-) (9.0). Price: $7. CyberAuction #392, Lot #8.

3477. MISCELLANEOUS. Agate. Hand cut banded agate. Beautiful coloring and pattern. No faceting. Probably old, but I'm not certain. 1/2". Mint (9.9). Price: $7. CyberAuction #420, Lot #24.

3478. MISCELLANEOUS. Agate. Hand cut agate. Nice faceting. Mostly brown with wavy white ribbons. Several original defects. Beauty. Germany, circa 1870-1915. 19/32". Mint(-) (9.0). Price: $7. CyberAuction #445, Lot #46.

3479. MISCELLANEOUS. Agate. Hand cut carnelian agate. Faint banding. Dark brown patch at either pole. Two small original gouges. Nice faceting. Germany, circa 1860-1920. 5/8". Mint(-) (9.0). Price: $4. CyberAuction #453, Lot #50.

3480. MISCELLANEOUS. Agate. Hand cut agate. Creamy and honey brown banding. A couple of tiny subsurface moons. Germany, circa 1850-1920. 19/32". Near Mint(+) (8.7). Price: $2. CyberAuction #485, Lot #7.

3481. MISCELLANEOUS. Agateware. Victorian button hook with a hand cut agate ornament. White metal buttonhook, with a claw at the top. Claw is grasping a light brown and white hand cut agate sphere. Agate is about 5/8" and Mint (9.9). Buttonhook is about 4" long and Mint(+) (9.0). Circa mid to late 1800s. England. Price: $120. CyberAuction #428, Lot #35.

3482. MISCELLANEOUS. Apparel. Baseball-type cap. Embroidered on front "Lost Your Marbles" with a colorful marble in the center of that. Six styles available. Bidding on one. Winner has choice of any or all. After you win, state the style(s) you want, remainder to unders. The styles The styles and lot numbers are: 1)blue denim with brown suede bill, 2) blue with brown piping, 3) blue with red piping, 4) green with jacquard bill, 5) blue with red bill, 6) green denim with khaki bill. Price: $12. CyberAuction #358, Lot #25.

3483. MISCELLANEOUS. Ashtray. Slag glass ashtray. Looks like Akro, but isn't. Ruddy oxblood red swirled in fluorescent cream green. About 3-1/2" diameter. One tiny rim chip. Price: $19. CyberAuction #469, Lot #36.

3484. MISCELLANEOUS. Ballot Box. Pine ballot box. Lifting top. Some minor scuffing on lid. Box is about 9" x 6" x 4". Handle is 5". Price: $33. CyberAuction #394, Lot #14.

3485. MISCELLANEOUS. Ballot Box. Pine ballot box. Lifting top. Some minor scuffing on lid. Box is about 9" x 6" x 4". Handle is 5". Price: $23. CyberAuction #346, Lot #30.

3486. MISCELLANEOUS. Bottle hanger. Poly bag with a cardboard advertising bottle hanger attached. Advertises Nehi Beverage. Bag contains Marble King catseyes. Two available, bidding on one. Winner has choice of either or both, remainder to under. Price: $4. CyberAuction #437, Lot #15.

3487. MISCELLANEOUS. Bottle hanger. Poly bag with a cardboard advertising bottle hanger attached. Advertises Nehi Beverage. Bag contains Marble King catseyes. Two available, bidding on one. Winner has choice of either or both, remainder to under. Price: $3. CyberAuction #406, Lot #35.

3488. MISCELLANEOUS. Bottle stopper. Very rare item. This a pewter bottle stopper with an onionskin on a rod. Pewter stopper with a cork surrounded bottom hole. When the bottle is placed on a shelf upright the onionskin falls on top of the hole to seal the bottle. When tipped the swirl falls out of the hole and the liquid can be poured. The onionskin was attached to a metal rod when hot. Probably English. S Stands about 3" high, about 1" wide at widest point. In great shape. Very difficult to find these. Last one from this consignor England, circa 1860-1915. Mint (9.5). Price: $370. CyberAuction #425, Lot #59.

3489. MISCELLANEOUS. Bottle stopper. Very rare item. This a pewter bottle stopper with a trapped handmade swirl. Pewter stopper with a cork surrounded bottom hole. Cage on top the holds the swirl. When the bottle is placed on a shelf upright the swirl falls on top of the hole to seal the bottle. When tipped the swirl falls out of the hole and the liquid can be

poured. The stopper rim reads "J.B. Williams Pat. Feb. 9. 1858". Probabl English. Swirl is a four band divided core swirl. Stands about 3" high, abou 1" wide at widest point. In great shape. Very difficult to find these. Englan circa 1860-1915. Mint (9.5). Price: $230. CyberAuction #418, Lot #60.

3490. MISCELLANEOUS. Brochure. Single sheet full color brochure fo "Museum Fur Glaskunst in Lauscha". This is the pamphlet for the glassmakir museum in Lauscha Germany. Front is a photo of many of the marble made there, including swirls, gooseberries, etc. Back describes the mu seum, and gives directions and a map. Consignor says that he got these i Germany about 10 years ago. There are eleven available, you are biddin on one. Winner has choice of any or all, remainder to under. Price: $ CyberAuction #481, Lot #13.

3491. MISCELLANEOUS. Character marble. Opaque blue marble. Printe "75th Anniversary National Marbles Tournament Wildwood NJ 1998". Abou 1". There are five marbles available. You are bidding on one Winner has choice of any or all, remainder to under. Consigned by Th National Marbles Tournament. All proceeds go directly to the Tournamer to defray costs. No commission is being charged on this sale. Price: $27 CyberAuction #354, Lot #32.

3492. MISCELLANEOUS. Character marble. Box of "12 Repro. Comi Strip Marbles by Bennett Cambridge, OHIO". White box with Xeroxe label on top. Label depicts the twelve original comic characters. Contair 3/4" modern Marble King two-patch. Each is screened with a different cha acter: Sandy, Moon, Skeezix, Annie, Andy, Koko, Betty Boop, Popeye, Mrs. Jiggs, Mutt, and Jeff. Fairly recent. Price: $24. CyberAuction #410, L #28.

3493. MISCELLANEOUS. Character marble. Yellow opaque. Advertise for Kevin's Marble Emporium, with the dragon logo. 31/32". Mint (9.9 Price: $15. CyberAuction #354, Lot #21.

3494. MISCELLANEOUS. Character marble. Opaque blue marble. Printe "75th Anniversary National Marbles Tournament Wildwood NJ 1998". Abou 1". Mint (9.9). Price: $14. CyberAuction #494, Lot #29.

3495. MISCELLANEOUS. Character marble. Original package c "Bullwinkle and Rocky Marbles". By Qualatex. Plastic blister pack on card board. Contains one Rocky and one Bullwinkle marble. Cardboard back ing has graphic of Rocky, Bullwinkle, Boris and Natasha on it. Game de scribed on back. 1988. Price: $12. CyberAuction #341, Lot #30.

3496. MISCELLANEOUS. Character marble. Opaque blue marble. Printe "75th Anniversary National Marbles Tournament Wildwood NJ 1998". Abou 1". Mint (9.9). There are two marbles available. You are bidding on one Winner has choice of any or all, remainder to under. Price: $12 CyberAuction #443, Lot #37.

3497. MISCELLANEOUS. Character marble. Opaque white marble. Ad vertisement for Dennis Webb's and Mark Randall's Greenberg's Guide t Marbles. Dated 1988. These were created in conjunction with the firs addition of the book. There are three marbles available. You are bidding o one. Winner has choice of any or all, remainder to under. Price: $10 CyberAuction #354, Lot #25.

3498. MISCELLANEOUS. Character marble. Opaque blue marble. Printe "75th Anniversary National Marbles Tournament Wildwood NJ 1998". Abou 1". Mint (9.9). Price: $8. CyberAuction #474, Lot #37.

3499. MISCELLANEOUS. Character marble. Original package c "Bullwinkle and Rocky Marbles". By Qualatex. Plastic blister pack on card board. Contains one Rocky and one Bullwinkle marble. Cardboard back ing has graphic of Rocky, Bullwinkle, Boris and Natasha on it. Game de scribed on back. 1988. Price: $7. CyberAuction #464, Lot #21.

3500. MISCELLANEOUS. Character marble. Opaque white machine made Imprint is "BERT" in black, in a green circle. These were produced for Ber Cohen about fifteen years ago. 31/32". Mint (9.9). Price: $6. CyberAuctio #344, Lot #25.

3501. MISCELLANEOUS. Character marble. Opaque white marble. Ad vertisement for Dennis Webb's and Mark Randall's Greenberg's Guide t Marbles. Dated 1988. These were created in conjunction with the firs addition of the book. There are four marbles available. You are bidding o one. Winner has choice of any or all, remainder to under. Price: $5 CyberAuction #356, Lot #24.

3502. MISCELLANEOUS. Character marble. Opaque white marble. Ad vertisement for Dennis Webb's and Mark Randall's Greenberg's Guide t Marbles. Dated 1988. These were created in conjunction with the firs addition of the book. There are three marbles available. You are bidding o one. Winner has choice of either or both, remainder to under. Price: $5. CyberAuction #375, Lot #11.

3503. MISCELLANEOUS. Character marble. Opaque white marble. Ad vertisement for Dennis Webb's and Mark Randall's Greenberg's Guide t Marbles. Dated 1988. 31/32". These were created in conjunction with the first addition of the book. Price: $5. CyberAuction #447, Lot #23.

3504. MISCELLANEOUS. Character marble. Opaque white marble. Printe in blue "Bob Hamon 1993". Advertisement for a contemporary maker. 7/ 8". Mint (9.9). Price: $4. CyberAuction #375, Lot #4.

3505. MISCELLANEOUS. Character marble. Opaque white marble. Printe in blue "Bob Hamon 1993". Advertisement for a contemporary maker. 7/ 8". Mint (9.9). Price: $4. CyberAuction #445, Lot #3.

3506. MISCELLANEOUS. Character marble. Transparent dark red marble. White printing "5c Coca-Cola". 15/16". Mint (9.0). Price: $3. CyberAuctio #349, Lot #38.

3507. MISCELLANEOUS. Character marble. Opaque white marble. Ad vertisement for Dennis Webb's and Mark Randall's Greenberg's Guide t Marbles. Dated 1988. These were created in conjunction with the first addition of the book. There are two marbles available. You are bidding on one. Winner has choice of any or all, remainder to under. Price: $3. CyberAuction #404, Lot #5.

3508. MISCELLANEOUS. Character marble. Opaque white marble. Advertisement for Dennis Webb's and Mark Randall's Greenberg's Guide to Marbles. Dated 1988. These were created in conjunction with the first addition of the book. There are two marbles available. You are bidding on one. Winner has choice of any or all, remainder to under. Price: $3. CyberAuction #449, Lot #5.

3509. MISCELLANEOUS. Character marble. Marble commemorating National Rolley Hole Marble Tournament. White base, blue printing. About 1". Mint (9.9). Price: $2. CyberAuction #364, Lot #17.

3510. MISCELLANEOUS. Character marble. Marble commemorating National Rolley Hole Marble Tournament. White base, blue printing. About 1". Mint (9.9). Price: $2. CyberAuction #447, Lot #16.

3511. MISCELLANEOUS. Character marble. Opaque white marble imprinted "Perot 96". About an 1" and Mint. Price: $1. CyberAuction #364, Lot #27.

3512. MISCELLANEOUS. Character marble. Opaque white marble imprinted "Perot 96". About an 1" and Mint. Price: $1. CyberAuction #408, Lot #16.

3513. MISCELLANEOUS. Character marble. Opaque white marble imprinted "Perot 96". About an 1" and Mint. Price: $1. CyberAuction #426, Lot #16.

3514. MISCELLANEOUS. Character marble. Opaque white marble imprinted "Perot 96". About an 1" and Mint. Price: $1. CyberAuction #490, Lot #27.

3515. MISCELLANEOUS. Character marble. Opaque white marble imprinted "Perot 96". About an 1" and Mint. Price: $1. CyberAuction #506, Lot #42.

3516. MISCELLANEOUS. Christmas Ornament. Hallmark Christmas Ornament dated 1997. Porcelain ornament. Depicts Norman Rockwell's "The Champion". In original box, unopened. Price: $15. CyberAuction #395, Lot #28.

3517. MISCELLANEOUS. Cigarette card. Cigarette card from "The Terrors of American and Their Doings" of Duke's Cigarettes. Front shows a boy shooting a marble. Printed "Marbles 'Knuckle down, Shoot hard across the box'". About 2-1/2" x 1-1/4". In great shape. Circa 1900. Mint (9.5). Price: $65. CyberAuction #356, Lot #33.

3518. MISCELLANEOUS. Cigarette card. English cigarette card. Issued by Nicolas Sarony & Co., New Bond Street, London W. From the Origin of Games series. Front pictures two cave men with Stonehenge behind them, playing marbles. Printed "Prehistoric Man Playing Marbles". Reverse discusses the origins of the game of marbles. In great shape. Early 1900s. Super example. Mint (9.7). Price: $60. CyberAuction #400, Lot #25.

3519. MISCELLANEOUS. Figurine. Glass figurine. Clown holding a marble. Very nice. This is Murano Glass. I saw a similar one appraised on one of the TV antique shows recently as being from the 1950s. I'm not sure if that is the age of this one or not, but still it's a really nice figurine. Italian, age unknown. 6" tall. Mint (9.9). Price: $70. CyberAuction #400, Lot #36.

3520. MISCELLANEOUS. Fisher Jewel Tray. Has design patent number only on the bottom. Marbles are fluorescent Vaseline yellow. Smooth bed. 3-1/4". Mint (9.5). Price: $34. CyberAuction #392, Lot #32.

3521. MISCELLANEOUS. Fisher Jewel Tray. Has design patent and patent number on the bottom. Textured bed. 3-1/4". Mint (9.5). There are two trays available. One has red marbles, one has green marbles. Winner has choice, remainder to under. Price: $34. CyberAuction #392, Lot #36.

3522. MISCELLANEOUS. Fisher Jewel Tray. Has patent number only on the bottom. Marbles are blue. Bottom is rusted. 3-1/4". Near Mint (8.6). Price: $29. CyberAuction #341, Lot #32.

3523. MISCELLANEOUS. Fisher Jewel Tray. Textured jewel tray. Has patent and design number on bottom. Creamy white opaque marbles. 3-1/4". Mint (9.7). There are two trays available. You are bidding on one. Winner has choice of either or both, remainder to under. Price: $27. CyberAuction #388, Lot #36.

3524. MISCELLANEOUS. Fisher Jewel Tray. Has patent number only on the bottom. Marbles are semi-opaque blue. Bottom is rusted. 3-1/4". Mint (9.7). Price: $22. CyberAuction #448, Lot #32.

3525. MISCELLANEOUS. Flower frog. Glass flower frog. Seven holes. Would hold 11/16" to 3/4"" marbles. About 3-1/2" diameter (sight). Mint. Price: $10. CyberAuction #473, Lot #34.

3526. MISCELLANEOUS. Flower frog. Glass flower frog. Good marble display piece. Eleven holes. Transparent clear glass. One minor chip at the bottom. About 4-1/2" diameter. Near Mint(+). Price: $6. CyberAuction #464, Lot #29.

3527. MISCELLANEOUS. Flower frog. Glass flower frog. Seven hole frog. Clear. Good for displaying marbles. About 2-1/2" diameter. Mint. Price: $4. CyberAuction #464, Lot #27.

3528. MISCELLANEOUS. Flower frog. Glass flower frog. Sixteen holes. Would hold 3/4" to 15/16" marbles. About 5" diameter (sight). Mint. Price: $4. CyberAuction #472, Lot #17.

3529. MISCELLANEOUS. Fortune telling. Thirty-two sided glass marble. Each facet has a different number embossed in it. This is used in a fortune telling game. You ask a question, roll the marble and then consult a key, where the number showing at the top of the marble is the answer to your question. This is the marble only, the box and key are missing. Still, they are harder to find. Embossed "Made in Czechoslovakia". 1-1/16". Mint (9.8). Price: $25. CyberAuction #482, Lot #39.

3530. MISCELLANEOUS. Fortune telling. Thirty-two sided glass marble. Each facet has a different number embossed in it. This is used in a fortune telling game. You ask a question, roll the marble and then consult a key, where the number showing at the top of the marble is the answer to your question. This is the marble only, the box and key are missing. Still, they are

harder to find. Marked "Made in Czechoslovakia". 3/4". Mint (9.8). Price: $23. CyberAuction #441, Lot #19.

3531. MISCELLANEOUS. Fortune telling. Thirty-two sided glass marble. Each facet has a different number embossed in it. This is used in a fortune telling game. You ask a question, roll the marble and then consult a key, where the number showing at the top of the marble is the answer to your question. This is the marble only, the box and key are missing. Still, they are harder to find. Probably European and pre-1903. 1-1/16". Mint (9.8). Price: $23. CyberAuction #447, Lot #40.

3532. MISCELLANEOUS. Fortune telling. Thirty-two sided glass marble. Each facet has a different number embossed in it. This is used in a fortune telling game. You ask a question, roll the marble and then consult a key, where the number showing at the top of the marble is the answer to your question. This is the marble only, the box and key are missing. Still, they are harder to find. Marked "Made in Czechoslovakia". 3/4". Mint (9.8). There are two examples available. You are bidding on one. Winner has choice of one or both, remainder to under. Price: $21. CyberAuction #400, Lot #27.

3533. MISCELLANEOUS. Fortune telling. Thirty-two sided glass marble. Each facet has a different number embossed in it. This is used in a fortune telling game. You ask a question, roll the marble and then consult a key, where the number showing at the top of the marble is the answer to your question. This is the marble only, the box and key are missing. Still, they are harder to find. Embossed "Made in Czechoslovakia". 1-1/16". Mint (9.8). Price: $21. CyberAuction #471, Lot #9.

3534. MISCELLANEOUS. Fortune telling. Thirty-two sided glass marble. Each facet has a different number embossed in it. This is used in a fortune telling game. You ask a question, roll the marble and then consult a key, where the number showing at the top of the marble is the answer to your question. This is the marble only, the box and key are missing. Still, they are harder to find. Probably European and pre-1903. 1-1/16". Mint (9.8). There are three examples available. You are bidding on one. Winner has choice of any or all, remainder to under. Price: $17. CyberAuction #396, Lot #34.

3535. MISCELLANEOUS. Fortune telling. Thirty-two sided glass marble. Each facet has a different number embossed in it. This is used in a fortune telling game. You ask a question, roll the marble and then consult a key, where the number showing at the top of the marble is the answer to your question. This is the marble only, the box and key are missing. Still, they are harder to find. Embossed "Made in Czechoslovakia". 1-1/16". Mint (9.8). Price: $15. CyberAuction #402, Lot #22.

3536. MISCELLANEOUS. Fortune telling. Thirty-two sided glass marble. Each facet has a different number embossed in it. This is used in a fortune telling game. You ask a question, roll the marble and then consult a key, where the number showing at the top of the marble is the answer to your question. This is the marble only, the box and key are missing. Still, they are harder to find. Embossed "Made in Czechoslovakia". 1-1/16". Mint (9.8). Price: $12. CyberAuction #454, Lot #47.

3537. MISCELLANEOUS. Game. Modern walnut solitaire board with thirty two peewee malachite marbles. Board is about 7-1/2". All Mint. Price: $100. CyberAuction #394, Lot #13.

3538. MISCELLANEOUS. Game. Skill-Ball Marble Game by Marx & Co. Metal ramp tray with scoring holes. In original box. Great graphics. 1930s. Some rubbing of the box edges. Tray in great shape. No marbles. Price: $23. CyberAuction #458, Lot #25.

3539. MISCELLANEOUS. Game. "Swingeroo" on original card. Wire cage with heavy cardboard handle, with three marbles trapped in it. Play a variety of games with it, all described on the card. From RENNOC Games and Toys. Circa 1955. Mint. Price: $19. CyberAuction #429, Lot #31.

3540. MISCELLANEOUS. Game. Boxed Chinese Checkers game. J. Pressman, No. 2801. Cardboard game board. Contains thirty six glass marbles. Some rubbing of the top. Red box top. Probably 1940s. Nice game. Two available, you are bidding on one. Winner has choice of either or both, remainder to under. Near Mint (8.6). Price: $14. CyberAuction #435, Lot #31.

3541. MISCELLANEOUS. Game. Hop-Over Puzzle. J. Pressman, No. 2991. Cardboard board with instructions. Four white game marbles and four black game marbles. Some rubbing of the top. Near Mint (8.6). Price: $13. CyberAuction #435, Lot #32.

3542. MISCELLANEOUS. Game. "Roll Them Thru Game". Small cardboard box with graphic of a boy playing the game. Contains a small cardboard "arch game" and three Champion Agates. Mint (9.5). Price: $12. CyberAuction #335, Lot #30.

3543. MISCELLANEOUS. Game. Bagatelle. Norwestern Products Poosh-M-Up Big-5. Put-N-Take, Base-Ball, Twenty-One, Pennants and Bagatelle, all in one. Pine frame. Metal pins and hoops on board. Steel balls. Has the metal stand for tilting it up on a table. The return track is a little bent, you'd probably have to remove the nails on one side of the frame, push it back, and then replace the nails. Glass top. In great shape. Probably 1930s. Price: $10. CyberAuction #409, Lot #33.

3544. MISCELLANEOUS. Game. J. Pressman Chinese Checkers. Small square cardboard box. Cardboard miniature Chinese checker game inside. No marbles. About 6" x 6" x 1". Near Mint (8.6). Price: $8. CyberAuction #406, Lot #32.

3545. MISCELLANEOUS. Game. Small marble game, although it might actually be a gumball machine. Pine and Plexiglas. Home-made. Marbles fill upper half. Turn knob and a marble falls and comes out a ramp. About 12" x 2" x 2". Very nice. Price: $5. CyberAuction #468, Lot #25.

3546. MISCELLANEOUS. Game board. Old General Grant Solitaire board. Mahogany. Great finish and patina. Would accommodate marbles up to 1" in diameter. Three stubby feet. Handwritten with a fountain pen on the back is "Solitaire Board A Present From Cranie". A beauty. About 10" diameter. Mint (9.7). Price: $160. CyberAuction #356, Lot #34.

3547. MISCELLANEOUS. Game board. Resin solitaire game board. Designed to look like ivory with a weathered patina. This one is inscribed with fruit bowls, wreaths and distelfinks on the top. Flowers and wreaths around the rim. I am not sure who made these. I've seen maybe a dozen or so in the past ten years. They are not that common. Also, I have seen almost no duplicates. About 10" diameter, very heavy. Green felt on base. Price: $140. CyberAuction #373, Lot #27.

3548. MISCELLANEOUS. Game board. Stunning solitaire game board. This is an outstanding English antique solitaire game board. Mahogany. Thirty-two holes to accommodate marbles from about 13/16" to about an 1". Has green quadrant and black stripes painted on it for "German Tactics". Gorgeous patina and in superb shape. The only damage is that one of the three small feet has two chunks out of it. Still, one of the nicest game boards I have ever seen. About 10-1/2" diameter. About 1" high. Near Mint(+) (8.9) (would be 9.9, if not for the damage to the one foot). Price: $125. CyberAuction #471, Lot #33.

3549. MISCELLANEOUS. Game board. Old solitaire board. Mahogany. Has three stubby feet. Original finish with a very nice patina. In great shape. About 9" diameter. England, circa 1870-1920. Mint (9.5). Price: $90. CyberAuction #503, Lot #43.

3550. MISCELLANEOUS. Game board. Old English solitaire board. On quadrant outlined in green for Fox and Geese. Black lines painted between each hole, again for the Fox and Geese game. No feet. Original finish, nice patina. Some scratching. About 10" diameter. Mint(-) (9.0). Price: $85. CyberAuction #504, Lot #45.

3551. MISCELLANEOUS. Game board. Old solitaire board. Mahogany. Has three stubby feet. Original finish with a very nice patina. In great shape. About 10" diameter, a bit taller than Lot #43. England, circa 1890-1920. Mint(-) (9.0). Price: $70. CyberAuction #503, Lot #44.

3552. MISCELLANEOUS. Game board. Hand turned mahogany solitaire board. Nicely finished, with some crazing overall on the finish. Probably English and early 1900s, possibly late 1800s. About 10" diameter. Mint(-). Price: $65. CyberAuction #464, Lot #22.

3553. MISCELLANEOUS. Game board. Antique solitaire board. Walnut. Larger size. Needs a good cleaning. The discard marble rim is painted green. Rest is unpainted. Three small feet. About 10" diameter. Nice. England, circa 1870-1910. Price: $60. CyberAuction #408, Lot #30.

3554. MISCELLANEOUS. Game board. Small walnut solitaire board. Nice small board. Older. This board is from England. There are the remnants of a French label on it (perhaps from a store). Scrawled on the back, probably in crayon very faintly visible now, in child's handwriting are a number of words, probably his/her name and address. Interesting. About 7" diameter. Mint (9.7). Price: $55. CyberAuction #508, Lot #44.

3555. MISCELLANEOUS. Game board. Nice solitaire board. Mahogany. Some pitting of the finish. About 9" diameter. No feet. English, very early 1900s. Price: $50. CyberAuction #465, Lot #30.

3556. MISCELLANEOUS. Game board. Mahogany old English solitaire board. Three stubby feet. Nice wood and finish. Some water stains and several penciled numbers on it. About 9" diameter. Near Mint(+). Price: $35. CyberAuction #507, Lot #26.

3557. MISCELLANEOUS. Gear shift knob. Blue and white slag. No metal insert or collar. A couple of tiny pits on the top. 2". Near Mint(+) (8.8). Price: $14. CyberAuction #428, Lot #32.

3558. MISCELLANEOUS. Gear shift knob. Blue and white slag. No metal insert or collar. A couple of tiny pits on the top. 2". Near Mint(+) (8.8). Price: $8. CyberAuction #466, Lot #23.

3559. MISCELLANEOUS. Golden rule marble. Plastic salmon orange marble. Metal band around equator with the Golden Rule. Comes in original plastic box with original paper insert. Circa 1960s. Price: $17. CyberAuction #388, Lot #33.

3560. MISCELLANEOUS. Golden rule marble. Plastic salmon orange marble. Metal band around equator with the Golden Rule. Comes in original plastic box with original paper insert. Circa 1960s. Price: $17. CyberAuction #449, Lot #29.

3561. MISCELLANEOUS. Golden rule marble. Plastic blue marble. Metal band around equator with the Golden Rule. Comes in original plastic box with original paper insert. Circa 1960s. Price: $14. CyberAuction #396, Lot #35.

3562. MISCELLANEOUS. Golden rule marble. Plastic green marble. Metal band around equator with the Golden Rule. Comes in original plastic box with original paper insert. Circa 1960s. Price: $12. CyberAuction #401, Lot #34.

3563. MISCELLANEOUS. Golden rule marble. Plastic salmon orange marble. Metal band around equator with the Golden Rule. Comes in original plastic box. No original paper insert. Circa 1960s. Price: $12. CyberAuction #494, Lot #24.

3564. MISCELLANEOUS. Golden rule marble. Plastic salmon orange marble. Metal band around equator with the Golden Rule. Comes in original plastic box. No original paper insert. Circa 1960s. Price: $7. CyberAuction #466, Lot #20.

3565. MISCELLANEOUS. Jewelry. Small brass pin with a Peltier Peerless Patch in it. These are generally believed to be late 1920's or early 1930's. Super example. Price: $50. CyberAuction #396, Lot #44.

3566. MISCELLANEOUS. Jewelry. Sterling silver tie bar. Has half a solid core swirl set in it. Handmade by Larry Castle. Marked "Sterling" and has his hallmark. Price: $37. CyberAuction #406, Lot #27.

3567. MISCELLANEOUS. Kaleidoscope. Glass kaleidoscope. Three mirror. Blue/white slag exterior. Loops will hold a marble from about 1" to about 1-1/2". Modern, about 3" diameter. Price: $24. CyberAuction #352, Lot #35.

3568. MISCELLANEOUS. Lamp finial. The piece that screws on the very top of a lampshade. Brass finial with a shooter Vitro modern parrot glued to the top of it. Price: $5. CyberAuction #404, Lot #2.

3569. MISCELLANEOUS. Lithograph. High quality lithograph of "Grandma Gives a Lesson". From 1951. This is one of the "calendar blanks" found a few years ago. Intended as a cover for a wall calendar. Top of the litho had a blank space for printing the name of the pharmacy or other business name. This on has been trimmed so that blank space is no longer present. Still, very nice and would look great matted and framed. I believe that less than fifty of these blanks were found a few years ago in Massachusetts. About 14" x 10". No damage, other than the trim. Price: $27. CyberAuction #475, Lot #13.

3570. MISCELLANEOUS. Magazine. May 10, 1937 issue of Life Magazine. Cover is a boy knuckling down. Originally sold as Lot #21 in CyberAuction #148 back in 1998. Mint. Price: $19. CyberAuction #475, Lot #12.

3571. MISCELLANEOUS. Magazine. Smithsonian magazine. April 1988. Cover story is Marbles. Great photo on the cover. Price: $15. CyberAuction #347, Lot #30.

3572. MISCELLANEOUS. Magazine. Smithsonian magazine. April 1988. Cover story is Marbles. Great photo on the cover. Small tear in upper right hand corner. Price: $15. CyberAuction #453, Lot #25.

3573. MISCELLANEOUS. Magazine. April 1977 issue of "Hobbies: The Magazine of Collectors". Cover story is "Marbles - Another Fun Hobby". Cover shows pictures of marbles (all handmade). Article is about a page long. This particular marble-related magazine is harder to find. Mint. Price: $12. CyberAuction #453, Lot #22.

3574. MISCELLANEOUS. Magazine. Collectors' Showcase magazine. August 1991. Cover story is Marbles. Great photo on the cover. Price: $11. CyberAuction #453, Lot #24.

3575. MISCELLANEOUS. Magazine article. Page 28 from the May 20, 1946 issue of Life. Describes a boy who swallowed marbles on a dare. Shows picture of a boy and the x-ray of his abdomen. Single sheet. Price: $1. CyberAuction #477, Lot #29.

3576. MISCELLANEOUS. Marble Pouch. Pink pouch. Printed in blue "Marbles". Graphic of a girl playing marbles at the beach. Printed on textile. Stamped "Japan". This is a rare girl's pouch. 5" x 3". Mint. 1950s or 1960s. Price: $25. CyberAuction #433, Lot #28.

3577. MISCELLANEOUS. Marble pouch. Actually, a marble purse. Very hard to find. Felt purse with a metal clasp on top. Printed on one side with "Marbles" and a dog sitting behind a Ringer ring. Green felt. The felt has begun to flake off the backing in a couple of spots. Still, very nice example. American, circa 1930s-1940s. 5" x 3". Near Mint(+) (8.7). Price: $29. CyberAuction #373, Lot #26.

3578. MISCELLANEOUS. Marble pouch. Black rubberized textile. Green piping. White drawstring. Printed on front is the head of a boy with a crown. Reads "Champion Glass Marbles". Wear on the piping. Dirty. 1930s. Near Mint (8.6). Price: $28. CyberAuction #404, Lot #26.

3579. MISCELLANEOUS. Marble pouch. Red felt on canvas. Front is printed in black "Marbles" and has a boy shooting marbles. Some felt flaking away at the top. No drawstring. 4-1/2" x 3" (sight). Near Mint(+) (8.7). Circa 1930s. Price: $27. CyberAuction #421, Lot #26.

3580. MISCELLANEOUS. Marble pouch. Six segment leather pouch, with drawstring. In great shape. Very nice bag. Probably 1930s. About 4" x 6". Mint (9.5). Price: $13. CyberAuction #464, Lot #25.

3581. MISCELLANEOUS. Marble pouch. Plastic pouch which came in the "Miner's Pouch" package. Came along with some Vitro All-Reds. Early 1960s. Red front, gray back. Printed "Marbles" with some marbles on it. Yellow drawstring. About 5" x 3". Mint (9.7). Price: $10. CyberAuction #386, Lot #22.

3582. MISCELLANEOUS. Marble pouch. Suede bottom two-thirds. Top third is red cloth. Nice drawstring. Dirty, but it is definitely old. Faded Indian head on it in black. 1930s-1940s. Mint(-). Price: $8. CyberAuction #432, Lot #23.

3583. MISCELLANEOUS. Marble pouch. Six segment leather bag. Has a small tear in one panel. Shoestring as the drawstring. Dirty. Circa 1930s-1940s. Near Mint (8.6). Price: $5. CyberAuction #435, Lot #33.

3584. MISCELLANEOUS. Marble pouch. Old green felt marble pouch with string. Small repair to one side in the stitching, repair is old. Probably 1950s or 1960s. Nice bag. Near Mint(+) (8.9). Price: $2. CyberAuction #389, Lot #29.

3585. MISCELLANEOUS. Marble pouch. Lot of two items. First is a plastic marble pouch from the 1960s. Nice graphics. Has drawstring, but some tears at the top. Other is a vinyl pouch with seventy five catseyes. 1980s or 1990s. Price: $2. CyberAuction #389, Lot #34.

3586. MISCELLANEOUS. Marble pouch. Plastic marble pouch, 1960s. No drawstring. Mint (9.6). Price: $2. CyberAuction #404, Lot #25.

3587. MISCELLANEOUS. Marble pouch. Plastic marble pouch, 1960s. No drawstring. Mint (9.6). Price: $2. CyberAuction #456, Lot #25.

3588. MISCELLANEOUS. Marble pouch. Blue and white "calico". Cloth drawstring. Homemade, probably 1940s or 1950s. From England. About 6" x 6". Nice. Price: $2. CyberAuction #464, Lot #23.

3589. MISCELLANEOUS. Marble shooter. One of the red spring loaded metal marble shooters. 1930s. About 4" long. Mint(-). Price: $17. CyberAuction #477, Lot #35.

3590. MISCELLANEOUS. Marble shooter. Metal marble shooter. Spring loaded. This is a red one. Some paint chipping. About 3-1/2" long. Circa 1930s. Near Mint(+) (8.7). Price: $13. CyberAuction #447, Lot #20.

3591. MISCELLANEOUS. Marble shooter. Metal marble shooter. Spring loaded. This is a blue one. About 3-1/2" long. Circa 1930s. Near Mint(+) (8.7). Price: $11. CyberAuction #341, Lot #33.

3592. MISCELLANEOUS. Marble shooter. Metal marble shooter. Spring loaded. This is a red one. Some paint chipping. About 3-1/2" long. Circa 1930s. Near Mint(+) (8.7). Price: $7. CyberAuction #392, Lot #30.

3593. MISCELLANEOUS. Milk cap. From Marble Farms in Syracuse NY. For Half and Half. Five available. Bidding on one. Winner has choice of any or all, remainder to under. Price: $1.50. CyberAuction #386, Lot #20.

3594. MISCELLANEOUS. Mineral. Hand cut tigereye. Brown with some purple. Very nice faceting. Very hard to find. Tiny hit mark near the top of one end. Age and origin unknown. 1-3/8". Mint(-) (9.0). Price: $120. CyberAuction #392, Lot #29.

3595. MISCELLANEOUS. Mineral. Gorgeous blue tigereye. Not sure if it is hand cut, but I think it is older. Beauty. Origin and age unknown. 1-3/8". Mint (9.7). Price: $50. CyberAuction #449, Lot #9.

3596. MISCELLANEOUS. Mineral. Interesting. Brown tigereye with lots of gray hematite (?) in it. Lots of shimmering. Machine ground. 1-3/16". Mint (9.9). Price: $37. CyberAuction #376, Lot #5.

3597. MISCELLANEOUS. Mineral. Purple goldstone sphere. Great shimmering. 13/16". Mint (9.9). Price: $30. CyberAuction #379, Lot #29.

3598. MISCELLANEOUS. Mineral. Purple goldstone sphere. Great shimmering. 25/32". Mint (9.9). Price: $25. CyberAuction #341, Lot #5.

3599. MISCELLANEOUS. Mineral. Gorgeous blue tigereye. Not sure if it is hand cut, but I think it is older. Beauty. Origin and age unknown. 1-3/8". Mint (9.7). Price: $22. CyberAuction #395, Lot #54.

3600. MISCELLANEOUS. Mineral. Gorgeous brown tigereye. Great shimmering. 11/16". Mint(-) (9.0). Price: $21. CyberAuction #355, Lot #40.

3601. MISCELLANEOUS. Mineral. Brown goldstone sphere. Great shimmering. 1-1/16". Mint (9.9). Price: $20. CyberAuction #402, Lot #26.

3602. MISCELLANEOUS. Mineral. Snowflake obsidian sphere. 1-15/16". Mint (9.9). Price: $20. CyberAuction #409, Lot #23.

3603. MISCELLANEOUS. Mineral. Purple goldstone sphere. Great shimmering. 7/8". Mint (9.9). Price: $19. CyberAuction #402, Lot #25.

3604. MISCELLANEOUS. Mineral. Snowflake obsidian sphere. Nice. Machine ground. 25/32". Mint (9.9). Price: $15. CyberAuction #376, Lot #34.

3605. MISCELLANEOUS. Mineral. Onyx sphere. Modern. Probably Mexican. 2-1/8". Mint (9.9). Price: $15. CyberAuction #391, Lot #20.

3606. MISCELLANEOUS. Mineral. Purple fluorite sphere. 1-15/16". Mint (9.9). Price: $15. CyberAuction #409, Lot #8.

3607. MISCELLANEOUS. Mineral. Goldstone (glass with copper flakes) sphere. 29/32". Mint (9.9). Price: $15. CyberAuction #497, Lot #40.

3608. MISCELLANEOUS. Mineral. Brown goldstone sphere. Great shimmering. 3/4". Mint (9.9). Consignor note: D15. Price: $13. CyberAuction #344, Lot #56.

3609. MISCELLANEOUS. Mineral. Tigereye. Brown. Nice shimmering. 25/32". Mint (9.8). Price: $12. CyberAuction #497, Lot #9.

3610. MISCELLANEOUS. Mineral. Very nice tigereye sphere. Nice shimmering to it. 25/32". Mint (9.9). Price: $11. CyberAuction #402, Lot #13.

3611. MISCELLANEOUS. Mineral. Brown tigereye sphere. Origin and age unknown. 17/32". Mint (9.9). Price: $11. CyberAuction #505, Lot #54.

3612. MISCELLANEOUS. Mineral. Dyed purple marble marble. The stone, marble. 1-9/16". Mint (9.7). Price: $10. CyberAuction #402, Lot #34.

3613. MISCELLANEOUS. Mineral. Picture Sandstone sphere. 2-3/4". Mint (9.9). Price: $10. CyberAuction #409, Lot #34.

3614. MISCELLANEOUS. Mineral. Tigereye with matrix. Probably fairly modern. Nice shimmering. 31/32". Mint (9.5). Price: $10. CyberAuction #441, Lot #9.

3615. MISCELLANEOUS. Mineral. Picture Sandstone sphere. 2-3/4". Mint (9.9). Price: $8. CyberAuction #437, Lot #27.

3616. MISCELLANEOUS. Mineral. Obsidian sphere. 1-15/16". Mint (9.9). Price: $8. CyberAuction #437, Lot #31.

3617. MISCELLANEOUS. Mineral. Malachite sphere. Modern. 27/32". Mint (9.7). Price: $8. CyberAuction #505, Lot #2.

3618. MISCELLANEOUS. Mineral. Some sort of stone sphere, probably marble. 1-5/8". Mint (9.9). Price: $7. CyberAuction #331, Lot #28.

3619. MISCELLANEOUS. Mineral. Machine ground. Green fluorite. 23/32". Mint (9.5). Price: $7. CyberAuction #354, Lot #1.

3620. MISCELLANEOUS. Mineral. Malachite sphere. Machine ground. 31/32". Mint (9.9). Price: $7. CyberAuction #392, Lot #26.

3621. MISCELLANEOUS. Mineral. Purple fluorite sphere. 1-15/16". Mint (9.9). Price: $7. CyberAuction #409, Lot #4.

3622. MISCELLANEOUS. Mineral. Onyx sphere. Probably Mexican. Modern. 2-1/16". Mint (9.9). Price: $7. CyberAuction #409, Lot #27.

3623. MISCELLANEOUS. Mineral. Tigereye with matrix. Probably fairly modern. Nice shimmering. 31/32". Mint (9.5). Price: $7. CyberAuction #410, Lot #11.

3624. MISCELLANEOUS. Mineral. Mineral sphere. Pink stone marble, cut into a sphere. Very pretty. 2". Mint (9.9). Price: $5. CyberAuction #457, Lot #21.

3625. MISCELLANEOUS. Mineral. Black and white sphere. The stone "marble". 1-15/16". Mint. Price: $4. CyberAuction #480, Lot #10.

3626. MISCELLANEOUS. Mineral. Some sort of agate. Agglomeration of brown, white, red, green. Modern. Machine cut. 25/32". Mint (9.9). Price: $3. CyberAuction #379, Lot #7.

3627. MISCELLANEOUS. Mineral. Jasper. Modern, machine cut. 25/32". Mint (9.9). Price: $2. CyberAuction #386, Lot #37.

3628. MISCELLANEOUS. Mineral. Onyx sphere. Mexican. Modern. 1-15/16". Mint. Four spheres available, you are bidding on one. Winner has choice of any or all, remainder to under. Price: $2. CyberAuction #480, Lot #5.

3629. MISCELLANEOUS. National Marble Tournament. This is a bronze circular medallion on a long ribbon. It is cast with the 75th Anniversary logo. Medallion is 2-3/8" in diameter. Less than a hundred of these were made. They were given out to staff members and participants. None was

ever sold to the public. Consigned by The National Marbles Tournament. All proceeds go directly to the Tournament to defray costs. No commission is being charged on this sale. Price: $70. CyberAuction #354, Lot #28.

3630. MISCELLANEOUS. National Marble Tournament. Small white terrycloth towel. Printed in red with the National Marbles Tournament logo and printing for the 76th Annual Tournament. 15" x 7" (sight). Mint (9.9).Consigned by The National Marbles Tournament. All proceeds go directly to the Tournament to defray costs. No commission is being charged on this sale. Price: $30. CyberAuction #354, Lot #33.

3631. MISCELLANEOUS. National Marble Tournament. Pin from the 75th Anniversary of the National Marbles Tournament. Tie tack type pin. Gelplastic front with the 75th Anniversary logo. In it's original poly packet. 27/32". Mint (9.9). There are three pins available. You are bidding on one. Winner has choice of any or all, remainder to under. Consigned by The National Marbles Tournament. All proceeds go directly to the Tournament to defray costs. No commission is being charged on this sale. Price: $19. CyberAuction #354, Lot #29.

3632. MISCELLANEOUS. National Marble Tournament. White cap. White braid on front. Has the 75th Anniversary logo on it. Mint (9.9). Consigned by The National Marbles Tournament. All proceeds go directly to the Tournament to defray costs. No commission is being charged on this sale. Consigned by The National Marbles Tournament. All proceeds go directly to the Tournament to defray costs. No commission is being charged on this sale. Price: $15. CyberAuction #354, Lot #36.

3633. MISCELLANEOUS. National Marble Tournament. Printed rule book with "The Official Rules of THE NATIONAL MARBLES TOURNAMENT" "The Game of Ringer". From the 76th Annual Tournament (1999). 8-1/2" x 5". Six pages plus cover. Mint (9.5).Consigned by The National Marbles Tournament. All proceeds go directly to the Tournament to defray costs. No commission is being charged on this sale. Price: $12. CyberAuction #354, Lot #35.

3634. MISCELLANEOUS. National Marble Tournament. Ballpoint pen. Imprinted "National Marbles Tournament Wildwood, NJ Sponsored by Jabo, Inc. Marble King, Inc. Ed Stanley Trophies". Two pens available. You are bidding on one. Winner has choice of either or both, remainder to under. Consigned by The National Marbles Tournament. All proceeds go directly to the Tournament to defray costs. No commission is being charged on this sale. Price: $11. CyberAuction #354, Lot #31.

3635. MISCELLANEOUS. National Marble Tournament. Commemorative postcard from the 75th National Marbles Tournament. Black and white postcard. Pictures the 1960 National Tournament. Overprinted with logo from the 1998 tournament (75th Anniversary). Back describes the picture. 6" x 4". Mint (9.9). There are four postcards available. You are bidding on one. Winner has choice of any or all, remainder to under. Consigned by The National Marbles Tournament. All proceeds go directly to the Tournament to defray costs. No commission is being charged on this sale. Price: $6. CyberAuction #354, Lot #34.

3636. MISCELLANEOUS. Necktie. Man's necktie. Blue background. Red, blue and white marbles on it, with white arcs. Older tie. Price: $10. CyberAuction #411, Lot #49.

3637. MISCELLANEOUS. Paperweight. This item and the vase in Lot 45 came with a consignment, so I've included them here. Perthshire paperweight. Poinsettia flower. Overlay cameo-cut exterior. Transparent clear glass. Diamond-cut base. There is a three dimensional red poinsettia in the glass with a signature millefiori cane where the stamen would be. Red petals, green leaves. Overlaid by white and then overlaid by blue. Large window cut on the top. Four medium windows and four small windows cut along the sides. Very nice. 2-1/4" diameter. Scotland, circa 1970-1985. Mint (9.9). Price: $65. CyberAuction #373, Lot #49.

3638. MISCELLANEOUS. Paperweight. Hollow Murano egg-shaped paperweight. Transparent clear with strands of white, blue and bands of golden lutz. Nicely made. Older weight, nice amount of age scratching on the base. Italian, circa 1940-1960. 2-1/4" high. Mint (9.9). Price: $42. CyberAuction #508, Lot #10.

3639. MISCELLANEOUS. Picture. Print of Norman Rockwell's "The Champion" decoupage on a pine plaque. From "Prints on Wood, Salem NY". Probably 1970s. About 9" x 7". Mint (9.9). Price: $8. CyberAuction #392, Lot #42.

3640. MISCELLANEOUS. Reflector. Circular metal vehicle reflector. Has seven cleareis as the reflector units. Each is about 1" diameter, transparent Vaseline yellow and very fluorescent. No manufacturer name. Some rusting. About 4" diameter. Near Mint (8.5). Price: $25. CyberAuction #345, Lot #30.

3641. MISCELLANEOUS. Reflector. Truck reflector. Uses seven red cleareis as the reflectors. About 4" x 4" (sight). Mint. 1930s. Price: $23. CyberAuction #433, Lot #27.

3642. MISCELLANEOUS. Reproduction medal. Sterling silver reproduction tournament medal. Front is "United States National Marble Championship Tournament". Back reads "School Championship Awarded to {blank}" by the Youngstown Telegram 1930". Stamped "Sterling". This is a modern reproduction, not an old medal. No ribbon. Two available, you are bidding on one. Winner has choice of either or both, remainder to under. Price: $17. CyberAuction #482, Lot #13.

3643. MISCELLANEOUS. Reproduction medal. Sterling silver reproduction tournament medal. Front is "United States National Marble Championship Tournament". Back reads "School Championship Awarded to {blank}" by the Youngstown Telegram 1930". Stamped "Sterling". This is a modern reproduction, not an old medal. No ribbon. Two available, you are bidding on one. Winner has choice of either or both, remainder to under. Price: $10. CyberAuction #428, Lot #49.

3644. MISCELLANEOUS. Shooter. Pink Mar-Bo-Gun with original store card. From Cardinal Rubber, Barberton OH. Late 1940s, early 1950s. About 10" long. Mint. There are two available, you are bidding on one. Winner has choice of either or both, remainder to under. Price: $40. CyberAuction #433, Lot #30.

3645. MISCELLANEOUS. Souvenir. Atomic Marble, souvenir of the Hanford Science Center. With original envelope. 1970s-1990s. Price: $5. CyberAuction #477, Lot #25.

3646. MISCELLANEOUS. Souvenir. Nuclear Waste Disposal marble from U.S. Department of Energy. On informative blister card. 1970s-1990s. Price: $5. CyberAuction #477, Lot #26.

3647. MISCELLANEOUS. Stamped cover. Letter size envelope bearing a Monaco stamp depicting two children playing marbles. Postmarked in Monaco, 9-5-89. Left side of the envelope is printed "First Day Cover" with Monaco coat of arms. Price: $12. CyberAuction #356, Lot #35.

3648. MISCELLANEOUS. Stamped cover. Business size envelope bearing a Belgian stamp depicting marbles. Postmarked in Brussels, 6-5-89. Left side of the envelope is rubber stamped with a mason jar containing marbles. Price: $10. CyberAuction #356, Lot #36.

3649. MISCELLANEOUS. Stamped cover. Letter size envelope bearing a Monaco stamp depicting two children playing marbles. Postmarked in Monaco, 9-5-89. Left side of the envelope is printed "First Day Cover" with Monaco coat of arms. Price: $8. CyberAuction #441, Lot #24.

3650. MISCELLANEOUS. Stamped cover. Business size envelope bearing a Belgian stamp depicting marbles. Postmarked in Brussels, 6-5-89. Left side of the envelope is rubber stamped with a mason jar containing marbles. Price: $6. CyberAuction #404, Lot #29.

3651. MISCELLANEOUS. Steelie. Nice steelie. Hollow marble. Nice "X" on surface. Some minor rust. American, age unknown. 5/8". Mint (9.5). Price: $12. CyberAuction #350, Lot #48.

3652. MISCELLANEOUS. Steelie. Nice steelie. Hollow marble. Nice "X" on surface. Some rust. American, age unknown. 9/16". Mint(-) (9.0). Price: $6. CyberAuction #473, Lot #39.

3653. MISCELLANEOUS. Tigereye. Very nice tigereye sphere. Nice shimmering to it. 31/32". Mint (9.9). Price: $45. CyberAuction #341, Lot #10.

3654. MISCELLANEOUS. Toothpick holder. Reproduction of a toothpick holder. Named "The Marble Shooter". Depicts a boy knuckling down. He carries a basket on his back in which you place the toothpicks. The original was produced around 1900 in France. This is a modern Czech reproduction. About 2-1/2" x 2-1/4". Mint. Blue glass. Price: $7. CyberAuction #367, Lot #26.

3655. MISCELLANEOUS. Tournament medal. Bronze medal. Obverse reads "United States National Marble Championship Tournament". Shows two boys shooting Ringer. Reverse reads "District Championship Awarded to Edward Murphy by The Springfield Union". Has a white and salmon silk ribbon with pinback. Medal and ribbon are in superior condition. Excellent example. Mint (9.7). Price: $285. CyberAuction #333, Lot #60.

3656. MISCELLANEOUS. Tournament medal. Hard to find tournament medal. Bronze. Octagonal rectangle. Front reads "United States Marble Shooting Championship Tournament" above a boy shooting at a Ringer circle, edged by olive branches. Reverse reads "School Championship Awarded to _____ by The Youngstown Telegram 1924". In great shape. Ribbon is old, but I don't think it is as old as the medal. Great patina on the medal. Outstanding. 1-7/16" x 1-1/8". Mint (9.7). Price: $285. CyberAuction #354, Lot #59.

3657. MISCELLANEOUS. Tournament medal. Bronze medal. Obverse reads "United States National Marble Championship Tournament". Shows two boys shooting Ringer. Reverse reads "District Championship Awarded to Edward Murphy by The Springfield Union". Has a white and salmon silk ribbon with pinback. Medal and ribbon are in superior condition. Excellent example. Mint (9.7). Price: $235. CyberAuction #379, Lot #45.

3658. MISCELLANEOUS. Tournament medal. Bronze medal. Obverse reads "National Marbles Tournament" "1939". Shows two boys shooting Ringer with a bleacher of cheering fans in the background. Eagle above them. Reverse reads "School Championship Awarded to [blank] by The Cleveland Press" The [blank] is a ribbon that can be engraved with the winners name. Has a white silk ribbon with pinback. Medal and ribbon are in superior condition. Pinback is stamped "Balfour". Excellent example. Mint (9.7). Price: $235. CyberAuction #406, Lot #56.

3659. MISCELLANEOUS. Tournament medal. Bronze medal. Obverse reads "United States National Marble Championship Tournament". Shows two boys shooting Ringer. Reverse reads "District Championship Awarded to Edward Murphy by The Springfield Union". Has a white and salmon silk ribbon with pinback. Medal and ribbon are in superior condition. Excellent example. Mint (9.7). Price: $235. CyberAuction #474, Lot #45.

3660. MISCELLANEOUS. Tournament medal. Bronze medal. Obverse reads "National Marbles Tournament" "1933". Shows two boys shooting Ringer with a bleacher of cheering fans in the background. Eagle above them. Reverse reads "1933 Philadelphia School and Playground Championship Awarded By The Evening Bulletin" (name of the medal manufacturer below that). Has a yellow and light blue silk ribbon with pinback. Ribbon faded and stained on front, reverse is fine. Nice example. Medal is Mint (9.9), ribbon is Near Mint (8.5). Price: $150. CyberAuction #363, Lot #59.

3661. MISCELLANEOUS. Tournament medal. Bronze medal. Obverse reads "National Marbles Tournament" "1933". Shows two boys shooting Ringer with a bleacher of cheering fans in the background. Eagle above them. Reverse reads "1933 Philadelphia School and Playground Championship Awarded By The Evening Bulletin" (name of the medal manufacturer below that). Has a yellow and light blue silk ribbon with pinback. Ribbon faded and stained on front, reverse is fine. Nice example. Medal is Mint (9.9), ribbon is Near Mint (8.5). Price: $150. CyberAuction #447, Lot #60.

3662. MISCELLANEOUS. Tournament pin. Small pinback. Green printing on white background. "Star-Times Player 1940 Marble Tournament". 7/8". Mint (9.7). Price: $22. CyberAuction #483, Lot #39.

3663. MISCELLANEOUS. Tournament pin. Small pinback. Green printing on white background. "Star-Times Player 1940 Marble Tournament". 7/8". Mint (9.7). Price: $22. CyberAuction #503, Lot #65.

3664. MISCELLANEOUS. Toy. A Limited Edition toy 1957 "International R-190 Full Rack Stake Truck" Printed on both sides with the Marble King name and the Marble King logo. Produced by Eastwood Collectibles, First Gear Inc. in 1995. 1/34 scale truck. Includes a bunch of Marble King patches. This is a heavy metal model truck. In the original box. These were produced for a very short period of time by a collectibles company from Pennsylvania. They are out of production and the company is sold out. A great item for a marble room. In the original box and shipping case. Heavy metal truck. 8" x 4" (sight). Mint (9.9). Price: $150. CyberAuction #333, Lot #30.

3665. MISCELLANEOUS. Toy. A Limited Edition toy 1957 "International R-190 Full Rack Stake Truck" Printed on both sides with the Marble King name and the Marble King logo. Produced by Eastwood Collectibles, First Gear Inc. in 1995. 1/34 scale truck. Includes a bunch of Marble King patches. This is a heavy metal model truck. In the original box. These were produced for a very short period of time by a collectibles company from Pennsylvania. They are out of production and the company is sold out. A great item for a marble room. In the original box and shipping case. Heavy metal truck. 8" x 4" (sight). Mint (9.9). Price: $120. CyberAuction #462, Lot #28.

3666. MISCELLANEOUS. Trade card. Very hard to find item. French trade card. Advertising on one side, image of children playing marbles on the other. Front shows three peasant boys playing marbles on a cobblestone street, probably in Paris. The other side is an advertisement in French. Appears to be an ad for a dry cleaner in Paris. Promising hygienic 24 hour dry-cleaning. He'll even pick up and deliver downtown. My guess is late 1800s. Cardboard. About 3" x 2". Mint (9.5). Price: $65. CyberAuction #339, Lot #55.

3667. MISCELLANEOUS. Trade card. Trade card depicting boy playing marbles. Advertises Porters Cough Balsam. Front of card has two panels. One depicts nanny holding a baby. Other depicts mother holding a baby while a boy plays marbles and a girl watches him. Front is in color. Back in black and white, advertises the product. In great shape. About 6" x 3". Late 1800s. Mint (9.5). Price: $40. CyberAuction #363, Lot #30.

3668. MISCELLANEOUS. Trade card. Depicts three French boys playing marbles. Printed "Au Grand Saint-Bernard 158 et 160, rue du Faubourg Saint-Antoine", "il oubhe tout pour faire une partie". French, circa 1900. About 2-1/2" x 4-1/2". Mint (9.7). Price: $32. CyberAuction #483, Lot #36.

3669. MISCELLANEOUS. Vase. Interesting item. This and the paperweight in Lot 49 came in a consignment, I popped them in here. The vase is a bulbous shape. Measures about 6" tall, 2" wide at top and bottom, about 4-1/2" wide at center. It's a cased "slump" glass. Clear glass containing pieces of slumped glass including a couple of latticinio canes. Opening at top is narrow and goes about two-thirds the way down the marble. Signed on the bottom "Mark Russell 2/81". Mint (9.9). Price: $65. CyberAuction #373, Lot #45.

3670. NON-GLASS HANDMADE. Bakelite. Very hard to find bakelite sphere. Red. Probably 1930's to 1940's. 27/32". Mint (9.9). Price: $17. CyberAuction #496, Lot #6.

3671. NON-GLASS HANDMADE. Bennington. Interesting marble. Pink background with lots of gray splotches. "Wrinkly" surface. Germany, circa 1850-1920. 13/16". Mint (9.9). Price: $100. CyberAuction #368, Lot #54.

3672. NON-GLASS HANDMADE. Bennington. Green bennington. Very nice, and hard to find. Germany, circa 1850-1900. 25/32". Mint (9.7). Price: $37. CyberAuction #377, Lot #40.

3673. NON-GLASS HANDMADE. Bennington. Pink background with lots of blue splotches. Germany, circa 1850-1920. 15/32". Mint (9.9). Price: $32. CyberAuction #377, Lot #50.

3674. NON-GLASS HANDMADE. Bennington. Black bennington. Hard to find. Germany, circa 1850-1920. 1-1/16". Near Mint(+) (8.9). Price: $27. CyberAuction #428, Lot #15.

3675. NON-GLASS HANDMADE. Bennington. Fancy bennington. Beautiful shooter. Germany, circa 1850-1920. 1-5/16". Mint (9.7). Price: $27. CyberAuction #475, Lot #19.

3676. NON-GLASS HANDMADE. Bennington. Fancy bennington. White background. Covered by blue and brown splotches. Germany, circa 1850-1920. 27/32". Mint (9.8). Price: $17. CyberAuction #482, Lot #1.

3677. NON-GLASS HANDMADE. Bennington. Fancy bennington. White background. Covered by blue and brown splotches. Germany, circa 1850-1920. 27/32". Mint (9.8). Price: $17. CyberAuction #499, Lot #13.

3678. NON-GLASS HANDMADE. Bennington. Fancy bennington. White background. Covered by blue and brown splotches. Germany, circa 1850-1920. 27/32". Mint (9.8). Price: $16. CyberAuction #418, Lot #13.

3679. NON-GLASS HANDMADE. Bennington. Shooter fancy bennington. White background with green and brown splotches on it. Germany, circa 1850-1920. 1-1/8". Mint (9.9). Price: $15. CyberAuction #427, Lot #41.

3680. NON-GLASS HANDMADE. Bennington. Blue bennington. Germany, circa 1850-1920. 1-7/16". Mint (9.8). Price: $13. CyberAuction #475, Lot #8.

3681. NON-GLASS HANDMADE. Bennington. Brown bennington. Germany, circa 1850-1920. 1-5/16". Mint (9.8). Price: $13. CyberAuction #475, Lot #10.

3682. NON-GLASS HANDMADE. Bennington. Large blue bennington. Great example. Germany, circa 1850-1920. 1-5/16". Mint (9.9). Price: $12. CyberAuction #428, Lot #1.

3683. NON-GLASS HANDMADE. Bennington. Fancy bennington. White

ckground with blue and brown splotches. Germany, circa 1850-1920. 3/
. Mint (9.9). Price: $6. CyberAuction #368, Lot #40.

584. NON-GLASS HANDMADE. Bennington. Shooter fancy bennington.
ermany, circa 1870-1915. 25/32". Mint (9.8). Price: $6. CyberAuction
493, Lot #5.

585. NON-GLASS HANDMADE. Carpet Ball. Very rare mocha ware car-
et ball. Swirled and smeared pattern of black, olive green, brown and
hite. In superior condition, completely undamaged. Stunning and ex-
emely rare (especially in this condition). Germany or England, circa 1860-
930. 3-1/4" (sight). Mint (9.9). Price: $460. CyberAuction #414, Lot #51.

586. NON-GLASS HANDMADE. Carpet Ball. Hard to find geometric
attern. Black and green concentric ring with bulls eye. One small area of
couple of tiny chips. Beauty. England, possibly Germany, circa 1870-
930. 3-1/4". Near Mint(+) (8.9). Price: $255. CyberAuction #400, Lot
35.

587. NON-GLASS HANDMADE. Carpet Ball. White background. Purple
ower design. Rare. Several very small chip spots, some crazing. Germany
England, circa 1850-1930. 3-1/4". Near Mint (8.6). Price: $130.
yberAuction #421, Lot #26.

588. NON-GLASS HANDMADE. Carpet Ball. Opaque white background.
ed patch at either end. Three red bands around circumference. Blue nu-
eral 4 on it. In great shape. Rare. 3". English, circa 1900-1930. Mint (9.6).
ice: $110. CyberAuction #385, Lot #36.

589. NON-GLASS HANDMADE. Carpet Ball. Brown crown and thistle
esign on white base. One small chipped area over one, rest is fine. En-
and, possibly Germany, circa 1870-1930. 3-1/4" (sight). Near Mint (8.5).
ice: $80. CyberAuction #416, Lot #30.

590. NON-GLASS HANDMADE. Carpet Ball. Jack ball. White porcelain
all. This was made in a mold and is hollow! Small seam around the equa-
r. Tiny hole in the bottom. Printed "Pat Oct 24, '93". In very nice shape.
ngland, circa 1890-1920. 2-3/4". Price: $80. CyberAuction #430, Lot #30.

591. NON-GLASS HANDMADE. Carpet Ball. White background. Inter-
ecting yellow lines design. Shows usage with a number of very tiny hit
arks. Germany or England, circa 1870-1930. 3-1/4" (sight). Near Mint
.6). Price: $55. CyberAuction #410, Lot #30.

592. NON-GLASS HANDMADE. Carpet Ball. Porcelain base. White back-
round. Covered by green stars. Odd design. It has been used and has
me flaking. This came from Scotland. Circa 1880-1940. About 3" diam-
er. Near Mint(-) (8.0). Price: $46. CyberAuction #472, Lot #18.

593. NON-GLASS HANDMADE. China. Rare Pennsylvania Dutch China.
paque white background. Six petal flower on either pole. Flowers are
anberry with black highlights. Green band around equator, with black
oops. A couple of typical air holes. A few very tiny spots where the glaze
nd underlying paint flaked off. Very tiny spots. I'm going to have to grade
below 9.0, because of this, but is views much better. Germany, circa
850-1900. 1-11/16". Near Mint(+) (8.9). Price: $875. CyberAuction #493,
ot #60.

594. NON-GLASS HANDMADE. China. Rare Pennsylvania Dutch china.
paque white background. Six five-petal flowers, one at each cardinal
oint. Each is a blue outline and blue center with green highlights. Some
inor hit spots where the glaze and color flaked off. All are tiny. These are
xtremely hard to find. Germany, circa 1850-1900. 1-13/16". Near Mint(+)
.7). Price: $700. CyberAuction #356, Lot #60.

595. NON-GLASS HANDMADE. China. Rare Pennsylvania Dutch china.
paque white background. A black, four-petal flower on either pole. Green
reath around the equator. The black has some sort of oxidation, making
art of it gray. Small hole on the surface (from manufacture) with a small
acture emanating from it. Pretty marble. These are rare. From same col-
ction as the one sold a few weeks ago. Germany, circa 1860-1920. 1-3/
". Near Mint (8.6). Price: $675. CyberAuction #366, Lot #60.

696. NON-GLASS HANDMADE. China. Hand painted unglazed large
hina. Each pole has a black bulls eye. The equator has four red donut hole
oses with green leaves. All the colors have some fading. Rare. Germany,
irca 1870-1915. 1-1/8". Mint(-) (9.2). Price: $210. CyberAuction #425,
ot #57.

697. NON-GLASS HANDMADE. China. Nice hand painted glazed china.
White background. Six bulls eyes on it. Two are light blue, two are black,
wo are gold. The gold are very faded, rest is fine. Gold are very rare ac-
ording to Carskadden and this is one of the largest I have seen. Germany,
irca 1860-1920. 1-1/16". Mint(-) (9.0). Price: $185. CyberAuction #398,
ot #35.

698. NON-GLASS HANDMADE. China. Hand painted unglazed china.
uper marble, hard to find design. Green pinwheel at each pole. Red tracks
round the equator, edged by four blue lines. Some minor fading. Ger-
any, circa 1870-1915. 1-1/16". Mint (9.6). Price: $180. CyberAuction
376, Lot #21.

699. NON-GLASS HANDMADE. China. An outstanding hand painted
hina. Each axis is a wide band, flanked on either side by two narrow
ands. One axis is black, one green, one orange/red. Stunning marble.
Germany, circa 1850-1920. 15/16". Mint (9.6). Price: $155. CyberAuction
418, Lot #49.

700. NON-GLASS HANDMADE. China. Nice hand painted glazed china.
White background. Six bulls eyes on it. Two are light blue, two are black,
wo are gold. The gold are very faded, rest is fine. Gold are very rare ac-
ording to Carskadden and this is one of the largest I have seen. Germany,
irca 1860-1920. 1-1/16". Mint(-) (9.0). Price: $135. CyberAuction #363,
ot #45.

701. NON-GLASS HANDMADE. China. Rare design. Unglazed hand
ainted china. Three red band around the equator. Yellow filled circle at
each pole. Ten black leaf petals on either hemisphere, running from the
ellow circle (flower center) to the equatorial red bands. Color in nice shape,

considering the marble is unglazed. Very rare design. Germany, circa 1860-
1920. 5/8". Mint (9.5). Price: $110. CyberAuction #362, Lot #60.

3702. NON-GLASS HANDMADE. China. Superb example. Hand painted
unglazed china. Three lines on each of the three axes. Each set is a wide
line, flanked by narrow lines. One axis each of black, green and red. In
great shape. Germany, circa 1850-1920. 1-1/8". Mint (9.7). Price: $110.
CyberAuction #373, Lot #44.

3703. NON-GLASS HANDMADE. China. Rare marble. Hand painted unglazed china. Three red bands around the equator. Green pinwheel on one
pole. Black Prussian Eagle on the other. All the colors are faded. Germany,
circa 1850-1920. 13/16". Mint(-) (9.0). Price: $110. CyberAuction
#427, Lot #43.

3704. NON-GLASS HANDMADE. China. Outstanding hand painted unglazed china. Green pinwheel leaf at each pole. Equator is black lines bound-
ing a ribbon of currant red tracks. The green is sharp and crisp, the equator
colors are slightly faded. Superb. Germany, circa 1850-1920. 1-1/8". Mint
(9.6). Price: $110. CyberAuction #428, Lot #58.

3705. NON-GLASS HANDMADE. China. Excellent and rare hand painted
glazed china. White background. One half of the marble is blue. Other half
is a light black concentric ring design. Rare design. Germany, circa 1860-
1920. 25/32". Mint (9.5). Price: $100. CyberAuction #344, Lot #58.

3706. NON-GLASS HANDMADE. China. Unglazed, painted china. Super
China (see similar marble on Page 21 of Marble Mania). Two pale lavender
lines painted around the equator. Light red image of a running horse on
either side. Very hard to find. Germany, circa 1870-1915. 13/16". Mint
(9.5). Price: $100. CyberAuction #388, Lot #53.

3707. NON-GLASS HANDMADE. China. Hand painted china for the top
of a cane, converted to a marble. Blue glaze with white panel on top. Panel
has two figures posing in a garden painted on it. Panel is edged in gold.
Blue has gold filigrees on it. Pinhole at bottom was filled a long time ago.
Some rubbing of the painting on the white. Very hard to find. Probably
French, possibly German, circa 1830-1900. 1-7/16". Near Mint(+) (8.9).
Price: $90. CyberAuction #437, Lot #57.

3708. NON-GLASS HANDMADE. China. Hand painted china. Rare marble. Unglazed, hand
painted. Large. White background. Three black bands around the equator.
Green pinwheel on one pole, pinkish purple pinwheel on the other pole.
Superb. Some very minor fading of the color, typical of unglazed chinas.
Very rare. Germany, circa 1850-1920. 1-1/4". Mint (9.6). Price: $80.
CyberAuction #504, Lot #73.

3709. NON-GLASS HANDMADE. China. Hand painted unglazed china.
In superb shape. Six bulls eyes. Equidistantly spaced on the six axes. Two
dark red, two dark green, two black. The two black are a little faded. The
other four are crisp. Stunning. Germany, circa 1870-1915. Germany, circa
1860-1920. 3/4". Mint (9.6). Price: $75. CyberAuction #345, Lot #60.

3710. NON-GLASS HANDMADE. China. Hand painted china for the top
of a cane, converted to a marble. Blue glaze with white panel on top. Panel
has two figures posing in a garden painted on it. Panel is edged in gold.
Blue has gold filigrees on it. Pinhole at bottom was filled a long time ago.
Some rubbing of the painting on the white. Very hard to find. Probably
French, possibly German, circa 1830-1900. 1-7/16". Near Mint(+) (8.9).
Price: $75. CyberAuction #406, Lot #50.

3711. NON-GLASS HANDMADE. China. Nice hand painted glazed china.
White background. Six bulls eyes on it. Two are light blue, two are green,
two are gold. The gold are very faded, rest is fine. Gold are very rare according to Carskadden and this is the largest one that I've ever seen. Germany, circa 1860-1920. 13/16". Mint(-) (9.0). Price: $65. CyberAuction
#339, Lot #14.

3712. NON-GLASS HANDMADE. China. Hand painted unglazed china.
One side has a bulls eye of light blue and two concentric rings of light blue.
Other side is a bulls eye of green and two concentric rings of the same
color. Red equatorial ribbon with two narrow ones. Faded. Germany, circa
18 60-1920. 3/4". Mint (9.5). Price: $61. CyberAuction #364, Lot #59.

3713. NON-GLASS HANDMADE. China. Hand painted glazed china. Super
coloring. Opaque white background. Blue bulls eye at one pole, green
bulls eye at other. Three red bands around equator. Very nice and hard to
find. Germany, circa 1870-1915. 11/16". Mint (9.7). Price: $60. CyberAuction
#342, Lot #55.

3714. NON-GLASS HANDMADE. China. Hand painted unglazed china.
Black bulls eye on one pole, green bulls eye on the other. Nice coloring.
Germany, circa 1870-1915. 25/32". Mint (9.5). Price: $55. CyberAuction
#377, Lot #32.

3715. NON-GLASS HANDMADE. China. Hand painted unglazed china.
Two red lines around the equator. Green oak leaf on either pole. Oak
leaves are the Victorian symbol of loyalty. Some original defects. Germany,
circa 1860-1920. 23/32". Mint(-) (9.0). Price: $55. CyberAuction #386,
Lot #40.

3716. NON-GLASS HANDMADE. China. Unglazed hand painted china.
Very nice china. Red pinwheel at either pole. Green lines of varying widths
around the equator. In great shape. Super marble. One flat spot. Germany,
circa 1860-1920. 23/32". Mint (9.5). Price: $47. CyberAuction #354, Lot
#53.

3717. NON-GLASS HANDMADE. China. Unglazed hand painted china.
Very nice china. Red pinwheel at either pole. Green lines of varying widths
around the equator. In great shape. Super marble. One flat spot. Germany,
circa 1860-1920. 23/32". Mint (9.5). Price: $47. CyberAuction #404, Lot
#32.

3718. NON-GLASS HANDMADE. China. Hand painted glazed china.
Faded green lines around two axes. Two quadrants have red leaves, two
have green leaves. Very slightly oval. Germany, circa 1850-1900. 1-1/8".
Mint(-) (9.0). Price: $45. CyberAuction #360, Lot #57.

3719. NON-GLASS HANDMADE. China. Nice unglazed hand painted china. Large marble with bright colors. Pink spiral on one side, blue crows-feet on the other. In great shape. Germany, circa 1880-1920. 1-1/16". Mint (9.8). Price: $43. CyberAuction #341, Lot #41.

3720. NON-GLASS HANDMADE. China. Unglazed, hand painted china. Four red lines around the equator. Three blue leaves at either pole. Germany, circa 1860-1920. 21/32". Mint (9.7). Price: $38. CyberAuction #371, Lot #19.

3721. NON-GLASS HANDMADE. China. Unglazed hand painted china. Each pole is a bulls eye of green with a spiral. Core is purple/red crow feet. Some fading. Also, some pencil scribbles on it. Germany, circa 1870-1915. 1-3/8". Mint(-) (9.0). Price: $37. CyberAuction #359, Lot #42.

3722. NON-GLASS HANDMADE. China. Hard to find subject. Unglazed, hand painted. Red helix around equator. Green branch of oak leaves (Victorian symbol of loyalty) on either pole. Germany, circa 1860-1920. 17/32". Mint (9.7). Price: $37. CyberAuction #406, Lot #47.

3723. NON-GLASS HANDMADE. China. Unglazed hand painted china. Equatorial red band with a narrow one above and below it. Another light blue band encircling them marble, perpendicular to the first (pole to pole), edged on either side by a narrow band of light blue. Some fading. Germany, circa 1860-1920. 11/16". Mint(-) (9.0). Price: $35. CyberAuction #398, Lot #15.

3724. NON-GLASS HANDMADE. China. Unglazed hand painted china. Equatorial red band with a narrow one above and below it. Another light blue band encircling them marble, perpendicular to the first (pole to pole), edged on either side by a narrow band of light blue. Some fading. Germany, circa 1860-1920. 11/16". Mint(-) (9.0). Price: $32. CyberAuction #365, Lot #33.

3725. NON-GLASS HANDMADE. China. Very nice hand painted glazed china. White background. Red helix on either pole. Green tracks around equator. Germany, circa 1850-1920. 1-1/16". Mint (9.5). Consignor note: B16. Price: $32. CyberAuction #423, Lot #38.

3726. NON-GLASS HANDMADE. China. Hand painted and glazed. Three bulls eyes. One red, one light blue, one gold. Carskadden describes gold as rare, in his book. Some rubbing of the gold, which is typical. Germany, circa 1850-1920. 21/32". Mint (9.6). Price: $32. CyberAuction #477, Lot #4.

3727. NON-GLASS HANDMADE. China. Glazed, hand painted china. White background. Three bulls eyes. One red, one light blue, one is very hard to find gold. Some fading of the gold. Germany, circa 1860-1920. 11/16". Mint (9.5). Price: $30. CyberAuction #362, Lot #41.

3728. NON-GLASS HANDMADE. China. Hand painted unglazed china. Purple concentric circles on each pole. Green leaves around the equator. Very nice marble. Germany, circa 1860-1920. 27/32". Mint (9.5). Price: $30. CyberAuction #383, Lot #37.

3729. NON-GLASS HANDMADE. China. Glazed, hand painted china. White background. Three bulls eyes. One red, one light blue, one is very hard to find gold. Some fading of the gold. Germany, circa 1860-1920. 11/16". Mint (9.5). Price: $30. CyberAuction #398, Lot #39.

3730. NON-GLASS HANDMADE. China. Hand painted glazed china. Large marble. Opaque white surface with random white lines and splotches of blue and green. One small unglazed spot. Large marble. Germany, circa 1860-1920. 1-3/16". Mint (9.8). Price: $29. CyberAuction #379, Lot #43.

3731. NON-GLASS HANDMADE. China. Hand painted and glazed. Three bulls eyes. One red, one light blue, one gold. Carskadden describes gold as rare, in his book. Some rubbing of the gold, which is typical. Germany, circa 1850-1920. 21/32". Mint (9.6). Price: $27. CyberAuction #439, Lot #50.

3732. NON-GLASS HANDMADE. China. Hand painted and glazed. Three bulls eyes. One red, one light blue, one gold. Carskadden describes gold as rare, in his book. Some rubbing of the gold, which is typical. Germany, circa 1850-1920. 21/32". Mint (9.6). Price: $27. CyberAuction #454, Lot #17.

3733. NON-GLASS HANDMADE. China. Odd china. Hand painted. Unglazed. Three black lines on each axis, creating eight quadrants. Two are painted in green, two are painted in yellow. Other four are unpainted. All the colors are faded. Germany, circa 1870-1915. 21/32". Near Mint(+) (8.9). Price: $25. CyberAuction #425, Lot #43.

3734. NON-GLASS HANDMADE. China. Hand painted unglazed china. Purple concentric circles on each pole. Green leaves around the equator. Very nice marble. Germany, circa 1860-1920. 27/32". Mint (9.5). Price: $24. CyberAuction #336, Lot #51.

3735. NON-GLASS HANDMADE. China. Hand painted unglazed china. Bulls eye design. Faded. Two bulls eyes each of red, green and black. Germany, circa 1870-1915. 1-1/16". Mint(-) (9.0). Price: $24. CyberAuction #337, Lot #54.

3736. NON-GLASS HANDMADE. China. Hand painted glazed china. White background. Three bulls eyes. One pink, one light green, one light blue. Germany, circa 1870-1915. 17/32". Mint (9.7). Price: $23. CyberAuction #419, Lot #38.

3737. NON-GLASS HANDMADE. China. Hand painted glazed china. Opaque white base. Three lines on each of the three axes. One group each of red, light blue and black. Germany, circa 1860-1920. 25/32". Mint (9.6). Price: $23. CyberAuction #471, Lot #38.

3738. NON-GLASS HANDMADE. China. Unglazed hand painted china. Six bulls eyes. Two red, two black, two green. Germany, circa 1860-1920. 9/16". Mint (9.9). Price: $22. CyberAuction #367, Lot #56.

3739. NON-GLASS HANDMADE. China. Glazed, hand painted china. White background. Three bulls eyes. One red, one light blue, one is very hard to find gold. Some fading of the gold. Germany, circa 1860-1920. 11/16". Mint (9.5). Price: $22. CyberAuction #434, Lot #38.

3740. NON-GLASS HANDMADE. China. Bulls eye motif. Six bulls eyes.

Very nice. Germany, circa 1850-1920. 23/32". Mint (9.7). Price: $2 CyberAuction #447, Lot #39.

3741. NON-GLASS HANDMADE. China. Glazed hand painted china. S bulls eyes. Four are red, two are black. Germany, circa 1870-1915. 3/4 Mint (9.8). Price: $21. CyberAuction #504, Lot #38.

3742. NON-GLASS HANDMADE. China. Hand painted unglazed chin. Each axis has four black lines on it. Widely spaced, almost a checkerboa pattern. Some smearing and fading. Germany, circa 1860-1920. 31/32 Mint(-) (9.0). Price: $20. CyberAuction #447, Lot #54.

3743. NON-GLASS HANDMADE. China. Bulls eye china. White bac ground. Three bulls eyes. One red, one blue, one black. Germany, circ 1860-1920. 1/2". Mint (9.9). Price: $17. CyberAuction #338, Lot #56.

3744. NON-GLASS HANDMADE. China. Hand painted glazed china. Re crow feet on one side. Blue helix on the other. Germany, circa 1850-192 3/4". Mint (9.5). Price: $17. CyberAuction #418, Lot #9.

3745. NON-GLASS HANDMADE. China. Hand painted glazed china. Re helix on one side. Five purple leaves on the other. Germany, circ 1860-1920. 13/16". Mint (9.9). Price: $16. CyberAuction #345, Lot #1

3746. NON-GLASS HANDMADE. China. Unglazed hand painted chin. Odd colors. Turquoise helix on one axis, orange helix on another. Ge many, circa 1870-1920. 5/8". Mint (9.5). Price: $15. CyberAuction #38 Lot #2.

3747. NON-GLASS HANDMADE. China. Hand painted glazed china. Tw black lines on one axis. Two orange lines on another axis. Germany, circ 1850-1900. 27/32". Mint (9.7). Price: $15. CyberAuction #414, Lot #1

3748. NON-GLASS HANDMADE. China. Hand painted glazed china. Two black lines around the equator. Five vane pinwheel on each pole Also, black. Some fading. Germany, circa 1860-1900. 19/32". Mint(-) (9.0 Price: $12. CyberAuction #338, Lot #48.

3749. NON-GLASS HANDMADE. China. Hand painted glazed china. White background. Red spiral on one side, green track on the other. Ge many, circa 1860-1920. 5/8". Mint (9.9). Price: $12. CyberAuction #47 Lot #18.

3750. NON-GLASS HANDMADE. China. Hand painted unglazed chin. Green spiral at each pole. Red crow feet around the equator. Exception. colors. Germany, circa 1850-1920. 19/32". Mint (9.9). Price: $11 CyberAuction #357, Lot #37.

3751. NON-GLASS HANDMADE. China. White background. One ax has a series of red strands. Another axis has a series of black strands. Som fading. Germany, circa 1870-1915. 15/16". Mint(-) (9.1). Price: $11 CyberAuction #382, Lot #21.

3752. NON-GLASS HANDMADE. China. Nice hand painted glazed china Intersecting lines on each of the three axes. One axis each of black, ligh blue and red. Dirt marks on the glaze, but no damage. Germany, circ 1850-1920. 1-3/16". Mint(-) (9.1). Price: $11. CyberAuction #454, Lo #44.

3753. NON-GLASS HANDMADE. China. Hand painted glazed china White background. Red spiral on one axis, green spiral on another, blac on a third. Some fading. Germany, circa 1850-1920. 1-1/16". Mint (9.5 Price: $11. CyberAuction #475, Lot #6.

3754. NON-GLASS HANDMADE. China. Nice hand painted glazed china Intersecting lines on each of the three axes. One axis each of black, ligh blue and red. Dirt marks on the glaze, but no damage. Germany, circ 1850-1920. 1-3/16". Mint(-) (9.1). Price: $10. CyberAuction #410, Lo #46.

3755. NON-GLASS HANDMADE. China. Hand painted and glazed. Re helix on one pole, three green leaves on the other. Germany, circa 1850 1920. 7/8". Mint (9.7). There are two marbles available, you are bidding o one. Winner has choice of either or both, remainder to under. Price: $1 CyberAuction #439, Lot #26.

3756. NON-GLASS HANDMADE. China. Nice hand painted china. Gree spiral on one axis, red spiral perpendicular to it. Germany, circa 1870 1915. 19/32". Mint (9.9). Price: $9. CyberAuction #339, Lot #40.

3757. NON-GLASS HANDMADE. China. Glazed hand painted china White background. Two lines on each of the three axes. One axis is red one is turquoise, one is black. Germany, circa 1850-1920. 5/8". Mint (9.7 Price: $9. CyberAuction #396, Lot #1.

3758. NON-GLASS HANDMADE. China. Hand painted glazed china White background. Six bulls eyes. Two each of red, black and green. Ur evenly distributed. Germany, circa 1870-1915. 19/32". Mint (9.9). Price $9. CyberAuction #471, Lot #35.

3759. NON-GLASS HANDMADE. China. Glazed hand painted china White background. Six bulls eyes. Two each of green, red and black. Ger many, circa 1860-1920. 17/32". Mint (9.4). Price: $7. CyberAuction #346 Lot #39.

3760. NON-GLASS HANDMADE. China. Hand painted unglazed china Faded colors. Helix on either pole and leaves around the equator. Ger many, circa 1860-1920. 3/4". Near Mint (8.5). Price: $6. CyberAuctio #482, Lot #27.

3761. NON-GLASS HANDMADE. China. Glazed hand painted china White background. Faded dark green helix on one pole. Three tiny re leaves on the other. Germany, circa 1870-1920. 5/8". Mint (9.5). Price: $5 CyberAuction #337, Lot #14.

3762. NON-GLASS HANDMADE. China. Hand painted glazed china White background. Blue lines on equator, red pinwheel at each pole Most of the design is rubbed off. Germany, circa 1870-1915. 11/16". Mint( ) (9.0). Price: $5. CyberAuction #460, Lot #19.

3763. NON-GLASS HANDMADE. China. Hand painted glazed china White background. Six bulls eyes. Two each of red, black and green. Un evenly distributed. Germany, circa 1870-1915. 19/32". Mint (9.9). Price $5. CyberAuction #479, Lot #28.

764. NON-GLASS HANDMADE. China. Glazed hand painted china. White background. Two bands on each of the three axes. One axis is red, one blue, one black. Some flaking of the glaze. Germany, circa 1870-1920. ¾". Near Mint (8.6). Price: $4. CyberAuction #392, Lot #40.

765. NON-GLASS HANDMADE. China. Hand painted glazed china. Red helix on one pole, black track on other. Germany, circa 1860-1920. 9/16". Mint(-) (9.0). Price: $4. CyberAuction #485, Lot #38.

766. NON-GLASS HANDMADE. China. Tiny pipe clay hand painted china. Blue helix around equator. Germany, circa 1870-1915. 7/16". Mint (9.9). Price: $3. CyberAuction #369, Lot #23.

767. NON-GLASS HANDMADE. China. Hand painted glazed china. White background. Green lines on one axis. Red lines on another. Somewhat oval. Germany, circa 1860-1920. 7/8". Mint(-) (9.0). Price: $3. CyberAuction #458, Lot #3.

768. NON-GLASS HANDMADE. China. Hand painted glazed china. White background. Red lines on one axis. Black lines on another. Germany, circa 1860-1920. 5/8". Mint (9.7). Price: $3. CyberAuction #474, Lot #8.

769. NON-GLASS HANDMADE. China. Hand painted glazed china. White background. Black track on one side, red spiral on other. Some fading. Germany, circa 1860-1920. 3/4". Mint(-) (9.0). Price: $2. CyberAuction #461, Lot #2.

770. NON-GLASS HANDMADE. China. Hand painted glazed china. White background. Red spiral on one axis, light green on another. Germany, circa 1850-1920. 21/32". Mint (9.9). Price: $2. CyberAuction #472, Lot #10.

771. NON-GLASS HANDMADE. China. Hand painted glazed china. White background. Two black bands on one axis, two red on another. Germany, circa 1860-1920. 5/8". Mint(-) (9.0). Price: $2. CyberAuction #485, Lot #40.

772. NON-GLASS HANDMADE. China. Hand painted glazed marble. White background. Green spiral on one axis, red spiral on another. Germany, circa 1860-1920. 21/32". Mint (9.5). Price: $2. CyberAuction #490, Lot #3.

773. NON-GLASS HANDMADE. China. Hand painted glazed china. Small black leaves on one side, red helix on other. Germany, circa 1870-1915. 9/32". Mint (9.5). Price: $2. CyberAuction #492, Lot #1.

774. NON-GLASS HANDMADE. China. Hand painted glazed china. White background. Black track on one side, red spiral on other. Some fading. Germany, circa 1860-1920. 3/4". Mint(-) (9.0). Price: $2. CyberAuction #496, Lot #29.

775. NON-GLASS HANDMADE. China. Hand painted glazed marble. White background. Green spiral on one axis, red spiral on another. Germany, circa 1860-1920. 21/32". Mint (9.5). Price: $1. CyberAuction #458, Lot #7.

776. NON-GLASS HANDMADE. China. Hand painted glazed china. White background. Black helix on one pole, red track on the other. Germany, circa 1860-1920. 3/4". Mint(-) (9.0). Price: $1. CyberAuction #458, Lot #10.

777. NON-GLASS HANDMADE. China. Hand painted glazed china. White background. Red lines on one axis. Black lines on another. Germany, circa 1860-1920. 5/8". Mint (9.7). Price: $.50. CyberAuction #457, Lot #31.

778. NON-GLASS HANDMADE. Clay. Large speckled brown earthenware marble. Probably used for a lawn bowling or similar game. Probably American. See Carskadden Colonial Marbles pages 55-57 for similar discussion. Very hard to find them this large. American, circa 1870-1930. 2-1/ .. Mint (9.9). Two marbles available, you are bidding on one. Winner has choice of either or both, remainder to under. Price: $44. CyberAuction #387, Lot #31.

779. NON-GLASS HANDMADE. Crockery. Painted crockery. Excellent. Natural base. Six vane red pinwheel on each pole. Equator has two red circles and one black one. Someone has written the initials "C G" in pencil in the center of one pinwheel. Germany, circa 1860-1920. 1-1/16". Mint (9.7). Price: $125. CyberAuction #462, Lot #55.

780. NON-GLASS HANDMADE. Crockery. Painted crockery. Excellent. Natural base. Six vane red pinwheel on each pole. Equator has two red circles and one black one. Someone has written the initials "C G" in pencil in the center of one pinwheel. Germany, circa 1860-1920. 1-1/16". Mint (9.7). Price: $110. CyberAuction #351, Lot #52.

781. NON-GLASS HANDMADE. Crockery. Hand painted glazed crockery. Large marble. Opaque white surface with random lines and splotches of blue and green. One small unglazed spot. Large marble. Germany, circa 1860-1920. 1-3/16". Mint (9.8). Price: $26. CyberAuction #442, Lot #47.

782. NON-GLASS HANDMADE. Crockery. Very nice shooter size lined crockery. Thin lines of blue and green swirled in white. Beauty. Germany, possibly American, circa 1860-1920. 7/8". Mint (9.9). Price: $19. CyberAuction #330, Lot #15.

783. NON-GLASS HANDMADE. Crockery. Hand painted, glazed crockery. White base with splotches of green and blue. Very nice. Possibly German or American, circa 1850-1920. 11/16". Mint (9.9). Price: $10. CyberAuction #340, Lot #13.

784. NON-GLASS HANDMADE. Crockery. Glazed, lined crockery. White base with blue and green swirls in it. Super example. Germany, circa 1850-1920. 19/32". Mint (9.7). Price: $7. CyberAuction #439, Lot #55.

785. NON-GLASS HANDMADE. Crockery. Very pretty lined crockery. Glazed. Smeared blue and green lines. Germany, possibly American, circa 1860-1920. 11/16". Mint (9.9). There are three available. You are bidding on one. Winner has choice of any or all, remainder to under. Price: $6. CyberAuction #335, Lot #37.

786. NON-GLASS HANDMADE. Crockery. Shooter lined crockery. Blue

and green lines in white. Some dirt. American, circa 1870-1920. 7/8". Near Mint(+) (8.9). Price: $6. CyberAuction #389, Lot #9.

3787. NON-GLASS HANDMADE. Crockery. Lined crockery. Tan background with smeared blue and green lines. unglazed. Some rough areas. Germany, circa 1870-1915. 27/32". Near Mint(+) (8.8). Price: $6. CyberAuction #390, Lot #37.

3788. NON-GLASS HANDMADE. Crockery. Lined crockery. Tan background with smeared blue and green lines. unglazed. Some rough areas. Germany, circa 1870-1915. 27/32". Near Mint(+) (8.8). Price: $6. CyberAuction #449, Lot #42.

3789. NON-GLASS HANDMADE. Crockery. Glazed lined crockery. Little white showing. Mostly green and blue. A few tiny chips. Germany, possibly American, circa 1850-1900. 11/16". Near Mint(+) (8.7). Price: $3. CyberAuction #362, Lot #37.

3790. NON-GLASS HANDMADE. Crockery. Smeared blue and green lines. unglazed. Tan background with smeared blue and green lines. unglazed. Some rough areas. Germany, circa 1870-1915. 27/32". Near Mint(+) (8.8). Price: $3. CyberAuction #474, Lot #15.

3791. NON-GLASS HANDMADE. Crockery. Glazed lined crockery. Opaque white with light green and blue lines. Lots of oven dirt on the surface. German or American, circa 1850-1920. 23/32". Mint (9.7). Price: $2. CyberAuction #371, Lot #2.

3792. NON-GLASS HANDMADE. Crockery. Glazed lined crockery. Opaque white with light green and blue lines. Lots of oven dirt on the surface. German or American, circa 1850-1920. 23/32". Mint (9.7). Price: $1. CyberAuction #451, Lot #44.

3793. NON-GLASS HANDMADE. Crockery. Glazed lined crockery. Opaque white with light green and blue lines. Lots of oven dirt on the surface. German or American, circa 1850-1920. 23/32". Mint (9.7). Price: $1. CyberAuction #474, Lot #27.

3794. NON-GLASS HANDMADE. Crockery. Gray crockery with some green and blue on it. Germany, circa 1850-1920. 5/8". Mint (9.5). Price: $1. CyberAuction #473, Lot #13.

3795. NON-GLASS HANDMADE. Handle. This is part of a cane or umbrella handle. The sphere on the top is very unusual. It is a glazed English pottery. Looping browns on white. What is unusual about this one is that it looks exactly like a Navarre transitional, but it is ceramic. The transitionals were designed to mimic agate, and this is the only Non-Glass sphere I've ever seen that was also designed to mimic agate. It probably has a screw in the bottom, which is attaching it to an approximately 3" length of hornbill cane. There is a nickel collar. The sphere has a couple of tiny hit marks in the glaze. Outstanding and rare. English, circa 1850-1900. 1-1/2". Near Mint(+) (8.9). Price: $90. CyberAuction #504, Lot #50.

3796. NON-GLASS HANDMADE. Limestone. Rare hand painted limestone. Limestone sphere. Painted with aqua bands on one axis and black bands on another. Very nice (a little dirty). Germany, circa 1850-1920. 11/16". Mint (9.5). Price: $17. CyberAuction #487, Lot #34.

3797. NON-GLASS HANDMADE. Mocha ware. Very rare marble. Mocha ware marbles themselves are rare, but when you do see them, they are as Carpet Balls. This one is a regular size playing marble. Swirled pattern of grainy white, light brown, dark brown, on a natural gray base. Glazed. This one has a tiny pit. Germany, circa 1850-1900. 3/4". Mint (9.5). Note: there were five marbles in total in this consignment, this is the second. Price: $135. CyberAuction #426, Lot #58.

3798. NON-GLASS HANDMADE. Mocha ware. Very rare marble. Mocha ware marbles themselves are rare, but when you do see them, they are as Carpet Balls. This one is a regular size playing marble. Swirled pattern of grainy white, light brown, dark brown and blue, on a natural gray base. Glazed. This one has a few small pits. Extremely rare. Germany, circa 1850-1900. 23/32". Mint(-) (9.0). Price: $100. CyberAuction #403, Lot #59.

3799. NON-GLASS HANDMADE. Mocha ware. Very rare marble. Mocha ware marbles themselves are rare, but when you do see them, they are as Carpet Balls. This one is a regular size playing marble. Swirled pattern of grainy white, light brown, dark brown, on a natural gray base. Glazed. This one has a tiny pit. Germany, circa 1850-1900. 3/4". Mint (9.5). Note: there were five marbles in total in this consignment, this is the second. Price: $85. CyberAuction #409, Lot #57.

3800. NON-GLASS HANDMADE. Original box. Original box of twelve metallic foil clays. Straw paper box with staples at corners. Printed on top "Germany No 380/32/12". Each marble is 3/16". Two green, Two blue, two gold, two purple, three red, one silver. All are metallic foil colored and Mint. Super set, hard to find. Germany, circa 1880-1920. Mint. Price: $260. CyberAuction #498, Lot #30.

3801. NON-GLASS HANDMADE. Pottery. One of the rarest pottery marbles you will find. This is a glazed English Dedham pottery sphere. Brown saltglaze. Darker brown on one side than the other. Accompanied by a signed letter from a well-known English pottery author and dealer, Mrs. Frances Gibson, attested to the sphere being an "English orange-peel 18th Century salt-glazed Rare Alley Taw". Very rare and important marble. England, circa 1750-1800. 1-9/16". Mint (9.9). Price: $321. CyberAuction #503, Lot #69.

3802. NON-GLASS HANDMADE. Steelie. Large handmade steelie. Nice "X". Probably from a Busy Andy game. 1". Mint (9.9). Price: $44. CyberAuction #497, Lot #24.

3803. NON-GLASS HANDMADE. Stone. Hard to find painted limestone. Nice white limestone with four concentric black rings. Very hard to find. Germany, circa 1850-1900. 13/16". Mint (9.5). Price: $20. CyberAuction #359, Lot #8.

3804. NON-GLASS HANDMADE. Stone. Hand cut limestone. Gray. Some banding. Very nice early example. Probably Germany, circa 1830-1870. 19/32". Mint (9.7). Consignor note: G38/. Price: $5. CyberAuction #423, Lot #4.

3805. NON-GLASS HANDMADE. Stone. Hand cut limestone. Gray. Some banding. Very nice early example. Probably Germany, circa 1830-1870. 19/32". Mint (9.7). Price: $5. CyberAuction #460, Lot #22.

3806. NON-GLASS HANDMADE. Stoneware. Very hard to find. Creamy white background with two wide blue splotches. Salt-glazed. American, circa 1850-1920. 1". Mint (9.9). Price: $55. CyberAuction #381, Lot #57.

3807. NON-GLASS HANDMADE. Stoneware. Glazed yellow stoneware marble. Looks like a dyed clay at first glance, but it is much denser. Harder to find. American, possibly German, circa 1850-1900. 11/16". Mint (9.9). Price: $20. CyberAuction #400, Lot #45.

3808. NON-GLASS HANDMADE. Stoneware. Salt-glazed beige stoneware with blue splotching around the equator. "Dimple" on one pole. Germany, possibly American, circa 1850-1920. 1". Mint (9.5). Price: $20. CyberAuction #506, Lot #43.

3809. NON-GLASS HANDMADE. Stoneware. Small salt-glazed stoneware. American, circa 1880-1920. 23/32". Mint (9.9). Price: $17. CyberAuction #476, Lot #11.

3810. NON-GLASS HANDMADE. Stoneware. Salt-glazed beige stoneware with blue splotching around the equator. "Dimple" on one pole. Germany, possibly American, circa 1850-1920. 1". Mint (9.5). Price: $17. CyberAuction #491, Lot #7.

3811. NON-GLASS HANDMADE. Stoneware. Salt glazed white background with light blue splotching. Germany, possibly American, circa 1850-1920. 1". Mint(-) (9.0). Price: $13. CyberAuction #506, Lot #44.

3812. NON-GLASS HANDMADE. Stoneware. Salt glazed white background with light blue splotching. Germany, possibly American, circa 1850-1920. 1". Mint(-) (9.0). Price: $12. CyberAuction #491, Lot #17.

3813. OTHER HANDMADE. Banded Transparent. Actually, a banded transparent. Superior example of this rare marble. Transparent very lightly tinted aqua base. Surface is completely covered with transparent, translucent and opaque stretched strands, bands and splotches of white, blue, yellow and green. Exceptional. Germany, circa 1870-1915. 25/32". Mint (9.7). Price: $310. CyberAuction #363, Lot #56.

3814. OTHER HANDMADE. Banded Opaque. Exceptional example of a banded opaque. Butterscotch brown semi-opaque base. Two panels of light transparent pink bands. In superb shape. Stunning. Germany, circa 1870-1915. 19/32". Mint (9.9). Price: $185. CyberAuction #418, Lot #21.

3815. OTHER HANDMADE. Banded Opaque. Semi-opaque white base. Two bands of teal covering about seventy percent of the marble. The teal is shiny, the white is satiny. This is intentional and not damage. Very nice. Germany, possibly American, circa 1880-1920. 11/16". Mint (9.7). Price: $150. CyberAuction #330, Lot #4.

3816. OTHER HANDMADE. Banded Opaque. Base is lightly tinted blue opaque white. Two bands of electric orange covering about forty percent of the surface. Very nice coloring. Top pontil has a small crease in it. Marble is out of round. Germany, circa 1870-1915. 21/32". Mint(-) (9.2). Price: $141. CyberAuction #420, Lot #38.

3817. OTHER HANDMADE. Banded Opaque. Base is lightly tinted blue opaque white. Two bands of electric orange covering about forty percent of the surface. Very nice coloring. Top pontil has a small crease in it. Marble is out of round. Germany, circa 1870-1915. 21/32". Mint(-) (9.2). Price: $140. CyberAuction #478, Lot #39.

3818. OTHER HANDMADE. Banded Opaque. Very unusual and rare banded opaque. Semi-opaque milky white base. Almost completely covered by slightly stretch splotches of turquoise, teal, yellow, white and blue. An air hole, some tiny and small subsurface moons, one small filled chip. Germany, circa 1870-1915. 29/32". Good(+) (7.7). Price: $135. CyberAuction #335, Lot #56.

3819. OTHER HANDMADE. Banded Opaque. Semi-opaque white base. Two bands of stretched blue covering about forty percent of the marble. One melt spot, one pit. Germany, circa 1870-1915. 21/32". Mint(-) (9.2). Price: $110. CyberAuction #394, Lot #45.

3820. OTHER HANDMADE. Banded Opaque. Very unusual marble. Semi-opaque light green base. Several white bands on one side, a narrow yellow band on the other. Colors go into the marble. Some light rubbing, but no damage. 23/32". Mint(-) (9.0). Price: $110. CyberAuction #419, Lot #11.

3821. OTHER HANDMADE. Banded Opaque. Semi-opaque white base. Two bands of stretched blue covering about forty percent of the marble. One melt spot, one pit. Germany, circa 1870-1915. 21/32". Mint(-) (9.2). Price: $110. CyberAuction #422, Lot #29.

3822. OTHER HANDMADE. Banded Opaque. Very rare example. Semi-opaque milky white base. Thin bands of blue, pink and white on the surface and in the marble. This looks like an early American cane-cut marble to me. Very rare. One tiny moon, one blown air hole. American, circa 1880-1910. 21/32". Near Mint(+) (8.8). Price: $110. CyberAuction #473, Lot #57.

3823. OTHER HANDMADE. Banded Opaque. Semi-opaque white base. Two bands of stretched green covering about thirty percent of the marble. No damage, but there is some light black on the surface, probably burnt carbon from manufacture. Germany, circa 1870-1915. 11/16". Mint(-) (9.0). Price: $95. CyberAuction #387, Lot #33.

3824. OTHER HANDMADE. Banded Opaque. Rare banded translucent. Opalescent translucent white base. Ghost core. Two bands on the surface. Each is pink strands. Covering about twenty five percent of the surface. One small chip. Rare. Germany, circa 1870-1915. 11/16". Near Mint (8.5). Price: $90. CyberAuction #353, Lot #52.

3825. OTHER HANDMADE. Banded Opaque. Rare marble. Semi-opaque blue base. Two white bands on it. Very rare base coloring. One tiny melt spot with a sand "seed" in the center. One elongated blown out air hole. Germany, possibly American, circa 1870-1915. 9/16". Mint(-) (9.0). Price: $85. CyberAuction #462, Lot #22.

3826. OTHER HANDMADE. Banded Opaque. Opaque white base. Thre[e] narrow pink bands. In great shape. Germany, circa 1870-1915. 19/32[?] Mint (9.7). Price: $80. CyberAuction #452, Lot #41.

3827. OTHER HANDMADE. Banded Opaque. Opaque white base. Tw[o] bands covering about seventy percent of the surface. Each is blues an[d] greens. A couple of tiny flakes and some tiny subsurface moons. German[?] circa 1870-1915. 25/32". Near Mint (8.3). Price: $71. CyberAuction #42[?], Lot #35.

3828. OTHER HANDMADE. Banded Opaque. Semi-opaque white bas[e]. Two bands of pink covering about forty percent of the marble. One dirt spotting. 23/32". Near Mint (8.6). Price: $65. CyberAuction #390, Lot #38.

3829. OTHER HANDMADE. Banded Opaque. Semi-opaque white bas[e]. Two narrow bands on it. One is dark blue, other is yellow. The yellow partial. Probably from near an end of the cane. Small cold roll line. Ge[r]many, possibly American, circa 1870-1915. 21/32". Mint (9.5). Price: $6[0] CyberAuction #410, Lot #13.

3830. OTHER HANDMADE. Banded Opaque. White base. One sma[ll] pink band. Some melted dirt on the bottom. No damage. Germany, circ[a] 1870-1915. 23/32". Mint (9.5). Price: $60. CyberAuction #506, Lot #2[?]

3831. OTHER HANDMADE. Banded Opaque. White base. One sma[ll] pink band. Some melted dirt on the bottom. No damage. Germany, circ[a] 1870-1915. 23/32". Mint (9.5). Price: $50. CyberAuction #489, Lot #[?]

3832. OTHER HANDMADE. Banded Opaque. Semi-opaque white base. Two bands covering about forty percent of the surface. Each is stretche[d] blue. One tiny subsurface moon. Germany, circa 1870-191[5] 21/32". Near Mint(+) (8.7). Price: $50. CyberAuction #491, Lot #52.

3833. OTHER HANDMADE. Banded Opaque. Opaque white base. Su[r]face almost completely covered by pink bands. Several tiny chips, in on[e] are. Germany, circa 1870-1915. 21/32". Near Mint (8.6). Price: $4[?] CyberAuction #487, Lot #7.

3834. OTHER HANDMADE. Banded Opaque. Base is very lightly tinte[d] blue. Two very narrow bands of blue and red. One tiny chip on a band an[d] some pinpricking. Germany, circa 1870-1915. 11/16". Near Mint(+) (8.[?] Price: $42. CyberAuction #388, Lot #44.

3835. OTHER HANDMADE. Banded Opaque. Semi-opaque white base. Two bands of pink covering about forty percent of the marble. One p[?] couple of small subsurface moons. Germany, circa 1870-1915. 21/32". Ne[ar] Mint (8.5). Price: $37. CyberAuction #382, Lot #58.

3836. OTHER HANDMADE. Banded Opaque. Semi-opaque white bas[e] with pink bands. Buffed. Germany, circa 1870-1915. 9/16". Price: $3[?] CyberAuction #469, Lot #10.

3837. OTHER HANDMADE. Banded Opaque. Semi-opaque white base with pink bands. One large flake, that I think might be from manufacturin[g] (melted edges). Some light wear on the surface. Germany, circa 1870-191[5] 13/16". Good(+) (7.9). Price: $36. CyberAuction #371, Lot #28.

3838. OTHER HANDMADE. Banded Opaque. Semi-opaque white bas[e] almost completely covered by transparent pink bands. One subsurface moo[n] and one large flake. Germany, circa 1870-1915. 27/32". Near Mint(-) (8.[?] Price: $35. CyberAuction #338, Lot #12.

3839. OTHER HANDMADE. Banded Opaque. Semi-opaque white bas[e] with a yellow strand on it and a partial, very thin black line. Odd. Two sma[ll] chips and some pitting. 23/32". Near Mint (8.3). Price: $35. CyberAuctio[n] #371, Lot #18.

3840. OTHER HANDMADE. Banded Opaque. Semi-opaque white bas[e] with a yellow strand on it and a partial, very thin black line. Odd. Two sma[ll] chips and some pitting. 23/32". Near Mint (8.3). Price: $34. CyberAuctio[n] #422, Lot #18.

3841. OTHER HANDMADE. Banded Opaque. Corkscrew type. One ha[lf] is semi-opaque white. Other half is transparent light green. Twisted like [a] corkscrew. Pitting overall on the white (the glass is softer). Several pits o[n] the green. Germany, possibly American, circa 1870-1915. 5/8". Good (7.[?] Price: $32. CyberAuction #421, Lot #22.

3842. OTHER HANDMADE. Banded Opaque. Opalescent semi-opaqu[e] white base. Two pink bands covering about forty percent of the marbl[e] Three small chips on one side. Germany, circa 1870-1915. 21/32". Good[+] (7.9). Price: $27. CyberAuction #397, Lot #38.

3843. OTHER HANDMADE. Banded Opaque. Semi-opaque white bas[e] Two bands of stretched blue and red covering about forty percent of th[e] surface. Pitting and very tiny chips. Germany, circa 1870-1915. 21/3[2] Good(+) (7.9). Price: $25. CyberAuction #483, Lot #9.

3844. OTHER HANDMADE. Banded Opaque. Semi-opaque white bas[e] Surface covered by transparent pink bands. Several small flakes and chip[s] Germany, circa 1870-1915. 11/16". Good(+) (7.9). Price: $23. CyberAuctio[n] #402, Lot #54.

3845. OTHER HANDMADE. Banded Opaque. Unusual marble. Sem[i]-opaque white base. Subsurface pink band. Some dirt spots and a few tin[y] and small chips on the surface. Germany, circa 1870-1915. 23/32". Goo[d] (7.5). Price: $22. CyberAuction #401, Lot #15.

3846. OTHER HANDMADE. Banded Opaque. Semi-opaque white bas[e] Surface covered by transparent pink bands. Several small flakes and chip[s] Germany, circa 1870-1915. 11/16". Good(+) (7.9). Price: $21. CyberAuctio[n] #401, Lot #58.

3847. OTHER HANDMADE. Banded Opaque. It's either a clambroth o[r] banded opaque. Semi-opaque white base. Two pink strands and one blac[k] strand on it. A piece has flaked off, still in the package. 5/8". Good (7.[?] Price: $17. CyberAuction #364, Lot #30.

3848. OTHER HANDMADE. Banded Opaque. Opaque white base. Tw[o] bands of stretched color covering about half the marble. Lots of tiny chi[ps] and pits. Germany, circa 1870-1915. 11/16". Good (-) (7.2). Price: $1[?] CyberAuction #399, Lot #18.

3849. OTHER HANDMADE. Banded Opaque. Blue base. Some whi[te]

146

ands and a red splotch. Overall chips and subsurface moons. Germany, ca 1870-1915. 5/8". Good(-) (7.0). Price: $14. CyberAuction #447, Lot 8.

3850. OTHER HANDMADE. Banded Opaque. It's either a clambroth or a banded opaque. Semi-opaque white base. Two pink strands and one black band on it. A piece has flaked off, still in the package. 5/8". Good (7.5). Price: $10. CyberAuction #451, Lot #21.

3851. OTHER HANDMADE. Cane piece. Cane piece for a black clambroth with white strands. Wow!!! Germany, circa 1870-1915. About 2" long. Near Mint(+) (8.7). Price: $120. CyberAuction #339, Lot #49.

3852. OTHER HANDMADE. Cane piece. Section of cane for a naked mellow latticinio core swirl. Very nice. 2-1/4" wide, 21/32" diameter. Mint (9). Price: $39. CyberAuction #363, Lot #6.

3853. OTHER HANDMADE. Cane piece. Cane piece for a black clambroth with white strands. Wow!!! Germany, circa 1870-1915. About 1-1/4"" long. Near Mint(+) (8.7). Price: $20. CyberAuction #364, Lot #39.

3854. OTHER HANDMADE. Cane piece. Segment of a millefiori cane. Probably for a paperweight or button, not a marble. About 2-1/2" long. Price: $20. CyberAuction #366, Lot #6.

3855. OTHER HANDMADE. Cane piece. Cane section for a handmade blue slag. Very hard to find. About 2" long. Mint. Price: $15. CyberAuction #408, Lot #13.

3856. OTHER HANDMADE. Cane piece. Section of a cane that was meant to be used as the stem of a goblet. Slightly blue tinted glass. Four white strands in the center. Subsurface cage of white strands. Note the precision of the spacing and twist in the cane, this is much more precise than you see in marble canes. Great care went into making this piece. Germany, circa 1830-1920. 15/32" x 3-3/4". Mint (9.5). Price: $12. CyberAuction #405, Lot #59.

3857. OTHER HANDMADE. Cane piece. Cane section for and Indian. About 2" long. Price: $10. CyberAuction #411, Lot #58.

3858. OTHER HANDMADE. Cane piece. Segment of a millefiori cane. Probably for a paperweight or button, not a marble. About 2-1/2" long. Price: $8. CyberAuction #368, Lot #21.

3859. OTHER HANDMADE. Cased clambroth. A type of cased clambroth. Technically it's a type of banded swirl. Transparent clear core. Opaque white layer on top of that core. Closely packed orange strands on top of the white. Then a clear outer layer. Very hard to find. Several small flakes and tiny subsurface moon. Germany, circa 1870-1915. 11/16". Near Mint (4). Price: $80. CyberAuction #375, Lot #44.

3860. OTHER HANDMADE. Clambroth. Stunning shooter. Opaque white base. Seventeen blue stripes. Pristine surface. Absolutely spectacular example, in as close to perfect shape as you can get. Germany, circa 1870-1915. 13/16". Mint (9.9). Price: $650. CyberAuction #356, Lot #59.

3861. OTHER HANDMADE. Clambroth. From near an end of the cane. Opaque white base. Six green strands and six purple strands. One panel of surface clear. No damage, some cold roll lines. Hard to find. Germany, circa 1870-1915. 25/32". Mint (9.6). Price: $300. CyberAuction #333, Lot #56.

3862. OTHER HANDMADE. Clambroth. Opaque white base. Twelve blue bands on it. One tiny additional bit of blue. In super shape. Germany, circa 1870-1915. 3/4". Mint (9.7). Price: $275. CyberAuction #479, Lot #56.

3863. OTHER HANDMADE. Clambroth. Opaque black base with seventeen complete white strands and one partial white strand. One very tiny pinprick. Superb marble. Germany, circa 1870-1915. 23/32". Mint(-) (9.2). Price: $240. CyberAuction #500, Lot #45.

3864. OTHER HANDMADE. Clambroth. Semi-opaque white base. Six black bands alternating with six pink bands. Equidistantly spaced. Very wellmade marble. One barely visible subsurface moon, two very tiny pits. Germany, circa 1870-1915. 11/16". Near Mint(+) (8.8). Price: $220. CyberAuction #330, Lot #56.

3865. OTHER HANDMADE. Clambroth. Beauty. Semi-opaque white base. Eight pink bands, four blue bands, four green bands. One small flake, a couple of pits. Very nice marble. Germany, circa 1870-1915. 23/32". Near Mint(+) (8.7). Price: $195. CyberAuction #336, Lot #59.

3866. OTHER HANDMADE. Clambroth. Very nice clambroth. Opaque black base. Seventeen white strands on the surface. Some tiny pits and flakes. Very nice marble. Germany, circa 1870-1915. 11/16". Near Mint(+) (7). Price: $170. CyberAuction #336, Lot #20.

3867. OTHER HANDMADE. Clambroth. Nice shooter. Opaque white base. Five blue strands and six green strands. Surface shows some wear and a few sparkles. Still a beauty. Germany, circa 1870-1915. 13/16". Near Mint(+) (7). Price: $150. CyberAuction #388, Lot #23.

3868. OTHER HANDMADE. Clambroth. Semi-opaque white base. Five pink bands and six green bands. One small melt spot, small fracture. Beauty. Germany, circa 1870-1915. 11/16". Near Mint (8.6). Price: $120. CyberAuction #418, Lot #57.

3869. OTHER HANDMADE. Clambroth. Semi-opaque white base. Surface layer is four green bands, four blue bands and seven pink bands. Two tiny chips, some pits. Germany, circa 1870-1915. 19/32". Near Mint(-) (8.2). Price: $111. CyberAuction #414, Lot #52.

3870. OTHER HANDMADE. Clambroth. Black based shooter clambroth. Seventeen white bands. Overall small chips. Germany, circa 1870-1915. 7/8". Good (7.4). Price: $103. CyberAuction #397, Lot #23.

3871. OTHER HANDMADE. Clambroth. Black based shooter clambroth. Seventeen white bands. Overall small chips. Germany, circa 1870-1915. 7/8". Good (7.4). Price: $90. CyberAuction #460, Lot #58.

3872. OTHER HANDMADE. Clambroth. Black based shooter clambroth. Seventeen white bands. Overall small chips. Germany, circa 1870-1915. 7/8". Good (7.4). Price: $80. CyberAuction #422, Lot #10.

3873. OTHER HANDMADE. Clambroth. Semi-opaque white base. Thir-teen baby blue bands. Odd color. Several tiny flakes. Germany, circa 1870-1915. 11/16". Near Mint(+) (8.7). Price: $70. CyberAuction #495, Lot #49.

3874. OTHER HANDMADE. Clambroth. Semi-opaque white base. Twelve pink bands. Two tiny flakes. Germany, circa 1870-1915. 21/32". Near Mint(+) (8.7). Price: $55. CyberAuction #491, Lot #42.

3875. OTHER HANDMADE. Clambroth. Black base clambroth with seventeen white strands. Some pitting and tiny and small chips. Germany, circa 1870-1915. 11/16". Good (7.6). Price: $50. CyberAuction #445, Lot #57.

3876. OTHER HANDMADE. Clambroth. Semi-opaque white base. Surface layer is pink bands. A chip, some subsurface moons. Germany, circa 1870-1915. 21/32". Good(+) (7.7). Price: $42. CyberAuction #446, Lot #5.

3877. OTHER HANDMADE. Clambroth. Large clambroth. Blue strands on white. Several large chips and overall other chipping. Germany, circa 1870-1915. 1-3/16". Collectible. Price: $42. CyberAuction #447, Lot #22.

3878. OTHER HANDMADE. Clambroth. Semi-opaque white base with pink strands. Overall chipping. Germany, circa 1870-1915. 9/16". Good (7.5). Price: $40. CyberAuction #337, Lot #56.

3879. OTHER HANDMADE. Clambroth. White base with an outer layer of green bands. Small chips, tiny chips, small subsurface moons. Germany, circa 1870-1915. 29/32". Good(-) (7.1). Consignor note: D2. Price: $40. CyberAuction #343, Lot #57.

3880. OTHER HANDMADE. Clambroth. Black base clambroth with seventeen white strands. Some pitting and tiny and small chips. Germany, circa 1870-1915. 11/16". Good (7.6). Price: $40. CyberAuction #365, Lot #58.

3881. OTHER HANDMADE. Clambroth. Opaque white base. Outer strands of pink, blue and green. Subsurface moon, a few tiny flakes and some flaking of the green. Germany, circa 1870-1915. 21/32". Good (7.6). Price: $39. CyberAuction #370, Lot #56.

3882. OTHER HANDMADE. Clambroth. Large clambroth. Blue strands on white. Several large chips and overall other chipping. Germany, circa 1870-1915. 1-3/16". Collectible. Price: $37. CyberAuction #375, Lot #15.

3883. OTHER HANDMADE. Clambroth. White base with blue bands and two green bands. Small chip, some haze. Germany, circa 1870-1915. 21/32". Good(+) (7.7). Price: $35. CyberAuction #382, Lot #56.

3884. OTHER HANDMADE. Clambroth. Hard to find shooter. Opaque white base. Blue stripes. Chip, overall hitting. Germany, circa 1870-1915. 15/16". Good (7.5). Price: $30. CyberAuction #469, Lot #5.

3885. OTHER HANDMADE. Clambroth. Rare marble. Blue base clambroth. Opaque blue base. White strands. Overall chips. Still, very difficult to find. Germany, circa 1870-1915. 11/16". Good (7.5). Price: $30. CyberAuction #469, Lot #7.

3886. OTHER HANDMADE. Clambroth. Rare marble. Blue base clambroth. Opaque blue base. White strands. Overall chips. Still, very difficult to find. Germany, circa 1870-1915. 11/16". Good (7.5). Price: $30. CyberAuction #496, Lot #18.

3887. OTHER HANDMADE. Clambroth. Semi-opaque white base. Pink bands. Overall chipping and pitting. Germany, circa 1870-1915. 3/4". Good(+) (7.9). Price: $21. CyberAuction #493, Lot #35.

3888. OTHER HANDMADE. Clambroth. Opaque white base. Fourteen blue strands. Shooter. Some chips, including a large one at the top. Rust stains. Germany, circa 1870-1915. 13/16". Good(-) (7.1). Price: $15. CyberAuction #492, Lot #14.

3889. OTHER HANDMADE. Clambroth. Opaque white base. Alternating bands of blue, green and pink. Heavily damaged. Germany, circa 1870-1915. 21/32". Good(-) (7.0). Price: $4. CyberAuction #468, Lot #5.

3890. OTHER HANDMADE. Clearie. Rare marble. Handmade corkscrew. Transparent aqua blue base with a translucent white band covering about one-fifth of the marble. Nice spiral from the twisting motion of making it. Two-pontil. Two subsurface moons on one side, some pitting. Germany, possibly American, circa 1880-1920. 11/16". Good(+) (7.9). Price: $55. CyberAuction #375, Lot #16.

3891. OTHER HANDMADE. Clearie. Large transparent clear shooter. Two pontil. Very nice. Germany, circa 1870-1915. 1-1/16". Mint (9.9). There are two marbles available. You are bidding on one. Winner has choice of either or both, remainder to under. Price: $42. CyberAuction #381, Lot #45.

3892. OTHER HANDMADE. Clearie. Large transparent clear shooter. Two pontil. Very nice. Germany, circa 1870-1915. 1-1/16". Mint (9.9). There are two marbles available. You are bidding on one. Winner has choice of either or both, remainder to under. Price: $42. CyberAuction #440, Lot #52.

3893. OTHER HANDMADE. Clearie. Very odd clear. Single pontil. Aqua base with loads of unmelted sand. Nub pontil. One subsurface moon. Rare. Germany, circa 1870-1915. 27/32". Near Mint(+) (8.8). Price: $29. CyberAuction #394, Lot #5.

3894. OTHER HANDMADE. Clearie. Two-pontil handmade clearie. Olive green. Beautiful. Two melt spots. Germany, circa 1870-1915. 23/32". Mint(-) (9.1). Price: $28. CyberAuction #348, Lot #5.

3895. OTHER HANDMADE. Clearie. Two-pontil transparent very pale amethyst clearie. A couple of pits. Germany, circa 18970-1915. 5/8". Mint(-) (9.0). There are two marbles available. You are bidding on one. Winner has choice of either or both, remainder to under. Price: $27. CyberAuction #377, Lot #7.

3896. OTHER HANDMADE. Clearie. Transparent clear two-pontil handmade marble. A couple of tiny sparkles, subsurface moon and tiny chips. Germany, circa 1870-1915. 1-1/16". Near Mint (8.5). Price: $20. CyberAuction #390, Lot #35.

3897. OTHER HANDMADE. Clearie. Transparent clear two-pontil hand-made marble. A couple of tiny sparkles, subsurface moon and tiny chips. Germany, circa 1870-1915. 1-1/16". Near Mint (8.5). Price: $20. CyberAuction #440, Lot #11.

3898. OTHER HANDMADE. Clearie. Transparent clear two-pontil hand-made marble. A couple of tiny sparkles, subsurface moon and tiny chips. Germany, circa 1870-1915. 1-1/16". Near Mint (8.5). Price: $20. CyberAuction #484, Lot #42.

3899. OTHER HANDMADE. Clearie. Two pontil handmade clearie. Trans-parent clear. Germany, circa 1870-1915. 5/8". Mint (9.7). Price: $17. CyberAuction #392, Lot #23.

3900. OTHER HANDMADE. Clearie. Large transparent clear clearie. Ground pontil. Some small air bubbles inside. Overall tiny subsurface moons. Origin and age unknown. 1-3/4". Good (7.4). Price: $17. CyberAuction #394, Lot #23.

3901. OTHER HANDMADE. Clearie. Transparent dark green clearie with a filament core. Nice. Germany, circa 1870-1915. 23/32". Mint (9.9). Price: $17. CyberAuction #406, Lot #46.

3902. OTHER HANDMADE. Clearie. Transparent dark green clearie with a filament core. Two-pontil. Nice. Germany, circa 1870-1915. 23/32". Mint (9.9). Price: $17. CyberAuction #486, Lot #33.

3903. OTHER HANDMADE. Clearie. Transparent dark green clearie with a filament core. Two-pontil. Nice. Germany, circa 1870-1915. 23/32". Mint (9.9). Price: $12. CyberAuction #437, Lot #58.

3904. OTHER HANDMADE. Clearie. Transparent clear two-pontil hand-made marble. Germany, possibly American, circa 1870-1915. 15/32". Mint (9.9). Price: $11. CyberAuction #436, Lot #41.

3905. OTHER HANDMADE. Clearie. Transparent pale blue marble. Streams of tiny air bubbles in the marble. Germany, circa 1870-1915. 15/32". Mint (9.5). Price: $10. CyberAuction #366, Lot #20.

3906. OTHER HANDMADE. Clearie. Transparent clearie. Ghost core. Lots of tiny air bubble. Looked like a mica at first glance. Very nice. Germany, circa 1870-1915. 17/32". Mint (9.5). Price: $9. CyberAuction #426, Lot #42.

3907. OTHER HANDMADE. Clearie. Two-pontil handmade transparent clear clearie. Germany, circa 1870-1915. 15/32". Mint (9.7). Price: $9. CyberAuction #429, Lot #44.

3908. OTHER HANDMADE. Clearie. Transparent clearie. Ghost core. Lots of tiny air bubble. Looked like a mica at first glance. Very nice. Germany, circa 1870-1915. 17/32". Mint (9.5). Price: $8. CyberAuction #366, Lot #5.

3909. OTHER HANDMADE. Clearie. Transparent clearie. Ghost core. Lots of tiny air bubble. Looked like a mica at first glance. Very nice. Germany, circa 1870-1915. 17/32". Mint (9.5). Price: $8. CyberAuction #408, Lot #8.

3910. OTHER HANDMADE. Clearie. Clearie. One pontil, broken off the rod. Overall pitting and scratching. American, circa 1880-1930. 3/4". Near Mint(-) (8.0). Price: $8. CyberAuction #440, Lot #27.

3911. OTHER HANDMADE. Clearie. Pale blue. Ghost core surrounding a filament core. Some haziness. Germany, circa 1870-1915. 25/32". Near Mint(-) (8.1). Price: $6. CyberAuction #370, Lot #14.

3912. OTHER HANDMADE. Clearie. Handmade two-pontil clearie. Trans-parent blue. Cold roll line on it and two tiny rough spots. German or Ameri-can, circa 1880-1920. 19/32". Near Mint(+) (8.7). Price: $6. CyberAuction #399, Lot #43.

3913. OTHER HANDMADE. Clearie. Two-pontil handmade green clear. Some tiny subsurface moons. Germany, circa 1870-1915. 13/16". Near Mint (8.3). Price: $6. CyberAuction #488, Lot #44.

3914. OTHER HANDMADE. Clearie. Single pontil transparent clear marble. Some tiny subsurface moons. Germany, circa 1870-1915. 1/2". Near Mint (8.6). Price: $4. CyberAuction #419, Lot #12.

3915. OTHER HANDMADE. Clearie. Two-pontil handmade green clear. Some tiny subsurface moons. Germany, circa 1870-1915. 13/16". Near Mint (8.3). Price: $4. CyberAuction #439, Lot #46.

3916. OTHER HANDMADE. Clearie. Transparent clear marble. Some air bubbles inside. Ground pontil bottom, no mold lines. Some pinpricks. Ori-gin and age unknown. 7/8". Near Mint(+) (8.9). There are three marbles available. You are bidding on one. Winner has choice of any or all, remain-der to under. Price: $2. CyberAuction #387, Lot #12.

3917. OTHER HANDMADE. Clearie. Two-pontil handmade clear. Some chips. Origin and age unknown. 1-9/16". Good(+) (7.9). Price: $2. CyberAuction #415, Lot #29.

3918. OTHER HANDMADE. Clearie. Transparent clear marble. Some air bubbles inside. Ground pontil bottom, no mold lines. Some pinpricks. Ori-gin and age unknown. 7/8". Near Mint(+) (8.9). There are three marbles available. You are bidding on one. Winner has choice of any or all, remain-der to under. Price: $2. CyberAuction #445, Lot #22.

3919. OTHER HANDMADE. Clearie. Two-pontil handmade clear. Some chips. Origin and age unknown. 1-9/16". Good(+) (7.9). Price: $2. CyberAuction #486, Lot #24.

3920. OTHER HANDMADE. Indian. Another of the maglite three hun-dred sixty degree Indians (there were several in the collection). Core is transparent dark blue. Surface completely covered by stretched bands of pink, white and blue, with some yellow and green. Beautiful and hard to find. Germany, circa 1870-1915. 23/32". Mint (9.7). Price: $435. CyberAuction #503, Lot #22.

3921. OTHER HANDMADE. Indian. Another of the three hundred sixty degree Indians from the English collection. This one is stunning and the only one of the half dozen in this color. Transparent dark blue maglite base. Surface is completely covered of a mixture of pink and yellow. Exceptional marble. Pristine surface. Germany, circa 1870-1915. 11/16". Mint (9.9). Price: $400. CyberAuction #503, Lot #64.

3922. OTHER HANDMADE. Indian. Three hundred sixty degree magl[ite] Indian. Rare. Transparent blue base. Cover is completely covered by a ve[ry] thick layer of stretched opaque white, transparent pink and transpare[nt] green bands. Stunning. A couple of tiny flakes of color missing. Germa[n] circa 1870-1915. 11/16". Mint (9.5). Price: $340. CyberAuction #502, L[ot] #75.

3923. OTHER HANDMADE. Indian. Another of the maglite three hu[n]-dred sixty degree Indians (there were several in the collection). Core [is] transparent dark blue. Four panel surface. Two panels of stretched pink a[nd] white, two of stretched blue and white. Beautiful and hard to find. Ge[r]-many, circa 1870-1915. 11/16". Mint (9.7). Price: $310. CyberAuction #50[3], Lot #1.

3924. OTHER HANDMADE. Indian. Another of the maglite three hu[n]-dred sixty degree Indians (this is the last one in the collection). Core [is] transparent dark blue. Four panel surface. Two panels of stretched gree[n] and white, two of stretched blue and white. Beautiful and hard to fi[nd] Germany, circa 1870-1915. 11/16". Mint (9.7). Price: $310. CyberAucti[on] #507, Lot #59.

3925. OTHER HANDMADE. Indian. Another of the maglite three hu[n]-dred sixty degree Indians (there were several in the collection). Core [is] transparent dark blue. Four-panel. Overall white. Two blue and two pi[nk] panels. Beautiful and hard to find. Germany, circa 1870-1915. 11/16". M[int] (9.8). Price: $300. CyberAuction #505, Lot #73.

3926. OTHER HANDMADE. Indian. Another of the maglite three hu[n]-dred sixty degree Indians (there were several in the collection). Core [is] transparent dark blue. Four panel surface. Two panels of stretched pink a[nd] white, two of stretched blue and white. Beautiful and hard to find. Tw[o] melt spots. Germany, circa 1870-1915. 11/16". Mint (9.5). Price: $28[?] CyberAuction #507, Lot #48.

3927. OTHER HANDMADE. Indian. Rare shooter maglite Indian. Ve[ry] dark transparent green base. Two bands covering about sixty percent of t[he] surface. One is light blue and white, other is pink and mustard. In gre[at] shape. Very rare. Germany, circa 1870-1915. 13/16". Mint (9.7). Pric[e] $270. CyberAuction #486, Lot #32.

3928. OTHER HANDMADE. Indian. Another of the maglite three hu[n]-dred sixty degree Indians (there were several in the collection). Core [is] transparent dark blue. Surface is stretched opaque white and transpare[nt] pink. Beautiful and hard to find. Germany, circa 1870-1915. 11/16". M[int] (9.9). Price: $260. CyberAuction #504, Lot #68.

3929. OTHER HANDMADE. Indian. Rare shooter maglite Indian. Ve[ry] dark transparent green base. Two bands covering about sixty percent of t[he] surface. One is light blue and white, other is pink and mustard. In gre[at] shape. Very rare. Germany, circa 1870-1915. 13/16". Mint (9.7). Pric[e] $255. CyberAuction #450, Lot #47.

3930. OTHER HANDMADE. Indian. Stunning maglite three hundred s[ixty] degree Indian. Transparent dark blue. Surface is almost completely cover[ed] by bands of pink, yellow and white. In great shape. Superb!!!! Germa[n] circa 1870-1915. 9/16". Mint (9.9). Price: $240. CyberAuction #366, L[ot] #50.

3931. OTHER HANDMADE. Indian. Another of the maglite three hu[n]-dred sixty degree Indians (there were several in the collection). Core [is] transparent dark blue. Six panel surface. Three panels of stretched gre[en] and white, three of stretched pink and white. Beautiful and hard to fi[nd] One dirt spot, one manufacturing flat spot. Germany, circa 1870-1915. 1[1/] 16". Mint(-) (9.0). Price: $210. CyberAuction #504, Lot #52.

3932. OTHER HANDMADE. Indian. Large Indian. Opaque black bas[e] Two bands covering about half the marble. Each is opaque blue wide[ly] edged by opaque white. One small flake, some pits. Very hard to find the[m] this large. Germany, circa 1870-1915. 29/32". Near Mint (8.5). Price: $2[00] CyberAuction #339, Lot #51.

3933. OTHER HANDMADE. Indian. Stunning three-hundred-sixty deg[ree] Indian. Opaque black base. Surface completely covered by white, blu[e] red, yellow and green bands. One tiny subsurface moon. Bright colo[rs] Beauty. Germany, circa 1870-1915. 11/16". Near Mint(+) (8.9). Price: $18[?] CyberAuction #448, Lot #38.

3934. OTHER HANDMADE. Indian. Very dark almost opaque ameth[yst] base. Two bands covering about sixty percent of the surface. One is m[us]-tard and pink. Other is mustard, green and blue. One small flake, a ti[ny] moon and a small manufacturing chip spot. Shooter though, very har[d to] find. 29/32". Near Mint (8.6). Price: $160. CyberAuction #366, Lot #5[?]

3935. OTHER HANDMADE. Indian. Maglite Indian. Transparent bl[ue] base. Two bands covering about seventy percent of the surface. Each [is] stretched white with yellow and pink. Not quite wet, but no dama[ge] Germany, circa 1870-1915. 3/4". Mint(-) (9.0). Price: $160. CyberAucti[on] #372, Lot #46.

3936. OTHER HANDMADE. Indian. You have to decide if you want to c[all] it a transparent Indian, or a banded swirl. Either way it is a superb mar[ble] Transparent very dark transparent aqua base. Four sets of banding on t[he] surface. Each is strands of green and white. Surface in great shape. Stu[n]-ning. Germany, circa 1870-1915. 29/32". Mint (9.8). Price: $15[?] CyberAuction #342, Lot #7.

3937. OTHER HANDMADE. Indian. Superb shooter transparent India[n] Transparent blue base. Two bands covering ninety percent of the surfac[e] Each is stretched flecks of white and yellow. Small subsurface moon right [at] the top. Superb. Germany, circa 1870-1915. 15/16". Near Mint(+) (8.[?]) Price: $150. CyberAuction #355, Lot #60.

3938. OTHER HANDMADE. Indian. Very nice shooter. Opaque black bas[e] Two bands covering about twenty percent of the surface. Both are subsur-face white strands, covered by transparent blue, edged by white. Surfa[ce] has some light pitting and rubbing. Germany, circa 1870-1915. 15/1[6"] Near Mint (8.6). Price: $140. CyberAuction #338, Lot #57.

39. OTHER HANDMADE. Indian. Another of the maglite three hundred sixty degree Indians (there were several in the collection). Core is ...nsparent dark blue. Surface completely covered by stretched bands of ...k and yellow. Beautiful and hard to find. One melt spot, one tiny spot ...he color flaked off down to the blue. Germany, circa 1870-1915. .../32". Mint(-) (9.1). Price: $130. CyberAuction #505, Lot #50.

40. OTHER HANDMADE. Indian. Rare maglite Indian. Translucent very ...rk green base. Some sort of core in it. Surface has two bands covering ...out forty percent. One is stretched yellow with some pink, other is ...etched white and light blue. One tiny subsurface moon. Nice shooter. ...ermany, circa 1870-1915. 27/32". Near Mint(+) (8.9). Price: $110. ...berAuction #369, Lot #54.

41. OTHER HANDMADE. Indian. Gorgeous example. Transparent dark ...ne base. Two bands covering about fifty percent of the marble. One ...nk is yellow, other is light blue. Beauty. Germany, circa 1870-1915. 21/ ...". Mint (9.6). Price: $110. CyberAuction #420, Lot #8.

42. OTHER HANDMADE. Indian. Four-panel three-sixty degree Indian. ...paque black base. Surface is almost completely covered by color. Two ...de panels are dark pink on mustard, one narrow panel is light blue, other ...rrow panel is light green, with some black showing through. Mint(-) ... Gorgeous. Germany, circa 1870-1915. 19/32". Mint(-) (9.0). Price: $110. ...berAuction #420, Lot #50.

43. OTHER HANDMADE. Indian. Very dark transparent purple base. ...ands covering about eighty percent of the surface. Pink, yellow, blue and ...een. In great shape. Germany, circa 1870-1915. 23/32". Mint (9.7). Price: ...10. CyberAuction #498, Lot #2.

44. OTHER HANDMADE. Indian. Shooter. Transparent very dark green ...se. Two bands covering about seventy five percent of the surface. One is ...ht blue and white, other is dark pink and yellow. Some minor seed de...cts in the glass, but no damage. 13/16". Mint(-) (9.0). Price: $100. ...berAuction #418, Lot #45.

45. OTHER HANDMADE. Indian. Purple maglite Indian. Dark transpar...t purple base. Outer layer is two bands covering about seventy percent ...the surface. Both sets are yellow and white. Germany, circa 1870-1915. ...32". Mint (9.7). Price: $100. CyberAuction #452, Lot #34.

46. OTHER HANDMADE. Indian. Rare. Opaque black base. Four bands ... white and gray. Very nice marble. In great shape. Germany, circa 1870-...15. 11/16". Mint (9.9). Price: $100. CyberAuction #467, Lot #46.

47. OTHER HANDMADE. Indian. Very unusual construction. Opaque ...ack base. Two panels covering about thirty percent of the surface. Each ...nel is two bands, next to each other. One panel has a band of green ...ged by white and a band of transparent pink on white strands, edged by ...llow. Other panel has a band of blue edged by white and a band of ...nsparent blue on white strands edged by white. In great shape. Super ...arble. Germany, circa 1870-1915. 11/16". Mint (9.9). Price: $95. ...berAuction #330, Lot #54.

48. OTHER HANDMADE. Indian. Transparent Indian. Transparent dark ...een base. Two bands covering about fifty percent of the surface. Both are ...qua, white and yellow. One melt spot, one blown air hole. Superb. Ger...any, circa 1870-1915. 11/16". Mint(-) (9.0). Price: $95. CyberAuction ...350, Lot #22.

49. OTHER HANDMADE. Indian. Very rare Indian. Opaque black base. ...even, evenly spaced, outer bands. Each is green, edged by red on one ...de, orange on the other. Super design. Very rare. One tiny subsurface ...oon, a couple of tiny flakes, some overall pinpricks. Consigned from ...ermany. Germany, circa 1870-1915. 11/16". Good(+) (7.9). Price: $93. ...yberAuction #349, Lot #60.

50. OTHER HANDMADE. Indian. Transparent dark maglite amethyst ...se. Two bands covering less than twenty percent of the surface. One is ...etched blue and white, other is yellow and white. One tiny chip. Ger...any, circa 1870-1915. 3/4". Near Mint(+) (8.9). Price: $90. CyberAuction ...345, Lot #21.

51. OTHER HANDMADE. Indian. Maglite Indian. Transparent amethyst ...se. Two bands of wispy yellow and white covering about forty percent of ...e surface. In great shape, with just one extremely tiny pinprick. Germany, ...rca 1870-1915. 15/32". Mint (9.4). Price: $90. CyberAuction #357, Lot ...51.

52. OTHER HANDMADE. Indian. Very dark transparent purple maglite ...se. Almost completely covered by stretched opaque white bands. Ger...any, circa 1870-1915. 11/16". Mint (9.5). Price: $90. CyberAuction #498, ...t #22.

53. OTHER HANDMADE. Indian. Opaque black base. Four bands of ...hite and olive green. Rare type. Germany, circa 1870-1915. One tiny ...ough spot. Germany, circa 1870-1915. 21/32". Mint(-) (9.0). Price: $89. ...yberAuction #356, Lot #12.

54. OTHER HANDMADE. Indian. Very dark almost opaque amethyst ...se. Two bands covering about sixty percent of the surface. One is mus...rd and pink. Other is mustard, green and blue. One small flake, a small ...oon and a small manufacturing chip spot. Shooter though, very hard to ...nd. 29/32". Near Mint (8.6). Price: $85. CyberAuction #336, Lot #49.

55. OTHER HANDMADE. Indian. Opaque black base. Two bands cov...ing over eighty percent of the surface. Both are mustard yellow, with ...me red. In great shape. Germany, circa 1870-1915. 9/16". Mint (9.7). ...rice: $80. CyberAuction #336, Lot #22.

56. OTHER HANDMADE. Indian. Opaque black base. Two bands cov...ring about twenty five percent of the marble. One is mustard yellow, other ...white. Both are stretched. Germany, circa 1870-1915. 21/32". Mint (9.9). ...20. CyberAuction #363, Lot #18.

57. OTHER HANDMADE. Indian. Transparent light purple base. Two ...ands covering about seventy five percent of the surface. Both are stretched ...ue, pink, white and yellow. Some color under the surface too. Some

scratches on one side. Germany, circa 1870-1915. 9/16". Mint(-) (9.1). Price: $75. CyberAuction #368, Lot #60.

3958. OTHER HANDMADE. Indian. Hard to find maglite Indian. Transparent very dark purple base. Two bands covering about seventy percent of the surface. One is blue and white, other is some blue and white and lights of air bubbles. Germany, circa 1870-1915. 9/16". Mint (9.7). Price: $75. CyberAuction #452, Lot #3.

3959. OTHER HANDMADE. Indian. Transparent dark blue base. Two bands covering over half the marble. Stretched white, blue, yellow, orange. Germany, circa 1870-1915. Air hole and very tiny flake. 25/32". Near Mint(+) (8.9). Price: $75. CyberAuction #500, Lot #13.

3960. OTHER HANDMADE. Indian. Opaque black base. Two bands covering about forty percent of the surface. One is yellow and white, one is light blue and white. In very nice shape. Germany, circa 1870-1915. 11/16". Mint (9.5). Price: $70. CyberAuction #372, Lot #58.

3961. OTHER HANDMADE. Indian. Transparent Indian. Very odd coloring. Transparent smoky base. Two bands covering about thirty percent of the surface. Both are blue, edged by white. Some scratching and pitting. Hard to find. Germany, circa 1870-1915. 21/32". Near Mint (8.6). Price: $65. CyberAuction #337, Lot #5.

3962. OTHER HANDMADE. Indian. Opaque black base. Two bands covering about seventy percent of the surface. One band is white and pink, other is white and mustard. Pristine surface. Gorgeous. Germany, circa 1870-1915. 19/32". Mint (9.9). Price: $65. CyberAuction #339, Lot #6.

3963. OTHER HANDMADE. Indian. Very interesting. Transparent dark blue base. Two bands covering about eighty percent of the surface. Each is white, yellow and pink. Very light haziness. Germany, circa 1870-1915. 9/16". Near Mint (8.6). Price: $65. CyberAuction #366, Lot #30.

3964. OTHER HANDMADE. Indian. I've classified this as a transparent Indian, although some might call it a banded swirl. Transparent brown base. Wispy white band in the core. Surface has two bands covering about seventy five percent of the marble. Each is stretched light yellow. One small flake and a tiny subsurface moon. 25/32". Near Mint(+) (8.7). Originally sold as Lot #133 in Block's Box Absentee Marble Auction #34. Price: $65. CyberAuction #383, Lot #1.

3965. OTHER HANDMADE. Indian. Opaque black base. Two white bands on it. Germany, circa 1870-1915. 1/2". Mint (9.9). Price: $60. CyberAuction #465, Lot #54.

3966. OTHER HANDMADE. Indian. Transparent bubble-filled very light green glass. Ghost core. A band of stretched yellow and a band of stretched white covering about sixty percent of the surface. Germany, possibly American, circa 1870-1920. 11/16". Mint(9.7). Price: $55. CyberAuction #404, Lot #24.

3967. OTHER HANDMADE. Indian. Opaque black base. Two bands covering about thirty percent of the surface. One is red and white, one is blue with white. Not quite wet. Germany, circa 1870-1915. 21/32". Mint(-) (9.2). Price: $55. CyberAuction #439, Lot #30.

3968. OTHER HANDMADE. Indian. Super transparent Indian, or banded transparent. Transparent blue base. Two bands covering about ninety percent of the surface. Each is stretched pink, yellow and white. One small chip, one larger area that appears to be a blown air hole, but might be a chip. Germany, circa 1870-1915. 25/32". Near Mint(-) (8.2). Price: $55. CyberAuction #490, Lot #45.

3969. OTHER HANDMADE. Indian. Opaque black base. Two bands covering about thirty percent of the surface. Each is transparent blue over white strands, edged by white. Germany, circa 1870-1915. 11/16". Mint (9.6). Price: $55. CyberAuction #491, Lot #36.

3970. OTHER HANDMADE. Indian. Opaque black base. Two bands covering about twenty percent of the surface. Both are white and blue. One sparkle, one tiny subsurface moon. Super looking marble. Germany, circa 1870-1915. 3/4". Near Mint(+) (8.9). Price: $50. CyberAuction #333, Lot #52.

3971. OTHER HANDMADE. Indian. Transparent bubble-filled very light green glass. Ghost core. A band of stretched yellow and a band of stretched white covering about sixty percent of the surface. Germany, possibly American, circa 1870-1920. 11/16". Mint(9.7). Price: $50. CyberAuction #342, Lot #5.

3972. OTHER HANDMADE. Indian. I've been calling this type transparent Indian, because the construction is exactly the same as an opaque Indian. Transparent bubble-filled very light green glass. A band of stretched yellow and a band of stretched white covering about fifty percent of the surface. Germany, possibly American, circa 1870-1920. 19/32". Mint (9.8). Price: $50. CyberAuction #425, Lot #17.

3973. OTHER HANDMADE. Indian. Super transparent Indian, or banded transparent. Transparent blue base. Two bands covering about ninety percent of the surface. Each is stretched pink, yellow and white. One small chip, one larger area that appears to be a blown air hole, but might be a chip. Germany, circa 1870-1915. 25/32". Near Mint(-) (8.2). Price: $50. CyberAuction #464, Lot #17.

3974. OTHER HANDMADE. Indian. Opaque black base. Two bands covering about thirty percent of the surface. Each is blue band on white strands, edged by white. A number of tiny moons. Nice shooter. Germany, circa 1870-1915. 7/8". Near Mint(-) (8.2). Price: $50. CyberAuction #489, Lot #10.

3975. OTHER HANDMADE. Indian. Transparent Indian. Transparent light amethyst base. Two bands of pink, yellow and white covering about eighty percent of the surface. Germany, circa 1870-1915. 9/16". Mint (9.6). Price: $48. CyberAuction #348, Lot #5.

3976. OTHER HANDMADE. Indian. Opaque black base. Band on one side covers about a quarter of the marble. That one is pink and yellow. One wide pink strand on the other side. One tiny subsurface moon, one very tiny chip. Germany, circa 1870-1915. 27/32". Near Mint(+) (8.7). Price: $48. CyberAuction #365, Lot #50.

3977. OTHER HANDMADE. Indian. Opaque black base. Two bands covering about forty percent of the surface. One is yellow and aqua. Other is aqua and white. Several tiny chips. Germany, circa 1870-1915. 21/32". Near Mint(+) (8.7). Price: $47. CyberAuction #341, Lot #58.

3978. OTHER HANDMADE. Indian. Opaque black base. Two bands covering about thirty percent of the surface. One is white strands, covered by transparent dark blue, edged by white. Other is white strands, covered by transparent dark green, edged on one side by white. In very nice shape. Germany, circa 1870-1915. 21/32". Mint (9.6). Price: $45. CyberAuction #354, Lot #49.

3979. OTHER HANDMADE. Indian. Transparent Indian. Transparent light blue base. Two bands of yellow and white covering about half the surface. One cold roll line around the marble. Germany, circa 1870-1915. 5/8". Mint (9.5). Price: $45. CyberAuction #375, Lot #8.

3980. OTHER HANDMADE. Indian. Hard to find maglite Indian. Transparent very dark purple base. Two bands covering almost ninety percent of the surface. One is blue and white stretched, the other is blue and yellow stretched. One barely noticeable flake on the blue and white, still a beauty. Germany, circa 1870-1915. 11/16". Near Mint(+) (8.7). Price: $45. CyberAuction #391, Lot #59.

3981. OTHER HANDMADE. Indian. Very unusual Indian. Maglite amethyst base. Two bands on the surface covering about thirty percent. Each is stretched red, blue, green and white. There is also a partial core (about three-quarters) in the marble that consists of the same coloring. Very unusual. Some pitting. Germany, circa 1870-1915. 5/8". Near Mint (8.4). Consignor note: C1. Price: $44. CyberAuction #343, Lot #38.

3982. OTHER HANDMADE. Indian. Opaque black base. Two bands covering about half the marble. One is light blue and white. other is yellow and light blue. Germany, circa 1870-1915. 23/32". Mint (9.7). Price: $44. CyberAuction #447, Lot #15.

3983. OTHER HANDMADE. Indian. Maglite. Transparent dark amethyst base. Two bands covering about seventy five percent of the surface. One is stretched yellow and pink. Other is stretched yellow and green. The green is "sick" and flaking. Small damage flake and some sparkles. Germany, circa 1870-1915. 3/4". Near Mint(-) (8.0). Price: $43. CyberAuction #364, Lot #57.

3984. OTHER HANDMADE. Indian. I've been calling this type transparent Indian, because the construction is exactly the same as an opaque Indian. Transparent bubble-filled very light green glass. A band of stretched yellow and a band of stretched white covering about eighty percent of the surface. Small ghost core with a few colored strands on it, that you can view through the open panel. One tiny air hole. Germany, possibly American, circa 1870-1920. 19/32". Mint(-) (9.2). Price: $42. CyberAuction #356, Lot #3.

3985. OTHER HANDMADE. Indian. Transparent bubble filled very light green base. One band of stretched white, one of stretched yellow. Germany, circa 1870-1915. 19/32". Mint (9.5). Price: $42. CyberAuction #469, Lot #51.

3986. OTHER HANDMADE. Indian. Opaque black base. Two bands covering about half the marble. One is light blue and white. other is yellow and light blue. Germany, circa 1870-1915. 23/32". Mint (9.7). Price: $40. CyberAuction #368, Lot #50.

3987. OTHER HANDMADE. Indian. Transparent light blue base. Two bands covering about seventy five percent of the surface. Left twist. Both are stretched pink, white and yellow. Some light haze. Germany, circa 1870-1915. 9/16". Near Mint (8.6). Price: $40. CyberAuction #370, Lot #60.

3988. OTHER HANDMADE. Indian. Opaque black base. Two bands of stretched white covering about forty percent of the surface. Small subsurface moon near the top. Germany, circa 1870-1915. 11/16". Near Mint(+) (8.9). Price: $40. CyberAuction #386, Lot #39.

3989. OTHER HANDMADE. Indian. Opaque black base. Two bands covering about thirty percent of the surface. Each is pink and blue on white strands, edged by white. One pit on one band. Beauty. Germany, circa 1870-1915. 111/6". Near Mint(+) (8.8). Price: $40. CyberAuction #388, Lot #49.

3990. OTHER HANDMADE. Indian. Opaque black base. Two bands covering about sixty percent of the marble. One is yellow and pink, other is light blue and white. One small flake and a little haze. Germany, circa 1870-1915. 5/8". Near Mint(+) (8.7). Price: $39. CyberAuction #355, Lot #13.

3991. OTHER HANDMADE. Indian. Opaque black base. Two bands covering about forty percent of the surface. Both are blue on white. One very tiny flake. Germany, circa 1870-1915. 5/8". Near Mint(+) (8.9). Price: $38. CyberAuction #340, Lot #48.

3992. OTHER HANDMADE. Indian. Rare four-panel three-hundred sixty degree Indian. Opaque black base. Two panels of pink and mustard, two of light blue. Tiny flake, small manufacturing flake, some melt spots, some haziness. Germany, circa 1870-1915. 11/16". Near Mint(-) (8.0). Price: $38. CyberAuction #402, Lot #46.

3993. OTHER HANDMADE. Indian. Opaque black base. Two bands covering about twenty percent of the surface. One is wider. It is red on yellow, edged by yellow and white. Other is narrow. Some green and white. Small flake. Germany, circa 1870-1915. 11/16". Near Mint(+) (8.7). Price: $38. CyberAuction #410, Lot #54.

3994. OTHER HANDMADE. Indian. First off cane transparent Indian. Transparent dark aqua base. Splotches of yellow, blue and white. Slightly flattened. One tiny chip on the pontil (no top pontil), a little haze. Germany, circa 1870-1915. 21/32". Near Mint (8.5). Price: $37. CyberAuction #350, Lot #59.

3995. OTHER HANDMADE. Indian. Cane piece from an Indian. Super. 3/4" x 7/8". Mint(-) (9.0). Price: $37. CyberAuction #369, Lot #13.

3996. OTHER HANDMADE. Indian. Rare four-panel. Opaque black base. Three hundred sixty degrees. Two surface panels of light blue, two surfa panels of pink and yellow. Overall haze and a chip. Germany, circa 187 1915. 23/32". Good (7.5). Price: $37. CyberAuction #397, Lot #10.

3997. OTHER HANDMADE. Indian. Transparent light blue base. Two ban covering about seventy five percent of the surface. Left twist. Germany, circa 187 1915. 9/16". Near Mint (8.6). Price: $37. CyberAuction #444, Lot #52

3998. OTHER HANDMADE. Indian. Opaque black base. Two bands stretched white covering about forty percent of the surface. Beautiful. Sm subsurface moon near the top. Germany, circa 1870-1915. 11/16". Ne Mint(+) (8.9). Price: $35. CyberAuction #338, Lot #51.

3999. OTHER HANDMADE. Indian. Opaque black base. Two bands cove ing about ninety percent of the surface. One is light blue and white, pink and mustard yellow. A little haze and a couple of pits. Germany, cir 1870-1915. 9/16". Near Mint (8.6). Price: $35. CyberAuction #446, L #21.

4000. OTHER HANDMADE. Indian. Opaque black base. Two bands co ering about thirty percent of the surface. One is yellow and white, one blue, white and yellow. Some pits and very light haze. Germany, circa 187 1915. 11/16". Near Mint (8.5). Price: $34. CyberAuction #353, Lot #4

4001. OTHER HANDMADE. Indian. Opaque black base. Two bands co ering about half the surface. One is light blue and white. Other is pink an yellow. One melt spot. Germany, circa 1870-1915. 11/16". Mint(-)(9.2 Price: $34. CyberAuction #419, Lot #15.

4002. OTHER HANDMADE. Indian. Opaque black base. Two bands stretched bright white, covering about forty percent of the surface. O elongated air bubble. Germany, circa 1870-1915. 19/32". Mint(-) (9.0 Price: $34. CyberAuction #473, Lot #49.

4003. OTHER HANDMADE. Indian. Opaque black base. Surface is most completely covered by strands of red, yellow, blue, white and gree Small subsurface moon, couple of pinpricks, not wet. Germany, circa 187 1915. 11/16". Good(+) (7.9). Price: $32. CyberAuction #364, Lot #46

4004. OTHER HANDMADE. Indian. Transparent three hundred sixty I dian, or a three hundred sixty banded swirl? You decide. Transparent lig green base. Completely covered by white bands of various shades, and a fe yellow strands. One small subsurface moon. Germany, circa 1870-1915. 1 32". Near Mint(+) (8.7). Price: $32. CyberAuction #365, Lot #56.

4005. OTHER HANDMADE. Indian. Opaque black base. Two bands co ering about eighty percent of the surface. One is light blue and white, oth is pink and yellow. Some pitting. Germany, circa 1870-1915. 19/32". Min) (9.0). Price: $32. CyberAuction #411, Lot #56.

4006. OTHER HANDMADE. Indian. Opaque black base. Two bands co ering about half the marble. Both are pink and yellow. Some minor lig haze, one tiny moon. Germany, circa 1870-1915. 23/32". Near Mint (8.5 Price: $32. CyberAuction #483, Lot #15.

4007. OTHER HANDMADE. Indian. I've classified this as a transpare Indian, although some might call it a banded swirl. Transparent light blu base. Surface has two bands covering about seventy percent of the marbl One stretched yellow, one stretched white. A couple of melt spots. 11/16 Mint(-) (9.0). Price: $32. CyberAuction #487, Lot #43.

4008. OTHER HANDMADE. Indian. Opaque black base. Colored bar covering about eighty-five percent of the surface. Band is stretched mu tard yellow, red, blue and white. A couple of small subsurface moons, or large melt spot, some pitting. Germany, circa 1870-1915. 25/32". Good(- (7.9). Price: $30. CyberAuction #396, Lot #8.

4009. OTHER HANDMADE. Indian. Opaque black base. Two bands co ering about thirty percent of the surface. One is blue on white strand edged by white. Other is green on white strands, edged by white. Subsu face moon and some pitting. Germany, circa 1870-1915. 5/8". Near Mi (8.3). Price: $28. CyberAuction #343, Lot #16.

4010. OTHER HANDMADE. Indian. Cane section from an Indian. Sligh flat at one end. Germany, circa 1870-1915. About 2" long, Mint (9.5 Price: $28. CyberAuction #372, Lot #56.

4011. OTHER HANDMADE. Indian. Shooter. Opaque black base. Tw bands covering almost ninety percent of the surface. One is green an white, one is pink and white. Misshapen. One tiny chip, some hazines some dirt spots. Germany, circa 1870-1915. 29/32". Good(+) (7.9). Pric $26. CyberAuction #481, Lot #16.

4012. OTHER HANDMADE. Indian. Opaque black base. Two bands co ering about thirty percent of the surface. Each is white strands, covered transparent dark blue, edged by yellow. Several tiny flakes and some pits. was a dug marble, there is still some dirt on it. Germany, circa 1870-191 21/32". Near Mint (8.4). Price: $25. CyberAuction #365, Lot #10.

4013. OTHER HANDMADE. Indian. Opaque black base. Two bands co ering about thirty percent of the surface. One is blue and white, other green and yellow. Some minor chips. Germany, circa 1870-1915. 5/ Near Mint(+) (8.0). Price: $24.95. CyberAuction #397, Lot #40.

4014. OTHER HANDMADE. Indian. Opaque black base. Two white na row bands on one side. Small chip. Germany, circa 1870-1915. 21/32 Near Mint(+) (8.7). Price: $24. CyberAuction #489, Lot #16.

4015. OTHER HANDMADE. Indian. Opaque black base. Four blue an white bands. Very interesting. Misshapen (elongated). Germany, circa 187 1915. 5/8". Mint (9.5). Price: $23. CyberAuction #488, Lot #8.

4016. OTHER HANDMADE. Indian. Four panel Indian. Opaque blac base. Colored bands covering about eighty percent of the surface. Two a pink on yellow. Two are light blue. Just one area of black showing. Overa light haze. Germany, circa 1870-1915. 23/32". Good(+) (7.9). Price: $2 CyberAuction #428, Lot #18.

017. OTHER HANDMADE. Indian. Black opaque base. Two bands covering about half the marble. One is white and light blue, one is pink and mustard yellow. Some very light haze on part of the marble. Germany, circa 1870-1915. 11/16". Near Mint(+) (8.7). Price: $22. CyberAuction #442, Lot #20.

018. OTHER HANDMADE. Indian. Opaque black base. Four blue and white bands. Very interesting. Misshapen (elongated). Germany, circa 1870-1915. 5/8". Mint (9.5). Price: $20. CyberAuction #405, Lot #26.

019. OTHER HANDMADE. Indian. Teardrop shaped. Opaque black base. Some lines of blue and black. One melt hole. Germany, circa 1870-1915. 13/32". Near Mint(+) (8.9). Price: $20. CyberAuction #408, Lot #43.

020. OTHER HANDMADE. Indian. Teardrop shaped. Opaque black base. Some lines of blue and black. One melt hole. Germany, circa 1870-1915. 13/32". Near Mint(+) (8.9). Price: $20. CyberAuction #426, Lot #22.

021. OTHER HANDMADE. Indian. Opaque black base. Four blue and white bands. Very interesting. Misshapen (elongated). Germany, circa 1870-1915. 5/8". Mint (9.5). Price: $20. CyberAuction #449, Lot #45.

022. OTHER HANDMADE. Indian. Cane piece from a transparent Indian. About 2" long. Mint (9.7). Price: $19. CyberAuction #367, Lot #12.

023. OTHER HANDMADE. Indian. Opaque black base. Two bands covering about thirty percent of the surface. Both are blue edged by white. A couple of tiny chips. Germany, circa 1870-1915. 5/8". Near Mint(-) (8.2). Price: $19. CyberAuction #419, Lot #49.

024. OTHER HANDMADE. Indian. I've been calling this type transparent Indian, because the construction is exactly the same as an opaque Indian. Transparent bubble-filled very light green glass. A band of stretched yellow and a band of stretched white covering about eighty percent of the surface. Small ghost core with a few colored strands on it, that you can view through the open panel. One flake. Germany, possibly American, circa 1870-1920. 21/32". Near Mint(+) (8.7). Price: $19. CyberAuction #436, Lot #33.

025. OTHER HANDMADE. Indian. Opaque black base. Two bands covering about thirty percent of the surface. Both are blue edged by white. A couple of tiny chips. Germany, circa 1870-1915. 5/8". Near Mint(-) (8.2). Price: $19. CyberAuction #460, Lot #5.

026. OTHER HANDMADE. Indian. Opaque black base. Two bands covering about sixty percent of the marble. One is pink and white, one is green and white. Hazy and some pits. Germany, circa 1870-1915. 3/4". Good(+) (5.7). Price: $19. CyberAuction #469, Lot #18.

027. OTHER HANDMADE. Indian. Black opaque base with one white band. Overall light pitting and tiny chips. Germany, circa 1870-1915. 5/8". Near Mint(-) (8.0). Price: $17. CyberAuction #341, Lot #17.

028. OTHER HANDMADE. Indian. Cane piece for an Indian swirl. About 1 inch long. Mint(-) (9.0). Price: $17. CyberAuction #370, Lot #3.

029. OTHER HANDMADE. Indian. Teardrop shaped. Opaque black base. Some lines of blue and black. One melt hole. Germany, circa 1870-1915. 13/32". Near Mint(+) (8.9). Price: $17. CyberAuction #482, Lot #16.

030. OTHER HANDMADE. Indian. Opaque black base. Two multicolor surface bands covering about thirty percent of the marble. Overall small chips and haze. Germany, circa 1870-1915. 23/32". Good (7.5). Price: $14. CyberAuction #445, Lot #20.

031. OTHER HANDMADE. Indian. Opaque black base. Two bands of pink, yellow and light blue, covering about sixty percent of the surface. Overall haze. Germany, circa 1870-1915. 25/32". Good (7.5). Price: $13. CyberAuction #401, Lot #24.

032. OTHER HANDMADE. Indian. Shooter with wide bands of color, but heavily damaged. Germany, circa 1870-1915. 31/32". Collectible. Price: $10. CyberAuction #416, Lot #35.

033. OTHER HANDMADE. Indian. Shooter with wide bands of color, but heavily damaged. Germany, circa 1870-1915. 31/32". Collectible. Price: $10. CyberAuction #456, Lot #45.

034. OTHER HANDMADE. Indian. Shooter with wide bands of color, but heavily damaged. Germany, circa 1870-1915. 31/32". Collectible. Price: $10. CyberAuction #484, Lot #11.

035. OTHER HANDMADE. Indian. Opaque black base. Two multicolor surface bands covering about thirty percent of the marble. Overall small chips and haze. Germany, circa 1870-1915. 23/32". Good (7.5). Price: $7. CyberAuction #372, Lot #14.

036. OTHER HANDMADE. Mica. Shooter red mica, one of the largest I have ever seen. Dark red, almost looks rust, but shine a light through it and you get a gorgeous currant-red color. Nice layer of subsurface mica. Small cold roll area at the top pontil. Beautifully faceted bottom pontil. In superb shape. Wow! Germany, circa 1870-1915. 31/32". Mint (9.5). Price: $2250. CyberAuction #373, Lot #60.

037. OTHER HANDMADE. Mica. Shooter red mica. Has a three-lobed translucent white core with mica on it. And a nice subsurface layer of mica. Gorgeous cherry red color. One small subsurface moon, not really that noticeable, a tiny subsurface moon (near the bottom pontil), a couple of very tiny flakes and pits. Germany, circa 1870-1915. 13/16". Near Mint (8.6). Price: $985. CyberAuction #410, Lot #60.

038. OTHER HANDMADE. Mica. Shooter red mica. Has a three-lobed translucent white core with mica on it. And a nice subsurface layer of mica. Gorgeous cherry red color. One small subsurface moon, not really that noticeable, a tiny subsurface moon (near the bottom pontil), a couple of very tiny flakes and pits. Germany, circa 1870-1915. 13/16". Near Mint (8.6). Price: $985. CyberAuction #430, Lot #60.

039. OTHER HANDMADE. Mica. Very pale pink mica. Beauty and rare. Germany, circa 1870-1915. 15/32". Mint (9.9). Price: $525. CyberAuction #357, Lot #42.

040. OTHER HANDMADE. Mica. One of the rarest mica marbles I have seen. Large blizzard yellow mica. Stunning bright yellow color. Very heavy layer of mica subsurface. Several tiny and small chips. The top is fine. The bottom fifth of the marble has been buffed, the bottom pontil is missing. Top pontil is present. Very rare. Germany, circa 1870-1915. 1-9/16". Near Mint(-) (8.0). Price: $500. CyberAuction #498, Lot #75.

4041. OTHER HANDMADE. Mica. Gorgeous and extremely rare shooter yellow mica. Nice mica layer. Some pits. Very rare. Germany, circa 1870-1915. 31/32". Near Mint(+) (8.7). Price: $485. CyberAuction #403, Lot #58.

4042. OTHER HANDMADE. Mica. Rare large mica. Aqua mica. Mica core. Slightly shrunken on two sides. One tiny chip, several tiny subsurface moons, some sparkles. Very rare in this size and color. Germany, circa 1870-1915. 1-9/16". Near Mint(-) (8.1). Price: $410. CyberAuction #487, Lot #54.

4043. OTHER HANDMADE. Mica. Transparent very dark amethyst base. Excellent subsurface layer mica. This is a very rare marble, in terms of color, probably rarer than red or yellow. Spectacular. Germany, circa 1870-1915. 21/32". Mint (9.9). Price: $350. CyberAuction #357, Lot #15.

4044. OTHER HANDMADE. Mica. Rare, large aqua mica with a blizzard subsurface layer of mica. Stunning. Buffed, but the pontil is pretty much intact. Germany, circa 1870-1915. 1-3/4". Mint(-) (9.2). Price: $290. CyberAuction #425, Lot #37.

4045. OTHER HANDMADE. Mica. Smokey gray with tons of mica. Superb. Germany, circa 1870-1915. 25/32". Mint (9.7). Price: $240. CyberAuction #501, Lot #68.

4046. OTHER HANDMADE. Mica. Amber yellow mica shooter. Not bright yellow, but a pleasing shade. Nice mica. Germany, circa 1870-1915. 7/8". Mint (9.9). Price: $210. CyberAuction #505, Lot #71.

4047. OTHER HANDMADE. Mica. Yellow mica. Mica core. Beautiful subsurface layer of mica. Stunning. In great shape. Germany, circa 1870-1915. 11/16". Mint (9.8).. Price: $205. CyberAuction #345, Lot #59.

4048. OTHER HANDMADE. Mica. Shooter yellow mica. Rare marble. Gorgeous. One melt spot. Germany, circa 1870-1915. 25/32". Mint(-) (9.2). Price: $200. CyberAuction #465, Lot #59.

4049. OTHER HANDMADE. Mica. Large green mica. Nice blizzard layer of mica. A couple of tiny subsurface moons, some tiny pits. Germany, circa 1870-1915. 1-5/16". Near Mint (8.6). Price: $200. CyberAuction #508, Lot #71.

4050. OTHER HANDMADE. Mica. Very nice mica. Nice yellow color. Ghost core. Nice mica layer. Germany, circa 1870-1915. 23/32". Mint (9.7). Price: $190. CyberAuction #508, Lot #67.

4051. OTHER HANDMADE. Mica. Transparent very dark indigo mica. Very hard to find. One melt spot. Beauty. Germany, circa 1870-1915. 11/16". Mint (9.4). Price: $180. CyberAuction #388, Lot #19.

4052. OTHER HANDMADE. Mica. Yellow mica. Mica core. Excellent subsurface layer of mica. Stunning. In great shape. Germany, circa 1870-1915. 21/32". Mint (9.5). Price: $160. CyberAuction #348, Lot #57.

4053. OTHER HANDMADE. Mica. Amethyst mica. Super mica core, shrunken on one side. Deep purple color. Very rare, larger example. One tiny melt spot. Germany, circa 1870-1915. 27/32". Mint(-) (9.2). Price: $155. CyberAuction #479, Lot #40.

4054. OTHER HANDMADE. Mica. Yellow mica. Gorgeous color with great mica. Germany, circa 1870-1915. 23/32". Mint (9.8). Price: $150. CyberAuction #396, Lot #41.

4055. OTHER HANDMADE. Mica. Dark brown mica. Shooter. Lots of mica. Superb. Germany, circa 1870-1915. 7/8". Mint (9.8). Price: $150. CyberAuction #504, Lot #9.

4056. OTHER HANDMADE. Mica. Golden amber shooter mica. Close to a yellow. Gorgeous. Germany, circa 1870-1915. 27/32". Mint (9.8). Price: $150. CyberAuction #504, Lot #33.

4057. OTHER HANDMADE. Mica. Gorgeous aqua shooter mica. Ghost core. Subsurface layer of mica. Two tiny melt pits. Stunning. Germany, circa 1870-1915. 13/16". Mint (9.5). Price: $145. CyberAuction #483, Lot #44.

4058. OTHER HANDMADE. Mica. Golden amber shooter mica. Close to a yellow. Gorgeous. Germany, circa 1870-1915. 27/32". Mint (9.9). Price: $140. CyberAuction #503, Lot #12.

4059. OTHER HANDMADE. Mica. Emerald green mica. Excellent subsurface layer of mica. One tiny melt spot. Great marble. Germany, circa 1870-1915. 1". Mint (9.6). Price: $130. CyberAuction #357, Lot #56.

4060. OTHER HANDMADE. Mica. Very hard to find yellow mica. Outstanding example of this type! Filament core with mica around it. Heavy layer of subsurface large mica , mostly on one side. Super marble. Germany, circa 1870-1915. 21/32". Mint (9.7). Price: $130. CyberAuction #374, Lot #58.

4061. OTHER HANDMADE. Mica. Yellow mica. Gorgeous color with great mica. Germany, circa 1870-1915. 19/32". Mint (9.7). Price: $130. CyberAuction #425, Lot #58.

4062. OTHER HANDMADE. Mica. Gorgeous aqua mica. A couple of tiny pinpricks. Nice shooter. Germany, circa 1870-1915. 13/16". Mint(-) (9.2). Price: $130. CyberAuction #487, Lot #51.

4063. OTHER HANDMADE. Mica. Yellow mica. Mica core. Excellent subsurface layer of mica. Stunning. In great shape, with one tiny melt spot. Germany, circa 1870-1915. 11/16". Mint(-) (9.2). Price: $120. CyberAuction #356, Lot #56.

4064. OTHER HANDMADE. Mica. Gorgeous large aqua mica. A beauty!!!! Several very tiny chips. Germany, circa 1870-1915. 1-1/16". Near Mint(+) (8.7). Price: $120. CyberAuction #393, Lot #57.

4065. OTHER HANDMADE. Mica. Hard to find amethyst mica. Gorgeous. Germany, circa 1870-1915. 5/8". Mint (9.9). Price: $120. CyberAuction #448, Lot #55.

4066. OTHER HANDMADE. Mica. Light amethyst mica. Gorgeous. Germany, circa 1870-1915. 1/2". Mint (9.8). Price: $120. CyberAuction #487, Lot #25.

4067. OTHER HANDMADE. Mica. Yellow mica. Very nice subsurface layer of mica and a mica core. There is one tiny melt spot. Hard to find. Germany, circa 1870-1915. 9/16". Mint (9.5). Price: $110. CyberAuction #363, Lot #47.

4068. OTHER HANDMADE. Mica. Yellow mica. Nice color, and nice mica flakes, with a mica core too. Germany, circa 1870-1915. 5/8". Mint (9.7).. Price: $110. CyberAuction #392, Lot #60.

4069. OTHER HANDMADE. Mica. Gorgeous shooter blue mica. Nice mica layer. A couple of very tiny pinpricks. Germany, circa 1870-1915. 31/32". Mint (9.3). Price: $110. CyberAuction #403, Lot #36.

4070. OTHER HANDMADE. Mica. Amethyst mica. Gorgeous. Germany, circa 1870-1915. 9/16". Mint (9.9). Price: $110. CyberAuction #421, Lot #50.

4071. OTHER HANDMADE. Mica. Amethyst mica. Gorgeous and hard to find. Germany, circa 1870-1915. 9/16". Mint (9.7). Price: $110. CyberAuction #452, Lot #49.

4072. OTHER HANDMADE. Mica. Semi-transparent purple mica. Gorgeous. Very rare color. Germany, circa 1870-1915. 9/16". Mint (9.9). Price: $110. CyberAuction #500, Lot #38.

4073. OTHER HANDMADE. Mica. Gorgeous emerald green mica. Single ribbon mica core and a subsurface layer of mica. Stunning. Germany, circa 1870-1915. 27/32". Mint (9.9). Price: $110. CyberAuction #504, Lot #41.

4074. OTHER HANDMADE. Mica. Emerald green mica. Thick mica core. Excellent subsurface layer of mica. One tiny melt spot. Great marble. Germany, circa 1870-1915. 1". Mint(-) (9.2). Price: $100. CyberAuction #360, Lot #34.

4075. OTHER HANDMADE. Mica. Dark amethyst mica. Hard color to find. Germany, circa 1870-1915. 9/16". Mint (9.9). Price: $95. CyberAuction #360, Lot #16.

4076. OTHER HANDMADE. Mica. Emerald green mica. Very nice subsurface layer of mica. Shrunken core. Great marble. Stunning. Some mica melted into the surface. Germany, circa 1870-1915. 31/32". Mint (9.8). Price: $95. CyberAuction #421, Lot #56.

4077. OTHER HANDMADE. Mica. Emerald green mica. Thick mica core. Excellent subsurface layer of mica. Two tiny melt spots. Great marble. Germany, circa 1870-1915. 1". Mint(-) (9.2). Price: $90. CyberAuction #356, Lot #47.

4078. OTHER HANDMADE. Mica. Gorgeous. Light aqua base. Superb layer of large mica flakes. Great coverage. Slightly shrunken on one side. Stunning. Some pinpricks. Germany, circa 1870-1915. 7/8". Near Mint (8.6). Price: $85. CyberAuction #377, Lot #18.

4079. OTHER HANDMADE. Mica. Shooter brown mica. Stunning. Germany, circa 1870-1915. 25/32". Mint (9.9). Price: $80. CyberAuction #347, Lot #57.

4080. OTHER HANDMADE. Mica. Emerald green mica. Very nice subsurface layer of mica. Shrunken core. Great marble. Stunning. A couple of tiny scratches. Germany, circa 1870-1915. 31/32". Mint (9.3). Price: $80. CyberAuction #354, Lot #8.

4081. OTHER HANDMADE. Mica. Amethyst mica. Beauty. Germany, circa 1870-1915. 1/2". Mint (9.9). Price: $80. CyberAuction #360, Lot #36.

4082. OTHER HANDMADE. Mica. Stunning aqua mica. Great color. Excellent core of mica. One melted white glass spot on it. Surface is pristine. Exceptional example!!! Germany, circa 1870-1915. 27/32". Mint (9.9). Price: $80. CyberAuction #377, Lot #55.

4083. OTHER HANDMADE. Mica. Gorgeous yellow mica. Beauty. Germany, circa 1870-1915. 5/8". Mint (9.7). Price: $80. CyberAuction #439, Lot #58.

4084. OTHER HANDMADE. Mica. Yellow mica. Nice color, and nice mica flakes, with a mica core too. Germany, circa 1870-1915. 5/8". Mint (9.7).. Price: $80. CyberAuction #446, Lot #58.

4085. OTHER HANDMADE. Mica. Purple mica. Hard to find color. Nice mica. Germany, circa 1870-1915. 9/16". Mint (9.8). Price: $80. CyberAuction #459, Lot #35.

4086. OTHER HANDMADE. Mica. Large clear mica. Ghost core with mica on it. Subsurface mica layer. Still has original inventory tag on it. Nicely faceted pontil. One tiny flake. Germany, circa 1870-1915. 1-1/4". Near Mint(+) (8.9). Price: $80. CyberAuction #505, Lot #65.

4087. OTHER HANDMADE. Mica. Emerald green mica. Very nice subsurface layer of mica. Great marble. Germany, circa 1870-1915. 15/16". Mint (9.7). Price: $75. CyberAuction #345, Lot #56.

4088. OTHER HANDMADE. Mica. Honey amber (almost yellow) mica. Gorgeous. Germany, circa 1870-1915. 9/16". Mint (9.9). Price: $75. CyberAuction #363, Lot #42.

4089. OTHER HANDMADE. Mica. Yellow mica. Very nice subsurface layer of mica. There is one blown out spot where the mica is almost at the surface. Hard to find. Germany, circa 1870-1915. 5/8". Mint(-) (9.0). Price: $75. CyberAuction #404, Lot #15.

4090. OTHER HANDMADE. Mica. Superb clear mica. Excellent subsurface layer of mica. Exceptional example. Germany, circa 1870-1915. 15/16". Mint (9.8). Price: $65. CyberAuction #354, Lot #52.

4091. OTHER HANDMADE. Mica. Clear mica. Absolutely gorgeous. Germany, circa 1870-1915. 7/8". Mint (9.9). Price: $65. CyberAuction #369, Lot #50.

4092. OTHER HANDMADE. Mica. Purple mica. Hard to find color. Nice mica. Germany, circa 1870-1915. 9/16". Mint (9.8). Price: $65. CyberAuction #467, Lot #51.

4093. OTHER HANDMADE. Mica. Amethyst mica. Nice layer of mica. Peewee. Germany, circa 1870-1915. 1/2". Mint (9.8). Price: $60. CyberAuction #441, Lot #57.

4094. OTHER HANDMADE. Mica. Gorgeous aqua mica. Nice mica core. Nice

subsurface layer of mica. Superb marble. Stunning. Germany, circa 187 1915. 27/32". Mint (9.8). Price: $60. CyberAuction #450, Lot #37.

4095. OTHER HANDMADE. Mica. Gorgeous light brown mica with a clea core. The core is open at the top. This is from near the very beginning of th cane. Wonderful example. One tiny melt chip. A beauty. Germany, circa 1870-1915. 7/8". Mint(-) (9.1). Price: $60. CyberAuction #505, Lot #2

4096. OTHER HANDMADE. Mica. Gorgeous shooter emerald green mic Germany, circa 1870-1915. 27/32". Mint (9.9). Price: $60. CyberAuctic #505, Lot #52.

4097. OTHER HANDMADE. Mica. Light brown mica. Gorgeous. One ti pit. Germany, circa 1870-1915. 7/8". Mint(-) (9.2). Price: $60. CyberAuctic #507, Lot #47.

4098. OTHER HANDMADE. Mica. Emerald green mica. Very nice subsu face layer of mica. One melt area. Great marble. Germany, circa 187 1915. 15/16". Mint (9.3). Price: $56. CyberAuction #351, Lot #50.

4099. OTHER HANDMADE. Mica. Transparent clear base. Shrunken mic core with great mica in it. One melt "seed", one tiny chip. Germany, circa 1870-1915. 31/32". Near Mint(+) (8.8). Price: $55. CyberAuction #34 Lot #45.

4100. OTHER HANDMADE. Mica. Clear mica shooter. Ghost core wi mica. Nice subsurface layer of mica. A couple of sparkles. Superb marble Germany, circa 1870-1915. 1". Mint(-) (9.0). Price: $55. CyberAuction #35 Lot #28.

4101. OTHER HANDMADE. Mica. Rare color. Pale Vaseline yellow (n fluorescent). Shooter. Mica core and excellent subsurface layer of mic Several subsurface moons. Germany, circa 1870-1915. 7/8". Near Mint(+ (8.1). Price: $55. CyberAuction #366, Lot #18.

4102. OTHER HANDMADE. Mica. Pale amethyst shooter. Gorgeous mic Great color. Some pinpricking. Germany, circa 1870-1915. 3/4". Ne Mint(+) (8.9). Price: $55. CyberAuction #381, Lot #33.

4103. OTHER HANDMADE. Mica. Gorgeous brown mica. Super mica the subsurface layer. In great shape. Excellent example. Germany, circ 1870-1915. 3/4". Mint (9.9). Price: $55. CyberAuction #400, Lot #24.

4104. OTHER HANDMADE. Mica. Interesting ribbon core mica. Emera green marble. Excellent core of mica, flattened on either side. Gorgeou Two tiny sparkles. Germany, circa 1870-1915. 25/32". Mint(-) (9.1). Pric $51. CyberAuction #366, Lot #15.

4105. OTHER HANDMADE. Mica. Clear mica shooter. Ghost core. Ve nice. Germany, circa 1870-1915. 27/32". Mint (9.7). Price: $5 CyberAuction #508, Lot #28.

4106. OTHER HANDMADE. Mica. Yellow mica. Excellent mica in it. Som very light haze on the surface, but no damage. Very nice. Germany, circ 1870-1915. 9/16". Near Mint(+) (8.9). Price: $50. CyberAuction #34 Lot #7.

4107. OTHER HANDMADE. Mica. Dark brown shooter. Nice layer of mic One very tiny moon, one small sparkle. Germany, circa 1870-1915. 1 16". Near Mint(+) (8.8). Price: $50. CyberAuction #363, Lot #20.

4108. OTHER HANDMADE. Mica. Amber yellow mica. Gorgeous marble!! Germany, circa 1870-1915. 9/16". Mint (9.9). Price: $50. CyberAuctic #448, Lot #40.

4109. OTHER HANDMADE. Mica. Clear mica. Green core. Nice coatin of mica, very close to the surface. One dirt line on the surface. German circa 1870-1915. 27/32". Mint (9.7). Price: $50. CyberAuction #502, Lc #59.

4110. OTHER HANDMADE. Mica. Emerald green shooter mica. Super Nicely ground pontil. Germany, circa 1870-1915. 27/32". Mint (9.9). Pric $50. CyberAuction #503, Lot #17.

4111. OTHER HANDMADE. Mica. Emerald green mica shooter. German circa 1870-1915. 13/16". Mint (9.9). Price: $50. CyberAuction #508, Lc #9.

4112. OTHER HANDMADE. Mica. Rare marble. Almost a mist with mic Transparent green base. Lots of bands of translucent blue stretched throug out it. Great layer of mica. One small chip, some pitting, some roughnes Germany, circa 1870-1915. 23/32". Near Mint(-) (8.2). Price: $4 CyberAuction #372, Lot #17.

4113. OTHER HANDMADE. Mica. Gorgeous aqua mica. Filament core Beauty. Germany, circa 1870-1915. 11/16". Mint (9.7). Two marbles avai able, you are bidding on one. Winner has choice of either or both, remain der to under. Price: $47. CyberAuction #452, Lot #24.

4114. OTHER HANDMADE. Mica. Brown mica. Shooter. Two small flake Germany, circa 1870-1915. 25/32". Near Mint(+) (8.7). Price: $4 CyberAuction #362, Lot #49.

4115. OTHER HANDMADE. Mica. Emerald green mica. Gorgeous shoote Large mica flakes. A couple of tiny pinpricks. Germany, circa 1870-1915 13/16". Mint(-) (9.2). Price: $46. CyberAuction #404, Lot #57.

4116. OTHER HANDMADE. Mica. Hard to find dark amethyst mica. Go geous. Germany, circa 1870-1915. 5/8". Mint (9.8). Price: $46. CyberAuctic #450, Lot #43.

4117. OTHER HANDMADE. Mica. Emerald green. Slightly shrunken core Beauty. Germany, circa 1870-1915. 13/16". Mint (9.9). Price: $46 CyberAuction #503, Lot #51.

4118. OTHER HANDMADE. Mica. Teal mica. Has some strands in it, ei ther very dark green or black. Germany, circa 1870-1915. 9/16 Mint (9.9). Price: $45. CyberAuction #344, Lot #57.

4119. OTHER HANDMADE. Mica. Aqua. Shrunken core of mica. Beauty Germany, circa 1870-1915. 1/2". Mint (9.7). Price: $45. CyberAuction #359 Lot #51.

4120. OTHER HANDMADE. Mica. Gorgeous aqua mica. Has a black core Excellent mica layer. Exceptional example. Germany, circa 1870-1915. 2 32". Mint (9.9). Price: $44. CyberAuction #351, Lot #57.

4121. OTHER HANDMADE. Mica. Very interesting mica. Transparent clea base. Subsurface blizzard layer of mica. Transparent brownish red band on top of the mica on one side, some of the bands in the core. Heavily polished. Germany, circa 1870-1915. 31/32". Price: $42. CyberAuction #337, Lot #55.

4122. OTHER HANDMADE. Mica. Gorgeous aqua mica. Nice layer of mica. Germany, circa 1870-1915. 19/32". Mint (9.9). Price: $42. CyberAuction #400, Lot #16.

4123. OTHER HANDMADE. Mica. Purple mica. Hard to find color. Nice mica. Several very tiny chips. Germany, circa 1870-1915. 21/32". Near Mint(+) (8.9). Price: $42. CyberAuction #406, Lot #41.

4124. OTHER HANDMADE. Mica. Single pontil mica. End of cane. Clear mica. Nice cloud of mica in the core, shrunken on one side. Slightly flattened marble. One tiny chip. Rare. Germany, circa 1870-1915. 3/4". Near Mint(+) (8.8). Price: $41. CyberAuction #332, Lot #6.

4125. OTHER HANDMADE. Mica. Amethyst mica. Beauty. Germany, circa 1870-1915. 17/32". Mint (9.7). Price: $41. CyberAuction #392, Lot #51.

4126. OTHER HANDMADE. Mica. Honey yellow amber mica. Shooter. Very nice color, but not bright yellow. Germany, circa 1870-1915. 25/32". Mint (9.7). Price: $40. CyberAuction #492, Lot #36.

4127. OTHER HANDMADE. Mica. Shooter emerald green mica. Gorgeous. One tiny sparkle. Germany, circa 1870-1915. 29/32". Mint(-) (9.2). Price: $40. CyberAuction #507, Lot #54.

4128. OTHER HANDMADE. Mica. Green mica. Very nice. Germany, 1870-1915. 3/4". Mint (9.8). Price: $39. CyberAuction #348, Lot #39.

4129. OTHER HANDMADE. Mica. Ice blue mica. Tons of mica in the marble. Gorgeous. Small flake. Germany, circa 1870-1915. 3/4". Near Mint(+) (8.9). Price: $38. CyberAuction #344, Lot #51.

4130. OTHER HANDMADE. Mica. Amethyst mica. Nice layer of mica. Two tiny pits. Germany, circa 1870-1915. 17/32". Mint(-) (9.0). Price: $38. CyberAuction #377, Lot #46.

4131. OTHER HANDMADE. Mica. Blue mica. Nice shrunken core of mica. Germany, circa 1870-1915. 3/4". Mint (9.9). Price: $37. CyberAuction #342, Lot #19.

4132. OTHER HANDMADE. Mica. Amethyst mica. Nice subsurface layer of mica and a nice core. Some pitting and light haze. Germany, circa 1870-1915. 3/4". Near Mint (8.4). Price: $37. CyberAuction #367, Lot #51.

4133. OTHER HANDMADE. Mica. Green mica. Nice subsurface layer of mica. Germany, circa 1870-1915. 25/32". Mint (9.7). Price: $36. CyberAuction #337, Lot #47.

4134. OTHER HANDMADE. Mica. Brown mica. Very nice marble. Mica core and sparse subsurface layer of mica. Germany, circa 1870-1915. 23/32". Mint (9.7). Price: $36. CyberAuction #342, Lot #39.

4135. OTHER HANDMADE. Mica. Amber yellow mica. Gorgeous marble. Germany, circa 1870-1915. 9/16". Mint (9.7). Price: $36. CyberAuction #471, Lot #57.

4136. OTHER HANDMADE. Mica. Amber yellow mica. Gorgeous marble. Germany, circa 1870-1915. 9/16". Mint (9.7). Price: $36. CyberAuction #496, Lot #3.

4137. OTHER HANDMADE. Mica. Emerald green shooter mica. Very nice marble. Germany, circa 1870-1915. 13/16". Mint (9.8). Price: $36. CyberAuction #498, Lot #10.

4138. OTHER HANDMADE. Mica. Blue mica. Gorgeous. Germany, circa 1870-1915. 23/32". Mint (9.9). Price: $36. CyberAuction #500, Lot #16.

4139. OTHER HANDMADE. Mica. Amber brown. Nice mica in it. Two tiny dirt melt spots, one glass melt spot. Germany, circa 1870-1915. 7/8". Mint(-) (9.2). Price: $36. CyberAuction #502, Lot #33.

4140. OTHER HANDMADE. Mica. Clear mica. Gorgeous. One small moon, one tiny manufacturing pit. Germany, circa 1870-1915. 7/8". Near Mint (8.6). Price: $35. CyberAuction #369, Lot #30.

4141. OTHER HANDMADE. Mica. Emerald green mica. Ribbon core of mica. Super. One tiny flake. Germany, circa 1870-1915. 11/16". Near Mint(+) (8.9). Price: $35. CyberAuction #385, Lot #51.

4142. OTHER HANDMADE. Mica. Shooter brown mica. Beautiful subsurface layer of mica. One large chip and a couple of very small subsurface moons. No pitting or other damage on the marble. Germany, circa 1870-1915. 1-3/16". Near Mint(-) (8.1). Price: $35. CyberAuction #391, Lot #39.

4143. OTHER HANDMADE. Mica. Honey amber mica. Not quite yellow, but close. Beautiful subsurface layer of mica. Germany, circa 1870-1915. 9/16". Mint (9.9). Price: $35. CyberAuction #478, Lot #10.

4144. OTHER HANDMADE. Mica. Emerald green shooter mica. A couple of pinpricks. Germany, circa 1870-1915. 7/8". Mint(-) (9.2). Price: $35. CyberAuction #500, Lot #6.

4145. OTHER HANDMADE. Mica. Gorgeous clear mica. Germany, circa 1870-1915. 3/4". Mint (9.9). Price: $35. CyberAuction #505, Lot #36.

4146. OTHER HANDMADE. Mica. Outstanding mica! Transparent clear base. Green core. Excellent subsurface layer of mica. There are several very long subsurface elongated air bubbles. There are two cold roll lines on the surface. They are on opposite sides of the marble. In my opinion, they are intentional crimps. The air bubbles and the crimps form a spiral type design. Very unusual. Two small subsurface moons, very noticeable. Excellent marble. Germany, circa 1870-1915. 25/32". Near Mint (8.6). Price: $34. CyberAuction #381, Lot #17.

4147. OTHER HANDMADE. Mica. Emerald green mica. Nice layer of mica. One small dirt spot on the surface. Germany, circa 1870-1915. 5/8". Mint (9.9). Price: $34. CyberAuction #400, Lot #6.

4148. OTHER HANDMADE. Mica. Transparent emerald green mica. Stunning. Ghost core. Germany, circa 1870-1915. 11/16". Mint (9.9). Price: $32. CyberAuction #354, Lot #22.

4149. OTHER HANDMADE. Mica. Peewee green mica. Gorgeous. Germany, circa 1870-1915. 1/2". Mint (9.5). Price: $32. CyberAuction #362, Lot #59.

4150. OTHER HANDMADE. Mica. Aqua mica. Very nice subsurface layer of mica. Beautiful color. One small chip. Germany, circa 1870-1915. 13/16". Near Mint(+) (8.7). Price: $32. CyberAuction #367, Lot #48.

4151. OTHER HANDMADE. Mica. Clear mica. Subsurface layer of finely ground mica. Nice marble. Germany, circa 1870-1915. 13/16". Mint(-) (9.1). Price: $32. CyberAuction #371, Lot #5.

4152. OTHER HANDMADE. Mica. Emerald green mica. Stunning. Germany, circa 1870-1915. Two tiny chips. 13/16". Near Mint(+) (8.9). Price: $32. CyberAuction #397, Lot #60.

4153. OTHER HANDMADE. Mica. Green mica. One manufacturing pit and several pinpricks. Germany, circa 1870-1915. 15/16". Mint(-) (9.0). Price: $32. CyberAuction #408, Lot #40.

4154. OTHER HANDMADE. Mica. Green mica. Gorgeous marble. Germany, circa 1870-1915. 21/32". Mint (9.9). Price: $32. CyberAuction #452, Lot #40.

4155. OTHER HANDMADE. Mica. Unusual. Emerald green. Two black bands as the core. Layer of mica around them, slightly shrunken on one side. Left hand twist. Super marble. Germany, circa 1870-1915. 11/16". Mint (9.8). Price: $32. CyberAuction #483, Lot #23.

4156. OTHER HANDMADE. Mica. Green shooter mica. One tiny flake. Germany, circa 1870-1915. 7/8". Mint(-) (9.0). Price: $32. CyberAuction #483, Lot #29.

4157. OTHER HANDMADE. Mica. Very dark transparent aqua. Large shooter. Superb mica core, shrunken on one side. Overall tiny chips, light haze and pits. Germany, circa 1870-1915. 29/32". Good (7.6). Price: $30. CyberAuction #372, Lot #9.

4158. OTHER HANDMADE. Mica. Green mica. One manufacturing pit and several pinpricks. Germany, circa 1870-1915. 15/16". Mint(-) (9.0). Price: $30. CyberAuction #392, Lot #12.

4159. OTHER HANDMADE. Mica. Very dark transparent aqua. Large shooter. Superb mica core, shrunken on one side. Overall tiny chips, light haze and pits. Germany, circa 1870-1915. 29/32". Good (7.6). Price: $30. CyberAuction #398, Lot #11.

4160. OTHER HANDMADE. Mica. Very dark transparent aqua. Large shooter. Superb mica core, shrunken on one side. Overall tiny chips, light haze and pits. Germany, circa 1870-1915. 29/32". Good (7.6). Price: $30. CyberAuction #430, Lot #8.

4161. OTHER HANDMADE. Mica. Teal mica. Gorgeous. Germany, circa 1870-1915. 13/16". Mint (9.9). Price: $30. CyberAuction #461, Lot #48.

4162. OTHER HANDMADE. Mica. Aqua mica. Stunning marble. Germany, circa 1870-1915. 21/32". Mint (9.9). Price: $30. CyberAuction #467, Lot #48.

4163. OTHER HANDMADE. Mica. Emerald green shooter mica. Superb! Germany, circa 1870-1915. 27/32". Mint (9.9). Price: $30. CyberAuction #503, Lot #8.

4164. OTHER HANDMADE. Mica. Light blue mica. Unusual color. Two air holes. Germany, circa 1870-1915. 3/4". Mint (9.5). Price: $30. CyberAuction #504, Lot #5.

4165. OTHER HANDMADE. Mica. Light green mica. Very pretty. Germany, circa 1870-1915. 19/32". Mint (9.9). Price: $28. CyberAuction #344, Lot #4.

4166. OTHER HANDMADE. Mica. Green mica. Gorgeous. Germany, circa 1870-1915. 5/8". Mint (9.9). There are three marbles available, you are bidding on one. Winner has choice of any or all. Price: $28. CyberAuction #377, Lot #42.

4167. OTHER HANDMADE. Mica. Gorgeous blue mica. Nice color. Large ghost core. Nice subsurface layer of mica. Germany, circa 1870-1915. 5/8". Mint (9.9). Price: $28. CyberAuction #385, Lot #26.

4168. OTHER HANDMADE. Mica. Emerald green mica. Ghost air bubble core with mica on it. Subsurface layer of mica. Beautiful marble. Germany, circa 1870-1915. 3/4". Mint (9.8). Price: $28. CyberAuction #450, Lot #16.

4169. OTHER HANDMADE. Mica. Aqua mica. One melt pit. Germany, circa 1870-1915. 5/8". Mint(-) (9.2). Price: $28. CyberAuction #479, Lot #15.

4170. OTHER HANDMADE. Mica. Transparent clear base. Excellent subsurface layer of mica. Germany, circa 1870-1915. 25/32". Mint (9.7). Price: $27. CyberAuction #330, Lot #44.

4171. OTHER HANDMADE. Mica. Clear mica. Has a transparent blue core!! Hard to find. One chip, one subsurface moon. Germany, circa 1870-1915. 21/32". Near Mint(-) (8.0). Price: $27. CyberAuction #335, Lot #23.

4172. OTHER HANDMADE. Mica. Turquoise blue with shrunken mica layer. Some big chunks of mica. Overall tiny and small subsurface moons and a couple of small chips. Interesting color. Germany, circa 1870-1915. 1-1/16". Good (7.5). Price: $27. CyberAuction #371, Lot #35.

4173. OTHER HANDMADE. Mica. Amber brown mica. Large mica flakes. Beauty. One tiny chip, some tiny pits. Germany, circa 1870-1915. 13/16". Near Mint(+) (8.7). Price: $27. CyberAuction #372, Lot #20.

4174. OTHER HANDMADE. Mica. Peewee brown mica. Light brown. Gorgeous. Germany, circa 1870-1915. 15/32". Mint (9.9). Price: $27. CyberAuction #381, Lot #37.

4175. OTHER HANDMADE. Mica. Gorgeous brown mica. Panelled. Two subsurface panels of mica. Unusual. Tiny subsurface moon and tiny melt chip. Germany, circa 1870-1915. 25/32". Near Mint(+) (8.7). Price: $27. CyberAuction #417, Lot #52.

4176. OTHER HANDMADE. Mica. Gorgeous emerald green mica. Beauty. Germany, circa 1870-1915. 11/16". Mint (9.7). There are three marbles available, you are bidding on one. Winner has choice of any or all, remainder to under. Price: $27. CyberAuction #452, Lot #13.

4177. OTHER HANDMADE. Mica. Gorgeous blue mica. Superb shooter. Three tiny flakes. Germany, circa 1870-1915. 7/8". Near Mint(+) (8.8). Price: $27. CyberAuction #473, Lot #52.

4178. OTHER HANDMADE. Mica. Blue mica. Gorgeous. Germany, circa 1870-1915. 21/32". Mint (9.9). Price: $27. CyberAuction #495, Lot #6.

4179. OTHER HANDMADE. Mica. Green mica. Very fine layer of light mica. One pit. Germany, circa 1870-1915. 3/4". Mint(-) (9.0). Price: $26. CyberAuction #363, Lot #39.

4180. OTHER HANDMADE. Mica. Blue mica. Core is mica, and a super subsurface layer of mica. Germany, circa 1870-1915. 11/16". Mint (9.9). Price: $26. CyberAuction #471, Lot #45.

4181. OTHER HANDMADE. Mica. Dark green mica. Very nice. Germany, circa 1870-1915. 9/16". Mint (9.6). Price: $26. CyberAuction #478, Lot #26.

4182. OTHER HANDMADE. Mica. Dark brown mica. Lots of mica flakes in it. Some surface rubbing. Germany, circa 1870-1915. 21/32". Mint(-) (9.0). Price: $25. CyberAuction #339, Lot #43.

4183. OTHER HANDMADE. Mica. Yellow mica. Nice color, and nice mica flakes. Two large subsurface moons and a number of small subsurface moons. Germany, circa 1870-1915. 19/32". Good(-) (7.2). Price: $25. CyberAuction #353, Lot #4.

4184. OTHER HANDMADE. Mica. Brown mica. Black filament in it. Great mica layer. Germany, circa 1870-1915. 9/16". Mint (9.9). Price: $25. CyberAuction #354, Lot #40.

4185. OTHER HANDMADE. Mica. Green mica. Super subsurface layer of finely ground mica. Superb marble. Germany, circa 1870-1915. 11/16". Mint (9.9). Price: $25. CyberAuction #357, Lot #22.

4186. OTHER HANDMADE. Mica. Clear mica. Super marble. Germany, circa 1870-1915. 5/8". Mint (9.7). Price: $25. CyberAuction #382, Lot #54.

4187. OTHER HANDMADE. Mica. Green mica. Nice one. Germany, circa 1870-1915. 19/32". Mint (9.9). Price: $25. CyberAuction #425, Lot #52.

4188. OTHER HANDMADE. Mica. Gorgeous emerald green mica. Beauty. Germany, circa 1870-1915. 11/16". Mint (9.7). Price: $25. CyberAuction #470, Lot #13.

4189. OTHER HANDMADE. Mica. Yellow mica. Nice color, and nice mica flakes. Two large subsurface moons and a number of small subsurface moons. Germany, circa 1870-1915. 19/32". Good(-) (7.2). Price: $25. CyberAuction #486, Lot #26.

4190. OTHER HANDMADE. Mica. Brown mica. Very dark. Excellent subsurface layer of large mica. Some tiny flakes and pits. Germany, circa 1870-1915. 25/32". Near Mint (8.5). Price: $24. CyberAuction #368, Lot #47.

4191. OTHER HANDMADE. Mica. Brown mica. Very nice. Germany, circa 1870-1915. 1/2". Mint (9.7). There are three marbles available, you are bidding on one. Winner has choice of any or all, remainder to under. Price: $24. CyberAuction #397, Lot #56.

4192. OTHER HANDMADE. Mica. Light amber brown (almost yellow) mica. Melted pontil top, ground pontil bottom. Very odd. Germany, circa 1870-1915. 9/16". Mint (9.8). Price: $24. CyberAuction #483, Lot #19.

4193. OTHER HANDMADE. Mica. Blue mica. Germany, circa 1870-1915. 19/32". Mint (9.9). Price: $24. CyberAuction #508, Lot #51.

4194. OTHER HANDMADE. Mica. Dark blue mica. Very nice mica core. One tiny melt spot and a scratch. Germany, circa 1870-1915. 25/32". Mint(-) (9.0). Price: $23. CyberAuction #332, Lot #22.

4195. OTHER HANDMADE. Mica. Yellowish brown mica. Very pretty color. Germany, circa 1870-1915. 15/32". Mint (9.9). Price: $23. CyberAuction #443, Lot #4.

4196. OTHER HANDMADE. Mica. Honey amber mica. Not quite yellow, but close. Beautiful subsurface layer of mica. Germany, circa 1870-1915. 9/16". Mint (9.9). There are three marbles available, you are bidding on one. Winner has choice of any or all, remainder to under. Price: $23. CyberAuction #450, Lot #29.

4197. OTHER HANDMADE. Mica. Emerald green mica. Gorgeous. Germany, circa 1870-1915. 21/32". Mint (9.9). Price: $23. CyberAuction #479, Lot #27.

4198. OTHER HANDMADE. Mica. Green mica. Very nice. A couple of pits. Germany, circa 1870-1915. 3/4". Mint(-) (9.0). Price: $23. CyberAuction #504, Lot #21.

4199. OTHER HANDMADE. Mica. Dark blue mica. Excellent subsurface layer. One tiny moon. Germany, circa 1870-1915. 27/32". Near Mint(+) (8.9). Price: $21. CyberAuction #330, Lot #36.

4200. OTHER HANDMADE. Mica. Blue mica. Gorgeous. One melt spot. Germany, circa 1870-1915. 5/8". Mint (9.5). Price: $21. CyberAuction #336, Lot #38.

4201. OTHER HANDMADE. Mica. Green mica. Nice subsurface layer. Some pits and pinpricks. Germany, circa 1870-1915. 27/32". Near Mint(+) (8.7). Price: $21. CyberAuction #364, Lot #60.

4202. OTHER HANDMADE. Mica. Aqua mica. Filament core surrounded by a ghost of mica. Nice subsurface layer of mica too. A beauty. A couple of tiny chips. Germany, circa 1870-1915. 3/4". Near Mint (8.6). Price: $21. CyberAuction #382, Lot #10.

4203. OTHER HANDMADE. Mica. Emerald green mica. Gorgeous. Germany, circa 1870-1915. 11/16". Mint (9.8). There are four marbles available, you are bidding on one. Winner has choice of any or all. Remainder to under. Price: $21. CyberAuction #391, Lot #46.

4204. OTHER HANDMADE. Mica. Blue mica. Germany, circa 1870-1915. 5/8". Mint (9.7). There are three marbles available. You are bidding on one. Winner has choice of any or all, remainder to under. Price: $21. CyberAuction #425, Lot #8.

4205. OTHER HANDMADE. Mica. Clear mica. Very nice subsurface layer of mica. Germany, circa 1870-1915. 11/16". Mint (9.8). Price: $21. CyberAuction #459, Lot #17.

4206. OTHER HANDMADE. Mica. Dark teal mica. Gorgeous color. One tiny melt spot. Germany, circa 1870-1915. 1/2". Mint(-) (9.2). Price: $21. CyberAuction #471, Lot #8.

4207. OTHER HANDMADE. Mica. Emerald green marble with mica cloud core. Super. Germany, circa 1870-1915. 21/32". Mint (9.8). Price: $21. CyberAuction #481, Lot #52.

4208. OTHER HANDMADE. Mica. Yellow mica. Nice color, and nice mica flakes. Two large subsurface moons and a number of small subsurface moons. Germany, circa 1870-1915. 19/32". Good(-) (7.2). Price: $20. CyberAuction #374, Lot #23.

4209. OTHER HANDMADE. Mica. Yellow mica. Nice color, and nice mica flakes. Two large subsurface moons and a number of small subsurface moons. Germany, circa 1870-1915. 19/32". Good(-) (7.2). Price: $20. CyberAuction #445, Lot #43.

4210. OTHER HANDMADE. Mica. Yellow/brown mica. Gorgeous. Germany, circa 1870-1915. 9/16". Mint (9.8). There are three marbles available, you are bidding on one. Winner has choice of any or all, remainder to under. Price: $20. CyberAuction #459, Lot #27.

4211. OTHER HANDMADE. Mica. Very lightly tinted green. Lots of mica. Germany, circa 1870-1915. 21/32". Mint (9.7). Price: $20. CyberAuction #503, Lot #56.

4212. OTHER HANDMADE. Mica. Green mica. Beautiful subsurface layer of mica. One pit. Beauty. Germany, circa 1870-1915. 11/16". Mint (9.5). Price: $19. CyberAuction #333, Lot #13.

4213. OTHER HANDMADE. Mica. Light blue mica. Loads of mica flakes. Some surface scratches. Germany, circa 1870-1915. 5/8". Mint(-) (9.0). Price: $19. CyberAuction #376, Lot #45.

4214. OTHER HANDMADE. Mica. Clear mica. Mica in core. Cold crease on it. Very nice. Germany, circa 1870-1915. 5/8". Mint (9.7). Price: $19. CyberAuction #382, Lot #5.

4215. OTHER HANDMADE. Mica. Green mica. Very nice. Filament core with ghost air bubbles around it. Nice mica subsurface layer. One pit. Germany, circa 1870-1915. 23/32". Mint(-) (9.2). Price: $19. CyberAuction #388, Lot #4.

4216. OTHER HANDMADE. Mica. Blue mica. Gorgeous. Germany, circa 1870-1915. 19/32". Mint (9.7). There are four marbles available. You are bidding on one. Winner has choice of any or all, remainder to under. Price: $19. CyberAuction #388, Lot #25.

4217. OTHER HANDMADE. Mica. Blue mica. Very shrunken core. Hard to find. Germany, circa 1870-1915. 19/32". Mint (9.8). Price: $19. CyberAuction #392, Lot #3.

4218. OTHER HANDMADE. Mica. Amber brown mica. Gorgeous. Germany, circa 1870-1915. 9/16". Mint (9.9). Price: $19. CyberAuction #448, Lot #19.

4219. OTHER HANDMADE. Mica. Superb emerald green mica. Beauty. Ghost core. Germany, circa 1870-1915. 21/32". Mint (9.8). Three marbles available, you are bidding on one. Winner has choice of any or all, remainder to under. Price: $19. CyberAuction #459, Lot #39.

4220. OTHER HANDMADE. Mica. Gorgeous emerald green mica. One pit. Germany, circa 1870-1915. 3/4". Mint(-) (9.0). Price: $19. CyberAuction #467, Lot #37.

4221. OTHER HANDMADE. Mica. Blue mica. Mica core and subsurface mica layer. Germany, circa 1870-1915. 5/8". Mint (9.7). Price: $19. CyberAuction #479, Lot #47.

4222. OTHER HANDMADE. Mica. Dark teal Mica. One small subsurface moon, one tiny moon. Germany, circa 1870-1915. 25/32". Near Mint(+) (8.7). Price: $19. CyberAuction #486, Lot #19.

4223. OTHER HANDMADE. Mica. Aqua mica. Beauty. Light aqua. Big mica flakes in the core and subsurface. One flat spot. Germany, circa 1870-1915. 5/8". Mint (9.6). Price: $19. CyberAuction #489, Lot #41.

4224. OTHER HANDMADE. Mica. Clear mica. Germany, circa 1870-1915. 9/16". Mint (9.7). Price: $19. CyberAuction #504, Lot #17.

4225. OTHER HANDMADE. Mica. Golden amber brown, almost yellow. Germany, circa 1870-1915. 9/16". Mint (9.9). Two marbles available, you are bidding on one. Winner has choice of either or both, remainder to under. Price: $18. CyberAuction #475, Lot #31.

4226. OTHER HANDMADE. Mica. Blue mica. Very pretty marble with nice mica in it. Germany, circa 1870-1915. 9/16". Mint (9.9). Price: $17. CyberAuction #339, Lot #17.

4227. OTHER HANDMADE. Mica. Green mica. Very nice. Germany, circa 1870-1915. 9/16". Mint (9.9). Price: $17. CyberAuction #341, Lot #48.

4228. OTHER HANDMADE. Mica. Green mica. Beauty. Germany, circa 1870-1915. 17/32". Mint (9.7). Price: $17. CyberAuction #351, Lot #30.

4229. OTHER HANDMADE. Mica. Blue mica. Some surface debris. Germany, circa 1870-1915. 19/32". Mint(-) (9.0). There are three marbles available. You are bidding on one. Winner has choice of any or all, remainder to under. Price: $17. CyberAuction #381, Lot #23.

4230. OTHER HANDMADE. Mica. Clear mica. Germany, circa 1870-1915. 1/2". Mint (9.9). There are four marbles available. You are bidding on one. Winner has choice of any or all, remainder to under. Price: $17. CyberAuction #381, Lot #43.

4231. OTHER HANDMADE. Mica. Aqua mica. Finely ground mica. One pit. Germany, circa 1870-1915. 11/16". Near Mint(+) (8.9). Price: $17. CyberAuction #382, Lot #50.

4232. OTHER HANDMADE. Mica. Green mica. Nice marble. Germany, circa 1870-1915. 21/32". Mint (9.8). There are three examples available, you are bidding on one. Winner has choice of any or all, remainder to under. Price: $17. CyberAuction #392, Lot #27.

4233. OTHER HANDMADE. Mica. Amethyst mica. Subsurface moon. Germany, circa 1870-1915. 19/32". Near Mint (8.5). Price: $17. CyberAuction #399, Lot #48.

4234. OTHER HANDMADE. Mica. Clear mica. Very nice layer of flakes. Germany, circa 1870-1915. 19/32". Mint (9.7). There are two marbles available, you are bidding on one. Winner has choice of either or both, remainder to under. Price: $17. CyberAuction #434, Lot #42.

4235. OTHER HANDMADE. Mica. Emerald green mica. Nice layer of mica. One small dirt spot on the surface. Germany, circa 1870-1915. 5/8". Mint (9.9). Price: $17. CyberAuction #440, Lot #50.

4236. OTHER HANDMADE. Mica. Emerald green mica. Gorgeous. Germany, circa 1870-1915. 11/16". Mint (9.8). There are two marbles available, you are bidding on one. Winner has choice of any or all. Remainder to under. Price: $17. CyberAuction #445, Lot #39.

4237. OTHER HANDMADE. Mica. Green mica. Beauty. Germany, circa 1870-1915. 11/16". Mint (9.8). There are three marbles available, you are bidding on one. Winner has choice of any or all, remainder to under. Price: $17. CyberAuction #448, Lot #8.

4238. OTHER HANDMADE. Mica. Clear mica. Very nice marble. Germany, circa 1870-1915. 21/32". Mint (9.6). There are two marbles available, you are bidding on one. Winner has choice of either or both, remainder to under. Price: $17. CyberAuction #452, Lot #7.

4239. OTHER HANDMADE. Mica. Emerald green mica. Gorgeous. Germany, circa 1870-1915. 5/8". Mint (9.9). There are three examples available, you are bidding on one. Winner has choice of any or all, remainder to under. Price: $17. CyberAuction #467, Lot #18.

4240. OTHER HANDMADE. Mica. Blue mica. Super example. One tiny pinprick. Germany, circa 1870-1915. 3/4". Mint (9.6). Price: $17. CyberAuction #467, Lot #22.

4241. OTHER HANDMADE. Mica. Gorgeous clear mica. Germany, circa 1870-1915. 11/16". Mint (9.8). Price: $17. CyberAuction #478, Lot #34.

4242. OTHER HANDMADE. Mica. Emerald green mica. Mica core and mica subsurface layer. Gorgeous. Germany, circa 1870-1915. 21/32". Mint (9.9). Price: $17. CyberAuction #489, Lot #25.

4243. OTHER HANDMADE. Mica. Honey amber mica. Beauty. Melt spot. Germany, circa 1870-1915. 9/16". Mint (9.6). Price: $17. CyberAuction #489, Lot #39.

4244. OTHER HANDMADE. Mica. Emerald green mica. Germany, circa 1870-1915. 5/8". Mint (9.9). Price: $17. CyberAuction #491, Lot #25.

4245. OTHER HANDMADE. Mica. Blue mica. Teardrop air bubble core. Shrunken mica. A couple of pinpricks. Germany, circa 1870-1915. 5/8". Mint(-) (9.1). Price: $17. CyberAuction #505, Lot #25.

4246. OTHER HANDMADE. Mica. Brown mica. Very nice. Several pits. Germany, circa 1870-1915. 5/8". Near Mint(+) (8.7). Price: $16. CyberAuction #382, Lot #16.

4247. OTHER HANDMADE. Mica. Peewee mica. Clear. Very thin green filament core. Subsurface layer of very finely ground mica. Sparse. Germany, circa 1870-1915. 15/32". Mint (9.7). Price: $15. CyberAuction #337, Lot #3.

4248. OTHER HANDMADE. Mica. Brown mica. Gorgeous. One pit. Germany, circa 1870-1915. 15/32". Near Mint(+) (8.9). Price: $15. CyberAuction #354, Lot #13.

4249. OTHER HANDMADE. Mica. Clear mica. Large mica flakes. Ghost core. Pitting on the surface. Germany, circa 1870-1915. 29/32". Near Mint (8.3). Price: $15. CyberAuction #355, Lot #9.

4250. OTHER HANDMADE. Mica. Brown mica. Nice flakes. A couple of pinpricks. Germany, circa 1870-1915. 17/32". Mint(-) (9.0). Price: $15. CyberAuction #376, Lot #26.

4251. OTHER HANDMADE. Mica. Aqua mica. Beauty. One tiny chip. Germany, circa 1870-1915. 5/8". Near Mint(+) (8.9). Price: $15. CyberAuction #382, Lot #20.

4252. OTHER HANDMADE. Mica. Nice aqua mica. Nice layer of mica. Small subsurface moon. Germany, circa 1870-1915. 9/16". Near Mint(+) (8.9). Price: $15. CyberAuction #400, Lot #26.

4253. OTHER HANDMADE. Mica. Clear mica. Ghost core with some mica. Subsurface mica layer. Germany, circa 1870-1915. 21/32". Mint (9.8). Price: $15. CyberAuction #418, Lot #18.

4254. OTHER HANDMADE. Mica. Stunning emerald green mica. Germany, circa 1870-1915. 11/16". Mint (9.9). Price: $15. CyberAuction #462, Lot #24.

4255. OTHER HANDMADE. Mica. Very light green mica. Very nice. A couple of tiny pinpricks. Germany, circa 1870-1915. 23/32". Mint(-) (9.0). Price: $15. CyberAuction #465, Lot #6.

4256. OTHER HANDMADE. Mica. Very dark blue mica. A couple of tiny pits. Germany, circa 1870-1915. 13/16". Mint(-) (9.0). Price: $15. CyberAuction #469, Lot #58.

4257. OTHER HANDMADE. Mica. Green mica. Filled with air bubbles. Very nice. Germany, circa 1870-1915. 17/32". Mint (9.6). Price: $15. CyberAuction #471, Lot #2.

4258. OTHER HANDMADE. Mica. Emerald green mica. Gorgeous. Germany, circa 1870-1915. 5/8". Mint (9.9). Price: $15. CyberAuction #485, Lot #51.

4259. OTHER HANDMADE. Mica. Emerald green mica shooter. Gorgeous. One small ding. Germany, circa 1870-1915. 13/16". Near Mint(+) (8.8). Price: $15. CyberAuction #491, Lot #46.

4260. OTHER HANDMADE. Mica. Blue mica. One pit. Germany, circa 1870-1915. 19/32". Mint(-) (9.1). Price: $15. CyberAuction #498, Lot #45.

4261. OTHER HANDMADE. Mica. Clear mica with tons of flakes of mica. Germany, circa 1870-1915. 11/16". Mint (9.7). Price: $15. CyberAuction #502, Lot #9.

4262. OTHER HANDMADE. Mica. Blue mica. Several small flakes and chips. Germany, circa 1870-1915. 25/32". Near Mint (8.5). There are two marbles available, you are bidding on one. Winner has choice of either or both, remainder to under. Price: $15. CyberAuction #502, Lot #23.

4263. OTHER HANDMADE. Mica. Clear mica. Mica core, mica subsurface layer. One tiny flat spot and a pit. Germany, circa 1870-1915. 29/32". Near Mint(+) (8.9). Price: $15. CyberAuction #507, Lot #39.

4264. OTHER HANDMADE. Mica. Light green. Very nice marble. Slightly malformed. Germany, circa 1870-1915. 19/32". Mint (9.7). Price: $13. CyberAuction #353, Lot #14.

4265. OTHER HANDMADE. Mica. Clear mica. Finely ground mica. Several small and tiny chips. Germany, circa 1870-1915. 25/32". Near Mint (8.3). Price: $13. CyberAuction #355, Lot #12.

4266. OTHER HANDMADE. Mica. Beautiful blue mica. A couple of small and tiny chips. Loads of mica. 5/8". Near Mint (8.3). Price: $13. CyberAuction #432, Lot #41.

4267. OTHER HANDMADE. Mica. Light green mica. Very nice. From near an end of the cane. One sparkle. Germany, circa 1870-1915. 25/32". Mint(-) (9.0). Price: $13. CyberAuction #488, Lot #39.

4268. OTHER HANDMADE. Mica. Emerald green mica. Gorgeous. Germany, circa 1870-1915. 5/8". Mint (9.9). Price: $13. CyberAuction #494, Lot #38.

4269. OTHER HANDMADE. Mica. Emerald green mica. Germany, circa 1870-1915. 5/8". Mint (9.7). Price: $13. CyberAuction #499, Lot #37.

4270. OTHER HANDMADE. Mica. Clear mica. Nice subsurface layer of mica. Filament core with some ghost bubbles. Germany, circa 1870-1915. 19/32". Mint (9.7). Price: $12. CyberAuction #388, Lot #17.

4271. OTHER HANDMADE. Mica. Green mica. Nice mica layer. Small chip. Germany, circa 1870-1915. 5/8". Near Mint (8.6). There are two marbles available, you are bidding on one. Winner has choice of either or both, remainder to under. Price: $12. CyberAuction #397, Lot #26.

4272. OTHER HANDMADE. Mica. Blue mica. Gorgeous. Germany, circa 1870-1915. 5/8". Mint (9.8). Price: $12. CyberAuction #414, Lot #24.

4273. OTHER HANDMADE. Mica. Clear mica. Ghost core with mica. Nice subsurface layer of mica. Two melt spots. Germany, circa 1870-1915. 5/8". Mint(-) (9.0). Price: $12. CyberAuction #430, Lot #44.

4274. OTHER HANDMADE. Mica. Blue mica. Gorgeous. Tiny melt spot. Germany, circa 1870-1915. 19/32". Mint(-) (9.1). There are two marbles available. You are bidding on one. Winner has choice of either or both, remainder to under. Price: $12. CyberAuction #432, Lot #9.

4275. OTHER HANDMADE. Mica. Clear mica. Germany, circa 1870-1915. 1/2". Mint (9.9). Price: $12. CyberAuction #439, Lot #33.

4276. OTHER HANDMADE. Mica. Gorgeous clear mica. Germany, circa 1870-1915. 11/16". Mint (9.8). Price: $12. CyberAuction #448, Lot #12.

4277. OTHER HANDMADE. Mica. Emerald green mica. Gorgeous. Germany, circa 1870-1915. 5/8". Mint (9.9). There are three marbles avail, you are bidding on one. Winner has choice of any or all, remainder to under. Price: $12. CyberAuction #485, Lot #12.

4278. OTHER HANDMADE. Mica. Emerald green mica. Germany, circa 1870-1915. 5/8". Mint (9.7). Price: $12. CyberAuction #486, Lot #35.

4279. OTHER HANDMADE. Mica. Clear mica. Very nice. Germany, circa 1870-1915. 5/8". Mint (9.8). Price: $12. CyberAuction #489, Lot #21.

4280. OTHER HANDMADE. Mica. Emerald green mica. Mica core and mica subsurface layer. Germany, circa 1870-1915. 5/8". Mint (9.9). Price: $12. CyberAuction #508, Lot #56.

4281. OTHER HANDMADE. Mica. Small blue mica. Very nice. Germany, circa 1870-1915. 1/2". Mint (9.8). Price: $11. CyberAuction #342, Lot #9.

4282. OTHER HANDMADE. Mica. Green mica. One tiny chip. Germany, circa 1870-1915. 19/32". Near Mint(+) (8.9). Price: $11. CyberAuction #346, Lot #55.

4283. OTHER HANDMADE. Mica. Light green mica. Nice layer of mica. Small chip, tiny subsurface moon. Germany, circa 1870-1915. 27/32". Near Mint (8.6). Price: $11. CyberAuction #358, Lot #57.

4284. OTHER HANDMADE. Mica. Blue mica. Small. Slightly flattened. Germany, circa 1870-1915. 17/32". Mint (9.7). Price: $11. CyberAuction #360, Lot #11.

4285. OTHER HANDMADE. Mica. Light blue mica. Some tiny chips and haze. Germany, circa 1870-1915. 25/32". Near Mint(-) (8.0). Price: $11. CyberAuction #370, Lot #46.

4286. OTHER HANDMADE. Mica. Clear mica. Very nice. Germany, circa 1870-1915. 17/32". Mint (9.7). There are five marbles available, you are bidding on one. Winner has choice of any or all, remainder to under. Price: $11. CyberAuction #384, Lot #53.

4287. OTHER HANDMADE. Mica. Clear mica. Germany, circa 1870-1915. 19/32". Mint (9.9). Price: $11. CyberAuction #415, Lot #12.

4288. OTHER HANDMADE. Mica. Blue mica. Germany, circa 1870-1915. 17/32". Mint (9.7). Price: $11. CyberAuction #465, Lot #41.

4289. OTHER HANDMADE. Mica. Blue mica. Some surface debris. Germany, circa 1870-1915. 19/32". Mint(-) (9.0). Price: $11. CyberAuction #474, Lot #13.

4290. OTHER HANDMADE. Mica. Very dark green mica. Germany, circa 1870-1915. 19/32". Mint (9.9). Price: $11. CyberAuction #476, Lot #34.

4291. OTHER HANDMADE. Mica. Germany, circa 1870-1915. 1/2". Mint (9.9). Price: $11. CyberAuction #482, Lot #9.

4292. OTHER HANDMADE. Mica. Green mica. Nice marble. Tiny chip. Germany, circa 1870-1915. 21/32". Near Mint (8.9). There are two examples available, you are bidding on one. Winner has choice of either or both, remainder to under. Price: $11. CyberAuction #495, Lot #17.

4293. OTHER HANDMADE. Mica. Clear mica. Small melt chip. Germany, circa 1870-1915. 5/8". Mint (-) (9.1). Price: $11. CyberAuction #501, Lot #12.

4294. OTHER HANDMADE. Mica. Clear mica. Gorgeous mica core and mica subsurface layer. Germany, circa 1870-1915. 9/16". Mint (9.6). Price: $10. CyberAuction #333, Lot #3.

4295. OTHER HANDMADE. Mica. Clear mica. From near an end of the cane. Partial cloud core. One small rough spot. Germany, circa 1870-1915. 19/32". Near Mint(+) (8.8). Price: $10. CyberAuction #347, Lot #4.

4296. OTHER HANDMADE. Mica. Blue mica. Ghost core. The surface has some pits and very tiny chips. Germany, circa 1870-1915. 21/32". Near Mint (8.6). Price: $10. CyberAuction #349, Lot #14.

4297. OTHER HANDMADE. Mica. Small, very dark green mica. Very nice marble. Two small subsurface moons. Germany, circa 1870-1915. 17/32". Near Mint (8.6). Price: $10. CyberAuction #353, Lot #11.

4298. OTHER HANDMADE. Mica. Blue mica. Some tiny chips. Germany, circa 1870-1915. 1/2". Near Mint (8.3). Price: $10. CyberAuction #372, Lot #38.

4299. OTHER HANDMADE. Mica. Clear mica. Germany, circa 1870-1915. 9/16". Mint (9.7). There are three marbles available, you are bidding on one. Winner has choice of any or all, remainder to under. Price: $10. CyberAuction #387, Lot #5.

4300. OTHER HANDMADE. Mica. Blue mica. A couple of tiny chips. Germany, circa 1870-1915. 5/8". Near Mint (8.6). There are four marbles available. You are bidding on one. Winner has choice of any or all, remainder to under. Price: $10. CyberAuction #389, Lot #6.

4301. OTHER HANDMADE. Mica. Clear mica. Ghost core with mica. Nice subsurface layer of mica. Two melt spots. Germany, circa 1870-1915. 5/8". Mint(-) (9.0). Price: $10. CyberAuction #396, Lot #47.

4302. OTHER HANDMADE. Mica. Dark green mica. Very nice. Germany, circa 1870-1915. 9/16". Mint (9.6). Price: $10. CyberAuction #410, Lot #53.

4303. OTHER HANDMADE. Mica. Clear mica. Big flakes of mica. One pit. Germany, circa 1870-1915. 19/32". Mint (9.3). Price: $10. CyberAuction #434, Lot #48.

4304. OTHER HANDMADE. Mica. Clear mica. Ghost core with burnt mica flakes on it. Subsurface mica layer. Interesting marble. One melt pit. Germany, circa 1870-1915. 25/32". Mint (9.5). Price: $10. CyberAuction #442, Lot #16.

4305. OTHER HANDMADE. Mica. Clear mica. Germany, circa 1870-1915. 1/2". Mint (9.9). Price: $10. CyberAuction #444, Lot #11.

4306. OTHER HANDMADE. Mica. Emerald green. Some tiny chips. Germany, circa 1870-1915. 11/16". Near Mint(+) (8.7). There are seven marbles available, you are bidding on one. Winner has choice of any or all, remainder to under. Price: $10. CyberAuction #463, Lot #28.

4307. OTHER HANDMADE. Mica. Light green mica. Very nice. From near an end of the cane. One sparkle. Germany, circa 1870-1915. 25/32". Mint(-) (9.0). Price: $10. CyberAuction #464, Lot #15.

4308. OTHER HANDMADE. Mica. Brown mica. Mica core and subsurface layer. Small chip. Germany, circa 1870-1915. 3/4". Near Mint(+) (8.7). Price: $10. CyberAuction #477, Lot #41.

4309. OTHER HANDMADE. Mica. Blue mica. One tiny chip. Germany, circa 1870-1915. 3/4". Near Mint(+) (8.9). Price: $10. CyberAuction #477, Lot #45.

4310. OTHER HANDMADE. Mica. Aqua mica. Beauty. Several tiny chips. Germany, circa 1870-1915. 11/16". Near Mint(+) (8.7). Price: $10. CyberAuction #477, Lot #56.

4311. OTHER HANDMADE. Mica. Transparent teal mica. Very nice. Several tiny rough spots. Germany, circa 1870-1915. 3/4". Near Mint(+) (8.9). Price: $10. CyberAuction #490, Lot #28.

4312. OTHER HANDMADE. Mica. Blue mica. One melt spot. Germany, circa 1870-1915. 9/16". Mint(-) (9.2). Price: $10. CyberAuction #493, Lot #47.

4313. OTHER HANDMADE. Mica. Emerald green. Some tiny chips. Germany, circa 1870-1915. 11/16". Near Mint(+) (8.7). There are five marbles available, you are bidding on one. Winner has choice of any or all, remainder to under. Price: $10. CyberAuction #494, Lot #19.

4314. OTHER HANDMADE. Mica. Emerald green mica. Nice mica core, slightly shrunken on one side. Germany, circa 1870-1915. 11/16". Mint (9.9). Price: $10. CyberAuction #495, Lot #29.

4315. OTHER HANDMADE. Mica. Blue mica. Nice mica flakes. One tiny area of pits. Germany, circa 1870-1915. 9/16". Mint(-) (9.0). Price: $9. CyberAuction #355, Lot #21.

4316. OTHER HANDMADE. Mica. Clear mica. Nice subsurface layer of mica. Filament core with some ghost bubbles. Germany, circa 1870-1915. 19/32". Mint (9.7). Price: $9. CyberAuction #440, Lot #44.

4317. OTHER HANDMADE. Mica. Cobalt blue mica. Deep cold roll line at one end. Germany, circa 1870-1915. 5/8". Mint (9.7). Price: $9. CyberAuction #491, Lot #24.

4318. OTHER HANDMADE. Mica. Emerald green mica. One tiny chip. Two tiny melt chips. Germany, circa 1870-1915. 11/16". Near Mint(+) (8.7). Price: $9. CyberAuction #505, Lot #42.

4319. OTHER HANDMADE. Mica. Clear mica. Some small subsurface moons. Germany, circa 1870-1915. 25/32". Near Mint(-) (8.0). Price: $8. CyberAuction #331, Lot #49.

4320. OTHER HANDMADE. Mica. Blue mica. Nice mica layer. Some tiny chips. Germany, circa 1870-1915. 23/32". Near Mint (8.4). Price: $8. CyberAuction #355, Lot #7.

4321. OTHER HANDMADE. Mica. Clear mica. Big flakes of mica. One pit. Germany, circa 1870-1915. 19/32". Mint (9.3). Price: $8. CyberAuction #388, Lot #1.

4322. OTHER HANDMADE. Mica. Clear mica. Some surface debris. Germany, circa 1870-1915. 19/32". Mint(-) (9.0). Price: $8. CyberAuction #444, Lot #34.

4323. OTHER HANDMADE. Mica. Beautiful blue mica. Small chip. 5/8". Near Mint (8.6). Price: $8. CyberAuction #446, Lot #3.

4324. OTHER HANDMADE. Mica. Light green mica. Very pretty. One melt spot. Germany, circa 1870-1915. 5/8". Mint(-) (9.2). Price: $8. CyberAuction #485, Lot #18.

4325. OTHER HANDMADE. Mica. Emerald green. Some tiny chips. Germany, circa 1870-1915. 11/16". Near Mint(+) (8.7). There are seven marbles

available, you are bidding on one. Winner has choice of any or all, remainder to under. Price: $8. CyberAuction #488, Lot #3.

4326. OTHER HANDMADE. Mica. Clear mica. Germany, circa 1870-1915. 1/2". Mint (9.7). Price: $8. CyberAuction #500, Lot #8.

4327. OTHER HANDMADE. Mica. Emerald green. Some tiny chips. Germany, circa 1870-1915. 11/16". Near Mint(+) (8.7). There are six marbles available. Winner has choice of any or all, remainder to under. Price: $8. CyberAuction #506, Lot #19.

4328. OTHER HANDMADE. Mica. Brown shooter mica. Large chip, elongated large air hole, small chip, some haze. Germany, circa 1870-1915. 3/4". Good (7.5). Price: $7. CyberAuction #364, Lot #14.

4329. OTHER HANDMADE. Mica. Beautiful blue mica. Small chip. 5/8". Near Mint (8.6). There are five marbles available, you are bidding on one. Winner has choice of any or all, remainder to under. Price: $7. CyberAuction #380, Lot #30.

4330. OTHER HANDMADE. Mica. Brown shooter mica. Nice mica layer. Overall flakes and pits. Germany, circa 1870-1915. 13/16". Good (7.4). Price: $7. CyberAuction #420, Lot #7.

4331. OTHER HANDMADE. Mica. Very lightly tinted blue. Green filament core. Nice mica subsurface layer. Transparent dark green band on the surface. Melt spot and some pits. Germany, circa 1870-1915. 23/32". Near Mint(+) (8.9). Price: $7. CyberAuction #438, Lot #11.

4332. OTHER HANDMADE. Mica. Green mica. Shrunken mica core. Two tiny sparkles. Germany, circa 1870-1915. 17/32". Mint(-) (9.0). Price: $7. CyberAuction #442, Lot #15.

4333. OTHER HANDMADE. Mica. Brown mica. One tiny manufacturing chip on it. Germany, circa 1870-1915. 21/32". Mint(-) (9.0). Price: $7. CyberAuction #442, Lot #21.

4334. OTHER HANDMADE. Mica. Aqua mica. One pit. Germany, circa 1870-1915. 21/32". Mint(-) (9.2). Price: $7. CyberAuction #442, Lot #32.

4335. OTHER HANDMADE. Mica. Transparent teal mica. Very nice. Several tiny rough spots. Germany, circa 1870-1915. 3/4". Near Mint(+) (8.9). Price: $7. CyberAuction #462, Lot #16.

4336. OTHER HANDMADE. Mica. Brown mica. A couple of tiny chips. Germany, circa 1870-1915. 1/2". Near Mint (8.5). There are four examples available, you are bidding on one. Winner has choice of any or all, remainder to under. Price: $6. CyberAuction #416, Lot #32.

4337. OTHER HANDMADE. Mica. Green mica. Gorgeous color. Filament core. Several tiny chips. Germany, circa 1870-1915. 25/32". Near Mint (8.3). Price: $6. CyberAuction #458, Lot #52.

4338. OTHER HANDMADE. Mica. Light brown mica. Tiny chips. Germany, circa 1870-1915. 9/16". Near Mint (8.3). Price: $6. CyberAuction #482, Lot #11.

4339. OTHER HANDMADE. Mica. Blue mica. Very nice mica layer. A couple of tiny flakes. Germany, circa 1870-1915. 21/32". Near Mint(+) (8.7). Price: $6. CyberAuction #491, Lot #1.

4340. OTHER HANDMADE. Mica. Emerald green. Some tiny chips. Germany, circa 1870-1915. 11/16". Near Mint(+) (8.7). There are seven marbles available, you are bidding on one. Winner has choice of any or all, remainder to under. Price: $5. CyberAuction #461, Lot #18.

4341. OTHER HANDMADE. Mica. Clear mica. Ghost core. One melt spot. Germany, circa 1870-1915. 19/32". Mint(-) (9.0). Price: $5. CyberAuction #465, Lot #46.

4342. OTHER HANDMADE. Mica. Dark teal Mica. One small subsurface moon, one tiny moon. Germany, circa 1870-1915. 25/32". Near Mint(+) (8.7). Price: $5. CyberAuction #468, Lot #37.

4343. OTHER HANDMADE. Mica. Aqua mica. Several subsurface moons. 11/16". Near Mint(-) (8.2). Price: $5. CyberAuction #496, Lot #35.

4344. OTHER HANDMADE. Mica. Light brown mica. Tiny chips. Germany, circa 1870-1915. 9/16". Near Mint (8.3). Price: $4. CyberAuction #372, Lot #50.

4345. OTHER HANDMADE. Mica. Honey amber mica. Some tiny pits. Germany, circa 1870-1915. 9/16". Near Mint(+) (8.7). Three marbles available, you are bidding on one. Winner has choice of any or all, remainder to under. Price: $4. CyberAuction #463, Lot #6.

4346. OTHER HANDMADE. Mica. Clear mica. Area of unmelted sand on one side. Large annealing fracture over it. Germany, circa 1870-1915. 21/32". Near Mint(+) (8.3). Price: $4. CyberAuction #463, Lot #43.

4347. OTHER HANDMADE. Mica. Blue mica, large flakes. Some tiny chips. Germany, circa 1870-1915. 5/8". Near Mint(-) (8.0). Price: $4. CyberAuction #502, Lot #46.

4348. OTHER HANDMADE. Mica. Clear mica. Some pits and haze. Germany, circa 1870-1915. 11/16". Near Mint (8.4). Price: $3. CyberAuction #410, Lot #2.

4349. OTHER HANDMADE. Mica. Blue mica. Some tiny chips. Germany, circa 1870-1915. 19/32". Near Mint (8.6). There are three marbles available, you are bidding on one. Winner has choice of any or all, remainder to under. Price: $3. CyberAuction #417, Lot #14.

4350. OTHER HANDMADE. Mica. Brown mica. Almost yellowish. Haziness and small chips. Germany, circa 1870-1915. 9/16". Good(-) (7.2). Price: $3. CyberAuction #451, Lot #8.

4351. OTHER HANDMADE. Mica. Clear mica. Nice mica layer. Green core with mica on it. Some light haze. Germany, circa 1870-1915. 11/16". Near Mint (8.6). Price: $3. CyberAuction #461, Lot #7.

4352. OTHER HANDMADE. Mica. Clear mica. Stretched air bubbles inside. Small chip on top pontil. Germany, circa 1870-1915. 13/16". Near Mint(+) (8.9). Price: $3. CyberAuction #469, Lot #15.

4353. OTHER HANDMADE. Mica. Clear mica. Very nice layer of flakes. Germany, circa 1870-1915. 19/32". Mint (9.7). There are four marbles available, you are bidding on one. Winner has choice of any or all, remainder to under. Price: $2. CyberAuction #389, Lot #22.

4354. OTHER HANDMADE. Mica. Brown mica. Hazy with some pitting. Germany, circa 1870-1915. 9/16". Good(+) (7.9). There are six marbles available. You are bidding on one. Winner has choice of any or all, remainder to under. Price: $2. CyberAuction #428, Lot #20.

4355. OTHER HANDMADE. Mica. Light brown mica. Tiny chips. Germany, circa 1870-1915. 9/16". Near Mint (8.3). Price: $2. CyberAuction #451, Lot #28.

4356. OTHER HANDMADE. Mica. Brown mica. Hazy with some pitting. Germany, circa 1870-1915. 9/16". Good(+) (7.9). There are six marbles available. You are bidding on one. Winner has choice of any or all, remainder to under. Price: $1. CyberAuction #455, Lot #20.

4357. OTHER HANDMADE. Mica. Very lightly tinted blue mica. Overall tiny chips. Germany, circa 1870-1915. 21/32". Good(+) (7.9). Price: $1. CyberAuction #458, Lot #26.

4358. OTHER HANDMADE. Mica. Aqua mica. Several subsurface moons. 11/16". Near Mint(-) (8.2). Price: $1. CyberAuction #463, Lot #14.

4359. OTHER HANDMADE. Mica. Clear mica. Very lightly hazy, one tiny chip. Germany, circa 1870-1915. 1/2". Near Mint (8.1). Price: $1. CyberAuction #491, Lot #8.

4360. OTHER HANDMADE. Mist. Extremely rare large Mist marble. Stunning and gorgeous. Transparent clear base. Narrow translucent green and white core. Two bands of stretched bright red strands and bands on the surface, covering about twenty percent of the surface. Stunning. English, possibly German, circa 1870-1920. 1-3/16". Mint (9.6). Price: $385. CyberAuction #400, Lot #52.

4361. OTHER HANDMADE. Mist. Exceptional and very rare marble. Large Mist. Transparent clear base. Ghost core. Subsurface layer of transparent green stretched splotches and bands. Surface has four bands on it. One bright yellow, one partial white, two red bands. Surface is in exceptional shape. Incredible marble, very rare. Germany, circa 1870-1915. 1-3/16". Mint (9.9). Price: $300. CyberAuction #487, Lot #60.

4362. OTHER HANDMADE. Mist. Transparent clear base. Subsurface layer of stretched blue with a couple of opaque white strands on the surface. One sparkle. Very rare. Germany, circa 1870-1915. 1-3/16". Mint(-) (9.0). Price: $235. CyberAuction #403, Lot #56.

4363. OTHER HANDMADE. Mist. Transparent clear base. Subsurface layer of stretched blue with a couple of opaque white strands on the surface. One sparkle. Very rare. Germany, circa 1870-1915. 1-3/16". Mint(-) (9.0). Price: $235. CyberAuction #454, Lot #50.

4364. OTHER HANDMADE. Mist. Transparent clear base. Subsurface layer of stretched blue with a couple of opaque white strands on the surface. One sparkle. Very rare. Germany, circa 1870-1915. 1-3/16". Mint(-) (9.0). Price: $235. CyberAuction #478, Lot #45.

4365. OTHER HANDMADE. Mist. I've classified it as a Mist, although it is odd. Transparent light blue base. Surface is almost completely covered by a layer of stretched opaque white splotches and bands. One pit. Germany, circa 1870-1915. 3/4". Mint (9.7). Price: $120. CyberAuction #487, Lot #29.

4366. OTHER HANDMADE. Mist. I'm going to call it a panelled mist for lack of a better category. Transparent base. Two subsurface bands covering about forty percent. Both are translucent yellow. Rare. Pretty. Germany, possibly England, circa 1870-1915. 21/32". Mint (9.9). Price: $115. CyberAuction #371, Lot #34.

4367. OTHER HANDMADE. Mist. Very nice Mist. Transparent clear base. Subsurface layer of transparent green bands and strands. Two panels of opaque white stretched bands. Excellent example. Germany, circa 1870-1915. 5/8". Mint (9.9). Price: $95. CyberAuction #508, Lot #58.

4368. OTHER HANDMADE. Mist. Super marble. Transparent clear base. Subsurface layer of packed transparent cobalt blue strands and one opaque orange band. Some minor rubs. Germany, circa 1870-1915. 21/32". Mint(-) (9.1). Price: $85. CyberAuction #450, Lot #26.

4369. OTHER HANDMADE. Mist. Transparent clear base. Subsurface layer of translucent white and blue bands. One melt hole. Germany, circa 1870-1915. 11/16". Mint(-) (9.0). Price: $80. CyberAuction #403, Lot #47.

4370. OTHER HANDMADE. Mist. Outstanding example. Transparent clear base. Subsurface layer is transparent green with translucent blue and opaque white bands. Melt spot and a couple of tiny sparkles. Germany, circa 1870-1915. 3/4". Mint (9.8). Price: $75. CyberAuction #462, Lot #13.

4371. OTHER HANDMADE. Mist. Transparent clear base. Subsurface layer is transparent blue bands and opaque white strands. Beauty. Germany, circa 1870-1915. 11/16". Mint (9.8). Price: $60. CyberAuction #452, Lot #45.

4372. OTHER HANDMADE. Mist. Unusual two-panel mist. Transparent clear base. One subsurface panel of stretched opaque white, one subsurface panel of stretched transparent green. Colors cover about eighty percent of the marble. Very odd. Germany, circa 1870-1915. 9/16". Mint (9.9). Price: $60. CyberAuction #504, Lot #6.

4373. OTHER HANDMADE. Mist. Interesting marble. Transparent clear base. Filament core. Two panels of ghost air bubbles in a layer above it (with two clear panels). Two panels of semi-opaque yellow in a layer above that, mirroring the clear panels. One pit. Germany, circa 1870-1915. 27/32". Mint (-) (9.0). Price: $55. CyberAuction #369, Lot #37.

4374. OTHER HANDMADE. Mist. I guess you could call it either a mist or a very odd onionskin. Transparent base. Subsurface layer consists mostly of band of very fine air bubbles creating a silvery effect. There are several bands of translucent blue or mustard yellow. In great shape. Very odd marble. Germany, circa 1870-1915. 19/32". Mint (9.9). Price: $55. CyberAuction #375, Lot #29.

4375. OTHER HANDMADE. Mist. Transparent clear base. Subsurface layer of transparent green bands and mica. One large burnt mica piece too. One small chip. Germany, circa 1870-1915. 3/4". Near Mint(+) (8.9). Price: $55. CyberAuction #388, Lot #46.

4376. OTHER HANDMADE. Mist. Gorgeous. Transparent clear base. Subsurface layer of transparent blue bands and strands with a nice sprinkling of mica. One pit. Super example. Germany, circa 1870-1915. 11/16". Mint(-) (9.0). Price: $55. CyberAuction #406, Lot #40.

4377. OTHER HANDMADE. Mist. Transparent clear base. Subsurface layer of very light transparent blue with loads of mica. Some pinpricks. Germany, circa 1870-1915. 11/16". Mint(-) (9.0). Price: $55. CyberAuction #508, Lot #69.

4378. OTHER HANDMADE. Mist. Transparent clear base. Subsurface layer of stretch blue with lots of mica. One small subsurface moon. A beauty. Germany, circa 1870-1915. 11/16". Near Mint(+) (8.8). Price: $50. CyberAuction #396, Lot #3.

4379. OTHER HANDMADE. Mist. One of the oddest mists I've seen. Transparent very lightly blue tinted glass. Subsurface layer is broad bands of tiny ghost air bubbles. With some mica. Several pits. Germany, circa 1870-1915. 5/8". Near Mint(+) (8.8). Price: $50. CyberAuction #398, Lot #10.

4380. OTHER HANDMADE. Mist. One of the oddest mists I've seen. Transparent very lightly blue tinted glass. Subsurface layer is broad bands of tiny ghost air bubbles. With some mica. Several pits. Germany, circa 1870-1915. 5/8". Near Mint(+) (8.8). Price: $50. CyberAuction #430, Lot #14.

4381. OTHER HANDMADE. Mist. Transparent clear base. Subsurface layer of transparent blue bands. Some mica. One melt spot, near the top, one pinprick. Germany, circa 1870-1915. 21/32". Mint (-) (9.2). Price: $50. CyberAuction #500, Lot #50.

4382. OTHER HANDMADE. Mist. Fascinating marble. Transparent very light green base. Subsurface wispy band of stretched transparent blue. A surface band of opaque white and a surface band of opaque orange/yellow. One melt chip, one tiny sparkle. Germany, circa 1870-1915. 21/32". Mint (-) (9.0). Price: $45. CyberAuction #504, Lot #4.

4383. OTHER HANDMADE. Mist. One of the oddest mists I've seen. Transparent very lightly blue tinted glass. Subsurface layer is broad bands of tiny ghost air bubbles. With some mica. Several pits. Germany, circa 1870-1915. 5/8". Near Mint(+) (8.8). Price: $42. CyberAuction #388, Lot #39.

4384. OTHER HANDMADE. Mist. Interesting. Transparent clear base. Large ghost core. Subsurface layer of transparent blue bands. A narrow yellow strand and a narrow white strand on the surface. Unground nub as the bottom pontil. Germany, circa 1870-1915. 19/32". Mint (9.8). Price: $37. CyberAuction #398, Lot #6.

4385. OTHER HANDMADE. Mist. Very odd mist. Transparent green base. Blue and white strands form a core. The outer layer is transparent blue bands subsurface on one side, and stretched opaque white and yellow bands on the surface on the other side. Small melt hole on the mist side. Germany, circa 1870-1915. 11/16". Mint(-) (9.0). Price: $37. CyberAuction #498, Lot #4.

4386. OTHER HANDMADE. Mist. Transparent clear base. Subsurface layer is some transparent green bands and opaque white strands. One small chip. Germany, circa 1870-1915. 19/32". Near Mint (8.5). Price: $36. CyberAuction #394, Lot #41.

4387. OTHER HANDMADE. Mist. Transparent clear base. Subsurface layer is some transparent green bands and opaque white strands. One small chip. Germany, circa 1870-1915. 19/32". Near Mint (8.5). Price: $36. CyberAuction #422, Lot #21.

4388. OTHER HANDMADE. Mist. Transparent clear base. Transparent narrow blue core. Two subsurface panels of translucent white. Germany, circa 1870-1915. 19/32". Mint (9.9). Price: $32. CyberAuction #369, Lot #14.

4389. OTHER HANDMADE. Mist. Transparent clear base. Subsurface layer of blue and white stretched bands and strands. The blue is translucent. One flake. Very nice. Germany, circa 1870-1915. 5/8". Near Mint(+) (8.7). Price: $32. CyberAuction #395, Lot #20.

4390. OTHER HANDMADE. Mist. Transparent clear base. Three subsurface panels. One blue, one white, one pink. A couple of subsurface moons. Germany, circa 1870-1915. 11/16". Good(+) (7.7). Price: $22. CyberAuction #411, Lot #53.

4391. OTHER HANDMADE. Mist. Unusual marble. Transparent clear base. Single white strand in the center. Middle layer is a layer of transparent light blue. Two bands on the surface. White strands for one and light yellow for the other. Tiny chip and tiny subsurface moon. Germany, circa 1870-1915. 1/2". Near Mint (8.6). Price: $11. CyberAuction #428, Lot #54.

4392. OTHER HANDMADE. Moonie. Two pontil handmade moonie. Opalescent semi-opaque white base. Surface has overall spider web crazing on it. This is intentional. Very unusual. Two tiny sparkles. Germany, circa 1870-1915. 9/16". Mint(-) (9.0). Price: $47. CyberAuction #429, Lot #1.

4393. OTHER HANDMADE. Opaque. Opaque dark green two-pontil marble. Odd color. Big. One tiny subsurface moon. Germany, possibly American, circa 1860-1920. 7/8". Near Mint(+) (8.9). Price: $140. CyberAuction #347, Lot #59.

4394. OTHER HANDMADE. Opaque. Two-pontil handmade marble. Semi-opaque opalescent green marble. Hard to find this type. Germany, circa 1870-1915. 21/32". Mint (9.7). Price: $80. CyberAuction #452, Lot #8.

4395. OTHER HANDMADE. Opaque. Very rare example. Semi-opaque white interior. Thick clear outer layer. Two-pontil. Very hard to find. A couple of pinpricks. Germany, possibly American, circa 1870-1915. 5/8". Mint(-) (9.2). Price: $75. CyberAuction #492, Lot #30.

4396. OTHER HANDMADE. Opaque. Fluorescent Vaseline yellow two-pontil handmade semi-opaque marble. Small flake and a couple of subsurface moons. Germany, circa 1870-1195. 3/4". Near Mint (8.5). Price: $73. CyberAuction #356, Lot #30.

4397. OTHER HANDMADE. Opaque. Opaque dark green two-pontil marble. Odd color. Big. One tiny subsurface moon. Germany, possibly

American, circa 1860-1920. 7/8". Near Mint(+) (8.9). Price: $70. CyberAuction #470, Lot #33.

4398. OTHER HANDMADE. Opaque. Semi-opaque blue two-pontil marble. In great shape. Superb. Germany, possibly American, circa 1870-1915. 25/32". Mint (9.6). Price: $56. CyberAuction #347, Lot #53.

4399. OTHER HANDMADE. Opaque. Translucent two-pontil handmade moonie with a ghost core. Opalescent white glass. Harder to find than the marble in Lot #3 of this auction. Germany, possibly American, circa 1870-1915. 17/32". Mint (9.9). Price: $55. CyberAuction #400, Lot #37.

4400. OTHER HANDMADE. Opaque. Semi-opaque rose pink marble. Two pontils. Rare. One tiny blown air hole. Super example. Germany, possibly American, circa 1870-1920. 23/32". Mint (9.4). Price: $55. CyberAuction #467, Lot #3.

4401. OTHER HANDMADE. Opaque. Opaque two-pontil light green marble. Has one tiny chip. Germany, circa 1870-1915. 11/16". Near Mint(+) (8.9). Price: $47. CyberAuction #356, Lot #46.

4402. OTHER HANDMADE. Opaque. Rare marble. Two-pontil opaque white marble. The base glass is actually satin glass, with a glazed exterior. The top pontil area is missing the glaze and you can see the satin glass. Gorgeous. Germany, circa 1870-1915. 19/32". Mint (9.9). Price: $42. CyberAuction #357, Lot #54.

4403. OTHER HANDMADE. Opaque. Very rare example. Semi-opaque white interior. Thick clear outer layer. Two-pontil. Very hard to find. A couple of pinpricks. Germany, possibly American, circa 1870-1915. 5/8". Mint(-) (9.2). Price: $42. CyberAuction #462, Lot #33.

4404. OTHER HANDMADE. Opaque. Actually a semi-opaque. Rare handmade "moonie". Two pontil semi-opaque opalescent marble. Beauty. The bottom pontil is ground. Germany, circa 1870-1915. 9/16". Mint (9.9). Price: $40. CyberAuction #336, Lot #14.

4405. OTHER HANDMADE. Opaque. Pale yellow two-pontil handmade marble. Appears to have a ruddy pink core. Slightly out of round. Germany, circa 1870-1915. 25/32". Mint(-) (9.2). Price: $40. CyberAuction #419, Lot #23.

4406. OTHER HANDMADE. Opaque. Opaque dark green two-pontil marble. Odd color. Big. One tiny subsurface moon. Germany, possibly American, circa 1860-1920. 7/8". Near Mint(+) (8.9). Price: $35. CyberAuction #440, Lot #56.

4407. OTHER HANDMADE. Opaque. Semi-opaque two-pontil rose colored marble. Some tiny pits. Germany, possibly American, circa 1870-1915. 11/16". Near Mint(+) (8.9). Price: $34. CyberAuction #345, Lot #37.

4408. OTHER HANDMADE. Opaque. Very interesting slate green/blue opaque. Very odd color. Two pontil. Several small and tiny subsurface moons. Germany, circa 1870-1915. 3/4". Near Mint (8.3). Price: $34. CyberAuction #354, Lot #41.

4409. OTHER HANDMADE. Opaque. Two pontil blue opaque. Germany, circa 1870-1915. 21/32". Mint (9.8). Price: $33. CyberAuction #354, Lot #46.

4410. OTHER HANDMADE. Opaque. Very unusual marble. End of cane semi-opaque. Bottom two-thirds are a cloudy semi-opaque white. Top third is a translucent white. Almost has a satin glass look to it. Very odd. Germany, possibly American, circa 1870-1915. 9/16". Mint (9.7). Price: $32. CyberAuction #374, Lot #54.

4411. OTHER HANDMADE. Opaque. Semi-opaque two-pontil handmade moonie. Opalescent white glass with unmelted sand in it. Hard to find. Germany, possibly American, circa 1870-1915. 9/16". Mint (9.9). Price: $32. CyberAuction #400, Lot #3.

4412. OTHER HANDMADE. Opaque. Opaque light blue opaque two-pontil. Beauty. A couple of tiny sparkles. Germany, circa 1870-1915. 25/32". Mint(-) (9.1). Price: $31. CyberAuction #366, Lot #37.

4413. OTHER HANDMADE. Opaque. Gorgeous dark pink opaque handmade. Polished, pontils are missing. Rare color, especially for the size. Germany, possibly American, circa 1870-1915. 1-5/8". Mint. Price: $30. CyberAuction #427, Lot #18.

4414. OTHER HANDMADE. Opaque. Semi-opaque opalescent rose pink two-pontil marble. One tiny chip. Beauty. Hard color to find. Germany, possibly American, circa 1880-1920. 5/8". Near Mint(+) (8.9). Price: $29. CyberAuction #377, Lot #48.

4415. OTHER HANDMADE. Opaque. Semi-opaque rose two-pontil marble. Hard color to find. Germany, possibly American, circa 1860-1920. 19/32". Mint (9.8). Price: $26. CyberAuction #330, Lot #46.

4416. OTHER HANDMADE. Opaque. Semi-opaque blue. Several tiny chips. Germany, circa 1870-1915. 3/4". Near Mint (8.5). Price: $25. CyberAuction #373, Lot #20.

4417. OTHER HANDMADE. Opaque. Semi-opaque two-pontil rose colored marble. Some tiny subsurface moons. Germany, possibly American, circa 1870-1915. 11/16". Near Mint(+) (8.7). Price: $21. CyberAuction #348, Lot #32.

4418. OTHER HANDMADE. Opaque. Semi-opaque various shaded bands of white. One melt spot. Two pontils. Very nice. Germany, circa 1870-1915. 5/8". Mint(-) (9.2). Price: $21. CyberAuction #357, Lot #40.

4419. OTHER HANDMADE. Opaque. Nice two-pontil opaque. Semi-opaque light blue. Gorgeous. One sparkle and some melted dirt. Germany, circa 1870-1915. 23/32". Near Mint(+) (8.9). Price: $13. CyberAuction #357, Lot #25.

4420. OTHER HANDMADE. Opaque. White translucent. Lots of unmelted sand in it. One rough spot, two tiny subsurface moons. Germany, circa 1870-1915. 13/16". Near Mint(+) (8.7). Price: $13. CyberAuction #371, Lot #7.

4421. OTHER HANDMADE. Opaque. Handmade white opaque. Odd because it is various shades of white. Not a ballot box marble. Two-pontil.

4422. OTHER HANDMADE. Opaque. Light blue two-pontil handmade opaque. Some light pitting on the surface. Large. Germany, possibly American, circa 1880-1920. 27/32". Near Mint (8.4). Price: $12. CyberAuction #430, Lot #17.

4423. OTHER HANDMADE. Opaque. Handmade white opaque. Odd because it is various shades of white. Not a ballot box marble. Two-pontil. One melt hole. Germany, circa 1870-1920. 19/32". Near Mint (9.5). Price: $12. CyberAuction #446, Lot #18.

4424. OTHER HANDMADE. Opaque. Light blue two-pontil handmade opaque. Some light pitting on the surface. Large. Germany, possibly American, circa 1880-1920. 27/32". Near Mint (8.4). Price: $11. CyberAuction #398, Lot #8.

4425. OTHER HANDMADE. Opaque. Two-pontil semi-opaque white marble. Germany, circa 1870-1915. 9/16". Mint (9.8). There are two marbles available, you are bidding on one. Winner has choice of either or both, remainder to under. Price: $7. CyberAuction #439, Lot #51.

4426. OTHER HANDMADE. Opaque. Two-pontil white handmade marble. Ballot box. Germany or American, circa 1870-1920. 9/16". Mint (9.7). There are seven marbles available, you are bidding on one. Winner has choice of any or all, remainder to under. Price: $4. CyberAuction #392, Lot #28.

4427. OTHER HANDMADE. Opaque. Opaque black two-pontil ballot box marble. Germany, circa 1870-1915. 9/16". Mint (9.8). Price: $3. CyberAuction #446, Lot #4.

4428. OTHER HANDMADE. Opaque. Opaque black two-pontil ballot box marble. Germany, circa 1870-1915. 9/16". Mint (9.8). Price: $2. CyberAuction #379, Lot #16.

4429. OTHER HANDMADE. Paper mache. Very rare marble. Paper mache marble. Repeating lightning bolt design of green, red, black and yellow. A small crack, typical of this type. Very rare!!! Probably Germany, circa 1850-1900. 3/4". Mint (9.7). Price: $365. CyberAuction #339, Lot #59.

4430. OTHER HANDMADE. Paper mache. Very rare marble. Paper mache marble. Repeating lightning bolt design of green, red and yellow. A small crack, typical of this type. Very rare!!! Probably Germany, circa 1850-1900. 7/8". Mint(-) (9.2). Price: $350. CyberAuction #366, Lot #55.

4431. OTHER HANDMADE. Paper mache. Very rare marble. Paper mache marble. Repeating lightning bolt design of green, red and yellow. A small crack, typical of this type. Very rare!!! Probably Germany, circa 1850-1900. 7/8". Mint(-) (9.2). Price: $300. CyberAuction #330, Lot #57.

4432. OTHER HANDMADE. Paperweight. One of the rarest handmades you will find. A star-type paperweight marble. Transparent clear base. Design consists of chunks of color. Chunks are pink, red, green, yellow and white. Four-vane core, with the color going from the center to the surface. But, in between each vane is a smaller vane, creating a second vane pattern that does not quite go to the surface. When viewed from the top, it creates an eight point star design. Extremely rare, rarer than most paperweights of the vane type, which are rare to begin with. Surface is exceptional. Germany, circa 1860-1920. 1-3/16". Mint (9.6). Price: $1,500. CyberAuction #504, Lot #75.

4433. OTHER HANDMADE. Slag. This can either be classified as a handmade slag or a caramel swirl. Gorgeous transparent caramel brown glass with random swirls of opaque white. In great shape. Very rare. One tiny spot on the surface where so me white has flaked off. Germany, possibly American, circa 1870-1910. 3/4". Mint (9.5). Price: $150. CyberAuction #479, Lot #52.

4434. OTHER HANDMADE. Slag. Dark purple glass with lots of lines of white. Rare design. In great shape. Germany, circa 1870-1915. 9/16". Mint (9.9). Price: $140. CyberAuction #373, Lot #28.

4435. OTHER HANDMADE. Slag. Rare marble. Opaque dark green with opaque white swirled in. Two pontil. One manufacturing chip. Hard marble to find. Germany, possibly American, circa 1880-1920. 11/16". Mint(-) (9.0). Price: $70. CyberAuction #374, Lot #52.

4436. OTHER HANDMADE. Slag. Dark transparent smoky gray base. Loads of white bands and strands in it and on it. Harder type to find. Two-pontil. Superb. Germany, possibly American, circa 1870-1915. 3/4". Mint (9.7). Price: $65. CyberAuction #421, Lot #54.

4437. OTHER HANDMADE. Slag. Handmade two-pontil slag. Black with white banding and swirl. Two very tiny chips, a tiny melt spot. Germany, circa 1870-1915. 11/16". Near Mint(+) (8.9). Price: $65. CyberAuction #487, Lot #11.

4438. OTHER HANDMADE. Slag. Two-pontil handmade slag. Opaque black with loads of white smeared in and on it. Germany, possibly American, circa 1870-1915. 11/16". Mint (9.8). Price: $51. CyberAuction #414, Lot #49.

4439. OTHER HANDMADE. Slag. Two-pontil handmade marble. Odd coloring. Translucent gray base with opaque white bands and swirls. Some tiny air holes and pinpricks. Germany, circa 1870-1915. 25/32". Mint(-) (9.0). Price: $32. CyberAuction #418, Lot #43.

4440. OTHER HANDMADE. Slag. Opaque very dark purple with white mixed in. Surface has some pits and pinpricks. Germany, circa 1870-1915. 29/32". Near Mint (8.4). Price: $22. CyberAuction #427, Lot #29.

4441. OTHER HANDMADE. Slag. Two pontil slag. Dark purple base with gray bands. Overall haze. German or American, circa 1870-1910. 29/32". Good (7.3). Price: $17. CyberAuction #401, Lot #27.

4442. OTHER HANDMADE. Slag. Two-pontil slag of dark brown and white. Heavily damaged. Germany, possibly American, circa 1870-1915. 1". Collectible. Price: $5. CyberAuction #389, Lot #15.

4443. OTHER HANDMADE. Slag. Two-pontil slag of dark brown and white. Heavily damaged. Germany, possibly American, circa 1870-1915. 1". Collectible. Price: $5. CyberAuction #447, Lot #7.

4444. OTHER HANDMADE. Slag. Two-pontil slag of dark brown and white. Heavily damaged. Germany, possibly American, circa 1870-1915. 1". Collectible. Price: $3. CyberAuction #492, Lot #7.

4445. OTHER HANDMADE. Slag. Two-pontil slag of dark brown and white. Heavily damaged. Germany, possibly American, circa 1870-1915. 1". Collectible. Price: $1. CyberAuction #466, Lot #28.

4446. OTHER HANDMADE. Submarine. Hard to find. Transparent dark purple base. Two bands on the surface covering about sixty percent of it. Each is a stretched white, yellow and pink. Two subsurface bands, under the open panels, of the same coloring. One sparkle. First that I have ever seen in purple glass!!! Germany, circa 1870-1915. 25/32". Mint(-) (9.0). Price: $550. CyberAuction #340, Lot #56.

4447. OTHER HANDMADE. Submarine. Larger version of the marble in Lot #26 in this auction. Transparent clear base. Subsurface panel of bright yellow, subsurface panel of gorgeous blue. One white band on the surface over the blue, two white bands on the surface over the yellow. Two tiny pits. Stunning. Germany, possibly Germany, circa 1870-1915. 29/32". Near Mint(+) (8.9). Price: $210. CyberAuction #491, Lot #41.

4448. OTHER HANDMADE. Submarine. Large submarine. From near an end of the cane. Transparent dark blue base. Two bands of stretched white strands and bands. One of those is partial. Two subsurface bands of the same coloring and style, set to mirror the spaces in the surface bands. Sparkle, two tiny subsurface moons, some very minor wear. Germany, circa 1870-1915. 31/32". Near Mint (8.6). Price: $165. CyberAuction #354, Lot #54.

4449. OTHER HANDMADE. Submarine. Very unusual. Transparent clear base. One wide band of stretched yellow, and one wide band of stretched white, with a little transparent clear green, covering about eighty percent of the surface. Through the two narrow open panels, you can see at the core a narrow band of stretched yellow and a narrow band of some stretched white, mirroring the open panels. Very intriguing. Germany, circa 1870-1915. 19/32". Mint (9.8). Price: $160. CyberAuction #354, Lot #56.

4450. OTHER HANDMADE. Submarine. For lack of a better categorization, I've called it a submarine. Transparent clear base. One subsurface panel of bright yellow. One subsurface panel of blue. Gorgeous and rare. Cold roll line. England, possibly Germany, circa 1870-1915. 9/16". Mint (9.7). Price: $90. CyberAuction #491, Lot #26.

4451. OTHER HANDMADE. Submarine. Very unusual example. Transparent clear base. Two wide subsurface panels of opaque white. The narrow clear spaces each have a band of transparent green deeper in the marble. Outstanding. One very tiny subsurface moon near the bottom pontil, otherwise undamaged and unused. Germany, circa 1870-1915. 21/32". Near Mint(+) (8.9). Price: $85. CyberAuction #420, Lot #25.

4452. OTHER HANDMADE. Submarine. A submarine of sorts, or perhaps a solid core swirl. Transparent clear base. Subsurface layer of bright yellow, covering half the marble. Superb. Germany, circa 1870-1915. 1/2". Mint (9.7). Price: $75. CyberAuction #481, Lot #58.

4453. OTHER HANDMADE. Submarine. I guess would categorize this as a type of submarine, or a type of mist? Transparent clear base. Two subsurface panels of stretched white. Germany, circa 1870-1915. 19/32". Mint (9.9). Price: $55. CyberAuction #505, Lot #40.

4454. OTHER HANDMADE. Submarine. Nice example. Transparent dark blue base. Two white bands on the surface. Two subsurface white bands, in the clear spaces. One blown-out air hole. Some very tiny pinpricking. Germany, circa 1870-1915. 21/32". Near Mint(+) (8.9). Price: $40. CyberAuction #463, Lot #30.

4455. OTHER HANDMADE. Submarine. A type of submarine. Transparent amethyst base. Ghost core. Two subsurface bands of stretched end of day white bands. The bands cover about sixty percent of the marble. One chip, one pit. Germany, circa 1870-1915. 5/8". Near Mint (8.4). Price: $36. CyberAuction #353, Lot #46.

4456. OTHER HANDMADE. Submarine. transparent blue base. Two white bands on the surface. One subsurface white band, inside one the clear panels. Other subsurface band is missing. One flake. Germany, circa 1870-1915. 5/8". Near Mint (8.6). Price: $35. CyberAuction #518, Lot #48.

4457. OTHER HANDMADE. Submarine. Transparent very light green base. Two surface bands, one yellow, one white. Two subsurface bands in the clear spaces, one yellow, one yellow and white. Overall tiny chips and haze. Germany, circa 1870-1915. 11/16". Good (7.5). Price: $19. CyberAuction #458, Lot #22.

4458. OTHER MACHINE MADE. Alley Agate. Shooter Alley Agate swirl. Orange swirls on white. Some flame tips. Gorgeous. American, circa 1935-1950. 3/4". Mint (9.9). Two nearly identical marbles available. Bidding on one. Winner has choice of either or both, remainder to under. Price: $23. CyberAuction #357, Lot #27.

4459. OTHER MACHINE MADE. Alley Agate. Two-color swirl. Light green on white. Nice swirling. 19/32". Mint (9.6). There are three marbles available, you are bidding on one. Winner has choice of any or all, remainder to under. Price: $2. CyberAuction #390, Lot #26.

4460. OTHER MACHINE MADE. Aventurine. Opaque green aventurine Very fiery. Probably Champion Agate. 1960s-1970s. 21/32". Mint (9.9). Price: $35. CyberAuction #333, Lot #12.

4461. OTHER MACHINE MADE. Aventurine. Solid opaque aventurine green marble. Dark green aventurine. Swirling pattern. Probably Champion Agate. These are hard to find. 21/32". Mint (9.9). Price: $35. CyberAuction #483, Lot #50.

4462. OTHER MACHINE MADE. Aventurine. Opaque white base with aventurine green swirls. Unidentified manufacturer, my guess is Champion or Alley. 5/8". Mint (9.5). Price: $17. CyberAuction #443, Lot #43.

4463. OTHER MACHINE MADE. Aventurine. Opaque white base with aventurine green swirls. Unidentified manufacturer, my guess is Champion or Alley. 5/8". Mint (9.9). Price: $15. CyberAuction #333, Lot #6.

4464. OTHER MACHINE MADE. Aventurine. Opaque white base with aventurine green swirls. Unidentified manufacturer, my guess is Champion or Alley. 5/8". Mint (9.9). Price: $15. CyberAuction #506, Lot #14.

4465. OTHER MACHINE MADE. Aventurine. Opaque white base with aventurine green swirls. Unidentified manufacturer, my guess is Champion or Alley. 9/16" Mint (9.9). Four marbles available, you are bidding on one. Winner has choice of any or all, remainder to under. Price: $14. CyberAuction #482, Lot #6.

4466. OTHER MACHINE MADE. Aventurine. Opaque white base with aventurine green swirls. Unidentified manufacturer, my guess is Champion or Alley. 5/8". Mint (9.9). Price: $13. CyberAuction #342, Lot #45.

4467. OTHER MACHINE MADE. Aventurine. Opaque white base with aventurine green swirls. Unidentified manufacturer, my guess is Champion or Alley. 5/8". Mint (9.5). Price: $11. CyberAuction #354, Lot #16.

4468. OTHER MACHINE MADE. Aventurine. Opaque white base with aventurine green swirls. Unidentified manufacturer, my guess is Champion or Alley. 19/32". Mint (9.9). Price: $11. CyberAuction #377, Lot #43.

4469. OTHER MACHINE MADE. Aventurine. Opaque white base with aventurine green swirls. Unidentified manufacturer, my guess is Champion or Alley. 9/16" Mint (9.9). Four marbles available, you are bidding on one. Winner has choice of any or all, remainder to under. Price: $11. CyberAuction #456, Lot #56.

4470. OTHER MACHINE MADE. Aventurine. Opaque white base with aventurine green swirls. Unidentified manufacturer, my guess is Champion or Alley. 5/8". Mint (9.9). Price: $10. CyberAuction #488, Lot #52.

4471. OTHER MACHINE MADE. Aventurine. Fiery aventurine green swirl in opaque white. Origin and age unknown. 21/32". Mint (9.9). Price: $10. CyberAuction #382, Lot #43.

4472. OTHER MACHINE MADE. Aventurine. Fiery aventurine green swirl in opaque white. Origin and age unknown. 21/32". Mint (9.9). Price: $10. CyberAuction #421, Lot #42.

4473. OTHER MACHINE MADE. Aventurine. Opaque white base with aventurine green swirls. Unidentified manufacturer, my guess is Champion or Alley. 5/8". Mint (9.9). Price: $10. CyberAuction #444, Lot #10.

4474. OTHER MACHINE MADE. Aventurine. Opaque white base with aventurine green swirls. Unidentified manufacturer, my guess is Champion or Alley. 5/8". Mint (9.9). Price: $10. CyberAuction #488, Lot #37.

4475. OTHER MACHINE MADE. Aventurine. Fiery green aventurine swirls on opaque white. Probably Champion Agate. 9/16". Mint (9.9). Price: $10. CyberAuction #508, Lot #46.

4476. OTHER MACHINE MADE. Aventurine. Probably Ravenswood, possibly Alley Agate. White base with blue swirls. Some thin dark aventurine swirls. One small flake. 29/32". Near Mint(+) (8.8). Price: $9. CyberAuction #369, Lot #21.

4477. OTHER MACHINE MADE. Aventurine. Fiery aventurine green swirl in opaque white. Origin and age unknown. 21/32". Mint (9.9). Price: $9. CyberAuction #460, Lot #55.

4478. OTHER MACHINE MADE. Aventurine. Fiery green aventurine swirls on white. American, circa 1950-1960. 9/16". Mint (9.8). Price: $8. CyberAuction #492, Lot #37.

4479. OTHER MACHINE MADE. Aventurine. Very light green base with transparent green swirls. Thin line of chunky black aventurine swirling the surface. Probably Heaton Agate. Some tiny chips. American, circa 1945-1955. 5/8". Near Mint (8.6). Price: $6. CyberAuction #372, Lot #39.

4480. OTHER MACHINE MADE. Bottle hanger. Bottle hanger bag. Advertises Ne-Hi Beverages. Poly bag contains fourteen Marble King catseyes. Probably produced by Marble King for the beverage company. 7" x 3" (sight). Mint (9.5). There are two bags available. You are bidding on one. Winner has choice of either or, remainder to under. Price: $17. CyberAuction #341, Lot #29.

4481. OTHER MACHINE MADE. Bottle hanger. Bottle hanger bag. Advertises Ne-Hi Beverages. Poly bag contains fourteen Marble King catseyes. Probably produced by Marble King for the beverage company. 7" x 3" (sight). Mint (9.5). There are two bags available. You are bidding on one. Winner has choice of either or, remainder to under. Price: $15. CyberAuction #394, Lot #11.

4482. OTHER MACHINE MADE. Bullet mold. Clearie. Made in a mold. Seamed with rough spot at either pole. Filled with air bubbles. Origin and age unknown. Two melt spots. 1-1/4". Mint(-) (9.0). Price: $21. CyberAuction #413, Lot #31.

4483. OTHER MACHINE MADE. Cairo Novelty. White, clear and pale blue swirl. Very nice. Couple of pinpricks. Cairo WV, circa 1945-1960. 21/32". Mint (9.3). Price: $13. CyberAuction #449, Lot #38.

4484. OTHER MACHINE MADE. Cairo Novelty. White, clear and pale blue swirl. Very nice. Couple of pinpricks. Cairo WV, circa 1945-1960. 21/32". Mint (9.3). Price: $3. CyberAuction #388, Lot #5.

4485. OTHER MACHINE MADE. Catseye. Nine vane catseye. Transparent clear base. Three yellow, three red and three green bands in the core. In great shape. Very well formed! Origin and age unknown. 5/8". Mint (9.9). Price: $13. CyberAuction #388, Lot #16.

4486. OTHER MACHINE MADE. Catseye. Nine vane catseye. Transparent clear base. Three red, three blue and three white bands in the core. In great shape. Very well formed! Origin and age unknown. 5/8". Mint (9.9). Price: $12. CyberAuction #360, Lot #7.

4487. OTHER MACHINE MADE. Catseye. Nine vane catseye. Transparent clear base. Three yellow, three white and three white bands in the core. In great shape. Very well formed! Origin and age unknown. 5/8". Mint (9.9). Price: $10. CyberAuction #336, Lot #1.

4488. OTHER MACHINE MADE. Catseye. Nine vane catseye. Transparent clear base. Three yellow, three white and three light blue bands in the core. In great shape. Very well formed! Origin and age unknown. 5/8". Mint

(9.9). Two marbles available. You are bidding on one. Winner has choice of either or both, remainder to under. Price: $10. CyberAuction #342, Lot #27.

4489. OTHER MACHINE MADE. Catseye. Nine vane catseye. Transparent clear base. Three yellow, three white and three blue bands in the core. Alternating bands. In great shape. Origin and age unknown. 5/8". Mint (9.9). Price: $10. CyberAuction #349, Lot #59.

4490. OTHER MACHINE MADE. Catseye. Nine vane catseye. Transparent clear base. Three red, three white and three light blue bands in the core. Origin and age unknown. 5/8". Mint (9.9). Price: $8. CyberAuction #346, Lot #54.

4491. OTHER MACHINE MADE. Catseye. Nine vane catseye. Transparent clear base. Three red, three white and three light blue bands in the core. Origin and age unknown. 5/8". Mint (9.9). Price: $7. CyberAuction #347, Lot #40.

4492. OTHER MACHINE MADE. Catseye. Nine vane catseye. Transparent clear base. Three red, three white and three light blue bands in the core. Origin and age unknown. 5/8". Mint (9.9). Price: $7. CyberAuction #404, Lot #13.

4493. OTHER MACHINE MADE. Catseye. Nine vane catseye. Transparent clear base. Three red, three white and three light blue bands in the core. Origin and age unknown. 5/8". Mint (9.9). Price: $7. CyberAuction #441, Lot #1.

4494. OTHER MACHINE MADE. Catseye. Nine vane catseye. Transparent clear base. Three red, three white and three light blue bands in the core. Origin and age unknown. 5/8". Mint (9.9). Price: $7. CyberAuction #456, Lot #41.

4495. OTHER MACHINE MADE. Catseye. Nine vane catseye. Transparent clear base. Three yellow, three red and three green bands in the core. In great shape. Very well formed! Origin and age unknown. 5/8". Mint (9.9). Price: $6. CyberAuction #370, Lot #53.

4496. OTHER MACHINE MADE. Catseye. Nine vane catseye. Transparent clear base. Three yellow, three white and three light blue bands in the core. In great shape. Very well formed! Origin and age unknown. 5/8". Mint (9.9). Price: $6. CyberAuction #372, Lot #15.

4497. OTHER MACHINE MADE. Catseye. Nine vane catseye. Transparent clear base. Three red, three blue and three white bands in the core. In great shape. Very well formed! Origin and age unknown. 5/8". Mint (9.9). Price: $5. CyberAuction #369, Lot #48.

4498. OTHER MACHINE MADE. Catseye. Nine vane catseye. Transparent clear base. Three red, three blue and three white bands in the core. In great shape. Very well formed! Origin and age unknown. 5/8". Mint (9.9). Price: $5. CyberAuction #447, Lot #2.

4499. OTHER MACHINE MADE. Catseye. Nine vane catseye. Transparent clear base. Three red, three white and three light blue bands in the core. Origin and age unknown. 5/8". Mint (9.9). Price: $2. CyberAuction #474, Lot #14.

4500. OTHER MACHINE MADE. Catseye. Nine vane catseye. Transparent clear base. Three red, three white and three light blue bands in the core. Origin and age unknown. 5/8". Mint (9.9). Price: $2. CyberAuction #494, Lot #17.

4501. OTHER MACHINE MADE. Champion Agate. Very hard to find furnace scraping marble. This is the much harder to find transparent brown, opaque blue and opaque bright yellow. Great colors and pattern. Tiny annealing fracture. American, 1975-1985. 5/8". Mint(-) (9.1). There are three marbles available, you are bidding on one. Winner has choice of any or all, remainder to under. Price: $46. CyberAuction #444, Lot #53.

4502. OTHER MACHINE MADE. Champion Agate. Real nice marble. Flame type swirl. Semi-opaque white base with olive green swirls. Some nice flames. There are some metallic highlights to the swirl. Pennsboro, WV, circa 1945-1960. 5/8". Mint (9.8). Price: $37. CyberAuction #342, Lot #16.

4503. OTHER MACHINE MADE. Champion Agate. Coral and white swirls in very, very light green. Pennsboro, WV, circa 1940-1960. 11/16". Mint (9.7). Price: $23. CyberAuction #481, Lot #7.

4504. OTHER MACHINE MADE. Champion Agate. Coral and green swirl. Transparent green base, nice coral swirl. Silver metallic swirl on the surface too! Pennsboro, WV, 1950-1960. 9/16". Mint (9.9). There are two marbles available. You are bidding on one. Winner has choice of either or both, remainder to under. Price: $20. CyberAuction #377, Lot #1.

4505. OTHER MACHINE MADE. Champion Agate. Very interesting. Almost a furnace scraping marble. Transparent clear base. Swirl of bright red and bright yellow, with some wispy white. Pennsboro, WV, circa 1960-1980. 5/8". Mint (9.9). Price: $19. CyberAuction #377, Lot #10.

4506. OTHER MACHINE MADE. Champion Agate. Beautiful three-color swirl. White, deep blue, rich red. Pennsboro, WV, circa 1960-1975. 19/32". Mint (9.9). Price: $19. CyberAuction #421, Lot #51.

4507. OTHER MACHINE MADE. Champion Agate. Champion Agate swirl. Light green base, coral and mercury red swirls. Pennsboro, WV, circa 1945-1955. 19/32". Mint (9.6). Price: $19. CyberAuction #431, Lot #18.

4508. OTHER MACHINE MADE. Champion Agate. Champion Agate oxblood swirl. Opaque white base with clear swirls, transparent light green swirls and loads of "oxblood" swirls. Some folding. Pennsboro, WV, 1940-1960. 5/8". Mint (9.5). Price: $18. CyberAuction #346, Lot #11.

4509. OTHER MACHINE MADE. Champion Agate. Coral and green swirl. Transparent green base, coral swirl. Cold roll line. Pennsboro, WV, 1950-1960. 9/16". Mint (9.6). Price: $17. CyberAuction #335, Lot #22.

4510. OTHER MACHINE MADE. Champion Agate. Nice metallic stripe. Two-tone blue swirl, with silver metallic striping. Pennsboro, WV, circa 1980-1990. 9/16". Mint (9.9). Price: $17. CyberAuction #345, Lot #18.

4511. OTHER MACHINE MADE. Champion Agate. Coral and green swirl.

Transparent green base, nice coral swirl. Silver metallic swirl on the surface too! Pennsboro, WV, 1950-1960. 9/16". Mint (9.9). Price: $17. CyberAuction #383, Lot #9.

4512. OTHER MACHINE MADE. Champion Agate. Coral and green swirl. Transparent green base, nice coral swirl. Silver metallic swirl on the surface too! Pennsboro, WV, 1950-1960. 9/16". Mint (9.9). Price: $17. CyberAuction #422, Lot #4.

4513. OTHER MACHINE MADE. Champion Agate. Hard to find furnace scraping marble. Yellow and black swirls in transparent brown. Great colors and pattern. Tiny annealing fracture. American, 1975-1985. 5/8". Mint(-) (9.1). Price: $17. CyberAuction #462, Lot #17.

4514. OTHER MACHINE MADE. Champion Agate. Opaque white and transparent green swirl. "Oxblood" edging the green. Outstanding example of this type. Pennsboro, WV, circa 1940-1960. 5/8". Mint (9.7). Price: $17. CyberAuction #483, Lot #11.

4515. OTHER MACHINE MADE. Champion Agate. Coral and green swirl. Semi-opaque green with pink coral swirls. Pennsboro, WV, circa 1945-1960. 9/16". Mint (9.7). Price: $15. CyberAuction #373, Lot #3.

4516. OTHER MACHINE MADE. Champion Agate. Coral and green swirl. Transparent green base, nice coral swirl. Silver metallic swirl on the surface too! Pennsboro, WV, 1950-1960. 9/16". Mint (9.9). There are two marbles available. You are bidding on one. Winner has choice of either or both, remainder to under. Price: $15. CyberAuction #421, Lot #2.

4517. OTHER MACHINE MADE. Champion Agate. Marble is very similar to coral and green swirls. Orange base. Brown and yellow swirls. Excellent example, odd color combination. Pennsboro, WV, circa 1935-1955. 19/32". Mint (9.9). Price: $13. CyberAuction #501, Lot #47.

4518. OTHER MACHINE MADE. Champion Agate. Coral and green swirl. Transparent green. Very nice. Pennsboro, WV, circa 1945-1960. 19/32". Mint (9.8). Price: $12. CyberAuction #385, Lot #6.

4519. OTHER MACHINE MADE. Champion Agate. Coral and green swirl. Transparent green base, nice coral swirl. Silver metallic swirl on the surface too! Pennsboro, WV, 1950-1960. 9/16". Mint (9.9). Price: $12. CyberAuction #460, Lot #53.

4520. OTHER MACHINE MADE. Champion Agate. Coral and green swirl. Transparent green base, nice coral swirl. Silver metallic swirl on the surface too! Pennsboro, WV, 1950-1960. 9/16". Mint (9.9). Price: $12. CyberAuction #494, Lot #1.

4521. OTHER MACHINE MADE. Champion Agate. Coral and green swirl. Transparent green with pink coral swirls. Pennsboro, WV, circa 1945-1960. 9/16". Mint (9.8). Price: $10. CyberAuction #496, Lot #15.

4522. OTHER MACHINE MADE. Champion Agate. Coral and green swirl. Transparent green base, anemic coral swirl. Some pitting. Pennsboro, WV, 1950-1960. 9/16". Near Mint(+) (8.7). Price: $8. CyberAuction #337, Lot #2.

4523. OTHER MACHINE MADE. Champion Agate. Coral and green swirl. Transparent green base, coral swirl. Excellent example! Pennsboro, WV, 1950-1960. 9/16". Mint (9.9). Price: $8. CyberAuction #342, Lot #43.

4524. OTHER MACHINE MADE. Champion Agate. Coral and green swirl. Transparent green base, anemic coral swirl. Tiny flake and a couple of pits. Pennsboro, WV, 1950-1960. 9/16". Near Mint(+) (8.7). Price: $7. CyberAuction #337, Lot #31.

4525. OTHER MACHINE MADE. Champion Agate. Poly bag with four shooter catseyes. Label is red printing on white. Four packages available. You are bidding on one. Winner has choice of any or all, remainder to under. Price: $7. CyberAuction #361, Lot #34.

4526. OTHER MACHINE MADE. Champion Agate. Coral and green. Semi-opaque green base with swirls of various colored coral on it. One very tiny abraded spot. Pennsboro, WV, circa 1945-1960. 9/16". Near Mint(+) (8.9). Price: $7. CyberAuction #376, Lot #6.

4527. OTHER MACHINE MADE. Champion Agate. Coral and green. Anemic coral and transparent green. Pennsboro, WV, circa 1950-1965. 19/32". Mint (9.9). Price: $7. CyberAuction #389, Lot #38.

4528. OTHER MACHINE MADE. Champion Agate. Coral and green swirl. Transparent green base, nice coral swirl. Pennsboro, WV, 1950-1960. 9/16". Mint (9.9). Price: $7. CyberAuction #421, Lot #20.

4529. OTHER MACHINE MADE. Champion Agate. Swirl. Red and white swirls in light green transparent with unmelted silica. Pennsboro, WV, 1950-1960. 5/8". Mint (9.9). Price: $7. CyberAuction #473, Lot #3.

4530. OTHER MACHINE MADE. Champion Agate. Coral and green swirl. Translucent green base, anemic coral swirl. Some pitting and a tiny flake. Pennsboro, WV, 1950-1960. 9/16". Near Mint (8.6). Price: $6. CyberAuction #337, Lot #38.

4531. OTHER MACHINE MADE. Champion Agate. Transparent cranberry red base with some electric yellow swirls. New Old Fashioned. 19/32". Mint (9.9). Price: $6. CyberAuction #503, Lot #32.

4532. OTHER MACHINE MADE. Champion Agate. Coral and green swirl. Transparent green with pink coral swirls. Pennsboro, WV, circa 1945-1960. 9/16". Mint (9.8). Price: $5. CyberAuction #462, Lot #48.

4533. OTHER MACHINE MADE. Champion Agate. Coral and transparent green. Pennsboro, WV, circa 1950-1970. 19/32". Mint (9.7). Price: $5. CyberAuction #493, Lot #2.

4534. OTHER MACHINE MADE. Champion Agate. Brown base with black and ruddy yellow swirls. Very odd. Pennsboro, WV, circa 1940-1955. 19/32". Mint (9.9). Price: $5. CyberAuction #501, Lot #66.

4535. OTHER MACHINE MADE. Champion Agate. Blue swirl with silver metallic. 9/16". Mint (9.9). Price: $4. CyberAuction #361, Lot #58.

4536. OTHER MACHINE MADE. Champion Agate. I believe it is Champion Agate. Very nice. Translucent milky white and clear base. Swirls of translucent green and translucent brown. Pretty. Pennsboro, WV, circa 1940-1955. 5/8". Mint (9.7). Price: $3. CyberAuction #346, Lot #48.

537. OTHER MACHINE MADE. Champion Agate. New Old-Fashioned. Orange/red base with bright yellow swirls. American, circa 1975-1990. 19/32". Mint (9.7). There are three marbles available, you are bidding on one. Winner has choice of any or all, remainder to under. Price: $3. CyberAuction #387, Lot #34.

538. OTHER MACHINE MADE. Champion Agate. New Old-Fashioned. Bright yellow on orange. Pennsboro, WV, circa 1970-1980. 5/8". Mint (9.9). Price: $3. CyberAuction #489, Lot #26.

539. OTHER MACHINE MADE. Champion Agate. Coral and green swirl. Semi-opaque green with pink coral swirls. One sparkle. Pennsboro, WV, circa 1945-1960. 9/16". Near Mint(+) (8.9). Price: $2. CyberAuction #368, Lot #2.

540. OTHER MACHINE MADE. Champion Agate. Transparent clear base with an interesting swirl of blue/white. Pennsboro, WV, circa 1965-1980. 9/32". Mint (9.9). Price: $2. CyberAuction #382, Lot #25.

541. OTHER MACHINE MADE. Champion Agate. Champion Agate. White base with transparent green swirls. Green is edged by oxblood. Very nice. Tiny subsurface moon. Pennsboro, WV, circa 1945-1955. 5/8". Near Mint(+) (8.9). Price: $2. CyberAuction #405, Lot #47.

542. OTHER MACHINE MADE. Champion Agate. New Old Fashioned. Electric yellow swirls on bright orange/red. 19/32". Mint (9.7). Price: $1. CyberAuction #405, Lot #48.

543. OTHER MACHINE MADE. Champion Agate. New Old Fashioned. Red, yellow and white. Shooter. Pennsboro, WV, circa 1975-1985. 13/16". Mint (9.7). There are two marbles available, you are bidding on one. Winner has choice of either or both, remainder to under. Price: $1. CyberAuction #416, Lot #33.

544. OTHER MACHINE MADE. Champion Agate. Transparent green swirl in ruddy brown. 19/32". Mint (9.7). There are four marbles available, you are bidding on one. Winner has choice of any or all, remainder to under. Price: $.20. CyberAuction #461, Lot #1.

545. OTHER MACHINE MADE. Czechoslovakian. One of the Czechoslovakian Guineas. Very hard to find. Transparent brown base. Colored splotches on it. Two-seam. A couple of tiny pits. Czechoslovakia, circa 1930-1940. 17/32". Near Mint(+) (8.9). Price: $175. CyberAuction #433, Lot #55.

546. OTHER MACHINE MADE. Czechoslovakian. One of the Czechoslovakian Guineas. Very hard to find. Transparent green base. Colored splotches on it. Two-seam. Small dimple on it. Czechoslovakia, circa 1930-1940. 5/8". Near Mint(+) (8.7). This is the last of this group. Price: $110. CyberAuction #467, Lot #12.

547. OTHER MACHINE MADE. Czechoslovakian. One of the Czechoslovakian Guineas. Very hard to find. Transparent green base. Colored splotches on it. Two-seam. Small dimple on it. Czechoslovakia, circa 1930-1940. 5/8". Near Mint(+) (8.9). Price: $100. CyberAuction #452, Lot #50.

548. OTHER MACHINE MADE. Foreign sparkler. Foreign sparkler. Transparent clear base. Wide vane inside of white with some blue, green, yellow and orange. Very nice. Probably Germany or Holland, circa 1930s. 3/4". Mint (9.5). Price: $44. CyberAuction #418, Lot #12.

549. OTHER MACHINE MADE. Foreign sparkler. Foreign sparkler. Transparent clear base. Wide vanes of blue and white. Some cold rolling. 25/32". Mint(-) (9.0). Price: $12. CyberAuction #333, Lot #18.

550. OTHER MACHINE MADE. Foreign sparkler. Foreign sparkler. Transparent clear base. Wide vane inside of white with some blue and orange. A couple of sparkles on it. Very nice. Probably Germany or Holland, circa 1930s. 11/16". Mint(-) (9.0). Two virtually identical marbles available. You are bidding on one. Winner has choice of either or both, remainder to under. Price: $10. CyberAuction #371, Lot #37.

551. OTHER MACHINE MADE. Foreign sparkler. Nice example. Transparent clear base. Ribbon of green, white and oxblood red in it. Probably German and circa 1960s. 21/32". Mint (9.8). Price: $15. CyberAuction #506, Lot #33.

552. OTHER MACHINE MADE. Foreign sparkler. Clear base. Ribbon vane of white, blue and "oxblood". Some pits. European, circa 1930-1940. 19/32". Near Mint(+) (8.7). Price: $14. CyberAuction #351, Lot #43.

553. OTHER MACHINE MADE. Foreign sparkler. Transparent clear base. Vanes of white and light blue. Two manufacturing dimples. Nice example. European, age unknown. 21/32". Mint(-) (9.1). Price: $13. CyberAuction #375, Lot #26.

554. OTHER MACHINE MADE. Foreign sparkler. European variety. Transparent clear base. Wide vane of white, pale green, pale yellow and oxblood. One tiny melt spot. 11/16". Mint (9.5). Price: $12. CyberAuction #363, Lot #43.

555. OTHER MACHINE MADE. Foreign sparkler. Transparent clear base. Vanes of yellow, orange, white, red and light blue. Two manufacturing dimples. Nice example. European, age unknown. 11/16". Mint(-) (9.2). Price: $12. CyberAuction #369, Lot #3.

556. OTHER MACHINE MADE. Foreign sparkler. Nice example. Transparent clear base. Ribbon of green, white and oxblood red in it. Probably German and circa 1960s. 21/32". Mint (9.8). Price: $12. CyberAuction #462, Lot #31.

557. OTHER MACHINE MADE. Foreign sparkler. Nice example. Transparent clear base. Ribbon of green, white and oxblood red in it. Probably German and circa 1960s. 21/32". Mint (9.8). Price: $12. CyberAuction #490, Lot #9.

558. OTHER MACHINE MADE. Foreign sparkler. Clear base. Ribbon vane of white, yellow, light blue and "oxblood". A couple of pits. European, circa 1930-1940. 19/32". Near Mint(+) (8.9). Price: $8. CyberAuction #346, Lot #7.

559. OTHER MACHINE MADE. Foreign sparkler. Foreign sparkler. Transparent clear base. Wide vane inside of orange and white. Either Vacor or European. 11/16". Mint (9.7). Price: $8. CyberAuction #478, Lot #15.

560. OTHER MACHINE MADE. Foreign sparkler. Clear base. Ribbon vane of white, green, yellow, light blue and "oxblood". Has a fracture. European, circa 1930-1940. 23/32". Near Mint (8.6). Price: $6. CyberAuction #364, Lot #40.

561. OTHER MACHINE MADE. Foreign sparkler. Transparent clear base. Vanes of orange and white. Nice example. Either Mexican or European, age unknown. 21/32". Mint (9.5). Price: $5. CyberAuction #342, Lot #12.

562. OTHER MACHINE MADE. Foreign sparkler. Foreign sparkler. Transparent clear base. Wide vane inside of orange and white. Either Vacor or European. 11/16". Mint (9.7). Price: $3. CyberAuction #374, Lot #1.

563. OTHER MACHINE MADE. Foreign sparkler. Transparent clear base. Wide vane inside of orange and white. Either Vacor or European. 11/16". Mint (9.7). Price: $3. CyberAuction #453, Lot #49.

564. OTHER MACHINE MADE. German. German swirl. White and clear base. Swirls of lavender and light green. A couple of pits. Germany, circa 1960s. 27/32". Mint(-) (9.2). Price: $28. CyberAuction #401, Lot #55.

565. OTHER MACHINE MADE. German. Striped transparent. Transparent pale green base with bands of white stripes in and on the marble. Exhibits the two seam pattern, similar to Master Marble Company marbles. Germany, age unknown. 15/16". Mint (9.6). Price: $24. CyberAuction #332, Lot #48.

566. OTHER MACHINE MADE. German. German swirl. White and clear base. Swirls of lavender and light green. A couple of pits. Germany, circa 1960s. 27/32". Mint(-) (9.2). Price: $22. CyberAuction #437, Lot #51.

567. OTHER MACHINE MADE. German. German swirl. White and clear base. Swirls of lavender and light green. A couple of pits. Germany, circa 1960s. 27/32". Mint(-) (9.2). Price: $22. CyberAuction #478, Lot #30.

568. OTHER MACHINE MADE. German. German swirl. White and clear base. Swirls of lavender and light green. A couple of pits. Germany, circa 1960s. 27/32". Mint(-) (9.2). Price: $22. CyberAuction #499, Lot #30.

569. OTHER MACHINE MADE. German. Striped opaque. Opaque white base with bands of translucent electric red stripes on the marble. Exhibits the two seam pattern, similar to Master Marble Company marbles, that is typical of German machine mades. One air hole. Much harder to find than the transparent ones. Germany, age unknown. 5/8". Mint(-) (9.1). Price: $17. CyberAuction #436, Lot #39.

570. OTHER MACHINE MADE. German. Striped transparent. Transparent clear base with bands of opaque white stripes in and on the marble. Exhibits the two seam pattern, similar to Master Marble Company marbles, that is typical of German machine mades. Two tiny subsurface moons. Germany, age unknown. 31/32". Near Mint(+) (8.8). Price: $15. CyberAuction #375, Lot #17.

571. OTHER MACHINE MADE. German. German swirl. White and clear base. Narrow swirls of lavender and light green. Germany, circa 1960s. 23/32". Mint(-) (9.2). Price: $15. CyberAuction #401, Lot #43.

572. OTHER MACHINE MADE. German. Striped transparent. Transparent clear base with bands of opaque white stripes in and on the marble. Exhibits the two seam pattern, similar to Master Marble Company marbles, that is typical of German machine mades. Germany, age unknown. 15/16". Near Mint(+) (8.9). Price: $12. CyberAuction #337, Lot #15.

573. OTHER MACHINE MADE. German. Striped transparent. Transparent green base with bands of opaque white stripes on the marble. Exhibits the two seam pattern, similar to Master Marble Company marbles, that is typical of German machine mades. 3/4". Mint (9.7). Price: $12. CyberAuction #341, Lot #18.

574. OTHER MACHINE MADE. German. Striped transparent. Transparent amber base with bands of opaque white stripes in and on the marble. Exhibits the two seam pattern, similar to Master Marble Company marbles, that is typical of German machine mades. One tiny flake, some pinpricks. Germany, age unknown. 25/32". Near Mint(+) (8.8). Price: $10. CyberAuction #447, Lot #38.

575. OTHER MACHINE MADE. German. Striped transparent. Transparent amber base with bands of opaque white stripes in and on the marble. Exhibits the two seam pattern, similar to Master Marble Company marbles, that is typical of German machine mades. One tiny flake, some pinpricks. Germany, age unknown. 25/32". Near Mint(+) (8.8). Price: $8. CyberAuction #374, Lot #20.

576. OTHER MACHINE MADE. German. Interesting. Clear base. Four subsurface bands. One each of white, orange, green and yellow. A type of catseye. Pitting. Probably 1960s. 13/16". Near Mint (8.5). Price: $8. CyberAuction #401, Lot #23.

577. OTHER MACHINE MADE. German. Striped transparent. Transparent brown base with bands of opaque white stripes on the marble. Exhibits the two seam pattern, similar to Master Marble Company marbles, that is typical of German machine mades. Germany, age unknown. 5/8". Mint (9.9). Price: $7. CyberAuction #418, Lot #13.

578. OTHER MACHINE MADE. German. Striped transparent. Transparent green base with bands of opaque white stripes on the marble. Exhibits the two seam pattern, similar to Master Marble Company marbles, that is typical of German machine mades. Two tiny subsurface moons. Germany, age unknown. 3/4". Near Mint(+) (8.8). Price: $6. CyberAuction #379, Lot #17.

579. OTHER MACHINE MADE. German. German swirl. White and clear base. Swirls of lavender and light green. A couple of tiny chips. Germany, circa 1960s. 21/32". Mint (8.6). Price: $6. CyberAuction #402, Lot #48.

580. OTHER MACHINE MADE. German. Striped transparent. Transparent green base with bands of opaque white stripes in and on the marble. Exhibits the two seam pattern, similar to Master Marble Company marbles, that is typical of German machine mades. Germany, age unknown. 5/8". Mint (9.9). Price: $5. CyberAuction #419, Lot #57.

4581. OTHER MACHINE MADE. German. Striped transparent. White completely covering transparent clear. Two seam. Germany, circa 1960s. 11/16". Mint (9.7). Price: $5. CyberAuction #463, Lot #15.

4582. OTHER MACHINE MADE. German. Striped transparent. Transparent green base with bands of opaque white stripes on the marble. Exhibits the two seam pattern, similar to Master Marble Company marbles, that is typical of German machine mades. Two tiny subsurface moons. Germany, age unknown. 3/4". Near Mint(+) (8.8). Price: $4. CyberAuction #442, Lot #46.

4583. OTHER MACHINE MADE. German. Striped transparent. White completely covering transparent clear. Two seam. One pit. Germany, circa 1960s. 23/32". Mint(-) (9.0). Price: $3. CyberAuction #444, Lot #3.

4584. OTHER MACHINE MADE. German. Striped transparent. Transparent orange base with bands of opaque white stripes in and on the marble. Exhibits the two seam pattern, similar to Master Marble Company marbles, that is typical of German machine mades. Two roller gouges. Germany, age unknown. 5/8". Near Mint(+) (8.8). Price: $2. CyberAuction #424, Lot #6.

4585. OTHER MACHINE MADE. German. Striped transparent. Transparent green base with bands of opaque white stripes in and on the marble. Exhibits the two seam pattern, similar to Master Marble Company marbles, that is typical of German machine mades. Germany, age unknown. 5/8". Mint (9.9). Price: $2. CyberAuction #460, Lot #12.

4586. OTHER MACHINE MADE. German. Striped transparent. White completely covering transparent clear. Two seam. Germany, circa 1960s. 11/16". Mint (9.7). Price: $2. CyberAuction #461, Lot #22.

4587. OTHER MACHINE MADE. German. Striped transparent. White in transparent green. Two seam. Germany, circa 1960s. 11/16". Mint (9.7). Price: $2. CyberAuction #461, Lot #42.

4588. OTHER MACHINE MADE. German. Striped transparent. Transparent green base with bands of opaque white stripes in and on the marble. Exhibits the two seam pattern, similar to Master Marble Company marbles, that is typical of German machine mades. Germany, age unknown. 5/8". Mint (9.9). Price: $2. CyberAuction #494, Lot #27.

4589. OTHER MACHINE MADE. German. Striped transparent. Transparent clear base with bands of opaque white stripes in and on the marble. Exhibits the two seam pattern, similar to Master Marble Company marbles, that is typical of German machine mades. Some pinpricks. Germany, age unknown. 25/32". Near Mint(+) (8.9). Price: $1. CyberAuction #427, Lot #15.

4590. OTHER MACHINE MADE. German. Striped transparent. White completely covering transparent clear. Two seam. Some dimples. Germany, circa 1960s. 23/32". Mint(-) (9.0). Price: $1. CyberAuction #459, Lot #37.

4591. OTHER MACHINE MADE. Heaton Agate. Original poly bag. Very hard to find. Cardboard label. Front reads "30 BIG SHOT 5 cents". Back reads "CAT EYES / Heaton Agate Co., Pennsboro, W. Va.". Printing is red on white, numbers in black. Bag in very nice shape. Mint (9.5). Price: $23. CyberAuction #398, Lot #23.

4592. OTHER MACHINE MADE. Heaton Agate. Early Heaton Agate. Red swirls on white. Looks like a Christensen Agate flame. A couple of sparkles. American, circa 1935-1945. 11/16". Near Mint(+) (8.7). Price: $7. CyberAuction #479, Lot #44.

4593. OTHER MACHINE MADE. Heaton Agate. Early Heaton. Green/white base with dark blue swirl. One sparkle. West Virginia, circa 1945-1955. 5/8". Mint(-) (9.0). Price: $2. CyberAuction #346, Lot #50.

4594. OTHER MACHINE MADE. Jackson Marble Company. Jobber box of Jackson Marble Company patches. Red on white diamond pattern. Two oval cutouts. Contains about thirty 5/8" Jackson Marble Company two-color patches. White base, blue patch on one end, orange/red patch on other. Everything Mint. Price: $27. CyberAuction #410, Lot #29.

4595. OTHER MACHINE MADE. Metallic. Superb metallic. Rare type. I believe it is a Heaton Agate swirl. Mustard yellow base. Transparent orange flame swirls edged by black on one side and shiny silver metallic on the other. Super marble. American, circa 1945-1955. 21/32". Mint (9.9). Price: $100. CyberAuction #330, Lot #39.

4596. OTHER MACHINE MADE. Metallic. Probably Champion Agate. These are hard to find. Baby blue base with silver metallic floating on the surface. Might be Vitro. 7/8". Mint (9.9). Price: $51. CyberAuction #360, Lot #23.

4597. OTHER MACHINE MADE. Metallic. Champion Agate. Blue base with silver metallic swirl. Pennsboro, WV, circa 1985-1990. 17/32". Mint (9.9). Price: $6. CyberAuction #381, Lot #44.

4598. OTHER MACHINE MADE. Metallic. Blue swirls with metallic blue swirl on it. Very nice. Champion Agate. Pennsboro, WV, circa 1975-1990. 9/16". Mint (9.9). There are three marbles available, you are bidding on one. Winner has choice of any or all, remainder to under. Price: $6. CyberAuction #388, Lot #29.

4599. OTHER MACHINE MADE. Metallic. Blue swirls with metallic blue swirl on it. Very nice. Champion Agate. Pennsboro, WV, circa 1975-1990. 9/16". Mint (9.9). There are two marbles available, you are bidding on one. Winner has choice of any or all, remainder to under. Price: $6. CyberAuction #440, Lot #16.

4600. OTHER MACHINE MADE. Original package. Very rare. Cardboard box. Stamped on one side "Certified Set Official Tournament Marbles Selected and Packed by Bob Conlin 10 Hampden Street Springfield, Mass. Phone 4-5869". Other side is a label for Tastyeast. Contains an assortment of very early Champion Agates and dyed clays. About 4" x 4". Mint. There are two available, you are bidding on one. Winner has choice of one or both, remainder to under. Price: $110. CyberAuction #433, Lot #29.

4601. OTHER MACHINE MADE. Original package. Original cardboard box. "CODEG Glass Marbles" "15 Pieces" "Foreign". Three oval cutouts on

the other side with graphics of various marbles. Very thin cardboard. Contains fifteen marbles. All are the same. Transparent non-fluorescent yellow base with two opaque white ribbons. Similar to an Acme Realer, but these are German. Marbles are 11/16" and Mint. Box is about 3" x 2" x 11/16" and Mint. Rare. English, probably circa 1930s. Price: $80. CyberAuction #504, Lot #44.

4602. OTHER MACHINE MADE. Original package. Very rare jobber box. This is an English sleeve containing German wire pulls. This is only the second original boxed set of wire pulls I have ever seen, the only other was a Dutch game sold in the CyberAuctions several years ago. The sleeve has one oval cut out. Reads "6 Giant Dazzlers / Monster Size Coloured Glass Marbles / CODEG / Foreign". CODEG is an English toy company. Contains six 15/16" Wire Pulls, in various colors. Marbles are Mint. Box is about 6" 1" x 1" and Mint(-). Very rare. 1950s or 1960s. Box is England, marbles are German. Price: $75. CyberAuction #505, Lot #31.

4603. OTHER MACHINE MADE. Original package. Rare original box. Yellow and red graphics. Thin cardboard, one oval. Reads "10 PIECES DAZZLERS GLASS MARBLES FOREIGN" End flap has a logo for ELGEE reading "TRADE MARK L.G. LTD. B.HAM FOREIGN". Contains catseyes and a ribbboned. Marbles are Japanese, the box is a jobber from Birmingham England. Pretty hard to find. My guess is 1950s. Box is about 2-1/2" x 1-1/4" x 9/16". Mint. Marbles are 9/16" and Mint. There are three available in this condition. You are bidding on one. Price: $31 CyberAuction #507, Lot #27.

4604. OTHER MACHINE MADE. Original package. Rare original box. Yellow and red graphics. Thin cardboard, one oval. Reads "10 PIECES DAZZLERS GLASS MARBLES FOREIGN" on both sides. End flap has a logo for ELGEE reading "TRADE MARK L.G. LTD. B.HAM FOREIGN". Contains catseyes and a ribbboned. Marbles are Japanese, the box is a jobber from Birmingham England. Pretty hard to find. My guess is 1950s. Box is about 2-1/2" x 1-1/4" x 9/16". Mint(-). Marbles are 9/16" and Mint. Price: $30. CyberAuction #502, Lot #32.

4605. OTHER MACHINE MADE. Original package. Odd bag. Cheese cloth bag printed "Ajax Marble Co. 36-Marbles 1-Shooter Columbus OH 5cents". Contains 9/16" brown earthenware marbles and a 7/8" natural clay. Printing on bag is faded. Looks like 1930s, but I've never seen it before. Price: $25. CyberAuction #392, Lot #34.

4606. OTHER MACHINE MADE. Original package. Mesh bag. Orange label. "Starkey's Beverages" "Drink Klicker". Contains Vitros. Small tear in bag. 1940s. Near Mint (8.5). Price: $17. CyberAuction #413, Lot #29.

4607. OTHER MACHINE MADE. Original package. Rare original box. Yellow and red graphics. Thin cardboard, one oval. Reads "10 PIECES DAZZLERS GLASS MARBLES FOREIGN" on both sides. End flap has a logo for ELGEE reading "TRADE MARK L.G. LTD. B.HAM FOREIGN". Contains catseyes and a ribbboned. Marbles are Japanese, the box is a jobber from Birmingham England. Pretty hard to find. My guess is 1950s. Box is about 2-1/2" x 1-1/4" x 9/16". Mint(-). Marbles are 9/16" and Mint. Box has some taped edges. There are three available in this condition, you are bidding on one. Price: $14. CyberAuction #507, Lot #28.

4608. OTHER MACHINE MADE. Original package. Poly bag of shooter catseyes. Red header label reads "20 pcs Santa Claus Brand Japan" with picture of Santa on it. Contains red and green four-vane catseyes. Nice bag. Circa 1960s. Price: $12. CyberAuction #339, Lot #31.

4609. OTHER MACHINE MADE. Original package. Small cardboard jobber box. Looks just like the Buddy boxes (see Lot #1 in this auction), but has "MARBLES" printed twice. About 4" x 3" x 5/8". Contains about twenty Champion Agates. About 5/8" and Mint. In nice shape. Price: $11. CyberAuction #480, Lot #1.

4610. OTHER MACHINE MADE. Original package. Small blue cardboard jobber box. "30 Marbles" and white stars on it. About 4" x 3" x 5/8". Contains about twenty Champion Agates. About 5/8" and Mint. In nice shape. Price: $11. CyberAuction #480, Lot #2.

4611. OTHER MACHINE MADE. Original package. Small red cardboard jobber box. "10c Marbles" and white stars on it. About 5" x 3" x 5/8". Contains about twenty five Champion Agates. About 5/8" and Mint. In nice shape. Price: $11. CyberAuction #480, Lot #3.

4612. OTHER MACHINE MADE. Original package. Original package of "Camel Cat's Eye Marbles". Orange paper header. Cellophane package very hard to find type. Contains Japanese catseyes. About 5" x 3". Mint (9.8). Price: $11. CyberAuction #481, Lot #20.

4613. OTHER MACHINE MADE. Original package. "Big Nickel Special" box from J. Pressman. Contains about thirty 1940s-1950s marbles. Top flap is torn, but present. Some other very minor tears. Near Mint (8.5). Price: $9. CyberAuction #426, Lot #30.

4614. OTHER MACHINE MADE. Original package. "Big Nickel Special" box from J. Pressman. Contains about thirty 1940s-1950s marbles. Top flap is torn, but present. Some other very minor tears. Near Mint (8.5). Price: $8. CyberAuction #395, Lot #29.

4615. OTHER MACHINE MADE. Original package. Poly bag. Header label reads "Gladiola Marble Cake Mix". Contains Vitro Agate Conquerors. Nice older poly bag. Near Mint(+) (8.7). Price: $8. CyberAuction #412, Lot #13.

4616. OTHER MACHINE MADE. Original package. Poly bag of catseye shooters. Label is red white and blue. Reads "Containing 6 Assorted Empire Made Coloured Glass Marbles" "A CODEG Production". English bags. Marbles are probably from Hong Kong, probably 1960s. Near Mint. Very thin poly. There are five bags available, you are bidding on one. Winner has choice of any or all, remainder to under. Each bag has a small tear. An opportunity to obtain English jobber bags. Price: $7. CyberAuction #502, Lot #45.

17. OTHER MACHINE MADE. Original package. Empty original red Jc Marbles box. About 4 x 3" x 5/8". Mint (9.5). Price: $3. CyberAuction 347, Lot #29.

18. OTHER MACHINE MADE. Original package. Small cardboard jobber box. Buddy box. About 4" x 3" x 3/4". Empty. Some crushing. Near Mint(+). Price: $2. CyberAuction #480, Lot #4.

19. OTHER MACHINE MADE. Original package. Poly bag of "20 count ats Eye Champion Marbles". Interesting header label. No country of origin, but I suspect it is Far East. Probably 1960s. Price: $1. CyberAuction 335, Lot #34.

20. OTHER MACHINE MADE. Original package. Poly bag. "Glass arbles" "Made in China Bee International 1987". Contains fifteen regular ze and one shooter. All are three vane catseyes, each vane a different color. Mint (9.5). Price: $1. CyberAuction #440, Lot #30.

21. OTHER MACHINE MADE. Oxblood. I am unsure who the manufacturer is of these. Possibly Champion, although the base colors look like rly Heaton. Opaque white and opaque powder blue. Thin oxblood swirl llowing the blue. Very nice. American, circa 1940-1950. 5/8". Mint (9.9). ice: $27. CyberAuction #470, Lot #12.

22. OTHER MACHINE MADE. Oxblood. I am unsure who the manufacturer is of these. Possibly Champion, although the base colors look like rly Heaton. Opaque white and opaque powder blue. Thin oxblood swirl llowing the blue. Very nice. American, circa 1940-1950. 5/8". Mint (9.9). ice: $22. CyberAuction #386, Lot #44.

23. OTHER MACHINE MADE. Oxblood. I am unsure who the manufacturer is of these. Possibly Champion, although the base colors look like rly Heaton. Opaque white and opaque powder blue. Thin oxblood swirl llowing the blue. Very nice. American, circa 1940-1950. 5/8". Mint (9.9). ice: $22. CyberAuction #430, Lot #45.

24. OTHER MACHINE MADE. Swirl. Stunning marble. Probably Cairo, ossibly early Heaton. Transparent blue swirls with opaque lavender. Gorous. American, circa 1935-1950. 5/8". Mint (9.8). Price: $65. yberAuction #373, Lot #10.

25. OTHER MACHINE MADE. Swirl. Probably European. Transparent ht green, translucent slate gray/gray and opaque white swirls. Very nice ooter. In real nice shape. Probably 1960s. 7/8". Mint (9.7). Price: $37. yberAuction #395, Lot #16.

26. OTHER MACHINE MADE. Swirl. I am not sure who made this marble, it it is stunning anyway. At first glance, it is a Christensen Agate, but the olors and glass are not right. I think it is Champion or Heaton, possibly ley. Green base about half covered with jet black swirls. A number of hall flames on it. American, circa 1930-1945. 21/32". Mint (9.7). Price: 25. CyberAuction #373, Lot #5.

27. OTHER MACHINE MADE. Swirl. I'm not sure who made this. It is nlike any I have seen. My guess is that it is a little bit older Vacor, although haven't seen this before. Transparent clear with swirls of yellow, orange nd blue. A couple of annealing fractures. Very pretty. 19/32". Mint(-) (9.0). ice: $22. CyberAuction #341, Lot #39.

28. OTHER MACHINE MADE. Swirl. Superb example of a calligraphy virl. Probably Alley Agate. Opaque white base. Thin opaque blue swirl ith numerous tiny flames. American, circa 1935-1950. 19/32". Mint (9.9). ice: $19. CyberAuction #351, Lot #37.

29. OTHER MACHINE MADE. Swirl. Interesting three color swirl. I suspect it is early Heaton Agate. Light blue base. Swirls of brown and black. A parkle. Very interesting. American, circa 1945-1960. 11/16". Mint(-) (9.0). ice: $17. CyberAuction #343, Lot #52.

30. OTHER MACHINE MADE. Swirl. Probably early Heaton Agate. Pale qua and white swirl with thin "oxblood" swirls on it. Super marble. American, circa 1940-1950. 9/16". Mint (9.7). Price: $17. CyberAuction #381, ot #52.

31. OTHER MACHINE MADE. Swirl. Outstanding three color swirl. I ink it is Cairo Novelty. White base with green and lavender swirls. 5/8". int (9.9). Price: $15. CyberAuction #355, Lot #4.

32. OTHER MACHINE MADE. Swirl. Early Heaton. Very light blue and hite swirl. American, circa 1945-1960. 21/32". Mint (9.8). Price: $13. yberAuction #381, Lot #22.

33. OTHER MACHINE MADE. Swirl. Probably Alley Agate. Blue on uish/white. Lots of flame tips. A couple of very tiny subsurface moons. 9/32". Near Mint(+) (8.7). Price: $9. CyberAuction #356, Lot #9.

34. OTHER MACHINE MADE. Swirl. Probably early Champion Agate. anslucent blue swirls in light green. Nice. Pennsboro, WV, circa 1945-960. 9/16". Mint (9.7). Price: $8. CyberAuction #381, Lot #8.

35. OTHER MACHINE MADE. Swirl. Champion Agate coral and transcent green swirl. Pennsboro, WV, circa 1955-1970. 9/16". Mint (9.9). ice: $8. CyberAuction #417, Lot #34.

36. OTHER MACHINE MADE. Swirl. Three color swirl. Not sure who ade it, perhaps Champion. But it is odd. Flame-type. Opaque white, ilky clear and transparent orange/brown. 5/8". Mint (9.7). Price: $7. yberAuction #336, Lot #25.

37. OTHER MACHINE MADE. Swirl. Probably early Heaton Agate. reen, blue and white swirls. One sparkle, not wet. Odd coloring. American, circa 1940-1950. 19/32". Near Mint(+) (8.9). Price: $6. CyberAuction 376, Lot #38.

38. OTHER MACHINE MADE. Swirl. I think it is Alley Agate. Opaque hite base. Transparent green swirl, edged by oxblood brown. A few sparkles. 9/32". Near Mint(+) (8.7). Price: $6. CyberAuction #441, Lot #36.

39. OTHER MACHINE MADE. Swirl. Not sure of the manufacturer. Peraps Ravenswood or Heaton. Gorgeous marble though. White, light green nd dark purple swirls. Some roughness and pitting. 11/16". Near Mint .3). Price: $6. CyberAuction #485, Lot #15.

40. OTHER MACHINE MADE. Swirl. Probably early Heaton Agate. Two

shades of yellow swirl on white. Gorgeous. American, circa 1940-1955. 19/32". Mint (9.9). Price: $4. CyberAuction #444, Lot #12.

4641. OTHER MACHINE MADE. Swirl. Probably very early Heaton Agate. White base with red swirls and thin brown swirls painted on the surface. Excellent example. 11/16". Mint (9.5). Price: $4. CyberAuction #495, Lot #2.

4642. OTHER MACHINE MADE. Swirl. Probably Champion Agate. Opaque white base with very light transparent green swirls and thin purple swirls. Overall pitting. 11/16". Price: $. CyberAuction #332, Lot #14.

4643. OTHER MACHINE MADE. Vacor de Mexico. Foreign sparkler. Shooter. A few sparkles. Mexico, circa 1980-1995. 1-1/16". Near Mint(+) (8.9). There are two marbles available. You are bidding on one. Winner has choice of either or both, remainder to under. Price: $9. CyberAuction #358, Lot #1.

4644. OTHER MACHINE MADE. Wire Pull. Transparent clear base. Filled with narrow white wire, narrow black wire, and loads of pieces of tiny unmelted sand and tiny air bubbles. Probably German, circa 1960s. 29/32". Mint (9.7). Price: $12. CyberAuction #346, Lot #40.

4645. OTHER MACHINE MADE. Wire Pull. Transparent clear base. Filled with narrow white wire, narrow blue wire, and some pieces of tiny unmelted sand and tiny air bubbles. Probably German, circa 1960s. 7/8". Mint (9.7). Price: $10. CyberAuction #335, Lot #45.

4646. OTHER MACHINE MADE. Wire Pull. Transparent clear base. Blue and white wire. Pit. Germany, circa 1960s. 15/16". Near Mint(+) (8.9). There are four marbles available, you are bidding on one. Winner has choice of any or all, remainder to under. Price: $2. CyberAuction #380, Lot #29.

4647. OTHER MACHINE MADE. Wire pull. Transparent clear with white and red wires. Some melt pits. Germany, probably 1950-1970. 1". Mint (9.3). Price: $13. CyberAuction #388, Lot #18.

4648. OTHER MACHINE MADE. Wire pull. Transparent clear with white and orange wires. Some cold roll lines. Germany, probably 1950-1970. 15/16". Mint (9.5). There are two marbles available. You are bidding on one. Winner has choice of either or both. Remainder to under. Price: $8. CyberAuction #373, Lot #1.

4649. OTHER MACHINE MADE. Wire pull. Transparent clear with white and red wires. Some melt pits. Germany, probably 1950-1970. 1". Mint (9.3). Price: $8. CyberAuction #440, Lot #8.

4650. OTHER MACHINE MADE. Wire pull. Transparent clear base with white wire. Shooter. Germany, circa 1960s. 15/16". Mint (9.7). There are four marbles available, you are bidding on one. Winner has choice of any or all, remainder to under. Price: $3. CyberAuction #381, Lot #1.

4651. OTHER MACHINE MADE. Wire pull. Transparent clear base. White and blue wire. Some pits. Germany, probably 1960s. 5/8". Near Mint(+) (8.9). Price: $2. CyberAuction #380, Lot #1.

4652. OTHER MACHINE MADE. Wire pull. Transparent clear base with white wire. Shooter. Germany, circa 1960s. 15/16". Mint (9.7). There are two marbles available, you are bidding on one. Winner has choice of any or all, remainder to under. Price: $2. CyberAuction #444, Lot #1.

4653. PELTIER GLASS COMPANY. Banana. Rare marble. Transparent clear base. White banana. Banana is surrounded by six transparent yellow bands. Ottawa, IL, circa 1935-1950. 9/16". Mint (9.9). Price: $65. CyberAuction #365, Lot #48.

4654. PELTIER GLASS COMPANY. Banana. Rare white banana in yellow glass. Cold dimple. Ottawa, IL, circa 1935-1960. 5/8". Mint (9.5). Price: $32. CyberAuction #493, Lot #59.

4655. PELTIER GLASS COMPANY. Bloodie. Early Bloodie. Opalescent semi-opaque white base. Cherry red translucent patch at each pole, same color ribbon around the equator. Thin ribbon running pole to pole from the patches. Very nice. Rare. Ottawa, IL, circa 1930-1935. 3/4". Mint (9.6). Price: $55. CyberAuction #444, Lot #4.

4656. PELTIER GLASS COMPANY. Bloodie. Shooter Bloodie. Opalescent semi-opaque white base. Four semi-opaque red/orange ribbons. In great shape. Hard to find them this large. Ottawa, IL, circa 1930-1945. 31/32". Mint (9.9). Price: $25. CyberAuction #410, Lot #12.

4657. PELTIER GLASS COMPANY. Bloodie. Translucent opalescent white base. Wide ribbon of translucent red. Beautiful shooter. Ottawa, IL, circa 1930-1945. 3/4". Mint (9.9). Price: $17. CyberAuction #459, Lot #44.

4658. PELTIER GLASS COMPANY. Bloodie. Interesting shooter. Opalescent translucent white base. Four yellow ribbons. One of the yellow ribbons has a red band on it. Small subsurface moon. Hard to find. Ottawa, IL, circa 1930-1945. 15/16". Near Mint(+) (8.9). Price: $15. CyberAuction #357, Lot #18.

4659. PELTIER GLASS COMPANY. Bloodie. Excellent example. Four-ribbon Rainbo. Translucent opalescent white base with four red ribbon. Ottawa, IL, circa 1930-1945. 19/32". Mint (9.9). Price: $12. CyberAuction #385, Lot #23.

4660. PELTIER GLASS COMPANY. Blue Galaxy. One of the rarest marbles. Six-ribbon, three-color National Line Rainbo Blue Galaxy. Blue base. Three wide, very fiery aventurine black ribbons. Three narrower opaque yellow ribbons. Several minor pits and one area of pitting. Extremely rare marble. Ottawa, IL, circa 1925-1935. 21/32". Near Mint (8.6). Price: $950. CyberAuction #504, Lot #74.

4661. PELTIER GLASS COMPANY. Blue Galaxy. Extremely rare three-color eight-ribbon National Line Rainbo Blue Galaxy. Opaque blue base. Four wide ribbons of red. Four narrow ribbons of aventurine black. One of the hardest machine mades to find, no National Line Rainbo collection is complete without it. This has a small annealing fracture, but no damage. Outstanding. Ottawa, IL, circa 1927-1935. 21/32". Mint(-) (9.0). Price: $725. CyberAuction #475, Lot #60.

4662. PELTIER GLASS COMPANY. Blue Zebra. Two-color four-ribbon National Line Rainbo Zebra. White base with four fiery aventurine black and blue ribbons. Blue highlights, but not completely blue. Ottawa, IL, circa 1927-1935. 21/32". Mint (9.9). Price: $46. CyberAuction #500, Lot #26.

4663. PELTIER GLASS COMPANY. Bumblebee. Miller Bumblebee. Opaque yellow base with wide black swirls. Superb! Ottawa, IL, circa 1925-1930. 5/8". Mint (9.9). Price: $130. CyberAuction #396, Lot #53.

4664. PELTIER GLASS COMPANY. Bumblebee. Miller Bumblebee. Opaque yellow base with wide black swirls. Superb! Ottawa, IL, circa 1925-1930. 5/8". Mint (9.9). Match to CyberAuction #396, Lot #53. Price: $120. CyberAuction #400, Lot #19.

4665. PELTIER GLASS COMPANY. Bumblebee. National Line Rainbo Bumblebee. Opaque yellow base with wide aventurine black ribbons. Nice aventurine in the black. Super. Ottawa, IL, circa 1927-1935. 19/32". Mint (9.9). Price: $66. CyberAuction #481, Lot #51.

4666. PELTIER GLASS COMPANY. Bumblebee. National Line Rainbo Bumblebee. Opaque yellow base with wide aventurine black ribbons. In great shape. Ottawa, IL, circa 1927-1935. 5/8". Mint (9.9). Price: $60. CyberAuction #373, Lot #41.

4667. PELTIER GLASS COMPANY. Bumblebee. National Line Rainbo Bumblebee. Opaque yellow base with wide aventurine black ribbons. Nice aventurine in the black. In great shape. Ottawa, IL, circa 1927-1935. 9/16". Mint (9.9). Price: $50. CyberAuction #339, Lot #12.

4668. PELTIER GLASS COMPANY. Bumblebee. National Line Rainbo Bumblebee. Opaque yellow base with wide aventurine black ribbons. Nice aventurine in the black. In great shape. Ottawa, IL, circa 1927-1935. 19/32". Mint (9.9). Price: $50. CyberAuction #500, Lot #46.

4669. PELTIER GLASS COMPANY. Bumblebee. National Line Rainbo Bumblebee. Opaque yellow base with wide aventurine black ribbons. Heavy aventurine in the black. Some air holes. Ottawa, IL, circa 1927-1935. 9/16". Mint(-) (9.0). Price: $44. CyberAuction #345, Lot #53.

4670. PELTIER GLASS COMPANY. Bumblebee. National Line Rainbo Bumblebee. Opaque yellow base with narrow black ribbons. Faint aventurine in the black. In great shape. Ottawa, IL, circa 1927-1935. 21/32". Mint (9.9). Price: $37. CyberAuction #363, Lot #50.

4671. PELTIER GLASS COMPANY. Bumblebee. National Line Rainbo Bumblebee. Opaque yellow base with wide aventurine black ribbons. One small moon. Ottawa, IL, circa 1927-1935. 9/16". Near Mint(+) (8.8). Price: $20. CyberAuction #366, Lot #26.

4672. PELTIER GLASS COMPANY. Bumblebee. Four-ribbon, two-color National Line Rainbo Bumblebee. Opaque yellow base with wide aventurine black ribbons. Nice aventurine in the black. One tiny flake. Ottawa, IL, circa 1927-1935. 9/16". Near Mint(+) (8.8). Price: $19. CyberAuction #471, Lot #23.

4673. PELTIER GLASS COMPANY. Champion Jr. Very unusual marble. A type of "Clown" Champion Jr. Transparent dark green base. Wide equatorial band of yellow, with white and some pink. Ottawa, IL, circa 1930-1945. 19/32". Mint (9.9). Price: $23. CyberAuction #421, Lot #4.

4674. PELTIER GLASS COMPANY. Champion Jr. Very unusual marble. A type of "Clown" Champion Jr. Transparent dark green base. Wide equatorial band of yellow, with white and some pink. One blown out air hole. Ottawa, IL, circa 1930-1945. 19/32". Near Mint(+) (8.9). Price: $12. CyberAuction #479, Lot #5.

4675. PELTIER GLASS COMPANY. Chocolate Cow. Peewee two color National Line Rainbo Chocolate Cow. Aventurine black ribbons on opaque cocoa brown. Not a lot of aventurine in the black. One of the harder cows to find. Some tiny chips and a small fold. Ottawa, IL, circa 1928-1935. 5/8". Near Mint (8.3). Price: $70. CyberAuction #347, Lot #22.

4676. PELTIER GLASS COMPANY. Christmas Tree. Stunning shooter. Three color National Line Rainbo Christmas Tree. Opaque white base with three red bands and three green bands. Outstanding example. Ottawa, IL, circa 1928-1935. 23/32". Mint (9.8). Price: $270. CyberAuction #366, Lot #59.

4677. PELTIER GLASS COMPANY. Christmas Tree. Three-color six-ribbon National Line Rainbo Christmas Tree. White base with two green ribbons and four red ribbons. Super marble, larger than you usually find and in very nice shape. Ottawa, IL, circa 1927-1935. 11/16". Mint (9.7). Price: $195. CyberAuction #467, Lot #55.

4678. PELTIER GLASS COMPANY. Christmas Tree. Shooter three-color six-ribbon National Line Rainbo Christmas Tree. White base with four green ribbons and two red ribbons. One very tiny melt pit. Ottawa, IL, circa 1925-1935. 23/32". Mint (9.6). Price: $165. CyberAuction #481, Lot #59.

4679. PELTIER GLASS COMPANY. Christmas Tree. Three-color National Line Rainbo Christmas Tree. Three red ribbons and three green ribbons on white. Outstanding example. Ottawa, IL, circa 1927-1935. 19/32". Mint (9.9). Price: $150. CyberAuction #356, Lot #53.

4680. PELTIER GLASS COMPANY. Christmas Tree. Three color National Line Rainbo Christmas Tree. Opaque white base. Four transparent red and two transparent green ribbons. Excellent pattern and a real beauty. Ottawa, IL, circa 1928-1935. 5/8". Mint (9.7). Price: $140. CyberAuction #377, Lot #24.

4681. PELTIER GLASS COMPANY. Christmas Tree. Rare eight-ribbon three-color National Line Rainbo Christmas Tree. Opaque creamy white base. Four red ribbons and four green ones. Some minor aventurine in a green. Ottawa, IL, circa 1925-1935. 21/32". Mint (9.6). Price: $140. CyberAuction #504, Lot #64.

4682. PELTIER GLASS COMPANY. Christmas Tree. Three-color six-ribbon National Line Rainbo Christmas Tree. Opaque white base. Four ribbons of red, two of green. Superb. One tiny sparkle. Ottawa, IL, circa 1927-1935. 21/32". Mint(-) (9.2). Price: $135. CyberAuction #385, Lot #50.

4683. PELTIER GLASS COMPANY. Christmas Tree. Three-color eight-ribbon National Line Rainbo Christmas Tree. White base with four green rib-

bons and four red ribbons. Super. Tiny fold seam. Ottawa, IL, circa 1927-1935. 5/8". Mint (9.7). Price: $130. CyberAuction #498, Lot #63.

4684. PELTIER GLASS COMPANY. Christmas Tree. Three-color eight-ribbon National Line Rainbo Christmas Tree. Stunning example. Creamy white base. Five brown/red ribbons, three green ribbons. Superior example. Pristine surface. Ottawa, IL, circa 1928-1935. 5/8". Mint (9.9). Price: $130. CyberAuction #503, Lot #62.

4685. PELTIER GLASS COMPANY. Christmas Tree. Three color National Line Rainbo Christmas Tree. Opaque white base. Four ribbons of red, two of green. Superb. One tiny subsurface. Ottawa, IL, circa 1927-1935. 5/8". Mint(-) (9.2). Price: $100. CyberAuction #360, Lot #59.

4686. PELTIER GLASS COMPANY. Christmas Tree. Three-color eight-ribbon Christmas Tree. Shooter. Opaque white base. Five transparent red ribbons, three transparent green ribbons. Heavily swirls. A couple of pinpricks. Ottawa, IL, circa 1925-1935. 23/32". Mint(-) (9.0). Price: $99. CyberAuction #507, Lot #51.

4687. PELTIER GLASS COMPANY. Christmas Tree. Six-ribbon three-color National Line Rainbo Christmas Tree. Opaque white base. Four transparent red and two transparent green ribbons. Excellent pattern and a real beauty. Ottawa, IL, circa 1928-1935. 19/32". Mint (9.7). Price: $80. CyberAuction #502, Lot #60.

4688. PELTIER GLASS COMPANY. Christmas Tree. Shooter three color National Line Rainbo Christmas Tree. White base with four green ribbons and two red ribbons. Some chipping. Ottawa, IL, circa 1927-1935. 27/32". Good(+) (7.9). Price: $60. CyberAuction #341, Lot #12.

4689. PELTIER GLASS COMPANY. Christmas Tree. Six-ribbon three-color National Line Rainbo Christmas Tree. White base with three green ribbons and three red ribbons. Some minor wear, no damage. Ottawa, IL, circa 1927-1935. 5/8". Mint(-) (9.0). Price: $60. CyberAuction #407, Lot #35.

4690. PELTIER GLASS COMPANY. Christmas Tree. Three-color eight-ribbon National Line Rainbo Christmas Tree. Opaque white base. Five transparent red and three transparent green ribbons. A couple of pits and some tiny haze. Ottawa, IL, circa 1928-1935. 5/8". Near Mint (8.5). Price: $56. CyberAuction #387, Lot #51.

4691. PELTIER GLASS COMPANY. Christmas Tree. Three color Rainbo Christmas Tree. Semi-opaque milky white base. Four transparent red bands and two transparent green bands. Pretty. Ottawa, IL, circa 1930-1945. 9/16". Mint (9.9). Price: $47. CyberAuction #341, Lot #57.

4692. PELTIER GLASS COMPANY. Christmas Tree. Three color National Line Rainbo Christmas Tree. Opaque white base. Four transparent red and two transparent green ribbons. Excellent pattern. Three tiny flakes. Ottawa, IL, circa 1928-1935. 11/16". Near Mint (8.6). Price: $45. CyberAuction #384, Lot #50.

4693. PELTIER GLASS COMPANY. Christmas Tree. Three-color six-ribbon National Line Rainbo Christmas Tree. Opaque white base. Four transparent red and two transparent green ribbons. Two sparkles. Ottawa, IL, circa 1928-1935. 5/8". Near Mint(+) (8.9). Price: $42. CyberAuction #370, Lot #54.

4694. PELTIER GLASS COMPANY. Christmas Tree. Three color Rainbo Christmas Tree. Semi-opaque milky white base. Four transparent red band and two transparent green bands. Pretty. Ottawa, IL, circa 1930-1945. 9/16". Mint (9.9). Price: $35. CyberAuction #387, Lot #38.

4695. PELTIER GLASS COMPANY. Christmas Tree. Three color National Line Rainbo Christmas Tree. Opaque white base. Four transparent red and two transparent green ribbons. Price: $. CyberAuction #389, Lot #21.

4696. PELTIER GLASS COMPANY. Christmas Tree. Shooter three color National Line Rainbo Christmas Tree. White base with four green ribbons and two red ribbons. Some pitting. Ottawa, IL, circa 1927-1935. 21/32". Near Mint (8.3). Price: $32. CyberAuction #402, Lot #7.

4697. PELTIER GLASS COMPANY. Christmas Tree. Three-color six-ribbon National Line Rainbo Christmas Tree. White base with four green ribbons and two red ribbons. Some pinpricking. Ottawa, IL, circa 1927-1935. 17/32". Near Mint (8.6). Price: $32. CyberAuction #432, Lot #60.

4698. PELTIER GLASS COMPANY. Christmas Tree. Shooter three-color eight-ribbon National Line Rainbo Christmas Tree. White base with four green ribbons and four red ribbons. Pits, tiny chips, tiny subsurface moon. Ottawa, IL, circa 1927-1935. 21/32". Near Mint(-) (8.2). Price: $30. CyberAuction #464, Lot #47.

4699. PELTIER GLASS COMPANY. Christmas Tree. Six-ribbon three-color National Line Rainbo Christmas Tree. White base. Four orange/red ribbons, two green ribbons. Tiny chips and tiny subsurface moon. Ottawa, IL, circa 1930-1940. 5/8". Near Mint (8.3). Price: $29. CyberAuction #477, Lot #38.

4700. PELTIER GLASS COMPANY. Christmas Tree. Four-ribbon three-color National Line Rainbo Christmas Tree. White base. Two transparent orange/red ribbons, two transparent green ribbons. Pit and tiny subsurface moon. Ottawa, IL, circa 1930-1940. 5/8". Near Mint(+) (8.7). Price: $25. CyberAuction #465, Lot #12.

4701. PELTIER GLASS COMPANY. Christmas Tree. Three color National Line Rainbo Christmas Tree. Opaque white base. Four transparent red and two transparent green ribbons. Price: $. CyberAuction #419, Lot #41.

4702. PELTIER GLASS COMPANY. Christmas Tree. Shooter three-color six-ribbon National Line Rainbo Christmas Tree. White base with four green ribbons and two red ribbons. Pits, tiny chips, tiny subsurface moons. Ottawa, IL, circa 1927-1935. 23/32". Good(+) (7.7). Price: $15. CyberAuction #431, Lot #2.

4703. PELTIER GLASS COMPANY. Clear Rainbo. Hard to find Clear Rainbo. Transparent clear base. One ribbon each opaque white, green, yellow and red. Annealing fracture in the marble (typical). Ottawa, IL, circa 1927-1935. 19/32". Mint(-) (9.0). Price: $60. CyberAuction #339, Lot #13.

4704. PELTIER GLASS COMPANY. Clear Rainbo. Hard to find Clear Rainbo

tiny pinpricks. Gorgeous. Ottawa, IL, circa 1927-1935. 23/32". Mint(-) (9.0). Price: \$80. CyberAuction #463, Lot #51.

4725. PELTIER GLASS COMPANY. Ketchup and Mustard. Eight-ribbon three-color National Line Rainbo Ketchup and Mustard. Opaque white base. Six red ribbons and two yellow ones. One pit. Ottawa, IL, circa 1930-1940. 11/16". Mint(-) (9.2). Price: \$75. CyberAuction #453, Lot #48.

4726. PELTIER GLASS COMPANY. Ketchup and Mustard. Eight-ribbon three-color National Line Rainbo Ketchup and Mustard. Opaque white base. Six red ribbons and two yellow ones. One pit. Ottawa, IL, circa 1930-1940. 11/16". Mint(-) (9.2). Price: \$70. CyberAuction #433, Lot #20.

4727. PELTIER GLASS COMPANY. Ketchup and Mustard. Eight-ribbon three-color National Line Rainbo Ketchup and Mustard. Opaque white base. Five red ribbons and three yellow ones. One pinprick. Ottawa, IL, circa 1930-1940. 9/16". Mint(-) (9.2). Price: \$45. CyberAuction #407, Lot #24.

4728. PELTIER GLASS COMPANY. Ketchup and Mustard. Three-color six-ribbon National Line Rainbo Ketchup and Mustard. Opaque white base. Four ribbons of red, two of yellow. One pinpricking. Ottawa, IL, circa 1927-1935. 5/8". Near Mint (8.6). Price: \$32. CyberAuction #370, Lot #55.

4729. PELTIER GLASS COMPANY. Ketchup and Mustard. Eight-ribbon three-color National Line Rainbo Ketchup and Mustard. Opaque white base. Five red ribbons and three yellow ones. Flake and a chip. Ottawa, IL, circa 1925-1935. 21/32". Good(+) (7.9). Price: \$17. CyberAuction #496, Lot #16.

4730. PELTIER GLASS COMPANY. Ketchup and Mustard. Eight-ribbon three-color National Line Rainbo Ketchup and Mustard. Opaque white base. Five red ribbons and three yellow ones. Flake and a chip. Ottawa, IL, circa 1925-1935. 21/32". Good(+) (7.9). Price: \$15. CyberAuction #464, Lot #3.

4731. PELTIER GLASS COMPANY. Ketchup and Mustard. Six-ribbon, three-color Ketchup and Mustard. White base. Four red ribbons, two yellow ribbons. Several tiny chips. Ottawa, IL, circa 1927-1935. 5/8". Near Mint(-) (8.1). Price: \$11. CyberAuction #477, Lot #8.

4732. PELTIER GLASS COMPANY. Ketchup and Mustard. Six-ribbon, three-color Ketchup and Mustard. White base. Four red ribbons, two yellow ribbons. Overall haze. Ottawa, IL, circa 1927-1935. 5/8". Good(-) (7.1). Price: \$2. CyberAuction #476, Lot #4.

4733. PELTIER GLASS COMPANY. Ketchup and Mustard. Six-ribbon, three-color Ketchup and Mustard. White base. Four red ribbons, two yellow ribbons. Overall haze. Ottawa, IL, circa 1927-1935. 5/8". Good(-) (7.1). Price: \$2. CyberAuction #499, Lot #26.

4734. PELTIER GLASS COMPANY. Liberty. Three-color National Line Rainbo Liberty. Super example. Opaque white base with three red ribbons and three blue ribbons. Ottawa, IL, circa 1927-1935. 19/32". Mint (9.9). Price: \$75. CyberAuction #355, Lot #52.

4735. PELTIER GLASS COMPANY. Liberty. Three-color six-ribbon Rainbo Line Rainbo Liberty. Nice example. Opaque white base with four red ribbons and two blue ribbons. Ottawa, IL, circa 1927-1935. 19/32". Near Mint(+) (8.8). Price: \$60. CyberAuction #385, Lot #15.

4736. PELTIER GLASS COMPANY. Liberty. Three-color six-ribbon Rainbo Liberty. Semi-opaque white base. Four red ribbons and two blue ribbons. Wide ribbons. One sparkle. Ottawa, IL, circa 1930-1945. 5/8". Near Mint(+) (8.9). Price: \$42. CyberAuction #476, Lot #45.

4737. PELTIER GLASS COMPANY. Liberty. Three-color Rainbo Liberty. Semi-opaque white base. Four transparent orange/red ribbons and two transparent dark blue ribbons. Ottawa, IL, circa 1930-1945. 19/32". Mint (9.7). Price: \$40. CyberAuction #387, Lot #57.

4738. PELTIER GLASS COMPANY. Liberty. Three color National Line Rainbo Liberty. White base. Ribbons of red and blue. Some pits and sparkles. Ottawa, IL, circa 1927-1935. 5/8". Near Mint(+) (8.9). Consignor note: D20. Price: \$36. CyberAuction #343, Lot #50.

4739. PELTIER GLASS COMPANY. Liberty. Three-color Rainbo Liberty. Semi-opaque white base. Four transparent orange/red and two transparent blue ribbons. Ottawa, IL, circa 1930-1945. 19/32". Mint (9.7). Price: \$36. CyberAuction #356, Lot #14.

4740. PELTIER GLASS COMPANY. Liberty. Three-color Rainbo Liberty shooter. Opaque white base. Four red ribbons and two blue ribbons. Ribbons are wide, covering almost all the white. Some small and tiny chips. Ottawa, IL, circa 1930-1945. 13/16". Good(+) (7.7). Price: \$36. CyberAuction #494, Lot #37.

4741. PELTIER GLASS COMPANY. Liberty. Six-ribbon three-color Rainbo. Semi-opaque white base. Four transparent red ribbons and two transparent blue. Ottawa, IL, circa 1927-1935. 5/8". Mint (9.9). Price: \$35. CyberAuction #381, Lot #39.

4742. PELTIER GLASS COMPANY. Liberty. Interesting coloring. Three color National Line Rainbo Liberty. Opaque white base. Four orange ribbons, one blue ribbon, one greenish/blue ribbon. Some tiny chips and sparkling. Ottawa, IL, circa 1927-1935. 11/16". Near Mint(-) (8.0). Price: \$25. CyberAuction #352, Lot #58.

4743. PELTIER GLASS COMPANY. Liberty. Three-color Rainbo Liberty. Semi-opaque white base. Four transparent orange/red ribbons and two transparent blue ribbons. Several tiny sparkles. Ottawa, IL, circa 1930-1945. 19/32". Near Mint(+) (8.9). Price: \$21. CyberAuction #449, Lot #58.

4744. PELTIER GLASS COMPANY. Liberty. Three color Rainbo Liberty. Opaque white base. Four transparent orange/red ribbons and three transparent blue ribbons. Ottawa, IL, circa 1930-1945. 19/32". Buffed. Price: \$19. CyberAuction #369, Lot #46.

4745. PELTIER GLASS COMPANY. Liberty. Three-color Rainbo Liberty. Semi-opaque white base. Four transparent orange/red ribbons and two

---

base. One ribbon each opaque white, blue, yellow and red. Superb. Ottawa, IL, circa 1927-1935. 19/32". Mint (9.8). Price: \$55. CyberAuction #384, Lot #55.

'05. PELTIER GLASS COMPANY. Clear Rainbo. Hard to find Clear Rainbo. Transparent clear base. One ribbon each opaque white, green, yellow and red. Superb. Ottawa, IL, circa 1927-1935. 19/32". Mint (9.8). Price: \$48. CyberAuction #499, Lot #36.

'06. PELTIER GLASS COMPANY. Clear Rainbo. Hard to find Clear Rainbo. Transparent clear base. One ribbon each opaque white, green, yellow and red. Tiny dimple at one end. Ottawa, IL, circa 1927-1935. 19/32". Mint (9.7). Price: \$44. CyberAuction #507, Lot #8.

'07. PELTIER GLASS COMPANY. Clear Rainbo. Hard to find Clear Rainbo. Transparent clear base. One ribbon each opaque white, green, yellow and red. Ottawa, IL, circa 1927-1935. 19/32". Mint (9.6). Price: \$35. CyberAuction #348, Lot #51.

'08. PELTIER GLASS COMPANY. Clear Rainbo. Transparent clear base with lots of unmelted sand. Two wide ribbons of red, two of white. A type of Sunset, but no air bubbles. Ottawa, IL, circa 1930-1945. 11/16". Mint (9.9). Price: \$26. CyberAuction #330, Lot #8.

'09. PELTIER GLASS COMPANY. Clear Rainbo. Hard to find Clear Rainbo. Transparent clear base. One ribbon each opaque white, blue, yellow and red. Small, typical, annealing fracture. Ottawa, IL, circa 1927-1935. 5/8". Mint(-) (9.0). Price: \$26. CyberAuction #495, Lot #51.

'10. PELTIER GLASS COMPANY. Clear Rainbo. Hard to find Clear Rainbo. Transparent clear base. One ribbon each opaque white, blue, yellow and white). Small annealing fracture, typical of this type. Ottawa, IL, circa 1927-1935. 19/32". Mint(-) (9.0). Price: \$22. CyberAuction #508, Lot #52.

'11. PELTIER GLASS COMPANY. Clear Rainbo. Hard to find Clear Rainbo. Transparent clear base. Two ribbons each opaque white, blue, and red. Ottawa, IL, circa 1927-1935. 19/32". Mint(-) (9.2). Price: \$17. CyberAuction #491, Lot #44.

'12. PELTIER GLASS COMPANY. Clear Rainbo. Hard to find Clear Rainbo. Transparent clear base. One ribbon each opaque white, blue, yellow and red. Small and tiny chips and flakes. Ottawa, IL, circa 1927-1935. 5/8". Good (7.5). Price: \$8. CyberAuction #355, Lot #37.

'13. PELTIER GLASS COMPANY. Clear Rainbo. Hard to find Clear Rainbo. Transparent clear base. One ribbon each opaque white, blue, yellow and red. Small and tiny chips and flakes. Ottawa, IL, circa 1927-1935. 5/8". Good (7.5). Price: \$8. CyberAuction #374, Lot #5.

'14. PELTIER GLASS COMPANY. Clear Rainbo. Hard to find Clear Rainbo. Transparent clear base. One ribbon each opaque white, blue, yellow and red. Small and tiny chips and flakes. Ottawa, IL, circa 1927-1935. 5/8". Good (7.5). Price: \$8. CyberAuction #445, Lot #38.

'15. PELTIER GLASS COMPANY. Flaming Dragon. Three color National Line Rainbo, sometimes referred to as a Flaming Dragon. Light green base. Thick ribbons of red mixed with orange/yellow. Several of the ribbons are very short. Ottawa, IL, circa 1925-1930. 21/32". Mint (9.7). Price: \$110. CyberAuction #330, Lot #6.

'16. PELTIER GLASS COMPANY. Golden Rebel. Three-color eight-ribbon National Line Rainbo Golden Rebel. Opaque yellow base. Five red ribbons and three aventurine black ribbons. Tiny flake, a couple of pinpricks. Stunning marble!!! Ottawa, IL, circa 1928-1935. 19/32". Near Mint(+) (8.7). Price: \$525. CyberAuction #498, Lot #71.

'17. PELTIER GLASS COMPANY. Golden Rebel. Three-color six-ribbon National Line Rainbo Golden Rebel. Opaque yellow base. Four red ribbons and two aventurine black ribbons. One very, very tiny flake. There is also aventurine in two of the red ribbons. Stunning marble!!! Ottawa, IL, circa 1928-1935. 19/32". Near Mint(+) (8.9). Price: \$370. CyberAuction #377, Lot #56.

'18. PELTIER GLASS COMPANY. Golden Rebel. Three-color eight-ribbon National Line Rainbo Golden Rebel. Shooter. Opaque yellow base. Four red ribbons, two aventurine black ribbons. The marble has been polished, one chip remnant remains. There is also one very small filled air hole. Still, very hard to find. Ottawa, IL, circa 1925-1935. 3/4". Price: \$200. CyberAuction #481, Lot #45.

'19. PELTIER GLASS COMPANY. Golden Rebel. Eight-ribbon three-color National Line Rainbo Golden Rebel. Very hard marble to find. Yellow base. Five red ribbons, three aventurine black ribbons. Some chipping, nothing very deep. Ottawa, IL, circa 1935-1945. 5/8". Good (7.4). Price: \$56. CyberAuction #493, Lot #33.

'20. PELTIER GLASS COMPANY. Graycoat. Six-ribbon three-color National Line Rainbo shooter. White base. Three red ribbons. Three ribbons gray on red. Stunning and rare. Ottawa, IL, circa 1927-1935. 23/32". Mint (9.9). Price: \$430. CyberAuction #381, Lot #58.

'21. PELTIER GLASS COMPANY. Ketchup and Mustard. Shooter three-color six-ribbon National Line Rainbo Ketchup and Mustard. Opaque white base. Four ribbons of yellow, two of red. A couple of tiny subsurface moons. Ottawa, IL, circa 1927-1935. 29/32". Near Mint(+) (8.8). Price: \$420. CyberAuction #373, Lot #56.

'22. PELTIER GLASS COMPANY. Ketchup and Mustard. Rare eight-ribbon three-color National Line Rainbo Ketchup and Mustard. Opaque white base. Five red ribbons and three yellow ones. Aventurine in two of the yellow ribbons, the other is very narrow. Ottawa, IL, circa 1925-1935. 5/8". Mint (9.8). Price: \$140. CyberAuction #504, Lot #56.

'23. PELTIER GLASS COMPANY. Ketchup and Mustard. Three-color six-ribbon National Line Rainbo Ketchup and Mustard. Opaque white base. Four ribbons of red, two of yellow. One sparkle. Ottawa, IL, circa 1927-1935. 21/32". Mint(-) (9.2). Price: \$80. CyberAuction #403, Lot #55.

'24. PELTIER GLASS COMPANY. Ketchup and Mustard. Six-ribbon three-color National Line Rainbo Ketchup and Mustard. Opaque white base. Four red ribbons and two yellow ones. Wide ribbons. A tiny sparkle and transparent blue ribbons. Several tiny sparkles. Ottawa, IL, circa 1930-1945. 19/32". Near Mint(+) (8.9). Price: $17. CyberAuction #373, Lot #16.

4746. PELTIER GLASS COMPANY. Liberty. Three-color six-ribbon National Line Rainbo Liberty. Semi-opaque white base. Four transparent orange/red ribbons and two transparent blue ribbons. Several small chips. Ottawa, IL, circa 1930-1945. 19/32". Near Mint (8.3). Price: $17. CyberAuction #477, Lot #21.

4747. PELTIER GLASS COMPANY. Liberty. Three-color National Line Rainbo Liberty. White base. Three wide ribbons of red. Three ribbons of blue. Some tiny chips and flakes. Ottawa, IL, circa 1927-1935. 11/16". Near Mint(-) (8.0). Price: $15. CyberAuction #485, Lot #11.

4748. PELTIER GLASS COMPANY. Liberty. Three-color, six-ribbon Rainbo Liberty. Semi-opaque white base. Four transparent orange/red ribbons and two transparent blue ribbons. Several small chips. Ottawa, IL, circa 1930-1945. 19/32". Near Mint (8.3). Price: $11. CyberAuction #382, Lot #51.

4749. PELTIER GLASS COMPANY. Liberty. Three-color National Line Rainbo Liberty. Opaque white base. Four transparent orange/red ribbons and two transparent blue ribbons. Ottawa, IL, circa 1930-1945. 19/32". Polished. Price: $11. CyberAuction #393, Lot #43.

4750. PELTIER GLASS COMPANY. Liberty. Opaque white base. Four red ribbons, two blue. Overall chipping. Ottawa, IL, circa 1927-1935. 5/8". Good (7.3). Price: $6. CyberAuction #376, Lot #13.

4751. PELTIER GLASS COMPANY. Liberty/Rebel hybrid. One of the rarest Peltiers I have ever seen. I guess you would call it a Liberty/Rebel hybrid. Six-ribbon, four-color National Line Rainbo. White base. Four translucent red ribbons. Two transparent blue ribbons, covered by aventurine black. Extremely rare. One tiny flake. Ottawa, IL, circa 1927-1935. 23/32". Near Mint(+) (8.9). Price: $325. CyberAuction #500, Lot #53.

4752. PELTIER GLASS COMPANY. Miller swirl. Very hard to find Miller swirl. Light opaque blue base covered with loads of red and very dark red. Stunning. Tiny air hole and a pinprick. Ottawa, IL, circa 1925-1930. 23/32". Mint(+) (9.2). Price: $180. CyberAuction #425, Lot #18.

4753. PELTIER GLASS COMPANY. Miller swirl. Very hard to find Miller swirl. Light opaque yellow base with light transparent green swirls. Stunning. A few very, very light pinpricks and hit spots (looks more like aventurine than damage). Very rare. Ottawa, IL, circa 1925-1930. 21/32". Near Mint(+) (8.9). Price: $150. CyberAuction #363, Lot #26.

4754. PELTIER GLASS COMPANY. Multicolor. Rare eight-ribbon. Transparent green base. Four green ribbons, two red, and two white. In great shape. Ottawa, IL, circa 1927-1935. 5/8". Mint (9.9). Price: $65. CyberAuction #342, Lot #28.

4755. PELTIER GLASS COMPANY. Multicolor. Odd coloring. Transparent dark green base. Two ribbons of red, two ribbons of light blue, one ribbon of white, one ribbon of yellow. Superb. Ottawa, IL, circa 1930-1945. 5/8". Mint (9.9). Price: $55. CyberAuction #416, Lot #42.

4756. PELTIER GLASS COMPANY. Multicolor. Transparent dark green base. Six ribbons. Two each of blue, salmon pink, and yellow. Harder to find coloring and design. Ottawa, IL, circa 1930-1945. 21/32". Mint (9.8). Price: $45. CyberAuction #436, Lot #42.

4757. PELTIER GLASS COMPANY. Multicolor. Interesting design. Transparent dark green base. Three ribbons of white, three of light blue. One thin ribbon of oxblood edging one the blue ribbons. Nice swirling. A couple of pinpricks. Ottawa, IL, circa 1930-1945. 21/32". Mint(-) (9.1). Price: $42. CyberAuction #363, Lot #21.

4758. PELTIER GLASS COMPANY. Multicolor. Transparent dark green base. Two ribbons each of salmon pink, white and blue. Ottawa, IL, circa 1930-1945. 21/32". Mint (9.9). Price: $42. CyberAuction #377, Lot #45.

4759. PELTIER GLASS COMPANY. Multicolor. Multicolor Miller Swirl. Transparent light green base. Swirls of orange, light blue and white. One small flake and a melt spot on it. Ottawa, IL, circa 1925-1930. 11/16". Near Mint (8.4). Price: $39. CyberAuction #345, Lot #58.

4760. PELTIER GLASS COMPANY. Multicolor. Very interesting. Transparent dark green base. Eight ribbons. Four red, two white, two light blue. Rare. One sparkle. Ottawa, IL, circa 1930-1945. 5/8". Mint(-) (9.0). Price: $39. CyberAuction #376, Lot #46.

4761. PELTIER GLASS COMPANY. Multicolor. Transparent light green base. Nice ribbons of white, orange and light blue. Ottawa, IL, circa 1925-1935. 5/8". Mint (9.8). Price: $35. CyberAuction #418, Lot #42.

4762. PELTIER GLASS COMPANY. Multicolor. Very interesting marble. Ribbon type. Transparent dark green base. Two blue ribbons, two salmon ribbons, one white and one yellow. Five-color are very hard to find. One tiny sparkle. Ottawa, IL, circa 1930-1940. 5/8". Mint(-) (9.2). Price: $32. CyberAuction #385, Lot #48.

4763. PELTIER GLASS COMPANY. Multicolor. Transparent green base. Six ribbons. Two each of yellow, white and light blue. Superior example. Ottawa, IL, circa 1930-1945. 21/32". Mint (9.8). Price: $32. CyberAuction #459, Lot #1.

4764. PELTIER GLASS COMPANY. Multicolor. Transparent light green base. Two wide ribbons each of red, white and light blue. Nice swirling. Ottawa, IL, circa 1930-1945. 11/16". Mint (9.9). Price: $31. CyberAuction #363, Lot #41.

4765. PELTIER GLASS COMPANY. Multicolor. Transparent light green base. Ribbons of light blue, white and yellow, with very tight swirling. Very nice. Ottawa, IL, circa 1927-1935. 5/8". Mint (9.7). Price: $30. CyberAuction #342, Lot #40.

4766. PELTIER GLASS COMPANY. Multicolor. Very interesting marble. Ribbon type. Transparent dark green base. Two blue ribbons, two salmon ribbons, one white and one yellow. Five-color are very hard to find. Ottawa, IL, circa 1930-1940. 5/8". Mint (9.9). Price: $30. CyberAuction #352, Lot #37.

4767. PELTIER GLASS COMPANY. Multicolor. Interesting coloring. Transparent light green base. Ribbons of salmon from each side. One very tiny subsurface moon. Ottawa, IL, circa 1930-1945. 5/8". Near Mint(+) (8.9). Price: $25. CyberAuction #373, Lot #29.

4768. PELTIER GLASS COMPANY. Multicolor. Swirl-type. Transparent dark green base. Two swirls each of orange, white and light blue. Ottawa, IL, circa 1925-1935. 21/32". Mint (9.9). Price: $22. CyberAuction #436, Lot #50.

4769. PELTIER GLASS COMPANY. Multicolor. Transparent green base. Orange, blue and white ribbons. Heavily swirled. Ottawa, IL, circa 1930-1940. 21/32". Mint (9.8). Price: $22. CyberAuction #462, Lot #14.

4770. PELTIER GLASS COMPANY. Multicolor. Very nice multicolor. Transparent green base. Two ribbons each of light blue, red and white. Nicely swirled. Ottawa, IL, circa 1930-1940. 21/32". Mint (9.7). Price: $1[?] CyberAuction #475, Lot #43.

4771. PELTIER GLASS COMPANY. Multicolor. Very nice multicolor. Transparent green base. Ribbons of red/orange (three), light blue (three), white (two). Narrow oxblood in one of the blue ribbons. Heavily swirled. Annealing fracture. Rare type. Ottawa, IL, circa 1930-1945. 23/32". Near Mint(-) (8.9). Price: $19. CyberAuction #485, Lot #39.

4772. PELTIER GLASS COMPANY. Multicolor. Shooter, hard to find. Transparent dark green base. Two ribbons each of orange, white and blue. Two air holes. Ottawa, IL, circa 1930-1945. 23/32". Mint (-) (9.0). Price: $1[?] CyberAuction #380, Lot #9.

4773. PELTIER GLASS COMPANY. Multicolor. Transparent green base. Two ribbons each of yellow, white and light blue. Beauty. Ottawa, IL, circa 1930-1945. 5/8". Mint (9.9). Price: $17. CyberAuction #388, Lot #43.

4774. PELTIER GLASS COMPANY. Multicolor. Gorgeous multicolor ribbon, in odder colors. Transparent dark green base. Two ribbons each of yellow, blue and salmon. Very nice. Ottawa, IL, circa 1930-1945. 19/32". Mint (9.9). Price: $17. CyberAuction #429, Lot #2.

4775. PELTIER GLASS COMPANY. Multicolor. Transparent green base. Six ribbons. Two each of salmon, white and blue ribbons. Ottawa, IL, circa 1930-1945. 19/32". Mint (9.9). Price: $17. CyberAuction #446, Lot #2[?]

4776. PELTIER GLASS COMPANY. Multicolor. Transparent green base. Two ribbons each of green, red and white. Very nice swirling. Gorgeous marble, harder to find colors. Ottawa, IL, circa 1925-1935. 21/32". Mint (9.7). Price: $15. CyberAuction #435, Lot #9.

4777. PELTIER GLASS COMPANY. Multicolor. Transparent green base. Swirled ribbons of white, green and red. Some pitting and a very light haze. Nicely swirled. Ottawa, IL, circa 1930-1945. 11/16". Near Mint (8.5). Price: $14. CyberAuction #354, Lot #43.

4778. PELTIER GLASS COMPANY. Multicolor. Super example. Transparent light green base. Almost completely covered by light blue, with some orange and white ribbons. One air hole, some pitting. Excellent. Ottawa, IL, circa 1930-1945. 21/32". Near Mint(+) (8.9). Price: $14. CyberAuction #369, Lot #12.

4779. PELTIER GLASS COMPANY. Multicolor. Transparent dark green base. Ribbons of red and white. Heavily swirled. Ottawa, IL, circa 1930-1945. 19/32". Mint (9.5). Price: $14. CyberAuction #502, Lot #22.

4780. PELTIER GLASS COMPANY. Multicolor. Transparent green base. Six ribbons. Two each of blue, light red and white. Ottawa, IL, circa 1930-1945. 21/32". Mint (9.7). Price: $13. CyberAuction #453, Lot #39.

4781. PELTIER GLASS COMPANY. Multicolor. Transparent dark green base. Bands of red, light blue and white. Nice. Ottawa, IL, circa 1930-1945. 11/16". Mint (9.9). Price: $12. CyberAuction #369, Lot #7.

4782. PELTIER GLASS COMPANY. Multicolor. Transparent light green base. Six ribbons. Two yellow, two light blue, two white. Nice pattern, in great shape. Ottawa, IL, circa 1930-1940. 11/16". Mint (9.7). Price: $1[?] CyberAuction #406, Lot #44.

4783. PELTIER GLASS COMPANY. Multicolor. Transparent dark green base. Two ribbons each of orange/yellow, pale white, light blue. Ottawa, IL, circa 1930-1940. 23/32". Mint (9.7). Consignor note: F22. Price: $1[?] CyberAuction #423, Lot #6.

4784. PELTIER GLASS COMPANY. Multicolor. Transparent light green base. Two ribbons each of white, yellow and light blue. Gorgeous. Ottawa, IL, circa 1930-1945. 21/32". Mint (9.8). Price: $11. CyberAuction #377, Lot #2.

4785. PELTIER GLASS COMPANY. Multicolor. Transparent green base. Almost completely covered by six ribbons. Two each of white, light blue and yellow. Ottawa, IL, circa 1930-1945. 21/32". Mint (9.6). Price: $1[?] CyberAuction #422, Lot #53.

4786. PELTIER GLASS COMPANY. Multicolor. Transparent dark green base. Four red ribbons, one white, one blue. Some cold lines. Interesting. Ottawa, IL, circa 1930-1945. 9/16". Mint(-) (9.1). Price: $10. CyberAuction #382, Lot #13.

4787. PELTIER GLASS COMPANY. Multicolor. Transparent green base. Six ribbons. Two each of red, light blue and white. Ottawa, IL, circa 1930-1945. 5/8". Mint (9.9). Price: $10. CyberAuction #385, Lot #1.

4788. PELTIER GLASS COMPANY. Multicolor. Transparent light green base. Almost completely covered by six ribbons. Two each of white, light blue and yellow. Ottawa, IL, circa 1930-1945. 21/32". Mint (9.6). Price: $1[?] CyberAuction #385, Lot #8.

4789. PELTIER GLASS COMPANY. Multicolor. Transparent light green base. Ribbons of light blue, yellow and white. Some tiny flakes. Ottawa, IL, circa 1930-1945. 21/32". Near Mint (8.6). Price: $9. CyberAuction #372, Lot #10.

4790. PELTIER GLASS COMPANY. Multicolor. Transparent dark green base. Six ribbons. Two blue, two white, two red. Ottawa, IL, circa 1935-1945. 11/16". Mint (9.9). Price: $9. CyberAuction #463, Lot #8.

4791. PELTIER GLASS COMPANY. Multicolor. Transparent green base. S[...]

ribbons. Two each of yellow, light blue, white. Ottawa, IL, circa 1935-1945. 9/16". Mint (9.7). Price: $9. CyberAuction #488, Lot #16.

4792. PELTIER GLASS COMPANY. Multicolor. Transparent light green base. Ribbons of yellow, light blue and white. One tiny subsurface moon. Ottawa, IL, circa 1930-1945. 11/16". Near Mint(+) (8.9). Price: $8. CyberAuction #369, Lot #17.

4793. PELTIER GLASS COMPANY. Multicolor. Transparent dark green base. Two ribbons each of red, white and light blue. Tiny flake and an air hole. Ottawa, IL, circa 1930-1945. 5/8". Near Mint(+) (8.9). Price: $8. CyberAuction #435, Lot #4.

4794. PELTIER GLASS COMPANY. Multicolor. Transparent dark green base. Six ribbons. Two each of white, salmon and blue. Ottawa, IL, circa 1935-1945. 11/16". Mint (9.9). Price: $8. CyberAuction #461, Lot #16.

4795. PELTIER GLASS COMPANY. Multicolor. Transparent dark green base. Six ribbons. Two each of salmon, white and blue ribbons. Ottawa, IL, circa 1930-1945. 19/32". Mint (9.9). Price: $7. CyberAuction #382, Lot #45.

4796. PELTIER GLASS COMPANY. Multicolor. Transparent dark green base. Two ribbons each of red, green and white. Couple of sparkles. Ottawa, IL, circa 1930-1945. 21/32". Near Mint(+) (8.9). Price: $6. CyberAuction #377, Lot #17.

4797. PELTIER GLASS COMPANY. Multicolor. Six-ribbon multicolor. Transparent dark green base. Two ribbons each of white, light blue and red. Ottawa, IL, circa 1930-1945. 19/32". Mint (9.7). There are four marbles available. You are bidding on one. Winner has choice of any or all, remainder to under. Price: $6. CyberAuction #384, Lot #3.

4798. PELTIER GLASS COMPANY. Multicolor. Six-ribbon multicolor. Transparent dark green base. Two ribbons each of white, light blue and red. Ottawa, IL, circa 1930-1945. 9/16". Mint (9.7). There are three marbles available. You are bidding on one. Winner has choice of any or all, remainder to under. Price: $6. CyberAuction #422, Lot #31.

4799. PELTIER GLASS COMPANY. Multicolor. Six-ribbon multicolor. Transparent dark green base. Two ribbons each of white, light blue and red. Ottawa, IL, circa 1930-1945. 19/32". Mint (9.7). There are two marbles available. You are bidding on one. Winner has choice of any or all, remainder to under. Price: $6. CyberAuction #422, Lot #43.

4800. PELTIER GLASS COMPANY. Multicolor. Transparent light green base. Two ribbons each of light blue, white and yellow. Nice swirling. Ottawa, IL, circa 1930-1945. 9/16". Mint (9.5). Price: $5. CyberAuction #382, Lot #15.

4801. PELTIER GLASS COMPANY. Multicolor. Six-ribbon multicolor. Transparent light green base. Two ribbons each of white, light blue and yellow. Ottawa, IL, circa 1930-1945. 19/32". Mint (9.7). There are two marbles available. You are bidding on one. Winner has choice of either or both, remainder to under. Price: $5. CyberAuction #384, Lot #7.

4802. PELTIER GLASS COMPANY. Multicolor. Six-ribbon multicolor. Transparent dark green base. Two ribbons each of white, light blue and red. Ottawa, IL, circa 1930-1945. 9/16". Mint (9.7). There are three marbles available. You are bidding on one. Winner has choice of any or all, remainder to under. Price: $5. CyberAuction #384, Lot #10.

4803. PELTIER GLASS COMPANY. Multicolor. Dark green transparent base. Two wide bands of blue and white, two bands of orange, two bands of orange/red. A tiny chip. Ottawa, IL, circa 1930-1940. 23/32". Near Mint(+) (8.9). Price: $5. CyberAuction #414, Lot #5.

4804. PELTIER GLASS COMPANY. Multicolor. Transparent green base. Six ribbons. Two each of blue, light red and white. Ottawa, IL, circa 1930-1945. 21/32". Mint (9.7). Price: $5. CyberAuction #433, Lot #15.

4805. PELTIER GLASS COMPANY. Multicolor. Six-ribbon multicolor. Transparent dark green base. Two ribbons each of white, light blue and red. Ottawa, IL, circa 1930-1945. 19/32". Mint (9.7). There are two marbles available. You are bidding on one. Winner has choice of any or all, remainder to under. Price: $5. CyberAuction #460, Lot #7.

4806. PELTIER GLASS COMPANY. Multicolor. Transparent dark green base. Two ribbons each of blue, white and orange/red. One subsurface moon. Ottawa, IL, circa 1930-1945. 11/16". Near Mint (8.9). Price: $4. CyberAuction #376, Lot #27.

4807. PELTIER GLASS COMPANY. Multicolor. Transparent dark green base. Two ribbons each of salmon pink, blue and white. One tiny sparkle. Ottawa, IL, circa 1930-1945. 19/32". Mint(-) (9.1). Price: $4. CyberAuction #381, Lot #24.

4808. PELTIER GLASS COMPANY. Multicolor. Transparent green base. Two ribbons each of salmon pink, white and yellow. Small flake, some pits. Not Mint. Ottawa, IL, circa 1930-1945. 11/16". Near Mint (8.4). Price: $3. CyberAuction #364, Lot #38.

4809. PELTIER GLASS COMPANY. Multicolor. Transparent green base. Three ribbons, three light blue ribbons, two white ribbons. Overall haze. Ottawa, IL, circa 1930-1940. 5/8". Near Mint(+) (8.2). Price: $2. CyberAuction #433, Lot #24.

4810. PELTIER GLASS COMPANY. Multicolor. Transparent green base. Six ribbons. Two each of orange, dark blue and white. One blown out air hole and one melt spot. Ottawa, IL, circa 1930-1945. 11/16". Mint(-) (9.1). Price: $2. CyberAuction #458, Lot #36.

4811. PELTIER GLASS COMPANY. Multicolor. Transparent light green base. Six bands. Two each of red, green and white. One sparkle. Ottawa, IL, circa 1930-1945. 5/8". Mint(-) (9.0). Price: $2. CyberAuction #496, Lot #30.

4812. PELTIER GLASS COMPANY. Multicolor. Very nice. Transparent dark green base. Two ribbons each of orange, blue and white. Heavily swirled. One subsurface moon. Ottawa, IL, circa 1930-1940. 11/16". Near Mint(+) (8.7). Price: $1. CyberAuction #457, Lot #1.

4813. PELTIER GLASS COMPANY. Multicolor. Transparent green base. Six ribbons. Two each of yellow, light blue, white. Ottawa, IL, circa 1935-1945. 9/16". Mint (9.7). Price: $1. CyberAuction #461, Lot #36.

4814. PELTIER GLASS COMPANY. Multicolor. Transparent light green base. Six bands. Two each of red, green and white. One sparkle. Ottawa, IL, circa 1930-1945. 5/8". Mint(-) (9.0). Price: $1. CyberAuction #463, Lot #5.

4815. PELTIER GLASS COMPANY. National Line Rainbo. Consignor refers to this as a "Red Devil". Two-color, six-ribbon National Line Rainbo shooter. Very large. Six red ribbons. Stunning and rare. Ottawa, IL, circa 1925-1930. 29/32". Mint (9.9). Price: $410. CyberAuction #381, Lot #51.

4816. PELTIER GLASS COMPANY. National Line Rainbo. One of the rarest National Line Rainbos I have ever seen. Five-color, six-ribbon National Line Rainbo. Doesn't have a name. Opaque white base. Three ribbons of translucent blue on aventurine opaque black. Light aventurine. Three ribbons of semi-opaque red on transparent brown. A beauty. One tiny air hole. Ottawa, IL, circa 1927-1935. 5/8". Mint (9.6). Price: $370. CyberAuction #441, Lot #60.

4817. PELTIER GLASS COMPANY. National Line Rainbo. One of the rarest National Line Rainbos I have ever seen. Five-color, six-ribbon National Line Rainbo. Doesn't have a name. Opaque white base. Three ribbons of translucent blue on aventurine opaque black. Light aventurine. Three ribbons of semi-opaque red on transparent brown. A beauty. One tiny air hole. Ottawa, IL, circa 1927-1935. 5/8". Mint (9.6). Price: $360. CyberAuction #401, Lot #60.

4818. PELTIER GLASS COMPANY. National Line Rainbo. This came with the "Red Devil" that was sold in CyberAuction 381. Two-color, six-ribbon National Line Rainbo shooter. Very large. Light blue base. Five yellow ribbons, one transparent dark brown ribbon. Very nice and hard to find. There are three tiny sparkles. Ottawa, IL, circa 1925-1930. 7/8". Near Mint(+) (8.9). Price: $260. CyberAuction #385, Lot #33.

4819. PELTIER GLASS COMPANY. National Line Rainbo. Two-color National Line Rainbo. Opaque yellow base. Four ribbons of red, varying widths. The widest ribbon has a layer of fiery golden aventurine. Superior example. Ottawa, IL, circa 1927-1935. 21/32". Mint (9.7). Price: $205. CyberAuction #356, Lot #25.

4820. PELTIER GLASS COMPANY. National Line Rainbo. Hard to find shooter marble. Two-color, four-ribbon, National Line Rainbo. Light blue base. Four red ribbons. One ribbon has gray around it. Tiny dimple at one ribbon, no damage on the marble. Large. Hard to find. Ottawa, IL, circa 1925-1935. 7/8". Mint (9.7). Price: $140. CyberAuction #459, Lot #23.

4821. PELTIER GLASS COMPANY. National Line Rainbo. Very nice three-color National Line Rainbo. Blue base. Four red bands and four semi-opaque black band between the reds. Very nice. Ottawa, IL, circa 1927-1935. 5/8". Mint (9.4). Price: $90. CyberAuction #348, Lot #33.

4822. PELTIER GLASS COMPANY. National Line Rainbo. Rare marble. Four ribbons. Light blue base. Each ribbon is red, edged by thin oxblood red. Very rare. One tiny subsurface moon. Ottawa, IL, circa 1927-1935. 5/8". Near Mint(+) (8.9). Price: $80. CyberAuction #335, Lot #59.

4823. PELTIER GLASS COMPANY. National Line Rainbo. Three-color, eight-ribbon National Line Rainbo Ketchup and Mustard. Opaque white base. Six red ribbons, two yellow ribbons. Super example. Ottawa, IL, circa 1930-1935. 21/32". Mint (9.6). Price: $80. CyberAuction #498, Lot #5.

4824. PELTIER GLASS COMPANY. National Line Rainbo. Mustard yellow base with four aventurine red ribbons. The aventurine is light and sparse, but it is there. One air hole. Rare. Ottawa, IL, circa 1927-1935. 21/32". Mint(-) (9.1). Price: $70. CyberAuction #359, Lot #37.

4825. PELTIER GLASS COMPANY. National Line Rainbo. Rare marble. Opaque mustard yellow base. Four wide ribbons of orange on yellow. Very nice marble. Ottawa, IL, circa 1927-1935. 11/16". Mint (9.8). Price: $65. CyberAuction #342, Lot #1.

4826. PELTIER GLASS COMPANY. National Line Rainbo. Three-color four-ribbon National Line Rainbo. Some collectors call these a Flaming Dragon. Personally, I don't do that, unless the base green is translucent or semi-transparent (see the Lot in the December 15 Absentee Marble Auction for an example). Light green opaque base. Four ribbons of red smeared on orange/yellow. Very hard to find. Couple of minor scuff marks. Ottawa, IL, circa 1930-1940. 21/32". Mint(-) (9.0). Price: $55. CyberAuction #502, Lot #25.

4827. PELTIER GLASS COMPANY. National Line Rainbo. Bifurcated three-color National Line Rainbo. One side is blue base, other side is green base. Four ribbons. Some pitting and sparkles. Ottawa, IL, circa 1927-1935. 21/32". Near Mint(+) (8.7). Price: $50. CyberAuction #345, Lot #16.

4828. PELTIER GLASS COMPANY. National Line Rainbo. Broken corkscrew design. Two-color, four-ribbon National Line Rainbo. Light blue base with brown ribbons. Ottawa, IL, circa 1927-1930. 21/32". Mint (9.8). Price: $47. CyberAuction #450, Lot #36.

4829. PELTIER GLASS COMPANY. National Line Rainbo. Two-color, four-ribbon National Line Rainbo. Opaque white base. Four orange ribbons. Hard to find coloring. In great shape. Ottawa, IL, circa 1925-1935. 5/8". Mint (9.9). Price: $47. CyberAuction #462, Lot #34.

4830. PELTIER GLASS COMPANY. National Line Rainbo. Odd four-ribbon three-color National Line Rainbo. Light blue base. Four ribbons of brown/red, edged by brown. Unusual. A couple of tiny sparkles. Ottawa, IL, circa 1927-1935. 5/8". Mint(-) (9.2). Price: $45. CyberAuction #354, Lot #55.

4831. PELTIER GLASS COMPANY. National Line Rainbo. I'm not sure what to call this, so I'll just describe it. Four ribbons. Heavily swirled. Light green base (opaque). Four ribbons of red mixed with orange/yellow. Each is edged by black. Not a burnt color, but distinctly black. No aventurine. Some pitting. Ottawa, IL, circa 1930-1935. 9/16". Near Mint(+) (8.9). Price: $40. CyberAuction #335, Lot #39.

4832. PELTIER GLASS COMPANY. National Line Rainbo. Three-color, six-ribbon National Line Rainbo. Six orange/red ribbons on light green. Gorgeous shooter size. Ottawa, IL, circa 1925-1935. 21/32". Mint (9.9). Price: $40. CyberAuction #479, Lot #22.

4833. PELTIER GLASS COMPANY. National Line Rainbo. Two color National Line Rainbo. Six red/brown ribbons on creamy white. Hard to find. A beauty. Ottawa, IL, circa 1925-1930. 21/32". Mint (9.9). Price: $37. CyberAuction #330, Lot #10.

4834. PELTIER GLASS COMPANY. National Line Rainbo. Gorgeous. Broken corkscrew. Light blue base. Four ribbons of gray/brown. One air hole. Beauty. Ottawa, IL, circa 1925-1935. 5/8". Mint (9.6). Price: $33. CyberAuction #366, Lot #43.

4835. PELTIER GLASS COMPANY. National Line Rainbo. Four-ribbon, two-color National Line Rainbo. Harder to find colors. Four two-tone red ribbons on mustard base. One air hole, but very wet. Gorgeous. Ottawa, IL, circa 1927-1935. 21/32". Mint (9.4). Price: $32. CyberAuction #429, Lot #36.

4836. PELTIER GLASS COMPANY. National Line Rainbo. Two-color four-ribbon National Line Rainbo. Four red/gray ribbons on light blue. Beauty. Ottawa, IL, circa 1927-1935. 9/16". Mint (9.9). Price: $31. CyberAuction #438, Lot #36.

4837. PELTIER GLASS COMPANY. National Line Rainbo. Two-color four-ribbon National Line Rainbo. Translucent red/brown ribbons on light green. Broken corkscrew pattern. Beauty. Ottawa, IL, circa 1927-1935. 5/8". Mint (9.9). Price: $30. CyberAuction #436, Lot #29.

4838. PELTIER GLASS COMPANY. National Line Rainbo. Two color National Line Rainbo. Four red ribbons on green. Ottawa, IL, circa 1925-1935. 19/32". Mint (9.7). Price: $29. CyberAuction #338, Lot #13.

4839. PELTIER GLASS COMPANY. National Line Rainbo. Two color National Line Rainbo. Very light gray base with four dark red ribbons. One small rough spot. Ottawa, IL, circa 1927-1935. 21/32". Near Mint(+) (8.9). Price: $28. CyberAuction #342, Lot #22.

4840. PELTIER GLASS COMPANY. National Line Rainbo. Four very fiery aventurine black ribbons on semi-opaque white. A real beauty. Two tiny flakes. Ottawa, IL, circa 1925-1935. 11/16". Near Mint(+) (8.8). Price: $27. CyberAuction #336, Lot #47.

4841. PELTIER GLASS COMPANY. National Line Rainbo. Odd marble. Blue base. Four ribbons. Each is a combination of red, yellow and black. Odd. A number of tiny pits and tiny chips. Ottawa, IL, circa 1927-1935. 19/32". Near Mint(-) (8.1). Price: $25. CyberAuction #343, Lot #37.

4842. PELTIER GLASS COMPANY. National Line Rainbo. Hard to find. Shooter. Transparent cherry red base with six semi-opaque white ribbons. Ottawa, IL, circa 1930-1935. 3/4". Mint(-) (9.0). Price: $25. CyberAuction #378, Lot #52.

4843. PELTIER GLASS COMPANY. National Line Rainbo. Four-ribbon, two-color National Line Rainbo. Light blue base. Broken corkscrew design. Red ribbons with gray edging. Very nice marble. One small air hole. Ottawa, IL, circa 1925-1930. 21/32". Mint (9.6). Price: $25. CyberAuction #436, Lot #15.

4844. PELTIER GLASS COMPANY. National Line Rainbo. Four-ribbon, two-color National Line Rainbo. Light blue base. Broken corkscrew design. Red ribbons with gray edging. Very nice marble. Several small and tiny air holes. Ottawa, IL, circa 1925-1930. 21/32". Mint(-) (9.0). Price: $24. CyberAuction #495, Lot #43.

4845. PELTIER GLASS COMPANY. National Line Rainbo. Two-color four-ribbon National Line Rainbo. Dark brown/red ribbons on blue. One air hole. Nice. Ottawa, IL, circa 1927-1935. 19/32". Mint(-) (9.0). Price: $23. CyberAuction #365, Lot #29.

4846. PELTIER GLASS COMPANY. National Line Rainbo. Two-color four-ribbon National Line Rainbo. Red/brown ribbons on green. Has a tiny unmelted piece of sand under one ribbon. Ottawa, IL, circa 1927-1935. 19/32". Mint(-) (9.0). Price: $23. CyberAuction #368, Lot #27.

4847. PELTIER GLASS COMPANY. National Line Rainbo. Two-color four-ribbon National Line Rainbo. Transparent green ribbons in yellow. Very nice. Ottawa, IL, circa 1927-1935. 5/8". Mint (9.7). Two marbles available. You are bidding on one. Winner has choice of either or both, remainder to under. Price: $23. CyberAuction #382, Lot #2.

4848. PELTIER GLASS COMPANY. National Line Rainbo. Two-color four-ribbon National Line Rainbo. Each ribbon is reddish/brown, edged by gray. Light blue base. Tiny sparkle. Ottawa, IL, circa 1927-1935. 5/8". Mint (9.3). Price: $23. CyberAuction #382, Lot #17.

4849. PELTIER GLASS COMPANY. National Line Rainbo. Some collectors refer to these as "Flaming Dragon". Light green base. Six ribbons, some short. Each is red on orange. Overall some tiny chips and pitting. Ottawa, IL, circa 1925-1935. 25/32". Good(+) (7.9). Price: $22. CyberAuction #344, Lot #24.

4850. PELTIER GLASS COMPANY. National Line Rainbo. Two-color six-ribbon National Line Rainbo. Red ribbons on light blue. Buffed. Ottawa, IL, circa 1927-1935. 5/8". Price: $22. CyberAuction #433, Lot #6.

4851. PELTIER GLASS COMPANY. National Line Rainbo. Two-color four-ribbon National Line Rainbo. Red ribbons on light blue. Overall pitting. Ottawa, IL, circa 1927-1940. 21/32". Near Mint(-) (8.0). Price: $21. CyberAuction #376, Lot #29.

4852. PELTIER GLASS COMPANY. National Line Rainbo. Two-color four-ribbon National Line Rainbo. Semi-opaque blue base. Four brown ribbons. Very nice. Ottawa, IL, circa 1930-1935. 9/16". Mint (9.7). Price: $21. CyberAuction #377, Lot #6.

4853. PELTIER GLASS COMPANY. National Line Rainbo. White base. Four red ribbons. Superb example. Ottawa, IL, circa 1927-1935. 21/32". Mint (9.9). Price: $20. CyberAuction #353, Lot #8.

4854. PELTIER GLASS COMPANY. National Line Rainbo. Blue base with red ribbons. Each ribbon is edged by black/gray. No aventurine. Two tiny chips. Ottawa, IL, circa 1927-1935. 5/8". Near Mint (8.5). Price: $19. CyberAuction #355, Lot #8.

4855. PELTIER GLASS COMPANY. National Line Rainbo. Two-color four-ribbon National Line Rainbo. Red ribbons on light blue. Two very tiny flakes. Ottawa, IL, circa 1927-1935. 5/8". Near Mint(+) (8.9). Price: $17. CyberAuction #364, Lot #53.

4856. PELTIER GLASS COMPANY. National Line Rainbo. Superior example of a broken corkscrew National Line Rainbo. Four red ribbons on light green. Ottawa, IL, circa 1925-1935. 9/16". Mint (9.7). Price: $17. CyberAuction #424, Lot #54.

4857. PELTIER GLASS COMPANY. National Line Rainbo. Two-color four-ribbon National Line Rainbo. Transparent green ribbons in pale light green. The green has light aventurine. There are some tiny pits and very tiny chips. Ottawa, IL, circa 1927-1935. 19/32". Near Mint(+) (8.7). Price: $17. CyberAuction #435, Lot #57.

4858. PELTIER GLASS COMPANY. National Line Rainbo. Two-color four-ribbon National Line Rainbo. White base with red ribbons. Nice marble. Ottawa, IL, circa 1927-1935. 21/32". Mint (9.9). Price: $15. CyberAuction #377, Lot #33.

4859. PELTIER GLASS COMPANY. National Line Rainbo. Two-color, four-ribbon, National Line Rainbo. Transparent dark green ribbons in opaque yellow. Some aventurine in the green, but light. A couple of pinpricks. Ottawa, IL, circa 1930-1940. 5/8". Mint(-) (9.0). Price: $15. CyberAuction #457, Lot #41.

4860. PELTIER GLASS COMPANY. National Line Rainbo. Six-ribbon, two-color National Line Rainbo. Light blue base. Four yellow ribbons, two very faint yellow ribbons (appear green). Ottawa, IL, circa 1930-1940. 5/8". Mint (9.7). Price: $15. CyberAuction #493, Lot #36.

4861. PELTIER GLASS COMPANY. National Line Rainbo. Two-color four-ribbon National Line Rainbo. Transparent green ribbons on yellow. Very nice marble. Ottawa, IL, circa 1925-1935. 21/32". Mint (9.8). Price: $14. CyberAuction #471, Lot #14.

4862. PELTIER GLASS COMPANY. National Line Rainbo. Two-color four-ribbon broken corkscrew National Line Rainbo. Four orangish-red ribbons on white. One air hole. Ottawa, IL, circa 1927-1940. 5/8". Mint(-) (9.2). Price: $13. CyberAuction #368, Lot #38.

4863. PELTIER GLASS COMPANY. National Line Rainbo. Two-color six-ribbon National Line Rainbo. Red ribbons on white. Heavily swirled. One tiny flake. Ottawa, IL, circa 1927-1935. 19/32". Near Mint(+) (8.9). Price: $13. CyberAuction #380, Lot #58.

4864. PELTIER GLASS COMPANY. National Line Rainbo. Two-color four-ribbon National Line Rainbo. Mustard base with four orange/red ribbons. Ottawa, IL, circa 1925-1935. 5/8". Mint (9.4). Price: $12. CyberAuction #385, Lot #3.

4865. PELTIER GLASS COMPANY. National Line Rainbo. Two-color four-ribbon National Line Rainbo. Mustard base with four orange/red ribbons. Ottawa, IL, circa 1925-1935. 5/8". Mint (9.4). Price: $12. CyberAuction #447, Lot #24.

4866. PELTIER GLASS COMPANY. National Line Rainbo. Two-color four-ribbon National Line Rainbo. Mustard base with four orange/red ribbons. Ottawa, IL, circa 1925-1935. 5/8". Mint (9.4). Price: $12. CyberAuction #474, Lot #2.

4867. PELTIER GLASS COMPANY. National Line Rainbo. Two-color four-ribbon National Line Rainbo. Brown/red ribbons on light green. One flake. Ottawa, IL, circa 1930-1935. 19/32". Near Mint(+) (8.7). Price: $11. CyberAuction #378, Lot #54.

4868. PELTIER GLASS COMPANY. National Line Rainbo. Two-color, four-ribbon, National Line Rainbo. Four transparent red ribbons in mustard yellow. Two tiny sparkles. Ottawa, IL, circa 1927-1935. 9/16". Mint(-) (9.0). Price: $11. CyberAuction #455, Lot #22.

4869. PELTIER GLASS COMPANY. National Line Rainbo. Four-ribbon two-color National Line Rainbo. Yellow ribbons on olive base. Polished. Ottawa, IL, circa 1930-1940. 3/4". Price: $10. CyberAuction #344, Lot #53.

4870. PELTIER GLASS COMPANY. National Line Rainbo. Two-color four-ribbon National Line Rainbo. Transparent red ribbons in mustard yellow. Very nice. One very tiny subsurface moon. Ottawa, IL, circa 1930-1940. 5/8". Near Mint(+) (8.9). Price: $10. CyberAuction #431, Lot #44.

4871. PELTIER GLASS COMPANY. National Line Rainbo. Two-color four-ribbon National Line Rainbo. Four wide brown ribbons on white. Several tiny sparkles. Ottawa, IL, circa 1927-1935. 5/8". Near Mint(+) (8.9). Price: $9. CyberAuction #372, Lot #44.

4872. PELTIER GLASS COMPANY. National Line Rainbo. Two-color, four-ribbon, National Line Rainbo. Four red ribbons on mustard yellow base. One tiny pit. Ottawa, IL, circa 1930-1935. 5/8". Mint(-) (9.0). Price: $9. CyberAuction #464, Lot #1.

4873. PELTIER GLASS COMPANY. National Line Rainbo. Two-color four-ribbon National Line Rainbo. Four transparent dark green ribbons in opaque white. Sparkle in one ribbon. Ottawa, IL, circa 1927-1935. 21/32". Mint(-) (9.0). Price: $8. CyberAuction #458, Lot #38.

4874. PELTIER GLASS COMPANY. National Line Rainbo. Two-color four-ribbon National Line Rainbo. Four transparent green ribbons in yellow. A couple of pits. Ottawa, IL, circa 1930-1940. 9/16". Near Mint (8.6). Price: $5. CyberAuction #463, Lot #53.

4875. PELTIER GLASS COMPANY. Original package. Original box of five comic marbles. Red box. Stamped "5-C" on the bottom. Box is in great shape. Contains Emma, Skeezix, Koko, Herbie and Bimbo. All marbles are in great shape (average to dark transfers). Super box and hard to find. Ottawa, IL, circa 1930-1935. Box is Mint (9.5). Marbles are Mint (9.9-9.7). Price: $825. CyberAuction #425, Lot #60.

4876. PELTIER GLASS COMPANY. Original package. Original box of five comic marbles. Red box. Stamped "5-C" on the bottom. Box is in great shape. Contains Emma, Skeezix, Koko, Herbie and Bimbo. All marbles are in great shape (average to dark transfers). Super box and hard to find. Ottawa, IL, circa 1930-1935. Box is Mint (9.5). Marbles are Mint (9.9-9.7). Price: $810. CyberAuction #400, Lot #60.

4877. PELTIER GLASS COMPANY. Original package. Original box of five comic marbles. Red box. Stamped "5-B" on the bottom. Box is in great shape. Contains Emma (blue patch, white base), Smitty (light transfer, red patch, white base), Koko (light transfer, black patch, white base), Herbie (light transfer, black patch, whit base) and Bimbo (green patch, white base). All marbles are in great shape. Super box and hard to find. Ottawa, IL, circa 1930-1935. Box is Mint (9.5). Marbles are Mint (9.9-9.7). Price: $800. CyberAuction #436, Lot #59.

4878. PELTIER GLASS COMPANY. Original package. Original box of five comic marbles. Red box. Box is in very nice shape (small tear in the bottom tab, some minor rubbing. Contains Emma (blue patch, white base), Smitty (light transfer, red patch, white base), Koko (light transfer, black patch, white base), Skeezix (blue patch, white base) and Bimbo (green patch, white base). All marbles are in great shape. Super box and hard to find. Ottawa, IL, circa 1930-1935. Box is Mint (9.5). Marbles are Mint (9.9-9.7). Price: $725. CyberAuction #455, Lot #60.

4879. PELTIER GLASS COMPANY. Original package. Original No. 5 box for five comic marbles. Red box. Box is in nice shape, with rubbing at the edges. Stamped 5-B on the bottom. There are no marbles, just the box. But, if you have the marbles, this is a great find. Ottawa, IL, circa 1930-1935. Mint (9.7). Price: $410. CyberAuction #458, Lot #60.

4880. PELTIER GLASS COMPANY. Original package. Original No. 5 box for five comic marbles. Red box. Box is in nice shape, with rubbing at the edges. Stamped 5-B on the bottom. There are no marbles, just the box. But, if you have the marbles, this is a great find. Ottawa, IL, circa 1930-1935. Mint (9.4). Price: $380. CyberAuction #495, Lot #33.

4881. PELTIER GLASS COMPANY. Original package. A very hard to find cube box for "100 Opaque Marbles" "Solid Color". This one is for green opaques and the word "GREEN" is stamped on it. Box has some wear and tiny tears. In very nice shape considering it is almost seventy five years old. About half filled with green opaque machine mades. Box is Near Mint(+), marbles are Mint. Hard to find. Price: $140. CyberAuction #441, Lot #28.

4882. PELTIER GLASS COMPANY. Original package. Box of "25 Prima Agates No. 50". This is a Gropper box. Tan paper over cardboard. Yellow label on the top. Box top is in great shape, box bottom has split corners. Includes twenty five Bloodie-type Rainbos. Each marble is orangish ribbons on semi-opaque white. Marbles 11/16". Box is about 3" x 3" x 3/4". Box top is Mint, bottom is Near Mint, marbles are Mint. I do not know if the marbles are original to the box. Price: $140. CyberAuction #455, Lot #50.

4883. PELTIER GLASS COMPANY. Original package. A very hard to find cube box for "100 Opaque Marbles" "Solid Color". This one is for green opaques and the word "GREEN" is stamped on it. Box has some wear and tiny tears. In very nice shape considering it is almost seventy five years old. About half filled with green opaque machine mades. Box is Near Mint(+), marbles are Mint. Hard to find. Price: $120. CyberAuction #385, Lot #28.

4884. PELTIER GLASS COMPANY. Original package. Box of "25 Prima Agates No. 50". This is a Gropper box. Tan paper over cardboard. Yellow label on the top. Box top is in great shape, box bottom has taped corners. Includes twenty five opaque black marbles. Marbles about 5/8". Box is about 3" x 3" x 3/4". Box top is Mint, bottom is Near Mint, marbles are Mint to Near Mint. I do not know if the marbles are original to the box. Price: $75. CyberAuction #373, Lot #25.

4885. PELTIER GLASS COMPANY. Original package. Poly bag with a Champion Jr. label. Contains Rainbos. About ten marbles. Orange label. Nice. There are two packages available, you are bidding on one. Winner has choice of either or both, remainder to under. Price: $15. CyberAuction #456, Lot #32.

4886. PELTIER GLASS COMPANY. Original package. Poly bag with a Champion Jr. label. Contains Rainbos. About ten marbles. Orange label. Nice. Price: $10. CyberAuction #448, Lot #31.

4887. PELTIER GLASS COMPANY. Original package. Poly bag with a Champion Jr. label. Contains Rainbos. About ten marbles. Orange label. Nice. There are two packages available, you are bidding on one. Winner has choice of either or both, remainder to under. Price: $7. CyberAuction #412, Lot #12.

4888. PELTIER GLASS COMPANY. Original package. Poly bag with a Champion Jr. label. Contains Rainbos. About ten marbles. Orange label. Nice. There are two packages available, you are bidding on one. Winner has choice of either or both, remainder to under. Price: $6. CyberAuction #419, Lot #25.

4889. PELTIER GLASS COMPANY. Original package. Poly bag. Green label. "Cat's Eye Champion". Contains nineteen Bananas. About 5" x 3". Mint. Price: $5. CyberAuction #476, Lot #22.

4890. PELTIER GLASS COMPANY. Patch. Not a Peerless Patch, later marble. Green base with blue patch. Ottawa, IL, circa 1930-1940. 19/32". Mint (9.9). There are three marbles available, you are bidding on one. Winner has choice of any or all, remainder to under. Price: $3. CyberAuction #473, Lot #37.

4891. PELTIER GLASS COMPANY. Peerless Patch. Yellow patch on green. Shooter. Hard to find. Ottawa, IL, circa 1925-1930. 23/32". Mint (9.7). Price: $29. CyberAuction #333, Lot #14.

4892. PELTIER GLASS COMPANY. Peerless Patch. Very hard to find "Superboy" Peerless Patch. Patch of yellow and red on blue. Rare marble. Ottawa, IL, circa 1925-1935. 5/8". Mint (9.7). Price: $27. CyberAuction #492, Lot #41.

4893. PELTIER GLASS COMPANY. Peerless Patch. Opaque white base,

aventurine black patch. Ottawa, IL, circa 1925-1930. 21/32". Mint (9.9). Price: $25. CyberAuction #362, Lot #50.

4894. PELTIER GLASS COMPANY. Peerless Patch. Shooter. Aventurine black patch on white. Beauty. Ottawa, IL, circa 1925-1930. 3/4". Mint (9.8). Price: $21. CyberAuction #353, Lot #57.

4895. PELTIER GLASS COMPANY. Peerless Patch. Aventurine black and white Peerless Patch. Black covers about half the marble. A few pinpricks. Ottawa, IL, circa 1925-1930. 23/32". Mint (9.4). Price: $21. CyberAuction #443, Lot #18.

4896. PELTIER GLASS COMPANY. Peerless Patch. Interesting Peerless Patch. Pale mustard base with a red patch. Narrow band of "burnt oxblood" on one edge of the patch. Ottawa, IL, circa 1925-1930. 11/16". Mint (9.7). Price: $17. CyberAuction #420, Lot #51.

4897. PELTIER GLASS COMPANY. Peerless Patch. Opalescent Peerless Patch. Hard to find. Opalescent milky white base. Black patch. No aventurine. Ottawa, IL, circa 1925-1930. 5/8". Mint (9.9). Price: $15. CyberAuction #348, Lot #20.

4898. PELTIER GLASS COMPANY. Peerless Patch. Aventurine black and white Peerless Patch. Black covers about half the marble. A few pinpricks. Ottawa, IL, circa 1925-1930. 23/32". Mint (9.4). Price: $15. CyberAuction #365, Lot #3.

4899. PELTIER GLASS COMPANY. Peerless Patch. Odd coloring. Pale orange base with a wide red patch. Ottawa, IL, circa 1925-1930. 21/32". Mint (9.6). Price: $15. CyberAuction #381, Lot #18.

4900. PELTIER GLASS COMPANY. Peerless Patch. Opaque white base. Aventurine black patch. Patch covers about half the marble. Fiery aventurine. Ottawa, IL, circa 1925-1930. 9/16". Mint (9.9). Price: $14. CyberAuction #365, Lot #11.

4901. PELTIER GLASS COMPANY. Peerless Patch. Red patch on aqua. About half red and half aqua. Some pits. Ottawa, IL, circa 1925-1930. 23/32". Mint(-) (9.0). Price: $13. CyberAuction #413, Lot #42.

4902. PELTIER GLASS COMPANY. Peerless Patch. Red patch on pale yellow. Odd color. Ottawa, IL, circa 1925-1930. 11/16". Mint (9.8). Price: $12. CyberAuction #418, Lot #7.

4903. PELTIER GLASS COMPANY. Peerless Patch. Opalescent white base with a black patch. One air hole (typical). Ottawa, IL, circa 1925-1930. 19/32". Mint (9.6). Price: $12. CyberAuction #421, Lot #40.

4904. PELTIER GLASS COMPANY. Peerless Patch. Opaque white base with an aventurine black patch. Light aventurine. Patch is almost half the marble. Some air holes in the patch. Ottawa, IL, circa 1925-1930. 21/32". Mint(-) (9.2). Price: $11. CyberAuction #330, Lot #35.

4905. PELTIER GLASS COMPANY. Peerless Patch. Opalescent white base with a black patch. One air hole (typical). Ottawa, IL, circa 1925-1930. 19/32". Mint (9.6). Price: $10. CyberAuction #482, Lot #12.

4906. PELTIER GLASS COMPANY. Peerless Patch. Rare coloring. Red patch on light chocolate brown. Ottawa, IL, circa 1925-1935. 19/32". Mint (9.9). Price: $10. CyberAuction #493, Lot #11.

4907. PELTIER GLASS COMPANY. Peerless Patch. Light blue base, yellow patch. Ottawa, IL, circa 1925-1930. 5/8". Mint (9.9). Price: $8. CyberAuction #362, Lot #40.

4908. PELTIER GLASS COMPANY. Peerless Patch. Opalescent white base with a black patch. One air hole (typical). Ottawa, IL, circa 1925-1930. 19/32". Mint (9.6). Price: $8. CyberAuction #381, Lot #29.

4909. PELTIER GLASS COMPANY. Peerless Patch. Light blue base. Yellow patch. Black patch brushed next to the yellow. One air hole. Ottawa, IL, circa 1925-1930. 9/16". Mint(-) (9.0). Price: $8. CyberAuction #393, Lot #52.

4910. PELTIER GLASS COMPANY. Peerless Patch. Opalescent white base with a black patch. One air hole (typical). Ottawa, IL, circa 1925-1930. 19/32". Mint (9.6). Price: $8. CyberAuction #454, Lot #31.

4911. PELTIER GLASS COMPANY. Peerless Patch. Rare coloring. Red patch on yellow (brighter yellow, not mustard yellow). A couple of tiny pits. Ottawa, IL, circa 1925-1935. 23/32". Mint(-) (9.0). Price: $8. CyberAuction #493, Lot #38.

4912. PELTIER GLASS COMPANY. Peerless Patch. White base, aventurine black patch. Light aventurine. Ottawa, IL, circa 1925-1930. 5/8". Mint (9.7). Price: $6. CyberAuction #433, Lot #5.

4913. PELTIER GLASS COMPANY. Peerless Patch. Aventurine black on white. Ottawa, IL, circa 1925-1930. 19/32". Mint (9.7). There are three marbles available. You are bidding on one. Winner has choice of any or all, remainder to under. Price: $5. CyberAuction #347, Lot #10.

4914. PELTIER GLASS COMPANY. Peerless Patch. Yellow patch on olive green base. Ottawa, IL, circa 1925-1930. 11/16". Mint (9.9). Price: $4. CyberAuction #424, Lot #21.

4915. PELTIER GLASS COMPANY. Peerless Patch. White base, red patch. Shooter. One tiny flake, one tiny air hole. Ottawa, IL, circa 1925-1930. 23/32". Near Mint(+) (8.9). Price: $4. CyberAuction #455, Lot #17.

4916. PELTIER GLASS COMPANY. Peerless Patch. Opaque white base. Black patch. No aventurine. Typical air hole in the black. Ottawa, IL, circa 1925-1935. 11/16". Mint (9.6). Price: $4. CyberAuction #483, Lot #26.

4917. PELTIER GLASS COMPANY. Peerless Patch. Red on aqua. A couple of tiny flakes. Ottawa, IL, circa 1925-1930. 23/32". Near Mint(+) (8.9). Price: $3. CyberAuction #417, Lot #2.

4918. PELTIER GLASS COMPANY. Peerless Patch. Red patch on aqua base. Ottawa, IL, circa 1925-1930. 19/32". Mint (9.9). Price: $3. CyberAuction #425, Lot #9.

4919. PELTIER GLASS COMPANY. Peerless Patch. Opalescent white base. Orange patch. Some tiny subsurface moons. Ottawa, IL, circa 1925-1930. 19/32". Near Mint(+) (8.7). Price: $3. CyberAuction #433, Lot #42.

4920. PELTIER GLASS COMPANY. Peerless Patch. Yellow patch on aqua. One air hole. Ottawa, IL, circa 1925-1935. 11/16". Mint (9.6). Price: $3. CyberAuction #463, Lot #3.

4921. PELTIER GLASS COMPANY. Peerless Patch. Red patch on white. Ottawa, IL, circa 1925-1930. 5/8". Mint (9.9). Price: $2. CyberAuction #436, Lot #26.

4922. PELTIER GLASS COMPANY. Peerless Patch. Yellow patch on light blue. 23/32". Mint (9.6). Two marbles available, you are bidding on one. Winner has choice of either or both, remainder to under. Price: $2. CyberAuction #469, Lot #14.

4923. PELTIER GLASS COMPANY. Peerless Patch. Two-tone red patch on light green. Air hole and subsurface moon. Ottawa, IL, circa 1925-1930. 9/16". Near Mint(+) (8.7). Price: $1. CyberAuction #433, Lot #14.

4924. PELTIER GLASS COMPANY. Peerless Patch. Yellow patch on light blue. One tiny subsurface moon. Ottawa, IL, circa 1925-1935. 5/8". Near Mint(+) (8.9). Price: $1. CyberAuction #457, Lot #4.

4925. PELTIER GLASS COMPANY. Picture Marble - comic. Black transfer of Kayo. White base, red patch marble. Transfer is average. Well centered. The white/red combination is rare for Kayo. Ottawa, IL, circa 1930-1935. 21/32". Mint (9.7). Price: $400. CyberAuction #428, Lot #60.

4926. PELTIER GLASS COMPANY. Picture Marble - comic. Black transfer of Kayo. White base, red patch marble. Transfer is a little light. Well centered. The white/red combination is rare for Kayo. Melt pits above figure. Ottawa, IL, circa 1930-1935. 21/32". Mint(-) (9.0). Price: $400. CyberAuction #495, Lot #41.

4927. PELTIER GLASS COMPANY. Picture Marble - comic. Black transfer of Kayo. White base, red patch marble. Transfer is average. Kayo's hat is on the red patch. The white/red combination is rare for Kayo. Ottawa, IL, circa 1930-1935. 21/32". Mint (9.7). Price: $345. CyberAuction #455, Lot #12.

4928. PELTIER GLASS COMPANY. Picture Marble - comic. Black transfer of Kayo. Marble is half red and half mustard yellow. Very odd. Very dark transfer. Well centered on the yellow. Very unusual color combination for Kayo. Tiny air hole in his hat. 21/32". Mint (9.5). Price: $335. CyberAuction #449, Lot #60.

4929. PELTIER GLASS COMPANY. Picture Marble - comic. Black transfer of Kayo. Marble is half red and half mustard yellow. Very odd. Very dark transfer. Well centered on the yellow. Very unusual color combination for Kayo. Tiny air hole in his hat. 21/32". Mint (9.5). Price: $310. CyberAuction #385, Lot #59.

4930. PELTIER GLASS COMPANY. Picture Marble - comic. Black transfer of Moon. Mustard base, green patch marble. Dark transfer, very well centered. Exceptional example. Ottawa, IL, circa 1930-1935. 21/32". Mint (9.9). Price: $295. CyberAuction #429, Lot #53.

4931. PELTIER GLASS COMPANY. Picture Marble - comic. Black transfer of Moon. Mustard base, light green patch. Average transfer. His collar just barely touches the green. Ottawa, IL, circa 1930-1935. 21/32". Mint (9.7). Price: $285. CyberAuction #425, Lot #41.

4932. PELTIER GLASS COMPANY. Picture Marble - comic. Black transfer of Betty. Mustard base with orange patch. Average transfer. Well centered. Marble color is very rare for any comic, not only Betty. Ottawa, IL, circa 1930-1935. 21/32". Mint (9.7). Price: $285. CyberAuction #438, Lot #48.

4933. PELTIER GLASS COMPANY. Picture Marble - comic. Very rare marble. Black transfer of Betty. Green base, yellow patch (reverse colors, rare). Light transfer. Well centered. Ottawa, IL, circa 193-1935. 21/32". Mint (9.9). Price: $275. CyberAuction #406, Lot #52.

4934. PELTIER GLASS COMPANY. Picture Marble - comic. Black transfer of Betty. White base, red patch marble. Rare color combination for Betty. Transfer is a little light, but is it very well centered. Ottawa, IL, circa 1930-1935. 21/32". Mint (9.7). Price: $275. CyberAuction #429, Lot #11.

4935. PELTIER GLASS COMPANY. Picture Marble - comic. Black transfer of Betty. Mustard yellow base, red patch. Odd color combination for Betty. Average transfer, just barely touches the red patch. Ottawa, IL, circa 1930-1935. 21/32". Mint (9.7). Price: $250. CyberAuction #450, Lot #15.

4936. PELTIER GLASS COMPANY. Picture Marble - comic. Black transfer of Kayo. Opaque white base, red patch marble. Light transfer. Well centered. Ottawa, IL, circa 1930-1935. 5/8". Mint (9.7). Price: $250. CyberAuction #498, Lot #47.

4937. PELTIER GLASS COMPANY. Picture Marble - comic. Very rare marble. Black transfer of Betty. Green base, yellow patch (reverse colors, rare). Light transfer. Well centered. Ottawa, IL, circa 193-1935. 21/32". Mint (9.9). Price: $235. CyberAuction #426, Lot #59.

4938. PELTIER GLASS COMPANY. Picture Marble - comic. Black transfer of Moon. Mustard yellow base, light green patch. Dark transfer. The name just barely touches the green patch. Ottawa, IL, circa 1930-1935. 21/32". Mint (9.9). Price: $210. CyberAuction #482, Lot #44.

4939. PELTIER GLASS COMPANY. Picture Marble - comic. Black transfer of Moon. Mustard yellow base, light green patch. Dark transfer. The name just barely touches the green patch. Ottawa, IL, circa 1930-1935. 21/32". Mint (9.9). Price: $200. CyberAuction #448, Lot #57.

4940. PELTIER GLASS COMPANY. Picture Marble - comic. Black transfer of Betty. White base, red patch marble. Harder to find color combination. Average transfer, well centered. Ottawa, IL, circa 1930-1935. 11/16". Mint (9.9). Price: $185. CyberAuction #448, Lot #43.

4941. PELTIER GLASS COMPANY. Picture Marble - comic. Black transfer of Koko. Olive green base, yellow patch. Average transfer, well centered. Ottawa, IL, circa 1930-1935. 21/32". Mint (9.9). Price: $185. CyberAuction #495, Lot #55.

4942. PELTIER GLASS COMPANY. Picture Marble - comic. Black transfer of Annie. Mustard base, red patch marble. Odd color combination for Annie. Light transfer. Top of head just touches the red. Ottawa, IL, circa 1930-1935. 21/32". Mint (9.7). Price: $175. CyberAuction #457, Lot #47.

4943. PELTIER GLASS COMPANY. Picture Marble - comic. Black transfer of Moon. Mustard base, light green patch. Light transfer. Well centered.

Tiny flake on back, couple of pinpricks. Ottawa, IL, circa 193-1935. 5/8" Near Mint(+) (8.8). Price: $130. CyberAuction #407, Lot #60.

4944. PELTIER GLASS COMPANY. Picture Marble - comic. Black transfer of Annie. White base, red patch marble. Transfer is a little light. Ottawa, IL, circa 1930-1935. 21/32". Mint (9.7). Price: $120. CyberAuction #490, Lot #44.

4945. PELTIER GLASS COMPANY. Picture Marble - comic. Black transfer of Annie. Mustard yellow base, red patch. Slightly light transfer, well centered. Odd color combination for Annie. Ottawa, IL, circa 1930-1935. 11 16". Mint (9.7). Price: $111. CyberAuction #450, Lot #34.

4946. PELTIER GLASS COMPANY. Picture Marble - comic. Black transfer of Emma. Mustard base, red patch marble. Average transfer. Well centered. Very odd marble color for Emma. Rare. Ottawa, IL, circa 1930-1935. 21 32". Mint (9.9). Price: $110. CyberAuction #425, Lot #50.

4947. PELTIER GLASS COMPANY. Picture Marble - comic. Black transfer of Sandy. Mustard base, red patch marble. Odd color combination for Sandy. The transfer is light, but well centered. Ottawa, IL, circa 1930-1935. 11 16". Mint (9.9). Price: $110. CyberAuction #508, Lot #61.

4948. PELTIER GLASS COMPANY. Picture Marble - comic. Black transfer of Sandy. White base, blue patch marble. Average transfer. Well centered. Ottawa, IL, circa 1930-1935. 5/8". Mint (9.9). Price: $100. CyberAuction #427, Lot #44.

4949. PELTIER GLASS COMPANY. Picture Marble - comic. Black transfer of Smitty. Mustard base, light green patch marble. Average transfer, nicely centered. Ottawa, IL, circa 1930-1935. 21/32". Mint (9.7). Price: $100 CyberAuction #508, Lot #29.

4950. PELTIER GLASS COMPANY. Picture Marble - comic. Black transfer of Bimbo. White base, transparent green patch. Well centered transfer Dark transfer. Ottawa, IL, circa 1930-1935. 11/16". Mint (9.7). Price: $90 CyberAuction #407, Lot #51.

4951. PELTIER GLASS COMPANY. Picture Marble - comic. Black transfer of Herbie. White base, aventurine black patch. Transfer is a little light. Well centered. 21/32". Mint (9.9). Price: $90. CyberAuction #428, Lot #6.

4952. PELTIER GLASS COMPANY. Picture Marble - comic. Black transfer of Smitty. White base, red patch marble. Top of head touches the red. Nice transfer. Ottawa, IL, circa 1930-1935. 11/16". Mint (9.7). Price: $90 CyberAuction #470, Lot #45.

4953. PELTIER GLASS COMPANY. Picture Marble - comic. Black transfer of Bimbo. Mustard base, red patch. Well centered transfer. Average transfer. Ottawa, IL, circa 1930-1935. 11/16". Mint (9.7). Price: $85. CyberAuction #407, Lot #58.

4954. PELTIER GLASS COMPANY. Picture Marble - comic. Black transfer of Bimbo. White base, transparent green patch. Well centered transfer Average transfer. One tiny subsurface piece of unmelted sand. Ottawa, IL, circa 1930-1935. 11/16". Mint (9.7). Price: $80. CyberAuction #359, Lot #59.

4955. PELTIER GLASS COMPANY. Picture Marble - comic. Black transfer of Sandy. White base, light blue patch marble. Transfer is on one edge of the white, but not touching the blue. Ottawa, IL, circa 1930-1935. 21/32". Mint (9.9). Price: $80. CyberAuction #439, Lot #59.

4956. PELTIER GLASS COMPANY. Picture Marble - comic. Black transfer of Annie. White base, red patch marble. Transfer is a little light. Ottawa, IL, circa 1930-1935. 21/32". Mint (9.9). Price: $80. CyberAuction #452, Lot #44.

4957. PELTIER GLASS COMPANY. Picture Marble - comic. Black transfer of Bimbo. Mustard base, red patch. Dark transfer, well centered. Ottawa, IL, circa 1927-1935. 21/32". Mint (9.9). Price: $80. CyberAuction #501, Lot #69.

4958. PELTIER GLASS COMPANY. Picture Marble - comic. Black transfer of Bimbo. White base, transparent green patch marble. Dark transfer, well centered. Some extraneous graphite on the marble. Tiny sparkle. Odd color combination for Bimbo. Ottawa, IL, circa 1930-1935. 11/16". Mint(-) (9.2). Price: $75. CyberAuction #495, Lot #30.

4959. PELTIER GLASS COMPANY. Picture Marble - comic. Black transfer of Bimbo. White base, transparent green base. Dark transfer. Well centered. Ottawa, IL, circa 1930-1935. 21/32". Mint (9.9). Price: $75. CyberAuction #498, Lot #38.

4960. PELTIER GLASS COMPANY. Picture Marble - comic. Black transfer of Smitty. Mustard base, light green patch. Average transfer. Hat just barely touches the green. Ottawa, IL, circa 1930-1935. 21/32". Mint (9.8). Price: $75. CyberAuction #500, Lot #28.

4961. PELTIER GLASS COMPANY. Picture Marble - comic. Black transfer of Bimbo. White base, transparent green patch marble. Dark transfer, well centered. Ottawa, IL, circa 1930-1935. 21/32". Mint (9.8). Price: $75. CyberAuction #500, Lot #35.

4962. PELTIER GLASS COMPANY. Picture Marble - comic. Black transfer of Bimbo. Mustard base, red patch. Dark transfer over the patch (which is large). Ottawa, IL, circa 1930-1935. 11/16". Mint (9.8). Price: $75. CyberAuction #505, Lot #43.

4963. PELTIER GLASS COMPANY. Picture Marble - comic. Black transfer of Andy. Mustard yellow base, light green patch. Dark transfer, but part of his neck is missing (the die must have been damaged). Ottawa, IL, circa 1930-1935. 21/32". Mint (9.6). Price: $70. CyberAuction #407, Lot #56.

4964. PELTIER GLASS COMPANY. Picture Marble - comic. Black transfer of Emma. Mustard base, red patch marble. Transfer is a little light. Well centered. Very odd marble color for Emma. Rare. Ottawa, IL, circa 1930-1935. 21/32". Mint (9.7). Price: $70. CyberAuction #455, Lot #23.

4965. PELTIER GLASS COMPANY. Picture Marble - comic. Black transfer of Smitty. Mustard base, light green patch marble. Dark transfer, well centered. Ottawa, IL, circa 1930-1935. 21/32". Mint (9.7). Price: $70. CyberAuction #501, Lot #11.

4966. PELTIER GLASS COMPANY. Picture Marble - comic. Black transfer of Smitty. Light green patch on mustard base. Dark transfer. Two tiny sparkles. Excellent example. Ottawa, IL, circa 1930-1935. 21/32". Mint (9.4). Price: $67. CyberAuction #357, Lot #53.

4967. PELTIER GLASS COMPANY. Picture Marble - comic. Black transfer of Skeezix. White base, light blue patch marble. Average transfer, well centered. Air hole on the white, but not near the transfer. Ottawa, IL, circa 1930-1935. 21/32". Mint(-) (9.0). Price: $67. CyberAuction #390, Lot #43.

4968. PELTIER GLASS COMPANY. Picture Marble - comic. Black transfer of Andy. Mustard yellow base, light green patch. Above average transfer, well centered. Ottawa, IL, circa 1930-1935. 21/32". Mint (9.9). Price: $65. CyberAuction #330, Lot #32.

4969. PELTIER GLASS COMPANY. Picture Marble - comic. Black transfer of Emma. Mustard base, red patch marble. Transfer is a little light. Well centered. Very odd marble color for Emma. Rare. Ottawa, IL, circa 1930-1935. 21/32". Mint (9.7). Price: $65. CyberAuction #458, Lot #59.

4970. PELTIER GLASS COMPANY. Picture Marble - comic. Black transfer of Andy. Mustard yellow base, light green patch. Dark transfer, but part of his neck is missing (the die must have been damaged). Ottawa, IL, circa 1930-1935. 21/32". Mint (9.6). Price: $60. CyberAuction #432, Lot #56.

4971. PELTIER GLASS COMPANY. Picture Marble - comic. Black transfer of Smitty. White base, red patch marble. Nice transfer. Top of head touches the red. Nice transfer. Ottawa, IL, circa 1930-1935. 11/16". Mint (9.7). Price: $60. CyberAuction #452, Lot #35.

4972. PELTIER GLASS COMPANY. Picture Marble - comic. Black transfer of Sandy. White base, light blue patch. Light transfer. Well centered. Ottawa, IL, circa 1930-1935. 21/32". Mint (9.7). Price: $60. CyberAuction #457, Lot #34.

4973. PELTIER GLASS COMPANY. Picture Marble - comic. Black transfer of Koko. White base, transparent green patch. Dark transfer. Well centered. Ottawa, IL, circa 1930-1935. 5/8". Mint (9.9). Price: $60. CyberAuction #498, Lot #25.

4974. PELTIER GLASS COMPANY. Picture Marble - comic. Black transfer of Smitty. Mustard base, light green patch marble. Dark transfer. Well centered. Ottawa, IL, circa 1930-1935. 11/16". Mint (9.8). Price: $60. CyberAuction #505, Lot #68.

4975. PELTIER GLASS COMPANY. Picture Marble - comic. Black transfer of Emma. Mustard base, red patch marble. Transfer is a little light. Well centered. Very odd marble color for Emma. Rare. Ottawa, IL, circa 1930-1935. 21/32". Mint (9.7). Price: $55. CyberAuction #458, Lot #41.

4976. PELTIER GLASS COMPANY. Picture Marble - comic. Black transfer of Bimbo. White base, transparent green patch. Average transfer. Ottawa, IL, circa 1930-1935. 21/32". Mint (9.8). Price: $50. CyberAuction #452, Lot #5.

4977. PELTIER GLASS COMPANY. Picture Marble - comic. Black transfer of Bimbo. Opaque white base, transparent green patch. Odd color marble for Bimbo. Dark transfer. Well centered. Ottawa, IL, circa 1930-1935. 21/32". Mint (9.9). Price: $50. CyberAuction #455, Lot #36.

4978. PELTIER GLASS COMPANY. Picture Marble - comic. Black transfer of Smitty. Mustard yellow base, light green patch. Dark transfer, well centered. Sparkle on the patch. Ottawa, IL, circa 1930-1935. 11/16". Mint(-) (9.0). Price: $50. CyberAuction #491, Lot #49.

4979. PELTIER GLASS COMPANY. Picture Marble - comic. Black transfer of Koko. White base, transparent green patch. Dark transfer. Well centered. Small subsurface air bubble on one side that looks like a moon, but is not. Ottawa, IL, circa 193-1935. 21/32". Mint (9.7). Price: $47. CyberAuction #371, Lot #39.

4980. PELTIER GLASS COMPANY. Picture Marble - comic. Black transfer of Emma. Opaque white base, light blue patch. Average transfer, well centered. Ottawa, IL, circa 1930-1935. 21/32". Mint (9.7). Price: $47. CyberAuction #470, Lot #11.

4981. PELTIER GLASS COMPANY. Picture Marble - comic. Black transfer of Koko. White base, transparent green patch. Dark transfer. Well centered. Ottawa, IL, circa 1930-1935. 5/8". Mint (9.9). Price: $46. CyberAuction #474, Lot #43.

4982. PELTIER GLASS COMPANY. Picture Marble - comic. Black transfer of Emma. Opaque white base, light blue patch. Average transfer, well centered. Ottawa, IL, circa 1930-1935. 21/32". Mint (9.8). Price: $45. CyberAuction #339, Lot #23.

4983. PELTIER GLASS COMPANY. Picture Marble - comic. Black transfer of Koko. White base, transparent green patch. Dark transfer. Well centered. Ottawa, IL, circa 193-1935. 21/32". Mint (9.7). Price: $45. CyberAuction #407, Lot #47.

4984. PELTIER GLASS COMPANY. Picture Marble - comic. Black transfer of Koko. White base with transparent green patch. Dark transfer. Off center but not touching the green. Ottawa, IL, circa 1930-1935. 21/32". Mint (9.9). Price: $45. CyberAuction #491, Lot #37.

4985. PELTIER GLASS COMPANY. Picture Marble - comic. Black transfer of Emma. White base, light blue patch marble. Dark transfer, but the nose and front of face touches the blue patch. Ottawa, IL, circa 1930-1935. 21/32". Mint (9.8). Price: $45. CyberAuction #498, Lot #11.

4986. PELTIER GLASS COMPANY. Picture Marble - comic. Black transfer of Koko. White base, transparent green patch. Average transfer. Top of hat almost touches green patch. Ottawa, IL, circa 1930-1935. 5/8". Mint (9.8). Price: $43. CyberAuction #508, Lot #4.

4987. PELTIER GLASS COMPANY. Picture Marble - comic. Black transfer of Emma. White base, light blue patch. Average transfer, well centered. Ottawa, IL, circa 1930-1935. 21/32". Mint (9.7). Price: $42. CyberAuction #358, Lot #48.

4988. PELTIER GLASS COMPANY. Picture Marble - comic. Black transfer of Emma. Opaque white base, light blue patch. Average transfer, well cen-

tered. Ottawa, IL, circa 1930-1935. 21/32". Mint (9.7). Price: $42. CyberAuction #404, Lot #42.

4989. PELTIER GLASS COMPANY. Picture Marble - comic. Black transfer of Emma. Opaque white base, light blue patch. Average transfer, well centered. Ottawa, IL, circa 1930-1935. 21/32". Mint (9.7). Price: $42. CyberAuction #449, Lot #44.

4990. PELTIER GLASS COMPANY. Picture Marble - comic. Black transfer of Bimbo. White base, transparent green patch. Average transfer. Ottawa, IL, circa 1930-1935. 21/32". Mint (9.8). Price: $42. CyberAuction #457, Lot #16.

4991. PELTIER GLASS COMPANY. Picture Marble - comic. Black transfer of Koko. White base, transparent green patch marble. Dark transfer. Well centered. Ottawa, IL, circa 1930-1935. 21/32". Mint (9.9). Price: $42. CyberAuction #494, Lot #15.

4992. PELTIER GLASS COMPANY. Picture Marble - comic. Black transfer of Emma. White base, light blue patch. Average transfer (top of hairdo is a little light). Well centered. Ottawa, IL, circa 1930-1935. 21/32". Mint (9.8). Price: $42. CyberAuction #500, Lot #9.

4993. PELTIER GLASS COMPANY. Picture Marble - comic. Black transfer of Emma. White base, blue patch. Dark transfer, well centered. Ottawa, IL, circa 1927-1935. 5/8". Mint (9.8). Price: $42. CyberAuction #501, Lot #26.

4994. PELTIER GLASS COMPANY. Picture Marble - comic. Black transfer of Koko. White base, transparent green patch. Average transfer. Ottawa, IL, circa 193-1935. 5/8". Mint (9.6). Price: $35. CyberAuction #392, Lot #43.

4995. PELTIER GLASS COMPANY. Picture Marble - comic. Black transfer of Koko. White base, transparent green patch marble. Well centered. Some extraneous graphite on it. One tiny sparkle on the back, one small blown air hole on the patch. Ottawa, IL, circa 1930-1935. 21/32". Mint(-) (9.0). Price: $35. CyberAuction #455, Lot #3.

4996. PELTIER GLASS COMPANY. Picture Marble - comic. Black transfer of Koko. White base, transparent green patch. Dark transfer. Well centered. Ottawa, IL, circa 1930-1935. 5/8". Mint (9.9). Price: $32. CyberAuction #458, Lot #8.

4997. PELTIER GLASS COMPANY. Picture Marble - comic. Black transfer of Emma. Opaque white base, light blue patch. Above average transfer, centered slightly low just touching the blue patch. Ottawa, IL, circa 1930-1935. 21/32". Mint (9.7). Price: $32. CyberAuction #494, Lot #31.

4998. PELTIER GLASS COMPANY. Rainbo. Interesting Rainbo. Light blue base. Four bands of mustard with aventurine strands in them. Ottawa, IL, circa 1940-1960. 11/16". Mint (9.7). Price: $38. CyberAuction #502, Lot #3.

4999. PELTIER GLASS COMPANY. Rainbo. Looks like a Bumblebee at first glance. However, under a maglite, you can see that it is very dark transparent brown base with four opaque yellow ribbons. Ottawa, IL, circa 1930-1940. 19/32". Mint (9.9). Price: $29. CyberAuction #348, Lot #49.

5000. PELTIER GLASS COMPANY. Rainbo. Interesting shooter size two-color Type 1 Rainbo. Opaque white base. Four blue ribbons. Excellent example. Ottawa, IL, circa 1930-1935. 7/8". Mint (9.9). Price: $28. CyberAuction #394, Lot #40.

5001. PELTIER GLASS COMPANY. Rainbo. Rainbo Champion Jr. sometimes referred to as a "Clown". Transparent green base with ribbons of red and ribbons of yellow. Pretty. Hard to find. One air hole. Ottawa, IL, circa 1935-1960. 19/32". Mint(-) (9.0). Price: $23. CyberAuction #391, Lot #53.

5002. PELTIER GLASS COMPANY. Rainbo. Rainbo Champion Jr. sometimes referred to as a "Clown". Transparent green base with ribbons of red and ribbons of yellow. Pretty. Hard to find. One tiny chip. Ottawa, IL, circa 1935-1960. 19/32". Near Mint(+) (8.9). Price: $20. CyberAuction #350, Lot #56.

5003. PELTIER GLASS COMPANY. Rainbo. Very odd. Fluorescent opaque Vaseline-type orangish base with four red ribbons. Ottawa, IL, circa 1930-1945. 9/16". Mint (9.7). Price: $17. CyberAuction #381, Lot #19.

5004. PELTIER GLASS COMPANY. Rainbo. Six-ribbon Rainbo. Semi-opaque white base. Six transparent blue ribbons. Ottawa, IL, circa 1930-1935. 19/32". Mint (9.9). Price: $17. CyberAuction #448, Lot #11.

5005. PELTIER GLASS COMPANY. Rainbo. Type of clear Rainbo. Would be a Sunset, but no tiny air bubbles. Transparent clear base with a very light green tint. Two ribbons of red and two of white. Interesting. Ottawa, IL, circa 1930-1945. 5/8". Mint (9.7). Price: $11. CyberAuction #373, Lot #15.

5006. PELTIER GLASS COMPANY. Rainbo. Two-color Type I Rainbo. Transparent blue base. Two opaque white equatorial ribbons, one white at the top, one at the bottom. Ottawa, IL, circa 1930-1935. 5/8". Mint (9.8). Price: $10. CyberAuction #365, Lot #32.

5007. PELTIER GLASS COMPANY. Rainbo. Hard to find transparent six-ribbon Rainbo. Transparent green base. Six semi-opaque white ribbons. Very nice. Ottawa, IL, circa 1930-1945. 5/8". Mint (9.9). Price: $10. CyberAuction #368, Lot #22.

5008. PELTIER GLASS COMPANY. Rainbo. Shooter Rainbo. White base, four blue ribbons. One panel is clear. Several sparkles. Ottawa, IL, circa 1930-1945. 27/32". Near Mint(+) (8.7). Price: $10. CyberAuction #397, Lot #37.

5009. PELTIER GLASS COMPANY. Rainbo. Harder to find type of Bloodie. Semi-opaque milky white base with opaque white, translucent red and semi-opaque red ribbons. Nice. Ottawa, IL, circa 1935-1950. 5/8". Mint (9.9). Price: $9. CyberAuction #351, Lot #6.

5010. PELTIER GLASS COMPANY. Rainbo. Very odd early Rainbo. Transparent very dark purple base with four white ribbons. Nice. Ottawa, IL, circa 1930-1940. 21/32". Mint (9.6). Price: $8. CyberAuction #377, Lot #4.

5011. PELTIER GLASS COMPANY. Rainbo. Odd Rainbo. Opalescent white base. Four transparent blue ribbon. One end is a transparent brown/green patch. Ottawa, IL, circa 1930-1945. 9/16". Mint (9.9). Price: $7. CyberAuction #393, Lot #32.

5012. PELTIER GLASS COMPANY. Rainbo. Semi-opaque white base. Four thin yellow ribbons, two with green on them. Unusual. One very tiny flake. Ottawa, IL, circa 1930-1940. 31/32". Near Mint(+) (8.9). Price: $6. CyberAuction #409, Lot #54.

5013. PELTIER GLASS COMPANY. Rainbo. Interesting marble. It's actually a Champion Jr. style Bloodie, not a Rainbo style Bloodie. Opalescent semi-opaque white base. A ribbon of smeared red wrapped around the equator (as opposed to four ribbons in the equator). Small air hole. Ottawa, IL, circa 1930-1945. 5/8". Mint(-) (9.1). Price: $5. CyberAuction #369, Lot #35.

5014. PELTIER GLASS COMPANY. Rainbo. Six ribbon Rainbo. Semi-opaque white base with six transparent blue ribbons. Nice. Ottawa, IL, circa 1930-1945. 5/8". Mint (9.9). Price: $4. CyberAuction #354, Lot #14.

5015. PELTIER GLASS COMPANY. Rebel. Exceptional example. Three-color six-ribbon National Line Rainbo Rebel. Opaque white base with four aventurine black ribbons and four red ribbons. Stunning marble. Ottawa, IL, circa 1927-1935. 23/32". Mint (9.7). Price: $300. CyberAuction #471, Lot #58.

5016. PELTIER GLASS COMPANY. Rebel. Three color National Line Rainbo Rebel. Opaque white base with two wide black ribbons and four wide red ribbons (varying shades). Almost no aventurine in the black. Stunning marble. Ottawa, IL, circa 1927-1935. 11/16". Mint (9.6). Price: $150. CyberAuction #363, Lot #55.

5017. PELTIER GLASS COMPANY. Rebel. Three-color six-ribbon National Line Rainbo Rebel. Opaque white base with four transparent red ribbons and two small black ribbons. No aventurine. Super condition. Ottawa, IL, circa 1927-1935. 5/8". Mint (9.9). Price: $95. CyberAuction #407, Lot #49.

5018. PELTIER GLASS COMPANY. Rebel. Odd three-color eight-ribbon National Line Rainbo Rebel. Opaque white base, five orange ribbons, three black ribbons. One black ribbon is very thin. No aventurine. One tiny flake. Odd coloring. Ottawa, IL, circa 1927-1935. 11/16". Near Mint(+) (8.9). Price: $71. CyberAuction #501, Lot #71.

5019. PELTIER GLASS COMPANY. Rebel. Six-ribbon three-color National Line Rainbo Rebel. Opaque white base. Four orange/red ribbons, two fiery aventurine black ribbons. Ottawa, IL, circa 1930-1935. 19/32". Mint (9.7). Price: $70. CyberAuction #505, Lot #61.

5020. PELTIER GLASS COMPANY. Rebel. Gorgeous example. Three-color six-ribbon National Line Rainbo Rebel. Opaque white base with two fiery aventurine black ribbons and four red ribbons. Beautiful marble. Air hole and some pinpricking. Ottawa, IL, circa 1927-1935. 9/16". Mint(-) (9.0). Price: $65. CyberAuction #496, Lot #44.

5021. PELTIER GLASS COMPANY. Rebel. Three-color six-ribbon National Line Rainbo Rebel. Opaque white base with two wide transparent red ribbons and four small black ribbons. Two small chips. Ottawa, IL, circa 1927-1935. 9/16". Near Mint (8.5). Price: $55. CyberAuction #385, Lot #42.

5022. PELTIER GLASS COMPANY. Rebel. Three-color six-ribbon National Line Rainbo Rebel. Opaque white base with two wide transparent red ribbons and four small black ribbons. Thin ribbons. Overall subsurface moons and pitting. Ottawa, IL, circa 1927-1935. 25/32". Good (7.4). Price: $27. CyberAuction #376, Lot #17.

5023. PELTIER GLASS COMPANY. Rebel. Three-color eight-ribbon National Line Rainbo Rebel. Opaque white base with five red ribbons and three aventurine black ribbons. Overall pitting. Ottawa, IL, circa 1927-1935. 21/32". Good(+) (7.9). Price: $15. CyberAuction #465, Lot #22.

5024. PELTIER GLASS COMPANY. Rebel. Three-color six-ribbon National Line Rainbo Rebel. Opaque white base with three wide transparent red ribbons and three aventurine black ribbons. Small chip, tiny subsurface moon. Ottawa, IL, circa 1927-1935. 21/32". Near Mint (8.3). Price: $15. CyberAuction #485, Lot #3.

5025. PELTIER GLASS COMPANY. Rebel. Eight-ribbon, three-color National Line Rainbo Rebel. White base. Five red ribbons, three aventurine black ribbons. Overall chipping. Ottawa, IL, circa 1925-1935. 5/8". Good(-) (7.3). Price: $11. CyberAuction #493, Lot #70.

5026. PELTIER GLASS COMPANY. Rebel. Three-color six-ribbon National Line Rainbo Rebel. Heavily swirled. No aventurine. Chips and flakes. Ottawa, IL, circa 1928-1935. 23/32". Good(-) (7.1). Price: $10. CyberAuction #411, Lot #17.

5027. PELTIER GLASS COMPANY. Red Zebra. Consignor refers to this as a "Red Devil", but it is really a Red Zebra. Two-color, six-ribbon National Line Rainbo shooter. Very large. White base with six red ribbons. Stunning and rare. Ottawa, IL, circa 1925-1930. 27/32". Mint (9.9). Price: $260. CyberAuction #418, Lot #58.

5028. PELTIER GLASS COMPANY. Red Zebra. Consignor refers to this as a "Red Devil", but it is really a Red Zebra. Two-color, six-ribbon National Line Rainbo shooter. Very large. White base with six red ribbons. Stunning and rare. Ottawa, IL, circa 1925-1930. 7/8". Mint (9.9). Price: $210. CyberAuction #448, Lot #41.

5029. PELTIER GLASS COMPANY. Red Zebra. Two-color four-ribbon National Line Rainbo. Red ribbons on white. Shooter. Ottawa, IL, circa 1930-1940. 29/32". Mint (9.9). Price: $24. CyberAuction #466, Lot #41.

5030. PELTIER GLASS COMPANY. Red Zebra. Two-color four-ribbon National Line Rainbo. Red ribbons on white. Shooter. Ottawa, IL, circa 1930-1940. 29/32". Mint (9.9). Price: $22. CyberAuction #419, Lot #51.

5031. PELTIER GLASS COMPANY. Red Zebra. Two-color four-ribbon National Line Rainbo. Red ribbons on white. Shooter. Lot so damage. Ottawa, IL, circa 1930-1940. 27/32". Good (7.5). Consignor note: G30. Price: $5. CyberAuction #423, Lot #1.

5032. PELTIER GLASS COMPANY. Slag. Hybrid Peltier slag. Aqua base with a little green mixed in. Nice feathering of the white. Very unusual coloring. Ottawa, IL, circa 1925-1930. 5/8". Mint (9.9). Price: $44. CyberAuction #330, Lot #26.

5033. PELTIER GLASS COMPANY. Slag. Aqua slag. Nice white feathering. Beauty. Ottawa, IL, circa 1925-1930. 21/32". Mint (9.6). Price: $25. CyberAuction #337, Lot #8.

5034. PELTIER GLASS COMPANY. Slag. Red slag. Very nice feathering. An air hole and a couple of tiny pits. Ottawa, IL, circa 1925-1930. 19/32". Mint(-) (9.2). Price: $19. CyberAuction #333, Lot #34.

5035. PELTIER GLASS COMPANY. Slag. Green slag. Nice white feathering. Ottawa, IL, circa 1925-1930. 19/32". Mint (9.7). Price: $19. CyberAuction #338, Lot #34.

5036. PELTIER GLASS COMPANY. Slag. Red slag. Nice white feathering. One small subsurface moo. Ottawa, IL, circa 1925-1930. 19/32". Near Mint(+) (8.7). Price: $15. CyberAuction #338, Lot #10.

5037. PELTIER GLASS COMPANY. Slag. Brown slag shooter. Hard to find size. Sparkle. Ottawa, IL, circa 1925-1930. 23/32". Near Mint(+) (8.9). Price: $15. CyberAuction #496, Lot #1.

5038. PELTIER GLASS COMPANY. Slag. Purple slag. One sparkle. Ottawa, IL, circa 1925-1930. 5/8". Mint(-) (9.0). Price: $14. CyberAuction #443, Lot #14.

5039. PELTIER GLASS COMPANY. Slag. Brown slag. Beautiful example. Two melt spots on it. Ottawa, IL, circa 1925-1930. 21/32". Mint(-) (9.0). Price: $13. CyberAuction #448, Lot #2.

5040. PELTIER GLASS COMPANY. Slag. Green slag. Nice white feathering. One tiny sparkle. Ottawa, IL, circa 1925-1935. 5/8". Mint(-) (9.1). Price: $12. CyberAuction #372, Lot #49.

5041. PELTIER GLASS COMPANY. Slag. Green slag with nice white feathering. Ottawa, IL, circa 1925-1930. 19/32". Mint (9.9). Price: $12. CyberAuction #418, Lot #19.

5042. PELTIER GLASS COMPANY. Slag. Brown slag. Very nice white feathering. Small chip. Ottawa, IL, circa 1927-1935. 11/16". Near Mint(+) (8.8). Price: $11. CyberAuction #335, Lot #55.

5043. PELTIER GLASS COMPANY. Slag. Aqua slag. One air hole. Ottawa, IL, circa 1925-1935. 5/8". Mint (9.3). Price: $11. CyberAuction #369, Lot #31.

5044. PELTIER GLASS COMPANY. Slag. Brown slag. Nice white feathering. Ottawa, IL, circa 1925-1935. 5/8". Mint (9.6). Consignor note: B13. Price: $11. CyberAuction #384, Lot #11.

5045. PELTIER GLASS COMPANY. Slag. Brown slag. Nice feathering. Ottawa, IL, circa 1925-1930. 21/32". Mint (9.9). Price: $10. CyberAuction #433, Lot #2.

5046. PELTIER GLASS COMPANY. Slag. Purple slag with white feathering. One tiny pit. Ottawa, IL, circa 1925-1930. 19/32". Mint(-) (9.2). Price: $9. CyberAuction #377, Lot #15.

5047. PELTIER GLASS COMPANY. Slag. Purple slag. One sparkle. Ottawa, IL, circa 1925-1930. 5/8". Mint(-) (9.0). Price: $9. CyberAuction #397, Lot #45.

5048. PELTIER GLASS COMPANY. Slag. Green slag. Nice white feathering. Pinprick. Ottawa, IL, circa 1925-1930. 19/32". Mint(-) (9.0). Price: $8. CyberAuction #360, Lot #13.

5049. PELTIER GLASS COMPANY. Slag. Brown slag. Nice white feathering. Ottawa, IL, circa 1925-1935. 5/8". Mint (9.6). Price: $8. CyberAuction #385, Lot #18.

5050. PELTIER GLASS COMPANY. Slag. Blue slag. Nice. Air hole and some pinpricks. Ottawa, IL, circa 1925-1930. 21/32". Near Mint(+) (8.8). Price: $8. CyberAuction #438, Lot #37.

5051. PELTIER GLASS COMPANY. Slag. Aqua slag. One air hole. Ottawa, IL, circa 1925-1935. 5/8". Mint (9.3). Price: $7. CyberAuction #444, Lot #45.

5052. PELTIER GLASS COMPANY. Slag. Aqua slag. Shooter size. Some pitting and dirt marks. Ottawa, IL, circa 1925-1930. 3/4". Near Mint (8.6). Price: $7. CyberAuction #456, Lot #52.

5053. PELTIER GLASS COMPANY. Slag. Aqua slag. Two melt flakes. Ottawa, IL, circa 1925-1930. 11/16". Near Mint(+) (8.9). Price: $6. CyberAuction #417, Lot #55.

5054. PELTIER GLASS COMPANY. Slag. Very hard to find two-seam fluorescent yellow slag. One chip. Ottawa, IL, circa 1925-1935. 21/32". Near Mint(+) (8.7). Price: $6. CyberAuction #465, Lot #2.

5055. PELTIER GLASS COMPANY. Slag. Green slag. Several tiny chips. Ottawa, IL, circa 1925-1930. 5/8". Near Mint (8.3). Price: $5. CyberAuction #405, Lot #33.

5056. PELTIER GLASS COMPANY. Slag. Aqua slag. Shooter size. Some pitting and dirt marks. Ottawa, IL, circa 1925-1930. 3/4". Near Mint (8.6). Price: $5. CyberAuction #416, Lot #2.

5057. PELTIER GLASS COMPANY. Slag. Green slag. Several tiny flakes. Ottawa, IL, circa 1925-1930. 19/32". Near Mint(-) (8.1). Price: $3. CyberAuction #435, Lot #12.

5058. PELTIER GLASS COMPANY. Slag. Green slag. Two seam. One tiny chip, some pits. Ottawa, IL, circa 1925-1930. 19/32". Near Mint(+) (8.7). Price: $1. CyberAuction #477, Lot #23.

5059. PELTIER GLASS COMPANY. Superboy. Three color National Line Rainbo Superboy. Opaque blue base. Four ribbons of red, three yellow. Also some black in between. Two tiny subsurface moons. Ottawa, IL, circa 1927-1935. 5/8". Near Mint(+) (8.8). Price: $100. CyberAuction #333, Lot #59.

5060. PELTIER GLASS COMPANY. Superboy. Three color National Line Rainbo Superboy. Opaque blue base. Six ribbons of yellow, with red floating on them. Several are very small or thin. One small flake, else in great shape. Large shooter. Rare marble. Ottawa, IL, circa 1927-1935. 3/4". Near Mint(+) (8.7). Price: $92. CyberAuction #354, Lot #57.

5061. PELTIER GLASS COMPANY. Superman. Shooter three-color six-ribbon National Line Rainbo Superman. Opaque light blue base. Four red ribbons and two yellow. A couple of very tiny flakes, in the same area. Ottawa, IL, circa 1927-1935. 23/32". Near Mint(+) (8.7). Price: $320. CyberAuction #373, Lot #52.

5062. PELTIER GLASS COMPANY. Superman. Three-color eight-ribbon National Line Rainbo Superman. Six red ribbons, two yellow ribbons. Varying thickness. In great shape. Ottawa, IL, circa 1927-1935. 21/32". Mint (9.8). Price: $235. CyberAuction #475, Lot #54.

5063. PELTIER GLASS COMPANY. Superman. Three-color six-ribbon National Line Rainbo Superman. Opaque light blue base. Yellow and red ribbons. Wide gray ribbons too. One tiny sparkle. Ottawa, IL, circa 1928-1935. 21/32". Mint(-) (9.2). Price: $185. CyberAuction #385, Lot #55.

5064. PELTIER GLASS COMPANY. Superman. Three-color six-ribbon National Line Rainbo Superman. Opaque light blue base. Three yellow and three red ribbons. Some gray in the red. No damage, but there are two tiny melt air holes that interestingly have some yellow highlights around them, under the surface. Very odd. In great shape. One tiny pinprick. Ottawa, IL, circa 1928-1935. 5/8". Mint (9.5). Price: $180. CyberAuction #387, Lot #60.

5065. PELTIER GLASS COMPANY. Superman. Light blue base. Four red ribbons, with some gray, two yellow ribbons. Some swirling and smearing. Several tiny subsurface moons. Still, a beauty. Ottawa, IL, circa 1925-1935. 5/8". Near Mint (8.6). Price: $135. CyberAuction #350, Lot #60.

5066. PELTIER GLASS COMPANY. Superman. Three color National Line Rainbo Superman. Opaque light blue base. Yellow and red ribbons. Wide gray ribbons too. A couple of tiny sparkles. Ottawa, IL, circa 1928-1935. 19/32". Mint(-) (9.0). Price: $130. CyberAuction #348, Lot #58.

5067. PELTIER GLASS COMPANY. Superman. Six-ribbon three-color National Line Rainbo Superman. Light blue base. Four red ribbons, with some gray, two yellow ribbons. One tiny flake. Ottawa, IL, circa 1925-1935. 11/16". Near Mint(+) (8.8). Price: $130. CyberAuction #407, Lot #46.

5068. PELTIER GLASS COMPANY. Superman. Light blue base. Four red ribbons, with some gray, two yellow ribbons. Lots of swirling and smearing. Several tiny flakes. Still, a beauty. Ottawa, IL, circa 1925-1935. 11/16". Near Mint (8.6). Price: $120. CyberAuction #339, Lot #16.

5069. PELTIER GLASS COMPANY. Superman. Shooter three-color six-ribbon National Line Rainbo Superman. Opaque light blue base. Four red ribbons and two yellow. Small chip and a couple of tiny rough spots. Still, views very well. Ottawa, IL, circa 1927-1935. 3/4". Near Mint (8.4). Price: $120. CyberAuction #384, Lot #59.

5070. PELTIER GLASS COMPANY. Superman. Light blue base. Six red ribbons, edged by gray, two yellow ribbons. Several tiny flakes and chips. Still, a beauty. Ottawa, IL, circa 1925-1935. 5/8". Near Mint(+) (8.7). Price: $100. CyberAuction #363, Lot #49.

5071. PELTIER GLASS COMPANY. Superman. Six-ribbon three-color National Line Rainbo Superman. Light blue base. Three red ribbons, with some gray, three yellow ribbons. Lots of swirling and smearing. Several tiny chips and flakes. Ottawa, IL, circa 1925-1935. 11/16". Near Mint (8.6). Price: $100. CyberAuction #408, Lot #44.

5072. PELTIER GLASS COMPANY. Superman. Six-ribbon three-color National Line Rainbo Superman. Light blue base. Four red ribbons, with some gray, two yellow ribbons. One tiny flake. Ottawa, IL, circa 1925-1935. 11/16". Near Mint(+) (8.8). Price: $100. CyberAuction #432, Lot #53.

5073. PELTIER GLASS COMPANY. Superman. Six-ribbon three-color National Line Rainbo Superman. Light blue base. Three red ribbons, with some gray, three yellow ribbons. Lots of swirling and smearing. Several tiny chips and flakes. Ottawa, IL, circa 1925-1935. 11/16". Near Mint (8.6). Price: $85. CyberAuction #389, Lot #59.

5074. PELTIER GLASS COMPANY. Superman. Light blue base. Six red ribbons, edged by gray, two yellow ribbons. Two blown air holes (one is chipped), on pit. Still, a beauty. Ottawa, IL, circa 1925-1935. 5/8". Near Mint (8.6). Price: $80. CyberAuction #422, Lot #60.

5075. PELTIER GLASS COMPANY. Superman. Three color National Line Rainbo Superman. Blue base. Yellow and red bands. Polished. 19/32". Price: $75. CyberAuction #344, Lot #2.

5076. PELTIER GLASS COMPANY. Superman. Three-color eight-ribbon National Line Rainbo Superman. Opaque light blue base. Yellow and red ribbons. Wide gray ribbons too. Pitting and a small chip. Ottawa, IL, circa 1928-1935. 11/16". Good(+) (7.9). Price: $70. CyberAuction #382, Lot #59.

5077. PELTIER GLASS COMPANY. Superman. Light blue base. Six red ribbons, edged by gray, two yellow ribbons. Two blown air holes (one is chipped), on pit. Still, a beauty. Ottawa, IL, circa 1925-1935. 5/8". Near Mint (8.6). Price: $65. CyberAuction #391, Lot #51.

5078. PELTIER GLASS COMPANY. Superman. Light blue base. Four red ribbons, with some gray, two yellow ribbons. Lots of swirling and smearing. Some tiny chips and flakes. Still, a beauty. Ottawa, IL, circa 1925-1935. 21/32". Near Mint(-) (8.1). Price: $65. CyberAuction #393, Lot #56.

5079. PELTIER GLASS COMPANY. Superman. Six-ribbon three-color National Line Rainbo Superman. Light blue base. Four red ribbons, with lots of gray, two yellow ribbons. Nice pattern. Several tiny chips and a little haze in spots. Ottawa, IL, circa 1925-1935. 19/32". Near Mint(-) (8.0). Price: $55. CyberAuction #431, Lot #40.

5080. PELTIER GLASS COMPANY. Tiger. Two-color four-ribbon National Line Rainbo Tiger. Orange base with black ribbons. No aventurine. One tiny manufacturing air hole. Stunning example. Ottawa, IL, circa 1928-1935. 11/16". Mint (9.7). Price: $80. CyberAuction #373, Lot #37.

5081. PELTIER GLASS COMPANY. Tiger. Two color National Line Rainbo Tiger. Orange base with four aventurine black ribbons. Excellent example. Ottawa, IL, circa 1927-1935. 19/32". Mint (9.9). Price: $55. CyberAuction #499, Lot #19.

5082. PELTIER GLASS COMPANY. Tiger. Two-color four-ribbon National Line Rainbo Tiger. Orange base with aventurine black ribbons. One small subsurface moon. Ottawa, IL, circa 1928-1935. 21/32". Near Mint(+) (8.8). Price: $45. CyberAuction #377, Lot #29.

5083. PELTIER GLASS COMPANY. Tiger. Two-color four-ribbon National Line Rainbo Tiger. Orange base with aventurine black ribbons. Two tiny chips. Ottawa, IL, circa 1928-1935. 19/32". Near Mint(+) (8.8). Price: $42. CyberAuction #463, Lot #33.

5084. PELTIER GLASS COMPANY. Tiger. Two-color four-ribbon National Line Rainbo Tiger. Orange base with aventurine black ribbons. One small subsurface moon. Ottawa, IL, circa 1928-1935. 21/32". Near Mint(+) (8.8). Price: $35. CyberAuction #376, Lot #15.

5085. PELTIER GLASS COMPANY. Tiger. Two color National Line Rainbo Tiger. Orange base with black ribbons. No aventurine. Some tiny pitting, but still very nice. Ottawa, IL, circa 1928-1935. 21/32". Mint(-) (9.1). Price: $32. CyberAuction #366, Lot #52.

5086. PELTIER GLASS COMPANY. Tiger. Two-color four-ribbon National Line Rainbo Tiger. Orange base with aventurine black ribbons. One small flake. Ottawa, IL, circa 1928-1935. 19/32". Near Mint(+) (8.8). Price: $27. CyberAuction #393, Lot #45.

5087. PELTIER GLASS COMPANY. Tiger. Two color National Line Rainbo Tiger. Bright orange base with aventurine black ribbons. Some small chips. Ottawa, IL, circa 1928-1935. 5/8". Near Mint(-) (8.0). Price: $17. CyberAuction #349, Lot #46.

5088. PELTIER GLASS COMPANY. Tiger. Two-color four-ribbon National Line Rainbo Tiger. Orange base with aventurine black ribbons. Several tiny chips in one spot. Ottawa, IL, circa 1928-1935. 5/8". Near Mint (8.5). Price: $15. CyberAuction #434, Lot #56.

5089. PELTIER GLASS COMPANY. Tiger. Two-color four-ribbon National Line Rainbo Tiger. Orange base with aventurine black ribbons. Several tiny chips in one spot. Ottawa, IL, circa 1928-1935. 5/8". Near Mint (8.5). Price: $9. CyberAuction #415, Lot #51.

5090. PELTIER GLASS COMPANY. Tricolor. Tricolor that looks like a multicolor. Transparent dark green base. Two wide ribbons each of orange and blue. Subsurface moon. Ottawa, IL, circa 1930-1945. 21/32". Near Mint(+) (8.7). Price: $2. CyberAuction #381, Lot #16.

5091. PELTIER GLASS COMPANY. Wasp. Two color National Line Rainbo Wasp. Red base with four aventurine black ribbons. Excellent example. Ottawa, IL, circa 1927-1935. 19/32". Mint (9.9). Price: $95. CyberAuction #498, Lot #61.

5092. PELTIER GLASS COMPANY. Wasp. Two color National Line Rainbo Wasp. Opaque red base with four black ribbons. Exceptional example, definitive for this type. Ottawa, IL, circa 1927-1935. 21/32". Mint (9.9). Price: $75. CyberAuction #448, Lot #48.

5093. PELTIER GLASS COMPANY. Wasp. Two color National Line Rainbo Wasp. Red base with four fiery aventurine black ribbons. Excellent example. Ottawa, IL, circa 1927-1935. 5/8". Mint (9.9). Price: $70. CyberAuction #508, Lot #68.

5094. PELTIER GLASS COMPANY. Wasp. Two color National Line Rainbo Wasp. Red base with four aventurine black ribbons. Excellent example. Ottawa, IL, circa 1927-1935. 19/32". Mint (9.9). Price: $60. CyberAuction #330, Lot #43.

5095. PELTIER GLASS COMPANY. Wasp. Two color National Line Rainbo Wasp. Opaque red base with four black ribbons. No aventurine. Two tiny air holes. Excellent. Ottawa, IL, circa 1927-1935. 9/16". Mint(-) (9.2). Price: $40. CyberAuction #341, Lot #38.

5096. PELTIER GLASS COMPANY. Wasp. Two-color four-ribbon National Line Rainbo Wasp. Ruddy red base. Four aventurine black ribbons. One very tiny chip, one small subsurface moon, a long scratch. Ottawa, IL, circa 1927-1935. 9/16". Near Mint (8.6). Price: $26. CyberAuction #365, Lot #53.

5097. PELTIER GLASS COMPANY. Wasp. Two-color four-ribbon National Line Rainbo Wasp. Ruddy red base. Four aventurine black ribbons. One very tiny chip, one small subsurface moon, a long scratch. Ottawa, IL, circa 1927-1935. 9/16". Near Mint (8.6). Price: $12. CyberAuction #432, Lot #37.

5098. PELTIER GLASS COMPANY. Zebra. Two-color six-ribbon National Line Rainbo Zebra. Opaque white base, six ribbons of very fiery black. Stunning example. Ottawa, IL, circa 1925-1935. 5/8". Mint (9.9). Price: $42. CyberAuction #368, Lot #12.

5099. PELTIER GLASS COMPANY. Zebra. Four-ribbon, two-color National Line Rainbo Zebra. Broken corkscrew pattern. Four aventurine black ribbons on white. Ottawa, IL, circa 1925-1935. 11/16". Mint (9.7). Price: $40. CyberAuction #429, Lot #47.

5100. PELTIER GLASS COMPANY. Zebra. Two-color four-ribbon National Line Rainbo Zebra. Four aventurine black ribbons on white. Fiery aventurine. Ottawa, IL, circa 1927-1935. 21/32". Mint (9.7). Price: $32. CyberAuction #428, Lot #41.

5101. PELTIER GLASS COMPANY. Zebra. Two color National Line Rainbo Zebra. Four black ribbons on opalescent white. One sparkle. Ottawa, IL, circa 1927-1935. 21/32". Mint(-) (9.2). Price: $32. CyberAuction #433, Lot #47.

5102. PELTIER GLASS COMPANY. Zebra. Two color National Line Rainbo Zebra. Opaque white base. Four ribbons of aventurine black. Ottawa, IL, circa 1927-1935. 9/16". Mint (9.9). Price: $26. CyberAuction #364, Lot #13.

5103. PELTIER GLASS COMPANY. Zebra. Two-color four-ribbon National Line Rainbo Zebra. Four aventurine black ribbons on white. Ottawa, IL, circa 1927-1935. 5/8". Mint (9.8). Price: $24. CyberAuction #370, Lot #48.

5104. PELTIER GLASS COMPANY. Zebra. Two color National Line Rainbo

Zebra. Broken corkscrew pattern. Four aventurine black ribbons on white. Ottawa, IL, circa 1927-1935. 5/8". Mint (9.7). Price: $24. CyberAuction #374, Lot #53.

5105. PELTIER GLASS COMPANY. Zebra. Two-color four-ribbon National Line Rainbo Zebra. Four aventurine black ribbons on white. Ottawa, IL, circa 1927-1935. 21/32". Mint (9.8). Price: $24. CyberAuction #418, Lot #40.

5106. PELTIER GLASS COMPANY. Zebra. Two color National Line Rainbo Zebra. Broken corkscrew pattern. Four aventurine black ribbons on white. Ottawa, IL, circa 1927-1935. 5/8". Mint (9.7). Price: $23. CyberAuction #356, Lot #2.

5107. PELTIER GLASS COMPANY. Zebra. Two-color four-ribbon National Line Rainbo Zebra. Four aventurine black ribbons on white. Ottawa, IL, circa 1927-1935. 21/32". Mint (9.8). Price: $23. CyberAuction #370, Lot #57.

5108. PELTIER GLASS COMPANY. Zebra. Two color National Line Rainbo Zebra. Four aventurine black ribbons on white. Ottawa, IL, circa 1927-1935. 5/8". Mint (9.7). Price: $21. CyberAuction #373, Lot #11.

5109. PELTIER GLASS COMPANY. Zebra. Four-ribbon, two-color National Line Rainbo Zebra. Black ribbons in white base. No aventurine. Ottawa, IL, circa 1927-1940. 21/32". Mint (9.7). Price: $21. CyberAuction #407, Lot #6.

5110. PELTIER GLASS COMPANY. Zebra. Two color National Line Rainbo Zebra. Broken corkscrew pattern. Four aventurine black ribbons on white. Ottawa, IL, circa 1927-1935. 5/8". Mint (9.7). Price: $21. CyberAuction #448, Lot #21.

5111. PELTIER GLASS COMPANY. Zebra. Two color National Line Rainbo Zebra. Four aventurine black ribbons on white. Ottawa, IL, circa 1927-1935. 21/32". Mint (9.8). Price: $20. CyberAuction #467, Lot #5.

5112. PELTIER GLASS COMPANY. Zebra. Two color National Line Rainbo Zebra. Four aventurine black ribbons on white. Ottawa, IL, circa 1927-1935. 5/8". Mint (9.7). Price: $19. CyberAuction #425, Lot #22.

5113. PELTIER GLASS COMPANY. Zebra. Two-color, four-ribbon, National Line Rainbo Zebra. Four black ribbons on opaque white. Beauty. Ottawa, IL, circa 1927-1935. 21/32". Mint (9.9). Price: $19. CyberAuction #455, Lot #37.

5114. PELTIER GLASS COMPANY. Zebra. Two-color four-ribbon National Line Rainbo Zebra. Four aventurine black ribbons on white. Ottawa, IL, circa 1927-1935. 5/8". Mint (9.8). Price: $19. CyberAuction #489, Lot #47.

5115. PELTIER GLASS COMPANY. Zebra. Two color National Line Rainbo Zebra. Four aventurine black ribbons on white. One tiny sparkle. Ottawa, IL, circa 1927-1935. 21/32". Mint(-) (9.2). Price: $18. CyberAuction #385, Lot #20.

5116. PELTIER GLASS COMPANY. Zebra. Two color National Line Rainbo Zebra. Four black ribbons on white. Very light aventurine. Ottawa, IL, circa 1927-1935. 11/16". Mint (9.7). Price: $17. CyberAuction #486, Lot #42.

5117. PELTIER GLASS COMPANY. Zebra. Two color National Line Rainbo Zebra. Four aventurine black ribbons on white. A few tiny air pits. Ottawa, IL, circa 1927-1935. 19/32". Mint(-) (9.0). Price: $15. CyberAuction #449, Lot #56.

5118. PELTIER GLASS COMPANY. Zebra. Two color National Line Rainbo Zebra. Four aventurine black ribbons on white. Several very tiny chips. Ottawa, IL, circa 1927-1935. 21/32". Near Mint(+) (8.8). Price: $15. CyberAuction #476, Lot #40.

5119. PELTIER GLASS COMPANY. Zebra. Two color National Line Rainbo Zebra. Four aventurine black ribbons on white. A few tiny air pits. Ottawa, IL, circa 1927-1935. 19/32". Mint(-) (9.0). Price: $12. CyberAuction #386, Lot #36.

5120. PELTIER GLASS COMPANY. Zebra. Two color National Line Rainbo Zebra. Four black ribbons on white. Very light aventurine. Ottawa, IL, circa 1927-1935. 11/16". Mint (9.7). Price: $12. CyberAuction #461, Lot #12.

5121. PELTIER GLASS COMPANY. Zebra. Two color National Line Rainbo Zebra. Four aventurine black ribbons on white. A few tiny air pits. Ottawa, IL, circa 1927-1935. 19/32". Mint(-) (9.0). Price: $12. CyberAuction #474, Lot #39.

5122. PELTIER GLASS COMPANY. Zebra. Two-color National Line Rainbo Zebra. Aventurine black ribbons on white. One small flake. Ottawa, IL, circa 1927-1935. 11/16". Near Mint(+) (8.9). Price: $11. CyberAuction #369, Lot #27.

5123. PELTIER GLASS COMPANY. Zebra. Two-color four-ribbon National Line Rainbo Zebra. Four aventurine black ribbons on white. Some aventurine. Some very slight haze. Highly swirled. Ottawa, IL, circa 1927-1935. 9/16". Near Mint(+) (8.7). Price: $10. CyberAuction #381, Lot #12.

5124. PELTIER GLASS COMPANY. Zebra. Two color National Line Rainbo Zebra. Four aventurine black ribbons on white. Some haze and an air hole. Ottawa, IL, circa 1927-1935. 21/32". Near Mint (8.5). Price: $10. CyberAuction #472, Lot #33.

5125. PELTIER GLASS COMPANY. Zebra. Two-color four-ribbon National Line Rainbo Zebra. Four aventurine black ribbons on white. Fiery aventurine. A couple of tiny chips. Ottawa, IL, circa 1927-1935. 5/8". Near Mint(+) (8.7). Price: $9. CyberAuction #381, Lot #6.

5126. PELTIER GLASS COMPANY. Zebra. Two color National Line Rainbo Zebra. Four aventurine black ribbons on white. Small chips. Ottawa, IL, circa 1927-1935. 23/32". Good(+) (7.9). Price: $7. CyberAuction #376, Lot #40.

5127. RAVENSWOOD NOVELTY WORKS. Catalogue. One of the four page "orange" catalogue sheets. 8" x 10". 1940s. Price: $11. CyberAuction #477, Lot #28.

5128. RAVENSWOOD NOVELTY WORKS. Original package. Original tan cardboard box. Diagonal oval cutout on the front. "MARBLES" printed

twice in red, "Assorted colors" in red and a red checkerboard pattern. Box is 5" x 3" x 5/8" (sight). Contains about thirty swirls (all are Ravenswood) Marbles are 5/8" and Mint. Box is Near Mint(+) (8.9) (some minor crushing and tears). There are four boxes available. You are bidding on one. Winner has choice of any or all, remainder to under. Price: $34. CyberAuction #349, Lot #28.

5129. RAVENSWOOD NOVELTY WORKS. Original package. Original tan cardboard box. Diagonal oval cutout on the front. "MARBLES" printed twice in red, "Assorted colors" in red and a red checkerboard pattern. Box is 5" x 3" x 5/8" (sight). Contains about thirty swirls (all are Ravenswood) Marbles are 5/8" and Mint. Box is Near Mint(+) (8.9) (some minor crushing and tears). There are four boxes available. You are bidding on one. Winner has choice of any or all, remainder to under. Price: $34. CyberAuction #350, Lot #30.

5130. RAVENSWOOD NOVELTY WORKS. Swirl. Blue and brown swirl Gorgeous. Ravenswood, WV, circa 1935-1945. 19/32". Mint (9.9). Price: $30. CyberAuction #483, Lot #45.

5131. RAVENSWOOD NOVELTY WORKS. Swirl. Two shades of blue swirl on brown. Hard to find. Ravenswood, WV, circa 1935-1950. 19/32". Mint (9.8). Price: $22. CyberAuction #475, Lot #5.

5132. RAVENSWOOD NOVELTY WORKS. Swirl. Green swirls on white Ravenswood, WV, circa 1940-1955. 15/16". Mint (9.9). Consignor note A11. Price: $15. CyberAuction #344, Lot #16.

5133. RAVENSWOOD NOVELTY WORKS. Swirl. Opaque white base. Blue and brown swirls. Nice. Ravenswood, WV, circa 1945-1960. 31/32". Mint (9.7). Price: $15. CyberAuction #360, Lot #31.

5134. RAVENSWOOD NOVELTY WORKS. Swirl. Brown/orange swirls on white. A little metallic smear. Ravenswood, WV, circa 1935-1950. 31/32". Mint (9.7). Price: $13. CyberAuction #410, Lot #1.

5135. RAVENSWOOD NOVELTY WORKS. Swirl. Three color swirl. Transparent brown and translucent blue on white. Ravenswood, WV, circa 1940-1955. 19/32". Mint (9.9). Price: $12. CyberAuction #440, Lot #24.

5136. RAVENSWOOD NOVELTY WORKS. Swirl. Yellow swirl on blue One tiny pit. Ravenswood, WV, circa 1945-1950. 1-1/16". Mint(-) (9.0) Price: $11. CyberAuction #417, Lot #42.

5137. RAVENSWOOD NOVELTY WORKS. Swirl. Very nice three color swirl. White base with blue and transparent brown swirls. Ravenswood WV, circa 1935-1950. 19/32". Mint (9.9). Price: $10. CyberAuction #390 Lot #36.

5138. RAVENSWOOD NOVELTY WORKS. Swirl. Blue and orange/brown on white. Beauty. Ravenswood, WV, circa 1935-1945. 19/32". Mint (9.9) Price: $10. CyberAuction #496, Lot #33.

5139. RAVENSWOOD NOVELTY WORKS. Swirl. Transparent and wispy white base. Translucent blue swirls. One sparkle. Ravenswood, WV, circa 1940-1950. 11/16". Near Mint(+) (8.9). Price: $8. CyberAuction #381 Lot #36.

5140. RAVENSWOOD NOVELTY WORKS. Swirl. Shooter swirl. Yellow swirls on light blue. One small manufacturing roll crease and a rough spot Ravenswood, WV, circa 1935-1950. 31/32". Near Mint(+) (8.9). Price: $6 CyberAuction #338, Lot #14.

5141. RAVENSWOOD NOVELTY WORKS. Swirl. Purple swirls on white 9/16". Mint (9.9). There are three marbles available. You are bidding on one. Winner has choice of any or all, remainder to under. Price: $5 CyberAuction #335, Lot #47.

5142. RAVENSWOOD NOVELTY WORKS. Swirl. Purple swirls on white Nice flame pattern. Ravenswood, WV, circa 1935-1950. 19/32". Mint (9.9) Price: $2. CyberAuction #439, Lot #34.

5143. RAVENSWOOD NOVELTY WORKS. Swirl. Very nice three color flame swirl. Several chips. Ravenswood, WV, circa 1935-1945. 11/16" Good(+) (7.9). Price: $2. CyberAuction #496, Lot #17.

5144. SULPHIDE. Hand painted sulphide. Rare marble. The figure is an angel, kneeling on one knee, cloth draped across other leg, holding a lyre or other harp-like instrument up to his right ear. Green ground, blue wings brown hair, black eyes and mouth. Very rare. Above average detail to figure. Some very shallow tiny air bubbles, but nothing covering much of the surface. Well centered. There are some air bubbles floating in the marble Some very tiny chips and pits. Super marble. Germany, circa 1870-1915 1-7/16". Near Mint(-) (8.2). Price: $1700. CyberAuction #436, Lot #60.

5145. SULPHIDE. Extremely rare figure. Consignor described it as Napoleon, I think it is George Washington. Whoever he is, it is very rare. Standing figure of a man in colonial garb, including trench coat and colonial hat One hand at side, one behind his back. Exceptional detail to the figure. No air bubbles. Set slightly off center. Surface has some very minor wear. Germany, circa 1870-1915. 1-11/16". Mint(-) (9.0). Price: $1700. CyberAuction #504, Lot #71.

5146. SULPHIDE. Extremely rare figure. Robin Hood. Man dressed in shirt with fringed collar and hem, calf length pants, and high boots, with a hat Looks just like Robin Hood. He is standing in front of a post with is legs spread wide apart and his hands clasped behind his back. Exceptional detail to the figure. Set a little high. The very bottom of the left foot broke off when it was inserted and is floating slightly in front of its original position. Very rare example, first time I've ever seen this one. Surface has a couple of very tiny pits. Germany, circa 1870-1915. 1-5/8". Mint(-) (9.2). Price: $1650. CyberAuction #479, Lot #59.

5147. SULPHIDE. Hand painted sulphide figure. Seated dog. Black spots, black facial features, green ground. Well centered, no air bubbles. Surface has some small and tiny moons. Would look great with a polish. Germany circa 1870-1915. 2-1/16". Good (7.5). Price: $1275. CyberAuction #500 Lot #56.

5148. SULPHIDE. Human figure, from the waist up, on a pedestal. Arms crossed over chest. Variously identified as Beethoven, Chopin, or a Euroɔean statesman. Exceptional detail. Large figure. Well-centered. Small air ɔubble on the back of the neck. Two small subsurface moons on the right ide of the marble, not in front or behind the figure. No other damage!!! xcellent pontil directly below the figure. Huge marble!!! A 1-7/8" polished xample sold in Block's Box Absentee Marble Auction #36 as Lot #31 for 787.50. This example is almost a half inch bigger and in far better shape!!! ɜermany, circa 1870-1915. 2-1/4". Near Mint(+) (8.7). Price: $1225. ɔyberAuction #373, Lot #58.

ɩ149. SULPHIDE. Rare figure of a running buffalo or bison. Excellent de-ail. No air bubbles. Well centered. The marble surface has some roughness nd a couple of tiny chips. It could be lightly buffed to reveal a beauty. ɜermany, circa 1870-1915. 2". Near Mint(-) (8.0). Price: $1200. ɔyberAuction #503, Lot #61.

ɩ150. SULPHIDE. Figure is a minstrel. Minstrel in fine dress with cap, lean-ng against a post, playing a guitar or mandolin. Rare figure. Well detailed. Vell centered. Lightly buffed, damage remains. Germany, circa 1870-1915. -7/16". Price: $825. CyberAuction #457, Lot #38.

ɩ151. SULPHIDE. Rare marble. Standing rooster in emerald green glass. /ery large figure. Exceptional detail. Well-centered. Small annealing frac-ure in glass behind neck (typical of this figure). Gorgeous emerald green ;lass. Surface has been buffed, however, chips remain. None too deep, but ou would have to do some polishing to remove them. Germany, circa 870-1915. 1-15/16". Price: $750. CyberAuction #457, Lot #50.

ɩ152. SULPHIDE. Figure is a minstrel. Minstrel in fine dress with cap, lean-ıg against a post, playing a guitar or mandolin. Rare figure. Well detailed. Vell centered. Lightly buffed, damage remains. Germany, circa 1870-1915. -7/16". Price: $750. CyberAuction #467, Lot #29.

ɩ153. SULPHIDE. Very rare figure. Minstrel. Man in an overcoat and a vide-brim hat, playing a stringed instrument, probably a mandolin or gui-ar. Excellent detail to the figure. Shallow air bubble around it. Well cen-ered. Surface has some pitting. Rare. Germany, circa 1870-1915. 1-11/ 6". Near Mint(-) (8.1). Price: $675. CyberAuction #455, Lot #58.

ɩ154. SULPHIDE. Usually referred to as the "obscene monkey". Seated nonkey, arm at right side. Left arm is crossed over chest and he is holding ıe top of his erection. This figure has exceptional detail. Amongst the best letail I have seen in any figure. Well centered, no air bubbles. One flat pot, several tiny sparkles. Absolutely exceptional example and a rare fig-ıre. Germany, circa 1870-1915. 1-5/8". Mint(-) (9.2). Price: $555. ɔyberAuction #421, Lot #59.

ɩ155. SULPHIDE. Figure is a girl in Victorian garb, with hat. Kneeling down olding a croquet mallet in one hand a croquet ball in the other. Excep-onal detail to the figure. This is a stunning example. Well centered. No air ubbles. Polished. Superior example. Germany circa 1870-1915. 2". Price: 500. CyberAuction #424, Lot #59.

ɩ156. SULPHIDE. Figure is a bust of Jenny Lind. Exceptional detail to the gure. Set off center. No air bubbles. Surface has an overall very light haze. very light buff will reveal a beauty. Germany, circa 1870-1915. 1-1/2". Near Mint (8.5). Price: $435. CyberAuction #351, Lot #60.

ɩ157. SULPHIDE. Exceptional figure of a parrot on a perch. Superior de-ail. Set slightly low. No air bubbles. Gorgeous marble!!!! A couple of tiny parkles. Small manufacturing chip on the pontil on the bottom where the narble was knocked off the punty rod. Germany, circa 1870-1915. 2-1/ 6". Mint(-) (9.2). Price: $435. CyberAuction #467, Lot #33.

ɩ158. SULPHIDE. Rare figure. Naked seated man with an odd face. Man is quatting on the ground. His right hand is on his right knee, his left hand is n his chest. Face is carved with a very wide grin, wide open eyes and a ulbous nose. Appears to be bald. You can tell he is naked by the portion of is rear end that is visible. Also, the muscles on his back shoulders (trap-zoids?) are very pronounced. Exceptional detail to the figure. No air bubbles. retty much well centered in the marble. Pontil on the bottom of the marble nicely ground. Front is very clean. There is a very tiny flake on the back nd a very tiny pit near the pontil. Remarkable! Germany, circa 1870-1915. -1/4". Near Mint(+) (8.8). Sold in an earlier auction, but bidder gave bad mail address. Price: $430. CyberAuction #430, Lot #24.

ɩ159. SULPHIDE. Figure is a French fairy tale character. A dog, dressed in rench clothing and a hat. Above average detail. No air bubbling. Figure is arge for the marble. Set slightly high. Excellent example of this figure. Ger-nany, circa 1870-1925. Polished. 2" (a hair under). Price: $410. ɔyberAuction #345, Lot #34.

ɩ160. SULPHIDE. Rare figure. Naked seated man with an odd face. Man is quatting on the ground. His right hand is on his right knee, his left hand is n his chest. Face is carved with a very wide grin, wide open eyes and a ulbous nose. Appears to be bald. You can tell he is naked by the portion of is rear end that is visible. Also, the muscles on his back shoulders (trap-zoids?) are very pronounced. Exceptional detail to the figure. No air bubbles. retty much well centered in the marble. Pontil on the bottom of the marble nicely ground. Front is very clean. There is a very tiny flake on the back nd a very tiny pit near the pontil. Remarkable! Germany, circa 1870-1915. -1/4". Near Mint(+) (8.8). Price: $410. CyberAuction #410, Lot #38.

ɩ161. SULPHIDE. Figure is a naked girl bathing. Seated figure. Has a sponge ı one hand at head, other hand on chest. Has a hair band hold her hair. xcellent detail. Super example of this figure. No air bubbles. Very well entered. Superb. Polished surface. Germany, circa 1870-1915. 1-5/8". Price: 410. CyberAuction #443, Lot #60.

ɩ162. SULPHIDE. Figure is the numeral #9. Excellent figure. Small air ubble on the back, nothing on the front. Set slightly low. The surface is ristine. Stunning. Germany, circa 1870-1915. 1-9/16". Mint (9.9). Price: 410. CyberAuction #444, Lot #24.

ɩ163. SULPHIDE. Figure of a fish in purple base glass. Above average letail to the figure. Small air bubble on one side. Well centered. Overall mall chips and flakes. Hard to find colored glass sulphide. Germany, circa 1870-1915. 2-1/16". Good (7.3). Price: $410. CyberAuction #444, Lot #29.

5164. SULPHIDE. Figure is a naked girl bathing. Seated figure. Has a sponge in one hand at head, other hand on chest. Has a hair band hold her hair. Excellent detail. Super example of this figure. No air bubbles. Very well centered. Superb. Polished surface. Germany, circa 1870-1915. 1-5/8". Price: $400. CyberAuction #451, Lot #60.

5165. SULPHIDE. Figure is a bust of Jenny Lind. Excellent detail. Very shallow tiny air bubbles. Figure is well centered. Hazy surface with a couple of tiny chips. Germany, circa 1870-1915. 1-11/16". Near Mint(-) (8.0). Price: $385. CyberAuction #433, Lot #60.

5166. SULPHIDE. Figure is a bust of Jenny Lind. Excellent detail. Very shallow tiny air bubbles. Figure is well centered. Hazy surface with a couple of tiny chips. Germany, circa 1870-1915. 1-11/16". Near Mint(-) (8.0). Price: $385. CyberAuction #453, Lot #17.

5167. SULPHIDE. Excellent figure. Girl in Victorian nightgown, seated, holding a large doll. Nice bow in the girl's hair. Excellent detail to the figure. No air bubbles. Well centered. Surface has been polished. Germany, circa 1870-1915. 1-5/8". Price: $360. CyberAuction #429, Lot #34.

5168. SULPHIDE. Figure is a reclining lioness. Rare figure. Average detail. No air bubbles. Well centered. One small melt flat spot, one tiny melt pit. Super marble. Germany, circa 1870-1915. 1-13/16". Mint (9.5). Price: $360. CyberAuction #432, Lot #33.

5169. SULPHIDE. Figure is a bust of Jenny Lind. Excellent detail. Very shallow air bubble on the left side of the bodice. Small part of the right side of the hair has detached slightly. Figure is slightly off-center. Polished surface. Germany, circa 1870-1915. 1-3/4". Polished. Price: $335. CyberAuction #406, Lot #49.

5170. SULPHIDE. Figure is a seated boy in a Victorian nightgown reading a book. Above average detail to the figure. No air bubbles. Well centered. Marble is polished. Germany, circa 1870-1915. 1-11/16". Price: $311. CyberAuction #433, Lot #36.

5171. SULPHIDE. Figure is a seated boy in a Victorian nightgown reading a book. Above average detail to the figure. No air bubbles. Well centered. Marble is polished. Germany, circa 1870-1915. 1-11/16". Price: $311. CyberAuction #454, Lot #21.

5172. SULPHIDE. Figure is a standing male lion in a defensive position. Excellent detail to the figure. No air bubbles. Slightly off center. Surface in great shape with just a couple of very tiny pinpricks. Germany, circa 1870-1915. 1-7/16". Mint (9.4). Price: $310. CyberAuction #442, Lot #35.

5173. SULPHIDE. Exceptional figure of a parrot on a perch. Superior detail. Set slightly low. No air bubbles. Gorgeous marble!!!! A couple of tiny sparkles. Small manufacturing chip on the pontil on the bottom where the marble was knocked off the punty rod. Germany, circa 1870-1915. 2-1/ 16". Mint(-) (9.2). Price: $300. CyberAuction #421, Lot #49.

5174. SULPHIDE. Figure is a wolverine, crouched in defensive mode with teeth bared. Large figure, well detailed. The figure did crack on insertion. A couple of tiny air bubbles floating in the marble, but nothing on the figure. Well-centered. Great surface, no blemishes or damage! Germany, circa 1870-1915. 1-7/8". Mint (9.9). Price: $285. CyberAuction #414, Lot #29.

5175. SULPHIDE. Figure of a floating angel. Naked male figure. Outstretched wings. Hands clasped over groin. No broken pieces on the figure (unusual). No air bubbling. Super detail. Exceptional figure. Well centered. Surface has one small area of chipping off to one side and a few tiny subsurface moons. Views reasonably well. Germany, circa 1870-1915. 1-7/8". Near Mint(-) (8.0). Price: $280. CyberAuction #374, Lot #60.

5176. SULPHIDE. Figure of a floating angel. Naked male figure. Outstretched wings. Hands clasped over groin. No broken pieces on the figure (unusual). No air bubbling. Super detail. Exceptional figure. Well centered. Surface has one small area of chipping off to one side and a few tiny subsurface moons. Views reasonably well. Germany, circa 1870-1915. 1-7/8". Near Mint(-) (8.0). Price: $280. CyberAuction #434, Lot #57.

5177. SULPHIDE. Base glass is pale blue. Figure is a standing bear, grasping a pole. Exceptional detail to the figure. No air bubbles, well centered. Outstanding. Several tiny chips on the back, some scratching, a couple of tiny subsurface moons. Views very nicely though, and an interesting pale colored sulphide. Germany, circa 1870-1915. 1-13/16". Near Mint(-) (8.2). Price: $275. CyberAuction #468, Lot #46.

5178. SULPHIDE. Figure is the Victorian boy kneeling and holding a sailboat. Excellent figure, well detailed. Set slightly high. No air bubbles. Surface has several small and tiny chips. Germany, circa 1870-1915. 1-1/2". Good(+) (7.9). Price: $275. CyberAuction #471, Lot #27.

5179. SULPHIDE. Figure is a standing lamb. Average detail. Well centered, no air bubbles. Base glass is tinted very slightly green. In superior shape. Germany, circa 1870-1915. 2-3/8". Mint (9.8). Price: $260. CyberAuction #385, Lot #45.

5180. SULPHIDE. Figure is a super three-dimensional figure of a spread-winged Prussian eagle. Outstanding figure. Wide outstretched wings and a head and neck sticking right up. Lots of depth to the figure. Excellent detail to figure. Off-center. Very shallow air bubble just on the small of the back. One floating air bubble in the marble itself. Exceptional piece of workmanship. It is surprising that there are not more obscuring air bubbles given the nooks and crannies in this figure. Surface has one melt spot where it touched another marble while hot and a tiny subsurface moon right at the top. Nothing interferes with viewing, but I have to grade it below Mint given the subsurface moon. Germany, circa 1870-1915. 1-3/4". Near Mint(+) (8.9). Price: $260. CyberAuction #414, Lot #56.

5181. SULPHIDE. Figure of the numeral #1. Excellent detail. No air bubbles. Off-center. Small subsurface moon, several tiny subsurface moons. Germany, circa 1870-1915. 1-9/16". Near Mint (8.4). Price: $260. CyberAuction #429, Lot #57.

5182. SULPHIDE. Figure is the numeral #9. Figure is very nice, with no air bubbles on it. Well centered. Some flakes on the surface. Germany, circa 1870-1915. 1-3/4". Good(+) (7.9). Price: $260. CyberAuction #442, Lot #23.

5183. SULPHIDE. Figure is a peasant boy seated on a stump. Excellent detail to the figure. No air bubbles. Set high. Polished surface. Germany, circa 1870-1915. 1-7/8". Price: $260. CyberAuction #469, Lot #33.

5184. SULPHIDE. Excellent figure. Girl in Victorian nightgown, seated, holding a large doll. Nice bow in the girl's hair. Excellent detail to the figure. No air bubbles. Well centered. Surface has been polished. Germany, circa 1870-1915. 1-5/8". Price: $260. CyberAuction #479, Lot #35.

5185. SULPHIDE. Huge figure of a whippet (dog) with collar. Seated on rear haunches. Exceptional detail, you can even see his ribs. Very well-centered. No air bubbles. One tiny melt spot and a sparkle. Excellent example of a sulphide. Germany, circa 1870-1915. 1-31/32". Mint(-) (9.0). Price: $250. CyberAuction #412, Lot #44.

5186. SULPHIDE. Figure is a man with one hand on his chest, other at his side. Average detail. Small air bubble on one side of the back. Large figure for the marble. Well centered. No air bubbles in the front. Some pitting. Germany, circa 1870-1915. 1-3/16". Near Mint (8.6). Price: $250. CyberAuction #413, Lot #50.

5187. SULPHIDE. Figure of a chicken in light blue glass. You can see veils of transparent light blue in the clear glass. Excellent detail to the figure. Off-center. Overall small chips and pitting. Could be polished to reveal a beauty. Germany, circa 1870-1915. 1-7/16". Good (7.5). Rare color. Price: $250. CyberAuction #448, Lot #28.

5188. SULPHIDE. Figure of a floating angel. Naked male figure. Outstretched wings. Hands clasped over groin. No broken pieces on the figure (unusual). No air bubbling. Super detail. Exceptional figure. Well centered. Surface has one small area of chipping off to one side and a few tiny subsurface moons. Views reasonably well. Germany, circa 1870-1915. 1-7/8". Near Mint(-) (8.0). Price: $250. CyberAuction #473, Lot #36.

5189. SULPHIDE. Figure of a floating angel. Naked male figure. Outstretched wings. Hands clasped over groin. No broken pieces on the figure (unusual). No air bubbling. Super detail. Exceptional figure. Well centered. Surface has one small area of chipping off to one side and a few tiny subsurface moons. Views reasonably well. Germany, circa 1870-1915. 1-7/8". Near Mint(-) (8.0). Price: $250. CyberAuction #496, Lot #43.

5190. SULPHIDE. Figure is the numeral #9. Excellent figure. Small air bubble on the back, nothing on the front. Set slightly low. The surface is pristine. Stunning. Germany, circa 1870-1915. 1-9/16". Mint (9.9). Price: $235. CyberAuction #472, Lot #45.

5191. SULPHIDE. Painted sulphide. Running small dog. Excellent detail, no air bubbles. Black painted tail. Set slightly off-center. Couple of tiny subsurface moons, overall pitting. Could use a good buff. Germany, circa 1870-1915. 1-1/4". Good(+) (7.9). Price: $230. CyberAuction #413, Lot #20.

5192. SULPHIDE. Figure is a standing horse. Superior example. Nice silvering, no air bubbles. Well centered. No cracks in the figure. Exceptional. Couple of tiny pits and some tiny scratches. Germany, circa 1870-1915. 1-5/8". Mint(-) (9.0). Price: $225. CyberAuction #366, Lot #51.

5193. SULPHIDE. Figure of the numeral #3. Excellent detail. Very well centered. Small air bubble on the back, but not the front (who looks at the back of a numeral anyhow?). Polished. Germany, circa 1870-1915. 1-9/16". Price: $225. CyberAuction #425, Lot #32.

5194. SULPHIDE. Figure is a standing horse. Superior example. Nice silvering, no air bubbles. Well centered. No cracks in the figure. Exceptional. Couple of tiny pits and some tiny scratches. Germany, circa 1870-1915. 1-5/8". Mint(-) (9.0). Price: $225. CyberAuction #447, Lot #36.

5195. SULPHIDE. Figure is a rearing horse on grass. Above average detail figure. No air bubbles. Set a little high. A scratch and a pit on the back of the marble. Excellent example of this figure. Germany, circa 1870-1915. 2-1/8". Mint(-) (9.0). Price: $225. CyberAuction #504, Lot #42.

5196. SULPHIDE. Figure is a razorback. Huge marble. Huge figure. Exceptional detail to the figure. Nice silvering. Very small air bubble under the figure. Well-centered. Surface has several tiny subsurface moons and pits. Nothing interferes with viewing the marble. Rare, due to the size, figure quality and condition. Germany, circa 1870-1915. 2-1/4". Near Mint (8.6). Price: $220. CyberAuction #369, Lot #59.

5197. SULPHIDE. Figure is Baby Moses in a basket. Figure cracked on insertion. Exceptional detail, well centered. No air bubbles. Overall pitting. Germany, circa 1870-1915. 1-3/4". Near Mint(-) (8.0). Price: $220. CyberAuction #448, Lot #33.

5198. SULPHIDE. Figure is a boy in Victorian garb with a cap, kneeling down, holding a pond sailor (toy sailboat). Average detail to the figure. Small air bubble on back, none on the front. Set very slightly high. Polished surface. Hard figure to find. Germany, circa 1870-1915. 1-7/8". Price: $210. CyberAuction #330, Lot #24.

5199. SULPHIDE. Figure of a standing cow. Outstanding detail to the figure. Large figure, well-centered, no air bubbles. Surface has several tiny to small subsurface moons. None detracts from viewing the figure, almost all are on the top or bottom. Huge marble!!!! 2-1/4". Near Mint (8.6). Price: $210. CyberAuction #351, Lot #49.

5200. SULPHIDE. Rare figure. Naked seated boy with a large marble (perhaps a very small ball) in his left hand. Large figure. Very three-dimensional. Excellent detail to the figure. Well-centered. No air bubbles. Unfortunately, the marble fractured. The fracture is directly under the figure, at it's base. The marble is fractured, not the figure. Also, a tiny fracture along the right arm. A couple of small subsurface moons and pits. The figure is still very viewable, but the marble is not perfect. Germany, circa 1870-1915. 1-3/4". Good (7.6). Price: $210. CyberAuction #357, Lot #35.

5201. SULPHIDE. Base glass is pale blue. Figure is a standing bear, grasping a pole. Exceptional detail to the figure. No air bubbles, well centered. Outstanding. Several tiny chips on the back, some scratching, a couple of tiny subsurface moons. Views very nicely though, and an interesting pal colored sulphide. Germany, circa 1870-1915. 1-13/16". Near Mint(-) (8.2 Price: $210. CyberAuction #418, Lot #54.

5202. SULPHIDE. Figure is a peasant boy seated on a stump. Excellent detail to the figure. No air bubbles. Set high. Polished surface. Germany, circa 1870-1915. 1-7/8". Price: $210. CyberAuction #444, Lot #28.

5203. SULPHIDE. Figure is the Victorian boy kneeling and holding a sai boat. Excellent figure, well detailed. Set slightly high. No air bubbles. Surface has several small and tiny chips. Germany, circa 1870-1915. 1-1/2 Good(+) (7.9). Price: $210. CyberAuction #451, Lot #36.

5204. SULPHIDE. Figure is a rearing horse on grass. Above average deta figure. No air bubbles. Set a little high. A scratch and a pit on the back of the marble. Excellent example of this figure. Germany, circa 1870-1915. 2-1/8". Mint(-) (9.0). Price: $210. CyberAuction #469, Lot #31.

5205. SULPHIDE. Figure is a naked girl bathing. Seated figure. Has a spong in one hand at head, other hand on chest. Has a hair band hold her ha Excellent detail. Super example of this figure. No air bubbles. Very we centered. Superb. Polished surface. Germany, circa 1870-1915. 1-5/8". Price $210. CyberAuction #475, Lot #20.

5206. SULPHIDE. Figure is an angel floating, outspread wings, hands claspe over groin. Nice large figure. Excellent detail. Tip of one wing is missin Well centered, no air bubbles on the figure. Polished. Germany, circa 1870-1915. 1-1/2". Price: $210. CyberAuction #490, Lot #41.

5207. SULPHIDE. Figure is a seated cat. Excellent detail to the figure. No air bubbles. Large figure. Well centered. One small melt spot on one side Very nice example. Germany, circa 1870-1915. 1-13/16". Mint(-) (9.0). Price $210. CyberAuction #507, Lot #52.

5208. SULPHIDE. Figure of Kate Greenaway. Excellent figure. Set a litt high in the marble. No air bubbling. Surface is polished, some damag remains. Germany, circa 1870-1915. 1-3/8". Price: $205. CyberAuctio #394, Lot #21.

5209. SULPHIDE. Perched eagle with partially outstretched wings. Excellent detail. Very shallow air bubble on the lower part of the breast on th front. Well-centered. Several tiny melt spots, a couple of tiny rub mark Germany, circa 1870-1915. 1-11/16". Mint(-) (9.0). Price: $200 CyberAuction #409, Lot #58.

5210. SULPHIDE. Figure is a rearing horse on grass. Above average deta figure. No air bubbles. Set a little high. A scratch and a pit on the back of the marble. Excellent example of this figure. Germany, circa 1870-1915. 2-1/8". Mint(-) (9.0). Price: $200. CyberAuction #417, Lot #24.

5211. SULPHIDE. Figure is the numeral #8. Excellent figure. Well centered. Small air bubble on back, no air bubble on front. Some tiny chip and tiny subsurface moons. Germany, circa 1870-1915. 1-9/16". Near Mint(-) (8.2). Price: $200. CyberAuction #448, Lot #35.

5212. SULPHIDE. Figure of the numeral #3. Excellent detail. Very well centered. Small air bubble on the back, but not the front (who looks at th back of a numeral anyhow?). Polished. Germany, circa 1870-1915. 1-9/16". Price: $200. CyberAuction #469, Lot #34.

5213. SULPHIDE. Figure is a Prussian Eagle. Perched on a branch, wing partially outstretched, head with long neck turned to one side. Above average detail. No air bubbles on the figure, but tiny air bubbles throughout th marble. Figure set slightly high. A couple of small chips on the side and th back. Some overall scratching. Very nice example of this figure. Large marble Germany, circa 1870-1915. 2-3/8". Near Mint(-) (8.0). Price: $195 CyberAuction #424, Lot #48.

5214. SULPHIDE. Figure is a Prussian Eagle. Perched on a branch, wing partially outstretched, head with long neck turned to one side. Above average detail. No air bubbles on the figure, but tiny air bubbles throughout th marble. Figure set slightly high. A couple of small chips on the side and th back. Some overall scratching. Very nice example of this figure. Large marble Germany, circa 1870-1915. 2-3/8". Near Mint(-) (8.0). Price: $195 CyberAuction #460, Lot #42.

5215. SULPHIDE. Figure is standing ram. Excellent detail. Well-centered No air bubbles. At first glance I thought the surface had been lightly buffed but further examination reveals that it is original. Outstanding condition!! Germany, circa 1870-1915. 1-13/16". Mint (9.9). Price: $190. CyberAuctio #414, Lot #27.

5216. SULPHIDE. Figure is a seated cat. Excellent detail to the figure. No air bubbles. Large figure. Well centered. One small melt spot on one side Very nice example. Germany, circa 1870-1915. 1-13/16". Mint(-) (9.0). Price $190. CyberAuction #418, Lot #39.

5217. SULPHIDE. Figure is a seated cat. Excellent detail to the figure. No air bubbles. Large figure. Well centered. One small melt spot on one side Very nice example. Germany, circa 1870-1915. 1-13/16". Mint(-) (9.0). Price $190. CyberAuction #460, Lot #40.

5218. SULPHIDE. Figure is a hen. Excellent detail. No air bubbles. Very well centered. A couple of very tiny subsurface moons. Super marble. Germany, circa 1870-1915. 1-7/8". Near Mint(+) (8.8). Price: $185 CyberAuction #410, Lot #58.

5219. SULPHIDE. Figure is a vulture. Rare figure. Excellent detail. No a bubbles around the figure, but one underneath it in the marble. Figure se high. Several small and tiny chips. Germany, circa 1870-1915. 1-9/16" Good(+) (7.9). Price: $185. CyberAuction #429, Lot #48.

5220. SULPHIDE. Figure is Babylonian bear grasping a pole. Excellent detail. No air bubbles. Well centered. Large figure. Marble has two tiny chip on the lower half, some pits and some minor haze. Very nice. Germany circa 1870-1915. 1-11/16". Near Mint(-) (8.0). Price: $185. CyberAuctio #431, Lot #46.

221. **SULPHIDE.** Figure of a running rabbit. Large figure. Above average etail. Very shallow air bubbles. Well centered. Surface has two barely isible tiny subsurface moons. Germany, circa 1870-1915. 2-1/8". Near Aint(+) (8.7). Price: $185. CyberAuction #436, Lot #23.
222. **SULPHIDE.** Figure is an angel floating, outspread wings, hands clasped ver groin. Nice large figure. Excellent detail. Tip of one wing is missing. Vell centered, no air bubbles on the figure. Polished. Germany, circa 1870-915. 1-1/2". Price: $185. CyberAuction #462, Lot #60.
223. **SULPHIDE.** Figure of a dog seated on its rear haunches. Excellent etail, set slightly back. No air bubbles. Surface is exceptional. 1-5/8". Mint .8). Price: $180. CyberAuction #386, Lot #41.
224. **SULPHIDE.** Figure is a standing horse. Excellent detail. Very shallow r bubble just under the belly on either side. No obscuring air bubbles. ery well centered. Surface is in great shape, just a few tiny rub spots and ny sparkles. Beauty. Germany, circa 1870-1915. 2-1/16". Near Mint(+) .9). Price: $180. CyberAuction #443, Lot #36.
225. **SULPHIDE.** Figure is a hare. Above average detail. Tall ears. The ears sually break off on these. Very shallow silvering air layer. Large figure. ightly off center. Subsurface moons on the marble. Germany, circa 1870-915. 2-3/8". Good(+) (7.9). Price: $180. CyberAuction #497, Lot #35.
226. **SULPHIDE.** Figure is a donkey. Average detail. Well centered. No air ubbles. Small marble. Harder to find. Surface in great shape. Germany, rca 1870-1915. 1-1/16". Mint (9.9). Price: $175. CyberAuction #424, ot #52.
227. **SULPHIDE.** Figure is a totem pole eagle. Excellent detail. Slightly off enter. No air bubbles. Surface has overall pitting. Germany, circa 1870-915. 2-1/16". Good(+) (7.9). Price: $175. CyberAuction #468, Lot #8.
228. **SULPHIDE.** Figure of a bear. Shallow air bubble on one side. Aver-ge detail. Well centered. Base glass is purple. May be sun-tinted, I don't now. Several tiny chips and flakes, light haze. Germany, circa 1870-1915. -7/16". Near Mint(-) (8.0). Price: $175. CyberAuction #499, Lot #10.
229. **SULPHIDE.** Figure of rearing horse. Excellent detail. Cracked during sertion. Small air bubble on part of each side. Well centered. Pontil is rectly on the bottom. Germany, circa 1870-1915. 2". Mint (9.8). Price: 170. CyberAuction #333, Lot #36.
230. **SULPHIDE.** Figure is a single hump camel. Excellent detail. Set slightly gh. One tiny subsurface moon, some pits. Hard to find. Germany, circa 370-1915. 1-7/8". Near Mint (8.4). Price: $170. CyberAuction #417, Lot 54.
231. **SULPHIDE.** Figure of a fish. Large figure. Above average detailing. et slightly off-center. Small air bubble on one side. Surface has one sparkle nd a couple of tiny pinpricks. Germany, circa 1870-1915. 2". Mint(-) (9.2). ice: $170. CyberAuction #418, Lot #27.
232. **SULPHIDE.** Figure of a seated goose. Long neck. The figure is very ell detailed. Well centered. Some annealing crazing cracks on the figure, ut not fractured. No air bubbles on the figure, but a couple floating in the wer half of the marble. Very odd figure, usually a figure with an append-e as long as this neck would have cracked or had an air bubble around it. ghtly buffed. Superb. Germany, circa 1870-1915. 1-5/16". Price: $170. yberAuction #418, Lot #47.
233. **SULPHIDE.** Figure is a pelican. Very rare. Slight fracturing of the ure. Base glass is very lightly tinted blue. Figure is well centered. Excel-nt detail. No air bubbles, but there is some odd cloudiness on one side of e marble. The surface has been polished, but not remelted. Germany, rca 1870-1915. 1-5/8". Price: $170. CyberAuction #421, Lot #43.
234. **SULPHIDE.** Figure is an owl with outstretched wings. Excellent de-il. Very hard to find, usually the wings break. This one is in great shape. ompletely fills the marble. A couple of tiny air bubbles in the marble, ne on the figure. Barely visible annealing fracture on one side of the arble. Several tiny hit marks and pits on the surface. One small cold roll e. Still, super figure. Germany, circa 1870-1915. 1-5/16". Near Mint (8.6). ice: $170. CyberAuction #425, Lot #53.
235. **SULPHIDE.** Figure is a reclining dog with collar. Excellent detail. perb silvering. Tiny air bubble on the bottom and on one side. A few her insertion air bubbles floating in the marble. Set slightly off center. ne sparkle. Excellent example. Germany, circa 1870-1915. 1-3/4". Mint(-9.2). Price: $160. CyberAuction #356, Lot #54.
236. **SULPHIDE.** Figure is a lizard crawling on a rock. Average detail. Off nter. No air bubbles. One tiny chip at the bottom, some pinpricks. Nice. ermany, circa 1870-1915. 1-5/16". Near Mint (8.6). Price: $160. yberAuction #416, Lot #37.
237. **SULPHIDE.** Cat begging on hind haunches. Average detail. No air bbles. Set slightly high in the marble. Three very tiny subsurface moons the top. Very nice marble. Germany, circa 1870-1915. 1-11/16". Near int(+) (8.8). Price: $160. CyberAuction #424, Lot #32.
238. **SULPHIDE.** Figure is a standing lamb. Average detail. Well centered, air bubbles. Base glass is tinted very slightly green. In superior shape. ermany, circa 1870-1915. 2-3/8". Mint (9.8). Price: $160. CyberAuction 440, Lot #32.
239. **SULPHIDE.** Figure is a vulture. Rare figure. Excellent detail. No air ibbles around the figure, but one underneath it in the marble. Figure set gh. Several small and tiny chips. Germany, circa 1870-1915. 1-9/16". ood(+) (7.9). Price: $160. CyberAuction #476, Lot #21.
240. **SULPHIDE.** Lightly amethyst glass. Seated bear. Small air bubble ider figure. Two tiny subsurface moons. 1-5/8". Near Mint(+) (8.7). Price: 60. CyberAuction #493, Lot #18.
241. **SULPHIDE.** Figure of a seated cat. Average detail to the figure. No bubbles. Well-centered. Figure cracked when inserted. Surface has one ry tiny sparkle, else it is pristine. Germany, circa 1870-1915. 1-13/16". int(-) (9.2). Price: $150. CyberAuction #414, Lot #53.
242. **SULPHIDE.** Figure of a standing male lion. Above average detail. No air bubbles. Well centered. Surface has a few very small subsurface moons, but nothing that really detracts from viewing. Germany, circa 1870-1915. 1-7/8". Near Mint (8.3). Price: $150. CyberAuction #435, Lot #51.
5243. **SULPHIDE.** Figure is a totem pole eagle. Excellent detail. Slightly off center. No air bubbles. Surface has overall pitting. Germany, circa 1870-1915. 2-1/16". Good(+) (7.9). Price: $150. CyberAuction #443, Lot #48.
5244. **SULPHIDE.** Figure is the numeral #4. Excellent figure. Small air bubble on the reverse of the figure, front is clean. Slightly off-center. Small chip, some pits, some haziness. Germany, circa 1870-1915. 1-5/8". Near Mint(-) (8.0). Price: $150. CyberAuction #446, Lot #57.
5245. **SULPHIDE.** Figure of a fish. Large figure. Above average detailing. Set slightly off-center. Small air bubble on one side. Surface has one sparkle and a couple of tiny pinpricks. Germany, circa 1870-1915. 2". Mint(-) (9.2). Price: $150. CyberAuction #468, Lot #15.
5246. **SULPHIDE.** Figure of the numeral #2. Large figure. No air bubbles. Well centered. Several chips on the marble. Germany, circa 1870-1915. 1-9/16". Good (7.4). Price: $150. CyberAuction #469, Lot #37.
5247. **SULPHIDE.** Figure is a flying duck. In full flight, with outstretched wings. Extremely rare figure. Excellent detail to the figure. Large for the marble. No air bubbles. Very well centered. Superb sulphide, but the surface is polished. Germany, circa 1870-1915. 1-13/16". Price: $150. CyberAuction #483, Lot #34.
5248. **SULPHIDE.** Figure of an elephant. Excellent detail to the figure. No air bubbles. Set slightly high. Polished. Germany, circa 1870-1915. 1-1/4". Price: $140. CyberAuction #355, Lot #56.
5249. **SULPHIDE.** Standing rooster. Excellent detail. No air bubbling. Well-centered. One tiny subsurface moon, two small melt spots. None interferes with viewing the figure. Excellent! Germany, circa 1870-1915. 1-3/4". Near Mint(+) (8.7). Price: $140. CyberAuction #409, Lot #49.
5250. **SULPHIDE.** Figure of standing male lion. Excellent detail. Slightly off-center. There are two small air bubbles on one side between the figure and the marble surface, but not on the figure itself. Several tiny chips, some haze. Germany, circa 1870-1915. 1-11/16". Near Mint(-) (8.0). Price: $140. CyberAuction #413, Lot #36.
5251. **SULPHIDE.** Figure of standing male lion. Excellent detail. Slightly off-center. There are two small air bubbles on one side between the figure and the marble surface, but not on the figure itself. Several tiny chips, some haze. Germany, circa 1870-1915. 1-11/16". Near Mint(-) (8.0). Price: $140. CyberAuction #430, Lot #26.
5252. **SULPHIDE.** Figure is a standing squirrel eating a nut. Excellent detail. Large figure. No air bubbles. Set slightly off center. Several tiny rub spots, a tiny subsurface moon. Germany, circa 1870-1915. 1-7/8". Near Mint(+) (8.8). Price: $140. CyberAuction #433, Lot #34.
5253. **SULPHIDE.** Figure is a seated duck. Above average detail. Very small air bubble laying on part of the back. Well centered. In super shape. Germany, circa 1870-1915. 1-11/16". Mint (9.7). Price: $140. CyberAuction #436, Lot #20.
5254. **SULPHIDE.** Rare figure. Naked seated boy with a large marble (perhaps a very small ball) in his left hand. Large figure. Very three-dimensional. Excellent detail to the figure. Well-centered. No air bubbles. Unfortunately, the marble fractured. The fracture is directly under the figure, at it's base. The marble is fractured, not the figure. Also, a tiny fracture along the right arm. A couple of small subsurface moons and pits. The figure is still very viewable, but the marble is not perfect. Germany, circa 1870-1915. 1-3/4". Good (7.6). Price: $140. CyberAuction #447, Lot #53.
5255. **SULPHIDE.** Figure is a donkey. Average detail. Well centered. No air bubbles. Small marble. Harder to find. Surface in great shape. Germany, circa 1870-1915. 1-1/16". Mint (9.9). Price: $140. CyberAuction #474, Lot #12.
5256. **SULPHIDE.** Figure of a fish. The fish is curved (unusual). Excellent detail. Some small air bubbles on the fish. Well centered. Marble is polished. Germany, circa 1870-1915. 1-11/16". Price: $135. CyberAuction #433, Lot #50.
5257. **SULPHIDE.** Figure of a fish. The fish is curved (unusual). Excellent detail. Some small air bubbles on the fish. Well centered. Marble is polished. Germany, circa 1870-1915. 1-11/16". Price: $135. CyberAuction #454, Lot #24.
5258. **SULPHIDE.** Figure is a singing songbird. Excellent detail to the figure. No air bubbles. Well-centered. One tiny sparkle, some pinpricks, some scratches. Still, a gorgeous example. Germany, circa 1870-1915. 2-1/8". Near Mint(+) (8.8). Price: $130. CyberAuction #420, Lot #32.
5259. **SULPHIDE.** Figure is a seated bunny rabbit. Average detail. Black eye and nose painted on one side, as well as two tiny black spots (one on the side, one on the base). Very shallow encasing air bubble. Tiny chip, tiny moon, some haze. Germany, circa 1870-1915. 1-3/8". Good(+) (7.8). Price: $130. CyberAuction #423, Lot #45.
5260. **SULPHIDE.** Figure is a llama. Above average detail. No air bubbles. Well centered. In great shape. Germany, circa 1870-1915. 1-1/2". Mint (9.7). Price: $130. CyberAuction #435, Lot #28.
5261. **SULPHIDE.** Figure is a Prussian Eagle. Perched on a branch, wings partially outstretched, head with long neck turned to one side. Above average detail. No air bubbles on the figure, but tiny air bubbles throughout the marble. Figure set slightly high. A couple of small chips on the side and the back. Some overall scratching. Very nice example of this figure. Large marble. Germany, circa 1870-1915. 2-3/8". Near Mint(-) (8.0). Price: $130. CyberAuction #507, Lot #31.
5262. **SULPHIDE.** Figure is the numeral #1. Excellent figure. Shallow air bubble on one side. Slightly off-center. Several small subsurface moons. Pontil is on the front of the marble. Germany, circa 1870-1915. 1-9/16". Good (7.4). Price: $120. CyberAuction #344, Lot #48.
5263. **SULPHIDE.** Figure is a razorback. Excellent detail to the figure. No

air bubbles. Well centered. Surface has a couple of very tiny chips and some pitting. Great figure though. Germany, circa 1870-1915. 1-11/16". Near Mint(-) (8.0). Price: $120. CyberAuction #413, Lot #33.
5264. SULPHIDE. Figure of a fish. Excellent detail! Well centered. Small air bubble on part of one side. Some tiny chips and pits. A beauty!!! Germany, circa 1870-1915. 1-9/16". Near Mint(+) (8.7). Price: $120. CyberAuction #416, Lot #18.
5265. SULPHIDE. Figure is a falcon. Above average detail. Well centered. Very small air bubble on one side. Surface has a couple of tiny sparkles. Germany, circa 1870-1915. 1-11/16". Near Mint(+) (8.9). Price: $120. CyberAuction #425, Lot #34.
5266. SULPHIDE. Figure is a begging bushy-tail cat. Average detail to figure. No air bubbles. Well centered. Surface in great shape. Germany, circa 1870-1915. 1-7/16". Mint (9.8). Price: $120. CyberAuction #443, Lot #24.
5267. SULPHIDE. Figure of a begging bear. Average detail. Air bubble on side of figure. Well centered. Surface has some pitting. Germany, circa 1870-1915. 2-5/16". Near Mint(-) (8.0). Price: $120. CyberAuction #456, Lot #25.
5268. SULPHIDE. Figure is a running rabbit. Above average detail. No air bubbling. Figure cracked on insertion. Well centered. A couple of very tiny flakes, some areas of very light rubbing. Views great. Very nice sulphide. Germany, circa 1870-1915. 1-3/4". Near Mint(+) (8.7). Price: $110. CyberAuction #410, Lot #33.
5269. SULPHIDE. Figure is a reclining rabbit with its head up. Above average detail to the figure. No air bubbles. Slightly off-center. Figure is a little small for the marble. Some tiny chips, a little haze. Germany, circa 1870-1915. 1-13/16". Good(+) (7.9). Price: $110. CyberAuction #415, Lot #52.
5270. SULPHIDE. Interesting figure. An organ-grinder monkey. Seated monkey wearing a hat with a tassel. Above average detail. Slightly off-center. No air bubbles. Surface has overall scratching and pinpricking. Needs a very light buff. Germany, circa 1870-1915. 1-3/16". Near Mint(-) (8.0). Price: $110. CyberAuction #418, Lot #59.
5271. SULPHIDE. Figure is a totem pole eagle. Above average detail. Small barely visible air bubble on the belly. Tip of one wing is missing. Well centered. Polished. Germany, circa 1870-1915. 1-9/16". Price: $110. CyberAuction #423, Lot #40.
5272. SULPHIDE. Base glass is very light teal. Figure is a standing male lion. Average detail. Air bubble on both sides. Well centered. Several large and small subsurface moons, a couple of tiny chips. Germany, circa 1870-1915. 1-3/4". Good (7.5). Price: $110. CyberAuction #428, Lot #28.
5273. SULPHIDE. Figure is a standing rooster. Excellent detail. Well centered. There is a very flat air bubble between the back of the head and the front of the tail (typical). Two very tiny subsurface moons on the side. Very nice example. Germany, circa 1870-1915. 1-11/16". Near Mint(+) (8.8). Price: $110. CyberAuction #428, Lot #34.
5274. SULPHIDE. Figure is baby Moses in the basket. Excellent detail, you can make out the entire baby's face. Nice reeded basket. Shallow air bubbling in the concavities of the figure, but not detracting from viewing. Chip on one side, some pits, but the figure still is very viewable from the top and the other side. Very nice, and hard to find. Germany, circa 1870-1915. 1-1/8". Good(+) (7.9). Price: $110. CyberAuction #428, Lot #48.
5275. SULPHIDE. Figure is a standing duck. Excellent detail for the figure. Very large figure for the marble size. Well centered. No air bubbles. Very light haze, a couple of very tiny shallow flakes. A very light buff will reveal a beauty (the pontil would even remain intact). Germany, circa 1870-1915. 1-1/2". Near Mint(-) (8.1). Price: $110. CyberAuction #431, Lot #16.
5276. SULPHIDE. Figure of the numeral #5. Figure set high in the marble. Small air bubble on the back side. Some small chips. Germany, circa 1870-1915. 1-9/16". Good(+) (7.9). Price: $110. CyberAuction #435, Lot #58.
5277. SULPHIDE. Figure is a running dog. Excellent detail to the figure. The figure cracked when inserted, but stayed together. Well centered. No air bubbles. Surface has overall pinpricks and some tiny and small chips. Germany, circa 1870-1915. 1-13/16". Good(+) (7.8). Price: $110. CyberAuction #442, Lot #33.
5278. SULPHIDE. Figure is a monkey seated on the ground. Exceptional detail to the figure. Surrounded by tiny air bubbles, but still very visible. Well centered. Surface has a few pits. Germany, circa 1870-1915. 2-1/8". Near Mint (8.4). Price: $110. CyberAuction #444, Lot #31.
5279. SULPHIDE. Figure of a perched parrot. Excellent detail to figure. No air bubbles. Well centered. Polished, some damage remains. Germany, circa 1870-1915. 1-11/16". Price: $110. CyberAuction #448, Lot #34.
5280. SULPHIDE. Unusual figure. Seated stork. At first glance looks like a duck, but it has a long bill. Perhaps it is an ibis, but I think it is a stork. Average detail to the figure. Well centered. Several small chips and pits. Germany, circa 1870-1915. 1-7/16". Near Mint(-) (8.0). Price: $110. CyberAuction #451, Lot #33.
5281. SULPHIDE. Figure of a standing male lion. Above average detail. No air bubbles. Well centered. Surface has a few very small subsurface moons, but nothing that really detracts from viewing. Germany, circa 1870-1915. 1-7/8". Near Mint (8.3). Price: $110. CyberAuction #453, Lot #23.
5282. SULPHIDE. Figure of the numeral #5. Figure set high in the marble. Small air bubble on the back side. Some small chips. Germany, circa 1870-1915. 1-9/16". Good(+) (7.9). Price: $110. CyberAuction #453, Lot #36.
5283. SULPHIDE. Figure of the numeral #2. Large figure. No air bubbles. Well centered. Several chips on the marble. Germany, circa 1870-1915. 1-9/16". Good (7.4). Price: $110. CyberAuction #456, Lot #7.
5284. SULPHIDE. Figure is a begging bushy-tail cat. Average detail to figure. No air bubbles. Well centered. Surface in great shape. Germany, circa 1870-1915. 1-7/16". Mint (9.8). Price: $110. CyberAuction #456, Lot #27.
5285. SULPHIDE. Figure is a totem pole eagle. Above average detail. Small barely visible air bubble on the belly. Tip of one wing is missing. Well centered. Polished. Germany, circa 1870-1915. 1-9/16". Price: $11[illegible] CyberAuction #456, Lot #31.
5286. SULPHIDE. Figure of a seated cat. Average detail to the figure. N[illegible] air bubbles. Well-centered. Figure cracked when inserted. Surface has o[illegible] very tiny sparkle, else it is pristine. Germany, circa 1870-1915. 1-13/1[illegible] Mint(-) (9.2). Price: $110. CyberAuction #472, Lot #42.
5287. SULPHIDE. Figure is the numeral #9. Figure is very nice, with no [illegible] bubbles on it. Well centered. Some flakes on the surface. Germany, ci[illegible] 1870-1915. 1-3/4". Good(+) (7.9). Price: $110. CyberAuction #473, L[illegible] #30.
5288. SULPHIDE. Figure is a monkey seated on the ground. Exceptio[illegible] detail to the figure. Surrounded by tiny air bubbles, but still very visib[illegible] Well centered. Surface has a few pits. Germany, circa 1870-1915. 2-1/[illegible] Near Mint (8.4). Price: $110. CyberAuction #473, Lot #32.
5289. SULPHIDE. Figure is a standing duck. Excellent detail for the figu[illegible] Very large figure for the marble size. Well centered. No air bubbles. Ve[illegible] light haze, a couple of very tiny shallow flakes. A very light buff will reve[illegible] a beauty (the pontil would even remain intact). Germany, circa 1870-191[illegible] 1-1/2". Near Mint(-) (8.1). Price: $110. CyberAuction #476, Lot #29.
5290. SULPHIDE. Figure of a bear. Shallow air bubble on one side. Av[illegible] age detail. Well centered. Base glass is purple. May be sun-tinted, I do[illegible] know. Several tiny chips and flakes, light haze. Germany, circa 1870-191[illegible] 1-7/16". Near Mint(-) (8.0). Price: $110. CyberAuction #477, Lot #42.
5291. SULPHIDE. Interesting figure. An organ-grinder monkey. Seat[illegible] monkey wearing a hat with a tassel. Above average detail. Slightly o[illegible] center. No air bubbles. Surface has overall scratching and pinpricking. Nee[illegible] a very light buff. Germany, circa 1870-1915. 1-3/16". Near Mint(-) (8.[illegible] Price: $110. CyberAuction #482, Lot #43.
5292. SULPHIDE. Figure of seated dog. Above average detail. No [illegible] bubbles. Set high. Surface in great shape. Germany, circa 1870-1915. 1-[illegible] 16". Mint (9.8). Price: $110. CyberAuction #489, Lot #56.
5293. SULPHIDE. Small marble. Figure is a running dog. Excellent det[illegible] Shallow air bubble on one side, but other side has better detail anyhow. [illegible] slightly forward in the marble. One sparkle. Germany, circa 1870-1915. [illegible] 1/16". Mint(-) (9.0). Price: $100. CyberAuction #412, Lot #18.
5294. SULPHIDE. Figure is a seated male lion. Exceptional detail. No [illegible] bubbles. Well-centered. Polished. Germany, circa 1870-1915. 1-7/16". Pri[illegible] $100. CyberAuction #415, Lot #57.
5295. SULPHIDE. Figure is a seated squirrel with an upraised tail. Excell[illegible] detail. Slightly off-center, no air bubbles. A few small and tiny chips a[illegible] subsurface moons. Still, views well. Germany, circa 1870-1915. 1-3/8". N[illegible] Mint(-) (8.2). Price: $100. CyberAuction #416, Lot #45.
5296. SULPHIDE. Small marble. Figure is a running dog. Excellent det[illegible] Shallow air bubble on one side, but other side has better detail anyhow. [illegible] slightly forward in the marble. One sparkle. Germany, circa 1870-1915. [illegible] 1/16". Mint(-) (9.0). Price: $100. CyberAuction #454, Lot #15.
5297. SULPHIDE. Figure is a seated squirrel with an upraised tail. Excell[illegible] detail. Slightly off-center, no air bubbles. A few small and tiny chips a[illegible] subsurface moons. Still, views well. Germany, circa 1870-1915. 1-3/8". N[illegible] Mint(-) (8.2). Price: $100. CyberAuction #471, Lot #29.
5298. SULPHIDE. Figure is a narrow figure of an owl. Average detail. W[illegible] centered. Very shallow air bubble on part of the back. Marble has so[illegible] surface pinpricks. Interesting and an odd figure. Germany, circa 1870-191[illegible] 1-11/16". Near Mint(+) (8.9). Price: $100. CyberAuction #472, Lot #[illegible]
5299. SULPHIDE. Figure of a seated cat. Excellent detail. Well center[illegible] Air bubble on one side of neck. Germany, circa 1870-1915. 1-13/16". M[illegible] (9.8). Price: $100. CyberAuction #501, Lot #60.
5300. SULPHIDE. Figure is a billy goat. Above average detail to the figu[illegible] Well centered, no air bubbles. Excellent. One small chip on the bottom [illegible] number of very shallow, small and tiny subsurface moons. Germany, cir[illegible] 1870-1915. 1-15/16". Near Mint(-) (8.0). Price: $95. CyberAuction #4[illegible] Lot #45.
5301. SULPHIDE. Figure is a seated frog. Very hard to find and this on[illegible] a really nice one. Average detail. Well centered. Very shallow small [illegible] bubble at the top and a similar one underneath. Views very well. Po[illegible] polished. Germany, circa 1870-1915. 1-5/8". Price: $95. CyberAucti[illegible] #428, Lot #53.
5302. SULPHIDE. Figure of a seated cat. Average detail to the figure. N[illegible] air bubbles. Well-centered. Figure cracked when inserted. Surface has o[illegible] very tiny sparkle, else it is pristine. Germany, circa 1870-1915. 1-13/1[illegible] Mint(-) (9.2). Price: $95. CyberAuction #499, Lot #22.
5303. SULPHIDE. Base glass is very light teal. Figure is a standing m[illegible] lion. Average detail. Air bubble on both sides. Well centered. Several la[illegible] and small subsurface moons, a couple of tiny chips. Germany, circa 18[illegible] 1915. 1-3/4". Good (7.5). Price: $90. CyberAuction #475, Lot #17.
5304. SULPHIDE. Seated cat. Average detail. Set low in marble. No [illegible] bubbles. Large marble. Two tiny chips, two small subsurface moons, all [illegible] the sides of the marble. Some pits. Germany, circa 1870-1915. 2". N[illegible] Mint(-) (8.1). Price: $90. CyberAuction #477, Lot #18.
5305. SULPHIDE. Figure of a grazing sheep. No air bubbles. Well ce[illegible] tered. Surface has no damage. Germany, circa 1870-1915. 1-1/2". M[illegible] (9.8). Price: $90. CyberAuction #492, Lot #24.
5306. SULPHIDE. Seated cat. Average detail. Set low in marble. No [illegible] bubbles. Large marble. Two tiny chips, two small subsurface moons, all [illegible] the sides of the marble. Some pits. Germany, circa 1870-1915. 2". N[illegible] Mint(-) (8.1). Price: $85. CyberAuction #417, Lot #22.
5307. SULPHIDE. Figure of a cow wearing a collar or yoke. Above avera[illegible] detail. No air bubbling. Nicely centered. One small chip at the botto[illegible] some minor scratching and rubbing. Germany, circa 1870-1915. 1-11/1[illegible] Near Mint (8.3). Price: $85. CyberAuction #446, Lot #50.
5308. SULPHIDE. Figure is a seated cow, chewing its cud. Excellent de[illegible]

o figure. Large figure for marble. Well centered. No air bubbles. Surface is original with a few sparkles (mostly on the top). Germany, circa 1870-1915. 1-1/4". Near Mint(+) (8.9). Price: $85. CyberAuction #471, Lot #25.

5309. SULPHIDE. Figure of a razorback hog. Exceptional detail to the figure. Large for the marble. No air bubbles. Well centered. Polished surface. One small chip remnant on the bottom that the polisher turned into a pontil. Germany, circa 1870-1915. 1-13/16". Price: $85. CyberAuction #497, Lot #55.

5310. SULPHIDE. Transparent pale pink glass. Figure is a grazing sheep. Average detail to the figure. Set off-center. Some subsurface moons. Germany, circa 1870-1915. 1-7/16". Near Mint(-) (8.1). Price: $80. CyberAuction #368, Lot #58.

5311. SULPHIDE. Figure of a seated male lion. Excellent detail to the figure. Well centered. A number of small chips and subsurface moons, but still views fine. 1-9/16". Good(+) (7.7). Price: $80. CyberAuction #383, Lot #21.

5312. SULPHIDE. Figure of a seated cat. Average detail. Figure is set high. No air bubbles. A couple of areas with tiny chips and pitting. Germany, circa 1870-1915. 1-7/16". Near Mint (8.6). Price: $80. CyberAuction #421, Lot #7.

5313. SULPHIDE. Figure is a narrow figure of an owl. Average detail. Well centered. Very shallow air bubble on part of the back. Marble has some surface pinpricks. Interesting and an odd figure. Germany, circa 1870-1915. 1-11/16". Near Mint(+) (8.9). Price: $80. CyberAuction #427, Lot #27.

5314. SULPHIDE. Figure of a standing cow. Average detail. No air bubbles. There is some white "debris" in the marble. Nice surface, with just a couple of very tiny pinpricks. Germany, circa 1870-1915. 1-3/8". Mint(-) (9.1). Price: $80. CyberAuction #432, Lot #24.

5315. SULPHIDE. Figure is a narrow frog, or possibly a lizard. Below average detail. No air bubbling. Nicely centered. Small chip, a couple of tiny subsurface moons, all on one side. Germany, circa 1870-1915. 1-1/4". Near Mint (8.5). Price: $80. CyberAuction #441, Lot #7.

5316. SULPHIDE. Figure is a standing rooster. Excellent detail to the figure. No air bubbles. Set slightly high. Surface has some very light haze with some tiny chips and flakes. Germany, circa 1870-1915. 1-15/16". Good (7.6). Price: $80. CyberAuction #442, Lot #31.

5317. SULPHIDE. Transparent pink glass. Figure is a grazing sheep. Average detail to the figure. Set off-center. Some subsurface moons. Germany, circa 1870-1915. 1-7/16". Near Mint(-) (8.1). Price: $80. CyberAuction #447, Lot #47.

5318. SULPHIDE. Figure is a standing sheep. Excellent detail. No air bubbles. Well centered. Surface has a tiny chip near the bottom, a couple of tiny pits, a tiny subsurface moon. The damage is unobtrusive and the marble views very well. Germany, circa 1870-1915. 1-1/2". Near Mint (8.5). Price: $80. CyberAuction #453, Lot #59.

5319. SULPHIDE. Figure is a seated cat. Average detail. Figure is set high. No air bubbles. A couple of areas with tiny chips and pitting. Germany, circa 1870-1915. 1-7/16". Near Mint (8.6). Price: $80. CyberAuction #460, Lot #46.

5320. SULPHIDE. Figure is a totem pole eagle. Above average detail. Small barely visible air bubble on the belly. Tip of one wing is missing. Well centered. Polished. Germany, circa 1870-1915. 1-9/16". Price: $80. CyberAuction #476, Lot #7.

5321. SULPHIDE. Figure of a warthog. The front of the snout is missing. Good detail. Set slightly low. No air bubbles. Small chip on top. Several small subsurface moons. Nothing interferes with viewing. Nice. Germany, circa 1870-1915. 1-9/16". Near Mint(-) (8.0). Price: $80. CyberAuction #478, Lot #25.

5322. SULPHIDE. Howling bear. Average detail. Small air bubble at bottom of one side. Nicely centered. Tiny chip on one side. Germany, circa 1870-1915. 1-3/8". Near Mint(+) (8.8). Price: $75. CyberAuction #339, Lot #27.

5323. SULPHIDE. Figure is a two-hump camel (rare). Figure has a crack. Also, shallow air bubble near the bottom of the figure on either side of it. Well-centered. Some roughness and pitting, mostly on one side. Germany, circa 1870-1915. 1-3/16". Near Mint(-) (8.0). Price: $75. CyberAuction #412, Lot #30.

5324. SULPHIDE. Figure is a papoose. Crude figure. No air bubbles. Well centered. Several very small moons and very small subsurface moons. Germany, circa 1870-1915. 1-9/16". Near Mint(-) (8.2). Price: $75. CyberAuction #425, Lot #36.

5325. SULPHIDE. Figure of a dog on its hind legs, begging. Below average detail to figure. No air bubbles. Large and well centered. Surface has some tiny chips and pits. Germany, circa 1870-1915. 1-3/4". Near Mint(-) (8.2). Price: $75. CyberAuction #427, Lot #22.

5326. SULPHIDE. Figure is a two-hump camel (rare). Figure has a crack. Also, shallow air bubble near the bottom of the figure on either side of it. Well-centered. Some roughness and pitting, mostly on one side. Germany, circa 1870-1915. 1-3/16". Near Mint(-) (8.0). Price: $75. CyberAuction #440, Lot #28.

5327. SULPHIDE. Figure is a running razorback hog. Excellent detail to figure. Extremely shallow silvering air layer. Off center. One tiny pit, one tiny sparkle. Germany, circa 1870-1915. 1-3/8". Mint(-) (9.0). Price: $70. CyberAuction #493, Lot #52.

5328. SULPHIDE. Figure is a reclining lamb. Average detail. Slightly off-center. No air bubbles. Surface has been buffed, some damage remains. Germany, circa 1870-1915. 1-1/4". Price: $65. CyberAuction #353, Lot #56.

5329. SULPHIDE. Figure of a warthog. The front of the snout is missing. Good detail. Set slightly low. No air bubbles. Small chip on top. Several small subsurface moons. Nothing interferes with viewing. Nice. Germany,

circa 1870-1915. 1-9/16". Near Mint(-) (8.0). Price: $65. CyberAuction #382, Lot #32.

5330. SULPHIDE. Figure of a standing sheep. Above average detail. Air bubble on one side. Base glass is slightly tinted bottle green. A few chips and a couple of tiny subsurface moons. A fracture on top. 1-7/16". Good(+) (7.9). Price: $65. CyberAuction #386, Lot #31.

5331. SULPHIDE. Figure is a narrow frog, or possibly a lizard. Below average detail. No air bubbling. Nicely centered. Small chip, a couple of tiny subsurface moons, all on one side. Germany, circa 1870-1915. 1-1/4". Near Mint (8.5). Price: $65. CyberAuction #410, Lot #15.

5332. SULPHIDE. Figure is a standing sheep. Excellent detail. No air bubbles. Well centered. Surface has a tiny chip near the bottom, a couple of tiny pits, a tiny subsurface moon. The damage is unobtrusive and the marble views very well. Germany, circa 1870-1915. 1-1/2". Near Mint (8.5). Price: $65. CyberAuction #432, Lot #49.

5333. SULPHIDE. Figure is a razorback. Excellent detail. No air bubbles. Well centered. Some small and tiny chips. Germany, circa 1870-1915. 1-13/16". Near Mint(-) (8.0). Price: $65. CyberAuction #439, Lot #15.

5334. SULPHIDE. Figure of a warthog. The front of the snout is missing. Good detail. Set slightly low. No air bubbles. Small chip on top. Several small subsurface moons. Nothing interferes with viewing. Nice. Germany, circa 1870-1915. 1-9/16". Near Mint(-) (8.0). Price: $65. CyberAuction #446, Lot #30.

5335. SULPHIDE. Figure of a standing sheep. Above average detail. Air bubble on one side. Base glass is slightly tinted bottle green. A few chips and a couple of tiny subsurface moons. A fracture on top. 1-7/16". Good(+) (7.9). Price: $65. CyberAuction #449, Lot #21.

5336. SULPHIDE. Figure of a standing cow. Average detail. No air bubbles. There is some white "debris" in the marble. Nice surface, with just a couple of very tiny pinpricks. Germany, circa 1870-1915. 1-3/8". Mint(-) (9.1). Price: $65. CyberAuction #454, Lot #29.

5337. SULPHIDE. Figure of a standing sheep. Above average detail. Air bubble on one side. Base glass is slightly tinted bottle green. A few chips and a couple of tiny subsurface moons. A fracture on top. 1-7/16". Good(+) (7.9). Price: $65. CyberAuction #466, Lot #31.

5338. SULPHIDE. Figure is a two-hump camel (rare). Figure has a crack. Also, shallow air bubble near the bottom of the figure on either side of it. Well-centered. Some roughness and pitting, mostly on one side. Germany, circa 1870-1915. 1-3/16". Near Mint(-) (8.0). Price: $65. CyberAuction #474, Lot #33.

5339. SULPHIDE. Figure of a standing sheep. Above average detail. Air bubble on one side. Base glass is slightly tinted bottle green. A few chips and a couple of tiny subsurface moons. A fracture on top. 1-7/16". Good(+) (7.9). Price: $65. CyberAuction #486, Lot #45.

5340. SULPHIDE. Parrot on a perch. Below average detail. Very shallow air bubble on one side. Slightly off center. Several tiny subsurface moons. Germany, circa 1870-1915. 1-5/16". Near Mint(+) (8.8). Price: $65. CyberAuction #492, Lot #32.

5341. SULPHIDE. Seated whippet dog. Excellent detail. No air bubbles. Set very slightly high. Polished surface. Germany, circa 1870-1915. 2-1/8". Price: $65. CyberAuction #493, Lot #15.

5342. SULPHIDE. Figure of a running horse. Hard figure to find. Average detail. Very shallow air bubble on one side, in the depressed areas. Well centered. Overall tiny pits and tiny chips. One moon on the top. Germany, circa 1870-1915. 1-1/4". Good(+) (7.9). Price: $65. CyberAuction #493, Lot #37.

5343. SULPHIDE. Figure of a standing cow. Large figure. Excellent detail. Very shallow silvering air bubbles. Well centered. Annealing fracture in the glass below the figure. Some pitting on one side, small subsurface moon on the back. Front views very well. Germany, circa 1870-1915. 1-1/2". Near Mint(+) (8.8). Price: $65. CyberAuction #501, Lot #14.

5344. SULPHIDE. Figure is a walking bear. Above average detail. Small air bubble on one side. Several small and tiny moons. Germany, circa 1870-1915. 1-9/16". Near Mint (8.4). Price: $61. CyberAuction #492, Lot #35.

5345. SULPHIDE. Figure appears to be a razorback. There is an air bubble around it. Average detail. Well centered. Surface has some scratching and pitting on one side. Germany, circa 1870-1915. 1-9/16". Near Mint(+) (8.7). Price: $60. CyberAuction #335, Lot #21.

5346. SULPHIDE. Figure of a begging bear. Average detail to the figure. Set slightly high. No air bubbling. Flat spot on the surface, and some pinpricking. Germany, circa 1870-1915. 1-5/8". Near Mint(+) (8.7). Price: $60. CyberAuction #409, Lot #9.

5347. SULPHIDE. Figure of a begging bear. Average detail to the figure. Set slightly high. No air bubbling. Flat spot on the surface, and some pinpricking. Germany, circa 1870-1915. 1-5/8". Near Mint(+) (8.7). Price: $60. CyberAuction #426, Lot #29.

5348. SULPHIDE. Figure of a pecking bird. Above average detail to the figure. Well centered. No air bubbles. Several small and tiny chips. Germany, circa 1870-1915. 1-1/2". Near Mint(-) (8.0). Price: $60. CyberAuction #427, Lot #6.

5349. SULPHIDE. Figure of a begging bear. Average detail to the figure. Set slightly high. No air bubbling. Flat spot on the surface, and some pinpricking. Germany, circa 1870-1915. 1-5/8". Near Mint(+) (8.7). Price: $60. CyberAuction #456, Lot #29.

5350. SULPHIDE. Figure is a seated goose. Hard to find figure. Long neck. Average detail. No air bubble. Well centered. Two very small subsurface moons, a couple of tiny pits. Germany, circa 1870-1915. 1-9/16". Near Mint (8.6). Price: $60. CyberAuction #493, Lot #21.

5351. SULPHIDE. Figure of a standing mule. Average detail. Slightly off-center. Small air bubble on one side. Chipping on one side of the marble, not where you view the figure. Germany, circa 1870-1915. 1-1/2". Good(+) (7.9). Price: $55. CyberAuction #371, Lot #21.

5352. SULPHIDE. Figure is a parrot. Average detail. No air bubbles. Set high. Some pitting and a few tiny rough spots. Germany, circa 1870-1915. 1-7/16". Near Mint(-) (8.0). Price: $55. CyberAuction #431, Lot #7.

5353. SULPHIDE. Figure is a spread winged eagle. Excellent detail. No air bubbles. Set high. Polished surface. Germany, circa 1870-1915. 1-11/16". Price: $55. CyberAuction #477, Lot #33.

5354. SULPHIDE. Figure is a donkey. Average detail. No air bubbles, nicely centered. Overall surface pitting. Germany, circa 1870-1915. 1-13/16". Near Mint(-) (8.1). Price: $55. CyberAuction #492, Lot #19.

5355. SULPHIDE. Figure of a seated dog. Small air bubble on one side of the figure. Slightly off center. One sparkle. Germany, circa 1870-1915. 1-9/16". Mint(-) (9.0). Price: $55. CyberAuction #492, Lot #22.

5356. SULPHIDE. Figure is a songbird. Average detail. Well centered. Small air bubble on one side. Some small melt chips and small subsurface moons. Germany, circa 1870-1915. 1-15/16". Near Mint (8.4). Price: $50. CyberAuction #439, Lot #12.

5357. SULPHIDE. Figure of a rooster. Excellent detail. No air bubbles. Well centered. Surface is buffed, pontil partially remains. Germany, circa 1870-1915. 1-1/2". Price: $50. CyberAuction #475, Lot #15.

5358. SULPHIDE. Standing lion. Average detail. No air bubbles. Set high. Polished surface with fake pontil. Germany, circa 1870-1915. 1-7/16". Price: $50. CyberAuction #480, Lot #46.

5359. SULPHIDE. Figure of a monkey walking on all fours. Short tail. Average detail. Small air bubble on one side. Slightly off center. Overall tiny moons and tiny subsurface moons. Germany, circa 1870-1915. 1-5/8". Good(+) (7.9). Price: $48. CyberAuction #394, Lot #40.

5360. SULPHIDE. Figure of a standing dog. Nice figure. Well detailed. No air bubbles on the figure, although there are some in the marble. Surface has a number of shallow flakes and chips. Germany, circa 1870-1915. 1-3/16". Good(+) (7.9). Price: $47. CyberAuction #394, Lot #36.

5361. SULPHIDE. Figure is a seated cow, chewing cud. Excellent detail, well centered, no air bubbles. Overall very light pitting and very light chips. Light polish will reveal a beautiful figure. Germany, circa 1870-1915. 1-1/2". Good(+) (7.9). Price: $47. CyberAuction #492, Lot #8.

5362. SULPHIDE. Seated cat. No air bubbles. Average detail. Set slightly forward. Surface has very minor haze and a couple of tiny chips. Germany, circa 1870-1915. 1-1/2". Near Mint(-) (8.1). Price: $47. CyberAuction #497, Lot #29.

5363. SULPHIDE. Figure of a running rabbit. Average detail. No air bubbles. Set slightly off center. Surface has several tiny moons and several tiny pits. Germany, circa 1870-1915. 1-3/16". Near Mint (8.6). Price: $47. CyberAuction #508, Lot #34.

5364. SULPHIDE. Figure is a bird pecking at the ground. Excellent detail. Set slightly back. No air bubbles. Surface has some tiny chips and tiny subsurface moons. Germany, circa 1870-1915. 1-3/8". Good (7.6). Price: $46. CyberAuction #415, Lot #25.

5365. SULPHIDE. Figure of a standing dog. Nice figure. Well detailed. No air bubbles on the figure, although there are some in the marble. Surface has a number of shallow flakes and chips. Germany, circa 1870-1915. 1-3/16". Good(+) (7.9). Price: $46. CyberAuction #434, Lot #31.

5366. SULPHIDE. Seated dog. Poor detail to figure. Small air bubble on it. Well centered. Two pits on surface. Germany, circa 1870-1915. 1-3/16". Near Mint(+) (8.9). Price: $46. CyberAuction #439, Lot #48.

5367. SULPHIDE. Figure of running rabbit. Average figure. Shallow air bubble on one side. Slightly off center. Several tiny pits. Germany, circa 1870-1915. 1-3/16" Near Mint (8.4). Price: $46. CyberAuction #446, Lot #38.

5368. SULPHIDE. Figure of a standing dog. Nice figure. Well detailed. No air bubbles on the figure, although there are some in the marble. Surface has a number of shallow flakes and chips. Germany, circa 1870-1915. 1-3/16". Good(+) (7.9). Price: $46. CyberAuction #484, Lot #35.

5369. SULPHIDE. Figure of a pig. Average detail. Very end of snout is missing. Tiny air bubble on one side. Well centered. Several tiny subsurface moons, none really in front of the figure. Germany, circa 1870-1915. 1-7/16". Near Mint (8.6). Price: $46. CyberAuction #492, Lot #3.

5370. SULPHIDE. Figure is a standing squirrel, eating a nut. Nicely detailed, no air bubbles. Set a little high. Surface has overall small and tiny chips. Germany, circa 1870-1915. 1-9/16". Good (7.6). Price: $45. CyberAuction #412, Lot #14.

5371. SULPHIDE. Figure is a standing squirrel, eating a nut. Nicely detailed, no air bubbles. Set a little high. Surface has overall small and tiny chips. Germany, circa 1870-1915. 1-9/16". Good (7.6). Price: $45. CyberAuction #437, Lot #34.

5372. SULPHIDE. Figure is a begging dog. Average detail. Small air bubble. Off center. Some small and tiny chips and roughness on surface. Germany, circa 1870-1915. 1-1/2". Good (7.6). Price: $45. CyberAuction #489, Lot #31.

5373. SULPHIDE. Figure of a begging dog. Above average detail to figure. Set off center. No air bubble. Surface has overall tiny chips. Germany, circa 1870-1915. 2". Good(+) (7.7). Price: $44. CyberAuction #499, Lot #25.

5374. SULPHIDE. Figure of an ape man on all fours. Poor detail to figure. Small figure. Well-centered. Shallow air bubble on either side of the figure. Marble is filled with very tiny air bubbles. One large flake on one side. A few pinpricks. 1-3/8". Near Mint (8.4). Price: $42. CyberAuction #390, Lot #25.

5375. SULPHIDE. Figure is the Victorian boy kneeling and holding a sailboat. Air bubble on the left front of the figure. The marble was originally damaged and has been coated with a polymer. 1-3/4". Reworked. Price: $42. CyberAuction #391, Lot #23.

5376. SULPHIDE. Figure is a bear standing on all fours, head tilted back slightly. Very front of the nose is missing. Average detail. Well centered. Some very shallow air bubble on the figure. Surface has some tiny chipping and subsurface moons. Germany, circa 1870-1915. 1-9/16". Good(+) (7.8). Price: $42. CyberAuction #430, Lot #36.

5377. SULPHIDE. Figure of a seated cat. Above average detail. Slightly off center. A chip and a number of small and tiny chips. Germany, circa 1870-1915. 1-7/16". Good(+) (7.9). Price: $42. CyberAuction #435, Lot #36.

5378. SULPHIDE. Figure is the Victorian boy kneeling and holding a sailboat. Air bubble on the left front of the figure. The marble was originally damaged and has been coated with a polymer. 1-3/4". Reworked. Price: $42. CyberAuction #445, Lot #37.

5379. SULPHIDE. Figure of a cow. Cracked in half on insertion, pieces separated. Excellent detail though. Well centered. Small subsurface moon, some pits. Germany, circa 1870-1915. 2". Near Mint (8.6). Price: $4_ CyberAuction #457, Lot #22.

5380. SULPHIDE. Figure is the Victorian boy kneeling and holding a sailboat. Air bubble on the left front of the figure. The marble was originally damaged and has been coated with a polymer. 1-3/4". Reworked. Price: $42. CyberAuction #466, Lot #40.

5381. SULPHIDE. Figure of a begging dog. Above average detail to figure. Set off center. No air bubble. Surface has overall tiny chips. Germany, circa 1870-1915. 2". Good(+) (7.7). Price: $42. CyberAuction #476, Lot #2_

5382. SULPHIDE. Figure of a running horse. Below average detail to the figure. Small for the marble. Shallow air bubble under the body on both sides. Well centered. Surface has a manufacturing flat spot on one side and some tiny chipping. Germany, circa 1870-1915. 1-5/16. Good (7.6). Pric_ $40. CyberAuction #374, Lot #16.

5383. SULPHIDE. Figure appears to be a wolverine. Slightly rose tinted glass. Well centered figure, no air bubbles. Overall tiny subsurface moons needs a light polish. Germany, circa 1870-1915. 2". Good (7.5). Price: $40. CyberAuction #397, Lot #42.

5384. SULPHIDE. Figure is a bear standing on all fours, head tilted back slightly. Very front of the nose is missing. Average detail. Well centered. Some very shallow air bubble on the figure. Surface has some tiny chipping and subsurface moons. Germany, circa 1870-1915. 1-9/16". Good(+) (7._ Price: $42. CyberAuction #398, Lot #24.

5385. SULPHIDE. Figure is a running wolf, or similar animal. Excellent detail. Well centered. Small air bubble on one side of it. Polished surface 1-5/16". Price: $40. CyberAuction #480, Lot #15.

5386. SULPHIDE. Figure of a seated cat. Above average detail. Slightly off center. A chip and a number of small and tiny chips. Germany, circa 1870-1915. 1-7/16". Good(+) (7.9). Price: $40. CyberAuction #486, Lot #2_

5387. SULPHIDE. Figure of a seated cow, chewing its cud. Average detail. No air bubbles. Well centered. A couple of tiny chips. Germany, circa 1870-1915. 1-7/16". Near Mint(+) (8.8). Price: $40. CyberAuction #493, L_ #28.

5388. SULPHIDE. Running squirrel. Small air bubble on back. Very nice detail. Well centered. Surface covered by small subsurface moons and tiny chips. Germany, circa 1870-1915. 1-3/16". Good(+) (7.7). Price: $3_ CyberAuction #489, Lot #23.

5389. SULPHIDE. Figure of a standing cow. Shallow air bubble on one side. Average detail. Well centered. Polished. Germany, circa 1870-191_ 1-5/8". Price: $36. CyberAuction #477, Lot #12.

5390. SULPHIDE. Figure of a seated cat. Above average detail. Slightly off center. A chip and a number of small and tiny chips. Germany, circa 1870-1915. 1-7/16". Good(+) (7.9). Price: $32. CyberAuction #475, Lot #18.

5391. SULPHIDE. Standing bushy-tail dog. Exceptional figure. Huge figure for the marble. No air bubbles. Very slightly high. A couple of tiny chips, some tiny subsurface moons, some scratching, mostly on one side. Germany, circa 1870-1915. 2-1/16". Near Mint(+) (8.0). Price: $32. CyberAuction #493, Lot #24.

5392. SULPHIDE. Running rabbit sulphide. The surface was damaged, but has been coated with a polymer of some sort. 1-1/4". Reworked. Price: $27. CyberAuction #391, Lot #14.

5393. SULPHIDE. Figure of a donkey. Below average figure. Well centered, no air bubbles. Chips on the back side, overall light haze. Germany, circa 1870-1915. 1-3/8". Good (7.5). Price: $26. CyberAuction #402, Lot #20.

5394. SULPHIDE. Figure of a donkey. Below average figure. Well centered, no air bubbles. Chips on the back side, overall light haze. Germany, circa 1870-1915. 1-3/8". Good (7.5). Price: $26. CyberAuction #440, Lot #42.

5395. SULPHIDE. Figure is a standing squirrel eating a nut. Figure broke into two pieces when inserted. Average detail. Off center. Surface has small and tiny subsurface moons. Germany, circa 1870-1915. 2". Good (7._ Price: $26. CyberAuction #442, Lot #12.

5396. SWIRL. Banded. Very rare marble. Large. Transparent dark cobalt blue base. Two light green bands on the marble, a third appears to be missing. Small flake, rest of the surface is in great shape. Super marble. Germany, circa 1870-1915. 1-5/16". Near Mint(+) (8.9). Price: $18_ CyberAuction #422, Lot #57.

5397. SWIRL. Banded. Very rare marble. Large. Transparent dark cobalt blue base. Two light green bands on the marble, a third appears to be missing. Small flake, rest of the surface is in great shape. Super marble. Germany, circa 1870-1915. 1-5/16". Near Mint(+) (8.9). Price: $16_ CyberAuction #400, Lot #11.

5398. SWIRL. Banded. Very rare end of cane (first off cane) banded swirl. Transparent clear base. About two-thirds of the surface is coated by speck_ of opaque white and opaque yellow (almost looks like paint spatter from spray can). Two small chips on the top and a small subsurface moon on th_

180

ide. Still, gorgeous and rare. Germany, circa 1870-1915. 11/16". Near Mint
(8.6). Price: $120. CyberAuction #363, Lot #54.

5399. SWIRL. Banded. Very unusual banded swirl. Transparent pale blue
tinted base filled with tiny air bubbles. There is one wide band on the
surface covering about one-third of it. The band is opaque white and opaque
yellow. A couple of very tiny manufacturing pits in the band. A beauty and
rare. Germany, circa 1870-1915. 13/16". Mint (9.5). Price: $100.
CyberAuction #374, Lot #43.

5400. SWIRL. Banded. Very similar to the previous lot. Transparent emerald green base. One side of the marble has a subsurface layer of stretched
white bands and strands. I guess you could call it a type of banded swirl, or
a type of submarine. Germany, circa 1870-1915. 23/32". Mint (9.9). Price:
$95. CyberAuction #338, Lot #55.

5401. SWIRL. Banded. Unusual coloring. Transparent emerald green base.
Three subsurface white bands. In great shape. Germany, circa 1870-1915.
13/32". Mint (9.9). Price: $70. CyberAuction #338, Lot #54.

5402. SWIRL. Banded. Very unusual banded swirl. Transparent pale blue
tinted base filled with tiny air bubbles. There is one wide band on the
surface covering about one third of it. The band is opaque white and opaque
yellow. A couple of very tiny manufacturing pits in the band. A beauty and
rare. Germany, circa 1870-1915. 13/16". Mint (9.5). Price: $50.
CyberAuction #345, Lot #9.

5403. SWIRL. Banded. I'm actually not sure what to classify this as. Unusual. Transparent clear base. Narrow core of translucent yellow and green,
surrounded by a ghost of tiny air bubbles. Subsurface layer of translucent
yellow, translucent green and opaque white, stretched bands and strands.
In pristine shape. Beauty. Germany, circa 1870-1915. 11/16". Mint (9.9).
Price: $55. CyberAuction #383, Lot #38.

5404. SWIRL. Banded. More properly, a banded end of day. Transparent
dark blue base. Surface almost completely covered by stretched opaque
white. Very pretty. Germany, circa 1870-1915. 1/2". Mint (9.7). Price: $55.
CyberAuction #481, Lot #23.

5405. SWIRL. Banded. Unusual. Really, a banded end of day, not a banded
swirl. Transparent clear base. Core has a small band of yellow and white
stretched flakes. Surface has a band of the same covering about half of it.
One melt chip, one tiny flake. Interesting. Germany, circa 1870-1915. 27/
32". Near Mint(+) (8.9). Price: $51. CyberAuction #372, Lot #16.

5406. SWIRL. Banded. Two-band banded swirl, or a two-panel Joseph
Coat, you decide. Transparent clear base. Each band is strands of electric
yellow, with a little blue and red. Pontils are fire-polished. Gorgeous. Germany, circa 1870-1920. 19/32". Mint (9.9). Price: $50. CyberAuction #504,
Lot #3.

5407. SWIRL. Banded. I've classified it as a banded swirl, but it has very
unusual construction. Three layer. Transparent clear base. Core is a couple
of blue and orange bands. Middle layer is four wide band
panels. Two are stretched blue and two are stretched red. Subsurface layer
of four wide band panels. Two are stretched orange and two are stretched
white. Small melt chip near bottom, small melt spot on side. Germany,
possibly England, circa 1870-1915. 11/16". Mint(-) (9.0). Price: $47.
CyberAuction #410, Lot #50.

5408. SWIRL. Banded. I'm going to categorize it as a banded swirl, but it is
very unusual. Transparent amethyst (almost a cranberry) base. Two bands
covering over three-quarters of the marble. The bands are light brown and
white, and go very far into the marble. Very unusual marble. Germany, circa
1870-1915. 1/2". Mint (9.9). Price: $45. CyberAuction #345, Lot #10.

5409. SWIRL. Banded. Very odd marble. Transparent light blue base. One
side is covered by bands of transparent caramel brown and opaque white.
Small melt flake, two tiny subsurface moons. Germany, circa 1870-1915.
13/32". Near Mint (8.6). Price: $45. CyberAuction #420, Lot #44.

5410. SWIRL. Banded. Banded swirl or Indian, you decide. Transparent
aqua base. Surface is covered with bands of yellow, pale white and blue.
One tiny subsurface moon by the bottom pontil. Germany, circa 1870-
1915. 5/8". Near Mint(+) (8.9). Price: $39. CyberAuction #420, Lot #57.

5411. SWIRL. Banded. Very odd marble. Transparent very dark blue base.
Has a very wide stretched, thick white band covering about two-thirds of
the marble. Very tiny subsurface moon. Real nice, and unusual. Germany,
circa 1870-1915. 17/32". Near Mint(+) (8.9). Price: $38. CyberAuction
#375, Lot #38.

5412. SWIRL. Banded. Transparent clear base. Subsurface strands of bright
red, bright blue and white. Gorgeous. A couple of pits. England, possibly
Germany, circa 1870-1915. 21/32". Near Mint(+) (8.9). Price: $38.
CyberAuction #401, Lot #48.

5413. SWIRL. Banded. Interesting. Very dark transparent blue base. Filled
with stretched very tiny air bubbles. Three subsurface bands of white and
red. Two tiny chips, one very tiny subsurface moon. Germany, circa 1870-
1915. 25/32". Near Mint (8.6). Price: $36. CyberAuction #376, Lot #7.

5414. SWIRL. Banded. Transparent clear base. Wide core of tiny air bubbles.
Two narrow white bands on the surface. Gorgeous. Germany, circa 1870-
1915. 9/16". Mint (9.9). Price: $35. CyberAuction #466, Lot #17.

5415. SWIRL. Banded. Very unusual marble. Transparent clear base. Two
subsurface bands covering about twenty percent of the marble. Each is light
green, orange and white strands. Germany, circa 1870-1915. 19/32". Mint
(9.9). Price: $35. CyberAuction #467, Lot #41.

5416. SWIRL. Banded. A type of Joseph Coat. Very nice. Transparent clear
base. Subsurface layer of faint yellow, light green and white strands. Vivid
colors, but faint. Germany, circa 1870-1915. 9/16". Mint (9.9). Price: $35.
CyberAuction #497, Lot #6.

5417. SWIRL. Banded. Very unusual marble. Translucent very light blue
base completely filled with tiny air bubbles. Three white strands in the
surface. Germany, circa 1870-1915. 19/32". Mint (9.9). Price: $35.
CyberAuction #503, Lot #20.

5418. SWIRL. Banded. You could call this either a three hundred sixty
degree banded swirl or a three hundred sixty degree transparent Indian.
Transparent pale aqua base. Completely covered by stretched bands of
yellow, aqua, red, white and green. Small flake. Germany, circa 1870-1915.
11/16". Near Mint (8.6). Price: $33. CyberAuction #368, Lot #24.

5419. SWIRL. Banded. Very odd marble. Transparent very dark blue base.
Has a very wide stretched, thick white band covering about two-thirds of
the marble. Very tiny subsurface moon. Real nice, and unusual. Germany,
circa 1870-1915. 17/32". Near Mint(+) (8.9). Price: $32. CyberAuction
#354, Lot #15.

5420. SWIRL. Banded. Transparent clear base. Some subsurface bands of
white, blue and red. Germany, circa 1870-1915. 13/16". Mint (9.9). Price:
$32. CyberAuction #503, Lot #13.

5421. SWIRL. Banded. Transparent dark blue base. Three surface bands of
bright white and yellow. Gorgeous. Germany, circa 1870-1915. 15/32".
Mint (9.9). Price: $31. CyberAuction #339, Lot #41.

5422. SWIRL. Banded. Transparent dark blue base with wide semi-opaque
white bands on it. Germany, circa 1870-1915. 21/32". Mint (9.9). Price:
$29. CyberAuction #335, Lot #17.

5423. SWIRL. Banded. Transparent brown base. One yellow strand and
two white strands on the surface. Germany, circa 1870-1915. 15/32". Mint
(9.9). Price: $28. CyberAuction #358, Lot #54.

5424. SWIRL. Banded. Transparent blue base. White white bands on the
surface. Germany, circa 1870-1915. 23/32". Mint (9.6). Price: $28.
CyberAuction #414, Lot #15.

5425. SWIRL. Banded. Transparent blue base. Several white strands in the
core. Some white strands and bands on the surface. In great shape! Germany, circa 1870-1915. 11/16". Mint (9.9). Price: $27. CyberAuction #387,
Lot #39.

5426. SWIRL. Banded. Transparent smoky base. Three subsurface multicolor
bands. Melt spot. Germany, circa 1870-1915. 25/32". Mint (9.6). Price:
$27. CyberAuction #502, Lot #37.

5427. SWIRL. Banded. Cobalt blue transparent base. Three subsurface
bands of various colors. One moon, on subsurface moon. Nice. Germany,
circa 1870-1915. 25/32". Near Mint (8.6). Price: $27. CyberAuction #502,
Lot #47.

5428. SWIRL. Banded. Unusual. Clear base. Three subsurface bright yellow bands on one side, two subsurface bright white bands on the other.
Germany, circa 1870-1915. 15/32". Mint (9.9). Price: $25. CyberAuction
#360, Lot #25.

5429. SWIRL. Banded. End of cane (first off cane) banded swirl. Light blue
base. Three red and blue bands. One red ends about halfway up the marble
and shoots out the side. Small melt spot. Rare. Germany, circa 1870-1915.
25/32". Mint (9.5). Price: $25. CyberAuction #410, Lot #7.

5430. SWIRL. Banded. Transparent dark green. Ghost core. One white
band. Two melt spots. Germany, circa 1870-1915. 13/16". Mint(-) (9.0).
Price: $25. CyberAuction #458, Lot #55.

5431. SWIRL. Banded. Transparent clear base. Wide core of tiny air bubbles.
Two narrow white bands on the surface. Gorgeous. Germany, circa 1870-
1915. 9/16". Mint (9.9). Price: $24. CyberAuction #366, Lot #40.

5432. SWIRL. Banded. Transparent clear base. Wide core of tiny air bubbles.
Two narrow white bands on the surface. Gorgeous. Germany, circa 1870-
1915. 9/16". Mint (9.9). Price: $24. CyberAuction #453, Lot #8.

5433. SWIRL. Banded. Transparent smoky olive green base. Four red bands
on the surface. Very nice. Germany, circa 1870-1915. 21/32". Mint (9.9).
Price: $23. CyberAuction #330, Lot #31.

5434. SWIRL. Banded. First off cane from a banded swirl. Transparent pale
green base with pastel colors swirled on it. Looped over. Some light haze.
Germany, circa 1870-1915. 21/32". Near Mint(+) (8.9). Price: $23.
CyberAuction #445, Lot #44.

5435. SWIRL. Banded. Dark transparent blue base. Two thin white bands
on the surface. One very tiny chip. Germany, circa 1870-1915. 27/32".
Near Mint(+) (8.9). Price: $23. CyberAuction #458, Lot #37.

5436. SWIRL. Banded. Cobalt blue transparent base. Several thin white
strands on the surface. Germany, circa 1870-1915. 9/16". Mint (9.7). Price:
$23. CyberAuction #501, Lot #52.

5437. SWIRL. Banded. Transparent blue base. Outer layer is four wide
strands on one side of the surface. Three are white, one is yellow. One melt
spot. Germany, circa 1870-1915. 21/32". Mint (9.5). Price: $22.
CyberAuction #377, Lot #3.

5438. SWIRL. Banded. I'm not sure what this is, except it is end of the
cane. Transparent clear base. Two opaque white bands travel halfway up
the interior of the marble. One tiny subsurface moon. Germany, circa 1870-
1915. 11/16". Near Mint(+) (8.7). Price: $22. CyberAuction #422, Lot
#20.

5439. SWIRL. Banded. Transparent light blue base. Outer layer is two surface bands. Each is wispy yellow and white. Nice marble. Germany, circa
1870-1915. 17/32". Mint (9.9). Price: $21. CyberAuction #339, Lot #47.

5440. SWIRL. Banded. Transparent clear base. Stretched surface bands of
white, purple and yellow. Germany, circa 1870-1915. 7/16". Mint (9.9).
Price: $21. CyberAuction #345, Lot #49.

5441. SWIRL. Banded. Gorgeous marble. Transparent clear base. Four subsurface bands. Two red, blue and yellow. Two red, blue and white. Sparkle.
Germany, circa 1870-1915. 13/16". Mint(-) (9.0). Price: $21. CyberAuction
#481, Lot #9.

5442. SWIRL. Banded. First off cane from a banded swirl. Transparent pale
green base with pastel colors swirled on it. Looped over. Some light haze.
Germany, circa 1870-1915. 21/32". Near Mint(+) (8.9). Price: $20.
CyberAuction #366, Lot #11.

5443. SWIRL. Banded. I'm not sure what this is, except it is end of the
cane. Transparent clear base. Two opaque white bands travel halfway up

the interior of the marble. One tiny subsurface moon. Germany, circa 1870-1915. 11/16". Near Mint(+) (8.7). Price: $20. CyberAuction #368, Lot #53.

5444. SWIRL. Banded. Transparent light olive green. Three narrow surface bands of yellow and white. Germany, circa 1870-1915. 11/16". Mint (9.9). Price: $19. CyberAuction #362, Lot #18.

5445. SWIRL. Banded. Transparent clear base. Two sets of opaque white bands and two sets of opaque yellow bands, painted on the surface. One air hole. Very nice. Germany, circa 1870-1915. 23/32". Mint (9.6). Price: $19. CyberAuction #446, Lot #53.

5446. SWIRL. Banded. Transparent clear base. Surface has four bands painted on. Each is white and yellow, with either a little blue or a little green. Small flake. Germany, circa 1870-1915. 25/32". Near Mint (8.6). Price: $19. CyberAuction #449, Lot #39.

5447. SWIRL. Banded. Transparent blue base. Three bands. Each is yellow and white. Germany, circa 1870-1915. 19/32". Mint (9.8). Price: $19. CyberAuction #469, Lot #3.

5448. SWIRL. Banded. Transparent clear base. Four outer bands. Each is orange, white and green. One tiny melt spot, one very tiny moon. Germany, circa 1870-1915. 19/32". Near Mint(+) (8.9). Price: $17. CyberAuction #334, Lot #18.

5449. SWIRL. Banded. Transparent clear base. Outer layer is four bands. Two white bands, two bright yellow bands. Germany, circa 1870-1915. 1/2". Mint (9.9). Price: $17. CyberAuction #357, Lot #19.

5450. SWIRL. Banded. Transparent clear base. Almost completely covered by stretched yellow and green. Subsurface moon, blown air hole, some pitting. Very hard to find. Germany, circa 1870-1915. 23/32". Near Mint (8.5). Price: $17. CyberAuction #359, Lot #41.

5451. SWIRL. Banded. Unusual. Transparent clear base. Filled with tiny air bubbles and unmelted sand. Surface has stretched bands of white and pale orange. One small subsurface moon. Germany, circa 1870-1915. 17/32". Near Mint(+) (8.7). Price: $17. CyberAuction #368, Lot #55.

5452. SWIRL. Banded. Transparent dark teal green base. Filament core. Three white bands on the surface. One tiny dirt seed pit. Germany, circa 1870-1915. 3/4". Mint(-) (9.1). Price: $17. CyberAuction #369, Lot #41.

5453. SWIRL. Banded. Transparent clear base. Two sets of opaque white bands and two sets of opaque yellow bands, painted on the surface. One air hole. Very nice. Germany, circa 1870-1915. 23/32". Mint (9.6). Price: $17. CyberAuction #404, Lot #8.

5454. SWIRL. Banded. Unusual. Clear base. Three subsurface bright yellow bands on one side, two subsurface bright white bands on the other. Germany, circa 1870-1915. 15/32". Mint (9.9). Price: $17. CyberAuction #440, Lot #51.

5455. SWIRL. Banded. Stunning and rare design. Six bands. Four are pink on white, turned to form vanes. Other two bands are two sets of blue narrow bands. Double twist. Tiny chip, several tiny moons, elongated air hole. Germany, circa 1870-1915. 27/32". Good(+) (7.9). Price: $17. CyberAuction #472, Lot #39.

5456. SWIRL. Banded. Smokey base. Some colored bands in the core. Subsurface layer of three bands. Each is a different multicolor scheme. Two tiny flakes, a tiny subsurface moon. Germany, circa 1870-1915. 13/16". Near Mint(+) (8.7). Price: $17. CyberAuction #502, Lot #51.

5457. SWIRL. Banded. Transparent clear base. Three bright yellow strands. Germany, circa 1870-1915. 17/32". Mint (9.9). Price: $17. CyberAuction #503, Lot #33.

5458. SWIRL. Banded. Transparent clear base. Four subsurface light blue bands. Peewee. Germany, circa 1870-1915. 1/2". Mint (9.9). Price: $16. CyberAuction #338, Lot #27.

5459. SWIRL. Banded. Transparent cobalt blue base. Wide band of stretched white on one side, partial band on the other. One small chip, some pits, not wet. Germany, circa 1870-1915. 3/4". Near Mint (8.3). Price: $15. CyberAuction #372, Lot #19.

5460. SWIRL. Banded. Transparent dark amethyst base. Three narrow bands on the surface of green and white. Several tiny chips. Germany, circa 1870-1915. 11/16". Near Mint (8.5). Price: $15. CyberAuction #376, Lot #32.

5461. SWIRL. Banded. Transparent green base. Four bands of white on the surface. One melt spot, one tiny subsurface moon. Germany, circa 1870-1915. 11/16". Near Mint(+) (8.9). Price: $15. CyberAuction #376, Lot #56.

5462. SWIRL. Banded. Transparent clear base. Four subsurface blue and white bands. Peewee. Germany, circa 1870-1915. 1/2". Mint (9.7). Price: $15. CyberAuction #383, Lot #36.

5463. SWIRL. Banded. Transparent lightly tinted blue base. Three surface bands of stretched yellow and white. Germany, circa 1870-1915. 23/32". Mint (9.5). Price: $15. CyberAuction #403, Lot #19.

5464. SWIRL. Banded. Transparent clear base. Ghost core. Outer layer is three bands of pink, yellow, blue and/or green strands. One melt spot. Germany, circa 1870-1915. 13/16". Mint(-) (9.0). Price: $15. CyberAuction #414, Lot #6.

5465. SWIRL. Banded. Nice. Transparent very dark blue base with some wispy white and yellow strands. Pontils were fire-polished, but that's original. Germany, circa 1870-1915. 9/16". Mint (9.5). Price: $15. CyberAuction #425, Lot #13.

5466. SWIRL. Banded. Transparent clear base. Ghost core. Outer layer is three bands of pink, yellow, blue and/or green strands. One melt spot. Germany, circa 1870-1915. 13/16". Mint(-) (9.0). Price: $15. CyberAuction #456, Lot #51.

5467. SWIRL. Banded. Ghost core. Transparent clear base. Three bands of stretched yellow, blue, light green, red, white. Small subsurface moon at the bottom pontil. Germany, circa 1870-1915. 13/16". Near Mint(+) (8.7). Price: $15. CyberAuction #507, Lot #17.

5468. SWIRL. Banded. transparent light blue base. Subsurface layer three bands. Each is stretched strands of red, white and light blue. Subsu face moons, tiny chips. Germany, circa 1870-1915. 25/32". Near Mint (8.0). Price: $15. CyberAuction #507, Lot #45.

5469. SWIRL. Banded. Transparent clear base. Surface has a white bar and two yellow bands. There is a ghost core with one white band and on black band in it. Germany, circa 1870-1915. 9/16". Mint (9.9). Price: $1 CyberAuction #350, Lot #1.

5470. SWIRL. Banded. Transparent cobalt blue base. Opaque white ri bon in core. One white band on surface. One melt spot. Germany, circa 1870-1915. 21/32". Mint(-) (9.2). Price: $14. CyberAuction #388, Lot #.

5471. SWIRL. Banded. Transparent clear base. One green strand and or yellow strand just under the surface. Interesting. Germany, circa 1870-191 17/32". Mint (9.9). Price: $13. CyberAuction #342, Lot #46.

5472. SWIRL. Banded. Transparent clear base. Four surface bands, sets white and green. Some pits, but overall very nice. Germany, circa 187 1915. 3/4". Near Mint(+) (8.7). Price: $13. CyberAuction #372, Lot #4

5473. SWIRL. Banded. End of cane (first off cane) marble. Transpare clear base. Subsurface blue and white band, subsurface purple band, short subsurface white band. Germany, circa 1870-1915. 21/32". Mint (9. Price: $13. CyberAuction #411, Lot #50.

5474. SWIRL. Banded. Transparent clear base. Four subsurface blue ar white bands. Peewee. Germany, circa 1870-1915. 1/2". Mint (9.7). Pric $13. CyberAuction #432, Lot #39.

5475. SWIRL. Banded. Transparent clear base. Three subsurface bands Each is red edged by white. Germany, circa 1870-1195. 19/32". Mint (9.8 Price: $13. CyberAuction #472, Lot #1.

5476. SWIRL. Banded. Transparent smoky gray base with a surface layer stretched white and yellow bands covering almost the entire marble. Ge many, circa 1870-1915. 9/16". Mint (9.7). Price: $12. CyberAuction #40 Lot #10.

5477. SWIRL. Banded. Transparent clear base. Outer layer is a yellow bar and a white band. One cold roll line. Germany, circa 1870-1915. 15/32 Mint (9.6). Price: $12. CyberAuction #466, Lot #5.

5478. SWIRL. Banded. Transparent clear base. Three bands of white ar light green. Germany, circa 1870-1915. One melt spot. 1/2". Mint (9.5 Price: $12. CyberAuction #469, Lot #40.

5479. SWIRL. Banded. Transparent clear base. Outer layer is three gre on white bands, and one wispy green band. Probably from near an end the cane. Germany, circa 1870-1915. 19/32". Mint (9.9). Price: $1 CyberAuction #470, Lot #17.

5480. SWIRL. Banded. Transparent clear base. Three subsurface band Each is red, blue and white. Germany, circa 1870-1915. 19/32". Mint (9.8 Price: $12. CyberAuction #473, Lot #2.

5481. SWIRL. Banded. Transparent clear base. Outer layer is three subs face white bands. A couple of white strands inside too. One tiny melt p Germany, circa 1870-1915. 11/16". Mint(-) (9.2). Price: $12. CyberAuctic #481, Lot #31.

5482. SWIRL. Banded. transparent clear base. Subsurface layer of thr bands. Each is stretched strands of red, white and light blue. One pit, tw sparkles. Germany, circa 1870-1915. 25/32". Near Mint(+) (8.8). Price $12. CyberAuction #507, Lot #3.

5483. SWIRL. Banded. Pale transparent aqua base. Green strand in cor One white strand on surface. Small melt chip. Germany, circa 1870-191 19/32". Mint(-) (9.0). Price: $12. CyberAuction #508, Lot #22.

5484. SWIRL. Banded. From near an end of the cane. Transparent ve lightly tinted green base. Two areas of banding. One is white and yello with some looping. Other is white narrow bands. One tiny subsurface moo Germany, circa 1870-1915. 19/32". Near Mint(+) (8.9). Price: $1 CyberAuction #339, Lot #10.

5485. SWIRL. Banded. Very light blue base. White strands on and und the surface. Beauty. Germany, circa 1870-1915. 15/32". Mint (9.8). Pric $11. CyberAuction #361, Lot #20.

5486. SWIRL. Banded. A type of gooseberry. Transparent gooseberry brow base. Subsurface layer of closely packed white bands. Poorly polishe Germany, circa 1870-1915. 11/16". Mint. Price: $11. CyberAuction #364, L #9.

5487. SWIRL. Banded. Transparent teal green base. Two subsurface whi bands. Some haze on one side. Subsurface moon at top. Germany, circ 1870-1915. 21/32". Near Mint (8.3). Price: $11. CyberAuction #368, L #41.

5488. SWIRL. Banded. Transparent slightly smoky base. Two bands on th marble. Both are white and yellow. Germany, circa 1870-1915. 9/16". Mi (9.7). Price: $11. CyberAuction #481, Lot #25.

5489. SWIRL. Banded. Transparent clear base. Outer layer has bands blue, yellow, orange and white. Subsurface moon and large open air ho Germany, circa 1870-1915. 1/2". Near Mint (8.6). Price: $10. CyberAuctic #390, Lot #27.

5490. SWIRL. Banded. End of cane (first off cane) banded swirl. Transpa ent clear base, some slightly stretched splotches of light blue and yellow c the surface. Misshapen, slight light haze. Germany, circa 1870-1915. 1 16". Near Mint (8.5). Price: $10. CyberAuction #408, Lot #29.

5491. SWIRL. Banded. Transparent clear base. Outer layer is a yellow bar and a white band. One cold roll line. Germany, circa 1870-1915. 15/32 Mint (9.6). Price: $10. CyberAuction #428, Lot #21.

5492. SWIRL. Banded. End of cane (first off cane) banded swirl. Transpa ent clear base, some slightly stretched splotches of light blue and yellow c the surface. Misshapen, slight light haze. Germany, circa 1870-1915. 1 16". Near Mint (8.5). Price: $10. CyberAuction #437, Lot #2.

5493. SWIRL. Banded. End of cane (first off cane) banded swirl. Transpa ent clear base, some slightly stretched splotches of light blue and yellow c he surface. Misshapen, slight light haze. Germany, circa 1870-1915. 13/16". Near Mint (8.5). Price: $10. CyberAuction #454, Lot #12.

5494. SWIRL. Banded. Nice marble. Transparent clear base. Ghost core. Two subsurface yellow bands. Two tiny flakes and a small melt spot. Germany, circa 1870-1915. 25/32". Near Mint (8.6). Price: $10. CyberAuction #458, Lot #13.

5495. SWIRL. Banded. Transparent very light blue base. Three bands of stretch wispy yellow and white. Germany, circa 1870-1915. 1/2". Mint (9.7). Price: $10. CyberAuction #481, Lot #27.

5496. SWIRL. Banded. Transparent clear base. Subsurface layer of three bands. Each is yellow, white and red strands of varying widths. Marble appears buffed. Germany, circa 1870-1915. 9/16". Price: $10. CyberAuction #483, Lot #18.

5497. SWIRL. Banded. End of cane (first off cane) banded swirl. Transparent clear base, some slightly stretched splotches of light blue and yellow on the surface. Misshapen, slight light haze. Germany, circa 1870-1915. 13/16". Near Mint (8.5). Price: $10. CyberAuction #486, Lot #34.

5498. SWIRL. Banded. Transparent clear base. Three bands of bright yellow and red. There are no pontils, but I don't think it has been worked on. I think the ends have been melted. England, possibly Germany, circa 1870-1915. 9/16". Mint (9.9). Price: $10. CyberAuction #497, Lot #16.

5499. SWIRL. Banded. Transparent light blue base. Two subsurface bands of white and brown. Germany, circa 1870-1915. 9/16". Mint (9.5). Price: $10. CyberAuction #501, Lot #31.

5500. SWIRL. Banded. Transparent clear base. Three subsurface bands. Each is light blue, yellow and red strands. Tiny moon. Germany, circa 1870-1915. 13/16". Near Mint(+) (8.8). Price: $10. CyberAuction #503, Lot #16.

5501. SWIRL. Banded. From near an end of the cane. Transparent clear base. Two white bands on one side, subsurface. Germany, circa 1870-1915. 3/16". Mint (9.8). Price: $9. CyberAuction #341, Lot #6.

5502. SWIRL. Banded. Transparent clear base. Outer layer is three green on white bands, and one wispy green band. Probably from near an end of the cane. Germany, circa 1870-1915. 19/32". Mint (9.9). Price: $9. CyberAuction #444, Lot #23.

5503. SWIRL. Banded. Transparent blue base. Two bands of wispy yellow and white on it. Some melt spots. Germany, circa 1870-1915. 1/2". Mint(-) (9.2). Price: $9. CyberAuction #455, Lot #48.

5504. SWIRL. Banded. Transparent clear base. Four subsurface blue and white bands. Peewee. Germany, circa 1870-1915. 1/2". Mint (9.7). Price: $8. CyberAuction #338, Lot #38.

5505. SWIRL. Banded. Transparent clear base. Three white strands on the surface. Germany, circa 1870-1915. 11/16". Mint (9.4). Price: $8. CyberAuction #405, Lot #4.

5506. SWIRL. Banded. Transparent clear base. Four subsurface white strands. Germany, circa 1870-1915. 5/8". Mint (9.6). Price: $8. CyberAuction #411, Lot #51.

5507. SWIRL. Banded. From near an end of the cane. Probably meant to be a solid core. Transparent clear base. One band of transparent pink in the marble, one band of blue just under the surface. Two tiny chips. Germany, circa 1870-1915. 13/16". Near Mint(+) (8.7). Price: $8. CyberAuction #458, Lot #21.

5508. SWIRL. Banded. Transparent clear base. Surface bands of bright yellow and some blue. Germany, circa 1870-1915. 15/32". Mint (9.9). Price: $8. CyberAuction #464, Lot #41.

5509. SWIRL. Banded. Transparent blue base. Four white strands. Not evenly spaced. A few tiny subsurface moons, pits and sparkles. Germany, circa 1870-1915. 23/32". Near Mint (8.3). Price: $8. CyberAuction #471, Lot #41.

5510. SWIRL. Banded. Transparent blue base. Three yellow bands. Polished. Germany, circa 1870-1915. 9/16". Price: $8. CyberAuction #487, Lot #23.

5511. SWIRL. Banded. Interesting marble. Transparent clear base. Subsurface layer is three bands of red and white strands. Two tiny melt spots. Germany, circa 1870-1915. 5/8". Mint(-) (9.1). Price: $7. CyberAuction #336, Lot #17.

5512. SWIRL. Banded. Transparent clear base. Four outer bands. Two yellow, two white. One small melt pit. Germany, circa 1870-1915. 5/8". Mint(-) (9.0). Price: $7. CyberAuction #485, Lot #16.

5513. SWIRL. Banded. Transparent clear base. Outer layer is two greenish yellow bands and one band of blue on white. One tiny flake. Germany, circa 1870-1915. 9/16". Near Mint(+) (8.7). Price: $6. CyberAuction #368, Lot #18.

5514. SWIRL. Banded. Transparent very light green/blue base. Two subsurface white strands. Peewee. One very tiny chip. 15/32". Near Mint(+) (8.9). Price: $6. CyberAuction #374, Lot #17.

5515. SWIRL. Banded. Light blue base. Two orange bands. Some pits and light haze. Germany, circa 1870-1915. 1/2". Near Mint(+) (8.7). Price: $4. CyberAuction #374, Lot #4.

5516. SWIRL. Banded. Transparent clear base. Three subsurface bands. A couple of tiny subsurface moons. 9/16". Near Mint(+) (8.7). Price: $2. CyberAuction #497, Lot #46.

5517. SWIRL. Banded. Transparent clear base. Three bands. Each is green and white. Germany, circa 1870-1915. 1/2". Mint (9.9). Price: $10. CyberAuction #476, Lot #35.

5518. SWIRL. Banded . Transparent clear base. Three bands. Each is green and white. Germany, circa 1870-1915. 1/2". Mint (9.9). Price: $10. CyberAuction #499, Lot #4.

5519. SWIRL. Butterscotch. Very hard marble to find. Semi-opaque brown butterscotch base. Bands of transparent pink on the surface. Germany, circa 1870-1915. 23/32". Mint (9.7). Price: $95. CyberAuction #386, Lot #14.

5520. SWIRL. Butterscotch. Very hard marble to find. Semi-opaque brown butterscotch base. Bands of transparent pink on the surface. One subsurface air bubble. Germany, circa 1870-1915. 11/16". Mint (9.5). Price: $55. CyberAuction #392, Lot #46.

5521. SWIRL. Butterscotch. Translucent orange/brown base. Pink transparent bands on the surface. Two very, very tiny chips. Germany, circa 1870-1915. 19/32". Near Mint(+) (8.7). Price: $45. CyberAuction #346, Lot #60.

5522. SWIRL. Butterscotch. Translucent orange/brown base. Pink transparent bands on the surface. Two very, very tiny chips. Germany, circa 1870-1915. 19/32". Near Mint(+) (8.7). Price: $42. CyberAuction #443, Lot #50.

5523. SWIRL. Butterscotch. Large shooter size. Transparent red base with bands of translucent creamy orange. Several small subsurface moons. Germany, circa 1870-1915. 27/32". Near Mint(-) (8.0). Price: $30. CyberAuction #372, Lot #3.

5524. SWIRL. Butterscotch. Large shooter size. Transparent red base with bands of translucent creamy orange. Several small subsurface moons. Germany, circa 1870-1915. 27/32". Near Mint(-) (8.0). Price: $30. CyberAuction #408, Lot #9.

5525. SWIRL. Butterscotch. Hard marble to find. Semi-opaque brown butterscotch base. Bands of transparent pink on the surface. Melt line. Both pontils have subsurface moons on them. Germany, circa 1870-1915. 11/16". Near Mint(-) (8.0). Price: $30. CyberAuction #420, Lot #52.

5526. SWIRL. Butterscotch. Semi-opaque mocha brown base. Translucent pink bands and a white strand on the surface. Two small sparkles, a couple of melted air holes. Germany, circa 1870-1915. 23/32". Near Mint(+) (8.7). Price: $29. CyberAuction #498, Lot #18.

5527. SWIRL. Butterscotch. Large shooter size. Transparent red base with bands of translucent creamy orange. Several small subsurface moons. Germany, circa 1870-1915. 27/32". Near Mint(-) (8.0). Price: $22. CyberAuction #426, Lot #3.

5528. SWIRL. Butterscotch. Semi-opaque brown base with surface pink bands. One tiny flake, some pitting. Germany, circa 1870-1915. 5/8". Near Mint(+) (8.9). Price: $19. CyberAuction #493, Lot #41.

5529. SWIRL. Cane piece. End of the cane for a solid core swirl. Super piece. One end has the colors shooting out. About 2-1/2". Price: $44. CyberAuction #348, Lot #36.

5530. SWIRL. Cane piece. Nice section of cane for a three layer solid core swirl. 1-1/8" wide, 2-1/8" long. Mint (9.5). Price: $41. CyberAuction #363, Lot #35.

5531. SWIRL. Cane piece. Section of cane from a solid core swirl. Nice piece. About 3" long. Germany, circa 1870-1915. Price: $27. CyberAuction #339, Lot #25.

5532. SWIRL. Cane piece. Cane section for a solid core swirl. About 5" long, 15/32" diameter. Germany, circa 1870-1915. Mint (9.7). Price: $27. CyberAuction #366, Lot #36.

5533. SWIRL. Cane piece. Cane section for a three layer solid core swirl. About 2" long. Nice. Mint. Price: $25. CyberAuction #341, Lot #50.

5534. SWIRL. Cane piece. Cane piece for a divided core swirl. About 2". Mint. Price: $22. CyberAuction #348, Lot #24.

5535. SWIRL. Cane piece. Cane section for a three layer solid core swirl. Nice. Germany, circa 1870-1915. 1-1/2" long, 19/32" diameter. Mint (9.5). Price: $20. CyberAuction #365, Lot #41.

5536. SWIRL. Cane piece. Cane piece for an orange latticinio core swirl. Nice. About 2" long. Germany, circa 1870-1915. Mint (9.5). Price: $19. CyberAuction #366, Lot #16.

5537. SWIRL. Cane piece. Cane piece from a white latticinio core swirl. About 1-1/2" long. Mint (9.5). Price: $11. CyberAuction #367, Lot #60.

5538. SWIRL. Cane piece. Small end of a cane. White latticinio core. Outer layer shows looping pattern. Hazy. Germany, circa 1870-1915. 13/16" x 1-1/2". Mint(-) (9.0). Price: $10. CyberAuction #405, Lot #9.

5539. SWIRL. Cane piece. Small end of a cane. White latticinio core. Outer layer shows looping pattern. Hazy. Germany, circa 1870-1915. 13/16" x 1-1/2". Mint(-) (9.0). Price: $10. CyberAuction #446, Lot #40.

5540. SWIRL. Cane piece. Cane piece for a divided core swirl. About an inch long and 5/8" wide. Mint (9.7). Price: $9. CyberAuction #368, Lot #49.

5541. SWIRL. Cane piece. Cane piece from a solid core swirl. About 2" long, very thin. Mint (9.5). Price: $8. CyberAuction #368, Lot #13.

5542. SWIRL. Cane piece. Cane piece from a solid core swirl. About 2" long, very thin. Mint (9.5). Price: $8. CyberAuction #422, Lot #3.

5543. SWIRL. Cane piece. Cane piece for a divided core swirl. About an inch long and 5/8" wide. Mint (9.7). Price: $8. CyberAuction #451, Lot #29.

5544. SWIRL. Cane piece. Small end of a cane. White latticinio core. Outer layer shows looping pattern. Hazy. Germany, circa 1870-1915. 13/16" x 1-1/2". Mint(-) (9.0). Price: $7. CyberAuction #477, Lot #14.

5545. SWIRL. Cane piece. Interesting color. Small cane piece for a banded swirl. Transparent cranberry base with some white surface strands. About an inch or so long. Mint (9.7). Price: $5. CyberAuction #368, Lot #28.

5546. SWIRL. Caramel. Rare marble. End of cane (first off cane) shooter caramel swirl. Transparent light brown base with bands and loops of opaque white in it. Some of the white shoots out the sides. Small flake, some pits, appears to have been very lightly buffed. Both pontils are intact. Germany, circa 1870-1915. 1-1/16". Price: $150. CyberAuction #406, Lot #48.

5547. SWIRL. Caramel. Transparent brown base with translucent white banding. One tiny melt spot. Germany, circa 1870-1915. 23/32". Mint(-) (9.2). Price: $85. CyberAuction #360, Lot #49.

5548. SWIRL. Caramel. Another caramel-type. Transparent gorgeous aqua base. Subsurface strands and bands of white, at various levels. One melt spot. Germany, circa 1870-1915. 3/4". Mint(-) (9.1). Price: $80. CyberAuction #342, Lot #54.

5549. SWIRL. Caramel. Blue caramel swirl. Same construction of a caramel swirl, but blue. Transparent blue base. Subsurface bands and loops of white. Germany, circa 1870-1915. 11/16". Mint (9.8). Price: $75. CyberAuction #414, Lot #44.

5550. SWIRL. Caramel. Transparent caramel brown base with some wispy white in it. Nice example. One melt spot. Germany, circa 1870-1915. 21/32". Mint (9.3). Price: $70. CyberAuction #337, Lot #60.

5551. SWIRL. Caramel. This is constructed the same as a caramel swirl, but the base glass is transparent green. Nice bands and swirls of wispy white in it. Germany, circa 1870-1915. 9/16". Mint (9.7). Price: $70. CyberAuction #383, Lot #39.

5552. SWIRL. Caramel. This is constructed the same as a caramel swirl, but the base glass is transparent green. Nice bands and swirls of wispy white in it. Germany, circa 1870-1915. 9/16". Mint (9.7). Price: $65. CyberAuction #342, Lot #25.

5553. SWIRL. Caramel. Dark transparent brown base with translucent white banding. One manufacturing pit. Germany, circa 1870-1915. 21/32". Mint(-) (9.2). Price: $51. CyberAuction #369, Lot #10.

5554. SWIRL. Caramel. Hard to find large example. Transparent very dark brown caramel base. Subsurface bands and loops of white. Overall haze, some tiny chipping. Germany, circa 1870-1915. 1-1/4". Good (7.6). Price: $47. CyberAuction #446, Lot #45.

5555. SWIRL. Caramel. Peewee. Nice example. Dark transparent brown base. Semi-opaque white strands and bands subsurface. A couple of pinpricks. Germany, circa 1870-1915. 1/2". Mint(-) (9.0). Price: $43. CyberAuction #390, Lot #4.

5556. SWIRL. Caramel. Dark transparent brown base with translucent white banding. Several tiny chips and moons. Germany, circa 1870-1915. 7/8". Near Mint(+) (8.2). Price: $42. CyberAuction #341, Lot #15.

5557. SWIRL. Caramel. Type of caramel swirl. Transparent emerald green base with subsurface bands of white. Overall haze. Germany, circa 1870-1915. 15/16". Good(+) (7.9). Price: $42. CyberAuction #368, Lot #43.

5558. SWIRL. Caramel. Hard to find large example. Transparent very dark brown caramel base. Subsurface bands and loops of white. Overall haze, some tiny chipping. Germany, circa 1870-1915. 1-1/4". Good (7.6). Price: $42. CyberAuction #382, Lot #23.

5559. SWIRL. Caramel. Very light honey amber brown base with translucent white banding. One flat melt area. Germany, circa 1870-1915. 11/16". Mint(-) (9.0). Price: $40. CyberAuction #399, Lot #52.

5560. SWIRL. Caramel. Dark transparent brown base with translucent white banding. Light haze. Germany, circa 1870-1915. 21/32". Near Mint(+) (8.0). Price: $27. CyberAuction #419, Lot #56.

5561. SWIRL. Caramel. Transparent brown base with translucent white banding. Several small subsurface moons. Germany, circa 1870-1915. 21/32". Near Mint(-) (8.2). Price: $25. CyberAuction #370, Lot #22.

5562. SWIRL. Caramel. Translucent butterscotch brown with bands of opaque white. Two small chips. Germany, circa 1870-1915. 21/32". Near Mint (8.5). Price: $25. CyberAuction #491, Lot #5.

5563. SWIRL. Caramel. Very dark brown base. Subsurface translucent white strands and bands. Some tiny subsurface moons and pits. Germany, circa 1870-1915. 21/32". Near Mint(+) (8.2). Price: $19. CyberAuction #420, Lot #10.

5564. SWIRL. Caramel. Same construction as a brown caramel, but it is green. Transparent green glass. Subsurface bands, strands and swirls of semi-opaque white. Some tiny chips and light haze. Germany, circa 1870-1915. 21/32". Near Mint(-) (8.1). Price: $19. CyberAuction #435, Lot #42.

5565. SWIRL. Caramel. Transparent brown base. Semi-opaque white strands and bands subsurface. Some unmelted sand. Small flake, small subsurface moon, some pinpricks. Germany, circa 1870-1915. 5/8". Good(+) (7.7). Price: $17. CyberAuction #396, Lot #17.

5566. SWIRL. Caramel. Dark transparent brown base with translucent white banding. Chips and pits. Germany, circa 1870-1915. 21/32". Good (7.6). Price: $17. CyberAuction #402, Lot #16.

5567. SWIRL. Caramel. Dark transparent brown base with translucent white banding. Chips and pits. Germany, circa 1870-1915. 3/4". Good(+) (7.8). Price: $17. CyberAuction #402, Lot #47.

5568. SWIRL. Caramel. Translucent dark brown base. Three wide subsurface bands of white. Subsurface moon at the bottom. Germany, circa 1870-1915. 11/16". Near Mint (8.5). Price: $15. CyberAuction #501, Lot #6.

5569. SWIRL. Caramel. Dark transparent brown base with translucent white banding. Chips and pits. Germany, circa 1870-1915. 21/32". Good (7.6). Price: $10. CyberAuction #401, Lot #10.

5570. SWIRL. Caramel. Dark transparent brown base with translucent white banding. Chips and pits. Germany, circa 1870-1915. 21/32". Good (7.6). Price: $10. CyberAuction #440, Lot #46.

5571. SWIRL. Caramel. Dark transparent brown base with translucent white banding. Chips and pits. Germany, circa 1870-1915. 21/32". Good (7.6). Price: $8. CyberAuction #454, Lot #35.

5572. SWIRL. Coreless. Very rare marble. Coreless swirl in translucent red base glass. Translucent currant red base. Three subsurface white bands. One tiny flake. Very rare. Germany, circa 1870-1915. 19/32". Near Mint(+) (8.7). Price: $235. CyberAuction #388, Lot #48.

5573. SWIRL. Coreless. One of the rarest and most unusual swirls I have ever seen. Transparent clear base. Outer layer is three bands. Each is the same construction. Each is a twisted yellow latticinio core, edged on either side by a band of white with pink and blue on it. The white bands are rotated ninety degrees, to give the impression that each of the three sets is an individual latticinio core with a double ribbon facing. The marble is from near end of the cane, so one is poorly constructed. But the other

two sets are outstanding. An exceptional marble. Several tiny chips. Germany, circa 1870-1915. 13/16". Near Mint (8.5). Price: $140. CyberAuction #467, Lot #21.

5574. SWIRL. Coreless. Rare marble (in the condition). Transparent emerald green base. Three subsurface bands. Each is pink (with a blue center band), edged by yellow. A couple of tiny flakes and a tiny subsurface moon. Damage is not visible except on close inspection. Super marble. Germany, circa 1870-1915. 3/4". Near Mint (8.6). Price: $85. CyberAuction #338, Lot #54.

5575. SWIRL. Coreless. Transparent emerald green base. Three subsurface bands of pink and yellow. Beauty. Several tiny subsurface moons, some rubbing. Germany, circa 1870-1915. 11/16". Near Mint(-) (8.0). Price: $35. CyberAuction #372, Lot #37.

5576. SWIRL. Coreless. Transparent clear base. Outer layer is three white bands and three blue on white bands. One small chip, two small subsurface moons. Germany, circa 1870-1915. 1-3/16". Near Mint(+) (8.1). Price: $33. CyberAuction #358, Lot #51.

5577. SWIRL. Coreless. Transparent blue base. Three wide subsurface panels of assorted colors. Beauty. Slightly flattened. One side flat spot, couple of pinpricks. Germany, circa 1870-1915. 13/16". Mint(-) (9.0). Price: $32. CyberAuction #360, Lot #19.

5578. SWIRL. Coreless. Clear base. Two subsurface orange/red bands, two subsurface white bands. Air bubble near center. Beauty. Germany, circa 1870-1915. 15/32". Mint (9.9). Price: $28. CyberAuction #360, Lot #14.

5579. SWIRL. Coreless. Gorgeous example. Transparent clear base. Two subsurface bands of bright red and white, one subsurface band of bright green and white. One pinprick on the surface. Germany, circa 1870-1915. 21/32". Mint(-) (9.2). Price: $27. CyberAuction #429, Lot #4.

5580. SWIRL. Coreless. Transparent very lightly tinted green base. Subsurface layer of four bands. Each is transparent green with white. One melt spot. Germany, circa 1870-1915. 25/32". Mint(-) (9.0). Price: $26. CyberAuction #459, Lot #15.

5581. SWIRL. Coreless. Superb coreless swirl. Transparent clear base. Three subsurface bands of pink and blue on white. One manufacturing pit, couple of tiny melt spots. Germany, circa 1870-1915. 21/32". Mint (9.3). Price: $24. CyberAuction #385, Lot #19.

5582. SWIRL. Coreless. Transparent light blue base. Three bands of white with a red center. Looks like there is a band missing. Small chip where the missing band is, pinprick on the other side. A beauty. Germany, circa 1870-1915. 21/32". Near Mint (8.6). Price: $23. CyberAuction #360, Lot #41.

5583. SWIRL. Coreless. Gorgeous coreless swirl. Transparent clear base. Four subsurface bands. Two are blue and white, two are green and yellow. One melt spot. Germany, circa 1870-1915. 1/2". Mint (-) (9.0). Price: $23. CyberAuction #387, Lot #41.

5584. SWIRL. Coreless. Unusual. Transparent clear base. Four subsurface bands. Two on each side of the marble. Two are pink on white, two are blue and green on white. Very nice marble. Two tiny chips. Germany, circa 1870-1915. 7/8". Near Mint(+) (8.7). Price: $23. CyberAuction #394, Lot #38.

5585. SWIRL. Coreless. Transparent clear base. Two bands of white on the surface, appears to be missing a third. Two melt flat spots. Germany, circa 1870-1911. 13/16". Mint(-) (9.0). Price: $17. CyberAuction #397, Lot #44.

5586. SWIRL. Coreless. Clear base. Four subsurface bands. Two are pink and white, two are green and white. Pinprick. Germany, circa 1870-1915. 21/32". Mint (9.4). Price: $15. CyberAuction #360, Lot #32.

5587. SWIRL. Coreless. Transparent clear base. Three subsurface bands. Each is orange and light green, with some blue and white. Germany, circa 1870-1915. 19/32". Mint (9.9). Price: $15. CyberAuction #365, Lot #6.

5588. SWIRL. Coreless. Transparent clear base. Three white subsurface bands alternating with three transparent blue subsurface bands. One tiny chip. Germany, circa 1870-1915. Near Mint(+) (8.8). 11/16". Price: $13. CyberAuction #356, Lot #39.

5589. SWIRL. Coreless. Transparent clear base. Four subsurface bands. Two are orange and light blue, two are orange and light green. Buffed damage remains, so do pontils. Germany, circa 1870-1915. 29/32". Price: $13. CyberAuction #371, Lot #16.

5590. SWIRL. Coreless. Transparent clear base. Four subsurface bands. Two are orange and light blue, two are orange and light green. Buffed damage remains, so do pontils. Germany, circa 1870-1915. 29/32". Price: $13. CyberAuction #453, Lot #44.

5591. SWIRL. Coreless. Transparent clear base. Four subsurface bands. Two are orange and light blue, two are orange and light green. Buffed damage remains, so do pontils. Germany, circa 1870-1915. 29/32". Price: $13. CyberAuction #470, Lot #36.

5592. SWIRL. Coreless. Transparent clear base. Subsurface layer is a band of pink on white, a band of blue on white, band of green on white, narrow band of pink. Germany, circa 1870-1915. 1/2". Mint (9.6). Price: $11. CyberAuction #436, Lot #4.

5593. SWIRL. Coreless. Transparent clear base. Outer layer is six bands. Three are blue and white, three are white. Germany, circa 1870-1915. 9/16". Mint (9.6). Price: $10. CyberAuction #410, Lot #51.

5594. SWIRL. Coreless. Transparent clear base. Subsurface layer of four white bands. A couple of pinpricks. Germany, circa 1870-1915. 21/32". Mint (9.6). Price: $10. CyberAuction #443, Lot #11.

5595. SWIRL. Coreless. Transparent clear base. Outer layer is six bands. Three are blue and white, three are white. Germany, circa 1870-1915. 9/16". Mint (9.6). Price: $10. CyberAuction #454, Lot #36.

5596. SWIRL. Coreless. Transparent clear base. Four subsurface bands. Two green and white, two blue and white. Some tiny and small chips. Germany, circa 1870-1915. 21/32". Near Mint(-) (8.0). Price: $9. CyberAuction #358, Lot #42.

5597. SWIRL. Coreless. Transparent clear base with four subsurface bands. Assortment of red, blue and white in the bands. Two small melt spots, one pit. Germany, circa 1870-1915. 19/32". Near Mint(+) (8.9). Price: $9. CyberAuction #361, Lot #59.
5598. SWIRL. Coreless. Transparent very lightly tinted blue base. Four subsurface bands of blue, white and green. Two tiny rough spots. Germany, circa 1870-1915. 19/32". Near Mint(+) (8.9). Price: $9. CyberAuction #362, Lot #3.
5599. SWIRL. Coreless. Transparent clear base. Four subsurface bands. Two are orange and light blue, two are orange and light green. Buffed, damage remains, so do pontils. Germany, circa 1870-1915. 29/32". Price: $9. CyberAuction #482, Lot #12.
5600. SWIRL. Coreless. Transparent clear base. Outer layer is six bands. Three are blue and white, three are white. Germany, circa 1870-1915. 9/16". Mint (9.6). Price: $8. CyberAuction #441, Lot #3.
5601. SWIRL. Coreless. Transparent clear base. Four subsurface bands. Two green and white, two blue and white. Some tiny and small chips. Germany, circa 1870-1915. 21/32". Near Mint(-) (8.0). Price: $4. CyberAuction #441, Lot #40.
5602. SWIRL. Coreless. Transparent clear base. Outer layer is three white bands and three blue and white bands. One chip. Germany, circa 1870-1915. 9/16". Near Mint (8.6). Price: $1. CyberAuction #451, Lot #13.
5603. SWIRL. Cornhusk. Interesting cornhusk from near the end of the cane. Transparent light brown base. Subsurface white band covering almost three-quarters of the marble. Germany, circa 1870-1915. 11/16". Mint (9.5). Price: $120. CyberAuction #445, Lot #55.
5604. SWIRL. Cornhusk. Cornhusk variety of a banded swirl. Transparent amber yellow base. Rare. Subsurface white band covering about one-quarter of the marble. One melt spot. In nice shape. Germany, circa 1870-1915. 9/16". Mint (9.5). Price: $65. CyberAuction #452, Lot #47.
5605. SWIRL. Cornhusk. First off cane. Transparent amber brown base. Opaque white band subsurface going about two-thirds of the way up the marble. Marble is misshapen and slightly flat. Germany, circa 1870-1915. 5/8". Mint (9.5). Price: $60. CyberAuction #348, Lot #41.
5606. SWIRL. Cornhusk. Cornhusk variety of a banded swirl. Transparent brown base. Subsurface white band covering about one-quarter of the marble. In nice shape. Germany, circa 1870-1915. 1/2". Mint (9.7). Price: $60. CyberAuction #458, Lot #58.
5607. SWIRL. Cornhusk. Interesting cornhusk from near the end of the cane. Transparent light brown base. Subsurface white band covering almost three-quarters of the marble. Germany, circa 1870-1915. 11/16". Mint (9.5). Price: $55. CyberAuction #366, Lot #19.
5608. SWIRL. Cornhusk. Cornhusk variety of a banded swirl. Transparent brown base. Subsurface white band covering about one-third of the marble. In nice shape. Germany, circa 1870-1915. 19/32". Mint (9.5). Price: $50. CyberAuction #410, Lot #10.
5609. SWIRL. Cornhusk. Cornhusk variety of a banded swirl. Transparent brown base. Subsurface white band covering about one-third of the marble. In nice shape, one small manufacturing pit and a dirt line. Germany, circa 1870-1915. 19/32". Mint (9.5). Price: $43. CyberAuction #450, Lot #40.
5610. SWIRL. Cornhusk. Cornhusk swirl. Transparent light brown base. Subsurface white band. One subsurface moon. Germany, circa 1870-1915. 5/8". Near Mint (8.3). Price: $27. CyberAuction #447, Lot #42.
5611. SWIRL. Cornhusk. Cornhusk variety of a banded swirl. Transparent brown base. Subsurface white band covering about one-third of the marble. Overall melt roughness, not finished properly. Not chipped. Germany, circa 1870-1915. 19/32". Mint(-) (9.0). Price: $23. CyberAuction #468, Lot #44.
5612. SWIRL. Cornhusk. Cornhusk swirl. Transparent light brown base. Subsurface white band. Two flakes, slightly misshapen. Germany, circa 1870-1915. 5/8". Near Mint (8.5). Price: $19. CyberAuction #399, Lot #46.
5613. SWIRL. Cornhusk. Transparent brown base with a wide subsurface opaque white band. Several small chips and overall pits and haze. Germany, circa 1870-1915. 13/16". Good (7.5). Price: $15. CyberAuction #397, Lot #21.
5614. SWIRL. Cornhusk. Cornhusk variety of a banded swirl. Transparent brown base. Subsurface white band covering about one-quarter of the marble. A few small chips. Germany, circa 1870-1915. 11/16". Good(+) (7.9). Price: $15. CyberAuction #464, Lot #10.
5615. SWIRL. Cornhusk. Cornhusk swirl. Transparent light brown base. Subsurface white band. One subsurface moon. Germany, circa 1870-1915. 5/8". Near Mint (8.3). Price: $12. CyberAuction #391, Lot #52.
5616. SWIRL. Custard. Pink custard swirl. Semi-opaque ruddy pink base. Surface has bands of transparent pink. Some tiny chipping and tiny pinpricking. Germany, circa 1870-1915. 5/8". Near Mint(-) (8.1). Price: $27. CyberAuction #487, Lot #14.
5617. SWIRL. Divided core. Rare and gorgeous four-layer large divided core swirl. Transparent clear base. Core is three bands. Each is pink and green on yellow. Next layer is three bands of transparent red. Next layer is three bands, each consisting of three white strands. Top layer is three bands. Each of those is pink and blue on white. All bands are equidistantly spaced. Superior design and workmanship to this marble. Truly made by a craftsperson. Nicely ground pontil. Surface has about eight tiny to small subsurface moons on one side and two small ones on the other. No surface glass missing however. Views very well. Very rare. Germany, circa 1870-1915. 2-1/8". Near Mint(-) (8.2). Price: $320. CyberAuction #432, Lot #19.
5618. SWIRL. Divided core. Very unusual core. Four-band core. Two are orange, green, white and yellow. Two are orange, blue, white and yellow. Outer layer is a cage of white strands. A couple of tiny chips, a couple of tiny subsurface moons, some pits. Surface has an "orange peel" texture. Large and odd. Germany, circa 1870-1915. 2-3/8". Near Mint(-) (8.1). Price: $315. CyberAuction #424, Lot #47.
5619. SWIRL. Divided core. Four band core. Two are pink, blue and white. Two are pink, green and yellow. Outer layer is two sets of white strands and two sets of yellow strands. Two very tiny subsurface moons and a couple of tiny pinpricks. Still, a gorgeous marble. Germany, circa 1870-1915. 2". Near Mint(+) (8.7). Price: $285. CyberAuction #508, Lot #37.
5620. SWIRL. Divided core. Four panel core. Each is pink on white, edged by blue and green. Outer layer is four sets of yellow strands. There are three barely visible subsurface moons and a tiny chip at the bottom pontil. Looks great though, you really have to look for the damage. Germany, circa 1870-1915. 1-7/8". Near Mint (8.6). Price: $260. CyberAuction #414, Lot #28.
5621. SWIRL. Divided core. Superior marble. Three band core. One band is orange strands on white, one is blue and orange strands on white, one is green and orange strands on white. Outer layer is three sets of strands. Two sets are orange, one is white. Surface has one very, very tiny pit. Exceptional marble, rare coloring. Germany, circa 1870-1915. 1-7/16". Mint (9.4). Price: $230. CyberAuction #338, Lot #59.
5622. SWIRL. Divided core. Base glass is tinted very lightly blue. Four band core. Each is pink and yellow on white. Outer layer is two sets of narrow pink bands on white, one set of narrow blue bands on white and one set of narrow green bands on white. A couple of tiny chips and an overall haze. Needs a good buff. Germany, circa 1870-1915. 2-3/8". Good (7.6). Price: $215. CyberAuction #415, Lot #28.
5623. SWIRL. Divided core. Interesting and beautiful. Three band core. One is pink on white, one is pink and blue on white, one is pink and green on yellow. Outer layer is three sets of white and yellow strands. Superb!!!! One tiny melt spot, a few small flat spots. Looks great. Germany, circa 1870-1915. 1-5/16". Mint (9.5). Price: $160. CyberAuction #366, Lot #44.
5624. SWIRL. Divided core. Three band core. Each is red, white and blue. Outer layer is three sets of yellow strands. In great shape with just a couple of small scratches. Superior example. Germany, circa 1870-1915. 1-5/8". Mint (9.6). Price: $160. CyberAuction #400, Lot #32.
5625. SWIRL. Divided core. Interesting and beautiful. Three band core. One is pink on white, one is pink and blue on white, one is pink and green on yellow. Outer layer is three sets of white and yellow strands. Superb!!!! One tiny melt spot, a few small flat spots. Looks great. Germany, circa 1870-1915. 1-5/16". Mint (9.5). Price: $155. CyberAuction #441, Lot #11.
5626. SWIRL. Divided core. Three band core. Each is a complex combination of pink, yellow, green and white. Outer layer is a cage of white strands. One very small chip, several small and tiny subsurface moons. Germany, circa 1870-1915. 2-1/16". Near Mint(-) (8.0). Price: $150. CyberAuction #423, Lot #30.
5627. SWIRL. Divided core. Nice larger marble. Three band core. Each is pink on yellow. Outer layer is six bands. Three are green on yellow, three are blue on white. Thick outer casing. Several very tiny rough spots where it rubbed against another marble. Germany, circa 1870-1915. 1-5/8". Near Mint(+) (8.9). Price: $140. CyberAuction #345, Lot #52.
5628. SWIRL. Divided core. Superb first-off-cane flower-type swirl. Three-layer swirl. Core is six bands. Middle layer is six pairs of white strands. Outer layer is eight bands. All the colors come shooting out the top. Outstanding. One small hazy spot. Some dirt. Germany, circa 1870-1915. 25/32". Near Mint(+) (8.9). Price: $140. CyberAuction #418, Lot #51.
5629. SWIRL. Divided core. Four band core. One is green on white, one is red on yellow, one is blue on white. Last we meant to be red on white, but only the white is faintly there. Outer layer is two sets of white strands and a set of yellow strands. Other set of yellow is missing. From near an end of the cane. Pristine surface, almost impossible to find in these larger ones. Germany, circa 1870-1915. 1-7/16". Mint (9.9). Price: $140. CyberAuction #503, Lot #57.
5630. SWIRL. Divided core. Four band core. Two are pink, blue and white. Two are pink, green and yellow. Outer layer is cage of white strands. Very nice marble. One tiny pit. Germany, circa 1870-1915. 1-1/16". Mint (9.4). Price: $130. CyberAuction #459, Lot #45.
5631. SWIRL. Divided core. Four band core. Each is pink and blue on white. Outer layer is four sets of yellow strands. Very lightly polished, but a beauty. Germany, circa 1870-1915. 1-13/16". Price: $120. CyberAuction #507, Lot #35.
5632. SWIRL. Divided core. Three band core. Each is white band with red on it. Edged by blue on one side and very fiery aventurine green on the other. Outer layer is three sets of yellow and white strands. Some scratching. Gorgeous marble!!! Germany, circa 1870-1915. 15/16". Near Mint(+) (8.9). Price: $110. CyberAuction #345, Lot #55.
5633. SWIRL. Divided core. Interesting and beautiful. Three band core. One is pink on white, one is pink and blue on white, one is pink and green on yellow. Outer layer is three sets of white and yellow strands. Superb!!!! One tiny melt spot, a few small flat spots. Looks great. Germany, circa 1870-1915. 1-5/16". Mint (9.5). Price: $110. CyberAuction #404, Lot #44.
5634. SWIRL. Divided core. Four band core. Each is pink and blue on white. Outer layer is four sets of yellow strands. Very lightly polished, but a beauty. Germany, circa 1870-1915. 1-13/16". Price: $110. CyberAuction #424, Lot #33.
5635. SWIRL. Divided core. Unusual marble. Six band core. Three are pink, yellow and white. Three are narrow blue bands. Outer layer is three sets of white strands. Small subsurface moon, several tiny subsurface moons, overall haze. Germany, circa 1870-1915. 1-3/4". Good(+) (7.7). Price: $110. CyberAuction #451, Lot #34.
5636. SWIRL. Divided core. Four band core. Each is pink and blue on white. Outer layer is four sets of yellow strands. Very lightly polished, but a beauty. Germany, circa 1870-1915. 1-13/16". Price: $110. CyberAuction #460, Lot #41.
5637. SWIRL. Divided core. Rare marble. From near an end of the cane. Transparent cobalt blue base. Two bands of white in the core, another

partial one. In great shape. Germany, circa 1870-1915. 17/32". Mint (9.9). Price: $95. CyberAuction #376, Lot #58.
5638. SWIRL. Divided core. Very rare marble. Divided core consisting of three bands of red latticinio strands. Or a red latticinio in divided form. Outer layer is three bands of blue and white mirroring the spaces in the core. One melt pit. Germany, possibly England, circa 1870-1915. 1/2". Mint(-) (9.2). Price: $95. CyberAuction #503, Lot #71.
5639. SWIRL. Divided core. Odd core. Four band core. Two bands are purple center band, edged by opaque white bands, flanked by transparent pink bands. Two bands are green center band, edged by opaque yellow bands, flanked by transparent pink bands. Each of the pink bands is coated with tiny air bubbles. Outer layer is two sets of yellow strands and two sets of white strands. One tiny subsurface moon. Rare. Germany, circa 1870-1915. 1-3/16". Near Mint(+) (8.9). Price: $90. CyberAuction #330, Lot #29.
5640. SWIRL. Divided core. Three band core. One is orange, green and blue on yellow. One is orange, lavender and yellow on white. Last is lavender, green and blue on white. Outer layer is three sets of yellow and white strands. A couple of very tiny chips/pits. Very odd coloring. Germany, circa 1870-1915. 1-5/16". Near Mint (8.5). Price: $90. CyberAuction #350, Lot #36.
5641. SWIRL. Divided core. Transparent brown base. Only two bands to the core. Each is white. Outer layer is six bands. Three are red and blue. Other three are red and yellow. One tiny subsurface moon. Germany, circa 1870-1915. 25/32". Near Mint(+) (8.9). Price: $80. CyberAuction #345, Lot #28.
5642. SWIRL. Divided core. Very interesting marble. Base glass is transparent clear and filled with tiny air bubbles. Four band core. Two bands are pink, blue and yellow on white. Two are pink, green, and yellow on white. Outer layer is two sets of white strands and two sets of yellow strands. Tiny subsurface moon, several tiny sparkles, one small blown air hole (near bottom). Germany, circa 1870-1915. 1-9/16". Near Mint (8.6). Price: $80. CyberAuction #421, Lot #11.
5643. SWIRL. Divided core. Amethyst base glass. Core is three bands. Each is blue bands on white. Outer layer is six pink on yellow bands. Surface very lightly buffed. Overall light damage remains. Pontils intact. Germany, circa 1870-1915. 1-11/16". Price: $80. CyberAuction #432, Lot #35.
5644. SWIRL. Divided core. Amethyst base glass. Core is three bands. Each is blue bands on white. Outer layer is six pink on yellow bands. Surface very lightly buffed. Overall light damage remains. Pontils intact. Germany, circa 1870-1915. 1-11/16". Price: $80. CyberAuction #468, Lot #14.
5645. SWIRL. Divided core. Four band core. Two are pink and green on yellow, two are pink and blue on white. Outer layer is two sets of yellow strands and two sets of white strands. One tiny subsurface moon, one tiny sparkle. Germany, circa 1870-1915. 1-9/16". Near Mint(+) (8.9). Price: $80. CyberAuction #479, Lot #48.
5646. SWIRL. Divided core. Four band core. Two are yellow and turquoise on white, two are pink and blue on white. Outer layer is four sets of white strands. Very pretty. One small manufacturing pit. Germany, circa 1870-1915. 1-1/16". Mint (9.6). Price: $75. CyberAuction #333, Lot #7.
5647. SWIRL. Divided core. From near an end of the cane. Was meant to be a four band core. One band of pink and white, one of green and white are present. One partial white also. Outer layer has several yellow and white strands. One side of the marble is filled with tiny, very thin pieces of a mica-like material (possibly razor thin pieces of mica, or of glass chips). Interesting effect, rare. Surface in great shape. Germany, circa 1870-1915. 1-3/16". Mint (9.7). Price: $75. CyberAuction #475, Lot #33.
5648. SWIRL. Divided core. Rare naked aventurine divided core. Transparent clear base. Four band core. Two bands are blue on white, two are very fiery aventurine green on white. Two melt spots. Stunning. Germany, circa 1870-1915. 9/16". Mint(-) (9.0). Price: $72. CyberAuction #335, Lot #2.
5649. SWIRL. Divided core. Four band core. Each band is wide. Two are red, blue and white. Two are green, yellow and red. Outer layer is four yellow strands alternating with four white strands. Some tiny melt holes, but no damage. Beauty. Germany, circa 1870-1915. 13/16". Mint (9.5). Price: $71. CyberAuction #467, Lot #1.
5650. SWIRL. Divided core. Three band core. Each is pink on white, edged by blue. Outer layer is three sets of yellow strands. Beautiful marble, very well executed. A couple of tiny pits. Germany, circa 1870-1915. 31/32". Mint(-) (9.0). Price: $70. CyberAuction #333, Lot #24.
5651. SWIRL. Divided core. Very interesting marble. Base glass is transparent clear and filled with tiny air bubbles. Four band core. Two bands are pink, blue and yellow on white. Two are pink, green, and yellow on white. Outer layer is two sets of white strands and two sets of yellow strands. Tiny subsurface moon, several tiny sparkles, one small blown air hole (near bottom). Germany, circa 1870-1915. 1-9/16". Near Mint (8.6). Price: $70. CyberAuction #466, Lot #22.
5652. SWIRL. Divided core. Four band core. Two are pink on yellow, one is green on white, one is blue on white. Outer layer is two sets of yellow strands and two sets of white strands. Tight twist. Gorgeous. Germany, circa 1870-1915. 3/4". Mint (9.9). Price: $70. CyberAuction #500, Lot #4.
5653. SWIRL. Divided core. Four band core. Two are pink, blue and white. Two are pink, green and yellow. Outer layer is two sets of yellow strands and two sets of white strands. Pretty marble. Some tiny chips and pitting. Some melted dirt on it. Germany, circa 1870-1915. 1-5/8". Near Mint(-) (8.1). Price: $65. CyberAuction #334, Lot #33.
5654. SWIRL. Divided core. One of the most unusual swirls I've ever seen. Three layer. Three band core. Each is the same pattern of red, green, blue, yellow and white. Middle layer is three sets of red and white strands. The surface is three-quarters covered by semi-opaque white, with just one small clear panel to view the interior. Slightly misshapen. One small flake. Germany, circa 1870-1915. 17/32". Near Mint (8.6). Price: $65. CyberAuction #341, Lot #42.
5655. SWIRL. Divided core. Three band core. Wide bands. Each is the same pattern of red, yellow and blue, edged by white. Outer layer is three sets of white and yellow strands. Germany, circa 1870-1915. 7/8". Mint (9.7). Price: $65. CyberAuction #357, Lot #49.
5656. SWIRL. Divided core. Very interesting. Four band core. Two pink on yellow, two pink on white. Outer layer is four bands. Two green on yellow, two blue on white. All bands (core and outer layer) are the same width and are evenly spaced. One pit. Germany, circa 1870-1915. 11/16". Mint(-) (9.2). Price: $65. CyberAuction #373, Lot #51.
5657. SWIRL. Divided core. Large. Three band core. Each is the same complex pattern of white, yellow, red, blue and green. Outer layer is three sets of yellow and white strands. Polished, but pontils are pretty much intact. Some damage remains. Germany, circa 1870-1915. 1-15/16". Price: $65. CyberAuction #387, Lot #24.
5658. SWIRL. Divided core. Yellow latticinio strands in three divided core bands. Outer layer is three bands. One each of blue on white, green on white, red on white. Subsurface moon and a sparkle. Hard to find this large. Germany, circa 1870-1915. 1-3/16". Near Mint (8.6). Price: $65. CyberAuction #393, Lot #55.
5659. SWIRL. Divided core. Pretty marble. Four band core. Two are pink on white, two are blue on white. Outer layer is four sets of yellow strands. Some surface pitting and a couple of very tiny subsurface moons. Germany, circa 1870-1915. 1-3/16". Near Mint (8.5). Price: $65. CyberAuction #434, Lot #46.
5660. SWIRL. Divided core. Superb divided core swirl. Three band core. Wide bands. One each of blue on white, green on yellow, pink on yellow. Outer layer is a cage of white strands. A real beauty. Germany, circa 1870-1915. 29/32". Mint (9.8). Price: $65. CyberAuction #459, Lot #16.
5661. SWIRL. Divided core. Exceptional divided core swirl. Three band core. One blue on white, one pink on white, one green on white. Outer layer is a cage of yellow strands. Thick outer casing. Superb. Germany, circa 1870-1915. 15/16". Mint (9.8). Price: $60. CyberAuction #337, Lot #24.
5662. SWIRL. Divided core. Four band core. Two are pink, blue and yellow on white, two are pink, green and yellow on white. Outer layer is four sets of white strands. Very nice marble. Germany, circa 1870-1915. 1-1/16". Mint (9.7). Price: $60. CyberAuction #337, Lot #44.
5663. SWIRL. Divided core. Three band core. Each is pink on white, edged by blue. Almost no spaces between the bands. Outer layer is three sets of yellow strands. One crease at the bottom pontil. Thick outer casing. Nice. Germany, circa 1870-1915. 1-1/4". Mint (9.6). Price: $60. CyberAuction #342, Lot #21.
5664. SWIRL. Divided core. Pretty marble. Four band core. Two are pink on white, two are blue on white. Outer layer is four sets of yellow strands. Some surface pitting and a couple of very tiny subsurface moons. Germany, circa 1870-1915. 1-3/16". Near Mint (8.5). Price: $60. CyberAuction #398, Lot #5.
5665. SWIRL. Divided core. Interesting marble. Teardrop air bubble center. Surrounded by four bands. Each is orange with blue center. Outer layer is four sets of white strands. Some tiny pinpricks. A beauty. Germany, circa 1870-1915. 1-3/16". Near Mint(+) (8.9). Price: $55. CyberAuction #334, Lot #4.
5666. SWIRL. Divided core. Four band core. All are same pattern of blue, pink, green, yellow and white. Outer layer is four sets of white strands. Several small and tiny flakes and chips, some scratching. Germany, circa 1870-1915. 1-13/16". Good(+) (7.9). Price: $55. CyberAuction #359, Lot #36.
5667. SWIRL. Divided core. Pretty marble. Four band core. Two are pink on white, two are blue on white. Outer layer is four sets of yellow strands. Some surface pitting and a couple of very tiny subsurface moons. Germany, circa 1870-1915. 1-3/16". Near Mint (8.5). Price: $55. CyberAuction #365, Lot #47.
5668. SWIRL. Divided core. Three band core. Each is a combination of pink, blue, yellow and green. Outer layer is three sets of yellow and white strands. Heavily polished. Germany, circa 1870-1915. 2". Price: $55. CyberAuction #397, Lot #31.
5669. SWIRL. Divided core. Three band core. Each is pink on white, edge by blue and green. Outer layer is three sets of yellow strands. A few tiny subsurface moons. Views very well. Germany, circa 1870-1915. 1-5/8". Near Mint (8.6). Price: $55. CyberAuction #414, Lot #30.
5670. SWIRL. Divided core. Three layer marble. Three band core. Each band is the same complex pattern of pink, green, blue, white and yellow. Middle layer is three sets of yellow strands, set to mirror the spaces in the core. Outer layer is three sets of white strands. Surface has been buffed. Pontils are pretty much intact, some damage remains. Germany, circa 1870-1915. 1-5/8". Buffed. Price: $55. CyberAuction #447, Lot #33.
5671. SWIRL. Divided core. Naked divided core swirl. Core is opaque white. Two orange bands, one green band, one blue band, on it. No outer layer. Superb. Very hard to find these larger ones as nakeds. One tiny subsurface moon near the bottom and a sparkle. Germany, circa 1870-1915. 1-1/16". Near Mint(+) (8.8). Price: $55. CyberAuction #495, Lot #48.
5672. SWIRL. Divided core. Four band core. Two are red and blue on white, two are red, blue and green on white. Outer layer is four sets of white strands. Gorgeous marble. One tiny flat spot. Germany, circa 1870-1915. 3/4". Mint (9.6). Price: $51. CyberAuction #353, Lot #22.
5673. SWIRL. Divided core. Four band core. Two are orange and yellow, one is green and yellow, one is blue and white. Bright colors. Outer layer is four sets of white strands. England, possibly Germany, circa 1870-1915. 13/16". Mint (9.7). Price: $51. CyberAuction #463, Lot #54.

5674. SWIRL. Divided core. Three band core. Each is pink on white, green on yellow, separated by blue. Outer layer is three sets of yellow and white strands. Small subsurface moons and a surface moon. Germany, circa 1870-1915. 1-11/16". Good(+) (7.8). Price: $50. CyberAuction #344, Lot #36.
5675. SWIRL. Divided core. Alternating yellow and white latticinio strands in divided form. Three band core. Outer layer is three bands, each is blue and white. Teardrop center. Several tiny sparkles, but still a super example. Germany, circa 1870-1915. 7/8". Near Mint(+) (8.9). Price: $50. CyberAuction #385, Lot #32.
5676. SWIRL. Divided core. Three band core. Gorgeous marble. Each band is red on yellow, next to green on white. Outer layer is three sets of yellow and white strands. Tiny subsurface moon, a couple of pits. Germany, circa 1870-1915. 1-3/16". Near Mint(+) (8.8). Price: $50. CyberAuction #447, Lot #49.
5677. SWIRL. Divided core. Three band core. Each is two transparent blue bands, edged by red, separated by white and edged by white. Outer layer is three sets of yellow strands. Left-hand twist. Rare in swirls. Germany, circa 1870-1915. 9/16". Mint (9.8). Price: $50. CyberAuction #483, Lot #30.
5678. SWIRL. Divided core. Four band core. Two are green on white, one red on white, one blue on white. Outer layer is two sets of yellow strands and two sets of white strands. Several small subsurface moons, a few tiny chips, some pits. Germany, circa 1870-1915. 1-7/8". Good(+) (7.9). Price: $47. CyberAuction #391, Lot #21.
5679. SWIRL. Divided core. Three band core. Each is orange, yellow, blue, green and white. Outer layer is three sets of yellow and white strands. Germany, possibly England, circa 1927-1935. 21/32". Mint (9.8). Price: $47. CyberAuction #491, Lot #20.
5680. SWIRL. Divided core. Super marble. Three band core. Very little space between bands. Each band is blue, white, red and green. Outer layer is three sets of orange strands. One pit. Beauty. Germany, circa 1870-1915. 1". Mint(-) (9.1). Price: $46. CyberAuction #345, Lot #44.
5681. SWIRL. Divided core. Gorgeous divided core, with hard to find coloring. Three band core. Each is red, white and very fiery aventurine green. Outer layer is three sets of yellow and white strands. One large air bubble under the surface on one side. England, possibly Germany, circa 1870-1920. 19/32". Mint (9.9). Price: $46. CyberAuction #353, Lot #7.
5682. SWIRL. Divided core. Three band core. Each is white with pink and yellow on it, edged by blue and green. Outer layer is three sets of white strands. Germany, circa 1870-1915. 25/32". Mint (9.9). Price: $46. CyberAuction #354, Lot #44.
5683. SWIRL. Divided core. End of cane (first off cane) flower-type. Three band core. Core and outer layer come shooting out of the top of the marble. Looks like a flower. Nice example. Some haziness. Germany, circa 1870-1915. 11/16". Good(+) (7.9). Price: $46. CyberAuction #368, Lot #57.
5684. SWIRL. Divided core. Four band core. Two are blue and pink on white. Two are pink and yellow on green. Outer layer is two sets of white strands and two sets of yellow strands. Polished, some moons remain. 2". Price: $46. CyberAuction #493, Lot #19.
5685. SWIRL. Divided core. Three band core. Each is orange on white and green on yellow. Outer layer is three sets of white strands. One tiny melt spot. Very nice. Germany, circa 1870-1915. 15/16". Mint (9.3). Price: $45. CyberAuction #342, Lot #51.
5686. SWIRL. Divided core. Four band core. Two are pink on yellow, one green on yellow, one blue on yellow. Outer layer is two sets of white strands and two sets of yellow strands. Two tiny subsurface moons, a couple of cold dimple spots. Germany, circa 1870-1915. 1-3/16". Near Mint (8.6). Price: $45. CyberAuction #357, Lot #39.
5687. SWIRL. Divided core. Bright English colors. Core is yellow, red and blue bands. Shoved to one side. Middle layer is red and blue bands. Outer layer is white strands. Two melt spots. England, circa 1880-1910. 23/32". Mint(-) (9.2). Price: $45. CyberAuction #433, Lot #21.
5688. SWIRL. Divided core. Gorgeous. Four band core. Two are bright red with pale white strands. Two are bright blue with yellow strands. Outer layer is two sets of orange strands and two sets of white strands. Germany, circa 1870-1915. 29/32". Mint (9.8). Price: $45. CyberAuction #503, Lot #54.
5689. SWIRL. Divided core. Three band core. Each is blue on white. Outer layer is three bands of pink on white. Outer bands are same width as the core bands. Stunning. Germany, circa 1870-1915. 21/32". Mint (9.9). Price: $44. CyberAuction #333, Lot #50.
5690. SWIRL. Divided core. Very hard to find. English colors. Naked divided core. Three band core. Each is bright blue, white, yellow, red and green. Germany, circa 1870-1920. 5/8". Mint (9.9). Price: $44. CyberAuction #338, Lot #17.
5691. SWIRL. Divided core. Very rare marble. Orange latticinio strands in divided form. Three bands. Outer layer is three bands. One each of pink on white, blue on white, green on white. No twist. There is a very thick casing of outer glass. Germany, circa 1870-1915. 11/16". Mint (9.7). Price: $44. CyberAuction #342, Lot #31.
5692. SWIRL. Divided core. Transparent base, lightly tinted blue. Four band core. Two bands are pink, blue and white. Two are pink, green and yellow. Outer layer is four sets of yellow and white strands. Several sparkles and tiny subsurface moons. Germany, circa 1870-1915. 1-1/4". Near Mint(-) (8.2). Price: $44. CyberAuction #348, Lot #34.
5693. SWIRL. Divided core. Four band core. Two are yellow on white, edged by blue. Two are orange, edged by white. Outer layer is a cage of eight white strands. Beauty. England, possibly Germany, circa 1870-1915. 27/32". Mint (9.9). Price: $44. CyberAuction #471, Lot #5.
5694. SWIRL. Divided core. Four band core. Two bands are pink, green, yellow and white. Two are pink, blue, yellow and white. Outer layer is a cage of white strands. Lightly buffed to remove haze, some damage remains. Germany, circa 1870-1915. 2-1/8". Price: $44. CyberAuction #492, Lot #38.
5695. SWIRL. Divided core. Three band core. Each is pink and blue on white. Outer layer is three sets of yellow and white strands. Super marble. Germany, circa 1870-1915. 3/4". Mint (9.9). Price: $43. CyberAuction #356, Lot #16.
5696. SWIRL. Divided core. Four band core. Two are blue, red and white. Other two are blue, yellow and green. Outer layer is two sets of white strands and two sets of yellow strands. Pitting, tiny chips and small subsurface moons. Germany, circa 1870-1915. 1-3/8". Near Mint(-) (8.0). Price: $42. CyberAuction #348, Lot #27.
5697. SWIRL. Divided core. English type. Three band core. Each band is the same pattern of red, blue, white, yellow and green. Outer layer is three sets of orange and white strands. Beauty. English, possibly German, circa 1880-1920. 5/8". Mint (9.7). Price: $42. CyberAuction #351, Lot #23.
5698. SWIRL. Divided core. Four band core. Two are pink on white, one is blue on white, one is green on white. Outer layer is four sets of yellow strands. Overall tiny chips and light haze. Germany, circa 1870-1915. 1-9/16". Good(-) (7.1). Price: $42. CyberAuction #352, Lot #36.
5699. SWIRL. Divided core. Four band core. Each is a different complex pattern. Outer layer is four bands. Two are yellow strands, two are white strands. Very nice. In great shape. Germany, circa 1870-1915. 3/4". Mint (9.8). Price: $42. CyberAuction #353, Lot #44.
5700. SWIRL. Divided core. Four band core. Two are pink on white, a green on white, a blue on white. Outer layer is four sets of yellow strands. Thick outer casing. Several very tiny chips. Beauty. Germany, circa 1870-1915. 29/32". Near Mint(+) (8.9). Price: $42. CyberAuction #373, Lot #42.
5701. SWIRL. Divided core. Very nice marbles. Four bands core. Two are pink on yellow, one is green on white, one is blue on white. Outer layer is three sets of three white strands, there is one set missing. Two tiny manufacturing pits, also marble is not wet. Germany, circa 1870-1915. 15/16". Mint(-) (9.0). Price: $42. CyberAuction #375, Lot #35.
5702. SWIRL. Divided core. Four band core. Two are pink on white, one is blue on white, one is green on white. Outer is four sets of yellow strands. One subsurface moon. Germany, circa 1870-1915. 15/16". Near Mint(+) (8.7). Price: $42. CyberAuction #376, Lot #14.
5703. SWIRL. Divided core. Four band core. From near an end of the cane. Two bands are red on yellow, one is blue on white, one is green on white. Outer layer is a set of white strands, a set of yellow strands, a white band and a small air bubble where the fourth yellow group would have been. Internal annealing fracture, two small subsurface moons. Still, a beauty. Germany, circa 1870-1915. 1-5/8". Near Mint(+) (8.7). Price: $42. CyberAuction #446, Lot #26.
5704. SWIRL. Divided core. Four band core. Two are pink and blue on white, two are pink and green on white. Outer layer is a cage of yellow strands. Outstanding. A couple of tiny chips. Germany, circa 1870-1915. 27/32". Near Mint(+) (8.7). Price: $42. CyberAuction #457, Lot #40.
5705. SWIRL. Divided core. Four band core. Two are pink and blue on white. Two are pink and green on yellow. Outer layer is four bands. Two each of the two inner color patterns. Unusual. One melt spot. Beauty. Germany, circa 1870-1915. 31/32". Mint (9.5). Price: $42. CyberAuction #473, Lot #17.
5706. SWIRL. Divided core. Very pretty marble, odd colors. Four band core. Two are yellow and white, edged by blue. Two are orange and white, edged by blue. Bright colors. Outer layer is two sets of yellow strands and two sets of white strands. Polished. Germany, possibly England, circa 1870-1915. 1-3/16". Price: $40. CyberAuction #332, Lot #35.
5707. SWIRL. Divided core. Four band core. Two are pink and blue on white. Two are pink and green on yellow. Outer layer is two sets of white strands and two sets of yellow strands. A few small subsurface moons and sparkles. Germany, circa 1870-1915. 1-9/16". Near Mint(-) (8.2). Price: $40. CyberAuction #334, Lot #35.
5708. SWIRL. Divided core. Three band core. Each is pink, green and blue, on white and yellow. Outer layer is a cage of white strands. One melt spot, a few tiny subsurface moons. Germany, circa 1870-1915. 1-9/16". Near Mint (8.5). Price: $40. CyberAuction #344, Lot #40.
5709. SWIRL. Divided core. Three band core. Two are pink on white, one is green on yellow. Outer layer is a cage of yellow strands. Stunning. Germany, circa 1870-1915. 21/32". Mint (9.8). Price: $40. CyberAuction #347, Lot #8.
5710. SWIRL. Divided core. Yellow latticinio strands in divided core form. Three band core. Outer layer is three bands of orange edged by white, set to mirror the spaces in the core. One melt spot, a few sparkles. Germany, circa 1870-1915. 27/32". Near Mint(+) (8.9). Price: $40. CyberAuction #356, Lot #43.
5711. SWIRL. Divided core. Three band naked divided core swirl, from near an end of the cane. Each band is pink and blue on white. One band is mostly on the surface of the marble, giving it the appearance of a double ribbon core swirl. One tiny chip, some small pitting. Germany, circa 1870-1915. 7/8". Near Mint (8.6). Price: $40. CyberAuction #366, Lot #38.
5712. SWIRL. Divided core. From near an end of the cane. Core consists of two white narrow bands, one blue narrow band, one green narrow band. Outer layer is one white narrow band and one yellow narrow band. Unmelted sand piece in the marble. One small elongated air hole. Germany, circa 1870-1915. 27/32". Mint(-) (9.0). Price: $40. CyberAuction #371, Lot #36.
5713. SWIRL. Divided core. Four very narrow bands. Two are yellow and two are white. Outer layer is two red on yellow, one green on white, one blue on white band. Several tiny and small subsurface moons. Germany,

5714. SWIRL. Divided core. Four band core. Two are blue on white, two are pink on yellow. Outer layer is two sets of white strands and two sets of yellow strands. A number of small subsurface moons. Germany, circa 1870-1915. 1-11/16". Good(+) (7.8). Price: $40. CyberAuction #382, Lot #33.

5715. SWIRL. Divided core. Four band core. Two are orange on white. Two are yellow on white, edged by blue. Outer layer is a cage of white strands. Beautiful marble. England, circa 1870-1915. 25/32". Mint (9.6). Price: $40. CyberAuction #462, Lot #45.

5716. SWIRL. Divided core. Naked divided core swirl. Three band core. Each is blue, pink and green on yellow and white. Superb. Germany, circa 1870-1915. 23/32". Mint (9.9). Price: $39. CyberAuction #335, Lot #52.

5717. SWIRL. Divided core. Four band core. Two are yellow and two are white. Outer layer is four bands. Two are orange/red and two are blue. In superb shape. Exceptional marble. England, possibly Germany, circa 1870-1915. 27/32". Mint (9.9). Price: $39. CyberAuction #479, Lot #25.

5718. SWIRL. Divided core. Three band divided core of latticinio strands. Each band is white and yellow strands. One band missing. Outer layer is four bands. Two are pink and blue on white, two are green and pink on yellow. Smokey base. Several tiny subsurface moons. Germany, circa 1870-1915. 1-7/16". Near Mint(-) (8.0). Price: $39. CyberAuction #493, Lot #25.

5719. SWIRL. Divided core. Three band core. Each is a different combination of blue, white, pink and yellow. Outer layer is three sets of yellow strands. One tiny subsurface moon, a couple of pits. Germany, circa 1870-1915. 1-5/16". Near Mint (8.6). Price: $38. CyberAuction #346, Lot #33.

5720. SWIRL. Divided core. Four band core. Two are pink and blue on white. One is pink and green on white. One is white with a little pink and green. Outer layer is two sets of white strands, and one set of yellow and white strand. Other yellow/white set is missing. Two tiny subsurface moons. Germany, circa 1870-1915. 1-3/16". Near Mint(+) (8.7). Price: $38. CyberAuction #349, Lot #56.

5721. SWIRL. Divided core. Four band core. Two are white, two are yellow. Outer layer is four bands. Two are green on white, two are blue on white. Several small and tiny subsurface moons. Germany, circa 1870-1915. 1-3/16". Near Mint (8.3). Price: $38. CyberAuction #349, Lot #58.

5722. SWIRL. Divided core. Naked divided core swirl. Very nice example. Core is slightly malformed. Two panels each of opaque orange, opaque yellow, opaque white and transparent purple. Very pretty. In great shape. Germany, circa 1870-1915. 21/32". Mint (9.9). Price: $38. CyberAuction #379, Lot #1.

5723. SWIRL. Divided core. Gorgeous marble. Six band core. Three are blue on white, three are pink on white. Outer layer is a cage of yellow strands. One small chip, a couple of tiny subsurface moons. Germany, circa 1870-1915. 29/32". Near Mint (8.6). Price: $38. CyberAuction #450, Lot #25.

5724. SWIRL. Divided core. Four band core. Two are pink, green and yellow. Two are pink, blue and white. The pink, green and yellow have annealing fractures on them. Outer layer is six sets of yellow strands. Cold roll line, couple of pinpricks. Super marble. Germany, circa 1870-1915. 15/16". Mint (-) (9.2). Price: $38. CyberAuction #489, Lot #8.

5725. SWIRL. Divided core. Four band core. Two are green on white, two are blue on white. Outer layer is four sets of white strands. Exceptional construction. Overall haze, one small flake. Buff will reveal a beauty. Germany, circa 1870-1915. 1-11/16". Good(+) (7.7). Price: $38. CyberAuction #493, Lot #29.

5726. SWIRL. Divided core. Four band core. Two are bright orange/red on white. One blue on white. Fourth is missing. Outer layer is three sets of bright orange/red strands. Again, a fourth set is missing. Beauty. Germany, possibly England, circa 1870-1915. 21/32". Mint (9.8). This marble matches the marble in Lot #34 in this auction. Buy the two for a matched pair. Price: $38. CyberAuction #495, Lot #22.

5727. SWIRL. Divided core. Gorgeous divided core swirl. Germany, circa 1870-1915. 1-7/16". Polished. Price: $37.42. CyberAuction #477, Lot #17.

5728. SWIRL. Divided core. Very interesting marble from near the end of the cane. Core has a wide band of blue, with some white. There is another band of blue closer to the surface. Several narrow bands of pink and yellow. One tiny subsurface moon. Germany, circa 1870-1915. 27/32". Near Mint(+) (8.8). Price: $37. CyberAuction #364, Lot #52.

5729. SWIRL. Divided core. Four band core. Two are pink and green on yellow, two are pink and blue on white. Outer layer is a cage of white strands. Tightly twisted. Germany, circa 1870-1915. 21/32". Mint (9.8). Price: $37. CyberAuction #403, Lot #6.

5730. SWIRL. Divided core. Three band core. Each is pink strands on white band. Outer layer is three turquoise on yellow bands, alternating with three sets of three yellow strands. A number of small and tiny chips, and some pitting. Germany, circa 1870-1915. 1-3/4". Good(+) (7.9). Price: $37. CyberAuction #445, Lot #35.

5731. SWIRL. Divided core. From end of cane. Four band core. One band each of pink on white, pink on yellow, green on yellow, green on white. Outer layer two sets of white strands and one set of yellow. Large looping smeared area on the surface of red and yellow. Germany, circa 1870-1915. 23/32". Mint (9.8). Price: $37. CyberAuction #498, Lot #28.

5732. SWIRL. Divided core. Three band core. Each is white and blue strands on orange/red. Outer layer is three sets of white strands. Tiny sparkle. Germany, circa 1870-1915. 1". Mint (9.3). Price: $37. CyberAuction #508, Lot #12.

5733. SWIRL. Divided core. Gorgeous. Core is four fat bands. Two are pink on white, one is blue on white, one is green on yellow. Outer layer is two sets of white strands, alternating with two sets of yellow strands. Tiny

5734. SWIRL. Divided core. Three band core. Each is pink and blue on white. Outer layer is three sets of yellow and white strands. Super marble. Germany, circa 1870-1915. 3/4". Mint (9.9). Price: $36. CyberAuction #44?, Lot #47.

5735. SWIRL. Divided core. Large divided core swirl. Three band core. Pink, green and yellow, blue, pink and white, pink, green and white. Outer layer is three sets of white strands. Small chip, couple of small subsurface moons. Germany, circa 1870-1915. 1-5/8". Near Mint(-) (8.1). Price: $36. CyberAuction #449, Lot #28.

5736. SWIRL. Divided core. Large divided core swirl. Three band core. Pink, green and yellow, blue, pink and white, pink, green and white. Outer layer is three sets of white strands. Small chip, couple of small subsurface moons. Germany, circa 1870-1915. 1-5/8". Near Mint(-) (8.1). Price: $36. CyberAuction #478, Lot #22.

5737. SWIRL. Divided core. Four band divided core. Two are pink and blue on white. Two are pink and green on yellow. Several very tiny subsurface moons. Germany, circa 1870-1915. 1-13/16". Near Mint (8.3). Price: $36. CyberAuction #493, Lot #17.

5738. SWIRL. Divided core. Four band core. Two bands are transparent pink on white, one is blue on white, one is green on yellow. Outer layer is four sets of strands. Two sets are white strands, two sets are yellow strands. Gorgeous marble. 29/32". Mint (9.8). Price: $35. CyberAuction #339, Lot #7.

5739. SWIRL. Divided core. Three band naked divided core swirl, from near an end of the cane. Each band is pink and blue on white. One band is mostly on the surface of the marble, giving it the appearance of a double ribbon core swirl. One tiny chip, some small pitting. Germany, circa 1870-1915. 7/8". Near Mint (8.6). Price: $35. CyberAuction #345, Lot #2.

5740. SWIRL. Divided core. Three band core. Two pink, one green. A green or blue is probably missing. Subsurface cage of white strands. Slightly misshapen. No damage. Germany, circa 1870-1915. 1-1/16". Mint (9.5). Price: $35. CyberAuction #366, Lot #34.

5741. SWIRL. Divided core. Three band core. Various combinations of orange/red, yellow, white and green. Outer layer is three bands. Each is orange and white strands. Odd marble. Very nice. Germany, circa 1870-1915. 25/32". Mint (9.8). Price: $35. CyberAuction #466, Lot #26.

5742. SWIRL. Divided core. Four band core. Each is pink on white. Outer layer is four sets of white strands. Several pits. Germany, circa 1870-1915. 31/32". Near Mint(+) (8.7). Price: $34. CyberAuction #375, Lot #5.

5743. SWIRL. Divided core. Three band core. Two are pink and green on yellow. One is pink and blue on white. Outer layer is three sets of white and yellow strands. Beauty. Some sparkles. One small manufacturing pit. Germany, circa 1870-1915. 3/4". Mint(-) (9.0). Price: $33. CyberAuction #331, Lot #10.

5744. SWIRL. Divided core. Three band core. Each is pink on yellow, blue on white, separated by green. Outer layer is three sets of white and red strands. Two tiny melt spots, one tiny manufacturing pit. Germany, circa 1870-1915. 7/8". Mint(-) (9.2). Price: $33. CyberAuction #368, Lot #45.

5745. SWIRL. Divided core. Four band core. Two are red on white, one blue on white, one green on white. Outer layer is four sets of yellow strands. One small flake, some pits. Very nice marble. Germany, circa 1870-1915. 1-1/4". Near Mint (8.6). Price: $33. CyberAuction #446, Lot #13.

5746. SWIRL. Divided core. Very interesting marble from near an end of the cane. I sell it if it was supposed to be a three-layer or two layer marble. Two blue bands in the core (one partial). On pink and green on yellow band floating above that. Three pink and blue on white, and a pink and green on yellow band, as he outer layer. Some melted air bubbles on the surface. No damage. Interesting marble. Germany, circa 1870-1915. 27/32". Mint (9.8). Price: $33. CyberAuction #471, Lot #4.

5747. SWIRL. Divided core. Four band core. Two are pink and green on yellow, two are pink and blue on white. Outer layer is a cage of white strands. Beauty. Germany, circa 1870-1915. 21/32". Mint (9.7). Price: $32. CyberAuction #337, Lot #27.

5748. SWIRL. Divided core. Four band core. Each is white, transparent pink, blue and transparent green. Outer layer is four sets of yellow bands. A couple of tiny pinpricks. Germany, circa 1870-1915. 29/32". Mint(-) (9.1). Price: $32. CyberAuction #345, Lot #43.

5749. SWIRL. Divided core. Superb. Three bands core. Each is the same pattern of pink and pale white on white. Outer layer is three sets of yellow strands. Germany, circa 1870-1915. 5/8". Mint (9.7). Price: $32. CyberAuction #347, Lot #12.

5750. SWIRL. Divided core. Three band core. Each is the same pattern of red, blue, green, yellow and white. Outer layer is three sets of yellow and white strands. Overall pitting. Germany, circa 1870-1915. 1-3/16". Good(+) (7.9). Price: $32. CyberAuction #352, Lot #38.

5751. SWIRL. Divided core. Very lightly tinted blue base. Four band core. Two are green and pink on yellow, two are pink and blue on white. Outer layer is two sets of white strands and two sets of yellow strands. Germany, circa 1870-1915. 7/8". Mint (9.6). Price: $32. CyberAuction #360, Lot #24.

5752. SWIRL. Divided core. Gorgeous. Core is four fat bands. Two are pink on white, one is blue on white, one is green on yellow. Outer layer is two sets of white strands, alternating with two sets of yellow strands. Tiny subsurface moon and two tiny pits. Germany, circa 1870-1915. 15/16". Near Mint(+) (8.7). Price: $32. CyberAuction #365, Lot #19.

5753. SWIRL. Divided core. Three band core. One is blue on white, one is green on white, one is purple on white. Outer layer is three sets of white and yellow strands. A number of small and tiny subsurface moons. Germany, circa 1870-1915. 1-3/16". Near Mint(-) (8.1). Price: $32. CyberAuction #368, Lot #25.

5754. SWIRL. Divided core. Three band core. Each is a blue, pink, yellow, green on white. Outer layer is three sets of yellow and white strands. Small subsurface moon and some pitting. 15/16". Near Mint (8.6). Price: $32. CyberAuction #390, Lot #29.

5755. SWIRL. Divided core. Three band core. Various combinations of orange/red, yellow, white and green. Outer layer is three bands. Each is orange and white strands. Odd marble. Very nice. Germany, circa 1870-1915. 25/32". Mint (9.8). Price: $32. CyberAuction #390, Lot #39.

5756. SWIRL. Divided core. Large divided core swirl. Three band core. Pink, green and yellow, blue, pink and white, pink, green and white. Outer layer is three sets of white strands. Small chip, couple of small subsurface moons. Germany, circa 1870-1915. 1-5/8". Near Mint(-) (8.1). Price: $32. CyberAuction #394, Lot #20.

5757. SWIRL. Divided core. Three band core. Each is a blue, pink, yellow, green on white. Outer layer is three sets of yellow and white strands. Small subsurface moon and some pitting. 15/16". Near Mint (8.6). Price: $32. CyberAuction #408, Lot #14.

5758. SWIRL. Divided core. Four band core. Two are red edged by white, one green edged by orange, one blue edged by orange. Outer layer is two sets of red strands and two sets of pale white strands. Rare coloring. One melt area near the bottom pontil, a couple of tiny melt pits elsewhere. Germany, possibly England, circa 1870-1915. 23/32". Mint(-) (9.1). Price: $32. CyberAuction #410, Lot #43.

5759. SWIRL. Divided core. Three band core. Each is pink, blue, green and white. Outer layer is three sets of white strands. Germany, circa 1870-1915. 27/32". Mint (9.6). Price: $32. CyberAuction #414, Lot #12.

5760. SWIRL. Divided core. Gorgeous. Core is four fat bands. Two are pink on white, one is blue on white, one is green on yellow. Outer layer is two sets of white strands, alternating with two sets of yellow strands. Tiny subsurface moon and two tiny pits. Germany, circa 1870-1915. 15/16". Near Mint(+) (8.7). Price: $32. CyberAuction #430, Lot #51.

5761. SWIRL. Divided core. Three band core. Various combinations of orange/red, yellow, white and green. Outer layer is three bands. Each is orange and white strands. Odd marble. Very nice. Germany, circa 1870-1915. 25/32". Mint (9.8). Price: $32. CyberAuction #449, Lot #43.

5762. SWIRL. Divided core. Four band core. Two are pink and blue on white. One is pink and green on white. One is white with a little pink and green. Outer layer is two sets of white strands, and one set of yellow and white strand. Other yellow/white set is missing. Two tiny subsurface moons. Germany, circa 1870-1915. 1-3/16". Near Mint(+) (8.7). Price: $32. CyberAuction #451, Lot #7.

5763. SWIRL. Divided core. Three band core. Each is a blue, pink, yellow, green on white. Outer layer is three sets of yellow and white strands. Small subsurface moon and some pitting. 15/16". Near Mint (8.6). Price: $32. CyberAuction #454, Lot #39.

5764. SWIRL. Divided core. Three band core. One each of blue/white, red/white, green/yellow. Outer layer is three sets of yellow and white strands. Almost identical to Lot #30 in this auction, slightly different outer series. Germany, circa 1870-1915. 25/32". Mint (9.8). Price: $32. CyberAuction #475, Lot #42.

5765. SWIRL. Divided core. Three band core. Each is red and green on yellow. Outer layer is three bands. Each is pink and blue on white. Super design. Two small melt spots. Germany, circa 1870-1915. 7/8". Mint(-) (9.2). Price: $32. CyberAuction #480, Lot #43.

5766. SWIRL. Divided core. Three band core. Each is pink, blue, green, yellow and white. Outer layer is three sets of yellow strands. Some tiny chips, tiny moons and tiny subsurface moons. Germany, circa 1870-1915. 1-13/16". Near Mint(-) (8.2). Price: $32. CyberAuction #492, Lot #31.

5767. SWIRL. Divided core. Three band core. Each is red and green on yellow. Outer layer is three bands. Each is pink and blue on white. Super design. Two small melt spots. Germany, circa 1870-1915. 7/8". Mint(-) (9.2). Price: $32. CyberAuction #499, Lot #41.

5768. SWIRL. Divided core. Three band core. Each is white band with light blue and dark red on it. Outer layer is three bands of yellow and white. Very interesting marble. Germany, circa 1870-1915. 25/32". Mint (9.7). Price: $32. CyberAuction #501, Lot #48.

5769. SWIRL. Divided core. Very nice marble. Four band core. Each is the same pattern of red, blue, green and white. Outer layer is four sets of white strands. Germany, possibly England, circa 1870-1920. 5/8". Mint (9.7). Price: $31. CyberAuction #338, Lot #26.

5770. SWIRL. Divided core. Alternating yellow and white latticinio strands in divided form. Three band core. Outer layer is three bands, each is blue and white. Teardrop center. Several tiny sparkles, but still a super example. Germany, circa 1870-1915. 7/8". Near Mint(+) (8.9). Price: $31. CyberAuction #347, Lot #17.

5771. SWIRL. Divided core. Four band core. Two are yellow, two are white. Outer layer is two bands of transparent pink on white, one band of transparent blue on white, one band of transparent green on white. Thick outer casing. Gorgeous. One very tiny subsurface moon. Germany, circa 1870-1915. 7/8". Near Mint(+) (8.9). Price: $31. CyberAuction #356, Lot #37.

5772. SWIRL. Divided core. Lot of two marbles. Both are four band core with a yellow cage outer layer. 1-9/16" & Good (7.6). 1-7/8" & Good(-) (7.2). Price: $31. CyberAuction #446, Lot #35.

5773. SWIRL. Divided core. Three band core. Each is a different pattern of red, blue, yellow, green and white. Outer layer is three sets of white and yellow strands. Germany, possibly England, circa 1870-1915. 13/16". Mint (9.9). Price: $31. CyberAuction #479, Lot #21.

5774. SWIRL. Divided core. Unusual. Four very wide bands. One each of pink on white, green on yellow, blue on white, white (no color). Outer layer is a cage of yellow strands. Gorgeous. One pinprick. Germany, circa 1870-1915. 3/4". Mint (9.6). Price: $31. CyberAuction #485, Lot #57.

5775. SWIRL. Divided core. Superb marble. Three band core. Each is pink, green and blue on white. Outer layer is three sets of white strands. Almost no twist. Germany, circa 1870-1915. 25/32". Mint (9.9). Price: $30. CyberAuction #330, Lot #11.

5776. SWIRL. Divided core. Three band core. Each is pink on white, edged by green. Outer layer is three sets of white strands. Beauty. Sparkle and a melt spot. Germany, circa 1870-1915. 13/16". Mint(-) (9.0). Price: $30. CyberAuction #335, Lot #46.

5777. SWIRL. Divided core. Four band core. Two are orange, blue and white. Two are green and orange. Outer layer is two sets of white strands and two sets of yellow strands. Tiny moon and small subsurface moon. Germany, circa 1870-1915. 1-3/16". Near Mint (8.5). Price: $30. CyberAuction #350, Lot #32.

5778. SWIRL. Divided core. Four band core. Two are pink on white, one blue on white, one turquoise on white. Outer layer is two sets of white strands and two sets of yellow strands. Gorgeous marble! Germany, circa 1870-1915. 19/32". Mint (9.8). Price: $30. CyberAuction #373, Lot #35.

5779. SWIRL. Divided core. Three band core. Each is a blue, pink, yellow, green on white. Outer layer is three sets of yellow and white strands. Small subsurface moon and some pitting. 15/16". Near Mint (8.6). Price: $30. CyberAuction #426, Lot #13.

5780. SWIRL. Divided core. English type. Four band core. Two are yellow, two are white. Outer layer is four bands. Two are red and two are blue. Very colorful. One tiny pit. England, possibly Germany, circa 1870-1915. 13/16". Mint(-) (9.2). Price: $30. CyberAuction #459, Lot #13.

5781. SWIRL. Divided core. Three band core. Blue on white, red on white, green on yellow. Outer layer is three sets of yellow strands. One tiny pinprick. Germany, circa 1870-1915. 13/16". Mint (9.6). Price: $30. CyberAuction #475, Lot #30.

5782. SWIRL. Divided core. English type. Four band core. Two are yellow, two are white. Outer layer is four bands. Two are red and two are blue. Very colorful. One tiny pit. England, possibly Germany, circa 1870-1915. 13/16". Mint(-) (9.2). Price: $30. CyberAuction #496, Lot #8.

5783. SWIRL. Divided core. Three band core. Each is orange, yellow, blue, green and white. Outer layer is three sets of yellow and white strands. Germany, possibly England, circa 1927-1935. 21/32". Mint (9.8). Price: $30. CyberAuction #506, Lot #45.

5784. SWIRL. Divided core. Naked divided core swirl. Very nice example. Core is slightly malformed. Two panels each of opaque orange, opaque yellow, opaque white and transparent purple. Very pretty. In great shape. Germany, circa 1870-1915. 21/32". Mint (9.9). Price: $29. CyberAuction #330, Lot #2.

5785. SWIRL. Divided core. Four band core. Two are pink on white, one green on white, one blue on white. Outer layer is four sets of yellow strands. Germany, circa 1870-1915. 1/2". Mint (9.9). Price: $29. CyberAuction #376, Lot #25.

5786. SWIRL. Divided core. Rare. Divided core swirl of latticinio strands. Four band core. Two are yellow strands, two are white strands. Outer layer is eight bands of two different color schemes. One pit. Germany, circa 1870-1915. 25/32". Mint(-) (9.0). Price: $29. CyberAuction #381, Lot #30.

5787. SWIRL. Divided core. Four band core. Two are pink and green on yellow. Two are pink and blue on white. Outer layer is two sets of yellow strands and two sets of white strands. Surface in great shape. Germany, circa 1870-1915. 27/32". Mint (9.7). Price: $29. CyberAuction #489, Lot #12.

5788. SWIRL. Divided core. Four band core. Two are bright orange/red on white. One blue on white. Fourth is missing. Outer layer is three sets of bright orange strands. Again, a fourth set is missing. Beauty. Germany, possibly England, circa 1870-1915. 21/32". Mint (9.8). This marble matches the marble in Lot #22 in this auction. Buy the two for a matched pair. Price: $29. CyberAuction #495, Lot #34.

5789. SWIRL. Divided core. Rare design. Naked three band divided core swirl. Each band is the same pattern. Left to right: blue band, white strand, orange strand, white strand, pink band. Gorgeous. Germany, circa 1870-1915. 15/32". Mint (9.8). Price: $28. CyberAuction #363, Lot #10.

5790. SWIRL. Divided core. Nice English colors. Core is four bands. Two are blue and orange, two are red and white. Outer layer is four sets of white strands. One small melt spot. England, possibly Germany, circa 1880-1920. 21/32". Mint(-) (9.0). Price: $28. CyberAuction #374, Lot #13.

5791. SWIRL. Divided core. Three wide bands. Each is the same pattern of blue, white, red, green and yellow. English type. Outer layer is three sets of yellow and white strands. England, possibly Germany, circa 1870-1920. 21/32". Mint (9.8). Price: $28. CyberAuction #392, Lot #17.

5792. SWIRL. Divided core. Three band core. Outer layer is three sets of yellow strands. Very heavily polished. Germany, circa 1870-1915. 1-9/16". Price: $28. CyberAuction #416, Lot #41.

5793. SWIRL. Divided core. Three band core. Each is pink on yellow, blue on white, separated by green. Outer layer is three sets of white and red strands. Two tiny melt spots, one tiny manufacturing pit. Germany, circa 1870-1915. 7/8". Mint(-) (9.2). Price: $28. CyberAuction #451, Lot #51.

5794. SWIRL. Divided core. Core is four fat bands. Two are pink on white, two are pink on yellow. Outer layer is a cage of white strands. Overall light haze, some tiny chips and pits. Germany, circa 1870-1915. 1-5/8". Good (7.4). Price: $28. CyberAuction #497, Lot #25.

5795. SWIRL. Divided core. Four band core. Each band is a combination of blue, red, green and yellow on white. Outer layer is a cage of red strands. Rare. 11/16". Mint (9.7). Price: $27. CyberAuction #333, Lot #11.

5796. SWIRL. Divided core. Four band core. Very interesting coloring and construction. Two bands are pink and yellow, one is blue and white, one is green and white. Outer layer is two sets of white strands and two sets of yellow strands. Several tiny subsurface moons. Germany, circa 1870-1915. 29/32". Near Mint (8.6). Price: $27. CyberAuction #335, Lot #58.

5797. SWIRL. Divided core. Three band core. Two are pink and blue on white, one is pink and green on yellow. Outer layer is two sets of yellow and white strands. Appears to be very lightly buffed, pontils are pretty much intact. Germany, circa 1870-1915. 1". Price: $27. CyberAuction #364, Lot #2.

5798. SWIRL. Divided core. Four band core. Each same design of pink, blue and white. Outer layer is four sets of white strands. Heavily polished, fake pontils added. Germany, circa 1870-1915. 1-7/8". Price: $27. CyberAuction #417, Lot #18.

5799. SWIRL. Divided core. Four band core. Each is a complex pattern of red, blue, white, yellow and green. Outer layer is four bands of yellow and white strands. Superb example. Germany, circa 1870-1915. 27/32". Mint (9.8). Price: $27. CyberAuction #462, Lot #9.

5800. SWIRL. Divided core. Beauty. Four band core. Wide bands. Pink, green and yellow on white. Outer layer is four sets of white strands. Germany, circa 1870-1915. 23/32". Mint (9.8). Price: $27. CyberAuction #473, Lot #53.

5801. SWIRL. Divided core. Three band core. Wide bands. One is pink on yellow, edged by green. One blue on white, edged by pink. One green on white, edged by blue. Outer layer is three sets of yellow strands. Very nice marble. Germany, circa 1870-1915. 13/16". Mint (9.9). Price: $27. CyberAuction #486, Lot #38.

5802. SWIRL. Divided core. Naked divided core swirl. Bright colors. Three band core. Bright orange, blue on white, bright yellow. No outer layer. One tiny sparkle. England, possibly Germany, circa 1870-1915. 1/2". Mint (9.6). Price: $27. CyberAuction #487, Lot #47.

5803. SWIRL. Divided core. English type. Three band core. Each is red, blue and white. Outer layer is three sets of yellow strands. Beauty. England, possibly Germany, circa 1880-1920. 5/8". Mint (9.7). Price: $26. CyberAuction #345, Lot #1.

5804. SWIRL. Divided core. From near the beginning of the cane. Was supposed to be a four band core, but only has three bands. One is pink, blue and yellow. One is pink and yellow (missing the blue). One is blue and white (the other blue and white band is missing. Four outer bands. Two are sets of white strands, two are sets of yellow strands. Several small and tiny subsurface moons. Still, looks great. 1". Near Mint (8.4). Price: $26. CyberAuction #394, Lot #29.

5805. SWIRL. Divided core. From near the beginning of the cane. Was supposed to be a four band core, but only has three bands. One is pink, blue and yellow. One is pink and yellow (missing the blue). One is blue and white (the other blue and white band is missing. Four outer bands. Two are sets of white strands, two are sets of yellow strands. Several small and tiny subsurface moons. Still, looks great. 1". Near Mint (8.4). Price: $26. CyberAuction #422, Lot #38.

5806. SWIRL. Divided core. Four band divided core. Two are pink on yellow, two are green on yellow. Outer layer is a cage of white narrow bands. One pinprick. Germany, circa 1870-1915. 13/16". Mint (9.5). Price: $26. CyberAuction #475, Lot #7.

5807. SWIRL. Divided core. Three band core. Wide bands. One is pink on yellow, edged by green. One blue on white, edged by pink. One green on white, edged by blue. Outer layer is three sets of yellow strands. Very nice marble. Germany, circa 1870-1915. 13/16". Mint (9.9). Price: $26. CyberAuction #475, Lot #22.

5808. SWIRL. Divided core. Four band divided core. Two are pink on yellow, two are green on yellow. Outer layer is a cage of white narrow bands. One pinprick. Germany, circa 1870-1915. 13/16". Mint (9.5). Price: $26. CyberAuction #486, Lot #44.

5809. SWIRL. Divided core. Three band core. Each is green, white and red. Beautiful. Outer layer is three sets of bright orange strands. Stunning. Germany, possibly England, circa 1870-1915. 5/8". Mint (9.9). Price: $26. CyberAuction #495, Lot #15.

5810. SWIRL. Divided core. Four band core. Two bands are pink on white, two are green on white. Outer layer is a cage of yellow strands. Small chip. Several pits. Germany, circa 1870-1915. 7/8". Near Mint (8.3). Price: $25. CyberAuction #337, Lot #58.

5811. SWIRL. Divided core. Three band core. Transparent very lightly tinted green base. Each core band is red, white and green. Outer layer is six sets of yellow strands. Interesting. Several tiny pinpricks. Germany, circa 1870-1915. 25/32". Mint(-) (9.1). Price: $25. CyberAuction #343, Lot #58.

5812. SWIRL. Divided core. Four band divided core swirl. Two are pink, green and yellow. Two are pink, blue and white. Outer layer is two sets of white strands and two sets of yellow strands. In great shape. Beauty. Germany, circa 1870-1915. 7/8". Mint (9.8). Price: $25. CyberAuction #355, Lot #1.

5813. SWIRL. Divided core. Four band core. Each is pink on white. Outer layer is four sets of white strands. Several pits. Germany, circa 1870-1915. 31/32". Near Mint(+) (8.7). Price: $25. CyberAuction #355, Lot #42.

5814. SWIRL. Divided core. Three band core. Two are pink and blue on white, two are pink and green on yellow. Outer layer is two sets of white strands and two sets of yellow strands. One tiny moon. Germany, circa 1870-1915. 3/4". Near Mint(+) (8.9). Price: $25. CyberAuction #365, Lot #37.

5815. SWIRL. Divided core. Three band core. Two are pink and green on yellow, two are pink and blue on white. Outer layer is two sets of yellow strands alternating with two sets of yellow strands. Overall pitting and roughness. 1-1/16". Near Mint(-) (8.1). Price: $25. CyberAuction #371, Lot #24.

5816. SWIRL. Divided core. Three band core. Each is the same pattern of pink, blue, green, yellow and white. Outer layer is three sets of yellow and white strands. Nicely constructed. One small subsurface moon, several tiny

subsurface moons. Still, pretty. Germany, circa 1870-1915. 1-3/16". Near Mint(+) (8.8). Price: $25. CyberAuction #428, Lot #12.

5817. SWIRL. Divided core. Four band core. Two are pink, yellow, blue and white. Two are pink, yellow, green and white. Outer layer is three sets of white strands. A couple of sparkles, but a beauty. Germany, circa 1870-1915. 15/16". Mint(-) (9.0). Price: $25. CyberAuction #434, Lot #32.

5818. SWIRL. Divided core. Three band core. Each is pink, blue, white and yellow. Outer layer is three bands of yellow and white strands. Several very tiny chips in one area. Germany, circa 1870-1915. 1-1/16". Near Mint (8.6). Price: $25. CyberAuction #440, Lot #23.

5819. SWIRL. Divided core. From near the beginning of the cane. Was supposed to be a four band core, but only has three bands. One is pink, blue and yellow. One is pink and yellow (missing the blue). One is blue and white (the other blue and white band is missing. Four outer bands. Two are sets of white strands, two are sets of yellow strands. Several small and tiny subsurface moons. Still, looks great. 1". Near Mint (8.4). Price: $25. CyberAuction #456, Lot #37.

5820. SWIRL. Divided core. Four band core. Two are yellow and green edged by red. Two are blue and white, edged by red. Outer layer is a cage of white strands. Heavy outer casing of clear. Some cold roll lines. Germany, circa 1870-1915. 7/8". Mint (9.6). Price: $25. CyberAuction #459, Lot #34.

5821. SWIRL. Divided core. Four band core. Each is blue stripe on white, edged by pink. Outer layer is a cage of yellow and white strands. Overall chips. Germany, circa 1870-1915. 2-1/4". Good(-) (7.1). Price: $25. CyberAuction #476, Lot #25.

5822. SWIRL. Divided core. Latticinio strands in divided form. Three bands. Each is yellow strands. Outer layer is three pink on white bands, mirroring the core spaces. Thick outer layer. Tiny chipping and one large chip. Germany, circa 1870-1915. 1-15/16". Good(-) (7.3). Price: $25. CyberAuction #477, Lot #39.

5823. SWIRL. Divided core. Three band core. Each is yellow, red and blue. Three sets of white strands. Germany, possibly England, circa 1870-1915. 21/32". Mint (9.9). Price: $25. CyberAuction #487, Lot #32.

5824. SWIRL. Divided core. Three band core. Each is blue and pink on yellow. Outer layer is three sets of yellow strands. Lightly buffed. Pontils intact, damage remains. Germany, circa 1870-1915. 1-1/8". Price: $24. CyberAuction #331, Lot #32.

5825. SWIRL. Divided core. Three band core. Each is red on white, edged by blue. Outer layer is three sets of white and yellow strands. Germany, circa 1870-1915. 5/8". Mint (9.8). Price: $24. CyberAuction #333, Lot #20.

5826. SWIRL. Divided core. Three band core. Each is red and white. Each band is turned slightly, vane-style. Outer layer is three sets of yellow strands. Odd coloring. Germany, circa 1870-1915. 3/4". Mint (9.7). Price: $24. CyberAuction #333, Lot #37.

5827. SWIRL. Divided core. Four band core. Each is the same pattern of pink, blue, yellow, green and white. Outer layer is three sets of white strands. Overall tiny chipping and pitting. Germany, circa 1870-1915. 1-3/16". Good (7.4). Price: $24. CyberAuction #347, Lot #23.

5828. SWIRL. Divided core. Superior example. Three band. One each of turquoise on white, blue on white, pink on white. Outer layer is three sets of white strands. Superb. Germany, circa 1870-1915. 21/32". Mint (9.9). Price: $24. CyberAuction #359, Lot #11.

5829. SWIRL. Divided core. Four band core. Two are pink bands on white, one is blue bands on white, one is green bands on white. Outer layer is two sets of white strands and two sets of yellow strands. Gorgeous. Germany, circa 1870-1915. 23/32". Mint (9.8). Price: $24. CyberAuction #369, Lot #45.

5830. SWIRL. Divided core. Gorgeous marble. Four band core. Two are pink on white, two are green on white. Outer layer is a cage of white strands. Ground pontil. Beauty. Germany, circa 1870-1915. 25/32". Mint (9.7). Price: $24. CyberAuction #429, Lot #6.

5831. SWIRL. Divided core. Four band core. Two are orange, blue and white. Two are green and orange. Outer layer is two sets of white strands and two sets of yellow strands. Tiny moon and small subsurface moon. Germany, circa 1870-1915. 1-3/16". Near Mint (8.5). Price: $24. CyberAuction #451, Lot #17.

5832. SWIRL. Divided core. Three layer marble. Four band core. Two are pink on white, one is green on yellow, one is blue on white. Outer layer is a cage of yellow strands in two separate layers. Tight twist. Beauty. One pit. Germany, circa 1870-1915. 11/16". Mint (9.5). Price: $23. CyberAuction #332, Lot #34.

5833. SWIRL. Divided core. Interesting three band core. Each is a transparent purple band, edged by yellow and blue. Surrounded by a small cage of white strands. Thick outer casing. Germany, circa 1870-1915. 5/8". Mint (9.7). Price: $23. CyberAuction #337, Lot #13.

5834. SWIRL. Divided core. Naked divided core swirl. Three band core. Wide core. Each band is white with blue strands, edged by pink. No outer layer. Two tiny chips, next to each other. Beauty. Germany, circa 1870-1915. 3/4". Near Mint(+) (8.9). Price: $23. CyberAuction #345, Lot #6.

5835. SWIRL. Divided core. Three band core. Each is the same pattern of blue, pink and green on white. Outer layer is three sets of yellow strands. Thick outer clear casing. Buffed, pontils remain. Germany, circa 1870-1915. 3/4". Mint. Price: $23. CyberAuction #362, Lot #58.

5836. SWIRL. Divided core. Very odd. Four band core. Two are semi-opaque white, two are opaque yellow. There are four bands floating just above the core. Two are orange and two are transparent green. No outer layer, thick outer casing of clear. A number of chips on the surface. Germany, circa 1870-1915. 29/32". Good (7.5). Price: $23. CyberAuction #398, Lot #19.

5837. SWIRL. Divided core. Naked divided core from near an end of the cane. Transparent clear base. Three yellow bands and two partial white bands in it. Germany, circa 1870-1915. 17/32". Mint (9.8). Price: $23. CyberAuction #455, Lot #49.

5838. SWIRL. Divided core. Three band core. From near an end of the cane. Pink on yellow, blue on white, green on white with "chunky" fiery aventurine. Outer layer is one set of yellow strands. One tiny chip. Germany, circa 1870-1915. 25/32". Near Mint(+) (8.9). Price: $23. CyberAuction #480, Lot #31.

5839. SWIRL. Divided core. Three band core. Each is red, green and blue, on white. Outer layer is three sets of white and yellow strands. Beautiful. Germany, possibly England, circa 1870-1915. 19/32". Mint (9.8). Price: $23. CyberAuction #483, Lot #6.

5840. SWIRL. Divided core. Stunning core. Three bands. Each is green, white, orange, yellow and black band. Outer layer is three sets of alternating orange and white strands. Germany, circa 1870-1915. 5/8". Mint (9.8). Price: $23. CyberAuction #495, Lot #25.

5841. SWIRL. Divided core. Four band core. Two are pink and blue on white. Two are pink and green on yellow. Outer layer is four sets of white and yellow strands. Very interesting color design. Germany, circa 1870-1915. 25/32". Mint (9.7). Price: $23. CyberAuction #508, Lot #32.

5842. SWIRL. Divided core. Latticinio strands in divided core form. Yellow latticinio. Outer layer is three bands. Each is blue and white. A small chip, some pitting, some haziness. Germany, circa 1870-1915. 15/16". Near Mint(-) (8.2). Price: $22. CyberAuction #337, Lot #22.

5843. SWIRL. Divided core. Nice marble. Three band core. One each of pink on white, green on white, blue on white. Outer layer is three sets of yellow strands. Tight twist. One tiny sparkle. Germany, circa 1870-1915. 21/32". Mint(-) (9.2). Price: $22. CyberAuction #353, Lot #3.

5844. SWIRL. Divided core. Three layer divided core. Three band core. Each is pink and blue bands on white. Middle layer is three sets of narrow bands of green on yellow. Outer layer is three sets of white strands. Small chip. Gorgeous. Germany, circa 1870-1915. 3/4". Near Mint (8.6). Price: $22. CyberAuction #358, Lot #58.

5845. SWIRL. Divided core. Three band core. Each is pink, green and yellow. Outer layer is three sets of white strands. One tiny sparkle. Germany, circa 1870-1915. 29/32". Mint(-) (9.1). Price: $22. CyberAuction #360, Lot #14.

5846. SWIRL. Divided core. Three band core. Each is pink, blue, white and yellow. Outer layer is three bands of yellow and white strands. Several very tiny chips in one area. Germany, circa 1870-1915. 1-1/16". Near Mint (8.6). Price: $22. CyberAuction #382, Lot #8.

5847. SWIRL. Divided core. Very lightly tinted blue base. Core is six bands. Three are green on white, three are blue on white. Outer layer is three sets of white strands. Almost no twist. Nice one. Manufacturing chip. Germany, circa 1870-1915. 21/32". Mint (9.5). Price: $22. CyberAuction #443, Lot #28.

5848. SWIRL. Divided core. Three band core. Red and green on yellow. Fiery aventurine on the green. Outer layer is three sets of white strands. Minor pinpricks. Germany, circa 1870-1915. 19/32". Near Mint(+) (8.9). Price: $22. CyberAuction #444, Lot #2.

5849. SWIRL. Divided core. Four band core. Two are white, two are yellow. Outer layer is four bands. Two are green on white, two are blue on white. Several small and tiny subsurface moons. Germany, circa 1870-1915. 1-3/16". Near Mint (8.3). Price: $22. CyberAuction #451, Lot #59.

5850. SWIRL. Divided core. Four band core. Two are on yellow, one is blue on white, one is green on white. Outer layer is two sets of white strands and one set of yellow strands. There is a second set of yellow strands missing. Germany, circa 1870-1915. 13/16". Mint (9.5). Price: $22. CyberAuction #455, Lot #46.

5851. SWIRL. Divided core. Four band core. Two bands each of a complex pattern. Outer layer is four sets of yellow strands. Some small chipping, mostly on one side. Germany, circa 1870-1915. 1-1/2". Good (7.4). Price: $22. CyberAuction #477, Lot #36.

5852. SWIRL. Divided core. Four band core. Two are pink on yellow, edged by blue. Two are pink on white, edged by blue. Outer layer is four sets of yellow strands. Beauty. One pit. Germany, circa 1870-1915. 29/32". Mint(-) (9.2). Price: $22. CyberAuction #481, Lot #21.

5853. SWIRL. Divided core. Three band core. One each of pink on yellow, green on white, blue on white. Outer layer is a cage of white strands. Germany, circa 1870-1915. 25/32". Mint (9.7). Price: $22. CyberAuction #494, Lot #28.

5854. SWIRL. Divided core. Three band core. One each of pink on white, blue on white, turquoise on white. Outer layer is three sets of white strands. Nice marble. Germany, circa 1870-1915. 29/32". Mint (9.6). Price: $22. CyberAuction #497, Lot #22.

5855. SWIRL. Divided core. Four band core. Two are white band. Two have pink and blue bands on it, two have pink and turquoise bands. Outer layer is four sets of yellow strands. Germany, circa 1870-1915. 11/16". Mint (9.9). Price: $22. CyberAuction #504, Lot #32.

5856. SWIRL. Divided core. Four band core. Two are pink, yellow and white. Two are blue, pink and yellow. Outer layer is two sets of yellow strands and two sets of white strands. Germany, circa 1870s-1915. 5/8". Mint (9.6). Price: $21. CyberAuction #354, Lot #37.

5857. SWIRL. Divided core. Three band divided core. Two are blue and pink on white, one is pink and green on yellow. Outer layer is three sets of white strands. Germany, circa 1870-1915. 1/2". Mint (9.9). Price: $21. CyberAuction #371, Lot #27.

5858. SWIRL. Divided core. Three band core. One each of pink and green on white, blue on white, green on yellow. Outer layer is three sets of yellow strands. Very nice. Germany, circa 1870-1915. 3/4". Mint (9.7). Price: $21. CyberAuction #452, Lot #1.

5859. SWIRL. Divided core. Three band core. Each is pink, blue, white and yellow. Outer layer is three bands of yellow and white strands. Several very tiny chips in one area. Germany, circa 1870-1915. 1-1/16". Near Mint (8.6). Price: $21. CyberAuction #453, Lot #47.

5860. SWIRL. Divided core. Three banded divided core. Each is red, blue, green and yellow. Outer layer is three sets of yellow and white strands. Germany, circa 1870-1915. 5/8". Mint (9.7). Price: $21. CyberAuction #479, Lot #17.

5861. SWIRL. Divided core. English type. Three band core. One each of light blue, yellow, white. Outer layer is six bands. Three light green, three red. One melt chip where the marble touched another when hot. England, possibly Germany, circa 1870-1915. 11/16". Mint(-) (9.0). Price: $21. CyberAuction #494, Lot #32.

5862. SWIRL. Divided core. Four band core. Two are green and white, two are white, yellow orange and blue. Outer layer is two sets of orange strands and two sets of white strands. One chip. Germany, circa 1870-1915. 29/32". Near Mint (8.6). Price: $20. CyberAuction #351, Lot #2.

5863. SWIRL. Divided core. Base is tinted slightly blue. Core is four bands. Two are red, blue and white. Two are green, yellow and red. Outer layer is four sets of white strands. One small chip, several pits. Germany, circa 1870-1915. 25/32". Near Mint (8.5). Price: $20. CyberAuction #351, Lot #34.

5864. SWIRL. Divided core. Three band core. Each is pink and green on white. Outer layer is three sets of white strands. Germany, circa 1870-1915. 15/32". Mint (9.7). Price: $20. CyberAuction #354, Lot #3.

5865. SWIRL. Divided core. Three band core. One each of green/yellow, pink/yellow, blue/white. Outer layer is six wispy strands. Thick outer casing of clear. Small subsurface moon, overall pitting. Germany, circa 1870-1915. 1-1/8". Good(+) (7.9). Price: $20. CyberAuction #419, Lot #1.

5866. SWIRL. Divided core. Narrow core. Three bands. Each is red and yellow. Outer layer is two bands of wispy yellow. Germany, circa 1870-1915. 25/32". Mint (9.6). Price: $20. CyberAuction #443, Lot #19.

5867. SWIRL. Divided core. Gorgeous marble. Three band core. One each of red on white, blue on white, green on white. Outer layer is three sets of yellow strands. One cold roll line. Germany, circa 1870-1915. 5/8". Mint (9.6). Price: $20. CyberAuction #467, Lot #23.

5868. SWIRL. Divided core. Four band core. Two are pink and white. One is blue, pink and white. One is blue, green and white. Outer layer is four sets of yellow strands. Germany, circa 1870-1915. 11/16". Mint (9.7). Price: $20. CyberAuction #467, Lot #43.

5869. SWIRL. Divided core. From near and end of the cane. Was intended as a four-band core. Two bands are missing. A blue, yellow and white is present. Parts of a pink and a green are there. Outer layer is four sets of white strands. One pinprick. Germany, circa 1870-1915. 29/32". Mint (9.5). Price: $20. CyberAuction #471, Lot #19.

5870. SWIRL. Divided core. From near and end of the cane. Was intended as a four-band core. Two bands are missing. A blue, yellow and white is present. Parts of a pink and a green are there. Outer layer is four sets of white strands. One pinprick. Germany, circa 1870-1915. 29/32". Mint (9.5). Price: $20. CyberAuction #486, Lot #15.

5871. SWIRL. Divided core. Three band core. One each of green/yellow, pink/yellow, blue/white. Outer layer is six wispy strands. Thick outer casing of clear. Small subsurface moon, overall pitting. Germany, circa 1870-1915. 1-1/8". Good(+) (7.9). Price: $20. CyberAuction #486, Lot #4.

5872. SWIRL. Divided core. Naked divided core swirl. Three bands. Each is green, white, red and yellow. All are bright colors. No outer layer. Germany, possibly England, circa 1870-1915. 5/8". Mint (9.7). Price: $20. CyberAuction #495, Lot #27.

5873. SWIRL. Divided core. Four band core. Two are blue and white, two are orange and white. One of the blue is partial. Outer layer is four sets of white strands. From near an end of the cane. In very nice shape. One melt spot. Germany, circa 1870-1915. 25/32". Mint(-) (9.2). Price: $19. CyberAuction #338, Lot #44.

5874. SWIRL. Divided core. English type marble. Four bands, set very closely together. Two are red, white and blue. Two are green, red and yellow. Outer layer is four sets of yellow and white strands. One set is missing. England, possibly Germany, circa 1870-1915. 21/32". Mint (9.9). Price: $19. CyberAuction #345, Lot #12.

5875. SWIRL. Divided core. Three band core. One is blue and white, one is pink and white, one it turquoise and white. Outer layer is a cage of white strands. Germany, circa 1870-1915. 23/32". Mint (9.7). Price: $19. CyberAuction #350, Lot #3.

5876. SWIRL. Divided core. From near an end of the cane. Core is six narrow bands. Three are pink on white, three are green on yellow. Several white strands as the outer layer. Everything is somewhat jumbled. Germany, circa 1870-1915. 17/32". Mint (9.7). Price: $19. CyberAuction #374, Lot #38.

5877. SWIRL. Divided core. Very interesting marble. Yellow latticinio in divided form. Three band core. Outer layer is three red and white bands. Slight blue tint to the base glass. Thick casing of clear. Beauty. Germany, circa 1870-1915. 11/16". Mint (9.6). Price: $19. CyberAuction #441, Lot #10.

5878. SWIRL. Divided core. Four band core. Two are pink and blue on white, two are pink and green on white. Outer layer is two sets of white strands and two sets of yellow strands. Tiny chip, some pits. Germany, circa 1870-1915. 1-1/16". Near Mint(-) (8.2). Price: $19. CyberAuction #442, Lot #13.

5879. SWIRL. Divided core. Three band core. Each is pink and blue on white. Outer layer is three sets of white strands. Germany, circa 1870-1915. 17/32". Mint (9.7). Price: $19. CyberAuction #443, Lot #34.

5880. SWIRL. Divided core. Three band core. Each is red, green and white.

Outer layer is three sets of white strands. Germany, circa 1870-1915. 21/32". Mint (9.9). Price: $19. CyberAuction #475, Lot #38.

5881. SWIRL. Divided core. Three band core. Each is pink, blue and green, on white. Outer layer is three sets of yellow and white strands. Germany, circa 1870-1915. 13/16". Mint (9.7). Price: $19. CyberAuction #476, Lot #8.

5882. SWIRL. Divided core. English colors. Three band core. Each is blue and white band on red, edged by olive green. Outer layer is three sets of yellow strands. Superb. England, possibly Germany, circa 1870-1915. 19/32". Mint (9.9). Price: $19. CyberAuction #483, Lot #14.

5883. SWIRL. Divided core. Three band core. Each is green, red, blue and yellow. Outer layer is three sets of white strands. Several tiny melt spots on one side. Germany, possibly England, circa 1870-1915. 5/8". Mint(-) (9.2). Price: $19. CyberAuction #495, Lot #42.

5884. SWIRL. Divided core. Four band divided core swirl. Two are blue on white, two are pink on white. Outer layer is four white strands. More than double twisted, so it looks caged. Slight cold roll line, some light haze. Germany, circa 1870-1915. 1-1/16". Near Mint (8.5). Price: $19. CyberAuction #497, Lot #38.

5885. SWIRL. Divided core. Four band core. Two are pink on white, one blue on white, one green on yellow. Outer layer is two sets of yellow strands and two sets of white strands. Germany, circa 1870-1915. 11/16". Mint (9.7). Price: $19. CyberAuction #502, Lot #8.

5886. SWIRL. Divided core. Four band core. Each band is blue on white. Outer layer is a cage of yellow strands. Thick outer casing. Very nice. One small subsurface moon, some pits. Germany, circa 1870-1915. 7/8". Near Mint (8.5). Price: $17. CyberAuction #331, Lot #47.

5887. SWIRL. Divided core. Three band core. Each is dark purple edged by white. Outer layer is three sets of white strands. Germany, circa 1870-1915. 17/32". Mint (9.8). Price: $17. CyberAuction #333, Lot #19.

5888. SWIRL. Divided core. Very interesting marble from near an end of the cane. Core is a couple of narrow bands of yellow, one has green on it. Outer layer is one white strands and two stretched green bands. From near an end of the core, very unusual. Germany, circa 1870-1915. 19/32". Mint (9.9). Price: $17. CyberAuction #335, Lot #13.

5889. SWIRL. Divided core. Naked divided core swirl. Four band core. Bands are packed close together. Two are pink and green on yellow, two are pink and blue on white. Very nice. One pit. Germany, circa 1870-1915. 19/32". Mint(-) (9.2). Price: $17. CyberAuction #338, Lot #39.

5890. SWIRL. Divided core. Transparent slightly milky base. Four band core. Two are pink on white, two are green on yellow. Outer layer is two sets of white strands and two sets of yellow strands. Several tiny moons and chips. Odd. Germany, circa 1870-1915. 1". Near Mint(-) (8.1). Price: $17. CyberAuction #346, Lot #51.

5891. SWIRL. Divided core. Three band core. One is light blue and orange on white, one is blue and pink on white and green, one is pink and green on yellow. Outer layer is three sets of yellow and white strands. Fracture on one side running pole to pole. Germany, circa 1870-1915. 1-1/16". Good(+) (7.9). Price: $17. CyberAuction #349, Lot #49.

5892. SWIRL. Divided core. Four band core. Two are pink and green on yellow. Two are pink and blue on white. Outer layer is four sets of yellow and white strands. Some pitting. Germany, circa 1870-1915. 27/32". Near Mint (8.6). Price: $17. CyberAuction #358, Lot #28.

5893. SWIRL. Divided core. Super naked divided core swirl. Four band core. Two bands of pink on yellow, one of blue on white, one of green on white. No outer layer. Superb. Germany, circa 1870-1915. 1/2". Mint (9.7). Price: $17. CyberAuction #359, Lot #12.

5894. SWIRL. Divided core. Very odd. Four band core. Two are semi-opaque white, two are opaque yellow. There are four bands floating just above the core. Two are orange and two are transparent green. No outer layer, thick outer casing of clear. A number of chips on the surface. Germany, circa 1870-1915. 29/32". Good (7.5). Price: $17. CyberAuction #367, Lot #5.

5895. SWIRL. Divided core. Four band core. Two bands are blue on white, two are pink on yellow. Outer layer is two white strands and two yellow strands. Some pits and sparkles. Germany, circa 1870-1915. 13/16". Near Mint(+) (8.7). Price: $17. CyberAuction #382, Lot #3.

5896. SWIRL. Divided core. Three band core. Each is blue and yellow on white, edged by blue. Wide bands. Outer layer is three sets of white strands. Overall small chips and subsurface moons. Germany, circa 1870-1915. 1-9/16". Good(-) (7.0). Price: $17. CyberAuction #382, Lot #31.

5897. SWIRL. Divided core. Three band core. Each is pink and blue on white. Outer layer is three sets of yellow strands. Germany, circa 1870-1915. 1/2". Mint (9.9). Price: $17. CyberAuction #388, Lot #42.

5898. SWIRL. Divided core. Four band core. Two are pink, yellow, blue and white. Two are pink, yellow, green and white. Outer layer is three sets of white strands. A couple of sparkles, but a beauty. Germany, circa 1870-1915. 15/16". Mint(-) (9.0). Price: $17. CyberAuction #399, Lot #16.

5899. SWIRL. Divided core. Very interesting marble. Yellow latticinio in divided form. Three band core. Outer layer is three red and white bands. Slight blue tint to the base glass. Thick casing of clear. Beauty. Germany, circa 1870-1915. 11/16". Mint (9.6). Price: $17. CyberAuction #402, Lot #28.

5900. SWIRL. Divided core. Three band core. Two are turquoise and pink on white, other is turquoise, blue and pink on white. Outer layer is three sets of white strands. Overall scratches. Germany, circa 1870-1915. 1-1/16". Near Mint(-) (8.2). Price: $17. CyberAuction #407, Lot #57.

5901. SWIRL. Divided core. Three band core. Each band is red, yellow, green, blue and white. Outer layer is three sets of white strands. Beauty. Germany, circa 1870-1915. 9/16". Mint (9.7). Price: $17. CyberAuction #414, Lot #43.

5902. SWIRL. Divided core. Three band core. Two are pink and blue on white. One is pink and green on yellow. Outer layer is six sets of yellow strands. One tiny melt spot. Super marble. Germany, circa 1870-1915. 23/32". Mint (9.5). Price: $17. CyberAuction #414, Lot #47.

5903. SWIRL. Divided core. Four band core. Bright colors. Two bands of red on white, one of blue on white, one of green on white. Outer layer is a cage of yellow strands. One melt area. Gorgeous. Germany, circa 1870-1915. 3/4". Mint(-) (9.2). Price: $17. CyberAuction #417, Lot #44.

5904. SWIRL. Divided core. English type. Three band core. Each is bright red and bright white. Outer layer is three sets of yellow strands. Two tiny sparkles. Gorgeous. England, possibly Germany, circa 1870-1920. 11/16" Mint(-) (9.0). Price: $17. CyberAuction #422, Lot #51.

5905. SWIRL. Divided core. Three band core. Odd. Two are pink and blue on white. Other is a white strand flanked by an orange/red band on each side. Outer layer is three sets of yellow and white strands. Germany, circa 1870-1915. 9/16". Mint (9.8). Price: $17. CyberAuction #424, Lot #40.

5906. SWIRL. Divided core. Four band core. Two are pink and yellow, one blue and white, one green and white. Outer layer is two sets of white strands and two sets of yellow strands. Small chips and overall haze. Germany, circa 1870-1915. 1-5/8". Good (7.5). Price: $17. CyberAuction #446, Lot #27.

5907. SWIRL. Divided core. Three band core. One each of blue on white, pink on white, green on white. Outer layer is three sets of yellow strands. Small manufacturing pit. Germany, circa 1870-1915. 25/32". Mint(-) (9.0) Price: $17. CyberAuction #451, Lot #22.

5908. SWIRL. Divided core. Three band core. One green on white, one pink on white, one blue on white. Outer layer is three sets of white strands. Out of round. Overall very light haze with some pitting and tiny chips. Germany, circa 1870-1915. 1-3/16". Good(+) (7.7). Price: $17 CyberAuction #451, Lot #41.

5909. SWIRL. Divided core. Four band core. Two are blue on white, two are green on white. Outer layer is four sets of white strands. Germany, circa 1870-1915. 21/32". Mint (9.9). Price: $17. CyberAuction #452, Lot #29.

5910. SWIRL. Divided core. Three band core. One each of pink on yellow, green on white, blue on white. Outer layer is a cage of white strands. Germany, circa 1870-1915. 25/32". Mint (9.7). Price: $17. CyberAuction #463, Lot #19.

5911. SWIRL. Divided core. English colors. Three band core. Each is green white, red, blue and yellow. Outer layer is three sets of yellow and white strands. Melt line on one side. Very pretty. England, possibly Germany circa 1870-1915. 19/32". Mint(-) (9.0). Price: $17. CyberAuction #487 Lot #15.

5912. SWIRL. Divided core. Four band core. Two bands are pink and turquoise on white, two are blue and pink on white. Outer layer is four sets of yellow strands. Small subsurface moon, some tiny pinpricks. Germany, circa 1870-1915. 15/16". Near Mint(+) (8.7). Price: $17. CyberAuction #491, Lot #48.

5913. SWIRL. Divided core. Lightly tinted blue base. Three band core. Each is yellow, pink and blue on white. Outer layer is three sets of white strands. Germany, circa 1870-1915. 1/2". Mint (9.9). Price: $17 CyberAuction #495, Lot #10.

5914. SWIRL. Divided core. Three band core. Each is red, green, blue white and yellow. Outer layer is three bands of red and white strands. Small fracture and a couple of small and tiny subsurface moons. Germany, circa 1870-1915. 29/32". Near Mint (8.3). Price: $17. CyberAuction #498, Lot #42.

5915. SWIRL. Divided core. Three band core. Each is the same complex pattern of yellow, orange and blue. Outer layer is three sets of yellow strands. Germany, circa 1870-1915. 11/16". Mint (9.9). Price: $17. CyberAuction #501, Lot #50.

5916. SWIRL. Divided core. Three band core. Each is ruddy red, blue and white. Outer layer is six bands of pale yellow on one side of the marble. A couple of tiny subsurface moons. Germany, circa 1870-1915. 1-1/16". Near Mint(+) (8.7). Price: $17. CyberAuction #502, Lot #26.

5917. SWIRL. Divided core. Four band core. Each is white band, pink central band, edged by blue. Outer layer is three sets of strands (one set is missing). Each set is a white strand and two blue strands. Very unusual. Germany, circa 1870-1915. 1/2". Mint (9.7). Price: $17. CyberAuction #504, Lot #35.

5918. SWIRL. Divided core. Four band core. Two yellow, two white. Outer layer is four strands. Two are pink on white, one blue on white, one green or white. One sparkle. Germany, circa 1870-1915. 25/32". Mint(-) (9.0). Price: $17. CyberAuction #508, Lot #26.

5919. SWIRL. Divided core. I think it was a naked divided core. From near an end of the cane. Three bands in the marbles. One blue on white, one green on white, one wispy yellow. Germany, circa 1870-1915. 27/32". Mint (9.4). Price: $16. CyberAuction #336, Lot #9.

5920. SWIRL. Divided core. Naked divided core swirl. Four bands. Two different schemes of pink, blue and white. No outer layer. A couple of pinpricks. Germany, circa 1870-1915. 5/8". Mint(-) (9.0). Price: $16. CyberAuction #347, Lot #9.

5921. SWIRL. Divided core. Four band core. Two are pink and blue on white. Other two are pink and green on yellow. Outer layer is two sets of yellow strands and two sets of white strands. One scratch. Germany, circa 1870-1915. 9/16". Mint(-) (9.1). Price: $16. CyberAuction #366, Lot #22.

5922. SWIRL. Divided core. Latticinio strands in divided form. Three bands of white latticinio. Outer layer is three transparent green bands, set to mirror the core bands. Thick outer casing. Germany, circa 1870-1915. 11/16". Mint (9.5). Price: $16. CyberAuction #428, Lot #38.

5923. SWIRL. Divided core. Four band core. Two red and white, one blue nd white, one green and white. Outer layer is four yellow strands. One nelt spot. Germany, circa 1870-1915. 5/8". Mint(-) (9.0). Price: $15. CyberAuction #333, Lot #45.

924. **SWIRL. Divided core.** Three band core. Each band is pink, blue and reen on white. Outer layer is three sets of white strands. One tiny sparkle. Germany, circa 1870-1915. 5/8". Mint(-) (9.2). Price: $15. CyberAuction #356, Lot #10.

925. **SWIRL. Divided core.** Beauty. Three band core. Each is a white and with light blue, pink and turquoise bands on it. Outer layer is three airs of white strands. One tiny subsurface moon. Germany, circa 1870-915. 3/4". Near Mint(+) (8.9). Price: $15. CyberAuction #357, Lot #44.

926. **SWIRL. Divided core.** English type. Three band core. Each is bright ed and bright white. Outer layer is three sets of yellow strands. Two tiny parkles. Gorgeous. England, possibly Germany, circa 1870-1920. 11/16". Mint(-) (9.0). Price: $15. CyberAuction #365, Lot #14.

927. **SWIRL. Divided core.** Three band core. Two are pink on white, dged by blue. Other is pink on white. Outer layer is a cage of white trands. One tiny subsurface moon. Germany, circa 1870-1915. 23/32". Near Mint(+) (8.9). Price: $15. CyberAuction #369, Lot #22.

928. **SWIRL. Divided core.** Naked divided core swirl. Three band core. ach is white, purple, orange and yellow. Germany, circa 1870-1915. 15/2". Mint (9.9). Price: $15. CyberAuction #369, Lot #28.

929. **SWIRL. Divided core.** Four band core. Two are green on white, two re blue on white. Outer layer is four sets of yellow strands. Germany, circa 870-1915. 15/32". Mint (9.9). Price: $15. CyberAuction #369, Lot #47.

930. **SWIRL. Divided core.** Three band core. Two are pink and blue on white, one is pink and green on white. Outer layer is a cage of yellow trands. One large melt spot. Very pretty. Germany, circa 1870-1915. 13/6". Mint(-) (9.0). Price: $15. CyberAuction #385, Lot #24.

931. **SWIRL. Divided core.** From near and end of the cane. Four band ore. Outer layer is two sets of yellow strands and one set of white strands. nother set of white strands is missing, and one of the yellow sets ends artway to the pontil. A little minor creasing at the bottom. Germany, circa 870-1915. 11/16". Mint(-) (9.1). Price: $15. CyberAuction #386, Lot #12.

932. **SWIRL. Divided core.** Slightly blue tinted base glass. Three band ore. Each is pink and blue on white. Outer layer is three sets of yellow trands. One tiny chip. Germany, circa 1870-1915. 23/32". Near Mint(+) 3.9). Price: $15. CyberAuction #409, Lot #37.

933. **SWIRL. Divided core.** Four band core. Odd core colors. Two are merald green edged by blue. Other two are lavender edged by pink. Outer yer is four sets of yellow strands. Melt spot and some melt pitting. Germany, circa 1870-1915. 21/32". Mint(-) (9.0). Price: $15. CyberAuction 413, Lot #19.

934. **SWIRL. Divided core.** Slightly blue tinted base glass. Three band ore. Each is pink and blue on white. Outer layer is three sets of yellow rands. One tiny chip. Germany, circa 1870-1915. 23/32". Near Mint(+) 3.9). Price: $15. CyberAuction #426, Lot #39.

935. **SWIRL. Divided core.** Four band core. Odd core colors. Two are merald green edged by blue. Other two are lavender edged by pink. Outer yer is four sets of yellow strands. Melt spot and some melt pitting. Germany, circa 1870-1915. 21/32". Mint(-) (9.0). Price: $15. CyberAuction 430, Lot #53.

936. **SWIRL. Divided core.** Three band core. Two are pink and blue on hite, one is pink and green on white. Outer layer is a cage of yellow rands. One large melt spot. Very pretty. Germany, circa 1870-1915. 13/6". Mint(-) (9.0). Price: $15. CyberAuction #441, Lot #42.

937. **SWIRL. Divided core.** Four band core. Two are pink and green on ellow, two are pink and blue on white. Outer layer is two sets of white rands alternating with two sets of yellow strands. Overall pitting and roughess. 1-1/16". Near Mint(-) (8.1). Price: $15. CyberAuction #451, Lot #47.

938. **SWIRL. Divided core.** Three band core. Very wide bands. One each f green on white, pink on white, blue on white. Outer layer is a cage of hite strands. Very unusual marble. One small flake. Germany, circa 1870-915. 25/32". Near Mint (8.6). Price: $15. CyberAuction #458, Lot #53.

939. **SWIRL. Divided core.** Three band core. One green on white, one ink on white, one blue on white. Outer layer is three sets of white strands. ut of round. Overall very light haze with some pitting and tiny chips. ermany, circa 1870-1915. 1-3/16". Good(+) (7.7). Price: $15. yberAuction #466, Lot #38.

940. **SWIRL. Divided core.** Three band core. One each of blue/yellow, d/yellow, green/yellow. Outer layer is three sets of white strands. One ery tiny flake, almost a pit. Gorgeous. England, circa 1870-1915. 11/16". ear Mint(+) (8.9). Price: $15. CyberAuction #473, Lot #20.

941. **SWIRL. Divided core.** Three band core. Each is transparent blue on paque white. Outer layer is three bands of red and white. Melt lines on ne side. Germany, possibly England, circa 1870-1915. 21/32". Mint(-) (9.0). ice: $15. CyberAuction #473, Lot #23.

942. **SWIRL. Divided core.** Three layer marble. Core is a band of pink on hite and a band of blue on white. Middle layer is an assortment of bands various combinations of blue, pink, green and white. Outer layer is two ts of yellow strands. From near an end of the cane, some of the design is issing. Two small moons, a sparkle, some pitting. Germany, circa 1870-915. 31/32". Near Mint (8.5). Price: $15. CyberAuction #478, Lot #4.

943. **SWIRL. Divided core.** Four band core. Each is pink and blue on hite. Outer layer is a cage of yellow strands. Germany, circa 1870-1915. 7/32". Mint (9.9). Price: $15. CyberAuction #478, Lot #19.

944. **SWIRL. Divided core.** Three band core. Blue on white, green on hite, red on white. Three outer bands of white strands. Germany, circa 870-1915. 25/32". Mint (9.6). Price: $15. CyberAuction #480, Lot #29.

945. **SWIRL. Divided core.** Four band core. Wide bands. Two are pink nd green on yellow. Two are pink and blue on white. Outer layer is a set of white strands, a set of yellow strands, a single yellow strand, and a missing white set. Melt crease at bottom pontil. Germany, circa 1880-1915. 3/4". Mint (9.5). Price: $15. CyberAuction #481, Lot #34.

5946. **SWIRL. Divided core.** Three band core. Three narrow bands of pink on white. Outer layer is three narrow bands of blue on white, set above the core spaces. Crease with dirt line on one side. Very pretty. Germany, circa 1870-1915. 21/32". Mint(-) (9.2). Price: $15. CyberAuction #489, Lot #50.

5947. **SWIRL. Divided core.** Three band core. Each is pink and blue on white. Outer layer is a cage of yellow strands. Some pits. Germany, circa 1870-1915. 27/32". Near Mint(+) (8.7). Price: $15. CyberAuction #500, Lot #29.

5948. **SWIRL. Divided core.** Beautiful. Four band core. Two are yellow and two are white. Outer layer is two orange bands, a light blue band, a green band. Beauty. Germany, circa 1870-1915. 1/2". Mint (9.9). Price: $15. CyberAuction #503, Lot #24.

5949. **SWIRL. Divided core.** Three band core. One each of pink on white, blue on white, green on yellow. Outer layer is two sets of white strands and two sets of yellow strands. Germany, circa 1870-1915. 5/8". Mint (9.7). Price: $15. CyberAuction #505, Lot #17.

5950. **SWIRL. Divided core.** Three band core. Three narrow bands of pink on white. Outer layer is three narrow bands of blue on white, set above the core spaces. Crease with dirt line on one side. Very pretty. Germany, circa 1870-1915. 21/32". Mint(-) (9.2). Price: $15. CyberAuction #506, Lot #25.

5951. **SWIRL. Divided core.** Three band core. Each is pink and blue on white. Outer layer is three sets of white strands. Germany, circa 1870-1915. 9/16". Mint (9.7). Price: $14. CyberAuction #336, Lot #4.

5952. **SWIRL. Divided core.** Four band core. Each are green and blue on white and yellow, in varying amounts. Outer layer is four sets of white strands. One pit. Germany, circa 1870-1915. 5/8". Near Mint(+) (8.9). Consignor note: A1. Price: $14. CyberAuction #344, Lot #19.

5953. **SWIRL. Divided core.** Three band core. One each of blue on white, pink on white, green on white. Outer layer is three sets of yellow strands. Small manufacturing pit. Germany, circa 1870-1915. 25/32". Mint(-) (9.0). Price: $14. CyberAuction #372, Lot #5.

5954. **SWIRL. Divided core.** Narrow core. Three bands. Each is red and yellow. Outer layer is two bands of wispy yellow. Germany, circa 1870-1915. 25/32". Mint (9.6). Price: $14. CyberAuction #381, Lot #20.

5955. **SWIRL. Divided core.** Four band core. One each of pink on yellow, blue on white, pink on white, green on yellow. Outer layer is four sets of yellow strands. Germany, circa 1870-1915. 5/8". Mint (9.9). Price: $14. CyberAuction #403, Lot #45.

5956. **SWIRL. Divided core.** Four band core. Each is pink and blue on white. Outer layer is a cage of yellow strands. Germany, circa 1870-1915. 17/32". Mint (9.9). Price: $14. CyberAuction #415, Lot #47.

5957. **SWIRL. Divided core.** Four band core. Two pink on yellow, one green on white, one blue on white. Outer layer is four sets of white strands. Germany, circa 1870-1915. 9/16". Mint (9.7). Price: $14. CyberAuction #423, Lot #24.

5958. **SWIRL. Divided core.** Three layer marble. Core is a band of pink on white and a band of blue on white. Middle layer is an assortment of bands in various combinations of blue, pink, green and white. Outer layer is two sets of yellow strands. From near an end of the cane, some of the design is missing. Two small moons, a sparkle, some pitting. Germany, circa 1870-1915. 31/32". Near Mint (8.5). Price: $14. CyberAuction #428, Lot #23.

5959. **SWIRL. Divided core.** Four band core. Two are pink, blue on white. Two are pink, green on yellow. Outer layer is four sets of yellow and white strands. Almost no twist. Germany, circa 1870-1915. 19/32". Mint(-) (9.1). Price: $14. CyberAuction #433, Lot #25.

5960. **SWIRL. Divided core.** English type. Three band core. One each of light blue, yellow, white. Outer layer is six bands. Three light green, three red. One melt chip where the marble touched another when hot. England, possibly Germany, circa 1870-1915. 11/16". Mint(-) (9.0). Price: $14. CyberAuction #461, Lot #3.

5961. **SWIRL. Divided core.** Four band core. Two are blue on white, two are pink and green on yellow. Outer layer is two sets of white strands and two sets of yellow strands. Germany, circa 1870-1915. 25/32". Mint (9.7). Price: $14. CyberAuction #503, Lot #5.

5962. **SWIRL. Divided core.** Very lightly tinted base glass. Three band core. Each is pink and green on white. Outer layer is three sets of white and yellow strands. Germany, circa 1870-1915. 9/16". Mint (9.7). Price: $13.50. CyberAuction #443, Lot #2.

5963. **SWIRL. Divided core.** Four wide bands. Two are pink on yellow, one blue on white, one green on white. Outer layer is two sets of white strands and two sets of yellow strands. Some pinpricking. Germany, circa 1870-1915. 17/32". Near Mint(+) (8.9). Price: $13.50. CyberAuction #443, Lot #15.

5964. **SWIRL. Divided core.** Very unusual marble. Four band core. Two are pink and green on yellow, one is pink and blue on white, one is pink and blue on yellow. Outer layer is four sets of bands, each is white latticinio strands floating just above the divided core. A couple of tiny pits and chips. Germany, circa 1870-1915. 5/8". Near Mint (8.6). Price: $13. CyberAuction #331, Lot #46.

5965. **SWIRL. Divided core.** Superb three layer swirl. Inner core is four bands. Two are green on yellow, two are blue on white. Middle layer is four bands, all pink on white, set to mirror the spaces in the core. Outer layer is four sets of yellow strands. Beauty. Germany, circa 1870-1915. Some pitting. 11/16". Near Mint(+) (8.7). Price: $13. CyberAuction #332, Lot #19.

5966. **SWIRL. Divided core.** Four band core. Each is a white band. One has blue and pink. One has pink and turquoise. One has just pink. One has pink, yellow and turquoise. Outer layer is two sets of yellow strands and two sets of white strands. Germany, circa 1870-1915. 3/4". Mint (9.7). Price: $13. CyberAuction #336, Lot #40.

5967. SWIRL. Divided core. Very interesting marble. White latticinio in divided form. Three band core. Just above that core is another layer which is three bands. One each of blue on white, red on white, green on white. Mirroring the spaces in the core. Thick casing of clear. Some pitting. Nice marble. Germany, circa 1870-1915. 11/16". Near Mint (8.4). Price: $13. CyberAuction #341, Lot #8.

5968. SWIRL. Divided core. Four band core. Two pink and blue on white, two pink and green on yellow. Outer layer is four sets of white strands. Germany, circa 1870-1915. 9/16". Mint (9.9). Price: $13. CyberAuction #347, Lot #15.

5969. SWIRL. Divided core. Latticinio strands in divided form. White strands. Three bands. Outer layer is two blue on white bands, another is missing. A couple of tiny subsurface moons. Germany, circa 1870-1915. 3/4". Near Mint(-) (8.2). Price: $13. CyberAuction #358, Lot #44.

5970. SWIRL. Divided core. Four band core. Two are pink and green on yellow. Two are pink and blue on white. Outer layer is two sets of white strands and two sets of yellow strands. One tiny chip, some pinpricks. Germany, circa 1870-1915. 13/16". Near Mint (8.6). Price: $13. CyberAuction #359, Lot #5.

5971. SWIRL. Divided core. Three band core. Each is pink, green, blue, yellow and white. Outer layer is three sets of yellow and white strands. In great shape. Germany, circa 1870-1915. 5/8". Mint (9.6). Price: $13. CyberAuction #359, Lot #7.

5972. SWIRL. Divided core. Four band core. Two are purple on white, one is green on white and one is blue on white. Outer layer is four sets of yellow strands. Pinpricks and some light haze. Germany, circa 1870-1915. 25/32". Near Mint (8.6). Price: $13. CyberAuction #368, Lot #11.

5973. SWIRL. Divided core. Three band core. Each is pink on white, with blue edges. Outer layer is a cage of yellow strands. A couple of tiny melt chips. Germany, circa 1870-1915. 23/32". Mint(-) (9.0). Price: $13. CyberAuction #373, Lot #9.

5974. SWIRL. Divided core. Four band core. Two are pink and green on yellow, two are pink and blue on white. Outer layer is a cage of yellow strands. One pit. Germany, circa 1870-1915. 11/16". Mint (-) (9.0). Price: $13. CyberAuction #403, Lot #15.

5975. SWIRL. Divided core. Very pretty. Four band core. Two are light green and blue on white, two are lavender and pink on white. Outer layer is four sets of yellow strands. One melt pit. Germany, circa 1870-1915. 5/8". Mint(-) (9.2). Price: $13. CyberAuction #413, Lot #41.

5976. SWIRL. Divided core. Four band core. Two are pink on white, two are blue on white. Outer layer is six narrow bands of pale yellow. Germany, circa 1870-1915. 11/16". Mint (9.7). Price: $13. CyberAuction #417, Lot #53.

5977. SWIRL. Divided core. Four band core. Each is pink and blue on white. Outer layer is four sets of yellow strands. Tightly twisted. Nicely faceted pontil. Germany, circa 1870-1915. 17/32". Mint (9.8). Price: $13. CyberAuction #421, Lot #6.

5978. SWIRL. Divided core. Four-band core. Two are pink on yellow, two are green on yellow. Outer layer is four sets of white strands. Germany, circa 1870-1915. 9/16". Mint (9.7). Price: $13. CyberAuction #423, Lot #21.

5979. SWIRL. Divided core. Three band core. Each is the same complex pattern of pink, yellow, pink, blue and green. Outer layer is three sets of yellow strands. Germany, circa 1870-1915. 15/32". Mint (9.6). Price: $13. CyberAuction #425, Lot #19.

5980. SWIRL. Divided core. Three band core. Appears to have been meant as a four-band core, but one band is missing. Two are pink, blue and white. One is green, pink and yellow. Outer layer is two sets of white strands. Germany, circa 1870-1915. 15/32". Mint (9.8). Price: $13. CyberAuction #425, Lot #38.

5981. SWIRL. Divided core. Three band core. Each is blue and yellow bands on white. Outer layer is three sets of yellow strands. One pit, one very tiny subsurface moon. Germany, circa 1870-1915. 1". Near Mint(+) (8.9). Price: $13. CyberAuction #442, Lot #42.

5982. SWIRL. Divided core. Four band core. One is pink and white, one is green on white, one is blue on white. Outer layer is a cage of yellow strands. Germany, circa 1870-1915. 11/16". Mint (9.8). Price: $13. CyberAuction #463, Lot #39.

5983. SWIRL. Divided core. Three band core. One is red, blue, green and white. Two are blue and white. Germany, circa 1870-1915. 9/16". Mint (9.9). Price: $13. CyberAuction #488, Lot #17.

5984. SWIRL. Divided core. Four band core. Two are pink, yellow and green. Two are pink, blue and white. Outer layer is two sets of white strands and two sets of yellow strands. A couple of pinpricks. Germany, circa 1870-1915. 25/32". Mint(-) (9.0). Price: $13. CyberAuction #503, Lot #2.

5985. SWIRL. Divided core. Four band core. Two are pink and green on yellow, two are pink and blue on white. Outer layer is four sets of yellow strands. Thick casing of clear glass. Some scratching. 11/16". Mint(-) (9.0). Price: $12. CyberAuction #331, Lot #13.

5986. SWIRL. Divided core. Four band core. Each is pink and green on yellow. Outer layer is four sets of white strands. Some sparkles. Germany, circa 1870-1915. 19/32". Mint(-) (9.0). Price: $12. CyberAuction #331, Lot #15.

5987. SWIRL. Divided core. Four band core. Two are pink and green on yellow, two are pink and blue on white. Outer layer is four sets of yellow strands. One tiny flake. Germany, circa 1870-1915. 21/32". Near Mint(+) (8.9). Price: $12. CyberAuction #331, Lot #42.

5988. SWIRL. Divided core. Naked divided core swirl. Three band. Each

is white strands, edged by red on one side. One band has green edging on the other side. Some pitting and tiny flakes on the surface. Germany, circa 1870-1915. 11/16". Near Mint(-) (8.0). Price: $12. CyberAuction #34, Lot #51.

5989. SWIRL. Divided core. Three band core. Each is the same complex pattern of pink, blue, white, green and yellow. Outer layer is three sets of white strands. Nicely constructed and executed. Two tiny chips. German, circa 1870-1915. 11/16". Near Mint (8.6). Price: $12. CyberAuction #35, Lot #5.

5990. SWIRL. Divided core. Four band core. Two pink on white, two blue on white. Outer layer is four sets of yellow strands. Germany, circa 1870-1915. 15/32". Mint (9.7). Price: $12. CyberAuction #366, Lot #7.

5991. SWIRL. Divided core. Three band core. One is pink on white, one is green and yellow on white, one is blue on white. Outer layer is three sets of yellow strands. Several small subsurface moons. Germany, circa 1870-1915. 13/16". Near Mint (8.6). Price: $12. CyberAuction #382, Lot #21.

5992. SWIRL. Divided core. Three wide bands. Almost no space between each. Each is pink, blue and green bands on white and yellow. Outer layer is three sets of yellow and white strands. A couple of pits. Germany, circa 1870-1915. 5/8". Near Mint(+) (8.9). Price: $12. CyberAuction #385, Lot #7.

5993. SWIRL. Divided core. Four band core. Odd coloring. Two of lavender and pink on yellow. Two of green and blue on white. Outer layer is four sets of yellow strands. Some melt spots. Germany, circa 1870-1915. 5/8". Mint(-) (9.1). Price: $12. CyberAuction #409, Lot #43.

5994. SWIRL. Divided core. Four band. Two are orange and yellow, two blue and white, two green and white. Outer layer is two sets of yellow strands and two sets of white strands. Some small chips on one side, other side is fine. Very nice. Germany, circa 1870-1915. 7/8". Near Mint(+) (8.9). Price: $12. CyberAuction #413, Lot #2.

5995. SWIRL. Divided core. Four band core. Each is blue, white, green and red. Outer layer is four sets of yellow strands. One melt pit, a couple of pinpricks. Germany, circa 1870-1915. 11/16". Mint(-) (9.0). Price: $12. CyberAuction #419, Lot #58.

5996. SWIRL. Divided core. From near an end of the cane. Four band core. One green on yellow, one pink on yellow, one very wispy pink on yellow, one narrow yellow (with no other color). Outer layer is one very short band of pink. No other decoration. Germany, circa 1870-1915. 16". Mint (9.7). Price: $12. CyberAuction #424, Lot #12.

5997. SWIRL. Divided core. Four band core. Two are pink on white, two are blue on white. Outer layer is four sets of white strands. Germany, circa 1870-1915. 15/32". Mint (9.9). Price: $12. CyberAuction #429, Lot #16.

5998. SWIRL. Divided core. Four band core. Each is a different color pattern. Blue, pink, green, white, yellow. Outer layer is four sets of white strands. Germany, circa 1870-1915. 5/8". Mint (9.7). Price: $12. CyberAuction #431, Lot #5.

5999. SWIRL. Divided core. Lightly blue tinted base glass. Four band core. Each is pink and green on yellow. Outer layer is four sets of white strands. No twist. Germany, circa 1870-1915. 19/32". Mint (9.7). Price: $12. CyberAuction #432, Lot #46.

6000. SWIRL. Divided core. Four band core. Two are pink and blue on white, two are pink and green on yellow. Outer layer is four sets of white strands. Germany, circa 1870-1915. 17/32". Mint (9.7). Price: $12. CyberAuction #439, Lot #38.

6001. SWIRL. Divided core. Four band. Two are orange and yellow, two blue and white, two green and white. Outer layer is two sets of yellow strands and two sets of white strands. Some small chips on one side, other side is fine. Very nice. Germany, circa 1870-1915. 7/8". Near Mint(+) (8.2). Price: $12. CyberAuction #447, Lot #5.

6002. SWIRL. Divided core. Four band core. Odd coloring. Two of lavender and pink on yellow. Two of green and blue on white. Outer layer is four sets of yellow strands. Some melt spots. Germany, circa 1870-1915. 5/8". Mint(-) (9.1). Price: $12. CyberAuction #454, Lot #40.

6003. SWIRL. Divided core. Three band core. Each band is red, green, yellow and blue. Outer layer is two sets of yellow and white strands. One set is missing. England, possibly Germany, circa 1870-1915. 19/32". Mint (9.7). Price: $12. CyberAuction #487, Lot #20.

6004. SWIRL. Divided core. Three band core. Each band is red, green, yellow and blue. Outer layer is two sets of yellow and white strands. One set is missing. England, possibly Germany, circa 1870-1915. 5/8". Mint (9.7). Price: $12. CyberAuction #487, Lot #39.

6005. SWIRL. Divided core. Four band core. Two are pink and blue on white, two are blue and white. The blue and white are riddled with annealing fractures. This is intentional. Outer layer is four sets of yellow strands. Germany, circa 1870-1915. 1/2". Mint (9.7). Price: $12. CyberAuction #494, Lot #20.

6006. SWIRL. Divided core. Four band core. Two are pink and green on yellow, two are pink and blue on white. Outer layer is two sets of yellow strands and two sets of yellow strands. Germany, circa 1870-1915. 5/8". Mint (9.7). Price: $12. CyberAuction #504, Lot #21.

6007. SWIRL. Divided core. Very rare marble. Divided core consisting of three bands of red latticinio. Or a red latticinio in divided form. Outer layer is three bands of blue and white mirroring the spaces in the core. Same as Lot 71 in CyberAuction 503, probably same cane (same consignor). Fractures and subsurface moon. Germany, possibly England, circa 1870-1915. 1/2". Good(-) (7.2). Price: $12. CyberAuction #507, Lot #43.

6008. SWIRL. Divided core. Three band core. Each is red and blue, with white. Outer layer is three sets of white strands. Very nice marble. Germany, circa 1870-1915. 5/8". Mint (9.8). Price: $12. CyberAuction #508, Lot #1.

009. SWIRL. Divided core. Three layer swirl. Inner core is three narrow ands of pink on yellow, Layer just above that is three narrow bands of blue n white. Outer layer is a cage of yellow strands. One small flake. Ger- nany, circa 1870-1915. 21/32". Near Mint(+) (8.9). Price: $11. CyberAuction #331, Lot #34.

010. SWIRL. Divided core. Three band core. Bands are very close to the urface. One is blue on white, one green on yellow, on pink on white. Outer layer is three sets of yellow strands, set to mirror the clear spaces. everal small melt spots. Germany, circa 1870-1915. 11/16". Mint(-) (9.0). rice: $11. CyberAuction #332, Lot #15.

011. SWIRL. Divided core. Three band core. Each is the same pattern of lue, pink and green on white and yellow. Outer layer is three sets of white trands. Some tiny pits. Germany, circa 1870-1915. 21/32". Near Mint(+) 3.8). Price: $11. CyberAuction #335, Lot #8.

012. SWIRL. Divided core. Intended as a naked divided core swirl. From ear an end of the cane. Three bands. Each is dark purple and white. Narrow bands, malformed core. One melt spot. Germany, circa 1870-1915. 1/32". Mint(-) (9.1). Price: $11. CyberAuction #345, Lot #46.

013. SWIRL. Divided core. Three band core. Each band is pink, yellow nd green, on white. Outer layer is three sets of yellow strands. Several pits. Germany, circa 1870-1915. 3/4". Near Mint(+) (8.7). Price: $11. CyberAuction #365, Lot #4.

014. SWIRL. Divided core. Four band core. Base glass is light blue. Two ands are blue on white, two are pink on white. Outer layer is four sets of white strands. One tiny chip. Germany, circa 1870-1915. 23/32". Near Mint(+) (8.9). Price: $11. CyberAuction #413, Lot #22.

015. SWIRL. Divided core. Six band core. Three are blue and white, hree are green and white. Outer layer is a cage of white strands. Germany, circa 1927-1935. 15/32". Mint (9.9). Price: $11. CyberAuction #414, Lot #10.

016. SWIRL. Divided core. Four band core. One each of pink on yellow, green on yellow, blue on white, pink on white. Outer layer is four sets of yellow strands. Tiny sparkle and a couple of tiny pits. Germany, circa 1870-1915. 25/32". Near Mint(+) (8.9). Price: $11. CyberAuction #428, Lot #46.

017. SWIRL. Divided core. Four band core. Two are blue white, two are pink and yellow. Outer layer is two sets of white strands and two sets of yellow strands. One tiny area of pinpricks. Germany, circa 1870-1915. 11/16". Mint(-) (9.0). Price: $11. CyberAuction #436, Lot #47.

018. SWIRL. Divided core. Three band core. Each band is pink, blue and green on white. Outer layer is three sets of white strands. One tiny sparkle. Germany, circa 1870-1915. 5/8". Mint(-) (9.2). Price: $11. CyberAuction #440, Lot #48.

019. SWIRL. Divided core. Four band core. Two are green and yellow, two are ruddy orange and white. Outer layer is two sets of white strands and two sets of yellow strands. A couple of small chips, a few small subsurface moons. Germany, circa 1870-1915. 1". Good(+) (7.8). Price: $11. CyberAuction #464, Lot #12.

020. SWIRL. Divided core. Four band core. Odd coloring. Two of lavender and pink on yellow. Two of green and blue on white. Outer layer is four sets of yellow strands. Some melt spots. Germany, circa 1870-1915. 5/8". Mint(-) (9.1). Price: $11. CyberAuction #466, Lot #2.

021. SWIRL. Divided core. Four band core. Two are pink and green on yellow, two are pink and blue on white. Outer layer is two sets of white strands alternating with two sets of yellow strands. Overall pitting and roughness. 1-1/16". Near Mint(-) (8.1). Price: $11. CyberAuction #466, Lot #12.

022. SWIRL. Divided core. Four band core. Odd core colors. Two are emerald green edged by blue. Other two are lavender edged by pink. Outer layer is four sets of yellow strands. Melt spot and some melt pitting. Germany, circa 1870-1915. 21/32". Mint(-) (9.0). Price: $11. CyberAuction #466, Lot #33.

023. SWIRL. Divided core. Four band core. Two are pink and blue on white, one is pink and green on yellow, one is pink and green on white. Outer layer is two sets of yellow strands and two sets of white strands. Two tiny chips, one melt hole. Germany, circa 1870-1915. 25/32". Near Mint (8.6). Price: $11. CyberAuction #477, Lot #22.

024. SWIRL. Divided core. Four band core. Two are pink and turquoise on white, two are pink and blue on white. Outer layer is four sets of white strands. One tiny chip. Germany, circa 1870-1915. 23/32". Near Mint(+) (8.9). Price: $11. CyberAuction #479, Lot #1.

025. SWIRL. Divided core. Three band core. One is light blue and orange on white, one is blue and pink on white and green, one is pink and green on yellow. Outer layer is three sets of yellow and white strands. Fracture on one side running pole to pole. Germany, circa 1870-1915. 1-1/16". Good(+) (7.9). Price: $11. CyberAuction #482, Lot #34.

026. SWIRL. Divided core. Three band core. Each band is red, green, yellow and blue. Outer layer is three sets of yellow and white strands. Melt lines on the surface. England, possibly Germany, circa 1870-1915. 19/32". Mint(-) (9.0). Price: $11. CyberAuction #487, Lot #24.

027. SWIRL. Divided core. Four band core. Two are blue and pink on white. Two are green and pink on white. Outer layer is four sets of yellow strands. Germany, circa 1870-1915. 5/8". Mint (9.7). Price: $11. CyberAuction #502, Lot #20.

028. SWIRL. Divided core. Four band core. Each is translucent white. Wide core. Outer layer is four sets of white strands/bands. One melt spot. Peewee. Germany, circa 1870-1915. 1/2". Mint(-) (9.0). Price: $10. CyberAuction #337, Lot #9.

029. SWIRL. Divided core. Three band core. Each is blue bands on white. Very nice marble. Outer layer is three sets of white strands. Small melt spot and some pitting. Germany, circa 1870-1915. 15/32". Near Mint(+) (8.9). Price: $10. CyberAuction #345, Lot #4.

6030. SWIRL. Divided core. Four band core. Wispy pink on white and blue on white. Outer layer is four sets of white strands. Cold roll lines. Germany, circa 1870-1915. 9/16". Mint (9.5). Price: $10. CyberAuction #359, Lot #3.

6031. SWIRL. Divided core. Four band core. Two are pink and blue on white, two are pink and turquoise on white. Outer layer is a cage of white strands. Four tiny pits and tiny melt spots. Germany, circa 1870-1915. 9/16". Near Mint(+) (8.9). Price: $10. CyberAuction #363, Lot #4.

6032. SWIRL. Divided core. Four band core. Two are green on yellow, two are pink and blue on white. Outer layer is two sets of white strands and two sets of yellow strands. Some pinpricking. Germany, circa 1870-1915. 9/16". Mint(-) (9.0). Price: $10. CyberAuction #388, Lot #8.

6033. SWIRL. Divided core. Four band core. Two are blue on white, two are red on yellow. Outer layer is two sets of yellow strands and two sets of white strands. Germany, circa 1870-1915. 19/32". Mint (9.8). Price: $10. CyberAuction #410, Lot #32.

6034. SWIRL. Divided core. Three band core. Pink and blue on white bands. Outer layer is three sets of white strands. Some pitting. Germany, circa 1870-1915. 13/16". Near Mint(-) (8.0). Price: $10. CyberAuction #412, Lot #8.

6035. SWIRL. Divided core. Three band core. Green on yellow, pink on yellow, blue on white. Outer layer is three sets of yellow strands. Melted dirt spot. Gorgeous. Germany, circa 1870-1915. 17/32". Mint (9.5). Price: $10. CyberAuction #412, Lot #37.

6036. SWIRL. Divided core. Four band core. Two are pink, blue and white. Two are pink, green, yellow and white. Outer layer is four sets of white and yellow strands. Germany, circa 1870-1915. 5/8". Mint (9.5). Price: $10. CyberAuction #413, Lot #45.

6037. SWIRL. Divided core. Four-band core. Two are pink on green, two are blue on white. Outer layer is a cage of white strands. Germany, circa 1870-1915. 5/8". Mint (9.6). Price: $10. CyberAuction #418, Lot #2.

6038. SWIRL. Divided core. Four band core. Two are pink on yellow, one is green on white, one is blue on white. Outer layer is two sets of yellow strands and two sets of white strands. Overall small and tiny subsurface moons. 1-7/16". Good (7.4). Price: $10. CyberAuction #442, Lot #11.

6039. SWIRL. Divided core. Three band core. Pink and blue on white bands. Outer layer is three sets of white strands. Some pitting. Germany, circa 1870-1915. 13/16". Near Mint(-) (8.0). Price: $10. CyberAuction #446, Lot #42.

6040. SWIRL. Divided core. Three band core. One is light blue and orange on white, one is blue and pink on white and green, one is pink and green on yellow. Outer layer is three sets of yellow and white strands. Fracture on one side running pole to pole. Germany, circa 1870-1915. 1-1/16". Good(+) (7.9). Price: $10. CyberAuction #451, Lot #58.

6041. SWIRL. Divided core. Three band core. Each is pink and blue on white. Outer layer is five bands of green, pink and yellow. Germany, circa 1870-1915. 9/16". Mint (9.7). Price: $10. CyberAuction #468, Lot #33.

6042. SWIRL. Divided core. Slightly blue tinted base glass. Three band core. Each is pink and blue on white. Outer layer is three sets of yellow strands. One tiny chip. Germany, circa 1870-1915. 23/32". Near Mint(+) (8.9). Price: $10. CyberAuction #474, Lot #5.

6043. SWIRL. Divided core. Four band core. Two are turquoise, pink and white, two are blue, pink and white. Outer layer is four sets of white strands. One tiny subsurface moon. Germany, circa 1870-1915. 17/32". Near Mint(+) (8.9). Price: $10. CyberAuction #478, Lot #1.

6044. SWIRL. Divided core. Four band core. Two are pink on yellow, one is green on white, one is blue on white. Outer layer is two sets of yellow strands and two sets of white strands. Overall small and tiny subsurface moons. 1-7/16". Good (7.4). Price: $10. CyberAuction #482, Lot #21.

6045. SWIRL. Divided core. Three-band divided core swirl. Each band is pink and yellow on white, edged by blue. Outer layer is three sets of white strands. Two small subsurface moons. Germany, circa 1870-1915. 29/32". Near Mint (8.5). Price: $10. CyberAuction #483, Lot #4.

6046. SWIRL. Divided core. Four band core. Two are pink and white, two are pink, green and yellow. Outer layer is two sets of white strands and two sets of yellow strands. Germany, circa 1870-1915. 17/32". Mint (9.7). Price: $10. CyberAuction #485, Lot #6.

6047. SWIRL. Divided core. Four band core. Two are pink and white, two are green and white. Outer layer is four sets of yellow strands. A couple of very tiny pinpricks (may be melt holes). Germany, circa 1870-1915. 15/32". Mint (9.5). Price: $10. CyberAuction #487, Lot #33.

6048. SWIRL. Divided core. From near an end of the cane. Supposed to be a four band core, but one band missing. One each of pink on white, blue on white, green on white. Outer layer is one white strand and two yellow strands. A melt area, melt chip. Germany, circa 1870-1915. 3/4". Mint(-) (9.2). Price: $10. CyberAuction #503, Lot #27.

6049. SWIRL. Divided core. Four band core. One each of red on yellow, blue on white, red on white, green on yellow. Outer layer is a cage of white strands. Germany, circa 1870-1915. 5/8". Mint (9.9). Price: $10. CyberAuction #503, Lot #58.

6050. SWIRL. Divided core. Four band divided core. One pink on yellow, one blue on white, one pink on white, one green on yellow. Outer layer is four sets of yellow strands. A couple of pits, and one side has melted dirt on it. Germany, circa 1870-1915. 21/32". Near Mint(+) (8.7). Price: $9. CyberAuction #332, Lot #4.

6051. SWIRL. Divided core. Was supposed to be a four band core. Each light blue and white. One band is partial. Outer layer is four sets of orange strands. Interesting. Couple of very tiny chips. Germany, circa 1870-1915. 9/16". Near Mint(+) (8.8). Price: $9. CyberAuction #352, Lot #12.

6052. SWIRL. Divided core. Four band core. Two are turquoise, pink and white, two are blue, pink and white. Outer layer is four sets of white strands.

One tiny subsurface moon. Germany, circa 1870-1915. 17/32". Near Mint(+) (8.9). Price: $9. CyberAuction #360, Lot #3.
6053. SWIRL. Divided core. Naked divided core swirl. Four band core. Three are pink and green on white, one is pink and blue on white. One sparkle, one pit. Germany, circa 1870-1915. 17/32". Near Mint(+) (8.9). Price: $9. CyberAuction #365, Lot #18.
6054. SWIRL. Divided core. Three layer marble. Three band core. Each is pink narrow bands on white. Middle layer is three bands of green and yellow, set vane-style. Outer layer is three sets of yellow strands. Superb construction and symmetry. Some scratching and tiny damage. Beauty. Germany, circa 1870-1915. 5/8". Near Mint(-) (8.2). Price: $9. CyberAuction #368, Lot #30.
6055. SWIRL. Divided core. Four band core. Two are pink on white, two are green on white. Outer layer is four sets of white strands. One flake. Germany, circa 1870-1915. 15/32". Near Mint(+) (8.7). Price: $9. CyberAuction #376, Lot #12.
6056. SWIRL. Divided core. Three band core. Each is the same pattern of pink, blue, white and yellow. Outer layer is three sets of white strands. Two melt pits. Very pretty. Germany, circa 1870-1915. 5/8". Near Mint(+) (8.9). Price: $9. CyberAuction #389, Lot #3.
6057. SWIRL. Divided core. Four band core. Two are turquoise, pink and white, two are blue, pink and white. Outer layer is four sets of white strands. One tiny subsurface moon. Germany, circa 1870-1915. 17/32". Near Mint(+) (8.9). Price: $9. CyberAuction #398, Lot #38.
6058. SWIRL. Divided core. Four band core. Two are red on yellow, one blue on white, one green on white. Outer layer is two sets of yellow strands and two sets of white strands. One tiny chip, else in great shape. Germany, circa 1870-1915. 7/8". Near Mint(+) (8.8). Price: $9. CyberAuction #409, Lot #14.
6059. SWIRL. Divided core. Eight band core. Four are blue on white, four are pink on yellow. Outer layer is two sets of yellow strands and two sets of white strands. Small flake. Germany, circa 1870-1915. 3/4". Near Mint(+) (8.7). Price: $9. CyberAuction #413, Lot #10.
6060. SWIRL. Divided core. Three band core. Each is the same complex color. Outer layer is three sets of white strands. One flat spot. Germany, circa 1870-1915. 9/16". Mint(-) (9.0). Price: $9. CyberAuction #423, Lot #10.
6061. SWIRL. Divided core. Four-band divided core swirl. Two bands are green, pink and white. Two are blue, pink and white. Outer layer is four sets of white strands. Germany, circa 1870-1915. 1/2". Mint (9.7). Price: $9. CyberAuction #425, Lot #23.
6062. SWIRL. Divided core. Four band core. Odd coloring. Two of lavender and pink on yellow. Two of green and blue on white. Outer layer is four sets of yellow strands. Some melt spots. Germany, circa 1870-1915. 5/8". Mint(-) (9.1). Price: $9. CyberAuction #426, Lot #1.
6063. SWIRL. Divided core. Four band core. Two are turquoise, pink and white, two are blue, pink and white. Outer layer is four sets of white strands. One tiny subsurface moon. Germany, circa 1870-1915. 17/32". Near Mint(+) (8.9). Price: $9. CyberAuction #430, Lot #3.
6064. SWIRL. Divided core. Four band core. Two are pink and blue on white, two are pink and turquoise on white. Outer layer is a cage of white strands. Four tiny pits and tiny melt spots. Germany, circa 1870-1915. 9/16". Near Mint(+) (8.9). Price: $9. CyberAuction #451, Lot #49.
6065. SWIRL. Divided core. Four band core. Two are green and yellow, two are pink and white. Outer layer is four sets of white strands. Germany, circa 1870-1915. 19/32". Mint(-) (9.0). Price: $9. CyberAuction #454, Lot #1.
6066. SWIRL. Divided core. Four band core. Two are pink, blue and white. Two are pink, green and yellow. Outer layer is four sets of yellow strands. One pit. Very lightly buffed, pontils are intact. Germany, circa 1870-1915. 13/16". Price: $9. CyberAuction #457, Lot #19.
6067. SWIRL. Divided core. Four bands, tightly packed. Dark red and white. Outer layer is four bands. Two dark red, blue and white. Two blue, yellow and white. Some tiny chips and flakes. Germany, circa 1870-1915. 11/16". Near Mint (8.3). Price: $9. CyberAuction #468, Lot #42.
6068. SWIRL. Divided core. Three band core. Each is pink on white, edged by blue. Outer layer is three sets of yellow strands. Thick outer casing. Two tiny chips. Germany, circa 1870-1915. 11/16". Near Mint(+) (8.9). Price: $9. CyberAuction #482, Lot #30.
6069. SWIRL. Divided core. Four band core. Two bands are pink on yellow and white, two are blue on white. Outer layer is four sets of yellow and white strands. Two tiny chips. Germany, circa 1870-1915. 1/2". Near Mint(+) (8.7). Price: $8. CyberAuction #365, Lot #2.
6070. SWIRL. Divided core. Naked divided core. Three band core. Each is blue and white on yellow. Two tiny chips. Germany, circa 1870-1915. 15/32". Near Mint (8.6). Price: $8. CyberAuction #367, Lot #4.
6071. SWIRL. Divided core. Four band core. Two are pink, blue and white. Two are pink, green and white. Outer layer is four sets of yellow strands. Well made. Several tiny subsurface moons. Germany, circa 1870-1915. 25/32". Near Mint(+) (8.7). Price: $8. CyberAuction #372, Lot #11.
6072. SWIRL. Divided core. Four band core. Two are pink and blue on white. Two are pink and green on yellow. Outer layer is two sets of white strands and two sets of yellow. Very nice. Small chip, pits, some haze. Germany, circa 1870-1915. 5/8". Near Mint (8.3). Price: $8. CyberAuction #382, Lot #1.
6073. SWIRL. Divided core. Four band core. Two are pink on yellow, one is blue on white, one is green on white. Outer layer is two sets of white strands, two sets of yellow strands. Some tiny chips and subsurface moons. Germany, circa 1870-1915. 25/32". Good(+) (7.9). Price: $8. CyberAuction #382, Lot #48.
6074. SWIRL. Divided core. Four band core. Two are blue on white, two are pink on yellow. Outer layer is two bands of yellow strands and two bands of white strands. Some unmelted sand in the marble. One tiny flak Germany, circa 1870-1915. 3/4". Near Mint(+) (8.7). Price: $8. CyberAucti #395, Lot #40.
6075. SWIRL. Divided core. English colors. Core is three bands. Red a orange, blue and yellow, green and yellow. Outer layer is three sets white strands. Some pitting. England, possibly Germany, circa 1870-191 19/32". Near Mint (8.4). Price: $8. CyberAuction #420, Lot #53.
6076. SWIRL. Divided core. Three band core. Each band is pink, yell and green, on white. Outer layer is three sets of yellow strands. Several pi Germany, circa 1870-1915. 3/4". Near Mint(+) (8.7). Price: $8. CyberAucti #451, Lot #2.
6077. SWIRL. Divided core. Three bands. Blue band on white. Very tigh twisted, looks like a solid core. Outer layer is three sets of bright yell strands. Heavy outer casing of clear. One flake, a couple of melt spo Germany, circa 1870-1915. 25/32". Near Mint (8.6). Price: $8. CyberAucti #458, Lot #31.
6078. SWIRL. Divided core. Four band core. Two are pink and yello two are green and yellow. Outer layer is four sets of white strands. Two m spots. Germany, circa 1870-1915. 19/32". Mint (9.5). Price: $8. CyberAucti #460, Lot #28.
6079. SWIRL. Divided core. Four band core. One band each of pink yellow, pink on white, green on yellow, blue on white. Outer layer is tw sets of white strands and two sets of yellow strands. Several small chip Germany, circa 1870-1915. 13/16". Good(+) (7.9). Price: $8. CyberAucti #464, Lot #14.
6080. SWIRL. Divided core. Four band. Two are orange and yellow, tw blue and white, two green and white. Outer layer is two sets of yello strands and two sets of white strands. Some small chips on one side, oth side is fine. Very nice. Germany, circa 1870-1915. 7/8". Near Mint(-) (8. Price: $8. CyberAuction #466, Lot #31.
6081. SWIRL. Divided core. Three band core. One each of pink on whit blue on white, green on yellow. Three sets of yellow strands. One p Germany, circa 1870-1915. 19/32". Near Mint(+) (8.9). Price: $ CyberAuction #468, Lot #4.
6082. SWIRL. Divided core. Four band core. One each of red on whit red on yellow, green on yellow, blue on white. Outer layer is four sets yellow strands. Tiny pit. Germany, circa 1870-1915. 25/32". Near Mint(- (8.9). Price: $8. CyberAuction #480, Lot #32.
6083. SWIRL. Divided core. Naked divided core. Three band core. Ea is blue and white on yellow. Two tiny chips. Germany, circa 1870-191 15/32". Near Mint (8.6). Price: $8. CyberAuction #482, Lot #26.
6084. SWIRL. Divided core. Four band core. Two are pink and yello two are blue and white. Outer layer is two pairs of white strands and tw pairs of yellow strands. Tiny annealing fracture on one core band. Ge many, circa 1870-1915. 15/32". Mint (9.7). Price: $8. CyberAuction #48 Lot #18.
6085. SWIRL. Divided core. Three band core. Each band is red, gree yellow and blue. Outer layer is three sets of yellow and white strand Some tiny pitting. England, possibly Germany, circa 1870-1915. 19/32 Near Mint(+) (8.9). Price: $8. CyberAuction #487, Lot #31.
6086. SWIRL. Divided core. Three band divided core. Each is pink, gree yellow and white. Outer layer is three sets of white strands. Some pittin Germany, circa 1870-1915. 25/32". Near Mint(+) (8.7). Price: $ CyberAuction #489, Lot #2.
6087. SWIRL. Divided core. Four band. Two are orange and yellow, tw blue and white, two green and white. Outer layer is two sets of yello strands and two sets of white strands. Some small chips on one side, oth side is fine. Very nice. Germany, circa 1870-1915. 7/8". Near Mint(-) (8. Price: $8. CyberAuction #494, Lot #5.
6088. SWIRL. Divided core. Three band core. One each of blue on whit green on white, pink on white. A few yellow strands on each band. Out layer is three sets of yellow strands. One melted dirt line on the surfac Germany, circa 1870-1915. 5/8". Mint(-) (9.0). Price: $8. CyberAucti #502, Lot #4.
6089. SWIRL. Divided core. Yellow latticinio in divided core form. Thre bands. Outer layer is three white bands. One each covered by green, blu and red. Rough spot and haziness. Germany, circa 1870-1915. 11/16 Near Mint(-) (8.0). Price: $7. CyberAuction #357, Lot #8.
6090. SWIRL. Divided core. Four band core. Two are turquoise on whit two are blue on white. Outer layer is four sets of white strands. Som pinpricks and dirt. Germany, circa 1870-1915. 9/16". Near Mint (8.5). Pric $7. CyberAuction #407, Lot #7.
6091. SWIRL. Divided core. Three band divided core swirl. Each band red on yellow and blue on white. Outer layer is three sets of white strand One melt spot, one very tiny flake. Germany, circa 1870-1915. 11/16 Near Mint(+) (8.8). Price: $7. CyberAuction #409, Lot #19.
6092. SWIRL. Divided core. Three band core. Each band is blue and pin on white. Outer layer is three sets of white and yellow strands. A couple pinpricks. Germany, circa 1870-1915. 9/16". Mint(-) (9.0). Price: $7 CyberAuction #411, Lot #45.
6093. SWIRL. Divided core. Three band core. Each is pink and green o yellow. Outer layer is three sets of yellow strands. Germany, circa 187 1915. 3/4". Buffed. Price: $7. CyberAuction #414, Lot #18.
6094. SWIRL. Divided core. Three band core. Each is pink on white, edge by blue. Outer layer is three sets of yellow strands. Thick outer casing. Tw tiny chips. Germany, circa 1870-1915. 11/16". Near Mint(+) (8.9). Pric $7. CyberAuction #414, Lot #41.
6095. SWIRL. Divided core. Naked divided core swirl. Six band cor Three are blue on white, three are pink on yellow. No outer layer. Small a hole, several pits. Germany, circa 1870-1915. 21/32". Near Mint(+) (8.9 Price: $7. CyberAuction #415, Lot #59.

096. SWIRL. Divided core. Four band core. Two are pink and yellow, two are green and yellow. Outer layer is four sets of white strands. Two melt spots. Germany, circa 1870-1915. 19/32". Mint (9.5). Price: $7. CyberAuction #421, Lot #16.

097. SWIRL. Divided core. Three band divided core swirl. Each band is red on yellow and blue on white. Outer layer is three sets of white strands. One melt spot, one very tiny flake. Germany, circa 1870-1915. 11/16". Near Mint(+) (8.8). Price: $7. CyberAuction #426, Lot #4.

098. SWIRL. Divided core. Latticinio strands in divided form. Three bands. Yellow strands. Outer layer is six bands. Three are opaque yellow, one each of green, red and blue. Melt pit and a tiny pit. Germany, circa 1870-1915. /16". Mint(-) (9.0). Price: $7. CyberAuction #435, Lot #38.

099. SWIRL. Divided core. Four band core. Two are pink, green, yellow and white. Two are pink, blue, yellow and white. Outer layer is two sets of white strands and two sets of yellow strands. Several dirt lines on the surface. Germany, circa 1870-1915. 19/32". Mint(-) (9.0). Price: $7. CyberAuction #438, Lot #16.

100. SWIRL. Divided core. Three band core. Each is a combination of pink, green, blue, yellow and white. Outer layer is a cage of white strands. Germany, circa 1870-1915. 21/32". Near Mint(-) (8.2). Price: $7. CyberAuction #451, Lot #52.

101. SWIRL. Divided core. Three band core. Each is pink on white, edged by blue. Outer layer is three sets of white strands. Thick outer casing. Two tiny chips. Germany, circa 1870-1915. 11/16". Near Mint(+) (8.9). Price: $7. CyberAuction #453, Lot #5.

102. SWIRL. Divided core. Three band core. Each band is narrow and is pink and blue on white. Outer layer is three sets of yellow strands. Melt spot and cold line. Several tiny chips. Germany, circa 1870-1915. 7/8". Near Mint (8.6). Price: $7. CyberAuction #491, Lot #2.

103. SWIRL. Divided core. Four band core. Two pink on white, one blue on white, one green on white. Outer layer is three sets of yellow strands. Tiny chip. Germany, circa 1870-1915. 3/4". Near Mint(+) (8.9). Price: $7. CyberAuction #501, Lot #30.

104. SWIRL. Divided core. Four band core. Two different complex color schemes. Outer layer is four sets of white strands. Some minor wear. Germany, circa 1870-1915. 1/2". Mint(-) (9.0). Price: $7. CyberAuction #505, Lot #10.

105. SWIRL. Divided core. Four band core. Two are pink on yellow, one blue on white, one green on white. Outer layer is two sets of yellow strands and two sets of white strands. Light surface haze. Tiny subsurface moons. Germany, circa 1870-1915. 27/32". Good(+) (7.9). Price: $6. CyberAuction #358, Lot #32.

106. SWIRL. Divided core. Three band core. Each is a combination of pink, green, blue, yellow and white. Outer layer is a cage of white strands. Germany, circa 1870-1915. 21/32". Near Mint(-) (8.2). Price: $6. CyberAuction #372, Lot #43.

107. SWIRL. Divided core. Three band core. Each is pink on white, edged by blue. Outer layer is two sets of yellow strands, an additional set is missing. Pretty. Several tiny pits. Germany, circa 1870-1915. 21/32". Near Mint(+) (8.9). Price: $6. CyberAuction #410, Lot #21.

108. SWIRL. Divided core. Four band core. Two are pink on yellow, two are green on yellow. Outer layer is a cage of white strands. Beautifully ground pontil. A couple of pinpricks on it. Germany, circa 1870-1915. 11/16". Near Mint(+) (8.8). Price: $6. CyberAuction #432, Lot #17.

109. SWIRL. Divided core. Three band core. Each is orange, edged by white. Outer layer is three sets of yellow strands. Buffed. 19/32". Price: $6. CyberAuction #441, Lot #8.

110. SWIRL. Divided core. Three band core. Each band is a combination of pink, yellow, white, blue and green. Outer layer is three sets of yellow strands. Several very shallow flakes, some pits. Germany, circa 1870-1915. 4". Near Mint (8.0). Price: $6. CyberAuction #441, Lot #15.

111. SWIRL. Divided core. Four band core. Blue on white. Outer layer is four sets of white strands. Several small chips. Germany, circa 1870-1915. 4". Near Mint (8.3). Price: $6. CyberAuction #454, Lot #32.

112. SWIRL. Divided core. Four band core. Two bands are pink on yellow and white, two are blue on white. Outer layer is four sets of yellow and white strands. Two tiny chips. Germany, circa 1870-1915. 1/2". Near Mint(+) (8.7). Price: $6. CyberAuction #470, Lot #16.

113. SWIRL. Divided core. Unusual. Four band core. Two are pink and blue on white, two are pink and green on white. The pink and green bands are partial. Outer layer is four strands of yellow strands. Melt chip and some pits. Germany, circa 1870-1915. 5/8". Near Mint(+) (8.7). Price: $6. CyberAuction #502, Lot #39.

114. SWIRL. Divided core. Three band core. Each band is the same complex color scheme. Outer layer is three sets of white and yellow strands. Tiny chips and subsurface moons. Germany, circa 1870-1915. 7/8". Good (6). Price: $5. CyberAuction #401, Lot #31.

115. SWIRL. Divided core. Three band core. Each band is a combination of pink, yellow, white, blue and green. Outer layer is three sets of yellow strands. Several very shallow flakes, some pits. Germany, circa 1870-1915. 4". Near Mint(-) (8.0). Price: $5. CyberAuction #410, Lot #19.

116. SWIRL. Divided core. Four band core. Two are green and yellow, two are pink and white. Outer layer is four sets of yellow strands. Germany, circa 1870-1915. 19/32". Mint(-) (9.0). Price: $5. CyberAuction #416, Lot #10.

117. SWIRL. Divided core. Four band core. Blue on white. Outer layer is four sets of white strands. Several small chips. Germany, circa 1870-1915. 4". Near Mint (8.3). Price: $5. CyberAuction #417, Lot #35.

118. SWIRL. Divided core. Four band core. Pink and white, pink and yellow, blue and white, green and yellow. Outer layer is two sets of white strands and two sets of yellow strands. One pit. Germany, circa 1870-1915. 16". Near Mint(+) (8.9). Price: $5. CyberAuction #430, Lot #7.

6119. SWIRL. Divided core. Naked divided core. Three band core. Each is blue and white on yellow. Two tiny chips. Germany, circa 1870-1915. 15/32". Near Mint (8.6). Price: $5. CyberAuction #451, Lot #27.

6120. SWIRL. Divided core. Four band core. One is green and white, one is blue and white, two are pink and white. Outer layer is two sets of yellow strands and two sets of white strands. Several chips on the surface. Germany, circa 1870-1915. 25/32". Near Mint(+) (8.0). Price: $5. CyberAuction #458, Lot #12.

6121. SWIRL. Divided core. Four band core. Each is a complex set of colors, including orange. Outer layer is four sets of yellow strands. A number of chips. Germany, circa 1870-1915. 31/32". Good (7.5). Price: $5. CyberAuction #472, Lot #24.

6122. SWIRL. Divided core. Excellent design, though damaged. Four band core. Each band is four latticinio strands. Two bands are two yellow strands, flanked by a white strand. Other two are two white strands, flanked by a green strand. Outer layer is two sets. Two are pink, blue and white. Two are pink, green and yellow. A number of small chips, but one clean side. Germany, circa 1870-1915. 7/8". Good(+) (7.9). Price: $5. CyberAuction #472, Lot #36.

6123. SWIRL. Divided core. Four band core. Two are green on yellow, two are pink and blue on white. Outer layer is two sets of white strands and two sets of yellow strands. Several tiny flakes. Germany, circa 1870-1915. 3/4". Near Mint (8.4). Price: $5. CyberAuction #505, Lot #21.

6124. SWIRL. Divided core. Three band core. Each is yellow, blue and red. Outer layer is three sets of yellow and white strands. Overall pitting. Germany, circa 1870-1915. 5/8". Near Mint (8.3). Price: $4. CyberAuction #332, Lot #2.

6125. SWIRL. Divided core. Pink and white, pink and yellow, blue and white, green and yellow. Outer layer is two sets of white strands and two sets of yellow strands. One pit. Germany, circa 1870-1915. 9/16". Near Mint(+) (8.9). Price: $4. CyberAuction #399, Lot #44.

6126. SWIRL. Divided core. Three band core. Each is orange, edged by white. Outer layer is three sets of yellow strands. Buffed. 19/32". Price: $4. CyberAuction #410, Lot #48.

6127. SWIRL. Divided core. Four band core. Two bands are pink on yellow and white, two are blue on white. Outer layer is four sets of yellow and white strands. Two tiny chips. Germany, circa 1870-1915. 1/2". Near Mint(+) (8.7). Price: $4. CyberAuction #451, Lot #5.

6128. SWIRL. Divided core. Four band core. Two are red on yellow, one green on white, one blue on white. Outer layer is a cage of alternating white and yellow strands (eight in all). Melt spot and tiny subsurface moons. Germany, circa 1870-1915. 25/32". Near Mint (8.4). Price: $4. CyberAuction #468, Lot #38.

6129. SWIRL. Divided core. Four band core, each in a different color combination. Some scratching. Germany, circa 1870-1915. 17/32". Near Mint(+) (8.7). Price: $3. CyberAuction #411, Lot #29.

6130. SWIRL. Divided core. Three band core. Each is yellow latticinio strands. Outer layer is three bands. Two blue on white, one green on white. Small and tiny subsurface moons. Germany, circa 1870-1915. 25/32". Good(+) (7.9). Price: $3. CyberAuction #473, Lot #6.

6131. SWIRL. Divided core. Transparent bubble filled base. Three band core. Each is pink and green on white. Outer layer is three sets of white strands. Some tiny chips. Germany, circa 1870-191.5 11/16". Good(+) (7.9). Price: $3. CyberAuction #486, Lot #16.

6132. SWIRL. Divided core. Four band core. Two are pink on white, two are green on white. Outer layer is four sets of yellow strands. Several subsurface moons. Germany, circa 1870-1915. 25/32". Good (7.3). Price: $2. CyberAuction #417, Lot #39.

6133. SWIRL. Divided core. English colors. Three band core. Each is white, yellow, blue, red and green. Outer layer is three sets of white strands. Overall pitting and tiny chips. Germany, circa 1870-1915. 5/8". Good(+) (7.9). Price: $2. CyberAuction #458, Lot #23.

6134. SWIRL. Divided core. Transparent bubble filled base. Three band core. Each is pink and green on white. Outer layer is three sets of white strands. Some tiny chips. Germany, circa 1870-191.5 11/16". Good(+) (7.9). Price: $2. CyberAuction #463, Lot #2.

6135. SWIRL. Divided core. Four band core. Two are orange and white, one is blue, one is green. Outer layer is two sets of white strands and two sets of yellow strands. Overall chipping. Germany, circa 1870-1915. 1". Good(-) (7.0). Price: $2. CyberAuction #464, Lot #19.

6136. SWIRL. Divided core. Three band core. One each of green on yellow, blue on white, pink on white. Outer layer is three sets of white strands. Some tiny pits. Germany, circa 1870-1915. 11/16". Near Mint (8.5). Price: $2. CyberAuction #476, Lot #9.

6137. SWIRL. Divided core. Three band core. Each is ruddy pink on white. Outer layer is four sets of white strands. Large annealing fracture. Germany, circa 1870-1915. 1/2". Mint(-) (9.0). Price: $2. CyberAuction #495, Lot #9.

6138. SWIRL. Divided core. Three band core. Each is light green and light pink on white. Outer layer is three sets of yellow strands. Germany, circa 1870-1915. 5/8". Price: $2. CyberAuction #497, Lot #4.

6139. SWIRL. Gooseberry. Transparent gooseberry amber base with thirteen subsurface white strands. One tiny melt spot. Beautiful marble. Germany, circa 1870-1915. 11/16". Mint(-) (9.2). Price: $90. CyberAuction #330, Lot #17.

6140. SWIRL. Gooseberry. Very unusual gooseberry from near an end of the cane. An amethyst base. Ghost core. There are eight wide strands on one side of the marble. Two-thirds of the marble has no strands. Melt nub on one side. Two tiny flakes near the bottom. Very unusual. Germany, circa 1870-1915. 23/32". Near Mint(+) (8.9). Price: $80. CyberAuction #404, Lot #36.

6141. SWIRL. Gooseberry. Very unusual gooseberry from near an end of the cane. An amethyst base. Ghost core. There are eight wide strands on one side of the marble. Two-thirds of the marble has no strands. Melt nub on one side. Two tiny flakes near the bottom. Very unusual. Germany, circa 1870-1915. 23/32". Near Mint(+) (8.9). Price: $70. CyberAuction #338, Lot #49.
6142. SWIRL. Gooseberry. Transparent gooseberry brown base. Subsurface layer of white strands. Some minor rubbing and flat spots. Germany, circa 1870-1915. 23/32". Mint(-) (9.0). Price: $65. CyberAuction #363, Lot #40.
6143. SWIRL. Gooseberry. Transparent gooseberry amber base with thirteen subsurface white strands. One flake. Beautiful marble. Germany, circa 1870-1915. 5/8". Near Mint (8.6). Price: $46. CyberAuction #395, Lot #55.
6144. SWIRL. Gooseberry. Transparent gooseberry amber base with subsurface white strands. Some chips, subsurface moons and flakes. Germany, circa 1870-1915. 25/32". Good(+) (7.7). Price: $27. CyberAuction #402, Lot #15.
6145. SWIRL. Gooseberry. This is a poorly constructed gooseberry. Transparent gooseberry honey amber base. White strands unevenly distributed under the surface, with a large number bunched together on one side. Several melt spots and a pit. Germany, circa 1870-1915. 21/32". Near Mint(+) (8.9). Price: $26. CyberAuction #425, Lot #4.
6146. SWIRL. Gooseberry. Transparent gooseberry amber base with subsurface white strands. Some chips and flakes. Germany, circa 1870-1915. 9/16". Good(+) (7.9). Price: $16. CyberAuction #401, Lot #18.
6147. SWIRL. Joseph Coat. Stunning, large example. Very rare. Transparent clear base. Surface bands of red, orange, yellow, lavender, blues, white, greens. Some minor clear bands. One small blown air hole. Absolutely stunning marble!!! Germany, possibly England, circa 1870-1915. 1". Mint(-) (9.2). Price: $700. CyberAuction #500, Lot #22.
6148. SWIRL. Joseph Coat. Gorgeous marble. English colors. Transparent clear base. Multicolor core. Outer layer is packed strands of bright green, bright orange, bright red, bright blue, dark blue and aventurine green. Superior example. Two very tiny melt spots. England, possibly Germany, circa 1870-1920. 25/32". Mint(-) (9.2). Price: $450. CyberAuction #462, Lot #53.
6149. SWIRL. Joseph Coat. Absolutely stunning and extremely rare marble. One of the nicest English Joseph Coats I've seen, large size, in superb condition. Transparent clear base. Subsurface layer is mostly packed yellow strands and bands, with red, green, and blue. All are very bright colors. Stunning. Surface in great shape. England, possibly Germany, circa 1870-1915. 15/16". Mint (9.8). Price: $375. CyberAuction #429, Lot #55.
6150. SWIRL. Joseph Coat. Very rare marble. Six-panel Joseph Coat swirl. Stunning. Transparent clear base. Single subsurface layer of color. Three bands of blue surrounding red. The space in between each band is packed red strands. Some yellow and green in with the blue bands too. Very bright colors. English, possibly German, circa 1870-1915. 21/32". Mint (9.8). Price: $200. CyberAuction #429, Lot #50.
6151. SWIRL. Joseph Coat. Transparent clear base. Subsurface layer is packed strands of orange, blue, yellow, white, green and red. Several tiny flat spots. A beauty and rare. Germany, circa 1870-1915. 27/32". Mint(-) (9.1). Price: $185. CyberAuction #392, Lot #54.
6152. SWIRL. Joseph Coat. Stunning marble. Transparent clear base. Colorful core. Subsurface layer of packed white, red, blue, purple, green, yellow and orange. Only one clear space where you can see the core. Bright colors. Very nice. Germany, possibly England, circa 1870-1915. 9/16". Mint (9.7). Price: $175. CyberAuction #455, Lot #5.
6153. SWIRL. Joseph Coat. Rare marble. Six-panel Joseph Coat swirl. Stunning. Transparent clear base. Single subsurface layer of color. Three bands of red, various widths. The space in between each band is packed blue, red and white strands. One tiny melt hole. Bright colors. This is the last of the group that we had for auction. English, possibly German, circa 1870-1915. 21/32". Mint (9.6). Price: $175. CyberAuction #467, Lot #58.
6154. SWIRL. Joseph Coat. Six-panel shooter. Transparent clear base. Subsurface layer is six panels. Three are light green and white. Some clear bands in those. Of the three others, one is red, blue and yellow. One is red, other is blue. Some clear bands there too. One melt flat spot. Rare type and size. Germany, possibly England, circa 1870-1915. 25/32". Mint (9.3). Price: $170. CyberAuction #491, Lot #53.
6155. SWIRL. Joseph Coat. Rare marble. Six-panel Joseph Coat swirl. Stunning. Transparent clear base. Single subsurface layer of color. Three bands of blue, various widths. The space in between each band is packed red strands. Bright colors. English, possibly German, circa 1870-1915. 21/32". Mint (9.8). Price: $160. CyberAuction #443, Lot #56.
6156. SWIRL. Joseph Coat. Super marble. Transparent clear base. Core is packed strands of orange, red, blue, white, green, yellow. Bright colors. Germany, possibly England, circa 1870-1915. 11/16". Mint (9.7). Price: $160. CyberAuction #455, Lot #14.
6157. SWIRL. Joseph Coat. Rare six-panel Joseph Coat swirl. Transparent clear base. Three panels are bright blue strands. Three panels are bright red strands. Stunning. Germany, 1870-1915. 5/8". Mint (9.8). Price: $150. CyberAuction #438, Lot #49.
6158. SWIRL. Joseph Coat. Hard to find shooter. Transparent clear base. Subsurface layer of strands of orange, yellow, light blue, white, yellow. Tiny sparkle, tiny melt chip. Germany, circa 1870-1915. 7/8". Mint(-) (9.1). Price: $150. CyberAuction #498, Lot #62.
6159. SWIRL. Joseph Coat. Gorgeous marble. English colors. Transparent clear base. Multicolor core. Outer layer is packed strands of bright green, bright orange, bright red, bright blue, dark blue and light green. Superior example. Two very tiny melt spots. England, possibly Germany, circa 1870-1920. 25/32". Mint(-) (9.2). Price: $150. CyberAuction #500, Lot #42.
6160. SWIRL. Joseph Coat. Very pretty marble. All bright colors, alm electric. Transparent clear base. Subsurface layer of packed red, pink, blu yellow and whit strands. Some clear spaces. Gorgeous. English, possib German, circa 1870-1915. 21/32". Mint (9.8). Price: $145. CyberAucti #433, Lot #58.
6161. SWIRL. Joseph Coat. Very rare "beach ball" type Joseph Co Transparent clear base. Subsurface layer is eight bands. Four are light gre four are dark red. The green are wider than the red. Each band is about t same width as its same color. In great shape. Rare. England, possibly G many, circa 1870-1915. 9/16". Mint (9.8). Price: $145. CyberAuction #4 Lot #48.
6162. SWIRL. Joseph Coat. Superb example. Transparent clear base. Su surface layer is packed bands of red, blue, white, green, orange. One ti sparkle. Germany, circa 1870-1915. 3/4". Mint(-) (9.1). Price: $14 CyberAuction #363, Lot #46.
6163. SWIRL. Joseph Coat. Very rare marble. Six-panel Joseph Coat sw Stunning. Transparent clear base. Single subsurface layer of color. Thr bands of blue surrounding red. The space in between each band is pack yellow strands. Very bright colors. English, possibly German, circa 187 1915. 5/8". Mint (9.8). Price: $140. CyberAuction #436, Lot #55.
6164. SWIRL. Joseph Coat. Seven band Joseph Coat. Transparent cle base. Seven complex bands of assorted colors. Well defined. Exceptio marble. Germany, possibly England, circa 1870-1915. 9/16". Mint (9. Price: $140. CyberAuction #503, Lot #68.
6165. SWIRL. Joseph Coat. Rare six-panel Joseph Coat swirl. Transpare clear base. Three panels are bright yellow strands. Three panels are bri red, blue and white strands. Stunning. Germany, 1870-1915. 5/8". M (9.9). Price: $135. CyberAuction #435, Lot #53.
6166. SWIRL. Joseph Coat. Transparent clear base. Core is packed stra and bands. No spaces. Predominately green, with some red, white, a blue. Several heavy fiery aventurine bands in the green. Rare. A pit and t tiny chips. Germany, circa 1870-1915. 11/16". Near Mint (8.6). Price: $1 CyberAuction #380, Lot #59.
6167. SWIRL. Joseph Coat. Transparent clear base. Eight subsurface ban Each is a different odd color with a colored strand in the center. Beauty a rare. England, possibly Germany, circa 1970-1915. 9/16". Mint (9.7). Pri $120. CyberAuction #450, Lot #22.
6168. SWIRL. Joseph Coat. Gorgeous marble. English colors. Transpare clear base. Multicolor core. Outer layer is packed strands of bright gre bright orange, bright red, bright blue, dark blue and light green. Super example. Two very tiny melt spots. England, possibly Germany, circa 187 1920. 25/32". Mint(-) (9.2). Price: $120. CyberAuction #482, Lot #42.
6169. SWIRL. Joseph Coat. Transparent clear base. Subsurface layer packed narrow bands of orange, blue, yellow, white, red and green. T long cold roll lines. Sparkle, two pinpricks. Beautiful marble. Germa circa 1870-1915. 3/4". Mint(-) (9.0). Price: $110. CyberAuction #432, #52.
6170. SWIRL. Joseph Coat. Transparent clear base. Subsurface layer packed narrow bands of orange, blue, yellow, white, red and green. T long cold roll lines. No damage. Beautiful marble. Germany, circa 187 1915. 3/4". Mint(-) (9.2). Price: $100. CyberAuction #388, Lot #52.
6171. SWIRL. Joseph Coat. Very pretty marble. All bright colors, alm electric. Transparent clear base. Subsurface layer of packed red, pink, blu yellow and whit strands. Some clear spaces. Gorgeous. English, possib German, circa 1870-1915. 21/32". Mint (9.6). Price: $100. CyberAucti #429, Lot #20.
6172. SWIRL. Joseph Coat. Transparent clear base. Subsurface layer pack strands. Bright colors. Green, yellow, red, orange, blue, white. So clear spaces. Gorgeous. Germany, possibly England, circa 1870-1915. 16". Mint (9.8). Price: $100. CyberAuction #452, Lot #43.
6173. SWIRL. Joseph Coat. Gorgeous Joseph Coat swirl. Transparent cle base. Outstanding bright colors for the subsurface layer. Germany, ci 1870-1915. 19/32". Mint (9.9). Price: $95. CyberAuction #411, Lot #5
6174. SWIRL. Joseph Coat. Transparent clear base. Subsurface layer orange bands with some white and blue. Gorgeous marble, very hard find. A couple of pinpricks. Germany, possibly England, circa 1870-191 13/16". Mint(-) (9.0). Price: $95. CyberAuction #497, Lot #59.
6175. SWIRL. Joseph Coat. Rare eight-panel Joseph Coat. Transparent cle base. Four panels are yellow and green, one is red and orange, two are r and blue, one is white. Outstanding. Germany, possibly England, circa 187 1915. 9/16". Mint (9.7). Price: $90. CyberAuction #457, Lot #49.
6176. SWIRL. Joseph Coat. Transparent clear base. Core is packed stran and bands. Some clear spaces. Blue, white, orange, red, green, yello Beauty. Germany, possibly England, circa 1870-1915. 19/32". Mint (9. Price: $90. CyberAuction #462, Lot #2.
6177. SWIRL. Joseph Coat. Unusual marble. Transparent clear base. Fo subsurface bands. Each is a different color combination using red, bl green and white. Germany, possibly England, circa 1870-1915. 9/16". M (9.9). Price: $90. CyberAuction #475, Lot #51.
6178. SWIRL. Joseph Coat. Beautiful Joseph Coat. Transparent clear ba Subsurface bands of orange, green, white, blue, red. Really a six pan Three narrow panels of blue and white. Two of red, green and orange. O of green and orange. A couple of very narrow clear bands. Super looki marble!!!. England, possibly Germany, circa 1870-1195. 9/16". Mint (9. Price: $90. CyberAuction #485, Lot #60.
6179. SWIRL. Joseph Coat. Transparent clear base. Subsurface layer colored bands and strands. Predominately bright red, with some yell and white. Germany, possibly England, circa 1870-1915. 19/32". Mint (9. Price: $90. CyberAuction #502, Lot #68.
6180. SWIRL. Joseph Coat. Transparent clear base. Subsurface layer predominately blue bands with some white and yellow. In great shape,

beauty. Germany, circa 1870-1915. 9/16". Mint (9.9). Price: $85. CyberAuction #354, Lot #51.

6181. SWIRL. Joseph Coat. Transparent clear base. Eight subsurface bands. Various colors. Beauty and rare. England, possibly Germany, circa 1970-1915. 9/16". Mint (9.6). Price: $85. CyberAuction #450, Lot #35.

6182. SWIRL. Joseph Coat. Very pretty marble of blue, white, red and green subsurface bands. England, possibly Germany, circa 1870-1920. 17/32". Mint (9.8). Price: $85. CyberAuction #478, Lot #41.

6183. SWIRL. Joseph Coat. Rare eight-panel Joseph Coat. Transparent clear base. Four panels are yellow and green, one is red and orange, two are red and blue, one is white. Outstanding. Germany, possibly England, circa 1870-1915. 9/16". Mint (9.7). Price: $85. CyberAuction #479, Lot #54.

6184. SWIRL. Joseph Coat. Transparent light blue base. Subsurface layer of packed color bands and strands. Various colors. Very nice. Germany, circa 1870-1915. 19/32". Mint (9.8). Price: $85. CyberAuction #508, Lot #45.

6185. SWIRL. Joseph Coat. Superb. Transparent clear base. Core is multicolor. Subsurface layer of multicolor bands and strands. Some clear spaces. One melt pit. Germany, circa 1870-1915. 17/32". Mint (9.5). Price: $80. CyberAuction #366, Lot #1.

6186. SWIRL. Joseph Coat. Transparent clear base. Core of some sort. Subsurface layer is packed strands and strands. Predominately orange, with some yellow, blue and green. One very tiny flake, a pinprick. Germany, circa 1870-1915. 7/8". Near Mint(+) (8.9). Price: $80. CyberAuction #463, Lot #52.

6187. SWIRL. Joseph Coat. Six-panel Joseph Coat. Transparent clear base. Three bands of bright blue and white, three panels of bright red. Germany, possibly England, circa 1870-1915. 19/32". Mint (9.9). Price: $80. CyberAuction #497, Lot #57.

6188. SWIRL. Joseph Coat. Very nice. Transparent clear base. Subsurface layer of packed red, blue, green, yellow, gray and clear strands. One very tiny flake. Gorgeous. Germany, circa 1870-1915. 11/16". Near Mint(+) (8.9). Price: $75. CyberAuction #385, Lot #52.

6189. SWIRL. Joseph Coat. Transparent clear base. Subsurface strands and bands of orange, blue, yellow, green and white. Earthy tones. Germany, circa 1870-1915. 19/32". Mint (9.9). Price: $75. CyberAuction #475, Lot #35.

6190. SWIRL. Joseph Coat. Rare eight-panel Joseph Coat. Transparent clear base. Four panels are yellow and green, one is red and orange, two are red and blue, one is white. Outstanding. Germany, possibly England, circa 1870-1915. 9/16". Mint (9.7). Price: $75. CyberAuction #495, Lot #12.

6191. SWIRL. Joseph Coat. Four-panel Joseph Coat. Transparent clear base. Two panels of bright red and two of bright yellow. Germany, possibly England, circa 1870-1915. 9/16". Mint (9.9). Price: $75. CyberAuction #500, Lot #33.

6192. SWIRL. Joseph Coat. Interesting six-panel example. Transparent clear base. Three panels of electric red, blue and some white. Each is separated by strands of electric red in various shades. Germany, circa 1870-1915. 19/32". Mint (9.9). Price: $75. CyberAuction #504, Lot #57.

6193. SWIRL. Joseph Coat. Stunning marble, although you might just call it a banded swirl. Transparent clear base. Two subsurface bands covering about half the marble. One is closely packed electric red strands. The other is closely packed electric yellow strands. Superb marble. Two sparkles. Germany, circa 1870-1915. 19/32". Mint(-) (9.0). Price: $70. CyberAuction #356, Lot #22.

6194. SWIRL. Joseph Coat. English colors. Transparent clear base. Subsurface layer of packed orange, red, yellow and white strands. Bright colors. England, possibly Germany, circa 1870-1915. 9/16". Mint (9.9). Price: $70. CyberAuction #425, Lot #55.

6195. SWIRL. Joseph Coat. Hard to find beginning of cane Joseph Coat swirl. Transparent clear base. One side has nicely packed strands of yellow, white and blue. Other side is loops of blue, white and some yellow. Hard to find. English, possibly German, circa 1870-1920. 11/16". Mint (9.6). Price: $70. CyberAuction #450, Lot #33.

6196. SWIRL. Joseph Coat. Transparent clear base. Colored core. Subsurface layer of stretched bands and strands. Some clear spaces. Blues, yellows, oranges, reds, greens, whites. From near an end of the cane, some of the colors are splotches. One small annealing fracture. Germany, circa 1870-1915. 13/16". Near Mint(+) (8.9). Price: $70. CyberAuction #465, Lot #56.

6197. SWIRL. Joseph Coat. Transparent clear base. Subsurface layer of "oxblood" red bands and white, blue and yellow strands. Some clear spaces. Two sparkles. Germany, circa 1870-1915. 11/16". Near Mint(+) (8.8). Price: $65. CyberAuction #501, Lot #67.

6198. SWIRL. Joseph Coat. Transparent clear base. Subsurface layer of packed bright colors. Black, blues, reds, oranges, yellows, greens. Some clear bands. Small melt chip. Some minor pitting. England, possibly Germany, circa 1870-1915. 11/16". Near Mint(+) (8.9). Price: $62. CyberAuction #506, Lot #29.

6199. SWIRL. Joseph Coat. Transparent clear bubble filled glass. Core of tightly packed strands. White, yellow, orange, green, blue, red. Germany, circa 1870-1915. 21/32". Mint (9.5). Price: $60. CyberAuction #425, Lot #21.

6200. SWIRL. Joseph Coat. Very pretty marble of blue, white, red and green subsurface bands. England, possibly Germany, circa 1870-1920. 17/32". Mint (9.8). Price: $60. CyberAuction #450, Lot #18.

6201. SWIRL. Joseph Coat. Transparent clear base. Subsurface layer of packed bright colors. Black, blues, reds, oranges, yellows, greens. Some clear bands. Small melt chip. Some minor pitting. England, possibly Germany, circa 1870-1915. 11/16". Near Mint(+) (8.9). Price: $60. CyberAuction #489, Lot #58.

6202. SWIRL. Joseph Coat. Transparent clear base. Subsurface layer of strands of electric red, white and blue. Lots of clear spaces. Germany, 1870-1915. 9/16". Mint (9.8). Price: $60. CyberAuction #501, Lot #21.

6203. SWIRL. Joseph Coat. I guess technically this is an onionskin, not a swirl. Transparent clear base. Subsurface layer of white. Packed bands on the white of orange, blue, light green, red, and yellow. Large elongated air hole melt area. Germany, possibly England, circa 1870-1915. 3/4". Near Mint(+) (8.7). Price: $55. CyberAuction #340, Lot #54.

6204. SWIRL. Joseph Coat. Transparent blue base. Colored bands in the core. Subsurface layer of bands of white, blue, orange, green. Germany, possibly England, circa 1870-1915. 9/16". Mint (9.7)l. Price: $55. CyberAuction #481, Lot #56.

6205. SWIRL. Joseph Coat. Base is lightly tinted blue. Subsurface layer of white, blue, yellow, red and green bands and strands. A few clear spaces. Two tiny moons. Germany, circa 1870-1915. 11/16". Near Mint(+) (8.7). Price: $50. CyberAuction #410, Lot #49.

6206. SWIRL. Joseph Coat. Transparent clear base. Subsurface layer is packed bands. White, orange, blue, yellow, green. Germany, circa 1870-1915. 5/8". Mint (9.7). Price: $50. CyberAuction #459, Lot #14.

6207. SWIRL. Joseph Coat. Transparent smoky base. Subsurface layer is closely packed bands. Yellow, blue, orange, red, white, some clear spaces. Earthy tones. Germany, circa 1870-1915. 19/32". Mint (9.8). Price: $50. CyberAuction #463, Lot #38.

6208. SWIRL. Joseph Coat. Transparent clear base. Subsurface layer of packed bands and strands. Predominately orange, but some yellow, red, blue and green. Earthy tones. One tiny pit. Germany, circa 1870-1915. 19/32". Mint(-) (9.0). Price: $50. CyberAuction #482, Lot #31.

6209. SWIRL. Joseph Coat. Transparent light blue base. Subsurface layer of packed bands and strands. White, orange, yellow, blue, green. Beautiful marble. Two pits. Germany, circa 1870-1915. 25/32". Near Mint(+) (8.9). Price: $50. CyberAuction #486, Lot #40.

6210. SWIRL. Joseph Coat. Light blue base. Subsurface layer is bands of yellow, red and blue. Some clear spaces. Germany, circa 1870-1915. 1/2". Mint (9.7). Price: $50. CyberAuction #487, Lot #37.

6211. SWIRL. Joseph Coat. Gorgeous six-panel Joseph Coat. Transparent clear base. Three opaque bands. One each of red/white, red/blue/white, red/yellow/blue/white. The alternating panels are translucent strands and bands of red. Bright colors. Germany, possibly England, circa 1870-1915. 9/16". Mint (9.3) (one tiny glass melt spot near bottom). Price: $50. CyberAuction #7.

6212. SWIRL. Joseph Coat. Transparent clear base. Orange core. Subsurface layer predominately of orange bands with blue, white, red and yellow. Some clear spaces. One melt spot. Germany, circa 1870-1915. 19/32". Mint(-) (9.2). Price: $47. CyberAuction #452, Lot #10.

6213. SWIRL. Joseph Coat. Transparent light blue base. Subsurface layer of packed bands and strands. White, orange, yellow, blue, green. Beautiful marble. Two pits. Germany, circa 1870-1915. 25/32". Near Mint(+) (8.9). Price: $47. CyberAuction #459, Lot #8.

6214. SWIRL. Joseph Coat. Transparent clear base. Core is packed strands of yellow, green, white, red, blue, orange. Beauty, one tiny pit. Germany, possibly England, circa 1870-1915. 19/32". Mint(-) (9.1). Price: $44. CyberAuction #498, Lot #64.

6215. SWIRL. Joseph Coat. Transparent clear base. Subsurface bands of yellow, red, white, blue and green. Gorgeous colors. Annealing fractures down one side. No external damage. Germany, circa 1870-1915. 5/8". Near Mint(+) (8.9). Price: $43. CyberAuction #403, Lot #52.

6216. SWIRL. Joseph Coat. Transparent clear base. Ghost core with dirt around it. Subsurface layer is pastel bands of white, light blue, light orange and light yellow. Melt spot on one side. Probably English, possibly German, circa 1870-1920. 9/16". Mint (9.6). Price: $42. CyberAuction #400, Lot #2.

6217. SWIRL. Joseph Coat. From near and end of the cane. Transparent dark blue base. Red, green and white subsurface bands. Large dimple fold on one side. Germany, circa 1870-1915. 9/16". Mint(-) (9.0). Price: $42. CyberAuction #443, Lot #10.

6218. SWIRL. Joseph Coat. Transparent clear base. Subsurface layer of packed bands and strands. Predominately orange, but some yellow, red, blue and green. Earthy tones. One tiny pit. Germany, circa 1870-1915. 19/32". Mint(-) (9.0). Price: $42. CyberAuction #457, Lot #45.

6219. SWIRL. Joseph Coat. Transparent clear base. Subsurface bands of yellow, red, white, blue and green. Gorgeous colors. Annealing fractures down one side. No external damage. Germany, circa 1870-1915. 5/8". Near Mint(+) (8.9). Price: $41. CyberAuction #449, Lot #57.

6220. SWIRL. Joseph Coat. Transparent clear base. Subsurface bands of yellow, red, white, blue and green. Gorgeous colors. Annealing fractures down one side. No external damage. Germany, circa 1870-1915. 5/8". Near Mint(+) (8.9). Price: $41. CyberAuction #478, Lot #9.

6221. SWIRL. Joseph Coat. Transparent light blue base. Subsurface bands orange, blue, white and yellow. Some spaces in the layer. Some pits. Germany, circa 1870-1915. 21/32". Near Mint (8.6). Price: $40. CyberAuction #420, Lot #6.

6222. SWIRL. Joseph Coat. Transparent clear base. Subsurface layer is closely packed bands and strands of orange, yellow, blue, and white. Some clear spaces. Germany, circa 1870-1915. 9/16". Mint (9.9). Price: $40. CyberAuction #448, Lot #53.

6223. SWIRL. Joseph Coat. Transparent clear base. Subsurface layer is packed strands. Oranges, whites, yellows, blues. One small flake, a few very tiny pit/chips. Germany, circa 1870-1915. 11/16". Near Mint(-) (8.2). Price: $38. CyberAuction #341, Lot #13.

6224. SWIRL. Joseph Coat. Transparent clear base. Subsurface strands of various colors. Lots of clear spaces. Nice. One tiny pit. Germany, circa 1870-1915. 9/16". Mint(-) (9.1). Price: $38. CyberAuction #441, Lot #12.

6225. SWIRL. Joseph Coat. Transparent clear base. Tightly packed subsurface layer of orange, white, yellow, green, light blue. Some clear bands. Germany, circa 1870-1915. 19/32". Mint (9.7). Price: $38. CyberAuction #485, Lot #49.

6226. SWIRL. Joseph Coat. Transparent clear base. Subsurface strands of various colors. Lots of clear spaces. Nice. One tiny pit. Germany, circa 1870-1915. 9/16". Mint(-) (9.1). Price: $36. CyberAuction #403, Lot #38.

6227. SWIRL. Joseph Coat. Transparent clear base. Subsurface layer of packed bands, with some clear spaces. Colors include red, blues, greens, white, yellow, black. Several tiny chips. England, possibly Germany, circa 1870-1915. 21/32". Near Mint (8.6). Price: $36. CyberAuction #488, Lot #36.

6228. SWIRL. Joseph Coat. Transparent clear base. Subsurface layer of bright light green and yellow bands and strands. Lots of clear. Germany, circa 1870-1915. 9/16". Mint (9.9). Price: $36. CyberAuction #501, Lot #65.

6229. SWIRL. Joseph Coat. Transparent clear base. Some subsurface strands of blue, orange, white, red, yellow. Some subsurface moons. Germany, circa 1870-1915. 7/8". Good (7.5). Price: $35. CyberAuction #401, Lot #45.

6230. SWIRL. Joseph Coat. Transparent clear base. Subsurface layer of packed bands, with some clear spaces. Colors include red, blues, greens, white, yellow, black. Several tiny chips. England, possibly Germany, circa 1870-1915. 21/32". Near Mint (8.6). Price: $35. CyberAuction #463, Lot #49.

6231. SWIRL. Joseph Coat. Joseph Coat type swirl. Transparent clear base. Two subsurface bands of multicolor strands. Covers about sixty percent of the marble. One subsurface moon. Germany, circa 1870-1915. 11/16". Near Mint(+) (8.7). Price: $33. CyberAuction #367, Lot #37.

6232. SWIRL. Joseph Coat. Transparent clear base. Several bands of color in the core. Subsurface layer of strands and bands of white, light orange, light blue, light green, with lots of clear spaces. One sparkle. Germany, circa 1870-1915. 11/16". Mint(-) (9.1). Price: $33. CyberAuction #505, Lot #29.

6233. SWIRL. Joseph Coat. Transparent clear base. Subsurface layer is packed strands of white, yellow, blue, pink, green and orange. Some clear strands too. A couple of very tiny pinpricks (may be melt spots). Rare peewee Joseph Coat. Germany, circa 1870-1915. 1/2". Mint (9.5). Price: $32. CyberAuction #487, Lot #10.

6234. SWIRL. Joseph Coat. Transparent clear base. Subsurface bands of yellow, red, white, blue and green. Gorgeous colors. Annealing fractures down one side. No external damage. Germany, circa 1870-1915. 5/8". Near Mint(+) (8.9). Price: $30. CyberAuction #495, Lot #31.

6235. SWIRL. Joseph Coat. Solid core of color bands. Subsurface layer of stretched bands and strands. Two wide clear spaces. Base glass is light blue. One small subsurface moon. Germany, circa 1870-1915. 13/16". Near Mint(+) (8.8). Price: $30. CyberAuction #507, Lot #19.

6236. SWIRL. Joseph Coat. Transparent blue tinted base. Subsurface layer of bands of white, blue, reds, oranges. Some pitting and haze. Germany, circa 1870-1915. 21/32". Near Mint(-) (8.0). Price: $28. CyberAuction #359, Lot #55.

6237. SWIRL. Joseph Coat. Transparent clear base. Subsurface bright red, blue, yellow, white and green bands and strands. A few clear strands. Several pits and tiny chips. Germany, possibly England, circa 1870-1915. 19/32". Near Mint (8.6). Price: $28. CyberAuction #501, Lot #61.

6238. SWIRL. Joseph Coat. Type of Joseph Coat. Transparent bubble filled glass. Two yellow bands in the core. Outer layer is bands of red, yellow, light blue and white. Mostly clear spaces. One tiny subsurface moon. Germany, circa 1870-1915. 25/32". Near Mint(+) (8.9). Price: $27. CyberAuction #502, Lot #2.

6239. SWIRL. Joseph Coat. Transparent clear base with multicolor subsurface bands. Misshapen (oblong), but not damaged. Germany, circa 1870-1915. 19/32". Mint(-) (9.0). Price: $26. CyberAuction #399, Lot #41.

6240. SWIRL. Joseph Coat. Transparent clear base. Subsurface layer is packed strands and bands of red, orange, yellow, blue and white. One tiny subsurface moon at the top. Germany, circa 1870-1915. 9/16". Near Mint(+) (8.7). Price: $25. CyberAuction #354, Lot #58.

6241. SWIRL. Joseph Coat. Four-panel Joseph Coat. Transparent clear base. Two narrow panels of red and light green. Two wide panels of light blue and light green. Thick outer casing of clear glass. A flake, some tiny flakes, some tiny chips and tiny pitting. Still, very unusual. Germany, possibly England, circa 1870-1915. 7/8". Good (7.6). Price: $25. CyberAuction #507, Lot #42.

6242. SWIRL. Joseph Coat. Transparent clear base. Colored core. Subsurface layer of packed bands and strands. Orange, white, blue, yellow. Some tiny chips. Germany, circa 1870-1915. 7/8". Good(+) (7.9). Price: $23. CyberAuction #469, Lot #23.

6243. SWIRL. Joseph Coat. Four-panel Joseph Coat. Transparent clear base. Two wide panels of bright white, two narrow panels of white. Polished, no pontils. Germany, circa 1870-1915. 9/16". Price: $23. CyberAuction #495, Lot #16.

6244. SWIRL. Joseph Coat. A couple of yellow strands in the core. Outer layer is stretched packed bands of light white and pale blue. Some clear spaces. A couple of tiny subsurface moons. Germany, circa 1870-1915. 13/16". Near Mint (8.3). Price: $23. CyberAuction #502, Lot #48.

6245. SWIRL. Joseph Coat. End of cane (first off cane) Joseph Coat. Rare. Transparent green with some subsurface bands ending halfway up the marble. Fractured. England, possibly Germany, circa 1870-1915. 19/32". Near Mint(-) (8.1). Price: $22. CyberAuction #401, Lot #47.

6246. SWIRL. Joseph Coat. Transparent clear base with multicolor subsurface bands. Misshapen (oblong), but not damaged. Germany, circa 1870-1915. 19/32". Mint(-) (9.0). Price: $22. CyberAuction #434, Lot #36.

6247. SWIRL. Joseph Coat. Joseph Coat type swirl. Transparent clear base. Two subsurface bands of multicolor strands. Covers about sixty percent of the marble. One subsurface moon. Germany, circa 1870-1915. 11/16". Near Mint(+) (8.7). Price: $22. CyberAuction #443, Lot #17.

6248. SWIRL. Joseph Coat. Transparent clear base with multicolor subsurface bands. Misshapen (oblong), but not damaged. Germany, circa 1870-1915. 19/32". Mint(-) (9.0). Price: $22. CyberAuction #453, Lot #45.

6249. SWIRL. Joseph Coat. Joseph Coat type swirl. Transparent clear base. Two subsurface bands of multicolor strands. Covers about sixty percent of the marble. One subsurface moon. Germany, circa 1870-1915. 11/16". Near Mint(+) (8.7). Price: $22. CyberAuction #482, Lot #14.

6250. SWIRL. Joseph Coat. Transparent clear base with multicolor subsurface bands. Misshapen (oblong), but not damaged. Germany, circa 1870-1915. 19/32". Mint(-) (9.0). Price: $22. CyberAuction #484, Lot #13.

6251. SWIRL. Joseph Coat. Transparent blue base. Subsurface layer of dark bands. Greens, blues, reds, whites. Overall very tiny subsurface moons. Germany, circa 1870-1915. 21/32". Near Mint(-) (8.1). Price: $19. CyberAuction #338, Lot #11.

6252. SWIRL. Joseph Coat. Transparent clear base. Subsurface packed bands of blue, red, yellow, green. Two tiny chips. Germany, circa 1870-1915. 1/2". Near Mint(+) (8.7). Price: $19. CyberAuction #487, Lot #41.

6253. SWIRL. Joseph Coat. Transparent clear base. Subsurface layer of bright yellow, red, white bands and strands with lots of clear spaces. Deep cold roll crease at top. Germany, circa 1870-1915. 9/16". Mint (9.5). Price: $17. CyberAuction #435, Lot #6.

6254. SWIRL. Joseph Coat. Transparent clear base. Subsurface bands of various colors. Some small clear spaces. One small subsurface moon. Germany, circa 1870-1915. 21/32". Near Mint (8.6). Price: $17. CyberAuction #457, Lot #13.

6255. SWIRL. Joseph Coat. Transparent clear base. Subsurface layer of light white, bright yellow and bright red strands. Clear spaces. Small flake. Germany, circa 1870-1915. 1/2". Near Mint (8.6). Price: $15. CyberAuction #487, Lot #44.

6256. SWIRL. Joseph Coat. Transparent clear base. Subsurface layer is predominately orange bands and strands, with some white and blue. Some clear spaces. A number of small chips. Germany, circa 1870-1915. 25/32". Good(-) (7.2). Price: $13. CyberAuction #456, Lot #13.

6257. SWIRL. Joseph Coat. Transparent clear base. Subsurface layer is predominately orange bands and strands, with some white and blue. Some clear spaces. A number of small chips. Germany, circa 1870-1915. 25/32". Good(-) (7.2). Price: $11. CyberAuction #402, Lot #57.

6258. SWIRL. Joseph Coat. Transparent clear base. Some blue strands in the core. Two panels covering about seventy five percent of the marble. Both panels are packed yellow, blue and white strands. Beauty. Germany, possibly England, circa 1870-1915. 11/16". Buffed. Price: $11. CyberAuction #410, Lot #57.

6259. SWIRL. Joseph Coat. Transparent clear base. Subsurface layer is bright orange, yellow, green, blue, white. Overall fractures. England, possibly Germany, circa 1870-1915. 11/16". Good (7.5). Price: $11. CyberAuction #413, Lot #47.

6260. SWIRL. Joseph Coat. Transparent clear base. Subsurface layer is predominately orange bands and strands, with some white and blue. Some clear spaces. A number of small chips. Germany, circa 1870-1915. 25/32". Good(-) (7.2). Price: $11. CyberAuction #437, Lot #5.

6261. SWIRL. Joseph Coat. Transparent clear base. Subsurface layer is orange, blue, green, yellow and white bands. Some clear spaces. Overall small chips. Germany, circa 1870-1915. 21/32". Good (-) (7.2). Price: $10. CyberAuction #402, Lot #59.

6262. SWIRL. Joseph Coat. Teardrop cane piece from a Joseph Coat swirl. Germany, circa 1870-1915. About 5/8". Mint (9.5). Price: $9. CyberAuction #411, Lot #3.

6263. SWIRL. Latticinio core. Huge marble in great shape. Three-layer marble from near the beginning of the cane. White latticinio core swirl. Middle layer is one band of green on white, one band of blue on white, and two bands of pink on white. Outer layer was intended to be six sets of strands. Three were supposed to be pairs of yellow, three were supposed to be pairs of white. However, two of the yellow pairs are partial and one white pair is missing entirely. Surface has one sparkle and some pinpricks from rubbing other marbles. Super example, very rare to find them this large in this nice of shape. Germany, circa 1870-1915. 2-1/16". Mint(-) (9.0). Price: $710. CyberAuction #467, Lot #31.

6264. SWIRL. Latticinio core. Very rare marble. True aqua base. White latticinio core. Outer layer is six sets of white strands. Stunning and very rare. A couple of sparkles on it. Germany, circa 1870-1915. 25/32". Mint(-) (9.0). Price: $505. CyberAuction #500, Lot #52.

6265. SWIRL. Latticinio core. Very rare marble. Latticinio core. The core is made up of two panels of latticinio strands and two panels of white strands. Each panel is separated by a red strands, so four strands in total. Outer layer is a cage of eight bands. Four are red on yellow, two are blue on white, one is green on white, last is very fiery aventurine green on white. Sold cold roll lines, a very tiny subsurface moon and a small annealing fracture on the green and white band. Still, stunning and gorgeous. Germany, circa 1870-1915. 1-1/2". Near Mint(+) (8.9). Price: $310. CyberAuction #342, Lot #60.

6266. SWIRL. Latticinio core. Base glass is very light tinted green. Yellow latticinio core. Core is misshapen. Outer layer is four white strands, two pink bands, one blue band. There is a pink band missing. In great shape. Germany, circa 1870-1915. 2-1/8". Mint (9.7). Price: $310. CyberAuction #388, Lot #54.

6267. SWIRL. Latticinio core. Stunning, large English swirl. Translucent white core. Outer layer is four sets of bands. Each consists of orange, red, white and green. Some tiny pinpricks, but nor real damage. Large. Stunning and superior. England, possibly Germany, circa 1870-1920. 1-9/16". Mint(-) (9.0). Price: $310. CyberAuction #400, Lot #57.

6268. SWIRL. Latticinio core. Super marble. Large. Opaque white core. Outer layer is six bands. Three are pink and yellow, three are blue and white. It was laid down on a rough surface when it was still hot. There is a dirt line on one side and a small dirt area on that side too. However, no damage or use marks. In great shape, given its size and age. Real beauty, you don't seem them this big in Mint condition very often. Germany, circa 1870-1915. 2". Mint(-) (9.0). Price: $300. CyberAuction #410, Lot #36.

6269. SWIRL. Latticinio core. Huge marble. Very tight yellow latticinio core (with an orangish hue). Outer layer is four bands. Two are pink and white, two are pink, blue and green. There is one sparkle and a couple of pinpricks. Still, in superb condition, given the size. Very clean. Germany, circa 1870-1915. 2-1/8". Near Mint(+) (8.9). Price: $285. CyberAuction #495, Lot #60.

6270. SWIRL. Latticinio core. Orange core encasing a trapped teardrop air bubble. Outer layer is six bands. Three are pink on yellow, three are blue on white. Several small and tiny subsurface moons, but no missing glass. Huge. Germany, circa 1870-1915. 2-3/8". Near Mint (8.3). Price: $270. CyberAuction #418, Lot #53.

6271. SWIRL. Latticinio core. Gorgeous three-layer. Yellow latticinio core. Middle layer is six bands. Three are blue on white, three are pink on yellow. Outer layer is six sets of white strands. A couple of tiny chips, overall pitting. Germany, circa 1870-1915. 2-1/2". Good(+) (7.9). Price: $270. CyberAuction #421, Lot #36.

6272. SWIRL. Latticinio core. White latticinio core swirl. Outer layer is four sets of two bands each. Two sets are pink, white and blue. Other two sets are pink, yellow and green. A couple of tiny shallow chips. Some overall pitting, not quite a haze. Germany, circa 1870-1915. 2-3/8". Near Mint(-) (8.0). Price: $260. CyberAuction #469, Lot #32.

6273. SWIRL. Latticinio core. White latticinio core. Outer layer is four bands. Each is an identical pattern of blue on white and pink on yellow bands. Surface has overall very, very light haze, with some subsurface moons and tiny chips. Huge marble. Germany, circa 1870-1915. 2-1/2". Good (7.5). Price: $235. CyberAuction #420, Lot #35.

6274. SWIRL. Latticinio core. Stunning three-layer. White latticinio core. Middle layer is six bands of pink. Outer layer is a cage of white strands. Large marble. Beauty. Several tiny chips, one small subsurface moon. Germany, circa 1870-1915. 2-1/8". Near Mint(-) (8.0). Price: $230. CyberAuction #413, Lot #38.

6275. SWIRL. Latticinio core. From near an end of the cane (last off cane). Base glass is lightly tinted blue. Yellow latticinio core. Several partial strands. Outer layer is six bands. Three are opaque white, three are transparent pink. Several tiny subsurface moons and some sparkles. Germany, circa 1870-1915. 2-3/8". Near Mint (8.3). Price: $230. CyberAuction #421, Lot #35.

6276. SWIRL. Latticinio core. Orange core encasing a trapped teardrop air bubble. Outer layer is six bands. Three are pink on yellow, three are blue on white. Several small and tiny subsurface moons, but no missing glass. Huge. Germany, circa 1870-1915. 2-3/8". Near Mint (8.3). Price: $220. CyberAuction #457, Lot #25.

6277. SWIRL. Latticinio core. White latticinio core swirl. Outer layer is four sets of two bands each. Two sets are pink, white and blue. Other two sets are pink, yellow and green. A couple of tiny shallow chips. Some overall pitting, not quite a haze. Germany, circa 1870-1915. 2-3/8". Near Mint(-) (8.0). Price: $210. CyberAuction #431, Lot #11.

6278. SWIRL. Latticinio core. Gorgeous marble. Exceptionally well constructed. White latticinio core. Outer layer is eight bands. Four are pink on white, four are green on yellow. Small subsurface moon, tiny subsurface moon, some pits, some sparkles. Germany, circa 1870-1915. 2-3/8". Near Mint(-) (8.1). Price: $205. CyberAuction #418, Lot #28.

6279. SWIRL. Latticinio core. Huge marble. Yellow latticinio core. Outer layer is four sets of two bands. Two sets are pink on white, one is green on white, one is blue on white. Gorgeous. One tiny subsurface moon, some sparkles. Huge and very hard to find. Germany, circa 1870-1915. 2-3/16". Near Mint(+) (8.9). Price: $205. CyberAuction #489, Lot #60.

6280. SWIRL. Latticinio core. First off cane marble. White latticinio core. Six outer bands. Three orange, three blue. Marble is folded over, looped design. Looks a little like a diaper fold. Gorgeous. Germany, circa 1870-1915. 11/16". Mint (9.9). Price: $200. CyberAuction #366, Lot #42.

6281. SWIRL. Latticinio core. Stunning three-layer. White latticinio core. Middle layer is six bands of pink. Outer layer is a cage of white strands. Large marble. Beauty. Several tiny chips, one small subsurface moon. Germany, circa 1870-1915. 2-1/8". Near Mint(-) (8.0). Price: $190. CyberAuction #456, Lot #8.

6282. SWIRL. Latticinio core. Very interesting marble, in great shape. Base glass is tinted green. Yellow latticinio core. Outer layer is four bands. Two are blue and white, two are green and white. Thick casing. Two sparkles. Superb. Germany, circa 1870-1915. 1-7/16". Mint(-) (9.0). Price: $185. CyberAuction #379, Lot #35.

6283. SWIRL. Latticinio core. Three layer marble. Red latticinio core. Middle layer is three yellow and three green strands, alternating. Outer layer is on blue strand. Super coloring, in great shape. Germany, circa 1870-1915. 21/32". Mint (9.8). Price: $180. CyberAuction #500, Lot #49.

6284. SWIRL. Latticinio core. Orange latticinio core swirl. Outer layer is four bands. wide. Two are purple and white, two are blue and white. Superb example. A beauty. Germany, circa 1870-1915. 7/8". Mint (9.7). Price: $175. CyberAuction #339, Lot #46.

6285. SWIRL. Latticinio core. Very interesting marble, in great shape. Base glass is tinted green. Yellow latticinio core. Outer layer is four bands. Two are blue and white, two are green and white. Thick casing. Two sparkles. Superb. Germany, circa 1870-1915. 1-7/16". Mint(-) (9.0). Price: $175. CyberAuction #356, Lot #32.

6286. SWIRL. Latticinio core. Exceptional marble. Alternating white and yellow latticinio core. Outer layer is four bands. Two are pink on white, edged by green. Two are pink on yellow, edged by green. One very tiny pinprick, one very tiny sparkle. Germany, circa 1870-1915. 1-1/2". Mint (9.5). Price: $170. CyberAuction #487, Lot #55.

6287. SWIRL. Latticinio core. Bright colors. White latticinio core. Outer layer is three red and three yellow bands. One small flat spot. This is an outstanding example. Certainly you could call it a definitive latticinio core swirl. One sparkle. Germany, possibly England, circa 1870-1915. 1-9/16". Mint(-) (9.0). Price: $160. CyberAuction #336, Lot #56.

6288. SWIRL. Latticinio core. Huge. White latticinio core swirl. Outer layer is three pink and blue on white bands, and three pink and green on yellow bands. Some pits and scratches, but no major or large damage. Very pretty. Germany, circa 1870-1915. 2-1/8". Near Mint (8.3). Price: $160. CyberAuction #365, Lot #36.

6289. SWIRL. Latticinio core. Large marble. White latticinio core. Outer layer is eight evenly spaced bands. Four are pink and yellow, two are blue and white, two are green and white. Exceptionally well made. Overall very light haze, two small moons. Germany, circa 1870-1915. 2-1/8". Near Mint(-) (8.0). Price: $160. CyberAuction #429, Lot #24.

6290. SWIRL. Latticinio core. Superb example. White latticinio core swirl. Outer layer is four bands. Two are blue flanked by bright red, two are green flanked by bright red. One melt hole near the top. Stunning. Slightly blue tinted base. Germany, circa 1870-1915. 1-5/16". Mint(-) (9.2). Price: $160. CyberAuction #429, Lot #60.

6291. SWIRL. Latticinio core. Red latticinio core. Excellent core. Outer layer is three transparent green bands and three opaque yellow strands. Germany, circa 1870-1915. 21/32". Mint (9.7). Price: $160. CyberAuction #504, Lot #61.

6292. SWIRL. Latticinio core. White latticinio core swirl. A gorgeous marble. Outer layer is four bands. Pink on white, pink on yellow, green on yellow, blue on white. In great shape with just some melted tiny air holes on the surface. Germany, circa 1870-1915. 1-1/2". Mint (9.7). Price: $150. CyberAuction #336, Lot #50.

6293. SWIRL. Latticinio core. Alternating green and white latticinio core. Base glass is very slightly tinted bottle green. There is a wide dark transparent purple band on part of the core. Outer layer is four bands. Two are dark purple and white. Two are red, blue and dark purple. Two small subsurface moons next to each other near the bottom pontil, and a couple of tiny sparkles. Rare marble. Germany, circa 1870-1915. 1-7/16". Near Mint (8.6). Price: $150. CyberAuction #374, Lot #31.

6294. SWIRL. Latticinio core. Nice large swirl. Base glass is tinted slightly blue. Yellow latticinio core. Outer layer is six bands. Three are pink on white, three are green on white. Several tiny subsurface moons, mostly clustered at the top pontil and a couple of tiny pits. In remarkable shape, given its size and age. Germany, circa 1870-1915. 1-15/16". Near Mint (8.6). Price: $150. CyberAuction #410, Lot #34.

6295. SWIRL. Latticinio core. Huge marble. White latticinio core swirl. Outer layer is four bands. Two are pink and green on yellow. Two are pink and blue on white. A couple of very small subsurface moons, a few sparkles, some melt spots. Very nice though. Germany, circa 1870-1915. 2-3/16". Near Mint(+) (8.7). Price: $150. CyberAuction #493, Lot #22.

6296. SWIRL. Latticinio core. Yellow latticinio core. Outer layer is six bands. Three are pink, blue and white. Three are pink, green and white. Thick outer casing. Lightly buffed, pontils are partially intact. Germany, circa 1870-1915. 2-1/8". Price: $135. CyberAuction #353, Lot #31.

6297. SWIRL. Latticinio core. Rare. Transparent olive green base. Yellow latticinio core. Outer layer is three sets of pink on white bands. In great shape. Germany, circa 1870-1915. 5/8". Mint (9.9). Price: $135. CyberAuction #377, Lot #53.

6298. SWIRL. Latticinio core. Orange latticinio core. Outer layer is three red and orange bands and three blue and white bands. Two small subsurface moons, next to each other. Rare marble. Germany, circa 1870-1915. 1-5/8". Near Mint (8.6). Price: $130. CyberAuction #335, Lot #50.

6299. SWIRL. Latticinio core. Large. White latticinio. Outer layer is six bands. Three are pale blue, three are red. Gorgeous marble. Germany, circa 1870-1915. 1-5/16". Mint (9.7). Price: $130. CyberAuction #381, Lot #48.

6300. SWIRL. Latticinio core. White latticinio core swirl. Outer layer is four bands. Two are pink and blue on white. Two are pink and green on yellow. One band has a chunk of unmelted sand in it. One tiny flat spot, one sparkle near the bottom pontil. Stunning example. Germany, circa 1870-1915. 1-9/16". Mint(-) (9.1). Price: $120. CyberAuction #338, Lot #33.

6301. SWIRL. Latticinio core. End of cane (last off cane) three-layer latticinio core. White core. Middle layer is a cage of pink, blue and green bands. Outer layer is a cage of yellow strands. The middle and outer layer end on one side just before the bottom pontil. One small chip, some small and tiny subsurface moons, some scratching. Beauty. Germany, circa 1870-1915. 1-3/4". Good(+) (7.7). Price: $120. CyberAuction #368, Lot #36.

6302. SWIRL. Latticinio core. Gorgeous marble. Bright orange latticinio core. Outer layer is six narrow bands. Three are white, one red, one blue and one black. Superior example!!!! English, possibly German, circa 1870-1915. 21/32". Mint (9.9). Price: $120. CyberAuction #436, Lot #51.

6303. SWIRL. Latticinio core. Large marble. White latticinio core. Outer layer is eight evenly spaced bands. Four are pink and yellow, two are blue and white, two are green and white. Exceptionally well made. Overall very light haze, two small moons. Germany, circa 1870-1915. 2-1/8". Near Mint(-) (8.0). Price: $120. CyberAuction #473, Lot #31.

6304. SWIRL. Latticinio core. Orange latticinio core. Outer layer is six bands. Three are green and white, three are blue and one. Two tiny melt pits. Gorgeous marble. Germany, circa 1870-1915. 1-3/16". Mint(-) (9.1). Price: $110. CyberAuction #351, Lot #53.

6305. SWIRL. Latticinio core. White latticinio core. Outer layer is four bands. Two are pink on white, edged by blue. Two are pink on yellow, edged by green. Huge marble. Four very small subsurface moons, on one side. Some sparkles. Still, a beauty. Germany, circa 1870-1915. 2-1/8". Near Mint (8.5). Price: $110. CyberAuction #492, Lot #21.

6306. SWIRL. Latticinio core. Yellow latticinio core swirl. Very interesting outer layer, Four bands. Two are white strands, edged by yellow. One is yellow strands edged by green on white. Last is yellow strands edged by blue on white. A couple of tiny subsurface moons. A beauty. Germany, circa 1870-1915. 1-11/16". Near Mint(+) (8.8). Price: $101. CyberAuction #414, Lot #31.

6307. SWIRL. Latticinio core. White latticinio core swirl. Outer layer is three green, white and yellow bands, and three pink, white and yellow bands. Heavy clear casing. There are several spots that are filled with a polymer or a resin (largest is 1/2"). Some other subsurface moons. Germany, circa 1870-1915. 2-5/16". Good(+) (7.9). Price: $95. CyberAuction #345, Lot #36.

6308. SWIRL. Latticinio core. White latticinio core swirl. Base glass is green tint. Outer layer is two blue, green and pink on white bands, and one blue, green and pink on yellow band. There is another band missing. Two tiny chips, a tiny rough spot, a sparkle. Very nice. Germany, circa 1870-1915. 1-5/8". Near Mint (8.3). Price: $95. CyberAuction #358, Lot #53.

6309. SWIRL. Latticinio core. Gorgeous marble, in great condition. Bright yellow latticinio core. Outer layer is six bands. Three white bands, one each of red, blue and green. Beautiful marble. Surface in great shape, with just one melt flat spot. Germany, possibly England, circa 1870-1915. 1-3/16". Mint(-) (9.2). Price: $95. CyberAuction #487, Lot #50.

6310. SWIRL. Latticinio core. White latticinio core swirl. Six band outer layer. Three are turquoise on white, three are pink on white. Stunning marble. Germany, circa 1870-1915. 27/32". Mint (9.7). Price: $95. CyberAuction #494, Lot #42.

6311. SWIRL. Latticinio core. White latticinio core swirl. Outer layer is four bands. Two are blue and red on yellow, two are green and red on yellow. Subsurface elongated air bubble. One very tiny chip, a couple of pinpricks. A beauty. Germany, circa 1870-1915. 1-1/2". Near Mint(+) (8.8). Price: $90. CyberAuction #393, Lot #59.

6312. SWIRL. Latticinio core. Very bright colors. Bright yellow latticinio core swirl. Outer layer is three bright red bands and three white bands. Stunning. A couple of tiny sparkles. England, possibly Germany, circa 1870-1915. 1-1/16". Mint(-) (9.1). Price: $85. CyberAuction #332, Lot #47.

6313. SWIRL. Latticinio core. Yellow latticinio core. Bright yellow. Outer layer is four bands. Two are pink and white, one blue and white, one green and white. Gorgeous. Germany, circa 1870-1915. 1-1/16". Mint (9.7). Price: $85. CyberAuction #348, Lot #37.

6314. SWIRL. Latticinio core. Orange latticinio core. Great coloring to the core. Outer layer is six bands. Each is blue, red and white. Some pits, one rough area. Beauty!!! Germany, circa 1870-1915. 31/32". Near Mint(+) (8.7). Price: $80. CyberAuction #336, Lot #48.

6315. SWIRL. Latticinio core. White latticinio core swirl. Outer layer is three green, white and yellow bands, and three pink, white and yellow bands. Heavy clear casing. There are several spots that are filled with a polymer or a resin (largest is 1/2"). Some other subsurface moons. Germany, circa 1870-1915. 2-5/16". Good(+) (7.9). Price: $80. CyberAuction #367, Lot #25.

6316. SWIRL. Latticinio core. Gorgeous marble. Bright white latticinio core. Outer layer is three shades of green on yellow, alternating with three bands of red on white. There are some pieces of unmelted silica floating in the marble. A dirt line, small chip, some pitting. Still, a beauty. Germany, circa 1870-1915. 1-7/16". Near Mint (8.3). Price: $80. CyberAuction #385, Lot #43.

6317. SWIRL. Latticinio core. Large marble. White latticinio core swirl. Outer layer is eight bands. Four are orange on white, two are blue on white, one is green on white, one is dark purple on white. A few very, very tiny flakes, a couple of tiny subsurface moons and some rubbing areas. Germany, circa 1870-1915. 1-13/16". Near Mint (8.2). Price: $80. CyberAuction #386, Lot #27.

6318. SWIRL. Latticinio core. White latticinio core swirl. Outer layer is four bands. Two are pink on yellow, one is blue on white, one is turquoise on white. Two tiny sparkles. Germany, circa 1870-1915. 1-3/8". Mint(-) (9.1). Price: $80. CyberAuction #387, Lot #23.

6319. SWIRL. Latticinio core. Orange latticinio core swirl. Outer layer is four bands: pink on white, green on white, blue on white, pink on yellow. In great shape. Hard to find this clean. Germany, circa 1870-1915. 7/8". Mint (9.8). Price: $80. CyberAuction #390, Lot #17.

6320. SWIRL. Latticinio core. White latticinio core swirl. Outer layer is three green, white and yellow bands, and three pink, white and yellow bands. Heavy clear casing. There are several spots that are filled with a polymer or a resin (largest is 1/2"). Some other subsurface moons. Germany, circa 1870-1915. 2-5/16". Good(+) (7.9). Price: $80. CyberAuction #404, Lot #19.

6321. SWIRL. Latticinio core. White latticinio core swirl. Outer layer is four bands. Two are pink on yellow, one is blue on white, one is turquoise on white. Two tiny sparkles. Germany, circa 1870-1915. 1-3/8". Mint(-) (9.1). Price: $80. CyberAuction #408, Lot #45.

6322. SWIRL. Latticinio core. Large marble. White latticinio core swirl. Outer layer is eight bands. Four are orange on white, two are blue on white, one is green on white, one is dark purple on white. A few very, very

6323. SWIRL. Latticinio core. White latticinio core swirl. Outer layer is three green, white and yellow bands, and three white and yellow bands. Heavy clear casing. There are several spots that are filled with a polymer or a resin (largest is 1/2"). Some other subsurface moons. Germany, circa 1870-1915. 2-5/16". Good(+) (7.9). Price: $80. CyberAuction #449, Lot #19.

6324. SWIRL. Latticinio core. Large marble. White latticinio core swirl. Outer layer is eight bands. Four are orange on white, two are blue on white, one is green on white, one is dark purple on white. A few very, very tiny flakes, a couple of tiny subsurface moons and some rubbing areas. Germany, circa 1870-1915. 1-13/16". Near Mint (8.2). Price: $80. CyberAuction #453, Lot #32.

6325. SWIRL. Latticinio core. Gorgeous marble. Bright white latticinio core. Outer layer is three bands of green on yellow, alternating with three bands of red on white. There are some pieces of unmelted silica floating in the marble. A dirt line, small chip, some pitting. Still, a beauty. Germany, circa 1870-1915. 1-7/16". Near Mint (8.3). Price: $80. CyberAuction #479, Lot #33.

6326. SWIRL. Latticinio core. Rare marble. You'd want to call it a gooseberry, but it has a core. Transparent olive green base (gooseberry type of green). Core is white latticinio. Outer layer is subsurface evenly spaced cage of white strands. One tiny melt spot. Very unusual. Germany, circa 1870-1915. 17/32". Mint(-) (9.2). Price: $76. CyberAuction #339, Lot #54.

6327. SWIRL. Latticinio core. White latticinio core swirl. Six band outer layer. Three are turquoise on white, three are pink on white. Stunning marble. Germany, circa 1870-1915. 27/32". Mint (9.7). Price: $75. CyberAuction #474, Lot #40.

6328. SWIRL. Latticinio core. Very lightly tinted blue. White core. Outer layer is six bands. All are blue on white. Filled with very tiny air bubbles. A couple of tiny subsurface moons. Germany, circa 1870-1915. 1-3/16". Near Mint(+) (8.9). Price: $70. CyberAuction #350, Lot #41.

6329. SWIRL. Latticinio core. Base glass is pale green. White latticinio core swirl. Outer layer is four bands of red and green. There is a very tiny subsurface moon near the bottom pontil. The equator is slightly dull. Germany, circa 1870-1915. 1-11/16". Near Mint(+) (8.7). Price: $70. CyberAuction #384, Lot #52.

6330. SWIRL. Latticinio core. Gorgeous. Odd colors. White latticinio core. Outer layer is six bands. Three are yellow, one orange, one blue, one two shades of turquoise. Germany, possibly English, circa 1870-1915. 7/8". (9.7). Price: $70. CyberAuction #413, Lot #57.

6331. SWIRL. Latticinio core. White latticinio core swirl. Outer layer is four bands. Two are orange on yellow, one is blue on white, one is green on white. Gorgeous. Germany, circa 1870-1915. 27/32". Mint (9.7). Price: $65. CyberAuction #332, Lot #49.

6332. SWIRL. Latticinio core. Orange latticinio core. Outer layer is four bands. Two are transparent dark purple. One is translucent white. One is bright opaque yellow. One pit. Stunning. Germany, circa 1870-1915. 7/8". Mint(-) (9.2). Price: $65. CyberAuction #337, Lot #7.

6333. SWIRL. Latticinio core. White latticinio core. Odd core. There is one yellow strand. Also, two white strands are covered by a transparent blue bands. Outer layer has four bands. Two are blue on white, two are pink and green on yellow. Surface is in great shape. Super marble. Germany, circa 1870-1915. 1-1/16". Mint (9.9). Price: $65. CyberAuction #338, Lot #15.

6334. SWIRL. Latticinio core. Transparent clear base with lots of tiny air bubbles. White latticinio core. Outer layer is three red bands and three light blue bands. A few pits and some roughness. Beauty. Germany, circa 1870-1915. 1-3/16". Near Mint(+) (8.7). Price: $65. CyberAuction #344, Lot #59.

6335. SWIRL. Latticinio core. Very lightly tinted green base. Very very light. White core. Outer layer is six bands. Three are red and white, three are green and white. Lots of tiny air bubbles in the marble. One sparkle. Germany, circa 1870-1915. 1-3/16". Mint(-) (9.0). Price: $65. CyberAuction #348, Lot #19.

6336. SWIRL. Latticinio core. Orange latticinio core swirl. Great color. Outer layer is three green bands and three yellow bands. One tiny pit and a tiny sparkle. Germany, circa 1870-1915. 31/32". Mint (-) (9.0). Price: $65. CyberAuction #410, Lot #41.

6337. SWIRL. Latticinio core. White latticinio core swirl. Outer layer is six bands. Three are blue. Three are red and white. Great coloring. Germany, possibly England, circa 1870-1915. 27/32". Mint (9.9). Price: $65. CyberAuction #459, Lot #51.

6338. SWIRL. Latticinio core. Beauty. White latticinio core. Outer layer is four bands. Two are orange, yellow and light blue. Two are orange, white and blue. One spot of melted glass. Superb. Germany, circa 1870-1915. 1-1/16". Mint (9.6). Price: $65. CyberAuction #467, Lot #6.

6339. SWIRL. Latticinio core. Bright yellow latticinio core. Outer layer is four bands. Two are blue edged by white, two are orange edged by white. England, possibly Germany, circa 1870-1915. 29/32". Mint (9.8). Price: $65. CyberAuction #471, Lot #13.

6340. SWIRL. Latticinio core. Very lightly tinted green base. Yellow latticinio core swirl. Outer layer is four bands. One green and yellow, one blue and white, one green, one blue. Germany, circa 1870-1915. 1". Mint (9.6). Price: $65. CyberAuction #505, Lot #44.

6341. SWIRL. Latticinio core. White latticinio core. Outer layer is four bands. Two are pink and blue on white, two are pink and green on white. One tiny subsurface moon and a couple of sparkles. Beautiful! Germany, circa 1870-1915. 1-1/4". Near Mint(+) (8.8). Price: $60. CyberAuction #332, Lot #31.

6342. SWIRL. Latticinio core. Alternating orange and light white core. Rare. Outer layer is four bands. Red/white, blue/white, green/white, orange/white. Very nice. Germany, circa 1870-1915. 19/32". Mint (9.9). Price: $60. CyberAuction #362, Lot #39.

6343. SWIRL. Latticinio core. White latticinio core swirl. Outer layer is four bands. Two are blue, white and purple. Two are yellow, blue, green and white. A beauty. Germany, circa 1870-1915. 1". Mint (9.4). Price: $60. CyberAuction #382, Lot #14.

6344. SWIRL. Latticinio core. One of the rarest latticinio core swirls I've seen. Core is two strands of blue, one of yellow, one of pale white, two of pale red. Outer layer is band of yellow and red and two thin strands of yellow. Small flake, some roughness. English, possibly German, circa 1870-1920. 7/8". Good (7.6). Price: $60. CyberAuction #422, Lot #30.

6345. SWIRL. Latticinio core. White latticinio core swirl. Outer layer is four bands. Two are pink on yellow, one is blue on white, one is turquoise on white. Two tiny sparkles. Germany, circa 1870-1915. 1-3/8". Mint(-) (9.1). Price: $60. CyberAuction #426, Lot #34.

6346. SWIRL. Latticinio core. Superb three layer English type colors. Inner core is very thin and is several strands of yellow and blue. Middle layer is solid with clear spaces. It's four panels: blue, red, green, yellow. Outer layer is two white strands and one yellow strand. Several small subsurface moons and a small fracture. England, possibly Germany, circa 1880-1920. 7/8". Near Mint(-) (8.1). Price: $60. CyberAuction #440, Lot #18.

6347. SWIRL. Latticinio core. Superb three layer English type colors. Inner core is very thin and is several strands of yellow and blue. Middle layer is solid with clear spaces. It's four panels: blue, red, green, yellow. Outer layer is two white strands and one yellow strand. Several small subsurface moons and a small fracture. England, possibly Germany, circa 1880-1920. 7/8". Near Mint(-) (8.1). Price: $60. CyberAuction #470, Lot #42.

6348. SWIRL. Latticinio core. White latticinio core. Outer layer is four bands. Two are blue and white, two are pink and yellow. Sparkle and a pit. Germany, circa 1870-1915. 1-5/16". Near Mint(+) (8.9). Price: $60. CyberAuction #489, Lot #42.

6349. SWIRL. Latticinio core. Very light green latticinio core. Outer layer is three orange bands and three white strands. One pit. Beauty. Germany, circa 1870-1915. 15/16". Mint(-) (9.0). Price: $60. CyberAuction #503, Lot #37.

6350. SWIRL. Latticinio core. Yellow latticinio core swirl. Outer layer is four bands. Two green and white, two pink and white. Heavily polished. Germany, circa 1870-1915. 1-15/16". Price: $56. CyberAuction #362, Lot #30.

6351. SWIRL. Latticinio core. Nice three layer. Yellow latticinio core. Middle layer is four bands. Two are pink, blue and white. Two are pink, green and white. Outer layer is four bands. Two are a pair of yellow strands, two are a pair of white strands. Polished, some damage remains. 1-7/8". Price: $55. CyberAuction #358, Lot #21.

6352. SWIRL. Latticinio core. Superb three layer English type colors. Inner core is very thin and is several strands of yellow and blue. Middle layer is solid with clear spaces. It's four panels: blue, red, green, yellow. Outer layer is two white strands and one yellow strand. Several small subsurface moons and a small fracture. England, possibly Germany, circa 1880-1920. 7/8". Near Mint(-) (8.1). Price: $55. CyberAuction #380, Lot #8.

6353. SWIRL. Latticinio core. White latticinio core swirl. Outer layer is three yellow bands and three blue bands. Very pretty. One small moon, otherwise no damage. Germany, circa 1870-1915. 1-5/16". Near Mint(+) (8.7). Price: $55. CyberAuction #387, Lot #35.

6354. SWIRL. Latticinio core. Yellow latticinio core. Outer layer is three white strands, one green band, one red band, one blue band. Long melt line on one side. One tiny subsurface moon. Germany, circa 1870-1915. 1-3/16". Near Mint(+) (8.9). Price: $55. CyberAuction #398, Lot #43.

6355. SWIRL. Latticinio core. Orange latticinio core. Nice bright color. Outer layer is four bands. Two are blue on white, two are green on white. Overall tiny and small chips and subsurface moons. Germany, circa 1870-1915. 1-3/16". Good(-) (7.2). Price: $55. CyberAuction #444, Lot #54.

6356. SWIRL. Latticinio core. Orange latticinio core. Nice coloring. Outer layer is six bands, blue on white. Beauty. Three very tiny sparkles/subsurface moons on one side. Germany, circa 1870-1915. 1". Near Mint(+) (8.9). Price: $55. CyberAuction #475, Lot #27.

6357. SWIRL. Latticinio core. Three-layer swirl. White latticinio core. Middle layer is four transparent green bands. Outer layer is four pink bands, edged by yellow. Polished. Germany, circa 1870-1915. 1-9/16". Price: $50. CyberAuction #331, Lot #26.

6358. SWIRL. Latticinio core. Yellow latticinio core. Outer layer is three white strands, one green band, one red band, one blue band. Long melt line on one side. One tiny subsurface moon. Germany, circa 1870-1915. 1-3/16". Near Mint(+) (8.9). Price: $50. CyberAuction #352, Lot #51.

6359. SWIRL. Latticinio core. Orange latticinio core. Bright orange. Outer layer is two orange bands and two blue on white bands. One manufacturing melt pit, overall pitting and tiny chips. 1-1/16". Good(+) (7.9). Price: $50. CyberAuction #379, Lot #40.

6360. SWIRL. Latticinio core. White latticinio core swirl. Outer layer is two bands of pink on white, two are blue and white. Thick outer casing. One moon, some pitting. Gorgeous. 1-9/16". Near Mint (8.4). Price: $50. CyberAuction #398, Lot #45.

6361. SWIRL. Latticinio core. One of the rarest latticinio core swirls I've seen. Core is two strands of blue, one of yellow, one of pale white, two of pale red. Outer layer is band of yellow and red and two thin strands of yellow. Small flake, some roughness. English, possibly German, circa 1870-1920. 7/8". Good (7.6). Price: $50. CyberAuction #401, Lot #46.

6362. SWIRL. Latticinio core. Red latticinio core. Has a slight orange hue to the red, but it is definitely red. Outer layer is six bands in two color patterns. In great shape. Germany, circa 1870-1915. 21/32". Mint (9.8). Price: $50. CyberAuction #426, Lot #49.

6363. SWIRL. Latticinio core. Three-layer latticinio core swirl. Base glass is sun-tinted amethyst. White latticinio core. Middle layer is two blue bands and two green bands. Outer layer is three pink and yellow bands and three pink and white bands. Polished, some damage remains. Germany, circa 1870-1915. 2-1/8". Price: $50. CyberAuction #434, Lot #19.

6364. SWIRL. Latticinio core. Orange latticinio core. Bright orange. Outer layer is two orange bands and two blue on white bands. One manufacturing melt pit, overall pitting and tiny chips. 1-1/16". Good(+) (7.9). Price: $50. CyberAuction #446, Lot #54.

6365. SWIRL. Latticinio core. White latticinio core swirl. Outer layer is five ruddy red bands and four white bands. Several pits, but a beauty! Germany, circa 1870-1915. 1-3/8". Near Mint(+) (8.7). Price: $50. CyberAuction #447, Lot #51.

6366. SWIRL. Latticinio core. White latticinio core. Outer layer is three orange/red bands and three yellow bands. Almost no twist. Superb example. Germany, circa 1870-1915. 27/32". Mint (9.8). Price: $50. CyberAuction #462, Lot #21.

6367. SWIRL. Latticinio core. Orange latticinio core. Outer layer is eight bands. Four are yellow, four are lavender and white. Superb. One melt spot. Germany, circa 1870-1915. 23/32". Mint(-) (9.2). Price: $50. CyberAuction #501, Lot #70.

6368. SWIRL. Latticinio core. Very lightly tinted blue. White core. Outer layer is six bands. Three are blue on white, three are pink on white. Filled with very tiny air bubbles. A couple of tiny subsurface moons. Germany, circa 1870-1915. 1-3/16". Near Mint(+) (8.9). Price: $49. CyberAuction #430, Lot #9.

6369. SWIRL. Latticinio core. Unusual coloring. Base is tinted slightly smoky. White latticinio core. Outer layer is two bands. Two are purple on yellow, edged by lavender. Other two are orange on white, edged by yellow. One melt spot, two tiny subsurface moons. England, possibly Germany, circa 1870-1920. 15/16". Near Mint(+) (8.7). Price: $49. CyberAuction #437, Lot #59.

6370. SWIRL. Latticinio core. English colors. Bright yellow and white alternating core. Outer layer is six bands. Three are green and white, three are red and blue. Gorgeous marble. Germany, circa 1870-1915. 11/16". Mint (9.6). Price: $48. CyberAuction #348, Lot #15.

6371. SWIRL. Latticinio core. White latticinio core swirl. Outer layer is six bands. Three are blue, and three are red. Some light very tiny chips, pitting and haze. Germany, circa 1870-1915. 1-9/16". Near Mint(-) (8.0). Price: $47. CyberAuction #337, Lot #34.

6372. SWIRL. Latticinio core. Very hard to find four-layer marble. White latticinio core. Next layer is three transparent red bands. Next is three transparent turquoise bands. Outer layer is three sets of yellow strands. All the layers are evenly space. Exceptional balance to the marble. This one is outstanding. One tiny moon. Germany, circa 1870-1915. 3/4". Near Mint(+) (8.9). Price: $47. CyberAuction #344, Lot #54.

6373. SWIRL. Latticinio core. Extremely rare end of cane latticinio core in cobalt blue glass. Multiple complete and partial white strands. No outer layer. The marble has been re-melted. I suspect that it was much larger at one point. Germany, circa 1870-1915. 27/32". Price: $47. CyberAuction #390, Lot #42.

6374. SWIRL. Latticinio core. Unusual coloring. Base is tinted slightly smoky. White latticinio core. Outer layer is two bands. Two are purple on yellow, edged by lavender. Other two are orange on white, edged by yellow. One melt spot, two tiny subsurface moons. England, possibly Germany, circa 1870-1920. 15/16". Near Mint(+) (8.7). Price: $47. CyberAuction #409, Lot #53.

6375. SWIRL. Latticinio core. Extremely rare end of cane latticinio core in cobalt blue glass. Multiple complete and partial white strands. No outer layer. The marble has been re-melted. I suspect that it was much larger at one point. Germany, circa 1870-1915. 27/32". Price: $47. CyberAuction #434, Lot #43.

6376. SWIRL. Latticinio core. Extremely rare end of cane latticinio core in cobalt blue glass. Multiple complete and partial white strands. No outer layer. The marble has been re-melted. I suspect that it was much larger at one point. Germany, circa 1870-1915. 27/32". Price: $47. CyberAuction #453, Lot #56.

6377. SWIRL. Latticinio core. Very lightly tinted blue base. White latticinio core swirl. Four band outer layer. Outer layer is four bands. Each is blue on white, one has an additional yellow. Two tiny subsurface moons. Germany, circa 1870-1915. 1-3/16". Near Mint(-) (8.7). Price: $46. CyberAuction #350, Lot #16.

6378. SWIRL. Latticinio core. White latticinio core swirl. Outer layer is two bands of pink on white, two are blue and white. Thick outer casing. One moon, some pitting. Gorgeous. 1-9/16". Near Mint (8.4). Price: $46. CyberAuction #367, Lot #27.

6379. SWIRL. Latticinio core. Yellow latticinio core. Outer layer is three white strands, one green band, one red band, one blue band. Long melt line on one side. One tiny subsurface moon. Germany, circa 1870-1915. 1-3/16". Near Mint(+) (8.9). Price: $46. CyberAuction #371, Lot #13.

6380. SWIRL. Latticinio core. Very lightly tinted blue. White core. Outer layer is six bands. Three are blue on white, three are pink on white. Filled with very tiny air bubbles. A couple of tiny subsurface moons. Germany, circa 1870-1915. 1-3/16". Near Mint(+) (8.9). Price: $46. CyberAuction #379, Lot #42.

6381. SWIRL. Latticinio core. Yellow latticinio core swirl. Outer layer is four bands. Two are pink and white, one is green and white, one is blue and white. Some sparkles and tiny pits. Germany, circa 1870-1915. 1-3/16". Near Mint(+) (8.8). Price: $46. CyberAuction #394, Lot #33.

6382. SWIRL. Latticinio core. Yellow latticinio core swirl. Outer layer is four bands. Two are pink and white, one is green and white, one is blue and white. Some sparkles and tiny pits. Germany, circa 1870-1915. 1-3/16". Near Mint(+) (8.8). Price: $46. CyberAuction #422, Lot #6.
6383. SWIRL. Latticinio core. White latticinio core. Outer layer is three orange/yellow bands and three green on yellow bands. Outstanding marble. England, possibly Germany, circa 1870-1915. 13/16". Mint (9.8). Price: $46. CyberAuction #467, Lot #35.
6384. SWIRL. Latticinio core. Exceptional example. White latticinio core. Outer layer is six wide bands. Three are red on white, three are turquoise on white. Thick outer clear casing. Very well made, a real beauty. One very tiny sparkle. Germany, possibly England, circa 1870-1915. 27/32". Mint (9.6). Price: $46. CyberAuction #485, Lot #55.
6385. SWIRL. Latticinio core. White latticinio core swirl. Outer layer is six bands. Three are orange and white, three are blue and yellow. One tiny moon. Beauty. Germany, circa 1870-1915. 31/32". Near Mint(+) (8.9). Price: $45. CyberAuction #330, Lot #7.
6386. SWIRL. Latticinio core. Three layer swirl. White latticinio core swirl. Middle layer is four wide bands. two are red on white, one is blue on white, one is green on white. Outer layer is four sets of yellow strands. One tiny manufacturing pit. 13/16". Mint (9.5). Price: $45. CyberAuction #333, Lot #54.
6387. SWIRL. Latticinio core. Yellow latticinio core. Outer layer is three opaque white bands and three transparent red bands. Tight twist. Heavily polished. Germany, circa 1870-1915. 1-7/16". Price: $45. CyberAuction #337, Lot #46.
6388. SWIRL. Latticinio core. Three layer swirl. White latticinio core. Middle layer is three yellow bands and three pink bands. Outer layer is a cage of white strands. Overall haze and some small subsurface moons. Excellent construction. A light buff will reveal a beauty. Germany, circa 1870-1915. 1-1/2". Good (7.6). Price: $45. CyberAuction #358, Lot #50.
6389. SWIRL. Latticinio core. White latticinio core swirl. Outer layer is five ruddy red bands and four white bands. Several pits, but a beauty! Germany, circa 1870-1915. 1-3/8". Near Mint(+) (8.7). Price: $45. CyberAuction #395, Lot #57.
6390. SWIRL. Latticinio core. End of cane (last off cane). Three layer. White latticinio core. Middle layer is six pink on white bands. Outer layer is six sets of yellow strands. Two outer layers have partial bands. Overall pitting and very light haze. Germany, circa 1870-1915. 1-1/16". Near Mint(-) (8.0). Price: $45. CyberAuction #437, Lot #49.
6391. SWIRL. Latticinio core. White latticinio core. Four outer bands. One each of white/blue. light green/blue, light green/orange-red, white/orange-red. Superb surface. Germany, circa 1870-1915. 7/8". Mint (9.9). Price: $45. CyberAuction #495, Lot #13.
6392. SWIRL. Latticinio core. Bright orange latticinio core. Outer layer is six bands. Three are blue and green, three are white and green. Super example. Germany, possibly England, circa 1870-1915. 19/32". Mint (9.7). Price: $45. CyberAuction #495, Lot #40.
6393. SWIRL. Latticinio core. Exceptional end of cane marble. Exhibits superior workmanship. White latticinio core. Outer layer is four bands. Two are pink, green and white. Two are blue, pink and white. The core ends halfway down the marble. The lower half of the core, for the same width of the latticinio, is an air bubble. The outer bands are the same width all the way down. Very difficult to make. Has one small subsurface moon. Germany, circa 1870-1915. 3/4". Near Mint(+) (8.7). Price: $44. CyberAuction #363, Lot #16.
6394. SWIRL. Latticinio core. Very lightly tinted blue. White core. Outer layer is six bands. Three are blue on white, three are pink on white. Filled with very tiny air bubbles. A couple of tiny subsurface moons. Germany, circa 1870-1915. 1-3/16". Near Mint(+) (8.9). Price: $42. CyberAuction #350, Lot #23.
6395. SWIRL. Latticinio core. Gorgeous. Yellow core. Outer layer is four bands. Two are green and white, two are blue and white. Germany, circa 1870-1915. 21/32". Mint (9.9). Price: $42. CyberAuction #351, Lot #42.
6396. SWIRL. Latticinio core. Yellow latticinio core. Outer layer is four wide bands. Two are pink on white, one blue on white, one green on white. Some sparkles, but well-balanced and a real nice marble. 31/32". Near Mint(+) (8.7). Price: $42. CyberAuction #376, Lot #5.
6397. SWIRL. Latticinio core. Yellow latticinio core swirl. Outer layer is two bands of orange and white, and two of blue and white. Two tiny subsurface moons and a couple of pinpricks. Very nice. Germany, circa 1870-1915. 31/32". Near Mint(+) (8.9). Price: $42. CyberAuction #403, Lot #8.
6398. SWIRL. Latticinio core. Gorgeous marble in English colors. Bright white latticinio core. Outer layer is three bright orange bands and three yellow bands. Some pinpricks. Beauty. England, possibly Germany, circa 1870-1915. 25/32". Mint(-) (9.0). Price: $42. CyberAuction #406, Lot #55.
6399. SWIRL. Latticinio core. Yellow latticinio core swirl. Outer layer is four bands. Two are pink and white, one is green and white, one is blue and white. Some sparkles and tiny pits. Germany, circa 1870-1915. 1-3/16". Near Mint(+) (8.8). Price: $42. CyberAuction #447, Lot #56.
6400. SWIRL. Latticinio core. White latticinio core swirl. Six band outer layer. Three are turquoise on white, three are pink on white. Stunning marble. Germany, circa 1870-1915. 27/32". Mint (9.7). Price: $42. CyberAuction #450, Lot #38.
6401. SWIRL. Latticinio core. Lightly blue tinted base glass. Yellow latticinio core. Outer layer is four bands. Each is white, edged by blue and red. Bottom pontil is an elongated melted nub. Some minor creasing from the bottom too. One pinprick. Germany, circa 1870-1915. 31/32". Mint (9.6). Price: $42. CyberAuction #471, Lot #22.
6402. SWIRL. Latticinio core. Superb three-layer latticinio core swirl. Yellow latticinio core. Middle layer is three bands of blue and yellow on baby blue. Outer layer is three bands of pink on white. A couple of tiny chips, but very unusual. England, possibly Germany, circa 1870-1915. 13/16". Near Mint(+) (8.9). Price: $42. CyberAuction #483, Lot #49.
6403. SWIRL. Latticinio core. White latticinio core. Outer layer is six bands. Three are blue, three are bright orange. A number of tiny moons and tiny subsurface moons. Germany, circa 1870-1915. 1-1/4". Near Mint(-) (8.1). Price: $42. CyberAuction #498, Lot #48.
6404. SWIRL. Latticinio core. Very unusual three-layer latticinio core swirl. White latticinio core. Middle layer is four pink bands. Outer layer is a cage of fourteen bands. Three yellow, three white, four red, four blue. Very nice design. Melt spot, tiny subsurface moon, several tiny sparkles. Germany, circa 1870-1915. 7/8". Near Mint (8.6). Price: $42. CyberAuction #505, Lot #62.
6405. SWIRL. Latticinio core. Very unusual three layer. Left-twist marble. Yellow latticinio core. Outer layer is four wide bands. Two are blue on white, two are turquoise on white. Floating in a layer above each band is a pink band. Gorgeous!!! Germany, circa 1870-1915. 19/32". Mint (9.9). Price: $41. CyberAuction #352, Lot #42.
6406. SWIRL. Latticinio core. Hard to find red latticinio core swirl. Outer layer is four bands. Two are blue and white, one is green and white, one is red, green and white. Overall small subsurface moons. Germany, circa 1870-1915. 5/8". Good (7.5). Price: $40. CyberAuction #340, Lot #14.
6407. SWIRL. Latticinio core. Yellow latticinio core swirl. Outer layer is four bands. Two are pink and white, one is green and white, one is blue and white. Some sparkles and tiny pits. Germany, circa 1870-1915. 1-3/16". Near Mint(+) (8.8). Price: $40. CyberAuction #347, Lot #6.
6408. SWIRL. Latticinio core. Red latticinio core. Has a slight orange hue to the red, but it is definitely red. Outer layer is six bands in two color patterns. In great shape. Germany, circa 1870-1915. 21/32". Mint (9.8). Price: $40. CyberAuction #408, Lot #4.
6409. SWIRL. Latticinio core. Exceptional end of cane marble. Exhibits superior workmanship. White latticinio core. Outer layer is four bands. Two are pink, green and white. Two are blue, pink and white. The core ends halfway down the marble. The lower half of the core, for the same width of the latticinio, is an air bubble. The outer bands are the same width all the way down. Very difficult to make. Has one small subsurface moon. Germany, circa 1870-1915. 3/4". Near Mint(+) (8.7). Price: $40. CyberAuction #440, Lot #43.
6410. SWIRL. Latticinio core. White latticinio core swirl. Outer layer is four bands. Two are red, yellow and blue. Two are red, white and blue. Superb marble. Germany, circa 1870-1915. 13/16". Mint (9.9). Price: $40. CyberAuction #459, Lot #20.
6411. SWIRL. Latticinio core. White latticinio core. Outer layer is six bands. Three are green on white, three are red. One very tiny subsurface moon. Gorgeous example of this type and size. Germany, circa 1870-1915. 1-1/16". Near Mint(+) (8.9). Price: $40. CyberAuction #475, Lot #53.
6412. SWIRL. Latticinio core. Three layer. Lightly blue tinted base. White latticinio core. Middle layer is four bands of transparent pink. Outer layer is a cage of strands. The strands are five red, five blue, four yellow, three white. Very interesting. Small melt spot, tiny pit, tiny sparkle. Germany, circa 1870-1915. 7/8". Mint(-) (9.0). Price: $40. CyberAuction #491, Lot #22.
6413. SWIRL. Latticinio core. Bright white latticinio core swirl. Outer layer is six bands. Three are blue, green and white. Three are yellow and red. Very nice. Germany, possibly England, circa 1870-1915. 19/32". Mint (9.9). Price: $40. CyberAuction #508, Lot #53.
6414. SWIRL. Latticinio core. Orange latticinio core. Outer layer is six bands. Three are blue edged by white, other three are pink edged by white. A couple of melt air hole pits, but no damage. Beauty and hard to find. Germany, circa 1870-1915. 11/16". Mint (9.8). Price: $39. CyberAuction #450, Lot #7.
6415. SWIRL. Latticinio core. Alternating white and yellow core. Outer layer is four bands. Two are blue, red and white. Two are red, green and yellow. Very nice marble. Germany, circa 1870-1915. A couple of tiny pits. Germany, circa 1870-1915. 15/16". Mint(-) (9.2). Price: $38. CyberAuction #344, Lot #50.
6416. SWIRL. Latticinio core. End of cane, last off cane. White latticinio core swirl. Outer layer is six bands. About half the marble is just clear glass, design ends. Super. Several tiny chips and subsurface moons. Germany, circa 1870-1915. 13/16". Near Mint (8.4). Price: $38. CyberAuction #434, Lot #34.
6417. SWIRL. Latticinio core. White latticinio core. Outer layer is six bands. Three are green and white. Three are orange and yellow. Germany, circa 1870-1915. 13/16". Mint (9.8). Price: $37. CyberAuction #351, Lot #44.
6418. SWIRL. Latticinio core. White latticinio core swirl. Outer layer is four pink on white bands, alternating with four blue bands. One small chip, overall haze. Germany, circa 1870-1915. 1-7/16". Good(+) (7.9). Price: $37. CyberAuction #353, Lot #24.
6419. SWIRL. Latticinio core. Transparent very lightly tinted blue base. Yellow latticinio core. Outer layer is four bands. Two are pink on white, two are blue on white. Very nice. One melt area. Germany, circa 1870-1915. 25/32". Mint(-) (9.0). Price: $37. CyberAuction #376, Lot #50.
6420. SWIRL. Latticinio core. Transparent very lightly tinted blue base. White core. Outer layer is three blue bands, alternating with three pink bands. One sparkle. Germany, circa 1870-1915. 15/16". Mint(-) (9.1). Price: $37. CyberAuction #376, Lot #53.
6421. SWIRL. Latticinio core. Orange latticinio core swirl. Outer layer is six sets of blue on white. Some subsurface moons. Germany, circa 1870-1915. 27/32". Near Mint(-) (8.0). Price: $37. CyberAuction #380, Lot #37.
6422. SWIRL. Latticinio core. Three-layer latticinio core swirl. Base glass is sun-tinted amethyst. White latticinio core. Middle layer is two blue bands

and two green bands. Outer layer is three pink and yellow bands and three pink and white bands. Polished, some damage remains. Germany, circa 1870-1915. 2-1/8". Price: $37. CyberAuction #397, Lot #27.

6423. SWIRL. Latticinio core. White latticinio core. Outer layer is four bands. One each of pink/white, pink/yellow, blue/white, green/white. Small chip and several tinier chips. Germany, circa 1870-1915. 1-5/8". Near Mint(-) 98.2). Price: $37. CyberAuction #417, Lot #20.

6424. SWIRL. Latticinio core. White latticinio core. Outer layer is six bands. Three pink, blue and white. Three pink, green and yellow. One tiny subsurface moon. One sparkle. Germany, circa 1870-1915. 1-1/8". Near Mint(+) (8.8). Price: $37. CyberAuction #445, Lot #47.

6425. SWIRL. Latticinio core. Alternating white and yellow latticinio core. Outer layer is four bands. Two are red and yellow, two are blue and white. Germany, circa 1870-1915. 13/16". Mint (9.8). Price: $37. CyberAuction #479, Lot #43.

6426. SWIRL. Latticinio core. White latticinio core. Very lightly tinted blue base. Outer layer is four bands. Two are blue and pink on white. Two are pink and green and yellow. Tight twist. Hazy and very slight chipping. Germany, circa 1870-1915. 1-5/8". Good(+) (7.9). Price: $37. CyberAuction #493, Lot #16.

6427. SWIRL. Latticinio core. White latticinio core swirl. Outer layer is four bands. Gorgeous marble. One pinprick. Germany, circa 1870-1915. 13/16". Mint(-) (9.2). Price: $37. CyberAuction #500, Lot #40.

6428. SWIRL. Latticinio core. Gorgeous three layer. White latticinio core. Middle layer is four bands. Two are pink on white, two are blue on white. Outer layer is four sets of yellow strands. Stunning marble. Well-designed and constructed. One pit. Germany, circa 1870-1915. 21/32". Mint(-) (9.2). Price: $36. CyberAuction #338, Lot #2.

6429. SWIRL. Latticinio core. Outer layer is four white strands, alternating with two bands of pink on white and one of green on white. There is a band missing. Germany, circa 1870-1915. 23/32". Mint (9.7). Price: $36. CyberAuction #342, Lot #26.

6430. SWIRL. Latticinio core. White latticinio core. Outer layer is four bands. Each band is a different color. Red/white, orange/white, blue/red/yellow, green/red/yellow. England, possibly Germany, circa 1870-1920. 21/32". Mint (9.8). Price: $36. CyberAuction #353, Lot #55.

6431. SWIRL. Latticinio core. Bright yellow latticinio core. Outer layer is four bands. Two are bright red and white, one is bright blue and yellow, one is bright green and yellow. English colors. England, possibly Germany, circa 1880-1920. 11/16". Mint (9.9). Price: $36. CyberAuction #360, Lot #30.

6432. SWIRL. Latticinio core. Interesting. Pale gooseberry amber base. White latticinio core (partial). Outer layer is three red bands and three pale green bands. One small subsurface moon. One tiny flake. Germany, circa 1870-1915. 19/32". Near Mint (8.6). Price: $36. CyberAuction #434, Lot #51.

6433. SWIRL. Latticinio core. Bubble filled base glass. White latticinio core. Outer layer is four bands. Two red, two green. Compare to Lot #57 in this auction for same marble with different outer colors. Superb. Germany, circa 1870-1915. 29/32". Mint (9.9). Price: $36. CyberAuction #463, Lot #56.

6434. SWIRL. Latticinio core. Alternating white and yellow latticinio core. Outer layer is four bands. Two are red on white, two are blue and yellow on white. Germany, circa 1870-1915. 25/32". Mint (9.6). Price: $36. CyberAuction #479, Lot #6.

6435. SWIRL. Latticinio core. White latticinio core swirl. Outer layer is three green, white and yellow bands, and three pink, white and yellow bands. Heavy clear casing. There are several spots that are filled with a polymer or a resin (largest is 1/2"). Some other subsurface moons. Germany, circa 1870-1915. 2-5/16". Good(+) (7.9). Price: $36. CyberAuction #488, Lot #25.

6436. SWIRL. Latticinio core. White latticinio core. Outer layer is six bands. Three are pink on yellow, three are green on white. Large marble. Several very tiny chips, some haziness. Germany, circa 1870-1915. 1-15/16". Good(+) (7.9). Price: $36. CyberAuction #492, Lot #34.

6437. SWIRL. Latticinio core. Very unusual swirl. Latticinio core is white strands on one side of it and yellow strands on the other half. Very odd. Outer layer is six bands. Three are opaque yellow. Others are one each of transparent blue, transparent green and transparent blue. One tiny melt spot. Rare. Germany, circa 1870-1915. 11/16". Mint (9.6). Price: $36. CyberAuction #498, Lot #26.

6438. SWIRL. Latticinio core. White latticinio core. Outer layer is four bands. Two are green on yellow, two are blue on white. Nice larger size. Several small and tiny subsurface moons. Germany, circa 1870-1915. 1-3/16". Near Mint (8.5). Price: $35. CyberAuction #340, Lot #11.

6439. SWIRL. Latticinio core. Base is very lightly tinted blue. Outer layer is four bands. Two are red, white and blue. Two are yellow, green and white. One tiny sparkle. Germany, circa 1870-1915. 15/16". Mint(-) (9.1). Price: $35. CyberAuction #351, Lot #19.

6440. SWIRL. Latticinio core. Very lightly tinted green. White latticinio core. Outer layer is two bands of orange on yellow, one blue on white, one green on white. Melt area, small chip, tiny chip, some pitting and haziness. Germany, circa 1870-1915. 1-3/8". Near Mint(-) (8.0). Price: $35. CyberAuction #355, Lot #11.

6441. SWIRL. Latticinio core. White latticinio core swirl. Outer layer is four bands. Two are pink, blue and white. Two are pink, green and yellow. Germany, circa 1870-1915. 3/4". Mint (9.9). Price: $35. CyberAuction #356, Lot #20.

6442. SWIRL. Latticinio core. White latticinio core swirl. Outer layer is two red bands, a green band and a blue band. In super condition. Exceptional example, definitive for its type. Germany, circa 1870-1915. 29/32". Mint (9.9). Price: $35. CyberAuction #407, Lot #54.

6443. SWIRL. Latticinio core. Yellow latticinio core swirl. Outer layer is four bands. Two are orange with white. Two are blue and white. Very similar to Lot #6 in this auction. Germany, possibly England. circa 1870-1915. 29/32". Mint (9.8). Price: $35. CyberAuction #471, Lot #6.

6444. SWIRL. Latticinio core. White latticinio core swirl. Outer layer is four bands. Two are red and yellow, two green and yellow. Very nicely made. Beauty. Germany, circa 1870-1915. 13/16". Mint (9.9). Price: $35. CyberAuction #475, Lot #49.

6445. SWIRL. Latticinio core. Three layer swirl. Double twisted. Yellow latticinio core is red on white bands. Outer layer is white strands. Surface haze and some damage. Germany, circa 1870-1915. 1-7/16". Good (7.5). Price: $35. CyberAuction #476, Lot #32.

6446. SWIRL. Latticinio core. Hard to find end of cane (last off cane) swirl. White latticinio core. Outer layer is four bands. Blue on white, pink on yellow, green on yellow, pink on white. Design ends about two-thirds down the marble. Two air holes (typical). One small melt chip. Germany, circa 1870-1915. 21/32". Mint(-) (9,0). Price: $35. CyberAuction #483, Lot #48.

6447. SWIRL. Latticinio core. White latticinio core. Outer layer is four red and blue bands (narrow), alternating with four white strands. Very pretty marble. Germany, circa 1870-1915. 3/4". Mint (9.5). Price: $34. CyberAuction #339, Lot #44.

6448. SWIRL. Latticinio core. White latticinio core. Outer layer is three bands. Each is pink, yellow and green. Gorgeous. Germany, circa 1870-1915. 21/32". Mint (9.9). Price: $34. CyberAuction #350, Lot #39.

6449. SWIRL. Latticinio core. White latticinio core. Outer layer is four bands. Two are orange and white, two are green and yellow. Germany, circa 1870-1915. 1/2". Mint (9.9). Price: $34. CyberAuction #387, Lot #32.

6450. SWIRL. Latticinio core. Three layer latticinio core. Middle layer is a cage of alternating green, red and blue narrow bands. Outer layer is a cage of narrow white bands. Marble was originally damaged and has been coated with a polymer. 1-13/16". Reworked. Price: $34. CyberAuction #426, Lot #26.

6451. SWIRL. Latticinio core. White latticinio core. Outer layer is three bands of blue and red, alternating with three bands of light aventurine green and red. One manufacturing melt pit. Germany, circa 1870-1915. 19/32". Mint(-) (9.2). Price: $34. CyberAuction #433, Lot #39.

6452. SWIRL. Latticinio core. Three layer latticinio core. Yellow latticinio core. Middle layer is a cage of alternating green, red and blue narrow bands. Outer layer is a cage of narrow white bands. Marble was originally damaged and has been coated with a polymer. 1-13/16". Reworked. Price: $34. CyberAuction #460, Lot #45.

6453. SWIRL. Latticinio core. White latticinio core. Outer layer is six bands. Three pink, blue and white. Three pink, green and yellow. One tiny subsurface moon. One sparkle. Germany, circa 1870-1915. 1-1/8". Near Mint(+) (8.8). Price: $33. CyberAuction #395, Lot #53.

6454. SWIRL. Latticinio core. Rare. Alternating orange and white latticinio core swirl. Outer layer is six bands. Two are blue and white, two are green and white, two are red and white. Annealing fracture, pole to pole. Germany, circa 1870-1915. 9/16" Mint(-) (9.0). Price: $33. CyberAuction #410, Lot #45.

6455. SWIRL. Latticinio core. Bubble filled base glass. White latticinio core. Outer layer is four bands. Two red, two blue. Compare to Lot #56 in this auction for same marble with different outer colors. Superb. Germany, circa 1870-1915. 29/32". Mint (9.8). Price: $33. CyberAuction #463, Lot #57.

6456. SWIRL. Latticinio core. Yellow latticinio core. Outer layer is four bands. Blue and pink on white. Heavily polished. Germany, circa 1870-1915. 1-1/8". Price: $32. CyberAuction #338, Lot #47.

6457. SWIRL. Latticinio core. White latticinio core. Outer layer is five bands. Two are red, orange and yellow. Two are green and yellow. One is yellow. One small moon, one tiny pit. Very pretty. Germany, circa 1870-1915. 1-1/16". Near Mint (8.6). Price: $32. CyberAuction #343, Lot #60.

6458. SWIRL. Latticinio core. White latticinio core swirl. Outer layer is four bands. Two are pink, blue, white and yellow. Other two are pink, blue and turquoise. Small manufacturing chip, small subsurface moon. Germany, circa 1870-1915. 1-1/8". Near Mint (8.6). Price: $32. CyberAuction #348, Lot #2.

6459. SWIRL. Latticinio core. Yellow latticinio core. Outer layer is two blue on white bands and one pink on white band. There is another missing pink and white band. Some sparkles and tiny subsurface moons. Germany, circa 1870-1915. 1-3/16". Near Mint (8.3). Price: $32. CyberAuction #348, Lot #29.

6460. SWIRL. Latticinio core. End of cane, last off cane. White latticinio core swirl. Outer layer is six bands. About half the marble is just clear glass, design ends. Super. Several tiny chips and subsurface moons. Germany, circa 1870-1915. 13/16". Near Mint (8.4). Price: $32. CyberAuction #359, Lot #53.

6461. SWIRL. Latticinio core. White latticinio core. Outer layer is four bands. Two are pink on white, two are green on yellow. Overall pitting and haze. Germany, circa 1870-1915. 1-9/16". Good(-) (7.2). Price: $32. CyberAuction #361, Lot #6.

6462. SWIRL. Latticinio core. Interesting. Pale gooseberry amber base. White latticinio core (partial). Outer layer is three red bands and three pale green bands. One small subsurface moon. One tiny flake. Germany, circa 1870-1915. 19/32". Near Mint (8.6). Price: $32. CyberAuction #376, Lot #9.

6463. SWIRL. Latticinio core. Three layer latticinio core. Yellow latticinio core. Middle layer is a cage of alternating green, red and blue narrow bands. Outer layer is a cage of narrow white bands. Marble was originally damaged and has been coated with a polymer. 1-13/16". Reworked. Price: $32. CyberAuction #391, Lot #24.

6464. SWIRL. Latticinio core. End of cane, last off cane. White latticinio core swirl. Outer layer is six bands. About half the marble is just clear glass, design ends. Super. Several tiny chips and subsurface moons. Germany, circa 1870-1915. 13/16". Near Mint (8.4). Price: $32. CyberAuction #398, Lot #13.

6465. SWIRL. Latticinio core. Three layer latticinio core. Yellow latticinio core. Middle layer is a cage of alternating green, red and blue narrow bands. Outer layer is a cage of narrow white bands. Marble was originally damaged and has been coated with a polymer. 1-13/16". Reworked. Price: $32. CyberAuction #408, Lot #41.

6466. SWIRL. Latticinio core. Beautiful white latticinio core swirl. Outer layer is six bands. Three are yellow, one blue, one orange, one green/light blue. Superb. Germany, possibly England, circa 1870-1915. 15/16". Mint (9.8). Price: $32. CyberAuction #409, Lot #47.

6467. SWIRL. Latticinio core. Beautiful white latticinio core swirl. Outer layer is six bands. Three are yellow, one blue, one orange, one green/light blue. Superb. Germany, possibly England, circa 1870-1915. 15/16". Mint (9.8). Price: $32. CyberAuction #426, Lot #15.

6468. SWIRL. Latticinio core. End of cane (last off cane). White latticinio core swirl. Outer layer is four bands. Two are blue and red on white, two are green and red on white. Design ends before bottom. Polished. Germany, circa 1870-1915. 1-3/8". Price: $32. CyberAuction #426, Lot #28.

6469. SWIRL. Latticinio core. White latticinio core swirl. Outer layer is three yellow strands and three transparent purple bands. Several tiny sparkles, all in one spot. A beauty. 29/32". Mint(-) (9.0). Price: $32. CyberAuction #426, Lot #46.

6470. SWIRL. Latticinio core. White latticinio core swirl. Outer layer is two red on yellow bands, one blue on white band, one green on white band. Germany, circa 1870-1915. 21/32". Mint (9.7). Price: $32. CyberAuction #433, Lot #49.

6471. SWIRL. Latticinio core. Gorgeous marble. White latticinio core. Outer layer is six bands. Three are red and yellow, three are green and yellow. Stunning. Germany, circa 1870-1915. 9/16". Mint (9.9). Price: $32. CyberAuction #448, Lot #17.

6472. SWIRL. Latticinio core. Stunning marble. Yellow latticinio core swirl. Outer layer is six bands. Three are pink on white, three are green on "lumpy" yellow. Tightly twisted. Several pits and pinpricks, but they are probably manufacturing. Superb marble. Germany, circa 1870-1915. 11/16". Mint(-) (9.0). Price: $32. CyberAuction #450, Lot #2.

6473. SWIRL. Latticinio core. Orange latticinio core swirl. Outer layer is four bands. Two pink and yellow, one blue and white, one green and white. Couple of melt pits, one small subsurface moon. Rare. Germany, circa 1870-1915. 11/16". Near Mint (8.6). Price: $32. CyberAuction #452, Lot #36.

6474. SWIRL. Latticinio core. Gorgeous marble. Yellow latticinio core. Outer layer is eight bands. Four are white, two are red, two are blue. Bright colors. England, possibly Germany, circa 1870-1915. 19/32". Mint (9.9). Price: $32. CyberAuction #455, Lot #28.

6475. SWIRL. Latticinio core. Bright yellow latticinio core. Outer layer is six bands. Three are blue on white, three are white. Germany, circa 1870-1915. 13/16". Mint (9.8). Price: $32. CyberAuction #459, Lot #22.

6476. SWIRL. Latticinio core. Bubble filled base glass. White latticinio core. Outer layer is four bands. Two red, one green, one blue. Superb. Germany, circa 1870-1915. 29/32". Mint (9.9). Price: $32. CyberAuction #471, Lot #7.

6477. SWIRL. Latticinio core. White latticinio core. Outer layer is four bands. Two are bright red and bright yellow. Two are green and bright yellow. A beauty. England, possibly Germany, circa 1870-1915. 25/32". Mint (9.7). Price: $32. CyberAuction #471, Lot #44.

6478. SWIRL. Latticinio core. End of cane (last off cane). White latticinio core swirl. Outer layer is four bands. Two are blue and red on white, two are green and red on white. Design ends before bottom. Polished. Germany, circa 1870-1915. 1-3/8". Price: $32. CyberAuction #478, Lot #28.

6479. SWIRL. Latticinio core. Unusual latticinio core swirl. The core is pale yellow strands. Outer layer is two red and white bands. One blue band. One fiery aventurine green band. One pit. Germany, circa 1870-1915. 19/32". Mint(-) (9.0). Price: $31. CyberAuction #345, Lot #15.

6480. SWIRL. Latticinio core. Alternating orange and pale white core. Outer layer is four bands. Two are very pale blue and orange. Other two are yellow and blue. Odd coloring. Germany, circa 1870-1915. 9/16". Mint (9.9). Price: $31. CyberAuction #410, Lot #16.

6481. SWIRL. Latticinio core. Yellow latticinio core swirl. Outer layer is three red bands and three white bands. Super marble. Germany, circa 1870-1915. 23/32". Mint (9.9). Price: $30. CyberAuction #330, Lot #40.

6482. SWIRL. Latticinio core. Yellow latticinio core swirl. Outer layer is a cage of baby blue strands. In great shape. Rare coloring. Germany, circa 1870-1915. 19/32". Mint (9.9). Price: $30. CyberAuction #331, Lot #9.

6483. SWIRL. Latticinio core. White latticinio core swirl. Outer layer is eight narrow bands. Four are yellow, two are orange, two are green on white. Nice bright colors. England, possibly Germany, circa 1880-1920. 7/8". Mint(-) (9.1). Price: $30. CyberAuction #336, Lot #26.

6484. SWIRL. Latticinio core. Yellow latticinio core. Outer layer is four bands of yellow, blue and white. The yellow is really a yellow/green color with almost fluorescent-looking qualities to it. Very odd color. Germany, circa 1870-1915. 21/32". Mint (9.7). Price: $30. CyberAuction #337, Lot #18.

6485. SWIRL. Latticinio core. Orange latticinio core swirl. Outer layer is three blue bands and three white bands. One small chip, a couple of small subsurface moons. Germany, circa 1870-1915. 7/8". Good(+) (7.9). Price: $30. CyberAuction #355, Lot #19.

6486. SWIRL. Latticinio core. White latticinio core swirl. Outer layer is three yellow strands and three transparent purple bands. Several tiny sparkles, all in one spot. A beauty. 29/32". Mint(-) (9.0). Price: $30. CyberAuction #383, Lot #3.

6487. SWIRL. Latticinio core. Gorgeous. White latticinio core. Outer layer is four bright yellow bands, two bright orange bands, two bands of green on white. One small melt pit, one tiny subsurface moon. Germany, circa 1870-1915. 29/32". Near Mint(+) (8.9). Price: $30. CyberAuction #390, Lot #41.

6488. SWIRL. Latticinio core. White latticinio core swirl. Outer layer is three yellow strands and three transparent purple bands. Several tiny sparkles all in one spot. A beauty. 29/32". Mint(-) (9.0). Price: $30. CyberAuction #408, Lot #38.

6489. SWIRL. Latticinio core. White latticinio core. Outer layer is six bands. Three are orange and red, three are blue and yellow. Surface has one tiny melt spot. England, possibly Germany, circa 1870-1915. 27/32". Mint(-) (9.2). Price: $30. CyberAuction #471, Lot #1.

6490. SWIRL. Latticinio core. White latticinio core. Outer layer is three blue and white bands, alternating with three pink, turquoise and white bands. Overall haziness and small chips. Germany, circa 1870-1915. 1-5/8". Collectible. Price: $30. CyberAuction #486, Lot #21.

6491. SWIRL. Latticinio core. Three layer latticinio core. Yellow latticinio core. Middle layer is a cage of alternating green, red and blue narrow bands. Outer layer is a cage of narrow white bands. Marble was originally damaged and has been coated with a polymer. 1-13/16". Reworked. Price: $30. CyberAuction #490, Lot #24.

6492. SWIRL. Latticinio core. Yellow latticinio core. Outer layer is six bands. Three are orange and blue, three are orange and green. One tiny chip, several pinpricks. Germany, circa 1870-1915. 1". Near Mint(+) (8.7). Price: $30. CyberAuction #499, Lot #9.

6493. SWIRL. Latticinio core. White latticinio core. Outer layer is six bands. Three yellow, one blue, one red, one green. Germany, circa 1870-1915. 19/32". Mint (9.9). Price: $30. CyberAuction #508, Lot #14.

6494. SWIRL. Latticinio core. White latticinio core. Outer layer is eight bands. Two red, two yellow, two white, one green, one blue. Beauty. Germany, circa 1870-1915. 11/16". Mint (9.7). Price: $30. CyberAuction #508, Lot #62.

6495. SWIRL. Latticinio core. White latticinio core swirl. Outer layer is three bands of pink on yellow and three bands of blue on white. Polished. Germany, circa 1870-1915. 1-3/8". Price: $29. CyberAuction #331, Lot #38.

6496. SWIRL. Latticinio core. Yellow latticinio core swirl. Outer layer is three pink and three white bands. Thick outer casing. A few melt air holes on the surface, but a beauty. Germany, circa 1870-1915. 13/16". Mint (9.6). Price: $29. CyberAuction #334, Lot #12.

6497. SWIRL. Latticinio core. Orange latticinio core. Nice bright color. Outer layer is four bands. Two are blue on white, two are green on white. Overall tiny and small chips and subsurface moons. Germany, circa 1870-1915. 1-3/16". Good(-) (7.2). Price: $29. CyberAuction #347, Lot #32.

6498. SWIRL. Latticinio core. Very lightly blue tinted base. Yellow latticinio, exhibiting a slight green hue because of the base glass. Outer layer is three bands of orange and white, and three of transparent green and white. One tiny chip. Very nice marble. Germany, circa 1870-1915. 7/8". Near Mint(+) (8.8). Price: $29. CyberAuction #374, Lot #29.

6499. SWIRL. Latticinio core. White latticinio core swirl. Outer layer is four bands. Two are pink on yellow, one green on white, one blue on white. Some tiny subsurface moons, overall pitting. Germany, circa 1870-1915. 1-1/4". Good(+) (7.9). Price: $29. CyberAuction #397, Lot #34.

6500. SWIRL. Latticinio core. End of cane (first-off-cane) latticinio core swirl. White core. Outer layer is two bands of blue on white and two of red on white. One side has partial bands. Annealing fracture. One pit. Germany, circa 1870-1915. 23/32". Near Mint(+) (8.9). Price: $29. CyberAuction #437, Lot #44.

6501. SWIRL. Latticinio core. Three layer. Gorgeous marble. White latticinio core. Middle layer is three sets of blue and red on white bands. Outer layer is three sets of green and red on white. Almost no twist. Gorgeous. Germany, circa 1870-1915. 11/16". Mint (9.7). Price: $29. CyberAuction #473, Lot #55.

6502. SWIRL. Latticinio core. Yellow latticinio core. Outer layer is six bands. Three are orange and blue, three are orange and green. One tiny chip, several pinpricks. Germany, circa 1870-1915. 1". Near Mint(+) (8.7). Price: $29. CyberAuction #477, Lot #11.

6503. SWIRL. Latticinio core. Yellow latticinio core swirl. Outer layer is four pairs of bands. Two pairs of pink on white, two of turquoise on white. Small melt flake. Germany, circa 1870-1915. 7/8". Mint (-) (9.0). Price: $29. CyberAuction #502, Lot #24.

6504. SWIRL. Latticinio core. White latticinio core. Eight outer bands. Four are transparent pink, two are pale opaque yellow, one transparent blue, one transparent green. Some sparkles and pitting. Germany, circa 1870-1915. 1-1/16". Near Mint(+) (8.7). Price: $28. CyberAuction #335, Lot #19.

6505. SWIRL. Latticinio core. Three layer. From near an end of the cane. Core is several white strands. Middle layer is three blue bands. Outer layer is two white bands with pink, green and yellow on them. One outer band appears to be missing. Not wet, but no damage. Germany, circa 1870-1915. 29/32". Mint(-) (9.0). Price: $28. CyberAuction #398, Lot #31.

6506. SWIRL. Latticinio core. White latticinio core swirl. Outer layer is four bands. Two are pink, blue, white and yellow. Other two are pink, blue and turquoise. Small manufacturing chip, small subsurface moon. Germany, circa 1870-1915. 1-1/8". Near Mint (8.6). Price: $28. CyberAuction #445, Lot #50.

6507. SWIRL. Latticinio core. Yellow latticinio core. Trapped air bubble. Outer layer is six bands. Three are green, three are lavender on green.

Beauty. Germany, possibly England, circa 1870-1915. 21/32". Mint (9.7). Price: $28. CyberAuction #464, Lot #32.

6508. SWIRL. Latticinio core. White latticinio core swirl. White latticinio core. Outer layer is six narrow bands. Three are blue on white, three are pink on white. In great shape. Gorgeous. Germany, circa 1870-1915. 21/32". Mint (9.9). Price: $27. CyberAuction #331, Lot #2.

6509. SWIRL. Latticinio core. White latticinio core swirl. Outer layer is three pink on yellow bands, and three green bands. One pit. A beauty. Germany, circa 1870-1915. 3/4". Mint(-) (9.0). Price: $27. CyberAuction #332, Lot #10.

6510. SWIRL. Latticinio core. From near the end of a cane. Yellow latticinio core. Outer layer is six bands. Each is blue, red, and white. Small smeared glass area at the bottom from near the end of the cane. A couple of small flakes. Germany, circa 1870-1915. 1". Near Mint (8.5). Price: $27. CyberAuction #334, Lot #50.

6511. SWIRL. Latticinio core. Several pale orange latticinio strands in the core. Outer layer is three wide bands of blue and white, alternating with three bands of ruddy orange and white. Almost all the bands are partial. From near the end of the cane. Germany, circa 1870-1915. 11/16". Mint (9.9). Price: $27. CyberAuction #342, Lot #2.

6512. SWIRL. Latticinio core. Pale white latticinio core. Outer layer is a cage of six red bands. Beauty. Germany, circa 1870-1915. 25/32". Mint (9.8). Price: $27. CyberAuction #342, Lot #37.

6513. SWIRL. Latticinio core. White latticinio core. Large piece of unmelted silica on the core. Outer layer is four bands. Two pink, green and yellow. Two pink, blue and white. Dirt line, some tiny pits and tiny subsurface moon. Germany, circa 1870-1915. 1-1/16". Near Mint (8.6). Price: $27. CyberAuction #347, Lot #55.

6514. SWIRL. Latticinio core. Translucent white latticinio core swirl. Outer layer is four bands. Two are one is blue, one is green on white. Beauty. Germany, circa 1870-1915. 5/8". Mint (9.9). Price: $27. CyberAuction #350, Lot #46.

6515. SWIRL. Latticinio core. White latticinio core swirl. From near an end of the cane. Outer layer is three bands. Two are orange/red and white. One is light green and yellow (very wide). Appears to be missing another green and yellow band. Germany, circa 1870-1915. 11/16". Mint (9.7). Price: $27. CyberAuction #363, Lot #37.

6516. SWIRL. Latticinio core. White latticinio core swirl. Outer layer is two purple on white bands alternating with two orange bands. Thick casing of clear glass. One melt spot, a tiny subsurface moon, some minor surface scratching. Very pretty. Germany, circa 1870-1915. 15/16". Near Mint(+) (8.9). Price: $27. CyberAuction #371, Lot #20.

6517. SWIRL. Latticinio core. Unusual latticinio core swirl. The core is pale yellow strands. Outer layer is two red and white bands. One blue band. One fiery aventurine green band. One pit. Germany, circa 1870-1915. 19/32". Mint(-) (9.0). Price: $27. CyberAuction #374, Lot #28.

6518. SWIRL. Latticinio core. White latticinio core. Outer layer is three blue and white bands, alternating with three pink, turquoise and white bands. Overall haziness and small chips. Germany, circa 1870-1915. 1-5/8". Collectible. Price: $27. CyberAuction #379, Lot #31.

6519. SWIRL. Latticinio core. White latticinio core. Outer layer is four bands. Two are pink and yellow, one is green and yellow, one is blue and white. Superb. Germany, circa 1870-1915. 11/16". Mint (9.7). Price: $27. CyberAuction #381, Lot #55.

6520. SWIRL. Latticinio core. Bright white core. Outer layer is four brightly colored bands. One pit. England, possibly Germany, circa 1870-1920. 19/32". Mint(-) (9.1). Price: $27. CyberAuction #382, Lot #52.

6521. SWIRL. Latticinio core. End of cane (last off cane). White latticinio core swirl. Outer layer is four bands. Two are blue and red on white, two are green and red on white. Design ends before bottom. Polished. Germany, circa 1870-1915. 1-3/8". Price: $27. CyberAuction #406, Lot #30.

6522. SWIRL. Latticinio core. End of cane (last off cane). Three layer. White latticinio core. Middle layer is six pink on white bands. Outer layer is six sets of yellow strands. Two outer layers have partial bands. Overall pitting and very light haze. Germany, circa 1870-1915. 1-1/16". Near Mint(-) (8.0). Price: $27. CyberAuction #406, Lot #37.

6523. SWIRL. Latticinio core. White latticinio core. Outer layer is three blue and white bands, alternating with three pink, turquoise and white bands. Overall haziness and small chips. Germany, circa 1870-1915. 1-5/8". Collectible. Price: $27. CyberAuction #440, Lot #35.

6524. SWIRL. Latticinio core. White latticinio core. Outer layer is three bands of red on yellow and three of blue on white. Surface was damaged. The marble was polished and then coated with a polymer. 1-11/16". Reworked. Price: $27. CyberAuction #449, Lot #30.

6525. SWIRL. Latticinio core. English colors. White latticinio core swirl. Outer layer is six bands. Three are bright yellow, one bright red, one green, one baby blue. One tiny flat spot. Beautiful marble. England, possibly Germany, circa 1870-1920. 9/16". Mint (9.7). Price: $27. CyberAuction #450, Lot #14.

6526. SWIRL. Latticinio core. English colors. White latticinio core swirl. Outer layer is six bands. Three are bright yellow, one bright red, one green, one baby blue. One tiny flat spot. Beautiful marble. England, possibly Germany, circa 1870-1920. 9/16". Mint (9.7). Price: $27. CyberAuction #482, Lot #32.

6527. SWIRL. Latticinio core. White latticinio core. Outer layer is three bright yellow and three bright orange bands. Gorgeous. English, possibly Germany, circa 1870-1915. 19/32". Mint (9.8). Price: $27. CyberAuction #491, Lot #12.

6528. SWIRL. Latticinio core. White latticinio core. Outer layer is six equidistantly spaced bands. Three yellow and three light green. Beauty. Ger-

many, circa 1870-1915. 11/16". Mint (9.9). Price: $27. CyberAuction #498, Lot #31.

6529. SWIRL. Latticinio core. Nice marble. White latticinio core swirl. Outer layer is a cage of three white bands and three orange bands. One tiny sparkle. Germany, circa 1870-1915. 29/32". Mint (-) (9.2). Price: $27. CyberAuction #501, Lot #19.

6530. SWIRL. Latticinio core. This is the first piece of a rod. Flattened, perhaps intended as drawer pull or other decorative piece. Yellow latticinio core. Six outer bands in two color schemes. Design shoots out the top. Flattened, resembles a flower. Very nice. Germany, circa 1870-1915. 1-1/2" diameter, about 3/4" high. Mint (9.5). Price: $26. CyberAuction #363, Lot #11.

6531. SWIRL. Latticinio core. White latticinio core swirl. Outer layer is two bands of blue on white, alternating with two bands of green on yellow. One melt pit. Gorgeous. 11/16". Mint(-) (9.2). Price: $26. CyberAuction #380, Lot #16.

6532. SWIRL. Latticinio core. White latticinio core. Outer layer is three pink on yellow bands and three blue on white bands. Small subsurface moon, manufacturing chip, and some very light haziness. Germany, circa 1870-1915. 1". Near Mint (8.6). Price: $26. CyberAuction #406, Lot #27.

6533. SWIRL. Latticinio core. End of cane (first-off-cane) latticinio core swirl. White core. Outer layer is two bands of blue on white and two of red on white. One side has partial bands. Annealing fracture. One pit. Germany, circa 1870-1915. 23/32". Near Mint(+) (8.9). Price: $26. CyberAuction #406, Lot #23.

6534. SWIRL. Latticinio core. Yellow latticinio core. Outer layer is eight bands. Four are white, two red and two blue. Bright colors. Gorgeous. Germany, circa 1870-1915. 9/16". Mint (9.9). Match to Lot #42 in this auction. Price: $26. CyberAuction #448, Lot #49.

6535. SWIRL. Latticinio core. Bright yellow latticinio core. Outer layer is eight bands. Four are white, two blue, two red. Very colorful. Germany, possibly England, circa 1870-1915. 9/16". Mint (9.9). Price: $26. CyberAuction #459, Lot #12.

6536. SWIRL. Latticinio core. Orange latticinio core. Outer layer is four bands. Two are green and white, two are blue and white. Several small chips. Germany, circa 1870-1915. 1". Near Mint(-) (8.0). Price: $26. CyberAuction #465, Lot #21.

6537. SWIRL. Latticinio core. White latticinio core swirl. Six band outer layer. Three are blue on white, three are red. Several small chips, subsurface moons and some scratching. Germany, circa 1870-1915. 1-3/8". Good(+) (7.8). Price: $25. CyberAuction #353, Lot #16.

6538. SWIRL. Latticinio core. Beauty. White latticinio core swirl. Outer layer is six bands. Three are red and white, three are green and yellow. A few pits. Germany, circa 1870-1915. 5/8". Mint(-) (9.1). Price: $25. CyberAuction #353, Lot #50.

6539. SWIRL. Latticinio core. Yellow latticinio core. Outer layer is two orange and white bands and two light blue and white bands. Beauty. Germany, circa 1870-1915. 19/32". Mint (9.7). Price: $25. CyberAuction #357, Lot #28.

6540. SWIRL. Latticinio core. Yellow latticinio core. Outer layer is four bands. Two pink and white, one blue and white, one green and white. Germany, circa 1870-1915. 15/32". Mint (9.7). Price: $25. CyberAuction #362, Lot #10.

6541. SWIRL. Latticinio core. White latticinio core. Outer layer is six bands. All narrow. Three are pink, blue and white. Three are pink, green and white. Germany, circa 1870-1915. 21/32". Mint (9.7). Price: $25. CyberAuction #363, Lot #32.

6542. SWIRL. Latticinio core. Orange latticinio core. Outer layer is four bands. Two are orange, white and blue. Two are orange, yellow and green. Overall tiny chipping with a few larger flakes. Germany, circa 1870-1915. 7/8". Good (7.4). Price: $25. CyberAuction #370, Lot #50.

6543. SWIRL. Latticinio core. Red latticinio core swirl. Outer layer is two red and blue bands and two red and green bands. Double twist. A couple of sparkles, overall pinpricking. Germany, circa 1870-1915. 23/32". Near Mint(-) (8.1). Price: $25. CyberAuction #402, Lot #60.

6544. SWIRL. Latticinio core. Hard to find yellow and white alternating core. Outer layer is six bands. Three are red, blue and white. Three are green, pink and yellow. Germany, circa 1870-1915. 5/8". Mint (9.9). Price: $25. CyberAuction #418, Lot #11.

6545. SWIRL. Latticinio core. White latticinio core swirl. Outer layer is two bands of red on white, and two of green on yellow. Gorgeous. Germany, circa 1870-1915. 9/16". Mint (9.9). Price: $25. CyberAuction #433, Lot #46.

6546. SWIRL. Latticinio core. English colors. White latticinio core. Outer layer is six bands. Three are baby blue, three are yellow. One manufacturing melt spot, one manufacturing pit, tiny annealing fracture in one band. Very pretty. Probably English, possibly German, circa 1870-1920. 19/32". Mint (9.5). Price: $25. CyberAuction #450, Lot #11.

6547. SWIRL. Latticinio core. Yellow latticinio core. Bright. Outer layer is eight bands. Four white, two red, two blue. Germany, possibly England, circa 1870-1915. 17/32". Mint (9.9). Price: $25. CyberAuction #452, Lot #22.

6548. SWIRL. Latticinio core. Gorgeous marble. White latticinio core. Outer layer is three red and three yellow bands. Gorgeous example. Small melt pit on one side. England, possibly Germany, circa 1870-1915. 27/32". Mint(-) (9.2). Price: $25. CyberAuction #467, Lot #15.

6549. SWIRL. Latticinio core. White latticinio core. Outer layer is six bands. Three orange and three lavender. Germany, circa 1870-1915. 11/16". Mint (9.7). Price: $25. CyberAuction #498, Lot #6.

6550. SWIRL. Latticinio core. Bright orange latticinio core. Outer layer is six bands of blue on white. A couple of pits. Germany, circa 1870-1915. 11/16". Near Mint(+) (8.7). Price: $25. CyberAuction #498, Lot #13.

6551. SWIRL. Latticinio core. Very thin, pale white latticinio core. Outer layer is three beads of transparent pink and three strands of opaque white. In very nice shape. Germany, circa 1870-1915. 21/32". Mint (9.9). Price: $24. CyberAuction #336, Lot #23.

6552. SWIRL. Latticinio core. White latticinio core swirl. Outer layer is four bands. Two are pink on yellow, one blue on white, one green on white. Germany, circa 1870-1915. A couple of sparkles. 7/8". Mint(-) (9.0). Price: $24. CyberAuction #346, Lot #41.

6553. SWIRL. Latticinio core. Orange latticinio core. Outer layer is three bands. Two are red, yellow and green. Two are red, white and blue. Some tiny and small chipping. Germany, circa 1870-1915. 7/8". Good(+) (7.9). Price: $24. CyberAuction #353, Lot #42.

6554. SWIRL. Latticinio core. White latticinio core. Outer layer is two blue and white bands, two green and white bands. Germany, circa 1870-1915. 7/16". Mint (9.9). Price: $24. CyberAuction #357, Lot #16.

6555. SWIRL. Latticinio core. Transparent clear base. Greenish tinted yellow strands. Outer layer is two bands of blue on white and two or pink on yellow. Germany, circa 1870-1915. 5/8". Mint (9.7). Price: $24. CyberAuction #380, Lot #47.

6556. SWIRL. Latticinio core. Yellow latticinio core swirl. Outer layer is seven bands. Three are opaque white, two are black, two are pink. Some small chips, pits and haziness. Germany, circa 1870-1915. 1-11/16". Good(+) (7.9). Price: $24. CyberAuction #446, Lot #25.

6557. SWIRL. Latticinio core. Transparent green base. Poorly formed white latticinio core with some stray white bands. One chip, some pitting and roughness. Germany, circa 1870-1915. 19/32". Near Mint (8.4). Price: $24. CyberAuction #449, Lot #31.

6558. SWIRL. Latticinio core. Very slightly blue tinted base. Yellow latticinio core. Outer layer is four bands. Two are red and white, two are blue and white. Two tiny melt spots, one sparkle. Very nice. Germany, circa 1870-1915. 29/32". Mint(-) (9.0). Price: $24. CyberAuction #449, Lot #47.

6559. SWIRL. Latticinio core. Gorgeous. White latticinio core. Outer layer is four bands. Each is yellow, green and powder blue, edged by red. Germany, circa 1870-1915. 19/32". Mint (9.8). Price: $24. CyberAuction #491, Lot #38.

6560. SWIRL. Latticinio core. Very light green base. Opaque white strands, only a partial core. Outer layer is two bands. Two are blue on white, two are orange/red on white. One tiny rough spot. Germany, circa 1870-1915. 27/32". Mint(-) (9.1). Price: $24. CyberAuction #508, Lot #49.

6561. SWIRL. Latticinio core. Peewee latticinio core. Germany, circa 1870-1915. 15/32". Mint (9.8). Price: $23. CyberAuction #347, Lot #19.

6562. SWIRL. Latticinio core. Alternating orange and white strands. Rare. Outer layer is two ruddy orange and blue bands and two blue on white bands. One pit. Germany, circa 1870-1915. 11/16". Mint(-) (9.2). Price: $23. CyberAuction #359, Lot #39.

6563. SWIRL. Latticinio core. White latticinio core. Outer layer is two orange and white bands, one red band, three dark blue and yellow. Gorgeous. Germany, circa 1870-1915. 23/32". Mint (9.8). Price: $23. CyberAuction #360, Lot #10.

6564. SWIRL. Latticinio core. Yellow latticinio core. Outer layer is four wide bands. Two pink and white, two turquoise and white. Germany, circa 1870-1915. 1/2". Mint (9.6). Price: $23. CyberAuction #381, Lot #14.

6565. SWIRL. Latticinio core. White latticinio core swirl. Outer layer is two bands of blue on white, alternating with two bands of green on yellow. One melt spot. Gorgeous. 11/16". Mint(-) (9.2). Price: $23. CyberAuction #442, Lot #51.

6566. SWIRL. Latticinio core. Orange latticinio core swirl. Outer layer is six sets of blue on white. Some subsurface moons. Germany, circa 1870-1915. 27/32". Near Mint(-) (8.0). Price: $23. CyberAuction #442, Lot #57.

6567. SWIRL. Latticinio core. White latticinio core. Outer layer is four wide bands. Two pink on white, one blue on white, one green on white. Outstanding example. Germany, circa 1870-1915. 11/16". Mint (9.9). Price: $23. CyberAuction #459, Lot #2.

6568. SWIRL. Latticinio core. Orange latticinio core. Core is not complete. Outer layer is three bands. Each is blue and white. Germany, circa 1870-1915. One tiny pit. 25/32". Mint(-) (9.2). Price: $23. CyberAuction #469, Lot #21.

6569. SWIRL. Latticinio core. Yellow latticinio core. Four outer bands. Two are pink and white, one is blue and white, one is green and white. A couple of pinpricks. Germany, circa 1870-1915. 11/16". Mint (-) (9.2). Price: $23. CyberAuction #469, Lot #26.

6570. SWIRL. Latticinio core. Yellow latticinio core. Outer layer is six bands. Three are orange and three are white. Germany, circa 1870-1915. 11/16". Mint (9.7). Price: $23. CyberAuction #475, Lot #25.

6571. SWIRL. Latticinio core. White latticinio core. Outer layer is three bands. One white, one blue, one red. Germany, circa 1870-1915. 27/32". Mint (9.8). Price: $23. CyberAuction #506, Lot #10.

6572. SWIRL. Latticinio core. Pale yellow latticinio core. Outer layer is three blue and white bands, alternating with three yellow and red bands. A couple of tiny pits and tiny subsurface moons. Germany, circa 1870-1915. 7/8". Near Mint (8.6). Price: $22. CyberAuction #337, Lot #16.

6573. SWIRL. Latticinio core. White latticinio core swirl. Outer layer is six bands. Three are blue, pink and white. Three are green, pink and yellow. Several small chips and some tiny ones. Germany, circa 1870-1915. 1-1/2". Good(+) (7.9). Price: $22. CyberAuction #340, Lot #27.

6574. SWIRL. Latticinio core. Yellow latticinio core. Outer layer is two bands of pink on white, one of green, one of blue. One pit. Very pretty. Germany, circa 1870-1915. 25/32". Mint(-) (9.0). Consignor note: B3. Price: $22. CyberAuction #344, Lot #23.

6575. SWIRL. Latticinio core. Yellow latticinio core. Six band outer layer.

Three are orange. Three are green on white. Peewee. Germany, circa 1870-1915. 15/32". Mint (9.6). Price: $22. CyberAuction #351, Lot #40.

6576. SWIRL. Latticinio core. Yellow latticinio core. Outer layer is three red on white bands and three blue on white bands. Large "cleave" fracture on one side, the piece looks like it was glued back on. Large chip and smaller chips. Germany, circa 1870-1915. 2-3/8". Collectible. Price: $22 CyberAuction #358, Lot #19.

6577. SWIRL. Latticinio core. Three layer. From near an end of the cane. Core is several white strands. Middle layer is three blue bands. Outer layer is two white bands with pink, green and yellow on them. One outer band appears to be missing. Not wet, but no damage. Germany, circa 1870-1915. 29/32". Mint(-) (9.0). Price: $22. CyberAuction #365, Lot #12.

6578. SWIRL. Latticinio core. Transparent green base. Poorly formed white latticinio core with some stray white bands. One chip, some pitting and roughness. Germany, circa 1870-1915. 19/32". Near Mint (8.4). Price: $22 CyberAuction #372, Lot #7.

6579. SWIRL. Latticinio core. Orange latticinio core. Outer layer is three green bands and three orange bands. Several subsurface moons. Germany, circa 1870-1915. 27/32". Good(+) (7.9). Price: $22 CyberAuction #376, Lot #39.

6580. SWIRL. Latticinio core. Yellow latticinio core. Outer layer is three blue bands alternating with three pink on yellow bands. Germany, circa 1870-1915. 25/32". Mint (9.7). Price: $22. CyberAuction #381, Lot #4.

6581. SWIRL. Latticinio core. White latticinio core. Outer layer is three bands of red on yellow and three of blue on white. Surface was damaged. The marble was polished and then coated with a polymer. 1-11/16". Reworked. Price: $22. CyberAuction #391, Lot #27.

6582. SWIRL. Latticinio core. Transparent green base. Poorly formed white latticinio core with some stray white bands. One chip, some pitting and roughness. Germany, circa 1870-1915. 19/32". Near Mint (8.4). Price: $22. CyberAuction #398, Lot #17.

6583. SWIRL. Latticinio core. Yellow latticinio core. Outer layer is three red on white bands and three blue on white bands. Large "cleave" fracture on one side, the piece looks like it was glued back on. Large chip and smaller chips. Germany, circa 1870-1915. 2-3/8". Collectible. Price: $22 CyberAuction #404, Lot #20.

6584. SWIRL. Latticinio core. White latticinio core swirl. Outer layer is eight bands. Two each of pink on yellow, green on white, white, blue. Almost no twist. Germany, circa 1870-1915. 21/32". Mint (9.7). Price: $22. CyberAuction #414, Lot #1.

6585. SWIRL. Latticinio core. White latticinio core swirl. Outer layer is two purple on white bands alternating with two orange bands. Thick casing of clear glass. One melt spot, a tiny subsurface moon, some minor surface scratching. Very pretty. Germany, circa 1870-1915. 15/16". Near Mint(+) (8.9). Price: $22. CyberAuction #422, Lot #32.

6586. SWIRL. Latticinio core. Yellow latticinio core. Outer layer is three red on white bands and three blue on white bands. Large "cleave" fracture on one side, the piece looks like it was glued back on. Large chip and smaller chips. Germany, circa 1870-1915. 2-3/8". Collectible. Price: $22. CyberAuction #430, Lot #27.

6587. SWIRL. Latticinio core. White latticinio core. Outer layer is two orange and white bands, one red band, three dark blue and yellow. Gorgeous. Germany, circa 1870-1915. 23/32". Mint (9.8). Price: $22. CyberAuction #440, Lot #53.

6588. SWIRL. Latticinio core. White latticinio core. Three band outer layer. Each is blue and pink on yellow. Germany, circa 1870-1915. 17/32". Mint (9.9). Price: $22. CyberAuction #443, Lot #44.

6589. SWIRL. Latticinio core. Yellow latticinio core. Outer layer is eight bands. Four are white, two red and two blue. Bright colors. Gorgeous. Germany, circa 1870-1915. 9/16". Mint (9.9). Match to lot #49 in this auction. Price: $22. CyberAuction #448, Lot #42.

6590. SWIRL. Latticinio core. First-off-cane yellow latticinio core. Flower-type. Colors come shooting out the top. Six outer bands, three red, three green. Some flakes and chips. Slightly flattened. Germany, circa 1870-1915. 9/16". Near Mint (8.4). Price: $22. CyberAuction #453, Lot #16.

6591. SWIRL. Latticinio core. Hard to find yellow and white alternating core. Outer layer is six bands. Three are red, blue and white. Three are green, pink and yellow. Melt hole on it. Germany, circa 1870-1915. 5/8". Mint(-) (9.2). Price: $22. CyberAuction #457, Lot #27.

6592. SWIRL. Latticinio core. White latticinio core. Outer layer is four bands. Two are orange and yellow, two are green and yellow. One pit. Germany, circa 1870-1915. 27/32". Mint(-) (9.0). Price: $22. CyberAuction #463, Lot #47.

6593. SWIRL. Latticinio core. White latticinio core. Outer layer is four bands. Two are pink and green on white, two are blue and green on white. A couple of pinpricks. Germany, circa 1870-1915. 1". Mint (-) (9.0). Price: $22. CyberAuction #469, Lot #48.

6594. SWIRL. Latticinio core. White latticinio core swirl. Outer layer is four bands. Two are pink strands on yellow, edged by green. Two are pink strands on white, edged by blue. Bright colors. English, possibly German. Circa 1870-1915. 5/8". Mint (9.9). Price: $22. CyberAuction #470, Lot #20.

6595. SWIRL. Latticinio core. White latticinio core. Outer layer is three bands. One white, one blue, one red. Germany, circa 1870-1915. 27/32". Mint (9.8). Price: $22. CyberAuction #488, Lot #27.

6596. SWIRL. Latticinio core. White latticinio core. Outer layer is four bands. Two are pink and green on white, two are blue and green on white. A couple of pinpricks. Germany, circa 1870-1915. 1". Mint (-) (9.0). Price: $22. CyberAuction #490, Lot #13.

6597. SWIRL. Latticinio core. From near the very beginning of the cane

ellow latticinio core. Outer layer is a complex set of four bands. Design ıds just before the top of the marble. Air hole and some melt spots. Ger- any, circa 1870-1915. 13/16". Mint(-) (9.2). Price: $22. CyberAuction 497, Lot #24.
598. **SWIRL. Latticinio core.** Light blue base. White latticinio core. Outer yer is six wide bands. Three pink on white, three turquoise on white. Dirt elt spot. Reverse twist top. Germany, circa 1870-1915. 11/16". Mint(-) .0). Price: $22. CyberAuction #501, Lot #56.
599. **SWIRL. Latticinio core.** Interesting design. Yellow latticinio core. uter layer is four bands. Pink on white, pink on yellow, blue on white, een on yellow. Each band is separated by a white and yellow strand. ıick outer casing. One small melt spot. Germany, circa 1870-1915. 11/ 5". Mint (9.5). Price: $21. CyberAuction #331, Lot #20.
500. **SWIRL. Latticinio core.** White latticinio core. Outer layer is four ınds. Two are pink on white, one is green on white, one is blue on white. ome tiny chips and haze. Germany, circa 1870-1915. 1-1/16". Good(+) .9). Price: $21. CyberAuction #347, Lot #41.
501. **SWIRL. Latticinio core.** White latticinio core swirl. Outer layer is ur bands. Two pink on white, one turquoise on white, one blue on white. ıick outer casing of clear. Germany, circa 1870-1915. 11/16". Mint (9.7). ice: $21. CyberAuction #350, Lot #20.
502. **SWIRL. Latticinio core.** Yellow latticinio core swirl. Outer layer is vo pink on yellow bands, two green on yellow bands. Germany, circa 370-1915. 21/32". Mint (9.7). Price: $21. CyberAuction #362, Lot #56.
503. **SWIRL. Latticinio core.** Pale yellow latticinio core. Outer layer is ur bands. Two are pink on white, one is blue on white, one is green on hite. Two small hazy areas, rest is in great shape. Germany, circa 1870- 915. 7/8". Near Mint(+) (8.8). Price: $21. CyberAuction #365, Lot #26.
504. **SWIRL. Latticinio core.** Alternating white and yellow core. Outer yer is three bands. Blue on white, green on white, pink on yellow. Some ıze. Germany, circa 1870-1915. 15/32". Near Mint (8.6). Price: $21. yberAuction #372, Lot #52.
505. **SWIRL. Latticinio core.** First-off-cane yellow latticinio core swirl. uter layer is two red and white bands, a partial red and white band, two een bands and a partial band. Some dirt spots. Misshapen. Still, very etty. Germany, circa 1870-1915. 5/8". Mint(-) (9.0). Price: $21. yberAuction #396, Lot #25.
506. **SWIRL. Latticinio core.** Three-layer white latticinio core swirl. Middle yer is two orange bands, one green band, one blue band. Outer layer is a ıge of white strands. A few pinpricks. Germany, circa 1870-1915. 25/32". int(-) (9.0). Price: $21. CyberAuction #412, Lot #29.
507. **SWIRL. Latticinio core.** White latticinio core. Outer layer is four ınds. Two blue on red, two green on light orange. One pit. Germany, rca 1870-1915. 25/32". Mint(-) (9.0). Price: $21. CyberAuction #417, ot #46.
508. **SWIRL. Latticinio core.** Odd coloring. Bright white core. Outer layer a blue and white band, a ruddy red and green band, a ruddy red band ıd a very wide ruddy red band. Cold roll line at the top. Germany, possi- y English, circa 1870-1915. 19/32". Mint (9.6). Price: $21. CyberAuction 435, Lot #44.
509. **SWIRL. Latticinio core.** Base glass is very lightly tinted blue. Yellow tticinio core that appears light green. Outer layer is three orange bands ıd three white bands. Germany, circa 1870-1915. 19/32". Mint (9.7). Price: 21. CyberAuction #443, Lot #7.
510. **SWIRL. Latticinio core.** Orange latticinio core. Outer layer is three ue bands alternating with three white bands. Surface has some chips. ermany, circa 1870-1915. 29/32". Good (7.5). Price: $21. CyberAuction 445, Lot #48.
511. **SWIRL. Latticinio core.** White latticinio core. Outer layer is four ınds. Two are blue and white. Two are green and white. Tiny flake, some npricking. Germany, circa 1870-1915. 1-1/16". Near Mint(+) (8.7). Price: 21. CyberAuction #458, Lot #5.
612. **SWIRL. Latticinio core.** Bright yellow latticinio core. Outer layer is ur bands. Each is dull red, white and blue. Almost no twist. Beauty. One nall moon. Germany, possibly England, circa 1870-1920. 13/16". Near int(+) (8.8). Price: $21. CyberAuction #464, Lot #8.
513. **SWIRL. Latticinio core.** White latticinio core. Outer layer is six bands. ıree blue, three white. A pit and some very light haze. Germany, circa 370-1915. 1-1/16". Near Mint(+) (8.9). Price: $21. CyberAuction #469, ot #44.
614. **SWIRL. Latticinio core.** White latticinio core. Outer layer is three ellow strands separated by three bands. The bands are green on yellow, ue on white, pink on yellow. One tiny melt pit. A beauty, super design. ermany, circa 1870-1915. 21/32". Mint (9.4). Price: $21. CyberAuction 481, Lot #44.
515. **SWIRL. Latticinio core.** Orange latticinio core. Outer layer is three ue bands alternating with three white bands. Surface has some chips. ermany, circa 1870-1915. 29/32". Good (7.5). Price: $21. CyberAuction 484, Lot #14.
616. **SWIRL. Latticinio core.** White latticinio core. Outer layer is three ellow strands separated by three bands. The bands are green on yellow, ue on white, pink on yellow. One tiny melt pit. A beauty, super design. ermany, circa 1870-1915. 21/32". Mint (9.4). Price: $21. CyberAuction 499, Lot #6.
617. **SWIRL. Latticinio core.** White latticinio core. Outer layer is four ınds. Two are blue and white, two are green and white. Slight haze. Some tting. Germany, circa 1870-1915. 1-1/2". Good(+) (7.9). Price: $21. yberAuction #499, Lot #20.
618. **SWIRL. Latticinio core.** Bright yellow latticinio core. Outer layer is vo sets of orange and red, and two sets of red, white and blue. Nice bright olors. Stunning coloring, but surface has some overall tiny flakes and chips. Probably England, possibly Germany, circa 1880-1915. 15/16". Good(+) (7.7). Price: $21. CyberAuction #506, Lot #38.
6619. **SWIRL. Latticinio core.** White latticinio core swirl. Outer layer is four bands. Two are red with yellow central strand, flanked by transparent green. Two are white and yellow strands, covered by transparent green. Excellent. Germany, circa 1870-1915. 27/32". Mint (9.7). Price: $21. CyberAuction #508, Lot #18.
6620. **SWIRL. Latticinio core.** Yellow latticinio core swirl. Outer layer is four bands. Two are pink and white. Two are blue, green and white. Super peewee. Germany, circa 1870-1915. 7/16". Mint (9.9). Price: $20. CyberAuction #351, Lot #38.
6621. **SWIRL. Latticinio core.** Very slightly blue tinted base. Yellow latticinio core. Outer layer is four bands. Two are red and white, two are blue and white. Two tiny melt spots, one sparkle. Very nice. Germany, circa 1870-1915. 29/32". Mint(-) (9.0). Price: $20. CyberAuction #372, Lot #21.
6622. **SWIRL. Latticinio core.** White latticinio core. Outer layer is four bands. Two are pink and yellow, two are green, purple and yellow. Very tiny chip, two tiny subsurface moons. Germany, circa 1870-1915. 29/32". Near Mint (8.6). Price: $20. CyberAuction #406, Lot #43.
6623. **SWIRL. Latticinio core.** White latticinio core. Outer layer is four bands. Two are pink and yellow, two are green, purple and yellow. Very tiny chip, two tiny subsurface moons. Germany, circa 1870-1915. 29/32". Near Mint (8.6). Price: $20. CyberAuction #426, Lot #51.
6624. **SWIRL. Latticinio core.** First-off-cane yellow latticinio core swirl. Outer layer is two red and white bands, a partial red and white band, two green bands and a partial band. Some dirt spots. Misshapen. Still, very pretty. Germany, circa 1870-1915. 5/8". Mint(-) (9.0). Price: $20. CyberAuction #434, Lot #37.
6625. **SWIRL. Latticinio core.** Very lightly tinted lavender base. White latticinio core. Four outer bands. Two are pink on white, one is green on white, one is blue on white. Germany, circa 1870-1915. 19/32". Mint (9.7). Price: $20. CyberAuction #443, Lot #13.
6626. **SWIRL. Latticinio core.** Yellow latticinio core. Outer layer is six bands. Three are blue and white, three are orange/red and yellow. Germany, circa 1870-1915. 19/32". Mint (9.7). Price: $20. CyberAuction #469, Lot #20.
6627. **SWIRL. Latticinio core.** Yellow latticinio core. Outer layer is two bands of pink on yellow and two bands of green on yellow. Germany, circa 1870-1915. 5/8". Mint (9.9). Price: $20. CyberAuction #478, Lot #29.
6628. **SWIRL. Latticinio core.** Base is very lightly tinted blue. White core. Outer layer is four bands. Two are red, white and blue. Two are yellow, green and white. One tiny sparkle. Germany, circa 1870-1915. 15/16". Mint(-) (9.1). Price: $20. CyberAuction #479, Lot #23.
6629. **SWIRL. Latticinio core.** White latticinio core. Outer layer is four bands. Two are pink and yellow, two are green, purple and yellow. Very tiny chip, two tiny subsurface moons. Germany, circa 1870-1915. 29/32". Near Mint (8.6). Price: $20. CyberAuction #484, Lot #40.
6630. **SWIRL. Latticinio core.** Gorgeous bright orange core. Some strands missing on one side. Four outer bands. Two blue and white, two light green and white. Beauty. Germany, circa 1870-1915. 21/32". Mint (9.9). Price: $20. CyberAuction #495, Lot #1.
6631. **SWIRL. Latticinio core.** Bright white latticinio core. Outer layer is six bands. Three narrow bright yellow, three blue on red. Germany, circa 1870-1915. 9/16". Mint (9.9). Price: $20. CyberAuction #501, Lot #39.
6632. **SWIRL. Latticinio core.** White latticinio core swirl. Outer layer is six bands. Three are blue and white, three are red and yellow. Germany, circa 1870-1915. 11/16". Mint (9.9). Price: $20. CyberAuction #508, Lot #5.
6633. **SWIRL. Latticinio core.** White latticinio core swirl. Outer layer is three yellow bands and three red bands. Germany, circa 1870-1915. 23/32". Mint (9.6). Price: $19. CyberAuction #339, Lot #15.
6634. **SWIRL. Latticinio core.** White latticinio core. Outer layer is six bands. Two are pink and yellow, two are green and yellow. One tiny scratch. Germany, circa 1870-1915. 25/32". Mint (9.5). Price: $19. CyberAuction #339, Lot #19.
6635. **SWIRL. Latticinio core.** Odd marble. Wispy white latticinio core. Outer layer is three narrow bands of red and blue. Thick casing of clear. Germany, circa 1870-1915. 1/2". Mint (9.9). Price: $19. CyberAuction #339, Lot #39.
6636. **SWIRL. Latticinio core.** Yellow latticinio core. Outer layer is three bands of blue on white, and three white strands. Germany, circa 1870-1915. 3/4". Mint (9.8). Price: $19. CyberAuction #342, Lot #23.
6637. **SWIRL. Latticinio core.** White latticinio core swirl. Outer layer is four bands. Two are green on yellow, two are pink on white. Germany, circa 1870-1915. 21/32". Mint (9.7). Price: $19. CyberAuction #347, Lot #51.
6638. **SWIRL. Latticinio core.** Transparent very lightly tinted blue base. Yellow core. Outer layer is four bands. Two red and white, one green and white, one blue and white. One melt spot. Germany, circa 1870-1915. 23/32". Mint(-) (9.2). Price: $19. CyberAuction #348, Lot #6.
6639. **SWIRL. Latticinio core.** White latticinio core. Outer layer is two blue on white bands and two pink on yellow bands. Germany, circa 1870-1915. 3/4". Mint (9.7). Price: $19. CyberAuction #355, Lot #15.
6640. **SWIRL. Latticinio core.** White latticinio core. Outer layer is four bands. Two are blue and white, two are green and white. Gorgeous. One pit. Germany, circa 1870-1915. 5/8". Mint(-) (9.0). Price: $19. CyberAuction #356, Lot #7.
6641. **SWIRL. Latticinio core.** From end of cane (last-off-cane). Yellow latticinio core. Partial core. Outer layer is two blue and white bands, one pink band, one green band. Germany, circa 1870-1915. 17/32". Mint (9.6). Price: $19. CyberAuction #360, Lot #5.
6642. **SWIRL. Latticinio core.** Transparent lightly tinted blue glass. White latticinio core. Outer layer is three yellow and pink band, alternating with

three white and blue bands. Very nice. Germany, circa 1870-1915. 19/32". Mint (9.8). Price: $19. CyberAuction #368, Lot #16.

6643. SWIRL. Latticinio core. White latticinio core swirl. Outer layer is three green and yellow bands and three pink and yellow bands. Gorgeous. Germany, circa 1870-1915. 9/16". Mint (9.9). Price: $19. CyberAuction #384, Lot #46.

6644. SWIRL. Latticinio core. Peewee. Light white latticinio core swirl. Outer layer is four bands. Two bands of green and white, two of light orange and white. Germany, circa 1870-1915. 1/2". Mint (9.9). Price: $19. CyberAuction #397, Lot #14.

6645. SWIRL. Latticinio core. First-off-cane yellow latticinio core swirl. Flower-type. Outer layer is four sets of pink on white bands. Colors come shooting out the top. Flattened somewhat. Overall haze. Germany, circa 1870-1915. 5/8". Near Mint(+) (8.1). Price: $19. CyberAuction #419, Lot #27.

6646. SWIRL. Latticinio core. White latticinio core. Outer layer is six bands. Three are red on white. Three are turquoise on white. Reverse twist top. Superior example, very well constructed. Several tiny melt pits and a tiny chip. Germany, circa 1870-1915. 25/32". Near Mint(+) (8.8). Price: $19. CyberAuction #435, Lot #59.

6647. SWIRL. Latticinio core. White latticinio core swirl. Outer layer is four bands. Two are pink on yellow, one is green on white, one is blue on white. Germany, circa 1870-1915. 21/32". Mint (9.6). Price: $19. CyberAuction #443, Lot #22.

6648. SWIRL. Latticinio core. White latticinio core. Outer layer is three pink on yellow bands and three blue on white bands. Small subsurface moon, manufacturing chip, and some very light haziness. Germany, circa 1870-1915. 1". Near Mint (8.6). Price: $19. CyberAuction #447, Lot #19.

6649. SWIRL. Latticinio core. White latticinio core swirl. Outer layer is four bands. Two are pink on yellow, two are blue on white. From near the very beginning of the cane. Germany, circa 1870-1915. 11/16". Mint (9.7). Price: $19. CyberAuction #451, Lot #39.

6650. SWIRL. Latticinio core. White latticinio core. Outer layer is four bands. Two are blue and white, two are green and white. Slight haze. Some pitting. Germany, circa 1870-1915. 1-1/2". Good(+) (7.9). Price: $19. CyberAuction #477, Lot #9.

6651. SWIRL. Latticinio core. Yellow latticinio core. Outer layer is three pink and blue bands, alternating with three pairs of yellow strands. One tiny sparkle. Germany, circa 1870-1915. 25/32". Mint(-) (9.2). Price: $19. CyberAuction #500, Lot #44.

6652. SWIRL. Latticinio core. White latticinio core swirl. Pale white strands. Outer layer is two orange bands and two blue bands. One large melt spot. Germany, circa 1870-1915. 11/16". Near Mint(+) (8.9). Price: $18. CyberAuction #336, Lot #24.

6653. SWIRL. Latticinio core. Orange latticinio core swirl. Outer layer is three light blue bands and three red bands edged by light blue. Overall light chips. Germany, circa 1870-1915. 13/16". Good (7.6). Price: $17. CyberAuction #331, Lot #43.

6654. SWIRL. Latticinio core. Pale white latticinio core. Outer layer is six bands. Three are red, and three are blue. Nice marble. Germany, circa 1870-1915. 5/8". Mint (9.7). Price: $17. CyberAuction #334, Lot #22.

6655. SWIRL. Latticinio core. White latticinio core. Net is not completely closed. Outer layer is four narrow bands. Two pink on yellow, one blue on white, one very dark green on white. One very tiny melt spot. Germany, circa 1870-1915. 11/16". Mint(-) (9.2). Price: $17. CyberAuction #336, Lot #15.

6656. SWIRL. Latticinio core. White latticinio core. Outer layer is six narrow bands of red and green. Interesting. Germany, circa 1870-1915. 11/16". Mint (9.7). Price: $17. CyberAuction #337, Lot #20.

6657. SWIRL. Latticinio core. Yellow latticinio core. Four outer bands. Two are pink on yellow, two are blue on white. One small chip. Germany, circa 1870-1915. 25/32". Near Mint(+) (8.7). Price: $17. CyberAuction #348, Lot #25.

6658. SWIRL. Latticinio core. Yellowish/orange. Outer layer is six bands. Three are green and white, three are red and white. Some tiny pitting. Germany, circa 1870-1915. 11/16". Near Mint(+) (8.9). Price: $17. CyberAuction #351, Lot #11.

6659. SWIRL. Latticinio core. Yellow latticinio core. Core is only partial. Outer layer is four bands. Two are pink and white, two are green and white. A few pinpricks. Germany, circa 1870-1915. 13/16". Mint(-) (9.0). Price: $17. CyberAuction #357, Lot #17.

6660. SWIRL. Latticinio core. Transparent very lightly tinted blue base. Yellow latticinio core. Outer layer is four bands. Two are blue, pink and white. Two are green, pink and white. Germany, circa 1870-1915. 19/32". Mint (9.9). Price: $17. CyberAuction #357, Lot #20.

6661. SWIRL. Latticinio core. Yellow latticinio core swirl. Outer layer is four bands of pink, blue and green, on white. Two small chips. Germany, circa 1870-1915. 29/32". Near Mint (8.3). Price: $17. CyberAuction #367, Lot #16.

6662. SWIRL. Latticinio core. Bright white latticinio core swirl. Outer layer is three bands. Two are orange, red and yellow. One is blue and white. Appears to be missing a fourth band. One tiny flat spot. England, possibly Germany, circa 1870-1920. 19/32". Mint (9.5). Price: $17. CyberAuction #373, Lot #31.

6663. SWIRL. Latticinio core. White latticinio core swirl. Outer layer is three pink bands and three yellow bands. Very nice. Germany, circa 1870-1915. 5/8". Mint (9.6). Price: $17. CyberAuction #380, Lot #54.

6664. SWIRL. Latticinio core. Orange latticinio core. Outer layer is three blue bands alternating with three white bands. Surface has some chips. Germany, circa 1870-1915. 29/32". Good (7.5). Price: $17. CyberAuction #386, Lot #1.

6665. SWIRL. Latticinio core. Rare color. Bright red core. Latticinio divided form. Outer layer is three bands of blue and white. Small chi■ small subsurface moon, overall pitting and haze. Germany, circa 187■ 1915. 25/32". Good(-) (7.1). Price: $17. CyberAuction #405, Lot #50.

6666. SWIRL. Latticinio core. White latticinio core. Three band close ■ the core. One each of pink on yellow, green on white, blue on white. Thi■ outer casing of clear. One melt spot. Germany, circa 1870-1915. 11/16■ Mint (9.5). Price: $17. CyberAuction #414, Lot #20.

6667. SWIRL. Latticinio core. Yellow latticinio core. Outer layer is tw■ bands of green on yellow and two of pink on yellow. Gorgeous. German■ circa 1870-1915. 5/8". Mint (9.9). Price: $17. CyberAuction #430, Lot #13.

6668. SWIRL. Latticinio core. White latticinio core swirl. Outer layer ■ four bands. Two are pink strands on yellow, edged by green. Two are ■ strands on white, edged by blue. Bright colors. English, possibly German■ circa 1870-1915. 5/8". Mint (9.8). Price: $17. CyberAuction #431, L■ #43.

6669. SWIRL. Latticinio core. Yellow latticinio core. Outer layer ■ two bands of pink on white and two of green on yellow. Germany, circ■ 1870-1915. 21/32". Mint (9.7). Price: $17. CyberAuction #433, Lot #5■

6670. SWIRL. Latticinio core. Yellow latticinio core. Six band outer laye■ Three are opaque yellow and three are transparent pink. Germany, circ■ 1870-1915. 19/32". Mint (9.8). Price: $17. CyberAuction #435, Lot #4■

6671. SWIRL. Latticinio core. White latticinio core. Outer layer ■ four bands. One each of pink on white, pink and blue on white, pink an■ green on yellow, blue and green on white. Odd coloring. Germany, circ■ 1870-1915. 5/8". Mint (9.8). Price: $17. CyberAuction #436, Lot #43.

6672. SWIRL. Latticinio core. White latticinio core. Outer layer ■ four bands. Two are orange, blue and white, two are orange, green an■ yellow. Surface has an almost satiny look to it. Germany, circa 1870-191■ 19/32". Mint (9.7). Price: $17. CyberAuction #443, Lot #6.

6673. SWIRL. Latticinio core. White latticinio core. Outer layer ■ four bands. Two are pink and yellow, one blue and white, one green an■ white. Germany, circa 1870-1915. 1/2". Mint (9.8). Price: $17. CyberAucti■ #443, Lot #19.

6674. SWIRL. Latticinio core. Yellow latticinio core. Outer layer is fo■ bands. Two red and yellow, two blue and white. Germany, circa 187■ 1915. One tiny pinprick. 25/32". Mint(-) (9.2). Price: $17. CyberAucti■ #467, Lot #10.

6675. SWIRL. Latticinio core. Bright yellow latticinio core. Outer layer ■ two sets of orange and red, and two sets of red, white and blue. Nice brig■ colors. Stunning coloring, but surface has some overall tiny flakes and chip■ Probably England, possibly Germany, circa 1880-1915. 15/16". Good(■ (7.7). Price: $17. CyberAuction #469, Lot #12.

6676. SWIRL. Latticinio core. White latticinio core swirl. Outer layer h■ three bands of red, blue and green, on white. One melt chip. German■ circa 1870-1915. 3/4". Mint(-) (9.0). Price: $17. CyberAuction #470, L■ #38.

6677. SWIRL. Latticinio core. Yellow latticinio core. Outer layer is thre■ red on white bands and three blue on white bands. Large "fractur■ on one side, the piece looks like it was glued back on. Large chip an■ smaller chips. Germany, circa 1870-1915. 2-3/8". Collectible. Price: $1■ CyberAuction #472, Lot #22.

6678. SWIRL. Latticinio core. Yellow latticinio core. Outer layer is fo■ bands. Two are blue, and orange. Two are green, white and orang■ Tiny chip, several tiny moons, couple of pits. Germany, circa 1870-191■ 1". Near Mint (8.3). Price: $17. CyberAuction #473, Lot #38.

6679. SWIRL. Latticinio core. Bright orange latticinio core. Outer layer ■ four bands. All are blue, white and pink. Melt area on one side. Beaut■ Germany, circa 1870-1915. 21/32". Mint(-) (9.1). Price: $17. CyberAucti■ #485, Lot #48.

6680. SWIRL. Latticinio core. Bright yellow latticinio core. Outer layer ■ two sets of orange and red, and two sets of red, white and blue. Nice brig■ colors. Stunning coloring, but surface has some overall tiny flakes and chip■ Probably England, possibly Germany, circa 1880-1915. 15/16". Good(■ (7.7). Price: $17. CyberAuction #490, Lot #33.

6681. SWIRL. Latticinio core. White latticinio core, not completely close■ Outer layer is six bands. Two are pink and blue on white, one is pink ■ white, two are pink on yellow, two are pink and green on yellow. On■ small subsurface moon. Germany, circa 1870-1915. 29/32". Ne■ Mint(+)(8.9). Price: $17. CyberAuction #491, Lot #40.

6682. SWIRL. Latticinio core. Yellow latticinio core. Outer layer is fou■ bands. Two are orange and white, two are lavender and white. Very simil■ to Lot #33 in this auction, but yellow core, not white core. Germany, circ■ 1870-1915. 11/16". Mint (9.7). Price: $17. CyberAuction #501, Lot #3■

6683. SWIRL. Latticinio core. White latticinio core. Outer layer is six band■ Three are orange and yellow, three are green and yellow. Germany, circ■ 1870-1915. 23/32". Mint (9.8). Price: $17. CyberAuction #501, Lot #4■

6684. SWIRL. Latticinio core. Transparent clear base with loads of ■ bubbles. Core is very pale blue strands with some yellow strands. Out■ layer is three wide bands of light blue and white bands. Two small subsu■ face moons. Germany, circa 1870-1915. 25/32". Near Mint(+) (8.7). Pric■ $17. CyberAuction #502, Lot #5.

6685. SWIRL. Latticinio core. Three layer. White latticinio core swirl. Midd■ layer is six pairs of bands. Three are blue pairs and three are pink pair■ Outer layer is three sets of yellow strands. Melt spot. Germany, circa 187■ 1915. 21/32". Mint (9.5). Price: $17. CyberAuction #502, Lot #71.

6686. SWIRL. Latticinio core. White latticinio core. Outer layer ■ four bands of pink and blue on white. Germany, circa 1870-1915. 15/32■ Mint (9.9). Price: $17. CyberAuction #503, Lot #53.

6687. SWIRL. Latticinio core. White latticinio core swirl. Outer layer

ur bands. Two are blue, red, green and white. Two are pink, yellow, een and white. Melt line and tiny sparkle. Very nice. Germany, circa 70-1915. 7/8". Mint(-) (9.0). Price: $17. CyberAuction #507, Lot #50.
88. **SWIRL. Latticinio core.** White latticinio core swirl. Outer layer is six nds. Three orange, three yellow. One tiny melt spot. Germany, circa 70-1915. 21/32". Mint (9.5). Price: $17. CyberAuction #508, Lot #7.
89. **SWIRL. Latticinio core.** White latticinio core. Outer layer is three de bands. Two are pink on white. One is pink and green on white. Deep lors. One tiny chip and a tiny rough spot. Germany, circa 1870-1915. 25/ ". Near Mint (8.6). Price: $16. CyberAuction #357, Lot #13.
90. **SWIRL. Latticinio core.** Translucent yellow core. Outer layer is three ts of transparent blue bands and three white strands. Cold roll marks at p. Germany, circa 1870-1915. 15/32". Mint (9.6). Price: $16. CyberAuction 375, Lot #40.
91. **SWIRL. Latticinio core.** Bright white latticinio core. Outer layer is six nds. Three green and three red. Germany, circa 1870-1915. 19/32". Mint 9). Price: $16. CyberAuction #501, Lot #37.
92. **SWIRL. Latticinio core.** White latticinio core swirl. Outer layer is o bands of blue on white, one of green on white, one of very dark green white. Germany, circa 1870-1915. 17/32". Mint (9.6). Price: $15. berAuction #337, Lot #23.
93. **SWIRL. Latticinio core.** White latticinio core. Outer layer is four nds. Two are pink and white, one is purple and white, one blue and nite. Heavily polished. Germany, circa 1870-1915. 3/4". Price: $15. berAuction #337, Lot #48.
94. **SWIRL. Latticinio core.** White latticinio core swirl. Six bands form e outer core. One each of transparent pink, opaque white, opaque blue, aque yellow, transparent green, transparent pink on opaque yellow. ffed, damage remains. Germany, circa 1870-1915. 29/32". Price: $15. berAuction #355, Lot #48.
95. **SWIRL. Latticinio core.** Yellow latticinio core. Outer layer is four nds. Two are green and white, two are blue and white. One rough spot. ermany, circa 1870-1915. 27/32". Near Mint(+) (8.9). Price: $15. berAuction #356, Lot #1.
96. **SWIRL. Latticinio core.** Yellow latticinio core. Outer layer is six bands. ree are blue and white, three are pink and white. Germany, circa 1870-15. 7/16". Mint (9.9). Price: $15. CyberAuction #357, Lot #11.
97. **SWIRL. Latticinio core.** Yellow latticinio core. Outer layer is three ue bands and three pink bands. Germany, circa 1870-1915. 15/32". Mint 9). Price: $15. CyberAuction #357, Lot #14.
98. **SWIRL. Latticinio core.** White latticinio core swirl. Outer layer is ee white bands and three blue bands. Germany, circa 1870-1915. 1/2". nt (9.9). Price: $15. CyberAuction #358, Lot #40.
99. **SWIRL. Latticinio core.** Alternating white and yellow latticinio core. uter layer is seven narrow bands. Two orange/ red, two yellow, one blue, e green, one white. Tiny chip. Germany, circa 1870-1915. 21/32". Near nt(+) (8.9). Price: $15. CyberAuction #360, Lot #48.
'00. **SWIRL. Latticinio core.** White latticinio core swirl. Outer layer is ght bands. Four are pink and white, two blue and white, two green and nite. Overall scratching, sparkles and tiny subsurface moon. Germany, ca 1870-1915. 27/32". Near Mint(-) (8.0). Price: $15. CyberAuction #364, t #43.
'01. **SWIRL. Latticinio core.** White latticinio core swirl. Outer layer is ur bands. Two are dark orange, two are green. Germany, circa 1870-15. 19/32". Mint (9.9). Price: $15. CyberAuction #373, Lot #17.
'02. **SWIRL. Latticinio core.** White latticinio core swirl. Outer layer is o bands of red and white, one band of blue, one of green. Germany, ca 1870-1915. 11/16". Mint (9.8). Price: $15. CyberAuction #381, Lot 27.
'03. **SWIRL. Latticinio core.** Yellowish orange latticinio core. Outer layer three red bands and three white bands. A couple of very tiny pinpricks. ermany, circa 1870-1915. 21/32". Mint(-) (9.1). Price: $15. CyberAuction 383, Lot #7.
'04. **SWIRL. Latticinio core.** Pale translucent white latticinio core. Outer yer is two bands of pink on yellow, two of blue on white, two of pale vender on yellow. Germany, circa 1870-1915. 15/32". Mint (9.9). Price: 5. CyberAuction #384, Lot #54.
'05. **SWIRL. Latticinio core.** Alternating yellow and white core. Outer yer is three sets of pastel bands. Germany, circa 1870-1915. 1/2". Mint 9). Price: $15. CyberAuction #403, Lot #12.
'06. **SWIRL. Latticinio core.** Odd coloring. White latticinio core. Outer yer is four bands. Two are light aqua with a yellow center. Two are orange/ d with a white center. Several tiny chips. Germany, circa 1870-1915. 29/ ". Near Mint (8.3). Price: $15. CyberAuction #406, Lot #10.
'07. **SWIRL. Latticinio core.** Yellow latticinio core. Outer layer is three nk narrow bands and three white narrow bands. Large pieces of unmelted ica on one side. Very tiny chip. Germany, circa 1870-1915. 3/4". Near nt(+) (8.9). Price: $15. CyberAuction #406, Lot #19.
'08. **SWIRL. Latticinio core.** This is the first piece off a rod. Flattened, rhaps intended as drawer pull or other decorative piece. White latticinio re. Four outer bands in two color schemes. Design shoots out the top. attened, resembles a flower. Very nice. Germany, circa 1870-1915. 1-1/ diameter, about 5/8" high. Mint (9.5). Price: $15. CyberAuction #411, t #41.
'09. **SWIRL. Latticinio core.** Yellow latticinio core. Outer layer is two nds of green on yellow and two of pink on yellow. Gorgeous. Germany, ca 1870-1915. 5/8". Mint (9.9). Price: $15. CyberAuction #413, Lot #4.
'10. **SWIRL. Latticinio core.** White latticinio core swirl. Outer layer is ur bands. Two blue and white, two pink and white. Several very tiny bsurface moons. Germany, circa 1870-1915. 29/32". Near Mint(+) (8.7). ce: $15. CyberAuction #417, Lot #9.
6711. **SWIRL. Latticinio core.** Very lightly tinted blue base. White latticinio core. Outer layer is two bands of brown and white and two bands of blue and white. Germany, circa 1870-1915. 9/16". Mint (9.7). Price: $15. CyberAuction #423, Lot #39.
6712. **SWIRL. Latticinio core.** Transparent clear base. Greenish tinted yellow strands. Outer layer is two bands of blue on white and two or pink on yellow. Germany, circa 1870-1915. 5/8". Mint (9.7). Price: $15. CyberAuction #442, Lot #55.
6713. **SWIRL. Latticinio core.** White latticinio core swirl. Outer layer is four bands. Two green, two pale yellow. Very nice. Germany, circa 1870-1915. 9/16". Mint (9.9). Price: $15. CyberAuction #443, Lot #1.
6714. **SWIRL. Latticinio core.** White latticinio core. Outer layer is four bands of pink and blue on white. Germany, circa 1870-1915. Slightly flattened. 15/32". Mint (9.6). Price: $15. CyberAuction #443, Lot #32.
6715. **SWIRL. Latticinio core.** White latticinio core. Two narrow blue bands, two narrow pink on yellow bands. Germany, circa 1870-1915. 1/2". Mint (9.9). Price: $15. CyberAuction #443, Lot #40.
6716. **SWIRL. Latticinio core.** White latticinio core. Odd outer layer. Six band outer layer. Three opaque white, one opaque orange/red, one opaque blue, one translucent purple. One tiny melt spot. Germany, possibly English, circa 1870-1915. 21/32". Mint (9.5). Price: $15. CyberAuction #456, Lot #39.
6717. **SWIRL. Latticinio core.** Yellow latticinio core. Outer layer is three white bands and three cranberry red bands. One tiny pit. Germany, circa 1870-1915. 5/8". Mint(-)(9.0). Price: $15. CyberAuction #474, Lot #32.
6718. **SWIRL. Latticinio core.** White latticinio core. Outer layer is six bands. Three yellow, one red, one light green, one light blue. Beauty. One melt spot. England, possibly Germany, circa 1870-1915. 9/16". Mint (9.4). Price: $15. CyberAuction #475, Lot #9.
6719. **SWIRL. Latticinio core.** Alternating yellow and white core. Outer layer is four bands. Two are blue and yellow, two are orange/red and white. Overall subsurface moons and rough spots. Germany, circa 1870-1915. 1-7/16". Good (7.4). Price: $15. CyberAuction #476, Lot #15.
6720. **SWIRL. Latticinio core.** White latticinio core swirl. Outer layer is three green bands and three orange/yellow bands. One sparkle. Beauty. Germany, circa 1870-1915. 13/16". Near Mint(+) (8.9). Price: $15. CyberAuction #479, Lot #4.
6721. **SWIRL. Latticinio core.** Yellow latticinio core. Outer layer is four bands. Two are red and white, two are blue and white. Heavy outer casing. Small chip on one side, tiny chip on other. Still, a beauty. Germany, circa 1870-1915. 13/16". Near Mint(-) (8.7). Price: $15. CyberAuction #481, Lot #46.
6722. **SWIRL. Latticinio core.** White latticinio core swirl. Outer layer is six bands. Three red and white, three blue and white. Germany, circa 1870-1915. 5/8". Mint (9.9). Price: $15. CyberAuction #483, Lot #1.
6723. **SWIRL. Latticinio core.** This is the first piece off a rod. Flattened, perhaps intended as drawer pull or other decorative piece. White latticinio core. Four outer bands in two color schemes. Design shoots out the top. Flattened, resembles a flower. Very nice. Germany, circa 1870-1915. 1-1/4" diameter, about 5/8" high. Mint (9.5). Price: $15. CyberAuction #484, Lot #26.
6724. **SWIRL. Latticinio core.** White latticinio core. Outer layer is six bands. Three yellow, one red, one light green, one light blue. Beauty. One melt spot. England, possibly Germany, circa 1870-1915. 9/16". Mint (9.4). Price: $15. CyberAuction #494, Lot #12.
6725. **SWIRL. Latticinio core.** Alternating yellow and white latticinio core. Outer layer is four bands. Two are pink on yellow, two are blue on white. Germany, circa 1870-1915. 1/2". Mint (9.8). Price: $15. CyberAuction #498, Lot #39.
6726. **SWIRL. Latticinio core.** Yellow latticinio core. Outer layer is four bands. One tiny subsurface moon. Germany, circa 1870-1915. 27/32". Near Mint(+) (8.9). Price: $15. CyberAuction #500, Lot #27.
6727. **SWIRL. Latticinio core.** Very lightly tinted green base. Yellow latticinio core, encasing a teardrop air bubble. Outer layer is four bands. Two are green on white, two are blue on white. A couple of tiny subsurface moons. Germany, circa 1870-1915. 7/8". Near Mint (8.6). Price: $15. CyberAuction #505, Lot #19.
6728. **SWIRL. Latticinio core.** White latticinio core. Four outer bands. Two light red, two blue. Germany, circa 1870-1915. 1/2". Mint (9.9). Price: $15. CyberAuction #505, Lot #48.
6729. **SWIRL. Latticinio core.** Very odd marble. Pale, thin white latticinio core swirl. Outer layer is three bands. Each is pink and blue on white. Thick clear outer casing. Some pinpricks and the surface is not completely wet. Germany, circa 1870-1915. 11/16". Near Mint(+) (8.9). Price: $14. CyberAuction #335, Lot #32.
6730. **SWIRL. Latticinio core.** White latticinio core swirl. Outer layer is three blue and red bands, alternating with three green and red bands. Germany, possibly English, circa 1870-1915. 9/16". Mint (9.8). Price: $14. CyberAuction #339, Lot #21.
6731. **SWIRL. Latticinio core.** White latticinio core. Outer layer is two blue and white bands, and two green and white bands. Small marble. Germany, circa 1870-1915. 1/2". Mint (9.9). Price: $14. CyberAuction #342, Lot #17.
6732. **SWIRL. Latticinio core.** Yellow latticinio core. Only a few strands in the core. Outer layer is four bands. Two are blue and white, two are pink and white. Germany, circa 1870-1915. 19/32". Mint (9.9). Price: $14. CyberAuction #357, Lot #2.
6733. **SWIRL. Latticinio core.** Yellow latticinio core. Outer layer is three bands of green on white. Several small and tiny chips. Germany, circa 1870-1915. 27/32". Near Mint (8.6). Price: $14. CyberAuction #359, Lot #16.
6734. **SWIRL. Latticinio core.** White latticinio core. Outer layer is three

bands of pink on white and three bands of blue. Nice peewee. Germany, circa 1870-1915. 15/32". Mint (9.9). Price: $14. CyberAuction #377, Lot #9.

6735. SWIRL. Latticinio core. White latticinio core. Outer layer is three yellow bands and three pink bands. Tight twist. Germany, circa 1870-1915. 9/16". Mint (9.7). Price: $14. CyberAuction #424, Lot #55.

6736. SWIRL. Latticinio core. Yellow latticinio core. Outer layer is two bands of green on yellow and two of pink on yellow. One tiny melt spot. Germany, circa 1870-1915. 5/8". Mint (9.6). Price: $14. CyberAuction #437, Lot #52.

6737. SWIRL. Latticinio core. White latticinio core swirl. Outer layer is five white strands and four blue on white strands. Germany, circa 1870-1915. 15/32". Mint (9.8). Price: $14. CyberAuction #443, Lot #29.

6738. SWIRL. Latticinio core. Very lightly tinted blue base glass. Translucent white latticinio core. Outer layer is four bands. Two are pink, green and white. Two are pink, blue and white. Beauty. One very tiny chip. Germany, circa 1870-1915. 29/32". Near Mint(+) (8.9). Price: $14. CyberAuction #458, Lot #39.

6739. SWIRL. Latticinio core. White latticinio core swirl. Outer layer is three bands. Pink and yellow, pink, green and yellow, pink, blue and white. Faint pink band where the fourth band would be. Several very tiny chips. Germany, circa 1870-1915. 7/8". Near Mint (8.6). Price: $14. CyberAuction #467, Lot #4.

6740. SWIRL. Latticinio core. Yellowish/green latticinio core. Outer layer is six bands. Three are blue and white, three are pink and yellow. One melt spot. Germany, circa 1870-1915. 13/16". Mint(-) (9.2). Price: $14. CyberAuction #472, Lot #37.

6741. SWIRL. Latticinio core. Stunning marble. White latticinio core swirl. Outer layer is a cage of strands. Yellow, white, bright red, bright blue. Tight twist. Beauty. Surface has a small chip, some tiny chips, and a dirt line. Germany, circa 1870-1915. 27/32". Near Mint(-) (8.0). Price: $14. CyberAuction #481, Lot #29.

6742. SWIRL. Latticinio core. Pale white latticinio core. Outer layer is two orange and dark green bands and two orange and gray/white bands. Odd coloring. Germany, circa 1870-1915. 11/16". Mint (9.7). Price: $13. CyberAuction #335, Lot #40.

6743. SWIRL. Latticinio core. White latticinio core swirl. Outer layer is three white bands and three transparent blue bands. Germany, circa 1870-1915. 23/32". Mint(-) (9.1). Price: $13. CyberAuction #336, Lot #11.

6744. SWIRL. Latticinio core. White latticinio core. Outer layer is eight bands. Four are transparent pink. Then one each of blue, yellow, green and white. Gorgeous. Nub bottom pontil. Some pitting. Germany, circa 1870-1915. 9/16". Near Mint(+) (8.7). Price: $13. CyberAuction #340, Lot #53.

6745. SWIRL. Latticinio core. White latticinio core. Outer layer is two bands of blue on white, and two of green on white. A couple of crease marks near the bottom. Germany, circa 1870-1915. 11/16". Mint (9.7). Consignor note: C6. Price: $13. CyberAuction #344, Lot #17.

6746. SWIRL. Latticinio core. Peewee white latticinio core. Germany, circa 1870-1915. 1/2". Mint(-) (9.0). Price: $13. CyberAuction #346, Lot #8.

6747. SWIRL. Latticinio core. White latticinio core swirl. Outer layer is six bands. Three green, three pink. One pink is near the core. Germany, circa 1870-1915. 21/32". Mint (9.8). Price: $13. CyberAuction #347, Lot #37.

6748. SWIRL. Latticinio core. White latticinio core. Outer layer is three bands. Each is pink and turquoise on white. Very slight wear. Germany, circa 1870-1915. 9/16". Near Mint(+) (8.9). Price: $13. CyberAuction #353, Lot #12.

6749. SWIRL. Latticinio core. White latticinio core. Outer layer is six bands. Three yellow, one blue, one red, one green. One tiny chip. Germany, circa 1870-1915. 1/2". Near Mint(+) (8.9). Price: $13. CyberAuction #358, Lot #34.

6750. SWIRL. Latticinio core. Yellow latticinio core. Outer layer is three orange narrow bands and three white narrow bands. One wide manufacturing melt line on the marble. Germany, circa 1870-1915. 11/16". Mint(-) (9.0). Price: $13. CyberAuction #359, Lot #19.

6751. SWIRL. Latticinio core. White latticinio core. Outer layer is four bands. Two blue and white, two pink and yellow. One hazy spot, some minor pitting. Germany, circa 1870-1915. 13/16". Near Mint(+) (8.7). Price: $13. CyberAuction #372, Lot #8.

6752. SWIRL. Latticinio core. Yellow latticinio core swirl. Outer layer is two bands of orange and white, one green and white, one blue and white. Germany, circa 1870-1915. 11/16". Mint (9.7). Price: $13. CyberAuction #402, Lot #14.

6753. SWIRL. Latticinio core. Yellow latticinio core. Outer layer is two bands of green on yellow and two of pink on yellow. One tiny melt spot. Germany, circa 1870-1915. 5/8". Mint (9.6). Price: $13. CyberAuction #406, Lot #20.

6754. SWIRL. Latticinio core. White latticinio core. Outer layer is four bands of yellow, pink and white. Germany, circa 1870-1915. 1/2". Mint (9.9). Price: $13. CyberAuction #410, Lot #26.

6755. SWIRL. Latticinio core. Yellow latticinio core. Outer layer is four bands. Two are lavender and white, one is blue and white, one is green and white. A couple of pits. Germany, circa 1870-1915. 5/8". Mint(-) (9.0). Price: $13. CyberAuction #419, Lot #48.

6756. SWIRL. Latticinio core. White latticinio core. Outer layer is five bands. Two pink, one green, one blue, one white. Germany, circa 1870-1915. 1/2". Mint (9.9). Price: $13. CyberAuction #429, Lot #18.

6757. SWIRL. Latticinio core. Orange latticinio core. Outer layer is six bands. Three are transparent blue, three are translucent white. Tiny subsurface moons on one side. Germany, circa 1870-1915. 1/2". Near Mint(+) (8.7). Price: $13. CyberAuction #429, Lot #37.

6758. SWIRL. Latticinio core. White latticinio core swirl. Outer layer i four bands. Two pink on yellow, one green on white, one blue on white Germany, circa 1870-1915. 9/16". Mint (9.9). Price: $13. CyberAuctio #435, Lot #13.

6759. SWIRL. Latticinio core. White latticinio core. Outer layer is thre pink bands and three white strands. Germany, circa 1870-1915. 1/2". Mir (9.9). Price: $13. CyberAuction #435, Lot #21.

6760. SWIRL. Latticinio core. Yellow latticinio core swirl. Outer layer is si bands. Three red and white, three blue and white. Germany, circa 1870 1915. 5/8". Mint (9.9). Price: $13. CyberAuction #435, Lot #25.

6761. SWIRL. Latticinio core. Very lightly blue tinted base. White latticini core. Outer layer is three bands of pink and green with yellow. German circa 1870-1915. 11/16". Mint (9.9). Price: $13. CyberAuction #436, Lo #35.

6762. SWIRL. Latticinio core. Base glass is tinted very lightly blue. Yello core, appearing slightly green. Four outer bands. Two pink on white, tw green on white. Germany, circa 1870-1915. 21/32". Mint (9.9). Price: $13 CyberAuction #439, Lot #25.

6763. SWIRL. Latticinio core. White latticinio core. Outer layer is eight bands. Four are pink and white, two blue and white, two green an white. Overall scratching, sparkles and tiny subsurface moon. German circa 1870-1915. 27/32". Near Mint(-) (8.0). Price: $13. CyberAuction #451 Lot #10.

6764. SWIRL. Latticinio core. White latticinio core. Outer layer is fou bands. Two are green edged by white, two are green edged by yellow Some small chips. Germany, circa 1870-1915. 1-1/16". Good(+) (7.7). Price $13. CyberAuction #464, Lot #36.

6765. SWIRL. Latticinio core. White latticinio core. Outer layer is six band Three red and three light green. Germany, circa 1870-1915. 9/16". Min (9.9). Price: $13. CyberAuction #483, Lot #8.

6766. SWIRL. Latticinio core. Yellow latticinio core. Outer layer is od Three bands (pink/white, blue/white, green/yellow) alternating with thre pairs of white strands. Tiny sparkle and a couple of tiny pinpricks. Ge many, circa 1870-1915. 11/16". Mint(-) (9.1). Price: $13. CyberAuctio #485, Lot #20.

6767. SWIRL. Latticinio core. Stunning marble. White latticinio core swir Outer layer is a cage of strands. Yellow, white, bright red, bright blue. Tigh twist. Beauty. Surface has a small chip, some tiny chips, and a dirt lin Germany, circa 1870-1915. 27/32". Near Mint(-) (8.0). Price: $13 CyberAuction #499, Lot #29.

6768. SWIRL. Latticinio core. Yellow latticinio core. Outer layer is thre translucent white bands and three transparent green bands. Germany, circ 1870-1915. 17/32". Mint (9.9). Price: $13. CyberAuction #501, Lot #27.

6769. SWIRL. Latticinio core. Yellow latticinio core. Outer layer if fou bands. Two pink and white, one green and white, one blue and white Small flake, small moon. Germany, circa 1870-1915. 29/32". Near Mir (8.5). Price: $13. CyberAuction #502, Lot #10.

6770. SWIRL. Latticinio core. White latticinio core. Outer layer is eigh bands. Four are pink on white, two blue on white, two turquoise on white Several tiny chips, and a little haze. Germany, circa 1870-1915. 15/16 Near Mint(-) (8.0). Price: $13. CyberAuction #506, Lot #46.

6771. SWIRL. Latticinio core. Yellow latticinio core swirl. Outer layer two bands of pink and blue on white, and two bands of pink and green o yellow. One manufacturing chip. Germany, circa 1870-1915. 21/32". Min) (9.2). Price: $12. CyberAuction #332, Lot #23.

6772. SWIRL. Latticinio core. White latticinio core swirl. Outer layer four bands. Two are green and white, two are green and yellow. One manu facturing gouge. Germany, circa 1870-1915. 15/32". Mint(-) (9.0). Pric $12. CyberAuction #345, Lot #41.

6773. SWIRL. Latticinio core. White latticinio core swirl. Outer layer is s lime green narrow bands. Germany, circa 1870-1915. 11/16". Mint (9.5 Price: $12. CyberAuction #347, Lot #43.

6774. SWIRL. Latticinio core. White latticinio core swirl. Outer layer two pink bands, one blue band, and one green band. Germany, circa 1870 1915. 9/16". Mint (9.9). Price: $12. CyberAuction #355, Lot #3.

6775. SWIRL. Latticinio core. White latticinio core. Outer layer is four narrow bands. Blue/white, pink/yellow, pink, green. Germany, circ 1870-1915. 17/32". Mint (9.8). Price: $12. CyberAuction #363, Lot #9.

6776. SWIRL. Latticinio core. White latticinio core. Outer layer is tw bands of purple flanked by yellow, and two bands of red flanked by white Beauty. Germany, circa 1870-1915. 19/32". Mint (9.9). Price: $12 CyberAuction #368, Lot #9.

6777. SWIRL. Latticinio core. White latticinio core swirl. Outer layer four bands. Two are pink and white, two are green and white. German circa 1870-1915. 1/2". Mint (9.9). Price: $12. CyberAuction #369, Lot #4.

6778. SWIRL. Latticinio core. White latticinio core swirl. Outer layer four complex colored bands alternating with four sets of yellow strand Rough spot and some pitting. Germany, circa 1870-1915. 5/8". Near Mir (8.5). Price: $12. CyberAuction #370, Lot #13.

6779. SWIRL. Latticinio core. Yellow latticinio core. Four outer bands Two green, pink/orange and yellow. Two blue, white and pink/orange. Sma pit and small melt dimple. Germany, circa 1870-1915. 9/16". Near Mint(+ (8.9). Price: $12. CyberAuction #375, Lot #33.

6780. SWIRL. Latticinio core. Translucent white latticinio core. Outer laye is two bands of blue on white, and two of green on white. Some pinprick Germany, circa 1870-1915. 3/4". Mint(-) (9.0). Price: $12. CyberAuction #380, Lot #50.

6781. SWIRL. Latticinio core. White latticinio core. Outer layer is fo bands. Three pink on white bands, three blue on white bands. Two me areas. Germany, circa 1870-1915. 5/8". Mint(-) (9.1). Price: $12 CyberAuction #382, Lot #44.

212

782. SWIRL. Latticinio core. Alternating pale yellow and white latticinio ore. Outer layer is two bands of blue, orange and white, and two bands of een, orange and white. Germany, circa 1870-1915. 1/2". Mint (9.7). Price: 2. CyberAuction #392, Lot #10.

783. SWIRL. Latticinio core. White latticinio core. Odd outer layer. Six and outer layer. Three opaque white, one opaque orange/red, one opaque ue, one translucent purple. One tiny melt spot. Germany, possibly En- ish, circa 1870-1915. 21/32". Mint (9.5). Price: $12. CyberAuction #400, ot #18.

784. SWIRL. Latticinio core. White latticinio core swirl. Outer layer has ree bands of red, blue and green, on white. One melt chip. Germany, rca 1870-1915. 3/4". Mint(-) (9.0). Price: $12. CyberAuction #409, Lot 39.

785. SWIRL. Latticinio core. White latticinio core swirl. Outer layer is ur bands. Two are pink on yellow, one blue on white, one green on hite. Beauty. Germany, circa 1870-1915. 11/16". Mint (9.9). Price: $12. yberAuction #413, Lot #43.

786. SWIRL. Latticinio core. Yellow latticinio core. Outer layer is two ands of pink on yellow and two bands of green on yellow. Germany, circa 370-1915. 5/8". Mint (9.9). Price: $12. CyberAuction #413, Lot #53.

787. SWIRL. Latticinio core. White latticinio core swirl. Outer layer has ree bands of red, blue and green, on white. One melt chip. Germany, rca 1870-1915. 3/4". Mint(-) (9.0). Price: $12. CyberAuction #426, Lot 6.

788. SWIRL. Latticinio core. White latticinio core swirl. Peewee. Ger- any, circa 1870-1915. 1/2". Mint (9.9). Price: $12. CyberAuction #430, ot #15.

789. SWIRL. Latticinio core. White latticinio core swirl. Outer layer is vo red bands, one green band, one blue band. Annealing fracture in the een band. A couple of pinpricks. Germany, circa 1870-1915. 25/32". lint(-) (9.1). Price: $12. CyberAuction #432, Lot #50.

790. SWIRL. Latticinio core. Yellow latticinio core swirl. Outer layer is ur bands. Each is pink and blue on white. Germany, circa 1870-1915. 19/ 2". Mint (9.9). Price: $12. CyberAuction #435, Lot #19.

791. SWIRL. Latticinio core. White latticinio core. Odd outer layer. Six and outer layer. Three opaque white, one opaque orange/red, one opaque ue, one translucent purple. One tiny melt spot. Germany, possibly En- ish, circa 1870-1915. 21/32". Mint (9.5). Price: $12. CyberAuction #437, ot #1.

792. SWIRL. Latticinio core. Translucent white/green latticinio core. Outer yer is four bands. Two blue on white, two pink on white. Some cold rolls. ermany, circa 1870-1915. 11/16". Mint (9.5). Price: $12. CyberAuction 439, Lot #5.

793. SWIRL. Latticinio core. Yellow latticinio core. Outer layer is one and of blue and green on white, and one band of pink and green on ellow. Appears to have a third band missing. Two melt spots. Germany, rca 1870-1915. 7/8". Mint(-) (9.1). Price: $12. CyberAuction #439, Lot 8.

794. SWIRL. Latticinio core. White latticinio core. Outer layer is six bands. hree are blue on white, three are pink on yellow. Looks like it was sup- osed to have a third layer. Very thick outer casing of clear. Flattened on ne side of the top. Very pretty though. Germany, circa 1870-1915. 29/32". int(-) (9.0). Price: $12. CyberAuction #446, Lot #12.

795. SWIRL. Latticinio core. Translucent white latticinio core. Outer layer two bands of blue on white, and two of green on white. Some pinpricks. ermany, circa 1870-1915. 3/4". Mint(-) (9.0). Price: $12. CyberAuction 446, Lot #49.

796. SWIRL. Latticinio core. White latticinio core swirl. Outer layer is ur bands. Two are pink, green and yellow. Two are pink, blue and white. couple of tiny sparkles. Germany, circa 1870-1915. 3/4". Mint(-) (9.0). rice: $12. CyberAuction #451, Lot #43.

797. SWIRL. Latticinio core. White latticinio core. Outer layer is four ands. Each is pink, blue, white, yellow, green. Cold roll line on it. Ger- any, circa 1870-1915. 3/4". Mint(-) (9.0). Price: $12. CyberAuction #458, ot #6.

798. SWIRL. Latticinio core. White latticinio core swirl. Outer layer is ur bands. Each is pink and blue. Gorgeous. One tiny chip. Germany, circa 370-1915. 9/16". Near Mint(+) (8.8). Price: $12. CyberAuction #459, ot #47.

799. SWIRL. Latticinio core. Base glass is very lightly tinted blue. White tticinio core. Outer layer is six bands. Three blue and three yellow. Very ice. Germany, circa 1870-1915. 9/16". Mint (9.9). Price: $12. CyberAuction 467, Lot #7.

800. SWIRL. Latticinio core. Base glass is very lightly tinted blue. Yellow tticinio core. Outer layer is four bands. Two are blue and white, two are uddy red. A couple of tiny pits and very tiny flakes. Germany, circa 1870- 915. 19/32". Near Mint(+) (8.9). Price: $12. CyberAuction #471, Lot 40.

801. SWIRL. Latticinio core. Pale yellow latticinio core. Outer layer is ree blue bands and three white bands. In beautiful shape. Germany, circa 870-1915. 7/8". Mint (9.7). Price: $12. CyberAuction #476, Lot #43.

802. SWIRL. Latticinio core. White latticinio core. Outer layer is five ands. Three are red, two are yellow. Missing one strand. Beauty. Ger- any, possibly England. 1870-1915. 17/32". Mint (9.8). Price: $12. yberAuction #483, Lot #10.

803. SWIRL. Latticinio core. Yellow latticinio core. Outer layer is one and of blue and green on white, and one band of pink and green on ellow. Appears to have a third band missing. Two melt spots. Germany, rca 1870-1915. 7/8". Mint(-) (9.1). Price: $12. CyberAuction #484, Lot 37.

804. SWIRL. Latticinio core. Translucent white latticinio core. Outer

is seven bands. Four light green, three transparent blue. Germany, circa 1870-1915. 15/32". Mint (9.9). Price: $12. CyberAuction #487, Lot #3.

6805. SWIRL. Latticinio core. White latticinio core. Outer layer is eight bands. Four are pink on white, two blue on white, two turquoise on white. Several tiny chips, and a little haze. Germany, circa 1870-1915. 15/16". Near Mint(-) (8.0). Price: $12. CyberAuction #491, Lot #30.

6806. SWIRL. Latticinio core. Pale yellow latticinio core. Outer layer is four bands. Two are blue on white, two are pink on yellow. One dirt line. Germany, circa 1870-1915. 3/4". Mint (9.5). Price: $12. CyberAuction #508, Lot #20.

6807. SWIRL. Latticinio core. Yellow latticinio core. Outer layer is three blue on white bands and three pink bands. One tiny sparkle. Germany, circa 1870-1915. 21/32". Near Mint(+) (8.9). Price: $11. CyberAuction #335, Lot #1.

6808. SWIRL. Latticinio core. White latticinio core. Outer layer is six bands. Three are blue on white, three are red on yellow. Milky glass on one side, it's from near an end of the cane. One small chip. Germany, circa 1870-1915. 25/32". Near Mint(+) (8.7). Price: $11. CyberAuction #344, Lot #52.

6809. SWIRL. Latticinio core. White latticinio core. Two are pink and yel- low, one is green, white and yellow, one is blue, yellow and white. One tiny melt spot and a couple of tiny pits. Germany, circa 1870-1915. 1/2". Near Mint(+) (8.9). Price: $11. CyberAuction #345, Lot #22.

6810. SWIRL. Latticinio core. White latticinio core swirl. Outer layer is three bands of green on white, alternating with three bands of pink on yellow. Very tiny pinpricks. Germany, circa 1870-1915. 11/16". Mint(-) (9.1). Price: $11. CyberAuction #356, Lot #45.

6811. SWIRL. Latticinio core. White latticinio core. Outer layer is six bands. Two are pink, one white, one green, one blue, one yellow. Tiny chip. Ger- many, circa 1870-1915. 11/16". Near Mint(+) (8.9). Price: $11. CyberAuction #364, Lot #7.

6812. SWIRL. Latticinio core. White latticinio core swirl. Outer layer is four bands. Two are pink, green and yellow. Two are pink, blue and white. A couple of tiny sparkles. Germany, circa 1870-1915. 3/4". Mint(-) (9.0). Price: $11. CyberAuction #367, Lot #57.

6813. SWIRL. Latticinio core. Pale yellow latticinio core. Outer layer is three bands. One green and white, one blue and white, one brown and white. Germany, circa 1870-1915. 1/2". Mint (9.7). Price: $11. CyberAuction #388, Lot #3.

6814. SWIRL. Latticinio core. White latticinio core. Outer layer is four bands. Germany, circa 1870-1915. 1/2". Mint (9.9). Price: $11. CyberAuction #397, Lot #52.

6815. SWIRL. Latticinio core. White latticinio core. Outer layer is four bands. Two red and yellow, two blue and white. Small piece of dirt in the marble. Germany, circa 1870-1915. 19/32". Mint (9.8). Price: $11. CyberAuction #405, Lot #14.

6816. SWIRL. Latticinio core. White latticinio core. Outer layer is four bands. Two are green and white, two are orange and white. Germany, circa 1870-1915. 1/2". Mint (9.7). Price: $11. CyberAuction #410, Lot #3.

6817. SWIRL. Latticinio core. White latticinio core. Outer layer is three bands of pink, blue and yellow. Germany, circa 1870-1915. 1/2". Mint (9.9). Price: $11. CyberAuction #416, Lot #13.

6818. SWIRL. Latticinio core. Yellow latticinio core. Outer layer is four bands. Two pink/white, one green/white, one blue/white. Several sparkles and one small subsurface moon. Germany, circa 1870-1915. 7/8". Near Mint (8.5). Price: $11. CyberAuction #417, Lot #41.

6819. SWIRL. Latticinio core. White latticinio core. Outer layer is four narrow bands. Two are pink, blue, green and white. Two are pink, green, yellow and white. Interesting. Germany, circa 1870-1915. 9/16". Mint (9.7). Price: $11. CyberAuction #420, Lot #55.

6820. SWIRL. Latticinio core. White latticinio core. Outer layer is four bands. Two pink on yellow, one green on white, one blue on white. Germany, circa 1870-1915. 9/16". Mint (9.9). Price: $11. CyberAuction #424, Lot #37.

6821. SWIRL. Latticinio core. White latticinio core. Outer layer is four bands. Two are pink and yellow, one is green and white, one is blue and white. Germany, circa 1870-1915. 15/32". Mint (9.9). Price: $11. CyberAuction #429, Lot #41.

6822. SWIRL. Latticinio core. White latticinio core. Six band outer layer. Three are opaque white and three are transparent pink. Germany, circa 1870-1915. 19/32". Mint (9.7). Price: $11. CyberAuction #435, Lot #46.

6823. SWIRL. Latticinio core. Very lightly tinted blue base. Yellow latticinio core. Outer layer is six bands. Three are pink on yellow, three are pink and blue on white. Germany, circa 1870-1915. 23/32". Mint (9.7). Price: $11. CyberAuction #442, Lot #14.

6824. SWIRL. Latticinio core. White latticinio core swirl. Outer layer is three blue bands and three white strands. Base glass is very lightly tinted blue. Germany, circa 1870-1915. 9/16". Mint (9.6). Price: $11. CyberAuction #442, Lot #27.

6825. SWIRL. Latticinio core. White latticinio core. Outer layer is four bands. One each of blue on white, pink on white, pink on yellow, green on yellow. Very nice. Germany, circa 1870-1915. 9/16". Mint (9.9). Price: $11. CyberAuction #452, Lot #17.

6826. SWIRL. Latticinio core. White latticinio core. Outer layer is six bands. Three are blue on white, three are yellow. Beautiful marble. Two tiny melt spots. Germany, circa 1870-1915. 9/16". Mint(-) (9.1). Price: $11. CyberAuction #455, Lot #18.

6827. SWIRL. Latticinio core. White latticinio core swirl. Outer layer is four bands. Two are pink on white, one is green on white, one is green and blue on white. One melt spot. Germany, circa 1870-1915. 11/16". Mint (9.7). Price: $11. CyberAuction #458, Lot #15.

6828. SWIRL. Latticinio core. Ghost latticinio core. Outer layer is four bands. Two are blue and two are red. Germany, circa 1870-1915. 19/32". Mint (9.9). Price: $11. CyberAuction #479, Lot #14.
6829. SWIRL. Latticinio core. White latticinio core. Outer layer is three bright yellow and three bright orange bands. One melt chip. English, possibly Germany, circa 1870-1915. 19/32". Mint(-) (9.0). Price: $11. CyberAuction #491, Lot #14.
6830. SWIRL. Latticinio core. White latticinio core swirl. Outer layer is six bands. Three are pink and yellow, three are green and yellow. Beauty. One tiny pit. Germany, circa 1870-1915. 9/16". Mint (9.5). Price: $11. CyberAuction #499, Lot #27.
6831. SWIRL. Latticinio core. White latticinio core swirl. Outer layer is four bands. All are pink on white, flanked by blue. Germany, circa 1870-1915. 1/2". Mint (9.9). Price: $11. CyberAuction #505, Lot #60.
6832. SWIRL. Latticinio core. White latticinio core swirl. Outer layer is four bands. Two are red, yellow and light green. Two are red, white and blue. However, rather than alternating, the two of the same color are next to each other. One small chip. Odd. Germany, circa 1870-1915. 21/32". Near Mint(+) (8.8). Price: $10. CyberAuction #331, Lot #40.
6833. SWIRL. Latticinio core. White latticinio core. Bubble filled glass. Outer layer is three red bands and three blue bands. Core is partial. One melt spot. Germany, circa 1870-1915. 11/16". Mint(-) (9.2). Price: $10. CyberAuction #360, Lot #1.
6834. SWIRL. Latticinio core. White latticinio core swirl. Outer layer is two bands (one or two are missing). One is pink and blue on white, other is very narrow with same colors. Some pinpricks. Germany, circa 1870-1915. 21/32". Mint(-) (9.0). Price: $10. CyberAuction #363, Lot #1.
6835. SWIRL. Latticinio core. White latticinio core. Outer layer is six pink on white bands. Some scratching. Germany, circa 1870-1915. 17/32". Near Mint(+) (8.7). Price: $10. CyberAuction #367, Lot #6.
6836. SWIRL. Latticinio core. White latticinio core swirl. Outer layer is four bands. Two are pink and yellow, two are blue and yellow. A couple of very tiny pinpricks. Germany, circa 1870-1915. 11/16". Mint (9.5). Price: $10. CyberAuction #373, Lot #22.
6837. SWIRL. Latticinio core. White latticinio core swirl. Outer layer is two bands of pink on yellow, one of turquoise on white, one of blue on white. Germany, circa 1870-1915. 1/2". Mint (9.7). Price: $10. CyberAuction #385, Lot #34.
6838. SWIRL. Latticinio core. End of cane, last off cane. White latticinio core swirl with one yellow strand. Outer layer is two bands of pink on yellow, one of blue on white, one of green on white. Very bottom has some excess glass. One small flake. Germany, circa 1870-1915. 9/16". Near Mint(+) (8.7). Price: $10. CyberAuction #386, Lot #30.
6839. SWIRL. Latticinio core. White latticinio core swirl. Outer layer is three bright yellow bands and three blue bands. Overall tiny chips and pits. Germany, circa 1870-1915. 1-3/16". Good (7.4). Price: $10. CyberAuction #391, Lot #9.
6840. SWIRL. Latticinio core. Base glass is tinted very lightly green. White latticinio core. Outer layer is three bands. Two brown on white, one green on white. Germany, circa 1870-1915. 11/16". Mint (9.7). Price: $10. CyberAuction #391, Lot #48.
6841. SWIRL. Latticinio core. White latticinio core. Outer layer is two pink on white bands and two green on yellow bands. Germany, circa 1870-1915. 1/2". Mint (9.9). Price: $10. CyberAuction #392, Lot #13.
6842. SWIRL. Latticinio core. White latticinio core swirl. Outer layer is four bands. Subsurface moon. Germany, circa 1870-1915. 1/2". Near Mint (8.6). Price: $10. CyberAuction #397, Lot #49.
6843. SWIRL. Latticinio core. Alternating white and yellow latticinio core swirl. Outer layer is four bands. Two blue and dark purple on white, two pink and green on yellow. Buffed, damage remains. Germany, circa 1870-1915. 13/16". Price: $10. CyberAuction #410, Lot #23.
6844. SWIRL. Latticinio core. White latticinio core. Six outer bands. Three are pink on yellow. Three are green. Germany, circa 170-1915. 9/16". Mint (9.9). Price: $10. CyberAuction #417, Lot #12.
6845. SWIRL. Latticinio core. Yellow latticinio core swirl. Outer layer is six narrow bands. Three are white, two blue on white, one green. Germany, circa 1870-1915. 11/16". Mint (9.9). Price: $10. CyberAuction #417, Lot #47.
6846. SWIRL. Latticinio core. Base glass is tinted blue. Yellow core, appears light green. Outer layer is four bands. Two are pink and white, one blue and white, one green and white. One melt spot. Germany, circa 1870-1915. 19/32". Mint (9.5). Price: $10. CyberAuction #421, Lot #39.
6847. SWIRL. Latticinio core. End of cane, last off cane. White latticinio core swirl with one yellow strand. Outer layer is two bands of pink on yellow, one of blue on white, one of green on white. Very bottom has some excess glass. One small flake. Germany, circa 1870-1915. 9/16". Near Mint(+) (8.7). Price: $10. CyberAuction #422, Lot #39.
6848. SWIRL. Latticinio core. White latticinio core swirl. Outer layer is three orange bands and three yellow bands. Germany, circa 1870-1915. 9/16". Mint (9.9). Price: $10. CyberAuction #423, Lot #12.
6849. SWIRL. Latticinio core. Yellow latticinio core. Outer layer is three white bands and three cranberry red bands. One tiny pit. Germany, circa 1870-1915. 5/8". Mint(-)(9.0). Price: $10. CyberAuction #428, Lot #52.
6850. SWIRL. Latticinio core. White latticinio core swirl. Outer layer is four bands. Germany, circa 1870-1915. 1/2". Mint (9.6). Price: $10. CyberAuction #430, Lot #40.
6851. SWIRL. Latticinio core. White latticinio core. Outer layer is three multi-color bands. Pretty. Germany, circa 1870-1915. 21/32". Mint (9.7). Price: $10. CyberAuction #431, Lot #21.
6852. SWIRL. Latticinio core. Yellow latticinio core swirl. Outer layer is three orange bands and three white bands. Germany, circa 1870-1915. 19/32". Mint (9.9). Price: $10. CyberAuction #440, Lot #6.
6853. SWIRL. Latticinio core. White latticinio core. Outer layer is thre bands. Each is pink and green on yellow. A couple of tiny subsurface moon Germany, circa 1870-1915. 11/16". Near Mint(+) (8.8). Price: $1(CyberAuction #443, Lot #38.
6854. SWIRL. Latticinio core. White latticinio core swirl. Outer layer two bands (one or two are missing). One is pink and blue on white, other very narrow with same colors. Some pinpricks. Germany, circa 1870-191 21/32". Mint(-) (9.0). Price: $10. CyberAuction #445, Lot #13.
6855. SWIRL. Latticinio core. From near an end of the cane. Several whi latticinio strands in the core. Outer layer is two blue band and on whi strand. Germany, circa 1870-1915. 19/32". Mint (9.9). Price: $1(CyberAuction #446, Lot #46.
6856. SWIRL. Latticinio core. White latticinio core. Outer layer is fo alternating bands of pink, green and white. Germany, circa 1870-1915. 2". Mint (9.7). Price: $10. CyberAuction #449, Lot #46.
6857. SWIRL. Latticinio core. White latticinio core swirl. Outer layer three bright yellow bands and three blue bands. Overall tiny chips and pit Germany, circa 1870-1915. 1-3/16". Good (7.4). Price: $10. CyberAuctio #453, Lot #51.
6858. SWIRL. Latticinio core. From near an end of the cane. White latticin core, but only a few strands. Outer layer is three bands, blue on whit green on white, pink on white. Germany, circa 1870-1915. 11/16". Mi (9.7). Price: $10. CyberAuction #454, Lot #14.
6859. SWIRL. Latticinio core. Three-layer swirl. Yellow latticinio cor Middle layer is three bands of pink and green on white. Outer layer is thre bands of pink and blue on white. Several tiny chips. Germany, circa 187(1915. 25/32". Near Mint (8.4). Price: $10. CyberAuction #458, Lot #47
6860. SWIRL. Latticinio core. Lightly tinted blue base. White latticin core. Outer layer is four bands. Two are pink and green on yellow, two a pink and blue on white. Beauty. Several tiny chips. Germany, circa 187(1915. 29/32". Near Mint (8.3). Price: $10. CyberAuction #458, Lot #4
6861. SWIRL. Latticinio core. White latticinio core swirl. Outer layer four bands. One each of red on white, red on yellow, green on yellow, blu on white. Germany, circa 1870-1915. 19/32". Mint (9.7). Price: $1(CyberAuction #459, Lot #10.
6862. SWIRL. Latticinio core. Alternating white and yellow translucer latticinio core. Outer layer is eight bands. Four red bands, two blue, tw green. Some pits. Germany, circa 1870-1915. 3/4". Near Mint(+) (8.9 Price: $10. CyberAuction #469, Lot #46.
6863. SWIRL. Latticinio core. First off cane white latticinio core swirl. Out layer is six bands. Three transparent red bands and three white band Colors shoot out the top. Several small chips. Germany, circa 1870-191 13/16". Near Mint(-) (8.2). Price: $10. CyberAuction #473, Lot #43.
6864. SWIRL. Latticinio core. White latticinio core swirl. Outer layer is s strands. Three are white, three are lime green on white. Germany, circ 1870-1915. 17/32". Mint (9.8). Price: $10. CyberAuction #475, Lot #3.
6865. SWIRL. Latticinio core. White latticinio core. Outer layer is thre narrow green bands and three yellow strands. Very nice. Germany, circ 1870-1915. 9/16". Mint (9.5). Price: $10. CyberAuction #481, Lot #36.
6866. SWIRL. Latticinio core. White latticinio core. Eight band outer laye Four yellow, two light orange, two light blue. One melt spot. England, pos sibly Germany, circa 1870-1915. 9/16". Mint (9.4). Price: $10. CyberAuctio #481, Lot #54.
6867. SWIRL. Latticinio core. White latticinio core swirl. Outer layer is s bands. Three are pink and yellow, three are green and yellow. Beauty. On tiny pit. Germany, circa 1870-1915. 9/16". Mint (9.5). Price: $1(CyberAuction #483, Lot #12.
6868. SWIRL. Latticinio core. End of cane, last off cane. White latticini core swirl with one yellow strand. Outer layer is two bands of pink o yellow, one of blue on white, one of green on white. Very bottom has som excess glass. One small flake. Germany, circa 1870-1915. 9/16". Ne Mint(+) (8.7). Price: $10. CyberAuction #488, Lot #33.
6869. SWIRL. Latticinio core. White latticinio core. Outer layer is fo bands. Two are green and white, two are blue and white. One melt spo Germany, circa 1870-1915. 25/32". Mint(-) (9.0). Price: $10. CyberAuctio #489, Lot #27.
6870. SWIRL. Latticinio core. Gorgeous. White latticinio core. Outer lay is three bright red bands and three bright yellow bands. One melt spo Germany, possibly England, circa 1870-1915. 5/8". Mint (-) (9.2). Pric $10. CyberAuction #491, Lot #32.
6871. SWIRL. Latticinio core. White latticinio core. Outer layer is thre bright yellow and three bright orange bands. One melt spot. English, poss bly Germany, circa 1870-1915. 19/32". Mint(-) (9.2). Price: $1(CyberAuction #491, Lot #34.
6872. SWIRL. Latticinio core. First off cane white latticinio core swirl. Out layer is six bands. Three transparent red bands and three white band Colors shoot out the top. Several small chips. Germany, circa 1870-191 13/16". Near Mint(-) (8.2). Price: $10. CyberAuction #496, Lot #19.
6873. SWIRL. Latticinio core. Yellow latticinio core. Outer layer is six band Germany, circa 1870-1915. 1/2". Mint (9.9). Price: $10. CyberAuction #50 Lot #12.
6874. SWIRL. Latticinio core. White latticinio core swirl. Outer layer is s bands. Three are yellow, one each of green, light red, and blue. German circa 1870-1915. 5/8". Mint (9.7). Price: $10. CyberAuction #504, L #14.
6875. SWIRL. Latticinio core. White latticinio core. Outer layer is fo bands. Two are green and white, two are blue and white. One melt spo Germany, circa 1870-1915. 25/32". Mint(-) (9.0). Price: $10. CyberAuctio #506, Lot #19.
6876. SWIRL. Latticinio core. White latticinio core swirl. Germany, circ 1870-1915. 1/2". Mint (9.7). Price: $10. CyberAuction #506, Lot #30.

877. SWIRL. Latticinio core. White latticinio core swirl. Outer layer is four bands. Two are red, one blue and one green. Small chip on top. Germany, circa 1870-1915. 9/16". Near Mint (8.6). Price: $9. CyberAuction #341, Lot #44.

878. SWIRL. Latticinio core. Peewee white latticinio core swirl. Germany, circa 1870-1915. 15/32". Mint(-) (9.0). Price: $9. CyberAuction #346, Lot #4.

879. SWIRL. Latticinio core. Peewee white latticinio core. Germany, circa 1870-1915. 1/2". Mint(-) (9.0). Price: $9. CyberAuction #346, Lot #12.

880. SWIRL. Latticinio core. Yellow latticinio core. Outer layer is four bands. Two are pink and white, one is blue and white, one is pink and white. Nice. One very tiny pinprick. Germany, circa 1870-1915. 11/16". Mint(-) (9.2). Price: $9. CyberAuction #357, Lot #5.

881. SWIRL. Latticinio core. Yellow latticinio core swirl. Outer layer is three bands. Two are blue on white, one is purple on white. Tiny subsurface moon. Germany, circa 1870-1915. 1/2". Near Mint(+) (8.9). Price: $9. CyberAuction #369, Lot #16.

882. SWIRL. Latticinio core. Yellow latticinio core. Outer layer is two pink and white bands and two blue and white bands. Germany, circa 1870-1915. 1/2". Mint (9.7). Price: $9. CyberAuction #388, Lot #6.

883. SWIRL. Latticinio core. White latticinio core. Outer layer is four alternating bands of pink, green and white. Germany, circa 1870-1915. 1/2". Mint (9.7). Price: $9. CyberAuction #392, Lot #15.

884. SWIRL. Latticinio core. White latticinio core swirl. Outer layer is four bands. Germany, circa 1870-1915. 1/2". Mint (9.6). Price: $9. CyberAuction #397, Lot #54.

885. SWIRL. Latticinio core. White latticinio core swirl. Outer layer is four bands. One yellow, pink and blue. Germany, circa 1870-1915. 1/2". Mint (9.9). Price: $9. CyberAuction #410, Lot #31.

886. SWIRL. Latticinio core. White latticinio core swirl. Germany, circa 1870-1915. 1/2". Mint (9.7). Price: $9. CyberAuction #417, Lot #10.

887. SWIRL. Latticinio core. Pale white latticinio core. Outer layer is two orange bands and two light blue on white bands. Germany, circa 1870-1915. 9/16". Mint (9.7). Price: $9. CyberAuction #433, Lot #48.

888. SWIRL. Latticinio core. White latticinio core. Outer layer is eight light blue bands and three white bands. A cold roll line on it. Germany, circa 1870-1915. 9/16". Mint(9.5). Price: $9. CyberAuction #436, Lot #6.

889. SWIRL. Latticinio core. White latticinio core. Outer layer is six bands. Three are blue and pink on white, three are pink and green on yellow. Germany, circa 1870-1915. 9/16". Mint (9.9). Price: $9. CyberAuction #439, Lot #45.

890. SWIRL. Latticinio core. White latticinio core. Outer layer is three bands. Each is pink and white with blue. Small hazy spot. Germany, circa 1870-1915. 9/16". Mint(-) (9.0). Price: $9. CyberAuction #451, Lot #40.

891. SWIRL. Latticinio core. Base glass is filled with very tiny air bubble. White latticinio core. Outer layer is three transparent green and pink on white bands and three transparent blue and pink on white bands. And one extra white strand. Germany, circa 1870-1915. 11/16". Mint (9.7). Price: $9. CyberAuction #453, Lot #38.

892. SWIRL. Latticinio core. White latticinio core swirl. Outer layer is seven bands. Three are light green, four are light red. Melt spot on the surface. Germany, circa 1870-1915. 9/16". Mint(-) (9.0). Price: $9. CyberAuction #455, Lot #35.

893. SWIRL. Latticinio core. Yellow latticinio core. Outer layer is four bands. Two are red and blue on yellow. Two are red and green on yellow. A couple of pinpricks, some sparkles, one tiny subsurface moon. Germany, circa 1870-1915. 29/32". Near Mint (8.6). Price: $9. CyberAuction #458, Lot #45.

894. SWIRL. Latticinio core. White latticinio core swirl. Outer layer is six bands. Three are pink and green on yellow, three are pink and blue on white. One tiny subsurface moon, one pit. Germany, circa 1870-1915. 25/32". Near Mint(+) (8.7). Price: $9. CyberAuction #461, Lot #14.

895. SWIRL. Latticinio core. White latticinio core swirl. Outer layer is four bands. Two are blue and white, two are red and green. Germany, circa 1870-1915. 21/32". Mint (9.7). Price: $9. CyberAuction #471, Lot #36.

896. SWIRL. Latticinio core. White latticinio core swirl. Outer layer is six bands. Three are green on white, three are pink on white. Several pits. Germany, circa 1870-1915. 21/32". Near Mint(+) (8.7). Price: $9. CyberAuction #477, Lot #47.

897. SWIRL. Latticinio core. Orangish red latticinio core. Four complex outer bands. Overall tiny pitting and tiny chipping. Germany, circa 1870-1915. 25/32". Good (7.5). Price: $9. CyberAuction #480, Lot #37.

898. SWIRL. Latticinio core. Alternating white and yellow core. Outer layer is six narrow colored bands. Germany, circa 1870-1915. 15/32". Mint (9.8). Price: $9. CyberAuction #485, Lot #22.

899. SWIRL. Latticinio core. Translucent white latticinio core. Outer layer is four bands of blue and pink on white. Germany, circa 1870-1915. 15/32". Mint (9.7). Price: $9. CyberAuction #487, Lot #8.

900. SWIRL. Latticinio core. White latticinio core. Four band outer layer. Two are orange on yellow, two are turquoise on white. Not quite wet, but no damage. Germany, circa 1870-1915. 23/32". Mint(-) (9.2). Price: $9. CyberAuction #489, Lot #1.

901. SWIRL. Latticinio core. White latticinio core swirl. Germany, circa 1870-1915. 1/2". Mint (9.7). Price: $9. CyberAuction #490, Lot #5.

902. SWIRL. Latticinio core. White latticinio core. Outer layer is four bands. Two are red on yellow, one blue on white, one green on white. Cold roll line. Germany, circa 1870-1915. 19/32". Mint (9.6). Price: $9. CyberAuction #491, Lot #4.

903. SWIRL. Latticinio core. White latticinio core. Outer layer is four bands. Two are blue, green and white. Two are pink, blue and white. Small

moon and tiny subsurface moons. Germany, circa 1870-1915. 31/32". Near Mint(-) (8.0). Price: $9. CyberAuction #493, Lot #12.

6904. SWIRL. Latticinio core. White latticinio core. Outer layer is four bands of blue on white. Germany, circa 1870-1915. 21/32". Mint (9.8). Price: $8. CyberAuction #411, Lot #54.

6905. SWIRL. Latticinio core. White latticinio core swirl. Peewee. Germany, circa 1870-1915. 1/2". Mint (9.9). Price: $8. CyberAuction #415, Lot #55.

6906. SWIRL. Latticinio core. White latticinio core. Outer layer is six bands. Three are pink and yellow, three are green and white. One flat melt spot. Germany, circa 1870-1915. 19/32". Mint (9.4). Price: $8. CyberAuction #421, Lot #9.

6907. SWIRL. Latticinio core. Yellow latticinio core. Outer layer is three white strands, one green, one red, one blue. Two small melt spots. Germany, circa 1870-1915. 9/16". Mint(-) (9.0). Price: $8. CyberAuction #423, Lot #42.

6908. SWIRL. Latticinio core. Base is very pale tinted blue. Small white latticinio core. Outer layer is three sets of orange/pink, white and blue bands. One melt spot. Germany, circa 1870-1915. 9/16". Mint (-) (9.0). Price: $8. CyberAuction #424, Lot #51.

6909. SWIRL. Latticinio core. Base glass is filled with very tiny air bubble. White latticinio core. Outer layer is three transparent green and pink on white bands and three transparent blue and pink on white bands. And one extra white strand. Germany, circa 1870-1915. 11/16". Mint (9.7). Price: $8. CyberAuction #432, Lot #4.

6910. SWIRL. Latticinio core. White latticinio core. Outer layer is two blue and green bands and two bands of pink on white. One melt spot. Germany, circa 1870-1915. 1/2". Mint(-) (9.2). Price: $8. CyberAuction #436, Lot #30.

6911. SWIRL. Latticinio core. White latticinio core swirl. Outer layer is three pink, green and white bands. Germany, circa 1870-1915. 9/16". Mint (9.8). Price: $8. CyberAuction #438, Lot #2.

6912. SWIRL. Latticinio core. From near an end of the cane. White latticinio core, but only a few strands. Outer layer is three bands, blue on white, green on white, pink on white. Germany, circa 1870-1915. 11/16". Mint (9.7). Price: $8. CyberAuction #439, Lot #1.

6913. SWIRL. Latticinio core. From near an end of the cane. A couple of wispy white latticinio strands. Outer layer is one blue band, one pink band, one green on white band. Germany, circa 1870-1915. 15/32". Mint (9.4). Price: $8. CyberAuction #443, Lot #42.

6914. SWIRL. Latticinio core. White latticinio core. Bubble filled glass. Outer layer is three red bands and three blue bands. Core is partial. One melt spot. Germany, circa 1870-1915. 11/16". Mint(-) (9.2). Price: $8. CyberAuction #451, Lot #19.

6915. SWIRL. Latticinio core. White latticinio core. Outer layer is four bands. Two are red, yellow and green, two are orange, yellow and blue. Some pitting. Germany, circa 1870-1915. 3/4". Near Mint (8.6). Price: $8. CyberAuction #458, Lot #32.

6916. SWIRL. Latticinio core. End of cane, last off cane. White latticinio core swirl with one yellow strand. Outer layer is two bands of blue on yellow, one of blue on white, one of green on white. Very bottom has some excess glass. One small flake. Germany, circa 1870-1915. 9/16". Near Mint(+) (8.7). Price: $8. CyberAuction #460, Lot #6.

6917. SWIRL. Latticinio core. White latticinio core. Outer layer is four bands. Two are blue, green and white. Two are pink, blue and white. Small moon and tiny subsurface moons. Germany, circa 1870-1915. 31/32". Near Mint(-) (8.0). Price: $8. CyberAuction #463, Lot #45.

6918. SWIRL. Latticinio core. White latticinio core swirl. Outer layer is three bright yellow bands and three blue bands. Overall tiny chips and pits. Germany, circa 1870-1915. 1-3/16". Good (7.4). Price: $8. CyberAuction #466, Lot #10.

6919. SWIRL. Latticinio core. Yellow latticinio core swirl. Core is misshapen and shoved to one side of the marble. Outer layer is four blue bands alternating with four yellow bands. Several tiny chips. Germany, circa 1870-1915. 27/32". Good(+) (7.9). Price: $8. CyberAuction #472, Lot #8.

6920. SWIRL. Latticinio core. White latticinio core. Outer layer is two white strands and three very faint blue bands. Large cloudy area, this is from near an end of the cane. Germany, circa 1870-1915. 9/16". Mint (9.5). Price: $8. CyberAuction #473, Lot #25.

6921. SWIRL. Latticinio core. White latticinio core. Six band outer core. Three are green, pink and white. Three are blue, pink and white. Germany, circa 1870-1915. 9/16". Mint (9.7). Price: $8. CyberAuction #475, Lot #36.

6922. SWIRL. Latticinio core. Was meant to be a yellow latticinio core swirl. Only two partial yellow strands in the core. Outer layer is partial colored bands and some yellow strands. Very odd. Germany, circa 1870-1915. 19/32". Mint (9.7). Price: $8. CyberAuction #481, Lot #12.

6923. SWIRL. Latticinio core. White latticinio core. Trapped air bubble. Outer layer is four complex bands. Germany, circa 1870-1915. 9/16". Mint (9.7). Price: $8. CyberAuction #486, Lot #12.

6924. SWIRL. Latticinio core swirl. White latticinio core swirl. Outer layer is four bands. One each of pink on yellow, pink on white, green on yellow, blue on white. There is an odd metallic stripe on the pink on yellow. Two tiny pits. Germany, circa 1870-1915. 15/32". Mint(-) (9.0). Price: $8. CyberAuction #487, Lot #2.

6925. SWIRL. Latticinio core. Peewee white latticinio core. Germany, circa 1870-1915. 1/2". Mint (9.9). Price: $8. CyberAuction #488, Lot #9.

6926. SWIRL. Latticinio core. Light latticinio core. Outer layer is four bands. Light pink, green and white. Germany, circa 1870-1915. 1/2". Mint (9.5). Price: $8. CyberAuction #489, Lot #3.

6927. SWIRL. Latticinio core. White latticinio core. Six band outer core. Three are green, pink and white. Three are blue, pink and white. Germany, circa 1870-1915. 9/16". Mint (9.7). Price: $8. CyberAuction #496, Lot #34.

6928. SWIRL. Latticinio core. Yellow latticinio core. Outer layer is three blue bands and three white bands. Germany, circa 1870-1915. 1/2". (9.7). Price: $8. CyberAuction #498, Lot #1.

6929. SWIRL. Latticinio core. White latticinio core swirl. Four band outer layer. Nice colors. In great shape. One tiny pinprick. Germany, circa 1870-1915. 19/32". Mint (9.5). Price: $8. CyberAuction #501, Lot #1.

6930. SWIRL. Latticinio core. Odd three-layer. White latticinio core swirl. Middle layer has one white strand. Outer layer is six bands in two different complex patterns. Germany, circa 1870-1915. 9/16". Mint (9.8). Price: $8. CyberAuction #501, Lot #3.

6931. SWIRL. Latticinio core. White latticinio core swirl. Outer layer is four bands. Two red and yellow, one green and white, one blue and white. One melt spot. Germany, circa 1870-1915. 21/32". Mint (-) (9.0). Price: $8. CyberAuction #501, Lot #46.

6932. SWIRL. Latticinio core. White latticinio core swirl. Germany, circa 1870-1915. 17/32". Mint (9.5). Price: $7. CyberAuction #347, Lot #39.

6933. SWIRL. Latticinio core. Yellow latticinio core. Outer layer is one white band, one blue band, one green band. Overall very light haze. Germany, circa 1870-1915. 5/8". Near Mint(-) (8.0). Price: $7. CyberAuction #352, Lot #44.

6934. SWIRL. Latticinio core. Yellow latticinio core. Two pits. Germany, circa 1870-1915. 17/32". Near Mint(+) (8.7). Price: $7. CyberAuction #361, Lot #13.

6935. SWIRL. Latticinio core. White latticinio core swirl. Outer layer is two green and white bands and two blue and white bands. Couple of pinpricks. Germany, circa 1870-1915. 21/32". Mint(-) (9.0). Price: $7. CyberAuction #399, Lot #50.

6936. SWIRL. Latticinio core. Lightly tinted blue base. White latticinio core. Three yellow bands and three red bands. A couple of small chips. Germany, circa 1870-1915. 11/16". Near Mint (8.6). Price: $7. CyberAuction #401, Lot #51.

6937. SWIRL. Latticinio core. White latticinio core swirl. Four outer bands. Two red, one blue, one green. Very nice. Germany, circa 1870-1915. 19/32". Mint (9.7). Price: $7. CyberAuction #405, Lot #1.

6938. SWIRL. Latticinio core. First-off-cane yellow latticinio core. Flower-type. Colors come shooting out the top. Yellow core. Six outer bands, three red, three green. Some flakes and chips. Slightly flattened. Germany, circa 1870-1915. 9/16". Near Mint (8.4). Price: $7. CyberAuction #405, Lot #2.

6939. SWIRL. Latticinio core. White latticinio core swirl. Outer layer is three blue bands and three yellow bands. One side has roughness, two tiny chips and a tiny subsurface moon. Other side views great. Germany, circa 1870-1915. 27/32". Near Mint(-) (8.0). Price: $7. CyberAuction #409, Lot #16.

6940. SWIRL. Latticinio core. Yellow latticinio core. Four bande outer layer. Two are red and white, one blue and white, one green and white. Cold roll lines at the top. Germany, circa 1870-1915. 21/32". Mint(-) (9.0). Price: $7. CyberAuction #411, Lot #19.

6941. SWIRL. Latticinio core. English colors. White core. Outer layer is six bands. Three green and white, three orange and white. Some pinpricks. England, possibly Germany, circa 1870-1915. 21/32". Near Mint(+) (8.9). Price: $7. CyberAuction #413, Lot #39.

6942. SWIRL. Latticinio core. White latticinio core swirl. Outer layer is three blue bands and three yellow bands. One side has roughness, two tiny chips and a tiny subsurface moon. Other side views great. Germany, circa 1870-1915. 27/32". Near Mint(-) (8.0). Price: $7. CyberAuction #426, Lot #24.

6943. SWIRL. Latticinio core. White latticinio core. Outer layer is three red and three blue bands. One tiny flake. Germany, circa 1870-1915. 1/2". Near Mint(+) (8.8). Price: $7. CyberAuction #429, Lot #7.

6944. SWIRL. Latticinio core. White latticinio core swirl. Outer layer is two green and white bands and two blue and white bands. Couple of pinpricks. Germany, circa 1870-1915. 21/32". Mint(-) (9.0). Price: $7. CyberAuction #430, Lot #4.

6945. SWIRL. Latticinio core. Yellow latticinio core. Outer layer is four bands. Two are orange and green on yellow, two are pink and blue on white. Melt line on one side of the marble. Germany, circa 1870-1915. 11/16". Mint (9.5). Price: $7. CyberAuction #442, Lot #43.

6946. SWIRL. Latticinio core. White latticinio core swirl. Outer layer is six bands. Three blue, three orange. Overall chips. Germany, circa 1870-1915. 31/32". Good (7.4). Price: $7. CyberAuction #461, Lot #28.

6947. SWIRL. Latticinio core. Yellow latticinio core. Outer layer is eight bands. Four are white, two blue, one pink, one air bubble. Overall chips. Germany, circa 1870-1915. 1-3/16". Good (7.6). Price: $7. CyberAuction #469, Lot #19.

6948. SWIRL. Latticinio core. White latticinio core. Outer layer is six bands. Three are red, three are green. Some pits and light subsurface moons. Germany, circa 1870-1915. 13/16". Near Mint (8.6). Price: $7. CyberAuction #469, Lot #24.

6949. SWIRL. Latticinio core. Very lightly tinted blue base. Core is extremely thin translucent white strands. Very unusual. Outer layer is four blue, green and white bands. A sparkle. Germany, circa 1870-1915. 19/32". Mint(-) (9.0). Price: $7. CyberAuction #485, Lot #26.

6950. SWIRL. Latticinio core. Amethyst base, probably sun-tint. White latticinio core. Outer layer is four blue bands and four white strands. Some tiny chips. Germany, circa 1870-1915. 21/32". Near Mint (8.4). Price: $7. CyberAuction #487, Lot #1.

6951. SWIRL. Latticinio core. White latticinio core swirl. Outer layer is six bands. Three blue, three orange. Overall chips. Germany, circa 1870-1915. 31/32". Good (7.4). Price: $7. CyberAuction #496, Lot #26.

6952. SWIRL. Latticinio core. White latticinio core. Outer layer is fo bands. Two orange and yellow, two lavender and white. Germany, circa 1870-1915. 21/32". Mint (9.5). Price: $7. CyberAuction #501, Lot #33.

6953. SWIRL. Latticinio core. From near an end of the cane. White latticinio core. Outer layer is one band of pink and blue on white and two of pi and green on yellow. Dirt line. Tight twist. Germany, circa 1870-1915. 1/2. Near Mint(+) (8.9). Price: $7. CyberAuction #503, Lot #48.

6954. SWIRL. Latticinio core. White latticinio core swirl. Outer layer bands in two different complex patterns. Melt spot and tiny sparkle. Germany, circa 1870-1915. 19/32". Mint(-) (9.0). Price: $7. CyberAuction #50 Lot #3.

6955. SWIRL. Latticinio core. White latticinio core swirl. Outer layer three bands. Each is pink on white with blue. Small hazy spot. Germany, circa 1870-1915. 9/16". Mint(-) (9.0). Price: $6. CyberAuction #372, Lot #24.

6956. SWIRL. Latticinio core. Pale white core. Four outer bands. Two re and yellow, one green and white, one blue and white. One tiny subsurfa moon. Germany, circa 1870-1915. 5/8". Near Mint(+) (8.9). Price: $ CyberAuction #405, Lot #8.

6957. SWIRL. Latticinio core. White latticinio core. Outer layer four multicolor bands. Germany, circa 1870-1915. 17/32". Mint (9.8). Pri $6. CyberAuction #408, Lot #32.

6958. SWIRL. Latticinio core. Yellow latticinio core. Outer layer is o white band, one blue band, one green band. Overall very light haze. Germany, circa 1870-1915. 5/8". Near Mint(-) (8.0). Price: $6. CyberAuctic #451, Lot #45.

6959. SWIRL. Latticinio core. White latticinio core. Outer layer is six band Three are yellow, one red, one blue, one green. Several melt spots on th Germany, circa 1870-1915. 17/32". Mint(-) (9.0). Price: $6. CyberAuctic #452, Lot #25.

6960. SWIRL. Latticinio core. White latticinio core swirl. Outer layer two bands (one or two are missing). One is pink and blue on white, other very narrow with same colors. Some pinpricks. Germany, circa 1870-191 21/32". Mint(-) (9.0). Price: $6. CyberAuction #474, Lot #16.

6961. SWIRL. Latticinio core. End of cane. White latticinio core. Outer lay is four bands. Two orange and two blue. Some jumbling. Germany, circa 1870-1915. 9/16". Mint(-) (9.2). Price: $6. CyberAuction #497, Lot #2.

6962. SWIRL. Latticinio core. White latticinio core swirl. Outer layer four bands. Two pink on white, two green on white. Cold roll line, som pinpricks. Germany, circa 1870-1915. 23/32". Near Mint(+) (8.9). Pric $6. CyberAuction #505, Lot #34.

6963. SWIRL. Latticinio core. White latticinio core. Four outer bands. Tw are blue, two are red. Some tiny chips. Germany, circa 1870-1915. 21/32 Near Mint(+) (8.8). Price: $6. CyberAuction #506, Lot #20.

6964. SWIRL. Latticinio core. Yellow latticinio core. Three outer bands dark purple. One tiny chip. Germany, circa 1870-1915. 9/16". Near Mint (8.9). Price: $6. CyberAuction #506, Lot #21.

6965. SWIRL. Latticinio core. White latticinio core. Outer layer three green strands and one red strand, all on the same side of the marble Germany, circa 1870-1915. 9/16". Mint (9.7). Price: $5. CyberAuction #39 Lot #34.

6966. SWIRL. Latticinio core. White latticinio core. Outer layer is thre pink and white bands and three pink and white bands. Some tiny pi Germany, circa 1870-1915. 21/32". Near Mint(+) (8.7). Price: $ CyberAuction #407, Lot #32.

6967. SWIRL. Latticinio core. White latticinio core swirl. Outer layer is s bands. Three are pink and blue on white, three are pink and green o yellow. Some pinpricks. Germany, circa 1870-1915. 5/8". Near Mint(+ (8.8). Price: $5. CyberAuction #411, Lot #30.

6968. SWIRL. Latticinio core. Yellow latticinio core. Outer layer is fo bands. Two are blue and white, two are green and white. Some tiny chip and subsurface moons. Germany, circa 1870-1915. 13/16". Good(+) (7.9 Price: $5. CyberAuction #417, Lot #1.

6969. SWIRL. Latticinio core. White latticinio core swirl. Outer layer is s bands. Three blue and three yellow. Several small melt chips. German circa 1870-1915. 25/32". Near Mint(+) (8.7). Price: $5. CyberAuction #41 Lot #3.

6970. SWIRL. Latticinio core. White latticinio core swirl. Outer layer three light blue bands and three orange/red bands. Two small flakes. Ge many, circa 1870-1915. 9/16". Near Mint (8.5). Price: $5. CyberAuctio #451, Lot #1.

6971. SWIRL. Latticinio core. White latticinio core. Outer layer is thre lavender and yellow bands, alternating with three blue and white band Slightly out of round. Germany, circa 1870-1915. 19/32". Mint (9.7). Price $5. CyberAuction #456, Lot #47.

6972. SWIRL. Latticinio core. Yellow latticinio core. Outer layer is fou bands. Two are pink on white, two are blue on white. Small subsurfac moon, tiny chip. Germany, circa 1870-1915. 21/32". Near Mint (8.4). Price $5. CyberAuction #458, Lot #4.

6973. SWIRL. Latticinio core. White latticinio core, with one yellow stranc Outer layer is four bands. Two are pink, green and white. One blue, gree and white. One green and white. A few tiny chips. Germany, circa 1870 1915. 25/32". Near Mint(-) (8.0). Price: $5. CyberAuction #458, Lot #1

6974. SWIRL. Latticinio core. White latticinio core. Outer layer is six band Three are pink on yellow, three are green on yellow. One tiny chip. Ger many, circa 1870-1915. 3/4". Near Mint(+) (8.9). Price: $5. CyberAuctic #458, Lot #33.

6975. SWIRL. Latticinio core. White latticinio core. Outer layer is six band Three blue, three light yellow. Some pitting and a small subsurface moor Germany, circa 1870-1915. 25/32". Near Mint(-) (8.0). Price: $5 CyberAuction #463, Lot #17.

216

6976. SWIRL. Latticinio core. Yellow latticinio core. Outer layer is six bands. Three blue and three white. Tiny subsurface moon, tiny pit. Germany, circa 1870-1915. 25/32". Near Mint (8.6). Price: $5. CyberAuction #468, Lot #2.

6977. SWIRL. Latticinio core. White latticinio core. Trapped air bubble. Outer layer is four complex bands. Germany, circa 1870-1915. 9/16". Mint (9.5). Price: $5. CyberAuction #468, Lot #30.

6978. SWIRL. Latticinio core. White latticinio core. Outer layer is six bands. Three are pink and yellow, three are green and yellow. Very nice. One tiny chip. Germany, circa 1870-1915. 9/16". Near Mint(+) (8.9). Price: $5. CyberAuction #469, Lot #52.

6979. SWIRL. Latticinio core. White latticinio core swirl. Outer layer is three light blue bands and three orange/red bands. Two small flakes. Germany, circa 1870-1915. 9/16". Near Mint (8.5). Price: $5. CyberAuction #482, Lot #9.

6980. SWIRL. Latticinio core. Slightly blue tinted glass. Core is very unusual. Transparent clear strands. Barely visible. Outer layer is six bands. Three blue on white, three green on white. A couple of pinpricks. Germany, circa 1870-1915. 19/32". Near Mint(+) (8.9). Price: $5. CyberAuction #485, Lot #9.

6981. SWIRL. Latticinio core. White latticinio core. Four outer bands. Two are blue, two are red. Some tiny chips. Germany, circa 1870-1915. 21/32". Near Mint(+) (8.8). Price: $5. CyberAuction #489, Lot #32.

6982. SWIRL. Latticinio core. Yellow latticinio core. Three outer bands of dark purple. One tiny chip. Germany, circa 1870-1915. 9/16". Near Mint(+) (8.9). Price: $5. CyberAuction #489, Lot #34.

6983. SWIRL. Latticinio core. White latticinio core. Outer layer is six bands. Three blue, three light yellow. Some pitting and a small subsurface moon. Germany, circa 1870-1915. 25/32". Near Mint(-) (8.0). Price: $5. CyberAuction #490, Lot #29.

6984. SWIRL. Latticinio core. From near an end of the cane. A couple of wispy white latticinio strands. Outer layer is one blue band, one pink band, one green on white band. Germany, circa 1870-1915. 15/32". Mint (9.4). Price: $5. CyberAuction #496, Lot #32.

6985. SWIRL. Latticinio core. White latticinio core swirl. Outer layer is three complex bands. Open air hole on the surface. Germany, circa 1870-1915. 15/32". Mint(-) (9.2). Price: $5. CyberAuction #498, Lot #50.

6986. SWIRL. Latticinio core. Slightly blue tinted glass. Core is very unusual. Transparent clear strands. Barely visible. Outer layer is six bands. Three blue on white, three green on white. A couple of pinpricks. Germany, circa 1870-1915. 19/32". Near Mint(+) (8.9). Price: $5. CyberAuction #499, Lot #1.

6987. SWIRL. Latticinio core. White latticinio core swirl. Outer layer is three light blue bands and three orange/red bands. Two small flakes. Germany, circa 1870-1915. 9/16". Near Mint (8.5). Price: $5. CyberAuction #499, Lot #5.

6988. SWIRL. Latticinio core. White latticinio core. Outer layer is four bands, two orange, two green. Tiny moon. Germany, circa 1870-1915. 9/16". Near Mint(+) (8.9). Price: $5. CyberAuction #501, Lot #17.

6989. SWIRL. Latticinio core. White latticinio core. Outer layer is three white bands alternating with three transparent pink bands. One side is wet, other side isn't. Germany, circa 1870-1915. 19/32". Mint(-) (9.0). Price: $5. CyberAuction #508, Lot #24.

6990. SWIRL. Latticinio core. Yellow latticinio core. Outer layer is three bands. One is pale pink on white, one is pale green on white, one is blue on white. Some subsurface moons. Germany, circa 1870-1915. 7/16". Near Mint (8.3). Price: $4. CyberAuction #367, Lot #7.

6991. SWIRL. Latticinio core. Yellow latticinio core. Outer layer is six bands. Three are orange and white, three are blue and white. Hazy. Germany, circa 1870-1915. 5/8". Near Mint (8.5). Price: $4. CyberAuction #411, Lot #11.

6992. SWIRL. Latticinio core. Alternating yellow and white core. Outer layer is four bands, two are blue, two are green. Surface has a flake and a couple of small chips. Germany, circa 1870-1915. 21/32". Good(+) (7.9). Price: $4. CyberAuction #431, Lot #17.

6993. SWIRL. Latticinio core. Yellow latticinio core. Outer layer is four bands. Two are blue and white, two are green and white. Some tiny chips and subsurface moons. Germany, circa 1870-1915. 13/16". Good(+) (7.9). Price: $4. CyberAuction #456, Lot #6.

6994. SWIRL. Latticinio core. Yellow latticinio core. Outer layer is four bands. Two are pink and white, one blue and white, one green and white. Some pitting. Germany, circa 1870-1915. 19/32". Mint (-) (9.0). Price: $4. CyberAuction #458, Lot #9.

6995. SWIRL. Latticinio core. Yellow latticinio core. Outer layer is four bands. Two are pink on white, two are blue on white. Tiny subsurface moon and tiny melt spots. Germany, circa 1870-1915. 21/32". Near Mint (8.6). Price: $4. CyberAuction #458, Lot #18.

6996. SWIRL. Latticinio core. Yellow latticinio core swirl. Outer layer is two blue and white bands and two green and white bands. Some pits. Germany, circa 1870-1915. 1/2". Near Mint(+) (8.9). Price: $4. CyberAuction #467, Lot #39.

6997. SWIRL. Latticinio core. Alternating yellow and white core. Outer layer is four bands, two are blue, two are green. Surface has a flake and a couple of small chips. Germany, circa 1870-1915. 21/32". Good(+) (7.9). Price: $4. CyberAuction #474, Lot #1.

6998. SWIRL. Latticinio core. From near an end of the cane. A couple of wispy white latticinio strands. Outer layer is one blue band, one pink band, one green on white band. Germany, circa 1870-1915. 15/32". Mint (9.4). Price: $4. CyberAuction #474, Lot #29.

6999. SWIRL. Latticinio core. White latticinio core swirl. Four outer bands. Three are pink on white, one is blue on white. One tiny chip.

Germany, circa 1870-1915. 9/16". Near Mint(+) (8.9). Price: $4. CyberAuction #475, Lot #1.

7000. SWIRL. Latticinio core. Pale yellow latticinio core. Outer layer is three dark purple bands and three white bands. Flake on the top. Still nice. Germany, circa 1870-1915. 19/32". Near Mint (8.5). Price: $3. CyberAuction #399, Lot #20.

7001. SWIRL. Latticinio core. White latticinio core. Outer layer is four bands. Two pink on yellow, two green on yellow. Some haze. Germany, circa 1870-1915. 5/8". Near Mint(+) (8.7). Price: $3. CyberAuction #411, Lot #57.

7002. SWIRL. Latticinio core. White latticinio core swirl. Outer layer is six bands. Three blue on white, three pink on yellow. Small flake. Germany, circa 1870-1915. 21/32". Near Mint (8.6). Price: $3. CyberAuction #418, Lot #6.

7003. SWIRL. Latticinio core. White latticinio core. Outer layer is three lavender and yellow bands, alternating with three blue and white bands. Slightly out of round. Germany, circa 1870-1915. 19/32". Mint (9.7). Price: $3. CyberAuction #419, Lot #4.

7004. SWIRL. Latticinio core. White latticinio core swirl. Outer layer is three sets of green, pink and white bands. A couple of tiny moons. Germany, circa 1870-1915. 21/32". Near Mint(+) (8.8). Price: $3. CyberAuction #438, Lot #5.

7005. SWIRL. Latticinio core. White latticinio core. Outer layer is two pink and yellow bands, one green and white band, one blue and white band. One sparkle. Germany, circa 1870-1915. 15/32". Near Mint(+) (8.9). Price: $3. CyberAuction #438, Lot #12.

7006. SWIRL. Latticinio core. White latticinio core. Outer layer is four bands. Two pink on yellow, two green on yellow. Some haze. Germany, circa 1870-1915. 5/8". Near Mint(+) (8.7). Price: $3. CyberAuction #449, Lot #41.

7007. SWIRL. Latticinio core. Yellow latticinio core. Outer layer is three bands. One is pale pink on white, one is pale green on white, one is blue on white. Some subsurface moons. Germany, circa 1870-1915. 7/16". Near Mint (8.3). Price: $3. CyberAuction #451, Lot #46.

7008. SWIRL. Latticinio core. White latticinio core. Outer layer is four bands. Two pink on yellow, two green on yellow. Some haze. Germany, circa 1870-1915. 5/8". Near Mint(+) (8.7). Price: $3. CyberAuction #478, Lot #31.

7009. SWIRL. Latticinio core. Yellow latticinio core. Outer layer is six bands. Three are orange and white, three are blue and white. Hazy. Germany, circa 1870-1915. 5/8". Near Mint (8.5). Price: $3. CyberAuction #484, Lot #41.

7010. SWIRL. Latticinio core. Very lightly tinted blue glass. White latticinio core. Outer layer is four bands. Blue/white, pink/white, green/yellow, blue/white. Several tiny chips. Germany, circa 1870-1915. 11/16". Near Mint(+) (8.8). Price: $3. CyberAuction #485, Lot #14.

7011. SWIRL. Latticinio core. Yellow latticinio core. Outer layer is three bands. Each is pink, green, blue and white. Several tiny chips. Germany, circa 1870-1915. 21/32". Near Mint(-) (8.2). Price: $2. CyberAuction #458, Lot #27.

7012. SWIRL. Latticinio core. White latticinio core. Outer layer is four pairs of bands. Each pair is the same. One pair each of pink on white, blue on white, green on yellow, pink on yellow. Overall tiny chips. Germany, circa 1870-1915. 23/32". Good(+) (7.9). Price: $1. CyberAuction #458, Lot #28.

7013. SWIRL. Latticinio core. White latticinio core swirl. Outer layer is four bands. Two are pink, blue and white. Two are pink, green and white. Some pitting. Germany, circa 1870-1915. 11/16". Near Mint (8.5). Price: $1. CyberAuction #458, Lot #44.

7014. SWIRL. Latticinio core. End of cane. White latticinio core swirl. Outer layer is one blue and white band and one green band. Subsurface moons and tiny chips. Germany, circa 1870-1915. 11/16". Good (7.5). Price: $1. CyberAuction #497, Lot #1.

7015. SWIRL. Latticinio core. White latticinio core. Hazy and subsurface moons. Germany, circa 1870-1915. 1/2". Good(+) (7.9). Price: $1. CyberAuction #501, Lot #23.

7016. SWIRL. Latticinio core. White latticinio core. Outer layer is four bands. Two pink, two blue. Overall pitting. Germany, circa 1870-1915. 5/8". Near Mint(-) (8.0). Price: $.25. CyberAuction #502, Lot #29.

7017. SWIRL. Latticinio core . White latticinio core swirl. Outer layer is two blue and white bands and one pink and white band. Appears to be missing one band. In very nice shape. Germany, circa 1870-1915. 25/32". Mint (9.7). Price: $19. CyberAuction #394, Lot #3.

7018. SWIRL. Peppermint. Hard to find shooter peppermint with mica. Transparent clear base. Opaque white subsurface layer. Six bands of pink. Two wide bands of blue. Nice mica sprinkling in the blue. Lightly buffed. Some damage remains, the pontils are intact. Rare shooter. Germany, circa 1870-1915. 25/32". Price: $325. CyberAuction #386, Lot #43.

7019. SWIRL. Peppermint. Transparent clear base. Subsurface layer of opaque white. Six pink bands and two wide blue bands. Mica in both blue bands. Several tiny flakes. Still, a beauty. Germany, circa 1870-1915. 11/16". Near Mint (8.6). Price: $210. CyberAuction #360, Lot #38.

7020. SWIRL. Peppermint. Transparent clear base. Subsurface layer of opaque white. Six pink bands and two wide blue bands. Mica in both blue bands. Several tiny flakes. Still, a beauty. Germany, circa 1870-1915. 11/16". Near Mint (8.6). Price: $210. CyberAuction #404, Lot #41.

7021. SWIRL. Peppermint. Transparent clear base. Subsurface layer of opaque white. Six pink bands and two wide blue bands. Mica in both blue bands. Several tiny flakes. Still, a beauty. Germany, circa 1870-1915. 11/16". Near Mint (8.6). Price: $210. CyberAuction #447, Lot #55.

7022. SWIRL. Peppermint. Transparent clear base. Subsurface layer of

opaque white. Six pink bands and two wide blue bands. Mica in both blue bands. Several tiny flakes. Still, a beauty. Germany, circa 1870-1915. 19/32". Near Mint (8.3). Price: $160. CyberAuction #504, Lot #25.
7023. SWIRL. Peppermint. Transparent clear base. Two wide blue bands, six narrow pink bands. A couple of thin clear spaces. In great shape. Germany, circa 1870-1915. 5/8". Mint (9.8). Price: $90. CyberAuction #410, Lot #17.
7024. SWIRL. Peppermint. Transparent clear base. Subsurface opaque white base. Four pink bands, two blue bands. 11/16". Mint (9.9). Price: $85. CyberAuction #335, Lot #60.
7025. SWIRL. Peppermint. Beach ball type peppermint. Transparent clear base. Opaque white subsurface layer. Two bands of pink and two of blue. All same width, and equidistantly spaced. Flake and some melt spots, some pinpricking. Germany, circa 1870-1915. 23/32". Near Mint(-) (8.1). Price: $75. CyberAuction #397, Lot #46.
7026. SWIRL. Peppermint. Beach ball type. Transparent clear base. Subsurface layer of white. Four equally sized and space bands. Two pink, two blue. Light haze. Germany, circa 1870-1915. 3/4". Near Mint (8.5). Price: $65. CyberAuction #372, Lot #23.
7027. SWIRL. Peppermint. Transparent clear base. Opaque white subsurface layer. Two wide transparent blue bands, four narrow transparent pink bands. One sparkle. Beauty. Germany, circa 1870-1915. 9/16". Mint(-) (9.0). Price: $65. CyberAuction #373, Lot #48.
7028. SWIRL. Peppermint. Transparent clear base. Opaque white subsurface layer. Two wide blue bands, four narrow pink bands. Germany, circa 1870-1915. 9/16". Mint (9.8). Price: $65. CyberAuction #377, Lot #57.
7029. SWIRL. Peppermint. Transparent clear base. Subsurface layer of opaque white. Four pink bands and two wide blue bands. Mica in both blue bands. Two melt spots. A beauty. Germany, circa 1870-1915. 9/16". Mint(-) (9.0). Price: $65. CyberAuction #385, Lot #54.
7030. SWIRL. Peppermint. Transparent clear base. Subsurface white layer. Six pink bands, two wide blue bands. Beauty. Green stripe in one of the blue bands. Some pits. Germany, circa 1870-1915. 21/32". Near Mint(+) (8.7). Price: $60. CyberAuction #459, Lot #55.
7031. SWIRL. Peppermint. Beach ball type. Transparent clear base. Opaque white subsurface layer. Three blue bands and three pink bands, all the same width, laying on the white. Hard to find. Two small flakes, a small subsurface moon, a couple of tiny pits and a small melt spot. Germany, circa 1870-1915. 21/32". Near Mint (8.5). Price: $50. CyberAuction #362, Lot #46.
7032. SWIRL. Peppermint. Transparent clear base. Subsurface white layer. Six pink bands, two wide blue bands. Small flake, some pitting. Germany, circa 1870-1915. 5/8". Near Mint (8.5). Price: $36. CyberAuction #396, Lot #10.
7033. SWIRL. Peppermint. Transparent clear base. Opaque white subsurface layer. Two wide transparent blue bands, six narrow transparent pink bands. One flake, some pits. Germany, circa 1870-1915. 5/8". Near Mint(-) (8.0). Price: $35. CyberAuction #391, Lot #44.
7034. SWIRL. Peppermint. Rarer type. Transparent clear base. Opaque white subsurface layer. Two blue bands and two pink bands. All bands are about the same size. Some small and tiny chips. Germany, circa 1870-1915. 25/32". Near Mint(-) (8.1). Price: $29. CyberAuction #477, Lot #15.
7035. SWIRL. Peppermint. Transparent clear base. Opaque white subsurface layer. Two blue bands. Three pink narrow bands on one white panel. One narrow pink band on the other partial white layer. Clear space in that panel. Polished. 5/8". Price: $29. CyberAuction #487, Lot #40.
7036. SWIRL. Peppermint. Transparent clear base. Subsurface white layer. Six pink bands, two wide blue bands. Some pitting. Germany, circa 1870-1915. 9/16". Near Mint (8.3). Price: $27. CyberAuction #455, Lot #10.
7037. SWIRL. Peppermint. Transparent clear base. Subsurface opaque white layer. Six pink bands, two wide blue bands. One small clear panel. A couple of tiny pits. Germany, circa 1870-1915. 21/32". Near Mint(+) (8.9). Price: $26. CyberAuction #491, Lot #9.
7038. SWIRL. Peppermint. Six pink bands, two blue bands. Missing part of one white panel. Heavily polished. Germany, circa 1870-1915. 5/8". Price: $25. CyberAuction #449, Lot #54.
7039. SWIRL. Peppermint. Transparent clear base. Subsurface opaque white layer. Two pink bands and two blue bands, equidistantly spaced. Two small melt chips, and a couple of pits. Germany, circa 1870-1915. 21/32". Near Mint (8.5). Price: $25. CyberAuction #483, Lot #13.
7040. SWIRL. Peppermint. Transparent clear base. Subsurface white layer. Six pink bands, two wide blue bands. Some fractures and surface haze. Germany, circa 1870-1915. 11/16". Good(+) (7.9). Price: $22. CyberAuction #402, Lot #55.
7041. SWIRL. Peppermint. Transparent clear base. Subsurface white layer. Five pink bands, two wide blue bands. Large clear open panel on one side. From near an end of the cane. Small fracture. Germany, circa 1870-1915. 5/8". Near Mint (8.3). Price: $21. CyberAuction #400, Lot #41.
7042. SWIRL. Peppermint. Transparent clear base. Opaque white subsurface layer. Two bands of pink and two bands of blue. All four bands are the same width and equidistantly spaced. Large fractures and a tiny chip. Marble is also not spherical. Germany, circa 1870-1915. 25/32". Good (7.3). Price: $17. CyberAuction #474, Lot #6.
7043. SWIRL. Peppermint. Transparent clear base. Subsurface white layer. Six pink bands, two wide blue bands. Some tiny chips. Germany, circa 1870-1915. 21/32". Near Mint(-) (8.0). Price: $17. CyberAuction #492, Lot #11.
7044. SWIRL. Peppermint. Transparent clear base. Subsurface white layer. Six pink bands, two wide blue bands. Some tiny chips. Germany, circa 1870-1915. 11/16". Near Mint(-) (8.0). Price: $17. CyberAuction #492, Lot #44.
7045. SWIRL. Peppermint. Transparent clear base. Subsurface white layer. Four pink bands, two wide blue bands. Some chips. Germany, circa 1870-1915. 11/16". Good(+) (7.9). Price: $15. CyberAuction #401, Lot #1.
7046. SWIRL. Peppermint. Transparent clear base. Opaque white subsurface layer. Two bands of pink and two bands of blue. All four bands are the same width and equidistantly spaced. Large fractures and a tiny chip. Marble is also not spherical. Germany, circa 1870-1915. 25/32". Good (7.3). Price: $15. CyberAuction #428, Lot #8.
7047. SWIRL. Peppermint. Transparent clear base. Subsurface white layer. Four pink bands, two wide blue bands. Polished. Germany, circa 1870-1915. 21/32". Price: $13. CyberAuction #493, Lot #39.
7048. SWIRL. Peppermint. Transparent clear base. Opaque white subsurface layer. Four pink bands, two blue bands. Overall haze. Germany, circa 1870-1915. 21/32". Good (7.6). Price: $12. CyberAuction #469, Lot #41.
7049. SWIRL. Peppermint. Six pink bands, two blue bands. Missing part of one white panel. Heavily polished. Germany, circa 1870-1915. 5/8". Price: $10. CyberAuction #395, Lot #38.
7050. SWIRL. Ribbon core. This is a stunning marble. Perhaps one of the finest pieces of workmanship I have ever seen in a handmade antique marble. Single ribbon core swirl. Yellow ribbon. Broad pink band in the center of each face. Edged by green. The outer layer is two sets of white strands, mirroring the ribbon faces. Double twisted. Perfectly symmetrical. Exceptional balance. Surface has a long dirt line, a tiny flake, a tiny chip and some pinpricking and scratching. If it were Mint, I would use the term "museum piece" to describe it. Still, it's an exceptional feat of workmanship. Germany, circa 1870-1915. 1-13/16". Near Mint (8.3). Price: $875. CyberAuction #385, Lot #39.
7051. SWIRL. Ribbon core. Extremely rare marble. Transparent cobalt blue base. White latticinio in ribbon core form. That is, it is a latticinio core, flattened on both sides to create a ribbon. The core is rare, in and of itself, however to find it in cobalt blue glass is almost impossible. Outer layer is two white and yellow bands, third is missing. Surface is pristine, with a nicely faceted pontil. Exceptional marble!!! Germany, circa 1870-1915. 27/32". Mint (9.9). Price: $775. CyberAuction #503, Lot #75.
7052. SWIRL. Ribbon core. Rare, large naked double ribbon core, consisting of latticinio strands. One ribbon is green central strand, flanked by yellow strands, flanked by pink covered white strands. Other side is a green central strand, with same flanking. Two tiny flat spots, a couple of tiny pinpricks and pits. Germany, circa 1870-1915. 1-11/16". Near Mint(+) (8.9). Price: $500. CyberAuction #504, Lot #70.
7053. SWIRL. Ribbon core. Naked double ribbon core swirl. Each ribbon is yellow and white strands, flanked on one side by a pink, white and blue band, and flanked on the other side by a pink, green and yellow band. Ribbons are mirror images. No outer layer. Several tiny subsurface moons and several sparkles. Rare. Germany, circa 1870-1915. 1-15/16". Near Mint(-) (8.2). Price: $352. CyberAuction #431, Lot #14.
7054. SWIRL. Ribbon core. Double ribbon core swirl. Large and rare. Each ribbon is a different pattern of pink, blue, green, yellow and green. Outer layer is two sets of yellow and white strands, mirroring the ribbon edges. A few very tiny chips, some pinpricking and haze. Germany, circa 1870-1915. 2-1/16". Near Mint(-) (8.0). Price: $325. CyberAuction #430, Lot #34.
7055. SWIRL. Ribbon core. Huge. Double ribbon core. Excellent design. One ribbon is green on yellow, flanked on either side by pink on white. Other ribbon is blue on white, flanked on either side by pink on yellow. Outer layer is a cage of white strands. One flake, one tiny melt spot. Excellent marble. Germany, circa 1870-1915. 2-1/8". Near Mint (8.6). Price: $300. CyberAuction #412, Lot #43.
7056. SWIRL. Ribbon core. Huge. Double ribbon core. Excellent design. One ribbon is green on yellow, flanked on either side by pink on white. Other ribbon is blue on white, flanked on either side by pink on yellow. Outer layer is a cage of white strands. One flake, one tiny melt spot. Excellent marble. Germany, circa 1870-1915. 2-1/16". Near Mint (8.6). Price: $300. CyberAuction #430, Lot #32.
7057. SWIRL. Ribbon core. Exceptional single ribbon core swirl. Fat ribbon. Opaque white. Red band on center of each face. Blue band on each edge. Outer layer is two sets of yellow strands, mirroring each face. Tiny melt pit, two tiny sparkles. Excellent marble, especially given the size. Germany, circa 1870-1915. 1-3/4". Mint(-) (9.0). Price: $285. CyberAuction #489, Lot #49.
7058. SWIRL. Ribbon core. Double ribbon core swirl. Large and rare. Each ribbon is a different pattern of pink, blue, green, yellow and green. Outer layer is two sets of yellow and white strands, mirroring the ribbon edges. A few very tiny chips, some pinpricking and haze. Germany, circa 1870-1915. 2-1/8". Near Mint(-) (8.0). Price: $260. CyberAuction #413, Lot #34.
7059. SWIRL. Ribbon core. Razor thin, double twist, naked single ribbon, filling the marble. Gorgeous colors and an excellent example. Tiny moon and some scratching and pinpricks. Germany, circa 1870-1915. 27/32". Near Mint(-) (8.2). Price: $210. CyberAuction #500, Lot #31.
7060. SWIRL. Ribbon core. Super three-layer ribbon core. Core is two ribbons. Both are blue, red, yellow, white and green. Two narrow bands of blue and red on white mirroring the ribbon edges. Outer layer is two sets of white and yellow strands mirroring the ribbon faces. Small chip, one small rough area, some scratching, several small air bubbles in the marble. Germany, circa 1870-1915. 1-3/4". Near Mint(-) (8.1). Price: $200. CyberAuction #382, Lot #49.
7061. SWIRL. Ribbon core. Stunning and very rare ribbon core swirl. Double ribbon. Each is white with red and blue bands on it. There are two narrow ribbons mirroring the edges of the larger ribbons. Each is yellow base with green and red. Outer layer is two sets of yellow strands mirroring the larger

ribbon faces. In super shape. Stunning example. Germany, circa 1870-1915. 27/32". Mint (9.8). Price: $175. CyberAuction #448, Lot #58.

7062. SWIRL. Ribbon core. Superb example. Single ribbon core swirl. Ribbon is a pink center band, flanked by white, flanked by yellow, edged by green. Outer layer is four evenly spaced bands. Two sets of white strands mirror the ribbon edges, two sets of yellow strands mirror the ribbon faces. Almost no twist. Two tiny melt holes. Outstanding. Germany, circa 1870-1915. 7/8". Mint(-) (9.2). Price: $165. CyberAuction #455, Lot #38.

7063. SWIRL. Ribbon core. Large naked double ribbon core. Rare. One ribbon is pink on yellow, flanked by white strands, flanked by green bands. Other ribbon is blue on white, flanked by yellow strands, flanked by pink bands. Several melt spots, a couple of tiny chips, a couple of tiny subsurface moons, a little bit of pitting. Very hard to find in this size. Germany, circa 1870-1915. 1-5/8". Near Mint(-) (8.0). Price: $155. CyberAuction #372, Lot #59.

7064. SWIRL. Ribbon core. Rare double ribbon core. Outstanding construction and very hard to find in these larger sizes. Two ribbons. One is pink stripes on white, other is blue stripes on white. Two outer bands. Each is yellow and white strands, floating above the ribbon faces. Several tiny subsurface moons and sparkles, still views remarkably well. Germany, circa 1870-1915. 1-1/2". Near Mint(-) (8.2). Price: $150. CyberAuction #357, Lot #33.

7065. SWIRL. Ribbon core. Three-layer double-ribbon core swirl. Exceptional example. Core is a double ribbon. One is pink and green on yellow. One is pink and blue on white. Middle layer is two bands, mirroring the ribbon edges. Each is pink on white. Outer layer is two sets of white strands, mirroring the ribbon faces. Surface in great shape. Superb example. Germany, circa 1870-1915. 13/16". Mint (9.8). Price: $120. CyberAuction #351, Lot #55.

7066. SWIRL. Ribbon core. Razor thin naked single ribbon. Pink, blue, yellow and white on one side. Green, pink, yellow and white on the other. Nicely twisted. Polished surface. Beauty. Germany, circa 1870-1915. 1-3/8". Price: $110. CyberAuction #480, Lot #14.

7067. SWIRL. Ribbon core. Double ribbon core. Beauty. One ribbon is blue bands on white, other is green bands on white. Two sets of white strands as the outer layer, mirroring the ribbon edges. Superior example. Hard to find. Germany, circa 1870-1915. 15/16". Mint (9.8). Price: $100. CyberAuction #333, Lot #39.

7068. SWIRL. Ribbon core. Very rare end of cane ribbon core in colored glass. Base glass is dark cobalt blue. Single ribbon of opaque white partially filling the core. Very rare. Nicely ground pontil. Germany, circa 1870-1915. 9/16". Mint (9.8). Price: $100. CyberAuction #383, Lot #4.

7069. SWIRL. Ribbon core. Double ribbon core swirl. One ribbon is red, white and green. Other is orange, white and blue. Malformed core. Outer layer is two sets of orange strands and two sets of white strands. Germany, circa 1870-1915. 1-3/16". Mint (9.7). Price: $95. CyberAuction #330, Lot #19.

7070. SWIRL. Ribbon core. Very rare end of cane ribbon core in colored glass. Base glass is dark cobalt blue. Single ribbon of opaque white partially filling the core. Very rare. Nicely ground pontil. Germany, circa 1870-1915. 9/16". Mint (9.8). Price: $95. CyberAuction #335, Lot #48.

7071. SWIRL. Ribbon core. This is a beauty and hard to find. Thin razor core. Pink, blue and yellow bands on white. Outer layer is two bands of green and pink on yellow, offsetting the ribbon edges. Really pretty marble. Polished. Germany, circa 1870-1915. 1-1/16". Price: $90. CyberAuction #335, Lot #38.

7072. SWIRL. Ribbon core. Single ribbon core swirl. Superb. Ribbon is opaque white. Narrow pink band on one face, the other face is covered by transparent pink with a white strand showing through the center. Blue strand floating above the face on the pink side. Yellow band just under the surface on the pink side too. Nothing on the white side. One dirt line. Superb example. Rare. Germany, circa 1870-1915. 7/8". Mint(9.1). Price: $90. CyberAuction #374, Lot #14.

7073. SWIRL. Ribbon core. Naked single ribbon core. Rare marble. Core is a thin ribbon. Opaque white with narrow bands of red. Heavily polished. Germany, circa 1870-1915. 1-5/16". Price: $80. CyberAuction #338, Lot #29.

7074. SWIRL. Ribbon core. Razor thin single ribbon core swirl. Ribbon is pink and yellow on white. Polished. Gorgeous. Germany, circa 1870-1915. 1-3/16". Price: $80. CyberAuction #477, Lot #58.

7075. SWIRL. Ribbon core. Superb single ribbon core swirl. Razor thin single ribbon. Blue, green and yellow on white. Outer layer is two bands of transparent pink strands mirroring the faces. A beauty. Surface has overall very tiny pitting. Germany, circa 1870-1915. 11/16". Near Mint (8.4). Price: $75. CyberAuction #385, Lot #11.

7076. SWIRL. Ribbon core. Hard to find large ribbon core. Single ribbon. It is a white band and a black band, flanked on either side by transparent pink. German flag colors. Some small and tiny subsurface moons. Germany, circa 1870-1915. 1-7/16". Good(+) (7.9). Price: $75. CyberAuction #397, Lot #47.

7077. SWIRL. Ribbon core. Hard to find large ribbon core. Single ribbon. It is a white band and a black band, flanked on either side by transparent pink. German flag colors. Some small and tiny subsurface moons. Germany, circa 1870-1915. 1-7/16". Good(+) (7.9). Price: $75. CyberAuction #430, Lot #56.

7078. SWIRL. Ribbon core. Interesting marble. Wide fat single ribbon. Opaque white core. Pink band in the center of each face, with a green on yellow band in the center of the pink. Ribbon is edged by blue. Outer layer is four sets of yellow and white strands. Two mirror the ribbon faces, two mirror the ribbon edges. A number of subsurface moons. Some pits. Germany, circa 1870-1915. 1-3/16". Good (7.6). Price: $70. CyberAuction #353, Lot #9.

7079. SWIRL. Ribbon core. Very interesting ribbon core. Good size. Three-layer. Double ribbon core. Each ribbon is yellow with pink and green on it. Middle layer is two sets of yellow strands mirroring the ribbon faces. Outer layer is two bands. One pink, blue and white. One green, pink and white. Mirroring the core edges. Polished. 1-3/8". Price: $70. CyberAuction #355, Lot #28.

7080. SWIRL. Ribbon core. Double ribbon core. Each is white ribbon covered by pink with blue bands. Outer layer is two sets of yellow strands, mirroring the ribbon faces. Gorgeous. Germany, circa 1870-1915. 23/32". Mint (9.7). Price: $70. CyberAuction #369, Lot #34.

7081. SWIRL. Ribbon core. Double ribbon core. One ribbon is white with pink and yellow. Other is white with turquoise and yellow. Outer layer is a cage of white strands. Two tiny flakes (might be melt areas). Very interesting marble. Germany, circa 1870-1915. 15/16". Near Mint(+) (8.9). Price: $65. CyberAuction #337, Lot #11.

7082. SWIRL. Ribbon core. Interesting marble. Wide fat single ribbon. Opaque white core. Pink band in the center of each face, with a green on yellow band in the center of the pink. Ribbon is edged by blue. Outer layer is four sets of yellow and white strands. Two mirror the ribbon faces, two mirror the ribbon edges. A number of subsurface moons. Some pits. Germany, circa 1870-1915. 1-3/16". Good (7.6). Price: $65. CyberAuction #358, Lot #43.

7083. SWIRL. Ribbon core. Exceptional and very rare ribbon core swirl. Opaque white ribbon core. There are two wide bands floating above the ribbon. Each is transparent green band, edged by yellow strands, flanked by wide transparent pink bands, edged by very narrow blue bands. The ribbon edge is mirrored by two narrow bands. Each is transparent pink on opaque white with a transparent blue bands, edged by white strands in the center. Almost no twist to it. A couple of tiny manufacturing pits. Very rare. Germany, circa 1870-1915. 11/16". Mint (9.6). Price: $65. CyberAuction #450, Lot #9.

7084. SWIRL. Ribbon core. Very odd marble. From near an end of the cane. Single ribbon. White ribbon, blue on one side, pink on the other. Outer layer is four bands. One each of pink on white, green on yellow, pink on white, white with no color. Gorgeous. Some melt spots. Germany, circa 1870-1915. 29/32". Mint(-) (9.2). Price: $60. CyberAuction #345, Lot #48.

7085. SWIRL. Ribbon core. Very interesting ribbon core. Double ribbon. One is green on yellow, edged by blue. Other is pink on yellow, edged by blue. The blue is separated from the bands. Interesting outer layer. Two sets of white strands mirroring the ribbon faces. Then, there are two bands, at the same level, mirroring the ribbon edges. One band is pink and green on yellow. Other is pink and blue on white. One small rough spot, some tiny pitting. Germany, circa 1870-1915. 7/8". Near Mint (8.4). Price: $55. CyberAuction #344, Lot #10.

7086. SWIRL. Ribbon core. Naked single ribbon core swirl. Opaque white core. Bands of pink and green on each face. Actually, one side is floating above the face. Several air holes and pits. Germany, circa 1870-1915. 27/32". Near Mint (8.6). Price: $55. CyberAuction #355, Lot #51.

7087. SWIRL. Ribbon core. Single ribbon core swirl. Razor thin ribbon. Complex pattern of pink, blue, green, white and yellow. Outer layer is two sets of white and yellow strands. One tiny pit. Germany, circa 1870-1915. 5/8". Mint(-) (9.0). Price: $50. CyberAuction #406, Lot #24.

7088. SWIRL. Ribbon core. English colors. Double ribbon core swirl. One ribbon is half red and white and half green and orange. Other ribbon is half blue and white, half red and yellow. Outer layer has one band of orange and white. Other band is missing. All are bright colors. Gorgeous marble. Small chip, several tiny subsurface moons. England, possibly Germany, circa 1870-1915. 1-1/4". Near Mint(-) (8.0). Price: $50. CyberAuction #487, Lot #21.

7089. SWIRL. Ribbon core. Interesting naked double ribbon core. Two subsurface ribbons of pink, green and blue on white. Melted dirt, tiny chip, some sparkles, scratching. Germany, circa 1870-1915. 25/32". Near Mint (8.4). Price: $50. CyberAuction #489, Lot #54.

7090. SWIRL. Ribbon core. Double ribbon core. Each ribbon is yellow on white. Floating above the face of one is a pink and green band. Floating above the face of the other is a green and pink band. Outer layer is two sets of yellow strands, floating above the ribbon faces. Polished. Germany, circa 1870-1915. 1-7/16". Price: $48.65. CyberAuction #477, Lot #32.

7091. SWIRL. Ribbon core. Rare marble, but damaged. Double ribbon. One is pink and green on yellow. Other is blue and pink on white. An outer band mirroring each edge of the ribbon. One is white strands, other is yellow strands. Large marble, almost impossible to find in this type. Very well constructed. Has overall subsurface moons and a couple of very shallow tiny chips. You're going to have to polish it or re-heat it, but rare. Germany, circa 1870-1915. 2". Good(-) (7.1). Price: $47. CyberAuction #374, Lot #34.

7092. SWIRL. Ribbon core. Stunning English swirl. Double ribbon core. One ribbon is blue and white. Other is red and yellow. Bright colors. Outer layer is two sets of yellow strands. In superb shape. Gorgeous. England, possibly Germany, circa 1870-1915. 5/8". Mint (9.9). Price: $45. CyberAuction #483, Lot #46.

7093. SWIRL. Ribbon core. Light blue base. Single ribbon. Opaque white, edged by pink, with blue and green bands on the face. Large air bubble on one side. Outer layer is two bands of yellow strands mirroring the faces. Germany, circa 1870-1915. 5/8". Mint (9.8). Price: $44. CyberAuction #383, Lot #28.

7094. SWIRL. Ribbon core. Naked double ribbon core. One ribbon is yellow strands edged by pink on one side and green on the other. Other is white strands edged by pink on one side and blue on the other. Rare marble. A couple of very tiny pinpricks. Germany, circa 1870-1915. 5/8". Mint(-) (9.0). Price: $42. CyberAuction #348, Lot #52.

7095. SWIRL. Ribbon core. Beautiful and large double ribbon core. This is an exceptional design, with a nice cage strand outer layer. Superb construction. The surface must have been damaged, it is now coated with a polymer. Germany, circa 1870-1915. 1-11/16". Reworked. Price: $42. CyberAuction #391, Lot #19.

7096. SWIRL. Ribbon core. Beautiful and large double ribbon core. This is an exceptional design, with a nice cage strand outer layer. Superb construction. The surface must have been damaged, it is now coated with a polymer. Germany, circa 1870-1915. 1-11/16". Reworked. Price: $42. CyberAuction #422, Lot #36.

7097. SWIRL. Ribbon core. Very interesting ribbon core. Double ribbon. One is green on yellow, edged by blue. Other is pink on yellow, edged by blue. The blue is separated from the ribbon. Interesting outer layer. Two sets of white strands mirroring the ribbon faces. Then, there are two bands, at the same level, mirroring the ribbon edges. One band is pink and green on yellow. Other is pink and blue on white. One small rough spot, some tiny pitting. Germany, circa 1870-1915. 7/8". Near Mint (8.4). Price: $42. CyberAuction #434, Lot #54.

7098. SWIRL. Ribbon core. Naked double ribbon core swirl. One ribbon is pink and green on yellow. Other is pink and blue on white. One melt spot. Germany, circa 1870-1915. 21/32". Mint(-) (9.0). Price: $41. CyberAuction #479, Lot #7.

7099. SWIRL. Ribbon core. Naked single ribbon core swirl. Ribbon is pink and blue on white on one side, and other side is pink and green on yellow. A teardrop air bubble floating above each face. Super. Super. Germany, circa 1870-1915. 17/32". Mint (9.8). Price: $40. CyberAuction #353, Lot #49.

7100. SWIRL. Ribbon core. Razor thin single ribbon core swirl. White ribbon. One side is orange and blue strands, other side is orange strands. Outer layer is a band of white strands on one edge and a band of yellow strands on the other. Overall haze, but no damage. Slightly flat on one side. Germany, circa 1870-1915. 1-3/16". Good (7.5). Price: $40. CyberAuction #408, Lot #34.

7101. SWIRL. Ribbon core. Razor thin single ribbon core swirl. White ribbon. One side is orange and blue strands, other side is orange strands. Outer layer is a band of white strands on one edge and a band of yellow strands on the other. Overall haze, but no damage. Slightly flat on one side. Germany, circa 1870-1915. 1-3/16". Good (7.5). Price: $40. CyberAuction #426, Lot #57.

7102. SWIRL. Ribbon core. Naked single ribbon core swirl. Blue, yellow, white and pink. Different pattern on each size. Excellent workmanship. Polished surface. Germany, circa 1870-1915. 1-3/8". Price: $40. CyberAuction #497, Lot #28.

7103. SWIRL. Ribbon core. Naked single ribbon core swirl. Opaque white ribbon. Two pink and one blue band on each face. Polished. Germany, circa 1870-1915. 27/32". Price: $38. CyberAuction #397, Lot #3.

7104. SWIRL. Ribbon core. Naked double ribbon core. Nice. Two ribbons. One is light yellow with pink and green. Other is white with pink and blue. Pretty. Overall light pitting. Germany, circa 1870-1915. 13/16". Good(+) (7.8). Price: $37. CyberAuction #383, Lot #41.

7105. SWIRL. Ribbon core. Stunning. Double ribbon core. Each is a yellow ribbon with green and pink on it. Outer layer is a cage of white strands. Germany, circa 1870-1915. 21/32". Mint (9.7). Price: $37. CyberAuction #412, Lot #35.

7106. SWIRL. Ribbon core. Naked single ribbon core swirl. Ribbon is white center flanked on one side by red and one side by black. Super ribbon. Two small chips. This is the coloring touted as the "Nazi Marbles" a while ago. Germany, circa 1870-1915. 7/8". Near Mint (8.6). Price: $37. CyberAuction #473, Lot #58.

7107. SWIRL. Ribbon core. Naked single ribbon core swirl. Polished surface. Germany, circa 1870-1915. 1-5/16". Price: $37. CyberAuction #477, Lot #46.

7108. SWIRL. Ribbon core. Razor thin single ribbon core swirl. White ribbon. One side is orange and blue strands, other side is orange strands. Outer layer is a band of white strands on one edge and a band of yellow strands on the other. Overall haze, but no damage. Slightly flat on one side. Germany, circa 1870-1915. 1-3/16". Good (7.5). Price: $37. CyberAuction #482, Lot #37.

7109. SWIRL. Ribbon core. Beautiful and large double ribbon core. This is an exceptional design, with a nice cage strand outer layer. Superb construction. The surface must have been damaged, it is now coated with a polymer. Germany, circa 1870-1915. 1-11/16". Reworked. Price: $36. CyberAuction #460, Lot #43.

7110. SWIRL. Ribbon core. Naked single ribbon core swirl. Opaque yellow ribbon. Pink and blue bands on it. Tiny chip, some very slight wear. Germany, circa 1870-1915. 11/16". Near Mint(+) (8.7). Price: $36. CyberAuction #472, Lot #41.

7111. SWIRL. Ribbon core. Beautiful and large double ribbon core. This is an exceptional design, with a nice cage strand outer layer. Superb construction. The surface must have been damaged, it is now coated with a polymer. Germany, circa 1870-1915. 1-11/16". Reworked. Price: $36. CyberAuction #494, Lot #23.

7112. SWIRL. Ribbon core. Single ribbon. Yellow ribbon with pink stripes and green edging. Outer layer is two sets of white strands, mirroring the ribbon faces. Polished. Germany, circa 1870-1915. 1-3/8". Price: $36. CyberAuction #497, Lot #32.

7113. SWIRL. Ribbon core. Naked ribbon core swirl. Beauty. Opaque white core. Has a wide blue band and two narrow pink bands on each side. A pit. Beauty. Germany, circa 1870-1915. 19/32". Mint (9.5). Price: $35. CyberAuction #338, Lot #7.

7114. SWIRL. Ribbon core. Naked single ribbon core swirl. Rare. Fat ribbon. Opaque white ribbon. One side is one blue band and two red bands. Other side is one turquoise band and two red bands. Some white space missing in the core. Some chips. Germany, circa 1870-1915. 27/32". Good(+) (7.8). Price: $35. CyberAuction #404, Lot #21.

7115. SWIRL. Ribbon core. Naked single ribbon core swirl. Rare. Fat ribbon. Opaque white ribbon. One side is one blue band and two red bands. Other side is one turquoise band and two red bands. Some white space missing in the core. Some chips. Germany, circa 1870-1915. 27/32". Good(+) (7.8). Price: $35. CyberAuction #449, Lot #49.

7116. SWIRL. Ribbon core. Double ribbon core swirl. Each ribbon is pink, blue and green, on yellow and white. Outer layer is two sets of yellow strands. Two small subsurface moons. Germany, circa 1870-1915. 29/32". Near Mint (8.6). Price: $35. CyberAuction #483, Lot #51.

7117. SWIRL. Ribbon core. Naked single ribbon core swirl. Rare. Fat ribbon. Opaque white ribbon. One side is one blue band and two red bands. Other side is one turquoise band and two red bands. Some white space missing in the core. Some chips. Germany, circa 1870-1915. 27/32". Good(+) (7.8). Price: $35. CyberAuction #486, Lot #13.

7118. SWIRL. Ribbon core. Naked single ribbon core swirl. Core is pink, yellow, green, blue and white. Two very thin outer strands. Odd twist. Germany, circa 1870-1915. 21/32". Mint (9.6). Price: $35. CyberAuction #489, Lot #29.

7119. SWIRL. Ribbon core. Double ribbon core swirl. Each is pink and blue on white and yellow. Outer layer is one set of white strands mirroring one ribbon face and one set of yellow strands mirroring the other ribbon face. Some light pinpricks. Germany, circa 1870-1915. 23/32". Mint(-) (9.0). Price: $33. CyberAuction #379, Lot #2.

7120. SWIRL. Ribbon core. Double ribbon core swirl. One is pink on white, one is blue on white. Outer layer is four bands. Two are white strands mirroring the ribbon face. Other two are turquoise and white band, mirroring the ribbon edges. Germany, circa 1870-1915. 17/32". Mint(-) (9.2). Price: $32. CyberAuction #346, Lot #43.

7121. SWIRL. Ribbon core. Single ribbon core swirl. Wide ribbon. Opaque white with pink band on the center and the face edges. Outer layer is two bands of yellow strands mirroring the ribbon faces. Lightly buffed. Pontil and damage remain. Germany, circa 1870-1915. 31/32". Price: $32. CyberAuction #367, Lot #2.

7122. SWIRL. Ribbon core. Single ribbon core swirl. Wide ribbon. Opaque white with pink band on the center and the face edges. Outer layer is two bands of yellow strands mirroring the ribbon faces. Lightly buffed. Pontil and damage remain. Germany, circa 1870-1915. 31/32". Price: $32. CyberAuction #398, Lot #9.

7123. SWIRL. Ribbon core. Single ribbon core swirl. Semi-opaque white core. One face has pink on it, other has blue on it. Outer layer is four sets of two white strands. Several tiny subsurface moons. Germany, circa 1870-1915. 29/32". Near Mint (8.6). Price: $32. CyberAuction #406, Lot #22.

7124. SWIRL. Ribbon core. Excellent example. Double ribbon core. Each ribbon is opaque white with pink and blue strands and bands. Two sets of white and yellow strands mirroring the ribbons. One tiny subsurface moon. Germany, circa 1870-1915. 23/32". Near Mint(+) (8.9). Price: $32. CyberAuction #445, Lot #49.

7125. SWIRL. Ribbon core. Double ribbon core swirl. Nice size marble. One ribbon is pink, blue and white. Other is pink, green and yellow. Outer layer is two sets of yellow and white strands. Overall subsurface moons. Germany, circa 1870-1915. 1-1/4". Good (7.6). Price: $30. CyberAuction #419, Lot #42.

7126. SWIRL. Ribbon core. Double ribbon core. Each is odd. Each ribbon is yellow strands edged on each side by a band of red and a band of black. German flag colors. Very interesting. Tiny subsurface moon right on the top pontil and a pit. Germany, circa 1870-1915. 23/32". Near Mint(+) (8.8). Price: $30. CyberAuction #430, Lot #41.

7127. SWIRL. Ribbon core. Single ribbon core swirl. Ribbon is pink band on white, edged by blue. Outer layer is a cage of yellow strands. Excellent example. One pit. Germany, circa 1870-1915. 11/16". Mint(-) (9.0). Price: $30. CyberAuction #479, Lot #30.

7128. SWIRL. Ribbon core. Rare first-off-cane flower-type ribbon core swirl. Transparent clear base. Single ribbon consisting of three multicolor bands. Outer layer is two bands on each side of the ribbon faces. All colors shoot out of the top of the marble. Several small and tiny chips. Germany, circa 1870-1915. 7/8". Good(+) (7.9). Price: $30. CyberAuction #498, Lot #65.

7129. SWIRL. Ribbon core. Naked single ribbon core. Opaque white ribbon. Two pink bands and one blue band on each side. Polished. Germany, circa 1870-1915. 11/16". Price: $29. CyberAuction #355, Lot #46.

7130. SWIRL. Ribbon core. Stunning naked single ribbon core swirl. Ribbon is transparent pink with yellow strands, flanked by white and then flanked by blue. Double twist. Surface is a little hazy. Beauty. Germany, circa 1870-1915. 17/32". Near Mint (8.6). Price: $29. CyberAuction #366, Lot #49.

7131. SWIRL. Ribbon core. Double ribbon core swirl. One is pink band on white, edged by blue. Other is pink bands on white, edged by green. Outer layer is a cage of alternating yellow and white strands. Germany, circa 1870-1915. 19/32". Mint (9.7). Price: $29. CyberAuction #433, Lot #43.

7132. SWIRL. Ribbon core. Very tightly twisted. Almost looks like an end of day ribbon. Transparent clear base. Two ribbons of dark green on yellow. Triple twisted. Tiny subsurface moon, some pitting, haziness. Germany, circa 1870-1915. 21/32". Good(+) (7.9). Price: $28. CyberAuction #365, Lot #15.

7133. SWIRL. Ribbon core. Ribbon core, odd type. Narrow yellow and red ribbon. Outer layer is two bands of yellow, red and white, and two bands of red and white. One pit. Germany, circa 1870-1915. 21/32". Mint(-) (9.2). Price: $28. CyberAuction #426, Lot #37.

220

7134. SWIRL. Ribbon core. Double ribbon core. One is pink on white, one is green on yellow. Shoved to one side. Outer layer is some blue bands, again on one side. In great shape. Germany, circa 1870-1915. 21/32". Mint (9.8). Price: $28. CyberAuction #499, Lot #18.

7135. SWIRL. Ribbon core. Naked single ribbon. Ribbon is transparent red and translucent blue. No outer layer. One sparkle, one manufacturing pit. Germany, circa 1870-1915. 17/32". Mint(-) (9.0). Price: $27. CyberAuction #344, Lot #14.

7136. SWIRL. Ribbon core. Double ribbon core swirl. Each is pink and blue on white and yellow. Outer layer is one set of white strands mirroring one ribbon face and one set of yellow strands mirroring the other ribbon face. Some light pinpricks. Germany, circa 1870-1915. 23/32". Mint(-) (9.0). Price: $27. CyberAuction #346, Lot #16.

7137. SWIRL. Ribbon core. From near an end of the cane. I think it was supposed to be a double ribbon core. Partial ribbons. One set of yellow strands. One tiny flake. Germany, circa 1870-1915. 7/8". Near Mint(+) (8.7). Price: $27. CyberAuction #390, Lot #31.

7138. SWIRL. Ribbon core. Double ribbon core. Each is odd. Each ribbon is yellow strands edged on each side by a band of red and a band of black. German flag colors. Very interesting. Tiny subsurface moon right on the top pontil, and a pit. Germany, circa 1870-1915. 23/32". Near Mint(+) (8.8). Price: $27. CyberAuction #399, Lot #54.

7139. SWIRL. Ribbon core. Single ribbon core swirl. Wide ribbon. Opaque white with pink band on the center and blue edges. Outer layer is two bands of yellow strands mirroring the ribbon faces. Lightly buffed. Pontils and damage remain. Germany, circa 1870-1915. 31/32". Price: $27. CyberAuction #434, Lot #1.

7140. SWIRL. Ribbon core. Single ribbon core swirl. Wide ribbon. Opaque white with pink band on the center and blue edges. Outer layer is two bands of yellow strands mirroring the ribbon faces. Lightly buffed. Pontils and damage remain. Germany, circa 1870-1915. 31/32". Price: $27. CyberAuction #470, Lot #8.

7141. SWIRL. Ribbon core. Double ribbon core. One is pink on white, one is green on yellow. Shoved to one side. Outer layer is some blue bands, again on one side. In great shape. Germany, circa 1870-1915. 21/32". Mint (9.8). Price: $27. CyberAuction #480, Lot #40.

7142. SWIRL. Ribbon core. Gorgeous English double ribbon core swirl. One ribbon is half bright red and half bright white. Other is half bright green and half bright yellow. Outer layer is one set of yellow strands and one set of white strands. Stunning marble. England, possibly Germany, circa 1870-1915. 19/32". Mint (9.8). Price: $27. CyberAuction #487, Lot #13.

7143. SWIRL. Ribbon core. Double ribbon core swirl. Nice size marble. One ribbon is pink, blue and white. Other is pink, green and yellow. Outer layer is two sets of white and yellow strands. Overall subsurface moons. Germany, circa 1870-1915. 1-1/4". Good (7.6). Price: $26. CyberAuction #482, Lot #18.

7144. SWIRL. Ribbon core. Double ribbon. Poorly formed core, but odd color. One ribbon is white and black. Other ribbon is yellow. Outer layer is white strands, yellow strands and air bubbles where the other strands should be. From near an end of the cane. Large melt chip near top. Germany, circa 1870-1915. 13/16". Mint(-) (9.0). Price: $24. CyberAuction #414, Lot #3.

7145. SWIRL. Ribbon core. Very interesting single ribbon core. Core is two narrow white bands, flanked by a red band and a black band. German flag colors. Melt flat spot on one side, two tiny melt pits on the other. Germany, circa 1870-1915. 11/16". Near Mint(+) (8.9). Price: $24. CyberAuction #430, Lot #47.

7146. SWIRL. Ribbon core. Naked single ribbon core. Ribbon is narrow and is transparent blue, edged on either side by white. Ribbon shoved to one side of the marble. Two tiny flakes and a tiny subsurface moon. Germany, circa 1870-1915. 9/16". Near Mint(+) (8.7). Price: $24. CyberAuction #449, Lot #35.

7147. SWIRL. Ribbon core. Double ribbon core swirl. One ribbon is green on white, one is blue on white. Outer layer is one band of a yellow strand and two white strands, mirroring the blue face. From near an end of the cane, design is shoved to one side. Three tiny melt spots. 21/32". Mint(-) (9.0). Price: $23. CyberAuction #346, Lot #31.

7148. SWIRL. Ribbon core. Single ribbon from near and of a cane. Poorly formed orange, red and pale yellow strands. Outer layer is two sets of yellow strands. Germany, circa 1870-1915. 11/16". Mint (9.8). Price: $23. CyberAuction #357, Lot #46.

7149. SWIRL. Ribbon core. Beautiful marble. Double ribbon core swirl. Each ribbon is the same complex pattern. White center with blue strands on it. Wide yellow flanking either side of the white. One yellow has red on it, other has green. Outer layer is four sets of strands. Two white strands with a blue strand mirroring both ribbon edges. Two yellow strands mirroring each ribbon face. Overall light pitting and chips. Germany, circa 1870-1915. 3/4". Near Mint(-) (8.0). Price: $23. CyberAuction #447, Lot #30.

7150. SWIRL. Ribbon core. Single ribbon core swirl. Opaque white ribbon. Green band on one edge, blue band on the other. Outer layer is two sets of yellow strands, mirroring the faces. Lots of tiny air bubbles in it. One small chip, one tiny melt chip. Germany, circa 1870-1915. 25/32". Near Mint (8.6). Price: $23. CyberAuction #453, Lot #3.

7151. SWIRL. Ribbon core. Double ribbon core swirl. White ribbons with complementary pink and blue strands. Outer layer is two sets of yellow strands, mirroring the ribbon faces. Germany, circa 1870-1915. 17/32". Mint (9.8). Price: $23. CyberAuction #500, Lot #24.

7152. SWIRL. Ribbon core. Double ribbon core. One ribbon is pink band on white, green center band (yellow-edged), with blue edging. Other is pink band on white, blue center band, with yellow and green edging. Clear space in that second band. Outer layer is two incomplete sets of white strands. Overall haziness with very light pitting and tiny flakes.

Germany, circa 1870-1915. 1-1/16". Good (7.6). Price: $22. CyberAuction #390, Lot #1.

7153. SWIRL. Ribbon core. Very interesting single ribbon core. Core is two narrow white bands, flanked by a red band and a black band. German flag colors. Melt flat spot on one side, two tiny melt pits on the other. Germany, circa 1870-1915. 11/16". Near Mint(+) (8.9). Price: $22. CyberAuction #399, Lot #22.

7154. SWIRL. Ribbon core. Single ribbon from near and of a cane. Poorly formed orange, red and pale yellow strands. Outer layer is two sets of yellow strands. Germany, Tiny subsurface moon near top pontil circa 1870-1915. 11/16". Near Mint(+) (8.9). Price: $22. CyberAuction #404, Lot #38.

7155. SWIRL. Ribbon core. Ribbon core, odd type. Narrow yellow and red ribbon. Outer layer is two bands of yellow, red and white, and two red and white. One pit. Germany, circa 1870-1915. 21/32". Mint(-) (9.2). Price: $22. CyberAuction #406, Lot #13.

7156. SWIRL. Ribbon core. Single ribbon from near and of a cane. Poorly formed orange, red and pale yellow strands. Outer layer is two sets of yellow strands. Germany, Tiny subsurface moon near top pontil Germany, circa 1870-1915. 11/16". Near Mint(+) (8.9). Price: $22. CyberAuction #440, Lot #36.

7157. SWIRL. Ribbon core. Double ribbon core swirl. One is pink on white, one is blue on white. Outer layer is four bands. Two are white strands, mirroring the ribbon face. Other two are turquoise and white band, mirroring ribbon edges. Germany, circa 1870-1915. 17/32". Mint(-) (9.2). Price: $22. CyberAuction #444, Lot #16.

7158. SWIRL. Ribbon core. Double ribbon core. One ribbon is pink band on white, green center band (yellow-edged), with blue edging. Other is pink band on white, blue center band, with yellow and green edging. Clear space in that second band. Outer layer is two incomplete sets of white strands. Overall haziness with very light pitting and tiny flakes. Germany, circa 1870-1915. 1-1/16". Good (7.6). Price: $22. CyberAuction #446, Lot #19.

7159. SWIRL. Ribbon core. Double ribbon core. One ribbon is pink band on white, green center band (yellow-edged), with blue edging. Other is pink band on white, blue center band, with yellow and green edging. Clear space in that second band. Outer layer is two incomplete sets of white strands. Overall haziness with very light pitting and tiny flakes. Germany, circa 1870-1915. 1-1/16". Good (7.6). Price: $22. CyberAuction #478, Lot #7.

7160. SWIRL. Ribbon core. Single ribbon core swirl. Opaque white ribbon. Green band on one edge, blue band on the other. Outer layer is two sets of yellow strands, mirroring the faces. Lots of tiny air bubbles in it. One small chip, one tiny melt chip. Germany, circa 1870-1915. 25/32". Near Mint (8.6). Price: $21. CyberAuction #372, Lot #18.

7161. SWIRL. Ribbon core. Excellent example. Double ribbon core. Each ribbon is opaque white with pink and blue strands and bands. Two sets of white and yellow strands mirroring the edges. One tiny subsurface moon. Germany, circa 1870-1915. 23/32". Near Mint(+) (8.9). Price: $21. CyberAuction #383, Lot #8.

7162. SWIRL. Ribbon core. Rare marble. Double ribbon core of latticinio strands. White latticinio. Outer layer is two bands. One is green on white, other is pink on yellow. Very nice. Some minor scratching. Germany, circa 1870-1915. 11/16". Near Mint(+) (8.9). Price: $21. CyberAuction #489, Lot #13.

7163. SWIRL. Ribbon core. Rare marble. Double ribbon core of latticinio strands. White latticinio. Outer layer is two bands. One is green on white, other is pink on yellow. Very nice. Some minor scratching. Germany, circa 1870-1915. 11/16". Near Mint(+) (8.9). Price: $21. CyberAuction #506, Lot #16.

7164. SWIRL. Ribbon core. End of cane (first off cane) single ribbon core swirl. Color is just in the bottom half of the marble. Overall haziness. Germany, circa 1870-1915. 17/32". Good (7.5). Price: $18. CyberAuction #350, Lot #14.

7165. SWIRL. Ribbon core. Very odd ribbon core. Double ribbon of pink strands on white, edged by blue. Edging the two clear spaces between the ribbons are two lines of "lumpy" yellow. It's the only way I can describe it. Not bands or strands, but just granulated yellow in a line. Outer layer is white strands on one side only. Melt line from pole to pole, a couple of tiny flakes, all confined to one side. Germany, circa 1870-1915. 11/16". Near Mint (8.6). Price: $18. CyberAuction #386, Lot #10.

7166. SWIRL. Ribbon core. Single ribbon core swirl. Yellow ribbon. Two green bands on each face, a red band on each edge. Outer layer is two sets of white strands mirroring each face. Some tiny chips and pitting. Germany, circa 1870-1915. 3/4". Near Mint(-) (8.0). Price: $18. CyberAuction #407, Lot #36.

7167. SWIRL. Ribbon core. Latticinio strands in ribbon core form. Double ribbon. One ribbon is yellow strands, one is white strands. Edged on either side by a wide band of transparent red. Some pitting, roughness and tiny chips. Germany, circa 1870-1915. 13/16". Good (7.6). Price: $17. CyberAuction #337, Lot #57.

7168. SWIRL. Ribbon core. Double ribbon core swirl. Naked. Both are white base. Various patterns of pink, green, yellow and blue on each. No outer layer. Some sparkles, pits and light scratching. Germany, circa 1870-1915. 11/16". Near Mint (8.6). Price: $17. CyberAuction #364, Lot #21.

7169. SWIRL. Ribbon core. Naked single ribbon core. Ribbon is narrow and is transparent blue, edged on either side by white. Ribbon shoved to one side of the marble. Two tiny flakes and a tiny subsurface moon. Germany, circa 1870-1915. 9/16". Near Mint(+) (8.7). Price: $17. CyberAuction #390, Lot #13.

7170. SWIRL. Ribbon core. Beautiful marble. Double ribbon core swirl.

Each ribbon is the same complex pattern. White center with blue strands on it. Wide yellow flanking either side of the white. One yellow has red on it, other has green. Outer layer is four sets of strands. Two white strands with a blue strand mirroring both ribbon edges. Two yellow strands mirroring each ribbon face. Overall light pitting and chips. Germany, circa 1870-1915. 3/4". Near Mint(-) (8.0). Price: $17. CyberAuction #394, Lot #9.

7171. SWIRL. Ribbon core. Naked double ribbon core. Each is bright blue, bright orange, bright yellow and bright white. No outer layer. Several small chips on the surface. England, possibly Germany, circa 1870-1915. 23/32". Good(+) (7.7). Price: $17. CyberAuction #413, Lot #7.

7172. SWIRL. Ribbon core. Superior design, some damage. Single ribbon of yellow strands. Two bands of white strands are set perpendicular to the yellow ribbon, to form the middle layer. Outer layer is four bands. Two are pink, blue and white. Two are pink, green and yellow. Two melt spots, one long fracture. Germany, circa 1870-1915. 19/32". Near Mint(+) (8.9). Price: $17. CyberAuction #473, Lot #12.

7173. SWIRL. Ribbon core. Superior design, some damage. Single ribbon of yellow strands. Two bands of white strands are set perpendicular to the yellow ribbon, to form the middle layer. Outer layer is four bands. Two are pink, blue and white. Two are pink, green and yellow. Two melt spots, one long fracture. Germany, circa 1870-1915. 19/32". Near Mint(+) (8.9). Price: $17. CyberAuction #493, Lot #49.

7174. SWIRL. Ribbon core. Double ribbon core. Each is a ribbon of opaque white, edged by red. There are two outer bands mirroring the ribbon edges. One opaque white edged by blue, one opaque white edged by turquoise. Surface buffed, damage remains. 13/16"". Price: $16. CyberAuction #383, Lot #34.

7175. SWIRL. Ribbon core. Double ribbon core. Each is a ribbon of opaque white, edged by red. There are two outer bands mirroring the ribbon edges. One opaque white edged by blue, one opaque white edged by turquoise. Surface buffed, damage remains. 13/16"". Price: $16. CyberAuction #422, Lot #12.

7176. SWIRL. Ribbon core. Single ribbon core swirl. From near an end of the cane. Fat opaque white core. Bands of pink and blue on it. Clear spaces in the core where the is white missing. Outer layer is a cage of yellow strands. One small pit. Germany, circa 1870-1915. 5/8". Near Mint(+) (8.9). Price: $15. CyberAuction #359, Lot #9.

7177. SWIRL. Ribbon core. Single ribbon core swirl. Ribbon is white. Pink, green and yellow on one side. Pink, blue and yellow on the other. Outer layer is two sets of white strands and two sets of yellow strands. Light haze. Germany, circa 1870-1915. 9/16". Near Mint (8.4). Price: $15. CyberAuction #367, Lot #45.

7178. SWIRL. Ribbon core. Single ribbon core naked swirl. Ribbon is opaque white with bands of pink and blue. Haziness on the marble. Germany, circa 1870-1915. 5/8". Near Mint(-) (8.1). Price: $15. CyberAuction #370, Lot #58.

7179. SWIRL. Ribbon core. Single ribbon. Opaque white. Blue bands on each face, pink bands on edges. Outer layer is two sets of yellow strands, mirroring the faces. Light haze. Germany, circa 1870-1915. 19/32". Near Mint (8.6). Price: $15. CyberAuction #407, Lot #45.

7180. SWIRL. Ribbon core. Double ribbon core swirl. One ribbon is red strands on yellow, other ribbon is blue strands on white. Outer layer is a set of yellow strands mirroring the white face and a set of white strands mirroring the yellow face. One small chip. Germany, circa 1870-1915. 23/32". Near Mint(+) (8.7). Price: $15. CyberAuction #431, Lot #34.

7181. SWIRL. Ribbon core. Double ribbon core swirl. Two ribbons of pink and blue on white. Two bands of green on yellow form the outer layer, mirroring the ribbon edges. A couple of tiny chips. Germany, circa 1870-1915. 5/8". Near Mint(+) (8.9). Price: $14. CyberAuction #497, Lot #17.

7182. SWIRL. Ribbon core. Single ribbon core. Opaque white core. Pink, blue and green bands on it. Outer layer is two sets of yellow strands, mirroring the ribbon faces. Some pitting. Germany, circa 1870-1915. 17/32". Near Mint(+) (8.7). Price: $12. CyberAuction #359, Lot #43.

7183. SWIRL. Ribbon core. Single ribbon core. Opaque white core. Pink, blue and green bands on it. Outer layer is two sets of yellow strands, mirroring the ribbon faces. Some pitting. Germany, circa 1870-1915. 17/32". Near Mint(+) (8.7). Price: $12. CyberAuction #398, Lot #2.

7184. SWIRL. Ribbon core. Single ribbon. Opaque white. Blue bands on each face, pink bands on edges. Outer layer is two sets of yellow strands, mirroring the faces. Light haze. Germany, circa 1870-1915. 19/32". Near Mint (8.6). Price: $12. CyberAuction #426, Lot #48.

7185. SWIRL. Ribbon core. End of cane (first off cane) marble. Double ribbon core. Colors shoot right out the top of the marble. Some light pitting, and the marble is somewhat flat. Germany, circa 1870-1915. 5/8". Near Mint (8.6). Price: $12. CyberAuction #437, Lot #55.

7186. SWIRL. Ribbon core. Single ribbon core. Opaque white core. Pink, blue and green bands on it. Outer layer is two sets of yellow strands, mirroring the ribbon faces. Some pitting. Germany, circa 1870-1915. 17/32". Near Mint(+) (8.7). Price: $12. CyberAuction #453, Lot #9.

7187. SWIRL. Ribbon core. Single ribbon. Opaque white. Blue bands on each face, pink bands on edges. Outer layer is two sets of yellow strands, mirroring the faces. Light haze. Germany, circa 1870-1915. 19/32". Near Mint (8.6). Price: $12. CyberAuction #456, Lot #4.

7188. SWIRL. Ribbon core. Double ribbon core swirl. One ribbon is red strands on yellow, other ribbon is blue strands on white. Outer layer is a set of yellow strands mirroring the white face and a set of white strands mirroring the yellow face. One small chip. Germany, circa 1870-1915. 23/32". Near Mint(+) (8.7). Price: $12. CyberAuction #466, Lot #16.

7189. SWIRL. Ribbon core. Single ribbon from near and of a cane. Poorly formed orange, red and pale yellow strands. Outer layer is two sets of yellow strands. Germany, Tiny subsurface moon near top pontil Germany, circa 1870-1915. 11/16". Near Mint(+) (8.9). Price: $12. CyberAuction #474, Lot #26.

7190. SWIRL. Ribbon core. Double ribbon core swirl. One is pink on white, one is blue on white. Outer layer is four bands. Two are white strands mirroring the ribbon face. Other two are turquoise and white band, mirroring ribbon edges. Germany, circa 1870-1915. 17/32". Mint(-) (9.2). Price: $12. CyberAuction #474, Lot #27.

7191. SWIRL. Ribbon core. Single ribbon from near and of a cane. Poorly formed orange, red and pale yellow strands. Outer layer is two sets of yellow strands. Germany, Tiny subsurface moon near top pontil Germany circa 1870-1915. 11/16". Near Mint(+) (8.9). Price: $12. CyberAuction #490, Lot #2.

7192. SWIRL. Ribbon core. Single ribbon from near and of a cane. Poorly formed orange, red and pale yellow strands. Outer layer is two sets of yellow strands. Germany, Tiny subsurface moon near top pontil Germany, circa 1870-1915. 11/16". Near Mint(+) (8.9). Price: $12. CyberAuction #506, Lot #26.

7193. SWIRL. Ribbon core. Interesting double ribbon core from near an end of the cane. One ribbon is yellow, white and pink. Other is a partial of green, white and pink. No outer layer. Some scratches. Germany, circa 1870-1915. 9/16". Near Mint(+) (8.7). Price: $11. CyberAuction #427, Lot #2.

7194. SWIRL. Ribbon core. Naked single ribbon core. Ribbon is green, blue, pink, yellow and white. Some striations on the surface. One tiny subsurface moon. Germany, circa 1870-1915. 9/16". Near Mint(+) (8.9). Price: $11. CyberAuction #427, Lot #37.

7195. SWIRL. Ribbon core. Single ribbon core swirl. Naked. Opaque white core. Two pink bands and a blue band on each face. Several flakes, some chipping. Germany, circa 1870-1915. 11/16". Good (7.3). Price: $10. CyberAuction #402, Lot #51.

7196. SWIRL. Ribbon core. End of cane (first off cane) marble. Double ribbon core. Colors shoot right out the top of the marble. Some light pitting, and the marble is somewhat flat. Germany, circa 1870-1915. 5/8". Near Mint (8.6). Price: $10. CyberAuction #411, Lot #1.

7197. SWIRL. Ribbon core. Double ribbon core. Each is a complex combination of pink, green, yellow, blue and white. Outer layer is two sets of white and yellow strands, mirroring the ribbon edges. Two tiny subsurface moons. Germany, circa 1870-1915. 19/32". Near Mint(+) (8.7). Price: $10. CyberAuction #419, Lot #2.

7198. SWIRL. Ribbon core. Naked single ribbon core. Light green, transparent blue, transparent purple, white. No outer layer. One cold roll line. Tiny flake. Germany, circa 1870-1915. 11/16". Near Mint(+) (8.8). Price: $10. CyberAuction #432, Lot #2.

7199. SWIRL. Ribbon core. Naked single ribbon core. Light green, transparent blue, transparent purple, white. No outer layer. One cold roll line. Tiny flake. Germany, circa 1870-1915. 11/16". Near Mint(+) (8.8). Price: $10. CyberAuction #453, Lot #55.

7200. SWIRL. Ribbon core. Naked double ribbon core. Two yellow bands in the core. No outer layer. Germany, circa 1870-1915. 17/32". Mint (9.6). Price: $10. CyberAuction #497, Lot #7.

7201. SWIRL. Ribbon core. Double ribbon core swirl. Each is a combination of green, blue, pink, yellow and white. Outer layer is two sets of yellow and white strands, mirroring the ribbon faces. Some light scratching. Germany, circa 18870-1915. 5/8". Near Mint(+) (8.7). Price: $9. CyberAuction #407, Lot #1.

7202. SWIRL. Ribbon core. Single ribbon core swirl. Ribbon is white with a red band on the center of each face and blue bands on the edges. The outer layer is two sets of yellow strands mirroring the ribbon faces. Excellent construction, but surface is frosted. 9/16". Good(+) (7.9). Price: $8. CyberAuction #349, Lot #8.

7203. SWIRL. Ribbon core. Double ribbon core swirl. Each is a combination of green, blue, pink, yellow and white. Outer layer is two sets of yellow and white strands, mirroring the ribbon faces. Some light scratching. Germany, circa 18870-1915. 5/8". Near Mint(+) (8.7). Price: $8. CyberAuction #437, Lot #4.

7204. SWIRL. Ribbon core. Single ribbon core swirl. Ribbon is white with a red band on the center of each face and blue bands on the edges. The outer layer is two sets of yellow strands mirroring the ribbon faces. Excellent construction, but surface is frosted. 9/16". Good(+) (7.9). Price: $6. CyberAuction #453, Lot #43.

7205. SWIRL. Ribbon core. Single ribbon core. Opaque yellow ribbon. Red and green band floating above each face. Outer layer is a cage of white strands. Poorly twisted. Hazy and minor chips. Germany, circa 1870-1915. 25/32". Good(+) (7.7). Price: $6. CyberAuction #490, Lot #18.

7206. SWIRL. Ribbon core. Single ribbon core. Opaque yellow ribbon. Red and green band floating above each face. Outer layer is a cage of white strands. Poorly twisted. Hazy and minor chips. Germany, circa 1870-1915. 25/32". Good(+) (7.7). Price: $5. CyberAuction #469, Lot #2.

7207. SWIRL. Solid core. Very large swirl. Three-layer. Opaque white core. Four bands floating above it. Two are pink, one blue, one green. Outer layer is four pairs of yellow strands. A couple of very tiny pinpricks. Stunning. Very hard to find them this large and especially in this kind of condition. Germany, circa 1870-1915. 2-3/16". Mint(-) (9.2). Price: $825. CyberAuction #505, Lot #69.

7208. SWIRL. Solid core. Exceptional lobed solid core swirl. Opaque white core. Four very deep lobes. Each trough is blue band on yellow band. Other yellow bands on the core. Each peak is a pink band. Outer layer is two sets of yellow strands and two sets of white strands. Superior marble. Two tiny chips, a couple of tiny subsurface moons, several small sparkles. But, no scratching or pinpricking. Germany, circa 1870-1915. 2-5/16". Near Mint(-) (8.2). Price: $360. CyberAuction #455, Lot #33.

7209. SWIRL. Solid core. Huge marble. Opaque white core. Outer layer is very interesting design. Four bands, separated by four strands. Two bands are pink flanking yellow, one is blue flanking yellow, one is green flanking yellow. Strands are yellow. Some small subsurface moons, but still a beauty. Germany, circa 1870-1915. 2-1/4". Near Mint(-) (8.2). Price: $285. CyberAuction #453, Lot #27.
7210. SWIRL. Solid core. Very unusual large marble. Base glass is slightly tinted pink. Opaque white core. Middle layer encases the core with a series of yellow bands, alternating with pink, blue or green bands. Outer layer is a cage of yellow strands. One small chip, several tiny chips, some tiny subsurface moons. Germany, circa 1870-1915. 2-1/16". Near Mint(-) (8.2). Price: $285. CyberAuction #468, Lot #12.
7211. SWIRL. Solid core. Huge marble. Opaque white core. Outer layer is very interesting design. Four bands, separated by four strands. Two bands are pink flanking yellow, one is blue flanking yellow, one is green flanking yellow. Strands are yellow. Some small subsurface moons, but still a beauty. Germany, circa 1870-1915. 2-3/8". Near Mint(-) (8.2). Price: $280. CyberAuction #412, Lot #45.
7212. SWIRL. Solid core. Very unusual large marble. Base glass is slightly tinted pink. Opaque white core. Middle layer encases the core with a series of yellow bands, alternating with pink, blue or green bands. Outer layer is a cage of yellow strands. One small chip, several tiny chips, some tiny subsurface moons. Germany, circa 1870-1915. 2-1/16". Near Mint(-) (8.2). Price: $260. CyberAuction #418, Lot #25.
7213. SWIRL. Solid core. Very nice large lobed solid core swirl. Core is opaque white. Three lobes. The trough of each is pink. There is a clear space in the core. Outer layer is three blue and white bands. Surface has overall very light scratches and pinpricks. Germany, circa 1870-1915. 1-7/8". Near Mint(-) (8.1). Price: $260. CyberAuction #455, Lot #31.
7214. SWIRL. Solid core. Very nice large lobed solid core swirl. Core is opaque white. Three lobes. The trough of each is pink. There is a clear space in the core. Outer layer is three blue and white bands. Surface has overall very light scratches and pinpricks. Germany, circa 1870-1915. 1-7/8". Near Mint(-) (8.1). Price: $250. CyberAuction #467, Lot #30.
7215. SWIRL. Solid core. Rare marble. Large lobed solid core. Opaque white core. Four very deep lobes. Blue band on each peak. Outer layer is eight bands. Four are green on yellow, four are pink on white. Super looking marble. One tiny flake, a few pits, one sparkle. Gorgeous. Germany, circa 1870-1915. 1-13/16". Near Mint(+) (8.8). Price: $250. CyberAuction #491, Lot #57.
7216. SWIRL. Solid core. Superbly constructed three-layer solid core swirl. Opaque white core. Middle layer is alternating bands of green, red and blue. Outer layer is a cage of yellow strands. Some very tiny chips, very tiny subsurface moons and pits. Germany, circa 1870-1915. 2-3/8". Near Mint(-) (8.2). Price: $210. CyberAuction #425, Lot #33.
7217. SWIRL. Solid core. Huge marble. Opaque white core. Outer layer is very interesting design. Four bands, separated by four strands. Two bands are pink flanking yellow, one is blue flanking yellow, one is green flanking yellow. Strands are yellow. Some small subsurface moons, but still a beauty. Germany, circa 1870-1915. 2-1/4". Near Mint(-) (8.2). Price: $210. CyberAuction #432, Lot #22.
7218. SWIRL. Solid core. Four-lobe three-layer solid core. Opaque white core. Four lobes. A blue band on two peaks, a pink band on the other two. No color in the troughs, rather, each has a teardrop air bubble. Middle layer is a cage of yellow strands. Outer layer is six bands. Three are pink, green and yellow. Three are pink, blue and white. Several tiny subsurface moons. Overall very light scratches. Germany, circa 1870-1915. 2-3/8". Good(+) (7.9). Price: $210. CyberAuction #498, Lot #43.
7219. SWIRL. Solid core. Superbly constructed three-layer solid core swirl. Opaque yellow core. Middle layer is alternating bands of green and red. Outer layer is a cage of white strands. One tiny chip and tiny subsurface moon. Some pitting. Germany, circa 1870-1915. 2-1/4". Near Mint (8.3). Very similar to Lot #33 in this auction, but reversed colors. Price: $200. CyberAuction #425, Lot #35.
7220. SWIRL. Solid core. Gorgeous three-layer solid core swirl. Opaque white core. Bands of blue, pink and green floating above the core. Outer layer is a cage of yellow strands. Huge. Two small subsurface moons near the bottom pontil, some very tiny chips and pits. Germany, circa 1870-1915. 2-1/8". Near Mint (8.6). Price: $185. CyberAuction #387, Lot #17.
7221. SWIRL. Solid core. White core. Had pink, blue and turquoise bands on it. Outer layer is a cage of yellow strands. Thick casing of outer clear glass. Some tiny chips, tiny subsurface moons and pitting. Germany, circa 1870-1915. 2". Good(+) (7.9). Price: $185. CyberAuction #421, Lot #33.
7222. SWIRL. Solid core. Stunning. Opaque yellow core. Four very deep lobes, almost to the core. Outer layer is five bands of pink on white (odd). Polished. Germany, circa 1870-1915. 2". Price: $185. CyberAuction #421, Lot #34.
7223. SWIRL. Solid core. Rare type. Opaque white core. Four lobes. Each trough is filled with transparent pink. There is a yellow strand floating above the pink in each lobe. Peaks are white. Tightly twisted. Outer layer is two sets of white strands and two sets of yellow strands. A number of tiny subsurface moons. Overall scratches. Needs a light buff. Germany, circa 1870-1915. 1-15/16". Good(+) (7.8). Price: $180. CyberAuction #364, Lot #35.
7224. SWIRL. Solid core. Very nice. Opaque white core. Bands of pink and blue on it. Outer layer is four sets of yellow strands. Several tiny chips and tiny subsurface moons. Germany, circa 1870-1915. 2". Near Mint (8.5). Price: $175. CyberAuction #417, Lot #27.
7225. SWIRL. Solid core. Very rare three-layer marble. Solid core swirl. Core is four panels. Two are yellow, two are white. Middle layer is a tight cage of pink (!!) strands, tightly packed together. Outer layer is three bands. One is white, one is blue and pink on white, one is green and pink on yellow. There is a band missing. From near an end of the cane. Very rare coloring. In great shape. Germany, circa 1870-1915. 11/16". Mint (9.7). Price: $160. CyberAuction #376, Lot #37.
7226. SWIRL. Solid core. Opaque white core. Two bands of blue and two of green on the core. Outer layer is three sets of white strands. One has three strands, one has two strands, one is a single strand. Interesting design. Some very light pitting on the surface and a couple of very tiny subsurface moons, but no significant damage. Germany, circa 1870-1915. 1-7/8". Near Mint(-) (8.1). Price: $150. CyberAuction #424, Lot #35.
7227. SWIRL. Solid core. Four-lobed solid core swirl. Rare marble. Opaque yellow core. Four very deep lobes, almost to the center. There is a dark green band in the trough of each lobe and a pink band on the peak of each lobe. Outer layer is four sets of white strands, mirroring the lobe troughs. Thick outer casing. Several small chips and subsurface moons, overall light haze. The damage is not deep and there is a thick outer casing. A polish would reveal a stunning marble. Germany, circa 1870-1915. 2-3/8". Good(-) (7.2). Price: $140. CyberAuction #382, Lot #35.
7228. SWIRL. Solid core. Very nice. Opaque white core. Bands of pink and blue on it. Outer layer is four sets of yellow strands. Several tiny chips and tiny subsurface moons. Germany, circa 1870-1915. 2". Near Mint (8.5). Price: $140. CyberAuction #454, Lot #28.
7229. SWIRL. Solid core. Stunning coloring to this marble. An absolutely exceptional example. Core is three light orange/red bands alternating with three light baby blue bands, each separated by bright yellow. Outer layer is a cage of white strands. Stunning marble! Germany, possibly England, circa 1870-1915. 29/32". Mint (9.8). Price: $135. CyberAuction #345, Lot #39.
7230. SWIRL. Solid core. Gorgeous example. Opaque yellow core. Outer layer is eight bands. Four light blue, two orange, two white. Gorgeous and large English swirl. Two tiny sparkles, one tiny annealing fracture. England, possibly Germany, circa 1870-1920. 1-1/4". Mint(-) (9.0). Price: $135. CyberAuction #448, Lot #51.
7231. SWIRL. Solid core. Large three-layer solid core. Opaque white core. Middle layer is twelve bands. All transparent. Six are pink, three are blue, three are green. Outer layer is four sets of yellow strands. Three tiny subsurface moons, one tiny moon. Superb marble, looks great. Excellent design and construction. Germany, circa 1870-1915. 1-15/16". Near Mint (8.6). Price: $130. CyberAuction #360, Lot #35.
7232. SWIRL. Solid core. Rare type. Opaque white core. Four lobes. Each trough is filled with transparent pink. There is a yellow strand floating above the pink in each lobe. Peaks are white. Tightly twisted. Outer layer is two sets of white strands and two sets of yellow strands. A number of tiny subsurface moons. Overall scratches. Needs a light buff. Germany, circa 1870-1915. 1-15/16". Good(+) (7.8). Price: $130. CyberAuction #470, Lot #23.
7233. SWIRL. Solid core. Superior example of an English type swirl. Opaque white core. Outer layer is a cage of fourteen bands. Three each of yellow, white, purple and orange/red. Also, one green and one light blue. Stunning. One sparkle. Rare marble. England, possibly Germany, circa 1870-1920. 29/32". Mint(-) (9.2). Price: $126. CyberAuction #406, Lot #58.
7234. SWIRL. Solid core. Three-layer solid core. Opaque white core. Floating in a layer above it are four bands. Each band is three narrow bands. Two sets are pink, one set is blue, one set is dark green. Outer layer is four sets of yellow strands. One tiny chip, a pit, a tiny subsurface moon, a couple of sparkles, some tiny pinpricks. Large. Germany, circa 1870-1915. 1-3/4". Near Mint (8.3). Price: $120. CyberAuction #416, Lot #36.
7235. SWIRL. Solid core. Three-layer solid core swirl. Opaque white core. Middle layer is a cage of pink and blue bands. Outer layer is three sets of yellow strands. Polished, some damage remains. 2-1/16". Price: $120. CyberAuction #420, Lot #36.
7236. SWIRL. Solid core. Three-layer solid core. Opaque white core. Floating in a layer above it are four bands. Each band is three narrow bands. Two sets are pink, one set is blue, one set is dark green. Outer layer is four sets of yellow strands. One tiny chip, a pit, a tiny subsurface moon, a couple of sparkles, some tiny pinpricks. Large. Germany, circa 1870-1915. 1-3/4". Near Mint (8.3). Price: $120. CyberAuction #430, Lot #28.
7237. SWIRL. Solid core. Super design. Three layer. Semi-opaque yellow core. Middle layer is a cage of white strands. Outer layer is six bands. Three are pink on white, three are blue on white. Couple o chip, some pitting, tiny subsurface moons, sparkles. Germany, circa 1870-1915. 1-7/8". Near Mint(-) (8.0). Price: $110. CyberAuction #352, Lot #26.
7238. SWIRL. Solid core. Three band core. Each is the same pattern of pink and blue on white. Outer layer is three sets of white strands. One tiny subsurface moon, one tiny chip. Germany, circa 1870-1915. 1-9/16". Near Mint(+) (8.7). Price: $110. CyberAuction #354, Lot #26.
7239. SWIRL. Solid core. Four panel core. Two are pink and green on yellow, two are pink and blue on white. Outer layer is four bands. Two are sets of yellow strands, two are sets of white strands. One very tiny subsurface moon, one very tiny rub spots. A beauty!!!! Germany, circa 1870-1915. 1-5/16". Near Mint(+) (8.9). Price: $110. CyberAuction #363, Lot #28.
7240. SWIRL. Solid core. Three-layer solid core swirl. Core is opaque white and opaque yellow bands of varying widths. Middle layer is four pairs of colored bands. two pairs are pink, one pair is blue, one pair is green. Outer layer is four sets of strands. Two are yellow, two are white. Buffed, with overall pitting and some subsurface moons. Germany, circa 1870-1915. 2-1/4". Price: $100. CyberAuction #420, Lot #26.
7241. SWIRL. Solid core. Three-layer solid core swirl. Core is opaque white and opaque yellow bands of varying widths. Middle layer is four pairs of colored bands. two pairs are pink, one pair is blue, one pair is green. Outer layer is four sets of strands. Two are yellow, two are white. Buffed, with overall pitting and some subsurface moons. Germany, circa 1870-1915. 2-1/4". Price: $100. CyberAuction #460, Lot #47.

7242. SWIRL. Solid core. Stunning marble. Three layer. Lobed solid core swirl. Opaque white core. Three very deep lobes. Pink strand on each peak, blue band in each trough. Middle layer is three pink on white bands. Outer layer is three green on white bands, mirroring the clear spaces in the middle layer. Core is obscured. Deep melt crease on one side. Gorgeous. Germany, circa 1870-1915. 23/32". Mint(-) (9.0). Price: $100. CyberAuction #503, Lot #38.
7243. SWIRL. Solid core. Three layer swirl. Fat white core. Has some yellow bands on it. Middle layer is four panels of bands. Two have three bands of pink, two have three bands of blue. Outer layer is four sets of yellow strands. Gorgeous marble. Melt chip on the top pontil. Germany, circa 1870-1915. 13/16". Mint (9.5). Price: $97. CyberAuction #498, Lot #37.
7244. SWIRL. Solid core. Naked solid core swirl. Core is alternating white, orange, green, blue and yellow bands. No outer layer. Gorgeous. Germany, circa 1870-1915. 7/8". Mint (9.9). Price: $86. CyberAuction #376, Lot #23.
7245. SWIRL. Solid core. Lobed solid core swirl. Opaque white core. Four lobes. Two have pink in the troughs, one has green in the trough, one has blue in the trough. Outer layer is four sets of yellow strands. Piece of melted sand on the surface, and a small subsurface moon. Germany, circa 1870-1915. 1-3/16". Near Mint(+) (8.8). Price: $80. CyberAuction #339, Lot #26.
7246. SWIRL. Solid core. Nice marble. Opaque white core. Three pink bands and three blue bands on it. Outer layer is a cage of yellow strands. One tiny chip, one sparkle, one small rough spot, some scratching. Germany, circa 1870-1915. 1-3/4". Near Mint (8.3). Price: $80. CyberAuction #359, Lot #34.
7247. SWIRL. Solid core. Beauty and rare coloring. Core is blue with white and yellow narrow bands on it. Outer layer is seven orange bands. Germany, circa 1870-1915. 21/32". Mint (9.9). Price: $77. CyberAuction #330, Lot #27.
7248. SWIRL. Solid core. Odd coloring. Green tinted base. Four panel core. Two panels are orange, light blue and white. Two are red, light blue and white. Outer layer is four bands. Each is a blue strand, flanked by a yellow strand on either side. Very unusual coloring. A number of sparkles and very tiny subsurface moons. Germany, circa 1870-1915. 1-3/8". Near Mint (8.4). Price: $75. CyberAuction #351, Lot #36.
7249. SWIRL. Solid core. Three layer. Outstanding example. Opaque yellow core. Middle layer is a cage of white strands. Outer layer is a cage of red strands. Thick outer casing. Tiny pits in a number of spots on the marble. Germany, circa 1870-1915. 1". Near Mint (8.3). Price: $75. CyberAuction #380, Lot #48.
7250. SWIRL. Solid core. Three layer. Outstanding example. Opaque yellow core. Middle layer is a cage of white strands. Outer layer is a cage of red strands. Thick outer casing. Tiny pits in a number of spots on the marble. Germany, circa 1870-1915. 1". Near Mint (8.3). Price: $75. CyberAuction #440, Lot #55.
7251. SWIRL. Solid core. Core consists of bands. Three each of blue, green, yellow and white. Alternating. Outer layer is a cage of red strands (unusual). Odd coloring. Gorgeous. Germany, possibly England, circa 1870-1915. 13/16". Mint (9.7). Price: $75. CyberAuction #483, Lot #42.
7252. SWIRL. Solid core. Stunning marble. Opaque yellow core. Cage of pink and yellow strands. So tightly packed that it is difficult to see inside the marble. A couple of pinpricks. Germany, circa 1870-1915. 5/8". Mint(-) (9.1). Price: $70. CyberAuction #333, Lot #28.
7253. SWIRL. Solid core. Rare colors. Core is transparent emerald green with wide strands of yellow and white on it. Outer layer is four bands of red edged by white. Heavily polished. Germany, circa 1870-1915. 1-5/16". Price: $70. CyberAuction #337, Lot #53.
7254. SWIRL. Solid core. Gorgeous three-layer solid core swirl. Opaque white core. Middle layer is a cage of alternating blue and pink strands. Outer layer is a cage of yellow strands. Superb. Germany, circa 1870-1915. 25/32". Mint (9.8). Price: $70. CyberAuction #459, Lot #49.
7255. SWIRL. Solid core. Nice English type. Green core. Six outer bands. Three are yellow and three are red. Flat melt spot at top. England, possibly Germany, circa 1870-1915. 11/16". Mint(-) (9.0). Price: $70. CyberAuction #462, Lot #41.
7256. SWIRL. Solid core. Opaque red core. Outer layer is a cage of six light blue bands and six white bands. Several sparkles. England, possibly Germany, circa 1870-1915. 21/32". Near Mint(+) (8.9). Price: $70. CyberAuction #465, Lot #51.
7257. SWIRL. Solid core. Gorgeous. Core is alternating red and bright yellow bands. Outer layer is four sets of white strands. One tiny melt spot. England, possibly Germany, circa 1870-1915. 13/16". Mint(-) (9.2). Price: $70. CyberAuction #471, Lot #15.
7258. SWIRL. Solid core. Naked solid core swirl. Transparent clear base. Core is two wide panels of white, with a wide orange band on each, separated by two narrow panels of transparent green. No outer layer. Very nice. A couple of tiny sparkles. Germany, circa 1870-1915. 1-1/16". Mint (9.5). Price: $70. CyberAuction #504, Lot #2.
7259. SWIRL. Solid core. Very nice large marble. Core is four panels. Each is white. Two have pink and blue on them, two have pink and green. Nice coloring. Outer layer is four sets of yellow and white strands. One tiny subsurface moon, several sparkles. Germany, circa 1870-1915. 1-9/16". Near Mint(+) (8.7). Price: $65. CyberAuction #392, Lot #56.
7260. SWIRL. Solid core. Beautiful marble. Transparent clear base. Opaque white core. Bands of pink, blue and turquoise on it. Outer layer is six sets of yellow strands. Exceptionally well constructed. Superior example. Germany, circa 1870-1915. 21/32". Mint (9.9). Price: $62. CyberAuction #462, Lot #18.
7261. SWIRL. Solid core. Base is tinted blue. Opaque white core. Four bands on the core. Two pink, two blue. Outer layer is four sets of yellow strands. Several tiny subsurface moons. Germany, circa 1870-1915. 1-3/16". Near Mint (8.5). Price: $60. CyberAuction #350, Lot #11.
7262. SWIRL. Solid core. Three layer. Outstanding example. Opaque yellow core. Middle layer is a cage of white strands. Outer layer is a cage of red strands. Thick outer casing. Tiny pits in a number of spots on the marble. Germany, circa 1870-1915. 1". Near Mint (8.3). Price: $60. CyberAuction #456, Lot #12.
7263. SWIRL. Solid core. English colors. Red solid core. Four outer bands. Two are white and blue. Two are yellow and green. Super marble. England, possibly Germany, circa 1870-1915. 27/32". Mint (9.8). Price: $60. CyberAuction #483, Lot #40.
7264. SWIRL. Solid core. Three-layer solid core swirl. Translucent white core. Middle layer is two blue bands and two pink bands. Outer layer is two pink on white bands and two pink on yellow bands. Stunning marble. Several tiny melt pits. Superb. Germany, possibly England, circa 1870-1915. 27/32". Mint(-) (9.1). Price: $60. CyberAuction #483, Lot #53.
7265. SWIRL. Solid core. Opaque white core. Three lobes. Blue band in the troughs, orange band on the peaks. Outer layer is three sets of yellow strands. Several tiny moons, but a beauty. Germany, circa 1870-1915. 1-1/4". Near Mint (8.6). Price: $60. CyberAuction #488, Lot #42.
7266. SWIRL. Solid core. Opaque white core. Slightly lobed. Two panels of green and two panels of blue in the troughs. Outer layer is four sets of yellow strands. One tiny sparkle. Superb example. Germany, circa 1870-1915. 1-1/16". Mint(-) (9.2). Price: $60. CyberAuction #506, Lot #40.
7267. SWIRL. Solid core. Three-layer solid core swirl. Core is opaque white and opaque yellow bands of varying widths. Middle layer is four pairs of colored bands. two pairs are pink, one pair is blue, one pair is green. Outer layer is four sets of strands. Two are yellow, two are white. Buffed, with overall pitting and some subsurface moons. Germany, circa 1870-1915. 2-1/4". Price: $60. CyberAuction #507, Lot #34.
7268. SWIRL. Solid core. Opaque white core. Bands of pink and blue on it. One open panel. Outer layer is a cage of white strands. Very tight twist. Super effect. Surface has a small chip, tiny chip and some very minor pinpricking. Germany, circa 1870-1915. 1-1/2". Near Mint (8.5). Price: $55. CyberAuction #332, Lot #40.
7269. SWIRL. Solid core. Three layer solid core swirl. Opaque white core. Middle layer is four bands. Two are turquoise and pink on yellow, two are pink and blue on white. Outer layer is four sets of two white strands and four sets of two yellow strands, creating a caged effect. Nice example. Some pitting and very tiny chipping. Germany, circa 1870-1915. 1-5/8". Near Mint(-) (8.1). Price: $55. CyberAuction #337, Lot #35.
7270. SWIRL. Solid core. Nice large marble. Four panel core in two complex patterns. Outer layer is four sets of white strands. Tiny subsurface moon. Some pitting. Germany, circa 1870-1915. 1-9/16". Near Mint(+) (8.7). Price: $55. CyberAuction #344, Lot #31.
7271. SWIRL. Solid core. Naked solid core swirl. Super marble. Core is alternating panels of blue, white and orange. No outer layer. Germany, circa 1870-1915. 7/8". Mint (9.9). Price: $55. CyberAuction #376, Lot #2.
7272. SWIRL. Solid core. Opaque yellow core. Two pink bands and two green bands on it. One open panel. Outer layer is four sets of white strands. One dirt line. Germany, circa 1870-1915. 29/32". Mint (9.5). Price: $55. CyberAuction #377, Lot #30.
7273. SWIRL. Solid core. Hard to find end of cane marble. Last off cane. Opaque white core. Two panels of red stripes, one of green, one of blue. Outer layer is four sets of yellow strands. The design ends just before the bottom of the marble. You can see into the inside of the core. The surface appears to have been very, very lightly buffed. Pitting remains and pontils are completely intact. A beauty. Germany, circa 1870-1915. 1-3/8". Price: $55. CyberAuction #387, Lot #46.
7274. SWIRL. Solid core. Opaque white core. Three lobes. Blue band in the troughs, orange band on the peaks. Outer layer is three sets of yellow strands. Several tiny moons, but a beauty. Germany, circa 1870-1915. 1-1/4". Near Mint (8.6). Price: $55. CyberAuction #463, Lot #29.
7275. SWIRL. Solid core. Three panel solid core. Each is a different color combination. The seam between two of the panels is not completely closed, creating a clear space to view the center. Outer layer is three sets of white strands. Some pitting. Germany, circa 1870-1915. 1-7/16". Near Mint(+) (8.9). Price: $55. CyberAuction #502, Lot #56.
7276. SWIRL. Solid core. Supposed to be a naked solid core swirl. Cork is two wide orange bands, a transparent blue band, a transparent green band and several narrow white bands. There are some open spaces. No outer layer. One tiny subsurface moon. Germany, circa 1870-1915. 1". Near Mint(+) (8.9). Price: $55. CyberAuction #505, Lot #64.
7277. SWIRL. Solid core. Beauty. Opaque yellow core with red strands on it. Outer layer is four sets of white strands. One pit. Germany, circa 1870-1915. 31/32". Mint(-) (9.2). Price: $50. CyberAuction #338, Lot #43.
7278. SWIRL. Solid core. Gorgeous and rare core, but not in too good of condition. Opaque blue core with white strands on it. Outer layer is six bands. Three are red, three are pale yellow/green. Very lightly buffed, damage remains. Germany, circa 1870-1915. 1". Price: $50. CyberAuction #340, Lot #20.
7279. SWIRL. Solid core. Opaque white core. Three shallow lobes. Blue band on each peak, pink band in each trough. Outer layer is three sets of yellow strands. Several tiny melt spots, no damage. Germany, circa 1870-1915. 1-1/16". Mint(-) (9.0). Price: $50. CyberAuction #398, Lot #16.
7280. SWIRL. Solid core. From near an end of the cane. Opaque white core. Some pink, green and yellow bands on it. Outer layer is two yellow bands on one side. One small area of haze. Very unusual. Germany, circa 1870-1915. 1-7/16". Near Mint (8.5). Price: $50. CyberAuction #414, Lot #26.

7281. SWIRL. Solid core. Three-layer solid core swirl. Opaque white core. Middle layer is eight transparent bands. Four pink, two blue, two green. Outer layer is eight yellow strands. Beauty. A couple of pinpricks. Germany, circa 1870-1915. 3/4". Mint (9.3). Price: $48. CyberAuction #373, Lot #47.
7282. SWIRL. Solid core. Opaque white core with two yellow bands in it. Alternating pink and blue bands on the core. Outer layer is four sets of yellow strands. One pit and one air hole. Germany, circa 1870-1915. 1-1/16". Mint(-) (9.1). Price: $47. CyberAuction #437, Lot #13.
7283. SWIRL. Solid core. Opaque white core. Slightly lobed. Two panels of green and two panels of blue in the troughs. Outer layer is four sets of yellow strands. One tiny sparkle. Superb example. Germany, circa 1870-1915. 1-1/16". Mint(-) (9.2). Price: $47. CyberAuction #467, Lot #19.
7284. SWIRL. Solid core. Opaque white core. Slightly lobed. Two panels of green and two panels of blue in the troughs. Outer layer is four sets of yellow strands. One tiny sparkle. Superb example. Germany, circa 1870-1915. 1-1/16". Mint(-) (9.2). Price: $47. CyberAuction #490, Lot #40.
7285. SWIRL. Solid core. Three-layer swirl. Opaque white core. Middle layer is two pairs of pink strands, one pair of blue strands, one pair of green strands. Outer layer is a cage of yellow strands. Germany, circa 1870-1915. 5/8". Mint (9.7). Price: $47. CyberAuction #498, Lot #34.
7286. SWIRL. Solid core. Naked solid core swirl. Four transparent purple bands alternating with two orange and two white bands. No outer layer. Germany, circa 1870-1915. 25/32". Mint (9.7). Price: $46. CyberAuction #377, Lot #25.
7287. SWIRL. Solid core. Peewee. Opaque white core. Four dark blue narrow bands sitting on it. Outer layer is a cage of pink on white narrow bands. Germany, circa 1870-1915. 15/32". Mint (9.9). Price: $45. CyberAuction #354, Lot #42.
7288. SWIRL. Solid core. Opaque white core. Open panel in it. Two bands of pink, one of blue, one of green on it. Outer layer is four sets of white strands. One line of melted dirt. Very nice. Germany, circa 1870-1915. 1". Mint(-) (9.2). Price: $45. CyberAuction #403, Lot #17.
7289. SWIRL. Solid core. Light green base glass. Opaque white core. Pink and blue bands on the core. Outer layer is a cage of yellow strands. Some overall small and tiny moons and subsurface moons. Nice marble. Germany, circa 1870-1915. 1-15/16". Good(+) (7.9). Price: $45. CyberAuction #493, Lot #14.
7290. SWIRL. Solid core. Rare color core. Transparent dark amethyst core with white strands on it. Outer layer is six bands. Three are red and three are blue. Some pitting and roughness on the surface. Germany, circa 1870-1915. 11/16". Near Mint(-) (8.1). Price: $42. CyberAuction #341, Lot #54.
7291. SWIRL. Solid core. Opaque white core. Three shallow lobes. Blue band on each peak, pink band in each trough. Outer layer is three sets of yellow strands. Several tiny melt spots, no damage. Germany, circa 1870-1915. 1-1/16". Mint(-) (9.0). Price: $42. CyberAuction #369, Lot #39.
7292. SWIRL. Solid core. Opaque white core with two yellow bands in it. Alternating pink and blue bands on the core. Outer layer is four sets of yellow strands. One pit and one air hole. Germany, circa 1870-1915. 1-1/16". Mint(-) (9.1). Price: $42. CyberAuction #406, Lot #15.
7293. SWIRL. Solid core. End of cane (first off cane) three-layer solid core swirl. Transparent clear base. Semi-opaque yellow core. Middle layer is pink, blue and green bands on white. Outer layer is sets of white strands. Colors come shooting out of the top (flower type). Very, very light haze on the surface, possibly manufacturing. One tiny pinprick. A beauty. Germany, circa 1870-1915. 21/32". Near Mint(+) (8.7). Price: $42. CyberAuction #447, Lot #14.
7294. SWIRL. Solid core. End of cane (first off cane) three-layer solid core swirl. Transparent clear base. Semi-opaque yellow core. Middle layer is pink, blue and green bands on white. Outer layer is sets of white strands. Colors come shooting out of the top (flower type). Very, very light haze on the surface, possibly manufacturing. One tiny pinprick. A beauty. Germany, circa 1870-1915. 21/32". Near Mint(+) (8.7). Price: $42. CyberAuction #484, Lot #29.
7295. SWIRL. Solid core. Odd coloring. Yellow core with baby blue strands on it. Outer layer is six bands. Three are bright red, three are white. English colors. A number of small subsurface moons. England, possibly Germany, circa 1870-1915. 1-9/16". Good(+) (7.7). Price: $42. CyberAuction #493, Lot #27.
7296. SWIRL. Solid core. Very brightly colored. Wispy yellow core. Bright blue, red, yellow and white outer bands. Germany, possibly England, circa 1870-1915. 9/16". Mint (9.9). Price: $42. CyberAuction #497, Lot #51.
7297. SWIRL. Solid core. Naked solid core swirl. Core is bands of transparent purple, separated by opaque orange and white bands. No outer layer. Very nice. Germany, circa 1870-1915. 11/16". Mint (9.7). Price: $41. CyberAuction #491, Lot #16.
7298. SWIRL. Solid core. Very pale light blue tinted base. Semi-opaque yellow core. Outer layer is five bands of blue on white. Looks like there was supposed to be another band, but it is missing. In great shape. Germany, circa 1870-1915. 29/32". Mint (9.9). Price: $40. CyberAuction #336, Lot #30.
7299. SWIRL. Solid core. Opaque white core. Two bands of pink, and two of blue. Outer layer is two sets of white strands and two sets of yellow strands. One tiny melt spot, one tiny scratch. Germany, circa 1870-1915. 1-1/16". Mint (9.5). Price: $40. CyberAuction #337, Lot #51.
7300. SWIRL. Solid core. White core. Bands of pink and blue on it. Outer layer is a cage of yellow strands. Germany, circa 1870-1915. 25/32". Mint (9.8). Price: $40. CyberAuction #345, Lot #31.
7301. SWIRL. Solid core. Opaque white core. Two narrow bands of light olive green. Outer layer is four bands. Two are orange/red and white. One is green and yellow. One is lavender and yellow. Gorgeous. Germany, circa 1870-1915. 19/32". Mint (9.9). Price: $40. CyberAuction #356, Lot #14.
7302. SWIRL. Solid core. Very pretty three layer marble. Opaque white core. Middle layer is a cage of yellow strands. Outer layer is four sets of two narrow bands. Two are pink, one set is turquoise, one set is blue. Almost no twist. Two tiny air holes. Superb. Germany, circa 1870-1915. 11/16". Mint (9.6). Price: $40. CyberAuction #356, Lot #49.
7303. SWIRL. Solid core. Outstanding end of cane marble (last off cane). Opaque white core. Pink and blue bands on it. Outer layer is a cage of yellow strands. Core ends about two-thirds of the way down. Remainder of the marble is milky clear glass. One air hole on the milky part. Super. Germany, circa 1870-1915. 11/16". Mint (9.3). Price: $40. CyberAuction #398, Lot #32.
7304. SWIRL. Solid core. Opaque white core. Bands of salmon pink floating on the core. Outer layer is a cage of alternating yellow and white strands. Germany, circa 1870-1915. 25/32". Mint (9.8). Price: $40. CyberAuction #491, Lot #27.
7305. SWIRL. Solid core. Gorgeous. Opaque white core. Alternating bands of pink and green on it. Outer layer is four sets of white strands. Cold roll marks and a couple of tiny sparkles. Germany, circa 1870-1915. 1". Mint(-) (9.0). Price: $39. CyberAuction #359, Lot #21.
7306. SWIRL. Solid core. Base glass is lightly tinted blue. Core is white. Three lobes. Light green band in each trough, blue band on each peak. Outer layer is three sets of white strands. Very unusual. Polished. 1". Price: $39. CyberAuction #374, Lot #37.
7307. SWIRL. Solid core. Very odd four-layer solid core swirl. Opaque white core. Next layer is two transparent narrow pink bands and two transparent narrow green bands. Next layer is four bands, two are pink on yellow, two are green on yellow. Outer layer is a band of pink on white with a strand of green on white on either side of it. Inner three layers are shoved to one side of the marble, outer layer is on the other side. From near an end of the cane. One melt spot, one tiny chip. Germany, circa 1870-1915. 27/32". Near Mint(+) (8.9). Price: $39. CyberAuction #499, Lot #33.
7308. SWIRL. Solid core. Naked solid core swirl. Alternating bands of transparent blue and opaque white. No outer layer. Germany, circa 1870-1915. 23/32". Mint (9.5). Price: $38.13. CyberAuction #370, Lot #30.
7309. SWIRL. Solid core. Interesting coloring. Translucent white core cased by transparent emerald green. Outer layer is a cage of six orange bands. Beautiful. Tiny subsurface moon and some sparkles. Germany, circa 1870-1915. 1/2". Near Mint (8.4). Price: $38. CyberAuction #340, Lot #51.
7310. SWIRL. Solid core. Outstanding end of cane marble (last off cane). Opaque white core. Pink and blue bands on it. Outer layer is a cage of yellow strands. Core ends about two-thirds of the way down. Remainder of the marble is milky clear glass. One air hole on the milky part. Super. Germany, circa 1870-1915. 11/16". Mint (9.3). Price: $38. CyberAuction #359, Lot #1.
7311. SWIRL. Solid core. Opaque white core. Outer layer is four bands. Two are yellow strands edged by pink, one is yellow strands edged by blue, one is yellow strands edged by green. Some tiny flakes, scratches and sparkles. Germany, circa 1870-1915. 1-3/8". Near Mint(-) (8.0). Price: $38. CyberAuction #364, Lot #32.
7312. SWIRL. Solid core. Base is a semi-transparent milky very light blue color. Multi-color core. Outer layer is three sets of white strands. Unusual. Germany, circa 1870-1915. 23/32". Mint (9.9). Price: $38. CyberAuction #437, Lot #42.
7313. SWIRL. Solid core. Opaque yellow core with alternating pink and green bands. Outer layer is four sets of white strands. Tight twist. One elongated spot of melted glass on the surface, but still a beauty. Germany, circa 1870-1915. 21/32". Mint (9.3). Price: $37. CyberAuction #348, Lot #12.
7314. SWIRL. Solid core. Core is four panels. Two are blue strand on white, edged by red. Other two are very lumpy yellow on transparent green. Outer layer is a cage of white strands. Nub bottom pontil. Germany, circa 1870-1915. 9/16". Mint (9.7). Price: $37. CyberAuction #348, Lot #50.
7315. SWIRL. Solid core. Lobed solid core. Superb marble. Opaque white core. Three lobes. Pink band in each trough, blue band on each peak. Outer layer is three sets of white strands. Superb. Germany, circa 1870-1915. 23/32". Mint (9.9). Price: $37. CyberAuction #358, Lot #52.
7316. SWIRL. Solid core. Base is a semi-transparent milky very light blue color. Multi-color core. Outer layer is three sets of white strands. Unusual. Germany, circa 1870-1915. 23/32". Mint (9.9). Price: $37. CyberAuction #368, Lot #48.
7317. SWIRL. Solid core. Base is a semi-transparent milky very light blue color. Multi-color core. Outer layer is three sets of white strands. Unusual. Germany, circa 1870-1915. 23/32". Mint (9.9). Price: $37. CyberAuction #408, Lot #17.
7318. SWIRL. Solid core. Super marble. English colors. Opaque white core. Outer layer is three lime green bands and three white bands. One melt spot. England, possibly Germany, circa 1927-1935. 11/16". Mint(-) (9.2). Price: $37. CyberAuction #413, Lot #55.
7319. SWIRL. Solid core. Interesting three-layer solid core swirl. Core is six alternating panels: three pink and three white. Middle layer is three bands of green, floating above the white panels. Outer layer is three sets of yellow strands, floating above the pink panels. Nice. Germany, circa 1870-1915. 25/32". Mint (9.5). Price: $37. CyberAuction #418, Lot #38.
7320. SWIRL. Solid core. Four panel core. Green bands on white, green and blue bands on white, two of pink bands on yellow. Outer layer is an alternating cage of yellow and white strands. Haziness and some pits. Germany, circa 1870-1915. 1-5/8". Good (7.5). Price: $37. CyberAuction #434, Lot #27.
7321. SWIRL. Solid core. Light green glass. Opaque white core. Outer layer is three bands. Two are blue and white, one is pink and white. One pinprick. Germany, circa 1870-1915. 5/8". Mint(-) (9.1). Price: $37. CyberAuction #439, Lot #56.

7322. SWIRL. Solid core. English colors. Very odd salmon peach core. Outer layer is six bands. Three are light olive green and three are white. Hard to find coloring. England, possibly Germany, circa 1870-1915. 9/16". Mint (9.8). Price: $37. CyberAuction #450, Lot #17.
7323. SWIRL. Solid core. English type. Opaque white core. Outer layer is eight bands. Four are blue and yellow, four are red and white. Very nice marble. England, possibly Germany, circa 1870-1915. 11/16". Mint (9.8). Price: $37. CyberAuction #462, Lot #38.
7324. SWIRL. Solid core. Opaque white core. Two pink bands and two blue bands on it. Outer layer is four green, pink and yellow bands, alternating with four sets of yellow strands. Very unusual. Pretty. Germany, circa 1870-1915. 3/4". Mint (9.6). Price: $36. CyberAuction #344, Lot #44.
7325. SWIRL. Solid core. Core is translucent and opaque white strands and bands, packed closely together. Outer layer is six bands. Three are yellow, three are blue. Super coloring. Surface has two small subsurface moons. Germany, circa 1870-1915. 29/32". Near Mint (8.5). Price: $36. CyberAuction #353, Lot #5.
7326. SWIRL. Solid core. Opaque white core. Two pink bands, one green band, one blue band, on it. Outer layer is four sets of yellow strands. Several small subsurface moons. Germany, circa 1870-1915. 1-7/16". Near Mint(-) (8.2). Price: $36. CyberAuction #493, Lot #23.
7327. SWIRL. Solid core. Opaque white core. Outer layer is two transparent blue bands and two transparent purple bands. Beauty. Germany, circa 1870-1915. 25/32". Mint (9.9). Price: $35. CyberAuction #330, Lot #9.
7328. SWIRL. Solid core. Three layer marble. White solid core. Middle layer is yellow strands. Outer layer is six bands. Three are blue and yellow. Three are pink and white. Very pretty. Several small chips. Germany, circa 1870-1915. 1-1/16". Near Mint(-) (8.0). Price: $35. CyberAuction #334, Lot #54.
7329. SWIRL. Solid core. Semi-opaque white core. Outer layer is six bands. Three are red and white, three are orange and green. In great shape. Super. One small melt spot. Germany, circa 1870-1915. 5/8". Mint (9.4). Price: $35. CyberAuction #348, Lot #13.
7330. SWIRL. Solid core. Gorgeous. Core is two panels of orange, edged by yellow and white, and two panels of transparent dark purple. Outer layer is two sets of yellow strands and two sets of white strands. Germany, circa 1870-1915. 11/16". Mint (9.9). Price: $35. CyberAuction #358, Lot #39.
7331. SWIRL. Solid core. Four panel core. Two are pink on white, two are blue on white. Outer layer is four sets of white strands. Germany, circa 1870-1915. 9/16". Mint (9.9). Price: $35. CyberAuction #360, Lot #46.
7332. SWIRL. Solid core. Solid core swirl. Semi-opaque white core. Outer layer is odd. Consists of (working way around marble) transparent pink band, yellow strand, yellow strand, transparent green band next to semi-opaque blue band, transparent pink band, semi-opaque blue band edged by a yellow strand. Peewee. Germany, circa 1870-1915. 15/32". Mint (9.9). Price: $35. CyberAuction #373, Lot #38.
7333. SWIRL. Solid core. Naked solid core swirl. Core is three panels of transparent blue and three of opaque white. No outer layer. Very similar to prior lot, but smaller and undamaged. Germany, circa 1870-1915. 11/16". Mint (9.9). Price: $35. CyberAuction #471, Lot #47.
7334. SWIRL. Solid core. Four panel core. Odd coloring. Two are bright orange and blue on white, two are bright red and green on white. Outer layer is four sets of bright orange strands. Germany, possibly England, circa 1870-1915. 21/32". Mint (9.9). Price: $35. CyberAuction #495, Lot #3.
7335. SWIRL. Solid core. Core is three panels. Each is the same pattern of pink, blue and green on white, edged by yellow. Outer layer is three sets of yellow strands. Bright colors. A couple of melt spots. England, possibly Germany, circa 1870-1915. 7/8". Mint(-) (9.0). Price: $34. CyberAuction #336, Lot #19.
7336. SWIRL. Solid core. Fascinating three layer swirl. Translucent yellow core. Surrounded by a cage of white strands. Outer layer is four bands. Two are green on white, two are blue on white. Very nice. Some tiny chipping. Germany, circa 1870-1915. 31/32". Near Mint(-) (8.1). Price: $34. CyberAuction #344, Lot #9.
7337. SWIRL. Solid core. Naked solid core swirl. Core is opaque white bands separated by transparent green and transparent purple bands. Odd coloring. One tiny pit. Germany, circa 1870-1915. 11/16". Mint (9.3). Price: $34. CyberAuction #348, Lot #10.
7338. SWIRL. Solid core. Solid core swirl. Opaque white core. Two blue bands and two pink bands on it. Outer layer is four sets of yellow strands. Polished, but a great marble. Germany, circa 1870-1915. 1-5/8". Price: $34. CyberAuction #355, Lot #36.
7339. SWIRL. Solid core. Opaque white core. Two wide blue bands and two wide red bands on the core. Four sets of yellow strands for the outer layer. Two melt pits. Germany, circa 1870-1915. 15/16". Mint(-) (9.2). Price: $34. CyberAuction #403, Lot #31.
7340. SWIRL. Solid core. Opaque white core. Two sets of pink and blue bands and one set of pink and green bands, on the core. Outer layer is three sets of yellow strands. One scratch. Germany, circa 1870-1915. 29/32". Mint(-) (9.2). Price: $34. CyberAuction #403, Lot #33.
7341. SWIRL. Solid core. Four panel core. Two are pink and blue on white. Two are very fiery aventurine green and pink on yellow. Outer layer is four yellow strands and four white strands. One very tiny chip and one pit. Germany, circa 1870-1915. 5/8". Near Mint(+) (8.9). Price: $34. CyberAuction #406, Lot #14.
7342. SWIRL. Solid core. English type. Opaque white core. Outer layer is six bands. Three yellow, three blue and orange. Some small subsurface moons and small flakes. England, possibly Germany, circa 1870-1920. 1-1/8". Good (7.4). Price: $34. CyberAuction #422, Lot #46.
7343. SWIRL. Solid core. Interesting colors. Opaque white core. Alternating lime green and blue strands on the core. Outer layer is a cage of sever yellow strands. Germany, circa 1870-1915. 9/16". Mint (9.7). Price: $34 CyberAuction #483, Lot #16.
7344. SWIRL. Solid core. Transparent smoky gray base. Technically, it's a three layer swirl, but the middle layer is so close to the core that it is hard to tell. Opaque white core. Middle layer is four bands. Two are pink and yellow, one is blue, one is green. Outer layer is four sets of strands. Two are white and two are yellow. Two sparkles and a pit. Germany, circa 1870-1915. 29/32". Near Mint(+) (8.9). Price: $33. CyberAuction #339, Lot #9
7345. SWIRL. Solid core. Core is alternating bands of opaque white and transparent green. Outer layer is four sets of yellow strands. Germany, circa 1870-1915. 11/16". Mint (9.7). Price: $33. CyberAuction #355, Lot #53
7346. SWIRL. Solid core. Four panel core. Two are pink and blue on white Two are very fiery aventurine green and pink on yellow. Outer layer is fou yellow strands and four white strands. One very tiny chip and one pit Germany, circa 1870-1915. 5/8". Near Mint(+) (8.9). Price: $33 CyberAuction #437, Lot #48.
7347. SWIRL. Solid core. Naked solid core swirl. Fat core. White core Two orange bands and two blue bands on it. No outer layer. One smal chip, a couple of tiny ones. Germany, circa 1870-1915. 31/32". Near Min (8.5). Price: $33. CyberAuction #463, Lot #34.
7348. SWIRL. Solid core. Opaque white core. Three bands on it, each i one blue band and two pink bands. There is a white space where a fourth set would have been. Outer layer is four sets of yellow strands. Surface is in nice shape. Germany, circa 1870-1915. 3/4". Mint (9.7). Price: $32 CyberAuction #331, Lot #3.
7349. SWIRL. Solid core. Base glass is lightly tinted blue. Core is white Three lobes. Light green band in each trough, blue band on each peak Outer layer is three sets of white strands. Very unusual. Polished. 1". Price $32. CyberAuction #355, Lot #30.
7350. SWIRL. Solid core. Naked solid core. Two blue bands and two orange bands, separated by white bands. No outer layer. Germany, circa 1870-1915. 11/16". Mint (9.8). Price: $32. CyberAuction #362, Lot #54
7351. SWIRL. Solid core. Three layer solid core swirl. Opaque white core Middle layer is four wide bands, almost obscuring the core. Two are pink strands, one blue strands, one green strands. Outer layer is a cage of yellow strands. In great shape, very nice. Germany, circa 1870-1915. 9/16". Mir (9.9). Price: $32. CyberAuction #363, Lot #23.
7352. SWIRL. Solid core. Opaque white core. Two pink bands on it, green band and a blue band. Outer layer is four sets of yellow strands Germany, circa 1870-1915. 21/32". Mint (9.9). Price: $32. CyberAuctio #366, Lot #12.
7353. SWIRL. Solid core. Core is bands of translucent white, green and blue. Outer layer is four sets of red strands. Germany, circa 1870-1915. 1 2". Mint (9.7). Price: $32. CyberAuction #372, Lot #45.
7354. SWIRL. Solid core. Naked solid core swirl. Two panels of orange one of green, one of blue, on white. No outer layer. One melt spot. Germany, circa 1870-1915. 11/16". Mint (9.5). Price: $32. CyberAuction #376 Lot #36.
7355. SWIRL. Solid core. Stunning three-layer solid core swirl. Semi-opaque white core, some clear panels. Middle layer is a cage of yellow strands Outer layer is four sets of two bands. Two sets are pink on white, one set is blue on yellow, one set is green on yellow. Stunning. Germany, circa 1870-1915. 19/32". Mint (9.7). Price: $32. CyberAuction #400, Lot #22.
7356. SWIRL. Solid core. Nice three-layer swirl. White solid core. Middle layer is a care of pink and blue narrow bands. Outer layer is six bands Three are red and yellow, three are red and green. Pit and cold roll line Germany, circa 1870-1915. 27/32". Mint(-) (9.0). Price: $32. CyberAuction #414, Lot #4.
7357. SWIRL. Solid core. Opaque yellow core. Outer layer is seven bands Three white, one white and light blue, two red and orange, one light green Very nice. Germany, possibly English, circa 1870-1915. 9/16". Mint (9.9 Price: $32. CyberAuction #452, Lot #39.
7358. SWIRL. Solid core. Opaque white core. Three blue bands and three orange bands on it. Outer layer is a cage of eight yellow strands. Very nice example. Germany, circa 1870-1915. 13/16". Mint (9.8). Price: $32 CyberAuction #462, Lot #7.
7359. SWIRL. Solid core. Naked solid core swirl. Core is alternating panels of blue and white. No outer layer. Small melt chip and small flat spot Germany, circa 1870-1915. 7/8". Mint(-) (9.0). Price: $32. CyberAuction #508, Lot #30.
7360. SWIRL. Solid core. Four panel core. Green bands on white, green and blue bands on white, two of pink bands on yellow. Outer layer is an alternating cage of yellow and white strands. Haziness and some pits. Germany, circa 1870-1915. 1-5/8". Good (7.5). Price: $31. CyberAuction #393 Lot #25.
7361. SWIRL. Solid core. Interesting naked solid core swirl. Three panels no spaces between them. Each is white base. One is blue, one orange/red one is green. No outer layer. Germany, circa 1870-1915. 1/2". Mint (9.9 Price: $30. CyberAuction #377, Lot #36.
7362. SWIRL. Solid core. Beauty. Opaque white base with blue stripes Outer layer is six bands. Three are red and white, three are yellow latticinio strands. Almost no twist. Lots of unmelted sand. A couple of tiny pits. Germany, circa 1870-1915. 13/16". Near Mint(+) (8.9). Price: $30 CyberAuction #473, Lot #28.
7363. SWIRL. Solid core. Opaque white core. Outer layer is six bands Three are yellow, one green, one red, one blue. Very nice marble. One melt chip. Germany, possibly England, circa 1870-1915. 11/16". Mint (9.2). Price: $30. CyberAuction #508, Lot #60.
7364. SWIRL. Solid core. Opaque white core. Four wide bands on it. Two are pink, one green, one blue. Outer layer is four sets of yellow strands

ermany, circa 1870-1915. 11/16". Mint (9.6). Price: $29. CyberAuction
348, Lot #21.

65. SWIRL. Solid core. Transparent clear base. Opaque white core. Four
nd on it. Two blue, two pink. Outer layer is a cage of yellow strands. Has
pit. Germany, circa 1870-1915. 3/4". Mint(-) (9.0). Price: $29. CyberAuction
350, Lot #55.

66. SWIRL. Solid core. Nice three-layer swirl. Opaque white core. Middle
er is a cage of pink strands. Outer layer is four bands. Two blue and
ite, two green and yellow. Germany, circa 1870-1915. 21/32". Mint (9.7).
ce: $29. CyberAuction #362, Lot #44.

67. SWIRL. Solid core. Naked solid core. Two orange bands, one purple
nd, one blue band, each separated by white bands. No outer layer. Ger-
any, circa 1870-1915. 9/16". Mint (9.8). Price: $29. CyberAuction #376,
t #47.

68. SWIRL. Solid core. Opaque white core. Narrow. Has three pink
nds and three blue strands on it. Outer layer is a cage of yellow strands.
veral subsurface moons. Germany, circa 1870-1915. 1-3/16". Near Mint(-
.0). Price: $29. CyberAuction #445, Lot #18.

69. SWIRL. Solid core. Superb coloring. Opaque white core. Outer
er is three orange bands and three purple on white bands. Super marble.
rmany, possibly English, circa 1870-1915. 11/16". Mint (9.7). Price: $28.
berAuction #332, Lot #13.

70. SWIRL. Solid core. Four band core. Might be a divided core with
bands very close together. Two are pink and yellow, two are blue and
. Outer layer four sets of yellow and white strands. Germany, circa
70-1915. 19/32". Mint (9.9). Price: $28. CyberAuction #356, Lot #18.

71. SWIRL. Solid core. White core. Two bands of orange, one of green,
e on it. Outer layer is a cage of yellow strands. One melt spot.
rmany, circa 1870-1915. 25/32". Mint(-) (9.0). Price: $28. CyberAuction
70, Lot #16.

72. SWIRL. Solid core. Naked solid core swirl. Core is opaque white
h blue strands on it. No outer layer. One elongated surface air bubble.
rmany, circa 1870-1915. 11/16". Near Mint(+) (8.9). Price: $28.
berAuction #414, Lot #39.

73. SWIRL. Solid core. Opaque white core. Outer layer is four bands.
o are yellow strands edged by pink, one is yellow strands edged by blue,
e is yellow strands edged by green. Some tiny flakes, scratches and
arkles. Germany, circa 1870-1915. 1-3/8". Near Mint(-) (8.0). Price: $28.
berAuction #451, Lot #31.

74. SWIRL. Solid core. Bright yellow core. Outer layer is three bands.
o are dark orange, one is light blue. Nice. Germany, possibly England,
ca 1870-1915. 19/32". Mint (9.9). Price: $28. CyberAuction #452, Lot
3.

75. SWIRL. Solid core. Opaque white core. Outer layer is eight bands.
ur red, two blue, two light green. England, possibly Germany, circa 1870-
15. 11/16". Mint (9.9). Price: $28. CyberAuction #459, Lot #40.

76. SWIRL. Solid core. Core is two orange panels, one transparent blue
d one transparent green, all separated by white. Outer layer is four nar-
w strands of yellow. Interesting. Germany, circa 1870-1915. 27/32". Mint
9). Price: $27. CyberAuction #337, Lot #50.

77. SWIRL. Solid core. Opaque white core. Two blue bands and two
k bands. Outer layer is a cage of yellow strands. In great shape. Ger-
any, circa 1870-1915. 5/8". Mint (9.9). Price: $27. CyberAuction #348,
t #9.

78. SWIRL. Solid core. Opaque yellow core. Three bands of green and
ee bands of pink on the surface. Outer layer is four white strands. Ger-
any, circa 1870-1915. 19/32". Mint (9.9). Price: $27. CyberAuction #356,
t #26.

79. SWIRL. Solid core. English type. Very unusual. Core is bands of
ue, orange, green and yellow. Has a clear panel. Outer layer is a wide
osurface band of green, blue, yellow, white and orange stretched splotches.
vers about one-quarter the marble. One large chip, several smaller ones.
gland, possibly Germany, circa 1870-1915. 31/32". Good(+) (7.9). Price:
7. CyberAuction #374, Lot #22.

80. SWIRL. Solid core. Outstanding solid core swirl. Opaque white core.
ter layer is two bands of red and white and two of green and white, all
the same side of the marble. One dirt line. Germany, possibly English,
ca 1870-1915. 3/4". Mint (9.7). Price: $27. CyberAuction #407, Lot #3.

81. SWIRL. Solid core. Interesting four-layer marble. Opaque white core.
ree transparent pink bands floating above the core. Three transparent
e bands floating in a layer above that. Outer layer is six sets of white
ands. One melt spot, one tiny subsurface moon. Germany, circa 1870-
15. 13/16". Near Mint(+) (8.9). Price: $27. CyberAuction #407, Lot
3.

82. SWIRL. Solid core. Naked solid core swirl. Core is alternating panels
blue and white. No outer layer. Surface has some melt holes on it. Ger-
any, circa 1870-1915. 11/16". Mint (9.5). Price: $27. CyberAuction #414,
t #34.

83. SWIRL. Solid core. Opaque white core. Outer layer is six bands.
ree are yellow, one light green, one light blue, one red. Gorgeous. Ger-
nd, possibly Germany, circa 1870-1915. 11/16". Mint (9.7). Price: $27.
berAuction #463, Lot #23.

84. SWIRL. Solid core. Naked solid core swirl. Core is four panels of
nsparent blue and four of opaque white. No outer layer. Very nice. One
elt chip, one tiny flake, one sparkle. Germany, circa 1870-1915. 25/32".
ar Mint(+) (8.7). Price: $27. CyberAuction #471, Lot #46.

85. SWIRL. Solid core. Core is three wide white panels and three nar-
w orange panels. Outer layer is eight bands. Four are blue and four are
t yellow. Germany, circa 1870-1915. 1/2". Mint (9.9). Price: $27.
berAuction #487, Lot #27.

86. SWIRL. Solid core. Three layer. Opaque white core. Middle layer is

two sets of pink bands, one set of green, one set of blue. Outer layer is a
cage of yellow strands. Double twist. Overall haziness. Germany, circa 1870-
1915. 1-7/16". Good(+) (7.8). Price: $27. CyberAuction #492, Lot #15.

7387. SWIRL. Solid core. Three layer swirl. Opaque yellow core. Middle
layer is three pink bands and three green bands. Outer layer is three sets of
white strands. Nice. Germany, circa 1870-1915. 11/16". Mint (9.7). Price:
$26. CyberAuction #347, Lot #13.

7388. SWIRL. Solid core. Very odd four-layer solid core swirl. Opaque
white core. Next layer is two transparent narrow pink bands and two transparent narrow green bands. Next layer is four bands, two are pink on yellow, two are green on yellow. Outer layer is a band of pink on white with a
strand of green on white on either side of it. Inner three layers are shoved to
one side of the marble, outer layer is on the other side. From near an end of
the cane. One melt spot, one tiny chip. Germany, circa 1870-1915. 27/32".
Near Mint(+) (8.9). Price: $26. CyberAuction #467, Lot #2.

7389. SWIRL. Solid core. Four panel core. Two orange and white, one
blue and yellow, one very dark green and yellow. Each panel is lobed.
Outer layer is three sets of white strands. A few small chips. Rare coloring.
Germany, circa 1870-1915. 31/32". Near Mint(-) (8.0). Price: $26.
CyberAuction #477, Lot #53.

7390. SWIRL. Solid core. Three-layer. Six-panel core. Three each of white
and yellow. Middle layer is three pink strands and three green strands.
Outer layer is three sets of white strands. Germany, circa 1870-1915. 5/8".
Mint (9.9). Price: $26. CyberAuction #502, Lot #43.

7391. SWIRL. Solid core. Peewee three layer swirl. Core is a mix of white
and yellow. Floating just above the core are two pink bands and two green
bands. Outer layer is four sets of white strands. Germany, circa 1870-1915.
15/32". Mint (9.7). Price: $25. CyberAuction #330, Lot #13.

7392. SWIRL. Solid core. Peewee. Opaque white core. Two bands of purple,
two of orange. Outer layer is stretched air bubbles, but no strands or bands.
Naked core. Germany, circa 1870-1915. 17/32". Mint (9.9). Price: $25.
CyberAuction #331, Lot #19.

7393. SWIRL. Solid core. Fat opaque white core. Outer layer is six bands.
Three are transparent green and three are transparent blue. Several tiny
subsurface moons. Germany, circa 1870-1915. 1". Near Mint(+) (8.7). Price:
$25. CyberAuction #337, Lot #26.

7394. SWIRL. Solid core. Three layer. Opaque white core. Middle layer is
three pink bands and three blue bands. Outer layer is three sets of yellow
strands. Some tiny pitting and very tiny chips. Germany, circa 1870-1915.
1". Near Mint(-) (8.0). Price: $25. CyberAuction #347, Lot #46.

7395. SWIRL. Solid core. Three-lobed opaque white core. Three
shallow lobes. Each has a blue and red band in the trough. Outer layer is
three sets of white strands. Germany, circa 1870-1915. 11/16". Mint (9.9).
Price: $25. CyberAuction #352, Lot #48.

7396. SWIRL. Solid core. Gorgeous marble. Opaque yellow core. Three
lobes. Green band in each trough, pink band on each peak. Outer layer is
three sets of white strands. A beauty. Several tiny flakes. Germany, circa
1870-1915. 23/32". Near Mint(+) (8.7). Price: $25. CyberAuction #362,
Lot #52.

7397. SWIRL. Solid core. Three layer solid core. Opaque white core. Four
bands floating just above the core. Two are pink, one is blue, on is green.
Outer layer is four sets of yellow strands. Tight twist. Germany, circa 1870-
1915. 21/32". Mint (9.6). Price: $25. CyberAuction #363, Lot #14.

7398. SWIRL. Solid core. Opaque white core. Narrow. Has three pink
bands and three blue strands on it. Outer layer is a cage of yellow strands.
Several subsurface moons. Germany, circa 1870-1915. 1-3/16". Near Mint(-
) (8.0). Price: $25. CyberAuction #370, Lot #1.

7399. SWIRL. Solid core. Naked solid core swirl. Alternating bands of
white, yellow, transparent blue and transparent green. No outer layer. Germany, circa 1870-1915. 1/2". Mint (9.8). Price: $25. CyberAuction #388,
Lot #31.

7400. SWIRL. Solid core. Gorgeous. Yellow core. Outer layer is a cage of
eight bands. Four are pink on white, two are blue on white, two are green
on white. Germany, circa 1870-1915. 19/32". Mint (9.8). Price: $25.
CyberAuction #421, Lot #47.

7401. SWIRL. Solid core. Opaque white core. One band each of red,
blue and green on it. Outer layer is three sets of yellow strands. One very
tiny subsurface moon at the top, some scratching. Germany, circa 1870-
1915. 31/32". Near Mint(+) (8.8). Price: $25. CyberAuction #425, Lot
#46.

7402. SWIRL. Solid core. Lobed solid core. Opaque white core. Four deep
lobes. Two have pink and green bands in the troughs, two have pink and
blue bands in the troughs. Outer layer is three sets of yellow strands and
one set of white strands. Nice marble. Germany, circa 1870-1915. 19/32".
Mint (9.6). Price: $25. CyberAuction #443, Lot #8.

7403. SWIRL. Solid core. Translucent white core. Six outer bands. Three
light orange and three light green. Germany, circa 1870-1915. 9/16". Mint
(9.7). Price: $25. CyberAuction #452, Lot #15.

7404. SWIRL. Solid core. English style. Opaque white core. Outer layer is
eight bands. Four are orange, four are light green. Outstanding example.
England, possibly Germany, circa 1870-1915. 11/16". Mint (9.9). Price:
$25. CyberAuction #459, Lot #6.

7405. SWIRL. Solid core. English type. Opaque white core. Outer layer is
seven bands. Two blue, two light green, on light orange, one light orange
and light green, one red. Very nice. England, possibly Germany, circa 1870-
1915. 11/16". Mint (9.8). Price: $25. CyberAuction #464, Lot #6.

7406. SWIRL. Solid core. Opaque white core. Outer layer is four yellow
bands and four red bands. England, possibly Germany, circa 1870-1915.
11/16". Mint (9.6). Price: $25. CyberAuction #465, Lot #17.

7407. SWIRL. Solid core. I've classified this as a solid core, but it is odd
construction. Transparent clear base. Bright yellow, partially closed core.

Several bright yellow outer strands. Odd. Germany, circa 1870-1915. 1/2". Mint (9.8). Price: $25. CyberAuction #480, Lot #42.

7408. SWIRL. Solid core. Opaque yellow core, three pink bands on it. Shrunken on one side. Outer layer is three sets of yellow strands. Tiny pit and some pinpricks. Germany, circa 1870-1915. 25/32". Near Mint(+) (8.7). Price: $25. CyberAuction #498, Lot #16.

7409. SWIRL. Solid core. Naked solid core. Opaque white core. Three pink bands and three blue bands, on the core. Subsurface moon. Germany, circa 1870-1915. 15/16". Near Mint(+) (8.7). Price: $25. CyberAuction #498, Lot #24.

7410. SWIRL. Solid core. Naked solid core swirl. Multicolor core. No outer layer. Germany, circa 1870-1915. 29/32". Near Mint (8.3). Price: $25. CyberAuction #499, Lot #12.

7411. SWIRL. Solid core. Naked solid core swirl. Core is alternating bands of transparent dark purple and opaque white. One manufacturing chip on the surface. Germany, circa 1870-1915. 11/16". Mint (-) (9.0). Price: $24. CyberAuction #344, Lot #5.

7412. SWIRL. Solid core. Opaque white base. Three bands on it. One pink, one turquoise, one blue. Outer layer is a cage of yellow strands. Germany, circa 1870-1915. 9/16". Mint (9.9). Price: $24. CyberAuction #350, Lot #53.

7413. SWIRL. Solid core. Super three layer peewee. Core is opaque white covered by transparent turquoise. Middle layer is a cage of white strands. Outer layer is three blue bands and three white bands. Some tiny subsurface moons. Germany, circa 1870-1915. 1/2". Near Mint(-) (8.0). Price: $24. CyberAuction #358, Lot #47.

7414. SWIRL. Solid core. Core is three transparent blue bands alternating with three opaque white bands. Outer layer is three sets of yellow strands. Germany, circa 1870-1915. 25/32". Mint (9.7). Price: $24. CyberAuction #377, Lot #5.

7415. SWIRL. Solid core. Four band core. Might be a divided core with the bands very close together. Two are pink and yellow, two are blue and white. Outer layer four sets of yellow and white strands. Germany, circa 1870-1915. 19/32". Mint (9.9). Price: $24. CyberAuction #441, Lot #37.

7416. SWIRL. Solid core. Core is three transparent blue bands alternating with three opaque white bands. Outer layer is three sets of yellow strands. Germany, circa 1870-1915. 25/32". Mint (9.7). Price: $24. CyberAuction #446, Lot #48.

7417. SWIRL. Solid core. Very pretty marble. Opaque white core. Three orange and three blue bands on it. Outer layer is four sets of yellow strands. In great shape. Germany, circa 1870-1915. 25/32". Mint (9.8). Price: $24. CyberAuction #462, Lot #1.

7418. SWIRL. Solid core. Naked solid core swirl. Core is four panels separated by four bands. Coloring is blue panel, white band, green panel, yellow band, blue panel white band, green panel, yellow band. No outer layer. Beauty. Germany, circa 1870-1915. 11/16". Mint (9.9). Price: $24. CyberAuction #475, Lot #29.

7419. SWIRL. Solid core. Translucent white core. Outer layer is six bands. Three are red and three are purple. Very pretty. One melt pit. Germany, circa 1870-1915. 21/32". Mint(-) (9.2). Price: $24. CyberAuction #495, Lot #46.

7420. SWIRL. Solid core. Opaque white core. Three pink bands, three green bands and two blue bands on the core. Outer layer is two sets of yellow strands and two sets of white strands. Germany, circa 1870-1915. 27/32". Mint (9.8). Price: $24. CyberAuction #503, Lot #34.

7421. SWIRL. Solid core. Pale blue base. Opaque white core. Two dark transparent blue bands and two transparent light turquoise bands. Nice marble. Germany, circa 1870-1915. 17/32". Mint (9.9). Price: $23. CyberAuction #335, Lot #27.

7422. SWIRL. Solid core. Opaque white core. Core has two blue panels and one green panel on it. The outer layer has two partial sets of yellow strands. Rest are missing. From near an end of the cane. A couple of sparkles. Germany, circa 1870-1915. 1". Near Mint(+) (8.9). Price: $23. CyberAuction #337, Lot #32.

7423. SWIRL. Solid core. Three layer. Opaque yellow core. Middle layer is four bands. Each band is two narrow bands. Two are red on white, one is blue on white, one is green on white. Outer layer is four sets of white strands. One small chip. Germany, circa 1870-1915. 21/32". Near Mint(+) (8.7). Price: $23. CyberAuction #342, Lot #44.

7424. SWIRL. Solid core. Solid core swirl. Four colored bands on it. Two pink, one blue, one green. Outer layer is four sets of yellow strands. Thick outer casing. Overall small and tiny chips. Germany, circa 1870-1915. 1-7/16". Good(+) (7.9). Consignor note: B18. Price: $23. CyberAuction #343, Lot #25.

7425. SWIRL. Solid core. Three layer solid core swirl. Opaque white core. Four bands floating as the middle layer. Two are from pink strands, one blue strands, one green strands. Outer layer is four sets of yellow strands. Almost no twist. Germany, circa 1870-1915. 11/16". Mint (9.7). Price: $23. CyberAuction #353, Lot #1.

7426. SWIRL. Solid core. Three layer. Opaque white core. Six bands floating just above the core. Three blue, two turquoise, one pink. Outer layer is three sets of white strands. Marble is filled with tiny air bubbles. One very, very tiny chip. Germany, circa 1870-1915. 7/8". Near Mint(+) (8.9). Price: $23. CyberAuction #354, Lot #11.

7427. SWIRL. Solid core. Naked solid core swirl. Core is two panels of blue and two of salmon, separated by white. No outer layer. Germany, circa 1870-1915. 9/16". Mint (9.8). Price: $23. CyberAuction #354, Lot #48.

7428. SWIRL. Solid core. Opaque white core. Three pink bands and three blue and pink bands on it. Outer layer is a cage of eight white strands. Thick outer casing. Small air hole. Germany, circa 1870-1915. 13/16". Mint(-) (9.2). Price: $23. CyberAuction #471, Lot #17.

7429. SWIRL. Solid core. Three layer. Opaque white core. Floating abov[e] it are two pink bands, one blue band, one green band. Outer layer is fo[ur] sets of yellow strands. Buffed. Germany, circa 1870-1915. 1-3/16". Pri[ce:] $23. CyberAuction #477, Lot #37.

7430. SWIRL. Solid core. Naked solid core swirl. Core is two bands eac[h] of lavender, orange, white, yellow. No outer layer. One melt pit. German[y] circa 1870-1915. 9/16". Mint (9.6). Price: $23. CyberAuction #481, L[ot] #38.

7431. SWIRL. Solid core. Opaque yellow core. Outer layer is three whi[te] bands and three red bands. One melt spot, one pit. Germany, circa 187[0-] 1915. 3/4". Mint(-) (9.1). Price: $23. CyberAuction #491, Lot #18.

7432. SWIRL. Solid core. Very lightly tinted blue base. Opaque white cor[e.] Pink bands on the core. Outer layer is a cage of white strands. One tin[y] rough pit. Germany, circa 1870-1915. 25/32". Near Mint(+) (8.9). Pri[ce:] $23. CyberAuction #491, Lot #28.

7433. SWIRL. Solid core. Opaque white core. Outer layer is six band[s.] Three are green and yellow, three are green and red. Germany, circa 187[0-] 1915. 21/32". Mint (9.9). Price: $23. CyberAuction #495, Lot #19.

7434. SWIRL. Solid core. Naked solid core swirl. Multicolor core. No out[er] layer. Germany, circa 1870-1915. 31/32". Near Mint (8.4). Price: $2[3.] CyberAuction #499, Lot #16.

7435. SWIRL. Solid core. Similar to Lot #13 in this auction. Opaque whi[te] core. Outer layer is three red and three green bands. One melt spot. Ge[r]many, possibly England, circa 1870-1915. 11/16". Mint (-) (9.2). Price: $2[3.] CyberAuction #332, Lot #17.

7436. SWIRL. Solid core. Three layer. Opaque white core. Middle layer [is] pink and blue bands. Outer layer is a cage of light yellow strands. One me[lt] spot. Germany, circa 1870-1915. 11/16". Mint(-) (9.2). Price: $2[3.] CyberAuction #333, Lot #22.

7437. SWIRL. Solid core. Opaque white core. Four bands on the cor[e.] Two pink, two blue. Outer layer is four sets of white strands. One melt sp[ot] and a tiny chip. Germany, circa 1870-1915. 27/32". Near Mint(+) (8.[9)] Price: $22. CyberAuction #358, Lot #27.

7438. SWIRL. Solid core. White solid core. Three lobes. Each has a pin[k] band in the trough and a blue band on the peak. Outer layer is three sets [of] yellow strands. Very nice. Germany, circa 1870-1915. 9/16". Mint (9.[9)] Price: $22. CyberAuction #362, Lot #42.

7439. SWIRL. Solid core. Beautiful three layer. Core is opaque white wi[th] pink coating. Middle layer is a cage of white strands. Outer layer is thr[ee] pink bands alternating with three green bands. Very light haze. Germa[ny,] circa 1870-1915. 11/16". Near Mint (8.6). Price: $22. CyberAuction #36[,] Lot #26.

7440. SWIRL. Solid core. Opaque white core. Covered by pink. One ye[l]low band on it. Outer layer is three bands of green on white, alternati[ng] with three sets of three yellow strands. One small flake. Germany, ci[rca] 1870-1915. 11/16". Near Mint (8.6). Price: $22. CyberAuction #364, L[ot] #56.

7441. SWIRL. Solid core. Lobed solid core swirl. Opaque white core. Thr[ee] deep lobes. Blue band on each peak, pink band in each trough. Out[er] layer is four sets of white and yellow strands. Germany, circa 1870-1915. 16". Mint (9.9). Price: $22. CyberAuction #369, Lot #20.

7442. SWIRL. Solid core. Opaque white core. Three light blue bands a[nd] three orange bands on it. Outer layer is three sets of yellow strands. Tw[o] sparkles and a melt spot. Germany, circa 1870-1915. 29/32". Near Mint(+[)] (8.9). Price: $22. CyberAuction #403, Lot #21.

7443. SWIRL. Solid core. Naked solid core swirl. Core is alternating band[s] White, orange, yellow, blue, white, orange, yellow, green. No outer lay[er.] One tiny melt chip, one tiny chip. Germany, circa 1870-1915. 29/32". Ne[ar] Mint(+) (8.8). Price: $22. CyberAuction #409, Lot #56.

7444. SWIRL. Solid core. Naked solid core swirl. Core is alternating pan[els] of orange, white, and blue. No outer layer. Beauty. Germany, circa 187[0-] 1915. 23/32". Mint (9.7). Price: $22. CyberAuction #412, Lot #10.

7445. SWIRL. Solid core. Semi-opaque white core. Outer layer is six ban[ds] and two strands. Three light green, three light orange, two red stran[ds.] Germany, circa 1870-1915. 9/16". Mint (9.7). Price: $22. CyberAucti[on] #448, Lot #3.

7446. SWIRL. Solid core. Opaque white core. Three light blue bands a[nd] three orange bands on it. Outer layer is three sets of yellow strands. Tw[o] sparkles and a melt spot. Germany, circa 1870-1915. 29/32". Near Mint(+[)] (8.9). Price: $22. CyberAuction #449, Lot #52.

7447. SWIRL. Solid core. Translucent white core. Outer layer is six band[s.] Three are light green, three are pink on yellow. Very nice. Germany, poss[i]bly English, circa 1870-1915. 9/16". Mint (9.9). Price: $22. CyberAuction #452, Lot #38.

7448. SWIRL. Solid core. English style. Opaque orange core. Outer layer [is] six bands. Three are white, three are light green. Outstanding exampl[e.] England, possibly Germany, circa 1870-1915. 9/16". Mint (9.9). Price: $2[2.] CyberAuction #459, Lot #7.

7449. SWIRL. Solid core. Opaque white core. Outer layer is six band[s.] Three are light green, three are yellow. England, possibly Germany, cir[ca] 1870-1915. 21/32". Mint (9.7). Price: $22. CyberAuction #465, Lot #3[ ]

7450. SWIRL. Solid core. Naked solid core swirl. Core is a twice repeati[ng] pattern of transparent blue, opaque white, opaque orange, opaque yello[w.] Germany, circa 1870-1915. 5/8". Mint (9.7). Price: $22. CyberAuction #47[,] Lot #20.

7451. SWIRL. Solid core. Naked solid core swirl. Core is alternating opaqu[e] yellow or white bands, with transparent blue in between. No outer lay[er.] Germany, circa 1870-1915. 1/2". Mint (9.7). Price: $22. CyberAuction #47[,] Lot #11.

7452. SWIRL. Solid core. Opaque white core. Three light blue bands a[nd] three orange bands on it. Outer layer is three sets of yellow strands. Tw[o] arkles and a melt spot. Germany, circa 1870-1915. 29/32". Near Mint(+) .9). Price: $22. CyberAuction #484, Lot #2.

453. SWIRL. Solid core. Three layer. Opaque white core. Middle layer is ree pink bands and three blue bands. Outer layer is three sets of yellow ands. Germany, circa 1870-1915. 5/8". Mint (9.7). Price: $22. berAuction #504, Lot #24.

454. SWIRL. Solid core. Four panel core. Each panel is white. Two are k and blue bands, two are green and pink bands. Outer layer are four ts of yellow strands. Germany, circa 1870-1915. 5/8". Mint (9.9). Price: 2. CyberAuction #504, Lot #31.

455. SWIRL. Solid core. Naked solid core. Opaque white core with red d blue alternating bands. Germany, circa 1870-1915. 5/8". Mint (9.9). ice: $21. CyberAuction #504, Lot #30.

456. SWIRL. Solid core. White core. Three blue and three turquoise bands the core. Outer layer is a cage of white strands. Germany, circa 1870-15. 1/2". Mint (9.6). Price: $21. CyberAuction #345, Lot #8.

457. SWIRL. Solid core. Three layer solid core. Beauty. Opaque white re. The middle layer is four sets of three bands. Two sets are pink, one is ue, one is turquoise. Outer layer is four sets of yellow strands. Gorgeous. couple of tiny sparkles. Germany, circa 1870-1915. 23/32". Mint(-) (9.1). ice: $21. CyberAuction #356, Lot #5.

458. SWIRL. Solid core. Opaque white core. Partially open. Outer layer six narrow bands in two color schemes. Germany, circa 1870-1915. 1/2". int (9.9). Price: $21. CyberAuction #365, Lot #45.

459. SWIRL. Solid core. Core is alternating panels of pink, blue and white, d pink, green and white. Outer layer is a cage of white strands. Two bsurface moons and some haziness. Germany, circa 1870-1915. 1-1/16". ear Mint (8.4). Price: $21. CyberAuction #367, Lot #55.

460. SWIRL. Solid core. Four band core. Each is green on white, sepa- ted by white. Outer layer is six orange strands. Tiny subsurface moon on e side. Germany, circa 1870-1915. 5/8". Near Mint(+) (8.9). Price: $21. berAuction #368, Lot #37.

461. SWIRL. Solid core. This is the first piece off a rod. Flattened, per- ps intended as drawer pull or other decorative piece. Solid core with an ter layer Design shoots out the top. Flattened, resembles a flower. Very ce. Germany, circa 1870-1915. 15/16", about 1/2" high. Mint (9.5). Price: 1. CyberAuction #370, Lot #26.

462. SWIRL. Solid core. Yellow core. Three panels of pink and two of ue on it. Outer layer is three sets of yellow strands. Germany, circa 1870- 15. 7/16". Mint (9.9). Price: $21. CyberAuction #439, Lot #52.

463. SWIRL. Solid core. Naked solid core swirl. Transparent purple bands, parated by yellow and white bands. One tiny melt spot. Germany, circa 70-1915. 11/16". Mint(-) (9.2). Price: $21. CyberAuction #445, Lot #16.

464. SWIRL. Solid core. Excellent three layer marble. Opaque white core th pink and green bands on it. Middle layer is four blue bands. Outer yer is four sets of yellow strands. One line of dirt, and several tiny chips on e other side. Germany, circa 1870-1915. 21/32". Near Mint (8.6). Price: 1. CyberAuction #449, Lot #37.

465. SWIRL. Solid core. Core is alternating panels of pink, blue and white, d pink, green and white. Outer layer is a cage of white strands. Two bsurface moons and some haziness. Germany, circa 1870-1915. 1-1/16". ar Mint (8.4). Price: $21. CyberAuction #451, Lot #42.

466. SWIRL. Solid core. Semi-opaque white base. Blue and red strands it. Outer layer is four sets of yellow strands. Germany, circa 1870-1915. 5/32". Mint (9.8). Price: $21. CyberAuction #466, Lot #3.

467. SWIRL. Solid core. White solid core swirl. Four panels of color strands it. Two sets of three pink strands, one set of three blue strands, one set of ree green strands. Outer layer is four sets of yellow strands. Small chip d pits. Germany, circa 1870-1915. 1-1/16". Near Mint (8.5). Price: $21. berAuction #497, Lot #3.

468. SWIRL. Solid core. Opaque white core. Outer layer is three orange d green bands and three purple and orange bands. Odd coloring. One y subsurface moon. Germany, circa 1870-1915. 25/32". Near Mint(+) .8). Price: $20. CyberAuction #333, Lot #43.

469. SWIRL. Solid core. Opaque white core. Two bands of pink on the re, one of blue, one of green. Outer layer is four sets of white strands. In eat shape. Germany, circ 1870-1915. 23/32". Mint (9.9). Price: $20. berAuction #336, Lot #7.

470. SWIRL. Solid core. Very nice marble, probably English. Opaque hite core. Outer layer is six bands. Three are red, two are baby blue, one light yellow. Very pretty. One tiny melt spot. Germany, circa 1880-1920. 16". Mint(-) (9.0). Price: $20. CyberAuction #345, Lot #7.

471. SWIRL. Solid core. Interesting. Core is two panels each of transpar- t dark blue, opaque white, transparent yellow on white. Outer layer is o orange strands, alternating with two pairs of white strands. Some pit- g, scratching and an extra melted glass spot. Germany, circa 1870-1915. 5/32". Near Mint (8.3). Price: $20. CyberAuction #364, Lot #41.

472. SWIRL. Solid core. Four lobes. Four lobes. Two peaks have a blue band. Two peaks have a pink band. No color in the troughs. Outer yer is four sets of yellow strands. Tightly twisted. Blown air hole and a tiny oon. Germany, circa 1870-1915. 3/4". Near Mint (8.6). Price: $20. yberAuction #367, Lot #39.

473. SWIRL. Solid core. Could be construed as a ribbon core, because it two bands in the same color scheme with two narrow clear panels sepa- ting them. But, I think the clear panels are part of the design. Each band yellow, white, orange, clear, blue and orange. Naked, no outer layer. Sev- al subsurface moons and a few chips. Rare. Germany, circa 1870-1915. . Near Mint(-) (8.0). Price: $20. CyberAuction #390, Lot #15.

474. SWIRL. Solid core. Three-layer solid core. Opaque white core. Three ue bands on the core. Three pink bands floating in a middle layer. Outer yer is three sets of yellow strands. Cold roll line, melt spot, one pit. Ger-

many, circa 1870-1915. 1". Near Mint(+) (8.8). Price: $20. CyberAuction #427, Lot #33.

7475. SWIRL. Solid core. Interesting four-layer marble. Opaque white core. Three transparent pink bands floating above the core. Three transparent blue bands floating in a layer above that. Outer layer is six sets of white strands. One melt spot, one tiny subsurface moon. Germany, circa 1870-1915. 13/16". Near Mint(+) (8.9). Price: $20. CyberAuction #432, Lot #44.

7476. SWIRL. Solid core. Opaque white core with cranberry pink stripes on it. Outer layer is four sets of white strands. Some pits. Germany, circa 1870-1915. 7/8". Near Mint(+) (8.8). Price: $20. CyberAuction #432, Lot #20.

7477. SWIRL. Solid core. Opaque white core. Outer layer is six bands. Three orange, three purple. Germany, possibly England, circa 1870-1915. 23/32". Mint (9.7). Price: $20. CyberAuction #465, Lot #11.

7478. SWIRL. Solid core. Opaque white core. Alternating pink and blue bands on the core. Outer layer is a cage of yellow strands. One tiny melt chip, one tiny subsurface moon. Germany, circa 1870-1915. 15/16". Near Mint(+) (8.9). Price: $20. CyberAuction #491, Lot #10.

7479. SWIRL. Solid core. White solid core swirl. Core has two red bands with yellow strand, one blue band with yellow strand and one green band with yellow strand, on it. Outer layer is four sets of yellow strands. Ger- many, circa 1870-1915. 9/16". Mint (9.9). Price: $20. CyberAuction #501, Lot #8.

7480. SWIRL. Solid core. White solid core swirl. Outer layer is six bands. Three yellow, one blue, one red, one black. Interesting marble. Several pinpricks. Germany, circa 1870-1915. 11/16". Mint(-) (9.0). Price: $20. CyberAuction #503, Lot #40.

7481. SWIRL. Solid core. Hard to find naked solid core swirl. Core is four panels of the same repeating pattern of transparent blue, opaque white, orange and yellow. No outer layer. A couple of tiny flakes. Germany, circa 1870-1915. 9/16". Near Mint(+) (8.8). Price: $19. CyberAuction #331, Lot #5.

7482. SWIRL. Solid core. Opaque white core. Pink bands on it. Outer layer is four bands of green on yellow. Germany, circa 1927-1935. 5/8". Mint (9.8). Price: $19. CyberAuction #333, Lot #26.

7483. SWIRL. Solid core. Opaque white core. Three bands on it. One red, one turquoise, one blue. Outer layer is three sets of yellow strands. Odd twist to it. Germany, circa 1870-1915. 1/2". Mint (9.9). Price: $19. CyberAuction #339, Lot #22.

7484. SWIRL. Solid core. Naked solid core swirl. Nice marble. Opaque white core. There are three bands on it. One yellow, one orange, one light blue. Misshapen core. Slightly flat spot. Germany, circa 1870-1915. 21/32". Mint(-) (9.0). Price: $19. CyberAuction #345, Lot #5.

7485. SWIRL. Solid core. Yellow core. Four shallow lobes. Pink band on each peak. Outer layer is a cage of yellow strands. Germany, circa 1870-1915. 5/8". Mint (9.5). Price: $19. CyberAuction #347, Lot #44.

7486. SWIRL. Solid core. Opaque white core with two bands of pink, one of green, one of blue. Outer layer is a cage of eleven yellow bands. Thick clear casing. Lots of glass bumps and air bubbles on the surface. Probably from near an end of the cane. Interesting marble. Germany, circa 1870-1915. 13/16". Near Mint(+) (8.9). Price: $19. CyberAuction #359, Lot #14.

7487. SWIRL. Solid core. Opaque white core. Three shallow lobes. Blue band in each trough, red band on each peak. Outer layer is a white strands (one yellow). Some tiny pits. Germany, circa 1870-1915. 11/16". Near Mint(+) (8.7). Price: $19. CyberAuction #364, Lot #5.

7488. SWIRL. Solid core. Opaque white core. Three bands on the core. One each of dark green, blue and red (narrow). Core is misshapen. Outer layer is two sets of yellow strands, a third set is missing. One small subsur- face moon. Germany, circa 1870-1915. 29/32". Near Mint(+) (8.7). Price: $19. CyberAuction #365, Lot #21.

7489. SWIRL. Solid core. Three layer. Opaque white core. Four bands floating above the core. Two are pink, one green, one blue. Outer layer is four sets of yellow strands. Germany, circa 1870-1915. 21/32". Mint (9.9). Price: $19. CyberAuction #366, Lot #32.

7490. SWIRL. Solid core. Naked solid core swirl. Transparent purple bands, separated by yellow and white bands. One tiny melt spot. Germany, circa 1870-1915. 11/16". Mint(-) (9.2). Price: $19. CyberAuction #369, Lot #6.

7491. SWIRL. Solid core. Three-layer solid core swirl. Opaque white core. Middle layer is three pairs of red narrow bands and three sets of green narrow bands. Outer layer is three sets of white strands. One pit. Germany, circa 1870-1915. 21/32". Mint(-) (9.2). Price: $19. CyberAuction #369, Lot #43.

7492. SWIRL. Solid core. Core is multicolored. Outer layer is a cage of yellow strands. One small subsurface moon. Germany, circa 1870-1915. 25/32". Near Mint (8.5). Price: $19. CyberAuction #370, Lot #40.

7493. SWIRL. Solid core. Three panels, each a different color scheme. Each panel is deeply lobed. Outer layer is three sets of yellow strands. Germany, circa 1870-1915. 15/32". Mint (9.9). Price: $19. CyberAuction #377, Lot #11.

7494. SWIRL. Solid core. White solid core. Outer layer is three bands of blue on white edged by bright orange, and two bands of bright orange. Missing one orange band. Slightly shrunken on one side. Gorgeous colors. One manufacturing chip. Very pretty. Germany, possibly England, circa 1870-1915. 11/16". Mint(-) (9.1). Price: $19. CyberAuction #379, Lot #26.

7495. SWIRL. Solid core. Opaque white core. Two bands of pink, one blue, one green, on the core. Outer layer is four sets of yellow strands. Germany, circa 1870-1915. 25/32". Mint(-) (9.0). Price: $19. CyberAuction #380, Lot #45.

7496. SWIRL. Solid core. Opaque white core. Three bands on the core.

One each of dark green, blue and red (narrow). Core is misshapen. Outer layer is two sets of yellow strands, a third set is missing. One small subsurface moon. Germany, circa 1870-1915. 29/32". Near Mint(+) (8.7). Price: $19. CyberAuction #398, Lot #28.

7497. SWIRL. Solid core. This is a solid core swirl with a partially closed core. Looks like a single ribbon. Naked, no outer layer. Core is a band of purple, blue, red and two bands of yellow. Missing part of the red and another yellow. Germany, circa 1870-1915. 25/32". Mint (9.7). Price: $19. CyberAuction #417, Lot #7.

7498. SWIRL. Solid core. Core is a combination of opaque white, transparent pink, green and yellow. Outer layer is three white strands. Germany, circa 1870-1915. 15/32". Mint (9.9). Price: $19. CyberAuction #422, Lot #44.

7499. SWIRL. Solid core. Opaque white core. Covered by bands of pink, blue and green. Outer layer is four sets of yellow strands (a couple are partial). Overall tiny chips and pits. Nothing is deep damage. Germany, circa 1870-1915. 1-5/16". Good (7.4). Price: $19. CyberAuction #428, Lot #10.

7500. SWIRL. Solid core. Opaque white core. Three bands on the core. One each of dark green, blue and red (narrow). Core is misshapen. Outer layer is two sets of yellow strands, a third set is missing. One small subsurface moon. Germany, circa 1870-1915. 29/32". Near Mint(+) (8.7). Price: $19. CyberAuction #430, Lot #20.

7501. SWIRL. Solid core. Bright yellow core with light pink strands on it. Outer layer is four sets of white strands. Germany, circa 1870-1915. 15/32". Mint (9.9). Price: $19. CyberAuction #441, Lot #44.

7502. SWIRL. Solid core. Opaque yellow core. Three bands of green and three bands of pink on the surface. Outer layer is four white strands. Germany, circa 1870-1915. 19/32". Mint (9.9). Price: $19. CyberAuction #441, Lot #46.

7503. SWIRL. Solid core. Opaque white core. Outer layer is three bands of blue on white and three of green on white. Germany, circa 1870-1915. 15/32". Mint (9.9). Price: $19. CyberAuction #444, Lot #47.

7504. SWIRL. Solid core. Three-lobed solid core swirl. Opaque white core. Pink band in trough, blue band on each peak. Outer layer is three sets of very thin yellow strands. Germany, circa 1870-1915. 19/32". Mint (9.7). Price: $19. CyberAuction #456, Lot #55.

7505. SWIRL. Solid core. Opaque white core. Six band outer layer. Three red, three yellow. Probably English. England, possibly Germany, circa 1870-1915. 9/16". Mint (9.8). Price: $19. CyberAuction #457, Lot #43.

7506. SWIRL. Solid core. Opaque white core. Six band outer layer. Three red, three yellow. Germany, possibly England, circa 1870-1915. 9/16". Mint (9.8). Price: $19. CyberAuction #459, Lot #42.

7507. SWIRL. Solid core. Opaque white core. Outer layer is six bands. Three are light blue. Three are orange and yellow. England, possibly Germany, circa 1870-1915. 21/32". Mint (9.8). Price: $19. CyberAuction #463, Lot #10.

7508. SWIRL. Solid core. Yellow core. Outer layer is six bands. Three are light green and three are white. A couple of melt spots. England, possibly Germany, circa 1870-1915. 11/16". Mint(-) (9.1). Price: $19. CyberAuction #463, Lot #21.

7509. SWIRL. Solid core. Looks like a fat single ribbon core swirl, but it is actually a solid core swirl that is not completely closed. Yellow core. Two green bands and one pink band on it. Three sets of equidistantly spaced white strands. Super. One melt pit. 13/16". Mint (9.5). Price: $19. CyberAuction #480, Lot #41.

7510. SWIRL. Solid core. English colors. Core is blue bands separated by white strands. Outer layer is four red bands and four yellow bands. Couple of melt pits. England, possibly Germany, circa 1870-1915. 9/16". Mint(-) (9.2). Price: $19. CyberAuction #483, Lot #25.

7511. SWIRL. Solid core. Three-layer. White middle. Middle layer is pink, green and blue bands. Outer layer is four sets of yellow strands. Small manufacturing pit. Germany, circa 1870-1915. 25/32". Mint(-) (9.2). Price: $19. CyberAuction #490, Lot #16.

7512. SWIRL. Solid core. Three panel core. Each is green, red, blue and white. Outer layer is three sets of orange and white strands. Germany, possibly England, circa 1870-1915. 21/32". Mint (9.7). Price: $19. CyberAuction #495, Lot #44.

7513. SWIRL. Solid core. Three layer marble. Opaque white core. Cage of pink strands floating above the core. Cage of yellow strands forms the outer layer. One pit. Germany, circa 1870-1915. 23/32". Near Mint(+) (8.9). Price: $19. CyberAuction #498, Lot #15.

7514. SWIRL. Solid core. Very unusual core. Alternating panels of translucent white and transparent light blue. Orange strands on the core. Outer layer is three sets of yellow strands. Germany, circa 1870-1915. 17/32". Mint (9.9). Price: $19. CyberAuction #500, Lot #2.

7515. SWIRL. Solid core. Opaque white core. Two bands of pink, one green, and one blue, on the core. Outer layer is a cage of yellow strands. Germany, circa 1870-1915. 5/8". Mint (9.9). Price: $19. CyberAuction #504, Lot #11.

7516. SWIRL. Solid core. Translucent white core. Outer layer is six bands. Three are yellow, three are blue. Germany, circa 1870-1915. 1/2". Mint (9.8). Price: $19. CyberAuction #504, Lot #39.

7517. SWIRL. Solid core. Opaque white core. Four bands on it. Two pink, one green, one blue. Outer layer is four sets of yellow strands. Germany, circa 1870-1915. 5/8". Mint (9.9). Price: $19. CyberAuction #504, Lot #54.

7518. SWIRL. Solid core. Three layer marble. Opaque white core. Middle layer is a cage of yellow strands. Outer layer is eight bands. Four are white and blue, four are yellow stands. One large melt spot. Peewee. Germany, circa 1870-1915. 7/16". Mint(-) (9.0). Price: $18. CyberAuction #351, Lot #28.

7519. SWIRL. Solid core. Opaque white core. Two panels of blue on pink and two of green on pink. Outer layer is a cage of yellow strands. Some scratches. Germany, circa 1870-1915. 21/32". Mint(-) (9.0). Price: $18. CyberAuction #367, Lot #53.

7520. SWIRL. Solid core. Three-layer marble. Opaque white core. Middle layer is pink and blue bands. Outer layer is cage of white strands. Germany, circa 1870-1915. 17/32". Mint (9.9). Price: $18. CyberAuction #41?, Lot #14.

7521. SWIRL. Solid core. Multicolor core. Partial and malformed. Outer layer is four sets of yellow and white strands. Two tiny melt spots, small subsurface moon, pinprick. Germany, circa 1870-1915. 15/16". Near Mint(+) (8.9). Price: $18. CyberAuction #451, Lot #56.

7522. SWIRL. Solid core. Lobed solid core swirl. Opaque white base. Four shallow lobes. Two lobes have blue strands in them, two have pink strands in them. No color on the peaks. Outer layer is a cage of white strands. One small manufacturing melt chip. Germany, circa 1870-1915. 3/4". Mint (9.2). Price: $18. CyberAuction #505, Lot #15.

7523. SWIRL. Solid core. Interesting marble. Yellow core, with one white stripe in the core. On the core are three bands of transparent pink. Outer layer was meant to be a cage of white strands, but about a quarter of them are missing off of one side. Cold roll line. Germany, circa 1870-1915. 1?/16". Mint(-) (9.0). Price: $17. CyberAuction #336, Lot #2.

7524. SWIRL. Solid core. Yellow core. Pink and green strands on it. Outer layer is a cage of white strands. Small chip at the top pontil. Germany, circa 1870-1915. 7/8". Near Mint(+) (8.7). Price: $17. CyberAuction #336, Lot #45.

7525. SWIRL. Solid core. Opaque white core. Four outer bands. Two are pink and two are blue. Germany, circa 1870-1915. 1/2". Mint(-) (9.0). Price: $17. CyberAuction #341, Lot #4.

7526. SWIRL. Solid core. Three layer. Opaque white core. Band of pink and band of blue floating above the core. Outer layer is four sets of yellow strands. Germany, circa 1870-1915. 15/32". Mint (9.7). Price: $17. CyberAuction #341, Lot #19.

7527. SWIRL. Solid core. Opaque white core. Outer layer is six bands. Three are light blue and yellow, three are orange and white. Interesting. Germany, circa 1870-1915. 21/32". Mint (9.8). Price: $17. CyberAuction #342, Lot #48.

7528. SWIRL. Solid core. Opaque white core with four bands on it. Two are pink, one blue, one turquoise. Outer layer is three sets of yellow strands. One set seems to be missing. Germany, circa 1870-1915. 25/32". Mint(-) (9.1). Price: $17. CyberAuction #347, Lot #3.

7529. SWIRL. Solid core. Semi-opaque yellow core. Outer layer is four bands. Two are orange edged by white, two are blue edged by white. Some pitting and tiny chips. Nice. Germany, circa 1870-1915. 11/16". Near Mint(-) (8.7). Price: $17. CyberAuction #348, Lot #1.

7530. SWIRL. Solid core. Peewee. Opaque white core. Four outer bands. Two are orange, two are blue and orange. Beauty. Germany, circa 1870-1915. 1/2". Mint (9.9). Price: $17. CyberAuction #351, Lot #9.

7531. SWIRL. Solid core. Three layer. Opaque yellow core. Four bands floating above that core. Two are green, two are pink. Outer layer is four sets of white strands. No twist. One tiny pit. Germany, circa 1870-1915. 21/32". Near Mint(+) (8.9). Price: $17. CyberAuction #353, Lot #20.

7532. SWIRL. Solid core. Yellow solid core. Four bands on it. Two pink bands, two green bands. Outer layer is four sets of white strands. Not white but no damage. Germany, circa 1870-1915. 17/32". Mint(-) (9.0). Price: $17. CyberAuction #358, Lot #45.

7533. SWIRL. Solid core. Bright yellow core with light pink strands on it. Outer layer is four sets of white strands. Germany, circa 1870-1915. 1?/32". Mint (9.9). Price: $17. CyberAuction #360, Lot #17.

7534. SWIRL. Solid core. Multicolor core. Partial and malformed. Outer layer is four sets of yellow and white strands. Two tiny melt spots, small subsurface moon, pinprick. Germany, circa 1870-1915. 15/16". Near Mint(+) (8.9). Price: $17. CyberAuction #360, Lot #20.

7535. SWIRL. Solid core. White core. Three very shallow lobes. Pink band in each trough, green band on each peak. Outer layer is three sets of yellow strands. Long air hole, a couple of pinpricks. Germany, circa 1870-1915. 25/32". Near Mint(+) (8.9). Price: $17. CyberAuction #360, Lot #27.

7536. SWIRL. Solid core. Nice three layer marble. Opaque white core. Four bands form the middle layer. Each is transparent blue and transparent pink. Outer layer is four sets of white strands. Germany, circa 1870-1915. 23/32". Mint (9.6). Price: $17. CyberAuction #361, Lot #60.

7537. SWIRL. Solid core. Naked solid core swirl. Two transparent blue panels and a transparent green panel, separated by opaque white bands. One pinprick. Germany, circa 1870-1915. 19/32". Mint (-) (9.0). Price: $17. CyberAuction #362, Lot #14.

7538. SWIRL. Solid core. Opaque white core. Floating above the core are two blue strands, one pink, one green. Outer layer is a cage of yellow strands. Germany, circa 1870-1915. 15/32". Mint (9.9). Price: $17. CyberAuction #365, Lot #23.

7539. SWIRL. Solid core. Four panel core. Various colors. Four lobes. Outer layer is four sets of two white strands. Very nice. Germany, circa 1870-1915. 1/2". Mint (9.7). Price: $17. CyberAuction #366, Lot #2.

7540. SWIRL. Solid core. Four panel core. Opaque white core. Two panels of pink bands, one of blue bands, one of green bands. Outer layer is four sets of yellow strands. Nice peewee. Germany, circa 1870-1915. 1/2". Mint (9.9). Price: $17. CyberAuction #368, Lot #7.

7541. SWIRL. Solid core. Translucent white core. Three pink bands and three blue on green bands, on the core. Outer layer is three sets of white and yellow strands. Germany, circa 1870-1915. 23/32". Mint (9.7). Price: $17. CyberAuction #368, Lot #15.

7542. SWIRL. Solid core. Opaque white core. Outer layer is three band of blue on white and three of green on white. Germany, circa 1870-1915. 15/32". Mint (9.9). Price: $17. CyberAuction #369, Lot #26.

7543. SWIRL. Solid core. Four panel core. One each of pink on white, blue on white, green on yellow, pink on yellow. Outer layer is two sets of yellow strands and to sets of white strands. Core is misshapen. One melt spot and one subsurface moon. Germany, circa 1870-1915. 31/32". Near Mint (8.6). Price: $17. CyberAuction #370, Lot #7.

7544. SWIRL. Solid core. Semi-opaque yellow core. Outer layer is four bands. Two are orange edged by white, two are blue edged by white. Some pitting and tiny chips. Nice. Germany, circa 1870-1915. 11/16". Near Mint(+) (8.7). Price: $17. CyberAuction #374, Lot #41.

7545. SWIRL. Solid core. Opaque white core with blue and red bands. Outer layer is yellow strands. Very misshapen. Germany, circa 1870-1915. 3/4". Mint(-) (9.0). Price: $17. CyberAuction #374, Lot #48.

7546. SWIRL. Solid core. Opaque white core. Three pink bands on it. Outer layer is three sets of yellow strands. Germany, circa 187-1915. 15/32". Mint (9.9). Price: $17. CyberAuction #377, Lot #13.

7547. SWIRL. Solid core. Opaque white core, only partially formed. Outer layer is three light blue bands. Germany, circa 1870-1915. 15/32". Mint (9.7). Price: $17. CyberAuction #377, Lot #34.

7548. SWIRL. Solid core. Opaque white core with four bands on it. Two are pink, one blue, one turquoise. Outer layer is three sets of yellow strands. One set seems to be missing. Germany, circa 1870-1915. 25/32". Mint(-) (9.1). Price: $17. CyberAuction #386, Lot #25.

7549. SWIRL. Solid core. Nice solid core composed of three panels, all the same color scheme. Outer layer is three sets of yellow and white strands. A couple of pits and melt spots on the surface. Large fracture running through the marble. Germany, circa 1870-1915. 1-3/4". Good (7.5). Price: $17. CyberAuction #387, Lot #19.

7550. SWIRL. Solid core. Semi-opaque yellow core. Outer layer is four bands. Two are orange edged by white, two are blue edged by white. Some pitting and tiny chips. Nice. Germany, circa 1870-1915. 11/16". Near Mint(+) (8.7). Price: $17. CyberAuction #398, Lot #4.

7551. SWIRL. Solid core. English type. Opaque white core. Outer layer is six bands. Three yellow, three blue and orange. Some small subsurface moons and small flakes. England, possibly Germany, circa 1870-1920. 1-1/8". Good (7.4). Price: $17. CyberAuction #401, Lot #13.

7552. SWIRL. Solid core. Opaque white core. Two bands of orange, one of blue and one of green, on the core. A yellow strands in the middle of each band. Outer layer is four sets of yellow strands. Germany, circa 1870-1915. 23/32". Mint (9.7). Price: $17. CyberAuction #403, Lot #23.

7553. SWIRL. Solid core. Three-layer solid core swirl. Opaque white core. Four pink bands, two blue and two green, floating above the core. Outer layer is four sets of yellow strands. One pinprick. Germany, circa 1870-1915. 3/4". Mint(-) (9.1). Price: $17. CyberAuction #403, Lot #26.

7554. SWIRL. Solid core. English colors. Opaque yellow core. Outer layer is four bands. Blue, light green, pale blue, blue. Overall tiny pits. England, possibly Germany, circa 1870-1920. 11/16". Near Mint(+) (8.8). Price: $17. CyberAuction #420, Lot #18.

7555. SWIRL. Solid core. Yellow core. Outer layer is six bands. Three are pink on white, three are blue on white. Germany, circa 1870-1915. 15/32". Mint (9.9). Price: $17. CyberAuction #425, Lot #6.

7556. SWIRL. Solid core. Naked solid core swirl. Opaque white core. Two bands of blue and two of orange on it. One pit. Germany, circa 1870-1915. 21/32". Mint(-) (9.0). Price: $17. CyberAuction #426, Lot #35.

7557. SWIRL. Solid core. White core. Outer layer is three pale pink bands and three pale blue bands. Germany, circa 1870-1915. 21/32". Mint (9.9). Price: $17. CyberAuction #431, Lot #41.

7558. SWIRL. Solid core. Very lightly tinted blue base. Opaque white core. Middle layer is pink bands floating above the core. Core is shrunken. Outer layer is a cage of white strands. Germany, circa 1870-1915. 9/16". Mint (9.7). Price: $17. CyberAuction #433, Lot #37.

7559. SWIRL. Solid core. Three-lobed solid core swirl. Opaque white core. Pink band in each trough, blue band on each peak. Outer layer is three sets of very thin yellow strands. Germany, circa 1870-1915. 19/32". Mint (9.7). Price: $17. CyberAuction #436, Lot #38.

7560. SWIRL. Solid core. Opaque white core with four bands on it. Two are pink, one blue, one turquoise. Outer layer is three sets of yellow strands. One set seems to be missing. Germany, circa 1870-1915. 25/32". Mint(-) (9.1). Price: $17. CyberAuction #440, Lot #4.

7561. SWIRL. Solid core. Opaque white core. Outer layer is six bands. Three are blue, three are pink on white. Germany, circa 1870-1915. 13/16". Mint (9.7). Price: $17. CyberAuction #442, Lot #4.

7562. SWIRL. Solid core. Nice solid core composed of three panels, all the same color scheme. Outer layer is three sets of yellow and white strands. A couple of pits and melt spots on the surface. Large fracture running through the marble. Germany, circa 1870-1915. 1-3/4". Good (7.5). Price: $17. CyberAuction #449, Lot #16.

7563. SWIRL. Solid core. Opaque white core. Two sets of blue bands and two of red, on the white. Also, one yellow band on the white. Outer layer is a cage of yellow strands. One dirt line, one tiny melt chip. Germany, circa 1870-1915. 25/32". Near Mint(+) (8.7). Price: $17. CyberAuction #453, Lot #1.

7564. SWIRL. Solid core. Three layer. White core. Middle layer is alternating pink and blue bands. Outer layer is a cage of yellow strands. One melt chips, some pinpricks. Germany, circa 1870-1915. 29/32". Mint(-) (9.0). Price: $17. CyberAuction #461, Lot #31.

7565. SWIRL. Solid core. Three-layer. White core. Middle layer is pink, green and blue bands. Outer layer is four sets of yellow strands. Small manufacturing pit. Germany, circa 1870-1915. 25/32". Mint(-) (9.2). Price: $17. CyberAuction #461, Lot #46.

7566. SWIRL. Solid core. Three-layer. Gorgeous. Opaque white core. Middle layer is strands of pink, blue and green, floating above the core. Outer layer is two sets of white strands and two sets of yellow strands. Two tiny pits or melt spots. Germany, circa 1870-1915. 25/32". Mint(-) (9.2). Price: $17. CyberAuction #464, Lot #20.

7567. SWIRL. Solid core. Opaque white core. Four bands. Two pink, one blue, one green. Core is slightly lobed. Outer layer is four sets of yellow strands. Germany, circa 1870-1915. 1/2". Mint (9.8). Price: $17. CyberAuction #467, Lot #9.

7568. SWIRL. Solid core. Very lightly tinted blue glass. Yellow core. Two pink bands and two green bands on it. Outer layer is a cage of white strands. One tiny melt chip. Germany, circa 1870-1915. 21/32". Mint(-) (9.2). Price: $17. CyberAuction #471, Lot #12.

7569. SWIRL. Solid core. Four-layer swirl. Opaque white core. Next layer is yellow strands. Next is red and blue bands. Outer layer is two yellow bands, several appear to be missing. Tiny chip, some pits. Germany, circa 1870-1915. 21/32". Near Mint (8.6). Price: $17. CyberAuction #476, Lot #37.

7570. SWIRL. Solid core. Opaque white core. Outer layer is six bands. Three are blue, three are pink on white. Germany, circa 1870-1915. 13/16". Mint (9.7). Price: $17. CyberAuction #484, Lot #32.

7571. SWIRL. Solid core. Opaque white core with four bands on it. Two are pink, one blue, one turquoise. Outer layer is three sets of yellow strands. One set seems to be missing. Germany, circa 1870-1915. 25/32". Mint(-) (9.1). Price: $17. CyberAuction #490, Lot #37.

7572. SWIRL. Solid core. Opaque white core. Not completely closed. Two pink bands, one blue band, one green band, on the core. Outer layer is four sets of yellow strands. Thick outer casing. A couple of small subsurface moons. Germany, circa 1870-1915. 1-1/16". Near Mint(+) (8.7). Price: $17. CyberAuction #493, Lot #43.

7573. SWIRL. Solid core. Three-layer. Gorgeous. Opaque white core. Middle layer is strands of pink, blue and green, floating above the core. Outer layer is two sets of white strands and two sets of yellow strands. Two tiny pits or melt spots. Germany, circa 1870-1915. 25/32". Mint(-) (9.2). Price: $17. CyberAuction #494, Lot #30.

7574. SWIRL. Solid core. Four panels. Each is a different pattern of green, blue, red, yellow and/or white. Tiny flat spot and a dirt spot. Bright colors. Germany, possibly England, circa 1870-1915. 21/32". Mint (9.3). Price: $17. CyberAuction #495, Lot #37.

7575. SWIRL. Solid core. Opaque white core. Covered by transparent pink. Outer layer is four sets of yellow strands. Some tiny pits. Germany, circa 1870-1915. 7/8". Near Mint(+) (8.7). Price: $17. CyberAuction #498, Lot #8.

7576. SWIRL. Solid core. White solid core swirl. Three deep lobes. Green band on each peak. Outer layer is a cage of yellow strands. Some pitting and haze. Light buff will reveal a beauty. Germany, circa 1870-1915. 31/32". Good(+) (7.9). Price: $17. CyberAuction #502, Lot #53.

7577. SWIRL. Solid core. Translucent yellow core. Outer layer is three orange bands and three white bands. Beauty. Germany, circa 1870-1915. 1/2". Mint (9.9). Price: $17. CyberAuction #503, Lot #21.

7578. SWIRL. Solid core. Peewee solid core swirl. Opaque white core. Three bands on it. One blue, one pink, one turquoise. Outer layer is three sets of yellow strands. Germany, circa 1870-1915. 15/32". Mint (9.9). Price: $16. CyberAuction #335, Lot #25.

7579. SWIRL. Solid core. Transparent slightly smoky tinted base. Opaque white core. Outer layer is six bands. Three are red and white, three are green and orange. Germany, circa 1870-1915. 11/16". Mint (9.7). Price: $16. CyberAuction #342, Lot #42.

7580. SWIRL. Solid core. Very odd marble. Opaque white core, covered by transparent pale pink. The core is surrounded by a cage of orange strands. No outer layer. Misshapen core. Pinhole poked into the top for about an 1/8" when the marble was molten, large dimple there. I believe this was the top of a hatpin at one point. Polished, some minor damage remains. Germany, circa 1870-1915. 11/16". Price: $16. CyberAuction #355, Lot #6.

7581. SWIRL. Solid core. Translucent white solid core swirl. Outer layer is three bands of blue and three bands of green. Very nice. Germany, circa 1870-1915. 5/8". Mint (9.8). Price: $16. CyberAuction #380, Lot #4.

7582. SWIRL. Solid core. Naked solid core swirl. Opaque white core with strands of pink, green and blue on it. No outer layer. A few pinpricks and pits. Germany, circa 1870-1915. 19/32". Near Mint(+) (8.8). Price: $15. CyberAuction #331, Lot #17.

7583. SWIRL. Solid core. Three layer. Opaque white core. Middle layer is three wide transparent pink bands. Outer layer is three sets of yellow strands. Pretty marble. Small subsurface moon, couple of tiny chips. Germany, circa 1870-1915. 3/4". Near Mint (8.5). Price: $15. CyberAuction #334, Lot #58.

7584. SWIRL. Solid core. Opaque white core. Two pink bands, one blue band, one green band on the core. Outer layer is a cage of yellow strands. Broken off nub as the bottom pontil. Germany, circa 1870-1915. 19/32". Mint (9.9). Price: $15. CyberAuction #339, Lot #4.

7585. SWIRL. Solid core. Opaque yellow core, with pink bands on it. Outer layer is four sets of yellow strands. One small chip, some tiny pits. Germany, circa 1870-1915. 21/32". Near Mint (8.5). Price: $. CyberAuction #343, Lot #53.

7586. SWIRL. Solid core. Opaque white base. Four very shallow lobes. Each has a pink band in the trough. Outer layer is four sets of yellow strands. Several tiny subsurface moons. Germany, circa 1870-1915. 11/16". Near Mint (8.6). Price: $15. CyberAuction #351, Lot #21.

7587. SWIRL. Solid core. Yellow solid core. Outer layer is six bands. Two are pink and white, two green on white, two blue on white. One tiny chip. Germany, circa 1870-1915. 23/32". Near Mint(+) (8.7). Price: $15. CyberAuction #353, Lot #36.

7588. SWIRL. Solid core. Opaque yellow core. Outer layer is four bands. Two are orange and white, two are blue and white (one is partial). Several pits. Germany, circa 1870-1915. 15/32". Near Mint(+) (8.9). Price: $15. CyberAuction #354, Lot #24.

7589. SWIRL. Solid core. Opaque white core. Three bands on it. One each of pink, blue and green. Outer layer is three sets of yellow strands. In great shape. Germany, circa 1870-1915. 1/2". Mint (9.9). Price: $15. CyberAuction #358, Lot #38.

7590. SWIRL. Solid core. Naked solid core swirl. Core is transparent blue panels alternating with translucent white panels. No outer layer. Beauty. Germany, circa 1870-1915. 17/32". Mint (9.7). Price: $15. CyberAuction #366, Lot #4.

7591. SWIRL. Solid core. Rare variant. Latticinio strands in solid core form. Core is four panels two are transparent red latticinio strands, one is transparent blue latticinio strands, one is transparent green latticinio. Outer layer is a cage of yellow strands. Overall light haze. Germany, circa 1870-1915. 17/32". Near Mint(-) (8.0). Price: $15. CyberAuction #368, Lot #20.

7592. SWIRL. Solid core. Opaque white core. Two bands of blue and two of pink on it. Outer layer is four sets of yellow strands. Two tiny chips. Germany, circa 1870-1915. 3/4". Near Mint (8.6). Price: $15. CyberAuction #368, Lot #26.

7593. SWIRL. Solid core. Opaque white core. Two pink bands, one blue, one green, on it. Outer layer is three groups of yellow strands. Germany, circa 1870-1915. 15/32". Mint (9.7). Price: $15. CyberAuction #373, Lot #4.

7594. SWIRL. Solid core. Yellow core. Two pink bands and two green bands on it. Outer layer is four sets of white strands. One tiny chip. Germany, circa 1870-1915. 1/2". Near Mint(+) (8.9). Price: $15. CyberAuction #377, Lot #23.

7595. SWIRL. Solid core. Lobed solid core. White core. Four shallow lobes. Two peaks have a green strand, two have a pink strand. Outer layer is four sets of yellow strands. Pretty. Germany, circa 1870-1915. 1/2". Mint (9.7). Price: $15. CyberAuction #399, Lot #24.

7596. SWIRL. Solid core. Core is opaque white with pink strands on it. Outer layer is cage of yellow strands. One melt spot, a couple of tiny pits. Germany, circa 1870-1915. 27/32". Near Mint(+) (8.9). Price: $15. CyberAuction #406, Lot #1.

7597. SWIRL. Solid core. Naked solid core swirl. Opaque white core. Two bands of blue and two of orange on it. One pit. Germany, circa 1870-1915. 21/32". Mint(-) (9.0). Price: $15. CyberAuction #409, Lot #35.

7598. SWIRL. Solid core. Naked solid core swirl. Core is a twice repeating pattern of transparent blue, opaque white, opaque orange, opaque yellow. Germany, circa 1870-1915. 5/8". Mint (9.7). Price: $15. CyberAuction #411, Lot #5.

7599. SWIRL. Solid core. Naked solid core swirl. Core is alternating bands of blue and white. No outer layer. Germany, circa 1870-1915. 9/16". Mint (9.7). Price: $15. CyberAuction #412, Lot #33.

7600. SWIRL. Solid core. Gorgeous. Opaque white core with some yellow on it. There are three bands of red and three of turquoise on the core. Outer layer is four sets of yellow strands. One melt pit. Germany, circa 1870-1915. 23/32". Mint(-) (9.0). Price: $15. CyberAuction #413, Lot #47.

7601. SWIRL. Solid core. Three-layer solid core swirl. White core. Middle layer is two bands of blue and two of pink. Outer layer is a cage of yellow strands. Germany, circa 1870-1915. 17/32". Mint (9.6). Price: $15. CyberAuction #438, Lot #45.

7602. SWIRL. Solid core. Opaque white core with blue bands. Outer layer is four bands of pink on yellow. Some small and tiny subsurface moons, slight haze. Germany, circa 1870-1915. 23/32". Good(+) (7.9). Price: $15. CyberAuction #451, Lot #15.

7603. SWIRL. Solid core. Semi-opaque yellow core. Outer layer is four bands. Two are orange edged by white, two are blue edged by white. Some pitting and tiny chips. Nice. Germany, circa 1870-1915. 11/16". Near Mint(+) (8.7). Price: $15. CyberAuction #453, Lot #54.

7604. SWIRL. Solid core. Opaque white core. Two panels of blue strands and two red strands. Outer layer is four sets of yellow strands. One pinprick, one sparkle. Germany, circa 1870-1915. 23/32". Mint(-) (9.2). Price: $15. CyberAuction #456, Lot #53.

7605. SWIRL. Solid core. Opaque white core. Outer layer is six bands. Three are light blue, three are pink and yellow. Melt spot and a small crease. England, possibly Germany, circa 1870-1915. 11/16". Mint(-) (9.0). Price: $15. CyberAuction #464, Lot #45.

7606. SWIRL. Solid core. Opaque white core. Bands of pink, blue and turquoise on it. Outer layer is six sets of yellow strands. Germany, circa 1870-1915. 21/32". Mint (9.7). Price: $15. CyberAuction #465, Lot #3.

7607. SWIRL. Solid core. Opaque white core. Two panels of pink and two of white on it. Outer layer is six sets of yellow strands. Germany, circa 1870-1915. Some tiny chips and flakes. 27/32". Near Mint (8.4). Price: $15. CyberAuction #465, Lot #19.

7608. SWIRL. Solid core. Nice solid core composed of three panels, all the same color scheme. Outer layer is three sets of yellow and white strands. A couple of pits and melt spots on the surface. Large fracture running through the marble. Germany, circa 1870-1915. 1-3/4". Good (7.5). Price: $15. CyberAuction #466, Lot #24.

7609. SWIRL. Solid core. Opaque white core. Two pink bands, one green band, one blue band. Outer layer is four sets of yellow strands. Germany, circa 1870-1915. 23/32". Mint (9.6). Price: $15. CyberAuction #469, Lot #25.

7610. SWIRL. Solid core. Very nice three-layer swirl. Translucent white core. Middle layer is two red bands and two blue bands. Outer layer is four bands. Two pink on white, two pink on yellow. Thick outer casing. Two tiny subsurface moons. Germany, circa 1870-1915. 27/32". Near Mint(+) (8.7). Price: $15. CyberAuction #479, Lot #3.

7611. SWIRL. Solid core. Yellow core. Two pink bands and two blue band Outer layer is four sets of white strands. One tiny air hole. Germany, circ 1870-1915. 3/4". Mint(-) (9.2). Price: $15. CyberAuction #480, Lot #35

7612. SWIRL. Solid core. Opaque white core. Two pink bands, one gree band, one blue band on the core. Outer layer is four sets of yellow strand Germany, circa 1870-1915. 11/16". Mint (9.8). Price: $15. CyberAuctio #481, Lot #4.

7613. SWIRL. Solid core. Naked solid core swirl. Three white panels c white. Two narrow blue and two narrow pink panels. One white pan missing. No outer layer. 1/2". Mint (9.7). Price: $15. CyberAuction #487 Lot #45.

7614. SWIRL. Solid core. Opaque white core. Outer layer is seven band Four blue and white, three red and green. Not uniformly distributed. Er gland, possibly Germany, circa 1870-1915. 5/8". Mint (9.8). Price: $15 CyberAuction #488, Lot #26.

7615. SWIRL. Solid core. Opaque white core. Blue and green bands on i Outer layer is four sets of orange and white strands. Several small chip Germany, circa 1870-1915. 1". Near Mint(-) (8.0). Price: $15. CyberAuctio #494, Lot #26.

7616. SWIRL. Solid core. White core. Outer layer is six bands. Three ar purple, three are light orange. One melt spot. Germany, circa 1870-191! 11/16". Mint(-) (9.2). Price: $15. CyberAuction #495, Lot #24.

7617. SWIRL. Solid core. Translucent white core. Outer layer is six band Three yellow/orange and three black. One melt chip, one sparkle. Ge many, circa 1870-1915. 29/32". Near Mint(+) (8.9). Price: $15 CyberAuction #497, Lot #8.

7618. SWIRL. Solid core. Broken cane. Opaque white core. Shrunken o one side. Outer layer is six bands. Several were broken before the cane wa completed. Interesting type. A number of small chips. Germany, circa 187(1915. 23/32". Good(-) (7.9). Price: $15. CyberAuction #497, Lot #10.

7619. SWIRL. Solid core. Opaque yellow core with green bands on i One pink strand on it, one pink strand floating above it. Outer layer is fou sets of white strands. Chunk of unmelted sand in it. One tiny sparkle. Ge many, circa 1870-1915. 25/32". Mint(-) (9.2). Price: $15. CyberAuctio #501, Lot #5.

7620. SWIRL. Solid core. Three layer. Opaque white core. Four pink band on the core. Middle layer is two green bands, two blue bands. Outer laye is a cage of yellow strands. One pit. Germany, circa 1870-1915. 5/8". Mint( ) (9.0). Price: $15. CyberAuction #503, Lot #46.

7621. SWIRL. Solid core. Opaque white core. Two bands of pink and tw of blue on it. Outer layer is four sets of yellow strands. Manufacturing col roll crease on the top. Germany, circa 1870-1915. 3/4". Mint (9.5). Price $14. CyberAuction #332, Lot #11.

7622. SWIRL. Solid core. Opaque yellow core. Four white strands on th core. Outer layer is four strands. Two bands are pink on yellow, two are blu on white. Two pits. Germany, circa 1870-1915. 21/32". Mint(-) (9.0). Price $14. CyberAuction #342, Lot #13.

7623. SWIRL. Solid core. Three layer swirl. Opaque white core. Pink band on it. Middle layer is blue and green bands. Outer layer is sets of yellov strands. A melt line on it and a dimple. Germany, circa 1870-1915. 21/32 Mint(-) (9.0). Price: $14. CyberAuction #372, Lot #2.

7624. SWIRL. Solid core. Core is partial. Orange and blue on white. Oute layer is two yellow strands. From near an end of the cane. Germany, circa 1870-1915. 5/8". Mint (9.7). Price: $14. CyberAuction #380, Lot #43.

7625. SWIRL. Solid core. Opaque white base. One wide olive band on it Outer layer is two blue bands and one red one. Super. Germany, circa 1870-1915. 5/8". Mint (9.7). Price: $14. CyberAuction #381, Lot #10.

7626. SWIRL. Solid core. Opaque white core. Two sets of blue bands and two of red, on the white. Also, one yellow band on the white. Outer laye is a cage of yellow strands. One melt chip, one sparkle. Germany, circa 1870-1915. 25/32". Near Mint(+) (8.7). Price: $14. CyberAuction #386 Lot #16.

7627. SWIRL. Solid core. Three layer swirl from near an end of the cane Opaque white core with pink bands on it. Middle layer is four blue bands Outer layer is three sets of white strands and two sets of yellow strands One other set of yellow strands is missing. Small air hole, small flake. Ger many, circa 1870-1915. 3/4". Near Mint(+) (8.8). Price: $14. CyberAuctior #406, Lot #3.

7628. SWIRL. Solid core. Three-layer swirl. Opaque white core. Middle layer is four light pink bands and four blue bands. Outer layer is two sets o yellow strands. Tiny flake and tiny chips. Germany, circa 1870-1915. 25, 32". Good(+) (7.9). Price: $14. CyberAuction #413, Lot #16.

7629. SWIRL. Solid core. Semi-opaque white core. Outer layer is six bands. Three light blue, three light red. Germany, circa 1870-1915. 9/16". Min (9.6). Price: $14. CyberAuction #448, Lot #1.

7630. SWIRL. Solid core. Yellow solid core. Outer layer is six bands. Three blue and three white. Some pits and sparkles. Germany, circa 1870-1915 25/32". Near Mint (8.7). Price: $14. CyberAuction #473, Lot #41.

7631. SWIRL. Solid core. Opaque white core. Three pink and yellow bands, three green bands. Outer layer is three sets of yellow strands. Polished. 1-7/ 16". Price: $14. CyberAuction #477, Lot #2.

7632. SWIRL. Solid core. Three-layer swirl. Opaque white core. Middle layer is four light pink bands and four blue bands. Outer layer is four sets o yellow strands. Tiny flake and tiny chips. Germany, circa 1870-1915. 25/ 32". Good(+) (7.9). Price: $14. CyberAuction #482, Lot #28.

7633. SWIRL. Solid core. White solid core swirl. Two pink bands, one blue band, one green band, on the core. Outer layer is four sets of white strands. Germany, circa 1870-1915. 15/32". Mint (9.7). Price: $14. CyberAuction #503, Lot #31.

7634. SWIRL. Solid core. Opaque white core. Outer layer is three wide orange bands and three wide yellow bands. Cold crease on it. Some minor pitting. Germany, circa 1870-1915. 11/16". Mint(-) (9.0). Price: $13. CyberAuction #331, Lot #6.

7635. SWIRL. Solid core. Three layer solid core. Nice. Translucent white base. Middle layer is four bands. Two are orange, two are blue. Outer layer is four sets of yellow strands. One small chip. Germany, circa 1870-1915. 11/16". Near Mint(+) (8.7). Price: $13. CyberAuction #338, Lot #41.

7636. SWIRL. Solid core. Opaque white core. Two bands of pink, one of blue and one of green on it. Core is flattened on one side. Outer layer is a cage of yellow strands. Pretty. Nub bottom pontil. Germany, circa 1870-1915. 9/16". Mint (9.9). Price: $13. CyberAuction #340, Lot #58.

7637. SWIRL. Solid core. Core is opaque yellow with some pink and blue on it. Some open areas. Outer layer is three sets of white and yellow strands. Germany, circa 1870-1915. 1/2". Mint (9.9). Price: $13. CyberAuction #342, Lot #3.

7638. SWIRL. Solid core. Opaque white core. Three deep lobes. Pink band in each lobe. Outer layer is three blue bands, mirroring the trough peaks, and three sets of yellow strands, mirroring the lobe troughs. Several pits and tiny chips. Germany, circa 1870-1915. 11/16". Near Mint (8.5). Price: $13. CyberAuction #344, Lot #38.

7639. SWIRL. Solid core. End of cane marble. Nice solid core. Flipped over and melted at the very top. Nub bottom pontil. Nice first off cane. Germany, circa 1870-1915. 5/8". Near Mint(-) (8.1). Price: $13. CyberAuction #349, Lot #44.

7640. SWIRL. Solid core. Opaque white core. Outer layer is five bands. Two are green and yellow, two are red and white. One red and white missing. Slightly olive green tint to the glass. Germany, circa 1870-1915. 21/32". Mint (9.7). Price: $13. CyberAuction #350, Lot #7.

7641. SWIRL. Solid core. Three layer solid core. Opaque white core. Middle layer is a complex pattern of four bands in various colors. Outer layer is four sets of yellow strands. One small chip, several tiny chips. Germany, circa 1870-1915. 5/8". Near Mint (8.6). Price: $13. CyberAuction #352, Lot #40.

7642. SWIRL. Solid core. Beauty. Opaque white core. Four wide transparent bands on the core. Two are pink, two are turquoise. Outer layer is two sets of yellow strands and two sets of white strands. One very tiny chip. Germany, circa 1870-1915. 11/16". Near Mint(+) (8.9). Price: $13. CyberAuction #357, Lot #23.

7643. SWIRL. Solid core. Opaque white core. Six panels of transparent blue on it. Outer layer is six bands of red. Several tiny pits and chips. Germany, circa 1870-1915. 3/4". Near Mint (8.3). Price: $13. CyberAuction #358, Lot #59.

7644. SWIRL. Solid core. Opaque white core. Three pink strands on it. Outer layer is three yellow strands, alternating with three blue, green and white strands. One subsurface moon. Germany, circa 1870-1915. 21/32". Near Mint(+) (8.9). Price: $13. CyberAuction #366, Lot #13.

7645. SWIRL. Solid core. Three layer marble. Opaque white core. Two pink bands and two blue bands floating above the core. Outer layer is two yellow strands and two pairs of yellow strands. Germany, circa 1870-1915. 9/16". Mint (9.9). Price: $13. CyberAuction #368, Lot #14.

7646. SWIRL. Solid core. Opaque white core with orange and gray bands. Outer layer is three sets of white strands. Very nice. Germany, circa 1870-1915. 9/16". Mint (9.7). Price: $13. CyberAuction #388, Lot #28.

7647. SWIRL. Solid core. Naked solid core swirl. Core is alternating bands of transparent blue, opaque yellow and opaque white. Several small and tiny chips. Germany, circa 1870-1915. 13/16". Good(+) (7.7). Price: $13. CyberAuction #397, Lot #19.

7648. SWIRL. Solid core. Opaque white core, not completely closed. Outer layer is four bands. Two are red, yellow and blue. Two are red, yellow and lavender. Very nice. Germany, circa 1870-1915. 21/32". Mint (9.9). Price: $13. CyberAuction #416, Lot #39.

7649. SWIRL. Solid core. Three layer swirl from near an end of the cane. Opaque white core with pink bands on it. Middle layer is four blue bands. Outer layer is three sets of white strands and two sets of yellow strands. One other set of yellow strands is missing. Small air hole, small flake. Germany, circa 1870-1915. 3/4". Near Mint(+) (8.8). Price: $13. CyberAuction #426, Lot #2.

7650. SWIRL. Solid core. Peewee. Opaque white core. Two bands of purple, two of orange. Outer layer is stretched air bubbles, but no strands or bands. Naked core. Germany, circa 1870-1915. 17/32". Mint (9.9). Price: $13. CyberAuction #440, Lot #13.

7651. SWIRL. Solid core. Opaque white core with orange and gray bands. Outer layer is three sets of white strands. Very nice. Germany, circa 1870-1915. 15/32". Mint (9.7). Price: $13. CyberAuction #440, Lot #17.

7652. SWIRL. Solid core. Opaque white core. Two pink bands on it and two turquoise bands. Outer layer is a cage of white strands. Distinct reverse twist at the top. Some scratches on one side. Germany, circa 1870-1915. 21/32". Near Mint(+) (8.9). Price: $13. CyberAuction #451, Lot #48.

7653. SWIRL. Solid core. Core is bands of translucent white, green and blue. Outer layer is four sets of red strands. Germany, circa 1870-1915. 1/2". Mint (9.7). Price: $13. CyberAuction #479, Lot #20.

7654. SWIRL. Solid core. Gorgeous. Opaque white core with some yellow on it. There are three bands of red and three of turquoise on the core. Outer layer is four sets of yellow strands. One melt spot. Germany, circa 1870-1915. 23/32". Mint(-) (9.2). Price: $13. CyberAuction #495, Lot #20.

7655. SWIRL. Solid core. Core is opaque white with strands of light green, pink and pale blue. Not completely closed. Outer layer is three sets of yellow strands. One melt hole and one small subsurface moon. Germany, circa 1870-1915. 11/16". Near Mint (8.5). Price: $12. CyberAuction #339, Lot #1.

7656. SWIRL. Solid core. Opaque white core. Four orange bands on it. Outer layer is three blue bands and three green bands. Pretty. One pinprick.

Germany, circa 1870-1915. 1/2". Near Mint(+) (8.9). Price: $12. CyberAuction #360, Lot #22.

7657. SWIRL. Solid core. Opaque white core. Outer layer is eight bands. Four pink, two green, two blue. Two tiny subsurface moons. Germany, circa 1870-1915. 1/2". Near Mint(+) (8.7). Price: $12. CyberAuction #364, Lot #48.

7658. SWIRL. Solid core. Core is a combination of opaque white, transparent pink, green and yellow. Outer layer is three white strands. Germany, circa 1870-1915. 15/32". Mint (9.9). Price: $12. CyberAuction #368, Lot #3.

7659. SWIRL. Solid core. Core is alternating narrow bands of transparent blue and opaque white. Outer layer is three sets of yellow strands. Nice marble. Core is misshapen. Germany, circa 1870-1915. 19/32". Mint (9.5). Price: $12. CyberAuction #368, Lot #39.

7660. SWIRL. Solid core. Four panel core. White core. Two panels of pink strands, one of blue strands, one of green strands. Outer layer is two sets of yellow strands and two sets of white. Some surface scratching. Germany, circa 1870-1915. 21/32". Near Mint(+) (8.9). Price: $12. CyberAuction #383, Lot #15.

7661. SWIRL. Solid core. Nice three-layer solid core swirl. Core is yellow. Has four panels of three green strands on it. Middle layer is four sets of white strands. Outer layer is four bands of blue and pink on white. Very well made, great construction. Two melt spots, some haze. Germany, circa 1870-1915. 3/4". Near Mint(-) (8.2). Price: $12. CyberAuction #399, Lot #37.

7662. SWIRL. Solid core. Core is a three panel design of blue, white, pink and yellow. Outer layer is a cage of yellow strands. Beauty. Germany, circa 1870-1915. 19/32". Mint (9.7). Price: $12. CyberAuction #408, Lot #5.

7663. SWIRL. Solid core. Opaque white core. One wide turquoise panel, two sets of two red bands, on it. Missing another turquoise panel. Outer layer is four sets of yellow strands. One pinprick. Germany, circa 1870-1915. 23/32". Mint(-) (9.2). Price: $12. CyberAuction #409, Lot #22.

7664. SWIRL. Solid core. Opaque white core. One wide turquoise panel, two sets of two red bands, on it. Missing another turquoise panel. Outer layer is four sets of yellow strands. One pinprick. Germany, circa 1870-1915. 23/32". Mint(-) (9.2). Price: $12. CyberAuction #426, Lot #8.

7665. SWIRL. Solid core. Semi-opaque white base. Blue and red strands on it. Outer layer is four sets of yellow strands. Germany, circa 1870-1915. 15/32". Mint (9.8). Price: $12. CyberAuction #428, Lot #57.

7666. SWIRL. Solid core. Nice three-layer solid core swirl. Core is yellow. Has four panels of three green strands on it. Middle layer is four sets of white strands. Outer layer is four bands of blue and pink on white. Very well made, great construction. Two melt spots, some haze. Germany, circa 1870-1915. 3/4". Near Mint(-) (8.2). Price: $12. CyberAuction #434, Lot #49.

7667. SWIRL. Solid core. Opaque white core. Two bands of pink, one green, one blue. Outer layer is two sets of yellow and two sets of white strands. Germany, circa 1870-1915. 11/16". Mint (9.9). Price: $12. CyberAuction #436, Lot #24.

7668. SWIRL. Solid core. Opaque white core. Three bands on it, one blue, one red and one turquoise. Outer layer is three sets of yellow strands. A number of tiny chips. Germany, circa 1870-1915. 3/4". Near Mint (8.3). Price: $12. CyberAuction #451, Lot #55.

7669. SWIRL. Solid core. Opaque white core. Three lobes. Lobe troughs have blue bands, lobe peaks have pink bands. Outer layer is three sets of yellow strands. Some scratching. Germany, circa 1870-1915. 17/32". Mint(-) (9.0). Price: $12. CyberAuction #456, Lot #14.

7670. SWIRL. Solid core. Opaque white core. Outer layer is six bands. Three yellow, three red. One pit. England, possibly Germany, circa 1870-1915. 11/16". Near Mint(+) (8.9). Price: $12. CyberAuction #463, Lot #32.

7671. SWIRL. Solid core. Opaque white core. Outer layer is seven bands. Four blue and white, three red and green. Not uniformly distributed. England, possibly Germany, circa 1870-1915. 5/8". Mint (9.8). Price: $12. CyberAuction #464, Lot #39.

7672. SWIRL. Solid core. Opaque white core. One wide turquoise panel, two sets of two red bands, on it. Missing another turquoise panel. Outer layer is four sets of yellow strands. One pinprick. Germany, circa 1870-1915. 23/32". Mint(-) (9.2). Price: $12. CyberAuction #466, Lot #36.

7673. SWIRL. Solid core. Opaque white core. Outer layer is six bands. Three are red. Three are blue and yellow. Two melt pits. Germany, possibly England, circa 1870-1915. 23/32". Mint(-) (9.0). Price: $12. CyberAuction #493, Lot #58.

7674. SWIRL. Solid core. Opaque white core. Two pink bands, one blue band, one green band, on the core. Outer layer is four sets of yellow strands. Germany, circa 1870-1915. 5/8". Mint (9.7). Price: $12. CyberAuction #503, Lot #50.

7675. SWIRL. Solid core. White solid core swirl. Outer layer is three pink and white narrow bands and three blue and white narrow bands. Small chip and a tiny pit. Germany, circa 1870-1915. 21/32". Near Mint(+) (8.7). Price: $11. CyberAuction #332, Lot #8.

7676. SWIRL. Solid core. White core. Four outer bands. Two pink, one blue, one green. One pit. Germany, circa 1870-1915. 5/8". Mint(-) (9.0). Price: $11. CyberAuction #346, Lot #38.

7677. SWIRL. Solid core. Opaque white core. Two blue and two green bands on it. Outer layer is four pairs of white strands. One tiny subsurface moon. Germany, circa 1870-1915. 1/2". Near Mint(+) (8.9). Price: $11. CyberAuction #364, Lot #3.

7678. SWIRL. Solid core. Opaque white core. Three bands on it, one blue, one red and one turquoise. Outer layer is three sets of yellow strands. A number of tiny chips. Germany, circa 1870-1915. 3/4". Near Mint (8.3). Price: $11. CyberAuction #372, Lot #1.

7679. SWIRL. Solid core. Odd three-layer solid core. Core is a thick layer of blue on white. Middle layer is a cage of white strands. Outer layer is three bands of pink on white. Reverse twist. Several tiny and small chips. Germany, circa 1870-1915. 19/32". Near Mint(-) (8.0). Price: $11. CyberAuction #372, Lot #22.
7680. SWIRL. Solid core. Three layer. Opaque white core. Strands of pink, blue and turquoise floating above it. Outer layer is a cage of yellow strands. Overall light scratches, oddly ground pontil. Germany, circa 1870-1915. 11/16". Near Mint (8.6). Price: $11. CyberAuction #410, Lot #25.
7681. SWIRL. Solid core. Three-layer solid core. Opaque white core. Middle layer is four blue bands and four pink bands. Outer layer is a cage of white strands. One melt spot and a pinprick. Germany, circa 1870-1915. 23/32". Mint(-) (9.0). Price: $11. CyberAuction #413, Lot #13.
7682. SWIRL. Solid core. Three-layer solid core swirl. Core is opaque white with pink bands. Middle layer is a cage of yellow strands. Outer layer is four bands. Two are pink and green on "lumpy" yellow, two are pink and blue on white. Some tiny chips. Germany, circa 1870-1915. 11/16". Near Mint(-) (8.0). Price: $11. CyberAuction #415, Lot #50.
7683. SWIRL. Solid core. Very odd core. I suspect it is a solid core that was not completely closed, although it could be a single ribbon. Three-layer marble anyhow. White core. Middle layer is a cage of blue, red and green bands. Outer layer is a cage of yellow strands. Germany, circa 1870-1915. Two pinpricks. 11/16". Mint(-) (9.0). Price: $11. CyberAuction #426, Lot #41.
7684. SWIRL. Solid core. Core is a repeating pattern of pink, green, blue and white. Outer layer is four sets of yellow strands. Germany, circa 1870-1915. 15/32". Mint (9.7). Price: $11. CyberAuction #427, Lot #16.
7685. SWIRL. Solid core. Base glass is tinted very lightly blue. Opaque white core. Middle layer is alternating blue and pink bands. Outer layer is two sets of white strands and two sets of yellow strands. Slightly flat top. Germany, circa 1870-1915. 5/8". Mint (9.5). Price: $11. CyberAuction #433, Lot #41.
7686. SWIRL. Solid core. White core. Two pink bands, one blue band, one green band on it. Outer layer is four sets of yellow strands. One melt spot. Germany, circa 1870-1915. 1/2". Mint (9.6). Price: $11. CyberAuction #436, Lot #2.
7687. SWIRL. Solid core. Opaque white core. Four panels on the core. Two are red bands, one is turquoise bands, one is blue bands. Outer layer is a wide cage of yellow strands. Some tiny chips and overall pits. Germany, circa 1870-1915. 27/32". Good(+) (7.9). Price: $11. CyberAuction #437, Lot #45.
7688. SWIRL. Solid core. This is a first off cane marble. I'm guessing it was a solid core. Transparent lightly blue tinted base. There is a tiny piece of yellow and blue that is folded over in the bottom half of the marble. Surface is frosted. 15/32". Good(+) (7.9). Price: $11. CyberAuction #441, Lot #38.
7689. SWIRL. Solid core. Lobed solid core swirl. Opaque white base. Three deep lobes. Pink band in each trough, blue band on each peak. Outer layer is three sets of yellow strands. A few tiny flakes and some very light haze. Germany, circa 1870-1915. 23/32". Near Mint(-) (8.0). Price: $11. CyberAuction #454, Lot #10.
7690. SWIRL. Solid core. Transparent clear base. Opaque white core. Six outer bands. Three yellow, one light green, one blue, one red. One tiny chip. England, possibly Germany, circa 1870-1915. 11/16". Near Mint(+) (8.9). Price: $11. CyberAuction #461, Lot #44.
7691. SW!RL. Solid core. Opaque white core. Pink and blue bands on it. Outer layer is a cage of fine white strands. Some pinpricking. Germany, circa 1870-1915. 9/16". Near Mint(+) (8.9). Price: $11. CyberAuction #468, Lot #41.
7692. SWIRL. Solid core. English colors. Core is only partially closed. Bands of red, green, white and blue. Outer layer is two sets of white and yellow strands. At least one additional set is missing. England, possibly Germany, circa 1870-1915. 5/8". Mint (9.7). Price: $11. CyberAuction #483, Lot #21.
7693. SWIRL. Solid core. Hard to find blue solid core. Some blue bands on the core. Outer layer is six bands. Three orange, three light yellow. Several pits on one side. Nice. England, possibly Germany, circa 1870-1915. 21/32". Near Mint (8.6). Price: $11. CyberAuction #485, Lot #8.
7694. SWIRL. Solid core. Semi-opaque yellow core. Outer layer is six bands. Three are transparent blue, three are opaque white. Several melt chips. Germany, circa 1870-1915. 25/32". Near Mint(+) (8.7). Price: $11. CyberAuction #498, Lot #60.
7695. SWIRL. Solid core. White core. Two pink, one green, one blue band on it. Outer layer is a cage of white strands. From near the end of the cane, part of the outer layer ends before the bottom of the marble. A couple of sparkles. Germany, circa 1870-1915. 3/4". Near Mint(+) (8.7). Price: $11. CyberAuction #501, Lot #10.
7696. SWIRL. Solid core. Translucent white solid core. Outer layer is four bands. Each is pink on white, edged by blue. Pinprick. Germany, circa 1870-1915. 1/2". Mint(-) (9.1). Price: $11. CyberAuction #504, Lot #36.
7697. SWIRL. Solid core. Opaque white core. Four bands on the core. Two pink, one blue, one green. Outer layer is a cage of yellow strands. Germany, circa 1870-1915. 5/8". Mint (9.8). Price: $11. CyberAuction #504, Lot #37.
7698. SWIRL. Solid core. Three layer solid core swirl. Opaque white core. Middle layer is four bands. Each consists of four strands. Two bands are pink, one blue, one green. Outer layer is three sets of yellow strands and three sets of white strands. Tiny pit and some overall light scratches. Germany, circa 1870-1915. 3/4". Near Mint(+) (8.8). Price: $11. CyberAuction #505, Lot #6.
7699. SWIRL. Solid core. Three layer. Opaque white core. Middle layer is pink, blue and green bands. Outer layer is four sets of yellow strands. One melt spot. Germany, circa 1870-1915. 5/8". Mint(-) (9.1). Price: $11. CyberAuction #505, Lot #46.
7700. SWIRL. Solid core. Opaque white core. Four panels on the core. Each consists of two bands. Two panels of pink, one of blue, one of turquoise. Outer layer is four sets of yellow strands. Beauty. Germany, circa 1870-1915. 11/16". Mint (9.7). Price: $10. CyberAuction #333, Lot #17.
7701. SWIRL. Solid core. Opaque white core. Outer layer is four bands. Two are transparent pink on white and two are transparent blue on white. One pit. Beauty. Germany, circa 1870-1915. 19/32". Mint (9.5). Price: $10. CyberAuction #338, Lot #9.
7702. SWIRL. Solid core. Three layer solid core. Fascinating marble. Transparent orange/red core. Middle layer is a cage of white strands floating just above the core. Outer layer is four bands. Two are green and yellow. Two are blue and white. Frosted surface. Germany, circa 1870-1915. 5/8". Good(+) (7.9). Price: $10. CyberAuction #349, Lot #1.
7703. SWIRL. Solid core. This is a first off cane marble. I'm guessing it was a solid core. Transparent lightly blue tinted base. There is a tiny piece of yellow and blue that is folded over in the bottom half of the marble. Surface is frosted. 15/32". Good(+) (7.9). Price: $10. CyberAuction #349, Lot #6.
7704. SWIRL. Solid core. Opaque white core. Two pink bands on it and two turquoise bands. Outer layer is a cage of white strands. Distinct reverse twist at the top. Some scratches on one side. Germany, circa 1870-1915. 21/32". Near Mint(+) (8.9). Price: $10. CyberAuction #367, Lot #44.
7705. SWIRL. Solid core. Opaque white core. Has two sets of pink bands, a set of green bands and a set of blue bands on the core. Outer layer is a cage of yellow strands. Some pinpricks. Germany, circa 1870-1915. 23/32". Near Mint(+) (8.7). Price: $10. CyberAuction #368, Lot #4.
7706. SWIRL. Solid core. Opaque white core with eight bands of color on it. Outer layer is a cage of yellow strands. Couple of pits and a rust spot. Germany, circa 1870-1915. 9/16". Near Mint(+) (8.8). Price: $10. CyberAuction #385, Lot #21.
7707. SWIRL. Solid core. English type colors. Core is two sets of repeating bands. White, blue, yellow, orange. Outer layer is four sets of yellow strands. Several small chips and small subsurface moons. Germany, circa 1870-1915. 7/8". Good(+) (7.9). Price: $10. CyberAuction #406, Lot #6.
7708. SWIRL. Solid core. Very odd core. I suspect it is a solid core that was not completely closed, although it could be a single ribbon. Three-layer marble anyhow. White core. Middle layer is a cage of blue, red and green bands. Outer layer is a cage of yellow strands. Germany, circa 1870-1915. Two pinpricks. 11/16". Mint(-) (9.0). Price: $10. CyberAuction #409, Lot #51.
7709. SWIRL. Solid core. Opaque white core. Two panels of blue strands and two of red strands. Outer layer is four sets of yellow strands. One pinprick, one sparkle. Germany, circa 1870-1915. 23/32". Mint(-) (9.2). Price: $10. CyberAuction #413, Lot #8.
7710. SWIRL. Solid core. Naked solid core swirl. Core is alternating panels of orange, blue, green and white. One dirt line and a tiny subsurface moon. Germany, circa 1870-1915. 1/2". Near Mint(+) (8.7). Price: $10. CyberAuction #419, Lot #8.
7711. SWIRL. Solid core. Three-layer. Excellent marble. Opaque white core. Middle layer is two red bands, one blue band and one green band. Outer layer is four sets of yellow strands. Dirt line, several small subsurface moons and some pitting. Germany, circa 1870-1915. 7/8". Near Mint(-) (8.0). Price: $10. CyberAuction #427, Lot #14.
7712. SWIRL. Solid core. Opaque white core. Two pink panels, one blue band, one green panel, on it. Outer layer is four sets of yellow strands. Germany, circa 1870-1915. 23/32". Mint (9.6). Price: $10. CyberAuction #431, Lot #36.
7713. SWIRL. Solid core. English type colors. Core is two sets of repeating bands. White, blue, yellow, orange. Outer layer is four sets of yellow strands. Several small chips and small subsurface moons. Germany, circa 1870-1915. 7/8". Good(+) (7.9). Price: $10. CyberAuction #437, Lot #10.
7714. SWIRL. Solid core. From near an end of the cane. Opaque yellow core. Shoved over to one side of the marble. Outer layer is three bands. One is blue and white, one is green and white (narrow), one is just a white strand. Some pinpricks. Germany, circa 1870-1915. 13/16". Near Mint(+) (8.8). Price: $10. CyberAuction #438, Lot #32.
7715. SWIRL. Solid core. Three-layer marble. Opaque white core. Middle layer is three wide transparent pink bands alternating with three wide transparent blue bands. Outer layer is three sets of yellow strands. Some pitting. Germany, circa 1870-1915. 13/16". Near Mint(+) (8.7). Price: $10. CyberAuction #458, Lot #43.
7716. SWIRL. Solid core. Opaque white core. Outer layer is six bands. Three are red and yellow. Three are blue and yellow. One tiny pit. Germany, possibly England, circa 1870-1915. 9/16". Mint(-) (9.2). Price: $10. CyberAuction #459, Lot #30.
7717. SWIRL. Solid core. Fat opaque white core. Blue and green bands on it. Outer layer is four sets of white and orange strands. Some chips. Germany, circa 1870-1915. 1". Good(+) (7.9). Price: $10. CyberAuction #461, Lot #34.
7718. SWIRL. Solid core. Naked solid core swirl. Core is eight bands. Two each of white, orange, light yellow and transparent purple. No outer layer. A number of small chips. Germany, circa 1870-1915. 31/32". Good(+) (7.9). Price: $10. CyberAuction #464, Lot #9.
7719. SWIRL. Solid core. Rare. Three-layer, three-lobed solid core. Opaque white core. Three very deep lobes. Green band on each peak. Middle layer is three bands of pink on yellow, mirroring the troughs. Outer layer is three sets of yellow strands, mirroring the peaks. A couple of large chips, haze. Germany, circa 1870-1915. 1-1/8". Good(-) (7.2). Price: $10. CyberAuction #468, Lot #29.

7720. SWIRL. Solid core. Opaque white core. Two green bands, two orange bands, on the core. Yellow strands on each band. Outer layer is four sets of yellow strands. Germany, circa 1870-1915. 23/32". Mint (9.5). Price: $10. CyberAuction #497, Lot #48.

7721. SWIRL. Solid core. Opaque white core with blue strands. Six outer bands. Germany, circa 1870-1915. 17/32". Mint (9.9). Price: $10. CyberAuction #500, Lot #20.

7722. SWIRL. Solid core. Yellow core with pink strands on it. Outer layer is a cage of white strands. Cold roll line on top. Germany, circa 1870-1915. 11/16". Mint (9.5). Price: $10. CyberAuction #502, Lot #6.

7723. SWIRL. Solid core. White solid core. Pink, blue and yellow bands on it. Outer layer is four sets of white strands. A couple of tiny chips. Germany, circa 1870-1915. 19/32". Near Mint(+) (8.7). Price: $9. CyberAuction #334, Lot #10.

7724. SWIRL. Solid core. Three layer solid core swirl. Opaque white core with pink bans on it. Three blue strands form the middle layer. Two sets of yellow strands form the outer layer (one set is missing. Surface has a little rubbing on it. Germany, circa 1870-1915. 17/32". Mint(-) (9.0). Price: $9. CyberAuction #340, Lot #42.

7725. SWIRL. Solid core. Three layer marble. Opaque white core with narrow pink bands on it. Three blue narrow bands as the middle layer. Outer layer is three sets of yellow strands. Tight twist. Germany, circa 1870-1915. 1/2". Mint (9.7). Price: $9. CyberAuction #368, Lot #34.

7726. SWIRL. Solid core. Four-lobed solid core swirl. Opaque white core. Four lobes. Pink band in each trough. Nothing on peaks. Outer layer is four sets of yellow strands. One rough area. Germany, circa 1870-1915. 9/16". Near Mint(+) (8.7). Price: $9. CyberAuction #420, Lot #3.

7727. SWIRL. Solid core. Opaque white base. Pink and green bands on the core. Outer layer is a cage of yellow strands. Several tiny chips. Germany, circa 1870-1915. 3/4". Near Mint(+) (8.1). Price: $9. CyberAuction #458, Lot #51.

7728. SWIRL. Solid core. Naked solid core swirl. Core is alternating bands of white and transparent blue. No outer layer. Surface has some pits and scratching. Germany, circa 1870-1915. 23/32". Near Mint (8.6). Price: $9. CyberAuction #460, Lot #20.

7729. SWIRL. Solid core. Opaque white core. Outer layer is six blue bands and six white bands. Polished with fake pontils. Germany, circa 1870-1915. 3/4". Price: $9. CyberAuction #487, Lot #26.

7730. SWIRL. Solid core. Opaque white core. Pink and blue bands on it. Outer layer is four sets of yellow strands. Cold roll line. Tiny melt spot. Germany, circa 1870-1915. 21/32". Mint (9.5). Price: $9. CyberAuction #492, Lot #42.

7731. SWIRL. Solid core. Naked solid core swirl. Core is eight bands. Two each of white, orange, light yellow and transparent purple. No outer layer. A number of small chips. Germany, circa 1870-1915. 31/32". Good(+) (7.9). Price: $9. CyberAuction #496, Lot #14.

7732. SWIRL. Solid core. Very nice. Semi-opaque white core. Outer layer is three red bands and three light green bands. Slightly misshapen. Germany, circa 1870-1915. 5/8". Mint(-) (9.2). Price: $9. CyberAuction #499, Lot #39.

7733. SWIRL. Solid core. Four panel core. Each is white. Two have pink strands on them, one has blue, one has turquoise strands. Outer layer is four sets of yellow strands. Germany, circa 1870-1915. 9/16". Mint (9.8). Price: $9. CyberAuction #504, Lot #1.

7734. SWIRL. Solid core. Translucent white solid core. Outer layer is four bands. Each is green and orange. Tiny flake, pinprick and a sparkle. Germany, circa 1870-1915. 27/32". Near Mint(+) (8.7). Price: $9. CyberAuction #505, Lot #38.

7735. SWIRL. Solid core. Opaque white core. Two wide bands of blue and two wide bands of pink. Outer layer is a cage of yellow strands. Tiny moon, pit and a sparkle. Germany, circa 1870-1915. 21/32". Near Mint(+) (8.9). Price: $8. CyberAuction #332, Lot #37.

7736. SWIRL. Solid core. Opaque white core. Four panels on it. Two wide pink, one narrow blue, one narrow green. Almost no white showing. Outer layer is four sets of white strands. A couple of tiny subsurface moons. Germany, circa 1870-1915. 9/16". Near Mint (8.6). Price: $8. CyberAuction #335, Lot #6.

7737. SWIRL. Solid core. White core. Two turquoise bands and two pink bands on it. Outer layer is four sets of yellow strands. Some scratching. Germany, circa 1870-1915. 15/32". Near Mint(+) (8.8). Price: $8. CyberAuction #344, Lot #3.

7738. SWIRL. Solid core. Opaque white core with three wide red bands on it. Outer layer is three narrow green on yellow bands. Overall haziness. Germany, circa 1870-1915. 5/8". Near Mint(-) (8.1). Price: $8. CyberAuction #346, Lot #47.

7739. SWIRL. Solid core. White core. Outer layer is a cage of alternating transparent green strands and opaque yellow strands. Some pitting. Germany, circa 1870-1915. 5/8". Near Mint (8.6). Price: $8. CyberAuction #355, Lot #49.

7740. SWIRL. Solid core. Opaque white core with blue bands. Outer layer is four bands of pink on yellow. Some small and tiny subsurface moons, slight haze. Germany, circa 1870-1915. 23/32". Good(+) (7.9). Price: $8. CyberAuction #364, Lot #15.

7741. SWIRL. Solid core. Naked solid core swirl. Four panels of orange, white, blue and yellow. One tiny chip. Germany, circa 1870-1915. 15/32". Near Mint(+) (8.7). Price: $8. CyberAuction #367, Lot #46.

7742. SWIRL. Solid core. Core is a complex repeating pattern of blue and green on white, separated by orange. Outer layer is two sets of yellow strands, there are probably two other sets missing. Two tiny subsurface moons right on the top pontil. Germany, circa 1870-1915. 9/16". Near Mint(+) (8.9). Price: $8. CyberAuction #368, Lot #1.

7743. SWIRL. Solid core. Opaque white core. Three shallow lobes. A pink band in each trough, a blue band floating above each peak. Outer layer is three sets of white strands. Some pinpricks. Germany, circa 1870-1915. 9/16". Near Mint(+) (8.8). Price: $8. CyberAuction #403, Lot #2.

7744. SWIRL. Solid core. Opaque white core. Four panels on the core. Two are red bands, one is turquoise bands, one is blue bands. Outer layer is a wide cage of yellow strands. Some tiny chips and overall pits. Germany, circa 1870-1915. 27/32". Good(+) (7.9). Price: $8. CyberAuction #407, Lot #5.

7745. SWIRL. Solid core. Opaque white core. Two panels of pink strands, one panel of blue strands, one panel of green strands. Outer layer is a cage of yellow strands. Some light haze. Germany, circa 1870-1915. 23/32". Near Mint (8.4). Price: $8. CyberAuction #407, Lot #18.

7746. SWIRL. Solid core. Opaque white core with one band each on it of yellow, pink, blue and green. Outer layer is two sets of yellow strands and two sets of white strands. Germany, circa 1870-1915. 17/32". Mint (9.7). Price: $8. CyberAuction #411, Lot #7.

7747. SWIRL. Solid core. Naked solid core swirl. Core is alternating bands of white and transparent blue. No outer layer. Surface has some pits and scratching. Germany, circa 1870-1915. 23/32". Near Mint (8.6). Price: $8. CyberAuction #419, Lot #52.

7748. SWIRL. Solid core. Opaque white core. Outer layer is three transparent pink bands and three narrow opaque yellow strands. Pit. Germany, circa 1870-1915. 5/8". Mint(-) (9.1). Price: $8. CyberAuction #432, Lot #54.

7749. SWIRL. Solid core. Very nice. Semi-opaque white core. Outer layer is three red bands and three light green bands. Slightly misshapen. Germany, circa 1870-1915. 5/8". Mint(-) (9.2). Price: $8. CyberAuction #433, Lot #7.

7750. SWIRL. Solid core. White core. One band each of green, blue and red on it. Outer layer is three sets of yellow strands. One pit. Germany, circa 1870-1915. 9/16". Mint(-) (9.0). Price: $8. CyberAuction #435, Lot #40.

7751. SWIRL. Solid core. Very nice. Semi-opaque white core. Outer layer is three red bands and three light green bands. Slightly misshapen. Germany, circa 1870-1915. 5/8". Mint(-) (9.2). Price: $8. CyberAuction #453, Lot #41.

7752. SWIRL. Solid core. Very nice. Semi-opaque white core. Outer layer is three red bands and three light green bands. Slightly misshapen. Germany, circa 1870-1915. 5/8". Mint(-) (9.2). Price: $8. CyberAuction #478, Lot #33.

7753. SWIRL. Solid core. Opaque white core with one band each on it of yellow, pink, blue and green. Outer layer is two sets of yellow strands and two sets of white strands. Germany, circa 1870-1915. 17/32". Mint (9.7). Price: $8. CyberAuction #484, Lot #34.

7754. SWIRL. Solid core. Opaque white core. Three pink bands and four blue strands on the core. Outer layer is three sets of white strands. A couple of sparkles. Germany, circa 1870-1915. 19/32". Mint (-) (9.0). Price: $8. CyberAuction #498, Lot #32.

7755. SWIRL. Solid core. Translucent white solid core. Outer layer is four bands of blue, red and yellow. One pit. Germany, circa 1870-1915. 1/2". Mint(-) (9.0). Price: $8. CyberAuction #502, Lot #1.

7756. SWIRL. Solid core. Three-layer marble. White solid core swirl. Middle layer is four pink bands, two blue and two green. Outer layer is two sets of yellow strands and two sets of white strands. Dirt melt line. Germany, circa 1870-1915. 21/32". Mint (9.5). Price: $8. CyberAuction #502, Lot #35.

7757. SWIRL. Solid core. Lobed solid core swirl. Opaque white core. Three lobes. Blue band in each trough, pink band on each peak. Outer layer is a cage of yellow strands. Cold roll crease, some surface scratching. Germany, circa 1870-1915. 27/32". Near Mint(+) (8.7). Price: $8. CyberAuction #505, Lot #4.

7758. SWIRL. Solid core. Opaque white core. Three shallow lobes. A pink band in each trough, a blue band floating above each peak. Outer layer is three sets of white strands. Some dirt. Germany, circa 1870-1915. 9/16". Mint(-) (9.0). Match to Lot #2 in this auction. Price: $8. CyberAuction #506, Lot #11.

7759. SWIRL. Solid core. Interesting. Pink and white core. Outer layer is three blue bands and three white bands, tightly twisted. A little hazy. Germany, circa 1870-1915. 1/2". Near Mint (8.6). Price: $7. CyberAuction #338, Lot #45.

7760. SWIRL. Solid core. Naked solid core swirl. Panels of green and blue, separated by white and yellow strands. No outer layer. Surface is hazy. Germany, circa 1870-1915. 5/8". Good(+) (7.8). Price: $7. CyberAuction #346, Lot #18.

7761. SWIRL. Solid core. Semi-opaque white core. Outer layer is four bands. One tiny chip. Germany, circa 1870-1915. 15/32". Near Mint(+) (8.7). Price: $7. CyberAuction #357, Lot #1.

7762. SWIRL. Solid core. Two pink bands, one blue band, one green band, separated by white bands. Outer layer is four sets of yellow strands. Several tiny flakes. Germany, circa 1870-1915. 15/32". Near Mint(+) (8.7). Price: $7. CyberAuction #377, Lot #21.

7763. SWIRL. Solid core. White core, partly open. Two pink bands and two blue bands on it. Four sets of yellow strands. Pits and scratches. Germany, circa 1870-1915. 19/32". Near Mint(+) (8.8). Price: $7. CyberAuction #382, Lot #9.

7764. SWIRL. Solid core. Naked solid core swirl. Alternating bands and strands of white, yellow, purple and blue. Some pitting. Germany, circa 1870-1915. 1/2". Near Mint(+) (8.9). Price: $7. CyberAuction #392, Lot #4.

7765. SWIRL. Solid core. Opaque white core. Three shallow lobes. A pink band in each trough, a blue band floating above each peak. Outer layer is three sets of white strands. Some dirt. Germany, circa 1870-1915. 9/16". Mint(-) (9.0). Match to Lot #2 in this auction. Price: $7. CyberAuction #403, Lot #28.

7766. SWIRL. Solid core. Core is four panels of alternating white, pink and blue. Outer layer is four sets of yellow strands. Some pinpricks. Germany, circa 1870-1915. 17/32". Near Mint(+) (8.7). Price: $7. CyberAuction #407, Lot #9.

7767. SWIRL. Solid core. Opaque white core. Core is covered by alternating pink and green bands. Outer layer is four sets of yellow strands. Fracture through the marble, and one small chip. Germany, circa 1870-1915. 3/4". Good(+) (7.7). Price: $7. CyberAuction #409, Lot #10.

7768. SWIRL. Solid core. Opaque white core. Three lobes. Lobe troughs have blue bands, lobe peaks have pink bands. Outer layer is three sets of yellow strands. Some scratching. Germany, circa 1870-1915. 17/32". Mint(-) (9.0). Price: $7. CyberAuction #420, Lot #1.

7769. SWIRL. Solid core. Opaque white core. Three shallow lobes. A pink band in each trough, a blue band floating above each peak. Outer layer is three sets of white strands. Some dirt. Germany, circa 1870-1915. 9/16". Mint(-) (9.0). Match to Lot #2 in this auction. Price: $7. CyberAuction #488, Lot #28.

7770. SWIRL. Solid core. From near an end of the cane. Opaque yellow core. Shoved over to one side of the marble. Outer layer is three bands. One is blue and white, one is green and white (narrow), one is just a white strand. Some pinpricks. Germany, circa 1870-1915. 13/16". Near Mint(+) (8.8). Price: $7. CyberAuction #494, Lot #14.

7771. SWIRL. Solid core. Translucent yellow core. Outer layer is six bands. Three are green on white, three are blue on white. Unusual core. Thick outer casing. Some tiny chips and flakes. Germany, circa 1870-1915. 25/32". Good (7.5). Price: $6. CyberAuction #347, Lot #2.

7772. SWIRL. Solid core. Core is six alternating panels of semi-opaque white and transparent blue. Outer layer is four sets of yellow strands. Light haze. Interesting core. Germany, circa 1870-1915. 5/8". Near Mint(-) (8.1). Price: $6. CyberAuction #352, Lot #8.

7773. SWIRL. Solid core. It's a 1-1/2" solid core swirl that is broken into about a half dozen pieces. I suppose you could glue it back together or have it repaired. Germany, circa 1870-1915. Price: $6. CyberAuction #352, Lot #28.

7774. SWIRL. Solid core. Opaque white core. Outer layer is three bands of pink and three of blue. Very nice. Two large melt spots. Germany, circa 1870-1915. 17/32". Mint(-) (9.0). Price: $6. CyberAuction #382, Lot #26.

7775. SWIRL. Solid core. Three-layer solid core. Opaque white core. Middle layer is eight bands of pink, blue, or green. Outer layer is a cage of white strands. Overall haze, pitting and small chips. Germany, circa 1870-1915. 7/8". Good(-) (7.2). Price: $6. CyberAuction #428, Lot #40.

7776. SWIRL. Solid core. Naked solid core swirl. Alternating bands and strands of white, yellow, purple and blue. Some pitting. Germany, circa 1870-1915. 1/2". Near Mint(+) (8.9). Price: $6. CyberAuction #445, Lot #51.

7777. SWIRL. Solid core. From near an end of the cane. Opaque yellow core. Shoved over to one side of the marble. Outer layer is three bands. One is blue and white, one is green and white (narrow), one is just a white strand. Some pinpricks. Germany, circa 1870-1915. 13/16". Near Mint(+) (8.8). Price: $6. CyberAuction #494, Lot #4.

7778. SWIRL. Solid core. Three layer solid core. White core. Middle layer is alternating bands of pink and blue. Outer layer is three sets of yellow strands. Buffed, fake pontil. Germany, circa 1870-1915. 23/32". Price: $6. CyberAuction #494, Lot #16.

7779. SWIRL. Solid core. Four lobe solid core. Opaque white core. Two troughs have pink and blue band in them, two have pink and green band in them. Outer layer is a cage of yellow strands. Tiny moon. Germany, circa 1870-1915. 5/8". Near Mint(+) (8.9). Price: $6. CyberAuction #503, Lot #1.

7780. SWIRL. Solid core. Super three layer solid core. Opaque white core. Middle layer is four panels. Each is three strands. Two panels are pink, one is blue, one is turquoise. Outer layer is a cage of yellow strands. Hazy and pits. Germany, circa 1870-1915. 21/32". Good(+) (8.0). Price: $5. CyberAuction #382, Lot #7.

7781. SWIRL. Solid core. Opaque white core with blue bands on it. Outer layer is a cage of white strands. Reverse twist top. Lightly buffed, damage remains. Germany, circa 1870-1915. 29/32". Price: $5. CyberAuction #417, Lot #38.

7782. SWIRL. Solid core. Opaque white core. Core is covered by alternating pink and green bands. Outer layer is four sets of yellow strands. Fracture through the marble, and one small chip. Germany, circa 1870-1915. 3/4". Good(+) (7.7). Price: $5. CyberAuction #426, Lot #44.

7783. SWIRL. Solid core. Opaque white core. Two orange bands on it, two blue bands on it. Outer layer is four sets of yellow strands. Some pitting on the marble. Germany, circa 1870-1915. 11/16". Near Mint (8.5). Price: $5. CyberAuction #444, Lot #7.

7784. SWIRL. Solid core. Solid core swirl. White core. Three wide bands on it. Two are blue and pink, one is green and pink. Outer layer is three sets of yellow strands. Two tiny chips, some tiny subsurface moons. Germany, circa 1870-1915. 11/16". Near Mint(-) (8.2). Price: $5. CyberAuction #454, Lot #33.

7785. SWIRL. Solid core. White core of narrow bands. Two transparent pink bands on it. Outer layer is three sets of white strands. Pretty. Small flake, large melted out dot. Germany, circa 1870-1915. 3/4". Near Mint(+) (8.7). Price: $5. CyberAuction #472, Lot #15.

7786. SWIRL. Solid core. Core is two white panels and an orange panel, separated by transparent blue panels. Outer layer is three sets of yellow strands. Several tiny flakes. Germany, circa 1870-1915. 11/16". Near Mint (8.5). Price: $5. CyberAuction #480, Lot #34.

7787. SWIRL. Solid core. Opaque white core with blue bands on it. Outer layer is a cage of white strands. Reverse twist top. Lightly buffed, damage remains. Germany, circa 1870-1915. 29/32". Price: $5. CyberAuction #484, Lot #10.

7788. SWIRL. Solid core. Opaque white core. Three pink and three green bands on it. Outer layer is three yellow strands. One sparkle. Germany, circa 1870-1915. 11/16". Near Mint(+) (8.9). Price: $5. CyberAuction #492, Lot #9.

7789. SWIRL. Solid core. Solid core swirl. White core. Three wide bands on it. Two are blue and pink, one is green and pink. Outer layer is three sets of yellow strands. Two tiny chips, some tiny subsurface moons. Germany, circa 1870-1915. 11/16". Near Mint(-) (8.2). Price: $4. CyberAuction #410, Lot #6.

7790. SWIRL. Solid core. White core. Three pink bands and three blue bands on it. Outer layer is a cage of white strands. Bottom pontil is ground. Tiny chip near the bottom pontil. Germany, circa 1870-1915. 19/32". Mint(+) (8.9). Price: $4. CyberAuction #433, Lot #17.

7791. SWIRL. Solid core. Three layer solid core. White core. Middle layer is alternating bands of pink and blue. Outer layer is three sets of yellow strands. Buffed, fake pontil. Germany, circa 1870-1915. 23/32". Price: $3. CyberAuction #472, Lot #9.

7792. SWIRL. Solid core. Translucent white core. Two blue bands and two red bands on it. Outer layer is one set of three white strands. Base glass is very lightly tinted blue. Some tiny chips and pitting. Germany, circa 1870-1915. 21/32". Near Mint (8.3). Price: $2. CyberAuction #485, Lot #46.

7793. TRANSITIONAL. Bullet Mold. Transparent brown clearie. Mold line around the equator with a pontil. One tiny flake. Probably American, probably 1910-1940. 3/4". Near Mint(+) (8.9). Price: $33. CyberAuction #506, Lot #36.

7794. TRANSITIONAL. Bullet Mold. Transparent brown clearie. Mold line around the equator with a pontil. One tiny flake. Probably American, probably 1910-1940. 3/4". Near Mint(+) (8.9). Price: $25. CyberAuction #348, Lot #22.

7795. TRANSITIONAL. Bullet Mold. Transparent brown clearie. Mold line around the equator with a pontil. One tiny flake. Probably American, probably 1910-1940. 3/4". Near Mint(+) (8.9). Price: $25. CyberAuction #440, Lot #3.

7796. TRANSITIONAL. Bullet Mold. Transparent brown clearie. Mold line around the equator with a pontil. One tiny flake. Probably American, probably 1910-1940. 3/4". Near Mint(+) (8.9). Price: $25. CyberAuction #490, Lot #15.

7797. TRANSITIONAL. Crease pontil. Hand gathered slag. Transparent clear with loads of white swirling. Long crease pontil on the bottom. Poor "9" on the top. Rare. American, circa 1910-1920. 25/32". Mint (9.7). Price: $40. CyberAuction #342, Lot #24.

7798. TRANSITIONAL. Crease pontil. Opaque white and red swirl. Hand gathered with a very nice "9". Long crease on bottom. In very nice shape. Probably American, probably circa 1910-1930. 11/16". Mint (9.7). Price: $27. CyberAuction #342, Lot #20.

7799. TRANSITIONAL. Crease pontil. Gorgeous example. Opaque white swirled with electric red. Thin crease mark on the bottom. Origin and age unknown. Probably American, early 1920s. 21/32". Mint (9.9). Price: $22. CyberAuction #422, Lot #15.

7800. TRANSITIONAL. Crease pontil. Opaque white and electric red swirl. Long crease on bottom. In very nice shape. Origin and age unknown. 23/32". Mint (9.6). Price: $19. CyberAuction #342, Lot #8.

7801. TRANSITIONAL. Crease pontil. Gorgeous example. Opaque white swirled with electric red. Thin crease mark on the bottom. Origin and age unknown. Probably American, early 1920s. 21/32". Mint (9.9). Price: $19. CyberAuction #366, Lot #39.

7802. TRANSITIONAL. Opaque white with red/orange swirling. Nice pontil. Beauty. Origin and age unknown, my guess is American, 1920-1930. 11/16". Mint (9.9). Price: $16. CyberAuction #359, Lot #10.

7803. TRANSITIONAL. Crease pontil. Brown slag. Nice crease pontil. Origin unconfirmed, either American or Japanese, circa 1910-1930. 9/16". Mint (9.7). Price: $15. CyberAuction #349, Lot #52.

7804. TRANSITIONAL. Crease pontil. Transparent green base with semi-opaque white swirls. Long crease pontil. Origin and age unknown. 5/8". Mint (9.7). Price: $11. CyberAuction #373, Lot #41.

7805. TRANSITIONAL. Crease pontil. Opaque white base with red swirling. Large crease pontil on each. Age and origin unknown, but my guess is American, circa 1920-1930. 21/32". Mint (9.7). There are three marbles available, you are bidding on one. Winner has choice of any or all, remainder to under. Price: $11. CyberAuction #390, Lot #28.

7806. TRANSITIONAL. Crease pontil. Light aqua base with opaque white swirls. Nice crease pontil. Origin and age are unknown. 11/16". Mint (9.7). There are three marbles available. You are bidding on one. Winner has choice of any or all, remainder to under. Price: $10. CyberAuction #377, Lot #27.

7807. TRANSITIONAL. Crease pontil. Opaque white base with red swirling. Large crease pontil. Age and origin unknown, but my guess is American, circa 1920-1930. 21/32". Mint (9.7). There are three examples available, you are bidding on one. Winner has choice of any or all, remainder to under. Price: $8. CyberAuction #422, Lot #41.

7808. TRANSITIONAL. Crease pontil. Transparent brown base with white swirling. Nice long crease pontil. One air hole. Origin and age unknown. 9/16". Mint(-) (9.0). Price: $7. CyberAuction #378, Lot #55.

7809. TRANSITIONAL. Crease pontil. Transparent brown base with white swirling. Nice long crease pontil. Several air holes. Origin and age unknown. 5/8". Mint(-) (9.0). Price: $7. CyberAuction #385, Lot #17.

7810. TRANSITIONAL. Crease pontil. Transparent brown base with white swirling. Nice long crease pontil. One air hole. Origin and age unknown. 19/32". Mint(-) (9.0). Price: $6. CyberAuction #376, Lot #1.

7811. TRANSITIONAL. Crease pontil. Opaque white base with red swirling. Large crease pontil. Age and origin unknown, but my guess is American, circa 1920-1930. 21/32". Mint (9.7). There are three examples available, you are bidding on one. Winner has choice of any or all, remainder to under. Price: $6. CyberAuction #390, Lot #18.

7812. TRANSITIONAL. Crease pontil. Transparent light green base with white swirling. Nice long crease pontil. One air hole. Origin and age unknown. 9/16". Mint(-) (9.0). Price: $6. CyberAuction #442, Lot #53.

7813. TRANSITIONAL. Crease pontil. Transparent light green base with white swirling. Nice long crease pontil. One air hole. Origin and age unknown. 9/16". Mint(-) (9.0). Consignor note: H19. Price: $5. CyberAuction #380, Lot #21.

7814. TRANSITIONAL. Crease pontil. Transparent blue base with white swirling. Nice long crease pontil. Origin and age unknown. 19/32". Mint (9.7). Price: $5. CyberAuction #391, Lot #12.

7815. TRANSITIONAL. Crease pontil. Opaque white and electric red swirl. Long crease on bottom. In very nice shape. Origin and age unknown. 19/32". Mint (9.6). Price: $5. CyberAuction #393, Lot #44.

7816. TRANSITIONAL. Crease pontil. Transparent blue base with white swirling. Nice long crease pontil. One sparkle. Origin and age unknown. 19/32". Mint(-) (9.0). Price: $3. CyberAuction #392, Lot #7.

7817. TRANSITIONAL. Crease pontil. Transparent green with opaque white swirls. Very nice crease pontil. Age and origin unknown. Probably American, 1920s. 5/8". Mint (9.5). Price: $3. CyberAuction #435, Lot #1.

7818. TRANSITIONAL. Crease pontil. Transparent blue base with white swirling. Nice long crease pontil. One air hole. Origin and age unknown. 19/32". Mint(-) (9.0). Price: $2. CyberAuction #389, Lot #10.

7819. TRANSITIONAL. Fold pontil. Nice brown slag. Large folded pontil at bottom. One air hole, one melt spot. Akron, OH, circa 1910-1915. 5/8". Mint(-) (9.0). Price: $20. CyberAuction #391, Lot #36.

7820. TRANSITIONAL. Ground pontil. Excellent and rare ground pontil transitional. Transparent clear base. Excellent hand gathered swirl of white and lavender. Nice "9" on the side of the marble (relative to the ground pontil). In superb shape. Exceptional example. American, circa 1880-1910. 13/16". Mint (9.9). Price: $230. CyberAuction #336, Lot #60.

7821. TRANSITIONAL. Ground pontil. Stunning marble. Aqua base with super white spiral. Gorgeous "9", with nice whiptail. Nicely ground pontil. Super example. American, circa 1880-1910. 5/8". Mint (9.9). Price: $180. CyberAuction #333, Lot #55.

7822. TRANSITIONAL. Ground pontil. Early single pontil slag. Almost all white, with some dark purple or black mixed in. Tiny ground pontil. Nice "9", hand gathered. One air hole. In great shape, given the age. American, possibly German, circa 1880-1910. 25/32". Mint (9.6). Price: $100. CyberAuction #342, Lot #41.

7823. TRANSITIONAL. Ground pontil. Beautiful example in super shape. Transparent cobalt blue with veils of ghost air bubbles in it. Surface in super shape. Nicely ground pontil. American, circa 1880-1910. 15/16". Mint (9.8). Price: $80. CyberAuction #471, Lot #55.

7824. TRANSITIONAL. Ground pontil. Beautiful example in super shape. Transparent cobalt blue with veils of ghost air bubbles in it. Surface in super shape. Nicely ground pontil. American, circa 1880-1910. 15/16". Mint (9.8). Price: $80. CyberAuction #494, Lot #45.

7825. TRANSITIONAL. Ground pontil. Gorgeous example. Aqua slag. Nice white spiral, nicely hand gathered. Beautiful ground pontil. American, circa 1880-1910. 9/16". Mint (9.8). Price: $75. CyberAuction #452, Lot #46.

7826. TRANSITIONAL. Ground pontil. Transparent blue base with white swirls and blankets on it. Nice swirled design on the top. Some overall light scratching. American, circa 1880-1910. 25/32". Near Mint(+) (8.7). Price: $70. CyberAuction #404, Lot #37.

7827. TRANSITIONAL. Ground pontil. Gorgeous aqua base with nice white swirling. Poor "9" but nice tail. Surface has been buffed, damage remains. American, circa 1880-1910. 27/32". Price: $65. CyberAuction #422, Lot #54.

7828. TRANSITIONAL. Ground pontil. Gorgeous aqua base with nice white swirling. Poor "9" but nice tail. Surface has been buffed, damage remains. American, circa 1880-1910. 27/32". Price: $60. CyberAuction #393, Lot #58.

7829. TRANSITIONAL. Ground pontil. Gorgeous example. Transparent purple glass with translucent white swirls. Gorgeous "9". Great ground pontil. Definitive example. Probably M.F. Christensen. One sparkle. Akron, OH, circa 1890-1910. 21/32". Mint(-) (9.0). Price: $60. CyberAuction #448, Lot #50.

7830. TRANSITIONAL. Ground pontil. Lavender and white slag. Nicely hand gathered. Nice ground pontil. Some pitting and very tiny chips. American, circa 1880-1910. 21/32". Near Mint(+) (8.7). Price: $47. CyberAuction #450, Lot #32.

7831. TRANSITIONAL. Ground pontil. Very nice example of a ground pontil transitional. Green and white slag. Wide "9". Nice swirling. Nicely ground pontil. One tiny chip near the bottom pontil. American, circa 1880-1910. 13/16". Near Mint(+) (8.9). Price: $42. CyberAuction #464, Lot #49.

7832. TRANSITIONAL. Ground pontil. Transparent green with nice wispy white spiral. Excellent "9", nicely ground pontil. Tiny flake on the pontil. American, circa 1880-1910. Interestingly, this came from an English collection. 27/32". Near Mint(+) (8.9). Price: $39. CyberAuction #502, Lot #58.

7833. TRANSITIONAL. Ground pontil. Green and white slag. Nicely hand gathered. Very nicely ground pontil. One very tiny subsurface moon. Ameri-

can, circa 1880-1910. 21/32". Near Mint(+) (8.8). Price: $38. CyberAuction #450, Lot #13.

7834. TRANSITIONAL. Ground pontil. Transparent dark blue base. White cloud near the pontil. Some wispy white swirling. Beautiful pontil. Probably M.F. Christensen. One sparkle, some rubbing. American, circa 1880-1910. 13/16". Mint(-) (9.0). Price: $36. CyberAuction #455, Lot #53.

7835. TRANSITIONAL. Ground pontil. Super, small marble. Lavender with thin white spiral. Nice ground pontil. One tiny chip. Very pretty. American, circa 1880-1910. 9/16". Near Mint(+) (8.9). Price: $32. CyberAuction #332, Lot #42.

7836. TRANSITIONAL. Ground pontil. Aqua slag with loads of white. Nicely ground pontil. Nice "9" at top. A couple of tiny chips and a couple of tiny pits. American, circa 1880-1910. 27/32". Near Mint(+) (8.7). Price: $32. CyberAuction #457, Lot #36.

7837. TRANSITIONAL. Ground pontil. Probably a Leighton, or else early Ohio manufacturer. Transparent clear. Small white and air bubble core at the bottom pontil. Pontil is nicely ground. A little very tiny roughness. Nice example, hard to find. American, circa 1880-1910. 13/16". Near Mint(+) (8.8). Price: $32. CyberAuction #467, Lot #27.

7838. TRANSITIONAL. Ground pontil. Probably a Leighton, or else early Ohio manufacturer. Transparent clear. Small white and air bubble core at the bottom pontil. Pontil is nicely ground. A little very tiny roughness. Nice example, hard to find. American, circa 1880-1910. 13/16". Near Mint(+) (8.8). Price: $32. CyberAuction #490, Lot #38.

7839. TRANSITIONAL. Ground pontil. Probably a Leighton, or else early Ohio manufacturer. Transparent clear. Small white and air bubble core at the bottom pontil. Pontil is nicely ground. A little very tiny roughness. Nice example, hard to find. American, circa 1880-1910. 13/16". Near Mint(+) (8.8). Price: $32. CyberAuction #506, Lot #41.

7840. TRANSITIONAL. Ground pontil. Brown slag. Gorgeous white spiral in it. Nicely ground pontil on bottom. Two manufacturing pinprick air holes. American, circa 1880-1910. 11/16". Mint (9.6). Price: $30. CyberAuction #429, Lot #3.

7841. TRANSITIONAL. Ground pontil. Blue slag. Nice "9" on top. Ground pontil. Some light scratching and a couple of tiny pinpricks. American, circa 1880-1910. 11/16". Near Mint(+) (8.9). Price: $26. CyberAuction #429, Lot #17.

7842. TRANSITIONAL. Ground pontil. Interesting marble. Predominately opaque white with transparent green mixed in. Very nicely ground pontil. Two blown out air holes. One "star" fracture. American, circa 1880-1910. 25/32". Near Mint (8.3). Price: $25. CyberAuction #397, Lot #4.

7843. TRANSITIONAL. Ground pontil. Very light aqua base with a thin white swirl in it. Buffed surface, but the pontil is intact. American, circa 1880-1910. 3/4". Price: $22. CyberAuction #428, Lot #24.

7844. TRANSITIONAL. Ground pontil. Hand gathered purple transparent with a semi-opaque white spiral. Ground pontil at bottom. Nice "9". Several tiny subsurface moons and some wear. Faceting on the pontil is gone. American, circa 1880-1910. 19/32". Near Mint(-) (8.0). Price: $21. CyberAuction #349, Lot #57.

7845. TRANSITIONAL. Ground pontil. Milky aqua base filled with swirled white. Very nice "9" swirl on the upper half of the marble. Nicely ground pontil. One tiny subsurface moon and some overall rubbing. American, circa 1880-1910. 21/32". Near Mint(-) (8.1). Price: $19. CyberAuction #383, Lot #40.

7846. TRANSITIONAL. Ground pontil. Light blue base with a superb white spiral. Overall haziness. American, circa 1880-1910. 3/4". Near Mint(-) (8.1). Price: $13. CyberAuction #332, Lot #21.

7847. TRANSITIONAL. Ground pontil. Transparent aqua base with some white swirls. Buffed, pontil is missing. American, circa 1880-1910. 25/32". Price: $10. CyberAuction #494, Lot #36.

7848. TRANSITIONAL. Ground pontil. Transparent green base with some white swirling. Hand gathered. Ground pontil on bottom. Consigned from Germany. Two small subsurface moons. Probably Germany, possibly America, circa 1880-1910. 11/16". Good(+) (7.9). Price: $9. CyberAuction #365, Lot #55.

7849. TRANSITIONAL. Leighton. Stunning and very rare Leighton oxblood transitional. One of the rarest marbles!! Transparent clear base, almost completely filled with oxblood, with some white swirls. Hand gathered. Tail flips over top. Bottom is a ground pontil with exceptional faceting. Surface is pristine. An unbelievable marble. Exceptionally rare opportunity. Amazing condition for a marble that is this rare to begin with. American, circa 1880-1910. 3/4". Mint (9.9). This was Lot #60 in CyberAuction #377, it has been consigned by the winning bidder in that auction. Price: $2550. CyberAuction #500, Lot #59.

7850. TRANSITIONAL. Leighton. Extremely rare and important hand gathered Brick! Solid oxblood red with a thin white and black swirl. Nice "9". Good tail. Large folded pontil. Tiny melt spot on top where it touched another marble. This type is very rarely seen. Exceptional condition. Extremely important marble from an historical perspective, and due to its rarity. Superb opportunity. Shiny, wet condition. American, circa 1880-1900. 27/32". Mint (9.7). Price: $2100. CyberAuction #483, Lot #59.

7851. TRANSITIONAL. Leighton. Stunning and very rare Leighton oxblood transitional. One of the rarest marbles!!! Transparent clear base, almost completely filled with oxblood, with some white swirls. Hand gathered. Tail flips over top. Bottom is a ground pontil with exceptional faceting. Surface is pristine. An unbelievable marble. Exceptionally rare opportunity. Amazing condition for a marble that is this rare to begin with. American, circa 1880-1910. 3/4". Mint (9.9). Price: $2050. CyberAuction #377, Lot #60.

7852. TRANSITIONAL. Leighton. Stunning Leighton transitional. Transparent clear and some milky white, swirled with blue, oxblood red and yellow. The blue and oxblood are on the upper half, the yellow is on the lower half. Absolutely stunning marble. Very rare. One small air hole. Wow! American, circa 1880-1910. 7/8". Mint (9.6). Price: $1100. CyberAuction #445, Lot #60.

7853. TRANSITIONAL. Leighton. Very rare Leighton transitional with oxblood. Transparent aqua base. Filled with wispy white swirls. Nice swirl of yellow and oxblood. Super ground pontil. Exceptional surface. Superior example!!! American, circa 1880-1910. 25/32". Mint (9.9). Price: $985. CyberAuction #434, Lot #60.

7854. TRANSITIONAL. Leighton. Stunning marble. Transitional. Transparent clear and some milky white, swirled with blue, oxblood red and yellow. The blue and oxblood are on the upper half, the yellow is on the lower half. Absolutely stunning marble. Very rare. One small air hole. Wow! American, circa 1880-1910. 7/8". Mint (9.6). Price: $935. CyberAuction #403, Lot #60.

7855. TRANSITIONAL. Leighton. Very rare Leighton transitional with oxblood. Transparent aqua base. Filled with wispy white swirls. Nice swirl of yellow and oxblood. Super ground pontil. Exceptional surface. Superior example!!! American, circa 1880-1910. 25/32". Mint (9.9). Price: $925. CyberAuction #400, Lot #58.

7856. TRANSITIONAL. Leighton. Stunning marble. Dark transparent blue base. Cobalt blue. Gorgeous swirls of electric yellow. Nicely ground pontil. Very rare. One tiny subsurface moon, one pit. American, circa 1880-1910. 15/16". Near Mint(+) (8.8). Price: $710. CyberAuction #436, Lot #58.

7857. TRANSITIONAL. Leighton. Superb example. Transparent bubble filled white base. Swirled bright yellow and white. Wide "9" at the top. Nicely ground pontil. Two blown air holes, one has roughness around it. American, circa 1880-1910. 31/32". Mint(-) (9.0). Price: $485. CyberAuction #508, Lot #74.

7858. TRANSITIONAL. Leighton. Stunning marble. Transparent green base. Swirls of white with some yellow and oxblood. Nice "9". Super ground pontil. Excellent example. One air hole. American, circa 1880-1910. 21/32". Mint (9.4). Price: $470. CyberAuction #373, Lot #59.

7859. TRANSITIONAL. Leighton. Superb example. Transparent clear with yellow swirled in and out. Exceptional "9". Nicely ground pontil. Gorgeous marble. One tiny subsurface moon. Hard to find over an inch. American, circa 1880-1910. 1-1/16". Near Mint(+) (8.9). Price: $435. CyberAuction #475, Lot #55.

7860. TRANSITIONAL. Leighton. Rare marble. Transparent clear base. Swirled bright yellow and white, with some green. Beautiful ground pontil. Two manufacturing melt chips. Still, stunning. American, circa 1880-1910. 31/32". Mint(-) (9.0). Price: $410. CyberAuction #406, Lot #54.

7861. TRANSITIONAL. Leighton. Superb Leighton transitional. Transparent clear base. Swirls of white, yellow and oxblood on the surface. Gorgeous. Super "9" and swirling on it. Some very light scratches, one very tiny melt spot. Excellent marble!!! American, circa 1880-1910. 27/32". Mint (-) (9.2). Price: $400. CyberAuction #424, Lot #58.

7862. TRANSITIONAL. Leighton. Milky white base. Nice swirl of white, yellow and oxblood. Excellent "9" on the top. Nicely ground pontil. American, circa 1880-1910. 3/4". Mint (9.6). Price: $360. CyberAuction #439, Lot #60.

7863. TRANSITIONAL. Leighton. Gorgeous. Transparent light blue base. Filled with translucent white. Excellent "9" swirl of white, yellow and oxblood on the top. Nice trailing tail. One small subsurface moon, one tiny chip, both on the sides of the marble, not on the color. Several tiny blown out air holes. One small melt spot right on the color. Still, a gorgeous marble. American, circa 1880-1910. 29/32". Near Mint (8.6). Price: $320. CyberAuction #421, Lot #60.

7864. TRANSITIONAL. Leighton. Superb Leighton transitional. Excellent marble with great surface. Transparent aqua base with excellent swirl of wispy white and very thin oxblood. Superb "9". Nicely ground pontil. Super marble!!!! American, circa 1880-1910. 13/16". Mint (9.8). Price: $310. CyberAuction #330, Lot #59.

7865. TRANSITIONAL. Leighton. Gorgeous marble. Transparent aqua base. Wispy white and yellow spiral. Nice ground pontil. White and yellow in the core too. Superb. One sparkle. American, circa 1880-1910. 15/16". Mint(-) (9.0). Price: $310. CyberAuction #465, Lot #60.

7866. TRANSITIONAL. Leighton. Rare Leighton. Large. Translucent milky white core with wispy white swirls. Swirls of bright yellow and bright baby blue. Nicely ground pontil. One blown out air hole, a couple of tiny sparkles. Rare marble. American, circa 1880-1910. 29/32". Near Mint(+) (8.9). Price: $300. CyberAuction #450, Lot #46.

7867. TRANSITIONAL. Leighton. Rare Leighton. Large. Translucent milky white core with wispy white swirls. Swirls of bright yellow and bright baby blue. Nicely ground pontil. One blown out air hole, a couple of tiny sparkles. Rare marble. American, circa 1880-1910. 29/32". Near Mint(+) (8.9). Price: $300. CyberAuction #466, Lot #45.

7868. TRANSITIONAL. Leighton. Gorgeous ground pontil transitional with oxblood. Transparent dark blue base. Wide opaque white spiral with a great "9" and a nice tail. Narrow oxblood swirl next to the white for part of the marble. Pontil is superb!!! Surface has two tiny subsurface moons and a couple of tiny air holes. Excellent example, very hard to find. American, circa 1880-1910. 15/16". Near Mint(+) (8.8). Price: $260. CyberAuction #357, Lot #59.

7869. TRANSITIONAL. Leighton. Beauty. Transparent very lightly tinted green base. Bright yellow and white swirling. Nicely ground pontil. One air hole. Superb!!!! American, circa 1880-1910. 27/32". Mint(-) (9.2). Price: $260. CyberAuction #414, Lot #54.

7870. TRANSITIONAL. Leighton. Very odd marble. Translucent clear with some milkiness to it and some unmelted sand. Nice oxblood "9", just on the top. No trailing tail or swirls. Nicely ground pontil. Excellent example.

American, circa 1880-1910. 9/16". Mint (9.7). Price: $250. CyberAuction #504, Lot #60.

7871. TRANSITIONAL. Leighton. Superb ground pontil Leighton transitional. Transparent clear base. One spiral of wispy white. In superb shape. American, circa 1880-1910. 13/16". Mint (9.9). Price: $185. CyberAuction #462, Lot #56.

7872. TRANSITIONAL. Leighton. Gorgeous and superb. Ground pontil transitional. Transparent clear base, filled with swirls of milky white, yellow, and tiny air bubbles. Surface is pristine. Stunning. American, circa 1880-1910. 11/16". Mint (9.8). Price: $160. CyberAuction #366, Lot #46.

7873. TRANSITIONAL. Leighton. Very nice Leighton ground pontil transitional. Milky white base with semi-opaque white swirls and semi-opaque lavender swirls. Hard to find. Nicely ground pontil. Good pattern. One tiny subsurface moon, some pits. American, circa 1880-1910. 27/32". Near Mint (8.6). Price: $150. CyberAuction #395, Lot #58.

7874. TRANSITIONAL. Leighton. Very hard to find type. Very pale sea foam green with loads of white swirling. Excellent "9", nicely ground pontil. Several small blown out air holes at the bottom and on top. Beauty. American, circa 1880-1910. 27/32". Near Mint(+) (8.9). From an English collection. Price: $120. CyberAuction #503, Lot #26.

7875. TRANSITIONAL. Leighton. Very nice Leighton. Bubble filled transparent base. Nice wispy yellow swirl on it. Nice "9". Ground tail. Not quite wet mint, but no damage. American, circa 1880-1910. 11/16". Mint(-) (9.1). Price: $80. CyberAuction #508, Lot #66.

7876. TRANSITIONAL. Leighton. Transparent clear base. Swirls of white and yellow. Ground pontil. Nicely swirled. Several very small chips. American, circa 1880-1910. 27/32". Good(+) (7.9). Price: $42. CyberAuction #485, Lot #47.

7877. TRANSITIONAL. Leighton. Transparent clear base with a white looping swirl. Excellent "9" and tail. Overall haziness with much transitional. American, circa 1880-1910. 25/32". Good(+) (7.9). Price: $8. CyberAuction #358, Lot #41.

7878. TRANSITIONAL. Melted pontil. Large Navarre transitional. Dark brown/purple glass. White spiral inside the marble. Nicely melted pontil. Superior, rare marble. American, circa 1880-1910. 1-5/16". Mint (9.7). Price: $200. CyberAuction #333, Lot #58.

7879. TRANSITIONAL. Melted pontil. Large Navarre melted pontil transitional. Very dark purple with wispy white. Large pontil. About a half dozen tiny subsurface moons. American, circa 1880-1910. 1-3/16". Near Mint(-) (8.0). Price: $80. CyberAuction #364, Lot #51.

7880. TRANSITIONAL. Melted pontil. Very dark purple with white swirl. Exceptional "9". Nicely melted pontil. American, circa 1880-1910. 11/16". Mint (9.7). Price: $65. CyberAuction #334, Lot #55.

7881. TRANSITIONAL. Melted pontil. Superb example. Dark transparent olive brown base with white swirling and looping in it. Loaded with very tiny air bubbles. Excellent melted pontil, glass is blackened around it. In great shape. American, circa 1880-1920. 1". Mint (9.8). Price: $60. CyberAuction #377, Lot #16.

7882. TRANSITIONAL. Melted pontil. Gorgeous Navarre. Slate green with white looping. Nicely melted pontil. Two tiny pits. Superb example. Navarre OH, circa 1880-1910. 27/32". Near Mint(+) (8.9)>. Price: $60. CyberAuction #392, Lot #50.

7883. TRANSITIONAL. Melted pontil. Excellent Navarre transitional. Semi-opaque brown base with some very light white in it. Loads of tiny air bubbles in it. Nicely melted pontil. One tiny subsurface moon. Excellent marble. American, circa 1880-1910. 31/32". Near Mint(+) (8.8). Price: $55. CyberAuction #418, Lot #48.

7884. TRANSITIONAL. Melted pontil. Very dark purple with lots of white swirls. Nice "9". Nicely melted pontil. American, circa 1880-1910. 11/16". Mint (9.9). Price: $45. CyberAuction #335, Lot #53.

7885. TRANSITIONAL. Melted pontil. Probably Navarre. Very dark purple base with white loops and swirls. Excellent pontil. Gorgeous. Several tiny pinpricks. American, circa 1880-1910. 23/32". Near Mint(+) (8.9). Price: $44. CyberAuction #420, Lot #56.

7886. TRANSITIONAL. Melted pontil. Navarre. Beautiful dark purple and white slag. Nice looping. Nice melted pontil. American, circa 1880-1910. 11/16". Mint (9.9). Price: $42. CyberAuction #374, Lot #47.

7887. TRANSITIONAL. Melted pontil. Purple with white looping. Probably Navarre. Long tail flipping back over the top of the marble. Nice pontil. Large blown out air hole on one side. American, circa 1880-1910. 27/32". Near Mint(+) (8.7). Price: $40. CyberAuction #371, Lot #43.

7888. TRANSITIONAL. Melted pontil. Outstanding example of a Navarre melted pontil transitional. Slate green base with white looping. Nicely melted pontil. Some minor annealing crazing, but no damage. Excellent example. American, circa 1880-1910. 23/32". Mint(-) (9.2). Price: $35. CyberAuction #410, Lot #8.

7889. TRANSITIONAL. Melted pontil. Very dark purple with white swirl. Nice "9". Nicely melted pontil. American, circa 1880-1910. 11/16". Mint (9.9). Price: $32. CyberAuction #357, Lot #43.

7890. TRANSITIONAL. Melted pontil. Navarre melted pontil transitional. Transparent olive green base. Swirls of white and unmelted glass. Large melted pontil. American, circa 1880-1910. 5/8". Mint (9.9). Price: $30. CyberAuction #350, Lot #58.

7891. TRANSITIONAL. Melted pontil. Superb melted pontil transitional. Almost a horizontal. Green and white slag. Great "9" on the top, spiraling down to a beautifully melted pontil. Some pinpricking and scratching on the surface. American, circa 1880-1910. 11/16". Near Mint(+) (8.9). Price: $28. CyberAuction #427, Lot #11.

7892. TRANSITIONAL. Melted pontil. Very dark purple with white swirl. Nice "9". Nicely melted pontil. American, circa 1880-1910. 21/32". Mint (9.9). Price: $25. CyberAuction #335, Lot #43.

7893. TRANSITIONAL. Melted pontil. Dark purple and white. Navarre. Nice swirling. Nice pontil. One tiny chip. American, circa 1880-1910. 11/16". Near Mint(+) (8.9). Price: $25. CyberAuction #360, Lot #51.

7894. TRANSITIONAL. Melted pontil. Light brown transparent base with semi-opaque swirl. The white is predominately in the lower half of the marble. Probably Navarre. Great pontil. American, circa 1880-1920. 11/16". Mint (9.9). Price: $24. CyberAuction #356, Lot #44.

7895. TRANSITIONAL. Melted pontil. Excellent design. Super "9" and great pontil. Green, white and a little very light brown. Small annealing fracture right at the top. Probably M.F. Christensen. American, circa 1880-1910. 21/32". Mint(-) (9.0). Price: $24. CyberAuction #410, Lot #5.

7896. TRANSITIONAL. Melted pontil. Transparent dark green with translucent white looping. Nice melted pontil. Navarre. Very nice. American, circa 1880-1910. 9/16". Mint (9.6). Price: $23. CyberAuction #353, Lot #47.

7897. TRANSITIONAL. Melted pontil. Nice Navarre melted pontil transitional. Excellent gray/green base with lots of swirled white. Nice "9" on the top. Nicely melted pontil. Two tiny rough spots. American, circa 1880-1910. 11/16". Near Mint(+) (8.7). Price: $21. CyberAuction #371, Lot #11.

7898. TRANSITIONAL. Melted pontil. Very dark purple with white swirl. Nice "9". Nicely melted pontil. American, circa 1880-1910. 21/32". Mint (9.7). Price: $20. CyberAuction #333, Lot #4.

7899. TRANSITIONAL. Melted pontil. Opaque black with white loops. Nicely melted pontil. Probably Navarre. Opaque black transitionals are unusual. Subsurface moon near the pontil. American, circa 1880-1910. 11/16". Near Mint(+) (8.9). Price: $16. CyberAuction #374, Lot #18.

7900. TRANSITIONAL. Melted pontil. Dark transparent blue with a wispy white swirl and tons of unmelted sand. Very nice melted pontil nub. Two tiny subsurface moons. Consigned from Germany. 5/8". Near Mint (8.6). Price: $12. CyberAuction #420, Lot #29.

7901. TRANSITIONAL. Melted pontil. Navarre melted pontil transitional. White and dark purple. American, circa 1880-1910. 5/8". Near Mint (8.3). Price: $8. CyberAuction #402, Lot #44.

7902. TRANSITIONAL. Melted pontil. Navarre melted pontil. Olive green with lots of white loops. Some chipping. American, circa 1880-1910. 21/32". Good(+) (7.9). Price: $2. CyberAuction #439, Lot #28.

7903. TRANSITIONAL. Pinch pontil. Transparent green base. Beautiful swirl of semi-opaque white. Nice "9", nice pontil. Probably American, circa 1900-1930. 5/8". Mint (9.9). Price: $27. CyberAuction #335, Lot #9.

7904. TRANSITIONAL. Pinch pontil. Opaque white and translucent bright orange swirls. Thin pinch pontil on the bottom. Unidentified maker. Probably 1920s to 1930s. 3/4". Mint (9.5). Price: $23. CyberAuction #379, Lot #41.

7905. TRANSITIONAL. Pinch pontil. Transparent dark brown with translucent white spiral. Nice pinch pontil. One melt spot. American, circa 1920-1930. 11/16". Mint(-) (9.2). Price: $20. CyberAuction #433, Lot #40.

7906. TRANSITIONAL. Pinch pontil. Opaque white and translucent bright red swirls. Nice "9" pattern. Thin pinch pontil on the bottom. Gorgeous example. Unidentified maker. Probably 1920s to 1930s. 9/16". Mint (9.8). Price: $17. CyberAuction #330, Lot #18.

7907. TRANSITIONAL. Pinch pontil. Opaque white and translucent bright orange swirls. Thin pinch pontil on the bottom. Unidentified maker. Probably 1920s to 1930s. 3/4". Mint (9.5). Price: $17. CyberAuction #333, Lot #40.

7908. TRANSITIONAL. Pinch pontil. Translucent blue and semi-opaque white. Nice swirling and tail. Thin pinch pontil on the bottom. Unidentified maker. Probably 1920s to 1930s. 11/16". Mint (9.7). Price: $17. CyberAuction #356, Lot #48.

7909. TRANSITIONAL. Pinch pontil. Opaque white and translucent bright red swirls. Thin pinch pontil on the bottom. Unidentified maker. Probably 1920s to 1930s. 11/16". Mint (9.6). Price: $15. CyberAuction #410, Lot #20.

7910. TRANSITIONAL. Pinch pontil. Opaque white and translucent bright red swirls. Thin pinch pontil on the bottom. One tiny sparkle. Unidentified maker. Probably 1920s to 1930s. 11/16". Mint(-) (9.2). Price: $15. CyberAuction #421, Lot #17.

7911. TRANSITIONAL. Pinch pontil. Opaque white and translucent bright orange swirls. Thin pinch pontil on the bottom. Open elongated air hole on the top. Unidentified maker. Probably 1920s to 1930s. 3/4". Mint(-) (9.1). Price: $15. CyberAuction #432, Lot #42.

7912. TRANSITIONAL. Pinch pontil. Opaque white and translucent bright red swirls. Some carbon melting on the red. Thin pinch pontil on the bottom. Unidentified maker. Probably 1920s to 1930s. 19/32". Mint (9.7). Price: $14. CyberAuction #360, Lot #18.

7913. TRANSITIONAL. Pinch pontil. Opaque white and translucent bright orange/red swirls. Thin pinch pontil on the bottom. Unidentified maker. Probably 1920s to 1930s. 11/16". Mint (9.7). Price: $13. CyberAuction #351, Lot #35.

7914. TRANSITIONAL. Pinch pontil. Opaque white and translucent bright red swirls. Thin pinch pontil on the bottom. One sparkle. Unidentified maker. Probably 1920s to 1930s. 3/4". Mint(-) (9.2). Price: $13. CyberAuction #409, Lot #48.

7915. TRANSITIONAL. Pinch pontil. Opaque white and translucent bright red swirls. Thin pinch pontil on the bottom. Unidentified maker. Probably 1920s to 1930s. 9/16". Mint (9.9). Price: $13. CyberAuction #466, Lot #15.

7916. TRANSITIONAL. Pinch pontil. Transparent blue with semi-opaque white swirls. Thin pinch pontil on the bottom. Unidentified maker. Probably 1920s to 1930s. 11/16". Mint (9.7). Price: $12. CyberAuction #357, Lot #9.

7917. TRANSITIONAL. Pinch pontil. Opaque white and translucent bright red swirls. Thin pinch pontil on the bottom. One tiny sparkle. Unidentified maker. Probably 1920s to 1930s. 11/16". Mint(-) (9.2). Price: $11. CyberAuction #381, Lot #2.

7918. TRANSITIONAL. Pinch pontil. Dark purple and white slag. Nice pinch pontil. Misshapen. American, circa 1900-1920. 21/32". Mint (9.5). Price: $11. CyberAuction #436, Lot #7.

7919. TRANSITIONAL. Pinch pontil. Opaque white and translucent bright red swirls. Thin pinch pontil on the bottom. Unidentified maker. Probably 1920s to 1930s. 11/16". Mint (9.7). Price: $11. CyberAuction #440, Lot #45.

7920. TRANSITIONAL. Pinch pontil. Opaque white and translucent bright red. Great hand gathered "9" on the top. Nice tail and pontil on the bottom. One tiny melt spot. Origin and age unknown, probably American, circa 1920s. 5/8". Mint (9.5). Price: $10. CyberAuction #357, Lot #21.

7921. TRANSITIONAL. Pinch pontil. Opaque white and translucent bright red swirls. Thin pinch pontil on the bottom. Unidentified maker. Probably 1920s to 1930s. 9/16". Mint (9.9). Price: $10. CyberAuction #381, Lot #25.

7922. TRANSITIONAL. Pinch pontil. Opaque white and brown spiral design. Nicely pinched pontil at the bottom. American, probably 1920-1930. 19/32". Mint (9.7). Price: $10. CyberAuction #410, Lot #9.

7923. TRANSITIONAL. Pinch pontil. Opaque white and translucent bright red swirls. Thin pinch pontil on the bottom. One tiny sparkle. Unidentified maker. Probably 1920s to 1930s. 11/16". Mint(-) (9.2). Price: $10. CyberAuction #427, Lot #36.

7924. TRANSITIONAL. Pinch pontil. Opaque white and translucent bright red swirls. Thin pinch pontil on the bottom. Unidentified maker. Probably 1920s to 1930s. 9/16". Mint (9.9). Price: $10. CyberAuction #444, Lot #9.

7925. TRANSITIONAL. Pinch pontil. Dark purple and white slag. Nice pinch pontil. Misshapen. American, circa 1900-1920. 21/32". Mint (9.5). Price: $10. CyberAuction #488, Lot #18.

7926. TRANSITIONAL. Pinch pontil. Opaque white and translucent bright red swirls. Thin pinch pontil on the bottom. One pinprick. Unidentified maker. Probably 1920s to 1930s. 11/16". Mint(-) (9.2). Price: $9. CyberAuction #428, Lot #55.

7927. TRANSITIONAL. Pinch pontil. Opaque white and translucent bright red swirls. Thin pinch pontil on the bottom. Some tiny chips and pits. Unidentified maker. Probably 1920s to 1930s. 11/16". Near Mint (8.4). Price: $7. CyberAuction #421, Lot #41.

7928. TRANSITIONAL. Pinch pontil. Opaque white and translucent bright red swirls. Thin pinch pontil on the bottom. One flake. Unidentified maker. Probably 1920s to 1930s. 9/16". Near Mint(+) (8.8). Price: $7. CyberAuction #456, Lot #54.

7929. TRANSITIONAL. Pinch pontil. Opaque white and translucent bright red swirls. Thin pinch pontil on the bottom. One flake. Unidentified maker. Probably 1920s to 1930s. 9/16". Near Mint(+) (8.8). Price: $5. CyberAuction #392, Lot #22.

7930. TRANSITIONAL. Pinch pontil. Swirls of electric translucent red in opaque white. Nice pontil. Looks like an American Agate. Chip and some pitting. American, circa 1920-1930. 11/16". Near Mint(-) (8.0). Price: $4. CyberAuction #372, Lot #55.

7931. TRANSITIONAL. Pinch pontil. Opaque white and translucent bright red swirls. Long pinch pontil on the bottom. Sparkle and a very tiny flake. Unidentified maker. Probably 1920s to 1930s. 11/16". Near Mint(+) (8.8). Price: $4. CyberAuction #429, Lot #12.

7932. TRANSITIONAL. Pinch pontil. Orange swirls on white. Buffed. 5/8". Price: $4. CyberAuction #477, Lot #54.

7933. TRANSITIONAL. Pinch pontil. Opaque white and translucent bright red swirls. Thin pinch pontil on the bottom. Some tiny chips and pits. Unidentified maker. Probably 1920s to 1930s. 11/16". Near Mint (8.4). Price: $3. CyberAuction #424, Lot #17.

7934. TRANSITIONAL. Regular pontil. Transparent aqua base with lots of unmelted sand in it. Yellow swirls on the surface. Nice regular pontil. Has one tiny air hole and some rubbing. This marble came from a Germany from a German consignor. My guess is that it is German and not American. Circa 1880-1920. 11/16". Mint(-) (9.0). Price: $50. CyberAuction #339, Lot #48.

7935. TRANSITIONAL. Regular pontil. Transparent clear base. Filled with unmelted sand. Small white spiral with a small cloud of air bubbles rising into the center from the pontil. Nice regular pontil. American, circa 1880-1910. 5/8". Mint (9.5). Price: $24. CyberAuction #371, Lot #30.

7936. VITRO AGATE COMPANY. All-Red. Nice marble. Opaque white base. Red patch on one pole, green on the other. There is an excellent red "V" in the green. Parkersburg, WV, circa 1965-1980. 7/8". Mint (9.9). Price: $15. CyberAuction #380, Lot #5.

7937. VITRO AGATE COMPANY. Catseye. Hard to find. Gladding-Vitro cage style. Transparent blue base with white ribbons. Shooter. Gorgeous. Parkersburg, WV, circa 1960-1970. 7/8". Mint (9.9). Price: $37. CyberAuction #381, Lot #47.

7938. VITRO AGATE COMPANY. Catseye. Beautiful hybrid shooter catseye. Transparent clear base. Five vanes. Yellow vanes with red edging. Gorgeous. Parkersburg, WV, circa 1955-1965. 7/8". Mint (9.9). Price: $29. CyberAuction #330, Lot #30.

7939. VITRO AGATE COMPANY. Catseye. Shooter hybrid catseye. Five yellow vanes with red and green highlights. Beauty. Parkersburg, WV, circa 1955-1970. 29/32". Mint (9.8). Price: $17. CyberAuction #414, Lot #40.

7940. VITRO AGATE COMPANY. Catseye. Shooter hybrid catseye. Gray vanes, edged with a little green. 7/8". Mint (9.7). Price: $9. CyberAuction #404, Lot #6.

7941. VITRO AGATE COMPANY. Catseye. Shooter hybrid catseye. Red, edged by gray. Sparkles. 7/8". Mint(-) (9.0). Price: $8. CyberAuction #453, Lot #46.

7942. VITRO AGATE COMPANY. Catseye. Shooter hybrid catseye. Red, edged by gray. Sparkles. 7/8". Mint(-) (9.0). Price: $7. CyberAuction #404, Lot #7.

7943. VITRO AGATE COMPANY. Catseye. Nice shooter hybrid catseye. Four vane. Each is yellow and green. One tiny moon. Parkersburg, WV, circa 1950-1965. 31/32". Near Mint(+) (8.9). Price: $6. CyberAuction #360, Lot #47.

7944. VITRO AGATE COMPANY. Catseye. Hybrid shooter catseye. Yellow vanes with orange highlights. Very pretty. Parkersburg, WV, circa 1960-1970. 7/8". Mint (9.9). Price: $6. CyberAuction #410, Lot #24.

7945. VITRO AGATE COMPANY. Catseye. Shooter hybrid catseye. Five vane. Green, blue and white. Nice. 27/32". Mint (9.4). Price: $5. CyberAuction #378, Lot #39.

7946. VITRO AGATE COMPANY. Catseye. Four vane hybrid catseye. Blue and white. Very nice. Parkersburg, WV, circa 1960-1970. 5/8". Mint (9.7). Price: $1. CyberAuction #362, Lot #6.

7947. VITRO AGATE COMPANY. Catseyes. Shooter hybrid cage style. Red, yellow and gray. Subsurface moon. Parkersburg, WV, circa 1970-1980. 7/8". Near Mint(+) (8.9). Price: $4. CyberAuction #355, Lot #47.

7948. VITRO AGATE COMPANY. Original package. Original box of Jabo-V's, Series II, Millennium Edition 2000. Distributed by Lost Your Marbles. These are Jabo-Vitro short runs. The distributor then goes through, picks out the Mint ones, cleans them, and packages them in these boxes. Silver printing on the box top. This one is a variety of color swirls. Very nice. Price: $23. CyberAuction #429, Lot #32.

7949. VITRO AGATE COMPANY. Original package. Original poly bag of "VITRO CAT EYES" "30 - 10 cents". Red and black printing on white label. Contains thirty Vitro catseyes, including many hybrids. In great shape. Parkersburg, WV, circa 1960-1965. Mint (9.9). Price: $21. CyberAuction #390, Lot #24.

7950. VITRO AGATE COMPANY. Original package. Original poly bag of "VITRO CAT EYES" "19 - 5 cents". Yellow and black printing on white label. Contains nineteen Vitro catseyes, including many hybrids. In great shape. Parkersburg, WV, circa 1955-1960. Mint (9.8). There are two packages available, you are bidding on one. Winner has choice of either or both, remainder to under. Price: $21. CyberAuction #499, Lot #24.

7951. VITRO AGATE COMPANY. Original package. Original box of Jabo-V's, Series II, Millennium Edition 2000. Distributed by Lost Your Marbles. These are Jabo-Vitro short runs. The distributor then goes through, picks out the Mint ones, cleans them, and packages them in these boxes. Silver printing on the box top. This one is a evenly divided between brown, light green and white swirls, and brown and white swirls. Very nice. Price: $19. CyberAuction #436, Lot #25.

7952. VITRO AGATE COMPANY. Original package. Original poly bag of "VITRO CAT EYES" "19 - 5 cents". Yellow and black printing on white label. Contains nineteen Vitro catseyes, including many hybrids. In great shape. Parkersburg, WV, circa 1955-1960. Mint (9.8). There are two packages available, you are bidding on one. Winner has choice of either or both, remainder to under. Price: $17. CyberAuction #467, Lot #28.

7953. VITRO AGATE COMPANY. Original package. Original box of "60 GAME MARBLES - No. 00". Full set of marbles. Box corners are taped. No stains. Near Mint(+) (8.9). Price: $15. CyberAuction #395, Lot #27.

7954. VITRO AGATE COMPANY. Original package. Original box of Jabo-V's, Series II, Millennium Edition 2000. Distributed by Lost Your Marbles. These are Jabo-Vitro short runs. The distributor then goes through, picks out the Mint ones, cleans them, and packages them in these boxes. Silver printing on the box top. This red/white and green/white swirls. Very nice. Price: $15. CyberAuction #429, Lot #33.

7955. VITRO AGATE COMPANY. Original package. Poly bag of forty six Vitro Agate modern patches. The header label is from Anacortes, WA. This is the last batch of Vitros produced before they were bought out by JABO. Header has some creasing. Circa mid 1990s. Mint(-) (9.2). Price: $13. CyberAuction #447, Lot #25.

7956. VITRO AGATE COMPANY. Original package. Original poly bag of "VITRO CAT EYES" "19 - 5 cents". Red and black printing on white label. Contains nineteen Vitro catseyes, including many hybrids. In great shape. Parkersburg, WV, circa 1960-1965. Near Mint(+) (8.7). Price: $12. CyberAuction #361, Lot #40.

7957. VITRO AGATE COMPANY. Original package. Early poly bag. Red on white header label. "19 VITRO-AGATES". Continues three color brushed patch on transparent clear. Parkersburg, WV, circa 1950-1960. 5" x 4". Mint (9.5). Price: $11. CyberAuction #357, Lot #29.

7958. VITRO AGATE COMPANY. Original package. Poly bag. "100 count Vitro Cat Eye". White label, blue printing. Contains a number of hybrids. 7" x 3" (sight). Mint(-) (9.2). Price: $11. CyberAuction #465, Lot #26.

7959. VITRO AGATE COMPANY. Original package. Early poly bag. Red on white header label. "19 VITRO-AGATES". Contains three color brushed patch on transparent clear (Tigereye). Parkersburg, WV, circa 1950-1960. 5" x 4". Mint (9.5). Two bags available. You are bidding on one. Winner has choice of one or both, remainder to under. Price: $10. CyberAuction #335, Lot #28.

7960. VITRO AGATE COMPANY. Original package. Poly bag of forty six Vitro Agate modern patches. The header label is from Anacortes, WA. This is the last batch of Vitros produced before they were bought out by JABO. Header has some creasing. Circa mid 1990s. Mint(-) (9.2). Price: $10. CyberAuction #365, Lot #30.

7961. VITRO AGATE COMPANY. Original package. Original poly bag of "10 count Five Star Brand Vitro Catseyes". Blue printing on white label. 5"

x 3". Mint (9.7). There are two bags available, you are bidding on one. Winner has choice of either or both, remainder to under. Price: $7. CyberAuction #409, Lot #31.

7962. VITRO AGATE COMPANY. Original package. Poly bag. White header label with red printing. "Exotic Glass Gems". 25 count. Red clearie shooters. Some damage to label. Near Mint(+) (8.8). Price: $4. CyberAuction #419, Lot #26.

7963. VITRO AGATE COMPANY. Oxblood. Very rare Vitro Agate oxblood patch. Transparent red base filled with tiny air bubbles. Patch of Vitro oxblood covering about half of the marble. A couple of minor pinpricks. Parkersburg, WV, circa 1945-1955. 19/32". Mint(-) (9.2). Price: $50. CyberAuction #374, Lot #39.

7964. VITRO AGATE COMPANY. Oxblood. Rare type. Patch oxblood. Four color. Clear base. Green and wispy white patch on one side. Loaded with oxblood on the other. Outstanding marble. Several tiny flakes. Parkersburg, WV, circa 1945-1950. 23/32". Near Mint(+) (8.7). Price: $34. CyberAuction #457, Lot #48.

7965. VITRO AGATE COMPANY. Oxblood. Transparent blue base with wispy white vanes. Has an oxblood stripe on the surface. Parkersburg, WV, circa 1950-1965. 9/16". Mint (9.7). Price: $21. CyberAuction #356, Lot #23.

7966. VITRO AGATE COMPANY. Oxblood. Transparent clear base. Wide patch of opaque light blue. Two patches of wispy oxblood. Both oxblood patches form "V"s. Pitting and tiny chips. Parkersburg, WV, circa 1945-1960. 15/16". Near Mint(-) (8.0). Price: $17. CyberAuction #505, Lot #41.

7967. VITRO AGATE COMPANY. Parrot. Beautiful example. Opaque white base. Patches of yellow, blue, lavender, green and brown/red. The yellow forms a super "V". Some scratches. Parkersburg, WV, circa 1950-1960. 29/32". Mint(-) (9.0). Price: $38. CyberAuction #426, Lot #52.

7968. VITRO AGATE COMPANY. Parrot. Beautiful example. Opaque white base. Patches of yellow, blue, lavender, green and brown/red. The yellow forms a super "V". Some scratches. Parkersburg, WV, circa 1950-1960. 29/32". Mint(-) (9.0). Price: $32. CyberAuction #396, Lot #48.

7969. VITRO AGATE COMPANY. Parrot. Modern parrot shooter. Semi-opaque white base with bands of yellow, green, blue, orange. Parkersburg, WV, circa 1965-1975. 7/8". Mint (9.9). Price: $12. CyberAuction #362, Lot #24.

7970. VITRO AGATE COMPANY. Parrot. Modern Parrot. Nice "V". Parkersburg, WV, circa 1965-1980. 7/8". Mint (9.7). Price: $9. CyberAuction #397, Lot #53.

7971. VITRO AGATE COMPANY. Parrot. Modern Parrot. Excellent coloring. Parkersburg, WV, circa 1970-1985. 19/32". Mint (9.9). There are two available. You are bidding on one. Winner has a choice of one or both. Remainder to under. Price: $8. CyberAuction #350, Lot #2.

7972. VITRO AGATE COMPANY. Parrot. Modern Parrot. Opaque white base. Patch of green, orange and thin one of blue. Stylized "V". Subsurface tiny moons. Parkersburg, WV, circa 1965-1980. 23/32". Near Mint (8.5). Price: $4. CyberAuction #372, Lot #51.

7973. VITRO AGATE COMPANY. Parrot. A type of Parrot (anemic Parrot?). White base. Wide patch of yellow and white patch of aventurine green. Nice. Has a couple of tiny flakes. Parkersburg, WV, circa 1955-1970. 29/32". Near Mint (8.5). Price: $2. CyberAuction #422, Lot #13.

7974. VITRO AGATE COMPANY. Parrot. A type of Parrot (anemic Parrot?). White base. Wide patch of yellow and white patch of aventurine green. Nice. Has a couple of tiny flakes. Parkersburg, WV, circa 1955-1970. 29/32". Near Mint (8.5). Price: $1. CyberAuction #389, Lot #20.

7975. VITRO AGATE COMPANY. Patch. I'm pretty sure that this type is Vitro. It is very hard to find. I've seen maybe half dozen examples in various colors during the past five years. Opaque creamy white base. Wide "V" of translucent baby blue and a mirroring opaque bright white. Parkersburg, WV, circa 1955-1965. 31/32". Mint (9.7). Price: $60. CyberAuction #374, Lot #56.

7976. VITRO AGATE COMPANY. Patch. Popeye Patch mimic. But, very unusual. Red, blue, white and clear. Super "V" on the outer blue patch. And a very nice "V" in the white and red patch, when viewed through the open clear panel. Highly unusual. Parkersburg, WV, circa 1945-1960. 23/32". Mint (9.7). Price: $13. CyberAuction #461, Lot #10.

7977. VITRO AGATE COMPANY. Patch. Interesting. Opaque white base. Surface is veneered with red. Has a nice "V" in lighter red. Odd. Parkersburg, WV, circa 1955-1975. 27/32". Mint (9.9). Price: $12. CyberAuction #456, Lot #43.

7978. VITRO AGATE COMPANY. Patch. Interesting. Opaque white base. Surface is veneered with red. Has a nice "V" in lighter red. Odd. Parkersburg, WV, circa 1955-1975. 27/32". Mint (9.9). Price: $7. CyberAuction #416, Lot #38.

7979. VITRO AGATE COMPANY. Patch. Nice three color patch with two nice "V"s on it. One is in wispy "oxblood". Some tiny pitting. Parkersburg, WV, circa 1950-1965. 27/32". Near Mint(+) (8.7). Price: $7. CyberAuction #505, Lot #28.

7980. VITRO AGATE COMPANY. Patch. Odd coloring. Nice lazy "V". Parkersburg, WV, circa 1965-1980. 3/4". Mint (9.7). Price: $5. CyberAuction #425, Lot #2.

7981. VITRO AGATE COMPANY. Patch. Modern Parrot. Opaque white base. Patch of orange and patch of green. Stylized "V" pattern in both patches. Parkersburg, WV, circa 1970-1985. 7/8". Mint (9.9). Price: $4. CyberAuction #345, Lot #43.

7982. VITRO AGATE COMPANY. Patch. Sparkler-type patch. Very nice. Parkersburg, WV, circa 1960-1980. 19/32". Mint (9.9). There are four marbles available. You are bidding on one. Winner has choice of any or all, remainder to under. Price: $4. CyberAuction #365, Lot #27.

7983. VITRO AGATE COMPANY. Patch. Early Vitro patch. Semi-opaque light green with a light blue patch. Nice. Parkersburg, WV, circa 1945-1955. 5/8". Mint (9.9). Price: $4. CyberAuction #376, Lot #4.

7984. VITRO AGATE COMPANY. Patch. Popeye patch mimic. Blue and yellow. Parkersburg, WV, circa 1970-1990. 19/32". Mint (9.7). Price: $4. CyberAuction #381, Lot #13.

7985. VITRO AGATE COMPANY. Patch. Vitro patch. Opaque white base. Green patch and a mustard yellow patch. One tiny subsurface moon. Parkersburg, WV, circa 1955-1970. 31/32". Near Mint(+) (8.9). Price: $2. CyberAuction #362, Lot #43.

7986. VITRO AGATE COMPANY. Patch. Popeye patch look-alike. Blue and yellow. Flat spot. Parkersburg, WV, circa 1955-1975. 19/32". Mint(-) (9.1). Price: $1. CyberAuction #419, Lot #13.

7987. VITRO AGATE COMPANY. Patch. Odd patch of blue on white and grey. I'm unsure of the age. 19/32". Mint (9.9). Consignor note: G50. Price: $1. CyberAuction #424, Lot #38.

7988. VITRO AGATE COMPANY. Patch and ribbon. At first I thought it was a Peltier or an odd Marble King, but I think it is Vitro. White base. Orange ribbon encircling the equator, orange patch at either pole. Age unknown. 19/32". Mint (9.9). Price: $3. CyberAuction #443, Lot #9.

7989. VITRO AGATE COMPANY. Patch oxblood. Rare marble. Transparent red base. Oxblood patch on one side. Parkersburg, WV, circa 1940-1955. 7/8". Mint (9.8). Price: $40. CyberAuction #465, Lot #40.

7990. VITRO AGATE COMPANY. Patch oxblood. I believe this is actually Vitro Agate and not Akro Agate. Shooter. Opaque white base. Orange band on one side. Oxblood band on the other. A couple of tiny subsurface moons.

Parkersburg, WV, circa 1940-1950. 1". Near Mint(+) (8.7). Price: $15. CyberAuction #362, Lot #19.

7991. VITRO AGATE COMPANY. Ribbon. One of the very hard to find eight-ribbon Vitros. Opaque black base with eight white ribbons. Hardest color to find. Parkersburg, WV, age unknown. 19/32". Mint (9.9). Price: $70. CyberAuction #481, Lot #53.

7992. VITRO AGATE COMPANY. Ribbon. One of the very hard to find eight-ribbon Vitros. Translucent very dark purple base with eight white ribbons. Parkersburg, WV, age unknown. 19/32". Mint (9.9). Price: $50. CyberAuction #337, Lot #19.

7993. VITRO AGATE COMPANY. Ribbon. This is very similar to the six-ribbon Vitros. Transparent clear base. Four ribbons and two patches of semi-opaque white. This is a rare marble. Parkersburg, WV, circa 1950-1965. 11/16". Mint (9.9). Price: $40. CyberAuction #436, Lot #37.

7994. VITRO AGATE COMPANY. Tigereye. Conqueror type. Transparent clear base. Opaque white equatorial ribbon. Yellow patch and purple patch. Parkersburg, WV, circa 1940-1950. 19/32". Mint (9.7). There are three marbles available. You are bidding on one. Winner has choice of any or all, remainder to under. Price: $3. CyberAuction #365, Lot #42.

7995. VITRO AGATE COMPANY. Whitie. Opaque white base. Aventurine green ribbon around equator. Two seam. 19/32". Mint (9.9). Price: $6. CyberAuction #378, Lot #37.

7996. VITRO AGATE COMPANY. Whitie. Opaque white base. Aventurine green ribbon around equator. Two seam. 19/32". Mint (9.9). Price: $3. CyberAuction #391, Lot #35.

Indices
Index One — Cross Reference of Auction/Lot to Listing Number

If you are interested in finding the listing for a particular lot in a particular CyberAuction this list is in CyberAuction/Lot order (CyberAuction_Lot ... Listing number). This is useful if you are trying to reconstruct a particular auction or to view trends over time.

39_59 ... 4429	342_29 ... 2268	345_7 ... 7470	347_38 ... 3386	350_6 ... 3224	352_26 ... 7237
39_60 ... 1928	342_30 ... 1310	345_8 ... 7456	347_39 ... 6932	350_7 ... 7640	352_28 ... 7773
40_5 ... 1526	342_31 ... 5691	345_9 ... 5402	347_40 ... 4491	350_9 ... 2329	352_35 ... 3567
40_10 ... 3466	342_32 ... 2041	345_10 ... 5408	347_41 ... 6600	350_10 ... 3170	352_36 ... 5698
40_11 ... 6438	342_33 ... 939	345_11 ... 1054	347_42 ... 1300	350_11 ... 7261	352_37 ... 4766
40_12 ... 1648	342_35 ... 1750	345_12 ... 5874	347_43 ... 6773	350_12 ... 948	352_38 ... 5750
40_13 ... 3783	342_36 ... 10	345_13 ... 3745	347_44 ... 7485	350_14 ... 7164	352_39 ... 3449
40_14 ... 6406	342_37 ... 6512	345_14 ... 2471	347_45 ... 3294	350_15 ... 1615	352_40 ... 7641
40_19 ... 3173	342_38 ... 1117	345_15 ... 6479	347_46 ... 7394	350_16 ... 6377	352_41 ... 2080
40_20 ... 7278	342_39 ... 4134	345_16 ... 4827	347_47 ... 1369	350_17 ... 3419	352_42 ... 6405
40_21 ... 198	342_40 ... 4765	345_18 ... 4510	347_48 ... 1731	350_18 ... 2343	352_43 ... 156
40_23 ... 376	342_41 ... 7822	345_19 ... 2415	347_49 ... 2654	350_19 ... 2088	352_44 ... 6933
40_27 ... 6573	342_42 ... 7579	345_20 ... 1612	347_50 ... 1102	350_20 ... 6601	352_45 ... 3439
40_31 ... 1639	342_43 ... 4523	345_21 ... 3950	347_51 ... 6637	350_21 ... 1347	352_47 ... 1514
40_42 ... 7724	342_44 ... 7423	345_22 ... 6809	347_52 ... 264	350_22 ... 3948	352_48 ... 7395
40_43 ... 3290	342_45 ... 4466	345_23 ... 218	347_53 ... 4398	350_23 ... 6394	352_49 ... 3365
40_45 ... 3203	342_46 ... 5471	345_24 ... 1336	347_54 ... 1346	350_27 ... 2693	352_50 ... 457
40_46 ... 2514	342_47 ... 1386	345_25 ... 2810	347_55 ... 6513	350_30 ... 5129	352_51 ... 6358
40_47 ... 1016	342_48 ... 7527	345_26 ... 1361	347_56 ... 1094	350_31 ... 2042	352_52 ... 233
40_48 ... 3991	342_49 ... 98	345_27 ... 1055	347_57 ... 4079	350_32 ... 5777	352_53 ... 1764
40_49 ... 2031	342_50 ... 876	345_28 ... 5641	347_58 ... 3348	350_36 ... 5640	352_54 ... 1400
40_50 ... 117	342_51 ... 5685	345_29 ... 3402	347_59 ... 4393	350_39 ... 6448	352_55 ... 2240
40_51 ... 7309	342_52 ... 116	345_30 ... 3640	347_60 ... 1925	350_40 ... 1988	352_56 ... 403
40_52 ... 591	342_53 ... 1173	345_31 ... 7300	348_1 ... 2559	350_41 ... 6328	352_57 ... 3406
40_53 ... 6744	342_54 ... 5548	345_32 ... 3291	348_2 ... 6458	350_43 ... 297	352_58 ... 4742
40_54 ... 6203	342_55 ... 3713	345_33 ... 5748	348_3 ... 431	350_44 ... 724	352_59 ... 2578
40_55 ... 1072	342_56 ... 2605	345_34 ... 5159	348_4 ... 2371	350_45 ... 3163	352_60 ... 185
40_56 ... 4446	342_57 ... 2970	345_35 ... 14	348_5 ... 3894	350_46 ... 6514	353_1 ... 7425
40_57 ... 351	342_58 ... 1217	345_36 ... 6307	348_6 ... 6638	350_47 ... 402	353_2 ... 434
40_58 ... 7636	342_60 ... 6265	345_37 ... 4407	348_7 ... 2273	350_48 ... 3651	353_3 ... 5843
40_59 ... 1494	343_12 ... 1518	345_39 ... 7229	348_8 ... 3058	350_49 ... 2087	353_4 ... 4183
40_60 ... 1305	343_13 ... 1301	345_40 ... 3274	348_9 ... 7377	350_50 ... 3239	353_5 ... 7325
41_4 ... 7525	343_15 ... 318	345_41 ... 6772	348_10 ... 7337	350_51 ... 2540	353_6 ... 3435
41_5 ... 3598	343_16 ... 4009	345_42 ... 2449	348_11 ... 983	350_53 ... 7412	353_7 ... 5681
41_6 ... 5501	343_25 ... 7424	345_43 ... 7981	348_12 ... 7313	350_54 ... 1441	353_8 ... 4853
41_8 ... 5967	343_37 ... 4841	345_44 ... 5680	348_13 ... 7329	350_55 ... 7365	353_9 ... 7078
41_10 ... 3653	343_38 ... 3981	345_45 ... 1773	348_14 ... 2093	350_56 ... 5002	353_10 ... 2089
41_12 ... 4688	343_39 ... 653	345_46 ... 6012	348_15 ... 6370	350_57 ... 2237	353_11 ... 4297
41_13 ... 6223	343_44 ... 1413	345_48 ... 7084	348_16 ... 1113	350_58 ... 7890	353_12 ... 6748
41_14 ... 262	343_49 ... 1393	345_49 ... 5440	348_17 ... 7529	350_59 ... 3994	353_14 ... 4264
41_15 ... 5556	343_50 ... 4738	345_50 ... 2309	348_18 ... 280	350_60 ... 5065	353_15 ... 3108
41_17 ... 4027	343_51 ... 2797	345_51 ... 3399	348_19 ... 6335	351_1 ... 432	353_16 ... 6537
41_18 ... 4573	343_52 ... 4629	345_52 ... 5627	348_20 ... 4897	351_2 ... 5862	353_17 ... 1138
41_19 ... 7526	343_53 ... 7585	345_53 ... 4669	348_21 ... 7364	351_3 ... 554	353_18 ... 2818
41_20 ... 390	343_54 ... 353	345_54 ... 1452	348_22 ... 7794	351_4 ... 3405	353_20 ... 7531
41_21 ... 2479	343_55 ... 2442	345_55 ... 5632	348_23 ... 3414	351_5 ... 433	353_21 ... 3394
41_25 ... 3212	343_56 ... 3068	345_56 ... 4087	348_24 ... 5534	351_6 ... 5009	353_22 ... 5672
41_28 ... 692	343_57 ... 3879	345_57 ... 2577	348_25 ... 6657	351_7 ... 641	353_23 ... 1611
41_29 ... 4480	343_58 ... 5811	345_58 ... 4759	348_26 ... 486	351_8 ... 3430	353_24 ... 6418
41_30 ... 3495	343_59 ... 2140	345_59 ... 4047	348_27 ... 5696	351_9 ... 7530	353_27 ... 2228
41_31 ... 3207	343_60 ... 6457	345_60 ... 3709	348_28 ... 3201	351_10 ... 3431	353_28 ... 2667
41_32 ... 3522	344_2 ... 5075	345_61 ... 3026	348_29 ... 6459	351_11 ... 6658	353_31 ... 6296
41_33 ... 3591	344_3 ... 7737	346_4 ... 6878	348_32 ... 4417	351_12 ... 714	353_32 ... 2694
41_35 ... 1818	344_4 ... 4165	346_7 ... 4558	348_33 ... 4821	351_13 ... 2636	353_34 ... 2641
41_37 ... 2924	344_5 ... 7411	346_8 ... 6746	348_34 ... 5692	351_14 ... 574	353_35 ... 435
41_38 ... 5095	344_6 ... 3444	346_9 ... 500	348_35 ... 3411	351_15 ... 1800	353_36 ... 7587
41_39 ... 4627	344_7 ... 4106	346_11 ... 4508	348_36 ... 5529	351_16 ... 3250	353_37 ... 3457
41_40 ... 217	344_8 ... 319	346_12 ... 6879	348_37 ... 6313	351_17 ... 3422	353_38 ... 62
41_41 ... 3719	344_9 ... 7336	346_16 ... 7136	348_39 ... 4128	351_18 ... 88	353_40 ... 4000
41_42 ... 5654	344_10 ... 7085	346_18 ... 7760	348_40 ... 320	351_19 ... 6439	353_41 ... 133
41_43 ... 201	344_12 ... 905	346_29 ... 3209	348_41 ... 5605	351_20 ... 1023	353_42 ... 6553
41_44 ... 6877	344_13 ... 3467	346_30 ... 3485	348_42 ... 209	351_21 ... 7586	353_44 ... 5699
41_45 ... 2037	344_14 ... 7135	346_31 ... 7147	348_43 ... 3338	351_22 ... 501	353_45 ... 603
41_46 ... 844	344_16 ... 5132	346_33 ... 5719	348_44 ... 626	351_23 ... 5697	353_46 ... 4455
41_47 ... 3382	344_17 ... 6745	346_35 ... 2034	348_45 ... 4099	351_24 ... 718	353_47 ... 7896
41_48 ... 4227	344_19 ... 5952	346_38 ... 7676	348_46 ... 812	351_25 ... 2085	353_48 ... 2825
41_49 ... 968	344_20 ... 651	346_39 ... 3759	348_47 ... 2811	351_26 ... 2625	353_49 ... 7099
41_50 ... 5533	344_21 ... 2420	346_40 ... 4644	348_48 ... 1450	351_27 ... 456	353_50 ... 6538
41_51 ... 263	344_22 ... 3177	346_41 ... 6552	348_49 ... 4999	351_28 ... 7518	353_51 ... 2137
41_52 ... 3404	344_23 ... 6574	346_43 ... 7120	348_50 ... 7314	351_29 ... 321	353_52 ... 3824
41_53 ... 879	344_24 ... 4849	346_44 ... 1622	348_51 ... 4707	351_30 ... 4228	353_53 ... 2687
41_54 ... 7290	344_25 ... 3500	346_45 ... 2539	348_52 ... 7094	351_31 ... 1237	353_54 ... 2
41_55 ... 352	344_30 ... 3213	346_47 ... 7738	348_53 ... 1278	351_32 ... 2349	353_55 ... 6430
41_56 ... 2400	344_31 ... 7270	346_48 ... 4536	348_54 ... 3235	351_33 ... 709	353_56 ... 5328
41_57 ... 4691	344_32 ... 898	346_50 ... 4593	348_55 ... 3975	351_34 ... 5863	353_57 ... 4894
41_58 ... 3977	344_34 ... 2677	346_51 ... 5890	348_56 ... 758	351_35 ... 7913	353_58 ... 1476
41_59 ... 2110	344_36 ... 5674	346_52 ... 982	348_57 ... 4052	351_36 ... 7248	353_59 ... 3312
41_60 ... 3335	344_37 ... 3097	346_53 ... 2721	348_58 ... 5066	351_37 ... 4628	353_60 ... 2160
42_1 ... 4825	344_38 ... 3705	346_54 ... 4490	348_59 ... 1918	351_38 ... 6620	354_1 ... 3619
42_2 ... 6511	344_39 ... 1510	346_55 ... 4282	348_60 ... 3028	351_39 ... 555	354_2 ... 880
42_3 ... 7637	344_40 ... 5708	346_56 ... 2391	349_1 ... 7702	351_40 ... 6575	354_3 ... 5864
42_4 ... 485	344_41 ... 84	346_57 ... 1433	349_2 ... 3145	351_41 ... 229	354_5 ... 2655
42_5 ... 3971	344_42 ... 2942	346_58 ... 3098	349_6 ... 7703	351_42 ... 6395	354_6 ... 1996
42_6 ... 232	344_43 ... 202	346_59 ... 1467	349_8 ... 7202	351_43 ... 4552	354_7 ... 3474
42_7 ... 3936	344_44 ... 7324	346_60 ... 5521	349_11 ... 845	351_44 ... 6417	354_8 ... 4080
42_8 ... 7800	344_45 ... 203	347_2 ... 7771	349_14 ... 4296	351_45 ... 974	354_10 ... 1513
42_9 ... 4281	344_47 ... 3236	347_3 ... 7528	349_28 ... 5128	351_46 ... 1709	354_11 ... 7426
42_10 ... 317	344_48 ... 5262	347_4 ... 4295	349_29 ... 3218	351_47 ... 298	354_12 ... 977
42_11 ... 3401	344_49 ... 1446	347_6 ... 6407	349_38 ... 3506	351_48 ... 963	354_13 ... 4248
42_12 ... 4561	344_50 ... 6415	347_8 ... 5709	349_44 ... 7639	351_49 ... 5199	354_14 ... 5014
42_13 ... 7622	344_51 ... 4129	347_9 ... 5920	349_46 ... 5087	351_50 ... 4098	354_15 ... 5419
42_14 ... 927	344_52 ... 6808	347_10 ... 4913	349_49 ... 5891	351_51 ... 2249	354_16 ... 4467
42_15 ... 2413	344_53 ... 4869	347_12 ... 5749	349_51 ... 5988	351_52 ... 3780	354_17 ... 2344
42_16 ... 4502	344_54 ... 6372	347_13 ... 7387	349_52 ... 7803	351_53 ... 6304	354_18 ... 3416
42_17 ... 6731	344_55 ... 792	347_14 ... 1618	349_53 ... 1831	351_54 ... 2025	354_21 ... 3493
42_18 ... 1110	344_56 ... 3608	347_15 ... 5968	349_54 ... 1127	351_55 ... 7065	354_22 ... 4148
42_19 ... 4131	344_57 ... 4118	347_17 ... 5770	349_56 ... 5720	351_56 ... 53	354_23 ... 322
42_20 ... 7798	344_58 ... 3705	347_18 ... 3424	349_57 ... 7844	351_57 ... 4120	354_24 ... 7588
42_21 ... 5663	344_59 ... 6334	347_19 ... 6561	349_58 ... 5721	351_58 ... 3030	354_25 ... 3497
42_22 ... 4839	344_60 ... 1940	347_22 ... 4675	349_59 ... 4489	351_59 ... 592	354_26 ... 7238
42_23 ... 6636	345_1 ... 5803	347_23 ... 5827	349_60 ... 3949	351_60 ... 5156	354_28 ... 3629
42_24 ... 7797	345_2 ... 5739	347_24 ... 1000	350_1 ... 5469	352_4 ... 2083	354_29 ... 3631
42_25 ... 5552	345_3 ... 2414	347_29 ... 4617	350_2 ... 7971	352_8 ... 7772	354_30 ... 3208
42_26 ... 5629	345_4 ... 6029	347_30 ... 3571	350_3 ... 5875	352_10 ... 1111	354_31 ... 3634
42_27 ... 4488	345_5 ... 7484	347_32 ... 6497	350_4 ... 3415	352_12 ... 6051	354_32 ... 3491
42_28 ... 4754	345_6 ... 5834	347_37 ... 6747	350_5 ... 5989	352_19 ... 2043	354_33 ... 3630

354_34 ... 3635	356_30 ... 4396	358_40 ... 6698	360_37 ... 235	363_20 ... 4107	365_26 ... 6603
354_35 ... 3633	356_31 ... 1547	358_41 ... 7877	360_38 ... 7019	363_21 ... 4757	365_27 ... 7982
354_36 ... 3632	356_32 ... 6285	358_42 ... 5596	360_39 ... 2066	363_22 ... 1751	365_29 ... 4845
354_37 ... 5856	356_33 ... 3517	358_43 ... 7082	360_40 ... 3446	363_23 ... 7351	365_30 ... 7960
354_38 ... 1745	356_34 ... 3546	358_44 ... 5969	360_41 ... 5582	363_24 ... 660	365_31 ... 2401
354_39 ... 3425	356_35 ... 3647	358_45 ... 7532	360_42 ... 1231	363_25 ... 1895	365_32 ... 5006
354_40 ... 4184	356_36 ... 3648	358_46 ... 1515	360_43 ... 5578	363_26 ... 4753	365_33 ... 3724
354_41 ... 4408	356_37 ... 5771	358_47 ... 7413	360_44 ... 1542	363_28 ... 7239	365_36 ... 6288
354_42 ... 7287	356_38 ... 3113	358_48 ... 4987	360_45 ... 3296	363_30 ... 3667	365_37 ... 5814
354_43 ... 4777	356_39 ... 5588	358_49 ... 3445	360_46 ... 7331	363_31 ... 1320	365_38 ... 906
354_44 ... 5682	356_40 ... 1466	358_50 ... 6388	360_47 ... 7943	363_32 ... 6541	365_39 ... 1661
354_45 ... 1139	356_41 ... 2696	358_51 ... 5576	360_48 ... 6699	363_33 ... 3146	365_41 ... 5535
354_46 ... 4409	356_42 ... 715	358_52 ... 7315	360_49 ... 5547	363_34 ... 1877	365_42 ... 7994
354_47 ... 3164	356_43 ... 5710	358_53 ... 6308	360_50 ... 2708	363_35 ... 5530	365_43 ... 2272
354_48 ... 7427	356_44 ... 7894	358_54 ... 5423	360_51 ... 7893	363_36 ... 2123	365_44 ... 1505
354_49 ... 3978	356_45 ... 6810	358_55 ... 2936	360_52 ... 2575	363_37 ... 6515	365_45 ... 7458
354_50 ... 2135	356_46 ... 4401	358_56 ... 1619	360_53 ... 1457	363_38 ... 825	365_46 ... 1024
354_51 ... 6180	356_47 ... 4077	358_57 ... 4283	360_54 ... 3056	363_39 ... 4179	365_47 ... 5667
354_52 ... 4090	356_48 ... 7908	358_58 ... 5844	360_55 ... 2250	363_40 ... 6142	365_48 ... 4653
354_53 ... 3716	356_49 ... 7302	358_59 ... 7643	360_56 ... 798	363_41 ... 4764	365_49 ... 1046
354_54 ... 4448	356_50 ... 2656	358_60 ... 1324	360_57 ... 3718	363_42 ... 4088	365_50 ... 3976
354_55 ... 4830	356_51 ... 716	359_1 ... 7310	360_58 ... 2974	363_43 ... 4554	365_51 ... 245
354_56 ... 4449	356_52 ... 2635	359_2 ... 3407	360_59 ... 4685	363_44 ... 3319	365_52 ... 2260
354_57 ... 5060	356_53 ... 4679	359_3 ... 6030	360_60 ... 2561	363_45 ... 3700	365_53 ... 5096
354_58 ... 6240	356_54 ... 5235	359_4 ... 899	361_5 ... 1886	363_46 ... 6162	365_54 ... 1692
354_59 ... 3656	356_55 ... 85	359_5 ... 5970	361_6 ... 6461	363_47 ... 4067	365_55 ... 7848
354_60 ... 3021	356_56 ... 4063	359_6 ... 299	361_9 ... 1890	363_48 ... 1561	365_56 ... 4004
355_1 ... 5812	356_57 ... 593	359_7 ... 5971	361_13 ... 6934	363_49 ... 5070	365_57 ... 1247
355_3 ... 6774	356_58 ... 2022	359_8 ... 3803	361_14 ... 516	363_50 ... 4670	365_58 ... 3880
355_4 ... 4631	356_59 ... 3860	359_9 ... 7176	361_16 ... 1893	363_51 ... 2231	365_59 ... 3393
355_5 ... 515	356_60 ... 3694	359_10 ... 7802	361_20 ... 5485	363_52 ... 89	365_60 ... 2768
355_6 ... 7580	357_1 ... 7761	359_11 ... 5828	361_22 ... 1952	363_53 ... 3327	366_1 ... 6185
355_7 ... 4320	357_2 ... 6732	359_12 ... 5893	361_34 ... 4525	363_54 ... 5398	366_2 ... 7539
355_8 ... 4854	357_3 ... 1109	359_13 ... 104	361_37 ... 31	363_55 ... 5016	366_3 ... 129
355_9 ... 4249	357_4 ... 2379	359_14 ... 7486	361_40 ... 7956	363_56 ... 3813	366_4 ... 7590
355_10 ... 1238	357_5 ... 6880	359_15 ... 3458	361_43 ... 1646	363_57 ... 3101	366_5 ... 3908
355_11 ... 6440	357_6 ... 723	359_16 ... 6733	361_47 ... 2729	363_59 ... 3660	366_6 ... 5990
355_12 ... 4265	357_7 ... 2472	359_17 ... 1509	361_51 ... 458	363_60 ... 2162	366_7 ... 2590
355_13 ... 3990	357_8 ... 6089	359_19 ... 6750	361_52 ... 1545	364_2 ... 5797	366_8 ... 2331
355_14 ... 1100	357_9 ... 7916	359_20 ... 3242	361_53 ... 3040	364_3 ... 7677	366_9 ... 753
355_15 ... 6639	357_10 ... 2380	359_21 ... 7305	361_54 ... 3230	364_5 ... 7487	366_10 ... 2965
355_16 ... 1150	357_11 ... 6696	359_28 ... 690	361_55 ... 2531	364_7 ... 6811	366_11 ... 5442
355_17 ... 2723	357_12 ... 377	359_29 ... 27	361_56 ... 419	364_9 ... 5486	366_12 ... 7352
355_18 ... 915	357_13 ... 6689	359_30 ... 44	361_57 ... 1544	364_11 ... 2839	366_13 ... 7644
355_19 ... 6485	357_14 ... 6697	359_34 ... 7246	361_58 ... 4535	364_13 ... 5102	366_14 ... 379
355_21 ... 4315	357_15 ... 4043	359_35 ... 2244	361_59 ... 5597	364_14 ... 4328	366_15 ... 4104
355_22 ... 1436	357_16 ... 6554	359_36 ... 5666	361_60 ... 7536	364_15 ... 7740	366_16 ... 5536
355_23 ... 3400	357_17 ... 6659	359_37 ... 4824	362_1 ... 1894	364_17 ... 3509	366_17 ... 1506
355_24 ... 2891	357_18 ... 4658	359_38 ... 1613	362_3 ... 5598	364_18 ... 159	366_18 ... 4101
355_25 ... 487	357_19 ... 5449	359_39 ... 6562	362_6 ... 7946	364_20 ... 3249	366_19 ... 5607
355_28 ... 7079	357_20 ... 6660	359_40 ... 1192	362_8 ... 1887	364_21 ... 7168	366_20 ... 3905
355_30 ... 7349	357_21 ... 7920	359_41 ... 5450	362_10 ... 6540	364_22 ... 1620	366_21 ... 236
355_31 ... 26	357_22 ... 4185	359_42 ... 3721	362_11 ... 1896	364_23 ... 1033	366_22 ... 5921
355_32 ... 3214	357_23 ... 7642	359_43 ... 7182	362_14 ... 7537	364_24 ... 2155	366_23 ... 779
355_34 ... 1861	357_24 ... 1334	359_45 ... 2783	362_17 ... 1897	364_26 ... 7439	366_24 ... 1899
355_36 ... 7338	357_25 ... 4419	359_46 ... 1128	362_18 ... 5444	364_27 ... 3511	366_25 ... 3451
355_37 ... 4712	357_26 ... 2637	359_47 ... 2489	362_19 ... 7990	364_28 ... 2094	366_26 ... 4671
355_39 ... 533	357_27 ... 4458	359_48 ... 1746	362_20 ... 1640	364_30 ... 3847	366_27 ... 2350
355_40 ... 3600	357_28 ... 6539	359_49 ... 2215	362_22 ... 556	364_32 ... 7311	366_28 ... 1945
355_41 ... 710	357_29 ... 7957	359_50 ... 3162	362_24 ... 7969	364_34 ... 1813	366_29 ... 813
355_42 ... 5813	357_31 ... 25	359_51 ... 4119	362_30 ... 6350	364_35 ... 7223	366_30 ... 3963
355_44 ... 3432	357_32 ... 46	359_52 ... 234	362_31 ... 2626	364_37 ... 725	366_31 ... 3370
355_45 ... 67	357_33 ... 7064	359_53 ... 6460	362_36 ... 38	364_38 ... 4808	366_32 ... 7489
355_46 ... 7129	357_34 ... 1453	359_54 ... 1461	362_37 ... 3789	364_39 ... 3853	366_33 ... 107
355_47 ... 7947	357_35 ... 5200	359_55 ... 6236	362_38 ... 1152	364_40 ... 4560	366_34 ... 5740
355_48 ... 6694	357_36 ... 3257	359_56 ... 281	362_39 ... 6342	364_41 ... 7471	366_35 ... 1657
355_49 ... 7739	357_37 ... 3750	359_57 ... 2798	362_40 ... 4907	364_42 ... 459	366_36 ... 5532
355_50 ... 2537	357_38 ... 1743	359_58 ... 2927	362_41 ... 3727	364_43 ... 6700	366_37 ... 4412
355_51 ... 7086	357_39 ... 5686	359_59 ... 4954	362_42 ... 7438	364_44 ... 1880	366_38 ... 5711
355_52 ... 4734	357_40 ... 4418	359_60 ... 2171	362_43 ... 7985	364_46 ... 4003	366_39 ... 7801
355_53 ... 7345	357_41 ... 174	360_1 ... 6833	362_44 ... 7366	364_48 ... 7657	366_40 ... 5431
355_54 ... 2345	357_42 ... 4039	360_2 ... 1943	362_45 ... 1953	364_49 ... 1633	366_41 ... 1490
355_55 ... 1071	357_43 ... 7889	360_3 ... 6052	362_46 ... 7031	364_50 ... 354	366_42 ... 6280
355_56 ... 5248	357_44 ... 5925	360_4 ... 78	362_47 ... 3229	364_51 ... 7879	366_43 ... 4834
355_57 ... 2987	357_45 ... 143	360_5 ... 6641	362_48 ... 1883	364_52 ... 5728	366_44 ... 5623
355_58 ... 2695	357_46 ... 7148	360_6 ... 1656	362_49 ... 4114	364_53 ... 4855	366_45 ... 7872
355_59 ... 995	357_47 ... 621	360_7 ... 4486	362_50 ... 4893	364_54 ... 2330	366_46 ... 2332
355_60 ... 3937	357_48 ... 2201	360_8 ... 2775	362_51 ... 1944	364_55 ... 378	366_47 ... 1075
356_1 ... 6695	357_49 ... 5655	360_9 ... 1961	362_52 ... 7396	364_56 ... 7440	366_48 ... 1716
356_2 ... 5106	357_50 ... 3251	360_10 ... 6563	362_53 ... 848	364_57 ... 3983	366_49 ... 7130
356_3 ... 3984	357_51 ... 3951	360_11 ... 4284	362_54 ... 7350	364_58 ... 2006	366_50 ... 3930
356_4 ... 4739	357_52 ... 2214	360_12 ... 1614	362_55 ... 620	364_59 ... 3712	366_51 ... 5192
356_5 ... 7457	357_53 ... 4966	360_13 ... 5048	362_56 ... 6602	364_60 ... 4201	366_52 ... 5085
356_6 ... 646	357_54 ... 4402	360_14 ... 5845	362_57 ... 1747	365_1 ... 1036	366_53 ... 2724
356_7 ... 6640	357_55 ... 100	360_15 ... 300	362_58 ... 5835	365_2 ... 6069	366_55 ... 4430
356_8 ... 181	357_56 ... 4059	360_16 ... 4075	362_59 ... 4149	365_3 ... 4898	366_56 ... 2169
356_9 ... 4633	357_57 ... 740	360_17 ... 7533	362_60 ... 3701	365_4 ... 6013	366_57 ... 1274
356_10 ... 5924	357_58 ... 1564	360_18 ... 7912	363_1 ... 6834	365_5 ... 323	366_58 ... 3934
356_11 ... 252	357_59 ... 7868	360_19 ... 5577	363_2 ... 370	365_6 ... 5587	366_59 ... 4676
356_12 ... 3953	357_60 ... 2969	360_20 ... 7534	363_3 ... 3450	365_7 ... 70	366_60 ... 3695
356_13 ... 3440	358_1 ... 4643	360_21 ... 1876	363_4 ... 6031	365_8 ... 1621	367_2 ... 7121
356_14 ... 7301	358_8 ... 80	360_22 ... 7656	363_5 ... 134	365_9 ... 138	367_4 ... 6070
356_15 ... 1352	358_15 ... 2707	360_23 ... 4596	363_6 ... 3852	365_10 ... 4012	367_5 ... 5894
356_16 ... 5695	358_19 ... 6576	360_24 ... 5751	363_7 ... 2678	365_11 ... 4900	367_6 ... 6835
356_17 ... 3436	358_21 ... 6351	360_25 ... 5428	363_8 ... 6775	365_12 ... 6577	367_7 ... 6990
356_18 ... 7370	358_24 ... 21	360_26 ... 3127	363_9 ... 3275	365_13 ... 436	367_10 ... 1519
356_19 ... 167	358_25 ... 3482	360_27 ... 7535	363_10 ... 5926	365_14 ... 5926	367_12 ... 4022
356_20 ... 6441	358_27 ... 7437	360_28 ... 1541	363_11 ... 6530	365_15 ... 7132	367_16 ... 6661
356_21 ... 966	358_28 ... 5892	360_29 ... 1406	363_12 ... 2732	365_16 ... 2154	367_17 ... 1884
356_22 ... 6193	358_30 ... 1722	360_30 ... 6431	363_13 ... 3059	365_17 ... 265	367_22 ... 1881
356_23 ... 7965	358_32 ... 6105	360_31 ... 5133	363_14 ... 7397	365_18 ... 6053	367_25 ... 6315
356_24 ... 3501	358_34 ... 6749	360_32 ... 5586	363_15 ... 69	365_19 ... 5752	367_26 ... 3654
356_25 ... 4819	358_35 ... 3139	360_33 ... 1610	363_16 ... 6393	365_21 ... 7488	367_27 ... 6378
356_26 ... 7378	358_36 ... 2657	360_34 ... 4074	363_17 ... 2289	365_23 ... 7538	367_28 ... 1553
356_28 ... 4100	358_38 ... 7589	360_35 ... 7231	363_18 ... 3956	365_25 ... 3231	367_37 ... 6231
356_29 ... 964	358_39 ... 7330	360_36 ... 4081	363_19 ... 2100		367_39 ... 7472

382_8 ... 3408
382_9 ... 7763
382_10 ... 4202
382_11 ... 461
382_13 ... 4786
382_14 ... 6343
382_15 ... 4800
382_16 ... 4246
382_17 ... 4848
382_20 ... 4251
382_21 ... 3751
382_23 ... 5558
382_24 ... 1649
382_25 ... 4540
382_26 ... 7774
382_27 ... 1382
382_28 ... 5991
382_29 ... 3182
382_31 ... 5896
382_32 ... 5329
382_33 ... 5714
382_34 ... 2649
382_35 ... 7227
382_36 ... 1538
382_38 ... 5846
382_39 ... 669
382_40 ... 2532
382_42 ... 2507
382_43 ... 4471
382_44 ... 6781
382_45 ... 4795
382_46 ... 2983
382_47 ... 3132
382_48 ... 6073
382_49 ... 7060
382_50 ... 4231
382_51 ... 4748
382_52 ... 6520
382_53 ... 1379
382_54 ... 4186
382_55 ... 2019
382_56 ... 3883
382_57 ... 672
382_58 ... 3835
382_59 ... 5076
382_60 ... 2921
383_1 ... 3964
383_2 ... 2610
383_3 ... 6486
383_4 ... 7068
383_7 ... 6703
383_8 ... 7161
383_9 ... 4511
383_11 ... 2978
383_15 ... 7660
383_16 ... 2096
383_18 ... 2304
383_20 ... 2840
383_21 ... 5311
383_23 ... 2849
383_28 ... 7093
383_29 ... 3397
383_34 ... 7174
383_36 ... 5462
383_37 ... 3728
383_38 ... 5403
383_39 ... 5551
383_40 ... 7845
383_41 ... 7104
383_43 ... 3095
383_44 ... 1495
383_45 ... 2910
384_3 ... 4797
384_7 ... 4801
384_10 ... 4802
384_11 ... 5044
384_19 ... 1140
384_23 ... 1540
384_26 ... 1766
384_39 ... 1972
384_40 ... 3246
384_41 ... 303
384_43 ... 894
384_44 ... 3412
384_45 ... 3085
384_46 ... 6643
384_48 ... 664
384_49 ... 2416
384_50 ... 4692
384_51 ... 1957
384_52 ... 6329
384_53 ... 4286
384_54 ... 6704
384_55 ... 4704
384_56 ... 2372
384_57 ... 629
384_58 ... 1491
384_59 ... 5069
384_60 ... 2979
385_1 ... 4787
385_2 ... 3746
385_3 ... 4864
385_4 ... 1958
385_5 ... 219
385_6 ... 4518
385_7 ... 5992
385_8 ... 4788
385_9 ... 2364
385_10 ... 3147
385_11 ... 7075
385_14 ... 3442
385_15 ... 4735
385_16 ... 2826
385_17 ... 7809
385_18 ... 5049
385_19 ... 5581
385_20 ... 5115
385_21 ... 7706
385_22 ... 1951
385_23 ... 4659
385_24 ... 5930
385_25 ... 3087
385_26 ... 4167
385_28 ... 3255
385_29 ... 4883
385_30 ... 1723
385_32 ... 5675
385_33 ... 4818
385_34 ... 6837
385_35 ... 1552
385_36 ... 3688
385_37 ... 3304
385_38 ... 1571
385_39 ... 7050
385_41 ... 2261
385_42 ... 5021
385_43 ... 6316
385_44 ... 3303
385_45 ... 5179
385_46 ... 2115
385_47 ... 2373
385_48 ... 4762
385_49 ... 2312
385_50 ... 4682
385_51 ... 4141
385_52 ... 6188
385_53 ... 744
385_54 ... 7029
385_55 ... 5063
385_56 ... 2606
385_57 ... 1197
385_58 ... 3025
385_59 ... 4929
385_60 ... 2565
386_1 ... 6664
386_4 ... 1805
386_7 ... 1520
386_10 ... 7165
386_11 ... 383
386_12 ... 5931
386_14 ... 5519
386_16 ... 7626
386_20 ... 3593
386_22 ... 3581
386_25 ... 7548
386_27 ... 6317
386_30 ... 6838
386_31 ... 5330
386_32 ... 1006
386_33 ... 1882
386_34 ... 1511
386_35 ... 2497
386_36 ... 5119
386_37 ... 3627
386_38 ... 2820
386_39 ... 3988
386_40 ... 3715
386_41 ... 5223
386_43 ... 7018
386_44 ... 4622
386_45 ... 2911
387_3 ... 2452
387_4 ... 3088
387_5 ... 4299
387_9 ... 3452
387_12 ... 3916
387_17 ... 7220
387_19 ... 7549
387_22 ... 1534
387_23 ... 6318
387_24 ... 5657
387_25 ... 1732
387_26 ... 2650
387_31 ... 3778
387_32 ... 6449
387_33 ... 3823
387_34 ... 4537
387_35 ... 6353
387_36 ... 722
387_37 ... 2183
387_38 ... 4694
387_39 ... 5425
387_40 ... 3358
387_41 ... 5583
387_42 ... 1370
387_43 ... 3031
387_46 ... 7273
387_47 ... 1366
387_48 ... 673
387_49 ... 2008
387_50 ... 601
387_51 ... 4690
387_52 ... 3282
387_53 ... 1153
387_54 ... 590
387_55 ... 206
387_56 ... 814
387_57 ... 4737
387_58 ... 738
387_59 ... 2994
387_60 ... 5064
388_1 ... 4321
388_2 ... 212
388_3 ... 6813
388_4 ... 4215
388_5 ... 4484
388_6 ... 6882
388_7 ... 861
388_8 ... 6032
388_9 ... 3133
388_10 ... 2541
388_11 ... 328
388_12 ... 2898
388_13 ... 5470
388_14 ... 3313
388_15 ... 2697
388_16 ... 4485
388_17 ... 4270
388_18 ... 4647
388_19 ... 4051
388_20 ... 826
388_21 ... 2421
388_22 ... 622
388_23 ... 3867
388_24 ... 190
388_25 ... 4216
388_28 ... 7646
388_29 ... 4598
388_31 ... 7399
388_33 ... 3559
388_34 ... 1555
388_35 ... 2167
388_36 ... 3523
388_37 ... 150
388_38 ... 1492
388_39 ... 4383
388_40 ... 315
388_41 ... 2688
388_42 ... 5897
388_43 ... 4773
388_44 ... 3834
388_45 ... 3178
388_46 ... 4375
388_47 ... 614
388_48 ... 5572
388_49 ... 3989
388_50 ... 2841
388_51 ... 763
388_52 ... 6170
388_53 ... 3706
388_54 ... 6266
388_55 ... 980
388_56 ... 2628
388_57 ... 1900
388_58 ... 2937
388_59 ... 1203
388_60 ... 3300
389_3 ... 6056
389_6 ... 4300
389_8 ... 1959
389_9 ... 3786
389_10 ... 7818
389_15 ... 4442
389_20 ... 7974
389_21 ... 4695
389_22 ... 4353
389_24 ... 1662
389_29 ... 3584
389_34 ... 3585
389_38 ... 4527
389_40 ... 3192
389_50 ... 437
389_51 ... 3426
389_52 ... 423
389_53 ... 2130
389_54 ... 1973
389_55 ... 1129
389_56 ... 151
389_57 ... 635
389_58 ... 3418
389_59 ... 5073
389_60 ... 1456
390_1 ... 7152
390_3 ... 2353
390_4 ... 5555
390_6 ... 2354
390_13 ... 7169
390_15 ... 7473
390_17 ... 6319
390_18 ... 7811
390_19 ... 2521
390_23 ... 2122
390_24 ... 7949
390_25 ... 5374
390_26 ... 4459
390_27 ... 5489
390_28 ... 7805
390_29 ... 5754
390_30 ... 3359
390_31 ... 7137
390_33 ... 2443
390_34 ... 6965
390_35 ... 3896
390_36 ... 5137
390_37 ... 3787
390_38 ... 3828
390_39 ... 5755
390_40 ... 329
390_41 ... 6487
390_42 ... 6373
390_43 ... 4967
390_44 ... 2246
390_45 ... 2975
391_7 ... 1061
391_8 ... 780
391_9 ... 6839
391_10 ... 3475
391_12 ... 7814
391_14 ... 5392
391_15 ... 804
391_17 ... 1565
391_19 ... 7095
391_20 ... 3605
391_21 ... 5678
391_22 ... 6581
391_23 ... 5375
391_24 ... 6463
391_25 ... 2709
391_26 ... 1719
391_30 ... 2943
391_31 ... 2710
391_32 ... 997
391_34 ... 1984
391_35 ... 7996
391_36 ... 7819
391_37 ... 3039
391_38 ... 3156
391_39 ... 4142
391_40 ... 1974
391_41 ... 3080
391_44 ... 7033
391_45 ... 1427
391_46 ... 4203
391_47 ... 424
391_48 ... 6840
391_49 ... 924
391_50 ... 2374
391_51 ... 5077
391_52 ... 5615
391_53 ... 5001
391_54 ... 2381
391_55 ... 1343
391_56 ... 1599
391_57 ... 152
391_58 ... 3360
391_59 ... 3980
391_60 ... 1328
392_1 ... 2738
392_2 ... 933
392_3 ... 4217
392_4 ... 7764
392_5 ... 3130
392_6 ... 2437
392_7 ... 7816
392_8 ... 3476
392_9 ... 3168
392_10 ... 6782
392_11 ... 220
392_12 ... 4158
392_13 ... 6841
392_14 ... 3324
392_15 ... 6883
392_16 ... 944
392_17 ... 5791
392_19 ... 2733
392_20 ... 3283
392_21 ... 3001
392_22 ... 7929
392_23 ... 3899
392_24 ... 766
392_26 ... 3620
392_27 ... 4232
392_28 ... 4426
392_29 ... 3594
392_30 ... 3592
392_31 ... 1771
392_32 ... 3520
392_34 ... 4605
392_35 ... 1470
392_36 ... 3521
392_37 ... 462
392_39 ... 645
392_40 ... 3764
392_41 ... 1010
392_42 ... 3639
392_43 ... 4994
392_44 ... 1019
392_45 ... 1363
392_46 ... 5520
392_47 ... 3069
392_48 ... 2719
392_49 ... 1550
392_50 ... 7882
392_51 ... 4125
392_52 ... 767
392_53 ... 3311
392_54 ... 6151
392_55 ... 996
392_56 ... 7259
392_57 ... 2928
392_58 ... 1903
392_59 ... 101
392_60 ... 4068
392_61 ... 1204
393_12 ... 1968
393_16 ... 2790
393_18 ... 3339
393_21 ... 2739
393_23 ... 1533
393_25 ... 7360
393_28 ... 1600
393_29 ... 2669
393_32 ... 5011
393_43 ... 4749
393_44 ... 7815
393_45 ... 5086
393_46 ... 463
393_49 ... 438
393_50 ... 587
393_51 ... 1969
393_52 ... 4909
393_53 ... 2365
393_54 ... 3083
393_55 ... 5658
393_56 ... 5078
393_57 ... 4064
393_58 ... 7828
393_59 ... 6311
393_60 ... 1713
394_3 ... 7017
394_5 ... 3893
394_9 ... 7170
394_11 ... 4481
394_13 ... 3537
394_14 ... 3484
394_20 ... 5756
394_21 ... 5208
394_23 ... 3900
394_27 ... 6532
394_29 ... 5804
394_31 ... 2613
394_33 ... 6381
394_34 ... 175
394_35 ... 2266
394_36 ... 5360
394_37 ... 3172
394_38 ... 5584
394_39 ... 2516
394_40 ... 5000
394_41 ... 4386
394_42 ... 2725
394_43 ... 2938
394_44 ... 595
394_45 ... 3819
395_3 ... 557
395_4 ... 687
395_5 ... 291
395_6 ... 520
395_8 ... 558
395_9 ... 3077
395_10 ... 1963
395_14 ... 464
395_15 ... 3137
395_16 ... 4625
395_18 ... 3161
395_19 ... 3437
395_20 ... 4389
395_21 ... 3325
395_23 ... 1964
395_27 ... 7953
395_28 ... 3516
395_29 ... 4614
395_30 ... 3259
395_32 ... 391
395_35 ... 1551
395_37 ... 636
395_38 ... 7049
395_39 ... 521
395_40 ... 6074
395_41 ... 488
395_42 ... 2800
395_43 ... 1263
395_44 ... 1243
395_45 ... 1259
395_46 ... 1265
395_47 ... 1266
395_48 ... 2125
395_49 ... 2939
395_50 ... 835
395_51 ... 2009
395_52 ... 987
395_53 ... 6453
395_54 ... 3599
395_55 ... 6143
395_56 ... 330
395_57 ... 6389
395_58 ... 7873
395_59 ... 1568
395_60 ... 2670
396_1 ... 3757
396_2 ... 489
396_3 ... 4378
396_4 ... 778
396_5 ... 3427
396_6 ... 881
396_7 ... 465
396_8 ... 4008
396_9 ... 3143
396_10 ... 7032
396_11 ... 3241
396_12 ... 1916
396_13 ... 776
396_14 ... 3247
396_15 ... 815
396_16 ... 3193
396_17 ... 5565
396_18 ... 920
396_19 ... 505
396_20 ... 3189
396_21 ... 2660
396_22 ... 805
396_23 ... 1242
396_24 ... 2679
396_25 ... 6605
396_26 ... 1232
396_27 ... 246
396_29 ... 2188
396_30 ... 3202
396_31 ... 3258
396_32 ... 2195
396_33 ... 2333
396_34 ... 3534
396_35 ... 3561
396_36 ... 1725
396_37 ... 2698
396_38 ... 213
396_39 ... 2280
396_40 ... 1626
396_41 ... 4054
396_42 ... 304
396_43 ... 2300
396_44 ... 3565
396_45 ... 2239
396_46 ... 1236
396_47 ... 4301
396_48 ... 7968
396_49 ... 800
396_50 ... 988
396_51 ... 1331
396_52 ... 2665
396_53 ... 4663
396_54 ... 3340
396_55 ... 1315
396_56 ... 2614
396_57 ... 1454
396_58 ... 2925
396_59 ... 1275
396_60 ... 2202
397_3 ... 7103
397_4 ... 7842
397_6 ... 2950
397_9 ... 3090
397_10 ... 3996
397_12 ... 6644
397_17 ... 2958
397_19 ... 7647
397_21 ... 5613
397_23 ... 3870
397_25 ... 2944
397_26 ... 4271
397_27 ... 6422
397_29 ... 2754
397_31 ... 3568
397_32 ... 2590
397_34 ... 6499
397_36 ... 2498
397_37 ... 5008
397_38 ... 3842
397_40 ... 4013
397_42 ... 5383
397_44 ... 5585
397_45 ... 5047
397_46 ... 7025
397_47 ... 7076
397_49 ... 6842
397_50 ... 991
397_51 ... 2594
397_52 ... 6814
397_53 ... 7970
397_54 ... 6884
397_55 ... 600
397_56 ... 4191
397_57 ... 649
397_58 ... 2210
397_59 ... 836
397_60 ... 4152
398_2 ... 7183
398_4 ... 7550
398_5 ... 5664
398_6 ... 4384
398_7 ... 2393
398_8 ... 4424
398_9 ... 7122
398_10 ... 4379
398_11 ... 4159
398_13 ... 6464

398_15 ... 3723	400_52 ... 4360	403_34 ... 2700	406_23 ... 6533	408_40 ... 4153	411_8 ... 3403
398_16 ... 7279	400_53 ... 87	403_35 ... 305	406_24 ... 7087	408_41 ... 6465	411_11 ... 6991
398_17 ... 6582	400_54 ... 3301	403_36 ... 4069	406_26 ... 2494	408_42 ... 781	411_12 ... 3006
398_18 ... 1885	400_55 ... 1273	403_37 ... 700	406_27 ... 3566	408_43 ... 4019	411_16 ... 2963
398_19 ... 5836	400_56 ... 1926	403_38 ... 6226	406_28 ... 1733	408_44 ... 5071	411_17 ... 5026
398_21 ... 28	400_57 ... 6267	403_39 ... 3321	406_29 ... 2177	408_45 ... 6321	411_19 ... 6940
398_23 ... 4591	400_58 ... 7855	403_41 ... 2629	406_30 ... 6521	409_4 ... 3621	411_29 ... 6129
398_24 ... 5384	400_59 ... 2562	403_43 ... 2366	406_31 ... 1573	409_5 ... 2887	411_30 ... 6967
398_27 ... 2615	400_60 ... 4876	403_44 ... 506	406_32 ... 3544	409_7 ... 2888	411_41 ... 6708
398_28 ... 7496	401_1 ... 7045	403_45 ... 5955	406_33 ... 688	409_8 ... 3606	411_45 ... 6092
398_31 ... 6505	401_4 ... 2544	403_46 ... 3306	406_35 ... 3487	409_9 ... 5346	411_49 ... 3636
398_32 ... 7303	401_5 ... 1965	403_47 ... 4369	406_37 ... 6522	409_10 ... 7767	411_50 ... 5473
398_35 ... 3697	401_8 ... 3160	403_48 ... 1902	406_38 ... 3322	409_12 ... 1852	411_51 ... 5506
398_36 ... 2968	401_10 ... 5569	403_49 ... 2282	406_39 ... 1321	409_14 ... 6058	411_53 ... 4390
398_38 ... 6057	401_11 ... 946	403_50 ... 168	406_40 ... 4376	409_16 ... 6939	411_54 ... 6904
398_39 ... 3729	401_12 ... 2960	403_51 ... 2301	406_41 ... 4123	409_19 ... 6091	411_56 ... 4005
398_40 ... 5733	401_13 ... 7551	403_52 ... 6215	406_42 ... 74	409_22 ... 7663	411_57 ... 7001
398_41 ... 522	401_15 ... 3845	403_54 ... 2933	406_43 ... 6622	409_23 ... 3602	411_58 ... 3857
398_42 ... 1891	401_18 ... 6146	403_55 ... 4723	406_44 ... 4782	409_27 ... 3622	411_59 ... 6173
398_43 ... 6354	401_20 ... 2499	403_56 ... 4362	406_45 ... 2236	409_31 ... 7961	411_60 ... 2956
398_45 ... 6360	401_23 ... 4576	403_57 ... 3307	406_46 ... 3901	409_32 ... 1835	412_2 ... 559
399_15 ... 1442	401_24 ... 4031	403_58 ... 4041	406_47 ... 3722	409_33 ... 3543	412_8 ... 6034
399_16 ... 5898	401_25 ... 1980	403_59 ... 3798	406_48 ... 5546	409_34 ... 3613	412_10 ... 7444
399_17 ... 1074	401_27 ... 4441	403_60 ... 7854	406_49 ... 5169	409_35 ... 7597	412_12 ... 4887
399_18 ... 3848	401_28 ... 3099	404_2 ... 3568	406_50 ... 3710	409_37 ... 5932	412_13 ... 4615
399_19 ... 1975	401_31 ... 6114	404_5 ... 3507	406_51 ... 2314	409_39 ... 6784	412_14 ... 5310
399_20 ... 7000	401_34 ... 3562	404_6 ... 7940	406_52 ... 4933	409_41 ... 1606	412_18 ... 5293
399_21 ... 940	401_43 ... 4571	404_7 ... 7942	406_53 ... 3323	409_43 ... 5993	412_19 ... 3167
399_22 ... 7153	401_45 ... 6229	404_8 ... 5453	406_54 ... 7860	409_46 ... 1842	412_22 ... 3277
399_23 ... 292	401_46 ... 6361	404_10 ... 3096	406_55 ... 6398	409_47 ... 6466	412_28 ... 936
399_24 ... 7595	401_47 ... 6245	404_12 ... 3216	406_56 ... 3658	409_48 ... 7914	412_29 ... 6606
399_32 ... 1794	401_48 ... 5412	404_13 ... 4492	406_57 ... 4115	409_49 ... 5249	412_30 ... 5323
399_36 ... 33	401_49 ... 1857	404_15 ... 4089	406_58 ... 7233	409_50 ... 357	412_31 ... 560
399_37 ... 7661	401_50 ... 2193	404_16 ... 163	406_59 ... 743	409_51 ... 7708	412_32 ... 3461
399_38 ... 1983	401_51 ... 6936	404_17 ... 1617	406_60 ... 3022	409_52 ... 1845	412_33 ... 7599
399_39 ... 2522	401_52 ... 2935	404_19 ... 6320	407_1 ... 7201	409_53 ... 6374	412_34 ... 392
399_40 ... 3428	401_53 ... 2735	404_20 ... 6583	407_2 ... 760	409_54 ... 5012	412_35 ... 7105
399_41 ... 6239	401_54 ... 2191	404_21 ... 7114	407_3 ... 7380	409_55 ... 1832	412_36 ... 3264
399_42 ... 405	401_55 ... 4564	404_22 ... 4421	407_5 ... 7744	409_56 ... 7443	412_37 ... 6035
399_43 ... 3912	401_57 ... 3017	404_23 ... 941	407_6 ... 5109	409_57 ... 3799	412_38 ... 1004
399_44 ... 6125	401_58 ... 3846	404_24 ... 3966	407_7 ... 6090	409_58 ... 5209	412_39 ... 909
399_45 ... 439	401_59 ... 3051	404_25 ... 3586	407_8 ... 950	409_59 ... 1464	412_40 ... 90
399_46 ... 5612	401_60 ... 4817	404_26 ... 3578	407_9 ... 7766	410_1 ... 5134	412_41 ... 2995
399_47 ... 945	402_2 ... 3007	404_27 ... 3219	407_10 ... 679	410_2 ... 4348	412_42 ... 1663
399_48 ... 4233	402_3 ... 2533	404_29 ... 3650	407_11 ... 761	410_3 ... 6816	412_43 ... 7055
399_49 ... 1047	402_7 ... 4696	404_31 ... 3284	407_12 ... 3287	410_4 ... 3470	412_44 ... 5185
399_50 ... 6935	402_11 ... 2951	404_32 ... 3717	407_13 ... 2864	410_5 ... 7895	412_45 ... 7211
399_51 ... 1318	402_13 ... 3610	404_33 ... 3225	407_14 ... 868	410_6 ... 7789	413_1 ... 207
399_52 ... 5559	402_14 ... 6752	404_35 ... 3244	407_15 ... 2830	410_7 ... 5429	413_2 ... 5994
399_53 ... 1389	402_15 ... 6144	404_36 ... 6140	407_18 ... 7745	410_8 ... 7888	413_4 ... 6709
399_54 ... 7138	402_16 ... 5566	404_37 ... 7826	407_21 ... 851	410_9 ... 7922	413_5 ... 561
399_55 ... 1244	402_17 ... 1948	404_38 ... 7154	407_22 ... 2481	410_10 ... 5608	413_7 ... 7171
399_56 ... 2699	402_19 ... 3138	404_39 ... 3352	407_23 ... 7381	410_11 ... 3623	413_8 ... 7709
399_57 ... 1253	402_20 ... 5393	404_40 ... 794	407_24 ... 4727	410_12 ... 4656	413_10 ... 6059
399_58 ... 2755	402_21 ... 1970	404_41 ... 7020	407_27 ... 2791	410_13 ... 3829	413_12 ... 3279
399_59 ... 1282	402_22 ... 3535	404_42 ... 4988	407_31 ... 79	410_14 ... 1383	413_13 ... 7681
399_60 ... 1483	402_24 ... 3093	404_43 ... 2394	407_32 ... 6966	410_15 ... 5331	413_14 ... 112
400_1 ... 3337	402_25 ... 3603	404_44 ... 5633	407_33 ... 668	410_16 ... 6480	413_16 ... 7628
400_2 ... 6216	402_26 ... 3601	404_45 ... 3036	407_35 ... 4689	410_17 ... 7023	413_19 ... 5933
400_3 ... 4411	402_28 ... 5899	405_1 ... 6937	407_36 ... 7166	410_18 ... 1341	413_20 ... 5191
400_4 ... 256	402_32 ... 1821	405_2 ... 6938	407_37 ... 958	410_19 ... 6115	413_22 ... 6014
400_5 ... 1754	402_34 ... 3612	405_4 ... 5505	407_41 ... 2809	410_20 ... 7909	413_27 ... 3353
400_6 ... 4147	402_44 ... 7901	405_6 ... 3091	407_42 ... 3	410_21 ... 6107	413_29 ... 4606
400_7 ... 895	402_46 ... 3992	405_8 ... 6956	407_43 ... 2769	410_22 ... 137	413_30 ... 694
400_8 ... 2734	402_47 ... 5567	405_9 ... 5538	407_44 ... 862	410_23 ... 6843	413_31 ... 4482
400_9 ... 1641	402_48 ... 4579	405_14 ... 6815	407_45 ... 7179	410_24 ... 7944	413_32 ... 1668
400_10 ... 1344	402_49 ... 3453	405_18 ... 928	407_46 ... 5067	410_25 ... 7680	413_33 ... 5263
400_11 ... 5397	402_51 ... 7195	405_23 ... 3008	407_47 ... 4983	410_26 ... 6754	413_34 ... 7058
400_12 ... 1206	402_54 ... 3844	405_26 ... 4018	407_48 ... 2534	410_27 ... 536	413_36 ... 5250
400_13 ... 1268	402_55 ... 7040	405_33 ... 5055	407_49 ... 5017	410_28 ... 3492	413_38 ... 6274
400_14 ... 2081	402_57 ... 6257	405_38 ... 2157	407_50 ... 3395	410_29 ... 4594	413_39 ... 6941
400_15 ... 105	402_58 ... 908	405_40 ... 3086	407_51 ... 4950	410_30 ... 3691	413_41 ... 5975
400_16 ... 4122	402_59 ... 6261	405_46 ... 2955	407_52 ... 2737	410_31 ... 6885	413_42 ... 4901
400_17 ... 882	402_60 ... 6543	405_47 ... 4541	407_53 ... 708	410_32 ... 6033	413_43 ... 6785
400_18 ... 6783	403_1 ... 2876	405_48 ... 4542	407_54 ... 6442	410_33 ... 5268	413_44 ... 1037
400_19 ... 4664	403_2 ... 7743	405_49 ... 764	407_55 ... 2850	410_34 ... 6294	413_45 ... 6036
400_20 ... 2375	403_3 ... 830	405_50 ... 6665	407_56 ... 4963	410_35 ... 2065	413_46 ... 3180
400_21 ... 1281	403_4 ... 2671	405_51 ... 3148	407_57 ... 5900	410_36 ... 6268	413_47 ... 6259
400_22 ... 7355	403_5 ... 331	405_52 ... 2959	407_58 ... 4953	410_37 ... 806	413_49 ... 999
400_23 ... 162	403_6 ... 5729	405_53 ... 1272	407_59 ... 2786	410_38 ... 5160	413_50 ... 5186
400_24 ... 4103	403_7 ... 372	405_55 ... 1291	407_60 ... 4943	410_39 ... 3276	413_51 ... 3014
400_25 ... 3518	403_8 ... 6397	405_56 ... 3019	408_1 ... 1981	410_40 ... 1670	413_52 ... 1422
400_26 ... 4252	403_9 ... 3320	405_58 ... 949	408_3 ... 441	410_41 ... 6336	413_53 ... 6786
400_27 ... 3532	403_10 ... 2281	405_59 ... 3856	408_4 ... 6408	410_42 ... 3387	413_54 ... 537
400_28 ... 3341	403_11 ... 247	405_60 ... 3254	408_5 ... 7662	410_43 ... 5758	413_55 ... 7318
400_29 ... 1226	403_12 ... 6705	406_1 ... 7596	408_7 ... 2720	410_44 ... 3297	413_56 ... 3263
400_30 ... 1717	403_13 ... 3333	406_2 ... 850	408_8 ... 3909	410_45 ... 6454	413_57 ... 6330
400_31 ... 1995	403_14 ... 238	406_3 ... 7627	408_9 ... 5524	410_46 ... 3754	413_58 ... 1005
400_32 ... 5624	403_15 ... 5974	406_4 ... 440	408_10 ... 5476	410_47 ... 3122	413_59 ... 7600
400_33 ... 3110	403_17 ... 7288	406_5 ... 2511	408_13 ... 3855	410_48 ... 6126	413_60 ... 1748
400_35 ... 3686	403_18 ... 95	406_6 ... 7707	408_14 ... 5757	410_49 ... 6205	414_1 ... 6584
400_36 ... 3519	403_19 ... 5463	406_7 ... 3355	408_15 ... 1401	410_50 ... 5407	414_2 ... 816
400_37 ... 4399	403_20 ... 3330	406_8 ... 535	408_16 ... 3512	410_51 ... 5593	414_3 ... 7144
400_38 ... 2068	403_21 ... 7442	406_9 ... 2313	408_17 ... 7317	410_52 ... 3308	414_4 ... 7356
400_39 ... 2680	403_22 ... 3248	406_10 ... 6706	408_20 ... 1503	410_53 ... 4302	414_5 ... 4803
400_40 ... 1303	403_23 ... 7552	406_11 ... 2863	408_26 ... 604	410_54 ... 3993	414_6 ... 5464
400_41 ... 7041	403_24 ... 1720	406_12 ... 934	408_28 ... 935	410_55 ... 1546	414_7 ... 972
400_42 ... 969	403_25 ... 425	406_13 ... 7155	408_29 ... 5490	410_56 ... 2846	414_8 ... 2444
400_43 ... 1901	403_26 ... 7553	406_14 ... 7341	408_30 ... 3553	410_57 ... 6258	414_9 ... 3383
400_44 ... 2922	403_27 ... 2756	406_15 ... 7292	408_32 ... 6957	410_58 ... 5218	414_10 ... 6015
400_45 ... 3807	403_28 ... 7765	406_16 ... 1065	408_34 ... 7100	410_59 ... 3013	414_11 ... 680
400_46 ... 1167	403_29 ... 3376	406_18 ... 732	408_35 ... 3078	410_60 ... 4037	414_12 ... 5759
400_47 ... 3318	403_30 ... 888	406_19 ... 6707	408_36 ... 2185	411_1 ... 7196	414_13 ... 1592
400_48 ... 759	403_31 ... 7339	406_20 ... 6753	408_37 ... 666	411_3 ... 6262	414_15 ... 5424
400_49 ... 2189	403_32 ... 356	406_21 ... 466	408_38 ... 6488	411_5 ... 7598	414_17 ... 3747
400_50 ... 745	403_33 ... 7340	406_22 ... 7123	408_39 ... 3114	411_7 ... 7746	414_18 ... 6093

414_19 ... 3334	417_33 ... 676	419_52 ... 7747	421_53 ... 124	425_7 ... 221	427_17 ... 385
414_20 ... 6666	417_34 ... 4635	419_53 ... 2038	421_54 ... 4436	425_8 ... 4204	427_18 ... 4413
414_21 ... 1001	417_35 ... 6117	419_54 ... 3136	421_55 ... 1714	425_9 ... 4918	427_20 ... 2683
414_22 ... 2395	417_38 ... 7781	419_56 ... 5560	421_56 ... 4076	425_10 ... 3447	427_21 ... 2035
414_23 ... 384	417_39 ... 6132	419_57 ... 4580	421_57 ... 2711	425_12 ... 222	427_22 ... 5325
414_24 ... 4272	417_40 ... 1069	419_58 ... 5995	421_58 ... 5175	425_13 ... 5465	427_23 ... 2315
414_25 ... 2165	417_41 ... 6818	419_59 ... 942	421_59 ... 5154	425_14 ... 3267	427_24 ... 1601
414_26 ... 7280	417_42 ... 5136	419_60 ... 2940	421_60 ... 7863	425_15 ... 2262	427_25 ... 2263
414_27 ... 5215	417_43 ... 2523	420_1 ... 7768	422_1 ... 2976	425_16 ... 2072	427_26 ... 2105
414_28 ... 5620	417_44 ... 5903	420_2 ... 938	422_2 ... 2090	425_17 ... 3972	427_27 ... 5313
414_29 ... 5174	417_45 ... 658	420_3 ... 7726	422_3 ... 5542	425_18 ... 4752	427_29 ... 4440
414_30 ... 5669	417_46 ... 6607	420_4 ... 2996	422_4 ... 4512	425_19 ... 5979	427_31 ... 2425
414_31 ... 6306	417_47 ... 6845	420_5 ... 282	422_6 ... 6382	425_20 ... 223	427_32 ... 1801
414_32 ... 1627	417_48 ... 871	420_6 ... 6221	422_10 ... 3872	425_21 ... 6199	427_33 ... 7474
414_33 ... 3373	417_50 ... 2175	420_7 ... 4330	422_12 ... 7175	425_22 ... 5112	427_34 ... 3272
414_34 ... 7382	417_51 ... 681	420_8 ... 3941	422_13 ... 7973	425_23 ... 6061	427_35 ... 3827
414_35 ... 3237	417_52 ... 4175	420_9 ... 3262	422_15 ... 7799	425_25 ... 30	427_36 ... 7923
414_36 ... 2549	417_53 ... 5976	420_10 ... 5563	422_18 ... 3840	425_26 ... 43	427_37 ... 7194
414_37 ... 1002	417_54 ... 5230	420_12 ... 675	422_20 ... 5438	425_27 ... 42	427_38 ... 307
414_38 ... 3385	417_55 ... 5053	420_14 ... 2182	422_21 ... 4387	425_28 ... 22	427_39 ... 2874
414_39 ... 7372	417_56 ... 1566	420_17 ... 3292	422_22 ... 2180	425_29 ... 49	427_40 ... 308
414_40 ... 3265	417_57 ... 3336	420_18 ... 7554	422_29 ... 3821	425_30 ... 13	427_41 ... 3679
414_41 ... 6094	417_59 ... 2981	420_19 ... 467	422_30 ... 6344	425_31 ... 1637	427_42 ... 2141
414_42 ... 1245	417_60 ... 1202	420_20 ... 2813	422_31 ... 4798	425_32 ... 5193	427_43 ... 3703
414_43 ... 5901	418_1 ... 2873	420_23 ... 929	422_32 ... 6585	425_33 ... 7216	427_44 ... 4948
414_44 ... 5549	418_2 ... 6037	420_24 ... 3477	422_34 ... 2682	425_34 ... 5265	427_45 ... 5300
414_45 ... 2500	418_4 ... 2422	420_25 ... 4451	422_36 ... 7096	425_35 ... 7219	428_1 ... 3682
414_46 ... 7939	418_5 ... 852	420_26 ... 7240	422_38 ... 5805	425_36 ... 5324	428_2 ... 3471
414_47 ... 5902	418_6 ... 7002	420_29 ... 7900	422_39 ... 6847	425_37 ... 4044	428_3 ... 2184
414_48 ... 3295	418_7 ... 4902	420_32 ... 5258	422_40 ... 1879	425_38 ... 5980	428_4 ... 1820
414_49 ... 4438	418_8 ... 2501	420_33 ... 2218	422_41 ... 7807	425_39 ... 2424	428_5 ... 192
414_51 ... 3685	418_9 ... 3744	420_34 ... 1628	422_43 ... 4799	425_40 ... 273	428_6 ... 4951
414_52 ... 3869	418_10 ... 819	420_35 ... 6273	422_44 ... 7498	425_41 ... 4931	428_8 ... 7046
414_53 ... 5241	418_11 ... 6544	420_36 ... 7235	422_46 ... 7342	425_42 ... 1251	428_9 ... 1271
414_54 ... 7869	418_12 ... 4548	420_38 ... 3816	422_48 ... 3343	425_43 ... 3733	428_10 ... 7499
414_55 ... 2161	418_13 ... 4577	420_39 ... 3150	422_49 ... 2612	425_44 ... 2689	428_11 ... 507
414_56 ... 5180	418_14 ... 7520	420_43 ... 925	422_50 ... 1596	425_45 ... 1026	428_12 ... 5816
414_57 ... 770	418_15 ... 523	420_44 ... 5409	422_51 ... 5904	425_46 ... 7401	428_13 ... 3269
414_58 ... 1908	418_18 ... 4253	420_45 ... 1029	422_52 ... 2977	425_47 ... 3331	428_15 ... 3674
414_59 ... 3020	418_19 ... 5041	420_46 ... 2855	422_53 ... 4785	425_48 ... 2012	428_17 ... 633
414_60 ... 1207	418_21 ... 3814	420_47 ... 283	422_54 ... 7827	425_49 ... 618	428_18 ... 4016
415_12 ... 4287	418_22 ... 785	420_48 ... 1744	422_55 ... 2945	425_50 ... 4946	428_19 ... 408
415_15 ... 3194	418_23 ... 3678	420_49 ... 684	422_56 ... 3302	425_51 ... 2355	428_20 ... 4354
415_25 ... 5364	418_24 ... 1724	420_50 ... 3942	422_57 ... 5396	425_52 ... 4187	428_21 ... 5491
415_27 ... 1535	418_25 ... 7212	420_51 ... 4896	422_58 ... 1562	425_53 ... 5234	428_22 ... 617
415_28 ... 5622	418_26 ... 2585	420_52 ... 5525	422_59 ... 2617	425_54 ... 3316	428_23 ... 5958
415_29 ... 3917	418_27 ... 5231	420_53 ... 6075	422_60 ... 5074	425_55 ... 6194	428_24 ... 7843
415_46 ... 859	418_28 ... 6278	420_54 ... 1269	423_1 ... 5031	425_56 ... 2073	428_27 ... 2305
415_47 ... 5956	418_29 ... 1694	420_55 ... 6819	423_4 ... 3804	425_57 ... 3696	428_28 ... 5272
415_48 ... 937	418_32 ... 17	420_56 ... 7885	423_6 ... 4783	425_58 ... 4061	428_29 ... 2269
415_49 ... 3342	418_33 ... 19	420_57 ... 5410	423_10 ... 6060	425_59 ... 3488	428_30 ... 1760
415_50 ... 7682	418_34 ... 20	420_58 ... 981	423_12 ... 6848	425_60 ... 4875	428_31 ... 2630
415_51 ... 5089	418_35 ... 35	420_59 ... 2777	423_21 ... 5978	426_1 ... 6062	428_32 ... 3557
415_52 ... 5269	418_36 ... 12	420_60 ... 3159	423_24 ... 5957	426_2 ... 7649	428_33 ... 2595
415_53 ... 1028	418_37 ... 2172	421_1 ... 184	423_27 ... 1715	426_3 ... 5527	428_34 ... 5273
415_54 ... 1650	418_38 ... 7319	421_2 ... 4516	423_30 ... 5626	426_4 ... 6097	428_35 ... 3481
415_55 ... 6905	418_39 ... 5216	421_3 ... 468	423_35 ... 1784	426_6 ... 6787	428_37 ... 3223
415_56 ... 538	418_40 ... 5105	421_4 ... 4673	423_36 ... 1721	426_7 ... 443	428_38 ... 5922
415_57 ... 5294	418_41 ... 2403	421_5 ... 1101	423_37 ... 3469	426_8 ... 7664	428_40 ... 7775
415_58 ... 817	418_42 ... 4761	421_6 ... 5977	423_38 ... 3725	426_11 ... 2801	428_41 ... 5100
415_59 ... 6095	418_43 ... 4439	421_7 ... 5312	423_39 ... 6711	426_13 ... 5779	428_42 ... 2524
415_60 ... 2616	418_44 ... 746	421_8 ... 820	423_40 ... 5271	426_15 ... 6467	428_43 ... 2097
416_2 ... 5056	418_45 ... 3944	421_9 ... 6906	423_41 ... 406	426_16 ... 3513	428_44 ... 469
416_10 ... 6116	418_46 ... 130	421_10 ... 60	423_42 ... 6907	426_18 ... 2771	428_45 ... 1673
416_12 ... 1092	418_47 ... 5232	421_11 ... 5642	423_45 ... 5259	426_22 ... 4020	428_46 ... 6016
416_13 ... 6817	418_48 ... 7883	421_12 ... 1654	424_6 ... 4584	426_24 ... 6942	428_47 ... 359
416_18 ... 5264	418_49 ... 3699	421_13 ... 257	424_8 ... 2557	426_25 ... 1982	428_48 ... 5274
416_20 ... 1767	418_50 ... 63	421_14 ... 3374	424_12 ... 5996	426_26 ... 6450	428_49 ... 3643
416_24 ... 332	418_51 ... 5628	421_15 ... 917	424_13 ... 3252	426_28 ... 6468	428_50 ... 2748
416_27 ... 2153	418_52 ... 3199	421_16 ... 6096	424_16 ... 199	426_29 ... 5347	428_51 ... 176
416_30 ... 3689	418_53 ... 6270	421_17 ... 7910	424_17 ... 7933	426_30 ... 4613	428_52 ... 6489
416_31 ... 333	418_54 ... 5201	421_18 ... 3454	424_20 ... 3281	426_33 ... 1734	428_53 ... 5301
416_32 ... 4336	418_55 ... 2638	421_19 ... 1034	424_21 ... 4914	426_34 ... 4365	428_54 ... 4391
416_33 ... 4543	418_56 ... 3050	421_20 ... 4528	424_32 ... 5237	426_35 ... 7556	428_55 ... 7926
416_35 ... 4032	418_57 ... 3868	421_21 ... 306	424_33 ... 5634	426_37 ... 7133	428_56 ... 2028
416_36 ... 7234	418_58 ... 5027	421_22 ... 3841	424_35 ... 7226	426_39 ... 5934	428_57 ... 7665
416_37 ... 5236	418_59 ... 5270	421_23 ... 2039	424_36 ... 2032	426_41 ... 7683	428_58 ... 3704
416_38 ... 7978	418_60 ... 3489	421_24 ... 39	424_37 ... 6820	426_42 ... 3906	428_59 ... 2908
416_39 ... 7648	419_1 ... 5865	421_25 ... 3579	424_38 ... 7987	426_43 ... 1846	428_60 ... 4925
416_40 ... 818	419_2 ... 7197	421_26 ... 3687	424_39 ... 334	426_44 ... 7782	429_1 ... 4392
416_41 ... 5792	419_4 ... 7003	421_27 ... 29	424_40 ... 5905	426_46 ... 6469	429_2 ... 4774
416_42 ... 4755	419_7 ... 952	421_28 ... 18	424_41 ... 3268	426_47 ... 1462	429_3 ... 7840
416_43 ... 2011	419_8 ... 7710	421_29 ... 36	424_43 ... 1164	426_48 ... 7184	429_4 ... 5579
416_44 ... 2230	419_11 ... 3820	421_30 ... 23	424_44 ... 3326	426_49 ... 6362	429_5 ... 1398
416_45 ... 5295	419_12 ... 3914	421_31 ... 41	424_45 ... 1785	426_50 ... 1847	429_6 ... 5830
417_1 ... 6968	419_13 ... 7986	421_32 ... 2219	424_46 ... 2512	426_51 ... 6623	429_7 ... 6943
417_2 ... 4917	419_15 ... 4001	421_33 ... 7221	424_47 ... 5618	426_52 ... 7967	429_8 ... 524
417_3 ... 6969	419_19 ... 2757	421_34 ... 7222	424_48 ... 5213	426_53 ... 2187	429_9 ... 3128
417_7 ... 7497	419_22 ... 954	421_35 ... 6275	424_49 ... 2870	426_54 ... 3315	429_10 ... 5997
417_9 ... 6710	419_23 ... 4405	421_36 ... 6271	424_50 ... 442	426_55 ... 1563	429_11 ... 4934
417_10 ... 6886	419_25 ... 4888	421_37 ... 1062	424_51 ... 6908	426_56 ... 602	429_12 ... 7931
417_11 ... 1240	419_26 ... 7962	421_38 ... 1697	424_52 ... 5226	426_57 ... 7101	429_13 ... 3118
417_12 ... 6844	419_27 ... 6645	421_39 ... 6846	424_53 ... 3271	426_58 ... 3797	429_14 ... 1629
417_14 ... 4349	419_32 ... 3220	421_40 ... 4903	424_54 ... 4856	426_59 ... 4937	429_16 ... 2802
417_15 ... 575	419_35 ... 1652	421_41 ... 7927	424_55 ... 6735	426_60 ... 3023	429_17 ... 7841
417_17 ... 3195	419_37 ... 3388	421_42 ... 4472	424_56 ... 358	427_2 ... 7193	429_18 ... 6756
417_18 ... 5798	419_38 ... 3736	421_43 ... 5233	424_57 ... 1698	427_3 ... 335	429_19 ... 75
417_20 ... 6423	419_41 ... 4701	421_44 ... 61	424_58 ... 7861	427_4 ... 2851	429_20 ... 6171
417_22 ... 5306	419_42 ... 7125	421_45 ... 539	424_59 ... 5155	427_6 ... 5348	429_21 ... 627
417_23 ... 1651	419_45 ... 634	421_46 ... 3372	424_60 ... 1211	427_9 ... 407	429_22 ... 1826
417_24 ... 5210	419_46 ... 2453	421_47 ... 7400	425_1 ... 490	427_11 ... 7891	429_24 ... 6289
417_26 ... 2044	419_47 ... 562	421_48 ... 2591	425_2 ... 7980	427_12 ... 2104	429_25 ... 37
417_27 ... 7224	419_48 ... 6755	421_49 ... 5173	425_3 ... 71	427_13 ... 3278	429_26 ... 45
417_28 ... 191	419_49 ... 4023	421_50 ... 4070	425_4 ... 6145	427_14 ... 7711	429_27 ... 40
417_29 ... 1025	419_50 ... 2423	421_51 ... 4506	425_5 ... 272	427_15 ... 4589	429_28 ... 24
417_30 ... 2474	419_51 ... 5030	421_52 ... 2681	425_6 ... 7555	427_16 ... 7684	429_29 ... 32

443_35 ... 2335
443_36 ... 5224
443_37 ... 3496
443_38 ... 6853
443_40 ... 6715
443_41 ... 828
443_42 ... 6913
443_43 ... 4462
443_44 ... 6588
443_45 ... 727
443_46 ... 702
443_47 ... 1576
443_48 ... 5243
443_49 ... 2713
443_50 ... 5522
443_51 ... 2741
443_52 ... 68
443_53 ... 2233
443_54 ... 2316
443_55 ... 984
443_56 ... 6155
443_57 ... 762
443_58 ... 2931
443_59 ... 1191
443_60 ... 5161
444_1 ... 4652
444_2 ... 5848
444_3 ... 4583
444_5 ... 4655
444_6 ... 3361
444_7 ... 7783
444_9 ... 7924
444_10 ... 4473
444_11 ... 4305
444_12 ... 4640
444_14 ... 2859
444_15 ... 2336
444_16 ... 7157
444_18 ... 2386
444_19 ... 2828
444_20 ... 526
444_21 ... 2779
444_22 ... 1087
444_23 ... 5502
444_24 ... 5162
444_28 ... 5202
444_29 ... 5163
444_31 ... 5278
444_34 ... 4322
444_35 ... 705
444_36 ... 2831
444_38 ... 3187
444_39 ... 2525
444_41 ... 2853
444_42 ... 2357
444_43 ... 2438
444_45 ... 5051
444_46 ... 2780
444_47 ... 7503
444_48 ... 2310
444_49 ... 2701
444_50 ... 3004
444_51 ... 2358
444_52 ... 3997
444_53 ... 4501
444_54 ... 6355
444_55 ... 2781
444_56 ... 3155
444_57 ... 2917
444_58 ... 2603
444_59 ... 3062
444_60 ... 3035
445_3 ... 3505
445_7 ... 1659
445_9 ... 2526
445_11 ... 2772
445_12 ... 2396
445_13 ... 6854
445_16 ... 7463
445_18 ... 7368
445_20 ... 4030
445_22 ... 3918
445_25 ... 693
445_29 ... 2814
445_35 ... 5730
445_37 ... 5378
445_38 ... 4714
445_39 ... 4236
445_40 ... 2387
445_41 ... 260
445_42 ... 2842
445_43 ... 4209
445_44 ... 5434
445_45 ... 2997
445_46 ... 3478
445_47 ... 6424
445_48 ... 6610
445_49 ... 7124
445_50 ... 6506
445_51 ... 7776
445_52 ... 1504
445_54 ... 3037
445_55 ... 5603
445_57 ... 3875
445_58 ... 2988
445_59 ... 7

445_60 ... 7852
446_1 ... 3217
446_3 ... 4323
446_4 ... 4427
446_5 ... 3876
446_7 ... 2804
446_8 ... 57
446_12 ... 6794
446_13 ... 5745
446_14 ... 1155
446_15 ... 93
446_16 ... 2545
446_18 ... 4423
446_19 ... 7158
446_21 ... 3999
446_23 ... 4775
446_25 ... 6556
446_26 ... 5703
446_27 ... 5906
446_29 ... 2829
446_30 ... 5334
446_32 ... 2652
446_35 ... 5772
446_38 ... 5367
446_40 ... 5539
446_42 ... 6039
446_43 ... 2731
446_44 ... 3141
446_45 ... 5554
446_46 ... 6855
446_48 ... 7416
446_49 ... 6795
446_50 ... 5307
446_51 ... 1471
446_52 ... 3472
446_53 ... 5445
446_54 ... 6364
446_55 ... 1112
446_56 ... 2793
446_57 ... 5244
446_58 ... 4084
446_59 ... 713
446_60 ... 2952
447_2 ... 4498
447_5 ... 6001
447_7 ... 4443
447_10 ... 473
447_11 ... 3234
447_14 ... 7293
447_15 ... 3982
447_16 ... 3510
447_17 ... 3084
447_18 ... 3849
447_19 ... 6648
447_20 ... 3590
447_22 ... 3877
447_23 ... 3503
447_24 ... 4865
447_25 ... 7955
447_28 ... 2126
447_29 ... 2581
447_31 ... 2742
447_33 ... 5670
447_34 ... 2406
447_36 ... 5194
447_37 ... 7149
447_38 ... 4574
447_39 ... 3740
447_40 ... 3531
447_42 ... 5610
447_47 ... 5317
447_48 ... 1602
447_49 ... 5676
447_51 ... 6365
447_52 ... 2284
447_53 ... 5254
447_54 ... 3742
447_55 ... 7021
447_56 ... 6399
447_57 ... 2640
447_58 ... 2010
447_59 ... 2993
447_60 ... 3661
448_1 ... 7629
448_2 ... 5039
448_3 ... 7445
448_4 ... 1056
448_5 ... 512
448_6 ... 2397
448_7 ... 1171
448_8 ... 4237
448_10 ... 126
448_11 ... 5004
448_12 ... 4276
448_13 ... 169
448_14 ... 336
448_15 ... 409
448_16 ... 2112
448_17 ... 6471
448_18 ... 3142
448_19 ... 4218
448_20 ... 1212
448_21 ... 5110
448_22 ... 1431
448_23 ... 284
448_24 ... 1014

448_25 ... 2496
448_26 ... 1607
448_27 ... 1762
448_28 ... 5187
448_29 ... 1865
448_31 ... 4886
448_32 ... 3524
448_33 ... 5197
448_34 ... 5279
448_35 ... 5211
448_36 ... 1752
448_37 ... 606
448_38 ... 3933
448_39 ... 493
448_40 ... 4108
448_41 ... 5028
448_42 ... 6589
448_43 ... 4940
448_44 ... 2457
448_45 ... 474
448_46 ... 1354
448_47 ... 1909
448_48 ... 5092
448_49 ... 6534
448_50 ... 7829
448_51 ... 7230
448_52 ... 1287
448_53 ... 6222
448_54 ... 960
448_55 ... 4065
448_56 ... 3048
448_57 ... 4939
448_58 ... 7061
448_59 ... 706
448_60 ... 2601
449_5 ... 3508
449_9 ... 3595
449_16 ... 7562
449_17 ... 1782
449_19 ... 6323
449_21 ... 5335
449_23 ... 2192
449_28 ... 5735
449_29 ... 3560
449_30 ... 6524
449_31 ... 6557
449_34 ... 3171
449_35 ... 7146
449_37 ... 7464
449_38 ... 4483
449_39 ... 5446
449_41 ... 7006
449_42 ... 3788
449_43 ... 5761
449_44 ... 4989
449_45 ... 4021
449_46 ... 6856
449_47 ... 6558
449_49 ... 7115
449_50 ... 2918
449_51 ... 3345
449_52 ... 7446
449_53 ... 1246
449_54 ... 7038
449_55 ... 3409
449_56 ... 5117
449_57 ... 6219
449_58 ... 4743
449_59 ... 2923
449_60 ... 4928
450_1 ... 1041
450_2 ... 6472
450_3 ... 2482
450_4 ... 2773
450_5 ... 1875
450_6 ... 544
450_7 ... 6414
450_8 ... 1031
450_9 ... 7083
450_10 ... 1449
450_11 ... 6546
450_12 ... 1848
450_13 ... 7833
450_14 ... 6525
450_15 ... 4935
450_16 ... 4168
450_17 ... 7322
450_18 ... 6200
450_19 ... 1332
450_20 ... 1866
450_21 ... 241
450_22 ... 6167
450_23 ... 2050
450_24 ... 2407
450_25 ... 5723
450_26 ... 4368
450_27 ... 610
450_28 ... 2794
450_29 ... 4196
450_30 ... 1778
450_31 ... 2743
450_32 ... 7830
450_33 ... 6195
450_34 ... 4945
450_35 ... 6181
450_36 ... 4828

450_37 ... 4094
450_38 ... 6400
450_39 ... 119
450_40 ... 5609
450_41 ... 1923
450_42 ... 961
450_43 ... 4116
450_44 ... 585
450_45 ... 2221
450_46 ... 7866
450_47 ... 3929
450_48 ... 6161
450_49 ... 3042
450_50 ... 2632
451_1 ... 6970
451_2 ... 6076
451_4 ... 3240
451_5 ... 6127
451_6 ... 3081
451_7 ... 5762
451_8 ... 4350
451_9 ... 362
451_10 ... 6763
451_12 ... 2055
451_13 ... 5602
451_14 ... 170
451_15 ... 7602
451_16 ... 410
451_17 ... 5831
451_18 ... 2056
451_19 ... 6914
451_21 ... 3850
451_22 ... 5907
451_26 ... 1665
451_27 ... 6119
451_28 ... 4355
451_29 ... 5543
451_31 ... 7373
451_32 ... 1594
451_33 ... 5280
451_34 ... 5635
451_36 ... 5203
451_39 ... 6649
451_40 ... 6890
451_41 ... 5908
451_42 ... 7465
451_43 ... 6796
451_44 ... 3792
451_45 ... 6958
451_46 ... 7007
451_47 ... 5937
451_48 ... 7652
451_49 ... 6064
451_50 ... 1093
451_51 ... 5793
451_52 ... 6100
451_53 ... 2542
451_54 ... 807
451_55 ... 7668
451_56 ... 7521
451_57 ... 1798
451_58 ... 6040
451_59 ... 5849
451_60 ... 5164
452_1 ... 5858
452_2 ... 444
452_3 ... 3958
452_4 ... 3120
452_5 ... 4976
452_6 ... 1438
452_7 ... 4238
452_8 ... 4394
452_9 ... 1364
452_10 ... 6212
452_11 ... 802
452_12 ... 2057
452_13 ... 4176
452_14 ... 1448
452_15 ... 7403
452_16 ... 411
452_17 ... 6825
452_18 ... 1384
452_19 ... 2368
452_20 ... 1434
452_21 ... 2458
452_22 ... 6547
452_23 ... 1796
452_24 ... 4113
452_25 ... 6959
452_26 ... 833
452_27 ... 2538
452_28 ... 1169
452_29 ... 5909
452_30 ... 1869
452_31 ... 3238
452_32 ... 2459
452_33 ... 7374
452_34 ... 3945
452_35 ... 4971
452_36 ... 6473
452_37 ... 2048
452_38 ... 7447
452_39 ... 7357
452_40 ... 4154
452_41 ... 3826
452_42 ... 985

452_43 ... 6172
452_44 ... 4956
452_45 ... 4371
452_46 ... 7825
452_47 ... 5604
452_48 ... 1930
452_49 ... 4071
452_50 ... 4547
453_1 ... 7563
453_3 ... 7150
453_4 ... 3226
453_5 ... 6101
453_7 ... 1528
453_8 ... 5432
453_9 ... 7186
453_14 ... 1807
453_16 ... 6590
453_17 ... 5166
453_20 ... 2131
453_22 ... 3573
453_23 ... 5281
453_24 ... 3574
453_25 ... 3572
453_27 ... 7209
453_31 ... 1532
453_32 ... 6324
453_34 ... 1797
453_36 ... 5282
453_38 ... 6891
453_39 ... 4780
453_41 ... 7751
453_42 ... 396
453_43 ... 7204
453_44 ... 5590
453_45 ... 6248
453_46 ... 7941
453_47 ... 5859
453_48 ... 4725
453_49 ... 4563
453_50 ... 3479
453_51 ... 6857
453_52 ... 1080
453_53 ... 2760
453_54 ... 7603
453_55 ... 7199
453_56 ... 6376
453_57 ... 2337
453_58 ... 1186
453_59 ... 5318
453_60 ... 1200
454_1 ... 6065
454_4 ... 2953
454_8 ... 1849
454_9 ... 1825
454_10 ... 7689
454_11 ... 1675
454_12 ... 5493
454_13 ... 2476
454_14 ... 6858
454_15 ... 5296
454_17 ... 3732
454_21 ... 2483
454_23 ... 2045
454_24 ... 5257
454_28 ... 7228
454_29 ... 5336
454_31 ... 4910
454_32 ... 6111
454_33 ... 7784
454_35 ... 5571
454_36 ... 5595
454_37 ... 1914
454_39 ... 5763
454_40 ... 6002
454_41 ... 3034
454_42 ... 3010
454_43 ... 2359
454_44 ... 3752
454_45 ... 1706
454_46 ... 1931
454_47 ... 3536
454_48 ... 2069
454_50 ... 4363
455_1 ... 1256
455_2 ... 1822
455_3 ... 4995
455_4 ... 930
455_5 ... 6152
455_6 ... 2519
455_7 ... 1119
455_8 ... 1213
455_9 ... 607
455_10 ... 7036
455_11 ... 1166
455_12 ... 4927
455_13 ... 1066
455_14 ... 6156
455_15 ... 1015
455_16 ... 3018
455_17 ... 4915
455_18 ... 6826
455_19 ... 285
455_20 ... 4356
455_21 ... 3456
455_22 ... 4868

455_23 ... 4964
455_24 ... 2058
455_26 ... 3190
455_27 ... 747
455_28 ... 6474
455_29 ... 475
455_30 ... 1727
455_31 ... 7213
455_32 ... 1597
455_33 ... 7208
455_34 ... 140
455_35 ... 6892
455_36 ... 4977
455_37 ... 5113
455_38 ... 7062
455_39 ... 910
455_40 ... 2761
455_41 ... 1329
455_42 ... 2164
455_44 ... 2744
455_45 ... 698
455_46 ... 5850
455_47 ... 3047
455_48 ... 5503
455_49 ... 5837
455_50 ... 4882
455_51 ... 1254
455_52 ... 990
455_53 ... 7834
455_54 ... 652
455_55 ... 2551
455_56 ... 1374
455_57 ... 872
455_58 ... 5153
455_59 ... 1924
455_60 ... 4878
456_4 ... 7187
456_5 ... 1854
456_6 ... 6993
456_7 ... 5283
456_8 ... 6281
456_10 ... 1660
456_12 ... 7262
456_13 ... 6256
456_14 ... 7669
456_15 ... 2985
456_20 ... 1106
456_25 ... 5267
456_27 ... 5284
456_28 ... 1763
456_29 ... 5349
456_30 ... 2702
456_31 ... 5285
456_32 ... 4885
456_33 ... 3587
456_35 ... 50
456_37 ... 5819
456_39 ... 6716
456_41 ... 4494
456_42 ... 1855
456_43 ... 7977
456_45 ... 4033
456_47 ... 6971
456_50 ... 3367
456_51 ... 5466
456_52 ... 5052
456_53 ... 7604
456_54 ... 7928
456_55 ... 7504
456_56 ... 4469
456_57 ... 2071
456_58 ... 1292
456_59 ... 2998
456_60 ... 1187
457_1 ... 4812
457_2 ... 953
457_4 ... 4924
457_5 ... 1440
457_6 ... 1068
457_7 ... 1214
457_8 ... 1045
457_9 ... 787
457_13 ... 6254
457_14 ... 1856
457_16 ... 4990
457_17 ... 2059
457_18 ... 1260
457_19 ... 6066
457_20 ... 3197
457_21 ... 3624
457_22 ... 5379
457_24 ... 3260
457_25 ... 6276
457_26 ... 412
457_27 ... 6591
457_28 ... 1067
457_29 ... 2762
457_30 ... 387
457_31 ... 3777
457_32 ... 1789
457_33 ... 1143
457_34 ... 4972
457_35 ... 7505
457_36 ... 7836
457_37 ... 1749
457_38 ... 5150

457_39 ... 445
457_40 ... 5704
457_41 ... 4859
457_42 ... 638
457_43 ... 2822
457_44 ... 3079
457_45 ... 6218
457_46 ... 3151
457_47 ... 4942
457_48 ... 7964
457_49 ... 6175
457_50 ... 5151
458_1 ... 3273
458_2 ... 2558
458_3 ... 3767
458_4 ... 6972
458_5 ... 6611
458_6 ... 6797
458_7 ... 3775
458_8 ... 4996
458_9 ... 6994
458_10 ... 3776
458_11 ... 890
458_12 ... 6120
458_13 ... 5494
458_14 ... 2552
458_15 ... 6827
458_16 ... 230
458_17 ... 2554
458_18 ... 6995
458_19 ... 135
458_20 ... 7476
458_21 ... 5507
458_22 ... 4457
458_23 ... 6133
458_24 ... 6973
458_25 ... 3538
458_26 ... 4357
458_27 ... 7011
458_28 ... 7012
458_31 ... 6077
458_32 ... 6915
458_33 ... 6974
458_34 ... 337
458_35 ... 2060
458_36 ... 4810
458_37 ... 5435
458_38 ... 4873
458_39 ... 6738
458_41 ... 4975
458_42 ... 1521
458_43 ... 7715
458_44 ... 7013
458_45 ... 6893
458_47 ... 6859
458_48 ... 4456
458_49 ... 6860
458_50 ... 891
458_51 ... 7727
458_52 ... 4337
458_53 ... 5938
458_54 ... 286
458_55 ... 5430
458_56 ... 1493
458_57 ... 3293
458_58 ... 5606
458_59 ... 4969
458_60 ... 4879
459_1 ... 4763
459_2 ... 6567
459_3 ... 171
459_4 ... 846
459_5 ... 565
459_6 ... 7404
459_7 ... 7448
459_8 ... 6213
459_9 ... 2860
459_10 ... 6861
459_11 ... 2460
459_12 ... 6535
459_13 ... 5780
459_14 ... 6206
459_15 ... 5580
459_16 ... 5660
459_17 ... 4205
459_18 ... 1608
459_19 ... 545
459_20 ... 6410
459_21 ... 993
459_22 ... 6475
459_23 ... 4820
459_24 ... 2063
459_25 ... 1017
459_26 ... 2461
459_27 ... 4210
459_28 ... 2446
459_29 ... 674
459_30 ... 7716
459_31 ... 2428
459_32 ... 654
459_33 ... 1840
459_34 ... 5820
459_35 ... 4085
459_36 ... 640
459_37 ... 4590
459_38 ... 2254

459_39 ... 4219
459_40 ... 7375
459_41 ... 2225
459_42 ... 7506
459_43 ... 2317
459_44 ... 4657
459_45 ... 5630
459_46 ... 2151
459_47 ... 6798
459_48 ... 2714
459_49 ... 7254
459_50 ... 3045
459_51 ... 6337
459_52 ... 136
459_53 ... 2582
459_54 ... 739
459_55 ... 7030
459_56 ... 52
459_58 ... 1178
459_59 ... 2584
459_60 ... 1919
460_5 ... 4025
460_6 ... 6916
460_7 ... 4805
460_10 ... 3346
460_11 ... 2745
460_12 ... 4585
460_19 ... 3762
460_20 ... 7728
460_22 ... 3805
460_23 ... 2986
460_27 ... 2823
460_28 ... 6078
460_32 ... 48
460_33 ... 1255
460_34 ... 1850
460_40 ... 5217
460_41 ... 5636
460_42 ... 5214
460_43 ... 7109
460_44 ... 2619
460_45 ... 6452
460_46 ... 5319
460_47 ... 7241
460_49 ... 2113
460_50 ... 476
460_51 ... 2439
460_52 ... 1498
460_53 ... 4519
460_54 ... 2882
460_55 ... 4477
460_56 ... 3448
460_57 ... 2555
460_58 ... 3871
460_59 ... 1737
460_60 ... 2999
461_1 ... 4544
461_2 ... 3769
461_3 ... 5960
461_4 ... 2052
461_6 ... 546
461_7 ... 4351
461_8 ... 2763
461_9 ... 2429
461_10 ... 7976
461_11 ... 274
461_12 ... 5120
461_14 ... 6894
461_15 ... 1420
461_16 ... 4794
461_17 ... 657
461_18 ... 4340
461_20 ... 2014
461_21 ... 2061
461_22 ... 4586
461_23 ... 2430
461_24 ... 3299
461_25 ... 127
461_26 ... 1049
461_28 ... 6946
461_30 ... 338
461_31 ... 7564
461_32 ... 2462
461_34 ... 7717
461_35 ... 3261
461_36 ... 4813
461_37 ... 2764
461_38 ... 578
461_41 ... 2484
461_42 ... 4587
461_43 ... 1130
461_44 ... 7690
461_45 ... 397
461_46 ... 7565
461_47 ... 231
461_48 ... 4161
461_49 ... 2765
461_50 ... 54
462_1 ... 7417
462_2 ... 6176
462_3 ... 144
462_5 ... 703
462_6 ... 2440
462_7 ... 7358
462_8 ... 1830
462_9 ... 5799

462_10 ... 96
462_11 ... 293
462_13 ... 4370
462_14 ... 4769
462_15 ... 363
462_16 ... 4335
462_17 ... 4513
462_18 ... 7260
462_19 ... 224
462_20 ... 2049
462_21 ... 6366
462_22 ... 3825
462_23 ... 275
462_24 ... 4254
462_26 ... 1985
462_27 ... 3057
462_28 ... 3665
462_31 ... 4556
462_32 ... 2567
462_33 ... 4403
462_34 ... 4829
462_35 ... 2715
462_36 ... 720
462_37 ... 3305
462_38 ... 7323
462_40 ... 2133
462_41 ... 7255
462_42 ... 120
462_43 ... 1409
462_44 ... 2288
462_45 ... 5715
462_46 ... 839
462_47 ... 596
462_48 ... 4532
462_49 ... 1904
462_50 ... 2338
462_51 ... 829
462_52 ... 967
462_53 ... 6148
462_54 ... 2204
462_55 ... 3779
462_56 ... 7871
462_57 ... 2916
462_58 ... 1176
462_59 ... 1938
462_60 ... 5222
463_1 ... 1391
463_2 ... 6134
463_3 ... 4920
463_4 ... 1345
463_5 ... 4814
463_6 ... 4345
463_7 ... 2899
463_8 ... 4790
463_10 ... 7507
463_11 ... 547
463_12 ... 428
463_14 ... 4358
463_15 ... 4581
463_16 ... 2897
463_17 ... 6975
463_19 ... 5910
463_21 ... 7508
463_22 ... 548
463_23 ... 7383
463_24 ... 477
463_25 ... 1753
463_28 ... 4306
463_29 ... 7274
463_30 ... 4454
463_32 ... 7670
463_33 ... 5083
463_34 ... 7347
463_35 ... 413
463_37 ... 2053
463_38 ... 6207
463_39 ... 5982
463_40 ... 364
463_41 ... 2408
463_42 ... 1669
463_43 ... 4346
463_44 ... 2848
463_45 ... 6917
463_46 ... 2064
463_47 ... 6592
463_48 ... 340
463_49 ... 6230
463_50 ... 2774
463_51 ... 4724
463_52 ... 6186
463_53 ... 4874
463_54 ... 5673
463_55 ... 772
463_56 ... 6433
463_57 ... 6455
463_58 ... 1707
463_60 ... 3061
464_1 ... 4872
464_2 ... 3420
464_3 ... 4730
464_4 ... 2796
464_5 ... 374
464_6 ... 7405
464_7 ... 81
464_8 ... 6612

464_9 ... 7718
464_10 ... 5614
464_11 ... 215
464_12 ... 6019
464_13 ... 276
464_14 ... 6079
464_15 ... 4307
464_17 ... 3973
464_19 ... 6135
464_20 ... 7566
464_21 ... 3499
464_22 ... 3552
464_23 ... 3588
464_25 ... 3580
464_27 ... 3527
464_29 ... 3526
464_31 ... 1987
464_32 ... 6507
464_36 ... 6764
464_37 ... 375
464_38 ... 2003
464_39 ... 7671
464_40 ... 1444
464_41 ... 5508
464_43 ... 2815
464_44 ... 113
464_45 ... 7605
464_46 ... 1484
464_47 ... 4698
464_48 ... 2805
464_49 ... 7831
464_50 ... 2234
465_1 ... 728
465_2 ... 5054
465_3 ... 7606
465_5 ... 446
465_6 ... 4255
465_7 ... 494
465_8 ... 2490
465_11 ... 7477
465_12 ... 4700
465_15 ... 1073
465_17 ... 7406
465_19 ... 7607
465_20 ... 1082
465_21 ... 6536
465_22 ... 5023
465_24 ... 959
465_26 ... 7958
465_28 ... 47
465_30 ... 3555
465_31 ... 2051
465_38 ... 7449
465_40 ... 7989
465_41 ... 4288
465_42 ... 248
465_43 ... 971
465_44 ... 193
465_45 ... 447
465_46 ... 4341
465_47 ... 599
465_49 ... 2318
465_50 ... 3362
465_51 ... 7256
465_52 ... 2264
465_53 ... 145
465_54 ... 3965
465_56 ... 6196
465_57 ... 1410
465_58 ... 1569
465_59 ... 4048
465_60 ... 7865
466_1 ... 2186
466_2 ... 6020
466_3 ... 7466
466_4 ... 2149
466_5 ... 5477
466_6 ... 2077
466_7 ... 3174
466_10 ... 6918
466_12 ... 6021
466_16 ... 7188
466_17 ... 5414
466_18 ... 1783
466_19 ... 2303
466_21 ... 3564
466_22 ... 5337
466_23 ... 5651
466_24 ... 3558
466_25 ... 7608
466_26 ... 2620
466_27 ... 5741
466_28 ... 2463
466_29 ... 4445
466_30 ... 478
466_31 ... 6080
466_33 ... 6022
466_34 ... 3429
466_36 ... 7672
466_38 ... 5939
466_39 ... 7915
466_40 ... 5380
466_41 ... 5029
466_42 ... 2197
466_43 ... 2020

466_44 ... 3024
466_45 ... 7867
467_1 ... 5649
467_2 ... 7388
467_3 ... 4400
467_4 ... 6739
467_5 ... 5111
467_6 ... 6338
467_7 ... 6799
467_8 ... 2144
467_9 ... 7567
467_10 ... 6674
467_12 ... 4546
467_13 ... 1581
467_14 ... 3092
467_15 ... 6548
467_16 ... 729
467_17 ... 2569
467_18 ... 4239
467_19 ... 7283
467_20 ... 194
467_21 ... 5573
467_22 ... 4240
467_23 ... 5867
467_24 ... 1261
467_25 ... 1455
467_26 ... 2346
467_27 ... 7837
467_28 ... 7952
467_29 ... 5152
467_30 ... 7214
467_31 ... 6263
467_33 ... 5157
467_34 ... 2576
467_35 ... 6383
467_36 ... 1011
467_37 ... 4220
467_38 ... 2431
467_39 ... 6996
467_40 ... 1097
467_41 ... 5415
467_42 ... 448
467_43 ... 5868
467_44 ... 3131
467_45 ... 1860
467_46 ... 3946
467_47 ... 566
467_48 ... 4162
467_49 ... 2079
467_50 ... 1283
467_51 ... 4092
467_53 ... 1333
467_54 ... 2205
467_55 ... 4677
467_56 ... 2212
467_57 ... 1179
467_58 ... 6153
467_59 ... 1286
468_2 ... 6976
468_4 ... 6081
468_5 ... 3889
468_6 ... 1841
468_7 ... 1655
468_8 ... 5227
468_12 ... 7210
468_14 ... 5644
468_15 ... 5245
468_23 ... 3545
468_29 ... 7719
468_30 ... 6977
468_33 ... 6041
468_34 ... 1543
468_37 ... 4342
468_38 ... 6128
468_39 ... 582
468_40 ... 2485
468_41 ... 7691
468_42 ... 6067
468_44 ... 5611
468_45 ... 2961
468_46 ... 5177
469_1 ... 567
469_2 ... 7206
469_3 ... 5447
469_5 ... 3884
469_7 ... 3885
469_10 ... 3836
469_12 ... 6675
469_14 ... 4922
469_15 ... 4352
469_18 ... 4026
469_19 ... 6947
469_20 ... 6626
469_21 ... 6568
469_23 ... 6242
469_24 ... 6948
469_25 ... 7609
469_26 ... 6569
469_30 ... 1786
469_31 ... 5204
469_32 ... 6272
469_33 ... 5183
469_34 ... 5212
469_35 ... 1605
469_36 ... 3483
469_37 ... 5246

469_40 ... 5478
469_41 ... 7048
469_42 ... 2833
469_43 ... 2948
469_44 ... 6613
469_45 ... 3100
469_46 ... 6862
469_48 ... 6593
469_49 ... 1403
469_50 ... 719
469_51 ... 3985
469_52 ... 6978
469_53 ... 1311
469_55 ... 82
469_56 ... 1828
469_57 ... 2306
469_58 ... 4256
469_59 ... 479
469_60 ... 341
470_2 ... 3286
470_4 ... 1262
470_6 ... 3184
470_8 ... 7140
470_10 ... 1666
470_11 ... 4980
470_12 ... 4621
470_13 ... 4188
470_14 ... 2816
470_16 ... 6112
470_17 ... 5479
470_18 ... 342
470_20 ... 6594
470_21 ... 2592
470_23 ... 7232
470_25 ... 2293
470_26 ... 495
470_27 ... 3793
470_30 ... 1096
470_31 ... 2806
470_32 ... 1947
470_33 ... 4397
470_35 ... 513
470_36 ... 5591
470_37 ... 975
470_38 ... 6676
470_39 ... 586
470_40 ... 2464
470_41 ... 1239
470_42 ... 6347
470_43 ... 3332
470_44 ... 2070
470_45 ... 4952
471_1 ... 6489
471_2 ... 4257
471_3 ... 277
471_4 ... 5746
471_5 ... 5693
471_6 ... 6443
471_7 ... 6476
471_8 ... 4206
471_9 ... 3533
471_10 ... 1872
471_11 ... 3063
471_12 ... 7568
471_13 ... 6339
471_14 ... 4861
471_15 ... 7257
471_16 ... 568
471_17 ... 7428
471_18 ... 3749
471_19 ... 5869
471_20 ... 3433
471_21 ... 1338
471_22 ... 6401
471_23 ... 4672
471_24 ... 2503
471_25 ... 5308
471_26 ... 1815
471_27 ... 5178
471_28 ... 1583
471_29 ... 5297
471_30 ... 1630
471_31 ... 2222
471_33 ... 3548
471_34 ... 1769
471_35 ... 3758
471_36 ... 6895
471_37 ... 1120
471_38 ... 3737
471_39 ... 2852
471_40 ... 6800
471_41 ... 5509
471_42 ... 2242
471_43 ... 2339
471_44 ... 6477
471_45 ... 4180
471_46 ... 7384
471_47 ... 7333
471_48 ... 1050
471_49 ... 1679
471_50 ... 2076
471_51 ... 647
471_52 ... 1404
471_53 ... 2913
471_54 ... 2596
471_55 ... 7823

471_56 ... 3102	474_33 ... 5338	477_14 ... 5544	479_35 ... 5184	482_1 ... 3676	484_29 ... 7294
471_57 ... 4135	474_36 ... 2504	477_15 ... 7034	479_36 ... 11	482_2 ... 4905	484_31 ... 1057
471_58 ... 5015	474_37 ... 3498	477_17 ... 5727	479_37 ... 1829	482_4 ... 1527	484_32 ... 7570
471_59 ... 1929	474_38 ... 2817	477_18 ... 5304	479_38 ... 2535	482_6 ... 4465	484_33 ... 1851
471_60 ... 2560	474_39 ... 5121	477_19 ... 1091	479_39 ... 989	482_7 ... 4291	484_34 ... 7753
472_1 ... 5475	474_40 ... 6327	477_21 ... 4746	479_40 ... 4053	482_8 ... 58	484_35 ... 5368
472_5 ... 1823	474_41 ... 1088	477_22 ... 6023	479_41 ... 1502	482_9 ... 6979	484_37 ... 6803
472_8 ... 6919	474_42 ... 2991	477_23 ... 5058	479_42 ... 1319	482_10 ... 2121	484_38 ... 2433
472_9 ... 7791	474_43 ... 4981	477_24 ... 1598	479_43 ... 6425	482_11 ... 4338	484_39 ... 3368
472_10 ... 3770	474_44 ... 2319	477_25 ... 3645	479_44 ... 4592	482_12 ... 5599	484_40 ... 6629
472_11 ... 1445	474_45 ... 3659	477_26 ... 3646	479_45 ... 2247	482_13 ... 3642	484_41 ... 7009
472_12 ... 1584	475_1 ... 6999	477_28 ... 5127	479_46 ... 287	482_14 ... 6249	484_42 ... 3898
472_13 ... 2893	475_2 ... 415	477_29 ... 3575	479_47 ... 4221	482_16 ... 4029	484_43 ... 2622
472_15 ... 3221	475_3 ... 6864	477_30 ... 1816	479_48 ... 5645	482_17 ... 911	484_44 ... 2075
472_17 ... 3528	475_4 ... 2409	477_32 ... 7090	479_49 ... 1912	482_18 ... 7143	484_45 ... 1868
472_18 ... 3692	475_5 ... 5131	477_33 ... 5353	479_50 ... 1188	482_19 ... 3380	485_1 ... 1185
472_19 ... 5298	475_6 ... 3753	477_34 ... 2194	479_51 ... 2653	482_21 ... 6044	485_3 ... 5024
472_22 ... 6677	475_7 ... 5806	477_35 ... 3589	479_52 ... 4433	482_23 ... 1603	485_4 ... 2547
472_23 ... 1537	475_8 ... 3680	477_36 ... 5851	479_53 ... 3055	482_26 ... 6083	485_5 ... 1437
472_24 ... 6121	475_9 ... 6718	477_37 ... 7429	479_54 ... 6183	482_27 ... 3760	485_6 ... 6046
472_25 ... 2091	475_10 ... 3681	477_38 ... 4699	479_55 ... 3104	482_28 ... 7632	485_7 ... 3480
472_28 ... 730	475_11 ... 7451	477_39 ... 5822	479_56 ... 3862	482_30 ... 6068	485_8 ... 7693
472_29 ... 2795	475_12 ... 3570	477_40 ... 1131	479_57 ... 1189	482_31 ... 6208	485_9 ... 1170
472_30 ... 1667	475_13 ... 3569	477_41 ... 4308	479_58 ... 1933	482_32 ... 6526	485_10 ... 2881
472_31 ... 496	475_14 ... 1787	477_42 ... 5290	479_59 ... 5146	482_33 ... 2843	485_11 ... 4747
472_33 ... 5124	475_15 ... 5357	477_45 ... 4309	479_60 ... 3012	482_34 ... 6025	485_12 ... 4277
472_36 ... 6122	475_17 ... 5303	477_46 ... 7107	480_1 ... 4609	482_35 ... 3289	485_13 ... 365
472_37 ... 6740	475_18 ... 5390	477_47 ... 6896	480_2 ... 4610	482_36 ... 2766	485_14 ... 7010
472_39 ... 5455	475_19 ... 3675	477_48 ... 1429	480_3 ... 4611	482_37 ... 7108	485_15 ... 4639
472_40 ... 2143	475_20 ... 5205	477_49 ... 1501	480_4 ... 4618	482_38 ... 2432	485_16 ... 5512
472_41 ... 7110	475_21 ... 1089	477_50 ... 1435	480_5 ... 3628	482_39 ... 3529	485_18 ... 4324
472_42 ... 5286	475_22 ... 5807	477_51 ... 2868	480_9 ... 1817	482_40 ... 2919	485_20 ... 6766
472_43 ... 1770	475_23 ... 2320	477_52 ... 630	480_10 ... 3625	482_41 ... 3317	485_21 ... 1154
472_44 ... 3089	475_24 ... 1586	477_53 ... 7389	480_14 ... 7066	482_42 ... 6168	485_22 ... 6898
472_45 ... 5190	475_25 ... 6570	477_54 ... 7932	480_15 ... 5385	482_43 ... 5291	485_23 ... 1395
473_1 ... 731	475_26 ... 527	477_55 ... 2546	480_29 ... 5944	482_44 ... 4938	485_24 ... 847
473_2 ... 5480	475_27 ... 6356	477_56 ... 4310	480_31 ... 5838	482_45 ... 2972	485_25 ... 6980
473_3 ... 4529	475_28 ... 1148	477_57 ... 3464	480_32 ... 6082	483_1 ... 6722	485_26 ... 6949
473_6 ... 6130	475_29 ... 7418	477_58 ... 7074	480_34 ... 7786	483_2 ... 1257	485_27 ... 83
473_7 ... 414	475_30 ... 5781	477_59 ... 3076	480_35 ... 7611	483_3 ... 450	485_30 ... 1556
473_9 ... 2553	475_31 ... 4225	477_60 ... 2024	480_37 ... 6897	483_4 ... 6045	485_32 ... 1690
473_10 ... 1121	475_32 ... 1647	478_1 ... 6043	480_38 ... 1799	483_5 ... 289	485_35 ... 1967
473_11 ... 2108	475_33 ... 5647	478_2 ... 2528	480_40 ... 7141	483_6 ... 5839	485_37 ... 3298
473_12 ... 7172	475_35 ... 6189	478_4 ... 5942	480_41 ... 7509	483_7 ... 808	485_38 ... 3765
473_13 ... 3794	475_36 ... 6921	478_6 ... 2181	480_42 ... 7407	483_8 ... 6765	485_39 ... 4771
473_14 ... 1063	475_37 ... 1499	478_7 ... 7159	480_43 ... 5765	483_9 ... 3843	485_40 ... 3771
473_15 ... 7785	475_38 ... 5880	478_9 ... 6220	480_44 ... 398	483_10 ... 6802	485_41 ... 569
473_16 ... 343	475_39 ... 2078	478_10 ... 4143	480_45 ... 1481	483_11 ... 4514	485_42 ... 92
473_17 ... 5705	475_40 ... 2290	478_15 ... 4559	480_46 ... 5358	483_12 ... 6867	485_43 ... 1103
473_20 ... 5940	475_41 ... 549	478_19 ... 5943	480_47 ... 2646	483_13 ... 7039	485_44 ... 2477
473_21 ... 1585	475_42 ... 5764	478_22 ... 5736	481_2 ... 3011	483_14 ... 5882	485_45 ... 97
473_23 ... 5941	475_43 ... 4770	478_24 ... 2746	481_3 ... 3144	483_15 ... 4006	485_46 ... 7792
473_24 ... 1827	475_45 ... 1939	478_25 ... 5321	481_4 ... 7612	483_16 ... 7343	485_47 ... 7876
473_25 ... 6920	475_46 ... 3054	478_26 ... 4181	481_5 ... 1264	483_17 ... 1137	485_48 ... 6679
473_26 ... 344	475_47 ... 3391	478_27 ... 2491	481_6 ... 2854	483_18 ... 5496	485_49 ... 6225
473_28 ... 7362	475_48 ... 2750	478_28 ... 6478	481_7 ... 4503	483_19 ... 4192	485_50 ... 3082
473_29 ... 1497	475_49 ... 6444	478_29 ... 6627	481_8 ... 873	483_20 ... 416	485_51 ... 4258
473_30 ... 5287	475_50 ... 1294	478_30 ... 4567	481_9 ... 5441	483_21 ... 7692	485_52 ... 783
473_31 ... 6303	475_51 ... 6177	478_31 ... 7008	481_10 ... 2880	483_22 ... 2255	485_53 ... 2465
473_32 ... 5288	475_52 ... 796	478_32 ... 1960	481_11 ... 1144	483_23 ... 4155	485_54 ... 998
473_34 ... 3525	475_53 ... 6411	478_33 ... 7752	481_12 ... 6922	483_24 ... 637	485_55 ... 6384
473_35 ... 1572	475_54 ... 5062	478_34 ... 4241	481_13 ... 3490	483_25 ... 7510	485_56 ... 165
473_36 ... 5188	475_55 ... 7859	478_36 ... 2912	481_14 ... 2824	483_27 ... 2248	485_57 ... 5774
473_37 ... 4890	475_56 ... 2633	478_37 ... 2015	481_15 ... 1522	483_29 ... 4156	485_58 ... 789
473_38 ... 6678	475_57 ... 1932	478_38 ... 3363	481_16 ... 4011	483_30 ... 5677	485_59 ... 1691
473_39 ... 3652	475_58 ... 1199	478_39 ... 3817	481_17 ... 2690	483_31 ... 821	485_60 ... 6178
473_40 ... 1194	475_59 ... 2174	478_40 ... 528	481_19 ... 497	483_32 ... 1523	486_12 ... 6923
473_41 ... 7630	475_60 ... 4661	478_41 ... 6182	481_20 ... 4612	483_33 ... 2564	486_13 ... 7117
473_42 ... 1162	476_4 ... 4732	478_42 ... 1350	481_21 ... 5852	483_34 ... 5247	486_15 ... 5870
473_43 ... 6863	476_7 ... 5320	478_43 ... 2982	481_22 ... 605	483_35 ... 1819	486_16 ... 6131
473_44 ... 1007	476_8 ... 5881	478_44 ... 1322	481_23 ... 5404	483_36 ... 3668	486_17 ... 2486
473_45 ... 2726	476_9 ... 6136	478_45 ... 4364	481_25 ... 5488	483_37 ... 782	486_18 ... 1309
473_47 ... 1428	476_11 ... 3809	479_1 ... 6024	481_26 ... 677	483_38 ... 2251	486_19 ... 4222
473_48 ... 2661	476_14 ... 2883	479_2 ... 278	481_27 ... 5495	483_39 ... 3662	486_21 ... 6490
473_49 ... 4002	476_15 ... 6719	479_3 ... 7610	481_28 ... 288	483_40 ... 7263	486_24 ... 3919
473_50 ... 1729	476_18 ... 2556	479_4 ... 6720	481_29 ... 6741	483_41 ... 3070	486_25 ... 5386
473_51 ... 2347	476_19 ... 1644	479_5 ... 4674	481_30 ... 1052	483_42 ... 7251	486_26 ... 4189
473_52 ... 4177	476_21 ... 5239	479_6 ... 6434	481_31 ... 5481	483_43 ... 656	486_27 ... 2321
473_53 ... 5800	476_22 ... 4889	479_7 ... 7098	481_32 ... 529	483_44 ... 4057	486_29 ... 609
473_54 ... 1368	476_23 ... 1874	479_8 ... 1385	481_33 ... 3119	483_45 ... 5130	486_31 ... 2894
473_55 ... 6501	476_24 ... 5381	479_9 ... 2377	481_34 ... 5945	483_46 ... 7092	486_32 ... 3927
473_56 ... 2176	476_25 ... 5821	479_10 ... 1755	481_35 ... 1151	483_47 ... 1677	486_33 ... 3902
473_57 ... 3822	476_26 ... 1788	479_11 ... 2360	481_36 ... 6865	483_48 ... 6446	486_34 ... 5497
473_58 ... 7106	476_28 ... 2258	479_12 ... 1012	481_37 ... 1252	483_49 ... 6402	486_35 ... 4278
473_59 ... 2067	476_29 ... 5289	479_13 ... 2417	481_38 ... 7430	483_50 ... 4461	486_36 ... 2322
473_60 ... 3052	476_32 ... 6445	479_14 ... 6828	481_39 ... 309	483_51 ... 7116	486_37 ... 451
474_1 ... 6997	476_33 ... 3075	479_15 ... 4169	481_40 ... 2869	483_52 ... 597	486_38 ... 5801
474_2 ... 4866	476_34 ... 4290	479_16 ... 1500	481_42 ... 2871	483_53 ... 7264	486_39 ... 1508
474_3 ... 2508	476_35 ... 5517	479_17 ... 5860	481_43 ... 2098	483_54 ... 2579	486_40 ... 6209
474_4 ... 7777	476_36 ... 1740	479_18 ... 2662	481_44 ... 6614	483_55 ... 1216	486_41 ... 5871
474_5 ... 6042	476_37 ... 7569	479_19 ... 449	481_45 ... 4718	483_56 ... 755	486_42 ... 5116
474_6 ... 7042	476_38 ... 665	479_20 ... 7653	481_46 ... 6721	483_57 ... 2209	486_43 ... 3309
474_7 ... 1290	476_39 ... 2877	479_21 ... 5773	481_47 ... 2621	483_58 ... 1927	486_44 ... 5808
474_8 ... 3768	476_40 ... 5118	479_22 ... 4832	481_48 ... 655	483_59 ... 7850	486_45 ... 5339
474_12 ... 5255	476_42 ... 1051	479_23 ... 6628	481_49 ... 3149	483_60 ... 2203	487_1 ... 6950
474_13 ... 4289	476_43 ... 6801	479_24 ... 1790	481_50 ... 2782	484_2 ... 7452	487_2 ... 6924
474_14 ... 4499	476_45 ... 4736	479_25 ... 5717	481_51 ... 4665	484_4 ... 2834	487_3 ... 6804
474_15 ... 3790	477_2 ... 7631	479_26 ... 76	481_52 ... 4207	484_8 ... 608	487_4 ... 2835
474_16 ... 6960	477_4 ... 3726	479_27 ... 4197	481_53 ... 7991	484_9 ... 1977	487_5 ... 294
474_18 ... 3438	477_5 ... 2527	479_28 ... 3763	481_54 ... 6866	484_10 ... 7787	487_6 ... 2505
474_19 ... 2890	477_6 ... 1843	479_29 ... 429	481_55 ... 788	484_11 ... 4034	487_7 ... 3833
474_20 ... 7450	477_7 ... 2550	479_30 ... 7127	481_56 ... 6204	484_13 ... 6250	487_8 ... 6899
474_26 ... 7189	477_8 ... 4731	479_31 ... 3371	481_57 ... 1934	484_14 ... 6615	487_9 ... 1580
474_27 ... 7190	477_9 ... 6650	479_32 ... 1631	481_58 ... 4452	484_21 ... 2229	487_10 ... 6233
474_29 ... 6998	477_11 ... 6502	479_33 ... 6325	481_59 ... 4678	484_26 ... 6723	487_11 ... 4437
474_32 ... 6717	477_12 ... 5389	479_34 ... 624	481_60 ... 2586		487_12 ... 2706

487_13 ... 7142
487_14 ... 5616
487_15 ... 5911
487_16 ... 366
487_17 ... 2291
487_18 ... 6084
487_19 ... 1836
487_20 ... 6003
487_21 ... 7088
487_22 ... 157
487_23 ... 5510
487_24 ... 6026
487_25 ... 4066
487_26 ... 7729
487_27 ... 7385
487_28 ... 530
487_29 ... 4365
487_30 ... 797
487_31 ... 6085
487_32 ... 5823
487_33 ... 6047
487_34 ... 3796
487_35 ... 2703
487_36 ... 1700
487_37 ... 6210
487_38 ... 417
487_39 ... 6004
487_40 ... 7035
487_41 ... 6252
487_42 ... 180
487_43 ... 4007
487_44 ... 6255
487_45 ... 7613
487_46 ... 111
487_47 ... 5802
487_48 ... 2129
487_49 ... 121
487_50 ... 6309
487_51 ... 4062
487_52 ... 1451
487_54 ... 4042
487_55 ... 6286
487_56 ... 1941
487_57 ... 2905
487_58 ... 737
487_59 ... 2572
487_60 ... 4361
488_3 ... 4325
488_8 ... 4015
488_9 ... 6925
488_12 ... 3421
488_13 ... 1021
488_16 ... 4791
488_17 ... 5983
488_18 ... 7925
488_19 ... 1145
488_25 ... 6435
488_26 ... 7614
488_27 ... 6595
488_28 ... 7769
488_29 ... 2410
488_30 ... 2434
488_33 ... 6868
488_34 ... 1058
488_35 ... 2861
488_36 ... 6227
488_37 ... 4474
488_38 ... 1844
488_39 ... 4267
488_40 ... 2340
488_41 ... 1524
488_42 ... 7265
488_43 ... 2727
488_44 ... 3913
488_45 ... 2597
489_1 ... 6900
489_2 ... 6086
489_3 ... 6926
489_4 ... 2529
489_6 ... 1955
489_7 ... 2466
489_8 ... 5724
489_9 ... 1070
489_10 ... 3974
489_11 ... 2388
489_12 ... 5787
489_13 ... 7162
489_15 ... 1557
489_16 ... 2492
489_17 ... 2957
489_19 ... 1149
489_20 ... 2878
489_21 ... 4279
489_22 ... 900
489_23 ... 5388
489_24 ... 1838
489_25 ... 4242
489_26 ... 4538
489_27 ... 6869
489_28 ... 1125
489_29 ... 7118
489_31 ... 5372
489_32 ... 6981
489_34 ... 6982
489_35 ... 1738
489_37 ... 842

489_38 ... 1682
489_39 ... 4243
489_40 ... 1387
489_41 ... 4223
489_42 ... 6348
489_43 ... 3831
489_44 ... 1355
489_45 ... 2807
489_46 ... 2117
489_47 ... 5114
489_48 ... 2926
489_49 ... 7057
489_50 ... 5946
489_51 ... 4014
489_52 ... 1339
489_53 ... 2265
489_54 ... 7089
489_55 ... 1687
489_56 ... 5292
489_57 ... 1588
489_58 ... 6201
489_59 ... 3049
489_60 ... 6279
490_2 ... 7191
490_3 ... 3772
490_4 ... 2704
490_5 ... 6901
490_6 ... 3434
490_7 ... 2398
490_9 ... 4557
490_10 ... 2361
490_11 ... 1978
490_12 ... 2467
490_13 ... 6596
490_14 ... 1559
490_15 ... 7796
490_16 ... 7511
490_18 ... 7205
490_19 ... 2435
490_20 ... 1688
490_22 ... 2150
490_24 ... 6491
490_26 ... 2054
490_27 ... 3514
490_28 ... 4311
490_29 ... 6983
490_32 ... 2441
490_33 ... 6680
490_35 ... 2369
490_36 ... 1681
490_37 ... 7571
490_38 ... 7838
490_39 ... 2914
490_40 ... 7284
490_41 ... 5206
490_42 ... 1485
490_43 ... 2907
490_44 ... 4944
490_45 ... 3968
491_1 ... 4339
491_2 ... 6102
491_3 ... 1356
491_4 ... 6902
491_5 ... 5562
491_6 ... 2705
491_7 ... 3810
491_8 ... 4359
491_9 ... 7037
491_10 ... 7478
491_11 ... 1578
491_12 ... 6527
491_13 ... 3053
491_14 ... 6829
491_15 ... 2111
491_16 ... 7297
491_17 ... 3812
491_18 ... 7431
491_19 ... 367
491_20 ... 5679
491_21 ... 822
491_22 ... 6412
491_23 ... 99
491_24 ... 4317
491_25 ... 1165
491_26 ... 4450
491_27 ... 7304
491_28 ... 7432
491_29 ... 1775
491_30 ... 6805
491_31 ... 310
491_32 ... 6870
491_33 ... 3126
491_34 ... 6871
491_35 ... 863
491_36 ... 3969
491_37 ... 4984
491_38 ... 6559
491_39 ... 1359
491_40 ... 6681
491_41 ... 4447
491_42 ... 3874
491_43 ... 1699
491_44 ... 4711
491_45 ... 2285
491_46 ... 4259
491_47 ... 1376

491_48 ... 5912
491_49 ... 4978
491_50 ... 2900
491_51 ... 594
491_52 ... 3832
491_53 ... 6154
491_54 ... 1205
491_55 ... 2602
491_56 ... 689
491_57 ... 7215
491_58 ... 3109
491_59 ... 1990
491_60 ... 2563
492_1 ... 3773
492_3 ... 5369
492_6 ... 2692
492_7 ... 4444
492_8 ... 5361
492_9 ... 7788
492_11 ... 7043
492_14 ... 3888
492_15 ... 2536
492_16 ... 3115
492_19 ... 5354
492_21 ... 6305
492_22 ... 5355
492_23 ... 1979
492_24 ... 5305
492_25 ... 7386
492_26 ... 3175
492_29 ... 452
492_30 ... 4395
492_31 ... 5766
492_32 ... 5340
492_33 ... 1558
492_34 ... 6436
492_35 ... 5344
492_36 ... 4126
492_37 ... 4478
492_38 ... 5694
492_39 ... 1989
492_40 ... 5359
492_41 ... 4892
492_42 ... 7730
492_44 ... 7044
492_45 ... 1683
493_2 ... 4533
493_5 ... 3684
493_8 ... 550
493_11 ... 4906
493_12 ... 6903
493_14 ... 7289
493_15 ... 5341
493_16 ... 6426
493_17 ... 5737
493_18 ... 5240
493_19 ... 5684
493_20 ... 1791
493_21 ... 5350
493_22 ... 6295
493_23 ... 7326
493_24 ... 5391
493_25 ... 5718
493_26 ... 2716
493_27 ... 7295
493_28 ... 5387
493_29 ... 5725
493_30 ... 1465
493_31 ... 733
493_32 ... 2691
493_33 ... 4719
493_35 ... 3887
493_36 ... 4860
493_37 ... 5342
493_38 ... 4911
493_39 ... 7047
493_40 ... 1132
493_41 ... 5528
493_42 ... 901
493_43 ... 7572
493_44 ... 5025
493_45 ... 1684
493_46 ... 790
493_47 ... 4312
493_49 ... 7173
493_50 ... 773
493_51 ... 1587
493_52 ... 5327
493_53 ... 701
493_54 ... 1685
493_55 ... 1423
493_56 ... 2286
493_57 ... 3112
493_58 ... 7673
493_59 ... 4654
493_60 ... 3693

494_1 ... 4520
494_2 ... 3364
494_3 ... 2062
494_4 ... 1059
494_5 ... 6087
494_7 ... 2198
494_8 ... 1812
494_9 ... 1040
494_11 ... 2106
494_12 ... 6724
494_14 ... 7770
494_15 ... 4991
494_16 ... 7778
494_17 ... 4500
494_19 ... 4313
494_20 ... 2118
494_23 ... 7111
494_24 ... 3563
494_25 ... 1516
494_26 ... 7615
494_27 ... 4588
494_28 ... 5853
494_29 ... 3494
494_30 ... 7573
494_31 ... 4997
494_32 ... 5861
494_34 ... 2107
494_36 ... 7847
494_37 ... 4740
494_38 ... 4268
494_39 ... 3198
494_40 ... 2506
494_41 ... 5
494_42 ... 6310
494_43 ... 2663
494_44 ... 1574
494_45 ... 7824
495_1 ... 6630
495_2 ... 4641
495_3 ... 7334
495_4 ... 3073
495_5 ... 2120
495_6 ... 4178
495_7 ... 6211
495_8 ... 1439
495_9 ... 6137
495_10 ... 5913
495_11 ... 1672
495_12 ... 6190
495_13 ... 6391
495_14 ... 1525
495_15 ... 5809
495_16 ... 6243
495_17 ... 4292
495_18 ... 1421
495_19 ... 7433
495_20 ... 7654
495_21 ... 1388
495_22 ... 5726
495_23 ... 1589
495_24 ... 7616
495_25 ... 5840
495_26 ... 1053
495_27 ... 5872
495_28 ... 583
495_29 ... 4314
495_30 ... 4958
495_31 ... 6234
495_32 ... 691
495_33 ... 4880
495_34 ... 5788
495_35 ... 1680
495_36 ... 2580
495_37 ... 7574
495_38 ... 2971
495_39 ... 1357
495_40 ... 6392
495_41 ... 4926
495_42 ... 5883
495_43 ... 4844
495_44 ... 7512
495_45 ... 2226
495_46 ... 7419
495_47 ... 2000
495_48 ... 5671
495_49 ... 3873
495_50 ... 1704
495_51 ... 4709
495_52 ... 2902
495_53 ... 1396
495_54 ... 2213
495_55 ... 4941
495_56 ... 2168
495_57 ... 3046
495_58 ... 2568
495_59 ... 1181
495_60 ... 6269
496_1 ... 5037
496_2 ... 1609
496_3 ... 4136
496_4 ... 2468
496_5 ... 2469
496_6 ... 3670
496_7 ... 2103
496_8 ... 5782
496_9 ... 2509
496_10 ... 1083
496_12 ... 2884
496_13 ... 2747
496_14 ... 7731
496_15 ... 4521
496_16 ... 4729
496_17 ... 5143
496_18 ... 3886
496_19 ... 6872
496_20 ... 1529

496_25 ... 1811
496_26 ... 6951
496_27 ... 1472
496_29 ... 3774
496_30 ... 4811
496_32 ... 6984
496_33 ... 5138
496_34 ... 6927
496_35 ... 4343
496_36 ... 311
496_37 ... 2836
496_38 ... 1549
496_39 ... 179
496_40 ... 1003
496_41 ... 1371
496_42 ... 2323
496_43 ... 5189
496_44 ... 5020
496_45 ... 2611
497_1 ... 7014
497_2 ... 6961
497_3 ... 7467
497_4 ... 6138
497_6 ... 5416
497_7 ... 7200
497_8 ... 7617
497_9 ... 3609
497_10 ... 7618
497_13 ... 570
497_15 ... 2964
497_16 ... 5498
497_17 ... 7181
497_21 ... 551
497_22 ... 5854
497_23 ... 480
497_24 ... 6597
497_25 ... 5794
497_26 ... 2865
497_27 ... 1862
497_28 ... 7102
497_29 ... 5362
497_32 ... 7112
497_33 ... 1833
497_35 ... 5225
497_36 ... 3222
497_37 ... 531
497_38 ... 5884
497_39 ... 579
497_40 ... 3607
497_41 ... 1064
497_43 ... 3802
497_46 ... 5516
497_47 ... 1530
497_48 ... 7720
497_49 ... 368
497_50 ... 1488
497_51 ... 7296
497_52 ... 481
497_53 ... 2875
497_54 ... 3064
497_55 ... 5309
497_56 ... 153
497_57 ... 6187
497_58 ... 1905
497_59 ... 6174
497_60 ... 2604
498_1 ... 6928
498_2 ... 3943
498_3 ... 498
498_4 ... 4385
498_5 ... 4823
498_6 ... 6549
498_7 ... 261
498_8 ... 7575
498_9 ... 801
498_10 ... 4137
498_11 ... 4985
498_12 ... 552
498_13 ... 6550
498_14 ... 2086
498_15 ... 7513
498_16 ... 7408
498_17 ... 1288
498_18 ... 5526
498_19 ... 571
498_20 ... 6005
498_21 ... 290
498_22 ... 3952
498_23 ... 388
498_24 ... 7409
498_25 ... 4973
498_26 ... 6437
498_27 ... 295
498_28 ... 5731
498_29 ... 1561
498_30 ... 3800
498_31 ... 6528
498_32 ... 7754
498_33 ... 225
498_34 ... 7285
498_35 ... 2099
498_36 ... 896
498_37 ... 7243
498_38 ... 4959
498_39 ... 6725
498_40 ... 1696

498_41 ... 226
498_42 ... 5914
498_43 ... 7218
498_44 ... 748
498_45 ... 4260
498_46 ... 1487
498_47 ... 4936
498_48 ... 6403
498_49 ... 965
498_50 ... 6985
498_51 ... 1284
498_52 ... 2903
498_53 ... 619
498_54 ... 2243
498_55 ... 345
498_56 ... 1296
498_57 ... 1579
498_58 ... 717
498_59 ... 1160
498_60 ... 7694
498_61 ... 5091
498_62 ... 6158
498_63 ... 4683
498_64 ... 6214
498_65 ... 7128
498_66 ... 1220
498_67 ... 2573
498_68 ... 588
498_69 ... 2901
498_70 ... 2029
498_71 ... 4716
498_72 ... 2574
498_73 ... 51
498_74 ... 1942
498_75 ... 4040
499_1 ... 6986
499_4 ... 5518
499_5 ... 6987
499_6 ... 6616
499_8 ... 2436
499_9 ... 6492
499_10 ... 5228
499_11 ... 2862
499_12 ... 7410
499_13 ... 3677
499_15 ... 59
499_16 ... 7434
499_18 ... 7134
499_19 ... 5081
499_20 ... 6617
499_21 ... 1604
499_22 ... 5302
499_23 ... 3205
499_24 ... 7950
499_25 ... 5373
499_26 ... 4733
499_27 ... 6830
499_28 ... 3357
499_29 ... 6767
499_30 ... 4568
499_31 ... 2543
499_32 ... 699
499_33 ... 7307
499_35 ... 2447
499_36 ... 4705
499_37 ... 4269
499_38 ... 1163
499_39 ... 7732
499_40 ... 584
499_41 ... 5767
499_42 ... 1168
499_43 ... 2607
499_44 ... 1182
499_45 ... 2989
500_1 ... 697
500_2 ... 7514
500_3 ... 976
500_4 ... 5652
500_5 ... 64
500_6 ... 4144
500_7 ... 210
500_8 ... 4326
500_9 ... 4992
500_10 ... 1477
500_11 ... 3106
500_12 ... 6873
500_13 ... 3959
500_14 ... 840
500_15 ... 1548
500_16 ... 4138
500_17 ... 853
500_18 ... 2199
500_19 ... 685
500_20 ... 7721
500_21 ... 902
500_22 ... 6147
500_23 ... 1380
500_24 ... 7151
500_25 ... 1792
500_26 ... 4662
500_27 ... 4256
500_28 ... 4960
500_29 ... 5947
500_30 ... 1570
500_31 ... 7059
500_32 ... 158

500_33 ... 6191	502_7 ... 885	503_53 ... 6686	505_12 ... 1645	507_20 ... 3354	508_74 ... 7857
500_35 ... 4961	502_8 ... 5885	503_54 ... 5688	505_13 ... 2866	507_22 ... 2487	508_75 ... 1920
500_36 ... 1863	502_9 ... 4261	503_55 ... 663	505_14 ... 514	507_23 ... 347	
500_37 ... 1221	502_10 ... 6769	503_56 ... 4211	505_15 ... 7522	507_25 ... 3256	
500_38 ... 4072	502_11 ... 1381	503_57 ... 5629	505_16 ... 2016	507_26 ... 3556	
500_39 ... 216	502_12 ... 2530	503_58 ... 6049	505_17 ... 5949	507_27 ... 4603	
500_40 ... 6427	502_13 ... 1809	503_59 ... 878	505_18 ... 316	507_28 ... 4607	
500_41 ... 141	502_14 ... 1392	503_60 ... 1458	505_19 ... 6727	507_30 ... 2587	
500_42 ... 6159	502_16 ... 2886	503_61 ... 5149	505_20 ... 195	507_31 ... 5261	
500_43 ... 3065	502_17 ... 671	503_62 ... 4684	505_21 ... 6123	507_33 ... 1739	
500_44 ... 6651	502_18 ... 947	503_63 ... 1335	505_22 ... 296	507_34 ... 7267	
500_45 ... 3863	502_20 ... 6027	503_64 ... 3921	505_23 ... 2510	507_35 ... 5631	
500_46 ... 4668	502_21 ... 1864	503_65 ... 3663	505_24 ... 196	507_37 ... 1837	
500_47 ... 2929	502_22 ... 4779	503_66 ... 2252	505_25 ... 4245	507_38 ... 2885	
500_48 ... 1312	502_23 ... 4262	503_67 ... 3066	505_26 ... 399	507_39 ... 4263	
500_49 ... 6283	502_24 ... 6503	503_68 ... 6164	505_27 ... 4095	507_41 ... 1340	
500_50 ... 4381	502_25 ... 4826	503_69 ... 3801	505_28 ... 7979	507_42 ... 6241	
500_51 ... 1279	502_26 ... 5916	503_70 ... 864	505_29 ... 6232	507_43 ... 6007	
500_52 ... 6264	502_27 ... 926	503_71 ... 5638	505_30 ... 1624	507_44 ... 1258	
500_53 ... 4751	502_28 ... 2200	503_72 ... 279	505_31 ... 4602	507_45 ... 5468	
500_54 ... 2163	502_29 ... 7016	503_73 ... 2664	505_32 ... 2341	507_46 ... 2127	
500_55 ... 2023	502_32 ... 4604	503_74 ... 1276	505_33 ... 369	507_47 ... 4097	
500_56 ... 5147	502_33 ... 4139	503_75 ... 7051	505_34 ... 6962	507_48 ... 3926	
500_57 ... 639	502_35 ... 7756	504_1 ... 2673	505_35 ... 832	507_50 ... 6687	
500_58 ... 2158	502_37 ... 5426	504_2 ... 7258	505_36 ... 4145	507_51 ... 4686	
500_59 ... 7849	502_39 ... 6113	504_3 ... 5406	505_37 ... 1793	507_52 ... 5207	
500_60 ... 2966	502_43 ... 7390	504_4 ... 4382	505_38 ... 7734	507_53 ... 2253	
501_1 ... 6929	502_45 ... 4616	504_5 ... 4164	505_39 ... 208	507_54 ... 4127	
501_2 ... 453	502_46 ... 4347	504_6 ... 4372	505_40 ... 4453	507_55 ... 2990	
501_3 ... 6930	502_47 ... 5427	504_7 ... 1219	505_41 ... 7966	507_56 ... 2600	
501_4 ... 1090	502_48 ... 6244	504_8 ... 2287	505_42 ... 4318	507_57 ... 110	
501_5 ... 7619	502_49 ... 1358	504_9 ... 4055	505_43 ... 4962	507_58 ... 2571	
501_6 ... 5568	502_51 ... 5456	504_10 ... 109	505_44 ... 6340	507_59 ... 3924	
501_7 ... 1693	502_52 ... 886	504_11 ... 7515	505_45 ... 1702	507_60 ... 3043	
501_8 ... 7479	502_53 ... 7576	504_12 ... 2324	505_46 ... 7699	508_1 ... 6008	
501_9 ... 931	502_55 ... 855	504_13 ... 106	505_47 ... 1108	508_2 ... 1834	
501_10 ... 7695	502_56 ... 7275	504_14 ... 6874	505_48 ... 6728	508_3 ... 6954	
501_11 ... 4965	502_57 ... 2152	504_16 ... 843	505_50 ... 3939	508_4 ... 4986	
501_12 ... 4293	502_58 ... 7832	504_17 ... 4224	505_51 ... 183	508_5 ... 6632	
501_13 ... 2124	502_59 ... 4109	504_18 ... 1839	505_52 ... 4096	508_6 ... 2488	
501_14 ... 5343	502_60 ... 4687	504_19 ... 7733	505_53 ... 1365	508_7 ... 6688	
501_15 ... 454	502_61 ... 1159	504_20 ... 3071	505_54 ... 3611	508_8 ... 1377	
501_16 ... 662	502_62 ... 2672	504_21 ... 4198	505_55 ... 482	508_9 ... 4111	
501_17 ... 6988	502_63 ... 768	504_22 ... 2116	505_56 ... 973	508_10 ... 1317	
501_18 ... 389	502_64 ... 1478	504_23 ... 661	505_57 ... 2718	508_11 ... 3398	
501_19 ... 6529	502_65 ... 1289	504_24 ... 7453	505_58 ... 147	508_12 ... 5732	
501_20 ... 2021	502_66 ... 2915	504_25 ... 7022	505_59 ... 2027	508_13 ... 1911	
501_21 ... 6202	502_67 ... 659	504_26 ... 824	505_60 ... 6831	508_14 ... 6493	
501_22 ... 1158	502_68 ... 6179	504_27 ... 2389	505_61 ... 5019	508_15 ... 2411	
501_23 ... 7015	502_69 ... 3067	504_28 ... 3347	505_62 ... 6404	508_16 ... 2308	
501_24 ... 1299	502_70 ... 2717	504_29 ... 6006	505_63 ... 1308	508_17 ... 197	
501_25 ... 4244	502_71 ... 6685	504_30 ... 1473	505_64 ... 7276	508_18 ... 6619	
501_26 ... 4993	502_72 ... 957	504_31 ... 7454	505_65 ... 4086	508_19 ... 483	
501_27 ... 6768	502_73 ... 2220	504_32 ... 5855	505_66 ... 769	508_20 ... 6806	
501_29 ... 854	502_74 ... 1210	504_33 ... 4056	505_67 ... 2599	508_21 ... 750	
501_30 ... 6103	502_75 ... 3922	504_34 ... 553	505_68 ... 4974	508_22 ... 5483	
501_31 ... 5499	503_1 ... 7779	504_35 ... 5917	505_69 ... 7207	508_23 ... 3379	
501_33 ... 6952	503_2 ... 5984	504_36 ... 7696	505_70 ... 86	508_24 ... 6989	
501_34 ... 884	503_3 ... 2837	504_37 ... 7697	505_71 ... 4046	508_25 ... 348	
501_35 ... 6682	503_4 ... 580	504_38 ... 3741	505_72 ... 784	508_26 ... 5918	
501_36 ... 3378	503_5 ... 5961	504_39 ... 7516	505_73 ... 3925	508_27 ... 3135	
501_37 ... 6691	503_6 ... 2788	504_40 ... 2271	505_74 ... 1180	508_28 ... 4105	
501_38 ... 249	503_7 ... 572	504_41 ... 4073	505_75 ... 2159	508_29 ... 4949	
501_39 ... 6631	503_8 ... 4163	504_42 ... 5195	506_3 ... 4327	508_30 ... 7359	
501_40 ... 1634	503_9 ... 2259	504_43 ... 1678	506_6 ... 3396	508_31 ... 418	
501_41 ... 91	503_10 ... 2217	504_44 ... 4601	506_8 ... 1146	508_32 ... 5841	
501_42 ... 6683	503_11 ... 1424	504_45 ... 3550	506_10 ... 6571	508_33 ... 1810	
501_43 ... 312	503_12 ... 4058	504_46 ... 3107	506_11 ... 7758	508_34 ... 5363	
501_44 ... 2685	503_13 ... 5420	504_47 ... 2583	506_14 ... 4464	508_35 ... 2624	
501_45 ... 1460	503_14 ... 2548	504_48 ... 742	506_15 ... 2588	508_36 ... 1474	
501_46 ... 6931	503_15 ... 155	504_49 ... 2390	506_16 ... 7163	508_37 ... 5619	
501_47 ... 4517	503_16 ... 5500	504_50 ... 3795	506_18 ... 2879	508_38 ... 2566	
501_48 ... 5768	503_17 ... 4110	504_51 ... 65	506_19 ... 6875	508_39 ... 1814	
501_49 ... 66	503_18 ... 2598	504_52 ... 3931	506_20 ... 6963	508_40 ... 3638	
501_50 ... 5915	503_19 ... 874	504_53 ... 856	506_21 ... 6964	508_41 ... 34	
501_51 ... 94	503_20 ... 5417	504_54 ... 7517	506_23 ... 1808	508_42 ... 8	
501_52 ... 5436	503_21 ... 7577	504_55 ... 3027	506_24 ... 3830	508_44 ... 3554	
501_53 ... 346	503_22 ... 3920	504_56 ... 4722	506_25 ... 5950	508_45 ... 6184	
501_54 ... 2270	503_23 ... 834	504_57 ... 6192	506_26 ... 7192	508_46 ... 4475	
501_55 ... 3392	503_24 ... 5948	504_58 ... 1277	506_29 ... 6198	508_47 ... 2348	
501_56 ... 6598	503_25 ... 2370	504_59 ... 2216	506_30 ... 6876	508_48 ... 1590	
501_57 ... 72	503_26 ... 7874	504_60 ... 7870	506_32 ... 2325	508_49 ... 6560	
501_58 ... 2787	503_27 ... 6048	504_61 ... 6291	506_33 ... 4551	508_50 ... 978	
501_59 ... 2026	503_28 ... 2513	504_62 ... 1316	506_34 ... 2362	508_51 ... 4193	
501_60 ... 5299	503_29 ... 823	504_63 ... 2623	506_36 ... 7793	508_52 ... 4710	
501_61 ... 6237	503_30 ... 2747	504_64 ... 4681	506_38 ... 6618	508_53 ... 6413	
501_62 ... 122	503_31 ... 7633	504_65 ... 615	506_39 ... 2307	508_54 ... 1776	
501_63 ... 2634	503_32 ... 4531	504_66 ... 2211	506_40 ... 7266	508_55 ... 400	
501_64 ... 1701	503_33 ... 5457	504_67 ... 1280	506_41 ... 7839	508_56 ... 4280	
501_65 ... 6228	503_34 ... 7420	504_68 ... 3928	506_42 ... 3515	508_57 ... 242	
501_66 ... 4534	503_35 ... 1742	504_69 ... 1195	506_43 ... 3808	508_58 ... 4367	
501_67 ... 6197	503_36 ... 1351	504_70 ... 7052	506_44 ... 3811	508_59 ... 1218	
501_68 ... 4045	503_37 ... 6349	504_71 ... 5145	506_45 ... 5783	508_60 ... 7363	
501_69 ... 4957	503_38 ... 7242	504_72 ... 1922	506_46 ... 6770	508_61 ... 4947	
501_70 ... 6367	503_40 ... 7480	504_73 ... 3708	506_48 ... 1183	508_62 ... 6494	
501_71 ... 5018	503_41 ... 2084	504_74 ... 4660	506_49 ... 2166	508_63 ... 1225	
501_72 ... 1567	503_42 ... 1867	504_75 ... 4432	506_50 ... 2223	508_64 ... 3072	
501_73 ... 2608	503_43 ... 3549	505_1 ... 625	507_1 ... 3923	508_65 ... 2208	
501_74 ... 1215	503_44 ... 3551	505_2 ... 3617	507_3 ... 5482	508_66 ... 7875	
501_75 ... 2207	503_46 ... 7620	505_3 ... 831	507_4 ... 912	508_67 ... 4050	
502_1 ... 7755	503_47 ... 892	505_4 ... 7757	507_6 ... 869	508_68 ... 5093	
502_2 ... 6238	503_48 ... 6953	505_5 ... 795	507_8 ... 4706	508_69 ... 4377	
502_3 ... 4998	503_49 ... 1686	505_6 ... 7698	507_11 ... 499	508_70 ... 1174	
502_4 ... 6088	503_50 ... 7674	505_9 ... 809	507_13 ... 858	508_71 ... 4049	
502_5 ... 6684	503_51 ... 4117	505_10 ... 6104	507_17 ... 5467	508_72 ... 707	
502_6 ... 7722	503_52 ... 1327	505_11 ... 670	507_19 ... 6235	508_73 ... 2570	

Index Two — Listing Numbers by Major Category and Subcategory

This index cross-references the first listing number for each major classification used in this book. (For instance, if you wanted to see all Akro Agate Company Flinties, they would start at listing number 606 and continue to listing number 610).